LAW and POLITICS

The author's approach is Anglo-American. Born in England, he was educated at Oxford and at Yale and practiced law in New York and in London before becoming professor of law at Yale and later provost at Tulane. His book, the product of a long period of research and reflection, makes a major contribution to the literature of British legal and political history and to an understanding of the contrasting contexts of the British and American appellate courts.

Robert Stevens is president of Haverford College.

STUDIES IN LEGAL HISTORY

Published by The University of North Carolina Press
in association with the
American Society for Legal History

LAW *and* POLITICS

The House of Lords as a
Judicial Body, 1800–1976

By ROBERT STEVENS

The University of North Carolina Press   *Chapel Hill*

© 1978 The University of North Carolina Press
All rights reserved
Manufactured in the United States of America
Library of Congress Catalog Card Number 78-8500
ISBN 0-8078-1321-4

Library of Congress Cataloging in Publication Data

Stevens, Robert Bocking.
  Law and politics.

  (Studies in legal history)
  Bibliography: p.
  Includes indexes.
  1. Great Britain. Parliament. House of Lords—
Jurisdiction. I. Title. II. Series.
KD7132.S73   342'.41'05   78-8500
ISBN 0-8078-1321-4

For my parents
and in memory of A. M. B.

ᴓ Contents

ᐧᐧᐧ Preface

A hundred years ago today the First Lords of Appeal in Ordinary took office. Their arrival—part of the English genius for compromise or part of a political deal, depending on one's perception—was scarcely noted by contemporaries. The survival and expansion of the law lords as the basis of the final appeal court in England has been little studied and their centenary marked only modestly. While this book is intended to examine the House of Lords as a judicial body in its broadest sense, an analysis of the role of the law lords over the last hundred years is its core.

This study of the House of Lords as a judicial body was originally delivered as a series of twelve lectures at Queen's University, Belfast.[1] In turning those lectures into this volume, I have both expanded them[2] and brought them up-to-date. I have also drawn on other writings and lectures. Some of chapter 2 and 3 was not originally part of the series but appeared as an article in the *Law Quarterly Review*[3], and part of the final chapter was originally delivered as a public lecture at the University of London.[4] Moreover, I have not hesitated to draw on other lectures

1. Since the genesis of this book is a series of lectures, I have allowed myself a considerable amount of lecturer's license in the use of technical terms. For instance, I often use "judgment" where technically I should use "speech," when referring to the fruits of their lordships' judicial labors. Similarly, I have not paid deference to the various ranks of the peerage—all law lords have normally been treated as barons, even if technically entitled to some loftier rank in the order of nobility. I have also allowed myself the privilege of omitting titles altogether after the first mention of any particular law lord. I have also eschewed the use of those somewhat precious legal phrases, such as "as he then was," often used in England in discussions of members of the bench.

2. Much of the expansion has taken the form of increased analysis of developments in substantive law, in an effort to make the book more intelligible to both lawyers and nonlawyers. Normally I have incorporated this discussion in the last chapter of each part, although where structure made it appropriate, I have dealt with it earlier.

3. Robert Stevens, "The Final Appeal" (1964). An earlier version of chapter 13 appeared as Robert Stevens, "Judicial Legislation and the Law Lords" in the *Irish Jurist* (1975).

4. Robert Stevens, "The Role of a Final Appeal Court in a Democracy," *Modern Law Review* (1965).

and papers, particularly those delivered at the London School of Economics, Southampton University, the State University of New York at Buffalo, Trinity College, Dublin, University College, London, and Warwick University. To all these institutions, but especially Queen's University, Belfast, I am most grateful.

In completing the research for this book I have tried to be exhaustive with respect to both the decisions of the House of Lords and the law lords who comprise its membership. I have, if not read, at least glanced at all the reported decisions of the House of Lords, and, in the House of Lords Record Office, I have sampled the unreported decisions from the 1830s until the present.[5] With few exceptions, I have read all the docuents written by or to any Lord of Appeal in Ordinary,[6] at least insofar as these materials are traceable through the British Museum and the National Manuscripts Commission; I have also attempted to read all the extralegal writings of the law lords, as well as an extended sample of the speeches of the law lords in the House sitting legislatively. In addition, I have talked at length to a number of the present and recent law lords.

Of course, a volume such as this could not have been written without considerable help from others. I have, for instance, been embarrassingly fortunate in terms of financial support. At different times my research was supported by the American Council of Learned Societies, the Ford Foundation, the Rockefeller Foundation, and the Social Science Research Council. My work on the legal process in England was generously supported by the Yale Law School from its Ford Foundation grant for international and comparative studies. For this and other less tangible forms of support, I should particularly like to thank the deans with whom I have served there—Eugene Rostow, Louis Pollak, Abraham Goldstein, and Harry Wellington.

I have also been particularly fortunate in having had, at different points, the help of various research assistants. Pride of place must go to Rosemary Martin-Jones, who worked with me one summer in New Haven and managed to bring some form of final order into the drafts and working papers that had formed the basis for the lectures. To her I am

---

5. When I have referred to these they appear under the rubric of "Opinions of their Lordships."

The implication of the English tradition, which continues to this day, of not reporting all decisions was commented on by Lord Sumner in *Palgrave, Brown & Co. v. S. S. Turid, (Owners)*, [1922] A.C. 397, 413: "I have often wondered what would happen, if some learned and industrious person compiled from the records and cases lodged by the parties in your Lordships' House, and the transcripts of your Lordships' opinions preserved in the Parliament Office, a selection of 'Unnoticed House of Lords Cases.' The results might be somewhat unexpected, but the decisions themselves, all courts, your Lordships' House included, would be bound to follow, wherever they apply."

6. In view of Heuston's exhaustive work, I made no attempt to read the papers of the Lord Chancellors. See R. F. V. Heuston, *Lives of the Lord Chancellors 1885–1940*.

especially grateful. But I should also like to thank others who helped with specific research tasks: David Charity, Christopher Cook, Jill Cotrell, Brian Knight, Nigel Lambert, and Roger Moore. The bulk of the source checking was done by Sarah Forster and Dwight Monson; Scott Baskin, Alicia Kershaw, Ken Klein, and Robert Messineo—all of the Yale Law School class of 1978—made vital contributions to the last few chapters and ensured that the book ultimately saw the light of day. They all have my profound thanks.

It is difficult to know how to thank adequately all those who directly and indirectly have influenced this research. I owe much to my former teachers, especially Alex Bickel, Grant Gilmore, Harry Lawson, and Myres McDougal. The New York Admiralty Bar and the Commercial Bar clustered in Essex Court in the Temple, in different ways gave me insights and understandings not available elsewhere at the American or English bars. In addition, over the years I have also benefited greatly from discussions with practitioners and fellow academics in both England and the United States. In connection with this, I should especially like to thank Brian Abel-Smith, Louis Blom-Cooper, Theo Chorley, Gavin Drewry, Charles Gray, William Gwyn, Rosalyn Higgins, Jack Jacob, Anthony Lester, Leon Lipson, Christopher McCrudden, Claire Palley, Leolin Price, Richard Titmuss, Bill Wedderburn, and Basil Yamey. Bruce Ackerman, Bill Cornish, Reuben Hasson, Bill Nelson, Rosemary Stevens, and William Twining all generously undertook the consuming task of reading the final draft in an effort to prevent errors and misinterpretations. The strength of my thanks for that unrewarding task—and the support each of the six has given me—is matched only by my insistence that the remaining errors and misinterpretations are all my own. Finally, since the historical themes loom large in this study, I should like to thank two persons from a much earlier era: Robert Duesbury, who brought me up in the Whig tradition of English history, and Bill Winter, who introduced me to the Tory.

I should also like to thank those who so generously gave me access to different sets of papers, particularly the National Trust, for access to the Hughenden (Disraeli) Papers; His Grace the Archbishop of Canterbury and E. G. W. Bill, the librarian of Lambeth Palace Library, Fulham, for access to the Selborne Papers; to Bodley's librarian at Oxford for access to the Asquith Papers; to the Hon. Mrs. (Isabel) Vaughan-Thompson for access to the Shaw Papers; to Sir Anthony Macnaghten for access to the Macnaghten Papers; to Lord O'Hagan for access to his great-grandfather's papers; and to Lady Trower for access to the Tomlin Papers. I must also thank the Public Record Office for their efficiency in giving me access to the papers of the Lord Chancellor's Office; the British Museum, especially with respect to early Parliamentary Papers; and finally M. F. Bond, former Clerk of the Records in the House of Lords, and Elizabeth Poysner, the assistant Clerk, in facilitating the research in connection with the unpublished opinions of the House of Lords.

The library staffs at both the Sterling Memorial Library and the Law School Library at Yale were unfailingly courteous and helpful, as were the librarians and staff at the United Oxford and Cambridge Universities Club in London where the penultimate draft of this book was written. Sandra Eisdorfer and Jan McInroy of The University of North Carolina Press were both painstaking and supportive. Last, but by no means least, I should like to thank the secretarial staff of Yale and Tulane universities, who worked with successive drafts of this book, especially Patricia Brown, Janette Pope, Anita Raeffer, Lydia Saxton, Barbara Schmitt, and Beverly Shinn. They retyped the book with patience, charm, and efficiency.

New Orleans
1 January 1977

ॐ *Prologue*

Take the fundamental question, what constitutes law? You will find some
text writers telling you that it is something different from what is decided
by the courts of Massachusetts or England, that it is a system of reason,
that it is deduction from principles of ethics or admitted axioms or what
not, which may or may not coincide with the decisions. But if we take the
view of our friend the bad man we shall find that he does not care two
straws for the axioms or deductions, but that he does want to know what
the Massachusetts or English courts are likely to do in fact. I am much of
his mind.

Oliver Wendell Holmes, Jr., *The Path of the Law*

At the time the research for this book was begun there was a widespread sentiment in England that the second appeal—that is, the judicial
appeal from the Court of Appeal to the House of Lords sitting in its
judicial rather than its legislative capacity—should be abolished. The
abolition was supported by many leading practitioners, led by Gerald
Gardiner,[1] who was about to become Lord Chancellor—that is, the
presiding officer in both the judicial and the legislative work of the Lords
and head of the judiciary—in Harold Wilson's Labour government of
1964. Premised on the intellectual and political assumptions that were
then current—especially the widely articulated view that even appeal
judges had a largely mechanistic function of declaring preexisting law—
it seemed not unreasonable to argue that a single appeal to the Court of
Appeal should be sufficient to determine whether the law had been applied "correctly," with a second appeal to the Lords being regarded as a
luxury.

In the last dozen years attitudes in political, legal, and intellectual
circles in England have undergone major changes. The House of Lords,
at least as a judicial body, is no longer living under the threat of imminent
demise,[2] and the idea that appeal judges are engaged in some form of

1. Gerald Gardiner and Andrew Martin, *Law Reform* NOW 16.
2. The reasons for this are analyzed in chap. 11. For a defense of the second appeal, see
Louis Blom-Cooper and Gavin Drewry, *Final Appeal.*

lawmaking is now widely accepted intellectually and politically. Yet the analysis of the role of the final appeal court in the British system of government has, as yet, been scarcely discussed. Examination of the development of the law by the law lords, not to mention the social and political attitudes of the law lords themselves, has been generally ignored by students of the legal or political scene.

These lectures, now given more permanent form in this book, attempt to fill the vacuum in the literature. They seek to assess the judicial role of the House of Lords as part of British society and of British government. They attempt, over a wider time frame, to describe and evaluate in policy terms the legal doctrines that the House developed. Despite the various claims that law is merely a logical application of precedent or principle to a new setting, this book argues that the final appeal court has had an important creative function within the English system of parliamentary and responsible government, although its function has been changing throughout the different periods.

In the lectures I set out to discover, from a historian's point of view, what, over time, have been seen as the relationships between law and politics in England. From a sociological point of view, the book begins to examine the relationship between the persona of the law lord, his attitudes and predispositions, and the development of the law. From a jurisprudential point of view, the book looks at the changing role of judges in making law in the light of political developments, or what in other societies would be called changes in the constitution. From the practicing lawyer's point of view, the lectures—and now this book—analyze the development of technical doctrines in the light of other historical factors.

For an Americanized English lawyer such tasks are not as easy as might be thought. The assumption from which my analysis begins, based on the tradition most strongly articulated judicially by Holmes and Cardozo about the inevitably creative function of final courts of appeal, is even today not fully accepted in England. The literature about the judicial process that in America threatens to render extinct doctrinal analysis is largely absent in the United Kingdom. Quantitative studies of the judiciary are effectively nonexistent. These facts, together with the virtual absence of any modern English legal history and the heavy doctrinal and linguistic emphasis of English legal philosophers and academic lawyers, mean that debates that in the United States are commonplace—for instance, the basic arguments about judicial restraint and judicial activism —are only dimly perceived in England. There are other difficulties, too. Politically and socially England has strong taboos about examining too closely the work of judges, while all commentators agree that law and the courts, and thus inevitably the House of Lords, play a far less vital political and social role than their counterparts in the United States.[3] Moreover, at a practical level, the system that has the law lords sitting in panels means that trends in judicial styles and policies are far less easy to detect in England than in this country, especially in the Supreme Court of the United States.

Yet, despite all these difficulties, the task of attempting to see how the appellate process in the Lords came to take on the role it did is a challenging one. The first theme of this volume is thus the interaction of law and politics. Despite the difficulties of analysis, the attempt to analyze the attitudes and predispositions of the judges and the effect these have had on their concepts of the judicial process and the development of the law is an equally provocative one. Of course, there are dangers, when dealing with judges recruited from a relatively homogeneous professional group, of being unduly attracted by those relatively few judges who have articulated their views on the judicial process or who have been particularly vigorous in their pursuit of some policy or another; but I have sought to strike a balance between the flamboyant and the mundane.

Other inevitable problems are raised in any study such as this, which intends to generalize about the role of the final appeal court, including the use of what Julius Stone has called "categories of indeterminate reference." The contradistinction of law and policy, while examined in detail at certain points, is inevitably sometimes used in a shorthand way. The same is true of such controversial concepts as formalism, the declaratory theory, judicial strategy, and even the categories developed in this book, such as substantive formalism. I justify the use of such concepts in this way on the ground that, while at their peripheries they all are open to competing interpretations, at their core they do have effective meanings, and the use of such core concepts is essential in the effort to develop an overall institutional study. Similarly, there are some concepts whose contents change over time: for instance, laissez-faire and utilitarianism, liberal and conservative. While I have at points stopped to examine these "intertemporal" problems, there are inevitable elidings of meaning as one moves from period to period.

As already suggested, such trade-offs are unavoidable in a historical study of a legal-political phenomenon. The purpose of this book, however, is more than an analytical historical study. The attempt to relate the jurisprudential style of the law lords to the political and social pressures

3. See, for instance, the extreme view of one of my former colleagues: "Given the relatively few cases that the court decides, the very limited range of legal innovation and development which it has permitted itself, the similarity of its role and membership to the appellate courts immediately below it, and the off-hand way in which the court gives expression to its pronouncements, it is very hard to see what real use the court has in British law"; Geoffrey Hazard, "Review" 259, 261.

of the period is carried down to the present, while the last chapter deals with the trends of future development. The final section as a whole seeks to establish various alternative models available for development within the English legal and political context. Such development of models, however, begins to emerge in the treatment of the judicial process over a 175-year period, and the current alternatives can be understood only in the context of the political, social, and legal forces that led to the evolution of the House of Lords as the final appeal court in the legal system of the United Kingdom. No starting point is perfect, but I would argue that England on the brink of the Napoleonic War is as convenient as any.

LAW and POLITICS

ONE

Introduction: Power and Professionalism, 1800—1844

Walter Bagehot elegantly described the difference between the formal and the effective parts of the British Constitution; although the form changed slowly, power might shift rapidly.[1] No more perfect example of the dichotomy between the formal and the effective in the Constitution could be found than the judicial functions of the House of Lords. To see judgment rendered in a judicial appeal to the House in 1977 is to witness a near-perfect reenactment of the scene as it must have appeared when Lord Eldon took his seat on the Woolsack in 1801. It is true that electric lights have appeared and peers are less elegantly dressed; but the prayers, the mace, the bewigged figures of the Lord Chancellor (still sitting on a woolsack, the symbol of England's medieval prosperity), the clerks, and the counsel have not changed. Indeed, counsel are still crowded into the totally inadequate facilities at the bar of the House. The motion for judgment—whether the "contents" or the "not contents" "have it"—has not changed;[2] even the printed case has survived in almost the same form.[3]

1. For Bagehot on the House of Lords as a judicial body, see Walter Bagehot, *The English Constitution* 168.
2. Louis Blom-Cooper and Gavin Drewry, *Final Appeal* 102.
3. The House of Lords Record Office has the printed "Cases" for appeals to the Lords from 1702 on. (They are referred to as early as 1698 in Standing Orders. By Standing Order 89, counsel was required to sign printed appeals to prevent "scandalous and frivolous" appeals.) In general these appeals are serious arguments rather than formal statements. Perhaps the need to convince a lay audience encouraged those who drafted the documents to write with precision and to spell out with some clarity the legal arguments to be made. The historian may perhaps legitimately express surprise that these cases should have degenerated in two and a half centuries into the frequently bland and uninformative documents of the 1970s. The cases of the first decade of the eighteenth century read much more like the forerunners of the "written brief," used in American appellate work for the last hundred years.

Yet the real power has changed almost entirely under the trappings. In 1800 the House of Lords was an equal partner (if not the senior partner) with the Monarchy and Commons in the governance of England. Today the Lords as a legislative body has at best a marginal effect on legislation; as a judicial body, the House of Lords does little more than provide a physical home for the salaried judges who form the final court of appeal. The actual hearing of appeals takes place in one of the committee rooms, which might just as well be clustered with the other Superior Courts rather than segregated in the Palace of Westminster.

The constituency of the law lords has also changed. No longer do they represent the aristocracy or oligarchy that the younger Pitt used to govern an apparently omnipotent England. Their constituency is now provided by the lawyers in the Inns of Courts and the judges of the Superior Courts sitting in the Royal Courts of Justice in the Strand. The Labour government of the mid-1970s, presiding over a seemingly economically exhausted nation, had little reason to consider the views of the law lords or, indeed, of the judiciary at large. The influence of the law lords, like that of the entire House of Lords, had declined precipitously in a nation that increasingly marched to the tune of "pure democracy." Class bitterness remained as the main legacy of the old power relationship, but the "real" part of the Constitution had moved on. What was left were 175 years of political accommodations and legal decisions, reflecting the social values and economic outlook of generations of law lords.

The prescient might sense the new power relationship in the politics of the seventeenth century. Although some have seen the Glorious Revolution of 1688 as "the triumph of the lawyers,"[4] in many ways it was a Pyrrhic victory. Although it was true that the legal profession earned the gratitude of the politicians during the civil strife of the seventeenth century, the lawyers themselves had laid the groundwork for destroying the political element in the law. The judges were no longer lions under the throne; by the time of the Act of Settlement in 1701 they had become lions under the mace. The common law courts could operate freely, but the word of parliamentary legislation was henceforth final. The American colonists and the founding fathers in the new United States might still see the virtue in fundamental rights and laws, but the ideas that the courts might question the wisdom of Parliament or that its acts might be judged unreasonable by some common law standard could no longer be sustained.[5] This subservience of the formal legal system to the political

4. See, e.g., Michael Landon, *The Triumph of the Lawyers*, chap. 7 and Conclusion.
5. On this, see J. W. Gough, *Fundamental Law in English Constitutional History*, chaps. 9, 10, and 11; and Geoffrey Marshall, *Constitutional Theory, passim.*

sovereign was nowhere better illustrated than in the final appeal to the Lords.

Until the very end of the eighteenth century, the judicial functions of the Lords were an integral part of the governance of England, and England was perhaps most usefully seen as a "mixed government."[6] The idea of mixed government was not the same as that which had concerned Montesquieu and, increasingly, the new United States: the separation of powers among the executive, judicial, and legislative. The English mix was most elegantly described by Blackstone. He saw sovereignty lodged in King, Lords, and Commons; and, as in so many other areas, he perceived the balance to be almost perfect. "For in no other shape could we be so certain of finding the three great qualities of government so well and so happily united. If the supreme power were lodged in any one of the three branches separately, we must be exposed to the inconveniences of either absolute monarchy, aristocracy, or democracy; and so want two of the three principal ingredients of good polity; either virtue, wisdom, or power."[7]

During the nineteenth century, however, various pressures were to change the serenity of the scene as depicted by Blackstone. Pure or "unmixed" democracy was to reappear with full force, and, as Edmund Burke had realized, a reformed House of Commons would have a profound effect on the rights and privileges of the Lords.[8] No longer would the mixture—which allowed the Lords to retain final control over judicial appeals from the United Kingdom while the Crown through the Privy Council retained control over final appeals from abroad—remain unquestioned. Unmixed democracy was to change the focus of debate from a balance among King, Lords, and Commons to a balance among executive, judicial, and legislative institutions. This transformation is the con-

6. To adopt Corrine Weston's useful, if inelegant, phraseology; Corrine C. Weston, *English Constitutional Theory and the House of Lords 1556–1832.*

7. William Blackstone, 1 *Commentaries on the Laws of England* 51. Of the appellate jurisdiction of the House, Blackstone noted:

To this authority . . . [they] succeeded of course, upon the dissolution of the *aula regia.* For, as the barons of parliament were constituent members of that court; and the rest of its jurisdiction was dealt out to other tribunals, over which the great officers who accompanied those barons were respectively delegated to preside; it followed, that the right of receiving appeals, and superintending all other jurisdictions, still remained in the residue of that noble assembly, from which every other great court was derived. They are, therefore in all causes, the last resort, from whose judgement no farther appeal is permitted; but every subordinate tribunal must conform to their determinations: The law reposing an entire confidence in the honour and conscience of the noble persons who compose this important assembly, that (if possible) they will make themselves masters of those questions upon which they undertake to decide [and, in all dubious cases, refer themselves to the opinions of the judges, who are summoned by writ to advise them]; since upon their decision all property must finally depend. [3 *Commentaries* 57–58]

The parenthetical words did not appear in the editions of the *Commentaries* published during Blackstone's life. They do appear in the 1799 American edition.

8. For Burke's views on constitutional reform, see Gerald W. Chapman, *Edmund Burke,* chap. 4; and J. S. Hoffman and Paul Levack, eds., *Burke's Politics,* chap. 5.

cern of the core of the book; but first the question must be asked, How did the Lords acquire the appellate jurisdiction in the first place?

The Basic Jurisdiction

Perhaps Blackstone's vision of the appellate process as that left with the sovereign—the King in Parliament—when other judicial functions had been delegated, is the most apposite. By the thirteenth century, the development of the common law had led to the delegation of judicial work at the trial level (and by the Tudor period even to the establishment of a hierarchy of judicial appeals), but the idea that a final appeal from the regular courts lay to Parliament was not seriously questioned after the fourteenth century.[9] Parliament recognized no subtle distinctions among its judicial, executive, and legislative functions. As the laws and customs of Parliament had developed, the appellate function was seen as no more and no less a part of the work of the political sovereign than those original (trial) aspects of its judicial work—impeachment and the hearing of felony charges against peers. The issues that remained to be worked out over the centuries went rather to the scope and the form of that jurisdiction.[10]

9. In 1377 all the judges agreed that error lay from the Court of Common Pleas to the King's Bench and then to Parliament. By 1410 Parliament was hearing such cases by issuing a writ of error. As early as 1400, probably for fear of political reprisals, the Commons had resolved that they wanted no part of the judicial functions of Parliament, and in 1485 the judges declared that jurisdiction in error belonged solely to the Lords and not to Parliament as a whole. In the seventeenth century, however, Lord Hale still thought the Commons had a legal right to share in the judicial functions; Matthew Hale, *The Jurisdiction of the Lord's House*, chap. 22. For a general discussion of how jurisdiction was centralized in the Lords rather than in the Commons, see William S. Holdsworth, 1 *History of English Law* 355 ff.

Indeed, an element of specialization had, by this period, crept into the Lords' handling of these cases. Originally a group known as "Legal Assistants" was used. See John F. MacQueen, *A Letter to Lord Lyndhurst*. After that practice fell into disuse, some cases were referred to selected peers called "receivers and tryers." This system was first introduced in 1305, according to Hale, but fell into disuse under the Tudors; Hale, *Jurisdiction*, chap. 12. However, the "receivers and tryers" apparently were still active in the 1620s. See "Receivers et Trieurs des Petitions," 3 *H.L. Jour.* (1620), at 7. The House was still discussing the possibility of reviving them in 1667, and they continued to be formally appointed until the 1880s; Holdsworth, 1 *History of English Law* 359. In 1621 a Standing Committee of the House was established "for the Examination and Decision of Questions of civil Judicature," and this committee was given the power to hear counsel for both parties. See John F. MacQueen, *The Appellate Jurisdiction of the House of Lords and Privy Council* 15.

10. For detailed discussion of the development of the House of Lords during these earlier stages, see Charles M. Denison and Charles H. Scott, *The Practice and Procedure of the House of Lords*; Holdsworth, *History of English Law*; Frederick W. Maitland, *The Constitutional History of the House of Lords*; Theodore F. Plucknett, *Concise History of the Common Law*; Harold Potter, *Historical Introduction to English Law*; J. Enoch Powell and Keith Wallis, *The House of Lords in the Middle Ages*; and Thomas Beven, "The Appellate Jurisdiction of the House of Lords" 155.

From the perspective of the peerage in 1800, almost certainly the most important aspect of the Lords' work was its original jurisdiction. Impeachment, a favorite with the lay peers, provided opportunities for intrigue and a rather sadistic public spectacle. In this spectacle many peers participated actively. At the end of the eighteenth century, the impeachment of Warren Hastings occupied no less than 148 days, spread over more than seven years. While the impeachment of Lord Melville in 1805 was to be the last such proceeding,[11] it took a significant time for this fact to be appreciated. There was, for instance, talk of impeaching Palmerston in the 1860s. So, too, the Lords took seriously their responsibilities for the felony trials of their own members,[12] a procedure that survived until the 1940s.

Impeachment and trial of peers, however, were only two of many judicial or quasi-judicial functions that the House of Lords performed. The Committee for Privileges, since it was charged with determining disputed peerage claims and thereby de facto determining the composition of the Lords, was the scene of many adversary disputes. If the disputes in that committee today seem less violent, that fact merely reflects the decline in the political importance of the Lords. By 1800 there were other quasi-judicial functions. Before a private bill was sent to the floor, adversary proceedings could be held before a committee or before two Superior Court judges designated for the purpose.[13] The typical lay peer might have little interest in hearings on private bills, but he could generally work up enthusiasm for the proceedings preparatory to the granting of a bill of divorce.[14] Indeed, until the requirement was abolished in 1857, such divorce "trials," like that of Queen Caroline,[15] vied with impeachments in terms of interest both to the peerage and to the public.

Compared with such attractive diversions for the typical lay peer, the appellate work of the Lords must have seemed dry fare. During the eighteenth century the bulk of the appellate work was Scottish.[16]

11. See *The Trial by Impeachment of Henry, Viscount Melville* (London, 1806).

12. Philip Marsden, *In Peril before Parliament*.

13. E.g., the Browne Estate Act was introduced 8 May 1714. It was at once referred to Mr. Baron Berry and Mr. Baron Price. No action was taken by the House until their report was available. This procedure was apparently uniform, and it still appeared to be standard practice fifty years later. See, for example, 32 *H.L. Jour.* (1769), *passim*.

14. In addition to the act of Parliament, the petitioner, until 1857, had to obtain an order *a vinculo et thoro* from the ecclesiastical courts and successfully bring an action for criminal conversation in the common law courts.

15. See *A Full Report of the Trial of Her Majesty Caroline* (London, 1820); J. Nightingale, *Report of the Proceedings before the House of Lords . . . against Her Majesty Caroline*.

16. Having developed its own political and legal structure based on the civil law (Roman law) system, Scotland retained these separate identities even after the union of the

Although many Scots regarded the assumption of jurisdiction by the House of Lords after the Act of Union of 1707 as an English usurpation of power, the appearance of their appeals had a profound effect on the House's operation. Apart from cases from the little-used Scottish Court of Exchequer, appeals from Scotland were treated as appeals rather than hearings by way of writ of error, which meant that they had to be heard de novo. This requirement of itself would have imposed a heavy burden on the House, but the most startling aspect of Scottish appeals was the Order of 19 April 1709, which provided that an appeal to the Lords gave an automatic stay of execution. The Scottish were not slow to take

---

Crowns of England and Scotland in 1603. It was not until a hundred years later during the reign of Anne that the political systems were largely fused. But were appeals a manifestation of the political or the legal? The Act of Union of 1707 expressly preserved the separate legal systems, saying nothing about appeals from the final Scottish courts—the Court of Session and the High Court of Justiciary.

Although the tradition of taking appeals to the Scottish Parliament was at the time a relatively novel one, the procedure caused much concern to the commissioners negotiating the union between the two countries. Although the Act of Union expressly excluded the right of appeal from Scottish courts to the courts at Westminster, it was apparently assumed that there would be some appeal to the new "Imperial" Parliament. At first the commissioners toyed with a project "to erect a Court in Scotland, delegated from the Peers of Great Britain, assembled in Parliament, to be named annually or triennially, or every session, or otherwise, as in the Treaty of Union should be agreed." When the difficulties of developing such a scheme became clear, all parties tacitly agreed that appeals would lie to Parliament at Westminster, although, as Defoe pointed out, nothing was said in the act of Union because the Scottish people would "never have tolerated" such a scheme if it had been spelled out. That assertion about the state of public opinion was rapidly confirmed.

In the first session of Parliament after the union, the Lords took jurisdiction in the case of *Earl of Roseberie* v. *Inglis*. The clerks of the Scottish Court of Session made life difficult for the earl—who took the appeal—by refusing to hand over the documents relating to the case, and the officials of the House of Lords were at something of a loss to know how to proceed when the documents eventually did appear. There was, however, no serious objection to the new jurisdiction, perhaps because its existence was not widely appreciated. It was not until *Greenshields* v. *Magistrates of Edinburgh*, Colles 427 (1710), that the jurisdiction became notorious, for in that case the House overruled a decision of the Court of Session, which in turn had upheld a ruling by the magistrates forbidding an Episcopalian clergyman from preaching. The result was less than welcome to some Scots.

However, no appeals had come from the final criminal court in Scotland, the High Court of Justiciary, to the Scottish Parliament. After the union an effort was made to take such appeals to Westminster, but the jurisdiction was not welcomed, and the notion that it might exist was rejected by Lord Mansfield in *Bywater* v. *R.*, 2 Paton 563 (H.L., Scot. 1781). For the more romantic side of this decision, see T. B. Smith, *British Justice* 68. For attempts to bring criminal appeals in sedition cases as late as 1793, see 2 Paton 571. Fox and Burke sat and voted in those cases. The Court of Session does have some criminal jurisdiction (virtually in abeyance), and from such there would be an appeal to the Lords.

On the development of the Scottish connection with the House of Lords, see Daniel Defoe, *History of the Union of Great Britain*; Denison and Scott, *Practice and Procedure*; Andrew Gibb, *Law from Over the Border*; MacQueen, *Appellate Jurisdiction*; Smith, *British Justice*; Arthur Stanley Turberville, *The House of Lords in the Eighteenth Century*. See also *Minutes of Evidence before the Select Committee on the Appellate Jurisdiction*, 1856, 1 H.L. *Sessional Papers* (1856), at 46, especially evidence of Lord Moncrieff at 79.

advantage of this arrangement, and by 1718 the number of appeals from Scotland had reached "alarming" proportions.[17]

So great was the burden that administrative changes had to be made.[18] Special days were set aside for judicial work, and legislative questions were not allowed to impede such hearings. Since the majority of Scottish appeals involved technical doctrines of an alien legal system— Scottish law being based on civilian or Roman law—by the mid-eighteenth century, it was at times difficult to ensure a quorum of lords for this type of work. As a result, eighteenth-century Lord Chancellors were left largely to their own devices in shaping Scottish law, and some historians have argued that the extent of this judicial work explains the ascendancy that lawyers such as Hardwicke and Mansfield achieved in the upper house.[19]

Next in terms of significance after the Scottish work came appeals from the English Chancery courts.[20] About these there was a touch of Gilbert and Sullivan. Out of the dim mists of the Middle Ages the Lord Chancellor, as "keeper of the King's Conscience," had developed his own jurisdiction, "supplemental" to the common law, known as Equity. At the end of the eighteenth century, however, even though the Lord Chancellor had assistants, only he was free to hear cases in court at first instance in Chancery, where Equity was administered. Yet appeals from the Lord Chancellor went to the Lords, to be heard by the Lord Chancellor, as presiding officer of the Lords—and to be heard again de novo.

17. Turberville, *House of Lords* 140–41, citing Sir John Lauder of Fountainhall.

18. Whereas the House had heard an average of 9 English appellate proceedings per year in the 1750s, this number had risen to an average of 22 in the 1770s. Between 1791 and 1800, the House received 302 appeals and decided 139, as well as 117 writs of error, of which it decided 23; 4 *H.L. Sessional Papers* (1836).

19. Turberville, *House of Lords* 9. For an interesting insight into contemporary views of the law lords and the jurisdiction of the House of Lords, see Boswell's *Life of Johnson*, especially at 457–58, 589–90. Boswell appears to have had considerable respect for the law lords of his time.

20. The Lords finally established their right to hear Equity appeals only in *Shirley* v. *Fagg*, 6 St. Tr. 1121 (H.L. 1675). Not only did the House of Commons oppose the extension, but so did most common lawyers, as well as Lord Chancellor Nottingham. Feeling between Lords and Commons was so strong, particularly after the Commons ordered the arrest of counsel in the case, that Parliament had to be prorogued twice. In 1677, however, Parliament met again and the Lords continued to hear Chancery appeals as if nothing had happened; the Commons ultimately conceded their right to do so. Lord Nottingham, however, was able to persuade the Lords not to claim jurisdiction over the Court of Delegates, which heard admiralty and ecclesiastical appeals, on the ground that such a claim would infringe an Elizabethan statute. See further on this struggle, Charles P. Cooper, *A Brief Account of Some of the Most Important Proceedings in Parliament, Relative to the Defects in the Administration of Justice in the Court of Chancery, the House of Lords and the Court of Commissioners of Bankruptcy* at 156 ff. For the earlier situation, see W. J. Jones, *The Elizabethan Court of Chancery* 290. For Lord Nottingham's views, see David E. C. Yale, ed., *Lord Nottingham's 'Manual of Chancery Practice' and 'Prolegomena of Chancery and Equity'* 184–85.

In this and in other respects, appeals from the basic English courts of common law were less time-consuming. The form of appeal—by way of writ of error that lay from the House to all inferior courts[21]—did not call for a rehearing. While there had been a steady flow of English appellate work to the Lords in the early eighteenth century,[22] the common law side of this work had almost died out by the end of that century. The reason, though not entirely clear, was probably related to the fact that Scottish appeals were already causing delays in all lists;[23] moreover, the Lords were also putting pressure on the bar not to bring appeals.[24] Increasingly, even common law appeals were effectively heard by the same judges as in the lower courts; not only were the common law judges called to advise the Lords, but de facto they were treated as hearers of the appeals.[25] Yet, by the end of the eighteenth century, perhaps because of the new problems thrown to the courts as the result of the Industrial Revolution, the number of English appeals again began to rise.[26] The House was slowly being recognized by the profession as a court of law,[27]

21. Contrary to the view expressed by most authorities, the House, through the writ of error, had as much control of points of law involved in criminal proceedings as it did in common law cases. See, for example, *Lookup* v. *R.*, 5 Bro. Parl. Cas. 332 (H.L. 1776), where a judgment of King's Bench was reversed because the indictment for perjury had been badly drawn; see also *Wilkes* v. *R.*, 4 Bro. Parl. Cas. 360 (H.L. 1769), where the House refused to quash an information filed by the Solicitor-General alleging a seditious libel.

22. In the three years 1712, 1713, and 1714, 18 Scottish appeals on writs of error were heard and 10 Irish proceedings (6 from Chancery and 4 from Exchequer). From England there were some 58 proceedings: 2 from Exchequer Chamber, 21 from Chancery, 6 from Exchequer, and 1 from Queen's Bench; Maurice F. Bond, ed., 10 *The Manuscripts of the House of Lords* (new ser., 1712–1714), at xxxvii.

Of the English appeals, 28 were affirmed, 3 remained to be decided, in 10 appeals there was a failure to prosecute, in 3 cases the decision of the lower court was varied, and in 13 cases there were reversals. One case was effectively a sequel to an earlier case; ibid. at xxxviii. In 2 cases the House divided; ibid. at xxxvii.

23. During the four sessions of Hardwicke's Chancellorship, for instance, (1753–55), although a third of his time was spent on judicial business, he heard only 4 writs of error from the English common law courts. There were 3 equity appeals; Horace Twiss, *The Public and Private Life of Lord Chancellor Eldon.*

24. For instance, on 19 Mar. 1714 counsel for the plaintiff in the case of *Pitt* v. *Aston* (James Cliffe and Jonathan Troughton) were examined at the bar of the House in connection with the signing of Pitt's frivolous appeal. They were "reprimanded at the bar on their knees"; Bond, *Manuscripts* 238.

25. Eighteenth-century statistics are available in the appendixes to various nineteenth-century committee reports, particularly those of 1808, 1810–11, 1812, 1823, and 1836. See 3 *H.C. Sessional Papers* (1808), at 129, 144; ibid. (1810–11), at 925; ibid. (1812), at 925; 2 ibid. (1812), at 343; 10 *H.L. Sessional Papers* (1823), Rep. 65, at 6; and 4 *H.L. Sessional Papers* (1836) (British Museum Numbering). Unfortunately, not only are the statistics incomplete but there are obvious inaccuracies and inconsistencies; 140 *Parl. Deb.*, H.L. (3d ser.), col. 1674 (3 Mar. 1856).

26. E.g., *Smith d. Dormer* v. *Parkhouse*, 6 Bro. Parl. Cas. 351; 125 Eng. Rep. 1197 (H.L. 1742) (construction of a will). Hardwicke called on Chief Justice Willes to deliver the opinion of the judges as the opinion of the court.

27. Pollock later wrote, "[T]he House of Lords, even late in the eighteenth century,

laying down basic principles of the common law (as, for instance, when it overthrew Mansfield's efforts to curb the force of the doctrine of consideration in contract),[28] and not merely as an undifferentiated political organ. Moreover, with the return of both Equity and common law appeals from Ireland with the Act of Union of 1801,[29] the broader scope of the appellate work was confirmed.

Clarification of the range of the appellate judicial work of the Lords by no means ensured the clarification of the function of the lay peers in the operation of that process. Whatever impact Montesquieu may have had on eighteenth-century intellectuals, he had no impact on the peers in the exercise of their office. Stability or "good ordering" was the basis of the governance of England, whether at the level of the justices of the peace in the exercise of their wide powers or of the peers of Parliament as they exercised their broad concepts of governing; and insofar as Blackstone was accurate in assimilating the Lords and aristocracy, then the aristocracy distinguished between their legislative and judicial functions only for administrative convenience.

Sir Matthew Hale, writing at the end of the seventeenth century, affirmed that "since the time that the whole decision of errors have been practiced in the house of lords by their votes, the judges have been always consulted withal, and their opinion held so sacred, that the lords have ever confirmed their judgements thereunto unless in cases where all the judges were parties to the former judgement, as in the case of ship money." Yet he also made a concession to reality, at least with respect to the reign of Charles II. "[I]t is grown a fashion in the lords' house for lords to patronize petitions: a course, that, if it were used by the judges of Westminster-hall, would be looked upon, even by parliament itself, as undecent, and carrying a probable imputation or temptation at least to partiality."[30]

Nor did the peers' interest in important appeals change as the Stuarts gave way to the Hanoverians. In 1697, some 107 peers were present at the hearing of the appeal in *Bertie* v. *Lord Falkland*;[31] 13 peers dissented in the Election case of *Ashby* v. *White* (1703).[32] In the years 1712–14,

---

was only coming to be regarded as a regular and ordinary court of justice"; Sir Frederick Pollock, Preface to 1 Rev. R. at xii (1891).

28. *Rann* v. *Hughes*, 4 Bro. Parl. Cas. 24 (H.L. 1778), reversing *Pillans* v. *Van Mierop*, 3 Burrow's R. 1663 (1765).

29. By the mid-fifteenth century it had been settled that writs of error from the King's Bench in Ireland might be taken either to the House of Lords or to the King's Bench in London. With devolution in 1783 the Irish House of Lords became the final appeal court for Ireland.

30. Hale, *Jurisdiction* 158, 201.

31. Colles 10.

32. Lord Raym. 938 (1703). For the constitutional implications of *Ashby* v. *White*, see Gough, *Fundamental Law* 177–78.

not only did the Lords reverse the lower courts in almost a third of the cases heard, but the lay peers were responsible for dividing the House twice.[33] In the *Douglas-Hamilton Case* in 1769[34] 107 peers attended and 6 dissented from Mansfield's opinion, while in *Bishop of London v. Ffytche* (1783),[35] the episcopal bench succeeded in reversing the lower court 19–18, by persuading the House not to follow the advice of the judges who had been summoned.

It is true that the Lords generally relied on the judges who had been summoned when a point of English law was concerned. Yet the significance of this should not be overstated. Just as the Lords looked on appeals as an integral part of their work, the summons of His Majesty's judges to attend the Lords was no meaningless gesture. Not only did the common law judges appear at the opening of Parliament, but they were frequently summoned to advise the House on appeals, particularly where a point of common law arose in an Equity appeal[36] and they were also assigned to report on each private bill that was brought before the House. Thus recognition of the peculiar nature of judicial appeals did not involve any commitment to, or even recognition of, the separation of powers.

Indeed, during the eighteenth century the appellate process was frequently reaffirmed as an integral part of the overall political sovereignty vested in the Lords. Already, by the 1690s, those bringing appeals had to produce enough printed cases outlining their legal arguments so that each peer might have a copy. Moreover, in the eighteenth century cases were obviously written for the benefit of a lay audience. Since the Lords shared with the Commons a strong repugnance to having their debates reported, they could see no reason for this prohibition not to apply equally to the reporting of judicial appeals. At the end of the seventeenth century the publication of Showers' Reports was held a breach of privilege, and as late as 1762 a similar threat was made when a text writer wished to cite decisions of the House. The first regular reports were those published by Josiah Brown late in the eighteenth century, but they were far from perfect since they largely ignored the reasoning in the speeches. Such defects caused little concern to the peers; they saw themselves as fulfilling their overall constitutional responsibilities.

33. In *Don v. Don*, a Scottish appeal concerned with an entailed estate, the Court of Session was affirmed by only 12–8. More dramatically, in *Roger v. Hewet*, 1713, after eleven of the common law judges had given conflicting legal interpretations on the delicate point of whether executors who were "papists" might also benefit under a will, the House solemnly upset the Lord Keeper's holding that the device was lawful by a vote of 53–22; Bond, *Manuscripts* 48 ff., 110.
34. Turberville, *House of Lords* 340.
35. 2 Bro. Parl. Cas. 211 (H.L. 1783).
36. E.g., *Roger v. Hewet*, 9 June 1713; Bond, *Manuscripts* 148 ff.

Administratively, however, the structures were changing. As the number of appeals grew, it became more apparent that the majority of peers took part actively in only the most important of cases; as already suggested, politically it was the original jurisdiction of the House, rather than the appellate, that took their fancy. Yet they regarded appellate work as an integral part of their parliamentary duties,[37] and they turned out to make up a quorum even for the most abstruse of Scottish appeals.[38] This sense of responsibility was not out of keeping with the age. The presiding judge of the House, the Lord Chancellor, was also Speaker of the House and a member of the cabinet. Ellenborough sat in the cabinet even while he was Chief Justice.

Appeals were in every sense a part of the political work of the House, regarded as part of the Blackstonian balance within the political sovereign. Nor was there any apparent dissatisfaction with the system. When the North American colonies rebelled, they at once established final appeal courts that emulated the House of Lords or at least the Privy Council. The 1777 constitution of New York provided for a final appeal to the Supreme Court of Errors and Impeachments, consisting of seven judges and eight senators.[39] In Connecticut the governor and the upper house served as the final court of appeal.[40] The federal Constitution envisaged the Supreme Court as an integral part of the political process, and, indeed, it was physically located in the Capitol building. Nor should it be forgotten that Chief Justice John Marshall would have preferred that there be an appeal from the Supreme Court to the Senate rather than allowing judges to be liable to impeachment. Even in the United States, the concept of the separation of powers achieved much of its currency in the nineteenth century rather than in the eighteenth.

In England, the significant political fact of the latter part of the

37. Turberville, *House of Lords* 10.
38. The flavor of this situation can be savored by looking at the Minutes of the Lords. Pieced together from documents lodged in the Lords Record Office, the minutes provide an appreciably fuller picture than the *House of Lords Journal*, although falling far short of *Hansard* or the *Parliamentary Debates*. The minutes from 1712 to 1714, for instance, show that there were some 100 active peers and the average daily attendance was 70. With such a relatively cohesive body, there was no serious problem about appeals being treated as anything but an integral part of the Lords' work. On 11 June 1713, when 5 appeals were heard, a House presided over by the Lord Chancellor was composed of 6 bishops, 3 dukes, 26 earls, 6 viscounts, and 20 barons—a total of 62 peers; Bond, *Manuscripts* at vii. By Standing Order 75 (1689) proxies could not be used in the judicial work of the House; ibid. 17.
39. N.Y. Const. art. 32 (1777). The judges on the other hand, as a Council of Revision, in turn had a direct influence on legislation. In New Jersey, the Governor in Council became the court of appeal of last resort. This latter arrangement was presumably influenced by the appellate jurisdiction of the Privy Council.
40. Dwight Loomis and J. Gilbert Calhoun, *The Judicial and Civil History of Connecticut*, chap. 10.

eighteenth century was the reappearance of the demand for pure democracy,[41] which was to take its most extreme forms in France and the North American colonies. In England it was to lead to the Reform Act of 1832 (and ultimately to the enfranchisements of 1867 and 1885), which permanently destroyed the political balance among King, Lords, and Commons. As part of that upset, the inherent right of the Lords to act as the final appeal court was questioned and the inevitable tension between politics and law developed. Whereas, in the United States, that force conveniently known as Jacksonian democracy helped relieve the tension between law and politics by making the judiciary heavily subject to the democratic process, England attempted to solve that dilemma by isolating the judiciary from the democratic process and developing a uniquely formalistic approach. The House of Lords, however, avoided the force of these pressures until early in the twentieth century. Up to that point, it remained at the center of tension between law and politics.

The Chancellorship of Eldon and the Pressures for Reform

Eldon became Chancellor in 1801 and held that office until 1827, with the exception of Erskine's brief tenure (1806–7). The quarter of a century during which Eldon presided over the Lords is not traditionally regarded as a period of reform, and the tradition is largely justified. Yet in those twenty-six years, admittedly often against the wishes of the Chancellor, vital changes were made, ultimately leading to the period of tension between the political and legal roles of the House that was to last for almost a hundred years. The first light breezes of utilitarianism were felt.

The early years of Eldon's Chancellorship differed little from those of his predecessors in the eighteenth century.[42] The assumption remained

41. During the English Civil War the House of Lords was almost preserved in order to serve as a final court of appeal. For a discussion of the 1649 debates, see Weston, *English Constitutional Theory* 58–59. The Hale Commission appointed in 1652 recommended the establishment of a final court of appeal consisting of two judges from the equity and common law courts and seven laymen appointed annually by Parliament. This body was to hear appeals from all courts; Donald Veall, *The Popular Movement for Law Reform 1640–1660*, at 190–91.

42. In 1800 the vestiges of original jurisdiction were still active. Peerage claims in the Committee for Privileges took a surprising amount of the time of the House; Twiss, 3 *Life of Eldon* 386. Impeachment was still alive, although the trial of Melville in 1805 turned out to be its last appearance. Equity appeals remained nothing more than "appeals from the Lord Chancellor in one place to the Lord Chancellor in another place"; ibid., 477. Writs of error to the common law courts were still rare, and although there was power to summon the judges to advise when such writs were issued, Eldon used such power sparingly; Van Vechten Veeder, "A Century of English Judicature" 730. Irish appeals were not heard again until 1802, and Scottish appeals continued to evoke little interest. The result was that the peers left Eldon to handle the appellate jurisdiction largely on his own, with the assistance of lay peers, although after the Union, he had the help of Lord Redesdale, Lord Chancellor of Ireland.

that the judicial work was the work of the whole House and not solely of the legally qualified peers. Although the cohesiveness of the House was weakening in the face of the extraordinary number of peerages created by the Younger Pitt, the idea of the appellate work as the responsibility of the whole House was not a fiction. When Eldon, sitting in the Court of Chancery, made an order concerning the orphan daughter of Lord Hugh Seymour, conflicting with the wishes of Mrs. Fitz-Herbert, the commoner wife of the Prince of Wales who was looking after the child, an appeal was taken to the Lords. The Prince of Wales canvassed hard among the peers and obtained promises of eighty to ninety votes. When the appeal came on, Eldon delivered a speech in favor of affirming his decision at first instance and then left the chamber. After his departure a crowded House overruled his decision by a voice vote.[43]

It would, in some ways, be satisfying to think that such decisions encouraged reform in the appellate process. The call for reform, however, had little or nothing to do with the English courts. It was part of a wider utilitarian movement directed primarily at other bodies. Writs of error from the common law courts accounted for only 1 of the cases decided in the 1801–2 session, while some 19 Equity appeals were heard. Yet the House was creaking under the burden of the appellate jurisdiction. Between 1802 and 1806 the House sat, on an average, over fifty days a year in hearing appellate cases.[44] It was not the fault of English litigants. In 1808 only 31 English cases were pending.[45] The pressure came from the other jurisdictions. After 1801, the return of Irish appeals added to the burden,[46] and the stream of Scottish appeals grew to a torrent. While the House heard a few English and Irish common law cases each year, it was forced to hear ten times as many Scottish cases,[47] although this effort had no impact on the ever-increasing number of petitions lodged. By 1808, 139 Scottish cases were waiting to be heard.[48]

Even at the height of the Napoleonic War such a state of affairs caused concern, and the House of Commons, in an interesting byplay of power, appointed a committee to look into the causes of the delay. The committee summoned the Scottish judges and investigated the procedure

43. Beven, "Appellate Jurisdiction" 368. See also Samuel Romilly, 2 *Life of Romilly* 114, 146. Eldon was also overruled in *Fletcher v. Lord Sondes*; cited, *Minutes, Select Committee* (1856), at 168.

44. E.g., 71 days in 1802, 41 each of the next two years, 47 in 1805, and 66 in 1806; *Minutes, Select Committee* (1856), at 168.

45. 12 appeals and 19 writs of error; ibid.

46. There were 1 or 2 Irish appeals each year, and by 1808 27 were pending: 26 appeals and 1 writ of error; ibid.

47. In both 1800 and 1801, there were 8, 20 in 1802, 14 in 1803, 10 in 1804, 9 in 1805, 14 in 1806; ibid.

48. 138 appeals and 1 writ of error; ibid.

in appeals.[49] Its report was sufficiently disturbing to lead to two legislative changes in 1808, both designed to curb Scottish appeals.[50] Yet these changes had no major effect on the number of appeals from north of the border. Although fewer such appeals were heard,[51] the number put down for hearing actually increased. By 1811, a year when the House of Lords decided some 23 cases, no less than 338 appeals were waiting to be heard, the vast majority from Scotland.[52] These figures may have been somewhat inflated,[53] but the situation was increasingly serious.

The apparently insatiable appetite on the part of the Scots to appear before the Lords eventually had an impact on the operations of the Court of Chancery. At that time, except for some limited functions of the Master of the Rolls, the Lord Chancellor was the sole judge on the Chancery side. As the length of time required to dispose of cases in the Lords grew,[54] delay in the Chancery Court, already suffering from Eldon's proverbial stalling tactics, grew chaotic. The Commons became agitated about the backlog of cases before both the Lords and the Chancery Court. In particular, Michael Angelo Taylor, a wealthy man who had at one time practiced at the bar and was by then an M.P., assigned himself the task of leading the movement for reform. Although Eldon affected to despise Taylor—he nicknamed him "the chicken"—Taylor's efforts were not ineffective.

As the result of the pressure, in 1811 Eldon was forced to appoint a Select Committee of the Lords to study the arrears in the Lords and Chancery.[55] In the same year Taylor persuaded the House of Commons

49. Ibid.

50. In the future, appeals were to be forbidden in interlocutory matters, unless the Court of Session gave leave or there was disagreement among its members; Court of Session Act of 1808, especially § 15. More important, Scottish judges were given discretion in deciding whether an appeal to the Lords should justify a stay of execution; Administration of Justice (Scotland) Act of 1808. Minor improvements in Scottish appeals to the Lords were also made by the Proceedings of the Court of Session (Scotland) Act of 1810, § 11.

51. Scottish appeals and writs of error heard: in 1808, 9; 1809, 7; 1810, 8; 1811, 7; 1812, 11; *Report of the Select Committee on the Appellate Jurisdiction of the House of Lords* 17 June 1823, 10 *H.L. Sessional Papers* (1823), Mss. 6 (British Museum Numbering).

52. *Report of the Committee to Inspect the Lords Journals* 1 (appointed 5 Mar. 1811), 2 *H.C. Sessional Papers* (1810–11), at 923.

53. *First Report from the Committee appointed to enquire into the Causes that retard the Decision of Suits in the High Court of Chancery* (18 June 1811) suggested that the number of cases waiting to be heard was 266, of which 203 were from Scotland (202 appeals, 1 writ of error), 36 from Ireland (35 appeals, 1 writ of error), and 27 from England (15 appeals, 12 writs of error); 3 *H.L. Sessional Papers* (1810–11), at 925.

54. The sharp increase in appeals coincided with a change of attitude in the presentation of appeals. Redesdale noted in 1812 that counsel's arguments to the Lords were now "much larger and more complex"; Twiss, 3 *Life of Eldon* 391.

55. 2 ibid. 67; *Report*, 44 *H.L. Sessional Papers* (1811), at 45.

to appoint a similar committee.[56] Although not a direct result of this pressure, early in 1812 an Appeals Committee of the Lords was set up. The committee was not intended to be a "court," but a committee of the House charged with the task of hearing certain preliminary points of procedure and petitions for leave to appeal in forma pauperis.[57] Taylor was still not satisfied. His Select Committee was reappointed and, reporting in June 1812, found 273 appeals outstanding.[58] The demand for reform was surprisingly strong. Ultimately, in December the Lord Chancellor of Ireland, Lord Redesdale, introduced a bill to provide for a new Equity judge, to be known as a Vice-Chancellor. He justified the move by saying that even if there were no further appeals to the Lords, twelve years would be required to work off the arrears.[59] Sir Samuel Romilly opposed the measure on the ground that it would be better to divide the work of the Lord Chancellor, separating his legal and political functions.[60] Courteney (later Earl of Devon) suggested the alternative of radically curtailing Scottish appeals. Despite these divisions, the act passed in 1813.[61] In the same year, the Standing Orders of the House were at last altered to provide that judicial business should be taken three days a week, on which days the House should sit at ten o'clock in the morning, rather than, as usual, only after noon.[62]

These changes had a salutary effect at first. The number of cases heard increased rapidly, from twenty-one in the 1812 session, to fifty-eight in the session of 1812–13, and to eighty-one in the session of 1813–14[63]—of which fifty-six were Scottish appeals.[64] In 1815 and

56. The committee suggested that the House of Lords should meet in the mornings for judicial business and that the Lord Chancellor should have help in the Chancery Court. Additionally, the committee recommended that the "cases" (the primitive form of written brief used in appeals to the Lords) setting out the arguments to be made, should be made more effective; *First Report from the Committee appointed to enquire into the Causes that retard the Decision of Suits in the High Court of Chancery*, 3 H.C. *Sessional Papers* (1811), at 925. As a result of this report the House rules were at least changed to require parties to appeals to print their cases to include pleadings and arguments. Standing Order 177 (12 July 1811). As has been seen, a form of printed case (sometimes with arguments) had been used from the end of the seventeenth century. The other changes recommended by the committee were not made at this time.

57. 20 Jan. 1812. The committee survives to this day.

58. Made up of 181 Scottish cases (including 2 writs of error), 62 Irish cases (including 5 writs of error), and 30 English cases (including 11 writs of error). *Second Report (13 June 1812)*, 2 H.C. *Sessional Papers* (1812), at 346. The committee again recommended that the House should sit in the mornings three days a week for judicial business.

59. Twiss, 2 *Life of Eldon* 238. By December, the number of appeals outstanding was 276.

60. Arthur Stanley Turberville, "The House of Lords as a Court of Law 1784–1837," at 189.

61. Twiss, 2 *Life of Eldon* 239.

62. Standing Order 182 (3 May 1813).

63. Appeals and Writs of Error 1790–1820, 4 H.L. *Sessional Papers* (1836).

64. Appendix to *Report of the Select Committee on the Appellate Jurisdiction of the House of Lords* (17 June 1823), 10 H.L. *Sessional Papers* (1823), at 167.

1819, further efforts were made to curb Scottish appeals where juries were involved.[65] Unfortunately, the progress was not kept up. The Vice-Chancellor arrangement was a failure. The first appointee, Sir John Plomer, was a poor choice, with the result that virtually every decision of his was appealed. Moreover, the Scots behaved as if the new attempt to curb appeals were a slur on Celtic honor. Despite the various changes made, their appeals continued unabated. Irish appeals and writs also showed an increase. Moreover, the House was at last taken seriously by English common lawyers. No less than seventy-seven writs of error from the common law courts were issued in 1811, and during the period from 1813 to 1823 the House heard on an average six English common law appeals a year, a threefold increase over the previous decade. Thus, in 1819 and 1821 Taylor returned to the cause of reform,[66] and in 1822 Lord Liverpool set up a Select Committee on the Appellate Jurisdiction under Lord Colchester, which reported in 1823.[67] With the increasing influence of the "Young Tories" in the cabinet it seemed that more radical reform might be in the air.

Although the proposed reforms relating to the English Chancery procedure had to wait until Brougham became Lord Chancellor, the suggestions for reforms in the Scottish courts were taken further under Eldon. Commissioners were appointed to advise on the feasibility of the reforms recommended by the Select Committee, and their report appeared in 1824.[68] The commissioners came down in favor of curtailing frivolous Scottish appeals, of which they not unnaturally unearthed numerous examples.[69] They also adopted the suggestion that the Lords be free to consult the judges of the Court of Session on points of law, but advised against the establishment of an intermediate court of appeal in Scotland. Some of the recommendations of the commissioners were given

65. 55 Geo. 3, c. 42, § 4 (1815); 59 Geo. 3, c. 35, § 3 (1819).

66. 39 *Parl. Deb.*, H.L. (1st ser.), col. 1261 (30 Mar. 1819); 5 ibid. (2d ser.), col. 1025 (30 May 1821).

67. This time, the committee found 225 appeals waiting to be heard, of which 151 were from Scotland. It recommended that the appellate jurisdiction of the Lords should be retained, but again called for reforms to be made, particularly in Scottish cases. Pleadings, the committee said, should be clearer, another intermediate court of appeal should be set up in Scotland, some decisions of the Court of Session should be made final, and the House should be entitled to advice from the Scottish judges on points of law. With respect to England, the committee recommended various changes in the Chancery jurisdiction, including abolishing appeals in interlocutory matters and taking away the jurisdiction in lunacy and bankruptcy from Chancery. Appeals from Chancery were also to be streamlined; *Report of the Select Committee on the Appellate Jurisdiction of the House of Lords,* 10 *H.L. Sessional Papers* (1823), rep. 65, at 6.

68. *Report of the Commissions Inquiring into the Forms of Process in the Courts of Law in Scotland* (18 Mar. 1824), 4 *H.L. Sessional Papers* (1824).

69. One had involved the sum of three shillings and sixpence, another the ownership of an ox, and a third the right of a clergyman to put his cow out to pasture. Examples of eighteenth-century cases are cited in MacQueen, *Letter to Lyndhurst* 20.

statutory effect in 1825, when Parliament provided that appeals in cases beginning before magistrates or sheriffs could go from the Court of Session to the Lords only on questions of law.[70]

With respect to the working of the House itself, the committee conceded there was no ideal solution and plumped for the "least objectionable." While rejecting the suggestion of a special Appellate Committee to hear all cases, it recommended that a Speaker, who would not necessarily be a peer, be appointed to preside over appeals. The presence of the quorum would be ensured by the attendance of four peers, to be chosen by ballot and compelled to attend under fine. Moreover, the House, thus constituted, was to meet five days a week and to sit from ten in the morning until four in the afternoon. This dramatic change in the Lords' procedure was achieved by an order of the House early in 1824,[71] providing that, with the exception of those peers who were able to bring themselves within exemptions for the aged, infirm, or absent, all peers should be liable to be drafted to hear appeals at the rate of three peers a day. The rules for balloting were carefully laid down, including the fifty-pound fine for nonattendance,[72] and the rota of lords was published at the beginning of each session.[73]

The impact of the new regime was remarkable. In 1823 the House heard some 27 cases, including 15 from Scotland, and at the end of that year 293 cases were waiting to be heard. In 1824, the first year of the rota system, the House sat five days a week for judicial business, making a total of seventy-eight days during the session. During this time 82 appeals, including 59 from Scotland, were heard, and at the end of the session only 170 cases remained to be decided.[74] The efforts during 1825 were even more impressive. Eighty-six cases were heard in eighty-nine days, and at the end of the year only 106 cases were outstanding.[75] In 1826 the pressure was somewhat relaxed,[76] and in the session of 1826–

70. Court of Session (Scotland) Act, § 4. Section 5 further restricted the right to appeal to the Lords in superlocutory matters. A statute of the same year provided for the printing of cases in Scottish appeals; 6 Geo. 4, c. 126, § 26.

71. Dated 19 March 1824, although the rota had come into effect the previous month. Already in 1823 the House had been required to sit 5 days a week for judicial business; Standing Order 200 (7 July 1823).

72. 10 *H.L. Sessional Papers* (1827), at 1.

73. E.g., Rota of Lords appointed to attend on the Hearing of Causes in Session 1824, 10 *H.L. Sessional Papers* (1824), at 1.

74. Of the 9 English cases, 5 were appeals and 4 writs of error; ibid. The Report of the Lords Commissioners to report on procedure in Scotland noted the large number of Scottish cases waiting to be heard by the Lords but also observed that "very material progress appears to have been made in reducing the Arrear"; 4 *H.L. Sessional Papers* (1824), at 415.

75. Rota of Lords appointed to attend on the Hearing of Causes in Session 1825, 16 *H.L. Sessional Papers* (1825), at 1.

76. The House sat for 59 days and decided 49 cases, including 38 Scottish ones. Remaining to be heard were 92 cases; Rota of Lords appointed to attend on the Hearing of Causes in Session 1826, 9 *H.L. Sessional Papers* (1826), at 1.

27 it was clear that the worst of the crisis was over.[77]

The lay peers had not taken kindly to this novel escapade.[78] Eldon, who disapproved of the scheme, was nevertheless amused by the antics it caused. Writing to Lady Bankes in February 1824, he noted:

Nothing of news picked up, either in Chancery or at the House of Lords where the afternoon was employed in balloting for Lords to attend Scotch causes, as long as they should endure this Session. It is amazing, in counting and calling them over, how many, looking fresh and lively, excused themselves as above seventy—how many figuring off daily in Hyde Park and the Green Park, could not, without fatal consequences bear three or four hours' confinement—unless it was confinement for 5 or 6 hours at White's or Boodle's at night. However, we fixed lords enough to serve till 12th July, at 3 Lords a day.[79]

The formal rota system, which lasted only a few years, might well have been passed off, regarded as a joke by the Chancellor, an inconvenience by the peers, and an unfortunate but necessary expedient by the legal profession (and perhaps by the litigants). It was not, however, to be brushed off so easily as that, for the scheme had made a fundamental and lasting difference to the House as an appellate body. The rota system provided clear evidence, if such was needed, of the increasing collapse of the old order. The constitutional implications were profound.

The Passing of the Old Order

By the late eighteenth century the assumptions about the inherent right of the peers to act as the final court of appeal were already being questioned. As the utilitarians, at the beginning of the nineteenth century, moved to reform the law and the courts, the lodging of the final appeal in the hereditary House seemed increasingly anachronistic. Yet this was but one aspect of the pressures facing the House. Politically, the reappearance of articulate advocates of "unmixed" democracy[80] had helped fuel the demand for reform of the House of Commons that, when achieved, would permanently destroy the balance of sovereignty between the two Houses and the Monarchy. In this extensive game the appellate process was but a small pawn, yet between the increasingly reformed and profes-

---

77. By 1828, only 44 cases were heard; 22 H.L. Sessional Papers (1834).
78. Denison and Scott, Practice and Procedure 1.
79. Twiss, 2 Life of Eldon 486.
80. Weston, English Constitutional Theory. See especially chap. 5, dealing with the anti-Lords attitudes and pamphleteering by Joseph Priestley (1733–1804), Thomas Paine (1737–1809), and William Godwin (1756–1836). Chap. 6 deals with the writings of John Cartwright (1740–1824) and Jeremy Bentham (1748–1832) and the events leading to the Great Reform Act. Cartwright's English Constitution Produced and Illustrated (1823) and Bentham's Parliamentary Reform (1818) and Constitutional Code (1827–41) were devastating critiques of the balanced constitution.

sionalized legal system on the one hand and the political sovereign on the other, the appellate powers of the Lords seemed to be a fulcrum.

This situation was not clear as the political push toward a more democratically oriented House of Commons grew in strength during the 1820s. Repeal of the Combination Acts and the granting of Catholic emancipation dominated the political scene in the late twenties and leaders of both parties found the country on the verge of revolution, even as the Canning administration of 1827 brought Lord Lyndhurst to the Woolsack to replace Eldon as Chancellor. The Lords itself had little feeling that the old order was passing, at least with respect to the appellate jurisdiction. Indeed, the establishment of the rota system in 1824 had been applauded by Lord Holland, because it showed that the judicial work was in fact part of the work of the whole House,[81] and the Select Committee had specifically eschewed a separate judicial committee. In theory the rota system was intended to ensure participation of the whole House.

The operation of the system, however, far from bringing all the peers into the decision-making process, made it obvious that the lay peers were mere ciphers.[82] Nothing could be more calculated to make the distinction between law and lay lords clearer than a system that, using the sanction of a severe fine, compelled the lay peers to sit to hear cases, not by the case, but by the day. Leahy described the system vividly:

Two peers are summoned in rotation from a list made out at the beginning of every session, and one different every day. As the Chancellor considers it his peculiar duty to attend to the case before the House, the other Lords, very justly, look upon themselves as only present for the purpose of producing the necessary quorum of appellate authority. The duty of attending appeals is distributed as evenly as can be done amongst all the members of the Peerage whose services are desirable; and, therefore, no individual peer attends a second time until all the other peers then in town have had a term at the work. If therefore the hearing of a case continues for three days, it is heard on the first day by Lords A. and B; or, more correctly speaking, they *are present at the hearing*. The Lords summoned for the second day will be Lords C. and D; and for the third, Lords E. and F. When the judgement comes to be delivered, the Lords present, besides the Lord Chancellor, will be Lords G. and H. The Chancellor, on this last occasion, recommends their Lordships to make a certain decree; and to that recommendation an immediate compliance is accorded by Lords G. and H., who in consequence of the arrangement above stated have not been present during any part of the hearing. If the Lord Chancellor or Deputy Speaker be not a peer,[83] he cannot in the House address their Lordships, and he is therefore obliged to whisper the

81. Speech by Lord Holland, 10 *Parl. Deb.*, H.L. (2d ser.), col. 835 (9 Mar 1824).

82. Denison and Scott, *Practice and Procedure* 1.

83. The reform of allowing a commoner speaker to preside in judicial hearings was instituted under Eldon, although extended under Lyndhurst.

decision into the ear of Lord G., who rises and recommends it for adoption to the Lords H. and I., who both agree with Lord G. in making the order, and etc.[84]

The system that solved the crisis caused by Scottish appeals also guaranteed that the participation of lay peers in the judicial affairs of the House was doomed and threw serious doubt on the purpose of an additional appeal beyond the regular courts.

As already suggested, such implications were by no means clear to the members of the House who assembled in 1827. At this time some 110 cases were waiting to be heard, 70 of them from Scotland.[85] Lyndhurst was in an even worse position than Eldon when hearing Scottish appeals, for he knew no Scottish law at all, and, according to the uncharitable Campbell, would have exposed himself to ridicule had he sought to speak ex cathedra in such cases.[86] There was little point in having peers assigned to sit as figureheads in Scottish cases if the presiding judge, the Lord Chancellor, was not in a position to dominate the proceedings.

Lyndhurst outlined his plans for dealing with the problem in a speech in the Lords in May 1827. His basic proposal was that Alexander, Lord Chief Baron of the Exchequer, and Leach, Master of the Rolls, should be granted a commission to preside in the Lords as Deputy Speakers, although neither was a peer. Alexander, a Scot by origin, would sit two days a week to hear Scottish appeals, and Leach one day a week to hear Equity appeals. Lyndhurst proposed presiding on the other two days in the week, while devoting his main attention to the Chancery Court.[87] Meanwhile, although the balloting procedure was dropped, a rota would provide the other members of the quorum.

Bringing in commoners to preside over peers was the logical outcome of the rota system, which had forced the lay peers into a subservient position. The lay peers were by then becoming conscious of the impact of

84. Leahy, in a pamphlet, c. 1824, cited, MacQueen, *Appellate Jurisdiction* 12. The operation of this remarkable system can be seen by looking at the rota for a typical week in 1824 shortly after the system began:

Monday, 23 Feb.	Tuesday, 24 Feb.	Wednesday, 25 Feb.
Earl of Wicklow	Earl Cowper	Duke of St. Albans
Earl Grosvenor	Earl of Verulam	Earl of Cardigan
Bishop of London	Lord Stowell	Earl of Tankerville

Thursday, 26 Feb.	Friday, 27 Feb.
Archbishop of Canterbury	Earl of Jersey
Lord Dacre	Viscount Gordon
Earl of Rosebery	Duke of Clarence

Taken from Rota of Lords appointed to attend on the Hearing of Causes in Session 1824, 10 Feb. 1824, 10 *H.L. Sessional Papers* (1824), at 1.

85. Theodore Martin, *Life of Lord Lyndhurst* 220.

86. John Campbell, "Lord Chancellor Lyndhurst," 8 *Lives of the Lord Chancellors* 43.

87. 17 *Parl. Deb.*, H.L. (2d ser.), cols. 573–74 (7 May 1827).

that system, and they were by no means enthusiastic about allowing Lyndhurst the commission he sought. The opposition and the anxiety that caused it were best expressed by Lord Holland, the leader of the Whigs, when he said that he "must object to noble lords using expressions, which seemed to convey the idea, that the learned law lords sat in the House to try and decide appeals. The right to try and decide appeals was not limited to any one noble lord, or to any particular peers in preference to the rest; but resided in every member of the House equally. . . . It was the duty of every man in that House, as a lord of Parliament, to sit and assist in the hearing of appeals."[88]

The House, however, ultimately fell in with Lyndhurst's wishes, after the Lord Chancellor promised that if the House did allow the commission "he would pledge himself, before the next session, to perfect a plan."[89] Whether his plan was to return the appellate jurisdiction to the House as a whole or whether he would have made the court more professional still, is not clear, for, as Campbell remarked, the pledge was never redeemed.[90] Nor was the lack of redemption surprising, for the House was about to suffer a major blow to its power and prerogatives by the reform of the Commons. The idea that the peers had an inherent right to sit as the final court of appeal was increasingly to be questioned; but outside the House much more was at stake.

Political and Professional Radicalism

During 1830 the Bourbons were toppled in France, and to many of the English upper and middle classes it seemed as if revolution were imminent in England. The general election of 1830, held as the result of the death of George IV, finally put an end to a series of Tory-dominated ministries. The new Whig administration under Grey was scarcely radical; indeed, many historians argue that it was the most aristocratic (and certainly the most landed) of the century. Grey was prepared for reform of the Commons since, being "aristocratic both by position and by nature . . . with a predilection for old institutions," he believed that major reform of the lower house would "assure some ground of resistance to further innovation."[91] This latter assumption could scarcely have been more inaccurate.

The first Reform Bill, introduced in March 1831, transferred 168 seats from the "rotten boroughs" and grossly overrepresented boroughs, giving them mainly to the new industrial towns. The franchise was to be made uniform, based on the ten-pound householder in the towns, while

88. Ibid., col. 575.
89. Ibid.
90. Campbell, "Lord Chancellor Lyndhurst" 53.
91. Cited, E. L. Woodward, *The Age of Reform 1815–1870*, at 76.

the counties retained the base of the forty-shilling freeholder. The bill, largely through Irish support, passed on its Second Reading by one vote, but when the government was defeated in committee, William IV dissolved Parliament. With a larger majority, the government had no difficulty in securing passage of a slightly weakened Reform Bill, but after days of debate, the second bill was thrown out by the Lords in October.

The riots that followed in Bristol, Derby, and Nottingham alarmed the established order, as did the formation of the National Political Union. In December the third Reform Bill was introduced, cutting to 141 the number of boroughs disenfranchised. Meanwhile the more radical members of the administration persuaded Grey to pressure the King to create peers to ensure passage. This was threat enough to persuade a group of Tory peers—the "hedgers," led by Lords Harrowby and Wharncliffe—to allow the bill through; it passed the Lords by nine votes. No sooner was passage achieved than Lyndhurst pushed through a motion in the Lords to delay the disenfranchisement clauses. In response to this move, Grey called on the King to create fifty peers. When William IV refused to make more than twenty, Grey, with some obvious relief, resigned.

For a week the Duke of Wellington struggled to put an administration together, but Peel, leader of those of a "conservative inclination" in the Commons, refused to join. The King was forced to reinstate Grey and also to agree to create enough peers to force the third Reform Bill through the Lords in undiluted form. Although the Tories accused the Whigs of conspiring with "unconstitutional" forces, the truth was that the political sovereignty within the constitution had been fundamentally altered. The King had had an administration forced on him and, more important still, the Monarchy had given the assurance that, if the Commons felt strongly enough, new creations would be used to swamp the existing peers. Blackstone's balanced sovereign had succumbed.[92]

Although the House of Lords was being politically coerced, it was also being subjected to a different form of assault by Grey's Lord Chancellor, Brougham. At this stage in his career, Brougham was perhaps most accurately seen as a utilitarian,[93] although it is not easy to char-

92. This introduction has been drawn primarily from ibid. 77–82; Geoffrey B. A. M. Finlayson, *Decade of Reform* 10–14.
93. In 1828 Brougham made a six-hour speech in the House of Commons in favor of law reform, concluding with the following words: "It was the boast of Augustus . . . that he found Rome of brick, and left it of marble; a praise not unworthy of a great prince, and to which the present reign also has its claims. But how much nobler will be the Sovereign's boast, when he shall have it to say, that he found law dear, and left it cheap; found it a sealed book—left it a living letter; found it the patrimony of the rich—left it the inheritance of the poor; found it the two-edged sword of craft and oppression—left it the staff of honesty and the shield of innocence"; Chester W. New, *The Life of Henry Brougham to 1830*, at 398. The speech had led to the appointment of at least two Royal Commissions; John Campbell, "Life of Lord Brougham," 8 *Lives of the Lord Chancellors* 398.

acterize him, for Henry, Lord Brougham and Vaux, was akin in spirit to his fellow Whig, Palmerston. He was at once both radical and conservative; eccentric to a degree that scandalized his enemies and horrified his friends; high-spirited and energetic; at one time both high-principled and unscrupulous; and totally unpredictable.[94] It was this remarkably complex, impossible, yet attractive, character who was to dominate law reform and the judicial process in the House of Lords for the next twenty years.

Brougham had first raised the question of appeals to the Lords in 1823,[95] and in the debates on the Court of Session Act in 1825 he had attacked Eldon strongly.[96] In the last year of Lyndhurst's Chancellorship, 1829, only thirty-six days had been taken up with judicial business, while only 25 cases were decided. When Lyndhurst ceased to be Chancellor there were therefore some 105 cases pending.[97] Brougham set to work with a vengeance to demolish the delays he found in the House and the Court of Chancery. He proceeded to sit seven hours a day in the House of Lords and then held late evening sessions in the Chancery Court. Although these techniques annoyed the legal profession[98] and shocked Eldon,[99] Brougham was able to decide 129 cases in the Lords in 1830 and 1831. In 1832 the House was able to limit its sittings for judicial business to three days a week,[100] and by 1834 there were no arrears at all.[101]

Brougham was working equally vigorously on his plans for legislative reform of law and the legal process. Not only did he encourage various statutory reforms in substantive law and procedure,[102] but he also introduced changes in other courts, all destined to have a considerable effect on the future of the House of Lords. In 1831 the bank-

94. Brougham is the model for Quicksilver in Samuel Warren's novel, *Ten Thousand a Year*. On Brougham, see also Walter Bagehot's "Lord Brougham," published in 1857 and reprinted in *Bagehot's Historical Essays* 159.

95. Twiss, 2 *Life of Eldon* 475.

96. Ibid. 479.

97. 22 *H.L. Sessional Papers* (1834).

98. Campbell, "Life of Lord Brougham" 402.

99. Twiss, 3 *Life of Eldon* 132.

100. MacQueen, *Appellate Jurisdiction* 30.

101. Campbell, "Life of Lord Brougham" 444.

102. E.g., abolition of fines and recoveries, enabling a tenant in tail to bar the entail by a single deed if the life tenant agreed; Fines and Recoveries Act of 1833. See also the changes made in the rights and liabilities of the heir; Administration of Estates Act of 1833, Dower Act of 1833, and the Inheritance Act of 1833.

Procedural reforms included the Uniformity of Process Act of 1832, which abolished many fictions in common law pleading, and the Civil Procedure Act of 1833, which delegated to the judges the power to draw up rules for pleading in the unfulfilled hope that this might strike a balance between the rules of special pleading and the vagueness of the general issue; William S. Holdsworth, "The New Rules of Pleading of the Hilary Term, 1834," at 261.

ruptcy jurisdiction was taken from the Chancery Court,[103] and in 1833 the Master of the Rolls was at last allowed to sit in open court.[104] These reforms freed the Chancellor from some of his work as a judge in original Equity causes. Brougham would, however, have gone further. In 1834 he introduced a bill to separate the legal and political functions of the Lord Chancellor so that the head of the judiciary would no longer also be Speaker in the Lords, but since by this time there were no judicial arrears in the Lords, Brougham was persuaded to abandon the project.[105] Seen, however, in the light of the political crisis that had centered around the powers of the Lords, this attempt to split the political and legal roles of the Lord Chancellor was an important indicator of future trends.

The general issue of appeals also attracted Brougham's attention. In 1830 he established a new court of Exchequer Chamber to replace the strange system of appeal courts of that name that had lumbered on from Elizabeth's days. The court of King's Bench lost its eclectic appellate jurisdiction; writs of error lying directly from the House of Lords to the courts of original jurisdiction were abolished; and Exchequer Chamber was made a mandatory intermediate appeal court from the three common law courts: King's Bench, Common Pleas, and Exchequer.[106] Brougham then turned his attention to the Court of Delegates, which since the sixteenth century had been the final court of appeal in ecclesiastical and admiralty cases. Composed of three common lawyers and three civilians, it had, largely through the reputation of the latter, fallen into a sad state of disrepair. In 1832 the court was abolished and its jurisdiction transferred to the Privy Council.[107]

This change brought the Privy Council—the basic organ of the executive, which had also retained extensive judicial functions—under Brougham's watchful eye.[108] Its overseas appellate jurisdiction survived not only the political turmoils of the seventeenth century,[109] but also the

103. 1 & 2 Will. 4, c. 56.

104. 3 & 4 Will. 4, c. 94—a reform that achieved less than it might have, since, as in the case of the Vice-Chancellor, causes before the Master of the Rolls might be reargued before the Lord Chancellor.

105. 25 *Parl. Deb.*, H.C. (3d ser.), col. 1260 (14 Aug. 1834); Campbell, "Life of Lord Brougham" 444.

106. Exchequer Chamber Act of 1830.

107. 2 & 3 Will. 4, c. 92.

108. On this episode and Brougham's later efforts to reform the Privy Council, see D. B. Swinfen, "Henry Brougham and the Judicial Committee of the Privy Council" 396.

109. Since the 1641 act abolishing the judicial functions of the Council had not applied to colonies (it prohibited "His Majesty or his Privy Council" from adjudicating upon questions relating to the "lands, tenements, heriditaments, goods or chattels of any of the subjects of the Kingdom)", appeals from overseas courts continued to come to the Privy Council. In 1667, the Council Committee for Trade and Plantations heard appeals from Jersey and Guernsey, and in 1696 a formal committee was set up to hear judicial appeals; Holdsworth, 1 *History of English Law* 516, and J. H. Smith, *Appeals to the Privy Council from the American Colonies.*

loss of the American colonies in the eighteenth.[110] Indeed, its work steadily increased over the years. By the 1790s it heard an average of 14 cases a year; by the 1820s it decided twice as many, and the number set down for hearing had trebled.[111] In his speech on legal reform in 1828 in the House of Commons, Brougham claimed that the Privy Council normally sat on only nine feast days for judicial business and that at that time some 517 cases were awaiting disposal. This attack no doubt encouraged a greater efficiency in the Council's judicial proceedings, for in 1828 and 1829 the number of appeals heard rose considerably;[112] but by 1833 the number heard by the council, other than petitions referred to counsel, had dropped to 7.[113] This gave Brougham his chance, and he succeeded in passing a bill to have the judicial functions of the Council firmly established in a Judicial Committee of the Privy Council.[114] Originally the bill had also provided for two paid judges of the Privy Council, to be chosen from retired Indian judges,[115] since appeals were increasingly coming from that part of the Empire, but this clause was modified by Parliament.[116]

By 1833, then, both the House of Lords and the Privy Council had taken on the more obvious guise of courts and were becoming increasingly independent of the legislative and executive organs whose names they bore. By 1834 the importance of these two new courts had become clear to the legal world in London. For the first time since the early eighteenth century, the House of Lords decided more English than Scottish cases,[117] and the Privy Council quintupled its work.[118] To Brougham

110. Until independence, the Privy Council exercised a considerable appeal jurisdiction from the thirteen colonies and the other British concessions abroad. Between 1696 and 1783, the Council heard some 1,500 appeals from 35 different jurisdictions; Smith, *Appeals* 658. Faulty administrative procedure and the absence of any reliable printed reports gave the Council a partially undeserved reputation as a poor appeal court with little standing in the colonies; ibid. 660. For Privy Council appeal statistics, 1790–1836, see 5 *H.L. Sessional Papers* (1836), at 239.

111. In 1827, 53 appeals were set down for hearing and 30 appeals decided; 4 *H.L. Sessional Papers* (1836), at 9.

112. In 1828, 55 appeals were heard; in 1829, 68; ibid.

113. At this time the Privy Council used counsel rather like official referees; 20 *H.L. Sessional Papers* (1841), at 519.

114. 3 & 4 Will. 4, c. 41.

115. 3 *Public Bills* (1833), at 427, 436.

116. There was already some suggestion that Brougham was inventing the posts for his friends, not excluding himself. In 1833, however, Sir Edward Hyde-East (formerly Chief Justice of Bengal) and Sir Alexander Johnson (formerly Chief Justice of Ceylon) were appointed to the Judicial Committee. On this, see Swinfen, "Brougham and Privy Council" 406.

117. Of the 49 cases heard, 29 were from England. Of these, 24 were appeals from Chancery; 22 *H.L. Sessional Papers* (1834). No doubt Brougham's midnight sittings in the Chancery Court and the emancipation of the Master of the Rolls accounted in part for this increase in Equity appeals.

118. Thirty-four ordinary appeals were heard, and 8 petitions were heard by counsel; 18 *H.L. Sessional Papers* (1841).

it was illogical that there should be two final appeal courts in London, with the House of Lords handling English, Irish, and Scottish appeals, while the Judicial Committee of the Privy Council handled the rapidly growing number of British jurisdictions abroad and domestic ecclesiastical and admiralty cases. Brougham therefore introduced a bill that in effect merged the two courts by providing that, with few exceptions, any appeal or writ of error to the House, as well as divorce proceedings before it, might be referred to the Judicial Committee of the Privy Council.[119] The measure was, however, never discussed,[120] for the Whig government fell in November 1834, an event attributed by Melbourne, who succeeded Grey as Prime Minister earlier in the year, partly to Brougham's unbecoming behavior.[121] Whatever the cause for the government's fall, Melbourne was determined not to return Brougham to the Woolsack when the Whigs returned to power after the Hundred Days of Peel's administration.

The Impact of the Great Reform Act

In political terms, the Reform Act of 1832 had its chief impact on the House of Commons. The new franchise heralded four decades of legislative reform, for the most part based on utilitarian principles. The old Tory party was dying. Peel with his Tamworth Manifesto of 1834 and his repeal of the Corn Laws in 1846 both built and destroyed a new conservative coalition; yet he was to lay the foundations of a new Conservative party that would be finally shaped by Disraeli.[122] The Whigs, too, slowly changed. By the 1870s the Liberal party was the party of the "Left," comprised of an unhappy alliance of Whigs, liberals, and radicals, bound together by no particular logic or beliefs.[123] It was little wonder that Queen Victoria and Anthony Trollope still hankered for coalitions.

119. The bill required either the Lord Chancellor or the Chief Justice of King's Bench to preside, but provided for a permanent Vice-President of the Council and gave the Council the power to summon the judges from any of the United Kingdom jurisdictions; H.L. Sessional Papers (1834), 1st part at 1265. Also reproduced in MacQueen, *Appellate Jurisdiction*, Appendix 12. And see Swinfen "Brougham and Privy Council" 406–7.

120. Charles M. Denison and Charles H. Scott, *House of Lords Appeal Practice* (London, 1879).

121. Brougham could not understand this suggestion. For Melbourne's increasingly blunt explanations, see David Cecil, *Melbourne* 234–35. *The Times* shared Melbourne's view. Campbell, "Life of Lord Brougham" 449.

122. Robert Blake, *The Conservative Party from Peel to Churchill*, chaps. 1 and 2.

123. Contrast, for instance, the typical utilitarian commitment in favor of legislating to implement the rubric of "the greatest happiness of the greatest number" with Melbourne's observation that making laws was "only a subsidiary and incidental duty of Parliament: the principal duty of Parliament is to consider the estimates for the public service, to retrench what is superfluous, to correct what is amiss, and to assist the Crown with those supplies and subsidies which it thinks right and necessary to afford"; cited, Woodward, *Age of Reform* 99.

Constitutionally, however, it was the House of Lords that had received the greatest blow. After the Monarchy had, in 1832, accepted responsibility for creating enough peers to impose the will of the majority in the Commons on the House of Lords, many felt there was no future for the House. Lyndhurst confided to Grenville that "there was no chance of the House of Lords surviving ten years,"[124] and, immediately after the 1832 Reform Act, it did seem as if the powers of the Lords were permanently truncated. When, for instance, in June 1833 Wellington persuaded the Lords to defeat the government on its policy toward Portugal, Grey ignored the vote; confidence within the Commons was enough to continue the administration.[125]

The Lords' morale, however, slowly returned and they discovered during the debates on the Municipal Corporations Bill of 1835 that they could savagely maul a Commons bill and prevail, unless it was a matter on which the Commons felt so strongly that they were prepared to have a constitutional confrontation. Indeed, in the late thirties and forties the Lords gave the impression of institutional consolidation. Although by then clearly less important than the Commons, the Lords were still prepared to obstruct and delay legislation on matters about which they felt strongly, while willing to jettison their less important privileges. Nowhere was this latter willingness more obvious than in the matter of the appellate jurisdiction. In 1834 the Lords for the last time decided an appeal without any law lord present;[126] in 1844 the convention that lay lords never vote was established.

No doubt this latter decision was not a clear and conscious one; other factors were at work. By the late thirties there were seven law lords—that is, former Lord Chancellors or ennobled judges;[127] a "professional" court was at last possible. The definition of a law lord was still vague,[128] but the duty of the lay lord was increasingly clear: he was to be

124. Philip W. Wilson, ed., 1 *The Greville Diary* 518.
125. Ibid. 517.
126. Holdsworth, 1 *History of English Law* 377; Twiss, 3 *Life of Eldon* 232–33. On 17 June 1834 the hearing of a writ of error began without a law lord present and with Lord Abingdon on the Woolsack. The common law judges attended and gave their opinions, and then the lay peers present spoke and voted; Turberville, "The House of Lords as Court of Law" 189 ff.
127. Melbourne at first put the Great Seal in commission, thus bringing chaos into the judicial business of the House, with Lyndhurst and Brougham presiding alternately. Brougham then engineered the promotion of Denman, Chief Justice of King's Bench, to the Lords and, to help with the work, Vice-Chancellor Shadwell sat as Deputy Speaker in 1835. Then in January 1836 Pepys was made Lord Chancellor with the title of Lord Cottenham, and the opportunity was also used to create Bickersteth, Master of the Rolls, a peer with the title of Lord Langdale. Shortly thereafter Best, Chief Justice of Common Pleas, was created Lord Wynford, although he sat irregularly. The House could, however, count on Lord Plunket, Lord Chancellor of Ireland.
128. William Courtenay, who became Earl of Devon in 1835, was treated as a law lord, speaking and voting in a number of important cases in the later 1830s. See, for

a nonvoting member of the quorum in appellate hearings.[129] Although it took fifty years for this last convention finally to be accepted, the increase in judicial work during this period[130] meant that the appellate functions became increasingly differentiated from the other work of the House. Until this point the House of Lords had made relatively little contribution to the common law of England and only a limited one to equity. Henceforth, with the adequate supply of law lords,[131] there was a much greater opportunity to shape English law, and even the reputation of the House in Scottish cases apparently improved somewhat during this period.

The presence of a quorum of law lords and the end of the need to require attendance of lay peers not unnaturally put into the minds of reformers the idea of giving statutory effect to this professionalized court. Soon after he became Chancellor in 1836, Lord Cottenham introduced two bills—the one relieving the Lord Chancellor of all his duties in the Court of Chancery, at the same time making him President of the Judicial Committee of the Privy Council; and the other enabling the House of Lords to sit throughout the year for judicial business, not merely during the legislative sessions. Despite the enthusiasm of a few reformers, the bills aroused opposition in the Lords and were easily negatived.[132] The

---

instance, his speech in the leading case of *Attwood v. Small*, 6 Cl. & F. 232, 327 (H.L. 1838). The final vote was 3–2 (Devon, Cottenham, Brougham; Lyndhurst, Wynford dissenting). The Earl of Devon had, however, held only minor judicial office (called to the bar, 1799; Commissioner of Bankrupts, 1802–17; Master in Chancery, 1817–26; and Clerk Assistant of the Parliaments, 1826–35); Robert Megarry, *Miscellany-at-Law* 11.

129. The ballot had by this time lapsed, but a modified form of the rota still existed. Lay peers were informed by letter from the Speaker of the days on which they were required to attend for judicial business; MacQueen, *Appellate Jurisdiction* 31.

130. In 1835 the House sat for 80 days for judicial business and heard 58 cases, 42 of them from Scotland. In the 5 years from 1840 to 1845, the pressure of work dropped somewhat, although with the change of ministries in 1841 there were some judicial arrears; to overcome this, the House for a while sat for 4 days a week; Campbell, "Life of Lord Lyndhurst" 138. The House sat for judicial business on an average 52 days a year, and heard some 35 cases—averaging 20 from Scotland, 9 from England, and 6 from Ireland; 20 *H.L. Sessional Papers* (1850). Also by this date the Appeals Committee was sitting about once a fortnight to deal with procedural issues; MacQueen, *Appellate Jurisdiction*.

131. In 1841, Lord Campbell became Lord Chancellor of Ireland and received a peerage. Since the Melbourne administration fell only six weeks after this event, he had thereafter little to do but sit in the House and Privy Council. Thus, the main appellate work was undertaken by Campbell, Lyndhurst, Brougham, and Cottenham. Although individually (especially Brougham) they may have left something to be desired, these law lords gave the House for the first time a reputation as a serious court of law; "a most satisfactory tribunal," said the critical Bethell (later Lord Westbury) of this period, speaking of the judicial functions of the House in 1844; *Minutes, Select Committee* (1856), at 1.

132. 35 *Parl. Deb.*, H.L. (3d ser.), col. 413 (13 June 1836). Some relief for the Chancellor was obtained by the appointment of two Vice-Chancellors in 1841; 5 Vict., c. 5 (1841). Their impact was, however, weakened by the transfer of the Equity Jurisdiction of the Exchequer to the Chancery Court.

ideas embodied in them, however, remained alive, and the idea of solving the problem of the House of Lords and Privy Council in one fell swoop looked increasingly attractive, especially since lay participation in the Judicial Committee of the Privy Council remained significant.[133]

In 1841 Brougham returned to the subject of reform of the Privy Council.[134] The following year Campbell developed a plan to merge the appellate function of the Lords and the Council.[135] Unlike Brougham's plan of the previous year, Campbell's suggested changes were debated at length. They were opposed by Lyndhurst, who was unconvinced of the need to unify the two final courts of appeal and, since the convention that lay peers not vote in legal appeals was not yet established, feared that a session in the autumn might involve political debates as well as deciding judicial issues.[136] Brougham also opposed the bills. He had twice proposed schemes to join the two courts, but in general, by this time he tended to vote with the Tories, and in particular, he was not fond of Campbell. The bill thus failed at its Second Reading.[137] Such politicking did not discourage Brougham from reintroducing, two years later, his plan for salaried judges of the Privy Council.[138]

133. Lord Wharncliffe, Peel's Lord President of the Council, 1841–46, sat in no less than 61 appeals; Judicial Committee Return, 26 Feb. 1856, 1 *H.L. Sessional Papers* (1856), Rep. 43, at 9.

134. He revived his scheme for paid judges in its Judicial Committee. In particular, he envisaged himself as President of the Judicial Committee, and his protégé, the Earl of Devon, as Vice-President, both offices to carry a salary; Campbell, "Life of Lord Brougham" 525. It was Brougham who, presiding over the Committee for Privileges, to everyone's surprise (including that of the petitioner), had revived the Earldom in favor of the Courtenay family. Since the government refused to support such a move, Brougham dropped his plan, and incidentally, spent less time hearing appeals in the Privy Council.

135. He resurrected the idea of transferring the jurisdiction of the Privy Council to the House of Lords. For this purpose Campbell introduced three bills: The first transferred the jurisdiction. The second allowed the House to sit throughout the year for judicial business as well as providing for the summoning of the Equity, ecclesiastical, and admiralty judges to give their opinions, in the same way that the common law judges had traditionally been summoned to the Lords. The third transferred Irish ecclesiastical and admiralty appeals to the Lords; 2 *H.L. Sessional Papers* (1842), at 9, 13, 197.

Of course, for much of modern legal history, there had been virtually no Equity judges to summon, and yet the common law judges could not be asked points of equity. For a fascinating way around that problem, see *Phipps* v. *Ackers*, 134 Eng. Rep. 453; [1558–1774] All E.R. 381n (1842). There the common law judges were invited to give their opinions on the common law about vested remainders subject to divestiture. The law lords then discussed whether the same rules would apply to an equitable interest and held that they did.

136. 70 *Parl. Deb.*, H.L. (3d ser.), cols. 1248, 1266; 72 ibid., c. 175.

137. *An Annual Register of World Events for 1842*, at 200.

138. His plan called for a permanent head of the Judicial Committee, at a salary of £2,000 per year, to be assisted by two persons with salaries of £1,500 and £1,200. The bill, although read a second time in the Lords, evoked considerable hostility: there was still a strong suspicion that Brougham intended forcing himself into the presidency of any new court. The bill was therefore referred to a Select Committee; 73 *Parl. Deb.*, H.L. (3d ser.), cols. 691 ff. (8 Mar. 1844). When it emerged, it no longer contained the

In that year, however, 1844, a far more significant event occurred. Daniel O'Connell, who had been a thorn in the side of English politicians since the late twenties, was arrested as a result of his political activities in Ireland. He was tried at the bar of the Queen's Bench in Dublin and convicted of conspiracy. He appealed by writ of error to the House, alleging a defect in the indictment. The hearing came on before five law lords—Brougham, Lyndhurst, Denman, Cottenham, and Campbell; and the twelve common law judges were also summoned to attend for their advice. The judges gave their opinion first, the majority denying error. The law lords then made their speeches; Brougham and Lyndhurst were in favor of upholding the conviction, the other three for reversal by allowing the writ of error. At this point the voice vote was held and various lay peers purported to vote with the minority of the law lords. A general debate then broke out. The Earl of Stradbroke, in particular, "having considered the matter most maturely," was anxious to deliver a speech. The Peel administration had foreseen the possibility of some such attempt on the part of lay peers, and although they stood to lose by the reversal, Peel, who was firm on the subject,[139] sent a senior member of the cabinet, Lord Wharncliffe, Lord President of the Privy Council,[140] down to the House to prevent a crisis. Wharncliffe counseled that:

[Y]our Lordships should not divide the House upon a question of this kind, when the opinion of the law Lords have been already given upon it. . . . In point of fact, my Lords, they constitute the Court of Appeal; and if noble Lords unlearned in the law should interfere to decide such questions by their votes instead of leaving them to the decision of the law Lords, I very much fear that the authority of this House as a Court of Justice would be greatly lessened. . . . It is far better that the character of this House as a Court of Appeal and a Court of Law should be maintained, even though the decision should, in the opinion of your Lordships, be objectionable, as being contrary to that of the Judges, and although it should

---

clauses dealing with paid judges, and those clauses dealing with procedural and administrative reform were then passed into law.

139. Before the decision by the Lords, Peel wrote to Sir James Graham (7 Apr. 1844): "On one point I have a very decided opinion. You ask 'Is the decision to be left to the Law Lords, or is a political vote to be taken?' I answer at once, the decision ought to be left to the Law Lords, and on no account a political vote be taken." After the decision, Peel wrote to Brougham (21 Sept. 1844), making it clear that his purpose was unshaken. "The permanent evil of overruling the majority of the Law Lords by the votes of unprofessional Peers would have been, I think, greater than the reversal of the sentence"; Charles S. Parker, ed., 3 *Sir Robert Peel*, 124–26.

140. As Lord President, Wharncliffe, a layman, frequently presided in judicial appeals in the Privy Council. Greville, who among other things was clerk to the Privy Council, opined that Wharncliffe "was very far from being a man of first-rate capacity, but he had good strong sense, liberal opinions, honesty, straight-forwardness, and courage. . . . Perhaps the moment in his life when he appeared to the greatest advantage was when he stood by in the House of Lords and prevented the Tory Peers from swamping the decision of the Law Lords in O'Connell's case"; Lytton Strachey and Roger Fulford, eds., 5 *The Greville Memoirs, 1814–1860*, at 268–69.

prove inconvenient in this particular instance; it is, I say, under such circumstances, better to concur in the opinion of the majority of the law Lords, than reverse the judgement of those persons who by their education and station must be best able to decide upon subjects of this nature, and who in reality constitute the Court of Law in this House.[141]

Wharncliffe was supported by the Marquis of Clanricarde and the Earl of Verulum. The lay peers thereupon withdrew, and the House of Lords as a professional court, distinct from the legislative functions of the House, was, for all practical purposes, established.[142]

It took time for the impact of Wharncliffe's actions to be appreciated. At first Brougham regretted that the lay peers had withdrawn,[143] but he then contented himself with demanding that the government create enough law lords to give it a majority in the House.[144] Meanwhile, many of the Tory peers were furious with Wharncliffe for his action: the man who had led the "hedgers" in 1832 was undermining yet another privilege of the lords. The anger, moreover, came not only from "ditchers" like Lords Redesdale and Stradbroke but also from more reasonable men like Lord Ashburton.[145]

The deed was, however, done. From 1844 on the convention was established. Lay peers may have been recruited to make up a quorum as late as the 1860s,[146] and for many years parties to appeals were still required to print enough copies of their case for each peer to have one; but after 1844 the lay peers had no vote. In the tradition that Bagehot was to describe, no legal change had been made in the formal structure. Even today the Appellate Committee acts as if it were the House of Lords, and lay peers have a legal right to vote. In the British hierarchy of

141. *O'Connell v. R.*, 11 Cl. & F. 155, 421–22; 8 Eng. Rep. 1061 (H.L. 1844).

142. On the *O'Connell* case generally, see MacQueen, *Letter to Lyndhurst* 10; Strachey and Fulford, 5 *Greville Memoirs*; and Campbell, "Life of Lord Lyndhurst" 143–46.

143. Strachey and Fulford, 5 *Greville Memoirs* 189.

144. Campbell, "Life of Lord Brougham" 531.

145. Strachey and Fulford, 5 *Greville Memoirs* 188–89.

146. R. E. Megarry, "Lay Peers in Appeals to the House of Lords" 22, 24. This, however, may have been in connection with the Committee for Privileges. There may have been a layman sitting to make up the quorum in *Rylands v. Fletcher*, L.R. 1 Ex. 265 (Ex. Cham. 1866); L.R. 3 H.L. 330 (1868). Both the Law Reports and the Handwritten Opinion (Judgment) in the Lords Record Office record the speeches by (and presence of) only the Lord Chancellor (Cairns) and Lord Cranworth. It is true, however, that the *House of Lords Journal* for 6 and 7 July records the presence (in the House) of Lord Colonsay.

In *in re Lord Kinross*, [1905] A.C. 468, the Committee for Privileges, Lord James dissenting, held that there was nothing to prevent a peer, who was a barrister, from practicing before the House. Lord Halsbury stated that "[t]he House, when sitting on appeals, is confined to the legal members of the House of Lords"; ibid. 469. Earl Spenser, a lay peer, recalled "very well when I was a mere boy I was called in one morning to make a quorum and I recollect sitting here and hearing appeals"; ibid. 476.

forms of social control, convention may be, however, stronger than law. Any vote a lay peer tried to record would be invalid.[147] Either democracy or utilitarianism triumphed.

147. The last layman who attempted to vote was Lord Denman, son of a Chief Justice of King's Bench, who purported to vote in *Bradlaugh* v. *Clarke*, 8 App. Cas. 354 (1883). His vote was ignored by the Lord Chancellor in the House and also in the report in the official *Law Reports*. But Sir Vernon Harcourt, the Home Secretary, in answer to a question in the Commons, seems to have conceded Denman's legal right to vote in an appeal. See Megarry, "Lay Peers in Appeals," and Herbert du Parcq, "The Final Court of Appeal" 1.

PART ONE

FROM O'CONNELL TO THE PARLIAMENT CRISIS 1844–1912

By 1830 the balanced constitution was effectively at an end, but the reallocation of powers within the political sovereign was to take another hundred years. In the years after the Reform Act of 1832, law and the legal system as a whole were both increasingly professionalized and, at the same time, dissociated from the political system. It seemed natural that the final appeal should be similarly handled. The first step had been taken in 1844 in *O'Connell* v. *R*. Total professionalization almost arrived in the 1870s when the remainder of the court system was restructured, but the restructuring was not extended to the Lords. A second constitutional crisis, that of 1910 and 1911, and a different kind of Lord Chancellor (Lord Haldane) were necessary to achieve such professionalization. Between the two great constitutional crises lay seven decades of tension between law and politics.

TWO

Law, Politics,
and the Appellate Jurisdiction

The Logic of Professionalism

At least for administrative convenience it was increasingly important that the appellate work of the House be undertaken by "law lords," for the nature of Parliament was changing. Melbourne—Victoria's early favorite minister—had taken the view that passing legislation was "only a subsidiary and incidental duty of Parliament." This approach to the Constitution was, however, alien to the leaders of the newly emerging Conservative and Liberal parties. Parliamentary sessions lengthened, and their basic purpose was increasingly that of passing legislation. Some specialization of function was essential to keep up with the spate of utilitarian reform; thus the deciding of disputes that only indirectly made law became more clearly distinguished from legislation, the primary purpose of which was to make law.

The general influence of Benthamite philosophy also meant that the judicial work of the Lords came to be judged by lawyers' standards: as a professional court it was judged by professional standards. The connection of the House of Lords as an appeal court with the House of Lords as a legislative body raised fundamental questions of appropriateness. There was growing interest from outside the House as to the court's procedure, its staffing, the cost of appeals, its role in developing law, and other problems. So long as the caliber of the court remained high, there was little overt hostility to its work by lawyers or other molders of public opinion. The late 1840s saw general satisfaction with the law lords.[1]

1. The main burden of the work in these years fell on Lords Cottenham (1846, 60 days; 1847, 62 days; 1847–48, 60 days; 1849, 34 days), Lyndhurst (1846, 34 days; 1847, 14 days; 1847–48, 7 days; 1849, 9 days), Brougham (1846, 69 days; 1847, 59 days;

Although they produced several bold decisions, there is no evidence of any hostility to the House represented by the law lords' making new law, at least in essentially "legal" areas. While the influence of utilitarian thought probably encouraged a more careful approach toward doctrine, the effect of procedural reforms, not to mention the advent of a mass of new legislation, may well have given the final appeal court even greater scope for judicial legislation.[2] Reform, however, was definitely in the air, especially with respect to the lower courts and the intermediate appeal courts.[3] The whole tendency of the law and the legal system was toward "rationalization," and the law lords deviated from their newly found professional standards only at the risk of aggravating demands for reform.

Concern about the caliber of the law lords began to manifest itself in 1850, when Cottenham resigned the Chancellorship, and, in the phraseology of the Constitution, the Great Seal—the symbol of the Lord Chancellorship—was once again "put into commission," rather than given to any one person. The shortage of reliable law lords rapidly became ap-

---

1847–48, 34 days; 1849, 32 days), and Campbell (1846, 70 days; 1847, 42 days; 1847–48, 56 days; 1849, 31 days). Lords Denman and Langdale sat occasionally; 8 *H.C. Sessional Papers* (1856), at 17.

2. On this, see chaps. 3 and 5. There was certainly no modern view of the judicial function. *The Times*, in reporting a nullity case in which Denman, Lyndhurst, and Campbell had sat with lay peers, revealed that the judges had consulted Brougham on the evidence although he had not sat; Sargeant Ballentine, *Some Experiences of a Barrister's Life* 83–84.

3. The County Courts Act of 1846 had at last established a regular system of permanent courts throughout the country to try minor civil cases. In 1848 the Court for Crown Cases Reserved finally established a reasonably tolerable system of appeals in the criminal cases and effectively ended the erratic criminal jurisdiction of the House of Lords. Once a regular system of criminal appeals was established there was less attraction in appealing to the House of Lords, where the only means of appeal was by way of writ of error. The technicalities of this writ were remarkable; *Report of the Royal Commission to Consider the Law Relating to Indictable Offenses*; Cd. 2345 (1879). The possibility of such appeals did, however, survive the 1848 act and was used in appeals from Ireland; e.g., *O'Brian v. R.*, 2 H.L.C. 465 (1849). It also survived the Common Law Procedure Act of 1852. Section 148 abolished formal writs of error in civil cases, but stated, "We are clearly of opinion that the section does not include indictments"; per Lord Chief Justice Campbell, *R. v. Searle*, 5 E. & B. 1 (1855). The writ of error in criminal cases even survived the Judicature Acts in a truncated form; Charles M. Denison and Charles H. Scott, *The Practice and Procedure of the House of Lords*. Effectively, however, the criminal jurisdiction of the House of Lords from 1848 to 1907 (Court of Criminal Appeal Act) was nonexistent.

In 1851 an intermediate Court of Appeal in Equity was established, although a plan to allow the Equity judges to be consulted by the Lords was not carried; 117 *Parl. Deb.*, H.L. (3d ser.), col. 1069 ff. (23 June 1851).

In 1852 the Common Law Procedure Act, perhaps the most important act of the century in the field of law reform, went a long way toward freeing the law from its medieval fetters of procedure, as well as making appeals to the Lords simpler. Except in criminal cases, appeals to the Lords were to be by way of petition; Common Law Procedure Act of 1852 § 148.

parent.[4] For the next two years the appellate function was again dominated by the energetic and increasingly enigmatic Brougham.[5] The year
1852 saw the creation of two new law lords: St. Leonards, who was Lord
Chancellor in Lord Derby's brief administration, and Cranworth, who
became Lord Aberdeen's Chancellor. For the next few years Brougham,
St. Leonards, and Cranworth carried out the House's judicial functions.[6]
The activities of this trio, however, were less than satisfactory. They
could rarely agree with one another, and their general demeanor left
much to be desired by way of judicial temperament.[7]

Dissatisfaction grew on all sides. All manner of defects were alleged.
The enormous cost of appeals to the Lords was publicized for the first
time, and discontent was voiced about a court that sat only for that part
of the year during which the legislature also happened to be sitting.
Concern was also expressed about the method of hearing appeals. Some
thought it no longer appropriate for the final appeal court to masquerade
as a legislature. Advocates of the scientific utilitarian view of law would
have been happy to see a single judgment of the final court rather than—
as was the custom—a series of frequently unrelated speeches. (In fairness,
reasoned speeches in each case were still a novelty.) What concerned
everyone, however, was the actual membership of the judiciary—in particular the changing composition of the legal members of the House, the
absence of a regular supply of law lords, the absence of a Scottish judge,
and the need to rely from time to time on the presence of lay peers who,

4. Lyndhurst was no longer available and Campbell, who succeeded Denman as Chief
Justice of King's Bench in that year, was only rarely so.

5. Brougham, who only two years previously had been toying with the idea of becoming a French citizen and entering the National Assembly after the revolution of 1848, was
in his element. He made himself de facto Chancellor and began hearing many cases alone,
save only for the nominal presence of two lay peers. In 1850 Brougham sat for 40 out of the
41 days on which cases were heard; Cottenham, 11; and Campbell, 10. No other law lord
appeared; 50 *H.L. Sessional Papers* (1856). The public outcry persuaded the government to
take the Great Seal out of commission, and Lord Truro became Chancellor. Brougham,
however, persuaded Truro to concentrate his efforts on the Court of Chancery, while he
himself proceeded in his erratic way to hear a great number of cases. "The number of cases
knocked off in the Lords has been considerable"; *Daily News*, cited 113 *Parl. Deb.*, H.L.
(3d ser.), col. 845 (6 Aug. 1850). On this period, see also John Campbell, "Life of Lord
Brougham," 8 *Lives of the Lord Chancellors, passim*.

In the following session Truro and Brougham ran the House together, Truro sitting on
each of the 39 days set aside for judicial business; 50 *H.L. Sessional Papers* (1856).

6. In 1852, of 48 days of judicial business, Brougham sat for 32 and St. Leonards for
43. 1852–53: of 80 days of business—Cranworth, 67; Brougham, 40; St. Leonards, 36.
1854: of 78 days of business—Cranworth, 78; Brougham, 71; St. Leonards, 43. 1854–55:
of 83 days of business—Cranworth, 82; Brougham, 58; St. Leonards, 48; ibid.

7. See generally Campbell, "Life of Lord Brougham" 579, and J. B. Atlay, 2 *Victorian
Chancellors* 47; and see specifically *Minutes of Evidence*, Select Committee on the Appellate Jurisdiction, 8 *H.L. Sessional Papers* (1856).

in those years when there was a shortage of law lords, still operated on the exotic rota system.[8]

Breaking point was finally reached in 1855. In that year, Sir Richard Bethell (later Lord Westbury), at that time Palmerston's Solicitor-General, declared in the Commons that the "judicial business was conducted before the Supreme Court of Appeal in a manner which would disgrace the lowest court of justice in the kingdom."[9] Even Lord Campbell, who had set himself up as defender of the House of Lords, was forced to confess later in the year that "the judicial business in the House of Lords could not go on another Session as it did in the last."[10] Once it was abundantly clear that the House of Lords was a significant force in English law and the English legal system, certain minimum standards had to be met. So long as the Lords had felt institutionally secure, they were prepared largely to ignore the appellate process. By the middle of the century, however, they felt politically less secure and were sensitive to change. Moreover, although utilitarian notions were sweeping the country, some still thought the House had a legitimate legislative function to exercise when deciding judicial appeals.[11] In their efforts at reform, the Palmerston administration had to wrestle with these problems—and more.

Advised by his Solicitor-General, Bethell, Palmerston first decided to solve the complaint about an inadequate judiciary by giving life peerages to various leading lawyers. Instead of assuming that fate would provide enough lawyer-peers, lawyers were to be whisked magically into the peerage. The first two such creations were to be Parke, a Baron (judge) of the Exchequer Court, and Dr. Lushington, a widely respected civilian (ecclesiastic and admiralty lawyer).[12] In January 1856 Parke—who, incidentally, had no children, thereby in theory making his elevation less offensive to the more conservative peers—received his Letters Patent as a life peer. At once violent opposition erupted from the conservatives in the Lords, led by Lord Derby, and the lawyers, led by Lord Campbell and

8. For a tabulation of the main objections to the appellate jurisdiction, see *Select Committee on the Appellate Jurisdiction, 20 May 1856* 1 H.L. *Sessional Papers* (1856), Rep. 46.

9. Cited, Campbell, "Life of Lord Brougham" 582.

10. Cited, Thomas A. Nash, 1 *Life of Lord Chancellor Westbury* 170.

11. This was no longer Brougham's position. Having regretted that the lay peers had not voted in O'Connell's case, by 1856 he opined, "Does not all the world know, except very illiterate persons indeed, that it is the law lords who really constitute the Court?" *Minutes*, Select Committee (1856), at 11.

12. Campbell alleges that Pemberton Leigh was first offered a peerage but he refused to be "pitchforked." A peerage was then offered to Lushington, "but who, having a large family and small means, could not accept an hereditary peerage. A life peerage being proposed, he said he could not stand the obloquy of being the first peer for life, but would not mind following in the wake of another. Baron Parke was fixed upon for the experiment, and in an evil hour he consented to its being made upon him"; John Campbell, 2 *Life of Lord Campbell* 338–39; Campbell, "Life of Lord Brougham" 582–83.

Lord Lyndhurst. Derby raised the matter at the beginning of the session, and the House of Lords discussed it at length in February. Lyndhurst was particularly incensed, asking what "has the profession of the law done to merit this indignity?" and, although Britain boasts no written Constitution nor any clear concepts of constitutionalism, alleged that the appointment was a "flagrant violation of the principles of the Constitution." On a motion of Lyndhurst's the matter was referred to the Committee for Privileges, which, relying on its implicit belief in the hereditary principle rather than on the precedents in favor of life peerages (or on the advice of the existing law lords), reported that there was no prerogative power to create life peers.[13] The rather quaint outcome of all this was that Parke was then given a hereditary peerage, with the title of Lord Wensleydale.[14] Dr. Lushington was given nothing.

The government subsequently sought to persuade the Lords to agree to statutory changes that would allow the creation of life peers. The attempt was to no avail, and the government was defeated again. This move served to renew demands by members of the House of Commons for the reform of the appeal systems.[15] At this point, however, the opponents of the reform in the Lords were split. It was possible to oppose dilution of the hereditary principle while being committed to reform of the courts. Derby, the Conservative leader in the Lords, did not want to see life peers created under the prerogative, but he did look for reform in the appellate functions of the Lords. Indeed, he supplied the Lords with a list of defects in the appellate jurisdiction[16] and added that if the choice became one of maintaining their jurisdiction at the expense of the proper administration of justice, he had no doubt that the House would choose the latter.[17] Campbell was annoyed by Derby's position, since he thought Derby had given too much ammunition to the enemy.[18] Derby, however, pressed on, and the House accepted his motion to set up a Select Committee to Study the Appellate Jurisdiction.

13. *An Annual Register of World Events for 1856*, at 85.

14. John F. MacQueen, *Report of the Debates on the Life Peerage Question in the House of Lords*. Lushington, who had not thus far been nominated as a life peer, was never elevated.

15. See especially the speech by Bowyer, 7 Mar. 1856, outlining the defects of the Lords and suggesting reforms; 140 *Parl. Deb.*, H.L. (3d ser.), cols. 2045 ff.

16. The list of defects was as follows: (1) small number of judges; (2) noncompulsory attendance; (3) uncertainty about the number of judges because of (2); (4) failure of justice, especially where the judges are divided and no judgment is given; (5) appeal from one judge in one capacity to some judge in another capacity; (6) tribunal sits only half a year; (7) not an adequate tribunal to decide Scottish appeals; ibid., cols. 1448 ff. (28 Feb. 1856).

17. Ibid.

18. John Campbell, "Life of Lord Lyndhurst," 8 *Lives of the Lord Chancellors* 195. See also 140 *Parl. Deb.*, H.L. (3d ser.), cols. 1465 ff. (28 Feb. 1856). He did, however, see some merit in Derby's idea of setting up a Judicial Committee of the Lords, which would sit in an adjoining room; ibid. at 1469.

The Select Committee mirrored the various forces swirling around the operation of the Lords as a final court of appeal. Lines were not clearly drawn. St. Leonards, Lord Chancellor in the Derby administration of 1852, thought that lay peers should still be free to vote in those cases where "they are just as competent to decide;"[19] and the fact that the O'Connell decision was only eight years old was reflected in the evidence to the committee.[20] If Derby were prepared to make noises attractive to the utilitarians, Romilly, a liberal reformer and by then Master of the Rolls, voiced skepticism about the formalism and professionalism generally associated with utilitarianism and unmixed democracy. His argument was that since "[a]ll courts, to some extent, make law; but Courts of Appeal more than any others," the final court should not be composed solely of lawyers, but should have two paid lay lords sitting with the three law lords.[21]

Derby's Select Committee had various delicate matters on its hands. Bethell's so-called courageous frankness[22] led the law lords, whose behavior had been criticized, to insist on appearing before the committee.[23] Bethell, however, also took on the last vestiges of the privilege of lay peers: the making up of a quorum: "[T]o those who come in, and know the constitution of the House of Lords, the only effect, I think, is this, it casts a ludicrousness upon the whole proceeding; upon those who are ignorant of the rule it also produces an evil result, because they come in and see what are called the lay lords, one of them probably reading a book, another writing letters; if they happen to sit together they are conversing; and upon an uninformed spectator the impression would be that they are not attending to their duty."[24] Bethell's solution was to

19. *Minutes, Select Committee* (1856), at 158.

20. The Earl of Caernarvon assumed that lay peers had "laid aside" their judicial function; ibid. 168. The majority of other witnesses assumed this was so, e.g., H. Malins, M.P., ibid. at 45; Sir Fitzroy Kelly, M.P., ibid. at 22; R. Palmer, Solicitor-General, ibid. at 61: "We have got so accustomed to the principle that was acted on in O'Connell's case, that the lay lords, in the exercise of their own sense of what is right, do not think fit to interfere, that we do not contemplate such an intervention." On the other hand, Lord Abinger assumed the lay peers could reappear (ibid. 169), as did Stuart, Vice-Chancellor, if they "suspected" the law lords, citing Sir William Follett as saying that O'Connell's case was "one of the greatest blows to the privilege of the Peerage"; ibid. 174.

21. Ibid. 159.

22. Nash, 1 *Life of Westbury* 149.

23. These particular peers were busy refuting the hints offered by witnesses that they attended irregularly, behaved unjudicially, and disagreed unreasonably. St. Leonards insisted that he got on well with Cranworth to the extent of agreeing with 71 out of 81 of Cranworth's judgments. He also insisted that if they disagreed they did reserve judgment— in at least half the cases. He also saw nothing wrong in affirmance of an appeal 1–1 and hinted that it was sometimes necessary to give a decision without giving reasons. Brougham was similarly anxious to preserve his reputation and clashed violently with Bethell; *Minutes, Select Committee* (1856), at 107, 147, 177.

24. Ibid. 11.

combine the House of Lords and the Judicial Committee of the Privy Council into one court, sitting throughout the year and staffed by an adequate number of professional judges.[25]

The committee, however, was by no means unanimous in its recommendations, although its final report was strongly in favor of reform. In particular, it felt that no appeal should be heard by fewer than three law lords. To ensure the attendance of this number, the committee suggested the appointment of two paid judges as Deputy Speakers of the Lords, to be created life peers. Although the committee rejected Derby's idea of a separate judicial committee to deal with appeals,[26] it did recommend that appeals should be heard at any time during the year and not merely during the legislative sessions.

The Select Committee reported in May and during the same month its recommendations were incorporated in a bill,[27] which was introduced by Cranworth at the end of the month.[28] The bill was welcomed by Campbell and Derby and opposed only by the more eccentric elements in the Lords.[29] It was soon on its way to the Commons,[30] but the spirit of compromise that had existed in the Lords did not survive in the Commons. At the First Reading the Conservative leader, Benjamin Disraeli, announced he would treat the bill as a government one and therefore fair game for party politics.[31] The House was nearing the end of the session, and the bill came under fire, not only from the conservatives,

25. The majority of the English witnesses took a similar view, although each had some favorite reform to propose. Roundell Palmer (later Lord Selborne) would have preferred a single opinion of the whole court.

The committee received confusing advice from the Scottish witnesses. They all seemed to agree that Scottish public opinion favored the continuation of appeals to the Lords; but they could not agree on whether there should be a Scottish member of the House. The Lord Justice-General, the Lord Advocate (Moncrieff), and the Dean of the Faculty (Inglis) all thought there should be a Scottish judge, but the Lord Justice Clerk (Hope) disagreed.

On the question of why there were so many Scottish appeals, views varied. The Lord Advocate suggested that the Scots regarded appeals to the Lords as a lottery; ibid. 85. Mr. Anderson, Q.C. (Scotland), denied that the Scots were more litigious than the English, "but when they go to law they are more persevering in their litigation"; ibid. 98. John Rolt, Q.C. (Scotland), claimed, "It is the consistency of our character; having taken up a view, we maintain it"; ibid. 75.

26. 140 *Parl. Deb.*, H.L. (3d ser.), cols. 1460 ff. (28 Feb. 1856).

27. 51 *H.L. Bills* (1856), at 1.

28. 142 *Parl. Deb.*, H.L. (3d ser.), col. 621 (26 May 1856). Cranworth felt, however, that a quorum of three could be provided without legislating for this.

29. Lord Denman considered the bill superfluous and ominously announced his willingness to sit to make up any quorum. Lord Redesdale opposed the idea of putting life peers on the same level as hereditary members of the Lords, while, at the Third Reading, Lord Dungannon argued that the provision for life peerages was unconstitutional in view of the earlier resolutions of the House and on the ground that the abandonment of the hereditary principle undermined the monarchy; ibid. 1085.

30. 1 *Public Bills* (1856), at 77.

31. 142 *Parl. Deb.*, H.L. (3d ser.), cols. 2078 ff. (1856).

who were shocked that the privileges of the Lords had been tampered with, but also from the radicals, who felt the bill had not gone far enough.[32] The prevailing mood of the House was that of either leaving the Lords alone or making a thorough job of reform; but, as Lord John Russell put it, "[D]o not fall between the two."

Despite this spirit, the bill limped through its Second Reading and reached the Committee Stage. Here the inadequacy of the compromise became all too clear. Neither reformers nor reactionaries were satisfied. Many members of the House had no strong views; the government gave little leadership, but everywhere there was condemnation of the aura of compromise that surrounded the bill. The most telling speech was made by William Gladstone,[33] who by this time was a convert to the liberal cause. If this speech was not enough to kill the bill, the reappearance of the bogey of the royal prerogative to create life peers was; the very social structure of England seemed under attack. Neither Palmerston nor his Solicitor-General was able to save the day, and the House voted to refer the bill to a Select Committee. "This Committee never met."[34] The tension between professionalism and privilege was all too clear. It was the beginning of the lull before the storm.

Democracy, Utilitarianism, and the House of Lords

The lull[35] was made possible partly by the increase in the number of law lords, caused mainly by the rapid change of ministries.[36] During

32. Bowyer felt the bill "inadequate"; ibid. 316. Palmer felt it "weak and unsatisfactory"; ibid. 455. The author of the 1870s legislation at this time thought the defects of the Lords "exaggerated" and felt there were great advantages for the administration of justice in having its "root and foundation head" in the House of Lords; ibid. 459. Cf. Lord Selborne (Roundell Palmer), 3 *Memorials Personal and Political 1865–1895*, at 307, where he says he supported Cranworth's bill but hinted that the Lords' jurisdiction might one day have to be taken away. Sir James Graham made a strong speech against the compromise attitude and would have preferred a stronger bill, while Whiteside believed there was no need for a bill at all.

33. The bill "is a compromise huddled up for the convenience of parties in some committee-room in another place, then brought down to the House of Commons, and presented to us for our acceptance in such a shape, and under such circumstances, that it is not too much to say that if we pass this Bill ... we shall be doing nothing short of abdicating our functions as legislators"; ibid. 600.

34. 51 *H.C. Sessional Papers* (1856), at 450.

35. Occasional questions were still asked about the appellate jurisdiction; e.g., on 17 Mar. 1857 Bowyer asked the Home Secretary whether the government would introduce a measure in the next session setting up an adequate final appeal court; 144 *Parl. Deb.*, H.L. (3d ser.), cols. 2397–98 (17 Mar. 1857).

36. In addition to Wensleydale (Parke), changes of administration brought Chelmsford and Westbury into the Lords and made Campbell regularly available. (Palmerston in 1859 was so desperate for a Chancellor that, to everyone's surprise, he appointed Campbell.) Brougham, fortunately, sat less frequently, and the House was strengthened by the promotion of Lord Colonsay, a Scottish judge, and Lord Kingsdown (Pemberton Leigh), who had

1856 the House caught up with its work; at the end of the year only ten cases were pending. Less satisfactory were the arrangements in the Privy Council, which, while not so professionalized[37] as the Lords, was increasingly competing for the services of the law lords as colonies grew in importance and became more prepared to send appeals to London.[38] The situation was kept in check because the law lords, aided by various procedural reforms,[39] concentrated on the work of the House: litigants before the Council had a less powerful constituency.[40]

The world was, however, changing. The utilitarians were at work in India, and 1867 saw the emergence of the first self-governing dominion, Canada, with the Privy Council acting as guardian of its constitution. The law lords had sometimes reviewed legislation indirectly while sitting in the Privy Council to determine whether it was consistent with the common law, but they were then faced for the first time with judicial

---

already distinguished himself while sitting as a Privy Councillor in the Judicial Committee of the Privy Council.

37. Laymen still played an active role in the work of the Judicial Committee. The Lord President of the Council sat as late as the 1860s, and in 1856, the Select Committee of the House of Lords on the Appellate Jurisdiction was told that when the Duke of Buccleuch, Lord President under Peel, doubted the wisdom of such an arrangement after sitting in an Indian appeal lasting 9 days, he was assured by Pemberton Leigh that he might "depend upon it, the natives of India would much rather have this case decided by a great Scotch Duke than by lawyers alone"; *Minutes, Select Committee* (1856), at 18. Apparently, both the Colonial and Home secretaries sometimes attended and spoke, but after 1833 they were not allowed to vote; ibid. 30. The bishops still formed an important lay element, and in appeals under the Church Discipline Act of 1840 they sat as judges, in other cases as assessors. Thus *Hebbert* v. *Purchas* (1870) was heard by two bishops and two lawyers; ibid. 26.

The report also examined the cost of appeals in the Privy Council. The Registrar of the Privy Council estimated the average cost of an appeal at £300; ibid. 22. There was also an examination of the history and practice of a unanimous opinion. The tradition of a unanimous opinion dated back to a ruling of Charles I, but the ecclesiastical appeals of the midnineteenth century put a strain on the system. Knight Bruce, L.J., registered a public dissent in the *Gorham* cases, and the Archbishops of Canterbury and York in the "Essays and Reviews" case. Unannounced dissents might, however, be recorded in a book provided for the purpose; ibid. 27.

Most of the work of the Judicial Committee came from India and was caused by "considerable appetite for litigation" on the part of the "natives" and by the reform of the Bengal courts in 1862, in the view of Sir Barnes Peacock, legal member of the Council in India and Chief Justice of the High Court in India; ibid. 53. Sir Henry Maine told how the early decisions of the Privy Council in Indian appeals had been largely legislative, laying down basic rules; ibid. 56.

38. In 1857, the Privy Council decided 68 cases and the House of Lords 25. By 1860, the numbers were more equal: 42 in the Privy Council and 49 in the Lords; but there were 81 cases pending before the Council and only 27 before the Lords.

39. Codification of the law was championed and made considerable progress in criminal law; e.g., Larceny Act of 1857. The House benefited directly from the reform of divorce law in 1857; no longer was there the requirement of an act of Parliament, granted only after a quasi-judicial hearing in the Lords, before a divorce could be granted. A Divorce Court was set up and, as with the new Probate Court, the House was concerned solely with appeals.

40. By 1865, 157 cases were pending before the Privy Council.

review in the sense of testing the legality of legislation, passed by the Federal Parliament in Ottawa, against a written constitution (the British North America Act of 1867) designed for a sovereign state. Yet, if judicial review is seen as inconsistent with pure democracy, responsibility with respect to Canada seemed to run against the tide. At home the march toward pure democracy seemed irresistible, and 1867 was its apotheosis.

Eighteen sixty-seven was also the year of publication of Bagehot's classic *English Constitution*. Bagehot believed that the idea of "checks and balances" was out-of-date.[41] The utilitarian solution for the final appeal was therefore simple: "I do not reckon the judicial function of the House of Lords as one of its true subsidiary functions, first because it does not in fact exercise it, next because I wish to see it in appearance deprived of it. The supreme court of the English people ought to be a great conspicuous tribunal, ought to rule all other courts, ought to have no competitor, ought to bring our law into unity, ought not to be hidden beneath the robes of a legislative assembly."[42]

It seemed then as if 1867 would be the high-water mark of intellectual liberalism with its belief in the separation of powers and the beginning of its decline in favor of the more radical tradition of naked democracy. In August 1867, after competition between Liberals and Conservatives, the second Reform Act doubled the electorate by enfranchising the working classes. At almost the same time the spirit of change in the legal structure was carried into the political arena by Roundell Palmer, a former Liberal Attorney-General. A dedicated advocate of the reform of the whole court system, Palmer made a speech in the House of Commons in that same year that led to the rapid establishment of a strong Royal Commission on the Judicature, under the chairmanship of Lord Cairns, the Conservative Chancellor, who became available with the fall of the Conservative administration and the coming into office of the new Gladstone administration.

Yet it may be that some of the appearances of reform were only superficial. Opposition to change by the aristocratic element, especially in the Lords, was a constant in British nineteenth-century history. Increasingly, however, as the century progressed, the reformers were more consciously seeking to replace a landed aristocracy with an aristocracy of talent. Pelling had attributed the pressures that led to the reform of the Civil Service in 1870 less to the pressure of utilitarianism and more to the fear that, after the 1867 act, the Civil Service might fall under the control of the masses as it had in the United States, especially during the Jacksonian period, with the attendant system of spoils.[43] Paternalism and an

41. Walter Bagehot, *The English Constitution* 2.
42. Ibid. 168.
43. Henry Pelling, *America and the British Left*.

effort to prevent direct control by the masses certainly influenced other legislation.[44]

Seen in the sweep of history, the movement to professionalize the judiciary, although not antidemocratic in the traditional political sense, was more similar to Jeffersonian than Jacksonian democracy. It was rule by the liberal aristocracy of talent, not by the voter; and there is considerable evidence to support this analysis. In his generally eulogistic *American Commonwealth*, James Bryce, whose politics were akin to those of Roundell Palmer, could not hide his horror of an elected judiciary.[45] Consciously or not, in the long run utilitarianism, as manifested in law reform, was to provide a bulwark against pure democracy, which might well expect judges, like politicians, either to be elected or at least to be responsive to the whims of the party. In the short run, it was the peers who were to provide that bulwark, at least insofar as they held out for the retention of the appellate jurisdiction.

Utilitarian Attack

Strong as the Judicature Commission seemed and chaotic as the appeal "system" was,[46] it was difficult for the commission's members to talk about the appellate courts frankly because of the delicate constitutional position of the Privy Council and the House of Lords. The *First Report of the Judicature Commission*, published in 1869, recommended the establishment of a single Supreme Court, comprising a High Court and a Court of Appeal. The High Court would contain five divisions representing the three old common law, equity, and civilian (Probate, Divorce, and Admiralty) courts. There would, with minor exceptions, be an appeal in every instance from the different divisions of the High Court

---

44. Forster, the President of the Board of Education, felt the need to "educate our masters"; hence, the Education Act of 1870; E. L. Woodward, *The Age of Reform 1815–1870*, at 462–63.

45. "In America suspicion (of the bench) has arisen only in States where popular election prevails. . . . The shortcomings of the Bench in these States do not therefore indicate unsoundness in the general tone either of the people or of the profession . . . but are the natural result of (the elective) system. . . . Thus we may note with satisfaction that the present tendency is not only to make judges more independent by lengthening their term of office but to withdraw their appointment from popular vote and restore it to the governor, from whom, as a responsible officer, the public may exact the utmost care in the selection of able and upright men"; James Bryce, 2 *The American Commonwealth* 624.

46. The whole process of appeals, although it had been vastly improved during the century, was still rightly described as chaotic. Equity appeals went from the Chancery courts to the Court of Appeal in Chancery and then to the Lords, or, if the appellant followed the correct procedure, they might leap the intermediate court and go directly to the Lords. Appeals from the three common law courts—Queen's Bench, Common Pleas, and Exchequer—went to the Exchequer Chamber and then to the Lords. From the Divorce Court appeal was to a full court of divorce judges and then to the Lords, although from the Probate Court there was a direct appeal to the Lords. Even when appeals were provided,

to the new Court of Appeal. A separate Royal Commission was sitting for Scotland; thus little mention was made of the Lords, which retained its jurisdiction over English, Scottish, and Irish appeals. The report noted, however, that "[it] may hereafter deserve consideration" whether the decisions of the new Court of Appeal should be made final unless either that court or the House of Lords gave leave to appeal.[47] If this plan were to be implemented the House would serve a limited specialized function. From this time forward there was general agreement about the Supreme Court concept; the arguments swirled around the form and location of the final appeal. Since the Supreme Court would have no connection with either house of Parliament, the idea that the House of Lords should retain the power to dispose finally of all cases and retain general supervision of the law would have to be justified anew.

By the time the commission made its first report, Gladstone had returned as Prime Minister, leading what many regarded as the most radical administration of the century. The first move to implement the suggestions of the Judicature Commission was made in 1870, when Lord Chancellor Hatherley[48] introduced the Appellate Jurisdiction Bill of 1870 to give general effect to the recommendations of the Royal Commission.[49] The bill provided for appeals to continue to the Lords, but there was to be a drastic change. The House was to choose a "Judicial Committee" at the beginning of each session, which might include commoner members of the Privy Council (and judges were by then freely made privy councillors), providing there was always a majority of peers.

The bill ran into a sea of trouble. Despite amendments,[50] the idea of a Judicial Committee of the Lords to hear appeals was not acceptable to

---

the system was erratic in determining which appeals might be taken as of right and which might be taken only with leave, and in some cases there was no right of appeal at all. Admiralty and ecclesiastical cases went to the Judicial Committee, as, of course, did appeals from all courts in what was then appropriately called the Empire.

47. *First Report of the Judicature Commission*, 25 H.C. *Sessional Papers* (1868–69), at 1. The report also recommended that if the respondent agreed and there were a point of law involved, an appeal might be made directly to the House of Lords from a court of first instance. Appeals to the Lords, said the commission, should be by petition, and every appeal should be in the nature of rehearing; ibid.

48. Gladstone had wanted to make Palmer (Selborne) his Lord Chancellor, but the latter refused to take office so long as Gladstone proposed to disestablish the Irish Church. (The disestablishment was achieved in 1869.) Selborne eventually became Chancellor in 1872. See Robert Stevens, "The Final Appeal" 346.

49. A unified High Court was to be established and a permanent Court of Appeal. The latter was to replace not only the courts of Exchequer Chamber, and Appeal in Chancery, but also the Court for Crown Cases Reserved, which since 1848 had served as a limited criminal appeals court. The new Court of Appeal was to be made up of four special judges, various ex officio judges, and three judges of the High Court on an annual rotating basis; 3 H.L. *Sessional Papers* (1870), at 37.

50. See amendments by Lord Chancellor and recommitment; ibid. 71.

many peers.[51] Moreover, the judges themselves refused to cooperate with Hatherley.[52] When invited to comment on the bill, they collectively announced: "[U]ntil the whole appellate jurisdiction, including that of the House of Lords and of the Judicial Committee of the Privy Council, shall be dealt with, the amounts of arrears in the latter being of a most formidable description, it will be impossible for the judges to offer any opinion or recommendations which shall be satisfactory to their minds."[53] The view of the judges prevailed. The reform of the House of Lords could wait.

In one sense there seemed little urgency. The Lords, while clearly by then the final court of appeal for England, was, in its work, still heavily weighted toward Scottish appeals.[54] In any event the House was handling its work load effectively,[55] although in the Privy Council the position was absurd. Even though the Judicial Committee had been hearing steadily more cases each year, the expansion of the Empire generally and the reform of the Indian courts in the 1860s, in particular, left a record number of overseas cases waiting to be heard. In 1869, 78 cases were heard, but at the end of the year no less than 329 were pending.[56] During 1870, Lord Kingsdown, who had borne much of the burden of Judicial Committee work, died; fewer cases were heard, and the pressure on the Judicial Committe became even stronger.[57] Clearly there was an urgency about facing this aspect of the appellate process.

During 1870, therefore, Lord Westbury, as Bethell had by then become,[58] harassed Hatherley into producing a bill that would provide a regular judiciary for the Privy Council,[59] but it made little progress.[60] Westbury's prodding of Hatherley was appreciably more successful the following year, 1871. Although a bill severely limiting appeals to the

51. E.g., speech by Lord Redesdale, 200 *Parl. Deb.*, H.L. (3d ser.), cols. 195 ff. (18 Mar. 1870).

52. The uncharitable might attribute some of the judicial lack of enthusiasm for the reforms to the judicial fear (based on fact) that Gladstone intended to cut the salaries of judges. See Stevens, "Final Appeal" 347–48.

53. Letter from the Lord Chief Justice to the Lord Chancellor, 13 May 1870, reprinted, 13 *H.L. Sessional Papers* (1870), at 309.

54. In 1869 the House heard 24 cases: 12 from England (5 Chancery, 6 Common Law, 1 Divorce), 8 from Scotland, and 4 from Ireland (all Chancery). Of the 51 cases in 1870, 19 came from England (13 Chancery, 6 Common Law), 31 from Scotland, and 1 from Ireland (Chancery); *Judicial Statistics* (1869–70).

55. The House heard 51 cases in 1870, leaving only some 34 pending.

56. *Judicial Statistics* (1869). In 1858, 52 cases had been pending, and in 1856, 157; *Judicial Statistics* (1857–58); *Judicial Statistics* (1865).

57. 61 cases were heard, 336 were pending at the end of the year; *Judicial Statistics* (1870).

58. Nash, 2 *Life of Westbury* 219.

59. It provided for 4 salaried judges to be added to the Judicial Committee: 2 chosen from the bar, and 2 from former Indian judges.

60. 203 *Parl. Deb.*, H.C. (3d ser.), cols. 1706 ff. (8 Aug. 1870).

Lords from the three United Kingdom jurisdictions[61] made almost no progress,[62] considerable ground was gained in the reform of the Privy Council. Somewhat against his inclinations, Hatherley introduced a bill to allow the appointment of four paid judges to the Privy Council . The scandal of the backlog of cases this time ensured passage of the bill,[63] but the salary of five thousand pounds proved not enough to tempt members of the English bench to accept such judgeships and led Gladstone into the stupid Collier affair.[64] The whole act was clearly no more than a make-shift.[65] Indeed, in establishing these judgeships, the act included a proviso that "they shall hold their offices subject to such arrangements as may be hereafter made by Parliament for the constitution of a supreme court of appellate jurisdiction." Suddenly everyone had ideas for reforming the final courts of appeal. "Surely the time had come when the House of Lords may be asked to give up a jurisdiction which it has only in name," said Chief Justice Cockburn,[66] while Westbury declared himself in favor of eliminating the jurisdiction of both the Lords and the Privy Council and making one final Imperial Court of Appeal.[67]

At the end of 1871, then, some reform in appeals had been achieved; but much, including the basic recommendations of the Royal Commission on the Judicature, still remained to be implemented. In 1872 there was further activity. Westbury, particularly incensed by the frivolity of some Scottish appeals, reintroduced the bill to limit appeals to the Lords if less than a thousand pounds was involved or the two lower courts agreed, arguing that "it has been said that law is a luxury; but as a luxury it should be restrained by sumptuary law."[68] For the government, Hatherley introduced the Supreme Court of Appeals Bill to set up a

61. House of Lords Appellate Jurisdiction Bill of 1871, 4 *H.L. Sessional Papers* (1871), at 365. It provided that no appeals could be taken to the Lords unless at least £1,000 were at stake, with exceptions for cases certified by judges and certain matrimonial matters. It also forbade appeals from any English, Scottish, or Irish appeal court where the appeal court had agreed with the decision of the lower court, unless the appeal court gave permission or a divorce was involved.

62. 207 *Parl. Deb.*, H.L. (3d ser.), cols. 208 ff. (19 June 1871).

63. Judicial Committee of the Privy Council Act of 1871.

64. One of the qualifications for appointment was being a judge of a Superior Court in England. Gladstone wished to appoint Collier, who was admirably qualified in every way, except that he had never been a judge of a Superior Court. Possibly on Palmer's advice, Gladstone made Collier a judge of the Court of Common Pleas for two days and then promoted him to the Privy Council. The reaction of the judges, the legal profession, and the opposition in Parliament was hostile; John Morley, 2 *Life of William Ewart Gladstone* 382–86; Nash, 2 *Life of Westbury* 222; Selborne, 1 *Memorials* 197. In passing, it is worth noting that this is the only mention made by Morley of any of the legal reforms of the 1870s. The reforms were mostly the work of Palmer (Selborne), whom Morley despised.

65. Nash, 2 *Life of Westbury* 221.

66. Selborne, 3 *Memorials* 307.

67. Nash, 2 *Life of Westbury* 235–36. The court was to be economical, easily accessible, and would sit throughout the year.

68. Ibid. 238.

statutory appeals court to handle the judicial functions of both the House of Lords and the Privy Council,[69] but the bill was not introduced until halfway through the session and looked uncommonly like another of Hatherley's insufficiently considered ideas.[70] Cairns, the former Conservative Chancellor and Chairman of the Royal Commission, was suspicious and suggested an alternative scheme for a final appeal court.[71] The upshot was that the bill was shelved for that session and a Select Committee was appointed to consider the matter further.[72]

The Select Committee of the House of Lords complemented the work of the Royal Commission by making a study of the House of Lords and the Privy Council, both of which had been formally outside the terms of reference of the Judicature Commission. The Privy Council, it emerged, had in fact been transformed by the appearance of paid judges.[73] Similarly, there had been far greater satisfaction with the Lords during the 1860s and 1870s than in the 1850s.[74] The Select Committee, by a narrow majority,[75] came down in favor of a joint Judicial Committee of the House of Lords and Privy Council, based on the Lord Chancellor and four salaried judges. The latter would be known as Lords of Appeal and would be both life peers and privy councillors. Various high judicial

69. 210 *Parl. Deb.*, H.L. (3d ser.), cols. 1228 ff. (15 Apr. 1872). Besides the ex officio members, the bill called for 5 permanent judges of the new appeals court.

70. See, e.g., Lord Cairns' conclusion, "I believe that this measure is a very hurried production"; ibid., col. 2001 (30 Apr. 1872).

71. The most striking difference in the Cairns plan was the inclusion of Scottish and Irish judges.

72. 210 *Parl. Deb.*, H.L. (3d ser.), col. 2012.

73. In 1871 the Judicial Committee sat for 102 days and decided 108 cases; Report of the Select Committee of the House of Lords on the Appellate Jurisdiction, 9 July 1872; Minutes of Evidence 31, 9 *H.L. Sessional Papers* (1872), at 149.

74. There was by then a plentiful supply of law lords, and everyone assumed that lay peers could no longer vote. Indeed, since about 1866 it had been unnecessary to have lay lords to make up a quorum; Minutes of Evidence, 9 *H.L. Sessional Papers* (1872), at 97, 100. The appointment of a Scottish law lord—Lord Colonsay—had given general satisfaction; e.g., per the Lord Advocate; ibid. 65; but it was still necessary to send for the common law judges on an average three times a year to advise the House in English appeals; ibid. 107. Appeals were also expensive. The average cost was £500 per party, largely represented by counsel's fees, although it was probably somewhat lower in Scottish cases; ibid. The delays of the 1840s and 1850s, however, had disappeared, and it was possible to have a case tried in the same session in which it was set down; ibid. 83. Scottish appeals were still often frivolous, and various witnesses suggested curbing appeals involving less than a certain sum. Other witnesses advocated a single appeal court covering both the House of Lords and the Privy Council (e.g., W. J. Farrer, a solicitor, ibid. 90). The Scottish witnesses all appeared to prefer their appeals to go to the Lords rather than any "English" court; e.g., ibid. 67, 88. The constitutional argument raised before the Select Committee of 1856, namely that it would be a violation of the Act of Union, which had provided that there should be no appeal to an English court, was repeated.

75. In fact, a majority of 2. Lord Ossington, in a letter to Selborne dated 17 Oct. 1872, thought that if the matter had been better handled, there would have been a majority for no second appeal at all; Letters, 12 Selborne Papers, Lambeth Palace Library, London.

officers would be ex officio members of the committee, and two former Indian judges were to act as assessors. The salaried judges would be under a duty to attend, and the committee might sit in divisions. The report also suggested that appeals below a certain value should come only with leave and that the new committee should sit throughout the year.

This solution—namely, a second appeal to an Imperial Court of Appeal, clothed with the trappings of the Lords and Privy Council—was not acceptable to Palmer, who became Lord Chancellor with the title of Lord Selborne during 1872. He was determined to push the reform of the judicature and in doing so to strip the Lords entirely of their judicial function.[76] Thus the Judicature Bill of 1873,[77] the most sweeping reform in the history of the English courts up to that time, followed to a large extent the recommendations of the Judicature Commission Report of 1869. A Supreme Court was envisaged, comprising a High Court and a Court of Appeal. Selborne did, however, depart from the recommendations of the commission in the matter of the composition and powers of the Court of Appeal. The bill proposed that this new court should be staffed, in addition to the ex officio judges, by nine permanent appeal judges. All appeals from England would go to this court and would go no further. Double appeals in English cases were abolished by ending appeals to the House of Lords entirely,[78] a solution "at which I did not arrive hastily, or even willingly."[79]

Instead of such a second appeal, it was provided that if a case were of sufficient importance or difficulty,[80] it might be transferred from an ordinary division of three judges of the Court of Appeal to be reheard by a larger or full court.[81] In this sense the nine judges would in major cases operate like the Supreme Court of the United States. The bill assumed that ecclesiastical, Scottish, and Irish appeals would continue as before, but Selborne envisaged that these also would ultimately be referred to his new court, and the bill allowed Scottish and Irish lawyers to become appeal judges.[82] The bill also specifically vested power in the Crown to

76. Gladstone also stressed the "urgency of judicial reconstruction"; Letter from Gladstone to Selborne, 4 Nov. 1872, Letters, 12 Selborne Papers, Lambeth Palace Library, London.

77. 5 *Public Bills* (1873), at 443.

78. Selborne was not satisfied with schemes that kept any semblance of the court's remaining a part of the House of Lords. "I do not propose to connect it, even nominally, with the House of Lords"; 214 *Parl. Deb.*, H.L. (3d ser.), col. 355 (13 Feb. 1873).

79. Selborne, 1 *Memorials* 307.

80. According to Selborne; ibid. 306.

81. § 50 of the bill and § 53 of the act provided that "[a]ny appeal which for any reason may be deemed fit to be re-argued before decision or to be reheard before final judgement may be so re-argued or reheard before a greater number of judges if the Court of Appeal think fit so to direct."

82. Among those allowed to be appointed as additional judges of the Court of Appeal

refer Privy Council appeals from the colonies to the Court of Appeal, and it was the government's intention to refer all such cases.

In introducing his bill, Selborne emphasized that he had never thought of second appeals as a "good system."[83] In his plan to abolish the appellate jurisdiction of the Lords he was supported by Hatherley and Chelmsford, who thought it desirable to have an appeal court, sitting regularly, composed of a fixed complement of judges. The bench and bar seemed in favor of the change,[84] and Selborne was strongly supported by *The Times* and the *Economist*.[85] The Conservative leader for the debates was Cairns. He was a stronger man than Selborne and was able to carry the other law lords with him,[86] as well as the natural conservative majority in the House of Lords. Fortunately for Selborne, Cairns was basically in favor of the reforms and was prepared to lend his support. On the appeal question, as a good conservative, he would have preferred strangling appeals by creating strong appeal courts in all three jurisdictions and putting a pecuniary limit on appeal instead of the outright abolition of the Lords' jurisdiction;[87] but even here he was willing to go

---

were persons qualified to be members of the Judicial Committee of the Privy Council, or persons who had held the office of Lord Justice-General or Lord Justice Clerk in Scotland, or Lord Chancellor or Lord Justice of Appeal in Ireland, "evidently foreseeing a time when their services may be required for the hearing of Scotch and Irish appeals," commented *The Times*; Leader, 27 Feb. 1873, at 9.

83. 214 *Parl. Deb.*, H.L. (3d ser.), col. 349 (13 Feb. 1873). In deference to the House he declared, "[T]here is not a man in it who would be more unwilling to do anything to derogate from the dignity of your Lordships' House in any respect whatever"; ibid., col. 351.

84. Selborne, 1 *Memorials* 308. Chief Baron Kelly wrote to Selborne, "[A]fter about 20 years' experience . . . in every description of cases before the House of Lords, I entirely concur in the wisdom of the 20th clause, putting an end to its appellate jurisdiction, at least as regards the High Court of Justice to be created under your Bill"; letter from Kelly to Selborne, 11 Feb. 1873, 12 Selborne Papers. Romilly, M.R., did, however, register considerable doubts about the desirability of putting an end to the appellate jurisdiction of the House; Confidential Memorandum, Romilly to Selborne, 12 Selborne Papers, Lambeth Palace Library, London.

85. E.g., Leader, *The Times*, 27 Feb. 1873, at 9. Westbury's views vacillated; in the end he was too ill to take part in the debates; Selborne, 1 *Memorials* 302.

86. *Economist*, 3 May 1873, at 524.

87. "I am strongly persuaded that the safe and easy way of dealing with this [the appellate jurisdiction of the House of Lords] is on the 'lines' suggested by the First Report of the Judcl. Comm., i.e., by erecting a very strong Ct. of Appeal in the Supreme Ct. and practically 'choking off' the power of appeal, 1st in a small case, 2nd where there is unanimity in the first two courts, 3rd leaving this court to gain public confidence, and this to lead to a cessation rather than a transfer of the jurisn. It is true that this wd. not meet the case of Scotland and Ireland, but much might be done in strengthening their appellate cts. at home, and there wd. be both reason and advantage in dealing with England first, where a formal reconstruction of the judicial system cannot be delayed"; Letter from Cairns to Selborne, 11 Oct. 1872, Letters, 12 Selborne Papers, Lambeth Palace Library, London.

After reading the bill, Cairns announced that he was generally in favor except on the question of appeals. "On the appellate question, I am glad you have not touched Scotland

along with Selborne's plan in the interests of judicial reform.[88]

Apart from a reference to a Select Committee on a point having nothing to do with appeals to the Lords, as Selborne noted, their lordships parted with the jurisdiction "with less difficulty than might have been expected."[89] The only serious opposition came from a group of backwoods peers, led by Lord Redesdale, the descendant of a Lord Chancellor of Ireland, and Lord Denman,[90] the son of a former Chief Justice of King's Bench, later to distinguish himself as the last layman to attempt to vote in a judicial hearing.[91] Although they paid deference to the work of the House as a court, their chief concern was undoubtedly for the privileges of the House at large and indirectly about the powers of the upper house. In defense of this position, they opposed the measure at all its stages.[92] Outright opposition was, however, slight, since the Conservative leaders made it clear that opposition would be a bad tactical move

and Ireland. I have a strong conviction that until the Scotch and Irish themselves express a desire for it, we have no right to take from them what they regard as an Imperial Tribunal, and to give them a municipal one." Cairns approved the plan to transfer Privy Council appeals to the new Court of Appeal. But he was still reluctant to see the jurisdiction of the House of Lords abolished outright. He continued to favor strangulation. He was particularly concerned with cases when the Court of Appeal was split. "I do not overlook that a further appeal to the House of Lords in such a case might fall to be decided by 2 or 3 law Peers, who again might differ; but the House of Lords on a third hearing has an enormous advantage in the complete discussions that have previously taken place before the first two courts. I own I should much rejoice if either by leaving open an appeal to the House of Lords when the Judges were divided, or when special leave was given, or in some other way, this difficulty could be avoided, for I have every urge and desire to support the measure in its appellate as well as in its general aspect"; letter from Cairns to Selborne, 3 Feb. 1873, Letters, 12 Selborne Papers. In the House, Cairns confirmed that "I am not ignorant of the danger of multiplying appeals, but my objection is that you may go too far in the other direction"; 214 *Parl. Deb.*, H.L. (3d ser.), col. 364 (13 Feb. 1873).

88. 214 *Parl. Deb.*, H.L. (3d ser.), cols. 361 ff. (13 Feb. 1873).

89. Selborne, 1 *Memorials* 305. Lord Cairns observed in his main speech in the House, "The great danger, in my opinion, has always been that some of your Lordships would be tempted to part with your appellate jurisdiction too easily"; 214 *Parl. Deb.*, H.L. (3d ser.), col. 363 (13 Feb. 1873).

90. He had, already in 1872, made his views clear in a letter to Disraeli. He alleged that he was responsible for saving the country £60,000 by successfully opposing the plan for paid life peers in 1856. He also strongly opposed putting "young lawyers" in the House of Lords, since "they introduce uncertainty into the highest court"; letter from Denman to Disraeli, 24 Mar. 1872, Hughenden Papers, B/XII/D/203, Hughenden, Hertfordshire.

91. In *Bradlaugh* v. *Clarke*, 8 App. Cas. 354 (1883). His vote was ignored; *The Times*, 10 April 1883, at 4. He had also attempted to vote in *Bain* v. *Fothergill*, L.R. 7 H.L. 158 (1874), but his vote was not counted; see 227 *Parl. Deb.*, H.L. (3d ser.), col. 913 (1876). Of this case he wrote to Disraeli, enclosing a press cutting of the decision and explaining that he had voted "in accordance with my right" since the speeches of Lords Chelmsford and Hatherley had been "contrary to justice." He also exploded against "Lord Selborne's unconstitutional Bill"; letter from Denman to Disraeli, 25 June 1874, Hughenden Papers, B/XXI/B/212, Hughenden, Hertfordshire. He may have tried to vote in some cases in 1875, since he wrote to Disraeli on 12 June 1875, complaining that his speeches were being suppressed; ibid., B/XXI/D/213.

92. 215 *Parl. Deb.*, H.L. (3d ser.), cols. 391 ff., 1463 (1 Apr. 1873).

from the political point of view.[93] Behind the scenes, however, the Conservative leaders were working to retain the broader notions of sovereignty associated with the Lords. While Salisbury was prepared to see the Court of Appeal as the final appeal court, he argued that its judges should remain members of the Lords. Not only did he feel that "legal strength is essential to the proper performance of its [the House's] duty" and "a fair reparation for stripping it of its ancient jurisdiction," but he also argued that by keeping the judges of the final appeal court as legislators "they are thereby saved from too technical and professional a spirit; and their decisions gain in breadth. Practically they have often to make law as judges, and they will do it all the better from having also to make it as legislators."[94] If Salisbury accepted utilitarian arguments about the structure of courts, he retained his traditional conservative view about judicial legislation.

In the Commons the debate was somewhat livelier. The liberals used the opportunity to castigate the failings of the Lords.[95] Meanwhile, a small group of Conservative M.P.'s attempted to stem any further diminution in the powers and dignity of the Lords.[96] Even this was not a strong feeling. For much of the debate on the Lords' jurisdiction, only twenty to thirty M.P.'s were present, and the amendments moved by William Charley, a Conservative back-bencher, opposing abolition of appeals to the Lords were not even pressed to a vote.[97] The reaction became extreme only when Gladstone, encouraged by Bouverie-Scott and always unable to steer a middle course, moved an amendment at the

93. Letters from Cairns to the Earl of Harrowby, 19 and 22 July 1873, 37 Harrowby Papers, National Manuscript Commission.

94. Letter from Salisbury to Selborne, 24 Feb. 1873, 12 Selborne Papers. Lambeth Palace Library, London.

95. In introducing the Judicature Bill, Sir John Coleridge declared, "For [my] part, [I] would say that if [the] Bill did nothing else but get rid of the House of Lords as a judicial tribunal it would be worthwhile to pass it"; 216 *Parl. Deb.*, H.L. (3d ser.), col. 649 (9 June 1873). The Solicitor-General, Sir George Jessel, noted that "[i]t [is] impossible to calculate upon the continued attendance of octogenarians"; ibid., col. 682. The main weaknesses were the irregular and short sittings, the expense of appeals, the changing composition of the House in legal matters, and the absence of a regular supply of talent to supplement what one member described as "a kind of Greenwich Pensioner"; ibid., col. 847 (12 June 1873).

96. Such members pointed out that the Judicature Commission had not recommended its abolition and the Select Committees of 1856 and 1872 had both recommended retention, while a somewhat rosy picture was painted of the high regard in which its decisions were held; Speech by Charley, ibid., cols. 654 ff. (9 June 1873). It was said to be both popular and economical, but one speaker who claimed such attributes also conceded the real danger in the reform was that it would weaken the overall power of the second chamber; Speech by Bourke, ibid., cols. 659 ff. Other speakers opposed the existence of three different appeal courts—the House of Lords, the Privy Council, and the new Court of Appeal—and the effect that the new court might have on Ireland and Scotland. But the objection, such as it was, was an emotional one, opposing any loss of dignity on the part of the peers; Speech by Newdegate, 217 *Parl. Deb.*, H.C. (3d ser.), col. 338 (14 July 1873).

97. 216 *Parl. Deb.*, H.C. (3d ser.), col. 900 (12 June 1873). The *Economist* described Charley's amendment as "absolutely lifeless . . . and . . . well known to be so"; 14 June

committee stage to send Irish and Scottish appeals to the new Court of Appeal rather than to the Lords.[98] Selborne, in introducing the bill into the House of Lords, had openly conceded that he left Irish appeals with the House of Lords for fear of stirring up a "hornet's nest," which the transfer of appeals to a new English court might appear to the Home Rulers; and he felt the Scots had not yet been sufficiently consulted to justify transferring their appeals to the new court.[99]

When Gladstone unwisely agreed to transfer all United Kingdom appeals to the court, he not only stirred up the Celtic wrath, but the opposition claimed that the amendment was a breach of the privileges of the House of Lords, in that bills and clauses affecting the right of peerage could be introduced only in the Lords.[100] The debate was heated and lasted several days. Although Gladstone denied the existence of such a privilege, it became clear that unless he yielded in the Commons, the House of Lords would later hold up the whole bill.[101] Appeals from Ireland and Scotland were therefore left with the Lords, although English appeals would no longer go there,[102] and the power to transfer the Privy Council jurisdiction to the Court of Appeal was retained.[103] The bill was given its Third Reading in both houses; the Royal Assent was received in August 1873;[104] and the act was set to come into force in November 1874.[105] Utilitarian concepts apparently had triumphed.

1873, at 713. *The Times* commented that Charley's amendment "needlessly delayed" the whole bill; Leader, 11 June 1873, at 11. Of efforts by Mr. Lopes and Sir R. Baggallay to save the Lords' jurisdiction, *The Times* said, "[T]hese speakers, and they who go with them, labor under the fatal weakness of trying to repulse an attack on an abandoned fortress"; Leader, 13 June 1873, at 9.

98. 216 *Parl. Deb.*, H.C. (3d ser.), cols. 1561 ff. (30 June 1873). In January, Gladstone had taken the line that he did "not suppose the Irish and Scotch appeals would long survive the withdrawal of English appeals to the tribunals"; letter from Gladstone to Selborne, Letters, 12 Selborne Papers, Lambeth Palace Library, London.

99. 214 *Parl. Deb.*, H.L. (3d ser.), col. 1738 (11 Mar. 1873). Such exclusions led *The Times* to talk of "the Lord Chancellor's timid legislation"; Leader, 1 July 1873, at 9.

100. Cairns raised the question in the House of Lords on 8 July; 217 *Parl. Deb.*, H.L. (3d ser.), cols. 10 ff. (8 July 1873). It is not clear whether Cairns was acting in his own interest, or was responding to emotional Conservative elements. His action earned him the distrust of the Liberal press, already exhausted by the behavior of the House of Lords. The *Economist* talked of "the forces of organized destruction which the Conservative ex-Chancellor commands," and noted that "the country will not forget that to win a momentary triumph the Conservative leaders did not hesitate to endanger the success of the great measure of the Session, the importance of which they do not deny, and to embroil the two Houses of Parliament in a sterile controversy"; 12 July 1873, at 836 ff.

101. See Leaders, *The Times*, 3 July at 11, 15 July at 9, 16 July at 9, all in 1873.

102. § 20 provided that there should be no appeal from the Court of Appeal to either the House of Lords or the Privy Council. The latter provision was necessary because Admiralty appeals had previously gone to the Privy Council.

103. § 21 gave power to transfer the jurisdiction of the Privy Council to the Court of Appeal by Order in Council.

104. Supreme Court of Judicature Act of 1873.

105. For the detailed provisions of the act and commentaries thereon, see Freeman

Oligarchic Counterattack

Throughout the period when the 1873 bill was being discussed, Gladstone's political position was almost untenable. Indeed, shortly after the Judicature Bill had been introduced his ministry resigned, having been defeated on the Irish University Bill, and Gladstone recommended to the Queen that Disraeli be invited to take office with a minority government. Disraeli, however, was too skillful a politician, and after a week out of office, Gladstone was forced to return. He did not seek a dissolution of the House, but allowed his government to limp along. He had already told the Queen that he was tired and felt his mandate exhausted; in fact, the largely nonpartisan Judicature Act was the only major legislation that emerged from his government during its remaining months. The Gladstone administration had by then been in office for more than five years and had offended vested interests ranging from the army to the brewers. The by-election results became steadily more hostile, and in February 1874 Gladstone's first administration finally came to an end. The ensuing general election brought in the Conservatives with a comfortable majority.[106]

Disraeli, the new Prime Minister, was faced with many more pressing problems than the appellate jurisdiction of the House of Lords. But the vicissitudes about its future form a fascinating chapter in the history of his ministry. The story is one of intrigue, legislation, and counterlegislation that virtually defies unraveling.[107] The main dramatis personae were Selborne, Cairns, Disraeli, and Charley. The Judicature Act of 1873 had been Selborne's. "It was the work of my own hand, without any assistance beyond what I derived from the labours of my predecessors; and it passed, substantially, in the form in which I proposed it."[108] Moreover, Selborne was prepared to use every device to keep the act in the terms in which it was passed. Only with respect to the appellate procedure did he stand any serious chance of having his work undone; for on most matters the act was bipartisan. Cairns, once again Lord Chancellor, had no particular love for the Lords as an appeal court, although, as has been seen, he would have preferred a strengthening of the intermediate appeal courts in all three jurisdictions in the hope that the Lords would then die a natural death; but since the Lords had given up their jurisdiction, he felt an obligation to take such abdication to its logical conclusion.[109]

Oliver Haynes, *The Supreme Court of Judicature Act, 1873.*

106. On the period generally, see R. C. K. Ensor, *England 1870–1914*, at 24 ff.

107. Sir George Bowyer thoughtfully noted that "when some future historian would come to write the history of the change in the laws of this country which they were now considering he would have some difficulty"; 224 *Parl. Deb.*, H.C. (3d ser.), cols. 1657–58 (10 June 1875).

108. Selborne, 1 *Memorials* 298.

109. Ibid. 309, 314.

Disraeli's views on the appellate jurisdiction were officially unknown. He had not spoken against the abolition of English appeals to the
Lords in 1873,[110] although he had opposed the amendment that would
have taken Irish and Scottish appeals from the Lords.[111] It would be in
accordance with his character to encourage retention of the House as the
final appeal court for all the jurisdictions.[112] One man, however, whose
views were clear was Charley. A "fair" lawyer with a "moderate" practice, but a man of some considerable arrogance, he had, as a Tory back-
bencher, led the opposition in the Commons to the abolition of appeals
to the Lords. A man of insignificance compared with Selborne, Cairns,
and Disraeli, perhaps even a pawn of the Prime Minister's, Charley was
nevertheless destined to play what seemed to him,[113] as it did to many
others, a vital part in the legislative changes of the next two years.

The return of the jurisdiction to the Lords was in no way obvious
when Disraeli formed his cabinet in February 1874, for at that point the
activities of Charley and his friends were not taken seriously by lawyers
of weight.[114] Indeed, the new administration celebrated its return by
taking Selborne's plan to its logical conclusion and totally abolishing
appeals to the Lords. During 1874 Cairns brought in a bill to end Irish
and Scottish appeals;[115] instead of going to the Lords, these appeals were
to go to the Court of Appeal, now grandiosely known as the Imperial
Court of Appeal.[116] Colonial and ecclesiastical appeals could also be
transferred from the Privy Council to the Imperial Court.[117] Cairns also

110. Despite Lord Denman's generous offer to lend Disraeli the notes his Lordship had
used for his speeches in the House of Lords; letter from Denman to Disraeli, 30 June 1873,
Hughenden Papers, B/XXI/D/208, Hughenden, Hertfordshire.

111. 216 *Parl. Deb.*, H.C. (3d ser.), cols. 1712 ff. (3 July 1873).

112. "Mr. Disraeli . . . we knew, had, all along, been in sympathy with our movement"; William T. Charley, *The Crusade Against the Constitution* 389.

113. For Charley's views of the events of those years, see ibid. and William T. Charley,
Mending and Ending the House of Lords.

114. A series of letters from Sir George Bowyer to *The Times* during the autumn of
1873 in favor of appeals to the Lords caused no response, although Bowyer was a Liberal;
16 and 28 Aug., 4 and 11 Sept., published in booklet form; George Bowyer, *The Appellate
Jurisdiction of the House of Lords and the New Court of Appeal.* Bowyer also bombarded
Disraeli with letters during these months. On 4 July 1873 he wrote that it was "intolerable
to have three courts of appeal" since "in no other country have the judges such a power of
making law"; Hughenden Papers, B/XXI/B/734, Hughenden, Hertfordshire. On 16 Aug.
1873 he wrote, "In my humble opinion Cairns and Palmer have led that House into a great
mistake the consequences of which will be very serious. . . . If we abolished all fictions what
would become of the Constitution? . . . Can anything be done or is it too late?" ibid.,
B/XXI/B/734. In any event, Bowyer was already estranged from the party, and in 1876 he
was expelled.

115. Supreme Court of Judicature Act (1873) Amendment Bill of 1874, 7 *Public Bills*
(1874), at 261.

116. § 3.

117. § 11. This extension required some broadening of the qualifications for appeal

clarified and extended Selborne's plan for rehearing. The Court of Appeal was to be clearly divided into three divisions, with the First Division established as the most senior division composed of five judges as opposed to the three in the other two divisions. The First Division was to be responsible for hearing all Irish and Scottish cases,[118] and for rehearing any English case if one of the other divisions disagreed.[119]

With the assistance of Hatherley and Selborne, together with former Liberal Attorney-General, Coleridge, by then Chief Justice and a member of the House of Lords, Cairns was able to push this relatively radical bill through the Lords; but it was by no means an easy passage. It was clear that in the intervening months support for appellate functions of the Lords had grown. Nor was the support confined to the emotional fringe that had attacked the 1873 proposals; more powerful forms of conservatism were at work. The elimination of the appellate functions was becoming linked with the idea of a general weakening in the Lords' powers and an attack on the hereditary system itself.

Cairns conceded that he had received a petition from some of the leading members of the English bar favoring some form of second appeal, but he insisted that the petition left open whether such appeal should take the form of an appeal to the Lords.[120] The Lord Justice Clerk of Scotland had announced that the Scots were not at all keen to see their cases go to this new "English" Court of Appeal, and this objection was seized on by many peers. There was also opposition from Liberal peers. O'Hagan, Gladstone's Lord Chancellor of Ireland, opposed the transfer of Irish appeals from the Lords,[121] and Penzance, a Liberal law lord, made several strong speeches, suggesting that since the First Division was in fact to act as a superior appeal court, the opportunity should be used to reinstate the Lords' jurisdiction on a rational basis.[122]

---

judges. Cairns was against a rigid quota system; 218 *Parl. Deb.*, H.L. (3d ser.), cols. 1808 ff. (7 May 1874). The bill therefore provided that the judges of the Court of Appeal might be chosen from the bench or bar of any of the three jurisdictions; § 5.

118. § 13.

119. § 12 (10), in referring to the Second and Third divisions provided that any decision by a division of the Court of Appeal "where the judges of such Divisional Court are not unanimous or where the decision of such Divisional Court reverses on any question of law a material part of the order or judgement appealed from, shall, if any party to such appeal so desire, be reheard before the first Divisional Court." The First Division was also to be arbiter of what amounted to a "question of law" or "a material part."

120. 219 *Parl. Deb.*, H.L. (3d ser.), col. 1370 (11 June 1874). He felt that by making the rehearing before the First Division as of right where another division was not unanimous, he had cured a serious omission in the 1873 act, which had left rehearings to the discretion of the judges; ibid., col. 1372.

121. 219 *Parl. Deb.*, H.L. (3d ser.), cols. 1387 ff. (11 June 1874).

122. E.g., ibid., col. 1037 ff. (5 June 1874).

Despite growing opposition, Cairns was able to muster a comfortable majority in the Lords for the new legislation,[123] and *The Times* noted confidently that the opposition to the transfer of Scottish and Irish appeals "proves to be weaker than had been anticipated."[124] As in 1873, there was vociferous opposition in the Commons,[125] but since the Liberal Opposition supported the measure, there was no difficulty in pushing the bill through.[126] It passed the Second Reading and the Committee Stage, and on 17 July *The Times* was able to predict that "the establishment of a new Imperial Court of Appeal, and the transfer to it of the functions hitherto exercised by the Judicial Committee of the Privy Council and the Judicial Committee of the House of Lords, must now be accepted as finally settled."[127]

With only the relatively unimportant Report Stage and the formal Third Reading remaining, such predictions must have seemed justified. But Disraeli was feeling pressure from outside the House,[128] and there was conflict in the cabinet. The obvious was not to be. Cairns found himself under attack in the cabinet meeting held on 24 July.[129] The following day, the Opposition, in the remarkable position of being more in favor of a government bill than the government itself, expressed concern. Sir Henry James asked the Attorney-General if the rumor that had been circulating that the government proposed dropping the bill were true.[130] The Attorney-General prevaricated and two days later James returned to the attack.[131] This time he received a reply from the Prime Minister. The rumor was true. The bill was to be dropped for that session.[132]

123. 52–23, a majority of 29.

124. *The Times*, 10 June 1874.

125. This time led chiefly by Sir George Bowyer, who had by then been reelected to the House. He relied strongly on a petition by the common law bar advocating appeals to the Lords and on the argument that the House of Lords had no constitutional right to vote away its jurisdiction; 221 *Parl. Deb.*, H.C. (3d ser.), cols. 133 ff. (16 July 1874).

126. It was piloted through the Commons by Sir Richard Baggallay, by then Attorney-General, who the previous year had opposed depriving the House of Lords of its jurisdiction.

127. *The Times*, 7 July 1874.

128. E.g., Bowyer to Disraeli, 8 June 1874: "Can you stop the *lamentable* course of Cairns regarding the appellate jurisdiction of the Lords? If you do this, you will have done a service *greater* than any Minister ever did to the Constitution. Cairns is under the influence and power of Palmer"; Hughenden Papers, B/XX I/B/736, Hughenden, Hertfordshire.

129. "I doubt whether, consistently with the expressions used yesterday . . . the Judicature Bill could now be gone on with"; letter from Cairns to Disraeli, 25 July 1874, ibid., B/XX/Ca/120.

130. 221 *Parl. Deb.*, H.C. (3d ser.), col. 705 (25 July 1874).

131. Ibid., col. 763 (27 July 1874).

132. Disraeli offered two reasons or excuses for this change of heart. First, the bill would impede more urgent legislation; second, the judges would not have produced their Rules of the Supreme Court under the 1873 act in time for them to be debated that session. What more urgent legislation the Prime Minister had in mind was not made clear. It was

The advocates of retention were overjoyed. "I am *delighted* that you have shaken the influence of Cairns," wrote Bowyer to Disraeli.[133] The Liberals were exasperated by Disraeli's behavior. "Worse than the Massacre of the Innocents—it was the murder of an adult," said Harcourt;[134] but they could do nothing.[135] On the very day of Disraeli's statement, a bill was introduced postponing the effective date of the 1873 Judicature Act from November 1874 to November 1875.[136] As Bowyer and Redesdale realized, the delay played into their hands.[137] Cairns henceforth was seen as the main enemy of their plan.[138] At this point Charley began the organization of a more militant movement to save the Lords' jurisdiction. He worked hard during the autumn of 1874, spurred on by the feeling that "the Prime Minister must, by his antecedents, still be opposed to its abolition."[139] By the end of the year the Committee for Preserving the House of Lords had come into being.[140]

---

assumed to be the Public Worship Bill, although the Attorney-General said there were two Real Property Bills of greater importance. As to the allegation that nothing could be done until the judges had drawn up the Rules, James insisted that the bill was in no way subject to the Rules; ibid., cols. 705, 789.

133. Letter, 27 July 1874, Hughenden Papers, B/XXI/B/737, Hughenden, Hertfordshire.

134. 221 *Parl. Deb.*, H.C. (3d ser.), cols. 788–89 (27 July 1874).

135. E.g., speech by James, ibid., col. 1039 (31 July 1874); speech by Selborne, ibid., H.L. (3d ser.), cols. 1383 ff.

136. The bill was pushed through all stages in both houses in a remarkably short time and became law on 7 Aug. 1874; Supreme Court of Judicature Act (1873) Suspension Bill of 1874, 7 *H.L. Sessional Papers* 317. House of Commons: First Reading, 4 Aug.; Second Reading (and committee negatived), 5 Aug.; Third Reading, 6 Aug.; Royal Assent, 7 Aug.

137. See speech by Bowyer, *Parl. Deb.*, H.C. (3d ser.), cols. 1222–23 (3 Aug. 1874); speech by Redesdale, ibid., H.L. (3d ser.), col. 1386 (6 Aug. 1874).

138. Bowyer was particularly upset by the friendly tone of certain exchanges between Selborne and Cairns early in August. In a letter to Disraeli, dated 7 Aug. 1874, Bowyer insisted that Cairns was still under the influence of Selborne and that the latter would not let him go back on his plans for the House of Lords. "Gladstone *hates* the House of Lords and therefore Palmer hates it also—they wish to humble it. They know that to deprive the House of Lords of its essential judicial character will be a great blow—and that it will lead to *other* changes in the constitution." Gladstone and Selborne were alleged to be "cleverly *managing* the Conservative Government"; letter from Bowyer to Disraeli, 7 Aug. 1874, Hughenden Papers, B/XXI/B/738, Hughenden, Hertfordshire.

139. Letter from Charley to Corry (Disraeli's secretary), 7 Apr. 1875, ibid., B/XXI/C/167. By November he had collected the signatures of nearly all the members of the Northern Circuit to a petition asking for the Lords to be retained as the final appeal court for the United Kingdom.

140. The first meeting of the committee was attended by Charley, Wortley, and Bowyer and was held in Bowyer's chambers. It was agreed to restrict membership to peers, M.P.'s, and Q.C.'s; meetings were held regularly at Wortley's house in St. James Place; Charley, *Crusade Against the Constitution* 387–88. Meanwhile, Bowyer persuaded all the benchers of the Inner Temple to sign a petition in favor of restoration of the jurisdiction, and Butt was charged with the task of organizing a petition in Ireland; letter from Bowyer to Disraeli, 18 Dec. 1874, Hughenden Papers, B/XXI/B/741, Hughenden, Hertfordshire. After stating these facts, he added, "I trust that all this will have an effect on the *Conservative* Government."

As the 1875 session got under way, Selborne was anxiously waiting to see what moves the government would make, for within the cabinet was further dissension.[141] Disraeli was, by this time, clearly in favor of retaining the Lords as the final court, although Cairns still regarded it as his duty to finish Selborne's work. For a while it looked as if Cairns' sense of obligation would overcome Disraeli's emotional urge to appease the vested interests in the Conservative party, for in February, Cairns reintroduced the Supreme Court of Judicature Act (1873) Amendment Bill,[142] in much the same form as its 1874 appearance. Selborne was obviously relieved and poured scorn on the attempts to improve and revive the Lords as a judicial body.[143] The impact of Charley's work was, however, becoming clear, for several distinguished lawyers and influential politicians had become members of his committee.[144] At the Second Reading,[145] not only Redesdale and Penzance attacked the abolition, but this time the influential Earl of Harrowby joined in. There was by then considerable contact between the committee and the politically active peers. Some members of the committee had been in touch with Disraeli.[146] On 4 March, at the Committee Stage, the Duke of Buccleuch announced that he would move to insert a clause that would in effect restore the appellate jurisdiction.[147] That evening Disraeli attended a meeting of disgruntled peers held at the Duke of Richmond's house. Of that meeting Disraeli wrote to the Queen that he had succeeded "so far as to induce them to take a prudent and moderate course for the moment, but their spirit was high and somewhat unmanageable. Peers, who, two

141. Letter from Cairns to Disraeli, 18 Feb. 1875, Hughenden Papers, B/XX/Ca/139, Hughenden, Hertfordshire.

142. 9 H.L. *Sessional Papers* (1875), at 41.

143. 222 *Parl. Deb.*, H.L. (3d ser.), cols. 150 ff. (9 Feb. 1875).

144. At this stage there were 109 members, including the peers; Hughenden Papers, B/XX/Ca/140a, Hughenden, Hertfordshire.

145. 222 *Parl. Deb.*, H.L. (3d ser.), col. 737 (23 Feb. 1875).

146. Bowyer, for instance, wrote again on 26 February, claiming that several peers realized "they committed a great error" in giving up the appellate jurisdiction. His somewhat extravagant letter may well have appealed to Disraeli. Its tone can be gathered from such phrases as "[t]he House of Lords is one of the *greatest* Supreme Courts of Appeal in Europe," "Cairns seems determined to stifle opinion by pressing on as fast as possible," and "the first step towards the downfall of the House of Lords"; Hughenden Papers, B/XXI/B/746, Hughenden, Hertfordshire.

A formal petition from the committee was relayed by Cairns to Disraeli on 27 February. It stated that since there was going to be a second appeal it might just as well be to the House of Lords. "It will be wiser to attempt, by removing any real defects, to secure for the suitors the moral weight and consideration which the present tribunal derives from its constitutional association, from its antiquity, and from its long career of successful adjudication." It was argued, moreover, that the jurisdiction "is not a question of mere privilege which the peers can of themselves surrender; but a duty and a function cast upon them by the laws of the Realm"; Petition, ibid., B/XX/Ca/140a.

147. 222 *Parl. Deb.*, H.L. (3d ser.), col. 1174 (4 Mar. 1875).

years ago, showed the greatest apathy on the subject, have become quite headstrong."[148]

The following day the die was cast. With Disraeli's connivance,[149] Spenser Walpole gave notice in the Commons of a resolution calling for one tribunal to hear appeals from the three United Kingdom jurisdictions and suggesting that the House of Lords be retained for that purpose.[150] On 8 March 1875, Cairns announced that the government had no alternative but to withdraw the bill introduced the previous month,[151] and the Earl of Derby justified the decision by arguing that if the bill had been forced to a vote, the government would have been defeated.[152] Selborne was disappointed and angry.[153] There was little, however, that he and his supporters could do.

Disraeli did not make his intentions clear at once. Some new scheme for appeals was to be introduced; almost everyone assumed it would involve a restoration of appeals to the Lords, but this was not absolutely certain. Advice poured in on all sides. Cairns was still unhappy, and there was further conflict in the cabinet. Disraeli wanted the full restoration of the Lords' jurisdiction at once, but Cairns "doubted the wisdom" of this.[154] One confused cabinet meeting followed another.[155] A week later it seemed that Cairns' more cautious approach had triumphed, although he wrote of the need "to proceed boldly and rapidly."[156] On 11 April Redesdale, representing the peers who had caballed at the Duke of Richmond's, called on Disraeli. The peers were angry that the Lords' jurisdic-

---

148. Quoted, George Buckle, 5 *Life of Disraeli* (London, 1929), at 375.

149. Ibid.; Charley wrote to Disraeli at the time asking if he might move the resolution; Hughenden Papers, B/XXI/C/166, Hughenden, Hertfordshire. Later the same day he telegraphed to say he thought it wiser if a more influential member moved; ibid., B/XXI/C/166a.

150. 222 *Parl. Deb.*, H.C. (3d ser.), col. 1284 (5 Mar. 1875).

151. Ibid., H.L. (3d ser.), cols. 1371–72, (8 Mar. 1875).

152. Ibid., cols. 1377–78.

153. He attacked the pressure-group politics of Charley's committee and tried to have Spenser Walpole's motion declared a breach of privilege; ibid., cols. 1372–75. At a City banquet, he alleged that the government had "succumbed to a coterie" and been "subdued by a clique"; cited, speech by Lord O'Hagan, 223 *Parl. Deb.*, H.L. (3d ser.), col. 109 (16 Apr. 1875).

The Times attributed the situation to a lack of leadership on the part of Cairns and Derby; Leader, *The Times*, 9 Mar. 1875, at 9. *The Times* did admit that the committee had been influential. "A self-elected committee meeting in some corner of St. James has overpowered the counsels of Parliament, and Lord Selborne was justified in saying that he knew not to what lengths such a mode of interference may be carried"; 4 Mar. 1875. *The Times* also conceded, "There can be no doubt that the policy embodied in these amendments is supported by a considerable and energetic body of lawyers in this country and by the preponderance of professional opinion both at the Scotch and Irish Bars"; ibid.

154. Letter from Cairns to Disraeli, 18 Mar. 1875, Hughenden Papers, B/XX/Ca/146, Hughenden, Hertfordshire.

155. Ibid., 21 Mar. 1875, ibid., B/XX/Ca/147.

156. Ibid., 26 Mar. 1875, ibid., B/XX/Ca/148.

tion had not been restored at once. Disraeli explained the cabinet complications and guaranteed an act to restore the jurisdiction the following
session if Redesdale would support, and use his influence to persuade
other peers to support, another delaying bill.[157] It was this interview that
settled the future structure of the English appellate system.

On 9 April 1875 Cairns introduced another bill into the Lords.[158]
All that was clear from Cairns' speech was that the government had
decided in principle that there should be a double or second appeal and
that appeals from England, Scotland, and Ireland should go to a single
tribunal.[159] To implement this change of principle, the bill cut down the
number of judges in the Court of Appeal to five ex officio and five
permanent ones.[160] It said nothing about Scottish and Irish appeals,
which would by default continue to go to the Lords; but it expressly
stated that those sections of the 1873 act, as amended by the 1874 act,
that provided for English appeals to the Lords to end in November 1875,
should have their implementation postponed until November 1876.[161]

The Conservative peers expressed their delight with the changes,
and clamored for the full restoration of the Lords' powers.[162] Both Hatherley and Selborne stressed the need to make the intermediate appeal
court as strong as possible to discourage appeals to the final court, which
they earnestly hoped would not be the House of Lords.[163] No new points
emerged from the debates in the Commons, but it was generally conceded that things "were in a great mess."[164] There can have been little
doubt in the minds of most Liberals what solution Disraeli would choose.
Charley's committee had done its work well.[165]

157. Letter from Redesdale to Disraeli, 31 Oct. 1875, ibid., B/XXI/R/70.
158. Supreme Court of Judicature Act (1873), Amendment Bill (1875) No. 11, 9 H.L.
Sessional Papers (1875), at 75. It was "so absolutely colorless and negative in its character
that it might have been accepted without a word of criticism," said The Times; Leader, 19
Apr. 1875, at 11. According to Cairns, the judges were more flattering. "All the judges
of all the courts at the breakfast this morning stated that they [consider] the new Judicature Bill the perfection of human wisdom"; letter from Cairns to Disraeli, 15 Apr. 1875,
Hughenden Papers, B/XX/Ca/150, Hughenden, Hertfordshire.
159. 223 Parl. Deb., H.L. (3d ser.), cols. 574–97 (9 Apr. 1875).
160. § 4.
161. § 2.
162. E.g., speech by Redesdale, 223 Parl. Deb., H.L. (3d ser.), cols. 1815–16 (29 Apr.
1875).
163. Ibid., cols. 1797–1815.
164. Speech by Morgan, 224 Parl. Deb., H.C. (3d ser.), col. 1653 (10 June 1875).
Government speakers defended the committee's activities, and the Opposition attacked
both government and committee. The bill received the Royal Assent on 11 Aug. 1875.
165. With Wortley as its chairman, the committee by then claimed 40 Q.C.'s, 35 peers
and 138 M.P.'s as members; ibid., cols. 1664–65. Charley individually and the committee
collectively bombarded the government that winter with demands that the jurisdiction of
the Lords be restored in full. Redesdale, who apparently thought that Cairns might still get
the better of the Prime Minister, reminded Disraeli of the promises made to the peers after
the meeting at the Duke of Richmond's remarking, "A good conservative fight at the

The activities of the existing final appeal courts helped. In 1875 the Judicial Committee of the Privy Council heard 89 cases, leaving only 109 pending at the end of the year. The House of Lords heard 46, leaving only 13 remaining.[166] Such figures provided excellent material for the antiabolitionists. In addition, much talk circulated about a change in public opinion in favor of retaining the Lords. As *The Times* pointed out, "There is no public opinion on the subject, any more than there is on the Transit of Venus,"[167] but it made an impressive argument.[168]

In November, Cairns circulated a confidential cabinet memorandum. The memorandum spelled out in greater detail the points the Lord Chancellor had made in introducing the April bill. The court of ultimate appeal should hear only cases that had passed through an intermediate court; it should be the final court for England, Scotland, and Ireland; and it should consist of an "adequate number of highly-trained judicial minds." It was by now politically necessary that the ultimate court should be the House of Lords; but various changes were thought to be necessary in the House.[169]

This memorandum formed the basis of the bill that Cairns introduced in 1876. The House of Lords was restored as the final court of appeal, but some modifications had been effected. The judicial sessions were no longer to be tied to the legislative sittings of the House, and all

---

beginning of the Session would be most popular, and there is the peculiar advantage attending one on this question that we shall have the support of many influential members of the Opposition"; e.g., letter from Charley to Corry (Disraeli's secretary), 7 Apr. 1875, Hughenden Papers, B/XXI/L/167, Hughenden, Hertfordshire; letter from Redesdale to Disraeli, 31 Oct. 1875, ibid., B/XXI/R/70.

166. *Judicial Statistics* (1875).

167. Leader, *The Times*, 15 June 1875, at 9.

168. For Charley's argument that he created the public opinion, see Charley, *Crusade Against the Constitution* 387. See also his letter to Corry (Disraeli's secretary), dated 12 Feb. 1876. "I have sometimes thought that Mr. Disraeli considered that my zeal in this subject outran my discretion and, if so, I heartily apologise for it. But enthusiasm was necessary to infuse life into what was, at first, a hopeless cause"; Hughenden Papers, B/XXI/C/170, Hughenden, Hertfordshire.

169. To give an impression of the separation of powers, the cabinet memorandum recommended that appeals no longer be addressed to the Lords, but to the sovereign in Parliament, just as colonial appeals went to the Queen in Council. Of the other specific objections to the Lords, four were spelled out: its inability to sit during prorogations, dissolutions, and adjournments; the absence of a regular supply of qualified lawyers; the absence of any security that nonlawyers would abstain; and the delay and expense involved. Cairns recommended that these be changed as far as possible and that a Judicial Committee of the House of Lords be set up, which would sit throughout the year in a separate courtroom; he suggested the Painted Chamber at Westminster. The judicial complement of the House would be ensured by the creation of paid law lords, who would sit either as the Judicial Committee of the House of Lords or as the Judicial Committee of the Privy Council, "[a]ccording to the nature of the business to be disposed of," since "the work to be done is not sufficient to give full employment to two separate tribunals"; Cabinet Memorandum, Court of Ultimate Appeal, Lord Chancellor's Office, File 1/1, Public Record Office.

appeals were to be addressed to the Queen in Parliament. Lords of Appeal in Ordinary were to be created, chosen from judges of the Supreme Courts or members of the bars of England, Scotland and Ireland of fifteen years' standing. Two Lords of Appeal would be appointed at first, then another after two of the salaried judges of the Privy Council, appointed under the 1871 act, died or resigned, and a fourth after the other two holders of such offices vacated them. The salary of six thousand pounds per annum was a thousand pounds more than the Lords Justices of Appeal in the Court of Appeal received, although the latter received a privy councillorship that both flattered them and ensured an adequate supply of judges for the Judicial Committee. Lords of Appeal were to be peers during their tenure of office. Holders or former holders of "high judicial office" who were peers were entitled to sit, and a quorum of three law lords was established.

The bill,[170] when introduced, was not seriously opposed. All the interested parties made their set speeches.[171] Selborne and Hatherley[172] thought the House could never be made an effective judicial body and criticized the existence of two final appeal courts.[173] Outside the House, the Charley Committee tried to use its influence to make the bill even more conservative.[174] It was business as usual. The bill received the Royal Assent in August 1876,[175] and the "new" House of Lords began

170. Appellate Jurisdiction of the House of Lords Bill, 3 *H.L. Sessional Papers* (1876), at 43.

171. Lord Moncrieff welcomed it on behalf of Scotland; 227 *Parl. Deb.*, H.L. (3d ser.), cols. 922–24 (25 Feb. 1876). Lord O'Hagan spoke on behalf of Ireland and Lord Redesdale on behalf of the committee; ibid., cols. 924, 1286–87 (Mar. 1876). Lord Cairns felt obliged to explain his apparent changes of heart, and Lord Selborne placed his view "once more, and finally, on record" and noted that "it did not come up to the best thing possible"; ibid., col. 203 ff. (11 Feb. 1876) and col. 909 (25 Feb. 1876).

172. Ibid., cols. 909 ff.

173. In the Commons, Disraeli and Charley blessed the bill; 229 *Parl. Deb.*, H.C. (3d ser.), col. 680 (12 June 1876). James and Harcourt cursed Charley and the Lords; ibid., cols. 1693, 1702.

174. The Committee for Preserving the House of Lords was reconstructed during the 1876 session. On 21 February it unanimously resolved "1st: that the Committee desired to express its thanks to the Lord Chancellor for presenting a Bill which preserves the appellate jurisdiction of the House of Lords, and 2nd: that the Chairman be requested to communicate this resolution to the Lord Chancellor and ask permission to offer any suggestions on the Bill that may occur to them from time to time"; Lord Chancellor's Office, File 1/3, Public Record Office. The committee held meetings at Wortley's house in St. James to discuss the bill. They purported to represent not only the profession, but the "better informed public." Wortley wrote to Cairns saying that in the view of the committee, it was essential that the House should not appear as a statutory court but as a continuation of the traditional jurisdiction. Among other things, he also thought that Lords of Appeal for the present should be chosen only from persons who were already members of the House of Lords; letter from Wortley to Cairns, 2 Mar. 1876, ibid. This document implies strongly that in the committee's view the judicial functions of the House were an excellent place to make law away from the vulgar glare of the voters.

175. Appellate Jurisdiction Act of 1876.

operations the following year, with one English and one Scottish Lord of Appeal, Lord Blackburn and Lord Gordon.[176]

The act meant different things to different people. To Redesdale it gave "the law a similar representation in this House to that which the Church has so long enjoyed."[177] But the typical observer was satisfied that the new court was not really the House of Lords.[178] To some the solution appeared to be a brilliant example of the English genius for compromise. Three years earlier, not only the system of double appeals had seemed doomed, but also the House of Lords as a judicial body. The compromise was to keep the name of the House of Lords but to make it in effect a court separate from the legislative body. The new judicial House of Lords bore many of the trimmings of the House, but it was a different body from the one that had previously heard appeals. While the compromise itself was in some ways harmless, the real purpose of the pressure groups behind the bill had been to bolster the peers as a branch of the legislature,[179] and the feeling that the appellate process itself should retain a legislative element remained strong. To achieve these ends conservatives had enlisted the natural conservative emotions of the legal profession to prevent serious tampering with the privileges of the peers. The judicial compromise was little more than a pawn in the political game. The appellate functions of the Lords remained at the fulcrum of the competing pressures of law and policy.

The End of an Era

It could be argued that politically the House of Lords was strengthened by passage of the Appellate Jurisdiction Act. That would probably be inaccurate except in limited formalistic terms, but in general, in the last decades of the nineteenth century, the Lords appeared to recover much of their confidence in their political rights and privileges. It was true that the Lords were outflanked by Gladstone when they attempted to defeat Cardwell's army reforms in 1871,[180] but as a legislative chamber they seemed increasingly unconcerned by earlier conventions. Only delicate negotiations between Gladstone and Disraeli prevented a show-

176. It was not easy to find a Scottish judge willing to sit regularly in London. Both Moncrieff and Inglis refused the appointment; letter from Cairns to Disraeli, 26 Aug. 1876, Hughenden Papers, B/XX/Ca/185, Hughenden, Hertfordshire.

177. 227 *Parl. Deb.*, H.L. (3d ser.), cols. 1286–87 (3 Mar. 1876).

178. *An Annual Register of World Events for 1876*, at 49. Maitland was more of a conservative: "[T]he House of Lords is one member of our supreme legislative body. But besides this it is a court of law. Such is the theory, and such, subject to some explanation, is the fact"; Frederick W. Maitland, *Justice and Police* 57.

179. Speech by Lord Elcho, cited, *The Times*, 15 June 1875.

180. On this, see Ensor, *England 1870–1914*, at 10–11.

down when Salisbury attempted to sabotage the 1885 Reform Bill.[181] While the first Home Rule Bill for Ireland, in 1886, never reached the Lords, the second Home Rule Bill, in 1893, was killed by that House by a massive majority.[182] Similarly, the Lords had no hesitation in mauling other bills during Gladstone's last administration;[183] and they made his successor Rosebery's administration impossible.[184]

As the Whigs had gradually abandoned the Liberals and adhered to the Conservatives, the Lords were increasingly seen as little more than an emanation of the Conservative party. Although ten years of Conservative administration (1895–1905) put no strain on a political system in which the hereditary upper house was effectively linked with the party in power, the reappearance of Sir Henry Campbell-Bannerman's Liberal administration in 1905, with its radical overtones, heralded a new political crisis. In 1906 the Lords killed the Education Bill and the Plural Voting Bill. They savaged the Land Bills of 1907 and they threatened to kill the Old Age Pension Bill in 1908. By the time they had rejected the 1908 Licensing Bill and the 1909 budget they had produced the great Parliament Crisis.[185] That crisis ended in 1911, with the Lords' losing their absolute right to veto legislation; in the future they could merely delay it. It was a decision that would have a profound effect on the judicial process in general and on the Lords' appellate process in particular.

The direct effect of the Parliament Crisis, and especially Lord Haldane's reaction to it, will be discussed later, but some of the political effects of the various Liberal administrations may be noted at this point. As long as legislation emphasized that strand of Benthamite thought described by Dicey as individualism,[186] there was little effort to exclude lawyers or the courts from decisions under the legislation or supervision over it. As legislation increasingly took on what Dicey called "collectivist" hues,[187] however, there was increasing willingness to exclude review of the legislation in the courts. While lawyers managed to maintain a role in workmen's compensation cases, the behavior of the Lords both legislatively and judicially led to the Trade Disputes Act of 1906, which attempted to put unions outside the law, or at least outside his purview of the courts.[188] David Lloyd George was not prepared to see judges involved

181. Ibid. 88.
182. Ibid. 211–12.
183. Including the Employers' Liability Legislation of 1894; ibid, 214.
184. Ibid. 216.
185. Ibid. 392–94, 408–9, 417.
186. Albert Venn Dicey, *Lectures on the Relation between Law and Public Opinion in England during the Nineteenth Century*, Lecture 6.
187. Ibid., Lecture 8.
188. For a discussion of the political implications of retaining the Lords for the final appeal, see Ensor, *England 1870–1914*, at 379.

in his new welfare programs; and the Chancellor of the Exchequer, Winston Churchill, spoke out vigorously against allowing the judges to make decisions where social policy was concerned.[189] The judges, especially the law lords, were poised to make an intellectually undistinguished, if politically wise, exit from those areas of the appellate process that appeared to politicians to involve policymaking. The logic of Benthamite utilitarianism was, at least in the English radical tradition, that judges should interpret the law scientifically, not creatively. By 1912, this message had reached the judicial members of the House of Lords.

Little of this withdrawal had surfaced, however, when the "new" judicial House of Lords met for the first time in 1877. Indeed, it seemed that every effort was made to keep the appellate process an integral part of the legislature.[190] By 1887, Lords of Appeal were given peerage for life rather than for the length of their judicial service. The Lord Chancellor remained an active politician as well as an active judge, sitting in the cabinet and presiding over the legislative and judicial functions in the Lords. Moreover, beginning under Cairns the Lord Chancellor's Office, manned solely by lawyers and operating somewhat outside the reformed structure of the Civil Service, acted as a kind of Ministry of Justice.[191] Indeed, it was almost impossible to overestimate the influence of Lord Chancellors. They not only appointed judges and promoted them (although technically Lords of Appeal were appointed by the Prime Minister), but it was they who decided which law lord should sit in which appeal in the Lords or Privy Council. If the appellate functions of the Lords were the focus of the interaction of law and politics, the Lord Chancellor was the person in whom the potential conflicts of legislator, judge, and civil servant were most intense.

Some changes were of course obvious almost from the beginning. Only after passage of the Appellate Jurisdiction Act of 1876 did the House of Lords finally become primarily an English court. For twenty years before the act, English appeals had been slowly drawing ahead of Scottish appeals in numbers (1860, twenty-seven English, nineteen Scottish; 1870, twenty English, fourteen Scottish; 1875, twenty-seven English, fourteen Scottish). But after the passage of the act this trend became pronounced.[192] By 1885 there were twenty-four English appeals and

189. Otto Kahn-Freund, "Labour Law" 232.

190. In fact, many of the trimmings that Cairns had suggested should go, did not. A Judicial Committee of the House was not formed, lay peers were never formally forbidden to vote, and the judicial functions of the House continued to be conducted in the Lords' chamber. (Changes along these lines have been a recent development.)

191. The Permanent Secretary of the Lord Chancellor's Office became the éminence grise of the legal system. Sir Kenneth Muir MacKenzie held that office from 1885 to 1915.

192. There were at least two aberrational years before 1900 when Scottish appeals exceeded English: 1884 (55 to 4) and 1890 (47 to 30).

seven Scottish, and by 1895, twenty-eight English and nine Scottish.[193] Within the English context, the psychological effect of the 1876 act was also to make the House much more of a common law court and less of an Equity one.[194]

Although in the last two decades of the nineteenth century and the first two of the twentieth century, "collectivist" legislation (and ultimately political wisdom or necessity on the part of the judges) began excluding the courts from even an interpretive role, that trend was far from obvious when the 1876 act came into operation in 1877. While affected by the economic crises of the times,[195] the County Courts and the High Court remained active in the prosperity of Victorian England.[196] This involvement included the House of Lords, where the kinds of appeals ranged over most of the matters covered by the legal system,[197]

193. Put another way, between 1876 and 1880, the House of Lords received an average of 60 cases a year, of which 31.2 were from England. For the period 1896–1900, the respective figures were 71.2 cases, of which 50.4 were from England; for 1906–10, 91.0 and 63.6, although not all the appeals were adjudicated; *Civil Judicial Statistics 1900*, Cd. 953, at 30–31; (1902); *Civil Judicial Statistics 1910*, Cd. 6047, at 24 (1912).

194. In 1860, of the English appeals, 18 had come from the Chancery courts and 9 from the common law courts. In 1870 the figures had been 13 and 6 and in 1875, 17 and 10. But the "new" House of Lords was seen as far less of an Equity preserve.

195. The depression that began in 1873 grew worse in 1876 and lasted until 1879; the depression that began in 1883 lasted until 1887; another depression hit its trough in 1893–94; Ensor, *England 1870–1914*, at 111–12, 282.

196. Between 1886 and 1910 the 5-year average of cases commenced (i.e., for which writs were issued) in the High Court actually fell from 83,308 to 75,286, but this figure rose in the County Courts from 1,042,114 to 1,359,450.

197. One can get some idea of these changes by sampling the work of the House each 14 years. 1882 was a typical year. There were 2 cases concerning trademarks, and 1 about patents; 1 action concerning a partnership, and 1 about a limited liability company, although at least 1 other case was concerned with the construction of a railway act. The 4 commercial cases were all concerned with shipping, primarily with the construction of charter parties and bills of lading. Bankruptcy and mortgage problems were each represented by 1 case. The affairs of the Victorian family were also the subject of litigation, and there were 3 cases on wills and trusts. Property and personal rights were much in evidence. The only tort cases were concerned with libel, nuisance, and trespass to a fishery. Fishery and other common rights were still a source of frequent litigation and in 1882 resulted in at least 1 other case. As in many years during the 1880s, 1 case involved liturgy of the church, and the year also produced 1 case on the distribution of booty to officers. Only 1 divorce case was heard for the year, concerning a problem of domicile. No tax or rating cases were heard, and the only social or administrative decision of the year involved the division of liability between a local authority and the central government when a pauper was transferred from prison to a lunatic asylum. Compared with 20 years earlier, the cases generally were more concerned with statutory interpretation, although primarily this involved the construction of private and local acts. The unreported cases of 1882 were concerned with a mortgage, a ship broker's commission, the interpretation of a statute, a will, an arbitration under the 1879 act, a contract involving the equal charges clause of a railway company, an action on promissory note, a claim of right, a private contract, a commercial contract, and a partnership deed. Of the 11 unreported cases, 2 were Scottish.

Compared with the position today, the House was a remarkably unanimous body. There were only 4 dissents in 1882 (1 in an unreported case), and this was excessive by the standards of the period. In 1881 there had been none, and in 1883 there was only 1. The

although, with the turn of the century, the House's work became more tort-oriented and to some extent constitutionally oriented.[198] The House also became much busier. Between 1901 and 1905 an average of 80 appeals each year was lodged in the House (55.2 from England) and for the next five years, 91 (63.6 from England). In 1909 the House heard no less than 108 appeals.[199]

The House was a busy court because no effective sifting mechanism was employed. There was an appeal as of right in all civil cases from England and Ireland, and from Scotland subject to those slight restrictions imposed early in the nineteenth century. Only in divorce cases were appeals limited to questions of law,[200] and under a few isolated statutes it had been held that no appeal lay.[201] In 1907 the English criminal juris-

---

atmosphere of judging was still relatively informal. During the early 1880s the average number of law lords sitting was still only 3 or 4, although isolated examples exist of as many as 8 being called together. Cases normally lasted at most 2 days, and in about half of them the opinions were given at the end of oral argument.

The appeal cases for 1896 comprise some 38 cases, and another 9 cases decided during that period went unreported. Of these 47 cases, many concerned the interpretation of private acts of Parliament, 2 being exclusively concerned with universities or highways. The bulk of the remaining cases was concerned with family affairs and, to a lesser extent, commercial law. There were 3 cases on wills, 1 on trusts, 2 on the construction of contracts, and 1 on mortgages, as well as cases on guardianship and married women's property. The area of contract was popular: 2 cases involved misrepresentation, and 2 involved the construction of deeds, while no less than 6 others were generally in the area of the construction of contracts. The Statute of Frauds and wagering each produced 1 case, and there were 2 cases on sales. In the area of commercial law, there was 1 case each on arbitration, bills of exchange, and bills of lading; there were 2 company law cases and 1 passing off and 1 patent action. No less than 5 cases were primarily concerned with practice and procedure. Three appeals were concerned with rates, and 2 tax cases were also heard. The only tort case was one of libel, although there was 1 decision under the Employer's Liability Act. The remaining miscellaneous cases covered landlord and tenant, the ownership of a fishery, and the interpretation of a customs statute.

198. During the period of a legal year beginning in October 1910, the work of the House had altered noticeably. In that year there were 5 property cases, covering various aspects of property; 16 tort cases, mainly concerned with workmen's compensation, but also covering liability for animals, nuisance, and conspiracy; 2 tax cases; 1 criminal appeal; 1 case in administrative law; 3 admiralty cases; 2 involving the interpretation of wills; some 14 cases on contracts, roughly a half being points of private contract, the remainder of a more commercial nature; 1 patent and 1 passing-off action; 1 company law point; and 2 cases involving procedural points.

199. In 1910, the House heard 74 cases in 87 days (57 from the Court of Appeal—41 affirmed and 16 reversed; 2 from the Court of Criminal Appeal; 13 from Scotland and 2 from Ireland). In addition the House heard 106 interlocutory petitions and allowed 6 petitions to bring in forma pauperis proceedings. The average taxed costs allowed to the successful party amounted to £448; *Civil Judicial Statistics*, 1910, at 24, 39. In 1900, the averaged taxed cost of an appeal was £354 (the highest being £1,826); *Civil Judicial Statistics*, 1900, at 20.

200. Supreme Court of Judicature Act of 1881. And see *Butchart* v. *Butchart*, [1901] A.C. 266.

201. It was held, for example, that no appeal lay from the Court of Session in Scotland for cases arising under the Workman's Compensation Act of 1897; *Osborne* v. *Barclay*

diction was restored to the House, subject to the granting of a fiat by the Attorney-General,[202] although there were no criminal appeals from Scotland. The House had also held that they would not entertain a purely hypothetical case.[203] For the most part, however, any civil case might be appealed as of right, and a large number of the appeals dealt primarily with factual disputes, with the result that the law lords were constantly complaining about the triviality of many of the appeals they heard.[204] Triviality at least partially explains the relative brevity of oral argument. In 1912 the Privy Council required only 101 days to hear 132 cases; and in 1908 the House heard 84 cases in 83 days, and 23 in forma pauperis petitions in 5 days. Despite assertions to the contrary, in 1912 still over half the judgments were given at the end of oral argument. The reserving of judgment came with later professionalization.

It was not, however, the work of the House that finally made it clear that four Lords of Appeal were not enough personnel to operate the system. The work of the Privy Council had been growing even faster than that of the Lords. After the 1871 reforms, the Judicial Committee of the Privy Council made great strides in cutting down the number of pending cases[205] and managed to keep abreast of its work in the 1880s. The fact was that from 1860, with isolated exceptional years, the Council had more cases than the Lords, and after the Judicature Acts it would have been unthinkable to use lay judges, while the Lords Justices found work enough in the Court of Appeal. Between 1876 and 1880 the Privy Council averaged 79.4 appeals lodged; between 1886 and 1890, 78.2; and between 1896 and 1900, 91.4. The situation was to become more dramatic yet. In 1900, the Judicial Committee heard 86 appeals,[206] 64

Curle & Co., [1901] A.C. 269. No appeal lay from a decision by Quarter Sessions fixing a police pension, *Kydd v. Liverpool Watch Comm.*, [1908] A.C. 327; nor from the Court of Appeal reviewing a decision of a judicial commission with reference to the distribution of purchase money on sales under the Irish Land Act of 1903; *Scottish Widows' Fund Life Assurance Soc'y v. Blennerhasset*, [1912] A.C. 281.

202. The Criminal Appeal Act of 1907 provided that if the Attorney-General gave his fiat, either the accused or the Crown might take an appeal from the Court of Criminal Appeal to the House of Lords. The first case heard under this system was *R. v. Ball*, [1911] A.C. 47 (1910), which was in fact an appeal by the Crown against the quashing of a conviction. The House restored the conviction in "off-the-cuff" speeches, although Lord Halsbury was far from happy with a system that allowed the restoration of a sentence, once quashed. These latter remarks were unreported. See Opinions of their Lordships, 1911.

203. *Glasgow Navigation Co. v. Iron Ore Co.*, [1910] A.C. 293 (Scot.).

204. E.g., Lord Shaw described a case as a "public scandal" when only £15 were at stake; *Watkins v. Wilson*, 55 Sol. J. 617 (H.L. 1911). Lord Macnaghten also categorized another case as "absolutely idle"; *Cockerill v. Middlesborough Co-operative Soc'y*, Opinions of their Lordships, (1912).

205. From 336 in 1870 to 109 in 1875.

206. 39 from India (23 affirmed, 16 reversed); 37 from colonial courts (17 affirmed, 18 reversed, 2 varied); 2 from the Channel Islands and 8 from consular courts (Zanzibar, Constantinople, China, and Japan); *Civil Judicial Statistics, 1900*, at 53.

petitions to appeal,[207] and various other matters.[208] In 1909 the House heard 108 cases and the Council heard 92,[209] while in 1910, when the House heard 74 appeals, the Council heard 78.[210] In the following years the crisis became even more acute. In 1911, the Privy Council sat for 101 days and decided 93 cases, while the House sat 87 days in deciding 74 cases. In 1912, the Privy Council heard 132 full appeals, the House was able to hear only 59, while the number of unadjudicated appeals began to rise.

In the middle of the nineteenth century it had been possible largely to ignore the operations of the Judicial Committee of the Privy Council. After the loss of the thirteen colonies, there was little enthusiasm for empire. Indeed, as late as the 1860s, Disraeli was talking about the colonies as "millstones round our neck." During the 1870s, however, the mood changed; the creation by the British North America Act of 1867 of the first dominion or commonwealth was ultimately hailed as a triumph and, by the time of Victoria's jubilee in 1887, England was engulfed in imperial jingoism.[211] If the Boer War served to dampen some of this enthusiasm, the importance of the administration of the Empire had been fully recognized, at least from the moment Joseph Chamberlain chose the Colonial Office rather than the Exchequer when Lord Salisbury formed his third administration in 1895.

As the self-governing dominions grew in numbers—Australia was added in 1900, New Zealand in 1907, South Africa in 1909—they became more articulate and made greater use of and demands on the Privy Council.[212] Once Cairns had destroyed the idea that after the Canadian Supreme Court had been established in 1875, there should be no further appeals to London,[213] the various Imperial Conferences, beginning in 1887, put pressure on the British government to ensure an adequate judiciary in the Privy Council. The first major public criticisms of the Judicial Committee had been heard in Canada in the 1880s.[214] Thus

207. Of which 39 were granted and 25 refused; ibid.
208. Including an application for a Letters Patent and a special reference that took 64 sitting days; ibid. 64.
209. In addition, the House had 89 appeals lodged and the Privy Council 142 (64 from India and 78 from the colonial courts).
210. *Civil Judicial Statistics, 1910*, at 24. Besides hearing 152 full-length appeals, the House also heard 106 interlocutory petitions and a number of in forma pauperis applications, while the Privy Council heard 74 petitions to appeal as well as a special reference.
211. John A. R. Marriott, *Modern England 1885–1932*, chap. 8.
212. In 1900 the Privy Council received 16 appeals from Canada, 27 from Australia, 11 from South Africa, and 6 from New Zealand; *Civil Judicial Statistics*, 1900, at 53. In 1910 the figures were Canada, 38; Australia, 16; South Africa, 8; New Zealand, 5; *Civil Judicial Statistics, 1910*, at 24.
213. Coen G. Pierson, *Canada and the Privy Council* 16–21.
214. One of the first problems was the relationship between the Judicial Committee of the Privy Council and Canadian criminal appeals. In the *Connors* case, 1885, an attempted

when Chamberlain, at the 1897 conference, broached the idea of economic union, if not of federation, the role of the courts took on added significance. In this atmosphere the first arrangements were made in 1895 to have "dominion" judges as opposed to ex-colonial judges sit with the law lords in the Privy Council,[215] and before long more dramatic gestures were being considered.

By 1900 the dominions and colonies were expressing considerable dissatisfaction about the somewhat random arrangements for staffing the Judicial Committee: the four Lords of Appeal and six judges of the Court of Appeal, various other English privy councillors who had held "high judicial office," two appointments under the 1833 act,[216] an Indian judge under the 1887 act, and up to five colonial and dominion judges under the 1895 act. Although by this time the urge to merge the House of Lords and Privy Council had largely evaporated, by 1900 a plan was developed to add four more Lords of Appeal to satisfy the demands of the self-governing colonies. Behind the scenes, Chamberlain, Lord Halsbury, and Sir Courtenay Ilbert (former Law Member of the Governor's Council in India and by then Parliamentary Draftsman) worked out a compromise.

---

appeal by a convicted murderer, the Attorney- and Solicitor-Generals (Webster and Gorst) advised the English cabinet that, while the 1867 act allowed Canada to abolish appeals in criminal cases, until the Canadian Parliament legislated, the right to appeal survived. Unfortunately, acting on the advice of the Canadian ministers, the Governor-General (the Marquis of Lansdowne) had refused Connors a stay of execution; Lord Chancellor's Office, 1/2, Public Record Office.

It was also at this point that the Judicial Committee, after an initial decision in *Russell v. The Queen*, 7 App. Cas. 829 (P.C. 1882), favoring the broad federal powers intended by the 1867 act, decided *Hodge v. The Queen*, 9 App. Cas. 117 (P.C. 1883), which appeared to espouse Mowat's theory of the coordinate relationship of the federal and provincial governments; Donald Creighton, *Canada's First Century 1867–1967*, at 49.

Meanwhile, the Australian judges were complaining because the Judicial Committee did not allow dissents, and at a meeting of the Australian State court judges in 1888, they voted "that their lordships be requested to obtain the necessary powers to enable them to deliver judgements individually if they see fit." Among those consulted by the Lord Chancellor, to whom the petition was referred, was Selborne. He wrote on 28 Nov. 1888: "I am extremely sorry to hear of a Colonial movement against the accustomed mode of delivering Privy Council Judgements; which I have always thought wise; and I think that a departure from it, much as you say certain Colonial Judges now desire, might tend to great discontents in India and in the Colonies in many cases in which there is now a satisfactory degree of acquiescence." Lord Bramwell (2 Dec. 1888) was less charitable: "I suppose the Australian judges think that sometimes their dignity would be saved by a minority opinion." None of the English and Scottish judges consulted was prepared to endorse the Australian view; Lord Chancellor's Office, 2/33, Public Record Office.

215. The 1833 act had provided for the appointment of 2 former colonial judges as members of the Council and 2 former Indian judges to be paid £400 per year. The 1871 act allowed 4 paid members to be chosen from among the judges of the English Superior Courts or from among the Chief Justices in Bengal, Madras, or Bombay. The 1887 act reduced to 1 the former Indian salaried judge under the 1833 act (and fixed his salary at £800). The 1895 act allowed up to 5 Canadian, Australian, and South African judges to be appointed as members of the Judicial Committee.

216. At that time Hobhouse and James.

Ilbert drafted a bill to add four more law lords, appointed for seven-year terms,[217] and it was assumed that four of the overseas judges appointed under the 1895 act would become Lords of Appeal.[218]

In July 1901, the Conference on the Final Court of Appeal met, chaired by David Mills, Minister of Justice in Canada. From the outset, the inherent absurdity of achieving agreement among such a heterogeneous group of emerging nations was plain. Mr. Justice Highes of the Supreme Court of Victoria insisted on pushing the merger of the Privy Council and the House of Lords,[219] a suggestion that Chamberlain thought "quite futile."[220] An unseemly debate ensued about who would pay for any new judges,[221] and tangential debates went on about allowing dissents in the reconstituted Privy Council.[222] It soon became clear that while there was dissatisfaction in the colonies and especially in the dominions, any new imperial court was liable to cause even more dissension than the Privy Council.[223] The Colonial Office, not surprisingly,

217. "Its object was probably to secure the existence of colonial Lords of Appeal who should be not too much out of touch with the course of law and justice in the colonies which they were to represent"; Lord Chancellor's Office, 2/179, Public Record Office.

218. With some horror, Ilbert reported, "[T]here would at least be a risk that a strong self-governing colony would claim a substantial voice in the appointment of a Lord of Appeal"; ibid.

219. There was some evidence that he had been put up to this by Edmund Barton, the Prime Minister of Australia; letter from Barton to Hughes, *Correspondence Relating to the Proposed Establishment of a Final Court of Colonial Appeal*, HMSO, 1901 at 24.

220. "To attempt a change of that kind, with all the difficulties attending it, when we are under the impression that a majority of the Colonies would object to the change, would be, of course, quite futile"; ibid., Conference Report, at 24.

221. Chamberlain noted, "I thought that possibly they might think it was a little *infra dig*, that a Judge appointed specially as the representative of a Colony should be paid for by the mother-country"; ibid. at 25.

222. New Zealand argued in favor. Sir James Prendergast, the former Chief Justice, argued, "An English judge first makes his reputation on the Bench, by his open pronouncements; he continues that reputation in the House of Lords; he continues to make his reputation, and that reaches us. If our appeals are to be disposed of by gentlemen who first made their reputation in India or in the Roman-Dutch colonies, and then have their mouths closed in the Privy Council, then we do not know by whom our cases are being disposed of"; ibid. 26.

Halsbury did not agree. "Lord Selborne took the very strongest view against it, and I am bound to say I think he was a good deal actuated by the difficulty of satisfying public opinion in India rather than in this country. The sort of notion was that the dissentient judges' opinion might be made the subject of great discussion in India, and would be rather likely to promote litigation. Some of the qualifications and disagreements that you occasionally find in the judgements in the House of Lords he thought might be very safely left to expert opinion in England to form a judgement upon, but he did not wish that, particularly by comparatively half-educated Hindoo lawyers."

223. The Canadian Privy Council had already resolved that "with the information they at present possess the creation of the four Colonial Law Lords suggested would not inspire any additional confidence in the Judicial Committee"; and the New Zealand representative announced at the conference: "In my opinion a Member or Members appointed from the Dominion of Canada or the Commonwealth of Australia or from South Africa would afford no better guarantee nor bring any further satisfaction to the Colony of New

reported that the views expressed at the conference were "too diverse" for any action to be taken. While reform of the Judicial Committee remained a perpetual agenda item at Imperial Conferences, its fate was uniform. Whatever the failings of the Privy Council, the powerful dominions were not prepared to risk the alternatives. At the 1907 conference, for instance, Canada once more defended the Judicial Committee.[224] It was to be business as usual.

The truth was, however, that allowing colonial judges to sit in the Privy Council made no real impact on the distressing work load of the law lords. In an effort to help, various administrations distributed peerages to senior judges during this period—for example, Brampton, Gorrell, James, Mersey, Parmoor, and Shand. Even that was not enough.[225] As the number of appeals presented to the Privy Council expanded dramatically in the first decade of the twentieth century, criticism of its work also grew. At the 1911 Imperial Conference, Loreburn promised the appointment of two additional Lords of Appeal to strengthen the Privy Council, especially since there was further talk of an "Imperial Court of Appeal."[226] Once again, however, although the project was by then being pushed by Australia and New Zealand, Canada opposed it.

The addition of two law lords was ultimately achieved by the Appellate Jurisdiction Act of 1913, but even this number was to prove insufficient, for the "quality" of the work of the House was beginning to change. Yet those additions were to prove significant. Indeed, with the Parliament Crisis (1909–11) and the beginning of Haldane's Chancellorship in 1912, the Appellate Jurisdiction Act of 1913 was to herald the beginning of a new phase in the work of the Lords.

_____

Zealand than is afforded by the presence of Great Britain or others under the existing laws at the hearing of appeals from New Zealand"; ibid.

224. Prime Minister Laurier said, "So far as Canada has any concern, we have an appeal to the Judicial Committee of the Privy Council; and it has, as a general rule, given very great satisfaction"; *Proceedings of the Imperial Conference*, Cd. 3524, at 210 (1907).

225. In 1908, Chief Justice Alverstone, who did not enjoy appellate work, wrote to Loreburn expressing his concern about the way things were going. "I venture to trouble you with a letter, a subject upon which although it does not directly concern me, I feel the greatest interest. I refer to the present condition of the appellate tribunals of the House of Lords and Privy Council. It is, in my judgement, impossible to exaggerate the importance to the country and to the empire that the Privy Council as well as the House of Lords as Courts of Appeal should be constituted in a manner which will command respect. I know how heavily this is felt in the colonies, and even with reference to appeals from our own Courts of Appeal"; cited, R. F. V. Heuston, *Lives of the Lord Chancellors 1885–1940*, at 148.

226. Haldane followed the Lord Chancellor's remarks with the observation that "[i]t is understood that this final Court of Appeal for the whole Empire is not merely to be of the strength of the existing one. We have agreed to strengthen it, and propose to add to it, as the Lord Chancellor said, two hand-picked lawyers"; *Proceedings of the Imperial Conference*, Cd. 5745, at 244 (1911).

THREE

Politics and Jurisprudence

The political and structural changes described in the previous chapter had an undeniable impact on the judicial approach to the appellate process. In the most general terms there was, during the nineteenth century, a march toward formalism. A utilitarianism that preached the need to make law scientific in order to curb judicial legislation could scarcely fail to have some effect on the way judges actually operated, and the general aura of laissez-faire was likewise calculated to keep judges—and others—away from policies and pursuits that savored of activism on the part of the state. The simplistic statement that Parliament made laws and judges applied them was increasingly accepted as formalist dogma. Theoretically, a judicial decision was rationalized only in terms of legal principles deduced from earlier cases. Different judges and different courts, however, moved at different paces in their acceptance of this.[1] The House of Lords moved appreciably more slowly than did the courts of first instance and the intermediate appeal courts toward any mechanistic approach to precedent that the apostles of utilitarianism might preach. The idea that the appellate functions of the Lords had important legislative implications survived well into the twentieth century.

The system of precedent is, of course, at the very core of the common law system. The idea that some part of the reasoning in earlier decisions (*rationes decidendi*), at least at the appeal level, is "binding" on

---

1. Although the situation was undoubtedly more "pluralistic" in the United States, conflicting assertions abound. Horwitz has argued that, freed from colonial restraints, the American judiciary embraced an instrumental approach during the federalist period, a path of virtue from which they were seduced only rather late in the century; Morton J. Horwitz, "The Emergence of an Instrumental Conception of American Law, 1780–1820," in *Law in American History*, ed. Donald Fleming and Bernard Baily (Boston, 1971), at 287. On this, see Robert Stevens, "Some Unexplored Avenues in Comparative Anglo-American Legal History" 1093.

later courts, is reflected in the concept of stare decisis; but how much of the earlier precedent and how serious the efforts to systematize such reasonings are frequently reflections of the intellectual (or at least judicial) tradition of the period. Those forces sometimes emphasize the fashion of looking primarily for principles in a line of earlier cases, sometimes treat each "relevant" case as a binding precedent, or sometimes look only for a case "on all fours." When one begins the analysis of judicial style, the study of literary style seems, in comparison, a relatively simple operation. Its implementation, at anything resembling a scientific level, is appreciably more difficult.

Lord Mansfield, lauded by some and accused by others for being what some would now call an instrumentalist, had a healthy respect of stare decisis,[2] while Eldon, generally associated with attempts to make the concept of precedent more formal, had a healthy belief in the need for flexibility.[3] If the House of Lords had basically accepted the presumption of stare decisis in decision making by early in the nineteenth century,[4] that assertion should cause no surprise. Despite some claims to the contrary, that most political of judicial bodies, the Supreme Court of the United States, was in a similar position. After the Chase impeachment in the first decade of the nineteenth century, "what carried the day, in a sense, was the John Marshall solution. The judges would take refuge in political decorum. The essence of their job would always be to make and interpret policy; but policy would be divorced from overt, partisan politics. Principles and policy would flow, at least ostensibly, from the logic of the law; they would not follow the naked give and take of the courthouse square. Justice would be blind; and it would wear a poker face."[5] Lawrence Friedman's description could, in many respects, be fairly adapted to the activities of the House of Lords. Indeed, the argument can be made that, for a significant part of the nineteenth century, the law

---

Karl Llewellyn claimed that the Grand Style prevailed roughly during the period 1820–60 and was then replaced by the Formal Style; Karl N. Llewellyn, *The Common Law Tradition,* e.g., at 35–44. This assertion, even as a generalization, must also be treated with caution. If the Grand Style was used by the New York Court for Impeachments and Errors and its 1846 successor, the Court of Appeals, it was most certainly not used by the Connecticut Supreme Court of Errors and Appeals; and if Chief Justice Shaw of the Supreme Judicial Court of Massachusetts was using the Grand Style, it was perhaps because he thought he was emulating the common law judges in Westminster Hall. In short, assertions about style, and hence about the approach to precedent, must be viewed with caution.

2. For the history of precedent up to the end of the eighteenth century, see L. Lewis, "The History of Judicial Precedent" and Carleton Kemp Allen, ed., *Law in the Making,* chap. 3.

3. Horace Twiss, 3 *The Public and Private Life of Lord Chancellor Eldon* 441 ff., gives a full account of Eldon's differing views on precedent.

4. Holdsworth believed it was established rather earlier; William S. Holdsworth, "Case Law" 180.

5. Lawrence M. Friedman, *A History of American Law* 116.

lords had more discretion in their decision-making process than the Supreme Court justices in Washington.

The Coming of a Doctrine

One of the problems in writing about the development of a formalistic system of precedent in the House of Lords is that, for much of the nineteenth century, there was considerable interweaving of two distinct issues: first, stare decisis—the theory behind the binding nature of statements of law in earlier decisions; and second, at a more practical and political level, how far the House was free, by legislation or resolution, to reverse a decision or order made by the House once it had been given. When one institution served as both a part of the legislature and a final appeal court, such confusion was inevitable.

Hale had argued that a petition of error was always available to ask the Lords to reconsider any particular decision, and apparently this was done in several instances in the seventeenth century.[6] By the end of the eighteenth century, however, Urquhart argued that once judgment had been entered by the House the case could not be reopened.[7] The House appeared to adopt the Urquhart position in *Stewart* v. *Agnew*[8] in 1823. In that case, the Deputy Speaker, Redesdale, made it clear that he was speaking solely of the specific review of an order already made.[9] Lord Chancellor Eldon, although obviously intending to discuss the same narrow topic, in fact spoke in terms that later generations could assume referred to stare decisis,[10] although Eldon was on record as holding that the House was not bound by its own prior decisions.[11] This flexibility for the future complemented Eldon's overall political view. The House of Lords was primarily a legislature, and the English concept of sovereignty did not allow the House to fetter its powers as to the future.

6. Charles M. Denison and Charles H. Scott, *The Practice and Procedure of the House of Lords* 119–25.

7. Thomas Malory Urquhart, *The Experienced Solicitor in Proceedings under the Appellate Jurisdiction of the Right Honorable the House of Lords on Appeals and Writs of Error, and the Jurisdiction Exercised by the House in Matters of Peerage.*

8. 1 Shaw 413 (H.L. 1823).

9. "[G]enerally speaking I take it to be a principle, that when a final judgement is once pronounced by a Court of competent jurisdiction, that Court has no right to alter its judgement, and it cannot be altered except by writ of error to a superior Court. If the decisions of this House, acting as a Court of ultimate resort, are subject to this sort of review, it would lead to mischief almost incalculable"; 426.

10. "In general, it is to be hoped that the decisions of the House are right, but whether right or wrong, it has been taken for granted that considerations of infinitely greater moment than the considerations which arise out of the particular mischief in particular cases, have led this House to determine that where a matter has been heard between the parties at the bar, and the House has given its decision upon the merits discussed by those parties, the House will not rehear the cause"; ibid. 432.

11. *Perry* v. *Whitehead*, 6 Ves. 544, 547 (1801).

The confusion of themes accelerated after *McGavin* v. *Stewart*,[12] in which Lord Wynford, in a Scottish appeal, ordered a new trial with a special jury, something unknown to Scottish law. Brougham, instead of seeking to vary the order, at once introduced a bill to amend the decision, although the problem was ultimately solved when the word "special" was dropped from the order.[13] Twenty years later the tables were turned. Brougham, in *Hutton* v. *Upfill*,[14] greatly upset the legal community with his decision on the vital question of the liability of shareholders to creditors in the winding up of a railway company. The case had begun before Brougham's brother, sitting as a Master, who held the shareholders liable as contributors; but the brother's decision was overruled by a Vice-Chancellor. Although Brougham alleged he had the concurrence of Cottenham,[15] he in fact sat alone when the appeal reached the Lords,[16] where he restored his brother's judgment in favor of the creditors. Campbell's response to this holding was to give Brougham a taste of his own medicine and to introduce a bill to reverse the specific decision. Campbell later wrote, "Apprehensions were entertained that an Act of Parliament would be necessary to set it right. But to save Brougham this disgrace, which he once proposed to put upon Lord Wynford, we contrived, during the next session of Parliament, by a little straining and ingenuity in a similar case to draw distinctions whereby the law on the subject was satisfactorily re-established."[17]

The result was that Campbell, who believed that the House could recall an earlier order (or overrule it by statute), but who believed that principles once laid down should not be reviewed, was party to *Bright* v. *Hutton*.[18] The facts and law could not have been closer to *Hutton* v. *Upfill*. The same railway company was involved, the same creditor, and an identical decision by Master Brougham. The liability of the shareholder was again the legal problem involved. The common law judges were called in to advise the Lords. Baron Parke, giving the unanimous view of the judges, found the law to be that the shareholder was liable to contribute, but solely because of the decision in the *Upfill* case, which

12. 5 Wilson & Shaw 807 (H.L., Scot. 1831).

13. John Campbell, "Life of Lord Brougham," 8 *Lives of the Lord Chancellors*, 401; J. W. Gordon, *The Appellate Jurisdiction of the House of Lords and of the Full Parliament* 22–23. See also Minutes of Evidence, Select Committee on the Appellate Jurisdiction, 20 May 1856, 1 *H.L. Sessional Papers* (1856), at 84.

14. 2 H.L.C. 674 (1850).

15. See *Bright* v. *Hutton*, 3 H.L.C. 341, 389 (1851).

16. He was, of course, surrounded by lay peers to make up the quorum. Lords Templemore and Dufferin attended the first day, Lords Erskine and Wharncliffe the second, and a third group on the last day. On this, see Alfred Denning, *From Precedent to Precedent* 36.

17. Campbell, "Life of Lord Brougham," 508.

18. 3 H.L.C. 341 (1851).

they regarded as wrongly decided but binding.[19] The law lords heeded the warning, but not the opinion, of the common law judges and over-ruled *Upfill*. St. Leonards, the Lord Chancellor, presided and stated the rights of the House in Eldonian terms: "[A]lthough you are bound by your own decisions as much as any Court would be bound, so that you could not reverse your own decision in a particular case, yet you are not bound by any rule of law which you may lay down, if upon a subsequent occasion you should find reason to differ from that rule; that is, that this House like every Court of Justice, possesses an inherent power to correct an error into which it may have fallen."[20]

Lord Campbell naturally objected, asserting "with great deference" that "a decision of this high Court, in point of law, is conclusive upon this House itself, as well as upon all inferior tribunals. I consider it the constitutional mode in which the law is declared, and that, after such a judgement has been pronounced, it can only be altered by an Act of the Legislature."[21] Both he and Cranworth purported to be able to distin-guish Upfill's case on the ground that the latter was limited to its facts[22] or involved a mixed question of fact or law.[23] Even Brougham was able to accept this formula. Such legal subtleties have commended themselves to later judges, but St. Leonards and the greater part of the legal profes-sion[24] regarded the *Bright* case as overruling the earlier decision. To them it seemed not unreasonable that the final court of appeal should be free to reverse decisions and rules of law it had laid down in earlier cases;[25] indeed, in *Coilsen* v. *Coilsen*, St. Leonards reiterated that power.[26]

Campbell, however, in theory if not in practice, continued to reflect the stricter concepts of stare decisis that already had overtaken the lower courts. In the following year (1853) he had more cause for complaint. In *Egerton* v. *Lord Brownlow*,[27] the House of Lords again ignored the advice of the common law judges who had been summoned; the law

19. "[W]e consider your Lordships' decision to be binding upon every inferior Court, and for that reason we answer the question in the affirmative; but for that case, we, upon other decisions, should have been of a contrary opinion"; ibid. 387.

20. Ibid. 388.

21. Ibid. 391.

22. Per Campbell, ibid. 391–92.

23. Per Cranworth, ibid. 393.

24. R. Malins, M.P., 1856, Minutes, Select Committee (1856), at 41.

25. A view strongly supported by Lords Loughborough and St. Leonards in *Glendowyn* v. *Maxwell*, 1 Macq. 791 (1854).

26. "It has been doubted by a noble and learned lord whether this House can correct any error which it has committed. I certainly hold that this House has the same power that every other judicial tribunal has to correct an error, if it has fallen into one, in subsequently applying the "law to other cases." Brougham noted, "[I]t is a *quaestio vexata* how far we may or may not disregard any one of our own judgements when applied to another cause"; 5 H.L.C. 581 (1855).

27. 4 H.L.C. 1 (1853).

lords generously extended the doctrine of public policy to strike down a clause in a will that purported to make the son's inheritance dependent on his acquiring the title of Duke of Bridgewater. Campbell regarded this as a disgraceful decision and alleged that the Lords, in their judicial capacity, were legislating rather than administering the law;[28] although the case did not specifically raise the question of the right of the House to overrule its own earlier decisions, it did so by implication, and Campbell's general position was ominous for St. Leonards' attitude. The appearance in the Lords of Baron Parke as Lord Wensleydale in 1856 gave Campbell the support of another advocate of a strict concept of precedent[29] and during the Chancellorship of Campbell (1859–61), the prominence of a formal position in favor of stare decisis was assured.

In *Attorney-General* v. *Dean of Windsor*, Romilly, sitting at first instance, while following a precedent of the Lords, had opined that the Lords themselves might overrule their own earlier decisions.[30] Presiding in the Lords when the case came on appeal, Campbell was given an opportunity to refute such a view categorically. "I feel it my duty to say that I think this expression is incorrect. By the constitution of this United Kingdom, the House of Lords is the Court of Appeal in the last resort, and its decisions are authoritative and conclusive declarations of the existing state of the law, and are binding upon itself when sitting judicially, as much as upon all inferior tribunals."[31] Although Lord Kingsdown reserved the point[32] and Lords Chelmsford[33] and Wensleydale did not mention it, the more formalistic Campbell view was fast becoming accepted.

In 1861 *Beamish* v. *Beamish*[34] reached the House of Lords. This

28. John Campbell, "Life of Lord Lyndhurst," 8 *Lives of the Lord Chancellors* 187. It is typical of Campbell's complex character that he was also capable of accusing English lawyers of being too narrow; ibid. 140, discussing *Johnstone* v. *Beattie*, 10 Cl. & F. 42 (1843).

29. Parke B.'s judgment in *Mirehouse* v. *Rennell*, 1 Cl. & F. 527, 546 (1833), is regarded as a classic statement of the modern doctrine of precedent.

30. "The decisions of the House are binding on me and upon all the courts except itself, . . . The House of Lords can, if it thinks fit, decline to apply the principle of that case to the present"; 24 Beavan 679, 715 (1858).

31. 8 H.L.C. 369, 390 (1860).

32. "[The question] with respect to the extent to which judicial decisions of your Lordships' House are binding on subsequent cases in the House itself, and all other English tribunals . . . open[s] [up] questions of great constitutional importance, the decision of which is not necessary in the present case. I allude to them now only for the purpose of saying that I desire to reserve my opinion upon them when they arise, entirely unprejudiced by anything which has passed in this discussion"; ibid. 458.

33. Chelmsford, however, said generally of precedent, "No case on this subject can, however, be a governing precedent for any other, because as it was admitted, the whole doctrine of charitable gifts ultimately resolves itself into the intention of the donor"; ibid. 437.

34. 9 H.L.C. 274 (1861).

case questioned the validity of a marriage at which no clergyman had been present (except, in the peculiar circumstances of this case, the bridegroom himself). The House held that this was the point decided in *R. v. Millis.*[35] In *Millis* a remarkable 1–1 decision of necessity affirmed the court below, holding that the presence of a clergyman was necessary. In the *Beamish* case the common law judges were again summoned and, although they showed little respect for the decision in *Millis*,[36] Lord Campbell knew his duty:

> If it were competent to me, I would now ask your Lordships to reconsider the doctrine laid down in R. v. Millis, particularly as the judges who were then consulted, complained of being hurried into giving an opinion without due time for deliberation . . . , [and the decision] was only pronounced on the technical rule of your Lordships' House, that where, upon a division, the numbers are equal, semper praesumitur pro negante.[37]
>
> But it is my duty to say that your Lordships are bound by this decision as much as if it had been pronounced nemine dissentiente, and that the rule of law which your Lordships lay down as the ground of your judgement, sitting judicially, as the last and supreme Court of Appeal for this empire, must be taken for law till altered by an Act of Parliament. . . . The law laid down as your ratio decidendi, being clearly binding on all inferior tribunals, and on all the rest of the Queen's subjects, if it were not considered as equally binding upon your Lordships, this House would be arrogating to itself the right of altering the law, and legislating by its own separate authority.[38]

While a refined formal theory of stare decisis was still some way away, the outlines of the approach were abundantly clear. In 1856 the legal profession still regarded the House of Lords, even in its appellate functions, as partially a legislative body, capable of overruling its earlier decisions and overtly changing the law. In that year Romilly and St. Leonards had argued before the Select Committee that there was still a role for lay peers in the House's appellate work, while, among others, they had also argued in favor of the House's right to resile from doctrines it had established earlier. By 1867, the House as a judicial body was generally expected—at least on the surface—to behave like any other English court and not to depart from its own earlier decisions, for fear that it might be exercising legislative functions,[39] and few suggested that any but the legally qualified were entitled to sit in appeals. It was in this context that the Lords' jurisdiction was "saved."

35. 10 Cl. & F. 534 (1844).
36. *Beamish* v. *Beamish* 9 H.L.C. 274 (1861).
37. Ibid. 338.
38. Ibid. Cranworth, Wensleydale, and Chelmsford appeared to concur.
39. For cases where stare decisis was still not thought to apply in the 1870s, see Denison and Scott *Practice and Procedure* 131–88.

The House of Lords after the Appellate Jurisdiction Act

The law lords—and especially the Lords of Appeal in Ordinary—who constituted the reformed House after 1876 were faced with an important political decision, namely, how to approach their task as members of the final court of appeal in a country that was increasingly becoming a "pure" democracy. Under the old regime, although the gradual professionalization of the judiciary had led to a steadily more stable approach to the functions of the House, a clear understanding of the role of a reformed final court of appeal was by no means established in 1876. The idea that the House had legislative functions even when sitting in its judicial capacity was still an acceptable one to conservative constitutionalists, although increasingly alien to utilitarian democracy.[40] While the concepts of utilitarian formalism might increasingly easily permeate the lower courts, such was not possible in the Lords.

The most obvious obstacle to a scientific formalism was the office of the Lord Chancellor itself. Some of the conflict between law and politics was patently obvious in the legislative and judicial functions of the office; but it was not the only obstacle. Until well into the twentieth century, most law lords felt free to speak out legislatively on virtually any issue. Indeed, they could justify that attitude on the ground that they had been left as members of the legislature for that very purpose. Yet even if the law lords themselves had sought to move out of the political fray, any chance to do so would have been undermined by the role that the Lord Chancellors of this period played in politics. Selborne (1880–85) and Cairns (1874–80) were national figures who ensured that important political battles were still fought in the Lords.[41] Halsbury (1885–86; 1886–92; 1895–1905) and Loreburn (1905–12) were also national figures, and although legislative power was by that period clearly ebbing from the Lords, those men dominated politics by their commitment to principle. Moreover, they were all active judges. While Lord Chancellor, the resilient Halsbury (he lived until he was ninety-eight) rarely failed to preside in the Lords in both its legislative and its judicial activities. Only ill health prevented Loreburn from being as pervasive in his activities.

One can judge the level of political commitment by the attitude of these Chancellors toward judicial appointments. Despite the eloquent and elegant defense by Robert Heuston,[42] there is little doubt that Hals-

---

40. Selborne, for instance, had still not fully accepted the Campbell position on stare decisis in *IRC v. Harrison*, L.R. 7 A.C. 1, 9 (1874).

41. So long as they dominated the Lords, both Liberals and Conservatives still used the upper house as a place to introduce government bills; John A. R. Marriott, *Second Chambers* 57.

42. R. F. V. Heuston, *Lives of the Lord Chancellors 1885–1940*, at 36–66. See also Halsbury's own defense; 330 *Parl. Deb.*, H.L. (3d ser.), cols. 1619 ff. (20 Nov. 1888).

bury appointed judges, both in the appeal courts and at first instance, as much for their political reliability and for political services performed as for any other reason.[43] Loreburn frowned on this practice, and even at the height of the radical reforms of Campbell-Bannerman's early years, he tried to ensure that justices of the peace, the lowest lay magistrates, were apolitical[44] and that High Court appointments were not (and were not seen as) political rewards.[45] Yet even Loreburn, when faced with the reality of judicial legislation in the House of Lords, was subject to rather different pressures. As Sir William Robson, the Attorney-General, noted of the House of Lords, in writing to Prime Minister Asquith at the time Robson was being made a law lord:

> The Lord Chancellor is no doubt anxious to exclude from his Court any appointment he believes to be political, but the political complexion of the Court cannot be altogether ignored especially in view of future developments. The tribunal would have to play a great part in disputes that are legal in form but political in fact, and it would be idle to deny the resolute bias of many of the judges—there and elsewhere. That bias will probably operate more than ever in cases that touch on labour, educational, constitutional and, for the future I might perhaps add, revenue questions.[46]

The power of the Lord Chancellors, however, went beyond their direct party political influence and the power to appoint judges. With respect to the appellate work of both the House of Lords and the Privy Council, it was they who determined the compositon of the panels of judges. Since this function was (and effectively still is) regarded as legitimate in the English political scene, it is unfair to complain that these panels were packed. Yet a political scientist might well so regard them. It is, for instance, possible to conceive that Bradlaugh, who had insisted on affirming rather than swearing in as an M.P., might not have persuaded the Lords to overrule the Court of Appeal's decision that he was liable to £355,000 in fines to common informers, had not the Liberal Selborne been presiding in *Bradlaugh v. Clarke*.[47] Yet even if one must be tentative

---

43. In the 1890s, Salisbury wrote to Halsbury that "[i]t is . . . the unwritten law of our party system; and there is no clearer statute in that unwritten law than the rule that party claims should always weigh very heavily in the disposal of the highest legal appointments. In dealing with them you cannot ignore the party system as you do in the choice of a general or an archbishop. It would be a breach of the tacit convention on which politicians and lawyers have worked the British Constitution together for the last 200 years"; Heuston, *Lives* 52.

44. Brian Abel-Smith and Robert Stevens, *Lawyers and the Courts* 96–97.

45. Haldane was severely criticized by his own party for failing to reward the faithful by appointment to the bench; Heuston, *Lives* 219.

46. Cited, ibid. 151.

47. 8 App. Cas. 354 (1883). Selborne was supported by Fitzgerald, a former Liberal M.P., and Watson, who, although a former Conservative politician, might be thought to have some sympathies with the Bradlaugh position. Blackburn dissented. See generally Walter L. Arnstein, *The Bradlaugh Case*, chap. 21. It was in this appeal that the last

about some of Selborne's panel packing, there was no doubt that Loreburn was often careful in the choosing of the law lords who were to sit in both the House of Lords and the Privy Council. It was by such careful selection that Loreburn helped to return some powers to the dominion government in Canadian appeals[48] and in English appeals ensured that the courts would abandon attempts to interfere directly with policy decisions by the executive.[49]

Sometimes, of course, the making up of panels, no matter who was Chancellor, was but a reflection of the vanities of the law lords;[50] Loreburn, however, was as tough a politician in his selection of panels as he was when presiding in debates. When, in *Colquhoun v. Faculty of Advocates*,[51] Loreburn found the law lords were divided 2–2, a situation that would have meant upholding the lower court decision of which he disapproved, he ordered the appeal reheard before seven law lords, the additional three proving more sympathetic to his viewpoint.[52] On the other hand, when, on a point of interpretation of land valuation under Lloyd George's 1911 budget provided another 2–2 decision, thereby upholding a Court of Appeal decision favorable to the government, Loreburn allowed it to stand. When the list of cases was juggled in order to bring on the English appeal before a Scottish appeal, on a parallel point, Lord Salvesen, the Scottish judge, was led to the conclusion that "politics had been allowed to affect the decision of the House of Lords, in a way that is far from creditable."[53]

While Salvesen knew of "no other example in my time," the Cabinet

---

attempt by a lay peer to vote was made—Lord Denman (the son of the Chief Justice) purporting to vote with Blackburn; David Tribe, *President Charles Bradlaugh M.P.* 224–25.

48. See chap. 5, at 180–81.

49. E.g., *Board of Educ. v. Rice*, [1911] A.C. 179.

50. The clerk to the Privy Council, Sir Almeric Fitzroy, described the difficulties of putting together a panel to hear *Duke of Northumberland v. Attorney-General*, [1905] A.C. 406:

A characteristic instance of the Lord Chancellor's (Halsbury's) humour occurred yesterday. An appeal by the Duke of Northumberland on some point touching estate duty was down for hearing in the House of Lords, whereupon Lord James, though of course not in so many words, intimated that his familiarity with Dukes would render it difficult for him to preserve an impartial mind. The Chancellor who was quite equal to the occasion, sent him to the Judicial Committee to hear an Indian appeal, which James hates as he knows nothing of Indian law and is reduced to a humiliating silence, and brought Davey to the House of Lords, who knowing the circumstances, took it as an intimation that he was not familiar with Dukes, which was wounding to his vanity. The Lord Chancellor scored by exchanging a weak lawyer for a strong one and flouted two colleagues, neither of whom he is particularly fond of. [Almeric Fitzroy, 1 *Memoirs* 248]

51. [1908] Sess. Cas. 10 (H.L.).

52. Hugh Macmillan, *A Man of Law's Tale* 116–18; A. A. Paterson, "Judges" 124.

53. Cited, Paterson, "Judges" 126.

Office records reveal at least two other examples. One of the earliest problems the new Campbell-Bannerman administration faced was disputes about the Cooper-Temple amendment to the 1902 Education Act, which had provided for limited state aid to church-affiliated schools. During the long vacation of 1906, the Court of Appeal handed down a decision refusing a mandamus to force an education authority to pay that part of teachers' salaries that reflected the time spent in giving religious instruction.[54] Augustine Birrell at once warned his cabinet colleagues that "as soon as Parliament meets the Government will be bombarded with questions about this case." Birell thus looked for advice to the legal member of the cabinet, Lord Chancellor Loreburn, and was able to report: "The Lord Chancellor, with whom I have had the advantage of a long talk on this subject, is strongly of the opinion (knowing nothing of the *legal* merits of the case, for he has studiously avoided reading the judgement in the Courts below or any of the comments thereupon) that as a matter of policy and fair play we should not only appeal, but also apply for an order expediting the hearing of the appeal, so that it may be disposed of without a moment's unnecessary delay."[55] Disposed of it was, moreover, four months later, with the Lord Chancellor presiding. A generally liberal House[56], chosen by the Chancellor, reversed the Court of Appeal. Loreburn delivered the leading speech, which he began by announcing that the question must be decided "upon the construction of the Act. We have nothing to do with the policy or with any unexpressed intentions of Parliament. Our duty is simply to ascertain the meaning of the Act as it stands."[57] Pure separation of powers rarely exists; such lack of separation was remarkable.

Just as in the appointment of judges, Halsbury used the political power of his office to influence judicial decisions most actively. In the important tax and charity case of *Inland Revenue Commissioners* v. *Pemsel*,[58] Halsbury held up the decision for sixteen months in an effort to break the majority against his position.[59] In *General Assembly of Free Church of Scotland* v. *Lord Overtoun*,[60] involving over two million pounds and the vast complexities of Scottish ecclesiastical history,[61] Halsbury engineered the reversal of a unanimous Court of Session decision,

54. *Attorney-General* v. *West Riding of Yorkshire County Council*, [1906] 2 K.B. 676 (C.A.).

55. Cabinet Office Papers, 1906, 37/83/73, Public Record Office.

56. Loreburn, Ashbourne, Macnaghten, Davey, and Atkinson.

57. *Attorney-General* v. *West Riding of Yorkshire County Council*, [1907] A.C. 29, 34 (1906).

58. [1891] A.C. 531.

59. Paterson, "Judges" 122.

60. [1904] A.C. 515 (Scot.).

61. Thomas Shaw, *Letters to Isabel* (1921), at 101.

partly by excluding the most knowledgeable Scottish judge.[62] After a hostile public reaction to the reversal, the government had to appoint a commission and in effect overrule the decision. By this time, however, Halsbury had managed to reactivate[63] the confusion of fifty years earlier —the relationship between the reversal of an earlier order or decision and the wider issue of stare decisis in the final appeal court.

There can be little doubt about the strength of Halsbury's statements. In *London Street Tramways Company* v. *London County Council* he declared that

a decision of this House once given upon a point of law is conclusive upon this House afterwards, and that it is impossible to raise that question again as if it was res integra and could be reargued, and so the House be asked to reverse its own decision. . . . My Lords, it is totally impossible, as it appears to me, to disregard the whole current of authority upon this subject, and to suppose that what some people call an "extraordinary case," an "unusual case," a case somewhat different from the common, in the opinion of each litigant in turn, is sufficient to justify the rehearing and rearguing before the final Court of Appeal of a question which has been already decided. Of course I do not deny that cases of individual hardship may arise, and there may be a current of opinion in the profession that such and such a judgement was erroneous; but what is that occasional interference with what is perhaps abstract justice as compared with the inconvenience —the disastrous inconvenience—of having each question subject to being reargued and the dealings of mankind rendered doubtful by reason of different decisions, so that in truth and in fact there would be no real final Court of Appeal?[64]

Halsbury put the matter in even more simplistic terms a few years later in the *Earldom of Norfolk Peerage Claim*.[65] "[T]o alter it [the law] or even modify it is the function of the Legislature, and not of your Lordships' House."[66]

In many ways, Halsbury's statements have been sadly misunderstood. The establishmentarian response to political and social pressures —namely, that politics and policy could be separated from the legal and administrative, which of necessity had to remain in the hands of the experts—had been slowly emerging since 1832. For instance, the *Law Quarterly Review*, in discussing the *London Street Tramways* case,

62. Paterson, "Judges" 122–23.

63. On the reaction to the decision, see Gordon, *Appellate Jurisdiction*, "Prefatory."

64. [1898] A.C. 375, 379.

65. [1907] A.C. 10, 12 (1906). See also Davey's remarks: "Whenever a Court or this House, acting judicially, declares the law, it is presumed to lay down what the law is and was, although it may have been misunderstood in former days, and this House is bound by its own declarations of the law in all matters within its jurisdiction. In fact, this House, exercising its judicial functions, has no jurisdiction or power to alter the law when once ascertained in a binding way"; ibid. 16–17.

66. For other statements by Halsbury of this strict view, see *Jacob* v. *Jacob*, Opinions of their Lordships, 1900; and *Pledge* v. *White*, [1896] A.C. 187.

thought Halsbury's principle "no great novelty" and disputed only his claim that it had been established for centuries. Sir Frederick Pollock, the editor of the *Review*, used Halsbury's words as evidence not that the House of Lords was not in the business of lawmaking but rather as evidence that "decisions of the House of Lords are, or may be, acts of legislation."[67]

Yet other oddities emerge about a decision that is invariably cited as the basis of the modern doctrine of stare decisis.[68] The most remarkable is that *London Street Tramways* was closer to a res judicata situation than the more conventional stare decisis aspect of precedent.[69] The rubric of the report reads:

House of Lords' Decision—*Res judicata*—Tramways,
Compulsory purchase of—Tramways Act 1870.

The London County Council had required the tramway company, for the second time, to sell to them some of the company's tramway operations. On the prior occasion when this had happened, the parties had had a dispute about the amount payable; and in the earlier decision in *London Street Tramways* v. *London County Council*,[70] the House of Lords decided that the price was to be the cost of construction less depreciation and that no account could be taken of profits. The only question then was whether there was any means of reviewing this judgment; clearly the decision had to be that there was not. There was, then, no question that the facts of the two cases were in the full sense of the word "identical," and, seen in this light, Halsbury's words were not remarkable.

Halsbury, however, probably intended his approach to have wider significance. For either political or possibly intellectual reasons, he was anxious to restate the formalistic theory of the basis of the English judicial function: namely, that English judges merely declared preexisting

67. 14 *Law Quarterly Review* 331–32 (1898). Pollock also opined, "It may be doubted whether at the present day even a reformer such as Bentham might not prefer the coherent legislation of the Courts to the ill-constructed statutes enacted by Parliamentary ignorance and incapacity; and the work of the Courts would be more coherent in proportion as its finality is recognised"; ibid. 331.

68. E.g., Rupert Cross, *Precedent in English Law* 105–7 (2d ed.).

69. Halsbury's statement indeed reveals some confusion of thought, not unique to this opinion. See also, for example, *Smith* v. *Cooke*, [1891] A.C. 297, 299; *Webb* v. *Outrim*, [1907] A.C. 81 (P.C. 1906).

70. (1894) A.C. 489. See also the *Edinburgh Street Tramways Co.* v. *Edinburgh Corporation*, [1894] A.C. 456 (Scot.). In the later *London Street Tramways* case, Sir Robert Reid (later Lord Loreburn) began his argument for the appellants: "This is in substance a petition to reconsider and overrule the decisions of this House in the *Edinburgh Street Tramways* and the *London Street Tramways* cases upon the constructions of s.43 of the Tramways Act, 1870. There are certain differences between the present facts and the facts in those cases, which are set out in the appellants' case, but they are comparatively unimportant." Counsel for the respondents was not called on and the House did not reserve judgment; [1898] A.C. 375, 376.

law. Such a pious hope was facilitated by Halsbury's simplistic view of life and language. He had predicted that the Interpretation Act of 1889 would "give the public a dictionary which will enable them to understand the language used in statutes."[71] In the same debate he established his linguistic position as being that "[t]here should be rule of law by statute, and then the question will simply be what is the construction to be placed upon this Act."[72] A Lord Chancellor who could believe that perhaps could take seriously the mechanistic view of the judicial process expounded in *London Street Tramways*.[73] If Halsbury represented the formal acceptance that even the highest courts in England took seriously the declaratory theory of law, his attitude also made it clear that, both politically and legally, the area reserved for judicial discretion remained large.

Halsbury's Theories: Practical Decisions and Practical Politics

It is often forgotten that Halsbury was a practicing judge, much of whose day-to-day appellate work had little relationship to his widely cited statements on precedent. In 1900, for instance, two years after *London Street Tramways*, Halsbury was faced with a novel issue in *De Nicols v. Curlier*.[74] The question was whether a Frenchwoman who had lived with her French husband in England, where the husband had acquired British nationality and disposed of all his property by will, could step in and, under the relevant French law of community property, claim one half of his movable property. The Court of Appeal had felt that it was bound by the decision in *Lashley v. Hogg*,[75] in which the House of Lords had decided that by Scottish law in this situation the widow's position was regulated by the will of the husband. Halsbury, however, came to the conclusion that the most satisfactory result in this case would be for the French law of community of goods still to regulate the position. He therefore took a tough line toward stare decisis. "My Lords, I

71. 338 *Parl. Deb.*, H.C. (3d ser.), col. 1567 (29 July 1889).
72. Ibid., col. 1568.
73. As evidence of the seriousness with which Halsbury purported to hold his views, one should recall his approval, in *Janson v. Driefontein Consol. Gold Mines*, [1902] A.C. 484, of Sargeant Marshall's pronouncement on public policy: "To avow or insinuate that it might, in any case, be proper for a judge to prevent a party from availing himself of an indisputable principle of law, in a Court of Justice, upon the ground of some notion of fancied policy or experience, is a new doctrine in Westminster Hall, and has a direct tendency to render all law vague and uncertain. A rule of law, once established, ought to remain the same until it be annulled by the Legislature, which alone has the power to decide on the policy or experience of repealing laws, or suffering them to remain in force." To this, Halsbury himself added, "I deny that any Court can invent a new head of public policy"; ibid. 491.
74. [1900] A.C. 21 (1899).
75. 4 Paton 581 (H.L., Scot. 1804).

should think that, in order to be binding on your Lordships, a previous decision must be in principle, and as applicable to the same circumstances, identical."[76] *Lashley* v. *Hogg*, since it concerned the slightly different provisions of Scottish law, was clearly not identical. "It follows, therefore, if I am right, that that case is not binding on your Lordships, and that we are at liberty to decide the question now in dispute in accordance with reason and common sense."[77] According to these dicta, then, reason and common sense had almost as strong a claim as analogy in the process of legal reasoning.

The Lord Chancellor, however, had an armory of devices for escaping the force of his own statements. He maintained that to be binding on the court, a former case had to be "identical" in principle and circumstances. Thus, in *Quinn* v. *Leatham*[78] Halsbury declared that

every judgement must be read as applicable to the particular facts proved, or assumed to be proved, since the generality of the expressions which may be found there are not intended to be expositions of the whole law, but governed and qualified by the particular facts of the case in which such expressions are to be found. The other [observation he wished to make] is that a case is only an authority for what it actually decides. I entirely deny that it can be quoted for a proposition that may seem to follow logically from it. Such a mode of reasoning assumes that the law is necessarily a logical code, whereas every lawyer must acknowledge that the law is not always logical at all.[79]

Two years later, in *Noakes* v. *Rice*, the Lord Chancellor accepted the idea that "whatever rule is laid down one can reduce it to something like an absurdity by taking an extreme case."[80]

By narrowing the concept of a rule of law and broadening the concept of fact, Lord Halsbury was able to do virtually anything,[81] although that insight did not prevent him from expressing considerable contempt for those members of the judiciary who attempted to state broad rules.[82]

76. [1900] A.C. 21, 27 (1899).

77. Ibid. 30.

78. [1901] A.C. 495 (Ire.).

79. Ibid. 506. Halsbury's remarks were preliminary to his discussion of *Allen* v. *Flood*, [1898] A.C. 1 (1897), in which he had dissented.

80. [1902] A.C. 24, 29 (1901).

81. See other comments by Lord Halsbury in *Barraclough* v. *Cooper*, [1908] 2 Ch. 121n, 124 (H.L. 1905); *Cross, Tetley & Co.* v. *Catterall*, [1926] 1 K.B. 488n (H.L. 1905) (workman's compensation); *Colls* v. *Home & Colonial Stores*, [1904] A.C. 179 (nuisance). "The test . . . depend[s] upon the surroundings and circumstances of light coming from other sources. . . . What may be called the uncertainty of the test may also be described as its elasticity"; ibid. 184–85. Once satisfied that there was no binding precedent, he had no hesitation in deciding according to the "canons of common sense."

82. *Smith & Co.* v. *Bedouin Steam Navigation Co.*, [1896] A.C. 70 (Scot. 1895). "I myself rather protest . . . against laying down any rules that are not applicable to the particular case as it comes before us"; ibid. 74. *Kingsbury* v. *Walter*, [1901] A.C. 187. "I am not disposed to indulge in general abstract propositions"; ibid. 188. In similar vein was

Indeed, during these years the ability of the Lords to "distinguish the undistinguished" and to shape the law to the needs of the time (as the law lords perceived it) remained largely untouched. The willingness to read early *rationes decidendi* narrowly and to escalate the importance of "facts" was only one aspect of this flexible approach. No matter how the composition of the Lords' panels changed, the flexibility remained; and no one more elegantly manipulated the system than Halsbury himself.[83] Yet, to understand fully the flexibility that Halsbury retained in the whole realm of the appellate system, one must recall the immense power he possessed in naming panels of judges, a power he did not hesitate to use in the hearing of trade union cases[84] during his last Chancellorship.

In *Allen* v. *Flood*,[85] in connection with a demarcation dispute, the defendant, the secretary of a local branch of the Boilermakers Society, had persuaded the plaintiff's employer to dismiss the plaintiff, without, however, breaching any contract between the employer and the plaintiff. It was not an easy case; yet it was a vital one for the unions, which at that time felt themselves to be fighting for survival on the margins of society. The Court of Appeal found for the plaintiff on the ground of conspiracy; the unions feared that they were about to be destroyed under the weight of the new scope of the test.

Halsbury felt equally concerned from his political standpoint, and he knew how to fight. He made it clear that he was in favor of upholding the appeal but, to his chagrin, found himself in a minority of two against a majority of five, including the Liberal law lords Herschell and Davey.

---

a remark of his in *Barraclough* v. *Cooper*, Opinions of their Lordships, 1905. "Speaking for myself, I must say that I am not fired with that ambition which appears to have prevailed in the mind of V.-C. Malins that it is possible to put the law into a perfectly satisfactory condition and to invent some canon of construction which shall prevent disputes over a will."

83. When it was a question of granting Lord Russell a judicial separation on the ground of his wife's cruelty, it was Herschell, Watson, Macnaghten, Shand, and Davey who refused to depart from the authorities; *Russell* v. *Russell*, [1897] A.C. 395. Lord Herschell announced, "I have no inclination towards a blind adherence to precedents. I am conscious that the law must be moulded by adapting it on established principles to the changing conditions which social development involves. But marital misconduct is unfortunately as old as matrimony itself. Great as have been the social changes which have characterized the last century in this respect, there has been no alternation—no new development. I think it is impossible to do otherwise than proceed upon the old lines"; ibid. 460–61. Halsbury, no less, led Hobhouse, Ashbourne, and Morris in revolt against the authorities with the rallying cry, "Can anyone conceive a Court enforcing cohabitation with such a woman?" Ibid. 425. Hobhouse said, "I cannot persuade myself that any judge would have felt himself so bound by precedent as to compel an innocent husband to take back a wife guilty of falsehood and persecution such as has characterised the conduct of the Countess in this case"; ibid. 427.

84. On this period generally, see, e.g., H. A. Clegg, Alan Fox, and A. F. Thompson, 1 *A History of British Trade Unionism since 1899*, chap. 8; Henry Pelling, *A History of British Trade Unionism*, chaps. 6 and 7; K. W. Wedderburn, *The Worker and the Law* 227 ff.

85. [1898] A.C. 1 (1897).

At this point, without consulting his fellow law lords, Halsbury summoned all the High Court judges to advise the House—a remarkable medieval throwback that had little justification and only one precedent since the appearance of Lords of Appeal in 1877. One can only assume that Halsbury, having appointed many of these judges for their political views, felt he could rely on them in his hour of need. He was not disappointed. They advised the House that the plaintiff indeed had a right of action in conspiracy. Yet Halsbury's moves may well have strengthened the resolve of the law lords.[86] A majority of six (the Liberals Herschell, Davey, and James, the Scots Watson and Shand, and even the middle-of-the-road conservative Macnaghten) found for the defendant.[87]

The decision in *Allen* v. *Flood* was greeted with jubilation among trade unionists[88] and relief among lawyers.[89] These feelings were, however, short-lived. Three years later the House decided *Quinn* v. *Leatham*.[90] The question before the House was pinpointed and caricatured by Shand. "The question now raised is really whether, in consequence of the decision of this House in the case of *Allen* v. *Flood*, and of the grounds on which that case was decided, it is now the law that where the acts complained of are in pursuance of a combination or conspiracy to injure or ruin another, and not to advance the parties' own trade interests, and injury has resulted, no action will lie, or, to put the question in a popular form whether the decision in *Allen* v. *Flood* has made boycotting lawful."[91] The most significant fact in the appeal was that Halsbury had chosen his hearing panel carefully. Herschell was dead, and the other two Liberals, Davey and James, were not invited to sit. On the other hand, Lord Brampton, who as Mr. Justice Hawkins had been one of the common law judges summoned to advise the Lords in *Allen* v. *Flood* and who had sided with Halsbury, was included.[92] Moreover, it was in this case

86. For a description of the incident, see Heuston, *Lives* 118–22; Paterson, "Judges" 121.

87. Halsbury found support from Ashbourne and Morris in his dissent that, incidentally, he refused to circulate before delivery, contrary to the custom in the Lords. Arguing that "the right to employ their labour as they will is a right both recognised by the law and sufficiently guarded by its provisions to make any undue interference with that right an actionable wrong" (at 71), he admitted, "My difference is founded on the belief that in denying these plaintiffs a remedy we are departing from the principles which have hitherto guided our courts in the preservation of individual liberty to all" (at 90). Ironically, much of the speech by the author of the *London Street Tramways* case reads like a statement of what the law ought to be, although superficially it has a "declaratory theory of law" ring.

88. See Clegg, Fox, and Thompson, *History of British Trade Unionism* 308–9.

89. See e.g., "Note," 14 *Law Quarterly Review* 1 (1898): "[W]e can only express in the fewest words our conviction that the House of Lords has never deserved better of the Common Law."

90. [1901] A.C. 495 (Ire.).

91. Ibid. 513.

92. Paterson, "Judges" 122.

that Halsbury observed, of *Allen* v. *Flood*, "A case is only an authority for what it actually decides. I entirely deny that it can be quoted for a proposition that may seem to follow logically from it."[93] The advocate of the strict rule of stare decisis was up to his tricks again. The result was foregone;[94] and the reaction, predictable.

Robert Reid, later Lord Loreburn, complained of the "loose and dangerous, one might almost say the slippery, language used in regard to the meaning of the term, 'conspiracy.' "[95] The *Law Quarterly Review*, an admirer of the decision, observed that "[i]t is idle to attack the result arrived at by the House on the ground that it is judge-made law, for in whatever way the House had decided, their judgement would have amounted to judicial legislation;"[96] in the High Court, one of Halsbury's least distinguished protégés, Grantham,[97] observed of *Allen* v. *Flood*, "[T]he House of Lords has been getting around [it] so there is little left of that case now."[98] The author of the narrow doctrine of precedent in *London Street Tramways* had not yet, however, finished.

The climax of Halsbury's assault on the unions came in *Taff Vale Railway Company* v. *Amalgamated Society of Railway Servants*, in 1901,[99] a direct fight between capital and labor for the support of the law. The question was the basic one of whether trade unions were liable in tort for loss arising from a strike. At first instance Mr. Justice Farwell —a Halsbury appointee—not only granted an injunction in favor of the railway company, but under the head of "further relief" he held the officers of the union personally liable in tort damages for inducing their members to breach a contract. The Court of Appeal reversed.[100] To the astonishment of the legal profession and the dismay of the unions, the

93. *Quinn* v. *Leatham*, [1901] A.C. 495, 506 (Ire.).

94. The answer was made to appear a simple one. In *Allen* v. *Flood* the element of conspiracy had been absent, so the presence of malice could make no difference, but in conspiracy, malice or intent to injure rather than the protection of one's own interests is the gist of the action. These ideas can be traced in the judgments in this case, although they are buried under a mass of other matter; ibid. 506–7. One thing at any rate was clear: the tort of civil conspiracy was slowly taking shape as a potent weapon in the attempt to counter trade unionism.

Halsbury was triumphant, and he made no effort to conceal that this was to a great extent a policy decision. "If upon these facts so found the plaintiff could have no remedy against those who had thus injured him, it could hardly be said that our jurisprudence was that of a civilized community, nor indeed do I understand that anyone has doubted that, before the decision in *Allen* v. *Flood* in this House, such fact[s] would have established a cause of action against the defendants"; ibid. 506.

95. 108 *Parl. Deb.*, H.L. (4th ser.), col. 307 (14 May 1902).

96. "Note," 18 *Law Quarterly Review* 5 (1902).

97. Grantham nearly achieved the distinction of being removed (i.e., impeached) after an address to both Houses; Heuston, *Lives* 257–58.

98. Cited, Wedderburn, *Worker and Law* 258–59.

99. See generally on the whole background, P. S. Bagnell, *The Railwaymen* 212 ff.

100. [1901] 1 K.B. 170, 176 (C.A.).

House held that a trade union could be sued in such a situation.[101] Having arranged for a sympathetic panel of law lords, Halsbury issued a brief opinion, the core of which stated simply that "[i]f the Legislature has created a thing which can own property, which can employ servants, and which can inflict injury, it must be taken, I think, to have implicitly given the power to make it suable in a Court of Law for injuries purposely done by its authority and procurement."[102]

This case must bear the distinction of being one of the politically unhappiest decisions that the House ever rendered. It permanently weakened the reputation of the law lords,[103] and the judgment had immediate and dramatic effect. As the *London Echo* said, "A strike under these conditions becomes nearly impossible, and without the ultimate right to strike—however cautious it may be in using it—a union is impotent."[104] The decision drove the unions to political action—specifically to the support of the Labour party[105]—and produced concrete results in the 1906 general election in the form of a massive Liberal landslide, with many of the M.P.'s in the category of "Lib-Labs."

The election returns left a political situation in which the passage of the Trade Disputes Act of 1906,[106] putting the unions largely outside the

101. *Taff Vale Ry.* v. *Amalgamated Soc'y of Ry. Servants*, [1901] A.C. 426 (Macnaghten, Shand, Brampton, Lindley).

102. Ibid. 436.

103. R. C. K. Ensor, *England 1870–1914* 379. As an appellate court the House also suffered in reputation. Instead of acting as a clarifying agency or even a reasoned advocate of judicial legislation, its behavior often sowed confusion and defied rational analysis—either legal or political. In 1903 Haldane, at that time a member of the House of Commons, wrote, "I should be very sorry to be called on to tell a trade union secretary how he could conduct a strike lawfully. The only answer I could give would be that, having regard to the diverging opinion of the judges, I did not know"; Richard Burdon Haldane, "The Labourer and the Law" 372.

104. 20 Dec. 1902. The Amalgamated Society of Railway Servants (ASRS) paid out £23,000 in damages, and an additional £19,000 in costs.

105. In the years 1903–5, despite rising prices, the number of strikes per year was only half that of any year between 1890 and 1900. See generally P. Poirer, *The Advent of the Labour Party*. The working classes needed a different weapon and were not slow to forge one. The material was close at hand. The Labour Representation Committee (LRC), something of an orphan since its creation in 1900, had its chance. As soon as the judgment of the House of Lords became known, the LRC sent out thousands of circulars to trade unionists all over the country, urging that the unions, attacked in workshop, courts, and press, had no refuge henceforth but the ballot box. The response was immediate. Previously 41 unions had been affiliated with the LRC. By the beginning of 1903 the number had risen to 127. This represented an increase in total trade union membership from 353,070 in 1901 to 847,315. This sudden flourishing produced concrete results in the general election of 1906. In 1902 the LRC had three representatives in Parliament; in the 1906 election no less than 29 were successful. Thus, with the 24 miners and Lib-Labs the total number of "labour" men in the House was 53. It can thus be argued that *Taff Vale* "made" the British Labour Party.

106. This was one of the first acts of the Liberal government under strong pressure from the Labour members; 6 Edw. 7, c. 47. The Liberals had been arguing in favor of such

ambit of the legal system, seemed logical. Halsbury was in despair. "I feel that this Bill is most unjust, and that it is contrary to the spirit of English liberty";[107] indeed, it was a "Bill for the purpose of legalising tyranny."[108] Loreburn, on the other hand, saw the legislation as the end of a four-year campaign. "This Bill proposes to place civil responsibility for conspiracy on the same footing as criminal, nothing more or less."[109] The strike was, at least in theory, to be outside the purview of the English judiciary.

When the act came to be considered in 1909 in *Conway* v. *Wade*,[110] Loreburn steered the Lords toward a via media.[111] Yet the Conservative law lords had one last hand to play, in respect to the political levy that the unions had begun to impose to support Labour M.P.'s. *Amalgamated Society of Railway Servants* v. *Osborne* (1910)[112] raised the validity of

---

a bill since May 1902. The conservative solution had been to appoint a Royal Commission. The majority report of that commission, signed by Dunedin, Cohen, and Webb, declared that the *Taff Vale* judgment "involved no new principle and was not inconsistent with the legislation of 1871" (Cd. 2825, 1906), but suggested further compromise legislation (see Clegg, Fox, and Thompson, *History of British Trade Unionism* 393). Lewis and Lushington, the minority, considered these proposals overgenerous to the unions. In any event, the Royal Commission's views were disregarded.

107. 166 *Parl. Deb.*, H.L. (4th ser.), col. 704 (4 Dec. 1906).

108. Ibid., col. 709.

109. Ibid., col. 694. For his previous attempts as Sir Robert Reid in the Commons, see 108 ibid., col. 305 (14 May 1902); 122 ibid., col. 244 (8 May 1903); 133 ibid., col. 979 (22 Apr. 1904). Loreburn had indeed made a valiant attempt to balance the scales prior to the act in *Denaby & Cadeby Main Collieries, Ltd.* v. *Yorkshire Miners' Ass'n*, [1906] A.C. 384, the sequel to *Yorkshire Miners' Ass'n* v. *Howden*, [1905] A.C. 256. The escape route was to find that the union had not induced an illegal strike.

110. [1909] A.C. 506.

111. There the defendant trade union official, acting without authority from his union, encouraged the plaintiff's employers to dismiss him, by threatening that otherwise the men would strike. Section 3 of the act conferred immunity from suit for procuring breach of contract, so long as it was "in contemplation or furtherance of a trade dispute." Here the jury found that the defendant's object was to compel the plaintiff to pay an 8-year-old fine imposed by the union. It was held that there was not a trade dispute. Loreburn said, "A mere personal quarrel or a grumbling or an agitation will not suffice. It must be something fairly definite and of real substance"; ibid. 510. The Court of Appeal had thought that the 1906 act gave protection and Farwell, L.J., had attacked the act in the name of Bacon's *Abridgement*, Blackstone, and the Book of Proverbs; "Note," 25 *Law Quarterly Review* 3–4 (1909).

112. [1910] A.C. 87 (1909). On this case, see especially William B. Gwyn, *Democracy and the Cost of Politics in Britain*, chap. 8.

The success of the Labour Representation Committee at the 1906 election had depended to a large extent on financial support from the unions. The decision of the LRC's third annual conference in 1903 to raise a levy on affiliated unions of 1d. per member per year made available in the first year £2,500 for the support of those M.P.'s the executive sponsored. At the same time it was declared that candidates and M.P.'s should strictly abstain from identifying themselves with, or promoting the interests of, any section of the Liberal or Conservative parties and that M.P.'s should abide by the majority vote of the group or resign.

This idea was attractive to many unions. In 1903 the Executive Committee of the ASRS approved changes in the rules that included a scheme for obligatory subscription of

the compulsory political levy on members of a trade union. The right to impose such a levy was upheld at first instance, but the Court of Appeal reversed the grounds that "any such agreement [to bind a candidate to a political party] is void as against public policy."[113] The appeal was heard by Halsbury, Macnaghten, Atkinson, James, and Shaw; Loreburn, the Lord Chancellor, having a clear conflict of interest,[114] did not sit. Thus Halsbury, who seemed unaware of the social changes that had led to an expansion of union functions,[115] had the upper hand; the appeal was dismissed, the rules being held to be ultra vires. Loreburn was obviously not amused by the decision,[116] and he lectured the cabinet[117] with the result that, once more, the legislature intervened.[118]

In the long run the result of the decision was to consolidate the position of the Parliamentary Labour party. In 1903 the trade union

---

1/- per member per year to a parliamentary fund. Osborne and the Walthamstow Branch were opposed to any such compulsory levy and came down firmly on the antisocialist side by carrying a resolution in favor of a union ballot on the question of affiliation to the LRC. The ASRS, however, still selected three socialist candidates, and Osborne's reply was a threat to test the legality of the compulsory political levy. The ASRS then took the opinions of Sir Robert Reid, Q.C. (later Lord Loreburn) and Sir Edward Clark, Q.C. (a Conservative), who both advised that there was nothing illegal about parliamentary levies so long as rules to provide for them were properly passed by the union membership. As far as the ASRS was concerned, if the opinions of two lawyers of opposite political views coincided on such a crucial issue, that was the end of the matter. The 1/- levy then came into force in 1905. When, however, the ASRS considered altering the rules to provide that "[a]ll candidates shall sign and accept the conditions of the Labour Party and be subject to the whip," Osborne took legal action.

113. Per Lord Justice Fletcher Moulton, [1909] 1 Ch. 163, at 186.

114. While "conflict of interest" is an integral part of the office of the Lord Chancellor (and thus apparently unexamined), in this case Loreburn, while at the bar, had given the original opinion on which the political levy had been based.

115. See Pelling, *History of British Trade Unionism* 131.

116. See Heuston, *Lives* 164–65, on the deliberations between Robson (the Attorney-General) and Loreburn about the decision. Loreburn thought Halsbury's judgment "loosely reasoned," and he regarded Shaw's statements about the pledge not to be part of the *ratio decidendi*; Cabinet Office Papers, 1910, 37/104/57, Public Record Office.

117. After the Trade Union Congress had voted 1,717,000 to 13,000 in favor of the overruling of the decision, the Chancellor of the Duchy of Lancaster (J. A. Pease) circulated a memorandum to the cabinet, noting, at 44, that the Lord Chancellor wanted the decision reversed and citing him to the effect that "I cannot see what considerations of morals or policy ought to prevent trade unions from making it a condition of membership that members shall subscribe for political purposes, always supposing that they become members with knowledge of the terms upon which they had joined." Herbert Samuel, by then Postmaster General, on the other hand, supported the decision. "[T]he efficiency and security of trade unions in the exercise of their industrial functions are not only untouched but are safeguarded by the disputed judgement"; Cabinet Office Papers, 1910, 37/103/42, Public Record Office.

118. Trade Union Act of 1913. After the decision, Winston Churchill noted the existence of "statements [which] have been made from the bench reflecting on the trade unions in language which is extremely ignorant and wholly out of touch with the general development of modern thought, and which has greatly complicated the administration of justice and created a sense of distrust in the ordinary administration of the law"; cited, TUC Parliamentary Commission, 9th Quarterly Report, June 1911.

M.P.'s committed to support the Labour Representation Committee were a small minority compared to the "Lib-Labs." By 1910 only three Lib-Labs survived, while there were fifty M.P.'s accepting the whip of the Labour party. The fact that one of the judges in the *Osborne* majority, Shaw, was a Liberal, had possibly helped to separate the trade unions from the Liberal party.[119] The need for some new judicial approach that might be embraced by judges of all persuasions was obvious. A more "apolitical" approach had long since been followed by the lower courts. In the Lords it was to be provided by Haldane after his appointment as Lord Chancellor in 1912. In the meantime, the nature of the judicial process had become an important ingredient in party politics.

Law Lords, High Court Judges, and Precedent

In one sense, to emphasize the Halsbury position with respect to precedent may be a distortion since other law lords, while perhaps less willing to articulate conflicting positions,[120] were inevitably adopting them. Thus although Herschell, as a Liberal Lord Chancellor, was frequently seen attempting to reduce principles to rules, at other times he could be found arguing in favor of leaving as much as possible to the realm of fact.[121] Loreburn was a master of emphasizing the strong element of fact and thereby leaving escape routes for the future.[122] Lord Watson, a Scottish Lord of Appeal, could, for example, say that the

119. For an example of what Heuston (*Lives* 1164) describes as "hypocrisy" in Shaw's opinion, see [1910] A.C. 87, 115: "[I]n regard to the member of Parliament himself, he too is to be free; he is not to be the paid mandatory of any man, or organisation of men, nor is he entitled to bind himself to subordinate his opinions on public questions to others, for wages, or at the peril of pecuniary loss; and any contract of this character would not be recognised by a Court of law, either for its enforcement or in respect of its breach."

120. But see Lord Watson's murmurings against a strict concept of stare decisis in *Nordenfelt* v. *Maxim Nordenfelt Guns & Ammunition Co.*, [1894] A.C. 535, 553.

121. For example, on the construction of wills he said, "I think there has been too much tendency in England . . . to evolve rigid rules from decided cases, and to apply previous decisions to the interpretations of wills which have subsequently to be construed, instead of endeavouring to ascertain by a study of the particular instrument what was the intention of the testator"; *Hickling* v. *Fair*, [1899] A.C. 15, 25 (Scot. 1897). See also *Reddaway* v. *Banham*, [1896] A.C. 199.

122. For example, *Polsue & Alfieri, Ltd.* v. *Rushmer*, [1907] A.C. 121, 122: "There is no question of law that I can see in this case." The tort of nuisance appeared to consist of a single proposition: "[W]hether an interference is actionable depends on the circumstances." See also *Kirkwood* v. *Gass*, [1910] A.C. 422, on construing the Moneylenders Act of 1900. "I do not propose to define what is meant by carrying on business. . . . It is always a question of fact"; ibid. 424.

Another example of his relatively flexible approach to old authorities is *West Ham Union* v. *Edmonton Union*, [1908] A.C. 1, 4–5 (1907). "Great importance is to be attached to old authorities, on the strength of which many transactions may have been adjusted and rights determined. But where they are plainly wrong, and especially where the subsequent course of judicial decisions has disclosed weakness in the reasoning on which they are based, and practical injustice in the consequences that must flow from them, I consider it as the duty of this House to overrule them, if it has not lost the right to do so by itself expressly

antiquity of a decision might make its authority and relevance suspect[123] but then on another occasion would follow a rule of antiquity, although he would "have desired if possible to decide otherwise."[124] Similarly, Lord Macnaghten, an Equity lawyer, would sometimes find himself reluctantly bound by decisions of antiquity,[125] but when pursuing a policy vigorously enough he favored confining existing decisions[126] and refused to go further than necessary in deciding the case before him.[127] Nor is there any reason to think that other law lords of this period behaved differently.[128] In short, the immediate practical effects of the protestations like Halsbury's in *London Street Tramways* were limited, although intellectually the statement may have encouraged the law lords to substitute

---

affirming them." See also in *Glasgow Corp.* v. *Lorimer*, [1911] A.C. 209, 215 (Scot. 1910): "[I]n my view decided cases are chiefly valuable when they establish a principle. Where they do not establish a principle, but merely record the application of a principle to a particular set of facts, they may be instructive as to the point of view from which the judge regards the facts; but they are of little importance from any other point of view."

123. E.g., in *Allen* v. *Flood*, [1898] A.C. 1, 101 (1897). "I am very far from suggesting that the antiquity of a decision furnishes a good objection to its weight; but it is a circumstance which certainly invites and requires careful consideration, unless the decision is clearly in point, and its principle has since been recognised and acted upon." He would also use the popular device of relegating questions to the realm of fact. See *San Paulo Ry.* v. *Carter*, [1896] A.C. 31, 39: "[T]he decision of this appeal does not involve any new controversy upon the construction of the Income Tax Acts. It depends, in my opinion, upon the answer which ought to be given to a single issue of fact."

124. *Pledge* v. *White*, [1896] A.C. 187, 191.

125. "My Lords, speaking for myself I agree with the conclusion at which the Lord Chancellor has arrived. That the law with regard to fixtures as between mortgagor and mortgagee is perfectly satisfactory, I should be sorry to affirm; but I am sure much mischief would be created if there were a departure at this stage from the law which has been looked upon as governing such transactions as this ever since the case of *Mather* v. *Frazer*"; *Reynolds* v. *Ashby & Son*, [1904] A.C. 466, 470–71. This constitutes the whole of his judgment. See also *Samuel* v. *Jarrah Timber & Wood Paving Corp.*, [1901] A.C. 323.

126. E.g., *Bradley* v. *Carritt*, [1903] A.C. 253, 259. "I must say, speaking for myself, that I am not sure that it would be a great misfortune if the operation of every decision were to be confined to the matter decided and the principles on which the decision rests. Harm, I think, is sometimes done by general expressions, even in praise of a principle which everybody admires in the abstract, when they are not necessary for the purpose in hand. Though true in themselves, they are apt to be misunderstood owing to the connection in which they are found."

127. E.g., *Saunderson* v. *Baron Von Radoch*, Opinions of their Lordships, 1905. "Your Lordships were asked to lay down a rule that would apply to all cases. I do not think it is possible to do that."

128. See for instance, ibid., where the question was whether the master's order with regard to some interrogatories had been proper, and counsel had specifically asked the court to lay down some rule that would be a guide for the future. James added, "It would be unwise to lay down any positive rule by way of definition as to the granting of these orders for interrogatories. Each case must be determined according to the discretion of the tribunal." Davey concurred, but thought there was a test: "Will the answer to the interrogatory which is objected to either tend to support the plaintiff's case or tend to enable him to destroy that of his adversary?" On a similar point, it was held in *Kent Coal Concessions* v. *Duguid*, [1910] A.C. 452, that in an appeal about a master's discretion as to a further affidavit of documents, no question of "principle" was involved.

narrow rules of law for broad principles and to label problems as "fact" rather than "law."[129] Certainly the jurisprudential underpinnings of the distinction between law and fact were not always easy to comprehend.[130]

Yet, contrasted with the lower courts, up to the Edwardian period, the law lords took a remarkably casual approach to precedent and stare decisis. By the time the superior courts were rationalized in the 1870s, the judges of what became the Supreme Court were more than accustomed to that aspect of formalism represented by the declaratory theory, namely, that they declared preexisting law. By that time there were a number of factors that made it easier to be more "scientific" about the law. The 1860s saw the establishment of the quasi-official law reports and the beginning of a parliamentary draftsmen's office. Each in its own way contributed to a new approach to the law. The decisions of the courts were by then reported far more systematically than they had ever been in the past, and the statutes that the courts were increasingly called upon to construe were drafted with unaccustomed precision. The same spirit encouraged at least some revival in legal education,[131] and the reformed lower courts undoubtedly aided the "scientific spirit."

129. For other examples, see *Johnstone* v. *Haviland*, [1896] A.C. 95, 104 (Scot.), concerning double portions in Scotland, where Herschell commented, "It comes then to be a question of fact to be determined in each case, whether there is enough to shew that he did not intend the disposition to be in satisfaction of his obligation, but did intend it to be a gift." Likewise, *Leigh* v. *Taylor*, [1902] A.C. 157 (1901), on fixtures. See especially 158–59.

The approach to negligence was similar. See Loreburn in *Toal* v. *North British Ry.*, [1908] A.C. 352, 355 (Scot.). "What was the duty of the railway company in this matter, and what they did or omitted to do, is for a jury to determine." A similar approach appeared in cases as widely separated as collision and libel. See, e.g., *The Draupner*, [1910] A.C. 450: "The only question is one of inference of fact." In *Linotype Co.* v. *British Empire Type Setting Co.*, Opinions of their Lordships, 1899, Halsbury said, "I am reluctant to quote authority since in actions for libel it is difficult if not impossible, to make one case an authority for another."

See also the insistence, even with respect to the taxation of insurance companies, that flexibility must be maintained. *Sun Ins. Office* v. *Clark*, [1912] A.C. 443, where Loreburn commented on the supposed rule laid down in *General Accident Fire & Life Assurance Co.* v. *McGowan*, [1908] A.C. 207 (Scot.): "I am equally anxious that your Lordships should not be supposed to have laid down that the method applied by the Commissioners in the present case has any universal application. If the Crown wishes in any future instance to dispute it the Crown can do so by evidence, and it is not to be presumed that it is either right or wrong"; ibid. 454.

130. See, for instance, Halsbury in *Reddaway* v. *Banham*, [1896] A.C. 199, 204, a passing-off case. "I believe in this case that the question turns upon a question of fact. The question of law is so constantly mixed up with the various questions of fact which arise on an inquiry of the character in which your Lordships have been engaged, that it is sometimes difficult when examining former decisions to disentangle what is decided as fact and what is laid down as a principle of law. . . . I believe the principle of law may be very plainly stated, and that is, that nobody has any right to represent his goods as the goods of somebody else." Compare *Cellular Clothing Co.* v. *Moxton & Murray*, [1899] A.C. 326 (Scot.), distinguishing *Reddaway* v. *Banham*.

131. London University had revived the teaching of law in the 1820s and 1830s. In the

Certainly, as the lower courts evolved during the century, the judges more steadily adopted the declaratory theory of law. These courts were, moreover, changing in different ways. The procedure of the courts had been massively reformed during the 1850s,[132] and the type of judge was changing. Whereas in the late eighteenth century the High Court judges had been chosen heavily from the same landed classes that dominated the Lords, by the mid-nineteenth century, sons of the professional classes predominated, with a strong element from the merchant class.[133] The new kind of judge was comfortable with utilitarian visions and a more mechanistic view of law. Lord Esher, Master of the Rolls in the reformed Court of Appeal, announced, "There is in fact no such thing as judge-made law, for the judges do not make the law," although he admitted, "[T]hey frequently have to apply existing law to circumstances as to which it has not previously been authoritatively laid down that such law is applicable";[134] and Mr. Justice Willes had already rejected with horror any idea that the bench might compete with Parliament, even where there was an allegation of fraud in inducing the passage of a private act of Parliament.[135]

By the time of the Reform Act of 1867, then, the declaratory theory of law was readily acceptable to the intellectual utilitarians who were increasingly occupying the bench. As already suggested, some of the attraction of the theory may have been more an enthusiasm for laissez-faire concepts than a wholehearted embracing of "formalism" assuming that formalism and the declaratory theory are treated as largely interchange-

---

1850s the older universities followed suit. The Inns of Court resumed the teaching of law in 1852, but the various plans to turn the Inns into true legal universities failed; Abel-Smith and Stevens *Lawyers and the Courts* 65–67.

132. William S. Holdsworth, 1 *History of English Law* 645–47.

133. Daniel Duman, "A Social and Occupational Analysis of the English Judiciary" 355. From 1770 to 1790 the figures are as follows: landed, 40 percent; professional, 40 percent; merchant, 2.5 percent; skilled artisan, 0 percent; unknown, 17.5 percent. For 1855–75 the respective figures are 15, 52, 19.2, 1.4, and 12.5 percent; ibid.

134. *Wellis & Co. v. Baddeley*, [1892] 2 Q.B. 324, 326 (C.A.).

135. "I would observe as to these Acts of Parliament that they are the law of the land; and we do not sit here as a court of appeal from Parliament. It was once said,—I think in Hobart,—that if an Act of Parliament were to create a man judge in his own case, the Court might disregard it. That dictum, however, stands as a warning rather than an authority to be followed. We sit here as servants of the Queen and the legislature. Are we to act as regents over what is done by Parliament with the consent of the Queen, Lords and Commons? I deny that any such authority exists. If an Act of Parliament has been obtained improperly, it is for the legislature to correct it by repealing it: but, so long as it exists as law, the Courts are bound to obey it. The proceedings here are judicial, not autocratic, which they would be if we could make laws instead of administering them"; *Lee v. Bude & Torrington Junction Ry.*, L.R. 6 C.P. 576, 582 (1871).

The House of Lords had frowned at a similar argument in *Edinburgh & Dalkeith Ry. v. Wauchope*, 8 Cl. & F. 710, 724 (1842).

able concepts. At another level it may be possible to link the development to conscious or subconscious desires to have the institutions of government controlled indirectly through an aristocracy of talent rather than directly by the electorate.[136] An even more dramatic interpretation is Max Weber's.

Weber attributed the English approach to law to the lawyers' guild system, which made the professional monopolies so successful that effective education was replaced by apprenticeship.[137] He also attributed the preservation of the formalistic system of adjudication to the desire by the establishment (the honoratories) to protect the "interests of the honoratories' own class or those of the class dominated by them."[138] Put somewhat more dramatically, Weber saw the formalistic system of decision making by the judiciary as a means of facilitating capitalism by entrenching vested interests in established doctrines.[139] Weber's modern disciples have had problems with his interpretation of the growth of formalism in England,[140] and even if his concept of formalism might be applied to the lower courts by the mid-nineteenth century, its application to the Lords could only come later. Yet it is tantalizingly attractive to explain Halsbury's outbursts—not to mention the outlook of those who came later—in Weberian terms.

Be that as it may, historically, with respect to all courts below the Lords, the pervasiveness of the more mechanistic, formalistic, or declaratory approach was profoundly interwoven with the English intellectual tradition. The newly reconstituted Oxford Law School was intensely utilitarian.[141] Its senior professors knew well enough the nature of the judicial process. Indeed, Maine's description of the role of the courts in *Ancient Law* (1861) still remains one of the most elegant descriptions of

136. See chap. 2.

137. "As soon as the monopoly was achieved, the lectures (at the Inns of Court) began to decline, to be ultimately discontinued altogether. Thereafter, training was purely empirical and practical and led, as in the craft guilds, to pronounced specialization. This kind of legal training naturally produced a formalistic treatment of the law, bound by precedent and analogies drawn from precedent"; Max Rheinstein, ed., *Max Weber on Law in Economy and Society* 201.

138. And to the absence of legal aid that prevented the economically deprived from using the system; ibid. 230. See also ibid. 318–53.

139. While Weber's interpretation was also neo-Marxist, it is surprisingly similar to the Hurst interpretation of the behavior of the American bench in the nineteenth century; namely, that by taking a laissez-faire, "hands-off" approach they encouraged the release of energy. See James W. Hurst, *Law and Conditions of Freedom in the Nineteenth Century United States*. For another interpretation of the role of formalism, see Duncan Kennedy, "Legal Formality" 351.

140. See Lawrence M. Friedman, "On Legalistic Reasoning—A Footnote to Weber," 148; Jerold Gubin, " 'The England Problem' and the Theory of Economic Development" (Program in Law and Modernization, Yale Law School, Working Paper No. 9, mimeograph, no date); David Trubek, "Toward a Social Theory of Law 1."

141. F. H. Lawson, *The Oxford Law School 1850–1965*, 3.

the judicial function.[142] Yet, in keeping with the changes in the courts, the utilitarian Liberals chose to emphasize the professional and to underplay the creative in the work of the judiciary.

This phenomenon was most elegantly illustrated by Albert Venn Dicey, who was Vinerian Professor at Oxford. In his *Introduction to the Study of the Law of the Constitution*, published in 1885—a work that was to be the guiding light of liberal intellectuals in the law for seventy-five years, Dicey not only praised the absence of constitutional and administrative law in England, but also downplayed any creative role for the judges,[143] because, like *droit administratif*, judicial legislation was inconsistent with his concept of the Rule of Law.[144] In his early work, Dicey carried judicial restraint to the point of assuming that judges were automatons.

Yet, by the end of his life Dicey no longer held the views that were to be so influential for much of the twentieth century in keeping law and policy seemingly distinct. Already alarmed by what he termed the "growth of collectivisim," Dicey, in his 1898 lectures at Harvard (published in 1905 as *Lectures on the Relation between Law and Public Opinion in England during the Nineteenth Century*), was far less willing to accept judge-made law as a minor form of "subordinate legislation, carried on with the assent and subject to the supremacies of Parliament."[145] By the turn of the century, the idea that judges might make law was far less of a problem for Dicey; indeed, he seemed to accept that "the best part of the law of England is judge-made law";[146] and whereas twenty years earlier he had talked of judge-made law primarily in the past tense, by 1905 he

142. "With respect to that great portion of our legal system which is enshrined in cases and recorded in law reports, we habitually employ a double language, and entertain, as it would appear, a double and inconsistent set of ideas. When a group of facts come before our English court for adjudication, the whole course of the discussion between the judge and the advocates assumes that no question is, or can be, raised which will call for the application of any principles but old ones, or of any distinctions but such as have long since been allowed. It is taken absolutely for granted that there is somewhere a rule of known law which will cover the facts of the dispute now litigated, and that, if such a rule be not discovered, it is only that the necessary patience, knowledge, or acumen is not forthcoming to detect it. Yet, the moment the judgment has been rendered and reported, we slide unconsciously or unavowedly into a new language and a new train of thought. We now admit that the new decision has modified the law. The rules applicable have, to use the very inaccurate expression sometimes employed, become more elastic. In fact, they have been changed. A clear addition has been made to the precedents, and the canon of law elicited by comparing the precedents is not the same with that which would have been obtained if the series of cases had been curtailed by a single example"; Henry Maine, *Ancient Law* 80–81. Sir Henry Maine was at this time Professor of Jurisprudence at Oxford.

143. E.g., the passing and unsatisfactory references at 58, 152, 369–70.

144. See especially at 321.

145. Albert Venn Dicey, *Introduction to the Study of the Law of the Constitution* 58. See also "The Science of Case Law" in Frederick Pollock, *Essays in Jurisprudence and Ethics* 237.

146. Albert Venn Dicey, *Lectures on the Relation between Law and Public Opinion in England during the Nineteenth Century* 359.

regarded it as very much alive and of considerable importance,[147] although admitting that there were differences in the types of law produced by the two branches of government.[148]

What may well have spurred Dicey's retreat from his unqualified support of the Rule of Law and parliamentary sovereignty, with its assumption of the unfettered power of naked democracy, was the fact that judges "have acquired the intellectual and moral tone of English lawyers. . . . They are for the most part persons of a conservative disposition."[149] For by this stage in his life, Dicey's enthusiasm for an electorate whose representatives in Parliament favored collectivist rather than individualist legislation was limited. He was shocked by the reaction to *Taff Vale* and horrified by the Parliament Act of 1911 and the third Home Rule Bill of 1914.[150] It was, however, too late. His earlier concepts of the Rule of Law, with its concomitants of parliamentary sovereignty and a passive judiciary, were to be the intellectual orthodoxy for the following decades. The march toward substantive formalism had begun.

147. "Nor let anyone imagine that judicial legislation is a kind of law-making which belongs wholly to the past, and which has been put an end to by the annual meeting and by the legislative activity of modern Parliaments. No doubt the law-making function of the Courts has been to a certain extent curtailed by the development of parliamentary authority. Throughout the whole of the nineteenth century, however, it has remained, and indeed continues to the present day, in operation. . . . Hence whole branches not of ancient but of very modern law have been built up, developed, or created by the action of the Courts"; ibid. 360–61.

148. *First*—Judicial legislation aims to a far greater extent than do enactments passed by Parliament, at the maintenance of the logic or the symmetry of the law. . . . *Secondly*—Judicial legislation aims rather at securing the certainty than at amending the differences of the law. . . . *Thirdly*—The ideas of expediency or policy accepted by the Courts may differ considerably from the ideas which, at a given time, having acquired predominant influence among the general public, guide parliamentary legislation"; ibid. 362–65.

149. Ibid. 362.

150. These changed views are most articulately expressed in the Introduction to the eighth edition of *Law of the Constitution*.

FOUR

Dramatis Personae[1]

Politically, the period between 1876 and 1912 was one of dramatic change; yet such was not obvious for its first two decades. The social composition of both political parties was not dissimilar. There were scarcely more radicals in Gladstone's administration from 1880 to 1885 than there had been "Tory Radicals" in Disraeli's government from 1874 to 1880. In both parties the great families were highly influential. In political matters, the country was still, for the most part, divided vertically. The attitudes of the governing class of this period, whether in Parliament or on the bench, were the essence of classical Victorianism. At the center of the lives of almost all these men was a burning religious conviction. They were evangelists in the broadest sense of the term, believing in salvation by works. Their remarkable emphasis on the Bible and their attempt to reject a seeking after pleasure during their mortal lives, which were merely a preparation for eternity, influenced their attitudes toward almost everything.[2] It influenced dissenters and Roman Catholics and all parties within the established church. Cairns was a low churchman and Selborne a high churchman, but both Lord Chancellors were diligent Sunday school teachers.

This religious conviction was matched in classical Victorianism by a

1. This chapter is concerned with the law lords after 1876. See J. B. Atlay, *Victorian Chancellors*, for Lord Chancellors up to Cairns. The only leading law lord of this earlier period not covered by a biography is Baron Parke (Lord Wensleydale). But see William S. Holdsworth, 15 *History of English Law* 486–92.

2. Typical is *Clarke v. Carfin Coal Co.*, [1891] A.C. 412, 420 (Scot.), in which the House held that under Scots law the parent of an illegitimate child had no action against anyone whose negligence caused the child's death, since the parent had no right to support by the child. Watson said, "It humbly appears to me that to impose upon illegitimate children, to whom the law denies the status of blood-relationship and all rights of succession, a liability to maintain parents who, in the most charitable view, have done them a great wrong, would be harsh and inequitable."

stern belief in economic and political laissez-faire. Institutions might be reformed to make them more efficient, but it was not permissible for the state to intervene to do what the individual should do for himself. For the state to interfere with the essential freedoms of the individual, no matter how theoretical those freedoms might be in practice, was condemned as collectivism. All men must be assumed to be equal in the eyes of the law, no matter how unequal they might be socially, economically, or educationally.[3] Although Dicey, somewhat emotionally, christened the period from 1865 to 1900 the "Period of Collectivism," twentieth-century commentators, speaking from a relative standpoint, understandably reserve such a label for a later period.

The pattern, in fact, began to change after the split in the Liberal party over Home Rule in 1886. That division led to the establishment of the Conservative ascendancy, for apart from a three-year break between 1892 and 1895 when the octogenarian Gladstone and the underestimated Rosebery led brief ministries and yet again failed to accomplish Home Rule, the Liberal party did not regain power until 1905. The last thirty years of the period, however, were to be very different from the first twenty. The latter years were chaotic ones: American visitors were horrified by the violence that pervaded so much of English life.[4] The country was racked by strikes in all basic industries—coal, steel, the docks, and railways.[5] Strikes often were ended by force; violence seemed to be as acceptable to the plotters in the Sydney Street Siege as it was to the Ulster Volunteers. While the Campbell-Bannerman administration of 1905 was perhaps the most radical the country had ever seen, the Lib-Lab coalition was breaking up, and there was, by the end of the period, a Parliamentary Labour party pledged to a socialist Britain. Many thought Lloyd George's budgets had sharpened class differences to breaking point; some, in 1912, thought England poised on the verge of revolution. In fact, the country was merely poised on the brink of war, a war that was to signal the death of liberal England.[6]

3. One of the basic beliefs of the supporters of the doctrine was that the person best fitted to take care of anyone was that person himself, a belief that Bramwell emphasized in his pamphlet, *Laissez-faire*. Inevitably, a doctrine to which so many of the foremost thinkers of the age subscribed had a marked effect on the law. As David Hughes Parry said, "For a century and a half the doctrine of *laissez-faire* had determined the general attitude of the Bench towards the law"; "Economic Theories in English Case Law" 195. The effect on the law was remarkable: "Many of our substantive legal rules, particularly in the realm of property and contract, are directly traceable to certain aspects of *laissez-faire* doctrine. 'Liberty of contract' and 'freedom of trade' are the favourite tunes of the nineteenth century common law judges"; ibid. 197. See also Albert Venn Dicey, *Lectures on the Relation between Law and Public Opinion in England during the Nineteenth Century*, Lecture 11.

4. Ben C. Roberts, "On the Origins and Resolutions of English Working Class Protest," 2 *Violence in America* 197 (Staff Report of the National Commission on the Causes and Prevention of Violence, 1969).

5. R. C. K. Ensor, *England 1870–1914*, chap. 13.

6. George Dangerfield, *The Strange Death of Liberal England*.

The political, social, and economic events of these decades undoubtedly had a profound effect on the attitudes of the judicial members of the Lords. The law lords of the 1870s or 1880s had no particular wish to compete with Parliament. After all, they were members of the upper house of Parliament and were men essentially akin to the members of the House of Commons. Many indeed had been members of that latter body. Yet the Commons was still an amateur, unsalaried body, while the reformed Civil Service was only slowly finding its feet. There was, in fact, a vacuum into which the judges, particularly the final court of appeal, had to step, if only with reluctance. That no more consciously activist move actually occurred was possibly a tribute to the deep belief on the part of the judges in that aspect of laissez-faire that regarded the minimum of state interference as the best form of government; if not that, their restraint was perhaps a conscious or subconscious political decision that the prestige, if not the power, of the judiciary would be enhanced by a deemphasis on judicial activism. Yet within the boundaries of the general reluctance to become involved in major problems of government, various shades of opinion could be discerned. Different legal backgrounds had given rise to different attitudes toward the role of the courts on the part of the law lords.

In contrast, during the 1890s and through the Edwardian period, the approach of the law lords began to change. The dominance of Equity lawyers on the Woolsack gave way to a new breed of common lawyers, while the centralist politics that had characterized the period of Cairns and Selborne gave way to the more active and generally more extreme politics of Halsbury and Loreburn. Judicial activism took on new meaning.

Manpower

When the "new" House of Lords met in 1877, at least three former Lord Chancellors were available, in addition to Cairns himself. Lord Chelmsford, the former Conservative Chancellor, occasionally sat, and the two most recent Liberal Chancellors—Hatherley and Selborne—sat regularly. The last two were high churchmen, and both politically fell into the no-man's-land between Whig and radical, although Hatherley[7] came from a decidedly radical background.[8] Better known as Page-Wood V.C., Hatherley achieved the post of Lord Chancellor, and that reluctantly, only because Palmer, who was the obvious candidate in the 1868 Liberal ministry, refused to take office so long as the government re-

7. W. R. W. Stephens, *Memoirs of Lord Hatherley*.
8. He was a deeply religious man, of whom Cairns said, "[A]s a judge, as a Christian, as a gentleman, and as a man this country has not seen and probably will not see anyone who is his superior"; ibid. 269.

mained committed to the disestablishment of the Irish church. Once this obstacle had been overcome by the doing of the "evil deed," Hatherley withdrew and Palmer took his seat on the Woolsack with the title of Selborne. Cairns,[9] who had become Chancellor in Disraeli's administration of 1874, to the disappointment of Chelmsford, who had been Derby's Chancellor and had hoped to be reappointed with the return of the Conservatives,[10] was akin in outlook to his predecessors. A reformer, Cairns, like Selborne, was an Equity lawyer of considerable ability.[11] In 1880 Selborne returned as the Liberal Chancellor in Gladstone's second administration. The group, in short, was a tightly knit one.

In the meantime, the first Lords of Appeal had been appointed. The first English Lord of Appeal, Blackburn (1876–87),[12] was, paradoxically, a Scot by birth, but he was by no means the last Scot to "represent" England. He had first been appointed to the English bench in 1859 by another Scot, Campbell, during his Lord Chancellorship.[13] Although unknown when he assumed the position, Blackburn rapidly demonstrated brilliance as a common lawyer, and he was an obvious choice as the first Lord of Appeal. By the time he retired in 1887 he was acknowledged to be the country's leading lawyer.[14] The other Lord of Appeal appointed under the 1876 act was Lord Gordon (1876–79), a Scottish judge.[15] Although an able lawyer, Gordon was never fully fit enough to undertake

9. Holdsworth, 16 *History of English Law* 105; Edward Monson, *Builders of Our Law during the Reign of Queen Victoria*; Van Vechten Veeder, "A Century of English Judicature" 786.

10. Lord Selborne (Roundell Palmer), 1 *Memorials Personal and Political 1865–1895*, at 77. Chelmsford complained he had been "dismissed with less courtesy than if he had been a butler."

11. Selborne, his political rival, paid a great tribute at the time of his death, mentioning his "great qualities and great virtues," although Selborne also said of Cairns, "[H]e yielded too easily to party influence, especially on questions relating to his native country Ireland"; 2 ibid. 158.

12. 1 *Dictionary of National Biography*, suppl. 203; Holdsworth, 15 *History of English Law* 492 ff.; Van Vechten Veeder, *Selected Essays in Anglo-American Legal History* 838 ff.

13. On the transference of Erle from Queen's Bench to be Chief Justice of Common Pleas. This appointment was received with surprise, as Blackburn was then virtually unknown; 1 *Dictionary of National Biography*, suppl. 203.

14. The Appellate Jurisdiction Act of 1887, which, in effect, created the first life peers, as opposed to peers during judicial tenure, was passed to enable Blackburn to sit and vote in the House after his resignation as a law lord. Herschell spoke in glowing terms of Blackburn on his retirement; 310 *Parl. Deb.*, H.L. (3d ser.), col. 748 (7 Feb. 1887). Lord FitzGerald added, "He was a great jurist, a strong and learned constitutional lawyer, with a mind so happily constituted that partiality was with him impossible; inflexible in his integrity, inexorable in his pursuit of justice, he dealt out even-handed justice to all suitors who came before him. He had throughout his long career performed with great success the duties of high office; and his name would be known to posterity as one who in his own life work, had well illustrated and enforced the principles of our own laws and the foundations of our Constitutional rights and liberties"; ibid.

15. 22 *Dictionary of National Biography* 177. "He was careful and accurate, if not a brilliant lawyer."

the work, and when he died, Lord Watson (1880–99), became the Scottish law lord.[16] Watson was the first of the line of vital Scottish law lords who have had an impact not only on the law of Scotland, but often, and more importantly, on the law of England and on the laws of the various Commonwealth jurisdictions whose appeals have come to the Privy Council. With Blackburn, Watson may be legitimately regarded as the intellectual leader of the period.

Under the 1876 act a third Lord of Appeal could be appointed when two of the salaried judgeships in the Privy Council under the 1871 act were vacant. This event occurred for the first time in 1882[17] when the first Irish Lord of Appeal, Lord FitzGerald, a common lawyer and former Liberal Member of Parliament, was appointed (1882–89);[18] he was replaced by Lord Morris and Killanin (1889–99).[19] In 1891, when the last vacancy occurred under the 1871 act, a fourth Lord of Appeal chosen was Lord Hannen (1891–93), who had been President

16. 1 *Dictionary of National Biography*, suppl. 1380–81. Veeder, *Selected Essays* 836. He was a Lord Advocate of less than 4 years' standing prior to his elevation.

17. Sir J. Colville and Sir M. Smith had retired.

18. In 1885 he was offered, but refused, the Lord Chancellorship of Ireland; R. F. V. Heuston, *Lives of the Lord Chancellors 1885–1940*, at 430. See 2 *Dictionary of National Biography*, suppl. 215. He had previously served as an Irish law officer and had refused an offer of the Chief Secretaryship of Ireland because of his desire to continue his professional career. "No fairer minded, abler, or more independent man sat upon the Irish Bench"; Lord Selborne, quoted, ibid. 216. He presided in the leading pro-provincial Canadian appeal, *Hodge v. The Queen*, 9 App. Cas. 117 (P.C. 1883).

19. He confessed that he was a conservative in legal matters. See 350 *Parl. Deb.*, H.L. (3d ser.), col. 125 (6 Feb. 1891). He belonged to an old Roman Catholic family. He was returned to Parliament as member for Galway in 1865. "Although of independent temperament and impatient of party ties he was distrustful of democracy, was devoted to the union and hostile to the cry of home rule"; 2 *Dictionary of National Biography*, 2d Suppl. 652. He was appointed Solicitor-General for Ireland in 1886 and Attorney-General in the same year. In 1887 he was raised to the Irish bench as a puisne judge in the Court of Common Pleas and became Lord Chief Justice of Ireland in 1887. See Maud Wynne, *An Irishman and His Family*.

Technical lawyers have regarded Morris as one of the least—if not the least—distinguished members of the House in these years. He did not pretend to be a great lawyer but simply made an honest attempt to judge a case on the merits as he saw them. He cared little for precedent, though he was a party to Halsbury's decision in *London Street Tramways Co. v. LCC* [1898] A.C. 375.

His concern for the spirit rather than the letter of the law resulted in his often being in a dissenting minority. E.g., *Grainger & Son v. Gough*, [1896] A.C. 325 at 342; *Russell v. Russell*, [1897] A.C. 395 at 461; *The Greta Holme*, [1897] A.C. 596; *Perth Gen. Station Comm. v. Ross*, [1897] A.C. 479 (Scot.); *North British Ry. v. Park Yard Co.*, [1898] A.C. 643 (Scot.). His judgments are written in a prose style that frequently animates the subject under discussion. His judgment in *Chadwich v. Manning*, [1896] A.C. 231 (P.C.) at 238, reads like a novel. See also his description of fraud in *Reddaway v. Banham*, [1896] A.C. 199, 221: "Fraud is infinite in variety, sometimes it is audacious and unblushing; sometimes it pays a sort of homage to virtues, and then it is modest and retiring; it would be honesty itself if it could only afford it. But fraud is fraud all the same."

of the Probate, Divorce, and Admiralty Division of the High Court since 1875.[20] Within three years, however, he was dead,[21] to be replaced by Lord Bowen (1893–94), who had been a Lord Justice of Appeal, but he in turn died in the following year.[22] His position was filled for a few months by Lord Russell before he became Lord Chief Justice; then Davey (1894–1907), a Chancery practitioner, was created a Lord of Appeal.[23] By this time Blackburn had retired, and his place as the English appeal judge was taken by an Equity lawyer, Lord Macnaghten (1887–1913), an Ulsterman and former Conservative M.P. for Antrim. *Truth* received this new appointment with satisfaction, expressing relief that it had been made by Salisbury rather than Halsbury,[24] whose appointments to the lower courts were far from satisfactory. The same review also suggested that were Macnaghten not so lazy he would be a liberal.[25]

Meanwhile, both the persons and the approaches of the Lord Chancellors were changing. When the Conservatives returned to power in 1885, Cairns was dead and Hardinge Giffard replaced him, taking the

20. James Hannen; b. 1821; father, wine merchant; educ. St. Paul's School, Heidelberg University; called to bar, 1848; unsuccessful Liberal candidate, 1865; Judge, Queen's Bench Court, 1868–72; Judge, Probate and Divorce Court, 1872–75; President, Probate, Divorce and Admiralty Division, 1875–91; Lord of Appeal, 1891–94; d. 1894.

21. His career as a law lord was interrupted when he was selected in 1892 to act as the U.K. nominee in the Bering Sea arbitration. General contemporary opinion of Hannen appears to have been high, although the following by Coleridge on Hannen's death is almost certainly exaggerated: "If there has been a greater English judge during the seventy-three years of my life than Lord Hannen, it has not been my good fortune to see him or know him"; ibid. 387.

22. The official law reports contain no separate opinion given by Bowen in the House of Lords. Bowen might have proved a distinguished law lord in that his talents were more suited to appellate work than work at first instance. "Without having the commanding force of character which procures for some men recognition as among the greatest judges of their day, Bowen was conspicuous among his contemporaries for the subtlety and rapidity of his perceptions, for his almost excessive power of refined distinction and for the elegant precision of his language"; 1 *Dictionary of National Biography*, suppl. 238–39. See also Henry Stewart Cunningham, *Lord Bowen*.

23. According to Heuston, formerly a not-very-successful or popular Solicitor-General; Heuston, *Lives* 104, 142. This view was not shared by many of his distinguished pupils. For details of Lord Russell's one-month tenure as a law lord, see R. Barry O'Brien, *The Life of Lord Russell of Killowan* 268–70.

24. Lord Salisbury saw the need to strengthen the Equity representation in the House. "It is a matter of great importance to strengthen the highest Court of Appeal by introducing into it the most eminent lawyers of the day; and I believe that in view of Lord Selborne's less frequent attendance, and the death of Lord Cairns, it is in respect of Equity hearings that the Court of Appeal specially requires reinforcing"; Letter from Salisbury to Macnaghten, 10 Feb. 1887, Macnaghten Papers, private possession, Bushmills, County Antrim, Northern Ireland.

25. *Manchester Examiner*, 14 Jan. 1887, noted that the electors of his Ulster constituency, Antrim, were none too pleased with him because he was not sufficient of an Ulsterman. However, he signed the Ulster Covenant in 1913. See Heuston, *Lives* 34–35.

title of Lord Halsbury. When the Liberals returned briefly in 1886[26] and again between 1895, the Great Seal was given to Lord Herschell. Halsbury and Herschell were different from their predecessors. Neither was an Equity lawyer; Herschell was a commercial lawyer and Halsbury primarily a criminal lawyer. More crucial, they were more partisan in their political views. Halsbury, while coming from a middle-class family, built on his Irish Protestant background and became a dedicated High Tory, with little of the reforming zeal of Cairns. Herschell, on the other hand, was the son of a Polish Jewish immigrant who had become a nonconformist preacher,[27] and for him "liberalism was a matter of profound conviction." In this respect these two Chancellors during the 1890s and 1900s were to represent the clash of high toryism and radicalism rather than the more classically Victorian skirmishes between Liberals and Conservatives.

During these early years of the "new" House of Lords, peerages were still given to distinguished senior judges who thus became law lords, although not Lords of Appeal. Among these, the most representative law lord was Lord Bramwell, a former judge in the Court of Appeal, who took an active part in the judicial affairs of the House from the time he was created a peer in 1882 until his death ten years later. He did not necessarily share the religious fervor of his fellow law lords, but his belief in laissez-faire was unshakable. In the early years of the period, Lord Penzance was still sitting. Lord O'Hagan, a common lawyer and the first Roman Catholic to be Lord Chancellor of Ireland since the reign of James II, was also prominent.[28] Lord Ashbourne,

26. Selborne declined a further term on the Woolsack, since he was unable to support the proposed Irish policy. "Selborne was surely one of the most consistent and honourable members of the Bar who have ever interested themselves in politics"; ibid. 101, 102. Selborne "shared with Lord James of Hereford the glorious distinction of being one of the two men who have refused the Great Seal of England for conscience sake"; Atlay, 2 *Victorian Chancellors* 405.

27. In later life, however, Herschell became a high church Anglican; Heuston, *Lives* 99.

28. 42 *Dictionary of National Biography* 53. He was appointed Solicitor-General for Ireland in 1861 and in 1862 Attorney-General. On the formation of the first Gladstone ministry in 1868, he was appointed Lord Chancellor of Ireland. He was raised to the peerage in 1870. In 1874 he resigned with the remainder of the ministry.

Intellectually, O'Hagan shared Blackburn's approach, particularly with respect to statutory construction. O'Hagan insisted that it was the task of the legislature alone to alter the law and of the courts merely to apply it. In his lone dissent in *River Wear Comm'rs* v. *Adamson*, 2 App. Cas. 743 (1877), he said, "Your Lordships, exercising your appellate jurisdiction, act as a Court of construction. You do not legislate, but ascertain the purpose of the Legislature; and if you can discover what that purpose was you are bound to enforce it, although you may not approve the motive from which it springs, or the objects which it aims to accomplish"; ibid. 756.

Yet in *Chatterson* v. *Cave*, he argued, "We should scrutinise carefully the terms of a Statute before we lend ourselves to administer it with ill results, and see whether it forces us inevitably to produce them"; 3 App. Cas. 483, 497 (1878).

another of Gladstone's appointments as Lord Chancellor of Ireland, was retained by the Conservative administration after the Home Rule split in 1886 and raised to the peerage; he also frequently took an active part in the deliberations of the House.[29]

When Halsbury began his third period on the Woolsack in 1895, he inherited a powerful quartet of Lords of Appeal—Davey, Macnaghten, Morris, and Watson. Yet, at the very moment when Halsbury was attempting to articulate a strict view of stare decisis, the new appointments during this period reflected the growing importance of political views and the fact that a man's party affiliations could facilitate his rise to the House. Thus when Watson died in 1899, the new Scottish Lord of Appeal was the Conservative politician Robertson (1899–1909). In 1900, to fill Morris' place, it is true that Salisbury appointed the largely apolitical Lindley (1899–1905),[30] but mainly because the Mastership of the Rolls was needed for the Attorney-General, Webster (later, with the title Lord Alverstone, Chief Justice). Moreover, when the Conservative government was breaking up in November 1905, the Prime Minister's patronage secretary put pressure on Halsbury to have Lindley resign[31] in order that a deserving Conservative politician might be rewarded. After Lindley agreed,[32] the vacant Lordship of Appeal was offered first to the Attorney-General (Finlay) and then, in a move designed to placate the Ulster Unionists, to Atkinson, the Irish Attorney-General, who was to sit as a Lord of Appeal until 1928.[33]

29. Loreburn later said of Ashbourne, "I have to keep him away . . . useless or worse." See Heuston, *Lives* 148. He in fact continued to sit occasionally until 1913.

Of this group, in some ways the most interesting was Lord Hobhouse who, after being a Charity Commissioner and law member of the Governor-General's Council in India, became a judicial member of the Privy Council in 1881. In 1885 he was given a peerage to help with the work of the House of Lords, but since he had never been a judge of an English Superior Court, he was held to be ineligible to sit. This statute was amended in 1887, and he then sat in 3 cases, including *Russell* v. *Russell*, [1897] A.C. 395; *Dictionary of National Biography 1901–1911*, at 272–73.

30. Lindley sat for 5 years, from 1900 to 1905, and was a valuable member of the court, although his confusion in *Quinn* v. *Leatham* pointed to some of the dangers of having a successful lawyer's lawyer in the final court of appeal. See especially [1901] A.C. 495, 534 (Ire.). "He [the plaintiff] had the ordinary rights as a British subject. He was at liberty to earn his own living in his own way, provided he did not violate some special law prohibiting him from so doing, and provided he did not infringe the rights of other people. This liberty involved liberty to deal with other persons who were willing to deal with him. This liberty is a right recognised by law; its correlative is the general duty of everyone not to prevent the free exercise of this liberty, except insofar as his own liberty of action may justify him in so doing." See Wesley Hohfeld, *Fundamental Legal Conceptions* 42, for a subtle analysis of this speech.

31. He was 75 and had had a fall. He in fact lived on until 1921; Heuston, *Lives* 62.

32. It was said of him on his retirement that "Lord Lindley has given us an almost unique example in our time of the highest distinction in the profession being attained by purely professional merit and without any kind of aid from political influence or claims on any party in the State"; "Note," 22 *Law Quarterly Review* 3 (1906).

33. Heuston, *Lives* 62.

The appearance of a Liberal Lord Chancellor in 1905 did nothing to change the situation. While Loreburn tried to "keep politics out" of appointments to the High Court, that did not apply to the Prime Minister's appointments of Lords of Appeal, at least after his first such nomination, when Lord Collins (1907–10), the former Master of the Rolls by then the presiding judge in the Court of Appeal, was appointed to replace Davey.[34] In 1909 Robertson died suddenly and Asquith, over the objections of Loreburn, appointed Thomas Shaw (1909–29), a Liberal M.P. and the Lord Advocate, as the new Scottish Lord of Appeal.[35] Loreburn and Asquith, however, did see eye to eye on the appointment of Robson the Attorney-General (1910–12) to replace Collins as a Lord of Appeal. By that time it was obvious that the Lords were, as Robson himself said, handling "disputes that are legal in form but political in fact."[36]

During the 1890s and the Edwardian period, the need for additional manpower became serious, especially as the pressure of appeals in the Privy Council increased. Lord Shand,[37] formerly of the Scottish bench,[38] was a regular but relatively silent attender between 1890 and his death in 1904. He had not been particularly prominent as a Liberal, although he had some progressive ideas on law reform.[39] Another frequent attender was Lord Brampton, who, the uncharitable said, had been made a peer to get him off the High Court bench. He had been a prominent (and reactionary) criminal judge and a well-known public figure.[40] Lord James of

34. Loreburn suggested Collins (who had been an unsuccessful Conservative candidate appointed to the bench by Halsbury) over Walters, the relatively inexperienced Attorney-General; ibid. 150, citing Sir Almeric Fitzoy's (Clerk to the Privy Council) observation, "The Chancellor's integrity is all the more to be commended [in] that no severe criticism need have been expected if the appointment had been decided by political considerations." Collins, by the time he was promoted to the House, was a sick man, and, although he sat quite frequently between 1907 and 1910, his contribution was small.

35. Heuston, *Lives* 149–50. Asquith, as a barrister, had grown up in the tradition that politics was the route to the bench; Roy Jenkins, *Asquith* 38.

36. Heuston, *Lives* 151. In 1912 Robson, worn out by overwork as Attorney-General, was replaced by another liberal, Moulton.

37. On his death, Halsbury said, "[W]ithout his assistance sometimes it would not have been easy to have had both Courts [Privy Council and House of Lords] going at the same time"; 131 *Parl. Deb.*, H.C. (4th ser.), col. 267 (7 Mar. 1904).

38. He was honest enough to admit when he was out of his depth on points of English law. "I cannot profess to have had any acquaintance with the Statute of 1837 prior to the discussion which has taken place today, or what seems to me the peculiar and special state of the law as it existed before the Statute"; *Mason v. Ogden*, [1903] A.C. 1 at 3 (1902), with reference to the Wills Act.

39. He was in favor of a Minister of Justice for the whole of Great Britain and outlined his plan before the Scots Law Society in 1874. In 1879 he outlined a social security scheme in a paper on "the liability of employers: a system of insurance by the mutual contribution of masters and workmen the best provision for accidents"; *Dictionary of National Biography*, Suppl' 2, at 295–96. He was Chairman of the Coal Industry Conciliation Board from 1894 and wrote frequently to *The Times* on Law Reform; ibid.

40. Although with some pretensions as a wit, he was a mean man and a poor civil lawyer; Richard Harris, ed., *Reminiscences of Sir Henry Hawkins.* Cf., for example,

Hereford, a Liberal, sat between 1896[41] and 1911, retaining the liberal outlook on social issues. Although by no means a great jurist, he had a judicial mind.[42] Lord Mersey[43] sat between 1910, when he retired from the Presidency of the Probate, Divorce, and Admiralty Divison, and 1929. Another Scottish judge, Lord Kinnear, also sat occasionally, as did the social reformer and former divorce judge, Gorrell Barnes (by then Lord Gorrell).[44]

Moving from the catalog of the judicial personnel to an effort to classify the approach of the law lords, at least from the establishment of the "new" House of Lords in 1877 to the end of Loreburn's Chancellorship in 1912, the most remarkable aspect is that in terms of personalities and judges—if not of articulation—the House became a much more political body during these years. By the Edwardian period, not only were the Chancellors more political, but so were the Equity lawyers, the common lawyers, and the Scottish judges. The declaratory theory was to ebb and flow as it partially reflected these changes.

The Equity Lawyers

In the thirty-five years under discussion, the House was remarkably Equity-oriented. Hatherley, Selborne, and Cairns were all Equity lawyers, as were three of the English Lords of Appeal—Macnaghten, Lindley, and Davey. Moreover, at least the first four of these represented the broadest

---

Dictionary of National Biography, suppl. 2, at 229: "As a civil judge he failed to convey the impression that to do justice between the parties was his single aim." Heuston describes him as "capricious, unfair and deceitful"; *Lives* 58.

His activities in the House of Lords testify to his weakness. His judgments are too long, his style verbose, and he never succeeded in fully grasping the principles of the civil law. See e.g., judgments in *Allen v. Flood*, [1898] A.C. 1 (1897); *Quinn v. Leatham*, [1901] A.C. 495, 515 (Ire.); *Taff Vale Ry. v. Amalgamated Soc'y of Ry. Servants*, [1901] A.C. 426, 441.

41. He was consoled with a peerage when Halsbury was reappointed as Lord Chancellor in 1895. James had been most anxious to have the appointment; Heuston, *Lives* 35. He had, however, twice turned down the Chancellorship under Gladstone because of his opposition to Home Rule; ibid. 102.

42. He remained a liberal in domestic matters. As arbitrator in industrial disputes he was Chairman of the Coal Conciliation Board from 1898 to 1909 and a great success. Sitting judicially, he tended to support the workers. See his dissents in *Houlder Line v. Griffin*, [1905] A.C. 220, 223; *Back v. Dick Kerr & Co.*, [1906] A.C. 325, 330; *Marshall v. S.S. Wild Rose (Owners)*, [1910] A.C. 486, 489. In the same vein, he was in the minority in favor of the trade union in *Yorkshire Miners' Ass'n v. Howden*, [1905] A.C. 256, 275. Rumor had it that he was Lord Randolph Churchill's homosexual partner.

43. Formerly Bigham J.

44. As Chairman of the Committee on County Courts that led to the County Courts Bill of 1909, he favored the extension of jurisdiction; 2 *Parl. Deb.*, H.L. (5th ser.), col. 743 (26 July 1909). He also favored giving the County Courts divorce jurisdiction. "The question we have now to consider is whether a large portion of the community should be left to feel that the remedies given by law are out of their reach while they are within the reach of persons with more means than they have"; ibid., col. 484 (14 July 1909).

type of Equity approach, not the narrow Equity that some perceived among twentieth-century Chancery practitioners. This was the Equity that stated broad principles and, in likening Equity to equity, sought to strike a balance in the world of laissez-faire.[45]

Cairns and Selborne were especially typical of the nineteenth-century Chancery approach. Concerned more with principles than with pedantic learning about causes of action, they were inclined to put principle before precedent. Although aware of the needs of stare decisis, they were also impressed with the importance of keeping the law in line with the needs of a changing society. Thus they stressed an intelligent and intelligible implementation of statutes, refusing to incarcerate the common law (or Scottish law) within rigid categories.

Selborne, for example, was anxious that the House should not be bound by mere obiter dicta in earlier decisions but only by general principles,[46] and in this regard his use of precedent was in particular contrast to that of his common law brethren, especially Blackburn, who felt the need to examine each precedent in detail. Nor did Selborne commit himself on the question of stare decisis in the way Blackburn did.[47] While alive to the desirability of certainty in the law, as his judgment in *Caledonian Railway Company* v. *Walker's Trustees* showed,[48] when previous

45. See, for instance, the Equity judges preventing excessive use of exemption clauses in *Henderson* v. *Stevenson*, L.R. 2 H.L. Sc. & Div. 470 (Scot. 1875).

46. And, as he said in *Dixon* v. *Caledonian & Glasgow & S.W. Ry.*, "I feel perfectly sure that that very learned judge would be the first to maintain that a dictum of that sort is not to be confounded with a judicial authority, when the question cannot have been presented in argument in the manner in which it would have been if it had been the real point to be decided"; 5 App. Cas. 820, 826 (Scot. 1880). See also *Sewell* v. *Burdick*, 10 App. Cas. 74, 81 (1884).

47. Although Selborne cited more cases than Cairns, he appeared to do so only where he thought it essential, and the citations were frequently subordinated to his discussion of principle. In *Cory* v. *Burr*, 8 App. Cas. 393, 395 (1883), for example, he stated the conclusion he would have reached in the absence of any authorities, then went on to show that, in fact, such cases as there were supported his conclusion.

In *Foakes* v. *Beer*, 9 App. Cas. 605 (1884), while Blackburn briefly discussed a dozen cases apart from *Pinnel's Case*, 5 Co. Rep. 117a (1602), Selborne relied on only 1 other case, mentioning 3 others only to dismiss them as irrelevant. *Maddison* v. *Alderson*, 8 App. Cas. 467 (1883), on the other hand, is an illustration of how well Selborne was capable of using earlier authorities in his judgments when he deemed it necessary.

48. "It is your Lordships' duty to maintain, as far as you possibly can, the authority of all former decisions of this House; and although later decisions may have interpreted and limited the application of earlier precedent, they ought not (without some unavoidable necessity) to be treated as conflicting. The reasons which learned Lords who concurred in a particular decision may have assigned for their opinions have not the same degree of authority with the decisions themselves. A judgement which is right, and consistent with sound principles, upon the facts and circumstances of the case which the House had to decide, need not be construed as laying down a rule for a substantially different state of facts and circumstances, though some propositions, wider than the case itself required, may appear to have received countenance from those who then advised the House"; 7 App. Cas. 259, 275 (Scot. 1882).

decisions appeared to conflict, Selborne would fall back on principle.[49] He showed a similar broad attitude toward the construction of statutes, calling on the House to bear in mind considerations of "reason and justice,"[50] although again admitting that certainty in the law should not be sacrificed to mere feelings of sympathy.[51]

Cairns is perhaps an even better example of a judge who argued primarily from principle and illustrated from precedents largely by way of conclusion. In *Cundy v. Lindsay and Company*,[52] for instance, Cairns approached the problem of mistake in contract from the point of view of *consensus ad idem*, discussing no cases, whereas his colleagues thought the facts as presented fell clearly within the scope of a previous authority. His attitude to the binding force of precedent was little more severe than Selborne's. Like Selborne, Cairns on occasion emphasized the duty of the judges to administer the law, regardless of sentiment,[53] although compared with later periods, his was a surprisingly relaxed approach.

A similar Equity mentality, although somewhat attenuated, was taken to the bench by Macnaghten. He too, by a subtle use of the canons of construction, was able to incorporate modern legislation into the legal system without involving himself in irrational decisions and without thwarting the will of the elected majority. He insisted that the legislature should have the sole responsibility for legislation, but at the same time that the law it made should be reasonably applied.[54] Yet Macnaghten

49. "In such a state of authority it is important to see how the matter stands in principle"; *Sewell v. Burdick*, 10 App. Cas. 74, 82 (1884).

50. "[I]n construing Acts of Parliament of this kind, and adjusting the general provisions in the general Act to the particular provisions of the special Act, consideration of reason and justice, and the universal analogy of such provisions in similar Acts of Parliament, are proper to be borne in mind, and ought to have much weight and force"; *Metropolitan Dist. Ry. v. Sharpe*, 5 App. Cas. 425, 433 (1880). See also *Caledonian Ry. v. North British Ry.*, 6 App. Cas. 114 (Scot. 1881). "The more literal construction ought not to prevail, if it is opposed to the intentions of the Legislature as apparent by the statute; and if the words are sufficiently flexible to admit of some other construction by which that intention will be better effectuated"; ibid. 122. Nevertheless there was a point beyond which he was not prepared to go. "It is never (as it seems to me) very safe ground, in the construction of a statute, to give weight to views of its policy, which are themselves open to doubt or controversy"; *Municipal Bldg. Soc'y v. Kent*, 9 App. Cas. 260, 273 (1884).

51. "It is your Lordships' duty to hold an even hand and to remember that you are bound by the law, and that you are not at liberty to place strained constructions upon it even from feelings of indulgence which you may entertain towards those whose liberty is in danger"; *Witham v. Vane*, Opinions of their Lordships, 1883 (Scot.).

52. 3 App. Cas. 459 (1878).

53. In *IRC v. Harrison*, L.R. 7 A.C. 1, 9 (1874), he refused to disturb two previous cases on the Succession Duty Act, for, as he said, "I think that with regard to statutes of that kind, above all others, it is desirable, not so much that the principle of the decision should be capable at all times of justification, as that the law should be settled, and should, when once settled, be maintained without any danger of vacillation or uncertainty."

54. In *Hamilton v. Baker*, 14 App. Cas. 209, 220 (1889), he refused to accept the argument that the House should follow a series of decisions in lower courts because they had been acted upon for a long time, although based on an erroneous view of a statute. "I am sensible of the inconvenience of disturbing a course of practice which has continued

was not entirely an Equity lawyer—perhaps a euphemism for saying that he was more cautious than either Selborne or Cairns, as shown by his reluctance to develop general equitable principles.[55] Even this statement, however, must be tempered, for Macnaghten was able to approach even income tax with a touch of common sense,[56] and in reworking the principles of the common law, he showed an ability to adapt them to changed business conditions, a skill best exemplified by his analysis of restraint of trade in *Nordenfelt*,[57] where he effectively brought in broad principles of Equity to replace common law formalism.

Despite his reputation for indolence, Macnaghten was elegant and witty; his best judgments are classics of elegant prose.[58] They are frequently beautifully constructed, with gracious linking of facts, premises, and principles.[59] Yet his reputation for good prose has sometimes impeded realization of his political sensitivity. His dissent in the *Free Church* case was both perceptive and realistic.[60] If, moreover, Macnaghten was less broad-gauged in his approach than either Cairns or Selborne, this tendency could be attributed to his rise through the judicial *cursus honorum*; a period in the lower courts is likely to curb some "freewheeling." This interpretation, incidentally, might also explain the "modified" Equity approach in Hatherley's speeches.[61]

---

unchallenged for such a length of time and which has been sanctioned by such high authority. But if it is really founded upon an erroneous construction of an Act of Parliament, there is no principle which precludes your Lordships from correcting the error. To hold that the matter is not open to review would be to give the effect of legislation to a decision contrary to the intention of the Legislature, merely because it has happened, for some reason or other, to remain unchallenged for a certain length of time"; ibid. 222. Yet, in the same case he also said, "Between the conflicting views I do not venture to express any opinion. I have only to state what in my judgement the law really is. It is for the legislature to alter the law if Parliament in its wisdom thinks an alteration desirable"; ibid. 227.

55. See *Blackburn* v. *Vigors*, in which he refused to extend the equitable doctrine of constructive notice, and in which he also said, "I apprehend that it is not the function of a Court of Justice to enforce or give effect to moral obligations which do not carry with them legal or equitable rights"; 12 App. Cas. 531, 543 (1887).

56. See chap. 5, at 170–72.

57. In one of the most brilliant speeches of his career, he substituted the equitable concept of reasonableness for the common law doctrine of partial restraint as the basis for enforcing contracts alleged to be in restraint of trade; *Nordenfelt* v. *Maxim Nordenfelt*, [1894] A.C. 535, 559. See especially at 564 and 565. At the time it was said of this case, "It is good to see that the Common Law is still capable of development even on familiar ground"; "Note," 11 *Law Quarterly Review* 2 (1895).

58. *A Selection of Lord Macnaghten's Judgments, 1887–1912.*

59. See especially *Simpson* v. *Attorney-General*, [1904] A.C. 476, 482. Note also *Lloyd* v. *Grace, Smith & Co.*, [1912] A.C. 716, 738.

60. He stressed the vast importance of the case (about 2 million pounds was at stake, apart from the question of principle), and concluded, "For my part I should hesitate long before I could give my voice for a decision which will I fear compel, or at any rate direct, her (the Free Church) to subordinate the Scriptures to the Westminster Confession of Faith"; *Free Church of Scotland* v. *Lord Overtoun*, [1904] A.C. 515, 643 (Scot.).

61. In *Muir* v. *City of Glasgow Bank & Liquidators*, 4 App. Cas. 337, 364 (Scot.

Davey, a Lord of Appeal from 1894 to 1907, represents a slightly different tradition. By the time he was appointed, the House—in appointments if not in judicial rhetoric—was becoming more political, and it was Davey the politician rather than Davey the Equity lawyer who made his mark. While he frequently delivered the leading speech when a will had to be disentangled or the law of mortgages explained, he is better remembered for various major dissents. In *Yorkshire Miners' Association* v. *Howden*[62] he dissented in favor of the trade union, an attitude also reflected in his strong and generally consistent support for the injured man in workmen's compensation cases. His other dissents came in cases where betting,[63] drink, and the Church of Rome were involved.[64] In-

---

1879), one of a series of cases arising as a result of the collapse of the bank, Lord Hatherley said, "Most anxiously does one scrutinise every case, especially every case presenting an appearance in any degree whatever of novelty, in order to see that the edge of justice is administered duly and not with undesirable sharpness. But, my Lords, the case really did appear to be one in which the Appellants must have been painfully conscious from the first opening that they had to struggle against that which had been settled and determined by the highest Court of Judicature, and which in reality, therefore, was not open to revision by any Court whatsoever."

This view was expressed again, although not quite so strongly, in *Charlton* v. *Attorney-General*, 4 App. Cas. 427, 442 (1879). "We are in a position in which we can without embarrassment uphold, as one would undoubtedly wish to do, the doctrine which has once been established by this House, and I confess I for one should feel it scarcely competent in us to reverse that doctrine, which is so established, not only by one, but by two or three cases."

Unfortunately, Hatherley's speeches sometimes lacked clarity. See e.g., *River Wear Comm'rs* v. *Adamson*, 2 App. Cas. 743, 752 (1877). It is interesting to note the subsequent treatment of this decision in *Great Western Ry.* v. *The Mostyn (Owners)*, [1928] A.C. 57 (1927). In the Court of Appeal Lord Justice Atkin, speaking of Hatherley's speech in *Adamson*, said, "Whether he really was concurring in the appeal being allowed, or the appeal being dismissed, or whether he was concurring in the opinion of Lord Cairns, I do not know, but if it was the latter he clearly stated his view with extreme doubt and hesitation"; [1927] P. 25 (C.A. 1926).

62. [1905] A.C. 256, at 267.

63. *Powell* v. *Kempton Park Racecourse*, [1899] A.C. 143, 183, was concerned with the Betting Act of 1853, and in it the majority decided that an inclosure on a racetrack frequented by bookmakers was not the sort of "betting establishment" that the act was designed to prohibit. Davey's views on betting were very strong indeed, and on this admittedly very doubtful question, he came down firmly on the side of his principles. He thought that the section was quite clear, the plain words, with the necessary omissions were "No ... place ... shall be ... used ... for the purpose of the owner ... or any person using the same ... betting with persons resorting thereto."

64. *Hope* v. *Campbell*, [1899] A.C. 1 (Scot. 1898), where the Pursuers were attempting to show that a relevant case for trial was made out, in an action upsetting a will, on the ground that the testator was insane. They averred that he was "subject to insane delusions ... he believed that he had a special and imperative duty to further the cause of total abstinence and to oppose the Church of Rome by devoting his pecuniary resources to these objects, in consequence of commands which he conceived he had received from the Deity by direct communications on various occasions"; ibid. 4.

The majority thought that a relevant case for trial was averred. Davey did not. "The question which I put to myself is whether, if these sentences ... were proved, they would necessarily amount to a finding of insanity and support the action. I answer, they might or

deed, seen in retrospect, he appears but a product of his liberal noncon-formist background.[65] To some he was a radical; to others, anathema. His character certainly did not endear him to those who fought success-fully against his appointment as Lord Chancellor in 1905.[66] Yet various areas of Equity still bear his stamp to this day.

The Common Lawyers

The dominant common lawyer of this period was Halsbury. While not a great lawyer,[67] he was a powerful personality.[68] A tough Tory when battling the trade unions,[69] his was a sympathetic voice for giving the

they might not. . . . They are quite susceptible of the meaning—and in my opinion it is the more natural meaning—that the testator conceived that in the philanthropic and religious ends which he aimed at in his lifetime, and in the disposal of his property, he was prompted by the direct command of the Almighty working upon his conscience. . . . You may call this an insane delusion if you will; but it is a delusion (if it be one) which has been shared by some of the greatest benefactors of the human race, who in obedience to such a call or command . . . have devoted their lives to mitigating the misery of the world and endeavour-ing to raise mankind to a higher life and a better conception of their duties on earth"; ibid. 23.

65. On Davey generally, see Edward Macnaghten, "The Late Lord Davey" 10.

66. See especially Heuston, *Lives* 142, particularly Asquith's vituperative view.

67. Yet he should not be underestimated. It is said that Halsbury was personally able to correct every contribution to his "Laws of England"; A. Wilson-Fox, *The Earl of Halsbury* 209. Halsbury had taken a "fourth" at Oxford.

68. His chief characteristic as a judge was his bluntness. A typical judicial reaction was, "It seems to me that this is a very plain case, and I am somewhat surprised that it should have been brought here"; *Skinner v. Northallerton County Court Judge*, [1899] A.C. 439, 440. Similarly, in *Earl Grey v. Attorney-General*, [1900] A.C. 124 (1899), an estate duty case, Halsbury began his judgment, "My Lords, there are some cases so extremely plain that it is difficult to give any better exposition of the question than that which the Statute itself provides"; ibid. 126.

On another occasion he had strong words to say about the way public bodies carried on business. In *Attorney-General v. Stewarts & Co.*, Opinions of their Lordships, 1901, the contracts in question were worth almost £100,000 and Halsbury could say, "I think it is to be regretted that where interests of this magnitude are involved the Courts should be vexed with the necessity of interpreting such irregular and unappropriate [*sic*] documents and should have out of them to spell some contract or another." And in *Hornsey Urban Dist. Council v. Vestry of St. Mary, Islington*, Opinions of their Lordships, 1902, he said, "Really it seems to me that this question however decided is a scandal, I can use no other phrase. . . . Here are the two public bodies. There is sought to be established a legal right, on the one side or the other, to stop up these sewers, which will cause a nuisance, or to leave things as they are, in which case nuisances from time to time will recur. That is the alternative . . . and instead of aiming at some *via media* by which some reasonable course might be adopted, the money of the ratepayers of both parishes is being wasted in this litigation which can come to nothing whatever happens . . . is it too late now to endeavour to do something?"

69. Halsbury in the Lords stigmatized the Trade Disputes Bill as being "contrary to the spirit of English liberty"; and of § 4, he "venture[d] to say that so disgraceful a section has never appeared in an English statute before . . . was there ever such a thing heard of in a civilised country?" 166 *Parl. Deb.*, H.L. (4th ser.), col. 705 (4 Dec. 1906). In fairness, it should be noted that many radicals, including the Webbs, were unhappy with this section;

workingman a fair deal under the Workmen's Compensation Acts.[70]
Such apparent inconsistencies reappeared in other aspects of the Chancellor's life. Halsbury, for instance, had little time for the failings of
fellow judges or businessmen, and he found it difficult to conceive that he
might be in the wrong;[71] yet he could be deeply concerned about reforming that branch of the law from which he had sprung—the criminal law.

Halsbury could be merciless in his criticism of the lower courts.
When the Divisional Court announced that it had "doubts, " Halsbury
had "not the least notion what they mean."[72] While paying respect to the
learned judges of the Court of Session in another case, he conceded that
he had "not been able to follow the reasoning by which they arrived at
their conclusions."[73] Litigants before the House were not allowed to
tarry long, and cases were dismissed out of hand on the ground that they
were "very simple" or "very plain."[74] Often "there was no room for
doubt."[75] The interpretation of legislation, if clear in Halsbury's opinion,[76] left no room for discussion.[77] Sophisticated interpretations of contracts were not encouraged.[78] In the House often only Halsbury delivered
a speech; sometimes the verdict came in the form of a terse sentence

---

William Beveridge, *Power and Influence* 51 ff. Intellectually, too, Harold Laski was
opposed; Kingsley Martin, *Harold Laski* 66.

70. There must have been some speculation as to how the Lord Chancellor was going
to approach an act about which in the Committee Stage in the Lords he had said that he
was "not enamoured of the drafting"; 51 *Parl. Deb.*, H.L. (4th ser.), col. 1004 (26 July
1897); and this at a time when he was vigorously supporting an amendment that gave the
workmen the ordinary right of appeal from the County Court judge up to the House of
Lords. Halsbury had refused to join in the earlier debates about whether the legislation was
"in accordance with Conservative principles."

71. "He had been a great political figure, and never wavered when he thought he was
in the right. His greatest fault, perhaps, was that he never thought he was in the wrong";
Edward Russell, *The Royal Conscience* 180.

72. *Hampton Urban Dist. Council v. Southwark & Vauxhall Water Co.*, [1900] A.C.
3, 4 (1899).

73. *Greville-Nugent v. Mackenzie*, [1900] A.C. 83, 86 (Scot. 1899).

74. E.g., *Seaton v. Burnand*, [1900] A.C. 135, 138 (1899); *Glasgow Corp. v. M'Ewan*,
[1900] A.C. 91, 95 (Scot. 1899).

75. *North Eastern Ry. v. Lord Hastings*, [1900] A.C. 260, 263 (1899).

76. He had no time for the man in the street's opinion (or on this occasion Loreburn's
and Atkinson's). "I am not much impressed by the question what the man in the street
would say if he were asked whether his remuneration was of such a character or no. The
man in the street by hypothesis is not dealing with such questions as are now vexing us in
construing this Act of Parliament. . . . For my own part I read the words simply as they are
and I think the natural and ordinary meaning of the words is that which the Court of
Appeal have adopted"; *Costello v. Owners of S.S. Pigeon*, [1913] A.C. 407, 413.

77. *Earl Grey v. Attorney-General*, [1900] A.C. 124 (1899); *Fielden Corp. v. Morley*,
[1900] A.C. 133 (1899).

78. "[A]s extraordinary a construction of a mere document as it has ever been my
fortune to hear argued"; *Veit v. Insland*, Opinions of their Lordships, 1890. See also
Barraclough v. Cooper, Opinions of their Lordships, 1905: "I repudiate the invocation of
any canon on construction here beyond the fact that I find enough in the language of this
instrument to show what, in my view, the testator meant."

rather than a reasoned speech; and during Halsbury's tenure the law lords often delivered their speeches at the end of counsel's argument rather than reserving judgment. Yet it was also Halsbury who was chiefly responsible for passage of the Criminal Evidence Act of 1898, allowing an accused man to testify, while he supported the Criminal Appeal Act of 1907, putting criminal appeals, for the first time, on a reasonably satisfactory basis.

Halsbury was a fascinating figure, both politically and legally. As a lawyer, he articulated a formalistic approach but practiced a flexible or functional one. This pattern allowed the final appeal court, at least in areas of private law, a distinguished period of development. Again, politically, there were remarkable conflicts. On some social reforms Halsbury showed hints of a Tory radicalism of which Disraeli or Joseph Chamberlain might have approved. Yet, in pure politics, Halsbury was a "ditcher," and his response to the Parliament Crisis of 1909–11 was no exception. He saw the crisis in simplistic terms. He fought to the last[79] and knew that the passage of the Parliament Act meant socialism. "[T]hus everyone who has nothing, and deserves to have nothing because he would not work, has a right to take away something from his neighbour, who has something because he worked, while the other had been idle and lazy. . . . If there is one thing of which I have the greatest horror it is the Government inspector employed to look after everything and everybody. The genius of this country is for voluntary and free effort."[80] By 1911, Halsbury represented an age that was passing.

Herschell, with his atypical Jewish immigrant background and lack of contacts, was in some ways the most interesting of the common lawyers.[81] A pupil of the great common law pleader Chitty, Herschell, after a slow start at the bar, entered the House of Commons on the radical wing of the Liberal party at a relatively young age and by 1880 he was Gladstone's Solicitor-General; in the following year he was offered the Lordship of Appeal that eventually went to FitzGerald. With Gladstone's return in 1886, Herschell became Lord Chancellor, a post he held again during the Gladstone and Rosebery administrations of the 1890s; and he continued sitting as a law lord until his death in 1899.

Intellectually, in terms of the English approach to law, Herschell is especially important. While Halsbury used theories of formalism to support his political positions, Herschell was the first Lord Chancellor who openly attempted to use formalism as a means to divert decisions from

79. Yet when the result was known, he took it with his customary good humor. His letters to his daughter immediately afterwards are full of joking references to "how hard[ly] Lady Halsbury was taking it." See Wilson-Fox, *Earl of Halsbury* 281–82.

80. Ibid. 214.

81. On Herschell, see Heuston, *Lives* 85–129.

the courts to the legislature. He announced that he would be satisfied if the courts could establish what the law was, leaving to Parliament the making of any changes in the law that might be necessary. As he said in *Salomon and Company* v. *Salomon*, "[W]e have to interpret the law not to make it."[82] He did admit that, on occasion, he might be prepared to depart from an earlier interpretation when it was manifestly wrong[83] and even strain the words of a statute slightly[84] if he felt that he would thereby better effectuate the clear intention of the legislature or avoid an injustice.[85] His basic approach to the function of the legislature, however, was noticeably more deferential than earlier Chancellors—even Liberal ones, and he relied upon precedent to a far greater extent than the Equity law lords. Herschell was the first Lord Chancellor after the 1885 Reform Act who had not held the office before; his behavior, not surprisingly, showed a greater deference to pure democracy than would have appeared seemly to a Cairns or a Halsbury.

Derry v. *Peek*,[86] establishing a narrow liability in tort for fraud, shows the importance that Herschell attached to authority,[87] even in a situation where he claimed he would have preferred a wider liability.[88]

82. [1897] A.C. 22, 46 (1896).

83. In one case he discussed the problem of a judgment long acted upon but based on an erroneous construction of a statute, saying, "At the same time if it could be established that the decision was manifestly erroneous, your Lordships would be bound to give effect to that view, and to hold that the statute must be construed according to its natural meaning, notwithstanding the interpretation which had so long ago been put upon it by eminent judges"; *Lancashire & Yorkshire Ry.* v. *Corporation of Bury*, 14 App. Cas. 417, 419–20 (1889).

Herschell insisted that a company promoting a private act of Parliament should be given only rights and powers that it did not possess at common law by clear words under the statute.

84. *Scottish Drainage & Improvement Co.* v. *Campbell*, 14 App. Cas. 139, 141 (Scot. 1889). He was aware of the problems of statutory interpretation. In the debates prior to the passing of the Interpretation Act, he said, "The question would be, what is the commonly-understood meaning of a term used. It is easy to say it shall mean so-and-so unless the contrary is expressed, but if you are to understand it, a plain interpretation of it should be given"; 338 *Parl. Deb.*, H.C. (3d ser.), col. 1568 (29 July 1889).

85. In *Lancashire & Yorkshire Ry.* v. *Bolton Union*, Herschell said, "My Lords, if such a construction of the Act or of the order necessarily led to any unjustice I can understand an effort being made, although it would be somewhat straining the language used, to give effect to the arguments which have been addressed to us by the learned counsel for the Appellants"; 15 App. Cas. 323, 332 (1890). See also *Bank of England* v. *Vagliano Bros.*, [1891] A.C. 107, 143.

86. Where he made what he himself described as "a close and critical examination of the earlier authorities"; 14 App. Cas. 337, 359 (1889).

87. He went carefully through the previous cases, including *Brownlie* v. *Campbell*, 5 App. Cas. 925 (Scot. 1880), and *Smith* v. *Chadwick*, 9 App. Cas. 187 (1884), in the House of Lords and extracted from them what he believed were the principles applicable.

88. "I have arrived with some reluctance at the conclusion to which I have felt myself compelled, for I think those who put before the public a prospectus to induce them to embark their money in a commercial enterprise ought to be vigilant to see that it contains such representations only as are in strict accordance with fact, and I should be very unwill-

Yet the nature of the appellate process inevitably caused inconsistencies in his position. For instance, he opposed the importation of equitable principles into the law, since such would tend to make the law flexible and discretionary. Yet it was still possible in 1892 for Bevan to complain in the *Law Quarterly Review* of Herschell's judgment in *Smith* v. *Baker* that "a proposition of enormous extent is advanced and without the faintest attempt to define its application. In Lord Cairns' days the opinions delivered in the House of Lords were on an altogether other plane."[89] In that particular case, his liberal sympathies for the worker may have overcome his apparent commitment to the declaratory theory.

Herschell, in fact, was unlikely to be remembered as a great analytical lawyer, and, especially in his later years, he was not always a particularly courteous judge.[90] Yet he remained an active politician to the bitter end, attacking the Salisbury government on its foreign policy, which, during these years, he felt was leading to some form of confrontation, as it ultimately did in the Boer War.[91] Even in his last years, he regarded the most important reforms as "one man, one vote," Home Rule for Ireland, and reform of the House of Lords. The incredible political pressures under which he lived in that House[92] inevitably caused him to neglect or

---

ing to give any countenance to the contrary idea. I think there is much to be said for the view that this moral duty ought to some extent be converted into a legal obligation, and that the want of reasonable care to see that statements, made under such circumstances are true, should be made an actionable wrong. But this is not a matter fit for discussion on the present occasion. If it is to be done the legislature must intervene and expressly give a right of action in respect of such a departure from duty. It ought not, I think to be done by straining the law, and holding that to be fraudulent which the tribunal feels cannot properly be so described"; *Derry* v. *Peek*, 14 App. Cas. 337, 376 (1889).

For further examples, see *Bank of England* v. *Vagliano Bros.*, [1891] A.C. 107, 143 ff., where Herschell emphasized the undesirability of disturbing a course of practice followed for a long time, although based on a decision in some respects unsatisfactory. "It is too late now to question the decision in *Robarts v. Tucker*. It has been acted upon and regarded as law though the decision certainly seems to have rested upon the assumption that it was possible for a banker to do that which would be, commercially speaking, absolutely impracticable, viz, to investigate the validity of all the endorsements before he complied with the directions of his customers and paid the bill"; ibid., 155.

He made remarks in a similar vein in *LCC* v. *Churchwardens of Parish of Erith*, [1893] A.C. 562, 599, and in *Tancred Arrol & Co.* v. *Steel Co. of Scotland*, 15 App. Cas. 125, 141 (1890).

89. "Note," 8 *Law Quarterly Review* 202, at 204 (1892). It should be noted, however, that in this case the plan of Herschell's judgment is similar to that often used by the Equity members of the House. He first discussed the problem from principle and then showed that the authorities supported the same conclusion.

90. In later years, Herschell frequently interrupted counsel, a characteristic that, tradition has it, gave rise to Lord Morris' exclamation during the hearing of *Allen* v. *Flood*, [1898] A.C. 1 (1897), "Now I can understand what is meant by molesting a man in his trade"; Heuston, *Lives* 110.

91. He described Conservative foreign policy as "[w]ar as a method of trade expansion." See Farrer Herschell, *The Political Situation*.

92. "What I maintain is that there never was such a preposterous second Chamber as

at least downplay the importance of his judicial duties, and this in turn may have made him more comfortable espousing a judicial philosophy that downplayed the importance of the judges.

This entanglement in the political work of the Lords also characterized that other Liberal Chancellor, Loreburn. (Halsbury, as the Conservative Chancellor, had the extraordinary advantage of a massive Tory majority in the Lords, and he could therefore devote more attention to judicial work). Indeed, the contrast between Halsbury and Loreburn could not have been greater. Loreburn's defense of the Trade Disputes Bill in 1906 was as low-key as Halsbury's had been assertive. His style was to point out that the reasoning of the House in the *Taff Vale*[93] case "was not the intention of the law, and the object of the present Bill was simply to restore the law to what it was intended and believed to be."[94] Similarly, he saw the Parliament Crisis of 1909–11 in terms of the distinction between the legal and the constitutional. "The knowledge that the House of Lords can at any time force a dissolution by throwing out the financial proposals of the Government would be of itself sufficient to make it necessary so to compose a Ministry that it can command the support of that House. This means a complete change in our system."[95]

Loreburn, as Speaker of the Lords, piloted through both the Trade Disputes Act and the Parliament Act, but the strain was even greater than that faced by Herschell and ultimately broke Loreburn physically. Surprisingly, Loreburn had managed to sit regularly as a judge, not only in common law cases,[96] but in a series of public law decisions. Thus, while fighting vigorously on the political front in the legislature,[97] he also sought to take balanced political positions in judicial decisions involving

---

the House of Lords under the present circumstances since the world began. . . . It may be said that I am prejudiced because I am one of a very few who fight a very unpleasant battle. I don't suppose anybody who is not a Member knows what it really means. We muster 15, 20 or 30 perhaps—our utmost number is 60—and we have against us 400 or 500, represented at a sitting say by 150 or 200. Nobody who has not fought that kind of battle can quite realise the situation. Though we may know perfectly well that our arguments are overwhelming we also know that we produce no more alteration or effect than we should if we were talking to that clock. It is not a pleasant situation"; ibid.

93. [1901] A.C. 426.

94. 133 *Parl. Deb.*, H.L. (3d ser.), cols. 979, 982.

95. On Loreburn, see generally Introduction to John Hartman Morgan, *The House of Lords and the Constitution.*

96. His judgments in common law were not particularly distinguished. In important cases he frequently concurred briefly. E.g., *Cavalier v. Pope*, [1906] A.C. 428 (liability of occupier); *Wallis, Son & Wells v. Pratt & Haynes*, [1911] A.C. 394 (sale of goods); *Lloyd v. Grace Smith & Co.*, [1912] A.C. 716 (vicarious liability). His presiding judgment in *E. Hulton & Co. v. Jones*, [1910] A.C. 20 (1909), imposing liability in libel, even when the defendant did not know of the existence of the plaintiff, was reversed by § 4 of the Defamation Act of 1952.

97. On Loreburn's career, see Heuston, *Lives* 133–82.

taxation,[98] trade disputes,[99] administrative law,[100] and the Canadian constitution.[101] Although lawyers might not look on Loreburn's decisons as particularly distinguished, in the light of the political turmoil of the time, his was a remarkable performance.

In some ways more typical of the legal system than the three common law Chancellors were the two common law judges, Blackburn and Bramwell, although the latter was never made a Lord of Appeal.

Having risen through the professional judiciary, Blackburn, in particular, was committed to a more professional, scientific, and formalistic view of law. Thus he frequently recorded his opposition to seeking the intention or policy behind an act; in his opinion the intent that was to guide the court in its legal reasoning was to be the intent discoverable exclusively from the words of the statute.[102] If the words of a statute were clear, that the court thought it unreasonable in operation was no justification for altering their effect.[103] Blackburn should not, however, be accused of being a blind adherent to the literal rule of statutory construction. He sensed the open-textured nature of language,[104] and on

98. See chap. 5.

99. *Conway v. Wade*, [1909] A.C. 506, 508.

100. *Board of Educ. v. Rice*, [1911] A.C. 179, 180.

101. *Attorney-General for Ontario v. Attorney-General for Canada*, [1912] A.C. 571 (P.C.). Loreburn's last appearance as a law lord was to oppose the harsh decision that the Privy Council was proposing in *in re Southern Rhodesia*, [1919] A.C. 217 (P.C. 1918). No dissent was, of course, at that time allowed. See Heuston, *Lives* 178.

102. He said, in *Justices of Lancashire v. Mayor of Rochdale*, 8 App. Cas. 494, 496 (1882), "The general rule of construction of Acts of Parliament is of course, as everyone knows, that we are to give effect to what we understand to be the intention of the Legislature; and we are to derive the intention of the Legislature from the words which they have used, construing them in the sense which such words ought to bear with reference to the subject-matter to which they are applied."

He admitted in *Ecclesiastical Comm'rs for England & Wales v. Rowe* that to talk of any "intention" was unreal. "But though I agree with Lord Justice Cotton that probably the attention of Parliament was never directed to the point, and that there was in one sense no intention either way, yet we must determine what is the intention indicated, following the usual rules of construction, by the words used"; 5 App. Cas. 736, 748 (1880).

See also *Pharmaceutical Soc'y v. London & Provincial Supply Ass'n*, 5 App. Cas. 857, 868 (1880); *Caledonian Ry. v. North British Ry.*, 6 App. Cas. 114, 126 (Scot. 1881).

103. 5 App. Cas. 736, 748–49.

104. He recognized that the cases that caused most difficulty were those where it was impossible simply to look for and apply the ordinary, natural, and grammatical meaning of the words in question. In discussing Lord Wensleydale's statement of the rule (which he called the "golden rule")—that the ordinary meaning could be modified only to avoid absurdity or inconsistency—Blackburn said, "I agree in that completely, but unfortunately in the cases in which there is real difficulty it does not help me much, because the cases in which there is real difficulty are those in which there is a controversy as to what the grammatical and ordinary sense of the words, used with reference to the subject-matter, is"; *Caledonian Ry. v. North British Ry.*, 6 App. Cas. 114, 131–32 (Scot. 1881).

See also "But though I think the reasonableness of a scheme is a very good reason for thinking that the legislature might have wished to adopt it, and therefore for construing the words used as shewing an intention to carry it out, if the words used will bear such a sense,

occasion discussed the necessity of construing words in relation to their subject matter, whether in an act of Parliament[105] or in some other instrument that was before the court.[106]

As a good lawyer, Blackburn had an ability to use precedents to achieve the ends he desired, but he paid deference to a more formalistic and rational view of the law than his Equity brethren. As he said in *Tiverton and North Devon Railway Company* v. *Loosemore*, "I believe it to be of more consequence that this point should be settled than how it is settled."[107] This style generally put precedent ahead of principle; he treated it as self-evident that the House was bound by its own decisions: "For I apprehend that after a position of law has been laid down judicially in this House it is no more competent for your Lordships to depart from it than it would be for an inferior tribunal to do so."[108] Yet before he became a law lord Blackburn had done much to develop the law, especially in the basic areas of contract.[109] Indeed, perhaps his greatest contributions had come before he reached the House of Lords.

Stylistically, Blackburn relied heavily on precedents in constructing

---

it affords no justification for introducing new words, or construing the words in a sense which they cannot bear"; *Trustees of Clyde Navigation* v. *Laird*, 8 App. Cas. 658, 668 (Scot. 1883). See also *Bradlaugh* v. *Clarke*, 8 App. Cas. 354, 373 (1883).

105. *Caledonian Ry.* v. *North British Ry.*, 6 App. Cas. 114, 131 (Scot. 1881). See also *River Wear Comm'rs* v. *Adamson*, 2 App. Cas. 743 (1877). "There is a legal proverb that hard cases make bad law; but I think there is truth in the retort that it is a bad law which makes hard cases. And I think that before deciding that the construction of the statute is such as to work this hardship, we ought to be sure that such is the construction, more especially when the hardship affects not only one individual but a whole class"; ibid. 770.

This latter decision, incidentally, has been cited as an example that the judges consistently tried to obstruct social legislation. It took a considerable amount of ingenuity to exclude the shipowners' liability in the face of a 3-year-old statute that said the "owner of every vessel . . . shall be answerable . . . for any damage . . . to the harbour, dock, or pier"; Alan Harding, *A Social History of English Law* 356.

106. "[B]ecause I take it to be clear that when you are construing words which apply to a particular subject matter you have to ask, and it is fair and legitimate to ask, not what those words mean in the abstract, if words can be said to mean anything in the abstract, but what is the intention which those words reasonably construed would show as applied to that subject matter. There are many instances in which the same words may reasonably have a meaning when applied to one thing different from what they would have when applied to another"; *McCredy* v. *Alexander*, Opinions of their Lordships, 1883. Also on the interpretation of contracts, see *Levy* v. *Lawes*, Opinions of their Lordships, 1879; and on the interpretation of deeds, *John Orr Ewing & Co.* v. *Orr Ewing*, 8 App. Cas. 822 (Scot. 1882).

107. 9 App. Cas. 480, 492 (1883).

108. *Metropolitan Ry.* v. *Jackson*, 3 App. Cas. 193, 209 (1877). "I take it that . . . this House has no more right than any other tribunal to depart from the principle of the decisions which have already been arrived at"; *Attorney-General* v. *Great Eastern Ry.*, 5 App. Cas. 473, 481 (1879). See also *Orr Ewing* v. *Colquhoun*, 2 App. Cas. 839 (Scot. 1879); and *Mortimore* v. *Mortimore*, 4 App. Cas. 448, 453 (1878).

109. See, for instance, *Taylor* v. *Caldwell*, 3 B. & S. 826; 122 Eng. Rep. 310 (Q.B. 1863); *Rylands* v. *Fletcher*, L.R. 1 Ex. 265 (Ex. Cham. 1866).

his speeches. In *Dalton v. Argus and Company*,[110] for example, a case concerning the acquisition of a right to support of a building, he carefully traced the doctrine back to the reign of Elizabeth. Yet, as a good lawyer and able judge, he did not allow his technical competence to override his "situation sense." He was still able to say, in *Baroness Wenlock v. River Dee Company*, "The law is proverbially uncertain. That cannot be helped. But I think I should unjustifiably add to the uncertainty if I set an example of adhering to my previous reasoning (even should I still think it better than that of noble and learned Lords who decided against it) in every case not precisely involving the very same point."[111] The final verdict about Blackburn's contribution to (or as critics might say, responsibility for) the "modern" concept of precedent has yet to be recorded; but his approach, in contrast with that of the Equity judges, was undoubtedly a major factor in putting the House's imprimatur on a formalistic approach that had already achieved currency in the lower courts.

While clearly a common lawyer, Bramwell was noticeably less restrained in his attitudes toward the law[112] and toward life itself. As a puisne judge of the Court of Exchequer, he had already made his views known when he had held picketing conducted in an intimidating fashion to be an indictable offense.[113] No one was more deeply imbued with the (inherently conflicting) concepts of Benthamite liberalism, and in his hands they were carried to extreme lengths. Even as a law lord Bramwell waged a vigorous campaign against any invasion of his concept of the freedom of contract, both in speeches in the Lords[114] and in letters to

110. 6 App. Cas. 740, 808 (1881). However, he sometimes refrained from citing cases if he felt it was unnecessary to do so to support a proposition. "For I take it, without citing cases, that it is now thoroughly well established that no action will lie for doing that which the legislature has authorised, if it be done without negligence, although it does occasion damages to anyone; but an action does lie for doing that which the legislature has authorised if it be done negligently"; *Geddis v. Proprietors of Bann Reservoir*, 3 App. Cas. 430, 455–56 (Scot. 1875).

111. 10 App. Cas. 354, 361 (1885).

112. See 1 *Dictionary of National Biography*, suppl. 256. Veeder, "Century of English Judicature" 778 ff. For a survey of his decisions in his 20 years on the Exchequer Bench and his five years as a Lord Justice of Appeal, see Charles Fairfield, *A Memoir of Lord Bramwell* 27 ff.

113. *R. v. Druitt*, 10 Cox. C.C. 600 (1867). Yet he professed to be in favor of trade unionism, 351 *Parl. Deb.*, H.L. (3d ser.), cols. 372–73 (6 Mar. 1891).

114. See for example, his comments on the Payment of Wages in Public Houses, etc. Bill, which he described as a most mischievous proposal. "This country was the most prosperous in the world. The people had more wealth, more comfort, and more happiness than the people of any other country he knew. If he were asked how that had been brought about, he would say that it was because the people had been left to themselves and had not been worried by Government, and he objected to the state of things being altered"; 276 *Parl. Deb.*, H.L. (3d ser.), col. 1569 (6 Mar. 1883). See also on Truck Bill, 319 ibid., cols. 255–56 (12 Aug. 1887); and on Employers' Liability Act, 332 ibid., col. 949 (21 Dec.

The Times; and he remained an ardent champion of the Liberty and Property Defense League. In 1884, the league published a pamphlet by Bramwell entitled *Laissez-Faire*, in which he argued for the minimum of state interference and pleaded, "Please govern me as little as possible."[115] Perhaps he had a sense of humor, for his hatred of collectivism almost matched his dislike for Equity and his ability to despise any sentimental weakening in the criminal law[116] by allowing defenses such as insanity.[117]

In terms of his attitude toward law, Bramwell would happily have abolished Equity with its notions of justice and its overtones of discretion.[118] His view of construction was equally firm. Only the literal approach might be adopted, whether the matter was one relating to statute or contract. On the former he said; "I think you must construe the Act of Parliament, not according to what possibly may have been the motives, if you can ascertain them, of those who passed it, but according to its language."[119] In keeping with this position, on occasion he insisted on

---

1888): "He cared not what the law was, so long as people were allowed to make their own bargains; but to say that such bargains should not be made, that master and man could not agree for higher wages, and no liability, or lower wages, and liability was preposterous."

115. His remark that, "I am a bit of a socialist," must be treated as high irony; Address, British Association, July 1888. More characteristic was his speech in 300 *Parl. Deb.*, H.L. (3d ser.), col. 655 (31 July 1885), on socialistic tendencies in recent legislation.

116. "[F]or the next twenty years the 'mad doctors' who either could not or would not understand that by the law of England some mad persons who commit crimes are responsible, and others are not, had no more formidable antagonist than Bramwell"; 1 *Dictionary of National Biography*, suppl. 256.

117. In 1872 he wrote to the *Spectator* on "The Object of the English Criminal Law," arguing against relaxation of penalties. A typical remark was his comment on kleptomania: "That is a disease which I am here to cure."

118. For example, in *Salt v. Marquis of Northampton*, [1892] A.C. 1 (1891), he had some uncomplimentary remarks to make on various equitable doctrines. On the equity of redemption he said, "Whether it would not have been better to have held people to their bargains, and taught them by experience not to make unwise ones, rather than relieve them when they had done so, may be doubtful. We should have been spared the double condition of things, legal rights and equitable rights, and a system of documents which do not mean what they say. But the piety or love of fees of those who administered equity has thought otherwise. And probably to undo this would be more costly and troublesome than to continue it"; ibid. 18–21.

Expressing his regret at having to arrive at the conclusion at which the majority arrived, he said that he thought the equitable doctrine prohibiting the fettering of the equity of redemption unreasonable. Cf. his judgment in *Ashbury Ry. Carriage & Iron Co. v. Riche*, L.R. 7 H.L. 653 (1875). See G. H. Powell, "*Bunch versus Great Western Railway Company*" 469. He was accused of being an advocate of the railway.

119. *Justices of Lancashire v. Corporation of Rochdale*, 8 App. Cas. 494, 501 (1882); and see 319 *Parl. Deb.*, H.L. (3d ser.), cols. 225–26 (12 Aug. 1887), where he had a disagreement with Halsbury as to what a proposed amendment in the Truck Bill meant. Bramwell construed it to mean master and servant could come to an effective special agreement. Halsbury said the amendment was not rendering unlawful anything contrary to the general policy of the act. Bramwell's retort was that "[t]he ascertainment of the true meaning of the Amendment was a pleasure that would have to be reserved until such time as his noble and learned friend and he were sitting judicially to interpret it"; ibid.

adhering to the words of a statute although all the other members of the House, following previous interpretative decisions, had come to the opposite conclusion.[120]

Despite his strictures about Equity, Bramwell's attitude to precedent was less strict than the logic of his position dictated. "I am prone to decide case on principles, and when I think I have got the right one I am apt (I hope I am not presumptuous) like Caliph Omar, to think authorities wrong or needless."[121] Typical of this attitude is his speech in *Derry* v. *Peek* in which he said, commenting on Herschell's judgment: "Now, I really am reluctant to cite authorities to shew that actual fraud must be established in such a case as this. It is one of the first things one learned and one has never heard it doubted until recently. I am very glad to think that my noble and learned friend . . . has taken the trouble to go into the authorities fully; but to some extent I deprecate it, because it seems to me somewhat to come within the principle Qui s'excuse s'accuse."[122] Bramwell was, however, far from advocating complete disregard of precedent,[123] for he was the quintessential common lawyer. Of Bramwell, one could say, perhaps fairly, that he saw every reason for adopting the declaratory theory of law but he would not personally have allowed its acceptance to inhibit his judicial style or personal predispositions.

Yet, just as by the end of the period the political judges were coming to predominate in the Equity tradition, the same was true in the common law tradition. This is perhaps most usefully illustrated by Robson. It may be that of all the law lords, Robson held the most radical opinions;[124] yet he remained a popular figure, with a wide circle of friends of all political

120. "The statute says the lease shall be deemed to be surrendered, your Lordships say it shall not, you do this to avoid an injustice and in doing so you cause another.

"I frankly own that if I had to advise anybody as to whether my opinion should be acted upon or the opinion of the noble and learned Lords who have addressed your Lordships, I should say undoubtedly the weight of authority is so against me that I must somehow or other be in the wrong, though I cannot see it"; *Hill* v. *East & West India Dock, Ltd.*, 9 App. Cas. 448, 459–60, 469 (1884).

Similarly, where the words are ambiguous in an instrument he said, "[W]e must look at the reasonable and probable thing"; *John Orr Ewing & Co.* v. *Orr Ewing*, 8 App. Cas. 822 (Scot. 1882).

121. Veeder, "Century of English Judicature" 785.

122. 14 App. Cas. 337, 346–47 (1889).

123. "But it is said that we are bound by the authority of *Last* v. *London Assurance Corporation* to hold otherwise. If I thought that that case decided otherwise, I would abide by it; it would be my duty to do so, and, I may say, my inclination, for it is much better that a wrong decision should be set right by legislation, than that idle distinctions should be made between it and other cases, and the law thrown into confusion"; *New York Life Ins. Co.* v. *Styles*, 14 App. Cas. 381, 396 (1889).

124. Although he did on occasion adopt a conservative line. See for example, his alliance with Halsbury in opposition to the extension of the jurisdiction of the County Courts; 9 *Parl. Deb.*, H.L. (5th ser.), col. 408 (12 July 1911). Even the most liberal of lawyers, however, has a tendency to be conservative where the interests of the legal profession are at stake.

persuasions.[125] He had been especially active during the crucial Liberal administration that was formed in December 1905. Indeed, it was the strain involved night after night on the front bench during the Committee Stage of Lloyd George's 1909 budget that broke his health; and when he was created Lord of Appeal in 1910, he had to endure two years of ill health until retirement was forced on him in 1912. Yet these two years suggested how valuable he could have been to the bench if only he had been appointed a law lord in the prime of his life.[126] The relationship of law and politics was indeed strange in Edwardian England.

The Scottish Tradition

Besides the Equity and the common law traditions, however, a third judicial tradition was at work. By 1876 representatives of the Scottish judiciary had appeared, bringing with them a broader attitude to the law than had been usual in England. Watson's importance in English cases became most marked after the retirement of Blackburn in 1887. Although a master of doctrine and by no means a judicial radical, Watson had a keen sense of the political and social conditions relating to the decision with which he was faced—a trait that was to become associated with the Scottish law lords. The approach played a vital role in his handling of appeals to the Lords. Nowhere was this more marked than in his observations on public policy in the *Nordenfelt* case.[127] In addition to his

125. See generally G. W. Keeton, *A Liberal Attorney-General*. A university contemporary recalled that, "though they abhorred his politics, they would have voted with him to a man whatever line he took." The same was not always true of the electors, for he lost his seat in the Commons in 1886 after supporting Gladstone's Home Rule policy. He joined the Liberal Imperialists in 1899 to support the South African War, and took a prominent part in the campaign of 1904–5 against the fiscal proposals of Chamberlain. In office he was first Solicitor-General and then Attorney-General in 1908. He steered the Trade Disputes Bill of 1906 and Lloyd George's budget of 1909 through the Commons.

126. As a judge, his clarity of expression and his judicial sense came into their own in cases like *Russell* v. *Amalgamated Soc'y of Carpenters & Joiners*, [1912] A.C. 421, 434.

127. "A series of decisions based upon grounds of public policy, however eminent the judges by whom they were delivered, cannot possess the same binding authority as decisions which deal with and formulate principles which are purely legal. The course of policy pursued by any country in relation to, and for promoting the interests of, its commerce must, as time advances and its commerce thrives, undergo change and development from various causes which are altogether independent of the action of its Courts. In England, at least, it is beyond the jurisdiction of her tribunals to mould and stereotype national policy. Their function when a case like the present is brought before them, is, in my opinion, not necessarily to accept what was held to have been the rule of policy a hundred or a hundred fifty years ago, but to ascertain, with as near an approach to accuracy as circumstances permit, what is the rule of policy for the then present time"; *Nordenfelt* v. *Maxim Nordenfelt Guns & Ammunition Co.*, [1894] A.C. 535, 553–54.

By the 1950s, this statement seemed sufficiently radical that it had to be "explained away" by the apologists of the orthodox approach. E.g., Carleton Kemp Allen, *Law in the Making*; Rupert Cross, *Precedent in English Law* 131–32, (1961 ed.), suggesting why it was

reputation in the Lords, Watson became a powerful figure in the Judicial Committee of the Privy Council. During the 1890s in particular, he was responsible for reversing the balance of power apparently intended by the drafters of the British North America Act to lie with the federal government by a series of decisions in favor of the provinces. Few law lords have exercised greater political power.[128]

Yet, Watson's successor, Robertson, was even more a politician. Indeed, Robertson would rather have been a politician than a lawyer but felt financially unable to be one.[129] Thus, in keeping with the tradition that had grown up among the Equity and common law lords, he frequently behaved like a politician while on the bench. This tendency was most blatant in his dissents with Atkinson, in favor of employers, as the Workmen's Compensation Acts came to be interpreted. Such dissents were scarcely surprising on Robertson's part, for in an age when, intellectually, socialism was increasingly readily accepted, Robertson, as Rector of Edinburgh University argued:

It is surely most desirable that the subject of Socialism should be studied and understood now, before it has got mixed up with party politics. ... of all subjects, Socialism must be studied to be understood in its practical proposals and ultimate consequences; and once these are realised, it is seen how essentially collectivism differs from a mere limitation of the old principle of laissez-faire. ... It [study of the subject] will above all inspire that kind of respect which is akin to amazement, for the boldness of this conception of a new ideal on which to fix the hopes of our race—a State in which man shall live by bread alone; in which, once for all, the human soul shall be given in exchange for rations; a state, of which slavery is not merely an institution but the corner stone and in which the gates of intellectual freedom are shut for ever on mankind.[130]

No juxtaposition could better symbolize the fact that, as the law lords tended to pay greater theoretical deference to the declaratory theory of law, these judges were, if anything, increasingly sensitive to the political realities. The 1876 act had made the Lords of Appeal political appointees; stare decisis provided a symbolic base to put them above politics. As long

---

not an exception to stare decisis; and Raymond Evershed, "The Judicial Process in 20th Century England" 761 ff.

128. Haldane later said "[A]s a result of a long series of decisions Lord Watson put clothing upon the bones of the Constitution, and so covered them over with living flesh that the Constitution of Canada took a new form. It is difficult to say what the extent of the debt was that Canada owes to Lord Watson, and there is no part of the Empire where his name is held in greater reverence"; Richard Burdon Haldane, "The Work for the Empire of the Judicial Committee of the Privy Council" 150. In view of the political hostility evoked in Canada by many of Haldane's decisions, the statement is uncritical.

129. Hugh Macmillan, *Law and Other Things*. According to Macmillan, he was a poor Lord President.

130. James Patrick Robertson, *The Duty of Educated Intellect to the State* 21–22.

as their work was primarily in private rather than public law the compromise worked, although a study of the substantive law of the period makes clear that law lords from the Equity, common law, and Scottish traditions contributed greatly to its acceptance. The new law lords turned out to have taken on some of the complexion of the aristocratic amateurs who had preceded them.

The Substantive Law

By the 1840s the House of Lords was finally regarded as a serious English court for common law as well as Equity cases; by the 1870s the House was predominantly an English court and, by 1900, predominantly a common law court. Indeed, despite the threats of abolition, the nineteenth century was a booming time for the appellate work of the House. The vast expansion of British industry and affluence brought new legislation to be interpreted, relating to companies, patents, and copyright; the expansion of trade brought contract law as a day-to-day responsibility of the House and presented doctrines that had to be adapted to the changing times. The rapid social changes also called for decisions about the allocation of risk, which were settled by the law of tort. As government grew, regulation appeared; the House had not only to settle problems raised by the attempt to regulate contracts, but also to consider controls over actions by the reformed local authorities and, ultimately, by the central government.

These later developments belong primarily to the last decades of the nineteenth century and the Edwardian period in the first decade of the twentieth. Between 1844 and 1876, however, the House did decide in a significant number of "leading" cases, many of considerable importance up to the present day.[1] During the 1840s, for instance, important advances were made in public international law.[2] Almost from the beginning of the railway age, the House had to wrestle with problems arising from the attempt to limit responsibility by contract (the so-called exemption clauses)[3] and, in the related field of industrial costs, the House put

1. C. H. S. Fifoot, *Judge and Jurist in the Reign of Victoria*, *passim*.
2. E.g., *Duke of Brunswick* v. *King of Hanover*, 2 H.L.C. (1848) (doctrine of sovereign immunity).
3. *Bristol & Exeter Ry.* v. *Collins*, 7 H.L.C. 194 (1859).

its imprimatur on common employment (the fellow servant rule) in 1850, thereby preventing the bringing of actions for most work-related injuries.[4] Meanwhile, on the Equity side, during the 1840s the House was moving to expand doctrines that were later to influence company (corporation) law,[5] as well as general equitable notions about negative, restrictive, or equitable covenants.[6]

During the 1850s, at a time when the judicial complement of the Lords was at its nadir,[7] the House gave a series of innovative decisions.[8] Brougham's operations, after all, produced two leading cases on the liability of shareholders to contribute in liquidation proceedings.[9] *Dimes v. Grand Junction Canal*[10] was a basic decision on natural justice, while *Scott v. Avery*[11] was an important decision on the power to oust the jurisdiction of the courts. Meanwhile, in the general area of contract, the House laid down significant new law in the areas of public policy[12] and the sale of nonexistent goods.[13]

With the greater supply of distinguished law lords during the 1860s, there was an even more noticeable tendency for the House to "legislate" in English appeals. It was during these years that the principles of the conflict of laws[14] were expanded, while the recently passed company and trademark legislation were used to expand other doctrines.[15] In tort, the House laid the basis of the modern doctrine of nuisance,[16] forged the idea of the vicarious liability of public corporations,[17] and coalesced the rules of strict liability into the doctrine that took its name from *Rylands v. Fletcher*.[18] In contract the House had to rethink matters ranging from

---

4. *Hutchinson v. York, Newcastle & Berwick Ry.*, 5 Ex. 343 (1850).

5. *Foss v. Harbottle*, 2 Hare 461; 67 Eng. Rep. 189 (1843).

6. *Tulk v. Moxhay*, 2 Phil. 774 (1848). They were later held to apply only to land; G. C. Cheshire and C. H. S. Fifoot, *Modern Contract Law* (London, 1972), 442. But see *Lord Strathcona S.S. Co. v. Dominion Coal Co.*, [1926] A.C. 108 (P.C. 1925) where the Privy Council applied the doctrine to a ship.

7. See chap. 2, at 38–41.

8. In a sense, of course, the Committee for Privileges decision in the *Wensleydale Peerage Case* falls within that category; 5 H.L.C. 958 (1856).

9. *Hutton v. Upfill*, 2 H.L.C. 674 (1850); *Bright v. Hutton*, 3 H.L.C. 341 (1852).

10. 3 H.L.C. 759 (1852).

11. 5 H.L.C. 811 (1855).

12. *Egerton v. Lord Brownlow*, 4 H.L.C. 1 (1853).

13. *Couturier v. Hastie*, 5 H.L.C. 673 (1856).

14. E.g., *Brook v. Brook*, 9 H.L.C. 193 (1861); *Doglioni v. Crispin*, L.R. 1 H.L. 301 (1866); *Shaw v. Gould*, L.R. 3 A.C. 55 (1868).

15. E.g., company law, *Oakes v. Turquand*, L.R. 2 A.C. 325 (1865); trademarks and passing off, *Leather Co. v. American Leather Co.*, 11 H.L.C. 523 (1865).

16. *St. Helens Smelting Co. v. Tipping*, 11 H.L.C. 642 (1865).

17. *Mersey Docks & Harbours Bd. v. Gibbs*, 11 H.L.C. 686 (1866).

18. L.R. 3 H.L. 330 (1868).

exemption clauses[19] to mistake,[20] while at the same time it further expounded broad principles of equity.[21]

The "new" House that appeared in 1877 was, if anything, heir to an expanding rather than a contracting view of judicial legislation—at least in those areas traditionally left by Parliament to the judges. Nor did the tradition of judicial legislation change in those private areas of the common law, although the rhetoric often did. The point at which the tradition and rhetoric both failed was in the area of public law.

Private Law: Incorporation and the Economy

Although it may be said that the structure of company law was largely settled by the Companies Act of 1862, the Lords of Appeal still had a series of problems to battle. In addition to the financial advantages already occurring with incorporation, the law lords—especially those from the common law tradition—seemed anxious to develop even greater attributes by insisting the corporate status established a "fictitious" person. Thus, for example, a limited company could not be prosecuted under the Pharmacy Acts as a "person" selling poisonous drugs.[22] This particular decision could easily be remedied by legislation, for the majority of the law lords had no doubt that a corporation could be subjected to fines.[23] Yet, in the following year the House unanimously decided that the garnishee process could not be invoked against a corporation,[24] a proposition not so easily overturned by Parliament. Bramwell, moreover, believed that a corporation ought not to be suable for libel or nuisance.[25] In the Lords, he sought to show that "a corporation is incapable of malice or of motive,"[26] and although the other law lords refused to decide the point,[27] the assertion caused difficulties in later decades. The

19. E.g., *Peek v. North Staffordshire Ry.*, 10 H.L.C. 473 (1862), interpreting the 1854 legislation allowing contracting out of liability. The House allowed it if "reasonable."

20. *Cooper v. Phibbs*, L.R. 2 A.C. 149 (Ire. 1867).

21. The broad principles of equity that the House developed in this period are perhaps its most remarkable feature, although many of them were restricted by later decisions. Apart from *Cooper v. Phibbs*, see decisions on recission for undue influence, *Williams v. Bayley*, L.R. 1 A.C. 200 (1866); misrepresentation, *Central Ry. of Venezuela v. Kirsch*, L.R. 2 H.L. 99 (1867); and the concept of estoppel, *Ramsden v. Dyson*, L.R. 1 H.L. 129 (1866).

22. *Pharmaceutical Soc'y v. London & Provincial Supply Ass'n*, 5 App. Cas. 857 (1880).

23. E.g., speech by Blackburn, ibid. 869.

24. *City of London v. London Joint Stock Bank*, 6 App. Cas. 393 (1881).

25. See speech by Bramwell, L. J., in *Pharmaceutical Soc'y v. London & Provincial Supply Ass'n*, 5 Q.B.D. 310, 313 (C.A. 1880).

26. *Abrath v. North Eastern Ry.*, 11 App. Cas. 247, 251 (1886). In this case of malicious prosecution, Bramwell felt that any remedy should be against the individual officers of the company.

27. See especially per Lord Selborne, ibid. 256.

House was also still plagued by the case of *Ashbury Railway Carriage and Iron Company* v. *Riche*,[28] which had applied the doctrine of ultra vires to the articles of a company,[29] although Selborne insisted that the concept be applied reasonably and not rigidly.[30]

Despite the philosophical ramifications of the fictitious person and the precedential difficulties produced by cases such as *Riche*, the House made a more determined effort to integrate the concept of a corporation into existing law and, at least when the "old" Equity judges sat, to supplement company law with broad principles of Equity. Thus in *Erlanger* v. *New Sombrero Phosphate Company*,[31] Selborne and Cairns imposed a fiduciary duty on the promoters of the company in their dealings with the company. In rescinding a contract for the purchase of an island, the House imposed on promoters of companies a duty that went far beyond anything provided by the Companies Acts up to that date.[32] Indeed, as the period wore on, a serious effort was made to develop company law along responsible lines.[33] Perhaps the best example of this attempt is *Trevor* v. *Whitworth*, in which, despite the power that a company was given in its memorandum to purchase its own shares, the House held such power ultra vires, as inconsistent with the tenor of the Companies Acts.[34]

In time, however, the common law tradition, represented by the doctrine of the fictitious person, and the Equity tradition of requiring quasi-fiduciary behavior of those who played the incorporation game

28. L.R. 7 H.L. 653 (1875).
29. The House felt obliged in principle to apply this theory to companies incorporated by special act of Parliament as well as to companies established under the Companies Act; *Attorney-General* v. *Great Eastern Ry.*, 5 App. Cas. 473 (1879); *Wenlock* v. *River Dee Co.*, 10 App. Cas. 354 (1885). See especially per Lord Blackburn, ibid. 358.
30. *Attorney-General* v. *Great Eastern Ry.*, 5 App. Cas. 473, 478 (1879).
31. 3 App. Cas. 1218 (1878).
32. The case was argued twice. On the second hearing it was heard by Cairns, Hatherley, Penzance, O'Hagan, Selborne, Blackburn, and Gordon.
33. Control was also exercised over directors, as in *Henderson* v. *Huntington Copper & Sulphate Co.*, Opinions of their Lordships, 1877. There the House applied the doctrine that a director must not enter into any contracts that caused his interests to conflict with those of his clients.
34. 12 App. Cas. 409 (1887). See especially the speeches of Herschell at 412, Watson at 421, and Macnaghten at 431.
Among the cases resulting from the collapse of the City of Glasgow Bank was one of some importance on the liability of corporations, *Houldsworth* v. *City of Glasgow Bank*, 5 App. Cas. 317 (Scot. 1880). The House held that the appellant could not recover damages from the company, although the fraudulent directors acting on the company's behalf were personally liable, unless the allotment of shares was also rescinded, which it was, on the facts, too late; L. C. B. Gower, *Modern Company Law*, 62–67.
There were frequently cases concerning points that required to be settled on the administration of company law, for example, *Birch* v. *Cropper*, 14 App. Cas. 525 (1889), on the distribution of assets on winding up and *Wright* v. *Horton*, 12 App. Cas. 371 (1887), on the registration of debentures.

were bound to conflict. The Judicature Act of 1873 had not only merged
Equity and common law, but had provided that in areas of conflict between the two, Equity was to prevail. Yet in the Lords, the style of the
common lawyer increasingly prevailed, especially after the Lord Chancellors began to be chosen more frequently from that branch of the law.
The conflict became clear when the House had to decide the limits to be
placed on incorporation as a means of evading or avoiding the law. The
House took the easy—or common law—way out.

In *Salomon and Company* v. *Salomon*[35] the Lords gave carte blanche
to incorporation. It was held that if a person turned himself into a limited liability company and that company failed, creditors had no means
by which they could obtain redress against the person who had incorporated himself. The Court of Appeal had been prepared to "lift the corporate veil" since the Lords Justices, who comprised that court under the
Judicature Acts, felt any other solution would be "contrary to the true
intent and meaning of the Companies Act." The House, however, insisted
on a rigid adherence to the letter of the law. "It seems to me impossible
to dispute that once the company is legally incorporated it must be
treated like any other independent person with its rights and liabilities
appropriate to itself,"[36] said Halsbury, who criticized the Lords Justices
who had allowed "what they have considered the inexpediency of permitting one man to be in influence and authority over the whole company . . . to encourage them in effect to add a clause to the relevant
Companies Acts."[37] The company was in the future to be sacrosanct.[38]
In many respects Halsbury's decision made the law easy to administer,
but in it lay the seeds of innumerable complicated economic problems for
the future.[39] As the result of Halsbury's common law approach, these

35. [1897] A.C. 22 (1896). See Gower, *Modern Company Law* 62–67, for a discussion and criticism of this decision; and see now also Tom Hadden, *Company Law and
Capitalism* 44–47.
36. [1897] A.C. 22, 30 (1896).
37. Ibid. 34.
38. See also per Macnaghten, ibid. 51.
39. One of the difficulties prescribed by a similar strict view of the independent existence of the limited company was illustrated by *Moss S.S. Co.* v. *Whinney*, [1912] A.C.
254. There a shipping company was held not entitled to exercise a lien clause in a bill of
lading against the receiver of a company for freight due from the company, since they were
different legal entities. Shaw and Mersey dissented.
There was perhaps a related reluctance to make natural persons liable for their acts in
respect of such artificial persons. See *Dovey* v. *Cory*, [1901] A.C. 477, where the House
held that a company director, who reasonably relied on the advice of the director of a bank
and paid dividends out of capital, was not liable to contribute in a winding up.
In contrast to this, outside the company proper, the House maintained firm control
over the behavior of promoters. E.g., *Glukstein* v. *Barnes*, [1900] A.C. 240. See especially
per Halsbury and Macnaghten, at 245, 248. So too within the company itself, the House
handled some rules effectively. Typical was that concerned with the discretion given to the

problems, when they arose, had to be tackled by increasingly detailed legislation[40] rather than by the expansion of Equity.

Commerce, Contract, and Free Will: The Victorian Perception[41]

Similarly, the House had to develop, or at least adapt, contract and commercial law to cope with the problems raised by an expanding economy. In this regard, the strength of the Equity representation among the law lords was particularly noticeable in the early years of the post-1876 period, and during that time equitable principles showed considerable resilience. In *Hughes* v. *Metropolitan Railway Company*,[42] Cairns restated, with some emphasis, the concepts of equitable estoppel. The breadth of his statement was remarkable,[43] and the speeches of both Cairns and Selborne were distinguished by their emphasis on basic principles, virtually unencumbered by precedents or even citations to earlier decisions.

Had the ascendancy of the law lords trained in the old school of Equity been maintained, it is arguable that much of the formalistic and legalistic tone of the later part of the period might not have developed. Slowly, however, during the 1880s, the influence of the common lawyers grew,[44] and with the rise in importance of Blackburn and Bramwell, and

---

court, under the Companies Acts, to sanction reductions of capital. See, for instance, *Poole* v. *National Bank of China*, [1907] A.C. 229.

40. E.g., Companies Acts of 1893 and 1911. The House was not always in tune with Parliament on company matters. See, for example, *ex parte Barnes*, [1896] A.C. 146, which undermined the Winding Up Act of 1890, with respect to fraudulent directors. "The conditions [laid down in the decision] are as impracticable as those prescribed by the fair Portia to Shylock for carving up Antonio"; "Note," *Law Quarterly Review* 199 (1896).

41. In this area it is now difficult to write without being influenced, consciously or unconsciously, by Grant Gilmore, *The Death of Contract*.

42. 2 App. Cas. 439 (1877)

43. "It is the first principle upon which all Courts of Equity proceed, that if parties who have entered into definite and distinct terms involving certain legal results—certain penalties or legal forfeiture—afterwards by their own act or with their own consent enter upon a course of negotiation which has the effect of leading one of the parties to suppose that the strict rights arising under the contract will not be enforced, or will be kept in suspense, or held in abeyance, the person who otherwise might have enforced those rights will not be allowed to enforce them where it would be inequitable having regard to the dealings which have thus taken place between the parties"; ibid. 448.

It was in reliance on this statement that Denning in *Central London Property Trust, Ltd.* v. *High Trees House, Ltd.* [1947] K.B. 130 (1946), was able to formulate his principle of "equitable estoppel."

44. A strategic case in this change of attitude is *Kendall* v. *Hamilton*, 4 App. Cas. 504 (1879), where the House held that the technical common law rule for suing on a joint contract should prevail over the more flexible, but less clearly defined, equitable principle. Penzance dissented. "I confess I am unwilling that your Lordships should confer the high sanction of this, the ultimate Court of Appeal, upon a rule of procedure which, without affecting to assert any just rights on the part of the Defendant, denies the aid of the law to enforce those of the Plaintiff. Procedure is but the machinery of the law after all—the

the appearance of more legalistically minded Chancery lawyers such as Macnaghten, the reliance on widely stated equitable principles diminished. Instead of being used to enforce broad standards in a general area of the law, equitable rules, as opposed to equitable remedies,[45] were used more often only in the more narrow substantive areas previously associated with the Court of Chancery itself.[46]

The ascendancy of the common law juristic approach might not have been so noticeable had it not coincided with the widening acceptance of laissez-faire principles as a basic policy, or at least assumption, by the judges. In contract, increasing judicial commitment to laissez-faire was reflected in developments such as the doctrines of *pacta sunt servanda* and caveat emptor.[47] The idea that parties should be bound by the terms of the agreement almost inevitably meant that exemption clauses excusing responsibility were generously interpreted. By such interpretation, incidentally, the House gave Britain's omnipotent merchant fleet wide protection at the same time that the Supreme Court in the United States—whose traders owned the cargoes—was seeking to restrict exemption clauses, particularly in shipping documents.[48] Moreover, begin-

---

channel and means whereby law is administered and justice reached. It strangely departs from its proper office when, in place of facilitating, it is permitted to obstruct, and even extinguish legal rights, and thus is made to govern where it ought to subserve"; ibid. 525.

45. *Adam* v. *Newbigging*, 13 App. Cas. 308 (1888), allowing rescission of a contract for innocent misrepresentation, is a wide and important decision on the breadth of equitable remedies and the implications that that might have in substantive law.

46. For instance, a high standard of behavior was required of agents. See *McPherson* v. *Watt*, 3 App. Cas. 254 (Scot. 1877), a Scottish case where the House held that a sale of property should be set aside where the vendor's solicitor arranged for a sale to his own brother, in which he was interested, without disclosing his interest. See especially speech by O'Hagan, ibid. 266.

47. The classical statement of the application of laissez-faire in contract was made by Master of the Rolls Jessel in the Court of Appeal: "[I]f there is one thing which more than another public policy requires, it is that men of full age and competent understanding shall have the utmost liberty of contracting, and that their contracts, when entered into freely and voluntarily, shall be held sacred and shall be enforced by Courts of justice"; *Printing & Numerical Registering Co.* v. *Sampson*, L.R. 19 Eq. 462, 465 (1875).

48. *Liverpool & Great Western Steam Co.* v. *Phoenix Ins. Co.*, 129 U.S. 397, 438–63 (1889). But in the House loss of cargo as the result of a collision and foundering was held by the Lords to fall clearly within an exception in a bill of lading covering "dangers and accidents of the sea"; *Thomas Wilson* v. *"Xantho" (Owners of Cargo)*, 12 App. Cas. 503 (1887). Rice ruined because rats gnawed a hole in a pipe, allowing seawater to escape into the cargo was held covered by an exception of "dangers and accidents of the sea"; *Hamilton, Fraser* v. *Pandorf & Co.*, 12 App. Cas. 518 (1887). The competing judicial approaches in the "owner" and "cargo" nations ultimately led to the Hague Convention on the Carriage of Goods by Sea in 1894. See Grant Gilmore and Charles Black, *Law of Admiralty*, chap. 3 (2d ed.).

Where a passenger ticket was concerned, apparently the House took a more liberal approach to exemption clauses, and refused to interfere with the finding of the jury that the plaintiff did not know that the writing on the ticket contained conditions so that insufficient notice of the conditions had been given; e.g., *Richardson, Spence & Co.* v. *Rowntree*,

ning with *Nordenfelt*,[49] the House established a policy that virtually prevented public policy in restraint of trade from ever being pleaded as a means of avoiding a contract. In this sense the courts refused to police the capitalist system.

In giving continued effect to the rule in *Pinnel's Case* in *Foakes* v. *Beer*,[50] the House exhibited another aspect of its reluctance to interfere with contractual rights once established. The payment of a lesser sum was not to be satisfaction of a debt for a greater amount.[51] Moreover, the common law having recently evolved the concept of the undisclosed principal—someone who might emerge and enforce an undisclosed agent's contract—the House insisted on construing its impact narrowly. Any other interpretation would have been out of keeping with the law lords' insistence on *consensus ad idem*. Thus, when an undisclosed principal sued a buyer for the price in a broken contract, the buyer was held not to be entitled to set off a debt owed by the agent.[52] The House had, so it seemed, little wish to soften the hard facts of Victorian business life. The economic effects of mistake, for instance, were to lie where they fell.[53]

In business, too, it was assumed that the effects of a fraud should be borne by the person who had suffered the loss, rather than by the person who had initially made the fraud possible. In *Cundy* v. *Lindsay and*

[1894] A.C. 217. Some explanation appears in the speech of Ashbourne. "The ticket in question in this case was for a steerage passenger—a class of people of the humblest description, many of whom have little education and some of them none"; ibid. 221. The message of collectivism was slowly being accepted. For the historical background, see Maldwyn A. Jones, "Immigrants, Steamships, and Governments," *passim*. For an overall view, see Oliver MacDonagh, *A Pattern of Government Growth*.

49. [1894] A.C. 535. But, while in general rejecting restraint-of-trade arguments, the House approved the limited protection that the common law gave to the seller of the goodwill of a business; *Trego* v. *Hunt*, [1896] A.C. 7 (1895).

50. 9 App. Cas. 605 (1884).

51. There was, perhaps surprisingly, a certain unwillingness to come to this decision; Selborne, for instance, said, "It might be (and indeed I think it would be) an improvement in our law, if a release or acquittance of the whole debt, on payment of any sum which the creditor might be content to receive by way of accord and satisfaction (though less than the whole), were held to be, generally, binding, though not under seal"; ibid. 613.

Blackburn had in fact prepared a dissenting judgment but did not read it on finding he was alone in his opinion, reluctantly accepting Coke's dictum in *Pinnel's Case*, of which he said, "I think however that it was originally a mistake"; at 622. Of the case, the *Law Quarterly Review* said, "A dogma of Coke's resting (it may be) originally upon a misconception of law, has been treated as having in effect nearly the weight of a statutory enactment"; 1 *Law Quarterly Review* 134 (1885).

52. *Cooke* v. *Eshelby*, 12 App. Cas. 271 (1887).

53. In *Soper* v. *Arnold*, 14 App. Cas. 429 (1889), a plaintiff had agreed to purchase a house, and a considerable sum had been paid on deposit. On his failure to pay the remainder the defendants sought to resell, only to discover that there was a flaw in their title. Alleging a common mistake, the plaintiff sought recovery of his deposit. "[G]roundless and almost absurd," declared Macnaghten. "[I]f there is a case in which a deposit is rightly and properly forfeited it is, I think, when a man enters into a contract to buy real property without taking the trouble to consider whether he can pay for it or not"; ibid. 438.

Company,[54] the bona fide purchaser of chattels from one who had fraudulently procured them from the manufacturer had a defeasible title. The House looked solely to see whether a contract had been made between the manufacturer and the dishonest middleman; finding that there had been none, the matter was treated as settled.[55] If there were a meeting of the minds, contracts were to be enforced at all costs; if there were no *consensus ad idem*, then the advocates of laissez-faire insisted there would be no contract.[56] Bramwell would have taken this dichotomy to remarkable lengths. He felt that if the acceptance of a bill of exchange had been obtained by fraud, the acceptor's bank should not be entitled to debit its customer's account. He held this view in spite of what appeared to be a broad statutory protection for the bank in such a situation. Fortunately for English law, the majority of the law lords refused to accept such an approach.[57]

Thus, although by the 1880s the Court of Appeal had acknowledged the need to imply terms into a contract to give "business efficacy" to it,[58] the spirit represented by that was alien to the House of Lords, which insisted on taking a peculiarly narrow view of the obligations of parties under the contract. When a public authority invited tenders for the erection of a bridge to the design and specification of the authority's engineer, the House held that there was no implied term that the bridge could be built according to such specifications.[59] The idea that businessmen should be protected in such situations evoked surprise.[60] Only in sales cases was the House prepared to imply warranties,[61] and even then,

54. 3 App. Cas. 459 (1878).
55. E.g., speech by Hatherley, ibid. 466. Cairns, ibid. 463, declared that the rules concerning such transactions were "well known." In fact, he reasoned from general principles and cited no precedents.
56. See speech by Cairns, ibid. 465. Bramwell was a strong advocate of the "meeting of the minds" theory. See, for example, his judgment in *British & American Telegraph Co.* v. *Colson*, L.R. 6 Ex. 108 (1871). In *Buchanan* v. *Duke of Hamilton & Brandon*, O'Hagan said, "For the purposes of a contract you must have a confluence of minds, and an identity of purpose"; Opinions of their Lordships, 1878.
57. *Bank of England* v. *Vagliano Bros.*, [1891] A.C. 107 (Halsbury, Selborne, Watson, Herschell, Macnaghten, and Morris; Bramwell and Field, dissenting).
58. *The Moorcock*, 14 P.D. 64 (C.A. 1889). See especially per Lord Justice Bowen at 68.
59. *Thorn* v. *Corporation of London*, 1 App. Cas. 120 (1876). The House did, however, appear to leave open the possibility of an action on a quantum meruit.
60. "If, as has been strongly contended upon this appeal, there can be found any warranty in such a contract as this, I apprehend it would be scarcely possible for any person whatever to enter upon any new work of any description; say the tubular bridge, for instance, which was originally a bold speculation, I believe, on the part of *Mr. Stephenson*. Any work of that kind, which must necessarily be in a great degree speculative, could scarcely be carried into effect if any person entering into a contract for the performance of that work with a contractor was to be supposed to have guaranteed to the contractor that the performance of it was possible"; ibid. 135, per Hatherley.
61. See *Drummond* v. *Van Ingen*, 12 App. Cas. 284 (1887), deciding that even in sales

much of the real protection for the purchaser lay in his right to demand "exact tender," which, as its name suggests, was a particularly technical requirement as to the discharge of contract developed by Blackburn within a year after his appointment as a Lord of Appeal.[62]

Indeed, throughout the area of contract during the period from 1880 to 1900 the law appears both formalistic and harsh. While in the matter of interpretation there was much talk about finding the intention of makers of contract, in practice this effort seemed to involve little more than reading the contract literally.[63] The Factors Act was read narrowly so that it did not cover the newly developing hire-purchase agreements.[64] If businessmen agreed to arbitrate, they could not then come running to court to have the agreement rescinded.[65] The court would refuse to interfere with the arbitrator so long as he was acting bona fide within his proper field. Thus the House declined to interfere with an arbitrator's award on the ground of exemption, refusing to accept the expression

---

by sample, there was still an implied term that the goods should be reasonably fit for the purpose for which they were supplied, at least where there were latent defects in the sample not discernible on examination.

62. Blackburn believed that "[i]f the description of the article tendered is different in any respect it is not the article bargained for, and the other party is not bound to take it"; *Bowes* v. *Shand*, 2 App. Cas. 455, 480 (1877). The House held that 2 contracts to carry in all 600 tons of rice "to be shipped at Madras—during the months of March and/or April, 1874, per *Rajah of Cochin*" was not satisfied when the major part of the cargo was in fact loaded during the last week of February.

63. As with the statutory language, Selborne sought to take a balanced view, declaring in one case, "I cannot help thinking that in construing such a mercantile contract as this, there is as much danger of error in extreme literalism as in too much latitude"; *M'Cowan* v. *Baine*, [1891] A.C. 401, 403 (Scot.). For the most part, however, the attitude of Bramwell, who dissented in this case, came to be accepted as the period went on: "[T]his seems to me to be a case (too common) in which there is a tendency to depart from the natural primary meaning of words, and add to or take from them—to hold that constructively words mean something different from what they say. It introduces uncertainty. No case is desperate when plain words may be disregarded"; ibid. 411. A typical reaction was that of Cairns in *Levy* v. *Lawes*: "I think it always a most excellent rule to adhere to the words of a contract, and not to import other words into it, or to put a fanciful construction upon it in accordance with a guess at what the parties may have intended"; Opinions of their Lordships, 1879.

64. Where the parties entered into an agreement for hire, the hirer having the option to terminate during the period of hire, but the subject of the agreement becoming his property if he paid all the installments, the House held that the hirer had not "agreed to buy goods" within § 9 of the Factors Act of 1889 and that, therefore, the owners could recover the goods from the pawnbroker with whom the hirer had pledged them. The case laid the foundations for the modern system of hire-purchase in that it enabled owners to avoid the Factors Act, and thus made such transactions far less of a risk; *Helby* v. *Matthews*, [1895] A.C. 471.

65. "The parties deliberately chose a reference, as they were entitled to do. They are entitled to shut out the ordinary judicial tribunals and they did so. They have got the decision of the judge they selected and they must abide by it and implement it"; per Gordon, *Hamilton, McCullock & Co.* v. *McEwan & McCullock*, Opinions of their Lordships, 1878 (Scot.).

"constructive exemption," used by the judges in some of the authorities cited. Appeals from arbitrators could be taken only on points of law and not on fact, and their lordships construed the concept of law narrowly.[66] As Jessel, the Master of the Rolls, had said, contracts that were entered into "freely and voluntarily" were to be held "sacred."

At the beginning of the twentieth century then, the law of contract as perceived by the House was, if not formalistic, at least strictly construed in keeping with the then-fashionable notion of laissez-faire as the manifestation of individual free will. Strictness in interpreting offer and acceptance was the order of the day.[67] The House sought to cling to the very words of agreements.[68] Exact tender remained the basis of performance,[69] and the House anxiously cut back on those aspects of the undisclosed principal that appeared inconsistent with the laissez-faire requirement of meeting of the minds.[70] Moreover, in the first few years of this century the House restated its narrow position on privity of contract.[71]

The Edwardian Court and Commercial Law

During the Edwardian period, however, there was a change of emphasis. In 1896 the House had held that there was a series of implied

66. *North & South Western Junction Ry.* v. *Brentford Union*, 13 App. Cas. 592 (1888), refusing to interfere with "so-called principles of valuation, which are simply formulae for arriving at the solution of the question of fact," per Watson, ibid. 594. See also speech by Halsbury, ibid. 593.

67. When a tobacco manufacturer, in order to gain a larger share of the market, offered to distribute to trade purchasers their entire profits for four years together with £200,000 per year, the House held the defendants bound by the "wild and extravagant" offer; *Ogdens, Ltd.* v. *Nelson*, [1905] A.C. 109 (1904).

68. For example, *North Eastern Ry.* v. *Lord Hastings*, [1900] A.C. 260, held that where a party leased land to a railway in return for a levy on any coal carried on the railway, the contract must be construed literally and the railway was liable to pay the dues on coal carried on their line but not over that part of it running through the plaintiff's land.

69. The shipowner also had no hope of being held not liable for lost goods if, in fact, he had signed for them; *Smith & Co.* v. *Bedouin Steam Navigation Co.*, [1896] A.C. 70 (Scot. 1895). See, for example, per Watson: "The rule of law applicable to this case appears to me to be settled beyond dispute"; ibid. 77. See also *Sandeman & Sons* v. *Tyzach & Branfoot S.S. Co.*, [1913] A.C. 680 (Scot.).

70. Thus the House illogically refused to extend the doctrine of the undisclosed principal to include later ratification of a specific contract even when the purported agent had made it clear at the time the contract was made that he was acting on the behalf of another; *Keighley, Maxsted & Co.* v. *Durant*, [1901] A.C. 240.

71. Charterers were not entitled to sue on an insurance policy effected by owners despite a term in the charterparty and the insurance policy that might be thought to have given them such a right; *Boston Fruit Co.* v. *British & Foreign Marine Ins. Co.*, [1906] A.C. 336. Only the tenant (and not even the tenant's wife) might sue for injuries resulting from defects in breach of a lease; *Cavalier* v. *Pope*, [1906] A.C. 428.

On the other hand, a producer of chalk agreeing to supply a cement manufacturer with all the chalk he might need for the manufacture of cement was held bound by the contract when the benefit of it was assigned by the original manufacturer; *Tolhurst* v. *Associated*

contracts between every competitor in a sailing race;[72] and Halsbury, no less, vigorously rejected the idea that all the terms of a contract necessarily existed within a written document when there was one.[73] For some time during this same period, the House appeared to toy with the idea of developing the concept of a collateral contract—a useful device for avoiding the terms of the main contract.[74] The idea of implying terms in interpreting the contract was also at last taken seriously. Breaking away from a series of earlier precedents, the House held that when a person sold a business and its goodwill, despite the silence of the written contract, a term could be implied to prevent the vendor's setting up a rival business.[75] Although deference was paid to the doctrine that "terms are not lightly or unnecessarily to be implied,"[76] Loreburn also made it clear that "terms are of course to be implied if it is necessary to give true effect to the express contract."[77] Thus it was held that under a c.i.f. (contract, insurance, freight) contract, although there was no express term, the seller

---

Portland Cement Mfrs., [1903] A.C. 414 (Macnaghten, Shand, and Lindley; Halsbury, *dubitante*; and Robertson, dissenting).

72. *Clarke v. Earl of Dunraven*, [1897] A.C. 59.

73. "If the learned judge means that the contract obligation would not exist unless it was to be found within the language of the written contract I am bound to say that I think that is contrary to the law. That is not the law.

"The written contract is only intended to codify and state in plain terms the bargain between the parties. You may by the operation of statements and representations made at the time so clothe the rest of your contract with an additional contract obligation that whether it is represented as an interpretation of the language of the contract or represented as something collateral is perhaps immaterial"; *Jacobs v. Scott*, Opinions of their Lordships, 1899.

74. In one case the House did use a collateral contract to enforce the sense of an agreement—*Schwale v. Rude*, Opinions of their Lordships, 1912—although the possibilities of this were largely blocked by *Heilbut, Symons & Co. v. Buckleton*, [1913] A.C. 30 (1912). There the House held that on the facts before them there was insufficient evidence to show that the defendants had warranted, to a plaintiff purchasing shares, that the company was a rubber company. In so holding, Moulton was able to weaken the idea that collateral contracts would offer remedies for innocent misrepresentation: "Such collateral contracts, the sole effect of which is to vary or add to the terms of the principal contract, are therefore viewed with suspicion by the law. They must be proved strictly. Not only the terms of such contracts but the existence of an animus contrahendi on the part of all the parties to them must be clearly shewn"; ibid. 47.

75. *Trego v. Hunt*, [1896] A.C. 7 (1895).

76. Per Loreburn in *Laire Motor Co. v. Albian Motor Co.*, Opinions of their Lordships, 1910. See also *Stewart v. Maclaine*, Opinions of their Lordships, 1899. "It is impossible for the court to import into the bargain something upon which the parties have not themselves agreed," holding that a lease did not by implication contain the articles or conditions usually inserted in leases of sheep farms on the estate in question. On at least one occasion it was laid down in very broad terms that a written contract could not be cut down by a parol agreement; *Mercantile Agency Co. v. Flitwick*, Opinions of their Lordships, 1897.

77. *Attorney-General v. Dublin Steam Packet Co.*, Opinions of their Lordships, 1909. There was held to be no implied term in a contract between the company and the Crown that the company should have sole and exclusive use of a certain pier.

was entitled to payment upon presentation of the documents, thereby aiding the smooth operation of modern commerce.[78] Even though Halsbury, in taking a more formalistic view in another case, insisted that "it would be most improper to depart from the contract they have made, and to make what we consider to be a fairer contract,"[79] a new approach was in the air.[80]

Indeed, in a wider sense also, the House adapted itself to the changes in commercial life. In the classical Victorian period the House had at times seemed disinterested in incorporating commercial law in the framework of the legal system. The Edwardian court was more flexible. New problems were faced with common sense. When the maker of a contract sought to rely on the literal wording of a contract, after what was in effect a frustrating event, Halsbury conceded, "[W]e have to determine . . . what is the real business meaning of the contract which has been made by the parties";[81] and the House refused to enforce the contract. The doctrine of frustration was thus moved further along the road to respectability. The House was also more reasonable in its interpretation of statutes designed to regulate the operation of the commercial system, rejecting, for instance, the argument that the new Moneylenders Act of 1900 should apply only to cases in which Equity would have given relief prior to the act.[82] Even in shipping contracts, which had been regarded as almost sacred by the Victorian court, the House began to import an element of "reasonableness" into their interpretations.[83]

This reaffirmation of basic principles of commercial justice was also

78. E. Clemens Horst Co. v. Diddell Bros., [1912] A.C. 18 (1911).

79. Elliott v. Crutchley, [1906] A.C. 7, 8·(1905).

80. See also a case like Cory Bros. v. Owners of Turkish S.S. "Mecca," [1897] A.C. 286, limiting the application of the rule in Clayton's case. This was in conformity with what the Law Quarterly Review described as the tendency to get to the real intention of the parties rather than rely on rigid presumptions; "Note," 13 Law Quarterly Review 333 (1897).

81. Elliott v. Crutchley, [1906] A.C. 7, 9 (1905). The contract was for the supply of food for catering aboard a vessel chartered for a review of the fleet. The plaintiff, the supplier, was entitled under the contract to £300, for which he was then suing. The contract provided "in the event of cancellation of the review before any expense is incurred by the caterer there shall be no liability on either side." In fact, the caterer had spent some £20 on providing cutlery. Held, despite the wording of the clause, he was not entitled to the £300.

82. Samuel v. Newbold, [1906] A.C. 461.

83. Thus, an owner who sought to rely on a term in a charterparty that gave the master the right to deliver goods at another port if the port of discharge was inaccessible was held not entitled to rely on the strict wording of the document when the port was blocked for only 3 days; S.S. Knutsford, Ltd. v. Tillmanns & Co., [1908] A.C. 406. Charterers of a ship under a time charter were held not entitled to rely on a clause exempting both owner and charterer from liability if the carrying out of the contract was hindered by strikes, when they knowingly sent the vessel to a strike-bound port; Brown v. Turner, Brightman & Co., [1912] A.C. 12 (1911).

evident in the House's dealings with the pressing problems of arbitration, particularly after the Arbitration Act of 1889. In the late nineteenth century, the view of the House had been that if the parties had directly or indirectly agreed to arbitrate, then they must live with their decision. During the early part of the twentieth century the emphasis was on ensuring that the process of arbitration operated fairly.[84] Even when the arbitration was once under way, there was also a distinctly greater willingness to supervise the activities of the arbitrators.[85] By overseeing the arbitral procedure in this way, the House was able to ensure the reliability of arbitration without unnecessarily interfering with its efficiency.

As further evidence that the law lords had become more flexible in commercial law, the House extended the canon of construction that exemption clauses[86] had to be construed against the party inserting them; in this way the House indirectly assisted in balancing the differing economic power of contracting parties. Shipowners were not entitled to rely on a confused exemption clause,[87] and a seller exempting warranties could sometimes still be sued for a breach of contract.[88]

Perhaps the most elegant judicial legislation by the Edwardian law lords, at least in commercial law, was at the junction of contract and property, represented by a balancing of the old equitable doctrine, which allowed no "clogs" on the equity of redemption in mortgages, and the need to allow modern companies to transact their businesses by raising

84. The House refused to hold that a term in a bill of lading incorporating the terms of the charterparty was sufficiently strong to include an agreement to arbitrate in the latter document; *T. W. Thomas & Co. v. Portsea S.S. Co.*, [1912] A.C. 1 (1911). See especially per Gorrell: "[T]here is a wide consideration which I think it is important to bear in mind in dealing with this class of case. The effect of deciding to stay this action would be that . . . either party is ousted from the jurisdiction of the Courts and compelled to decide all questions by means of arbitration"; ibid. 9.

85. Even if the parties were not within the jurisdiction, arbitrators might properly be called before the courts and compelled to choose an umpire. Haldane, for instance, had no doubt that it was up to the courts to integrate arbitration with the general legal system. "What ought to be the practice in cases of this kind must be determined in accordance with the principles which I have indicated; I have no doubt as to the competence of the Court to work them out;" *Taylor v. Denny, Mott & Dickson, Ltd.*, [1912] A.C. 666, 671.

The House insisted that a right of appeal on a point of law stated by an arbitrator lay right up to the final appeal court. *British Westinghouse Elec. & Mfg. Co. v. Underground Elec. Ry.*, [1912] A.C. 673.

Equally, the court was prepared to interfere with the behavior of arbitrators, and it invalidated awards where the arbitrator was in a position of both judge and witness in *Bristol Corp. v. John Aird & Co.*, [1913] A.C. 241, or where the arbitration was in danger of being influenced by one of the parties in *Hickman & Co. v. Roberts*, [1912] A.C. 229.

86. On the limitation of liability in admiralty, the House took an ambivalent view. In *Clarke v. Earl of Dunraven*, [1897] A.C. 59, the House allowed the protection of the act to be displaced by an implied contract. In *Sir John Jackson, Ltd. v. Owners of S.S. Blanche*, [1908] A.C. 126, however, they extended the act to cover a charterer.

87. *Nelson Line (Liverpool), Ltd. v. James Nelson & Sons, (No. 2)*, [1908] A.C. 16 (1907).

88. *Wallis, Son & Wells v. Pratt & Haynes*, [1911] A.C. 394.

money through the new form of floating charge, the debenture. In 1902 the House had no doubt that the mortgaging of a pub so that the manager had to buy all his beer from the mortgagee was a clog on the equity of redemption.[89] The following year, the House held that a mortgagee could not recover on a covenant in the mortgage deed requiring the mortgagor (the holder of most of the shares in a tea company) to sell all the company's tea through the mortgagee, who was a tea broker.[90] This time, however, it was a close decision: two Equity law lords[91] persuading the reluctant Scot, Robertson, to join them to protect the equitable principle.[92] The next year the point came up again in *Samuel* v. *Jarrah Timber and Wood Paving Corporation*.[93] By this time even Macnaghten, who the previous year had had no doubts, was regretting that the House could not escape its own earlier decision,[94] while Halsbury had come to the conclusion that Equity's refusal to allow any clogs on the equity of redemption was inconsistent with the sanctity of contract.[95] Lindley, no

89. *Noakes* v. *Rice*, [1902] A.C. 24 (1901).

90. *Bradley* v. *Carritt*, [1903] A.C. 253.

91. Macnaghten said, "[E]quity will not permit any device or contrivance designed or calculated to prevent or impede redemption. . . . Can you impose on the equity of redemption a fetter operating indirectly, when you cannot, as it is admitted, impose a fetter which operates directly? . . . I should have thought that that question answered itself—you cannot do indirectly that which you must not do directly"; ibid. 261. Davey was no less equivocal. "On payment of the principal, interest, and costs, together with any bonus or anything in the nature of a bonus which has been properly stipulated for, and has become payable, the mortgage contract comes to an end, and the mortgagor is entitled to get his property back, unaltered in character, condition, and incidents, and is henceforth relieved from the burden imposed upon him by the contract"; ibid. 266.

92. Not with any great enthusiasm. See, for instance, ibid. 270. "[W]hen I turn to the law of the case, I speak with much more diffidence, for the system of jurisprudence in which I was trained does not in the matter of mortgages impose any restraint on free contracts."

The dissenters were Shand and Lindley. Although an Equity judge, the latter could not bring himself to believe that "it is part of the law of this country that mortgagors and mortgagees cannot make what bargains they like with each other so long as such bargains are not inconsistent with the right of the mortgagor to redeem the property mortgaged by discharging the debt or obligation to secure which the mortgage was effected"; ibid. 279–80.

93. [1901] A.C. 323.

94. "The law undoubtedly is that a condition such as that in question, if legal and binding at all, must come to an end on repayment of the loan. . . . Speaking for myself, I should not be sorry if your Lordships could see your way to modify it so as to prevent its being used as a means of evading a fair bargain come to between persons dealing at arms' length and negotiating on equal terms. . . . At the same time I quite feel the difficulty of interfering with any rule that has prevailed for so long"; ibid. 326–27.

95. "I regret that the state of the authorities leaves me no alternative other than to affirm the judgement of Kekewich J. and the Court of Appeal. A perfectly fair bargain made between two parties to it, each of whom was quite sensible of what they were doing, is not to be performed because at the same time a mortgage arrangement was made between them. . . . [A] line of authorities going back for more than a century has decided that such an arrangement as that which was here arrived at is contrary to a principle of equity, the sense or reason of which I am not able to appreciate"; ibid. 325.

doubt feeling that the struggle was hopeless, concurred, following the precedents in *Noakes* v. *Rice* and *Bradley* v. *Carritt*. In short, all the law lords in *Samuel* felt that the law was in an unsatisfactory state but claimed they could not see their way clear to modify it. The *Law Quarterly Review*, somewhat mischievously, noted, "[U]nder the dogma of the House of Lords infallibility delivered by Lord Campbell and reverentially received by Lord Halsbury, *Bradley* v. *Carritt* must stand as unimpeachable law."[96]

Yet, looking ahead to the first year of Haldane's Chancellorship, the *Law Quarterly Review* need not have worried, if worried it was. In *G. and C. Kreglinger* v. *New Patagonia Meat and Cold Storage Company*,[97] apart from the fact that a floating charge was involved, rather than some other kind of mortgage, the facts were virtually indistinguishable[98] from those in *Bradley* v. *Carritt*. Despite the similarity to the earlier cases, Haldane refused to be fazed; he adopted the hue of his native Scotland and decided that principle had to take priority over precedent.

> In questions of this kind the binding force of previous decisions, unless the facts are indistinguishable, depends on whether they establish a principle. To follow previous authorities, so far as they lay down principles, is essential if the law is to be preserved from becoming unsettled and vague. In this respect the previous decisions of a Court of co-ordinate jurisdiction are more binding in a system of jurisprudence such as ours than in systems where the paramount authority is that of a code. But when a previous case has not laid down any new principle but has merely decided that a particular set of facts illustrates an existing rule, there are few more fertile sources of fallacy than to search in it for what is simple resemblance in circumstances, and to erect a previous decision into a governing precedent merely on this account. To look for anything except the principle established or recognised by previous decisions is really to weaken and not to strengthen the importance of precedent. The consideration of cases which turn on particular facts may often be useful for edification, but it can rarely yield authoritative guidance.[99]

96. "Note," 19 *Law Quarterly Review* 248 (1903).

97. [1914] A.C. 25 (1913).

98. A firm of wool brokers had lent £10,000 to a meat-preserving company, secured a floating charge, one of the terms being that for 5 years the company would sell all their sheepskins to the lenders. The agreement allowed the company to pay off the loan at any time by giving 1 month's notice, which they did after 3 years. The lenders claimed that they were still entitled to the sheepskins, that is, to exercise their option of preemption, notwithstanding the repayment of the loan.

99. *G. & C. Kreglinger* v. *New Patagonia Meat & Cold Storage Co.*, [1914] A.C. 25, 39–40 (1913). Haldane was then in a position to say of *Noakes* v. *Rice* and *Bradley* v. *Carritt*: "These cases, which related to circumstances differing widely from those before us, have been disposed of finally, and we are not concerned with them excepting insofar as they may have thrown fresh light on questions of principle"; ibid. 40. In fact, none of the law lords attempted to distinguish *Bradley* v. *Carritt* on the facts. Haldane suggested that the bargain might be thought of as being collateral to the mortgage, and severable from it, an argument not raised in *Bradley* v. *Carritt*. "In the case before the House your Lordships arrive at the conclusion that the agreement for an option to purchase the respondent's

It remained only for the new Equity law lord to restate a suitable principle.[100] The law lords of this period continued the practice of elegantly distinguishing the undistinguished.

Property, Progress, and Risk

Just as the years after 1876—or, more accurately, the Edwardian period—saw a slow freeing up of the strict "meeting of the minds" concept associated with the laissez-faire view of contract, so there was a similar—albeit slow—breaking down of the laissez-faire reluctance to impose liability in tort as well as a relaxation of the early strict approach to the preservation of private property.

In the early years of the period, the majority of tort actions heard by the House related to the general area of the preservation of property— the tort of nuisance and its related manifestations. The protection accorded property was, moreover, broad. The House allowed an action of trespass when one mine lessee so altered the course of a stream that injury to another mine lessee ensued.[101] Damage to property resulting from subsidence was also remedied even in the absence of negligence.[102] Landlords who granted mining leases were protected by the House, and terms were implied to prevent the mines' being worked in a way that would injure the reversion.[103] Where iron-smelting operations interfered with the enjoyment of substantial estates, the House had no qualms

---

sheepskins was not in substance a fetter on the exercise of their right to redeem, but was in the nature of a collateral bargain the entering into which was a preliminary and separate condition of the loan, the decided cases cease to present any great difficulty"; ibid. 39. Haldane argued that a case is not an authority for a point that was passed over sub silentio.

The coup was to dispose of Davey's statement of principle as being merely "dicta," and to prefer Lindley's remarks in his dissenting judgment. "I think that the tendency of Lord Lindley's conclusion is the one which is most consonant with principle, and I see no valid reason why this House should not act in accordance with it in the case now under consideration"; ibid. 43–44.

100. Parker formulated the proposition "that there is now no rule in equity which precludes a mortgagee, whether the mortgage be made upon the occasion of a loan or other wise, from stipulating for any collateral advantage, provided such collateral advantage is not either (1) unfair and unconscionable, or (2) in the nature of a penalty clogging the equity of redemption, or (3) inconsistent with or repugnant to the contractual and equitable right to redeem"; ibid. 61. Halsbury, Mersey, and Atkinson merely concurred.

101. *Fletcher* v. *Smith*, 2 App. Cas. 781 (1877). The case was distinguished from *Wilson* v. *Waddell*, 2 App. Cas. 95 (1876), where the defendant was held not liable for water trickling by gravitation and percolation, or for unnatural use of his land. A case similar to *Fletcher* v. *Smith* was *Musgrave* v. *Smith*, Opinions of their Lordships, 1877, where the defendant had diverted a stream on his land, which caused damage to the plaintiff's mine. The finding of the jury that the new channel was insufficient was upheld by the House.

102. *Darley Main Colliery Co.* v. *Mitchell*, 11 App. Cas. 127 (1886). It is noteworthy that the majority in this case included Bramwell.

103. *Davis* v. *Treharne*, 6 App. Cas. 460 (1881).

about prohibiting them.[104] On the other hand, where a landowner had a "lawful" right to do what he did, for instance, to dig a well,[105] he did not lose that right merely because his act was "malicious."[106] Intellectual property—such as copyright—was increasingly protected.[107] At the same time, although the law lords were uncomfortable with the government's compulsorily purchasing land, where private parties were concerned the House seemed to have little difficulty in allowing a wide exercise of powers of eminent domain under a statute.[108] Conversely, trustees hand-

104. *Shotts Iron Co.* v. *Inglis*, 7 App. Cas. 518 (Scot. 1882). A high degree of responsibility was also required of property owners whose property was subject to obligations to other property owners. In *Dalton* v. *Argus & Co.*, 6 App. Cas. 740 (1881), one of the three cases after the Judicature Act in which the High Court judges were sent for by the House, it was decided that a right of lateral support could be acquired by prescription. Such an obligation was so strong that it could not be delegated and if the servant of an independent contractor employed by the defendant did an act that injured the party wall, the defendant was personally liable even if the act was outside the scope of the contract between the defendant and the contractor; *Hughes* v. *Percival*, 8 App. Cas. 443 (1883). Blackburn, however, was reluctant to make the liability an absolute one; ibid. 446.

105. *Bradford Corp.* v. *Pickles*, [1895] A.C. 587. See also *Wilson* v. *Waddell*, 2 App. Cas. 95 (1876).

106. Macnaghten said, "It is the act, not the motive for the act, that must be regarded. If the act, apart from the motive, gives rise to damage without legal injury, the motive, however reprehensible it may be, will not supply that element"; *Bradford Corp.* v. *Pickles*, [1895] A.C. 587, 601. Halsbury added, "This is not a case in which the state of mind of the person doing the act can affect the right to do it. If it was a lawful act, however ill the motive might be, he had a right to do it. Motives and intention in such a question as is now before your Lordships seem to me to be absolutely irrelevant"; ibid. 594.

A later Scottish law lord, Lord Keith of Avonholm, questioned whether this was in accordance with Scottish law and whether it might be held not binding in future Scottish cases in the House of Lords. "It is a widely held view among many eminent Scottish lawyers that Lord Watson's proposition is not in accordance with the law of Scotland"; *The Spirit of the Law of Scotland* 14–15. See also a similar reaction in "Note," 11 *Law Quarterly Review* 108 (1895).

107. *Caird* v. *Sime*, 12 App. Cas. 326 (Scot. 1887), held that a professor giving his lectures did not communicate them to the world at large and was therefore entitled to prevent others from publishing them without his consent. While the patent cases were conflicting in attitude, there was a general trend in favor of protecting and encouraging the inventor. In *Badische Anilin und Soda Fabrik* v. *Levinstein*, 12 App. Cas. 710 (1887), a patent was upheld in the face of the argument that it had not been proved to be useful. Herschell noted, in rejecting this particular argument, "[T]here are abundant perils already in the path of every inventor, and I am not disposed to add to their number unless compelled to do so"; ibid. 720.

108. A Scottish presbytery, given a right to acquire land compulsorily under a private enabling act, was held entitled to enforce its powers although it followed no particular formula; *Walker* v. *Presbytery of Arbroath*, 2 App. Cas. 79 (Scot. 1876). O'Hagan said, "We can only interfere if there has been some flagrant violation of the fundamental principles of justice, resulting in substantial wrong to an individual, which it would be contrary to the universal course of legal tribunals to allow"; ibid. 89.

A railway company, authorized by an act to purchase land to carry out the purposes of the railway, which included the carrying of cattle, bought land near one of its stations as a cattle yard. This constituted a nuisance, and occupiers of neighboring houses sought an injunction. The House held that in the absence of negligence, since such activities were incidental to the activities statutorily authorized, the remedy was not available; *London, Brighton & South Coast Ry.* v. *Truman*, 11 App. Cas. 45 (1885).

ling the property of others were held to the highest levels of account-ability.[109]

Although physical property was protected vigorously, the House was much less comfortable with damage to other types of property. The law lords were, for instance, far more ambivalent about imposing liability for personal injury. The laissez-faire mentality was reflected in two directions: a general reluctance to impose liability and an insistence when it was imposed that it should be based on fault. Although vicarious liability —the responsibility of employers for the acts of their employees—had been established before the period began and the various strands of strict liability had been gathered together in *Rylands* v. *Fletcher*,[110] the law lords of the late Victorian era made considerable efforts to weaken strict liability, since it imposed liability without fault.[111] Bramwell would have happily rejected the concept of vicarious liability as well.[112] Even liability of occupiers and employers, however, was kept at a minimum, mainly through the use of contributory negligence. In the early years of the period, there was some willingness to take a flexible approach to this concept.[113] By the time of *Wakelin* v. *London and South Western Railway Company*,[114] however, the House held that when a body was found on a railway line, in such a way that the accident was equally consistent

109. See the highest levels of accountability in *Learoyd* v. *Whitely*, 12 App. Cas. 727 (1887); *Knox* v. *Mackinnon*, 13 App. Cas. 753 (Scot. 1888); *Rae* v. *Meek*, 14 App. Cas. 558 (Scot. 1889). The liability was not, however, absolute. See *Andrews* v. *M'Guffog*, 11 App. Cas. 313 (Scot. 1886).

110. L.R. 3 H.L. 330 (1868). The rule is generally stated in the words used by Blackburn when the case was in the Exchequer Chamber; L.R. 1 Ex. 265, 279 (Ex. Cham. 1866).

111. E.g., see especially per Blackburn in *Darley Main Colliery Co.* v. *Mitchell*, 11 App. Cas. 127, 135 (1886).

112. Bramwell, it seems, would have been prepared to put the clock back on this matter, when he dissented in favor of the appellants in *Great Western Ry.* v. *Bunch*, 13 App. Cas. 31, 48 (1888). A commentator noted, "Admirers of Lord Bramwell—and among this class must be placed every lawyer and layman who respects honesty, vigour, common sense, and humour—must regret the extent to which his Lordship is increasingly becoming the advocate of every company. On grounds which in themselves are defensible enough, Lord Bramwell objects to the law of England with regard to the liability of employers, and appears to be incapable of fairly applying a principle of law which he believes to be unfair"; George Powell, "*Bunch* v. *Great Western Railway Company*" 469.

113. In 1876, the House restated the doctrine of "the last clear chance" and refused to find a plaintiff company contributorily negligent when it failed to exercise due diligence after the defendant's negligent act; *Radley* v. *London & North Western Ry.*, 1 App. Cas. 754 (1876). In an Irish appeal in 1878, it was held that where there was contradictory evidence about whether or not the plaintiff had been negligent, the question might properly be left to the jury; *Dublin, Wicklow & Wexford Ry.* v. *Slattery*, 3 App. Cas. 1155 (Ire. 1878). By this time, however, the hostility to such a broad approach had become clear. The vote was 5–3, the minority including Hatherley, Coleridge, and Blackburn. They felt that where the evidence was inconsistent, the judge was entitled to direct a verdict for the defendant. Soon the minority view was to become the majority one.

114. 12 App. Cas. 41 (1886).

with both negligence and contributory negligence, then there was not enough evidence to send the case to the jury. Halsbury, who presided, articulated the narrow view, making it clear that any other decision would make nonsense of the burden of proof requiring the plaintiff to prove his case.[115] Once established, this attitude toward contributory negligence prevailed, the House finding that either no duty was owed or the right to sue had been forfeited by the contributory negligence of the plaintiff.[116] The law lords varied in their belief in the moral justifiability of the doctrine. Bramwell thought it excellent;[117] Blackburn, although he had participated in its development, had reservations.[118]

While the narrow view of occupiers' liability survived into the twentieth century,[119] as the years passed and the number of liberal law lords increased, a greater willingness to impose liability appeared to develop. The wide immunity given to occupiers began to be eroded.[120] The trend

115. Ibid., especially at 45.

116. A typical case is *Walker* v. *Midland Ry.*, Opinions of their Lordships, 1886. The House held, by a majority, that an innkeeper could not be held liable when a guest fell down a serving well while intoxicated. Selborne said, "I think it impossible to hold that the general duty of an innkeeper to take proper care for the safety of his guests extends to every room in the house, at all hours of night or day, irrespective of the question whether any such guests may have a right, or some unreasonable cause, to be there."

FitzGerald (with Ashbourne) dissented. He would have imposed a wider duty on the innkeeper. "The duty of the innkeeper is not to provide for the safety of such of his guests as are sharp, prudent, and strictly sober, but to provide reasonably for the safety of all that he receives into his own house as guests, amongst whom may be the dull, the stupid, the short sighted and people who have taken alcohol and who are ignorant of the ways of a great hotel."

117. Charles Fairfield, *A Memoir of Lord Bramwell*.

118. "If both parties are guilty of neglect of duty, so that the accident would not have happened if either had done his duty, it might not be unreasonable that the damage should be apportioned according to the degree of fault of each party and such is, I believe, the civil law. The maritime law, as administered in the Courts of Admiralty, in such a case divides the damages equally between them; but by the common law, which is what we have to administer, the damage lies where it falls, and neither the person who is himself to blame nor his representatives can recover though the Defendant may be as much or more to blame. It is not for us to inquire which of these rules is the more just and equitable"; *South Eastern Ry.* v. *Smitherman*, Opinions of their Lordships, 1886.

119. See especially, *Cavalier* v. *Pope*, [1906] A.C. 428, holding that the wife of a tenant might not sue the landlord for injuries suffered by reason of dilapidations in the premises demised, even though the landlord had specifically assumed responsibility for repairs. The House reasoned that since she was not a party to the lease she could not sue on it; and that she could not sue as an invitee since the defendants were not occupiers. Two years later, the House held that a similar doctrine applied in Scotland; *Cameron* v. *Young*, [1908] A.C. 176 (Scot.).

120. In *Cooke* v. *Midland Great Western Ry. of Ireland*, [1909] A.C. 229, (Ire.), the House overruled the Irish Court of Appeal, and held that where a trespassing child was injured playing on a turntable, there was sufficient evidence of negligence to go to a jury when the company's servant knew that children played on the turntable.

The owner of a field, who knowingly kept a dangerous horse in it, was held responsible for injuries to a plaintiff injured by the animal, the House refusing to categorize someone taking a walk as a trespasser; *Lowery* v. *Walker*, [1911] A.C. 10 (1910). A similarly wide view of negligence was taken when the plaintiff was in contractual relations with the

toward an expanding tort responsibility was reflected in a series of decisions on statutory negligence. Tortious liability under a statute first emerged clearly in the 1880s. Where negligence was proved the House had little difficulty in allowing a civil action for damages if a breach of such a statutory obligation occurred. Failure on the part of persons building a reservoir to carry out their duty to dredge streams that removed overflow water was held a clear breach of statutory duty and therefore grounds for an action in tort.[121] Where, however, no negligence was proved, the House, as in *Milnes v. Corporation of Huddersfield*,[122] tended to split.

The narrow scope of statutory negligence at the end of the nineteenth century was in large part a reflection of Blackburn's strong belief in "fault."[123] By the early twentieth century, however, with Blackburn and Bramwell gone, a more expansive approach was afoot. The House held that the obligation imposed on tramways by various Tramways Acts to keep the highway between the rails in a fit and safe condition was not only a duty owed to the public, but also one that might be enforced by an individual injured through negligent maintenance.[124] Wider still was the decision in *Shrimpton v. Hertfordshire County Council*.[125] In this case an education authority was held liable when it was negligent in performing its statutory duty to provide school buses; indeed the speeches of

---

defendant; e.g., *Toal v. North British Ry.*, [1908] A.C. 352 (Scot.). The House also frowned on the idea of invoking "inevitable accident" when a horse-drawn carriage collided with the increasingly popular motor car on a highway, and substituted a finding of negligence; *Robertson v. Griffith*, Opinions of their Lordships, 1912. Slowly the idea of *res ipsa loquitur* was coming to be accepted.

121. *Geddis v. Proprietors of Bann Reservoir*, 3 App. Cas. 430 (1878).

122. 11 App. Cas. 511 (1886). Under the Waterworks Clauses Act, the town waterworks undertaking was required "to provide . . . a supply of pure and wholesome water, sufficient for the domestic use of all the inhabitants of the town who should be entitled to demand a supply and should be willing to pay water-rate for the same." The undertaking made its own by-laws that provided that the pipes between the mains and consumers' houses should be made of lead. Although the water in the mains was pure, it reacted with lead, and as the result of this the plaintiff, a consumer, was poisoned and brought an action alleging breach of a statutory obligation. The majority (Blackburn, Bramwell, FitzGerald, Halsbury, and Ashbourne) found that, having complied with the obligation to provide pure water in the mains, the legal responsibilities of the defendants were satisfied. As Bramwell put it, "The pipe is bad, but the water is good. The plaintiff, therefore, has failed to make out his case"; ibid. 532. Selborne and Watson dissented, not on the ground that negligence had been proved, but purely on the ground of a breach of a statutory obligation.

123. Where an act provided that a waterworks "should be bound to make good to X and her heirs, all damages which may be occasioned to her or them, by reason of or in consequence of any bursting, or flow, or escape of water from any reservoir, or aquaduct, or pipe, or other work connected therewith," Blackburn held that the plaintiff must fail if the damage was occasioned by an act of God. He was prepared to take the view that a "reasonable" construction of the statute included a requirement of negligence; *Countess of Rothes v. Kirkcaldy & Dysart Waterworks Comm'n*, 7 App. Cas. 694, 700 (Scot. 1882).

124. *Ogston v. Aberdeen Dist. Tramways Co.*, [1897] A.C. 111 (Scot. 1896).

125. 9 L.G.R. 397 (1911).

some of the lords suggested that a duty such as this could not be avoided by employing a competent independent contractor. The law was making tentative steps toward imposing a strict duty in at least some types of statutory negligence.

Meanwhile, the effect of economic conditions meant that negligence, instead of being a mere ingredient in contract and certain specific torts, was increasingly being treated as an independent concept, en route to becoming an independent tort. Before negligence could, however, provide protection for workmen in the twentieth century, it had to shake off some of the nineteenth-century connotations it had acquired. The Employers' Liability Act of 1880 had curbed some of the worst excesses of the fellow servant or common employment concept,[126] but other barriers still existed, often created by the strict laissez-faire law lords. One of the most threatening of these was the concept of *volenti non fit injuria*. In *Membury* v. *Great Western Railway Company*,[127] the company employed an independent workman as a shunter, when possible supplying him with boys to assist him. Without such assistance, the operation was hazardous. Having been refused assistance on one day, the plaintiff continued his duties and was injured. The company was held not liable, not only because they were found not to have been negligent, but also, according to Halsbury and Bramwell, because the plaintiff was found to have consented (been *volens*) to the risk.[128] The law lords did not doubt that their approach was the right and proper one. Bramwell was able to expand the views he had set forth in his pamphlets and speeches, making it clear that, in his eyes, unless there was physical constraint, it was impossible to say that a workman engaged on the job was anything but *volens*. "The master says here is the work, do it or let it alone. If you do it, I pay you; if not, I do not. If he has engaged him, he says, I discharge you if you do not do it: I think I am right; if wrong, I am liable to an action. The master says this, the servant does the work and earns his wages, and is paid, but is hurt. On what principle or reason or justice should the master be liable to him in respect of that hurt?"[129]

Had the Bramwell view become settled law, it would have been

126. David Hanes, *The First British Workmen's Compensation Act*, 1897, at 20–21.

127. 14 App. Cas. 179 (1889).

128. A majority of the judges in fact based their speeches on the ground that there was no negligence on the part of the defendant. Bramwell, however, relied on both grounds— the absence of negligence and the finding of *volens*. "What I am saying is not obiter, not a needless expression of opinion on a matter not relevant to the decision. There are two answers to the plaintiff and I decide against him on both: on one as much as on the other"; ibid. 187.

129. Ibid. 188. A bill abolishing the doctrine entirely was passed by the House of Commons in 1893, but did not pass the Lords. Herschell supported the bill but despaired of convincing Selborne that no contracting out must be permitted; 19 *Parl. Deb.*, H.L. (4th ser.), col. 772 (8 Dec. 1898).

difficult for any workman to have sued his employers successfully for negligence. The possible implications of such a wide impact of *volenti* were clear even to the judges of this period. The naked Bramwell view was finally rejected in *Smith* v. *Baker and Sons*,[130] in which a workman, engaged to drill holes in rock, had been injured by a stone falling from a crane swinging over his head. The Court of Appeal had held that the *volenti* doctrine prevented Smith from recovering damages. In the House of Lords only Bramwell took that view. Dissenting, he insisted that "the plaintiff had no claim in law or morality."[131] Bramwell stood firm against any change. "Let us hold to the law. If we want to be charitable, gratify ourselves out of our own pockets."[132] Halsbury[133] showed some sympathy with the Bramwell view, but the majority of the law lords refused to give an extended application to the *volenti* doctrine.[134]

Bramwell, not unnaturally, was also a strong advocate of the doctrine of common employment,[135] and although in *Smith* v. *Baker and Sons* he insisted that he was not motivated by "any prejudice against the Employers' Liability Act,"[136] had his speech been supported by a majority, the effect would have been to return the law to its pre-1880 state. It was no doubt of some consolation to Bramwell that common employment still existed in some areas.[137] In the same year as *Smith* v. *Baker and Sons*, however, the House, in *Johnson* v. *Lindsay*,[138] struck another blow at common employment by refusing to apply the doctrine if the two workmen were working for different contractors on the same building site.[139] Bramwell, since he had doubts even about vicarious liability, continued in his urge to curb liability, seeking to restrict the concept of the "scope of the employment" that gave rise to vicarious liability.[140] In this position he had some support.[141]

130. [1891] A.C. 325.
131. Ibid. 339.
132. Ibid. 346.
133. Ibid. 333.
134. Watson's reaction was typical. He thought that to affirm the Court of Appeal would in effect take away the statutory remedy provided by the Employers' Liability Act of 1880; ibid.
135. E.g., Bramwell's letter to the *Economist*, 28 Aug. 1880, cited, Fairfield, *Memoir of Bramwell* 343. See also ibid. 336 ff.; 332 *Parl. Deb.*, H.L. (3d ser.), cols. 947–49 (21 Dec. 1888).
136. [1891] A.C. 325, 339.
137. For example, see *Hedley* v. *Pinkney & Sons' S.S. Co.*, [1894] A.C. 222.
138. (No. 1), [1891] A.C. 371.
139. Ibid., especially at 385. Watson in particular made it clear that he proposed limiting the doctrine as far as possible.
140. Together with Morris he dissented on this point in *The Apollo*, [1891] A.C. 499. The majority found that the owners of a ship might sue the harbor authorities when their ship was damaged as the result of relying on the representation of the harbor master that it was safe to use a dock as a dry dock. Bramwell was unable to find any duty or, on the part of the harbor master, any "authority to undertake any duty of care"; ibid. 512.
141. In a case in 1894, for instance, *Cobb* v. *Great Western Ry.*, [1894] A.C. 419, the

The reluctance to extend liability in tort, however, went well beyond those areas that would now fall under the rubric of negligence. In deceit, conspiracy, and libel, for much of the period the judicial policy was to restrict liability. Fraud had already been narrowly construed by the advocates of laissez-faire in contract decisions,[142] but the narrowness of their concept was not fully clear until the tort of deceit case—*Derry* v. *Peek*.[143] In this case the House refused to impose liability on directors who falsely claimed in a prospectus that they were authorized to run steam carriages on their tramway. The decision firmly established in English law that no action for deceit could lie if the defendants believed in the truth of their statements.[144] So strongly, in fact, were the speeches expressed[145] that it was also thought that no liability for any statements could be held unless fraud or a contract were proved.[146]

Parliament was far from happy with the decision and proceeded to pass the Directors' Liability Act of 1890, reversing the main conclusions of *Derry* v. *Peek*. The House thereafter held as fraudulent various activities that, although not fraudulent in the common law meaning of the word, were "deemed to be fraudulent" by the act, causing Lindley to complain in one case that "to be compelled by Act of Parliament to treat an honest man as if he were fraudulent is at all times painful."[147] Yet, in related areas where Parliament had legislated, the House reaffirmed a narrow view of fraud;[148] and naturally outside the ambit of parliamen-

---

House refused to hold the respondents liable in negligence when the plaintiff was robbed in a train crowded, so the plaintiff alleged, as a result of the defendant's negligence. There were other decisions of this kind that, by later standards, seemed to give vicarious liability a narrow base.

142. In *Smith* v. *Chadwick*, 9 App. Cas. 187 (1884), a prospectus of a company alleged that "the present value of the turnover on output of the entire works is over £1,000,000 sterling per annum." In fact the works had never in one year produced that value of goods, although it was true that it was capable of producing such a volume. When the plaintiff sought to recover damages for losses incurred by taking shares while relying on these statements, his claim was unanimously rejected. Most of the law lords found that the words were capable of being interpreted in two ways, and that the plaintiff had failed to prove that he had interpreted the words in the false sense. Bramwell found that there was not enough evidence to show fraud on the part of the defendants.

A similar attitude prevailed in *Coaks* v. *Boswell*, 11 App. Cas. 232 (1886), where the House refused to set aside a sale authorized by the court merely because all the facts were not made available to the judge authorizing the purchaser to bid. "[Y]ou cannot find the purchasers guilty of fraud because you may think there was too great facility in giving its sanction to the purchaser on the part of the Court"; ibid. 24.

143. 14 App. Cas. 337 (1889).

144. See especially per Bramwell: "Now, I really am reluctant to cite authorities to show that actual fraud must be established in such a case as this. It is one of the first things one learns, and one has never heard it doubted until recently"; ibid. 346.

145. Ibid. 247.

146. *Le Lievre* v. *Gould*, [1893] 1 Q.B. 491 (C.A.).

147. *Shepheard* v. *Broome*, [1904] A.C. 342, 346.

148. Even where the Companies Act required certain disclosures that were not made, a

tary control, the same narrow approach prevailed. Thus, in a case where a timber merchant's clerk fraudulently sold timber belonging to his employer, the House held that the bona fide purchasers had no title to it since the employers had not held out the clerk as being authorized to sell;[149] and, in *Ruben* v. *Great Fingall Consolidated*,[150] the House went so far as to hold that a company was not liable for shares fraudulently issued by the secretary of the company to innocent persons.[151]

Such a view of the responsibility (or rather the lack of responsibility) of the employer for the fraud of his servant appeared to be a return to the strongest traditions of classical Victorianism. But having taken this firm line on fraud, the House almost at once resiled from it.[152] The vital reversal of view again came in the Edwardian period—in 1912—after the influence of Blackburn, Bramwell, and (effectively) Halsbury had ended. In *Lloyd* v. *Grace, Smith and Company*,[153] the House affirmed that a master was in fact liable for the frauds of his servant committed in the course of the latter's employment. The vital issue was the definition of the scope of employment, and it was held to be immaterial whether the frauds were committed for the benefit of the employer or of the servant. The earlier cases were restricted, some earlier dicta of Davey's were overruled, and the House held that a solicitor was liable for the fraud of his clerk in transferring a client's property into his own name. Macnaghten, in one of his masterly surveys of the authorities, found prece-

---

conservatively constituted House refused to allow an action for damages where the plaintiff was unable to prove that he would not have subscribed for the shares had he known of the undisclosed contract; *MacLeay* v. *Tait*, [1906] A.C. 24 (1905) (Halsbury, Robertson, and Lindley).

149. *Farquharson Bros. & Co.* v. *King & Co.*, [1902] A.C. 325. See especially Halsbury: "A servant has stolen his master's goods, and the question arises whether the persons who have received those goods innocently can set up a title against the master. I believe that is enough to dispose of this case"; ibid. 329.

150. [1906] A.C. 439.

151. It was held that the company, not having held the secretary out as having any authority beyond that of delivering authorized shares, was not liable when the secretary handed over forged ones. A fraudulent act could not be imputed to a master, since it was not made in the course of employment. Loreburn, presiding, declared, "I cannot see upon what principle your Lordships can hold that the defendants are liable in this action"; 443. The law looked clearly settled. Davey recorded, "In my opinion it would be a matter of reproach if the law were otherwise"; ibid. 446. James was more sympathetic to the plaintiff; ibid. 447.

152. In 1907 the House held that an employer was liable for the acts of a servant, within the scope of his employment, which, together with the knowledge of the employer, amounted to fraud; *Pearson & Son* v. *Dublin Corp.*, [1907] A.C. 351 (Ire.). A company was also stopped from relying on a clause in its statements that checks must be paid to it when, having allowed their travelers to be paid in cash, one absconded with such a payment; *International Sponge Importers, Ltd.* v. *Andrew Watt & Sons*, [1911] A.C. 279. The House also allowed recovery of sums paid as the result of a fraudulent misrepresentation; *Refuge Assurance Co.* v. *Kettlewell*, [1909] A.C. 243.

153. [1912] A.C. 716.

dent and principle to justify his view of the liability of the defendants. He, however, like the other law lords, was impressed by the need to provide a remedy. He felt that if liability was to be put upon one of two innocent parties, it should be put on the one best able to protect himself and take out insurance.[154] In this sense his speech sounds more modern than those of many of his successors.

Throughout the period the approach to the tort of conspiracy, at least where businessmen were concerned, was narrow. (It was, of course, this same tort that Halsbury used to undermine the unions.) Just as freedom of contract discouraged any interference with bargains, even if their purpose might be restraint of trade, so the law of tort also mirrored the belief in the public desirability of allowing a maximum amount of freedom or, more properly, a minimum amount of state (including judicial) control. The most famous example of this approach during the period was *Mogul Steamship Company v. McGregor and Company*.[155] In that case the House refused to offer any remedy to a shipping company that had been driven out of business by a competing ring of shipping companies that had carried goods below cost with the express purpose of driving the first company out of business.[156] The idea that the tort of conspiracy might be used here was rejected vigorously by the House. In essence the House could find no act that might be labeled "unlawful" on the part of the defendant. The approach was clear. "All are free to trade upon what terms they will,"[157] said Halsbury. Indeed, all the law lords

154. "So much for the case as it stands upon the authorities. But putting aside the authorities altogether, I must say that it would be absolutely shocking to my mind if Mr. Smith were not held liable for the fraud of his agent in the present case. When Mrs. Lloyd put herself in the hands of the firm how was she to know what the exact position of Sandles was? . . . Who is to suffer from this man's fraud? The person who relied on Mr. Smith's accredited representative, or Mr. Smith, who put this rogue in his own place and clothed him with his own authority? If Sandles had been a partner in fact, Mr. Smith would have been liable for the fraud of Sandles as his agent. It is a hardship to be liable for the fraud of your partner. But that is the law under the Partnership Act. It is less a hardship for a principal to be held liable for the fraud of his agent or confidential servant. You can hardly ask your partner for a guarantee of his honesty; but there are such things as fidelity policies. You can insure the honesty of the person you employ in a confidential situation or you can make your confidential agent obtain a fidelity policy"; ibid. 738–39.

155. [1892] A.C. 25 (1891) (Halsbury, Watson, Bramwell, Macnaghten, Morris, Field, and Hannen).

156. They had also offered aggregated rebates and had put pressure on agents not to handle goods for the plaintiffs.

157. *Mogul S.S. Co. v. McGregor & Co.*, [1892] A.C. 25, 38 (1891). Halsbury adopted the language of Lord Justice Bowen in the Court of Appeal. "All commercial men with capital are acquainted with the ordinary expedient of sowing one year a crop of apparently unfruitful prices, in order by driving competition away to reap a fuller harvest of profit in the future; and until the present argument at the Bar it may be doubted whether shipowners or merchants were ever deemed to be bound by law to conform to some imaginary 'normal' standard of freights or prices, or that law courts had a right to say to them in respect of their competitive tariffs: 'Thus far shalt thou go, and no further' "; ibid. 37.

were equally shocked at this attempt to use the courts to regulate trade, although precedents for such intervention could be cited. The official view was put crisply by Watson. "I cannot for a moment suppose that it is the proper function of English courts of law to fix the lowest prices at which traders can sell or hire, for the purpose of protecting or extending their business, without committing a legal wrong which will subject them to liability in damages."[158] Moreover, the House preferred not to reactivate the tort of conspiracy, at least with respect to businessmen, during the Edwardian period. The possible importance of conspiracy was scotched in two appeals, one from Ireland[159] and the other fought out between two business interests in the City.[160] In both the House made it clear that the plaintiff had to prove "a design, common to the defendant and to others, to damage the plaintiff, without just cause or excuse" and that "a conclusion of that kind is not to be arrived at by a light conjecture."[161] The breadth of protection of lawful business interests was such that the bringing of a successful conspiracy action was virtually impossible.

One can, however, discern some movement in the tort of defamation. In the 1880s there was obvious reluctance to impose liablity for statements.[162] The Edwardian period saw a gradual easing of that narrow position, culminating in *Hulton and Company* v. *Jones,*[163] where damages were awarded even when the defendants were ignorant of the existence of the plaintiff. In this area, then, as in others, the newer law lords had gone some way to undermine the strong laissez-faire influence of Halsbury, Blackburn, and Bramwell. Compared with the radical social

158. Ibid. 43. The House was similarly concerned to limit liability where slander of goods was concerned. In *White* v. *Mellin,* [1895] A.C. 154, they refused to find for the plaintiff where the defendant had sold the plaintiff's "Infants' Food" with a label attached stating that the defendant's "food for infants and invalids" was far more nutritious and healthful than any other.

159. *Sweeney* v. *Coote,* [1907] A.C. 221 (Ire.) (allegation by schoolmistress of conspiracy among parents to have her dismissed).

160. *Wyler* v. *Lewis,* Opinions of their Lordships, 1910.

161. *Sweeney* v. *Coote,* [1907] A.C. 221, 222 (Ire.), per Loreburn.

162. When a large brewery announced that it would "not receive in payment cheques drawn on any of the branches of the" X bank, there was a run on the bank since it was assumed the bank was in danger of becoming insolvent. The House, with the exception of Penzance, refused to find an innuendo, and it was held that there was no case to go to a jury; *Capital & Counties Bank* v. *Henty,* 7 App. Cas. 741 (1882).

Legislatively, Selborne, who sat in this case, admitted he did not, in general, want defamation extended; 354 *Parl. Deb..,* H.L. (3d ser.), col. 1709 (29 June 1891).

See also Halsbury's stern views in *Nevill* v. *Fine Art & Gen. Ins. Co.,* [1897] A.C. 68, 72 (1896); and *Linotype Co.* v. *British Empire Type Setting Co.,* Opinions of their Lordships, 1899. "If the only meaning which a reasonable man would attach to these words amounted to a mere criticism of the machine as a mechanical appliance it is not an actionable wrong to publish such a criticism. I think that principle is well established and I do not think it requires any authority to establish it."

163. [1910] A.C. 20 (1909).

policies of the Campbell-Bannerman and Asquith governments, the steps were small indeed; yet by legal standards, these changes represented an important acceptance by the law lords of responsibility for keeping the common law, if not in line with, at least not totally out of touch with, the outside world.

Regulation of the Economy

If the law lords were able slowly to adapt the policies underlying the doctrines of the common law, they were far less comfortable dealing with those policies that lay behind parliamentary enactments. They in theory behaved toward statutes as they did in theory toward precedent and refused publicly to go behind the formal statements in the statute book. Just as it was impossible, however, to achieve a mechanical jurisprudence, so it was psychologically impossible to make decisions about legislation without some effort to comprehend or disregard what policies Parliament had attempted to pursue. It may be that in many areas of the law the law lords sought to be as objective as possible, to apply legal logic, and to adhere to neutral principles; but such judicial virtues were not easily achieved when Parliament legislated with specific reference to areas traditionally associated with judicial supervision. The problems that arose when the judges came to working out the Employers' Liability Act of 1880 and the Directors' Liability Act of 1890 have already been noted; but, to the law lords brought up in the laissez-faire tradition, almost the most difficult statutes to interpret were those that purported to regulate the economy.[164]

Some sense of things to come appeared in cases where local authorities were seeking to exercise police power. In *Metropolitan Asylum District* v. *Hill*[165] the House held that an act that gave the poor law board power to purchase land and, *inter alia*, build hospitals, did not give the board the right to create a nuisance. Thus, an injunction could be issued against the board to prevent it from using land so acquired as a fever hospital. Blackburn held that only express words or an implication of necessity could take away the private rights of individuals,[166] while Wat-

---

164. For some sense of the underlying attitudes, see Dicey's attitude toward protection of consumers and disapproval of acts, such as the Adulteration of Food Act of 1860, which "defend all citizens from dangers which certainly might be warded off, though at the cost of a great deal of trouble, by individual energy and circumspection, and these enactments rest upon the idea (which is thoroughly congenial to collectivism) that the State is a better judge than a man himself of his own interest, or at any rate of the right way to pursue it"; Albert Venn Dicey, *Lectures on the Relation between Law and Opinion in England during the Nineteenth Century* 262–63 (1905 ed.).

165. 6 App. Cas. 193 (1881). See Gwendoline Ayers, *England's First State Hospitals and the Metropolitan Asylums Board, 1867–1930.*

166. Ibid. 202 ff.

son felt that, if the terms of a statute were permissive rather than manda-tory, the implication was that the powers had to be exercised in strict conformity with private rights.[167]

This reluctance to allow the state to intervene where private property was concerned hindered the integrated development of social legislation that, as Dicey pointed out with some excitement, was an increasing feature of this period. By a narrow construction of the word "width," the House prevented the full implementation of bylaws, made under the Public Health Act of 1875, to ensure that new roads were built to an adequate size.[168] Another decision made difficult the collection of rates allowed by the Towns Improvement Clauses Act of 1847 for paving streets, by refusing to allow such local taxes when any earlier improve-ment had been made.[169] Efforts to control the general line of buildings, a concept then gaining acceptance in the development of town planning, were also subject to stringent and restrictive control.[170]

It would be wrong to suggest that the law lords sought to impede all such municipal reforms; their assistance was forthcoming in some cases.[171] All too often, however, their approach was unconstructive in that it was narrow and technical, rather than helpful in laying down basic principles as a guide to the future development of administrative law.[172] In these years, there was little doubt that where the state was involved, laissez-faire attitudes led to a strong presumption in favor of protecting private rights, particularly the right to property.[173] The broad

167. Ibid. 209 ff. Some of the law lords were prepared to extend this idea to powers of compulsory purchase given to private parties. Cf. *Knowles & Sons* v. *Lancashire & Yorkshire Ry.*, 14 App. Cas. 248 (1889), especially speech by Macnaghten at 255: "You cannot attribute to Parliament an intention to confiscate private property, unless the language of the enactment will admit of no other meaning."

168. *Robinson* v. *Barton Local Bd.*, 8 App. Cas. 798 (1883). For an example of the assessing of compensation under the Public Health Act of 1875, see *Brierley Hill Local Bd.* v. *Pearsall*, 9 App. Cas. 595 (1884).

169. *Mayor of Portsmouth* v. *Smith*, 10 App. Cas. 364 (1885).

170. Under the Metropolis Management Amendment Act of 1862, *Barlow* v. *Vestry of St. Mary Abbots, Kensington*, 11 App. Cas. 257 (1886).

171. E.g., *Spackman* v. *Plumstead Bd. of Works*, 10 App. Cas. 229 (1885), holding that a magistrate had no jurisdiction to interfere with an architect's certificate fixing the "general line of buildings" under the Metropolis Management Amendment Act of 1862, and that the magistrate should have convicted.

172. In *Lang* v. *Kerr, Anderson & Co.*, 3 App. Cas. 529 (Scot. 1878), the House had to consider a Glasgow Police Act, under which the Master of Works could require occupiers and proprietors of land, *inter alia*, to fence land and keep buildings in good repair to prevent their becoming dangerous. The law lords refused to hold that an owner could be compelled to put up a fence to protect persons who had a right of way along his land from falling into the river. This was not the purpose contemplated by the act, which was to keep the public out from the property, not to protect them once they were in.

173. For an extrajudicial example of this attitude, see Selborne's almost hysterical outburst in the House in the debate of the Evicted Tenants Commission (Ireland) Act; 11 *Parl. Deb.*, H.L. (4th ser.), cols. 1422–32 (28 Apr. 1893). "Nothing equally unconstitu-tional had been done by any Government since the reign of James II. . . . This was a Royal

views of the judicial process, still alive in common law cases, were not carried over into statutory interpretation. This pattern was especially true in the public law area.

Thus regulation was handled no better. Under the various Railway and Canal Traffic Acts, the judiciary, either directly or indirectly, was called to determine whether contracts between carriers and the public were "just and reasonable." The law lords freely commented on the political hostility to this type of legislation,[174] and there was little doubt that they shared some of that hostility.[175] In one case Bramwell was almost beside himself when presented with "a contract made by a fishmonger and a carrier of fish who know their business, and whether it is just and reasonable is to be settled by me who am neither fishmonger nor carrier, nor with any knowledge of their business." In that case the Court of Appeal had found that the contract was unreasonable since the plaintiff had no real choice for transporting the fish.[176] Blackburn declared this view to be "not legitimate reasoning."[177] Bramwell had "never heard anything like it before—it is the most extraordinary proposition that I have ever heard in my life. The assumption that he is obliged to do it because he cannot otherwise compete with his fellow-fishmongers is the most gratuitous one that was ever invented in this world."[178] In a similar case Bramwell severely attacked the "shocking" behavior of the plaintiff for trying to "wriggle" out of a contract, an "invitation to dishonesty" encouraged by "the mischievous operation of a law which avoids an agreement voluntarily entered into."[179] In later Victorian England, con-

---

Commission issued by the sole authority of the Crown, without any sanction whatever from Parliament to inquire into the private concerns and the exercise of the property rights of individual members of the community, with a view to overrule those property rights and to undo that which had been done in the due and regular course of law according to some scheme which this Royal Commission was to suggest"; ibid., col. 1422.

174. E.g., per Blackburn, *Manchester, Sheffield, & Lincolnshire Ry. v. Brown*, 8 App. Cas. 703, 710 (1883).

175. "I cannot understand how it could have been supposed necessary, that it should be referred to a judge to say whether an agreement between carriers, of whose business he knows nothing, and fishmongers, of whose business he equally knows nothing, is reasonable or not. If it is a question, it is one of fact; and evidence should be given to show that the fishmonger and carrier did not understand their business but made an unjust and unreasonable contract"; ibid. 718.

176. 10 Q.B.D. 250 (1882).

177. 8 App. Cas. 703, 713 (1883).

178. Ibid. 719-20. He concluded with this thought: "I really do not understand how such a conclusion could have been come to, except by some generous feeling that railway companies ought to be kept for the benefit of fishmongers"; ibid. 720.

179. *Great Western Ry. v. McCarthy*, 12 App. Cas. 218, 240 (1887). "The fact that it has been voluntarily entered into by them is the strongest possible proof that it is a reasonable agreement, and . . . I should require the strongest possible evidence, or something more even than a possibility, to show me that that was an unreasonable agreement"; per Bramwell, 8 App. Cas. 703, 718-19 (1883).

tracts, once made, had to be kept; and economic inequality was no concern of the law or at least of the law lords.

Likewise, the state's increasing interference with contracts of employment did not appeal to all the judiciary.[180] Yet, in terms of undermining legislative policies, perhaps the most dramatic example was the Privy Council's effective dismantling of the Canadian and Australian efforts to institute antitrust laws to prevent anticompetitive behavior by corporations. The law lords could not comprehend the American view of laissez-faire that allowed the legislature to establish—and the courts to police—the ground rules of competition. To the English law lords freedom *of* contract meant freedom *to* contract.

In the 1909 Canadian appeal, *United Shoe Machinery Company of Canada v. Brunet*,[181] the defendants had leased machines from the plaintiffs, who had a virtual monopoly of shoe machinery in Canada, and were being sued by the plaintiff for using ancillary machines not supplied by the plaintiff in contravention of a "tying clause." To the argument, accepted by the Quebec courts, that the agreements were void as being in restraint of trade, Atkinson, delivering the opinion of the Judicial Committee, happily took on the mantle of Bramwell.[182] The idea that the courts should be called in to handle such a situation was anathema to the law lords: "If the monopoly established by the appellants and their mode of carrying on their business be as oppressive as is alleged (upon which their Lordships express no opinion), then the evil, if it exists, may be

---

180. In *Netherseal Colliery Co. v. Bourne*, 14 App. Cas. 228 (1889), dealing with the interpretation of that part of the Coal Mine Regulation Act that prevented mine owners and employees from contracting that a deduction should be made from the miners' wages according to the amount of slack mined, Macnaghten took the balanced view: "In the case of persons employed in mines the legislature has thought good to impose a fetter on freedom of contract between masters and men. Parliament would legislate to little purpose if the objects of its care might supplement or undo the work of legislation by making a definition clause of their own"; ibid. 247. But the other members of the House, including Bramwell and FitzGerald, expressed regret at having to implement the legislation even had Macnaghten conceded that he was "by no means sure that in this case the men are not taking advantage of the provisions of the Act to escape from a bargain which they entered into or confirmed with their eyes open; which was fair in itself, and of which they have taken all the benefit"; ibid. For a more sympathetic view, see O'Hagan in *Doolan v. Midland Ry.*, 2 App. Cas. 792, 811–13 (Ire. 1877).

181. [1909] A.C. 330 (P.C.).

182. "By virtue of the privilege which the law secures to all traders, namely, that they shall be left free to conduct their own trade in the manner which they deem best for their own interests, so long as that manner is not in itself illegal, the respondents are at liberty to hire or not to hire the appellants' machines, as they choose, irrespective altogether of the injury their refusal to deal may inflict on others. The same privilege entitles the appellants to dispose of the products they manufacture on any terms not in themselves illegal, or not to dispose of their products at all, as they may deem best in their own interest, irrespective of the like consequences. This privilege is, indeed, the very essence of that freedom of trade in the name and in the interest of which the respondents claim to escape from the obligations of their contracts"; ibid. 342–43.

capable of cure by legislation or by competition, but in their view not by litigation. It is not for them to suggest what form the legislation should take, or by what methods the necessary competition should be established. These matters, may, they think, be safely left to the ingenuity and enterprise of the Canadian people."[183]

If such a dictum was intended to encourage legislation on such matters, it was misleading. Australia had passed various Australian Industries Preservation Acts, the validity of which was tested before the Privy Council in 1913.[184] The acts were modeled to a large extent on the United States Sherman Act and purported to make criminal those contracts made "with intent to restrain trade or commerce to the detriment of the public." In an action by the Crown to recover penalties and obtain an injunction with respect to a price-fixing arrangement between a group of colliery owners and a group of shipowners, the Privy Council refused to find that such contracts, which would have been unenforceable at common law as being in restraint of trade, would necessarily be to "the detriment of the public" and so in violation of the act. In so doing, Parker made clear the basic economic approach of the court:

[I]t was proved that the prices prevailing when negotiations for this agreement commenced were disastrously low owing to the "cut-throat" competition which had prevailed for some years. . . .
It can never, in their Lordships' opinion, be of real benefit to the consumers of coal that colliery proprietors should carry on their business at a loss, or that any profit they make should depend on the miners' wages being reduced to a minimum. Where these conditions prevail, the less remunerative collieries will be closed down, there will be great loss of capital, miners will be thrown out of employment, less coal will be produced, and prices will consequently rise until it becomes possible to reopen the closed collieries or open other seams. The consumers of coal will lose in the long run if the colliery proprietors do not make fair profits or the miners do not receive fair wages. There is in this respect a solidarity of interest between all members of the public. The Crown, therefore, cannot in their Lordships' opinion, rely on the mere intention to raise prices as proving an intention to injure the public.[185]

Workmen's Compensation Legislation

If the law lords found it virtually impossible to allow the state room to regulate commercial relationships, the House of Lords was somewhat

183. Ibid. 344.
184. *Attorney-General For Australia* v. *Adelaide S.S. Co.*, [1913] A.C. 781 (P.C.).
185. Ibid. 809. Doctrinally the Privy Council weakened the test laid down in Nordenfelt's case, [1894] A.C. 535, by pointing out that they were "not aware of any case in which a restraint though reasonable in the interests of the parties has been held unenforceable because it involved some injury to the public"; ibid. 795. After this it was extremely difficult to prove that, if the agreement were reasonable as between the parties, it could be held void as being contrary to the public interest.

more open-minded when it came to implementing the workmen's compensation legislation.[186] The idea behind workmen's compensation was that the employer should be the insurer of the continued bodily integrity of his men. Irrespective of fault on the part of anyone, the employer was to be liable to compensate a man for injuries from accidents arising "out of and in the course of his employment." Subsequently a similar liability was imposed on the employer in respect to certain prescribed industrial diseases.

The original act was intended to be virtually self-executing. In theory, the employer and the injured man would look to this scheme of the act, a doctor would be consulted, and the amount of compensation payable would be agreed upon. An arbitration procedure was provided (in practice in the person of the local County Court judge) in case any question arose that was not settled by agreement. Halsbury in the legislative debates in the House of Lords demanded that there should be a right of appeal from the decision of the arbitrator to the Court of Appeal and thence to the House of Lords; the effect of providing judicial supervision meant the chances of keeping the procedure simple were remote. The loose and simple phraseology lent itself to fine arguments, and the profession was not slow to take advantage of the opportunities offered; thus more cases were fought, often on facts virtually identical to those in a previous case. Davey, who was more used to the technicalities of Chancery, once referred to "this extraordinarily ill-drawn Act,"[187] while on another occasion, Robertson complained that "the arguments seem to me to be entirely over the heads of Parliament, of employers and of workmen."[188]

It is to Halsbury's credit that he was in the forefront in holding that "extremely refined notions"[189] were to be eschewed. He attempted to

186. Even after passage of the Employers' Liability Act of 1880, which restricted the scope of common unemployment, the increasing labor lobby demanded further legislation, particularly after *Griffith* v. *Earl of Dudley*, 9 Q.B.D. 357 (1881), allowed contracting out of the 1880 act. Chamberlain, while in the Gladstone administration of 1883–85, strongly championed the workers' cause in his "Unauthorized Program" and, after the Liberal split, Chamberlain championed a compensation program from the Conservative benches. After the Lords had mauled the Liberals' Employers' Liability Bill of 1893, compensation seemed the only solution. Thus, in 1897, the Salisbury administration introduced the Workmen's Compensation Bill; Hanes, *Workmen's Compensation Act, passim.*

187. *Lysons* v. *Andrew Knowles & Sons*, [1901] A.C. 79, 95 (1900). This prompted the reply, "It does not seem to have occurred to the noble and learned Lords that they are themselves answerable as legislators for the defects which they censure as judges"; "Note," 17 *Law Quarterly Review* 112 (1901).

188. *Fenton* v. *Thorley & Co.*, [1903] A.C. 443, 452.

189. *Main Colliery Co.* v. *Davies*, [1900] A.C. 358, 362. For Halsbury, "These extremely refined notions as applicable to the administration of this Act, creating some hypothetical standard within which the judge is obliged to act, would not to my mind be likely to conduce to the clear administration of the law"; ibid. 362–63.

limit cases to their facts,[190] and his decisions in workmen's compensation cases show that his vigorous attacks on the unions did not necessarily reflect a lack of sympathy with workingmen as such.[191] Indeed, he came close to laying down something akin to a presumption in favor of the workman in actions brought under the act.[192] Other law lords took even stronger tacks. Macnaghten referred to the act as "the workmens' charter,"[193] while for Loreburn it was a commonplace that "this Act is a remedial Act, and, like all such Acts, should be construed beneficially."[194]

As already suggested, the fact that the language of the acts was intended to be simple did not mean that it appeared simple to the law lords, and to some extent their perspective toward interpretation was colored by their view of the legislation. In *Cooper and Crane* v. *Wright*[195] Robertson complained of "[having to patch] up certain statutory enactments which are incoherent and almost contradictory," while in *McDermott* v. *S.S. Tintoretto (Owners)* Loreburn could say, "I feel no hesitation in reading such words into the statute.... In this case it is necessary, in order to avoid a plain frustration of the obvious intention of the Legislature."[196] In keeping with this approach, during the Edwardian period it was the politically

190. Once again, Halsbury was a strong advocate of treating as factual as many issues as possible. See *New Monckton Collieries* v. *Keeling*, [1911] A.C. 648: "It is a question of fact whether a particular person is a dependent or not." *Barnes* v. *Nunnery Colliery Co.*, [1912] A.C. 44, 46 (1911): "[T]he more I see of these cases under the Workmen's Compensation Act, the more I feel that nearly all of them are in reality pure questions of fact." In *Cross, Tetley & Co.* v. *Catterall*, Opinions of their Lordships, 1905, Halsbury did suggest the test that "[i]n order to be in the employment you must say at some point or another that the man was actually doing something on his employer's behalf," but he reaffirmed that it was merely a question of fact.

191. "It appears to me that the statute deliberately and designedly avoided anything like technology. I should judge from the language and the mode in which the statute has been enacted that it contemplated what would be a horror to the mind of a lawyer, namely, that there should not be any lawyers employed at all, and that the man who was injured should be able to go himself say, I claim so much, and then that he should be able to go to the county court judge and say, Now please to hear this case, because my employer will not give me what I have claimed. It appears to me that that is the meaning and construction of the whole statute, and that is what the Legislature intended, and that is the reason why it avoided any technical phrases"; *Powell* v. *Main Colliery Co.*, [1900] A.C. 366, 371–72.

He also advocated a broad form of statutory interpretation; *Brintons, Ltd.* v. *Turvey*, [1905] A.C. 230, 232–34.

192. His view was that the leading enactment was contained in § 1 (1) "If in any employment to which this Act applies personal injury by accident arising out of and in the course of employment is caused to a workman, his employer shall, subject as hereinafter mentioned, be liable to pay compensation." The words that followed "in accordance with the First Schedule of this act" described the mode by which compensation was to be calculated and did not cut down the plain words of the act; *Lysons* v. *Andrew Knowles & Sons*, [1901] A.C. 79, 85 (1900). See also at 86, "the leading enactment [provides] that every workman is entitled to compensation."

193. *Ball* v. *William Hunt & Sons*, [1912] A.C. 496, 500.

194. *Bist* v. *London & South West Ry.*, [1907] A.C. 209, 211.

195. [1902] A.C. 302, 306.

196. [1911] A.C. 35, 39 (1910).

conscious law lords who prevented the professional judges in the Court of Appeal from undermining the legislation by formalistic decisions.[197]

The broadest interpretation given by the House during this period was to the central phrase—"accident arising out of and in the course of the employment." For example, a rupture caused by trying to turn a wheel on a machine was held to be an accident,[198] as was contracting anthrax from a bacillus in wool.[199] A majority, led by Loreburn, decided that death from an aneurism that burst while the worker was tightening a nut with a spanner, without applying any particular strain, was an accident arising out of employment.[200] Even the death of a teacher as a result of a premeditated attack by his pupils was held to fall within the provisions of the act.[201] The burden of proving serious and willful misconduct

197. *Powell v. Main Colliery Co.*, [1900] A.C. 366, concerned the interpretation of § 2 (1): any "claim for compensation" had to be made within six months of the accident. The workman had given notice of the accident, and handed in a written demand for compensation, within six months, but his request for arbitration in the County Court was filed after six months. The Court of Appeal held that the proceedings were out of time. The House of Lords refused to read the words "claim for compensation" in any technical legal sense, as meaning the first step in legal proceedings. Halsbury, Shand, Davey, Brampton, and Robertson concurred; Morris dissented. The *Law Quarterly Review* said of this case, "Plain men will think that the House of Lords ... did a good deed by construing the Workmen's Compensation Act in accordance with its general beneficent intention and common sense"; "Note," 16 *Law Quarterly Review* 317 (1900).

In *Hoddinott v. Newton, Chambers & Co.*, [1901] A.C. 49 (1900), the Court of Appeal had said that work done on a building after it was meant to be completed was "alteration" rather than "construction or repair," and that a "staging" was not scaffolding. The House of Lords thought this definitely "too narrow a view." Shand and Lindley dissented.

The act said that compensation was to be calculated by reference to "average weekly earnings," a term that fell to be interpreted in *Lysons v. Andrew Knowles & Sons*, [1901] A.C. 79 (1900), where the man had been employed for only two days. The Court of Appeal held he was entitled to nothing, since he had no "average weekly earnings" until he had been employed for at least two weeks. The House of Lords said that this was to put too technical a meaning on the word "average." Men who were employed by the day for only a few days at a time could not be excluded from the benefits of the act by an implication of this sort.

198. *Fenton v. Thorley & Co.*, [1903] A.C. 443. Macnaghten defined an accident as "denoting an unlooked-for mishap or untoward event which is not expected or designed"; ibid. 448.

199. *Brintons, Ltd. v. Turvey*, [1905] A.C. 230. Halsbury warned the House that "we must be on our guard that we are not misled by medical phrases to alter the proper application of the phrase 'accident causing injury'; because the injury inflicted by accident sets up a condition of things which medical men describe as disease"; ibid. 233. Compare *Ismay Inrie & Co. v. Williamson*, [1908] A.C. 437, where a stoker who suffered from heatstroke was held to have died by accident. (Macnaghten dissented.)

200. *Clover, Clayton & Co. v. Hughes*, [1910] A.C. 242.

201. *Trim Joint Dist. School Bd. v. Kelly*, [1914] A.C. 667 (Ire.). The welcome this case received was somewhat qualified. "We rather think the opinion of the majority gives effect to the present case, to what Parliament did mean; but we also think it attains that end by doing such violence to the words of the Act as may prove a dangerous example"; "Note," 31 *Law Quarterly Review* 8 (1915).

was placed firmly on the employer,[202] and this responsibility was not easily displaced. The maxim *actio personalis moritur cum persona* was held to have no place in cases under the Workmen's Compensation Act, and where the sole dependent of a man killed in circumstances entitling the widow to compensation died herself two days after the accident, it was decided that the right of action passed to her executor.[203] Perhaps even more startling in view of the articulated morality of the period, it was held that in the case of a man who had admitted that he was the father of a child *en ventre sa mère* and had promised to marry the mother but was killed at work before the child was born, the child was nevertheless a "dependent" and entitled to compensation.[204]

It would, of course, be seriously misleading to suggest that law lords of such contrasting political views were unanimously proemployee. Disagreements did occur. It would be tempting to say that the lords split according to their politics, Conservatives favoring the employer and Liberals the worker, but this would be too facile a generalization. The most that can be said is that the Liberals, such as Loreburn (who had once said, "This was a humane Bill; let it remain a humane Bill")[205] and James,[206] usually favored the employee. Shaw[207] at least during this period was less consistent, as were the Conservatives. Some sense of these trends may be seen in a series of cases concerning seamen who fell over-

202. *Johnson v. Marshall, Sons & Co.*, [1906] A.C. 409.

203. *United Collieries, Ltd. v. Simpson*, [1909] A.C. 383.

204. *Orrell Colliery Co.* v. *Schofield*, [1909] A.C. 433; followed and extended in *Lloyd v. Powell Duffryn Steam Coal Co.*, [1914] A.C. 733.

205. 167 *Parl. Deb.*, H.L. (4th ser.), col. 1196 (18 Dec. 1906). Loreburn paid lip service to the normal burden of proof in civil cases and the orthodox canons of statutory construction. *E.g.*, "It is commonplace to say, of course one must be very sorry for people who suffer and may get no redress; but we are bound to administer the law, and I think we should be wanting in our duty if we did not do in cases of this kind the same as we are compelled to do in other kinds of cases"; *Barnabus v. Bersham Colliery Co.*, Opinions of their Lordships, 1910. Also, "My Lords, this appeal may serve to remind us of a truth sometimes forgotten, that this House sitting judicially does not sit for the purpose of hearing appeals against Acts of Parliament, or of providing by judicial construction what ought to be in an Act, but simply of construing what the Act says. We are considering here not what the Act ought to have said, but what it does say"; *Vickers, Sons & Maxim, Ltd.* v. *Evans*, [1910] A.C. 444, 445. In the same case he said, "[W]e are not entitled to read words into an Act of Parliament unless clear reason for it is to be found within the four corners of the Act itself."

206. See, for example, his dissent with Loreburn in *Back* v. *Dick Kerr & Co.*, [1906] A.C. 325; James had already come down firmly on the side of the workman by dissenting, with a somewhat facetious argument, in *Houlder Line v. Griffin*, [1905] A.C. 220, 225. He was even, in theory, prepared to find that there had been no "serious and willful misconduct" in a case where an engine driver had mounted the tender of his engine while it was in motion, in breach of a well-known rule; *Bist v. London & South Western Ry.*, [1907] A.C. 209, 213.

207. See, e.g., *Marshall v. S.S. Wild Rose (Owners)*, [1910] A.C. 486, where he sided with Atkinson and Mersey.

board in unexplained circumstances, although the tangle of these cases is forbidding. Little attempt then was made to distinguish the cases; it was simply a question of which group predominated on the panel, and this matter was all too frequently disguised by emphasizing the "factual" element in the process.[208] Twenty years later, Dunedin was to explain the decisions during those years in realist terms. "The conclusion I have come to is that there is to be found in the cases what I may call two opposing tendencies of construction, and I think that this case depends on which of the two opposing tendencies commends itself to your Lordships. To mention names I think it will certainly be found that the protagonist of one tendency is Lord Loreburn and of the other Lord Atkinson."[209]

Overall, the House no doubt fought hard to make sense of the Workmen's Compensation Acts. The idea that cases should be decided on their facts was admirable in many respects,[210] yet the solution inevitably encouraged litigation. The attempt to use simpler language in the act, because of the English tradition of statutory interpretation, in fact made implementation more difficult. Bearing this in mind, however, the House's treatment of the acts emerges as a laudable effort to give legal meaning and actual efficacy to legislation foreign to the law lords' previous experience. Certainly if appeals had stopped at the Court of

208. In *Marshall* v. *S.S. Wild Rose*, an engineer employed on a trawler went on deck one night to cool himself. His body was found next morning in the water near the rail where he had been in the habit of sitting in hot weather. In the absence of any evidence to show how the death happened, the majority (Lords Atkinson, Shaw, and Mersey) held that the accident had not arisen "out of and in the course of employment." It might have been in the course of employment, but there was no evidence on which to base a finding that it had arisen out of the employment. Atkinson thought that it might have been different if the ship had been at sea, but it was in harbor at the time. Loreburn and James dissented, on the ground that since the man was employed to be on board the ship, and falling overboard accidentally was a risk incidental to that employment, then the accident had arisen out of the employment.

Then in *Swansea Vale (Owners)* v. *Rice*, [1912] A.C. 238, it was held that when a seaman on duty as officer of the watch disappeared, in the absence of any evidence at all, the accident could still be held to have arisen out of his employment. Loreburn did not attempt to distinguish *Marshall* v. *S.S. Wild Rose*, but added "cases are valuable insofar as they contain principles of law. They are also of use to shew the way in which judges regard facts. In that case they are only used as valuable illustrations"; at 239. Shaw, however, thought that there was a valid distinction, since in this case the sailor had been on duty.

Finally in *Lendrum* v. *Ayr Steam Shipping Co.*, [1915] A.C. 217, where a steward on a boat in harbor was drowned, the accident was held to have arisen out of the employment. Loreburn repeated his previous observations, and Parker concurred. Shaw, also concurring, rested his decision on the fact that the man was given to vomiting and it was that that took him to the ship's side. Atkinson and Dunedin dissented.

209. *Simpson* v. *London, Midland & Scottish Ry.*, [1931] A.C. 351, 357 (Scot.).

210. For further examples, see the definition of "accident" in *Fenton* v. *Thorley & Co.*, [1903] A.C. 443; "earnings" in *Abram Coal Co.* v. *Southern*, [1903] A.C. 306; "serious and willful misconduct" in *Johnson* v. *Marshall, Sons & Co.*, [1906] A.C. 409 (especially per James at 412), and *George* v. *Glasgow Coal Co.*, [1909] A.C. 123, 128 (Scot. 1908) (per Robertson).

Appeal, appreciably more unfairness would have been evident in the operation of the system of workmen's compensation.

Taxation

The same "balanced" approach characterized the early decisions on taxation. The rate of income tax was low;[211] Cairns[212] and Bramwell[213] both insisted that tax statutes had to be treated like any other statute; the overall approach did not seem to favor one side or the other,[214] a tradition carried over into related decisions, like Macnaghten's reworking of the concept of charity in the *Pemsel* case.[215] Yet, as the period progressed, political and social changes brought a different and less easily justified style of interpretation to tax cases.

The rise of collectivism was marked by a fundamental change in taxation. In 1894 Harcourt made the estate tax, first introduced in 1889, into an effective and important source of revenue. Meanwhile, the rate of income tax was steadily increasing, receiving considerable impetus during the periods that Asquith and Lloyd George spent at the Treasury. All this added a new and vital aspect to tax cases which appeared with increasing frequency in the calendar of the House. Increasingly, law lords developed their own philosophies with respect to tax cases, generally mirroring their political views. As has been suggested, in 1900 tax statutes were still handled much as any other legislaton. By the outbreak of World War I, they were treated virtually as penal statutues and were not

---

At some level, however, a line had to be drawn. See, for example, Loreburn's warning to be careful to distinguish fact from law in *Kitchencham v. S.S. Johannesburg (Owners)*, [1911] A.C. 410. It was said that his words "ought to be set in letters of gold over the doors of every County Court and of the Court of Appeal"; "Note," 27 *Law Quarterly Review* 381 (1911). This time Loreburn held against the employee.

211. The standard tax rates on the pound during this period were 1876, 2d; 1886, 8d; 1896, 8d; and 1906, 1/–. From B. R. Mitchell, *Abstract of British Historical Statistics* 428–29.

212. In *Cox v. Rabbits*, 3 App. Cas. 473, 478 (1878), Cairns said, "[A] Taxing Act must be construed strictly; you must find words to impose the tax, and if words are not found which impose the tax, it is not to be imposed."

213. *Trustees of Clyde Navigation v. Laird*, 8 App. Cas. 658, 673 (Scot. 1883).

214. Cf. *Coltness Iron Co. v. Black*, 6 App. Cas. 315 (Scot. 1881); *Colquhoun v. Brooks*, 14 App. Cas. 493 (1889).

215. *Commissioners for Special Purposes of Income Tax v. Pemsel*, [1891] A.C. 531, 574. Concurring, Macnaghten gave a long and careful speech in which he rejected the narrow test, suggested by counsel for the appellant, of the popular use of the word "charity"—the relief of poverty. He said that the phrase used in the legal sense, which he laid down, was to be seen in broad terms. He admitted as charitable purposes not only the relief of the poor but also the advance of education and of religion and "other purposes beneficial to the community, not falling under any of the preceding heads." Moreover, he expressed his satisfaction at being able to decide for the respondents, as otherwise charitable foundations previously given remission of income tax would find themselves subject to heavy liabilities.

"enforced against" a taxpayer unless his behavior came within the "very wording" of the statute. The House had come to protect a man's income even more vigorously than it had his land, and in so doing had undermined an important plank in the Liberal program of social equality.

At the turn of the century the House was strongly under the dominance of Halsbury who, despite his conservatism, at that time saw nothing particularly desirable in helping a man avoid his share of taxation. In deciding tax cases, therefore, he took a "common sense" look at the taxing statute, and if he found the statute fairly applied, he found for the Crown. He refused to take a narrow view of the meaning of a tax category,[216] although he was most satisfied when a case plainly fell within the relevant statute.[217] While he was on record as encouraging the court to look at the words rather than the intent of the Income Tax Acts,[218] the majority of his pronouncements were in favor of taking a broad look at the acts. Indeed, in many cases, Halsbury specifically called on the House to look to the intent of the tax statutes[219] or to look to the scheme of the taxing statutes to make sure they applied a sensible test.[220] He also advised looking to the substance rather than the form of transaction.[221]

If anything, the tendency to construe tax statutes narrowly was more obvious among the reputedly more liberal law lords. Herschell, for instance, demanded that words in a taxing statute should be clear.[222] Macnaghten, from a more conservative standpoint, also expressed simi-

216. *Lord Sudeley* v. *Attorney-General*, [1897] A.C. 11 (1896).

217. *Earl Grey* v. *Attorney-General*, [1900] A.C. 124 (1899); *Ashton Gas Co.* v. *Attorney-General*, [1906] A.C. 10, 12 (1905).

218. "[T]he question in this case seems to me to depend upon the actual words used by the legislature, and I deprecate a construction which passes by the actual words and seeks to limit the words by what is supposed to be something equivalent to the language used by the Legislature"; per Halsbury, *Gresham Life Assurance Soc'y Ltd.* v. *Bishop*, [1902] A.C. 287, 290–91.

219. E.g., *Secretary of State in Council of India* v. *Scoble*, [1903] A.C. 299, 302. "I think it cannot be doubted, upon the language and the whole purport and meaning of the Income Tax Acts, that it never was intended to tax capital—as income at all events."

220. E.g., *Attorney-General* v. *Beech*, [1899] A.C. 53, 58 (1898).

221. E.g., *Attorney-General* v. *Montagu*, [1904] A.C. 316. Halsbury began his speech, "My Lords, in this case, with the greatest respect for the learned judges in the Court of Appeal, I think they have allowed validity to be given to what is mere form and not substance. If one looks at the whole arrangement, the substance of the matter was this—not that there should be a mere contractual relation between the remainderman and the lady who was entitled to this property, but that the property should remain hers as between those two persons, and that she should never have one farthing less than she was entitled to"; ibid. 318.

See also his remarks in *Duke of Northumberland* v. *Attorney-General*, [1905] A.C. 406, 409: "[A] succession within the Act once established, no manipulation of the parties afterwards can get rid of it." For an account of how Halsbury succeeded in offending both James and Davey in marshaling the Lords to hear this case, see p. 86n.

222. E.g., *IRC* v. *Tod*, [1898] A.C. 399, 410 (Scot.).

lar views,[223] although at other times he appeared to be in favor of taking a broad approach to tax problems.[224] Despite these slightly different approaches, the result put tax statutes in basically the same position as any other legislation. The court construed the acts neither particularly narrowly nor particularly broadly and in most cases effectively carried out the wishes of the legislature, at the same time keeping the general structure of doctrines in the area of tax law reasonably rational and coherent.[225]

With the advent of the Liberal administration at the end of 1905 and with the active interest Loreburn took in the judicial work of the House, it seemed that, the pendulum might swing, if anything, in favor of the Crown; and indeed, a series of decisions in the early years of his Chancellorship did take a view strongly in favor of the Revenue authorities.[226] Time and again Loreburn insisted on looking at "the substance" of the transaction[227] or finding out what "in reality" was the position.[228] The

223. E.g., *Earl Cowley* v. *IRC*, [1899] A.C. 198, 210 ff. Macnaghten's view that the heads of liability under §§ 1 and 2 of the Finance Act of 1894 are mutually exclusive was overruled by the House in *Public Trustee* v. *IRC*, [1960] A.C. 398 (1959).

224. E.g., *LCC* v. *Attorney-General*, [1901] A.C. 26, 35–40 (1900).

225. For typical cases during the period, see, for the Crown: *Lord Revelstoke* v. *IRC*, [1898] A.C. 565 (stamp duty); *Grant* v. *Langston*, [1900] A.C. 383 (Scot.), (house tax); *Midland Ry.* v. *Attorney-General*, [1902] A.C. 171 (stamp duty); *Scottish Provident Institution* v. *Allan*, [1903] A.C. 129 (income tax); *Eastbourne Corp.* v. *Attorney-General*, [1904] A.C. 155 (stamp duty). For the taxpayer see *Lord Wolverton* v. *Attorney-General*, [1898] A.C. 535 (succession duty); *IRC* v. *Muller & Co.*, [1901] A.C. 217 (stamp duty; see especially dissent of Halsbury in favor of the Crown at 238); *IRC* v. *Priestly*, [1901] A.C. 208 (Ire.) (estate duty); *Winans* v. *Attorney-General*, [1904] A.C. 287 (estate duty).

226. E.g., the House refused to allow a hotel company to deduct from its profits damages paid to a customer injured by negligence in one of its hotels; *Strong & Co.* v. *Woodifield*, [1906] A.C. 448. See per Loreburn at 452. An equally stern view was taken about the behavior of companies. The test of residence for companies was made the functional one of "where its real business is carried on" rather than the formalistic test of where its registered office was situated; *De Beers Consol. Mines, Ltd.* v. *Howe*, [1906] A.C. 455, per Loreburn, at 458. Companies were likewise held liable to pay stamp duty in England on a sale in France of property situated in England. Any other interpretation would be "unreasonable" since "a trip across the Channel would afford ready means of evading duty"; *IRC* v. *Maple & Co.*, [1908] A.C. 22, 26 (1907), per Macnaghten. The assets of insurance companies were subject to strict scrutiny and were not allowed to be manipulated to avoid tax responsibilities; *General Accident, Fire & Life Assurance Co.* v. *McGowan*, [1908] A.C. 207 (Scot.); but cf. *Sun Ins. Office* v. *Clark*, [1912] A.C. 443.

227. In *London & India Docks Co.* v. *Attorney-General*, [1909] A.C. 7 (1908), a company sought to evade stamp duty on the "issue of debenture stock" by "modifying the rights" rather than issuing stock. To the argument that this was not an issue of stock, Loreburn made the categorical reply, "It is quite clear to my mind that it was. The stock now in existence had no existence at all until after the Act passed; something different existed, different both in amount and in security. Whatever words were by the ingenuity of the draftsman used, the fact is that the debenture stock which is now held by its owners must have been issued"; ibid. at 12.

228. In *Blakiston* v. *Cooper*, [1909] A.C. 104 (1908), the House held that an Easter offering to a clergyman was, "in reality," "profits accruing to him by reason of his office" and therefore liable to income tax; ibid. 107. Per Loreburn. The Loreburn view, which

judicial change and serious conflict on tax matters appear to have arisen chiefly at the time of the Parliament Crisis (1909–11). This kind of development was not surprising. The tax implications of pure democracy became fully clear to the landed and wealthy classes only during this period, particularly with the passage of Lloyd George's 1909 budget. This event and the other crises in the legislative activities of the House of Lords were quickly reflected in the behavior of the judicial branch.

The impending clash of approach in the judicial arena first became evident in *Attorney-General v. Duke of Richmond, Gordon and Lennox* in 1909.[229] No doubt the judicial reaction was partially the result of the increasing subtlety of draftsmen. In this case a Scottish settler encumbered a settled estate with bonds in favor of later holders for the sole purpose of avoiding estate duty. The question at stake was whether such bonds were created "for full consideration in money or money's worth wholly for the deceased's own use and benefit." Collins and Shaw could not believe that this was their purpose. Collins[230] refused to approve the transaction because it violated "the true interpretation of the section. Looking, as we are entitled to do, at the transaction as a whole . . . it was part of the arrangement. . . . In point of fact, the property was at once resettled as nearly as possible on the old lines. I cannot think that a claim thus manufactured can be held good."[231] Shaw took a similar view. He too felt that the behavior of the settlor could not come within the wording of the section; more important, he held that the substance of the arrangement clashed with the spirit of the section.[232]

---

appeared to be shared by other of the more liberal law lords, was perhaps most firmly stated in *Great Northern, Piccadilly & Brompton Ry.* v. *Attorney-General*, [1909] A.C. 1 (1908). There a company sought to rely on a private act to exonerate itself from liability for stamp duty. Loreburn would have none of this and declared that "[t]he Courts will take every means of defeating an attempt . . . to affect the rights of the Crown or of other persons who have not been brought in"; ibid. 6.

229. [1909] A.C. 466.

230. "[E]ven if the grammatical construction put on the section by the Court below be adopted, I am far from satisfied that 'full consideration in money or money's worth' was received by the deceased in return for the incumbrances. In fact, if it had been, it might have defeated the main purpose of the transaction, which involved a diminution in the value of the estate to be left in the hands of the settlor at the close of the transaction"; ibid. 482.

231. Ibid. 481–82.

232. "[I]n order to arrive at a just determination upon the elements for consideration presented by this clause it is necessary to consider not merely the transaction of creating incumbrances by itself, but the entire transaction of which they form a part. I think that this must be done if mistake is to be avoided"; ibid. 483. After an examination of the facts he decided that the "[s]aving of estate duty (I purposely do not use the term evasion or even avoidance of estate duty) formed the object and purpose of the transaction"; ibid. 486. After looking at the different formal arrangements, he concluded, "To view these, so inter-related, as if they were in isolation, would be for me . . . to shut out the light, to lose their true meaning, and to produce a risk of failure to get down to the reality and substance of the case. I think that the creation of these incumbrances was not

On this occasion Atkinson and Macnaghten argued the conservative and legalistic approach. For Atkinson the problem was simple:

> It is admitted that the motive which prompted the late Duke to enter into these transactions was to relieve from the payment of estate duty those estates which upon his death would pass to another or to others. That motive does not, however, vitiate the transaction, no more than it vitiates a voluntary alienation of property made with the same purpose and object twelve months before a donor's death. Just as there is nothing illegal or immoral in making such a gift, or in living for twelve months afterwards so as to make it an effectual means of escape from death duties, so there is, in my opinion, nothing illegal or immoral in making the dispositions of property which were made in this case.[233]

Loreburn, presiding, no doubt found himself in a quandary. As Speaker of the House of Lords he was at this time both fighting for Lloyd George's budget and presiding over the debates on it. Perhaps he felt that politically it would be unwise to provoke still further the hostility of the Tory peers. His one-paragraph speech concluded, "It is not my province either to censure or to commend the transaction itself. It was within the law and without dishonesty. If this case has disclosed a way by which

---

for the use and benefit of the late Duke of Richmond and Gordon, but was simply a part of a plan for saving death duties to his heirs. I do not think that the scheme was in this case accomplished without a contravention of the letter as well as a very plain violation of the spirit of the statute"; ibid. 487.

233. Ibid. 475. He continued:

I further think that the case must be determined solely with regard to the legal rights and interest which the respective parties had acquired in October, 1897, the date of execution of the impeached securities. What they did afterwards, how they chose to dispose of these legal interests or to exercise those legal rights, is, in my view, irrelevant. It might have been legitimate to inquire into these matters subsequent, if the transactions which were concluded on that day had been impeached as unreal, colourable or sham transactions; but they have been admitted to be real and genuine in their character, and, if so, all the subsequent dealing with the estate and the interest created in it lie outside the field of inquiry, even though by their operation they practically restore the status quo ante. The question for decision, therefore, simply resolves itself into this: Were the incumbrances which were in fact created in October, 1897, to use the words of Section 7, Subsection 1(a), of the statute, "created bona fide for full consideration in money or money's worth, wholly for the deceased (Duke's) own use and benefit." [Ibid. 475–76]

Macnaghten allied himself with this view and attempted to justify it in moral terms.

If the construction for which the appellant contends be right, a man who burdens his property to portion his daughter, to educate or advance his son, to save a friend from ruin, to effect some lasting improvements on his estate which cannot give an immediate return, or to promote some benevolent object or some object of real or supposed public utility, to endow a hospital, for instance, or save a famous picture for his country, cannot hope for an allowance from the Commissioners of Inland Revenue. This concession is reserved for the man who spends on himself alone, for the prodigal, the gambler, and such like. I cannot bring myself to think that the Legislature deliberately intended to put a premium on extravagance purely selfish, and to penalise expenditure on objects generally considered more worthy. [Ibid. 473]

See also Macnaghten: "The Duke acted on the advice of his solicitor, conceiving, rightly or wrongly, that he was not under any obligation, legal or moral, to keep his property in a form peculiarly and unnecessarily obnoxious to an impost which I am afraid many people still think unequal and unfair"; ibid. 471.

settled property may largely escape the estate duty, that is an affair for the Legislature to consider, in which the Courts of law have no concern."[234] Whatever inspired this change of approach in the Lord Chancellor is not certain; but it is clear that his vote on this occasion had a profound impact on the interpretation of tax laws in the United Kingdom.

Some of the implications of the Duke of Richmond's case became manifest two years later in *Smith* v. *Lion Brewery, Limited*[235] and in two Australian appeals to the Privy Council also decided in 1911. In one of the latter, Macnaghten let it be known that his conversion to a strict interpretation of tax statutes was permanent. "No one may act in contravention of the law. But no one is bound to leave his property at the mercy of the revenue authorities if he can legally escape their grasp."[236] Having so concluded, the Judicial Committee refused to find that various property manipulations amounted to a conspiracy to defraud the Revenue. Atkinson, giving judgment in the second Australian appeal, refused to make shareholders liable when a company failed in its duty to deduct tax from dividends. "[I]t is not permissible to twist . . . words from their ordinary meaning and construe them in a strained or unnatural sense in order to extend the liability of the subject to taxation not imposed upon him by plain and unambiguous enactment, however beneficial in the interest of the revenue such a course might be."[237] In tax cases the

234. Ibid. 470.

235. [1911] A.C. 150. The House then had to decide whether a brewery company was entitled to deduct compensation from its profits, as being an expense "wholly and exclusively laid out or expended for the purposes of their trade." The compensation was a levy imposed on all brewers by the Licensing Act of 1904 to compensate persons who lost licenses as part of a policy of reducing the number of public houses. Both liberals and conservatives purported to take a legalistic view of the approach to the law. For instance, Loreburn noted, "We are here only concerned with the construction of an Act of Parliament"; ibid. 155; and Halsbury confirmed that "by the Act of Parliament [we are] confined to expressing our view whether by law such and such a deduction could possibly be made"; ibid. 157. Yet, below the surface there were strong "cross-currents of feeling" reflected in the view of the substantive problem. In a 2–2 vote the conservative law lords felt strongly that the levy should be deductible, the liberal law lords that it should not.

236. *Commissioner of Stamp Duties for New South Wales* v. *Byrnes*, [1911] A.C. 386, 392 (P.C.). A similar view had been expressed by the Privy Council in *Simms* v. *Registrar of Probates*, [1900] A.C. 323 (P.C.), in connection with Australian antievasion provisions in succession duty legislation. Hobhouse leant in favor of an honest settlor and held that only sham transactions were within the terms of the statute, saying, "Where there are two meanings each adequately satisfying the language and great harshness is produced by one of them, that has legitimate influence in inclining the mind to the other. Now, if the word evade be taken to signify some contrivance between donor and donee, that which is pointed out as the greatest harshness of the enactment would be removed or substantially reduced, seeing that the donee would be a party to the transaction which causes loss to him. It is more probable that the Legislature should have intended to use the word in that interpretation which least offends our sense of justice"; ibid. 335.

237. *Golden Horseshoe Estates Co.* v. *Crown*, [1911] A.C. 480, 488 (P.C.).

burden was now clearly on the Revenue. A rational approach to tax leg-islation was, indirectly, another casualty of the Parliament Crisis.

The formalistic approach toward tax legislation that the law lords developed turned English tax law for decades to come into a type of crossword puzzle, with the courts and the legislature playing an often unseemly game of cat and mouse. Politically and economically the se-manticism of the English judicial approach to tax problems that de-veloped during these years, although in later years sometimes quaintly dressed up as the protection of civil liberties, in fact enabled the ex-tremely wealthy to avoid the undisputed rigors of the English tax system. Indeed, among the wealthy, only the ignorant or the obstinate failed to derive some benefit from the formalistic approach to interpretation that began in the Edwardian period; and the later decisions based on this approach undoubtedly thwarted the kind of redistribution of wealth that Harcourt and Lloyd George had predicted in their budgets.[238]

In so many ways then, the law lords' treatment of taxation was the model that Weber would have expected. The senior English (and occa-sional Scottish and Irish) judges, although springing from the middle and professional classes, had been consciously absorbed into the House of Lords, which remained, somewhat misleadingly, the most obvious mani-festation of the aristocratic tradition. Caught up in that tradition, the lawyers behaved as might be expected. They reflected, sometimes more obviously than the lay peers, a concern with the protection of property and a distrust of coercion by government. Even where the law lords did "move with the times," they bent elegantly in the directions Weber would have expected—largely to protect the incomes of the established sections of society. It was only in the relatively rare constitutional law cases that other policies were more obviously at work.

Constitutional Law

Dominated by Dicey's notion that the Rule of Law treated public and private law questions alike,[239] the House of Lords produced during this period few cases that might legitimately be described as constitu-

---

238. The literature on the distribution of wealth and income is collected in A. B. Atkinson, *Unequal Shares*. While the data are conflicting, in Britain the top 1 percent own more than a quarter (probably rather more) and the top 5 percent, more than a half of the nation's wealth. (In comparative terms, while the distribution of income is similar in the United States and Britain, the top 1 percent own 21 percent of the wealth in the United States and over 40 percent in England.)

Over time there has been some change. In 1911–13, it was estimated that 5 percent of the British population owned 87 percent of the total wealth. By 1954, that proportion had fallen to 71 percent; by 1960, it had risen to 75 percent, ibid. 19–21.

239. Albert Venn Dicey, *Introduction to the Study of the Law of the Constitution* 189–91.

tional in nature. It is in some ways surprising that the reformed and gradually expanding Civil Service did not stimulate some kind of reaction, and ultimately litigation, on the part of those who perceived the passing of power from the legislature and judiciary to the executive;[240] but that was not to be. Thus the future (or almost nonfuture) of English administrative law came to be determined not by Bramwell, Blackburn, or Halsbury but by two Liberal Lord Chancellors who, under the guise of a formalist tradition, ensured absolute sovereignty for majority government in Parliament, untrammeled by any serious judicial supervision. The tone was set by Herschell in 1894, in *Institute of Patent Agents* v. *Lockwood*.[241] The case concerned the validity of rules made by the Board of Trade concerning fees, under the Patents, Designs, Trade Marks Act. The House held that such rules were *intra vires* the act, although power to make them was not specifically given by the legislation. Herschell, however, went further, opining that, if the formal requirements of the act as to laying before Parliament were met, the delegated legislation would be completely protected from judicial scrutiny. Only Morris dissented, restating the Tory position that there should be a presumption against excluding the courts.

The cases that might test the foundations of administrative law really began to flow only during Loreburn's period on the Woolsack. The Education Act of 1902 finally put education under the county and borough councils, including voluntary or nonprovided schools. The governors of such schools were to provide the buildings and choose the teachers, but the cost of upkeep was to be borne by the local authorities out of the rates (local property taxes). The Church of England and the Roman Catholic Church, both of which had large numbers of schools, were delighted; the nonconformists, who had none, were not. The latter started a series of cases designed to test the legality of the new statute; but Loreburn stood firm.[242]

It was also under Loreburn's direction that the House sought to strike a balance in judicial control of the executive. Thus, although the

---

240. E.g., John A. R. Marriott, *English Political Institutions*.

241. [1894] A.C. 347.

242. Thus in maintained but nonprovided schools, the House held that a local authority was compelled to defray the cost of providing religious instruction, thus confirming that the schools brought into the public sector were to be fully supported; *Attorney-General* v. *West Riding of Yorkshire County Council*, [1907] A.C. 29 (1906). The House even held that in a nonprovided school that was maintained, the local authority was required to pay the salaries of employees other than teachers (caretaker and cleaner); *Gillow* v. *Durham County Council*, [1913] A.C. 54 (1912). Of this decision it was said at the time that "it can only be read by one free from prejudices, religious or other, with the deepest regret"; "Note," 29 *Law Quarterly Review* 116 (1913).

For a less sensitive decision about early social security legislation, see *Murphy* v. *R.*, [1911] A.C. 401 (Ire.).

law lords refused to apply their power to declare bylaws unreasonable where a local authority was clearly acting within the discretion granted by Parliament, James made a plea that "we should be careful to say we do not shut out the power of review within certain limits."[243] Not only did the House seem to realize a need to retain some judicial control over procedural matters, while largely disclaiming any power over policy,[244] but it adopted a balanced view of what was required of a government in making a decision.

This equilibrium between what, in American terminology, would be called procedural and substantive due process, was most elegantly illustrated in *Board of Education* v. *Rice*,[245] one of the more sophisticated decisions delivered by the House during this period. While agreeing that the Board's decision should be reviewed, Loreburn, presiding, gently chided the Court of Appeal for failing to distinguish between, on the one hand, the procedural requirement that the board not violate "natural justice"[246] but follow specific procedures—all appropriate responsibilities of the courts—and, on the other hand, the exercise of policies themselves, supervision of which was no responsibility of the courts. "In the coil in which this quarrel, simple as it is in itself, has been entangled, this distinction may have been somewhat overlooked."[247] Shaw even went so far as to suggest, in discussing the general problem of how far local authorities were required to achieve a balance between the "maintained"

243. *Del Prato* v. *Provost of Patrick*, [1907] A.C. 153, 157.

244. See, for instance, the decisions on "line of building" certificates, refusing to interfere with the decision of the planning architect, even where some variations had been allowed: *Lilley* v. *LCC*, [1910] A.C. 1 (1909); *Fleming* v. *LCC*, [1911] A.C. 1 (1910).

245. [1911] A.C. 179.

246. "Comparatively recent statutes have extended, if they have not originated, the practice of imposing upon departments or officers of State the duty of deciding or determining questions of various kinds. In the present instance, as in many others, what comes for determination is sometimes a matter to be settled by discretion, involving no law. It will, I suppose, usually be of an administrative kind; but sometimes it will involve matter of law as well as matter of fact, or even depend upon matter of law alone. In such cases the Board of Education will have to ascertain the law and also to ascertain the facts. I need not add that in doing either they must act in good faith and fairly listen to both sides, for that is a duty lying upon everyone who decides anything. But I do not think they are bound to treat such a question as though it were a trial. They have no power to administer an oath, and need not examine witnesses. They can obtain information in a way they think best, always giving a fair opportunity to those who are parties in the controversy for correcting or contradicting any relevant statement prejudicial to their view. Provided this is done, there is no appeal from the . . . Board. . . . The Board have, of course, no jurisdiction to decide abstract questions of law, but only to determine actual concrete differences that may arise, and as they arise, between the managers and the local education authority. The Board is in the nature of an arbitral tribunal, and a Court of law has no jurisdiction to hear appeals from the determination either upon law or upon fact. But if the Court is satisfied either that the Board have not acted judicially in the way I have described, or have not determined the question which they are required by the Act to determine, then there is a remedy by mandamus and certiorari"; ibid. 182.

247. Ibid. 183.

and the "provided" schools, that the courts inevitably faced issues like the "reasonable classification" test of the Fourteenth Amendment's equal protection doctrine.[248]

The new Liberal law lords were in the ascendant;[249] only Halsbury survived to represent the Tory viewpoint. By this time past his prime, he appeared unable to comprehend either the Loreburn or the Shaw arguments. He was prepared to attack the executive head-on.[250] Only in the colonies, apparently, was Halsbury willing to see an unrestrained use of executive power.[251] At home, the counterattack on the executive had come too late. Dicey announced that *Rice* undermined the Rule of Law by having given judicial power to the education commissioners, but by this time his was a cry from another era.

Politically, no doubt both pro and con positions could be argued as to whether the courts had been wise to begin their retreat from the realm of administrative law. Yet, jurisprudentially, it can be maintained that the style and tradition of English judges made them poor public lawyers; the English judiciary was not at its best balancing competing political theories while producing analytical legal reasoning. Nowhere was this particular defect more apparent than in the Privy Council's handling of the Canadian constitution.

As has already been noted, the early decisions appeared to support what had been assumed to be the intention of the 1867 act, namely to make the Federal Government, by section 91, the predominant power in the Dominion of Canada.[252] Beginning in the 1890s, however, and associated with the influence of Watson, came a series of cases that effectively made the provincial powers under section 92 coordinate with the federal

248. "[W]here the circumstances are the same, discrimination primarily requires justification. But . . . a state of complete similarity—in the varying conditions as to schools, staffs, localities and otherwise—may be most infrequent, and to apply the same standard to dissimilar circumstances is in my humble judgement itself such a discrimination as would also require justification"; ibid. 187.

249. The case was heard by Loreburn, Halsbury, Atkinson, Shaw, and Mersey.

250. "The duty of the education authority was to keep the schools efficient; this duty they neglected and did not keep the schools efficient. The local education authority assumed to itself an absolute autocratic authority as to what schools they would keep efficient, and I cannot doubt for myself that they thought they were entitled to starve the Church schools and give advantages to the provided schools which they would not grant to the Church Schools. It is impossible to resist the conclusion that this was done from hostility to the Church Schools. . . . I quite agree with the Lord Chancellor, that it would be absurd to cavil at some differences between one school and another, and upon a mere difference between what was provided for one and another. We are far removed from such a question here"; *Board of Educ.* v. *Rice*, [1911] A.C. 179, 185–86.

251. In the Privy Council, however, Halsbury was agreeing to the ousting of the jurisdiction of the ordinary courts when martial law was in force. See *in re Marais*, [1902] A.C. 51 (P.C. 1901); *Tilonko* v. *Attorney-General of Natal*, [1907] A.C. 93 (P.C. 1906).

252. See per Sir Montague Smith in *Russell* v. *The Queen*, 7 App. Cas. 829 (P.C. 1882).

powers.[253] While the 1939 O'Connor Report attributed to this period the deviation from the intention of the founders of the confederation,[254] in fact by supporting the provinces the Privy Council had acquired itself a strong lobby for the retention of appeals to London—the provincial governments. By the time of the 1911 Imperial Conference, one of the representatives of French Canada announced that "[a]s to Canada there is no part of Canada more pleased with the decisions of the Privy Council than the Province of Quebec."[255] It was high praise for Watson.[256]

By this time, however, Loreburn was in command, and he saw that the membership of the Judicial Committee was organized in such a way that, in keeping with his own centralist approach, it was more sympathetic to the Ottawa government. In a series of cases in 1906 Macnaghten appeared to prop up dominion powers,[257] and the trend continued.[258] This apparent change of direction led to criticism of the work of the Judicial Committee in the provincial capitals, a criticism that had previously been limited to criminal appeals.[259] In contrast with Watson's opinions, which had tended to treat the 1867 act like any other legislation, Loreburn was expansive. He called on the Privy Council to interpret the legislation broadly, since Canada had a "completely self-governing Constitution founded upon a written organic instrument."[260] By the end

253. E.g., see especially Watson in *Tennant v. Union Bank of Canada*, [1894] A.C. 31 (P.C. 1893). *Attorney-General for Ontario v. Attorney-General for Canada*, [1894] A.C. 189 (P.C.); *City of Winnipeg v. Barrett*, [1892] A.C. 445 (P.C.); *Brewers and Maltsters' Ass'n of Ontario v. Attorney-General for Ontario*, [1897] A.C. 231 (P.C.). On Watson, see Coen G. Pierson, *Canada and the Privy Council* 33–37; Edward McWhinney, *Judicial Review in the English Speaking World* 64–65. For a defense of Watson's work in the light of the intention of "the fathers," see Bora Laskin, *Canadian Constitutional Law* 16. In defense of the Privy Council it has also been argued that in general, when the Conservatives were in power, the Council tended to support central government and to do the reverse when the Liberals were in power.

254. Senate of Canada, Sess. of 1939, Report Persuant to Resolutions of the Senate to the Honorable Mr. Speaker by the Parliamentary Counsel relating to the Enactments of the British North America Act, 1867, any lack of consonance between its terms and judicial construction of them and cognate matters, at 11–13.

For a criticism of the reasoning of the O'Connor Report, see G. P. Browne, *The Judicial Committee and the British North America Act* 58–72.

255. *Proceedings of the Imperial Conference*, Cd. 5745, at 232–33 (1911).

256. Pierson, *Canada and the Privy Council* 43.

257. *Attorney-General for British Columbia v. Canadian Pac. Ry.*, [1906] A.C. 204 (P.C. 1905); *Attorney-General for Canada v. Cain*, [1906] A.C. 542; *Grand Trunk Ry. v. Attorney-General for Canada*, [1907] A.C. 65 (P.C. 1906).

258. *Toronto Corp. v. Canadian Pac. Ry.*, [1907] A.C. 54 (P.C. 1906); *Woodruff v. Attorney-General for Ontario*, [1908] A.C. 508 (P.C.); *La Companie Hydraulique de St. François v. Continental Heat & Light Co.*, [1909] A.C. 194 (P.C. 1908); *Dominion of Canada v. Province of Ontario*, [1910] A.C. 637 (P.C.). In the last of these cases, Loreburn presided and delivered a strong pro-dominion opinion.

259. Pierson, *Canada and the Privy Council* 37, 45.

260. *Attorney-General for Ontario v. Attorney-General for Canada*, [1912] A.C. 571, 583 (P.C.).

of Loreburn's Chancellorship growing criticism came from Montreal and Toronto rather than Ottawa.[261] It was the kind of political criticism, however, that the law lords were least able to handle.

For some, the idea that constitutional cases frequently involved the balancing of interests other than legal ones never won acceptance. The Commonwealth of Australia Act of 1900 allowed for less leeway to the Judicial Committee than the British North America Act had; but some appeals still came to the Privy Council. In delivering judgment in a 1907 Australian appeal, *Webb* v. *Outrim*,[262] Halsbury was brought face-to-face with the concept of judicial review. He found it remarkably difficult to accept. "That is a novelty to me. I thought an Act of Parliament was an Act of Parliament and you cannot go beyond it. . . . I do not know what an unconstitutional act means."[263] As the Privy Council had been operating the doctrine of judicial review for forty years since the passage of the British North America Act, such thought can barely have brought much comfort to the Judicial Committee's customers.[264] The tension between law and politics had international repercussions.

261. Pierson, *Canada and the Privy Council* 46–48.
262. [1907] A.C. 81 (P.C. 1906).
263. Ibid.
264. The *Law Quarterly Review* said at the time, "[T]he constitutional mystery derived by Lord Halsbury from the assent of the Crown seems to us as illusory as it is obscure"; "Note," 23 *Law Quarterly Review* 130 (1907). It was later described, more bluntly, as a "major blunder"; William K. Hancock, *Survey of British Commonwealth Affairs 1937* 566.

THE RISE OF THE PROFESSIONALS
1912—1940

The period between 1844 and 1912, covered by part I, chronicled the appellate functions of the House of Lords, as they reflected the tensions between law and politics. It was a period during which the legal tended to prevail over the political, at least in the judicial work of the Lords. Nevertheless, while the lower and intermediate appeal courts were dominated by a professionalized judiciary handling doctrines that were increasingly regarded as self-contained and apolitical, the Lords remained under the influence of political Lord Chancellors, staffed by Lords of Appeal who were generally chosen for their political rather than their professional success. Certainly there was increasing discussion in the Lords about legal doctrines being objective and derived from the logic of the common law; and, at its core this was an undoubted truth. Those who ran the House of Lords and Privy Council, however, were well aware that the appeals that reached them were not dealing with core situations, but with those competing policies and doctrines inevitably operating at the penumbra. Both in administration and in decision making, the political predominated over the professional.

During the period with which part II is concerned, the situation was reversed. Beginning with the Parliament Act of 1911, Haldane's Chancellorship of 1912, and the Appellate Jurisdiction Act of 1913 and ending with the onset of World War II, these years witnessed the reversal of the relative importance of law and politics in the Lords. The remarkable constitutional position of the Lord Chancellor and the fact that the judges were members of a legislative body meant that a strong element of the political remained; but "the law," with its emphasis on objectivity and logic, became increasingly important. Not only were judges chosen more frequently from the professional judiciary, but they emphasized the more "scientific" spirit of the English tradition. The internal self-sufficiency of the law was more readily accepted; political decisions were more carefully eschewed; and by 1940 the approach that had helped preserve the lower courts from the rigors of political control, namely the declaratory theory of law, was not only about to be taken seriously by the law lords but also to be given a terrifying aura of certainty. Thus while legislation was used increasingly as a means of social control in the country at large, law—as understood by the English judges—was confined within increasingly narrow intellectual and practical bounds. This period, in truth, represented a remarkable change in the balance of political and intellectual forces.

SIX

Law, Politics, and the Ambit of Decision

The period between 1912 and 1940 was an uneasy time in English history. In 1912 the country was bitterly divided. Among politicians the Parliament Crisis had left a remarkable residue of hatred. The Marconi scandal, which implicated several members of the Asquith administration, appeared to herald a new low in political ethics. Despite the passage of the National Insurance Act of 1911, which was to prove the basis of what became the welfare state, the labor troubles of the Edwardian period continued; violence was rife and class hatreds were hardening in a way that would be almost immune to later healing. After the failure of Gladstone's attempts to grant Home Rule, Ireland was on the verge of revolution. The Conservative party, having lost much of the Tory radicalism of Disraeli and Chamberlain, seemed committed to attempts to sidetrack naked democracy, while the Liberal party was finally disintegrating. Having gradually shed the Whigs, the conflict between the laissez-faire Liberals—the heirs of utilitarian thought—and the radicals was inevitable. In turn, however, the Liberals were being usurped by the Lib-Labs and a socialist Labour party as the party of the Left.[1] The strange death of liberal England was at hand.

The Liberal government remained in power until 1915 under Asquith; however, that was to be the last Liberal administration in British history. Asquith's and then Lloyd George's coalition carried on until 1922 when the purely Conservative administrations of Bonar Law and Baldwin came to power. With the final split of the Liberals after the 1922

1. On this, see George Dangerfield, *The Strange Death of Liberal England*; and especially Introduction by Paul Johnson at 9–12. See also Arthur Marwick, *Britain in the Century of Total War* 85 ff.

election, the only alternative to the Conservatives was the Labour party. Thus, in January 1924 MacDonald formed a minority Labour administration, which was replaced in November of that year by a Conservative administration under Baldwin. In June 1929 MacDonald returned, but with the Crisis of 1931 his Labour administration gave way to a National government that survived (under MacDonald until 1935, Baldwin until 1937, and thereafter Chamberlain) until Chamberlain formed his War Cabinet at the outbreak of war in 1939.

Economically and socially little distinguished the years between the two world wars from the sad scene that had characterized England in the summer of 1914. World War I, which succeeding generations would come to regard with diminishing enthusiasm, had occupied and exhausted the energies of Britain for more than four years. When the war ended, a brief spell of prosperity gave way to a period of economic and social disruption without parallel in twentieth-century British history. Labor relations deteriorated rapidly, beginning with the National Coal Strike in 1921 and culminating in the General Strike of 1926. Although in the end the unions were crushed and several years of formal industrial peace followed, the labor relations that resulted were understandably bitter. Unemployment increased as the years went on; 1929 brought the Wall Street crash, which initiated a series of economic disasters for Britain that, if not as extreme as those in the United States, certainly marked the thirties as a period of deep depression. Unemployment and poverty gave rise to apathy and hostility. Labour and Conservative parties were divided; the split in the Liberal party was never to heal. The National government not only seemed incapable of making an active effort to speed recovery at home, but also allowed its foreign policy to be perceived as appeasement.[2]

The Structure of Appeals

At the 1911 Imperial Conference, the British government had made firm commitments to improve arrangements for hearing appeals in the Privy Council by creating two additional Lords of Appeal.[3] After some delay a bill was introduced to allow an increase in the number of "colo-

---

2. On the period generally, see C. L. Mowat, *Britain between the Wars 1918–1940*; A. J. P. Taylor, *English History 1914–1945*; and Robert Rhodes James, *The British Revolution*, part 2. For a lighthearted, albeit depressing, description of these interwar years, see Robert Graves and Anthony Hodge, *The Long Week-End*.

3. "[T]hat they should add to the highest court of appeal, both for the United Kingdom, and the Dominions and Colonies, by selecting two English judges of the finest quality; that the quorum should be fixed at, say, five, and that the court should sit successively in the House of Lords for United Kingdom appeals and in the Privy Council for appeal from the Dominions and Colonies"; *Proceedings of the Imperial Conference*, Cd. 5745, at 222–23 (1911).

nial" judicial members of the Council, under the 1895 act, from five to seven[4] and to increase the number of Lords of Appeal from four to six. Yet, even these additions were not sufficient to assuage growing doubts in the dominions. In Canada further rumblings were being heard that the right to appeal to London was an extravagance, coupled with irritation at any suggestion that the dominion was not free to end appeals. The Lord Chancellor's Office was uncomfortable.[5]

Yet there was little the office could do. Haldane pushed through the 1913 act over opposition in Parliament and immediately appointed Dunedin (1913–32) and Sumner (1913–30) as Lords of Appeal. Additionally, Sir Alfred Cripps was made Lord Parmoor in 1914 and Lord Justice Buckley was made Lord Wrenbury in 1915 on the understanding that they would act as full-time, unsalaried law lords.[6] The appeals, however, still flooded in. In 1913 the House of Lords sat for 115 days hearing sixty-four appeals and the Privy Council for 124 days to hear ninety-two cases. Far from having the same panel sitting alternately in Lords and Council as he had hoped,[7] Haldane was faced with such a backlog of

4. New Zealand felt it had not been fairly represented under the 1895 legislation. It was anxious to have Sir Joshua Williams appointed. He was, on 14 May 1914. Almeric Fitzroy, 2 *Memoirs* 549.

5. The *Montreal Star* (7 Mar. 1913) upset Sir Kenneth Muir Mackenzie by arguing that while "the right of appeal to an impartial tribunal has been of the greatest value to us in delicate constitutional questions—especially those in which race and religion are involved," it was inappropriate in cases where corporations were involved. (It may not be irrelevant that Loreburn's decisions upholding federal power under § 91 had been largely corporation cases). The *Star* also dismissed the argument that it was not open to Canada to abolish appeals. "[T]his sort of talk, leaving the impression that Canadian law for Canadians is made by somebody outside of Canada, is more mischievous when forced upon a democratic community such as ours"; Lord Chancellor's Office, 2/287, Public Record Office.

6. Richard Burdon Haldane, *An Autobiography* 269–70.

7. The Clerk of the Privy Council, after noting that Australia and New Zealand were more reasonable at the 1911 Imperial Conference than they had been in 1907 in their demands for merging the Privy Council and the House of Lords, recorded that Loreburn agreed to "the introduction of a more flexible system in the distribution of the judicial power available, to create what will be in effect one Supreme Court sitting in two divisions. No doubt his concessions in form had been brought about by the influence of Haldane and Asquith (both being present), who have on different occasions subscribed to the principle"; Fitzroy, 2 *Memoirs* 448–49.

The Imperial Conference of 1917 once more took up the issue of judicial appeals. Fitzroy summarized the situation in the following terms: On Hughes' (Australia)

resolution on the subject of a Supreme Court of Appeal . . . everyone subscribed to the theory of such a court, but with no concrete expression of the idea before then, they declined to commit themselves to its urgency. The only fruitful result of the discussion was the testimony elicited from the representatives of Canada, New Zealand, South Africa and India to the extremely satisfactory way in which the Judicial Committee did its work. . . . The two obstacles to the realization of Mr. Hughes' dream of "one Supreme Tribunal for all Appellants resident within the Empire," however attractive in appearance are (1) a matter of finance—will the Dominion contribute to its cost on an adequate scale?—and (2) a matter of repute—will a court largely recruited from Dominion Judges enjoy the confidence of British litigants either at home or beyond the seas? [Ibid. 679]

cases that he reconciled himself to having the Privy Council sit in two panels or divisions.[8] The law officers gave their opinion that this might not be done without legislation;[9] an act legitimating the arrangement was pushed through in 1915.[10] By 1916, the Lords of Appeal were often staffing three appellate panels. In the Lords, the panel was supplemented by other law lords, while in the Privy Council the law lords manned panels helped by those appointed under the 1833, 1884, 1895, and 1913 acts. Although efficiency was increased by these arrangements, the idea of a cohesive final court of appeal, which had been the goal of the reformers in the 1870s, was further from realization than ever.

By 1917, when the House sat for 110 days[11] to hear 47 cases, a new phenomenon was appearing: cases were taking longer to argue. Under the Chancellorships of Halsbury and Loreburn cases had, on average, taken between 1 and 1½ days to hear.[12] By the 1920s the norm was two days per appeal.[13] Although the increasing length of time required per case was not as pronounced in the Privy Council, the number of appeals was forbidding. In 1917 the 116 appeals took 164 days to hear, so that the Council sat in divisions on 29 days. By 1920 142 appeals took 175 days, including 62 days of sitting in divisions. In that year alone the final appeal courts, if the Appellate Committee work of the Lords with respect to in forma pauperis proceedings is included, sat for 299 days and heard 226 cases. For this work six salaried law lords provided the core of three panels. The arrangement was perhaps not the ideal setting for distinguished judicial contributions.[14]

Meanwhile, personnel changes had occurred. On the death of Parker, Cave (1918–22) was appointed a Lord of Appeal, while the vacancy left by Moulton went to Carson (1921–29). With the appointment of Cave as Lord Chancellor in 1922, Blanesburgh (1923–37) became a Lord of Appeal. The Appellate Jurisdiction Act of 1929 increased the number of

8. With the outbreak of war the Privy Council had the additional burden of hearing "prize" cases from the English courts. By 1915, there were 28 prize cases waiting to be heard; Lord Chancellor's Office, 2/92, Public Record Office.

9. Sir Rufus Isaacs (Attorney-General) and Sir John Simon (Solicitor-General); Lord Chancellor's Office; 2/287, Public Record Office. Two years later (5 Dec. 1915) Loreburn wrote to Buckmaster saying that he could see no reason, in law or practice, why the Judicial Committee should not sit in two divisions; Lord Chancellor's Office, 2/292, Public Record Office.

10. Judicial Committee Act of 1915; Lord Chancellor's Office, 2/292 Public Record Office. The committee began sitting in two divisions on 14 Feb. 1916. The second division began by hearing prize cases.

11. And also 5 days as the Appellate Committee to hear in forma pauperis petitions.

12. In 1900, the House heard 67 cases in 86 days; in 1905, 75 in 96; in 1910, 74 in 87; in 1915, 66 in 122.

13. In 1920 the House heard 74 cases in 119 days; in 1925, 60 in 113.

14. See W. Ivor Jennings, "Appeals to the Privy Council and the Statute of Westminster" 173.

Lords of Appeal by one, bringing it to seven. Moreover, between 1928 and 1932, there was, with one exception, a complete change in the complement of the Lords of Appeal. Atkinson retired in 1928, to be replaced by Atkin (1928–44). In 1929 Carson and Shaw retired, to be replaced and augmented by Tomlin (1929–35), Russell of Killowen (1929–46), and Thankerton (1929–48). In 1930 Sumner resigned and was replaced by Macmillan (1930–47). Wright was appointed in 1932 (1932–35, 1937–47).

By 1930, however, the phenomenon of longer hearings had reached the Privy Council. In that year, the 100 appeals took no less than 239 sitting days and, for the first time, the Judicial Committee sat in three divisions. With the increasing independence of the dominions, reflected politically in the 1931 Statute of Westminster, the solution was not to cut back on Privy Council appeals, many of which already came only with leave, but rather to abolish the absolute right in all cases of appeal to the Lords.[15] This move was recommended in the Second Report, in 1933, of the Business of the Courts Committee, under the Chairmanship of Lord Hanworth. The basic recommendation of the committee was that the right of appeal should be possible only with the permission of either the Court of Appeal or the House of Lords itself.

The suggestion was enacted into law in 1934.[16] Rather surprisingly, the proponents of the measure supported it more in terms of preventing injustice by protecting poor litigants who had won in the lower courts, than by arguments about the nature of the appellate process.[17] Only Lord Chancellor Sankey went further, with the remark, "[T]here are some who would like to lay the axe to the root and to abolish either the Court of Appeal or your Lordships' House. Whatever the future may have in store for us, the method is not at the moment practical politics. It

15. Statutes had, occasionally, limited this right of appeal. For instance § 108(2)(b) of the Bankruptcy Act of 1914, allowed appeals only with leave of the Court of Appeal.

There were, of course, no criminal appeals from Scotland, and criminal appeals from England were limited to those allowed by the 1907 act (appeals were allowed from the Court of Criminal Appeal only with the fiat of the Attorney-General).

16. Administration of Justice (Appeals) Act of 1934. See Louis Blom-Cooper and Gavin Drewry, *Final Appeal* 117 ff.

17. Atkin thought that the requirement of leave would prevent rich corporations and powerful government departments from terrorizing litigants with threats of appeal; Administration of Justice Bill, 92 *Parl. Deb.*, H.L. (5th ser.), col. 794 (5 June 1934). Hanworth talked darkly of cases brought for purposes other than reversing the judgment. "There are some cases which I have in mind, over the past few years; in respect of which certainly an appeal ought not to have been brought, but an appeal was brought for purposes . . . other than that of trying to put a wrong decision right. . . . in one case . . . the decision to go to the House of Lords was decided upon simply and solely for the purposes of delay." This view was echoed by Sankey, the Lord Chancellor, who added that "the most frequent complaint against our legal system . . . [was] the multiplicity of opportunities of appeal"; ibid., col. 797.

is not our way to make violent changes in the administration of the law. At present the Court of Appeal acts as a sieve for the House of Lords."[18] For the immediate future, however, appeals might be taken only with the permission of the Court of Appeal or the Appellate Committee of the Lords.[19]

In this restructured House, there were further changes of personnel. In 1935, Tomlin died and Wright resigned to become Master of the Rolls. In their places Maugham (1935–38, 1939–41) and Roche (1935–38) were appointed. After the resignation of Blanesburgh in 1937, Wright returned as a Lord of Appeal, while with the death of Roche in 1938 and the elevation of Maugham to the Woolsack, two other Lords of Appeal were appointed: Romer (1938–44) and Porter (1938–54). These judges participated in a somewhat different appellate process. The effect of the 1934 act and of the economic condition of the country was to reduce the number of appeals. Between 1935 and 1939 the number of cases heard by the Lords was appreciably lower—from a high of 49 in 1936 to a low of 35 in 1937, and contrary to earlier indications, a significant number of cases was filtered out.[20] More important, either the tempo of the House had changed or the new legislation (and the depression) allowed it to change. By the late thirties cases were taking an average of more than 2 days each to be heard,[21] and the House became even more an English court.[22] This more reflective attitude to decision making appeared to extend to the Privy Council; cases there, for the first time, began to average 2 days or more for hearing,[23] while their number declined.[24] The

18. Ibid., col. 790.

19. The Appellate Committee had existed since 1812, for deciding procedural issues, primarily in forma pauperis proceedings. By the 1930s, it functioned much like the regular House, except that there were normally only three members, it did not reserve judgment, and customarily did not give an opinion. The situation is largely the same today. Since the committee technically sits in camera, counsel are not heard as of right, although in practice the committee hears either barristers or solicitors. See Blom-Cooper and Drewry, *Final Appeal* 101.

20. In 1935 the Appeals Committee allowed 1 petition to appeal and rejected 10; in 1936 the figures were 3 and 7; in 1938, 3 and 5; in 1939, 3 and 19.

21. 1935, 48 cases were heard in 110 days; 1936, 49 in 112; 1937, 35 in 77; 1938, 42 in 91.

22. In 1905, the House heard 51 cases from the Court of Appeal, 23 from the Court of Session, and 1 from the Court of Appeal of Ireland. In 1915, the figures were 45, 17, and 4. In 1925, the figures were 45, 13, and 2 (although by this time Irish appeals came only from the Court of Appeal of Northern Ireland). In 1935, the figures were 36, 11, and 0, with 1 appeal from the Court of Criminal Appeal.

23. In 1930, 100 appeals were heard in 239 days; in 1932, 93 in 237 days; in 1933, 88 in 202 days; in 1936, 98 in 242 days; in 1938, 81 in 160 days.

24. From the time of Confederation, there had been some doubts about appeals from Canada, but the first persistent hostility to the work of the Judicial Committee came after passage of the Union of South Africa Act in 1909. South Africa's dislike of the appellate jurisdiction, however, paled into insignificance when compared with that of the Irish Free State, which had the Judicial Committee substituted for the House of Lords as its final

result was that whereas the law lords in 1920 had sat for 296 days to hear 206 cases in the two courts, in 1935, 142 cases took 327 days.[25] That fascinating transformation of the appellate process in a mere fifteen years was to have significant jurisprudential importance.

The Legal Temper of the Times

Fundamental changes rarely occur dramatically. It took time for the law lords to view themselves primarily as judges. The behavior of Lord Chancellor and Lords of Appeal did not change overnight; yet the arrival of Haldane did represent a new approach, and this, coupled with the emasculating of the Lords as a legislative body by the Parliament Act of 1911 and the diluting of the law lords by the Appellate Jurisdiction Acts of 1913 and 1929, represented a new direction. By the time Simon became Lord Chancellor in 1940 the legal temper of the times had changed; the House of Lords was no more than a second appeal court.

Although fundamental changes are not telegraphed, the advantage of hindsight enables one to record these developments. The shifts were not so clear at the time. Loreburn had been under attack by Liberal M.P.'s for appointing High Court judges irrespective of party;[26] Haldane not only continued this tradition but carried it further, appointing professional judges as Lords of Appeal as well. For Haldane, however, as a liberal intellectual, this move was only a beginning. He was prepared to accept politically what he recognized as impossible intellectually—a clear distinction between law and politics—and to attempt to implement it. Thus both in office and as Chairman of the Royal Commission on the Machinery of Government, Haldane advocated dividing the duties of Lord Chancellor so that a Minister of Justice would handle the legal work of the Home Office and the Lord Chancellor's Office and the Lord Chancellor would attend primarily to his judicial work.[27]

---

appeal court by the "Treaty" of 1922. The Irish fought to have the right to abolish appeals to the Privy Council established at the 1926 Imperial Conference, but eventually agreed to a plan by Birkenhead to put their demand off until the next conference. At the 1930 Imperial Conference, the Irish Free State was supported not only by South Africa but ultimately by Canada; and the right to abolish appeals was conceded by the Statute of Westminster of 1931; D. W. Harkness, *The Restless Dominion* 112–14, 138–39, 165–66, 203–7, 251–52.

The abolition of appeals to the Privy Council followed in the 1930s; Irish Free State: *Moore* v. *Attorney-General of the Irish Free State*, [1935] A.C. 484 (P.C.); Canadian criminal appeals: *British Coal Corp.* v. *The King*, [1935] A.C. 500 (P.C.). See Blom-Cooper and Drewry, *Final Appeal* 82–83.

25. Gavin Drewry, "One Appeal Too Many" 445.

26. Peter Rowland, *The Last Liberal Government: The Promised Land 1905–1910.* See also Peter Rowland, *The Last Liberal Government: Unfinished Business 1911–1914* at 3, 168.

27. Brian Abel-Smith and Robert Stevens, *Lawyers and the Courts* 131.

While the period provided its fair share of undistinguished Chancellors, the Haldane "hiving off" approach was continued by other Liberal and Labour Chancellors, particularly Lord Sankey. Politics, needless to say, did not suddenly disappear from the legal scene. The Lord Chancellor maintained his position as the embodiment of judicial, executive, and legislative roles. Since the Lords of Appeal were appointed by the Prime Minister (although normally with the approval of the Chancellor), politics was still apparent. (Lloyd George, for instance, saw no reason for politics and judicial appointments to be separated.) Moreover, Chancellors still had that mysterious power of choosing which law lords were to hear particular cases in the Lords and Privy Council. Haldane, for example, chose a group of four Liberal law lords to hear *Local Government Board* v. *Arlidge*,[28] the decision that removed any serious threat that the courts might exercise even procedural due process over departments of the central government. Hailsham did not disguise the fact that, by the late thirties, he was choosing panels in such a way as to discourage Atkin from "making law"; and there is evidence to suggest that Haldane, Sankey, and Hailsham all chose their Privy Council panels in order to further their own particular concerns about the dominion-provincial relationship in Canada.[29]

Such events, however, were deviations from the form, if not the substance, of the period. As part of the law-policy dichotomy, the courts and the legal establishment began to work more closely with Parliament. Throughout the 1920s Parliament became involved again with the procedure of the courts[30] and in 1925 passed the massive codification and reform of doctrine related to land law. Indeed, reforming doctrine, even in private law areas, was increasingly seen as the province of Parliament. In the early thirties, Sankey saw it as one of the responsibilities of the Lord Chancellor's Office to keep Parliament supplied with a "shopping list" of substantive law reforms that were needed.

It would be misleading to talk of a cooperative relationship between the appeal courts and Parliament. The judges, by this time perhaps more in the Court of Appeal than in the House of Lords,[31] still at times railed against the policies of Parliament or vented their furies on what they perceived to be the incompetence of the parliamentary draftsmen. In general, however, it was accepted that Parliament could and should be the institution to make changes in the law. This assumption undoubtedly had a reverse Thayerian effect. In the United States Thayer had argued

28. [1915] A.C. 120 (1914) (Haldane, Shaw, Moulton, Parmoor).
29. Abel-Smith and Stevens, *Lawyers and the Courts* 119.
30. Ibid. 101–3.
31. Ibid. 121.

that judicial review tended to make legislatures irresponsible;[32] by 1940 there was some evidence that the law lords were abandoning responsiblity for even interstitial legislation in the common law while reading statutes with increasing formality. When Parliament was prepared to right irrational decisions on an annual basis, as they were in tax law by the Finance Acts, little harm was perhaps done. In other areas increasing problems arose, and these were to assume major proportions in the years after 1940.

All these transitions were, however, slow. At least until the late twenties, the predominantly political Lords of Appeal—Atkinson, Shaw, Sumner, and Carson—were in the ascendant. Not until the thirties did the professional judges, led by Atkin, Wright, and Macmillan, take control; and only then did the House manage to avoid tackling difficult public law questions. During the twenties, on the other hand, the House had allowed itself to become embroiled in various "unseemly" appeals— at least that would be the view of those who espoused the law-policy distinction. Moreover, during that decade, equally unseemly things were happening elsewhere in the legal system.[33] Lloyd George treated the office of Lord Chief Justice with the same scrupulousness that he applied in distributing other patronage.[34] At the time of the General Strike, Sir John Simon in the House of Commons and Mr. Justice Astbury in the courts announced that the strike was a conspiracy at common law and illegal, and in 1928 the Lord Chief Justice, Hewart, discovered "that there [was] a long-standing plot (hatched among part of the civil service and fostered by Royal Commissions) to alter the position of the judiciary."[35]

The reaction to the Hewart outburst was significant in terms of the climate of the times. The government responded by appointing the Committee on Ministers' Powers. This body found, not surprisingly, that, beginning especially with the Liberal administration of 1905, an increasing amount of social legislation excluded the jurisdiction of the courts entirely, while disputes under the legislation were handled by tribunals

32. In J. B. Thayer, "The Origin and Scope of the American Doctrine of Constitutional Law" 129. Most usefully discussed in Alexander M. Bickel, *The Least Dangerous Branch* 21–23, 35–44.

33. Twice during the period under discussion there were suggestions that judicial salaries be cut. In 1921, when Lloyd George thought about cutting the salaries of judges, Birkenhead was outraged and announced they were "under paid"; Lord Chancellor's Office, 2/480, Public Record Office. In the 1930s, as part of the "Geddes axe" that cut public servants' salaries, an effort was made to include the judges. They were outraged and avoided both the indignity and the sacrifice. Abel-Smith and Stevens, *Lawyers and the Courts* 127–29.

34. Ibid. 130.

35. R. M. Jackson, *The Machinery of Justice in England* 213. Gordon B. Hewart's book, *The New Depotism*, was published in London in 1929.

outside the scope of the regular courts. Rather than urge reconciliation, however, the committee blessed the dichotomy between legal decisions (the rightful province of the regular courts) and policy decisions (the domain of the executive and tribunals). It was Dicey's original concept of the Rule of Law carried to the outer limit.[36] The committee apparently had no doubts that a line could be drawn between a judicial decision "which disposes of the whole matter by a finding upon the facts in dispute and an application of the law of the land to the facts so found" and a quasi-judicial situation (not appropriate for the judges) where such process was replaced by "administrative action" that might involve "consideration of public policy" or "discretion."[37] The report assumed the objectivity of legal rules and the feasibility of interpreting statutes "impartially." Formalism (and in particular the declaratory theory of law) had achieved public and political respectability.[38]

The seeds of the mechanistic or formalistic view of the judicial (including the appellate) process fell on fertile ground. The social structure of England provided a unity of interest among the legal profession, the Civil Service, and the bulk of successful politicians. Drawn primarily from the same class and normally sharing a similar educational background, the members of such groups were unlikely publicly to criticize an arrangement that protected the judiciary from political attack even if they appreciated that the convention was based on premises that could not stand rigorous intellectual analysis.

In other countries, rigorous analysis might have been provided by academic lawyers. Such was not the case in England. Both Dicey[39] and Weber,[40] in their different ways, realized that in England power and prestige in the profession belonged to the leading practitioners, not to the academics. Those going to the bar read "Greats" or history at Oxford or Cambridge. The early legal academics—Maine, Bryce, Dicey, Anson, and Pollock at Oxford and Maitland at Cambridge—did not produce serious successors. Those who came after saw their role as rationalizing the words of the judges rather than questioning them. Sir William Holdsworth, the leading legal academic of this later period, was reported as holding the view that "the law teacher ought not to encourage criticism

36. Of Dicey's theory, the committee opined, "[O]n the maintenance of the principles evolved by that process the liberty of the subject and the protection of his rights depend"; *Report of the Committee on Ministers' Powers*, Cmd. 4060, at 73 (1932).

37. Ibid. 74, 81.

38. Laski dissented and wrote to Holmes to explain that "my fight was the old one against regarding a judge as an automatic slot-machine into whom you put the statute and from whom you get a construction in which there is no articulate major premise"; Letter from Laski to Holmes, 8 Mar. 1932, M. de W. Howe, ed., *Holmes-Laski Letters* 1368.

39. Albert Venn Dicey, *Introduction to the Study of the Law of the Constitution*.

40. Max Weber, *Max Weber on Law in Economy and Society*.

of the judiciary in an age of scepticism," a speech of which Harold Laski said that Holdsworth gave the impression "of a desire on his part to fall flat on his face before a law lord."[41]

Little happened to counteract this antiintellectual approach.[42] The provincial universities had not lived up to their early promise and, so far as law was concerned, provided basically only service teaching for solicitors' articled clerks. The intellectual revolution, which on the Continent and in the United States had brought into being the social sciences, left England, with the possible exception of London University,[43] untouched; and in terms of the government of England, London University was still not important. Thus such intellectual effort as there was in the thirties was directed toward a refining of the mechanical approach to jurisprudence. The seminal work on the judicial process was Goodhart's essay, "Determining the Ratio Decidendi of a Case."[44] In this essay the Professor of Jurisprudence at Oxford sought to lay down a series of tests so that a single case, subjected to these formulae, would yield up its exact *ratio decidendi*. Although ignored by leading American scholars and derided by the Realists,[45] the essay was not only taken seriously in England but was treated as the starting point for all discussion of precedent for several legal generations.[46]

The fact that the English judiciary had seemingly been put "above politics" of course had many advantages. The judges enjoyed both the sense that they were respected[47] and also the sense that they were largely immune from criticism; indeed, it is also not without significance that during this period the idea crystallized that criticism of judges might amount to contempt of court.[48] More important, having established the

41. Howe, *Holmes-Laski Letters* 1398.

42. Laski did persuade Sankey to appoint a Committee on Legal Education under Atkin, but the lethargy was too great for it to achieve anything; Abel-Smith and Stevens, *Lawyers and the Courts* 184–85.

43. And particularly the London School of Economics.

44. Arthur L. Goodhart, *Essays in Jurisprudence and the Common Law* 1. (The essay was first published in 40 *Yale Law Journal* 161 [1930].)

In another article ("Case Law in England and America"), Goodhart was sufficiently convinced of the "scientific precision of the binding nature of precedents under the English system," that he felt it was not meaningful to talk about "distinguishing away" earlier precedents. See Goodhart, *Essays* 53–55, and Gerald Dworkin, "*Stare Decisis* in the House of Lords" 163.

45. Jerome Frank, "When 'Omer Smote 'is Bloomin' Lyre" 367.

46. See, for instance, Rupert Cross, *Precedent in English Law* 67–76 (2d ed.).

47. By 1936, even Hewart was prepared to admit that "His Majesty's Judges are satisfied with the almost universal admiration in which they are held"; see Jackson, *Machinery of Justice* 302.

48. The idea that contempt of court might apply to criticism of judges can be traced to the feeling of judicial solidarity that led the judges to resurrect the power to protect Mr. Justice Darling, one of Halsbury's least successful appointments; Abel-Smith and Stevens, *Lawyers and the Courts* 126.

sanctity of pure law, successive governments had few qualms in passing new functions of government to bodies totally unrelated to the regular courts.[49] In short, the regular courts became increasingly irrelevant as government intervention became the order of the day in Britain. At the same time, however, the depoliticization of the judiciary gave the government an important new political weapon. When a political crisis was peculiarly complex and difficult to solve, an "impartial" judge could always be appointed who would come up with an "objective" solution. Judges had always been employed occasionally to investigate and to recommend,[50] but by the 1920s and 1930s, judges were appointed to solve all manner of matters. Shaw could handle the Dock Strike of 1919,[51] Sankey, as a High Court judge, could be used to project the future of the coal industry;[52] and Scott could be called upon to worry about the growth of the executive power.[53] Most remarkable, however, was the increase in this constitutional phenomenon. In the reign of Edward VII the use of judges in such situations was increasing; by the forties it was increasingly the norm.[54]

The House of Lords as a judicial body during the period 1912 to 1940 could not avoid being affected by these attitudes and roles. All law lords, no matter what their background, exhibited an increasing tendency to articulate a declaratory theory of law and to insist that the judicial function, even in the final appeal court, was primarily the formalistic or mechanical one of restating existing doctrines.[55] Yet behind this facade, far more complex influences and ideas were at work. The House, as the influence of political law lords declined, was slowly, unevenly, and frequently ungraciously, moving away from the basic area of constitutional law and "playing possum" in those areas of public law

49. The 1905 Liberal administration had introduced trade boards in 1909 to determine remuneration in certain industries, as well as making use of the tribunal system under the National Insurance Act. But the process accelerated during the period under discussion. E.g., in 1919 an Industrial Court, where members were appointed by the Minister of Labour, was established to arbitrate wage claims. Under the Road Traffic Act of 1930, commissioners were appointed to license buses and coaches, while the Road and Rail Traffic Act of 1933, extended their responsibility to cover the carriage of goods.

50. E.g., Dunedin after *Taff Vale Ry.* v. *Amalgamated Soc'y of Ry. Servants*, [1901] A.C. 426.

51. Taylor, *English History* 141.

52. Ibid. 140. To the surprise of the government the majority recommended nationalization.

53. Sir Leslie Scott was Chairman (from 1931) of the Committee on Ministers' Powers. See *Report of the Committee on Ministers' Powers*, Cmd. 4060 (1932).

54. Between 1900 and 1907, 97 royal commissions and 12 departmental committees were appointed, 16 of the 59 being chaired by judges. Between 1945 and 1954 there were 11 royal commissions and 22 departmental committees. Of those 33 bodies, 11 were chaired by judges.

55. See Carleton Kemp Allen, "Precedent and Logic" 320.

from which it could not withdraw. Yet in private law, behind the same formula that insisted on the judicial inability to make law, the House—and particularly the professional judges—rapidly and forcefully developed many areas of tort and contract. The tension focused less and less on the relationship between law and politics and to a greater extent on the definition of public and private law.[56]

The Tragedy of Public Law

The period between 1912 and 1940 was thus not distinguished for its public law. Constitutional law was particularly arid.[57] Perhaps the most useful development during the period was that the House was less involved in constitutional issues. In part this was the result of the decision in *Local Government Board* v. *Arlidge*[58] at the outset of the period. *Arlidge* took the Loreburn approach in *Rice*,[59] which had pointed toward the retention of judicial review over procedural due process while avoiding attempts to control substantive due process, to a more dramatic conclusion. The style and purpose of the two Chancellors were indeed different. Whereas Loreburn was a radical and a politician, Haldane was an intellectual and a lawyer; and while Loreburn was anxious to protect both legislation and the common law from Conservative attack, Haldane was anxious to remove law from politics even if it involved the danger of making law irrelevant to the operation of the modern state.[60]

In *Arlidge*, the issue was how far the courts would interfere with the clearance order made by a local authority on a house that the authority had found unfit for human habitation. The Housing and Town Planning Act of 1909 gave a right of appeal to the Local Government Board, the only requirement being that before dismissing the appeal the board was required to hold a local inquiry.[61] Faced with an attempt to quash the confirmation of an order, the House, through Shaw, held that to require disclosure of the report and to insist that the applicant be heard in person "would be inconsistent, as I say, with efficiency, with practice, and with the true theory of complete parliamentary responsibility for departmental action."[62]

56. Frankfurter and Landis provided, for 1925, an enlightening contrast among the House of Lords, the Privy Council, and the highest courts in New York, Wisconsin, and Colorado. See Appendixes 1 and 2.

57. For a survey, see E. C. S. Wade, "Constitutional Law" 235.

58. [1915] A.C. 120 (1914). See Albert Venn Dicey, "The Development of Administrative Law in England" 148.

59. *Board of Educ.* v. *Rice*, [1911] A.C. 179; and see chap. 5, at 178–79.

60. Dicey, *Introduction* 148.

61. All the other rules for the appeal could be decided by the board.

62. [1915] A.C. 120, 137 (1914). He continued, "The judgements of the majority of the Court below appear to me, if I may say so with respect, to be dominated by the idea

Indeed, the panel of law lords—all of whom were or had been active Liberal politicians—seemed to be saying that responsible government made administrative law, even in the residual procedural sense, unnecessary. "My Lords, how can the judiciary be blind to the well-known facts applicable not only to the constitution but to the working of such branches of the Executive? The department is represented in Parliament by its responsible head. On the one hand he manages its affairs with such assistance as the Treasury sanctions, and on the other he becomes answerable in Parliament for every departmental act."[63] The fear that the courts might interfere with the actual workings of government had obsessed the liberals since the series of trade union cases a few years earlier; they responded by justifying Dicey's claim (and subconscious fear) that there was no *droit administratif* in England.

The die was cast. When, during the 1930s, *Minister of Health* v. *R., ex parte Yaffé*[64] examined another slum clearance scheme and defects in the scheme were discovered, it was held that, once the order was confirmed by the minister, any defects had automatically been cured.[65] In short, the courts had made a major retreat from those areas where policy conflicts could probably not be avoided. For the remainder of the period, at least as far as English constitutional law was concerned, the courts were involved only with skirmishes.

---

that the analogy of judicial methods and procedure should apply to departmental action. Judicial methods may, in many points of administration, be entirely unsuitable, and produce delays, expense, and public and private injury. . . . [W]hen a central administrative board deals with an appeal from a local authority it must do its best to act justly, and to reach just ends by just means. . . . But that the judiciary should presume to impose its own methods on administrative or executive officers is a usurpation"; ibid., 137–38.

63. Per Shaw, [1915] A.C. 120, 136 (1914), Haldane was perhaps a little more willing to retain judicial control:

They must deal with the question referred to them without bias, and they must give to each of the parties the opportunity of adequately presenting the case made. The decision must be come to in the spirit and with the sense of responsibility of a tribunal whose duty it is to mete out justice. But it does not follow that the procedure of every such tribunal must be the same. In the case of a Court of law tradition in this country has prescribed certain principles to which in the main the procedure must conform. But what that procedure is to be in detail must depend on the nature of the tribunal. In modern times it has become increasingly common for Parliament to give an appeal in matters which really pertain to administration, rather than to exercise of the judicial functions of an ordinary Court, to authorities whose functions are administrative and not in the ordinary sense judicial. Such a body as the Local Government Board has the duty of enforcing obligations on the individual which are imposed in the interests of the community. Its character is that of an organisation with executive functions. In this it resembles other great departments of the State. When, therefore, Parliament entrusts it with judicial duties, Parliament must be taken, in the absence of any declaration to the contrary, to have intended it to follow the procedure which is its own, and is necessary if it is to be capable of doing its work efficiently. [Ibid. 132]

64. [1931] A.C. 494.
65. Russell, who would have had little in common with the Liberal politicians who decided *Arlidge*, dissented; ibid. 536. (The majority was composed of Dunedin, Warrington, Tomlin, and Thankerton.)

Most of the constitutional battles, not unnaturally, revolved around the major political events. World War I produced its share of cases on personal liberty, foreign businesses, and compensation for acts of war.[66] *R. v. Halliday ex parte Zadig*[67] held that section 1(1) of the Defense of the Realm Consolidation Act of 1914, which allowed the King in Council to "issue regulations for securing the public safety and defense of the realm," was broad enough to encompass delegated legislation that suspended habeas corpus with respect to persons deemed to be of "hostile origins and associations." Intellectually, the appeal is interesting chiefly because of the vigorous dissent by Shaw. The owner of property was, however, rather more fortunate. In *Attorney-General v. De Keyser's Royal Hotel, Limited*,[68] the House held that, although the owner of requisitioned property was not entitled to rent for a hotel seized under the royal prerogative, on the facts of that particular case he was entitled to compensation under an 1842 act.

Foreign corporations caused problems both during and after the war. *Daimler Company v. Continental Tyre and Rubber Company (Great Britain)*[69] led even some of the more cautious members of the House to "lift the corporate veil" and so refuse to allow a corporation they then determined was an alien to sue in the English courts.[70] A differently constituted court, however, in *Rodriguez v. Speyer Brothers*[71] held, by a majority, that the principle that enemy aliens might not sue in the English courts did not apply to an action winding up a partnership on the outbreak of war.

The "Irish problem," which after the tragedy of 1916 led finally to the creation of the Irish Free State (and incidentally also to the abolition of Irish appeals to the Lords except for the six counties of Ulster that remained as part of the United Kingdom), also threw up its own series of problems. In *Johnstone v. Pedlar*,[72] the House held that the plea of act of state as a defense did not justify seizing, in the name of the Crown, the money of an American citizen who took part in the 1916 uprising; and in *Secretary of State for Home Affairs v. O'Brien*,[73] a case arising out of the attempt to deport someone held by the Irish Free State, the House held

66. T. E. Scrutton, "War and the Law" 116.

67. [1917] A.C. 260.

68. [1920] A.C. 508.

69. [1916] 2 A.C. 307.

70. Halsbury, Mersey, Kinnear, Atkinson, Shand, Parker, and Sumner may fairly be put into this category. Shaw and Parmoor, normally less cautious, opted for the narrower ground that the secretary had no authority to initiate the proceeding. E.g., see Shaw, ibid. 328 ff.

71. [1919] A.C. 59 (1918). The majority consisted of three Liberals—Finlay, Haldane, and Parmoor; the minority, of two Conservatives—Atkinson and Sumner.

72. [1921] 2 A.C. 262 (Ire.).

73. [1923] A.C. 603.

there could be no appeal from the granting, by the Court of Appeal, of a writ of habeas corpus.

It was in the Privy Council, however, that the law lords had the opportunity to exercise any urge they may have had to influence constitutional developments. Important appeals were by this time coming from countries other than India and the "old" dominions. In 1919, in *in re Southern Rhodesia*,[74] the Judicial Committee gave massive reparations, which many felt were undeserved, to the British South Africa Company.[75] In West Africa, partly as the result of the rise of an indigenous legal profession, there was litigation of various constitutional issues.[76] It was from Australia and especially Canada, however, that the most important constitutional appeals continued to come. With respect to Canada, Haldane saw as one of his most important tasks on becoming Chancellor the restoration of the powers of the provinces that Watson had so vigorously espoused and that Loreburn's Chancellorship had somewhat eroded.[77] In fact, Haldane went further in limiting the federal power under section 91 of the British North America Act than even Watson had gone, by developing the theory that the trade and commerce power was available to the dominion only in an emergency.[78] Moreover, Haldane's loyal

74. [1919] A.C. 217 (P.C. 1918).
75. On this see Claire Palley, *The Constitutional History and Law of Southern Rhodesia 1888–1965 with Special Reference to Imperial Control*, especially chap. 10.
See also, Fitzroy, 2 *Memoirs* 680. "I went to the Council-chamber to hear Lord Sumner deliver judgement in the Rhodesia lands case: he unravelled the complicated issue with great skill, and pronounced the whole decision of the Court in terms of impressive weight; on the whole the finding is a distinct advantage to the company. Lord Loreburn, who presided at the hearing, dissented from his colleagues, and, while agreeing with them that the company had no possessory title, would not have given a penny for the expenses of administration."
76. See, for instance, the use of habeus corpus in Nigeria: *Eshugbayi Eleko v. Government of Nigeria*, [1928] A.C. 459 (P.C.); *Eshugbayi Eleko v. Government of Nigeria No. (2)*, [1931] A.C. 662 (P.C.).
77. Haldane's "ambition is to sit on those appeals from the self-governing Dominions which raise judicial problems of the highest constitutional import, and so, as I reminded him, take up the great task of Watson"; Fitzroy, 2 *Memoirs* 441–42. On Haldane's intellectual debt to Watson, see Richard Burdon Haldane, "The Work for the Empire of the Judicial Committee of the Privy Council" 143.
78. See especially *in re Board of Commerce Act, 1919 and Combines and Fair Prices Act, 1919*, [1922] 1 A.C. 191 (P.C. 1920); *Toronto Elec. Comm'rs v. Snider*, [1925] A.C. 396 (P.C.).
Haldane took the view that Canada was not a true federation since the 1867 act had created a new federal government as well as new provincial governments; *Attorney-General for Australia v. Colonial Sugar Ref. Co.*, [1914] A.C. 237, 252–54 (P.C.). Haldane both restricted § 91 to matters of national interest that did not touch on the powers of the provinces under § 92, and gave very considerable protection to "property and civil rights," which had the effect of curbing the federal power to legislate. See R. F. V. Heuston, *Lives of the Lord Chancellors 1885–1940* 216–17.

attendance on the Judicial Committee over many years[79] ensured that the provincial bias, once restored, became entrenched.[80]

Sankey, who became Chancellor in 1929, did make a limited effort to return some power to the dominion government. Unlike Watson and Haldane's articulated position, Sankey shared Loreburn's view that a constitution was not just another statute. In reversing the Supreme Court of Canada and holding that women could be appointed to the Canadian Senate, Sankey noted that "the British North America Act planted in Canada a living tree capable of growth and expansion within its natural limits. . . . Their Lordships do not conceive it to be the duty of this Board—it is certainly not their desire—to cut down the provisions of the Act by a narrow and technical construction, but rather to give it a large and liberal interpretation."[81] Thus Sankey was prepared to do what Haldane was not,[82] and, in the context of the Statute of Westminster, to allow Canada to abolish criminal appeals.[83] Sankey also presided in the decision that held air navigation to be exclusively within the power of the dominion,[84] and shortly thereafter broadcasting was held to be exclusively a federal matter.[85]

Yet the work of Watson and Haldane was sufficiently entrenched that attempts to change direction fundamentally and to give greater power to the dominion, which most scholars thought was the intention of the framers of the confederation, were unlikely to have more than limited success. Moreover, Hailsham, when he became Chancellor in 1935, saw little with which to disagree in the Watson-Haldane approach.[86] Thus when Canadian Prime Minister Bennett's Conservative government passed its "New Deal" legislation in 1934 and 1935, the Privy Council solemnly struck down vital parts of it. During November

79. On this see Sir Claud Schuster, "Lord Haldane as Lord Chancellor," in *Viscount Haldane of Cloan*, ed. Gray (London, 1929) at 30. See also Heuston, *Lives* 216.

80. The only major decision upholding the dominion power was *Attorney-General for Ontario* v. *Attorney-General for Canada*, [1925] A.C. 750 (P.C.).

81. *Edwards* v. *Attorney-General for Canada*, [1930] A.C. 124, 136 (P.C. 1929).

82. *Nadan* v. *The King*, [1926] A.C. 482 (P.C.).

83. *British Coal Corp.* v. *The King*, [1935] A.C. 500 (P.C.). For the context of the Statute of Westminster, see especially Hector Hughes, *National Sovereignty and Judicial Autonomy in the British Commonwealth of Nations*.

84. *In re Regulation & Control of Aeronautics in Canada*, [1932] A.C. 54 (P.C. 1931).

85. *In re Regulation & Control of Radio Communications in Canada*, [1932] A.C. 304 (P.C.).

86. "It is possible, though it cannot be proved, that the desire of Mr. Ramsey MacDonald in 1935 to safeguard his son's political career, and the anxiety of Lord Hailsham to leave the lower office for the more exalted and better paid position on the Woolsack—circumstances which sent Lord Sankey into retirement—invalidated a large part of the Canadian 'New Deal' "; W. Ivor Jennings, "Constitutional Interpretation—the Experience of Canada" at 1, 36.

1936 the Judicial Committee[87] heard five related appeals and gave judgment on them in January 1937. Atkin, who presided, announced that, unlike Sankey's "living tree," "[w]hile the ship of state now sails on longer ventures and into foreign water she still retains the watertight compartments which are an essential part of her original structure."[88] The result of the "watertight compartments" was that, in a single day, the Judicial Committee struck down the efforts of the Ottawa government to implement the ILO (International Labor Organization) conventions by providing minimum wage laws and by limiting hours of work,[89] the unemployment and social insurance legislation,[90] and federal marketing boards.[91] Only the relatively unimportant provisions with respect to unfair trade practices survived.[92] After this mayhem,[93] it was merely a matter of time before appeals were abolished; indeed, had not World War II broken out in 1939, Canada would have taken this step in 1940.[94] Perhaps the remarkable thing was that appeals had survived for eighty years after independence.[95]

It was also during this period that the Australian constitution came in for more detailed and formalistic interpretation. The original assumption in 1900 had been that the Commonwealth of Australia Act would be interpreted as a constitution, rather than just another statute, but that attitude had begun to fade by 1920.[96] During the 1930s the Privy Council encouraged a more formalistic approach by its interpretations of section 92 of the 1900 act. The purpose of the section had been to abolish

87. Atkin, Thankerton, Macmillan, Wright, and Sir Sidney Rowlatt. Wright may have dissented in at least one of these cases. See Robert Anderson Wright, "Obituary for the Rt. Hon. Sir Lyman Poore Duff, G.C.M.G." 1123. F. R. Scott, "Labour Conventions Case" 114.

88. *Attorney-General for Canada* v. *Attorney-General for Ontario*, [1937] A.C. 326, 354 (P.C.).

89. Ibid. 326.

90. Ibid. 355.

91. *Attorney-General for British Columbia* v. *Attorney-General for Canada*, [1937] A.C. 368, 391 (P.C.).

92. Ibid. 368; *Attorney-General for Ontario* v. *Attorney-General for Canada*, [1937] A.C. 405 (P.C.).

93. On these cases, see also Paul Freund, *The Supreme Court of the United States* 107–8. For a more sympathetic interpretation, see G. P. Browne, *The Judicial Committee and the British North America Act*, passim.

94. Coen G. Pierson, *Canada and the Privy Council* 69 ff.

95. The appeals, written on vital issues that affect Canada to this day, were often heard in a day and decided shortly thereafter without the benefit of written briefs. Few of the law lords had ever visited Canada, although Haldane had been there for two days; Haldane, *Autobiography* 279. Moreover the "colonials" were heavily patronized by the English. For instance, the Clerk of the Privy Council, Fitzroy, noted in his diary, of Sir Charles Fitzpatrick, Chief Justice of Canada, "Fitzpatrick is much above the usual type of colonial lawyer, a man of polished manners, intelligent address and not without distinct judicial virtue"; Fitzroy, 2 *Memoirs* 490.

96. See Edward McWhinney, *Judicial Review in the English Speaking World* 72.

customs barriers between the states.[97] First the Australian judges used this guide to eliminate state quotas on agricultural products, but then the Privy Council in the 1930s struck down both state and federal agricultural quotas to leave a legal vacuum in such matters.[98] Although Lord Wright later came close to apologizing publicly for the decision,[99] it laid the basis for the rather bizarre laissez-faire decision in the 1949 *Bank Nationalization* case.[100] If, in general, during this period the Privy Council was the recipient of many laudatory statements, especially from those who were engaged in its operation,[101] in retrospect it may be seriously questioned whether much of this praise was not misconceived.[102]

In any event, this heady stuff of constitutional law had no serious counterpart in the air of English law. Public law in the United Kingdom might involve issues of international law: what, for instance amounted to a sovereign state?[103] There was, however, no question of going behind the Foreign Office certificate, even with the fluidity of the situation created by the Spanish civil war.[104] Meanwhile, with the central government departments effectively protected by *Arlidge*, the law lords might readily establish and announce their views on public affairs only through the control of activities of local authorities or when some area of private law, like charities, called for their views on the public interest.

The courts still had the power to control the activities of local authorities through the use of the ultra vires power. In *Roberts v. Hopwood*[105] the House was asked to decide whether the payment by the Poplar Borough Council of four pounds per week wages to its lowest-grade employees was ultra vires.[106] The district auditor found that such

---

97. "On the imposition of uniform duties of customs: trade, commerce and intercourse among the States whether by means of internal carriage or ocean navigation shall be absolutely free."

98. *James v. South Australia*, 40 Commw. L.R. 1 (1927); *James v. Cowan*, [1932] A.C. 542 (P.C.); *James v. Commonwealth of Australia*, [1936] A.C. 578 (P.C.).

99. Robert Anderson Wright, "Section 92—A Problem Piece" 145, 159.

100. *Commonwealth of Australia v. Bank of New South Wales*, [1950] A.C. 235 (P.C. 1949).

101. E.g., per Haldane, *Hull v. McKenna*, [1926] Ir. R. 402; address by Morton, Thirty-First Annual Meeting, Canadian Bar Association, 32 *Proceedings* 107 (1949); Barnett Hollander, *Colonial Justice*.

102. By the 1930s there was increasing dissatisfaction with the Privy Council's Indian work. See G. H. Gadbois, "Evolution of the Federal Court of India" 19.
Similarly, the Privy Council caused increasing dissatisfaction in the Roman-Dutch jurisdictions. See especially *Pearl Assurance v. Union of South Africa Gov't.*, [1934] A.C. 570 (P.C.); "Note," 51 *Law Quarterly Review* 274 (1935); "Note," 52 *South African Law Journal* 277 (1935).

103. E.g., *Duff Dev. Corp. v. Government of Kelantan*, [1924] A.C. 797.

104. *Compania Naviera Vascongada v. S.S. Cristina*, [1938] A.C. 485; *Spanish Republican v. S.S. "Arantzazu Mendi,"* [1939] A.C. 256.

105. [1925] A.C. 578.

106. See Brian Keith-Lucas, "Popularism" 52; Harold Laski, *Essays in Law and Government*, chap. 9.

payments were not wages but gratuities, since the cost of living had fallen by a quarter during the year, and the wages were therefore far in excess of what the workers could command in the marketplace. The councillors, who had been surcharged, argued that the wages were those that should be paid by model employers. The House, reversing the Court of Appeal,[107] came down unanimously on the side of ratepayers against the views of the Council. While probably justified in law, some of the law lords unwisely allowed their intemperate political views to show, a situation that, according to Laski, might be "fatal to the esteem in which judges should be held. . . . It is an easy step from the *Poplar* judgement to the conclusion that the House of Lords is, in entire good faith, the unconscious servant of a single class in the community."[108]

On other occasions the law lords gave clues, in private law cases, about how they might behave if they had more latitude in public law. The law lords showed increasing religious toleration in holding in *Bourne* v. *Keane*[109] that a gift to say masses for the dead might be a charity and therefore indirectly be entitled to a public subsidy by escaping taxation. In *Bowman* v. *Secular Society, Limited*[110] the House went even further, by holding that an agnostic organization was not only not an illegal organization, but might receive gifts. Yet at other times and in other situations the law lords exhibited, if not a more conservative, at least a more conventional approach. In *in re Viscountess Rhondda*,[111] Birkenhead led the Committee for Privileges to the conclusion that the Sex Disqualification (Removal) Act of 1919 did not apply to the House of Lords, while in the libel case of *Sutherland* v. *Stopes*,[112] some of the law lords allowed their hostility to birth control to become all too apparent.

In one sense tax law did not give an opportunity for the law lords to exhibit their attitudes toward public affairs. By the end of Loreburn's tenure as Lord Chancellor, the approach to tax law was largely settled as a formalistic one, although Loreburn had fought at least partially against an arid system whose tax avoidance potential he appreciated. Even though he was a Liberal, Haldane's view of the role of the courts was noticeably more legalistic, and his instinct was to sympathize with a narrow interpretation of statutes.[113] A broader view was still being taken

107. [1924] 2 K.B. 695 (C.A.) (Lords Justices Scrutton and Atkin; Lord Justice Bankes, dissenting).

108. Laski, *Essays* 219–20. Laski, who taught at the Harvard Law School before moving to the London School of Economics, writing almost at the same time as Goodhart, began this essay with the observation, "The fiction that judges do not legislate has long since been abandoned by all who care for a conscious and realistic jurisprudence."

109. [1919] A.C. 815.

110. [1917] A.C. 406.

111. [1922] 2 A.C. 339.

112. [1925] A.C. 47 (1924).

113. He expressed his views most clearly in *IRC* v. *Herbert*, [1913] A.C. 326, 332

by Liberal law lords such as Shaw[114] but a powerful advocate had been added to the supporters of a strict interpretation of tax legislation in the person of Moulton.[115] There was at least one uncomfortable 2–2 split in a tax decision,[116] but by 1914 the future approach to tax law was settled. In *Attorney-General* v. *Milne*,[117] the House was forced to construe various sections in the 1909–10 Finance Act, to determine whether settled estate duty was payable, as was general estate duty, in dispositions made within three years of the death of the settlor. The decision was 3–1 in favor of the view that it was not, although Parliament apparently intended the opposite result. The majority expressed the strictest view toward taxing statutes. Said Haldane, presiding:

> It may be that, if probabilities, apart from the words used, are to be looked at, there is, on the construction which the Court of Appeal have put on the statute, a casus omissus which the Legislature was unlikely to have contemplated. But, my Lords, all we are permitted to look at is the language used. If it has a natural meaning we cannot depart from that meaning unless, reading the statute as a whole, the context directs us to do so. Speculation as to a different construction having been contemplated by those who framed the Act is inadmissible, above all in a statute which imposes taxation.[118]

All but one of the other lords took the same line.[119] Only Dunedin, the recently appointed Scottish law lord, dissented. His argument was summarized in a passage in which he said:

> I quite bow to the rule as to taxing statutes. But after all, the question is what the words mean, and the expressions used must be given fair play. If, as here, where the word "passes" is used in any section except the 5th you are bound to give it

---

(Scot.). "The duty of a court of law is simply to take the statute it has to construe as it stands, and to construe its words according to their natural significance. While reference may be made to the state of the law, and the material facts and events with which it is apparent that Parliament was dealing, it is not admissible to speculate on the probable opinions and motives of those who framed the legislation, excepting in so far as these appear from the language of the statute."

114. See ibid. 349: "I desire to state broadly that I do not think a Finance Act in the United Kingdom ought to be—unless that be logically compelled—diverted from its plain financial object and meaning by considerations which do not touch general finance but affect merely the feudal conveyancing of land in Scotland."

115. See ibid. 357. See also the speech of Moulton in *Earl Fitzwilliam* v. *IRC*, [1914] A.C. 753, 762.

116. In *Lumsden* v. *IRC*, [1914] A.C. 877, the breakdown was odd. Haldane and Shaw found for the Revenue; Moulton and Parmoor for the taxpayer.

117. [1914] A.C. 765.

118. Ibid. 771.

119. The conservative Atkinson was even firmer. "To succeed the Crown must bring the case within the letter of that enactment. It is not enough to bring the case within the spirit of it, or to shew that if the section be not construed as the Crown contends it should be construed[,] property which ought to be taxed will escape taxation. . . . These evils, if such they be, must, if they exist, be cured by legislation. Judicial tribunals must in interpreting these taxing Acts stick to the letter of the statute"; ibid. 771–72.

the extended meaning in order to make sense, I think it is not giving the words fair play suddenly to revert to another meaning in § 5, a section which is inextricably intertwined with the other sections, and which, if construed as that argument would construe it, leaves a perfectly obvious casus improvisus; for why should a will bring liability for the duty—other dispositions bring none?"[120]

By then, however, even Dunedin's approach was that of *vox clamantis in deserto.*

The narrow approach to tax statutes continued during the twenties.[121] The 1930 budget, however, facing an international financial crisis, ignored the preaching of Keynes, and included wholesale tax increases;[122] but it also included measures to prevent tax evasion by large taxpayers. As the tax rate rose, a natural human instinct for the preservation of material possessions was enough to ensure that during the 1930s investment schemes, surtax avoidance schemes, and estate duty schemes came into their own. This development meant that the House of Lords, sitting judicially, would sooner or later be presented with problems where it would have to decide, on apparently objective grounds, whether such devices amounted to illegal evasions or were merely legal avoidances. The relationship between the judicial functions of the Lords and the taxing functions of Parliament, as represented by the annual Finance Acts, became even more complex. By 1935, in *Inland Revenue Commissioners* v. *Duke of Westminster*[123] the House appeared to have taken its obsession both with literal interpretation and with form as opposed to substance to an extreme.

With the rise in the tax rates, the Duke of Westminster, in lieu of salaries, entered into covenants with his "servants and retainers." The covenants were to last for seven years, or the joint lives of the Duke and the servant, and while legally the servant was still free to claim wages for services rendered, in fact the servants gave the Duke's solicitors undertakings that they would not seek more than the covenanted amounts. The result of this maneuver was basically that the Duke claimed to be

---

The most recently appointed law lord, Parker, shared this view. "The Finance Act is a taxing statute, and if the Crown claims a duty thereunder it must shew that such duty is imposed by clear and unambiguous words"; ibid. 781.

120. Ibid. 778.

121. E.g., *Nevill* v. *IRC*, [1924] A.C. 385; *Foulsham* v. *Pickles*, [1925] A.C. 458; *IRC* v. *Fisher's Executors*, [1926] A.C. 395.

122. The Snowden budget of the Labour government increased the basic tax rate to 4/6 in £; and increased the rate of supertax and estate duty.

123. *IRC* v. *Duke of Westminster*, [1936] A.C. 1 (1935).

The Duke was apparently not particularly grateful for the generous tax treatment awarded him. He remained a supporter of Hitler, giving a grand party at the Savoy to celebrate the invasion of Poland. As His Grace was leaving, he met a downcast Churchill, whom he cheerfully greeted as a "Jew-lover"; William Stevenson, *A Man Called Intrepid* 46.

able to deduct the amount of the covenanted payments from his total income for the purposes of surtax. In other words, he argued that his new device had transformed salaries that would have to be paid out of taxed increase into covenanted gifts that were treated like charitable deductions. The Revenue authorities not unnaturally disagreed,[124] arguing that the covenanted payments were, in substance, wages or salaries. Yet when the Revenue argued that in tax cases the courts might ignore the legal position and look at "the substance of the matter,"[125] the argument brought a swift reaction from the majority of four law lords.[126] Only Atkin was prepared to examine the substance of the transactions.

The actual conscious or subconscious motives of the law lords in the Westminster case provide a fertile field for speculation, but its effects were clear. The case finally gave the balance of advantage to those with resources sufficient to hire the best legal talent, who might then camouflage the substance of their transaction under some formal disguise.[127] It did not, of course, mean that the taxpayer always won in litigation.[128] It did, however, signal that tax litigation had become an arid, semantic (and often antisocial) vicious circle, and frequently the result of this was a windfall for the taxpayer.[129] Worse still, the attitude that led the judges

124. Asserting that the payments were "pure income profit, and therefore taxable under a different schedule." See G. S. A. Wheatcroft, 1 *British Tax Encyclopedia*, para. 1-330.

125. See Wheatcroft on the subject of tax avoidance and evasion; 1 *British Tax Encyclopedia*, paras. 1-017, 1-018, 1-69.

126. Despite the fact that the argument was not unknown in English tax law. See *Helby v. Matthews*, [1895] A.C. 471, 475; *IRC v. Blott*, [1921] 2 A.C. 171, 201; *IRC v. Fisher's Executors*, [1926] A.C. 395, 410; and see Barry Pinson, *Revenue Law* § 39:03.

127. As a leading tax expert noted in a somewhat elliptical remark, which nevertheless captured the spirit of the period, judicial opinion did not, in general, view "lawful tax avoidance with disfavour"; Wheatcroft, 1 *British Tax Encyclopedia*, para 1-070.

128. *IRC v. Crossman*, [1937] A.C. 26 (1936), was unfair to the taxpayer. That appeal concerned the valuation of a testator's shares, which were subject to rigid restrictions affecting alienation and transfer. According to § 7(5) of the Finance Act of 1894, such shares had to be valued for estate duty according to a "price which . . . such property would fetch in the open market." The personal representatives of the deceased were naturally contending for a lower price because of the restrictions, whereas the Revenue argued that such restrictions did not affect the intrinsic value of the shares. The major question facing the House was whether or not to recognize the fact that the transfer restrictions had the effect of lowering the price of such shares. The majority of the House (Hailsham, Blanesburgh, and Roche) decided that the restrictions were only a further ingredient in the whole bundle of ingredients that made up the share—such as the right to receive dividends and transmission of shares and that it was therefore wrong to consider the value to be that of a restricted price fixed under the articles.

The dissenters looked more to the substance of the transaction. E.g., per Macmillan, "I am of the opinion that neither the rights of pre-emption nor any of the other conditions and restrictions inherently affecting the alienation of these shares can justifiably be left out of account when conceiving them to be exposed for sale in the open market"; ibid. 70. See also Russell, ibid. 68.

129. For instance, the House insisted that if property were assessed under Schedule A (real property assessment), any profits or rents from the property beyond those caught by

to examine form rather than substance proved remarkably difficult to undo even when the legislature did intervene.[130] It was perhaps not surprising that, despite the formal rate of tax in Britain, the effective rate was noticeably less severe, while the apparently ferocious estate duty rate had almost no redistributive effect.[131]

Beyond constitutional and tax cases, however, the other public and quasi-public law areas were probably more satisfactory. Many felt the House's entry into criminal law (subject to the strict filter provided by the 1907 act) was successful. *Director of Public Prosecutions* v. *Beard*[132] and *Woolmington* v. *Director of Public Prosectuions*,[133] respectively restated the law with respect to drunkenness and manslaughter, both matters of increasing importance with the wider use of the automobile. Meanwhile, workmen's compensation cases continued to come to the House with great regularity. While the conservative law lords occasionally exhibited hostility to the system of compensation,[134] in general the House guarded the legislation from formalistic interpretation. Any hint, for instance, that workmen might be allowed to contract out, was repelled,[135] while the House also maintained its earlier position that the acts should be treated "factually" rather than encumbered with doctrine in order that the original purpose of protecting workmen might be maintained.[136] In the 1930s the House went further and began the process of linking protection of the worker with expanding liability in tort as a

---

Schedule A could not be included in the income schedule (B). The Schedule A taxation, even if it covered only a small part of the real value, was exhaustive; *Fry* v. *Salisbury House Estates*, [1930] A.C. 432; *Whelan* v. *Leney & Co.*, [1936] A.C. 363; *Neumann* v. *IRC*, [1934] A.C. 215. However, the Revenue persuaded the House that some of the fruits of a *Fry* situation might be assessed for surtax.

For a formalistic interpretation with respect to the stamp tax, see *Stanyforth* v. *IRC*, [1930] A.C. 339.

130. Parliament began its post-1945 attempt to force judges to look at the substance of this transaction in § 28 of the Finance Act of 1960. See, for instance, Lord Justice Danckwerts, in *IRC* v. *Cleary*, [1966] Ch. 365 (C.A.):

Section 28 is a highly artificial section and not all easy to follow in its complicated language. The objects are clear: to enable the Inland Revenue Commissioners to out-manoevre the ingenuity of wealthy taxpayers in arranging their business affairs so as to avoid or minimize tax. How delightful it must be to a taxing officer to have the power to counteract "a tax advantage," which a person is in a position to obtain, or has obtained, by assessments or other adjustments! The section is indeed a tax collector's dream. Gone was the old principle that a citizen was entitled to arrange his affairs so as to minimize his liability to tax. I sympathise with the sisters, who will suffer such heavy demands for tax. All taxation is confiscation and this is a very severe case.

131. See Richard Titmuss, *Income Distribution and Social Change, passim.*

132. [1920] A.C. 479 (murder committed during a drunken rape).

133. [1935] A.C. 462. T. Unger, "Silence as Admission of Guilt" 70, 71.

134. E.g., Carson, dissenting in *Russell* v. *Rudd*, [1923] A.C. 309, 315; Atkinson in *Ocean Coal Co.* v. *Davies*, [1927] A.C. 271, 281, 283, (1926).

135. *Russell* v. *Rudd*, [1923] A.C. 309.

136. E.g., *Stephen* v. *Cooper*, [1929] A.C. 570 (Scot.).

whole, with the result that, since that time, these areas of law have been more properly treated as part of the law of tort.

The Triumph of Private Law

If one makes the generalization that in public law the House distinguished itself chiefly by keeping out of the area and, if the work of the law lords in tax law emphasized the inadequacies of the judiciary in handling social policies, in private law the situation could scarcely have been more different. It is true that, with the additional Lords of Appeal (from four to seven) and with the relatively large number of former Lord Chancellors available as the result of the changes of ministries, it became more difficult to generalize as the membership of panels of judges changed rapidly. Overall, however, the trend was more than clear in private law. After a shaky beginning, the House of Lords moved into a golden period in private law. During the 1930s the Grand Style made a brief return, only to be cut short during World War II.

While by no means approaching contract in the spirit that produced such doctrines as strict tender, the early years of the period, as far as contract went, reflected more an urge to restate existing principles than an intent to break new ground. *Dunlop Pneumatic Tyre Company* v. *Selfridge and Company*,[137] was a classic restatement of the view that only parties to a contract might sue on it,[138] which, in that case meant that a manufacturer might not enforce terms of an agreement as to the resale price of goods supplied, when there was no contract between the manufacturer and retailer. Nothing in the House's thinking, however, showed any hint that price fixing might be in restraint of trade and so would violate public policy. Similarly, the House saw nothing wrong in *North-Western Salt Company* v. *Electrolytic Alkali Company*[139] with enforcing a contract that fixed prices throughout the salt industry. In fact, Haldane had little doubt that where businessmen were concerned the law regarded "the parties as the best judges of what is reasonable."[140]

---

137. [1915] A.C. 847. See G. C. Cheshire, C. H. S. Fifoot, and M. P. Furmston, *The Law of Contract* 66, 431–32.

138. Haldane said, "In the law of England certain principles are fundamental. One is that only a person who is a party to a contract can sue on it. Our law knows nothing of a *jus quaesitum tertii* arising by way of contract. Such a right may be conferred by way of property, as, for example, under a trust, but it cannot be conferred on a stranger to a contract as a right to enforce the contract *in personam*"; [1915] A.C. 847, 853; and see Theo Chorley, "Liberal Trends in Present Day Commercial Law" p. 272.

139. [1914] A.C. 461. In *Mason* v. *Provident Clothing & Supply Co.*, [1913] A.C. 724, a Liberal House (Haldane, Shaw, Moulton, Dunedin) refused to enforce restraints against a door-to-door salesman.

140. [1914] A.C. 461, 471. Haldane was no believer in that aspect of laissez-faire that lauded competition, but rather in that aspect of laissez-faire that believed in not intervening in the economy. "Unquestionably the combination in question was one the purpose of

Also during these early years the House rejected any idea that a representation made before the contract was complete could either be a term of the contract or give rise to a collateral contract.[141] In *Sinclair* v. *Brougham*,[142] moreover, Haldane and Sumner between them not only rejected any general concept of restitution in English law but also restricted quasi contract within narrow limits.[143]

Slowly, however, a different spirit emerged in the work of the House. It is true that the House never fully appreciated the changes that had occurred in the equality—or rather inequality—of bargaining power,[144] although in *Dunlop Pneumatic Tyre Company* v. *New Garage and Motor Company*,[145] the House attacked the worst excesses of penalty clauses masquerading as liquidated damages. The approach to restraint of trade cases also changed slowly,[146] and the law lords began the process of

---

which was to regulate supply and keep up prices. But an ill-regulated supply and unremunerative prices may, in point of fact, be disadvantageous to the public. Such a state of things may, if it is not controlled, drive manufacturers out of business, or lower wages, or so cause unemployment and labour disturbance"; ibid. 469.

141. *Heilbut, Symons & Co.* v. *Buckleton*, [1913] A.C. 30 (1912). Again it was Haldane who set the tone of the proceedings. He took the view that representations of fact could only be terms of the contract "if the context so requires"; ibid. 36–39. The case also helped cut off the growing remedy by way of collateral contract that, as was seen in chap. 5, had been developing in the Edwardian period.

142. [1914] A.C. 398. Halsbury had already set his face against the concept of restitution, for "it seems to me a very formidable proposition indeed to say that any Court has a right to enforce what may seem to them to be just, apart from common law or statute. . . . I cannot understand how it can be asserted that it is part of the common law that where one person gets some advantage from the act of another a right of contribution towards the expense from that act arises on behalf of the person who has done it." Thus when a vessel had been damaged as the result of an insurable risk, underwriters could not claim a contribution from the owner who used the period the vessel had to spend in dry dock to have a classification survey made; *Ruabon S.S. Co.* v. *London Assurance*, [1900] A.C. 6, 9 (1899). Similarly, a ship repairer was held entitled to recover nothing when he performed the repairs in a way other than the authorized one; *Forman & Co.* v. *The Ship "Liddlesdale"*, [1906] A.C. 190 (P.C.). "It seems hard that the plaintiffs should not be paid for work which they have done; but such is the effect of contracting to work for a lump sum and failing to do the work"; per Hobhouse, ibid. 205.

143. Although an effective remedy was given to the depositors in a bankrupt building society on the facts, it was held that no remedy could be given by way of quasi contract or restitution unless "the law could consistently impute to the defendant at least the fiction of a promise"; [1914] A.C. 398; per Haldane at 417. For an even stronger attack on any such principle, see per Sumner, ibid. 455–56.

144. E.g., *Dawsons, Ltd.* v. *Bonnin*, [1922] All E.R. 38 (H.L.); *Macuara* v. *Northern Assurance Co.*, [1925] A.C. 619 (Ire.).

145. [1915] A.C. 79 (1914). See also *Watts, Watts & Co.* v. *Mitsui & Co.*, [1917] A.C. 227, especially per Finlay at 234.

146. In *Fitch* v. *Dewes*, [1921] 2 A.C. 158, the House enforced a contract of employment between a solicitor and his managing clerk with a provision restricting the latter's later employment within a seven-mile radius. More surprisingly, the House struck down a milk cooperative scheme, including an exclusive sale arrangement, on the ground it was in restraint of trade; *McEllistrim* v. *Ballymacelligott Co-operative Agricultural & Dairy Soc'y*, [1919] A.C. 548 (Ire.).

ameliorating the strict doctrine of privity of contract by emphasizing the principle, inherited from Equity, that allowed an action by a stranger to the contract if it could be shown that one of the parties had contracted as trustee.[147] Indeed, in *Elder, Dempster and Company v. Paterson, Zochonis and Company*,[148] the House may have gone further than it intended when, in developing a doctrine of vicarious immunity, it allowed a shipowner to rely on exemption clauses inserted by a charterer when a shipper sued for damage to his goods.[149] The same may be said of the Privy Council when, in *Lord Strathcona Steamship Company v. Dominion Coal Company*,[150] the doctrine of negative or equitable covenants was applied to a vessel so that a purchaser with notice was bound by a preexisting charter party. Again it was a doctrine that later courts either ignored or restricted.[151]

World War I forced the House of Lords to consider the doctrine of impossibility or commercial frustration on various occasions; when would the courts hold a valid contract no longer binding because external circumstances had changed too dramatically? The House responded, in keeping with its hostility to solutions that savored of anything so vague as an equitable solution, by expanding its concept of the implied term, which Halsbury, absorbing the concept developed by the Court of Appeal, had popularized. As Loreburn explained it in *F. A. Tamplin Steamship Company v. Anglo-Mexican Petroleum Products Company*,[152] "[A] Court can and ought to examine the contract and the circumstances in which it was made, not of course, to vary, but only to explain it, in order to see whether or not from the nature of it the parties must have made their bargain on the footing that a particular thing or state of things would continue to exist. And if they must have done so, then a term to that effect will be implied, though it be not expressed in the contract." With such a start, the House then had to work out when an event was sufficiently severe to amount to a frustrating one,[153] although as time

---

147. Thus the House held that a charterer was trustee for the broker who negotiated a charter party; *Les Affreteurs Réunis S.A. v. Walford, Leopold (London), Ltd.*, [1919] A.C. 801. See also *Performing Rights Soc'y v. London Theatre of Varieties*, [1924] A.C. 1 (1923). For the application of the doctrine in a Canadian appeal see *Vanderpitte v. Preferred Accident Ins. Corp.*, [1933] A.C. 70 (P.C. 1932).

148. [1924] A.C. 522.

149. The doctrine was substantially restricted in *Midland Silicones, Ltd. v. Scruttons, Ltd.*, [1962] A.C. 446 (1961).

150. [1926] A.C. 108 (P.C. 1925).

151. E.g., *Greenhalgh v. Mallard*, [1943] 2 All E.R. 234, 239 (H.L.).

152. [1916] 2 A.C. 397, 403.

153. An apparently permanent requisition of a contractor was sufficient, while the temporary interruption of a twelve-month charterparty was not. Cf. *Metropolitan Water Bd. v. Dick, Kerr & Co.*, [1918] A.C. 199 (1917); and *Bank Line, Ltd. v. Arthur Capel & Co.*, [1919] A.C. 435 (1918).

went on the law lords seemed increasingly aware that what they were in fact doing was imposing a fair or just solution.[154]

Yet while the twenties brought a gradual expansion in both approach and doctrine, it was in the thirties that major strides were made, during the time when the House contained two masters of contract: Atkin and Wright. In this period Atkin performed for English contract law what Cardozo, at the same time, was doing for American. Atkin balanced the need for stability and predictability with the importance of change and the needs of business in remaking whole doctrines, such as that of mistake in *Bell* v. *Lever Brothers*.[155] Meanwhile, Wright was arguing the un-English position that it was unreasonable to expect to develop contract doctrines that applied to all types of factual situations.[156] Overall there was, by this time, in total contradistinction to the nineteenth-century insistence on the absolute need for acceptance to be in the exact terms of the offer, a more flexible approach to the making of the contracts.[157] Meanwhile, after having downplayed the principle of public policy for many years, the law lords in the 1930s began the process of revitalizing it as another weapon for either enforcing or refusing to enforce contractual relationships.[158]

154. Even Sumner, who liked his rules "hard," had realized by the time *Bank Line, Ltd.* v. *Arthur Capel & Co.* was decided that the doctrine was, at best, based on a "presumed common intention"; [1919] A.C. 435, 455 (1918). Later, he went so far as to admit that frustration was "a device by which the rules as to absolute contracts are reconciled with a special exception which justice demands"; *Hirji Mulji* v. *Cheong Yue S.S. Co.*, [1926] A.C. 497, 510 (P.C.). This approach was carried to its extreme by Wright in *Joseph Constantine S.S. Line, Ltd.* v. *Imperial Smelting Corp.*, [1942] A.C. 154, 185 (1941).

155. [1932] A.C. 161 (1931). There the House refused to rescind compensation agreements made to "buy out" the contracts of senior executives when, after the payments were made, it emerged that the executives were in violation of their contracts of employment and thus might have been dismissed without the payment of any compensation. The majority (Blanesburgh, Atkin, Thankerton) held that mutual mistake was not available because there was mistake only as to the quality and not as to the subject matter of the service contracts. The minority (Hailsham, Warrington) would have allowed rescission.

156. *Luxor (Eastbourne), Ltd.* v. *Cooper*, [1941] A.C. 108, 129 (1940).

157. In *Hillas & Co.* v. *Arcos, Ltd.*, [1932] All E.R. 494 (H.L.), in which the basic question was whether an option to purchase further "standards of timber" could be construed as a contract in the light of previous dealings, or whether the option was not intended to bind either party, being merely a basis for a future agreement, the House decided that an intention to be bound could be spelled out of the arrangement. This was apparently balanced by the rather strict holding in *Arcos* v. *Ronaasen & Son*, [1933] A.C. 470, namely, that goods could be rejected, even if of merchantable quality, if they did not correspond to the description in the contract. Yet *Luxor, Ltd.* v. *Cooper*, [1941] A.C. 108 (1940), at the very end of the period, seemed to be restating the broad scope of the first *Arcos* decision.

158. In *Fender* v. *St. John-Mildmay*, [1938] A.C. 1 (1937), a promise of marriage, made between decree nisi and the decree absolute, was held enforceable, although a promise to marry made by a married person was void as contrary to public policy. The doctrine of public policy was raised once again in *Beresford* v. *Royal Ins. Co.*, [1938] A.C. 586, where it was held that the personal representatives of the deceased could not recover policy

The opening up of tort began even earlier.[159] At the very time Haldane was beating back attempts to weaken the privity of contract doctrine, he was in fact party to the decision in *Nocton* v. *Lord Ashburton*[160] that allowed a client to sue his solicitor for mala fides short of fraud. Since contract had not been pleaded and the tort of negligence, independent of contract, was not yet available, and because *Derry* v. *Peek* had defined deceit narrowly, the decision required all of Haldane's legal dexterity. In an elegant speech, he argued that *Derry* v. *Peek* had decided only the question of deceit.[161] It was therefore open to the House to find that the plaintiff was entitled to recover, not in deceit nor for breach of contract, but for a misrepresentation in breach of duty imposed by the court in such special relationships as the one between solicitors and clients.

Nocton v. *Lord Ashburton* was in the tradition of extending liability, even for financial loss, which had regained momentum in *Lloyd* v. *Grace, Smith and Company*. In the interwar years, however, the most dramatic developments came in the area of remedying loss resulting from physical injury; indeed, during this time the House of Lords finally developed an independent tort of negligence, unencumbered by any requirement of contract and unburdened by any notions of "dangerous chattels" or remnants of nuisance. The concept of negligence, though by no means strange to the common law, had not before been subjected to rigorous analysis as a functional remedy in its own right, and it would have been a bold lawyer indeed who, in 1930, would have dared to plead negligence without reliance upon some other cause of action or at least some other legal concept. Negligence had always had its place in the law "as an element in some more complex relationship or in some specialised breach of duty." The impact of *Donoghue* v. *Stevenson*[162] was to establish the existence and breach of a duty of care untrammeled by other considerations.

Of course, the decision did not come out of this air nor was it merely *in nubibus*. The House, at least from 1929 on had been moving toward the decision; and, as was to happen again,[163] the House used Scottish

---

moneys where the assured had committed suicide while sane, on the ground that it would be contrary to public policy to assist what would be the fruits of crime, committed by the assured. Both cases gave the Lords not only an opportunity to display their own personal predispositions, but also a platform to discuss the role of the judges generally.

159. See generally Wolfgang Friedmann, "Modern Trends in the Law of Torts" 39.

160. [1914] 2 A.C. 932.

161. The decision represented a conscious effort on Haldane's part to undo the worst excesses of *Derry* v. *Peek*; M. de W. Howe, ed., *Holmes-Pollock Letters* 322.

162. [1932] A.C. 562 (Scot.). On the long-term historical implications of the decision, see R. F. V. Heuston, "*Donoghue* v. *Stevenson* in Retrospect" 1.

163. For instance, during the fifties and sixties Scottish decisions appeared to play the same role, for example, in the erosion of the law on Crown privilege.

cases to "feel out" major changes in the common law. Thus, in *Oliver v. Saddler and Company*,[164] the Scottish pursuer (plaintiff) argued that she was entitled to damages for the negligence of respondents in not providing a "duty of reasonable inspection."[165] The appellant rested her case on a simple breach of "a duty of ordinary care—regardless of any contractual position; the respondents attempted to bring the question within a contract of gratuitous hire . . . the liability under which is no higher than the disclosure of known defects."[166] Buckmaster, who was to dissent in *Donoghue v. Stevenson*, found that "the duty owed . . . is said to arise out of a combination of special circumstances which require close examination," but concluded that "these circumstances did disclose a duty cast on the respondents to take proper steps to see that the ropes were safe."[167] In 1930, the House took another tentative step forward in *Excelsior Wire Rope Company v. Callan*,[168] a case that involved children injured by machinery while on the land of another. Although the Lords spoke the language of the occupiers' liability, their generalizations went rather further.[169]

These cases paved the way for *Donoghue v. Stevenson*, in which the Lords—again, incidentally, in a Scottish appeal—drew the responsibili-

164. [1929] A.C. 584 (Scot.).

165. The pursuer was the widow of a workman employed by a porterage company. That company, for convenience, was gratuitously allowed to use slings provided by the stevedoring company. The stevedores had employees to inspect the slings, but one broke, killing the pursuer's husband.

166. [1929] A.C. 584, 590 (Scot.).

167. Ibid. 588, 590. Atkin's speech in *Oliver v. Saddler* is logically precedent to the formulation in *Donoghue*. After discussing the question of contractual bailment and distinguishing *Caledonia Ry. v. Mulholland*, [1898] A.C. 216 (Scot.) which almost persuaded Dunedin to decide the other way (at 598), he found himself of the opinion that the respondents "owed a duty to the porters to take reasonable care to see that the sling was in a fit condition to take the weight of the load" (at 596). He continued with more familiar words. "They provided a sling to be used . . . knowing that the latter [porters] would have no reasonable opportunity of examining the sling, and intending that they should rely on examination by themselves." However, Dunedin, although persuaded not to dissent, was fully aware of the implications of the decision, particularly Atkin's speech, and was careful to "express emphatically the very narrow limits within which any judgement is confined, for I cannot help feeling that this decision might be drawn into a precedent for what it does not warrant"; ibid. 598.

168. [1930] A.C. 404.

169. It cannot be said that the case fell strictly under the head of occupiers' liability, for the appellants were "not occupiers," to quote Dunedin; but he insisted that this did not remove the case "from the category of those cases where the land was in the occupation of the persons owning a dangerous machine." Warrington also felt that the question whether the children were invitees "is not a question which need engage our attention in this case" and it seemed to him "quite plain that there was a duty upon the present appellants." Atkin was equally emphatic that the duties of occupiers and the precise difference between invitees and occupiers and others were not relevant. "[I]t appears to me that they owed a duty to these children to take reasonable precautions to see that the children were not injured"; ibid. 413.

ties of the negligent actor in broad terms.[170] The implications of the case are perhaps best seen in Atkins' words:

The question is whether the manufacturer of an article of drink sold by him to a distributor, in circumstances which prevent the distributor or the ultimate purchaser or consumer from discovering by inspection any defect is under any legal duty to the ultimate purchaser or consumer to take reasonable care that the article is free from defect likely to cause injury to health . . .

The law of both countries appears to be that in order to support an action for damages for negligence the complainant has to show that he has been injured by the breach of a duty owed to him in the circumstances by the defendant to take reasonable care to avoid such injury. . . . We are solely concerned with the question whether, as a matter of law in the circumstances alleged, the defender owed any duty to the pursuer to take care. . . .

You must take reasonable care to avoid acts or omissions which you can reasonably foresee would be likely to injure your neighbour. Who, then, in law is my neighbour? The answer seems to be—persons who are so closely and directly affected by my act that I ought reasonably to have them in contemplation as being so affected when I am directing my mind to the arts or omissions which are called in question.[171]

After the decision, the House was certainly not overwhelmed by a welter of cases demanding that *Donoghue* be applied in their particular fact situation. Nor was the case widely applied in the lower courts.[172] Yet its immense psychological importance is undeniable. The decision was a major example of judicial legislation.[173] The scope of negligence gradually widened, being applied to situations that before 1932 would have caused difficulties[174] and, more important, being applied in a broad and

170. The decision has been neatly summarized by Heuston in four propositions: (1) That negligence is a distinct tort. (2) That the absence of privity of contract between plaintiff and defendant does not preclude liability in tort. (3) Manufacturers of products owe a duty of care to the ultimate consumer or user. (4) The criterion for the existence of a duty in the law of negligence is whether the defendant ought reasonably to have foreseen that his acts or omissions would be likely to result in damage to the plaintiff. He argued, however, that only two of the propositions "can truly be said to form part of the ratio" and these two were "judicial legislation of the highest order." R. F. V. Heuston, "*Donoghue* v. *Stevenson* in Retrospect" 1, 9, 24.

171. [1932] A.C. 562, 578–80 (Scot.). "A manufacturer of products which he sells in such a form as to show that he intends them to reach the ultimate consumer in the form in which they left him with no reasonable possibility of intermediate examination, and with the knowledge that the absence of reasonable care in the preparation or putting up of the products will result in an injury to the consumer's life or property owes a duty to the consumer to take that reasonable care"; ibid. 599.

172. In the tenth edition of Salmond, *Donoghue* v. *Stevenson* was still treated in the chapter on "Liability for Dangerous Chattels"; W. T. S. Stallybrass, ed., *Salmond's Law of Torts*.

173. Diplock later noted that "no lawyer really supposes that such decisions as *Donoghue* v. *Stevenson* did not change the law just as much as the Law Reform (Contributory Negligence) Act, 1945"; Sir Kenneth Diplock, *The Courts as Legislators* 2.

174. E.g., sulfur in the underpants; *Grant* v. *Australia Knitting Mills*, [1936] A.C. 85 (P.C. 1935). See especially Wright, ibid. at 103.

untrammeled way.[175] The ambience created by the new doctrine undoubtedly made it easier both to raise new heads of damages as was done in *Rose* v. *Ford*[176] and even to develop new areas of responsibility for employers—particularly the "safe system of work." In tort, perhaps even more than in contract, the House had experienced its most creative phase during the thirties.

175. E.g., *Manchester Corp.* v. *Markland*, [1936] A.C. 360; *Lindsey County Council* v. *Marshall*, [1937] A.C. 97 (1936), per Lord Wright: "The existence of the duty seems to follow from the general rules of the law of negligence. Now that the forms of action have been abolished and it is recognised that negligence is an independent tort, it is not necessary to consider if the duty is to be based on contract or whether it is based simply on the relationship between the parties"; *ibid.* 121.

176. [1937] A.C. 826.

The Political Tradition:
The Lord Chancellors, 1912–1940

Although the years 1912 to 1940 mark the decline of the political judges,—that is, judges appointed in recognition of political affiliation —they were still an integral part of the appellate scene until the 1930s and, in the case of the Lord Chancellors, of course, throughout the period. Yet even within the category of politicians, subtle variations were becoming clear. With the developments in party politics came a change in the attitudes of Chancellors: it was possible to observe different trends in the judicial outlook of Liberal and Labour Lord Chancellors on the one hand and Conservatives on the other.

The Liberal Intellectuals

At least three Chancellors fell into the category of liberal intellectuals: Asquith's Chancellor from 1912 to 1915—Haldane—who later served as MacDonald's Chancellor in the 1924 Labour administration; Asquith's Chancellor during the coalition government that lasted from May 1915 to December 1916—Buckmaster; and MacDonald's Chancellor during the second Labour administration (1929–31) and his National government (1931–35)—Sankey. These three men labored in what were hostile environments. As presiding officers in the legislative sessions of the Lords they faced massive built-in majorities in favor of the Conservative opposition; as heads of the judiciary they faced an inherently, if not consciously, conservative brotherhood of judges and lawyers; yet, in their roles as cabinet members they were normally regarded as "rightist" representatives of a particular interest group—the law. Theirs was not an easy position, and if these liberal intellectuals tended to take jurisprudential positions that were not intellectually distinguished, it can be understood partly in terms of the conflicting social, professional, and political pressures they had to withstand.

No one better typifies these problems than Lord Haldane.[1] He had some reason to think that he might be Lord Chancellor in 1905,[2] when Campbell-Bannerman was forming his administration, but instead he became Secretary of State for War. Yet, when Loreburn was clearly too exhausted and irritable to go on in 1912,[3] for a while it looked as if Reading might become Lord Chancellor.[4] Haldane was given little credit —then or later during World War I—for all his efforts in the War Office.[5] Indeed, the man did not strike warmth in men's hearts; he was never particularly popular.[6] He was, in many respects, a paradigm "scapegoat."

Loreburn had been a radical and an antiimperialist. Haldane belonged to a different tradition. An intellectual, he could believe in classical liberal reforms, yet even Loreburn could say to him, "[Y]ou have always been an imperialist 'au fond.'"[7] Haldane, however, pushed through his reforms in the law, as he had done with the army reforms. With the passage of the Appellate Jurisdiction Act of 1913 he was able to reduce by half the delay in the hearing of cases before the Privy Council.[8] He took an active part in Indian appeals,[9] and he insisted on presiding in all important

1. Richard Burdon; Edinburgh, 1856; father, writer to the Signet; educ., Edinburgh Academy, Edinburgh University, Gottingen; called to (English) bar, 1879; Q.C., 1890; M.P. (Liberal) East Lothian, 1885–1911; Secretary of State, War Office, 1905–12; Lord Chancellor, 1912–15 and 1924 (Labour); d. 1928.
On Haldane, see *Dictionary of National Biography, 1921–1930*, at 380; Richard Burdon Haldane, *An Autobiography*; R. F. V. Heuston, *Lives of the Lord Chancellors 1885–1940*, at 185–240; Stephen E. Koss, *Lord Haldane*; Roderick Maurice, *Haldane*.

2. Heuston, *Lives* 139–44.

3. See ibid. 165–66; Peter Rowland, *The Last Liberal Government: Unfinished Business 1911–1914.*

4. Sir Rufus Isaacs, the Attorney-General, greatly wanted the appointment and assumed the only reason he was not getting it was that he was Jewish. Sir John Simon, the Solicitor-General, who was sensitive because he was often mistaken for being Jewish rather than Welsh (see Simon, *Retrospect* 15, 88–89), irritated Asquith further by writing a memorandum on why there was no impediment to a Jew's becoming Lord Chancellor; Rowland, *Unfinished Business* 168.
There is every indication that Asquith had never considered anyone other than Haldane, but Reading's feelings were assuaged by his being included in the cabinet.

5. On these events, see especially Koss, *Lord Haldane*, chaps. 2, 5. See also Charles E. Wilson, *Haldane and the Machinery of Government.*

6. The press was relieved to see him out of the War Office and into the Woolsack; Koss, *Lord Haldane* 96. *John Bull* commented, "He can never say 'no' in under 20 minutes! Still he knows something about law." *The National Review* was crueller: "He was always a prodigious gas-bag but never a great lawyer"; ibid.

7. Koss, ibid. See also Heuston, *Lives* 174–75.

8. Maurice, 1 *Haldane* 325.

9. Heuston, *Lives* 225.

constitutional appeals,[10] and in the case of Canada's allocating power in favor of the provinces.[11] Meanwhile at home, less sensitive to political nuances than his predecessor, he continued to ignore political connections in making appointments to the High Court bench.[12] (These, incidentally, included both Atkin and Sankey.) A new concept of judicial appointments was, however, afoot; for Haldane sought to extend this system to the Lords of Appeal. Indeed, Haldane would have carried his concept of the separation of powers still further, for he was anxious to divide the judicial and political functions of the Lord Chancellor.[13] In this his views were akin to those of the utilitarian liberals from Brougham to Gardiner, views that so far have not been endorsed by the pragmatic guardians of the British Constitution.

There was, however, something not only cold but also inconsistent about Haldane. The man who wanted to take politics out of the judicial work of the Chancellor and to depoliticize judicial appointments in other regards used the political power of the Chancellorship to the full. His domination of Canadian appeals has already been noted, and he did not hesitate to send the Australian constitution off on another track.[14] At the

10. Between 1912 and 1929 there were 41 cases from Canada involving judicial review. Haldane sat in 32 of them, delivering judgment in 19.

11. He had had an immense practice before the House of Lords and Privy Council, as a result of which he had come to know the personalities of the individual law lords quite well; e.g., Heuston, *Lives* 189–90. He was counsel in the "watershed" case in which Watson finally demoted the residual powers of the dominion, effectively leaving the Federal government with only its enumerated powers; *Attorney-General for Ontario* v. *Attorney-General for Canada*, [1896] A.C. 348 (P.C.); and see Heuston, *Lives* 216–17.

12. Haldane saw it slightly differently. "With Asquith's cordial assent we decided that in filling the vacancies we would appoint only on the footing of high legal and professional qualification"; *Autobiography* 270.

13. Sir Claud Schuster, Permanent Secretary to the Lord Chancellor, records the scheme Haldane had for reforming the office of Lord Chancellor:

It appeared to Haldane indefensible that the mass of judicial patronage appertaining to the Lord Chancellor should be administered by a Minister who did not sit in the House of Commons, and he regarded the enforced seclusion of the Lord Chancellor from that Assembly as a barrier against the concentration of the judicial offices which was in his view urgently required. It appeared to him, therefore, that the solution of the problem lay in the creation of a Ministry of Justice, whose political chief would normally sit in the lower chamber. It would follow that the judicial duties of the lower chamber would be separated from the administration and the title would devolve on a permanent judge, who would be President of the Imperial Court of Appeal and of the Supreme Court of Justice. [Claud Schuster, "Lord Haldane of Cloan"]

For Haldane's own description of his plan, see *Autobiography* 270–72. He drafted a bill to implement his reform of the organization of the House of Lords in 1924.

14. His approach to the Australian constitution was more flexible. In part there was some moral obligation on the law lords not to be formalists about the Commonwealth of Australia Act, for during the parliamentary debates on the legislation, Davey had claimed he had no doubt that the Privy Council would regard it as a "treaty for the purpose of reconciling conflicting interests"; 85 *Parl. Deb.*, H.L. (4th ser.), col. 28 (29 June 1900).

Thus in *Attorney-General for Australia* v. *Colonial Sugar Ref. Co.*, [1914] A.C. 237

same time he chose panels or positions carefully when vital domestic issues were being litigated before the House of Lords. It was Haldane, for example, who orchestrated the substantial departure of the courts from any attempt to control the central executive in *Local Government Board v. Arlidge*.[15] Although not packing the panel so obviously,[16] he presided over another test of section 4 of the Trade Disputes Act of 1906. Haldane originally considered complete union immunity from actions for damages to be a legal monstrosity,[17] but later he was able to view the development with equanimity.[18] Thus in *Vacher and Sons v. London Society of Compositors*,[19] the House unanimously held that the trade union immunity from action applied even in a libel case where there was no trade dispute. In the decision Haldane took that formalistic approach to statutory interpretation that was to characterize the liberal intellectual's response to politically sensitive legislation:

I do not propose to speculate on what the motive of Parliament was. The topic is not one on which judges can profitably or properly enter. Their province is the very different one of construing the language in which the Legislature has finally expressed its conclusions, and if they undertake the other province which belongs to those who, in making the laws, have to endeavor to interpret the desire of the country, they are in danger of going astray in a labyrinth to the character of which they have no sufficient guide.[20]

In other areas, Haldane chose a similar route in order to avoid conflict even when, as in the case of tax law, his position tended to play

---

(P.C.), Haldane held, in contrast with Canada where the powers of federal legislation were derived from a reconstruction of all powers previously existing, the powers of the Australian federal legislature were derived from partial surrender of power by the states. With respect to this decision, a note in the *Law Quarterly Review* waxed almost lyrical: "The opinion delivered by Lord Haldane will be a classical document in the history of federal institutions as well as a leading authority in Australia"; "Note" 30 *Law Quarterly Review* 138 (1914).

15. [1915] A.C. 120 (1914).

16. *Arlidge* was decided by four liberals; *Vacher* by three liberals (Haldane, Shaw, and Moulton), a liberal conservative (Macnaghten), and a conservative (Atkinson).

17. See H. A. Clegg, Alan Fox and A. F. Thompson, *A History of British Trade Unionism since 1899*, at 393.

18. In the debate on the immunity of trade unions, he described the 1906 act as "passed to deal with a balance of evils"; 13 *Parl. Deb.* (H.L.), (5th ser.), col. 388 (22 Jan. 1913).

19. [1913] A.C. 107 (1912).

20. Ibid. 113. For other examples of this approach to statutory interpretation, see, for example, *Arlidge*, [1915] A.C. 120, 130 (1914): "Which of these opinions was right can only be determined by referring to the language of the Legislature. Here, as in other cases, we have simply to construe that language and to abstain from guessing at what Parliament had in its mind, excepting so far as the language enables us to do so." See also *Watney, Combe, Reid & Co. v. Berners*, [1915] A.C. 885, 891: "My Lords, I am of opinion that the Courts below have gone further than is legitimate in conjecturing what Parliament intended. The intention must be found in the language finally adopted in the statutes under construction, and in that language alone."

into the hands of more conservative elements in society.[21] Having talked himself into this formalistic position, Haldane had to offer an alternative formulation. Thus he was forced to concede that "general words may in certain cases properly be interpreted as having a meaning or scope other than the literal or usual meaning. They may be so interpreted where the scheme appearing from the language of the Legislature, read in its entirety, points to consistency as requiring modification of what would be the meaning apart from any context, or apart from the general law."[22] Intellectually, no doubt, Haldane justified under this broader contextual approach his view of Workmen's Compensation Act cases—namely, that "the fundamental conception is that of insurance in the true sense,"[23] while his dissent in *in re Viscountess Rhondda*, where he argued that the 1919 Sex Disqualification (Removal) Act had given the Viscountess a right to sit in the Lords, exhibited the reverse argument.[24]

The apparently conflicting tendencies showed even in Haldane's approach to common law. In some ways he could not have been a greater supporter of conventional common law doctrines. It was Haldane who led the restatement of the strict doctrines of privity of contract[25] and drew a narrow line around those representations that would be treated as part of the contract.[26] Yet it was also Haldane who helped develop the doctrine of commercial frustration[27] and when in the *Speyer* case he found no "crystallized" doctrine with respect to enemy aliens and the breakup of a partnership, he announced that "under these circumstances I am of opinion that it is open to us, as a supreme tribunal unfettered by any decision of its own, to look at the reason of the rule invoked."[28] His view of judicial creativity in this case could scarcely have been more generous.[29] Perhaps fueled by Haldane's background at the Chancery

---

21. See, however, his dissent in *Nevill v. IRC*, [1924] A.C. 385, where he was prepared to read an ambiguity in favor of the Crown; ibid. 394. This may, however, have been an isolated situation. Cf. *IRC v. Blott*, [1921] 2 A.C. 171, 182.

22. *Watney, Combe, Reid & Co. v. Berners*, [1915] A.C. 885, 891.

23. *Trim Joint Dist. School Bd. v. Kelly*, [1914] A.C. 667, 675–76 (Ire.).

24. "General words have, of course, on occasions been given by the Courts restricted interpretation. But that has been only when the scheme of the statute read as a whole, or the special character of the purpose as expressed by the legislature in the statute itself or in some other statute or law on which it bears, indicates such a restriction as intended by the legislature itself. Now here, the very title of the Act negatives this"; [1922] 2 A.C. 339, 383.

25. *Dunlop Pneumatic Tyre Co. v. Selfridge & Co.*, [1915] A.C. 847, 853.

26. *Heilbut, Symons & Co. v. Buckleton*, [1913] A.C. 30, 34–39 (1912).

27. *F. A. Tamplin S.S. Co. v. Anglo-Mexican Petroleum Prod. Co.*, [1916] 2 A.C. 397, 406; *Bank Line, Ltd. v. Arthur Capel & Co.*, [1919] A.C. 435 (1918).

28. *Rodriguez v. Speyer Bros.*, [1919] A.C. 59, 86 (1918).

29. "I think that there are many things of which the judges are bound to take judicial notice which lie outside the law properly so called, and among those things are what is called public policy and the changes which take place in it. The law itself may become modified by this obligation of the judges"; ibid. 79.

Bar, this approach was carried over into other areas. For instance, in *Kreglinger* v. *New Patagonia Meat and Cold Storage Company*,[30] he balanced the interests of mortgages and contracts; in *Nocton* v. *Lord Ashburton*,[31] he developed a quasi-fiduciary relationship to avoid the narrow common law concept of deceit; and in *Sinclair* v. *Brougham*,[32] while rejecting a broad remedy in restitution, he provided a solution through the equitable doctrine of tracing.

Overall, however, Haldane was the first in a line of liberal intellectual law lords who sought to lead the House, and hence the legal system, away from any semblance of competition with the political system. Haldane was both an active politician and a distinguished intellectual;[33] on the bench he was a scholarly judge, clearly aware of the implications of the decision-making process in which he was engaged. Yet he regarded it as important to articulate positions that not only strongly underplayed the creative function of the final appeal court, but frequently insisted that it had none. Thus a Chancellor who did not hesitate to use the political power of his office to reshape English administrative law or the Canadian constitution claimed little or no control over the interpretation of statutes on the development of the common law. The primacy of the declaratory theory was almost established; for the future it was to become as crucial to see what the law lords actually did as to pay attention to what they said they were doing.

With the coming of World War I, Haldane, whose training after Edinburgh had been in Germany, had become a political liability in an irrational period when any German connection was seen as a potential threat. Forced out by the May Crisis of 1915,[34] Haldane drifted toward the Labour party,[35] ultimately becoming Chancellor in MacDonald's Labour administration of 1924.[36] In the meantime, in 1915, he had been

---

30. [1914] A.C. 25 (1913): "[B]efore I refer to the decisions of this House which the Courts below have considered to cover the case, I will state what I conceive to be the broad principles which must govern it"; ibid. 35.

31. [1914] A.C. 932.

32. [1914] A.C. 398.

33. See Trevor O. Lloyd, *Empire to Welfare State* 27.

34. Koss, *Lord Haldane*, chap. 5 ("British attitudes to things German").

35. Of this change in politics he wrote:

There seemed to have set in a period of stagnation in the mind of the Liberal Party—it had no definite tasks such as fell to it in 1906, and it appeared to be lacking in fresh ideas. Towards the solution of social problems it was making but little progress. . . . [T]here was a growing Labour organisation to be taken into account . . . its program at least fitted in with the educational work on which I had been engaged . . . what seemed wisest was accordingly to continue rather aloof from Liberal organisations and to get such a contact with Labour as would enable me to understand it. I began to speak at Labour meetings and to see a good deal of Labour members. [Haldane, *Autobiography* 328–30]

36. Ramsay MacDonald asked him to help in forming a government, and Haldane asked for the Lord Chancellorship, though on condition that he be allowed to confine

replaced as Asquith's Chancellor by Buckmaster,[37] a man of much the same ilk as Haldane intellectually, and a person whom Asquith chose for his coalition Chancellor in preference to the Conservatives Sumner and Finlay, after it had been offered to Sir John Simon.[38]

Although similar to Haldane, Buckmaster was not the latter's intellectual equal. In Buckmaster's hands the declaratory theory became not a convenient political device, but more of a deadening judicial outlook. It was said, after his death, that he carried out his judicial duties "under the compulsion of a stern sense of duty and the recognition, when sitting as a judge in the highest tribunals of the empire, that justice, which had always been the ruling motive of his life, was now best served by statement of the law as it was."[39] Caution was the watchword of his judicial work.

Even in politics some thought Buckmaster too much the lawyer and too little the liberal.[40] On the bench (he sat as a former Lord Chancellor until his death in 1934) he gave occasional hints of social concern, but he never allowed these seriously to imperil his responsibility, as he saw it, to restate the law as it already existed and not to deviate from the ordinary meaning of statutory language. Thus, Hailsham's attempt to weaken workmen's compensation laws by importing the "added peril" doctrine was disposed of by relying "upon the words of the Act of Parliament."[41] The responsibilities of the courts were clear:

It is unnecessary to emphasise again the fact that it is the business of this House to administer the law and not to amend or express opinions about the wisdom of Acts of Parliament. If the words of a statute are obscure and ambiguous then the House is bound to consider which is the most rational view of their construction in order to determine what might be assumed to have been intended; but if the

---

himself to the administrative side. He insisted on returning to the Treasury £4,000 out of his annual salary of £10,000; Heuston, *Lives* 233.

37. Stanley Owen Buckmaster; b. 1861; father, self-educated inspector in the Department of Sciences and Art; educ., Aldenham and Christ Church, Oxford (Second, Mathematics) called to bar, 1884 (common law, later transferred to Chancery); M.P. (Lib.) Cambridge, 1906–10; Keithley, 1911–15; Solicitor-General, 1913; d. 1934; *Dictionary of National Biography 1931–1940*, at 119–21.

38. Heuston, *Lives* 265. *The Times* commented that it was "a reward for tolerable success at the Bar, and diligent but commonplace party services"; ibid. 267.

39. *Dictionary of National Biography 1931–1940*, at 119.

40. His maiden speech as an M.P., defending Mr. Justice Grantham—a shamelessly Tory judge—was motivated, in part at least, by "the sacred duty to maintain in every possible way the dignity and prestige of the High Court judges." His generous spirit also led him to defend the ministers involved in the Marconi scandals; Heuston, *Lives* 258.

His liberalism extended to opposition to capital punishment, to support of divorce law reform (he had particular interest in this; unhappily married, he had a well-known actress as his mistress), and he favored a negotiated peace during World War I.

41. *Thomas v. Ocean Coal Co.*, [1933] A.C. 100, 109 (1932).

words are unambiguous and plain it is no part of the duty of this House to say: "The result of this is something which we do not regard as reasonable and therefore we shall try to give it some other interpretation."[42]

So, while he did hold that gifts for the saying of masses[43] and gifts to the Secular Society were charities,[44] Buckmaster was able to do this in the most conventional way. He similarly insisted that in documents "plain words should be given their plain meaning."[45] Despite his political liberalism, he helped to confirm the position that tax statutes should be read narrowly like penal statutes,[46] at the same time encouraging the myth that somehow the statutory draftsmen rather than the judges (and especially the law lords) were responsible for the highly formalistic approach to tax law.[47] Indeed, it is almost ironic that Sumner, in one case, went so far as to suggest that Buckmaster's speech was influenced by "compassion."[48] As Dunedin said, after Buckmaster's death, "I have not and I never have had any sympathy with Buckmaster's political ideas and performances and I think him to be a sentimentalist—unless he is sitting on his arse on the bench; there he is one of the most learned, one of the most

42. *Ruston & Hornsby, Ltd.* v. *Goodman*, [1933] A.C. 150, 153 (1932).

43. Yet, it was not easy for Buckmaster. He insisted that "the principles of the common law do not change, though their application is capable of indefinite variation with the changing habits and customs of mankind. If void by the common law, therefore, it must always have been so." For the Chancery lawyer, the overruling of an 1835 lower court decision was not easy. Fortunately, he was able to convince himself that the earlier decision had been "legally" incorrect. His pleasure was obvious. "[I]t is the Roman Catholic religion which may have suffered by the effect of the authority, and I see no reason why what I regard as a misstatement of the law should be perpetuated in violence to the convictions of those who accept the teachings of the Roman Church"; *Bourne* v. *Keane*, [1919] A.C. 815, 863, 871.

44. *Bowman* v. *Secular Soc'y, Ltd.*, [1917] A.C. 406, 470–71; see note by R. E. Megarry, "Contemplative Nuns in Eire and England" 424.

45. *Boyce* v. *Wasbrough*, [1922] 1 A.C. 425, 439. "And confusion is often caused and litigation multiplied by attempting to impose upon clear language a meaning depending upon the assumptions of what any party must be supposed to have meant. The only way of testing that intention is to see what has been said"; ibid. 139–40. See also *King* v. *David Allen & Sons*, [1916] A.C. 54, 59.

46. "It is, I think, important to remember the rule, which the Courts ought to obey, that, where it is desired to impose a new burden by way of taxation, it is essential that this intention should be stated in plain terms. The Courts cannot assent to the view that if a section in a taxing statute is of doubtful and ambiguous meaning, it is possible out of that ambiguity to extract a new and added obligation not formerly cast upon the taxpayer"; *Greenwood* v. *Smidth & Co.*, [1922] 1 A.C. 417, 423. See also *Ormond Inv. Co.* v. *Betts*, [1928] A.C. 143, 151 (1927).

47. "I do not pretend that the opinion I hold rests on any firm logical foundation. Logic is out of place in these questions, and the embarrassment that I feel is increased with the knowledge that my views are not shared by other members of the House, but this fact is not surprising. It is not easy to penetrate the tangled confusion of these Acts of Parliament, and though we have entered the labyrinth together, we have unfortunately found exit by different paths"; *Great Western Ry.* v. *Bater*, [1922] 2 A.C. 1, 11.

48. In *Mersey Docks and Harbours Bd.* v. *Procter*, [1923] A.C. 253.

acute, and the fairest judge I ever sat with; and he will leave much in the books."[49]

In retrospect, however, what characterized Buckmaster was caution, which, in public law after the excursions of the Edwardian period, may have been desirable. Presiding, for example, in *Roberts v. Hopwood*,[50] he set a tone of caution and restraint not followed by his colleagues. In private law, the caution put him increasingly out of touch with what was becoming the spirit of the times. In *Beck and Company v. Szymanowski and Company*,[51] the majority[52] began development of what later became known as "fundamental breach" of the contract, in this situation allowing a buyer to ignore a fourteen-day limit on claims when the seller had "sold short." Buckmaster would have no part of any such interference with the sanctity of contract.

It was in tort that the great strides were being made and in tort that Buckmaster stood most firmly for the status quo. Yet one must admit consistency in Buckmaster's positions. In refusing to treat trespassing children as anything but trespassers vis-à-vis occupiers, he found himself "bound by the authorities" in *Addie and Sons (Collieries) v. Dumbreck* and he warned the world "to keep clearly in mind the distinction between a moral and a legal obligation."[53] He went along in *Oliver v. Saddler*[54] while denying that any of the dicta in *Heaven v. Pender* were of value to him.[55] His reputation for caution, however, was firmly established by his

49. *Dictionary of National Biography 1931–1940*, at 119–20. Whether he left "much in the books" is an open question. His judgments are, however, still regarded as important in some areas of equity, e.g., secret trusts, *Blackwell v. Blackwell*, [1929] A.C. 318.

50. [1925] A.C. 578. Buckmaster had no wish to place too many fetters on the local authority. "The discretion thus imposed is a very wide one, and I agree . . . that when such a discretion is conferred upon a local authority the Courts ought to show great reluctance before they attempt to determine how, in their opinion, the discretion ought to be exercised"; ibid. 588. He felt bound, however, to interfere, as the affidavit on behalf of the Council "states that 4 [pounds] a week was to be the minimum wage for adult labour, that is without the least regard to what that labour might be. It standardised men and women not according to the duties they performed, but according to the fact that they were adults. It is this that leads me to think that their action cannot be supported"; ibid. 589–90.

In the area of public law, however, Buckmaster refused to extend § four of the Trade Disputes Act of 1906 and voted to enforce a trade union membership agreement, apparently feeling that the courts should retain jurisdiction in the area; *Amalgamated Soc'y of Carpenters Cabinet Makers & Joiners v. Braithwaite*, [1922] 2 A.C. 440, 451: "To construe a rule is not directly to enforce any agreement between the members, and I am unable to see any reason why the words of the statute should be so extended as to exclude a trade union from obtaining the advantage of having obscure words construed by a wholly independent and impartial tribunal."

51. [1924] A.C. 43 (1923).

52. Atkinson, Shaw, Wrenbury.

53. [1929] A.C. 358, 379 (Scot.).

54. [1929] A.C. 584, 588 (Scot.).

55. 11 Q.B.D. 503 (C.A. 1883).

dissent in *Donoghue* v. *Stevenson*. His fears were clear. "There can be no special duty attaching to the manufacturer of food apart from that implied by contract or imposed by statute. If such a duty exists, it seems to me it must cover the construction of every article, and I cannot see any reason why it should not apply to the construction of a house. If one step, why not fifty?"[56] Having made a thorough examination of the precedents, he felt his task was done. " In my view . . . the authorities are against the appellant's contention, and, apart from authority, it is difficult to see how any common law proposition can be formulated to support her claim."[57] There was a certain charming, albeit destructive, simplicity about Buckmaster's judicial style. It was overwhelmed by the strength of Atkin and Wright in the thirties, although Buckmaster's approach was to become orthodoxy during and after World War II.

It was, in fact, during the thirties that the third of the liberal intellectuals—Sankey[58]—served as Lord Chancellor. Sankey, although important as a reformer, sought to implement change through legislation rather than litigation. He was MacDonald's Chancellor for some six years from 1929 to 1935, part of the most significant period in the judicial history of the House of Lords, but Sankey's contribution to decisions in the House was limited. His true interest lay in politics; and his politics were, in their way, remarkable.

He had begun life as a Conservative, but had been appointed a puisne judge by Haldane, whom he greatly admired.[59] The most important event in Sankey's political life, however, was his appointment in 1919 as Chairman of the Coal Industry Commission.[60] The final report of the commission came as a shock to the government, for one of its major recommendations was that "[t]he present system of ownership and working in the coal industry stands condemned, and some other system must be substituted for it, either nationalisation or a method of unification by national purchase and/or joint control."[61]

If the decision came as a shock to the Conservatives, it delighted MacDonald, for Sankey did not conceal his disappointment that his suggestions for nationalization were not implemented.[62] Many thought

56. [1932] A.C. 562, 577 (Scot.).

57. Ibid. See also R. F. V. Heuston, "*Donoghue* v. *Stevenson* in Retrospect" 1. See ibid. 3–4 for Pollock's interpretation of Buckmaster's behavior.

58. John Sankey; b. 1866; father, partner in firm of drapers and undertakers; educ., Lancing and Jesus College, Oxford (Second, History; Third, B.C.L.); called to bar, 1892; K.C. 1909; Judge, King's Bench Division, 1914–28; Lord Justice, 1928–29; Lord Chancellor, 1929–35; d. 1948; *Dictionary of National Biography 1941–1950*, at 757–58.

59. See Sankey, Haldane Memorial Lecture, 1929.

60. See C. L. Mowat, *Britain between the Wars 1918–1940*, at 31 ff.

61. *Report of the Commission on the Coal Industry*, Cmd. 359 (1919), Recommendation 9. See now also Heuston, *Lives* 504–5.

62. Obituary, *The Times*, 9 Feb. 1948.

that he would be made Lord Chancellor in the Labour government in 1924, but Haldane was unwilling to stand aside. Sankey was, however, a natural choice for Chancellor in 1929, and he clearly enjoyed the position, particularly its political aspect. Thus, MacDonald refused to move Sankey from the Woolsack in 1931 on the collapse of the Labour administration and the formation of a National one; and in 1934 when Chamberlain tried to force a cabinet shuffle that would have brought Hailsham in to replace Sankey, the latter resisted fiercely[63] and so retained his position. When in the following year, MacDonald gave way to Baldwin as Prime Minister, there was again a promise that Sankey would be retained as Chancellor—a promise that was not, however, kept.[64]

It was Sankey's thirst for politics—including his crucial work in the field of law reform where he insisted "that legal reform must not be intermittant, but should be part of a permanent policy"[65]—that resulted in his making such a small contribution to private law, at least through the appellate process.[66] Ironically, however, the pattern of parliamentary law reform initiated by him enabled the law lords of the forties and fifties to be casual about their responsibilities for developing the law. Yet Sankey's judicial contribution must not be dismissed as negligible. In areas of the law where the public interest was at stake, he was capable of taking an active and important part. His interventions in workmen's compensation cases were decisive,[67] while his speech in *Woolmington v. Director of Public Prosecutions*[68] was one of the major additions made in the House of Lords to criminal law.

Moreover, Sankey's work in Commonwealth affairs was important and sophisticated. In the Privy Council, he understood better than his contemporaries those nuances of political life necessary to the handling of constitutional cases. He sensed how the British North America Act should work, calling it a "living tree."[69] He understood the need for a federal rather than a provincial solution to the pressing social problems of the thirties.[70] The Statute of Westminster of 1931 was heavily influ-

---

63. Ian McLeod, *Neville Chamberlain* 166.

64. Mowat, *Britain between the Wars* 534. He was replaced by Hailsham.

65. A. L. Goodhart, cited, Heuston, *Lives* 530.

66. *Dictionary of National Biography 1941–1950*, at 757–58.

67. E.g., *Shotts Iron Co. v. Fordyce*, [1930] A.C. 503, 507 (Scot.).

68. [1935] A.C. 462. See, for instance, his style at 481: "Throughout the web of English Criminal Law one golden thread is always to be seen. It is the duty of the prosecution to prove the prisoner's guilt—subject to what I have already said as to the degree of insanity and subject also to any statutory exemption."

69. See chap. 6, at 201.

70. *In re Regulation & Control of Aeronautics in Canada*, [1932] A.C. 54, 62 (P.C. 1931). See also Edward McWhinney, *Judicial Review in the English Speaking World* 66; and see *Edwards v. Attorney-General for Canada*, [1930] A.C. 124 (P.C. 1929). The position was, of course, abandoned in 1937.

enced by his thinking and represented a sensitive compromise for settling the tensions that had grown up in the "old" Commonwealth. Sitting judicially in the Privy Council, he implemented the spirit of the statute by allowing Ireland and Canada to abolish appeals.[71] He was trusted by Indian politicians and lawyers alike, and he allied himself with Ghandi to overcome the (legally) conservative outlook of lawyers like Nehru, in the battle to establish a Federal Supreme Court in India.[72]

The style of the liberal intellectual judge was changing. If the Haldane-Buckmaster approach was the new orthodoxy, then progress had to come from the legislature and it was logical for the Chancellor's efforts to be directed primarily at that body. This had been Sankey's approach. Such an assumption was not, however, necessarily shared by the Conservative Chancellors, although, for different reasons, they arrived at a similar jurisprudential position.

The Conservative Chancellors

The reasons the Liberal and Labour Chancellors had for arguing for a formalistic approach to law are not difficult to discover. Operating in a basically hostile environment, they were best served politically by transferring work away from the regular courts, while encouraging those courts, in handling the work that remained, to emphasize formalistic legal logic. No amount of legal logic could exclude creativity entirely, but if judges made a bona fide effort to restate existing doctrine or develop the law only by invisible increments, the chances of decisions being given that might clash with the views of the elected majority were at least reduced.

The Conservative Chancellors, however, were also in general moving in the same direction, although some of them without the enthusiasm of their Liberal or Labour contemporaries; and their motives were probably somewhat different. Perhaps some viewed the declaratory theory as a useful device behind which law could be developed, if necessary, in directions of which the legislature might not have approved; others, motivated by professional concerns, undoubtedly saw a formalistic approach as a necessary part of the legal system's responsibility for certainty and predictability. Still others, no doubt, concerned with protecting the "integrity" of the judiciary, saw in the assertion that judges were largely mechanical appliers of rules and statutes a way of preventing the bench

71. E.g., *Moore* v. *Attorney-General of the Irish Free State*, [1935] A.C. 484 (P.C.); *British Coal Corp.* v. *The King*, [1935] A.C. 500 (P.C.). The latter, of course, related only to criminal appeals from Canada.

72. At the 1931 Round Table Conference, he argued that a "Federal Court is an essential element" in any future quasi-independent India; G. H. Gadbois, "Evolution of the Federal Court of India" 19, 30.

from being drawn into political debates at a time of national crisis. Strands of all of these motives may be discerned among the six Conservative Chancellors of the period.

When Buckmaster was removed from the Chancellorship, Lloyd George, in forming his coalition, gave the post to Finlay,[73] a physician turned barrister. Beginning as a Liberal and admirer of Gladstone, he opposed Home Rule and ultimately, as a Unionist, became one of his former leader's bêtes-noires. After serving as a Conservative law officer from 1895 to 1905, he returned to a remarkably successful practice at the bar. When the "Welsh wizard" was looking for a wartime Chancellor in 1916, Finlay seemed an ideal candidate, particularly as he was prepared to "do a deal" that involved his not drawing the generous Lord Chancellor's pension on retirement. Finlay appeared not to mind being excluded from the War Cabinet and showed only slight public irritation when, at the dissolution in 1918, he received a letter from Lloyd George telling him he had been dropped from office.[74]

The chief problem with Finlay was his age; when he was appointed Lord Chancellor he was already seventy-four and past his prime. Heuston reports that the general feeling was that "neither in pace nor in quality did he improve any tribunal over which he presided."[75] The Permanent Secretary of the Lord Chancellor's Office obviously suffered agonies with him[76] and Birkenhead said of his work as an appeal judge, "He is not the man he was" and "[T]he great powers he once possessed are now gradually leaving him."[77] Indeed, if one looks only at his work as Chancellor, the evidence is not impressive; and his period after office is even sadder. He refused to accept the Birkenhead position that law lords should not speak out on political issues and, with Sumner, insisted on defending General Dyer after the "Amritsar Massacre," when British troops fired into an Indian crowd, killing 379 persons. It was perhaps fortunate for British jurisprudence that his final years were spent in the relative obscurity of the Permanent Court of International Justice at the Hague.

In fairness, in commercial law, while not distinguished, Finlay's speeches are not unreasonable. He was willing to tolerate the growth of commercial frustration[78] and to be flexible about third parties who were

73. Robert Finlay; b. Scotland, 1842; father, physician; educ., Edinburgh Academy, Edinburgh University (M.D. 1864); called to English bar, 1867 (common law, later moved to Chancery and admiralty); M.P., Inverness Burghs, 1885–92 and 1895–1906; 1910–16, M.P., Edinburgh and St. Andrews University; Attorney-General, 1895–1900; Lord Chancellor, 1916–19; d. 1929; *Dictionary of National Biography 1922–1930*, at 305–6.

74. Heuston, *Lives* 313–47.

75. Ibid. 339, although Heuston does question somewhat the second part of the statement.

76. Ibid.

77. Ibid., 343–44.

78. See *Metropolitan Water Bd. v. Dick, Kerr & Co.*, [1918] A.C. 119 (1917); *Bank*

suing on a contract,[79] and he rarely encumbered his opinions with excessive authority.[80] The decisions that are chiefly remembered are those in which some political, social, or economic issue was directly or indirectly at stake, for in those cases he was frequently unable to resist speaking out on sensitive issues, or at least allowing them to appear too obviously in his judgments.

In *Halliday*'s case,[81] where habeas corpus was suspended by delegated legislation, Finlay was apparently prepared to go to any lengths in suspending civil liberties to help the war effort.

It was not, as I understand the argument, contended that the words of the statute are not in their natural meaning wide enough to authorise such a regulation as reg. 14B, but it was strongly contended that some limitation must be put upon these words, as an unrestricted interpretation might involve extreme consequences, such as, it was suggested, the infliction of the punishment of death without trial.

It appears to me to be a sufficient answer to this argument that it may be necessary in a time of great public danger to entrust great powers to His Majesty in Council, and that Parliament may do so feeling certain that such powers will be reasonably exercised.[82]

Line, Ltd. v. *Arthur Capel & Co.*, [1919] A.C. 435 (1918) (in which he had to distinguish the *Tamplin* case, ibid. 442–43), both decided during his term on the Woolsack. He was, however, the one dissenter in *Tennants (Lancashire), Ltd.* v. *C. S. Wilson Co.*, [1917] A.C. 495, 504: "It appears to me to be clear that a mere shortage of supply is not enough unless it prevents or hinders the manufacture or delivery of the magnesium chloride in question."

79. *Les Affreteurs Réunis S.A.* v. *Leopold Walford, Ltd.*, [1919] A.C. 801. See per Finlay, ibid. 811: "[C]lause 29 in part, at all events, must have been, I think entered into by those who were parties to the charterparty on behalf of the broker . . . [W]e must regard the charterer as having entered into that bargain in the interests of the broker and as a trustee for the broker."

Finlay also sat in *Elder, Dempster & Co.* v. *Paterson, Zochonis & Co.*, [1924] A.C. 522. He dissented only with respect to the scope of the exemption clause. His basic view was, "It would be absurd that the owner of the goods could get rid of the protective clauses of the bill of lading, in respect of all stowage, by suing the owner of the ship in tort"; ibid. 548.

80. In *Walford* he cited no authority; in *Metropolitan Water Bd.* v. *Dick, Kerr & Co.*, [1918] A.C. 119 (1917), he referred to authorities only in the last paragraph and then dismissed them either as not laying down any principle or as being wrongly decided; in *Adam* v. *Ward*, [1917] A.C. 309, on privilege and libel, he cited no cases.

81. R. v. *Halliday, ex parte Zadig*, [1917] A.C. 260.

82. Ibid. 268–69. This urge to defer to the executive existed in time of peace as well. See, with respect to sovereign immunity, *Duff Dev. Corp.* v. *Government of Kelantan*, [1924] A.C. 797, 815: "There is no ground for saying that because the question involves considerations of law these must be determined by the Courts. The answer of the King, through the appropriate department, settles the matter whether it depends on fact or on law."

When the question was whether a contract to pay the police for giving special protection was void as being illegal or against public policy, he noted, "Of course, if it were illegal to take such payments no amount of sanction by Government Departments would legalise what was against the law. But the fact that the Home Office has regulated such payments

In the *Bowman* case he argued that the crime of blasphemy still survived, since "any purpose hostile to Christianity is illegal."[83] In a libel action brought by Marie Stopes, a pioneer in birth control, his behavior was decidedly unjudicial. Her position was, he said, "revolting to the healthy instincts of human nature," and her books "have a most deplorable effect upon the young of both sexes."[84] Nor were his strong views limited to social mores. At the age of eighty-five Finlay presided in the Privy Council and dealt a crippling blow to the Commercial Trusts Act of 1910—the New Zealand version of the American antitrust law— for, as Finlay put it, "[I]t is not for this tribunal, nor for any tribunal, to adjudicate as between conflicting theories of political economy."[85]

Decisions such as these were scarcely distinguished contributions by the senior appeal judge. But in some ways their lack of distinction was compounded by Finlay's erratic endorsement of the declaratory theory. At times he would announce that legislation was for Parliament and not for the courts,[86] while at other times he would seem excessively concerned with the history of some doctrine and, having discovered the history, he would assume that such discovery settled the matter.[87] In still

---

goes a long way to show that there is nothing illegal about them"; *Glasbrook Bros.* v. *Glamorganshire County Council*, [1925] A.C. 270, 286 (1924).

On the other hand, in keeping with Diceyan concepts of the Rule of Law, in *Johnstone* v. *Pedlar*, [1921] 2 A.C. 262 (Ire.), the House unanimously rejected the argument that Act of State was a good defense when pleaded by an officer of the Crown in an action brought by an alien for acts done in the United Kingdom. Finlay strongly supported the decision; see especially ibid. 273.

83. *Bowman* v. *Secular Soc'y, Ltd.*, [1917] A.C. 406. The core of his dissent is as follows: "[W]e have to deal not with a rule of public policy which might fluctuate with the opinions of the age, but with a definite rule of law to the effect that any purpose hostile to Christianity is illegal. The opinion of the age may influence the application of this rule but cannot affect the rule itself. It can never be the duty of a Court of Law to begin by inquiring what is the spirit of the age and in supposed conformity with it to decide what the law is"; ibid. 432.

84. *Sutherland* v. *Stopes*, [1925] A.C. 47, 68 (1924). Finlay went on to attack the plaintiff for using the title Dr. when she was "only" a Ph.D.

At first instance, before the Lord Chief Justice, the plaintiff had been awarded £100 damages for the defendant's statement that Stopes had taken advantage of the ignorance of the poor to experiment on them. The House held that the words were, in fact, fair comment and refused to order a new trial since there had been no substantial miscarriage of justice.

85. *Crown Milling* v. *The King*, [1927] A.C. 394, 402 (P.C.). Illogically, in a restraint of trade case he recognized the policy of the law that "requires that every man shall be at liberty to work for himself, and shall not be at liberty to deprive himself or the State of his labour, skill, or talent, by any contract that he enters into"; *McEllistrim* v. *Ballymacelligott Co-operative Agricultural & Dairy Soc'y*, [1919] A.C. 548, 571 (Ire.).

86. For example, in *Edwards* v. *Porter*, [1925] A.C. 1, 18 (1924), Finlay expressed caution about developments that might be construed as being inconsistent with the language of legislation.

87. E.g., *Lord Advocate* v. *Jaffrey*, [1921] 1 A.C. 146, 157 (Scot. 1920), on the identity of domicile between husband and wife: "As to the existence of the rule, there is no doubt. It

other situations he seemed obsessed with the need to maintain symmetry.[88] If Finlay did not deserve all the unkind things that were said of him, there is no doubt that as an appeal judge he was undistinguished.

Undistinguished is not a word that could fairly be used of Finlay's successor after the "coupon" election of 1918—F. E. Smith, Lord Birkenhead, one of the most complex and controversial Chancellors of all times. He worked hard as Lord Chancellor, which one suspects must have interested him less than the "real" world, and thus survived until Lloyd George's fall in 1922.[89] A combination of a High Tory and a "wheeler-dealer," Birkenhead was publicly a vigorous opponent of the unions and Home Rule and the person who, behind the scenes, negotiated deals with union leaders and Irish nationalists. This style spilled over into his private life. He had one of the finest minds that ever came to the bar and was Lord Chancellor at forty-three. Yet, especially in his later years, he drank heavily, failed to file income tax returns, was both obsessed with money[90] and heavily in debt, had various rather sordid sexual adventures, was caught plagiarizing in his writings, while among his closest associates[91] he numbered Lloyd George's "bagman" for the sale of honors.[92]

While Birkenhead was a brilliant lawyer and as a law officer had every reasonable expectation of succeeding to the Woolsack, his appointment was not popular. *The Times* thought his promotion was "carrying a joke too far";[93] and his opinions certainly give a sense of the reasons for the discontent. It is clear that he was aware of his own ability, both

---

would be at once undesirable and mischievous to enter into an examination"; and *Attorney-General v. National Provincial & Union Bank of England*, [1924] A.C. 262, 269: "For reasons which have a root in the history of English law, special immunities are extended to charitable gifts which do not apply to gifts of other kinds, and I do not think it can be properly contended that gifts for a patriotic purpose are intended to share in these immunities."

88. E.g., *Neville v. London Express Newspapers, Ltd.*, [1919] A.C. 368.

89. Frederick Edwin Smith, b. 1872; father, provincial barrister who became mayor of Birkenhead; educ., Birkenhead School, Liverpool Univ., Wadham College Oxford (First, Jurisprudence); called to bar, 1899; 1906 Conservative M.P. for Liverpool (Walton); Solicitor-General, 1915; Attorney-General, 1915–18; Lord Chancellor, 1918–22; Secretary of State for India, 1922–24; d. 1930; *Dictionary of National Biography 1922–1930*, at 782–89.

90. In 1921 he circulated what may be one of the most arrogant cabinet papers of all time, the strong implication being that, as in the eighteenth century it was incumbent on the state to allow Lord Chancellors to amass a fortune while in office, they should be paid a fortune in the twentieth. He found the salary of £10,000 for being Lord Chancellor and £4,000 for being Speaker, together with an automatic pension of £4,000, totally inadequate; Lord Chancellor's Office, 2/480, Public Record Office. Nor was Birkenhead one to render unpaid judicial service after his retirement; Heuston, *Lives* 396.

91. Heuston, *Lives* 353–402. See also *Dictionary of National Biography* 782. Lord Birkenhead (Frederick Edwin Smith), *The Life of F. E. Smith, First Earl of Birkenhead*.

92. Tom Cullen, *Maundy Gregory*, especially at 132–37.

93. Heuston, *Lives* 381.

from the number of unreserved opinions he delivered[94] and the frequency with which he found, like Halsbury, that the answers to questions before the House were "quite plain," whether or not the lower courts or his fellow law lords shared his view.[95] His somewhat patronizing attitude to dissenters[96] cannot have endeared him to his judicial brethren, although there is little doubt that he was a powerful Chancellor, able on most occasions to enforce his own views; while the fears of some members of the legal profession that Birkenhead was not sufficient of a lawyer were soon allayed by his pronouncements from the bench. In cases such as *Director of Public Prosecutions* v. *Beard*[97] his was the only reasoned speech,[98] and this pattern was repeated elsewhere.[99]

Superficially, there was little to distinguish Birkenhead from what was becoming the orthodox view of the judicial process.[100] "We approach the matter in this House without responsibility for the genesis of the rule. We have not to ask whether we should ourselves have laid it down; still less to consider whether changed social conditions have undermined its authority. We find the rule living and authoritative. We find its application to legitimacy proceedings everywhere conceded. Our task therefore is to determine whether evidence inadmissible in such proceedings is admissible in Divorce. It is a simple, a limited, but an important task."[101] The legislature could change the rule if it wished, but it was rarely a part of his duty as a judge to do so and certainly none of his duty to consider the implications of a decision.[102] Just as it was the judicial

---

94. E.g., *Fitch* v. *Dewes*, [1921] 2 A.C. 158; *Les Affreteurs Réunis S.A.* v. *Leopold Walford, Ltd.*, [1919] A.C. 801; *Fried Krupp Aktiengesellschaft* v. *Orconera Iron Ore Co.*, [1919] W.N. 50, Opinions of their Lordships, 1919.

95. E.g., *McCawley* v. *The King*, [1920] A.C. 691, 704, 709 (P.C.); *in re Viscountess Rhondda*, [1922] 2 A.C. 339; *Secretary of State for Home Affairs* v. *O'Brien*, [1923] A.C. 603.

96. See *in re Viscountess Rhondda*, [1922] 2 A.C. 339, 376, on Haldane's and Wrenbury's dissents.

97. [1920] A.C. 479.

98. After this decision the *Law Quarterly Review* said, "Lord Birkenhead's judicial utterances in the House of Lords have by this time conclusively disposed of the apprehensions entertained in some quarters that in his period of controversial politics he had forgotten his law"; "Note," 36 *Law Quarterly Review* 202 (1920).

99. There is a tradition that Birkenhead did not write all the speeches delivered in his name. For instance, his speech in *Admiralty Comm'rs* v. *S.S. Volute (Owners)*, [1922] 1 A.C. 129, 130, is thought by many to have been drafted by Phillimore. See Robert Anderson Wright, "Contributory Negligence" 2, 17.

100. Similarly, although a politician himself, Birkenhead followed the Haldane line on judicial appointments. He even went to the extent of clashing with Lloyd George over the latter's attempts to influence judicial appointments; Heuston, *Lives* 383.

101. *Russell* v. *Russell*, [1924] A.C. 687, 698. See also *Rutherford* v. *Richardson*, [1923] A.C. 1, 12 (1922).

102. *Sutters* v. *Briggs*, [1922] 1 A.C. 1 (1921), holding that the loser of a bet on a horse race could recover from the banker who received the check for collection: "My Lords, this appeal, in my opinion, fails. The consequences of this view will no doubt be extremely

purpose to "avoid law making" if possible, so it was the task of the courts to apply the "ordinary meaning of words" in a statute.[103] With this narrow view also went a distaste on Birkenhead's part for anything savoring of judicial review.[104]

This is, of course, only part of the story, for Birkenhead (like so many of his contemporaries and his successors) always found it permissible to take a bold line if it accorded with strong personal views. In *Bourne* v. *Keane*,[105] he led the House into reversing a well-accepted principle in the law of charities.[106] Sometimes, moreover, Birkenhead publicly congratulated himself on some piece of interstitial legislation. In the *O'Brien* case, for example, he held out strongly against the Home Secretary's right to appeal from a decision in habeas corpus proceedings in favor of the subject: "I cannot refrain from expressing my satisfaction that the lacuna, if there was one, in the decision in *Cox's Case* has been happily filled by the present decision in a manner which effectively car-

---

inconvenient to many persons. But this is not a matter proper to influence the House unless in a doubtful case affording foothold for balanced speculations as to the probable intention of the Legislature. Where, as here, the legal issues are not open to serious doubt our duty is to express a decision and leave the remedy (if one be resolved upon) to others"; ibid. 8.

103. Where the question was whether a charge could be imposed under the Treaty of Peace Order of 1919, he denied that some restriction should be made on general words to exclude property subject to restraint on anticipation. "[W]e must apply the ordinary rule of construction, that the words are to be read in their ordinary sense, and in their full sense, unless there be something in the context to limit their meaning"; *Public Trustee* v. *Wolf*, [1923] A.C. 544, 558.

See also *Coman* v. *Governors of the Rotunda Hosp.*, [1921] 1 A.C. 1, 11 (Ire. 1920), on the point that the court should look at the whole scheme of the act (a taxing statute).

104. In an important opinion in the Privy Council on the power of the Queensland legislature to pass legislation inconsistent with its constitution, *McCawley* v. *The King*, [1920] A.C. 691, 704 (P.C.), he revealed a bias in favor of what he described as "uncontrolled constitutions," such as that of Great Britain. Yet he was aware of the evolutionary nature of constitutional law. "The doctrine that the King, having created a peer, cannot direct that he shall not be summoned to Parliament had become settled constitutional law in the course of the seventeenth century. As is so often the case, it represents not in truth the statement of a legal doctrine, but the result of a constitutional struggle"; *in re Viscountess Rhondda*, [1922] 2 A.C. 339, 353.

105. [1919] A.C. 815.

106. "Great importance is to be attached to old authorities, on the strength of which many transactions may have been adjusted and rights determined. But where they are plainly wrong and especially where the subsequent course of judicial decisions has disclosed weakness in the reasoning on which they were based, and practical injustice in the consequences that must flow from them, I consider it is the duty of this House to overrule them, if it has not lost the right to do so by itself expressly affirming them.

"In my view it is undoubtedly true that ancient decisions are not to be lightly disturbed when men have accepted them and regulated their dispositions in reliance upon them. And this doctrine is especially deserving of respect in cases where title has passed from man to man in reliance upon a sustained trend of judicial opinion.

"But this, my Lords, is not the present case. If my view is well founded citizens of this country have for generations mistakenly held themselves precluded from making these dispositions. I cannot conceive that it is my function as a judge of the Supreme Appellate Court of this country to make error perpetual in a matter of this kind"; ibid. 859–60.

ries out the evolutionary development of the constitutional liberty of the subject."[107]

His approach to statutory interpretation showed the same antithetical tendencies reflecting both a duty to follow the legislature and his delight that such constraint had been avoided.[108] Yet, no matter how incisive his opinions, there was a tendency toward superficiality, in the sense that within a single judgment Birkenhead could both express reluctance about stating a principle any more widely than absolutely necessary for the decision and indulge in a broad discussion of the policy underlying the rule.[109] One even has the feeling that Birkenhead was sometimes unaware of his innovations.

Birkenhead is not an easy man to characterize. His career was, in the strict sense, meteoric. He never fulfilled his potential as a lawyer and a judge, not through any lack of ability but through lack of application. After he left the cabinet, he refused to sit as a law lord and in 1928 he refused an invitation to return to the Woolsack.[110] He perhaps represented a new phenomenon in English public life, an outstanding lawyer who found the judicial work of the House too trivial to retain his interest. After Haldane, the Lord Chancellorship was seen far less as the pinnacle of a political career, although still the goal of a lawyer or judge with political ambitions.

When the coalition finally broke up in 1922, Bonar Law's support-

107. *Secretary of State for Home Affairs* v. *O'Brien*, [1923] A.C. 603, 614.

108. In the *Rhondda* case, [1922] 2 A.C. 339, he was first a little impatient about not being able to look at the parliamentary history of the Sex Disqualification Act. "On many grounds I regret this circumstance, for that history would upon its personal side have been worthy of the massive irony of Gibbon. I am, however, debarred from the entertainment of speculating upon the grounds which have disabled a noble and learned friend of mine from discovering in his legislative capacity that which he so plainly discerns when he applies his judicial self to the same subject matter"; ibid. 349. He then delivered a homily on the rules of construction:

The words of the statute are to be construed so as to ascertain the mind of the Legislature from the natural and grammatical meaning of the words which it has used, and in so construing them the existing state of the law, the mischiefs to be remedied, and the defects to be amended, may legitimately be looked at together with the general scheme of the Act. There can be no doubt that whatever the words mean, and whether or not they be taken in their most literal sense and must be construed so as to remove all possible disqualification, they are words as vague and general as can be found in any Act of Parliament. What we have to ask ourselves is whether the legislature, when dealing with a constitutional question of the utmost gravity, and effecting a revolutionary change in the privileges of this House, and dealing with and binding His Majesty's prerogative, has seen fit to do so by words which can be thus described. [Ibid. 365]

109. E.g., *Fitch* v. *Dewes*, [1921] 2 A.C. 158, 163, 165.

110. See, for instance, *Les Affreteurs Réunis S.A.* v. *Leopold Walford, Ltd.*, [1919] A.C. 801. "It appears to me plain that for convenience, and under long established practice, the broker in such cases, in effect, nominates the charterer to contract on his behalf, influenced probably by the circumstance that there is always a contract between charterer and owner in which this stipulation, which is to inure to the benefit of the broker, may very conveniently be inserted"; ibid. 806–7.

ers felt unable to accept Birkenhead as Chancellor, although prepared to allow him the India Office, and the search for an acceptable Tory Chancellor was on. After Pollock (Hanworth) turned it down, the field was seemingly limited to Sumner and Cave. Sumner, however, had shown what many felt to be unjudicial qualities in his vigorous support of General Dyer after the Amritsar Massacre. Although Cave (along with Finlay and Carson) had been chastised by Birkenhead for speaking out on Home Rule while he was a law lord[111] (itself further evidence of the professionalization of the Lords of Appeal), the choice ultimately fell to him. Except for the nine-month interlude of a Labour administration, Cave remained on the Woolsack until 1928.[112]

Cave, who had had a competent, but not outstanding career at the Chancery Bar, entered Parliament at the relatively late age of fifty, ultimately becoming Solicitor-General in 1915 and Home Secretary when Lloyd George came to power in 1916. In 1918 he became a Lord of Appeal and it was assumed that his political career was over, since his political instincts were not particularly acute.[113] Indeed, he himself appeared to see the bench as a retreat from politics and controversy, and it was natural that he would view the role of the judges in apolitical and noncreative terms; this tone colored his judgments both as a Lord of Appeal and as Lord Chancellor. He saw his function as a law lord strictly as that of an arbitrator and not as a legislator or policymaker. Thus, on the question of whether a state was entitled to sovereign immunity he said, "[W]here such a question arises it is desirable that it should be

111. Apparently Cave was encouraged to take this position by his wife and mother. Indeed, his wife and mother were extremely ambitious for him. See Viscountess Cave, Preface to A. Cave, *Three Journeys* at x. "My husband came to that delectable scarlet seat on which in dreams, throughout the ages, I had ever kept a single eye."

For his views on the Irish question, see George Cave, "The Constitutional Issue" in *Against Home Rule*, ed. Rosenbaum (1912), at 106.

112. George Cave; b. 1856; father, Liberal M.P.; educ., Merchant Taylors and St. John's College, Oxford (First, "Greats"); Unionist M.P. for Surrey (Kingston), 1906; Attorney-General, 1914; House Secretary, 1916–19; Lord of Appeal, 1918–22; Lord Chancellor, 1922–24, 1924–28; d. 1928; *Dictionary of National Biography, 1921–1930,* at 164.

See also Charles Mallet, *Lord Cave;* Heuston, *Lives* 408–48.

113. In 1918 he caused confusion by holding the offices of Home Secretary and Lord of Appeal simultaneously for a few weeks; Heuston, *Lives* 420. There is, in fact, a streak of political naiveté in Cave's political actions. For instance, while Speaker of the House of Lords he found himself the center of a controversy. In 1926 the Labour peers, though a small minority, tried to obstruct and prolong the debates on industrial legislation. On the advice of Lord Salisbury, Cave took the unprecedented action of accepting a motion and refusing to allow debate on it. To act without a precedent was unusual for Cave, though his action was eventually vindicated, the uproar it caused must have convinced him that the best policy is to do what has been done before; Heuston, *Lives* 435–36; Mallet, *Cave* 285–327. Shortly before his death in 1928 he wrote to the Prime Minister explaining that he had made a mistake in a Privy Council decision in which he had given judgment. See *Wigg v. Attorney-General of the Irish Free State,* [1927] A.C. 679 (P.C.). The case was reheard; Heuston, *Lives* 440–43.

determined, not by the Courts, which must decide on legal principles only, but by the Government of the country."[114] One of his favorite phrases when rejecting a proposition of law was "I know of no authority";[115] and he was equally concerned about the welfare of *stare decisis*. Phrases such as "I should say that the ruling has grown reverend by age and is not now to be broken in upon"[116] and "I think that it is far too late either to question the principle or to endeavour to whittle it away"[117] were part of his style.[118]

The same rather formalistic approach characterized his interpretation of statutes. With respect to most statutes he did not allow his views to inhibit reasonable interpretation,[119] but he had no hesitation, especially in his later years, in having his position make nonsense of tax legislation. In *Nevill v. Inland Revenue Commissioners* he admitted that he accorded tax statutes special treatment. "It may well be that this result was not foreseen by the framers of § 4 and 5 of the Act, but in construing a taxing Act regard must be had not to what one might expect to find in the Act but to the words of the Act themselves."[120] This ap-

---

114. *Duff Dev. Corp.* v. *Government of Kelantan*, [1924] A.C. 797, 808.

115. See, e.g., *in re Clifford & O'Sullivan*, [1921] 2 A.C. 570, 583 (Ire.); *Ambatielos* v. *Anton Jurgens Margarine Works*, [1923] A.C. 175, 183; *Commonwealth Shipping Representative* v. *P. & O. Branch Service*, [1923] A.C. 191, 197 (1922); *Swift & Co.* v. *Board of Trade*, [1925] A.C. 520, 532; *Lord Advocate* v. *Jaffrey*, [1921] 1 A.C. 146, 158 (Scot. 1920) (reaffirming unity of domicile of husband and wife). Speaking of testimony of his fellow law lords, Mallet reports that "some noted also his attachment to precedent, his distrust of evolution and change"; Mallet, *Cave* 226.

116. *Ward* v. *Van der Loeff*, [1924] A.C. 653, 664.

117. Ibid. 665. Contrast his commonsense attitude in *Samuel & Co.* v. *Dumas*, [1924] A.C. 431, 446–47: "Apart from authority . . . there seems to me to be something absurd in saying that when a ship is scuttled by her crew her loss is not caused by the act of scuttling but by the invasion of water which results from it."

118. Although Cave would cite a number of precedents in every speech, his judgments were clear, concise, and rarely long; e.g., *Sorrell* v. *Smith*, [1925] A.C. 700, and *Levene* v. *IRC*, [1928] A.C. 217. It is even arguable that he used his concise style on occasion to serve him as a means of avoiding earlier precedents, which, by the logic of his own position, should have been regarded as binding. Thus, in *Elder, Dempster & Co.* v. *Paterson, Zochonis & Co.*, [1924] A.C. 522, in which he presided, Cave ignored *Dunlop Pneumatic Tyre* v. *Selfridge* in dealing, in a few lines, with what, it is arguable, should have been treated as a privity of contract problem. "It may be that the owners were not directly parties to the contract; but they took possession of the goods . . . on behalf of and as the agents of the charterers, and so can claim the same protection as their principals"; ibid. 534. The decision is criticized in *Midland Silicones* v. *Scruttons*, [1962] A.C. 446, 468 (1961). The opinions of the other law lords were preferred to that of Cave; ibid. 477–78, e.g., per Simonds at 481.

119. See e.g., *Russell* v. *Rudd*, [1923] A.C. 309; *Salford Guardians* v. *Dewhurst*, [1926] A.C. 619, 626: "I base my decision on the scope and purposes of the statute." For his use of presumption, see *Frome United Breweries Co.* v. *Bath Justices*, [1926] A.C. 586, 590.

120. *Nevill* v. *IRC*, [1924] A.C. 385, 399. See also *Bradbury* v. *English Sewing Cotton Co.*, [1923] A.C. 744, 754.

proach did not mean that Cave invariably found against the Crown,[121] but he did so in a significant number of cases,[122] even if, on occasion, it meant ignoring the strict wording of the provision and looking to the "scheme of the Act."[123] At times it seemed as if the only civil liberty that Cave and his contemporaries cared about seriously was the right of those who could afford the appropriate legal advice to pass the burden of taxation to those who had less skilled or no advice.

It goes without saying that the mere articulation of a declaratory theory did not alter the nature of the appellate process, and from time to time Cave's "inarticulate major premises," as Mr. Justice Holmes would have called them,[124] showed through. He was entirely unable in *Sutherland* v. *Stopes* to hide his prejudices about birth control.[125] He could also sometimes be moved by a sense of justice[126] and, as a humane person, he on occasion would attempt to ameliorate the effect of his decisions.[127] Nor was he always timid.[128] Yet if the law, as he perceived it, was clear, he considered it his duty to apply it regardless of results, although he would do what he could to mitigate its harshness.[129]

Evaluation of Cave is not easy. He was a member of the House of Lords for some nine years, thus his behavior toward the judicial process

121. *Brown* v. *National Provident Institution*, [1921] 2 A.C. 222, 241–42. Uncharacteristically, Cave not only dissented in favor of the Crown, but talked in what appeared to be functional terms about the interpretation of statutes. See also *Swedish Cent. Ry.* v. *Thompson*, [1925] A.C. 495.

122. Other examples of hostility to the executive can be found in *Foulsham* v. *Pickles*, [1925] A.C. 458, 465; *IRC* v. *Lysaght*, [1928] A.C. 234, 241 (dissent); *IRC* v. *Fisher's Executors*, [1926] A.C. 395, 397.

123. *Whitney* v. *IRC*, [1926] A.C. 37 (1925).

124. Oliver Wendell Holmes, Jr., "The Path of the Law" 457.

125. [1925] A.C. 47 (1924). See, for instance, ibid. 56–58, although he began in a highly objective manner. See especially at 55.

126. See, e.g., his dissenting judgment in *Edwards* v. *Porter*, [1925] A.C. 1, 14 (1924), where, finding *Seroka* v. *Kattenburg*, 17 Q.B.D. 177 (1886), unhelpful, he had to appeal to "justice." This was an unusual case in that Cave actually swept away an old rule because the explanation for it (the previously existing legal unity of spouses) had by then gone. His views were later passed into law in the Law Reform (Married Women and Joint Tortfeasors) Act of 1935.

127. In *Mersey Docks & Harbours Bd.* v. *Procter*, [1923] A.C. 253, 263, he gave no costs against the widow with respect to the appeals either to the Court of Appeal or to the House, as she "has been a great sufferer." Dissenting in *Jones* v. *Waring & Gillow, Ltd.*, [1926] A.C. 670, 685, where the House had to choose between two innocent victims of fraud, he would not permit the successful party to recover more than the amount necessary to cover his loss.

128. In *Russell* v. *Rudd*, [1923] A.C. 309, 315, he overruled a number of Court of Appeal decisions, though he quickly reinforced his opinion with respectable precedents supporting his views. In *Swedish Cent. Ry.* v. *Thompson*, [1925] A.C. 495, finding himself without any positive authorities (see especially ibid. 505), he managed to struggle on and hold that a company was capable of having more than one residence at a time.

129. See, e.g., *Duff Dev. Corp.* v. *Government of Kelantan*, [1924] A.C. 797, 810, and *Mersey Docks and Harbours Bd.* v. *Procter*, [1923] A.C. 253, 263.

inevitably helped set the tone for later decades; yet his vision of the appellate process provided little rationale or justification for a second appeal. He was conservative in the broader sense, having no particular interest in law reform through either litigation or legislation.[130] He was a personally generous man,[131] yet totally out of touch with the attitudes of working-class England.[132] He was the archetypal English twentieth-century judge.

On Cave's resignation in 1928, the Chancellorship passed to Lord Hailsham.[133] The new Chancellor was a Conservative of the old school, whose career (and often his views) were akin to those of another Irish Protestant, Halsbury. Hailsham came to the bar relatively late and was still not a Member of Parliament when he became Attorney-General, in 1922, at age fifty. Once in the House, however, he became an active parliamentarian. He was bitter in his attacks on the Labour administration of 1924, and ultimately his partisan zeal acquired him the Chancel-

---

130. He did, however, begin reforms in the machinery for the administration of justice; Mallet, *Cave* 257–83. Most important of all, he was Lord Chancellor at the time of the massive reforms in land law in 1925. Here he was at home, as in the days when he had been a Chancery barrister, applying himself to details. The inspiration and the initiation of the reforms were rightly claimed by Haldane and Birkenhead. See Heuston, *Lives* 447–48.

131. He was interested in charities throughout his life. He also was responsible for bringing the decision in *Archer-Shee* v. *Baker*, [1927] A.C. 844, before the House of Commons and urged compensation for the wrongful dismissal of the naval cadet; Mallet, *Cave* 151.

In *Ward* v. *Laverty*, [1925] A.C. 101 (Ire. 1924) he affirmed the modern-sounding view that the overriding consideration when determining the custody of children was the welfare of the child.

132. In 1927 it was he who piloted the Trade Disputes and Trade Unions Bill through the Lords, legislation that sought to restrict trade unions and (indirectly) the Labour party after the General Strike. Of the bill, Cave said, "This Bill makes no attack on trade unions or on trade unionism. Still less can it be harmful to any workman. We seek only to defend . . . the ordinary folk in the mass, and especially the quiet and willing worker against injustice and oppression"; Mallet, *Cave* 308.

Further evidence of Cave's mistrust and misunderstanding of the claims of organized labor can be found in the Cave Commission Report on the Trade Boards Acts, in which, contrary to the views of the Whitley Committee, it was argued that trade boards should not be used to reinforce and foster collective bargaining, Report on Trade Board Acts. Cmd. 1645 (1922). See generally F. Bayliss, *British Wage Councils* 20–25.

In the light of this it was not surprising that Cave's attitude toward the problems of unemployment seems harsh by today's standards. See Mallet, *Cave* 268. It was perhaps fortunate that Cave was little concerned in his judicial capacity with decisions involving the unions or trade disputes. But see his discussion of picketing in *Glasbrook Bros.* v. *Glamorganshire County Council*, [1925] A.C. 270, 276 (1924).

133. Douglas McGarel Hogg; b. 1872; father "a philanthropist" who financed his philanthropy through his merchant's business; educ., Eton; called to bar, 1902; K.C., 1917; Attorney-General, 1920; M.P. (Cons.), St. Marylebone, 1922–28; Lord Chancellor, 1928–29; Secretary of State for War, 1931–35; Lord Chancellor, 1935–38; Lord President of Council, 1938–39; d. 1950; *Dictionary of National Biography 1941–1950*, at 400.

See "The Duties of a Lord Chancellor" (Presidential Address to Holdsworth Club, Birmingham, 1936). See also Mowat, *Britain between the Wars* 309, 323; *The Times*, 17 Aug. 1950.

lorship in 1928. With the return of a Labour government in 1929, he led the opposition in the House of Lords while at the same time taking an active interest in its judicial affairs. When the first National government was formed by MacDonald in August 1931, the Prime Minister vetoed the inclusion of Hailsham on the ground that Hailsham was "particularly obnoxious" to the Labour party; not only had Hailsham harried the two Labour administrations, he had also been one of the leading advocates of a belligerent attitude toward the unions at the time of the General Strike. In the government formed late in 1931, however, MacDonald yielded and Hailsham became Secretary of State for War, a post he held until resuming the Lord Chancellorship in 1935. Hailsham thus had two periods of active judicial work in the Lords. The first was from his appointment as Chancellor in 1928 until his reentry into the cabinet in 1931. The second period of regular judicial work was between 1935 and 1938, the occasion of his second Chancellorship.

Judicially, Hailsham's contribution to the development of the common law was not outstanding. He was responsible for some useful developments in the law of torts—for instance, his effort to limit contributory negligence to cases of "substantial contributory negligence" (although some would argue that he made the situation worse)[134]—but he failed to put his mark on the appellate work of the Lords.[135] In his second Chancellorship, Hailsham may have made some efforts to redress the balance between revenue authorities and the taxpayer;[136] but his judicial reputation is often dominated by his views on workmen's compensation. In a period increasingly attuned to the idea of compensation, not only under legislation but in tort as a whole, he adhered rigidly to concepts of fault that tended to be harsh toward the workman. He reaffirmed the doctrine of "added peril,"[137] he insisted on the finality of doctors' certificates, and he was hostile to the idea of considering market conditions in assessing compensation.[138] Thirty years earlier such views might have been regarded as reflecting the norm; but in the more liberal judicial climate of the 1930s they marked Hailsham as a reactionary in policymaking.

Heuston has described Hailsham as "a typical representative of English Conservatism of a kind which his fellow-countrymen once greatly

134. "[H]e had not the deep interest in the analysis of legal principles which marks the great jurist"; Heuston, *Lives* 482.

135. *Swadling* v. *Cooper*, [1931] A.C. 1, 5 (1930). Hailsham delivered a speech on behalf of all the law lords: Dunedin, Buckmaster, Warrington, and Thankerton.

136. E.g., *IRC* v. *Crossman*, [1937] A.C. 26, 32 (1936). But such a case could equally be explained in terms of Hailsham's rigidity of mind, rather than any effort—conscious or unconscious—to redress balances.

137. *Stephen* v. *Cooper*, [1929] A.C. 570 (Scot.). "[T]he injury sustained by the appellant was due to an accident caused by an added peril due to his own conduct"; ibid. 573.

138. *White* v. *London & North Eastern Ry.*, [1931] A.C. 52, 55 (1930).

admired";[139] and indeed he was typical. He had the robust common sense of a "good common lawyer," and he was also no mean intellect. He was, like most "good common lawyers," conservative by instinct and conservative by training. He was never fully aware, even while in the cabinet, of what was going on in domestic or foreign affairs, although he never allowed such ignorance to interfere with his views. He would have made an admirable King's Bench judge, but he probably did not have the qualities that make a great appeal judge. Among these qualities is a commitment to appellate work. Hailsham gave the impression, however, of being more interested in the political than the legal side of his work, something that is understandable in view of the fact that some thought he might have become Prime Minister had he stayed in the Commons. Indeed, while Lord Chancellor, he served as Deputy Prime Minister and undertook various assignments abroad; thus he sat less often than his predecessors in appellate work.[140]

Hailsham, like most of his contemporaries, had no clear philosophy about the judicial process. Indeed, he seemed to have given little thought to the role of a final appeal court. He appeared incapable, for instance, of appreciating the political element necessarily present in the interpretation of a constitution. Indeed, it is he who must bear at least some of the blame for those Privy Council decisions in which most of the Canadian "New Deal" legislation was struck down,[141] and it can even be argued that he was the *causa causans* of the final Canadian decision to abolish appeals to Downing Street.[142]

If one were to look merely at Hailsham's conservative disposition and premises and to record his inability to appreciate the role of the courts in constitutional matters, such observations would not distinguish him from the vast majority of English judges. What is perhaps saddest is that, during the most sophisticated period in the House of Lords as a judicial body, he failed to understand the rationale that Atkin was seek-

139. Heuston, *Lives* 494.

140. Hailsham wrote to Atkin apologizing for his inability to sit because of political work and illness. "I can only say again how sorry I am that I should leave my colleagues to carry the burden of this judicial work unassisted by their official head"; ibid. 487.

141. After the hearing of these appeals, but before the decision was given, Hailsham wrote to Atkin, who was presiding:

I think that you and I are both agreed as to the paramount importance of retaining the Appeal to the Privy Council from the Dominions of the Crown and as to the importance of constituting a board which will inspire confidence by its decision in all parts of the Empire. I am glad to tell you that I have recently heard indirectly that no less than four of the Canadian Counsel which were engaged in the recent Privy Council Appeal have severally expressed the greatest possible satisfaction as to the constitution of the Board, so that obviously you were all impressing as I felt sure you would do. . . . I expect the decisions, when given, will carry conviction, which after all is the best test of the strength of the tribunal. [Ibid. 487]

142. For some of Hailsham's difficulties in dealing with "the rising tide of nationalism in the Dominions," see ibid. 486–87.

ing to spell out for the House, especially its potential role in developing the common law. A letter from Hailsham to Sankey is all too revealing. He was urging the former Chancellor to sit in a particular appeal.[143] "Roche cannot sit as he was in the Court of Appeal, and I shall normally therefore be only left with Atkin, who is rather apt to take the opportunity of making the law as it ought to be, instead of administering it as it is. I am really rather anxious as to what may be formulated as the Common Law doctrine; Atkin is naturally apt to be followed by his fellow law lords of the Chancery or Scottish Bar on a Common Law point, and I should really value your assistance, in order to elucidate what the Common Law really is."[144]

In ways such as these, Hailsham helped to eviscerate the spirit and purpose of the House of Lords. *Addie and Sons* v. *Dumbreck*[145] offered the opportunity to soften slightly the rigidity of the distinctions relating to occupiers' liability that had emanated from Mr. Justice Willes in 1866 and 1867.[146] These standards, which were originally intended to be flexible, became first rigid and then fossilized by a harsh application of the English doctrines of precedent.[147] In *Addie* during his first Chancellorship, the Scottish courts had refused to apply the rigid tests, at least in this case where a child was involved and what would now be called an "attractive nuisance" was present. The House, led by Hailsham and egged on by that éminence grise, the editor of *Law Quarterly Review* (Pollock),[148] in a speech that looked solely to precedent,[149] willingly held the child a trespasser and thus owed no duty of care. In this way Hailsham played into the hands of those who were to lead the House in the forties and fifties.

Although a strong man, Hailsham in some respects let the power and prestige of the office of Lord Chancellor drift. He did not maintain the pressure of law reform work developed by Sankey, and he did not give the leadership to the judiciary that the office of Lord Chancellor made possible. Yet Hailsham appears as a giant when contrasted with the last two Chancellors of the period, Maugham and Caldecote.

143. *Lindsey County Council* v. *Marshall*, [1937] A.C. 97 (1936). Sankey sat with Hailsham; and although Atkin did not sit the case went in favor of the plaintiff. The strong concurring speech of Wright in particular helped to limit the previous apparently almost limitless immunity of hospitals. Russell was *dubitante*.

144. Heuston, *Lives* 531.

145. [1929] A.C. 358 (Scot.).

146. *Gautret* v. *Egerton*, L.R. 2 C.P. 371 (1867); *Indermaur* v. *Dames*, L.R. 2 C.P. 311 (1867).

147. Kenneth Diplock, "The Courts as Legislators" 8.

148. M. de W. Howe, ed., *Holmes-Pollock Letters*.

149. With this decision should be contrasted—both on facts and on judicial approach —*Excelsior Wire Rope Co.* v. *Callan*, [1930] A.C. 404.

As both law lord and Lord Chancellor, Maugham was unimpressive.[150] He was essentially apolitical, at least in the English sense, which assimilates being apolitical with innate (and sometimes antiintellectual) conservatism. He had served both in the Chancery Division and in the Court of Appeal before becoming a Lord of Appeal in 1935. His appointment as Lord Chancellor in 1938 caused some surprise, particularly to his colleagues. (Heuston goes so far as to say that the appointment was made "to the astonishment of the political and legal world.")[151] Maugham's term of office, although brief, was predictably undistinguished[152] except possibly by his strong defense of the Munich agreement.[153] Indeed, it is arguable that he carried to the Woolsack all the worst failings and prejudices of the least distinguished type of English judge. He was preoccupied by status and money and his autobiography, written, it is true, when he was an octogenarian, is often nauseating in its extreme materialism.[154] Worse still, he was equally obsessive in his noisy demands for the independence (financial and otherwise) of the judiciary.[155] This particular subject was undoubtedly one on which the Lord Chancellor had the right and the duty to speak out. Yet Maugham's claims were both arrogant and unsophisticated; he gave the impression that judges were England's last line of defense against the surging armies of democracy.

Although, like the other Lord Chancellors of the period, Maugham found little time to sit while he held the Great Seal, he was also twice a Lord of Appeal in Ordinary (1935–38, 1939–41). From the present perspective, his views on the common law appear somewhat pedantic and in marked contrast to the broader approaches of the better-known law lords of the period. Where artificial persons were concerned, he refused to concede that a foreign company might be wound up in England after being dissolved in its place of incorporation.[156] In other ways

150. Frederick Herbert; b. Paris 1866; father, solicitor; educ., Dover College; Trinity Hall, Cambridge (First, Mathematics); called to bar, 1890; K.C., 1913; Judge, Chancery Division, 1928–34; Lord Justice, 1934–38; Lord Chancellor, 1938–39; Lord of Appeal, 1939–41; d. 1958; *Dictionary of National Biography 1951–1960*, at 718. See also Obituary, *The Times*, 24 Mar. 1958; F. H. Maugham, *At the End of the Day*; and Robin Maugham, *Somerset and All the Maughams*.

151. Heuston, *Lives* 553.

152. A notable exception was his sponsorship of the Evidence Act of 1938. See F. H. Maugham, *The Problem of Judicial Proof*. See also Heuston, *Lives* 555–57.

153. Mowat, *Britain between the Wars* 619; F. H. Maugham, *The Truth about the Munich Crisis*. For a qualified defense, see Heuston, *Lives* 557–60.

154. Brian Abel-Smith and Robert Stevens, *Lawyers and the Courts* 128–29 and 290–91. For his remarkably reactionary view of the English class structure even by the standards of an earlier period, see Maugham, *End of the Day* 565–66.

155. E.g., Maugham, *End of the Day* 335–36, 353–59.

156. "If the artificial person is destroyed in its country of origin, the country whose law creates it as a person, it appears to me it is destroyed everywhere as a person"; dissenting in *Russian & English Bank* v. *Baring Bros. & Co.*, [1936] A.C. 405, 440.

he allowed the urge for legal logic to overcome the needs of the business community and the problems of other sections of the community. He was not, for instance, prepared to find the existence of a contract where "on hire purchase terms" was not further defined.[157] In keeping with this attitude of a limited scope for the courts, he opposed the judicialization of contracts of employment[158] and only rarely did he deviate from a narrow formalistic approach.[159]

Beyond that, it is difficult to generalize about Maugham. His important speeches were few and far between. In the majority of cases he was satisfied with an exhaustive and not always particularly intelligible discussion of the facts of the case in question, with a minimum of legal analysis and almost no discussion of general principles. He was perhaps at his least impressive in *Liversidge* v. *Anderson*,[160] the *R.* v. *Halliday* of World War II.[161] His speech, although coming from the high priest of judicial independence, deferred to the executive in a way that none of the other members of the majority did. "To my mind this is so clearly a matter for executive discretion and nothing else that I cannot myself believe that those responsible for the Order in Council could have contemplated for a moment the possibility of the action of the Secretary of State being subject to the discussion, criticism and control of a judge in a court of law."[162] In many respects such a speech was the mark of the man.

157. *Scammell & Nephew, Ltd.,* v. *Ouston,* [1941] A.C. 251, 256 (1940). He regretted that "there are few, if any, topics on which there seems to be a greater difference of judicial opinion than those which relate to the question whether as the result of informal letters or like documents a binding contract has been arrived at"; ibid. 254.

158. E.g., *London Passenger Transp. Bd.* v. *Moscrip,* [1942] A.C. 332, where the House refused to find that a term in a contract of employment allowing an employee to bring a union official to represent him at a hearing of disciplinary charges was anything more than a privilege. See per Maugham, ibid. 342.

159. Perhaps the most famous example of this was his reluctance to accept the doctrine of sovereign immunity. "My lords, I have indicated my unwillingness to follow what I must admit to be the recent current of authority in our Courts as regards State-owned trading ships. In what follows I shall merely be indicating the opinion I have formed—one which I believe is shared by many judges and by nearly all persons engaged in maritime pursuits— that it is high time steps were taken to put an end to a state of things which in addition to being anomalous is most unjust to our own nationals"; *Compania Naviera Vascongada* v. *S.S. Cristina,* [1938] A.C. 485, 521.

160. [1942] A.C. 206 (1941).

161. This is a view that Heuston disputes. "After a period of uncertainty, it is now perfectly clear that Maugham's judgment in *Liversidge* v. *Anderson* was a masterly piece of constitutional law. There is no ground for suggesting he in any way departed from the judicial desire to do justice impartially between Crown and subject"; Heuston, *Lives* 565–66.

162. [1942] A.C. 206, 220 (1941). It can also be argued that Heuston's defense of the way Maugham behaved over Atkin's dissent in *Liversidge* is overly charitable. After writing a letter to *The Times* to refute some of the things he alleged Atkin had implied, Maugham proceeded to make a speech on the subject at a legislative session of the House of Lords. He justified his behavior on the rather strange ground that it was his duty as presiding law lord

About Caldecote[163] there is need to say little. He held the office of Chancellor for only a brief period and was generally agreed to have been one of its least distinguished incumbents. As Thomas Inskip, politician, he had been noted chiefly for his opposition to change in the Book of Common Prayer and his enthusiastic support of the Munich agreement. After an undistinguished period as Minister for the Co-ordination of Defense, he moved to the Chancellorship,[164] and when Churchill's wartime politics called for Simon in the cabinet, Caldecote became Lord Chief Justice. On his record as a law lord, there is perhaps fortunately not sufficient information to judge him.[165] Indeed, the Chancellorships of Maugham and Caldecote were the culmination of a long period when, instead of providing a role model for the judges, successive Chancellors either had not articulated a clear role for the appellate work of the House or had somewhat mindlessly regurgitated what sounded acceptable to the typical High Court judge. This approach was to be reflected increasingly in those appointed as Lords of Appeal.

---

to protect the Attorney-General (Somervell). With respect to this, even Heuston concedes that Maugham behaved "rather impulsively." See R. F. V. Heuston, "*Liversidge v. Anderson* in Retrospect" 33.

163. Thomas Walker Hobar Inskip; b. 1876; father, solicitor; educ., Clifton and King's College, Cambridge; called to bar, 1899; K.C., 1914; M.P. (Cons.) Bristol, 1918–29; Fareham, 1931–39; Solicitor-General, 1922–28; Attorney-General, 1928–29; Solicitor-General, 1931–32; Attorney-General, 1932–36; Minister for Co-ordination of Defense, 1936–39; Secretary of State for the Dominions, 1939; Lord Chancellor, 1939–40; Lord Chief Justice, 1940–46; d. 1947; *Dictionary of National Biography 1941–1950*, at 421–22.

164. Churchill himself remarked that Baldwin had necessarily to appoint a man of abilities inferior to himself. Michael Foot gave wide currency to a quip that no such surprising appointment had been made since the Emperor Caligula appointed his horse a consul. "The *Annual Register* in more measured language stated that Inskip's abilities had never been regarded as more than mediocre, nor could he lay claim to any great administrative experience"; Heuston, *Lives* 589.

165. He was certainly not amused by Atkin's speech in *Liversidge v. Anderson*. His letter was perhaps the strangest Atkin received from a judge.

It was rather a shock to me to read your criticism of judges who you think, have taken the wrong view about Regulation 18B. What shocked me was to be told that when I am face to face with claims affecting the liberty of the subject I am more executive minded than the executive. That is to say that I am no different from the judges who in Stuart days did what the Executive wanted. . . . I cannot believe you meant to say what your language suggests. If you could correct the impression which your words have given, it would be an immense relief to all of us. This sentence from your speech has already been used and twisted by people who wholly misunderstand the nature of the question in Liversidge's case, in order to defame the judges. I beg you won't think I write out of any concern for my own reputation. What I am concerned about is the effect upon the reputation of the Bench for impartiality already produced by your words. [R. F. V. Heuston, "*Liversidge v. Anderson* in Retrospect" 33]

Competing Traditions

In the rather bland environment that the law lords created, it was often the "political" law lords who provided an element of interest, frequently being far more willing to discuss the appellate process and to shape the law by incorporating policies they thought appropriate. To some extent, of course, to draw a line between the political and professional judges has that same element of artificiality as to draw a line between the law and politics; yet at its core this distinction has meaning. Atkinson and Shaw were appointed by Balfour and Asquith because they were party men and party men were needed to ensure that the appellate functions of the House were handled from the appropriate political viewpoint. Parmoor and Carson would never have reached the Lords but for their politics. Moulton and Sumner both came up the judicial hierarchy, but the former's prior political work and the latter's subsequent political predilections justify their inclusion here. Beyond this point the line is no doubt hazy: Dunedin and Macmillan both have some claim to be included, although with them, as with others, different forces seem at least as important in developing their judicial philosophies. Those who were primarily politicians, however, had their own driving force.

The Political Law Lords: Shaw Revisited

Among the Liberal and Labour law lords, perhaps the most interesting was Lord Shaw.[1] It is not easy to write about him. He was disliked by many contemporaries even in his own party, including Loreburn, As-

1. Thomas Shaw; b. 1850; father, baker; educ., Dunfermline High School, Edinburgh University; Faculty of Advocates, 1875; M.P. (Lib.) for Hawick Burghs, 1892–1909; Solicitor-General, Scotland, 1894–95; Lord Advocate, 1905–9; Lord of Appeal, 1909–29; created Lord Craigmyle, 1929; d. 1937; *Dictionary of National Biography 1931–1940*, at 806.

quith, and Haldane;[2] Macmillan's account of his life in the *Dictionary of National Biography* is vicious;[3] and no doubt much of the hostility was justified. There is considerable evidence to support Macmillan's assertion that, on hearing of Robertson's death, Shaw "abandoned his client at a critical stage" in a divorce case before the Court of Session in order to lobby the Prime Minister in London.[4] Loreburn opposed his appointment on the ground that "he was not a lawyer of stature and that he simply wished to 'cut a figure' in the House of Lords."[5] Lords of Appeal are, however, appointed by Prime Ministers, and Asquith granted Shaw his wish. Yet within a few weeks it appeared that Loreburn was right. In the *Osborne* case, the outcome of which was particularly important to the Asquith administration, Shaw helped strike down the union's political levy that was coupled with the requirement that subsidized M.P.'s accept the Labour whip. Shaw attempted to emulate Lord Justice Farwell's invocation in the Court of Appeal of Burke's address to the electors of Bristol, but in Shaw's mouth the sentiments sounded sententious and pretentious.[6] It was only a matter of time before the decision was reversed by legislation;[7] although the political damage was permanent. The decision had underscored the split between liberalism and socialism. It was also in these early months that Shaw irritated the Liberals who had appointed him by vacillating in his decisions on workmen's compensation,[8] while confirming the worst suspicions of the Conservatives with his decisions on taxation.[9]

Yet such undistinguished behavior was not the whole story. Shaw was undoubtedly an ambitious man, but Macmillan went too far in impugning his ethics and legal competence.[10] No doubt a more able

2. See R. F. V. Heuston, *Lives of the Lord Chancellors 1885–1940*, at 149–50.

3. *Dictionary of National Biography 1931–1940*, at 807.

4. His family still disputes the veracity of this, but the Asquith Papers appear to confirm it; Asquith Papers, Bodleian Library, Oxford.

5. Heuston, *Lives* 149.

6. *Amalgamated Soc'y of Ry. Servants v. Osborne*, [1910] A.C. 87, 115 (1909): "In regard to the Member of Parliament himself, he too is to be free; he is not to be the paid mandatory of any man, or organisation of man, nor is he entitled to bind himself to subordinate his opinions in public question to others, for wages, or at the peril of pecuniary loss; and any contract of this character would not be recognised by a court of law, either for its enforcement or in respect of its breach."

7. Trade Union Act of 1913. Directly related was the payment of M.P.'s, which began in 1912.

8. *Kerr v. Ayr Steam Shipping Co.*, [1915] A.C. 217, 231 (Scot. 1914); *Ocean Coal Co. v. Davies*, [1927] A.C. 271, 285 (1926).

9. *Westminster School v. Reith*, [1915] A.C. 259 (1914), when he dissented with Parmoor. The majority held that certain school buildings were not assessable to house duty. Shaw and Parmoor thought they were.

10. E.g., "The generous and democratic fraternity of the Parliament House is always ready to extend a welcome to ability, however humble in origin, but at the price of conformity with its high professional standards. This price Shaw was not invariably disposed

lawyer than Shaw, Macmillan was nevertheless an insensitive and arrogant man, and his views reveal more than a trace of the Scottish aristocrat's (or would-be aristocrat's) contempt for the poverty-stricken baker's boy who made good.[11] Shaw was not a great analytical lawyer, but in the inventory of skills required of a good appellate judge it can be argued that adequate analytic skills are sufficient and that political wisdom and common sense are more important than outstanding analytical skills. Shaw did have political sense[12] and political courage. Although he believed in a division between the tasks of politician and judge, his whole attitude toward law was more that of a politician than a lawyer. A Liberal Home Ruler, he was also an ardent supporter of the League of Nations,[13] a firm believer in the Empire,[14] an opponent of capital punishment,[15] and an advocate of cheaper education.[16] He had come down firmly against the South African war, taking the view that it was blatantly unjust and that a great empire like Britain should be patient with its recalcitrant colonies. He became violently unpopular as a result, his practice at the bar diminished, and on one occasion an angry mob tried to storm his house.[17] Most aspiring law lords avoided venturing out on such limbs.

Shaw was to be accused of being emotional.[18] There was certainly an element of the emotional in *Osborne* and perhaps in Shaw's vigorous dissent in *R. v. Halliday*, in favor of liberty of the subject.[19] Yet Shaw did feel strongly on issues of personal liberty, as his various speeches con-

---

to pay. . . . He . . . soon acquired a considerable practice, especially in jury trials, civil and criminal, which provided a more congenial sphere for the exercise of his gift of advocacy than the more exacting tasks of legal argument. . . . It cannot be said that he made any distinctive contribution to the law"; *Dictionary of National Biography 1931–1940*, at 807.

11. See Shaw's autobiographical works: Thomas Shaw, *Letters to Isabel* (1921 and 1936 eds.), and *The Other Bundle*. See also the brief biography by his son: A. Shaw, *Thomas Shaw*. Macmillan says of the autobiography, "So far as it purports to narrate facts and to convey impressions it must be read with considerable reservations"; *Dictionary of National Biography 1931–1940*, at 808.

12. See Thomas Shaw, *Other Bundle* 70; Thomas Shaw, *Letters to Isabel* 71 (1936 ed.), where he showed little enthusiasm for his early work at the bar. "[T]he law was my living: these other things, the movements of public affairs, they were my life."

13. See 30 *Parl. Deb.*, H.L. (5th ser.), col. 412 (26 June 1918), when he was President of the League of Nations Society; A. Shaw, *Thomas Shaw*, chap. 3.

14. See, e.g., Thomas Shaw, *Law of the Kinsmen* 131–74.

15. Thomas Shaw, *Letters to Isabel* (1936 ed.) at 44–45.

16. Ibid. (1921 ed.) at 144–70.

17. Ibid. 25–26. He, however, supported World War I, considering it to be a principled struggle.

18. Comparing him with Dunedin, Wright said, "If, between the two, it must be said that Lord Dunedin had the greater reputation, the contrast is easily explained. . . . Lord Shaw's law was touched with emotion, Dunedin's was law pure and simple, touched, if by anything, by common sense"; Lord Wright (Robert Anderson), "Lord Dunedin" 317.

19. [1917] A.C. 260. He refused to believe that Parliament had impliedly repealed

firm,[20] and *Halliday*'s case was, in many respects, more outrageous than *Liversidge* v. *Anderson*, its equivalent in World War II. Although Atkin, the dissenter in the latter case, felt some of the same opprobrium that was directed at Shaw, when Pollock dismissed Shaw's speech as an "emotional outburst,"[21] it was to some extent a reprimand by an insider toward a nonmember of "the Club." In other cases where more "acceptable" law lords spoke with feeling—for example, *Sutherland* v. *Stopes*—Shaw spoke with dignity and restraint.[22]

Indeed, Shaw, who was appointed as a Lord of Appeal before he was fifty, matured in office. With his political background and unencumbered by the narrowing effect of service on the lower courts, he came to

---

habeas corpus, which constituted "a suspension and a breach of those fundamental constitutional rights which are protective of British liberty":

When—so is the logic of the argument—Parliament took elaborate pains to make a legal course and a legal remedy plain to the subject as to all the regulations which were stated in detail, there was one thing which Parliament did not disclose, but left Courts of law to imply—namely that Parliament, all the time and intentionally, left another deadly weapon in the hands of the Government of the day under which the remainder of these very Acts, not to speak of the entire body of the laws of these islands protective of liberty, would be avoided. As occasion served the Government of the day, despotic force could be wielded, and that whole fabric of protection be gone. My Lords, I do not believe Parliament ever intended anything of the kind. [Ibid. 285]

He returned to the attack again and again. E.g., "Under this the Government becomes a Committee of Public Safety. But its powers as such are far more arbitrary than those of the most famous Committee of Public Safety known to history.... The only law remaining is that which the Bench must accept from the mouth of the Government: '*Hoc volo, sic jubeo; sic pro ratione voluntas*'"; [1917] A.C. 260, 285.

20. Shaw was consistent in his concern with the liberties of the subject. See *Daimler Co.* v. *Continental Tyre & Rubber Co.*, [1916] 2 A.C. 307, 311: "Courts of law should give a strict interpretation to statutory provisions of this character—an interpretation which in any case of dubiety or ambiguity shall be favorable to the liberty of the subject"; *Secretary of State for Home Affairs* v. *O'Brien*, [1923] A.C. 603, 646: "There is hardly any great historical occasion on which a government might not plead its views of the public good and the public convenience as an excuse for a violent deprivation from the subject of those rights in which he is secured by law. In declining jurisdiction in this case, your Lordships are not doing more than affirming a settled principle and declining to permit an invasion of constitutional right"; and *Scott* v. *Scott*, [1913] A.C. 417, 477, refusing to call on a judge to hear a case in camera: "To remit the maintenance of a constitutional right to the region of judicial discretion is to shift the foundations of freedom from rock to sand."

21. M. de W. Howe, ed., *Holmes-Pollock Letters* 244–45. However, the *Law Quarterly Review* said, "[N]otwithstanding the respect justly due to the concurrent opinions of Lord Finlay, Lord Dunedin, Lord Atkinson, and Lord Wrenbury, we doubt whether the future editors or successors of Anson and Dicey, weighing the whole matter in cold blood when the stress of war is past, will be satisfied that Lord Shaw's dissent was unfounded"; "Note," 33 *Law Quarterly Review* 206 (1917).

22. *Sutherland* v. *Stopes*, [1925] A.C. 47 (1924): "[I]n thus declining to enter upon a matter of deep contest in the medical and sociological and moral spheres, or even to be induced to express or indicate any view or inclination of mind thereon, I am simply paying the respect which is due to the correct ambit of a purely judicial task. This appeal presents questions of law, and in my opinion must accordingly on that footing alone be disposed of"; ibid. 73. See also *Herd* v. *Weardale Steel, Coal & Coke Co.*, [1915] A.C. 67, 75–76 (1914); and *in re Clifford & O'Sullivan*, [1921] 2 A.C. 570 (Ire.).

be a sensitive appeal judge, even if he was not appreciated by those lawyers accustomed to the more formalistic and analytical performances of the professional judges. Yet Shaw had a subtle sense of the judicial process and of its possibilities and pitfalls. Unlike most of his contemporaries Shaw publicly acknowledged that a great responsibility rested with the courts. He was quick to agree that the provinces of legislator and judge should ideally be separate.[23] Indeed, during his years as a law lord, he rarely spoke in legislative debates.[24] Yet he was enough of a realist to see that there could be in practice no rigid separation of powers. "The *casus improvisus* is always with us: and in ninety-nine cases out of a hundred it must be settled before Parliament can turn. The appeal is made not to laws, for there are none, but to law: call it what you like— the common law, the principles of jurisprudence—anything from the *jus divinum* to common sense, from *recta ratio* to a square deal: it is on and by and with that stuff that judges have to work, and they must do so not as bondmen but as free."[25]

In keeping with his view of the inevitably creative role of the final appeal court, Shaw was more sophisticated about the relationship of legislation and litigation than were most of his contemporaries. He refused to join in the chorus of complaints about parliamentary drafting,[26] since he regarded the judicial work of the House of Lords and the legislative role of Parliament as complementing one another. The final appeal could shape legislation by construction, although it should avoid evisceration.[27] In interpreting he believed "that artificiality should be eschewed, and that the interpreter should remain on friendly terms with

23. Thomas Shaw, *Other Bundle* 171–75.

24. The two most notable occasions on which he broke this silence were in 1916 when he felt it his duty to speak in support of the Military Service Bill, 20 *Parl. Deb.*, H.L. (5th ser.), col. 985 (25 Jan. 1916); and in 1918 in support of the League of Nations, 30 *Parl. Deb.*, H.L. (5th ser.), col. 412 (26 June 1918).

25. Thomas Shaw, *Legislature and Judiciary* 13–14.

26. "In our day judicial observations from the bench as to inartistic drafting grow fortunately fewer, under the force of this juster and more generous consideration; and the causticity of comment upon Parliamentary labours—which so often equated with slenderness of Parliamentary experience—is passing away"; ibid. 62.

27. "In these times apparently the statute is to be eviscerated by conceptions *not* of the judges who made the law, but their conceptions of what was the true and correct line of policy which must be supposed to have been in the minds, and conditioned words, of those who made the statute. I humbly think this to be both legally and constitutionally unsound, even though it be put forward under the guise of construction. Parliament can and does change its own mind, and it will not under the constitution allow that the judiciary should change its mind for it.

"My Lords, in my opinion, we best adhere to both legal and constitutional principle when we affirm the statute, and decline to accept—unless it be where there is the clearest judicial decision to that effect—a vital and fundamental alternative which should deeply cut into the comprehensive words plainly employed by the legislature"; *Great Western Ry. v. The Mostyn (Owners)*, [1928] A.C. 57, 87–88 (1927).

good sense, and keep up throughout his operations and comments the closest intimacy with the text itself."[28] When Shaw felt his judicial brethren were tampering with the spirit of legislation, he did not hesitate to speak out and call on Parliament to remedy what he perceived as an undesirable change of direction.[29]

Shaw's realism about the nature of the appellate process thus made it possible for him to be frank about the direction in which law should be developed. "[T]o keep the law from sterility, capable of moving alertly to the call of justice, unafraid of novelty of method or interpretation, fitting with the movement of the times, that is part of the intelligence of a truly progressive community."[30] As far as statutes are concerned, one can see his interest in the spirit of legislation in workmen's compensation and taxation cases. After an erratic beginning, Shaw attempted to ensure that the former category of legislation was interpreted in the spirit in which it had been passed, namely for the benefit of workmen.[31] In particular, he feared that the scope of the acts might be unduly cut down if an extensive body of case law were imposed upon them.[32] Whenever possible, he would hold that the dispute was one of fact for the arbitrator,[33] and

28. Thomas Shaw, *Legislature and Judiciary* 33. He added, "I should personally prefer that the obsolete even in statute were liable to condemnation by a judgment on desuetude, rather than, by refinement, be evaded or if possible whittled away"; ibid. 47–48.

29. "[T]he denial of compensation for his injuries is a defeat not only of the intention but of the terms of the Workmen's Compensation Act. I desire . . . to call the attention of the legislature to the position of peril in which large classes of His Majesty's subjects may be placed by the decision about to be announced from the Woolsack. . . . It is because I humbly but strongly feel that Parliament did not mean this, that I have ventured to suggest that the case demands the attention of the Legislature"; *St. Helens Colliery* v. *Hewitson*, [1924] A.C. 59, 89–90 (1923). The legislature eventually responded. See National Insurance (Industrial Injuries) Act of 1946, § 9.

In *Bevan* v. *Nixon's Navigation Co.*, [1929] A.C. 44 (1928), he again dissented firmly. "[T]he judgement of the Court of Appeal . . . *pro tanto* defeats the main object of the Workmen's Compensation Acts, and it unduly and improperly reduces the scale of compensation awarded therein"; ibid. 53.

30. Thomas Shaw, *Law of the Kinsman* 141. See also ibid. 100; and *Other Bundle* 239.

31. E.g., *Anchor Line* v. *Mohad*, [1922] 1 A.C. 146, 156 (1921); *Russell* v. *Rudd*, [1923] A.C. 309; *Costello* v. *Addie & Sons' Collieries*, [1922] 1 A.C. 164 (Scot. 1921); *Coltness Iron Co.* v. *Baillie*, [1922] 1 A.C. 170 (Scot. 1921). He decided against the worker in *Ocean Coal Co.* v. *Davies*, [1927] A.C. 271 (1926); and *Stephen* v. *Cooper*, [1929] A.C. 570, 574 (Scot.).

32. See *Stephen* v. *Cooper*, [1929] A.C. 570, 578 (Scot.): "[T]here are no inconsiderable dangers of an erroneous development of the law by making added peril a sole test and therefrom a settled and conclusive category of cases which are excluded from the 'remedial' operation of the Workmen's Compensation Act."

33. *Manton* v. *Cantwell*, [1920] A.C. 781, 792–93 (Ire.): "I decline to be bound by any general propositions of so-called principle or law in cases of which this is an example. . . . [I]n such cases the question is always, or nearly always, a question of degree and of fact." See also *Stephen* v. *Cooper*, [1929] A.C. 570, 579–80 (Scot.); *Kerr* v. *Ayr S.S. Co.*, [1915] A.C. 217, 232, 234 (Scot. 1914). The decision of the arbitrator was overruled in *Dennis* v. *A. J. White & Co.*, [1917] A.C. 479, 491, because not to do so would "stultify

when he felt that the House was deviating from the spirit of the acts he did not hesitate to dissent vigorously. Shaw's position singled him out from the other law lords who were thought by the mass of working-class England to be biased against the lower classes and their aspirations. Shaw, however, had been moved by the early strikers' marches, and the unions were impressed by the positions he took in workmen's compensation and related legislation,[34] with the result that he was chosen to be president of the Inquiry into Dock Wages in 1920.[35]

It was with these broad approaches that Shaw faced issues of taxation and constitutional law. He recognized the need to look to the purpose of tax laws if the redistributive purpose of the legislation were to be implemented. As soon as he arrived in the Lords in 1909, he argued in favor of looking to the spirit rather than the letter of the legislation. In *Attorney-General* v. *Duke of Richmond, Gordon and Lennox*, he made the case for looking at "the entire transaction,"[36] and in 1913 he was still fighting a rearguard action.[37] He eventually lost that battle, but in a different political context he was party to Loreburn's and Haldane's decisions that put the central executive largely beyond the scope of review by the regular courts. In *Board of Education* v. *Rice* Shaw was sensitive to the needs of procedural due process and began to spell out lines of development for the rational exercise of discretion.[38] In *Local Government Board* v. *Arlidge* he took a functional approach, justifying the judicial retreat in terms of the working of cabinet government and responsible democracy.[39] Although *Rice* might have been the more ele-

---

the statute." In *Coyle* v. *John Watson, Ltd.*, [1915] A.C. 15 (Scot. 1914), and *Trim Joint Dist. School Bd.* v. *Kelly* [1914] A.C. 667 (Ire.), he was party to extending the meaning of "accident," in the latter case going well beyond the ordinary understanding of the term.

34. In *Churm* v. *Dalton Main Collieries, Ltd.*, [1916] 1 A.C. 612, Shaw began his judgment with a statement of the mischief that he considered the Coal Mines (Minimum Wage) Act of 1912 was intended to rectify—the considerable fluctuations in the output of each miner according to working conditions:

There may be obstacles to the getting of coal, or much trouble in the texture of the seam. The man may labour severely for the removal of these, but the output of coal be small, and all ordinary measure of wages to labour be lost. All this may occur without fault on either side, and it may yet be highly expedient to maintain the system of payment by piece work.

How to avoid the resultant insecurity, a risk which imperils subsistence to the workmen employed underground? There can in my mind, be no doubt that this was the problem to which the Minimum Wage Act was addressed.

35. Shaw discusses his experiences in connection with this in *Letters to Isabel* (1921 ed.) 298. For Ernest Bevin's view (he was the "dockers K.C."), see Alan Bullock, *The Life and Times of Ernest Bevin* 116–42; and see generally C. L. Mowat, *Britain between the Wars, 1918–1940*, at 38.

36. [1909] A.C. 466, 475.

37. *IRC* v. *Herbert*, [1913] A.C. 326, 349 (Scot.).

38. [1911] A.C. 179.

39. [1915] A.C. 120, 135 (1914).

gant solution in the long run, *Arlidge* made good political sense in the short run.

It would be wrong, moreover, to think of Shaw as concerned only with public law or those areas of private law where some policy bordering on the political was involved. While not an outstanding analytic lawyer, to take as an example only one area of private law—contract— he showed a sense of responsibility for adapting that area of the law as decisions came up to the Lords. He sensed the need to equalize bargaining power.[40] He did not hesitate to exercise the court's inherent power to control the development of contract through the doctrine of public policy.[41] His business sense led him to help extend the doctrine of commercial frustration[42] and to take a commonsense approach to damages,[43] while his civil law background led him to flirt with the idea of extending restrictive covenants to the commercial field.[44] In contract law there is no doubt that Shaw would have been outclassed intellectually by Atkin and Wright, yet his spirit was akin to theirs and his contribution has been unfairly denigrated over the years.

The Political Law Lords: The Other Lib-Labs

The contrast between Shaw and the second of the Liberal law lords, Moulton,[45] could scarcely be greater. Moulton, who replaced Robson, in

40. His attitude is typified by his agreement with the majority decision in *Beck & Co. v. Szymanowski & Co.,* [1924] A.C. 43, 51 (1923): "But in my opinion the clause can never be used so as to convert goods undelivered into goods delivered or to warrant an implication to the effect that non-delivery in length or small measure was included in the objections which should, within the time fixed, be made to goods delivered. I am totally unable to make such an implication out of anything in the bargain between these parties— an implication which would seriously affect the security of business dealings." See also, on exception clauses, his decision in *Great Western Ry.* v. *Wills,* [1917] A.C. 148, 162.

41. E.g., in *Hyman* v. *Hyman,* [1929] A.C. 601, 614, Shaw held that a wife could not contract out of her right to alimony. "This indulgence is claimed in the name of the sanctity of contract. But in my opinion the law of England would not uphold the sanctity of any contract the plain object and effect of which is to undermine the sanctity of marriage, for this would be contrary to and subversive of one of the fundamental elements upon which society itself is based"; ibid. 622. See also *Mason* v. *Provident Clothing & Supply Co.,* [1913] A.C. 724, 738, where Shaw involved the doctrine vigorously to prevent a door-to-door salesman from being deprived of his livelihood.

42. See *Bank Line, Ltd.* v. *Arthur Capel & Co.,* [1919] A.C. 435 (1918); cf. *Horlock* v. *Beal,* [1916] 1 A.C. 486, 514. "Such cases, no doubt, will take their rank among the many desolating circumstances which demand remedial attention at the hand of parliament or the Executive Power."

43. *In re R. & H. Hall, Ltd., and W. H. Pinn (Junior) and Co.'s Arbitration,* [1928] All E.R. 763 (H.L.).

44. *Lord Strathcona S.S. Co.* v. *Dominion Coal Co.,* [1926] A.C. 108, 112 (P.C. 1925).

45. Fletcher Moulton; b. 1844; father, Methodist clergyman; educ., Kingswood School, London Univ., Cambridge (First, Mathematics); called to bar, 1873 (Patents Bar); Liberal M.P., 1885 (Battersea-Chapham), 1899–1906 (Lancaster); Lord Justice, 1906–12; Lord of

1912, was a nineteenth-century liberal rather than a radical, an imperialist who believed in free trade. Unlike Shaw, Moulton was an intellectual who had practiced in the rarefied atmosphere of the patent bar and had spent six years in the Court of Appeal. Moreover, he fitted into the "professional model" in the sense that he was sixty-eight when he was made a Lord of Appeal and then spent most of his period as a law lord serving as head of the Explosives Department at the War Office.

His approach to law, given those credentials, was predictable. He thought law ought to play a relatively small part in the life of society and that other forms of social control were to be preferred.[46] Persons who did not stand on their legal rights were to be admired.[47] The functions of the courts should be passive or even mechanistic.[48] He believed wholeheartedly in the importance of stare decisis;[49] statutes, once enacted by the legislature, were to be treated as sacrosanct.[50] So, in *Arlidge*,[51] when the other Liberal law lords were explaining, partly in functional terms, why

Appeal, 1912–21; d. 1921; *Dictionary of National Biography 1912–1921*, at 392–94. See also F. Moulton, *Life of Lord Moulton*.

46. In a speech entitled "Law and Manners," delivered in 1912, Moulton expressed his views on the scope of law, drawing a distinction between positive (enforceable) law and manners (unenforceable). "Positive law should not extend to every sphere of human conduct." He hated unnecessary or excessive legislation—first, as an undue and dangerous infraction of individual liberty, and second, because the results obtained by such legislation "did not better the true spirit of the people—rather it worsened it by removing the need for self-discipline"; Moulton, *Life of Lord Moulton* 96–99.

47. For example, in *Herd v. Weardale Steel, Coal & Coke Co.*, [1915] A.C. 67, 76 (1914), he expressed the hope that it would never be the lot of the courts to have to decide the question of the strict legal rights of a worker who, due to sudden illness or injury, wished to leave a mine before the contract time for raising the lift. "In honour of human nature it must be said that when cases like this occur it is in the highest degree rare to find people standing on their strict contractual rights." See also *Coltness Iron Co. v. Dobbie*, [1920] A.C. 916, 954 (Scot.).

48. As a barrister he had not set much store by recitation of cases and once advised a pupil that "the most valuable cases to remember are those that have been wrongly decided." But on the bench he took a stricter view of the judicial function. Once when he suggested to counsel that there was no precedent for the views being propounded, counsel's answer was that "the Common Law is the mother of precedents." "Yes, but she is a mother who is now past the age of child-bearing" was Moulton's reply; Moulton, *Life of Moulton* 69.

49. E.g., *British & Foreign Ins. Co. v. Wilson Shipping Co.*, [1921] 1 A.C. 188, 207–8 (1920).

50. E.g., "[T]he way in which this is to be done is a matter for the legislature and not for the Courts of law. Our duty is loyalty to see that those laws are followed, and not to allow ourselves to be turned aside from this our plain duty by arguments as to whether their provisions might wisely be altered in either direction, still less to be influenced by appeals to our feelings by suggestions that they may bear hardly on the individual or the community in any particular case"; *Everett v. Griffiths*, [1921] 1 A.C. 631, 693. See also *Vacher & Sons v. London Soc'y of Compositors*, [1913] A.C. 107, 130 (1912): "The argument *ab inconvenienti* is one which requires to be used with great caution. There is a danger that it may degrade into mere judicial criticism."

51. *Local Government Board v. Arlidge*, [1915] A.C. 120 (1914).

the courts should not be involved in control of the executive, Moulton argued:

Parliament has wisely laid down certain rules to be observed in the performance of its functions in those matters and those rules must be observed because they are imposed by statute, and for no other reason, and whether they give much or little opportunity for what I may call quasi-litigious procedure depends solely on what Parliament has thought right. These rules are beyond the criticism of the Courts, and it is not their business to add to or take away from them, or even to discuss whether in the opinion of the individual members of the Court they are adequate or not.[52]

For Moulton, the decision seemed agreeable in that it made the line between law and policy easier to draw.

His decisions fell within the scope of this approach. Moulton took a formalistic approach to tax law.[53] Indeed, he managed to help undermine the progressive tax legislation being developed by the Liberals during the period,[54] and it is said that he killed Lloyd George's land value tax with his satire.[55] Moulton's tough analytic position gave further credence to his denial that any "sentimental consideration" could have any weight in a question of "pure law,"[56] although it is arguable that lurking beneath his judgments are classical notions of the market as allocator of resources,[57] as well as concepts such as equality of sacrifice[58] and fairness in procedure.[59] Moulton, however, was a "modern" judge. His premises were well hidden, and his other commitments meant that his judicial contribution in the Lords could not easily be singled out for analysis.

Lord Parmoor[60] in spirit falls somewhere between Shaw and Moulton. Constitutionally, Parmoor's role was even more reminiscent of Gil-

52. Ibid. 150.
53. Almost mathematical, in fact. E.g., *IRC* v. *Herbert*, [1913] A.C. 326 (Scot.). For an example of his mathematical skills in a nontax case, see *S.S. Orduna (Owners)* v. *Shipping Controller*, [1921] 1 A.C. 250, 256 (1920), dissenting, where by working out the relative speeds and related matters, he had a clear understanding of the positions of the ships at each moment.
54. *Lumsden* v. *IRC*, [1914] A.C. 877, 905–6, 917 (criticizing the draftsman). However, his view did not prevail since the House was evenly split and the decision of the Court of Appeal stood.
55. Wright, "Lord Dunedin" 317.
56. *Herd* v. *Weardale Steel*, [1915] A.C. 67, 77 (1914).
57. *Coltness Iron Co.* v. *Dobbie*, [1920] A.C. 916, 954 (Scot.).
58. *Attorney-General* v. *De Keyser's Royal Hotel, Ltd.*, [1920] A.C. 508, 554.
59. E.g., *Mason* v. *Provident Clothing & Supply Co.*, [1913] A.C. 724, 745; *North-Western Salt Co.* v. *Electrolytic Alkali Co.*, [1914] A.C. 461, 476–77.
60. Charles Cripps; b. 1852; father, ecclesiastical lawyer; educ., Winchester and New College, Oxford (four "Firsts"); called to bar, 1877 (Parliamentary Bar); Unionist M.P. for Stroud, 1895–1900, Stretford, 1901–6, Buckinghamshire, 1910–14; cr. Lord Parmoor, 1914; Lord President, 1924, 1929–31; d. 1941; *Dictionary of National Biography 1941–1950*, at 186. See also Charles Cripps (Lord Parmoor), *A Retrospect*.

bert and Sullivan than the office of the Lord Chancellor itself. Despite the two additional law lords provided by the Appellate Jurisdiction Act of 1913, Haldane still found himself short of judicial personnel. In 1914 Asquith agreed to Cripps' becoming Lord Parmoor and a member of the Privy Council to render full-time unpaid judicial service.[61] Parmoor agreed to this in return for the privilege of remaining an active politician, and he availed himself of that privilege. Although regarded as a left-wing liberal, Parmoor had been elected to Parliament in 1895 as a Conservative and ended his career as Lord President of the Council in the Labour governments of 1924 and 1929–31, having spent much of his time as Labour leader in the Lords. Nevertheless, except for the time he was actually a cabinet minister, he continued to sit regularly as a law lord and to comment vigorously on social and political issues. It was little wonder that when Birkenhead reprimanded the Lords of Appeal for speaking out on political matters, they pointed to Parmoor's activities,[62] only to be told that his behavior was acceptable because litigants regarded Parmoor as "above party."[63]

Parmoor was both an intellectual and an iconoclast, holding views that set him considerably apart from the legal profession at large. He opposed World War I, considering it incompatible with Christian morality;[64] he agreed to join the first Labour government mainly because it was pledged to support the League of Nations,[65] although by then he was also in sympathy with other socialist policies.[66] The driving force of his life, however, was his Christian faith,[67] which came in the high-church established variety, and he sought to make the "rules of law accord with the highest principles of religion."[68] At the same time, as an intellectual,

61. For instance, he hardly missed a sitting of the Judicial Committee of the Privy Council during the war and was heavily concerned with prize cases; Cripps, *Retrospect* 84–85.

62. E.g., per Carson, 49 *Parl. Deb.*, H.L. (5th ser.), col. 93 (29 Mar. 1922).

63. *Dictionary of National Biography 1941–1950*, at 187. See also Balfour's view, in Heuston, *Lives* 325; Cripps, *Retrospect* 83.

64. Ibid., chap. 6.

65. He was one of the delegates to the Assembly of the League of Nations in Geneva in 1924 and made an important contribution to drafting the Protocol for the Pacific Settlement of International Disputes. See ibid., chap. 9.

66. He was an advocate of free universal and compulsory education; ibid., chap. 5. After reversing his earlier position, he became an advocate of Home Rule. He was also anxious to solve unemployment; 59 *Parl. Deb.*, H.L. (5th ser.), col. 870 (19 Mar. 1924).

67. Cripps, *Retrospect*, chap. 5.

68. "Unless the rules of law accord with the highest principles of religion and morality, they fail in their object. I do not mean by this that the ambit of law is as wide as that of religion or morality but so far as the law extends it should always strive to be in accord with the highest conception of duty which prevails at the time.

"The nearer that the enforcement of legal duty approaches to the Christian ideal, the more hope is there for the morality of mankind, and for the honourable peace among nations"; Charles Cripps (Lord Parmoor), *Do Well and Right and Let the World Sink* 16.

he attempted to draw a clear line between his political views and his judicial work.[69] Thus in *Lumsden* v. *Inland Revenue Commissioners*, he announced, "A statute is the expression of the will of the Legislature, and it is the duty of the Courts to give effect to the language in which the will of the Legislature has been expressed. It is not the function of Courts of law to entertain questions of policy, and I am unable to give any weight to arguments based on the consideration whether a particular interpretation is more favourable to the Crown or to the subject."[70]

It would be incorrect, however, to conclude that Parmoor had not thought about the appellate process. He had, and he felt that Selborne's plan for a single appeal had been right. "The test of a judicial system depends primarily on the judges of First Instance." The expense of a multiplicity of appeals "often means the denial of equality of justice to a poor litigant" and could not ensure that the ultimate decision would be correct.[71] He insisted on impartiality and even deplored the printed "cases" used in appeals to the Lords because he feared too many law lords had made up their minds before counsel had begun hearing the appeal.[72] At the same time he was painfully aware that "although the House of Lords as a judicial body should carefully avoid all risk of legislative action, yet, in fact, the decisions do come very near legislation in certain cases."[73]

Moreover, despite all his protestations, when there was a choice

69. The law "should not be open to the caprice of panic but administered in strong hands without desire for approbation and above all divorced from the competing cries of party warfare"; Cripps, *Retrospect* 4.

70. He continued by saying that ordinary words must be interpreted in their natural sense, technical words in their acquired sense, as far as possible all should be construed so as to make a consistent enactment of the whole. He concluded triumphantly and perhaps overoptimistically, for there was a clear split in the House, that in that case the enactment was consistent, the aim clear, and the language not difficult; *Lumsden* v. *IRC*, [1914] A.C. 877, 924.

On another occasion he said, "It was argued on behalf of the appellant that it would be convenient, and add to the protection of workmen in dangerous trades, to place a liability on the owner of a ship. A Court cannot consider such matters in a question of ultra vires, and I think that it is essential to draw a distinction between matters of legislation and matters of judicial interpretation, and that your Lordships are only concerned with a question of construction"; *Mackey* v. *James Henry Monks (Preston) Ltd.*, [1918] A.C. 59, 96 (Ire. 1917).

71. Cripps, *Retrospect* 71–76.

72. "One of the worst characteristics of a judge is his inability to listen to an argument which is not in accord with his preconceived opinion, or to give due weight to a principle which at first sight appears to him untenable. This has often seemed to me to be a permanent disadvantage in appeals to the House of Lords, where each Law Lord has had a full opportunity of considering the evidence and forming judgements thereon before the parties themselves are heard in argument"; Cripps, *Retrospect* 71. Parmoor may have been seriously overestimating the value of the printed cases, which are little more than pleadings together with the opinion of the lower courts.

73. Ibid. 75.

open to the court, Parmoor's personal beliefs and attitudes came to the fore. He was quick to detect and resent injustice, particularly toward minorities.[74] He detested World War I, as well as the opportunities it provided for setting up special tribunals[75] and extending the royal prerogative.[76] In his view, "Law and arbitrary power are in eternal enmity."[77] It is, therefore, not surprising that in *Attorney-General v. De Keyser's Royal Hotel*[78] he held that compensation had to be paid when property was confiscated, arguing that the Crown's claim "was redolent of the days of Charles I,"[79] while his general requirement of procedural due process had become clear in *Local Government Board v. Arlidge*.[80] Parmoor's hatred of religious intolerance and knowledge of ecclesiastical matters are clearly illustrated by *Bourne v. Keane*.[81] In workmen's compensation cases, he showed himself almost without exception[82] to be on the side of the worker.[83] In a quieter way, he was, in fact, a more consistent champion of the injured employee than Shaw,[84] and, in general,

74. Especially conscientious objectors. E.g., 21 *Parl. Deb.*, H.L. (5th ser.), col. 1085 (18 May 1916), and 22 ibid., col. 480 (29 June 1916).

75. E.g., 18 ibid., col. 68 (11 Mar. 1915).

76. See, e.g., Cripps, *Retrospect* 3: "I think it is as important now as it was in the days of Bracton, that the action of Government should be kept within its legitimate sphere and that the rule of law, without which there is no justice, should be carefully maintained."

77. Ibid.

78. [1920] A.C. 508, 566 ff.

79. Cripps, *Retrospect* 46.

80. [1915] A.C. 120, 142 (1914). See also ibid., 143–44; and *Attorney-General v. Royal Mail Steam Packet Co.*, [1922] 2 A.C. 279, 295, dissenting against the Crown.

81. [1919] A.C. 815. In a long speech, he carefully reviewed all the cases and statutes and also the doctrines of the Roman Catholic Church, and, with obvious satisfaction, concluded, "[T]he appeal should be allowed with costs, and persons professing the Roman Catholic religion will no longer be debarred from making bequests for masses for the souls of the dead, in conformity with a sacred and sacramental rite, which is an essential and integral part of a service of great solemnity in the liturgy of the Roman Catholic Church"; ibid. 917. From the point of view of the strict rule of stare decisis, Parmoor kept his conscience clear on the basis that the House was really only overruling one erroneous decision; ibid. 915.

82. In *Charles R. Davidson & Co. v. M'Robb*, [1918] A.C. 304, 333 (Scot.), he decided against the worker. The case dealt with injury while absent on leave for own purposes.

83. E.g., *Smith v. Fife Coal Co.*, [1914] A.C. 723, 732 (Scot.); *Coyle v. John Watson, Ltd.*, [1915] A.C. 15 (Scot. 1914); *Kerr v. Ayr S.S. Co.*, [1915] A.C. 217, 235 (Scot. 1914); *Glasgow Coal Co., v. Welsh*, [1916] 2 A.C. 10; *Great Western Ry. v. Helps*, [1918] A.C. 141, 146 (1917).

84. For example, he dissented, together with Loreburn, in favor of the worker in *Herbert v. Samuel Fox & Co.*, [1916] 1 A.C. 405, 416, while Shaw was in the majority. In the important cases of *Thom v. Sinclair*, [1917] A.C. 127, 144, and *Dennis v. A. J. White & Co.*, [1917] A.C. 479, 494, he joined with Shaw and the majority in supporting the employees' claims.

He also supported cooperatives. In *McEllistrim v. Ballymacelligott Co-operative Agricultural & Dairy Soc'y*, [1919] A.C. 548, 598 (Ire.), he dissented vigorously, holding that the rules of the society were not in restraint of trade and arguing that the contract of

one can see a shift in his views from a laissez-faire view of society[85] to a neocollectivist approach.[86] Parmoor was, at the very least, an intriguing appellate judge.

The Political Law Lords: The Conservatives

The Conservative law lords found the orthodox approach attractive, as has been seen, for a variety of reasons. Atkinson[87] is a prime example of the species.[88] He was no great lawyer and he was not a loved man. Indeed, the kindest thing that people said about him was that he was a "good common lawyer"; but Atkinson certainly had had a large practice at the Irish bar. He was a loyal Protestant, a loyal unionist, and a long-time Irish law officer. Shortly before the demise of the Conservative administration in 1905, Lindley was persuaded to retire and a search for a loyal Conservative to appoint as a Lord of Appeal was begun. After Finlay and others had turned down the job, it was offered to Atkinson.[89] He remained a law lord until 1928, yet he cannot have felt secure. Efforts were made to remove him in 1915 when some job had to be found for Campbell;[90] and in 1928 Atkinson was finally persuaded to retire in order to appease Quebec opposition to the Privy Council. It was hinted

---

membership of such a society was of a distinctive character, which should be treated differently from other types of contracts.

The only trade union case with which he had to deal was *Larkin* v. *Long*, [1915] A.C. 814, 838 (Ire.), when perhaps his sympathy for trade unionism was not so strong as in later years. He decided against the union. On the other hand, he did not agree with Mr. Justice Asbury's view that the General Strike was illegal. He also opposed the Trade Disputes and Trade Unions Bill in 1926. On the other hand, during the political crisis of 1931, he was one of those in the cabinet who supported a reduction in unemployment payments. Mowat, *Britain between the Wars* 392; 68 Parl. Deb.., H.L. (5th ser.), cols. 49, 52, 524 (4 July 1927).

85. In early decisions he took a conventional view of *pacta sunt servanda* in contract. E.g., *Dunlop Pneumatic Tyre Co.* v. *New Garage & Motor Co.*, [1915] A.C. 79, 101, (1914); *Horlock* v. *Beal*, [1916] 1 A.C. 486, 515.

86. On the question of raising agricultural wages in 1914, he said, "I deprecate interference"; 15 Parl. Deb., H.L. (5th ser.), col. 971 (2 Apr. 1914). However, by 1924 he was piloting the Agriculture Minimum Wage Bill through the Lords and in 1936 he wrote, "A drastic change in the treatment of agriculture and agricultural labour provided the means whereby the unfair inequality of existing social conditions—themselves a consequence of economic competition—might be remedied."

87. John Atkinson; b. 1844; father, physician; educ., Royal Belfast Academical Institution and Queen's College, Galway (First, Honours); called to bar (King's Inn, Dublin), 1862; practiced on Munster Circuit; Solicitor-General for Ireland, 1889; Attorney-General for Ireland, 1892; Conservative M.P. for N. Londonderry, 1895–1905; Lord of Appeal, 1905–28; d. 1932; *Dictionary of National Biography 1931–1940*, at 24.

88. Atkinson appears to have written nothing outside his judicial speeches. He spoke little in the House. He had no children or friends. It is said that, on his death, the Lord Chancellor's Office had difficulty tracing his wife in order to pay her his pension.

89. Heuston, *Lives* 62.

90. Ibid. 270, 273.

to him that his departure would represent at least one "old fogy" gone.[91]

There is little to separate Atkinson in terms of jurisprudential attitudes from an increasing number of his contemporaries. He espoused the law-is-the-law-is-the-law approach[92] and had no doubt that there was always one "proper construction of the statute."[93] In the Edwardian period he was one of the major forces in ensuring that English tax would become formalistic.[94] Although he was prepared to read tax statutes with the presumption that they did not bite unless the factual situation in issue was expressly covered, he was not eager to apply another canon of statutory construction, namely, that legislation should be presumed not to have infringed civil liberties.[95] Indeed, he was not particularly enthusiastic about civil liberties in either war or peace.[96]

In short, Atkinson was generally able to give effect to his "inarticulate major premises" without having to spell out what these premises were. By taking a narrow approach to precedent and statutory interpretation he was able to implement the premises without articulating them. That is not to suggest that he was deliberately partial; *Bourne* v. *Keane* is clear evidence of his striving for judicial impartiality.[97] When legislation

91. Ibid. 303–4.

92. "This rule of our law, like many others of our rules of law, was, no doubt, originally based upon, and embodied, certain views of public policy; but in this case, as in many others, the principles of public policy so adopted have, as numerous authorities conclusively show, crystallised, as it were, into strict and rigid rules of law to be applied, to use Lord Stowell's words, 'with rigour.' If that be so, as I think it clearly is, then the cases establish that it is wholly illegitimate for any judicial tribunal, which may disapprove of the principles of public policy so embodied in the rigid rule, to disregard that rule in any particular case, and base its decision on other principles of public policy of which it more approves. To do so would be to usurp the prerogative and powers of the legislature, since it is the function of the legislature not of judicial tribunals, to discard the principles embodied in such rules, and in its enactments embody others which it prefers"; *Rodriguez* v. *Speyer Bros.*, [1919] A.C. 59, 90 (1918) (dissent).

See also *Kerr* v. *Ayr S.S. Co.*, [1915] A.C. 217, 230–31 (Scot. 1914).

93. *G. Gibson & Co.* v. *Wishart*, [1915] A.C. 18, 26 (Scot. 1914).

94. See especially *Attorney-General* v. *Duke of Richmond, Gordon and Lennox*, [1909] A.C. 466, 475; *Golden Horseshoe Estates Co.* v. *Crown*, [1911] A.C. 480, 488 (P.C.); *Attorney-General* v. *Milne*, [1914] A.C. 765, 771–72.

95. "For myself I must say that I never could appreciate the contention that statutes invading the liberty of the subject should be construed after one manner, and statutes not invading it after another, that certain words should in the first class have a meaning put on them different from what the same words would have put upon them when used in the second"; *R.* v. *Halliday, ex parte Zadig*, [1917] A.C. 260, 274.

96. He was the lone dissenter in *Secretary of State for Home Affairs* v. *O'Brien*, [1923] A.C. 603, 622, taking the view that the Crown should have the right to appeal to the Lords from the Court of Appeal decision granting an order of habeas corpus. There is evidence, however, that where the civil right involved property, he was more prepared to support it; *Johnstone* v. *Pedlar*, [1921] 2 A.C. 262, 278 (Ire.). See also *Attorney-General* v. *De Keyser's Royal Hotel, Ltd.*, [1920] A.C. 508, 531; *Roberts* v. *Hopwood*, [1925] A.C. 578, 590; and see also his dissent in *Swift & Co.* v. *Board of Trade*, [1925] A.C. 520, 533.

97. Atkinson was, indeed, magnanimous: "I think it is too late in the day to hold in this country that a religious ceremony, believed by millions of the Roman Catholics of

ran afoul of his biases, however, the internal conflict was apparent in his decision. Dunedin noted this with respect to workmen's compensation.[98] While Atkinson did not always decide against the workmen,[99] he showed a clear bias in that direction;[100] he could also be vitriolic about what he regarded as benevolent interpretations of the legislation.[101]

His most scathing political outburst, however, came in *Roberts* v. *Hopwood*, where he denounced the "model" employment policies of the Poplar Borough Council. "The council would, in my view, fail in their duty if, in administering funds which did not belong to their members alone, they put aside all these aids to the ascertainment of what was just and reasonable remuneration to give for the services rendered to them, and allowed themselves to be guided in preference by some eccentric principles of socialistic philanthropy, or by a feminist ambition to secure the equality of the sexes in the matter of wages in the world of labour."[102] He compared the happier prewar position in Poplar when "the vanity of appearing as model employers . . . had not then, apparently, taken possession of the council, nor had the council become such ardent feminists as to bring about, at the expense of the ratepayers whose money they administered, sex equality in the labour market."[103] Irrespective of the "correctness" of the decision, these were strong words for one who, at other times, prided himself on judicial restraint.

Atkinson was, in general, a cautious man[104] who chose, if possible, narrow solutions.[105] He purported to see only a mechanistic role for the Lords, although he apparently never considered publicly what role the

Christendom to be a solemn and sacred sacrament, is merely a superstitious rite." He even felt the House was performing a "worthy task" in shattering the precedents; *Bourne* v. *Keane*, [1919] A.C. 815, 894–95.

98. *Simpson* v. *London, Midland & Scottish Ry.*, [1931] A.C. 351, 357 (Scot.).

99. See, e.g., *Mackey* v. *James Henry Monks, Ltd.*, [1918] A.C. 59, 77 (Ire. 1917) (opposing Parmoor and Wrenbury).

He voted in favor of the union in *Amalgamated Soc'y of Carpenters* v. *Braithwaite*, [1922] 2 A.C. 440, 453.

100. See, for instance, his early decisions in *Paquin, Ltd.* v. *Beauclerk*, [1906] A.C. 148, 166 (1905); *Jolly* v. *Kine*, [1907] A.C. 1, 6 (1906); *London & India Docks Co.* v. *Thames Steam Tug & Lighterage Co.*, [1909] A.C. 15, 20 (1908); *Clover, Clayton & Co.* v. *Hughes*, [1910] A.C. 242, 250; *Richard Evans & Co.* v. *Astley*, [1911] A.C. 674, 679; *Costello* v. *S.S. Pigeon (Owners of)*, [1913] A.C. 407; *Herbert* v. *Samuel Fox & Co.*, [1916] 1 A.C. 405, 408; *Kerr* v. *Ayr S.S. Co.*, [1915] A.C. 217, 224 (Scot. 1914). Atkinson's speech in this last case attempted to hamper the working of the acts by applying facets of the law of tort to the acts themselves.

101. In *Ocean Coal Co.* v. *Davies*, [1927] A.C. 271, 281, 283 (1926), interpreting § 14 of the Workmen's Compensation Act of 1923.

102. [1925] A.C. 578, 594.

103. Ibid. 591–92.

104. E.g., *Daimler Co.* v. *Continental Tyre & Rubber Co.*, [1916] 2 A.C. 307, 317.

105. But occasionally he was ambitious. See, for example, his dissent in *F. A. Tamplin S.S. Co.* v. *Anglo-Mexican Petroleum Prod. Co.*, [1916] 2 A.C. 397, 422.

appeal judges played in the legal process or in the Constitution. Although the Atkinson approach was overshadowed by the judicial glamour of the thirties, it was a position that was to bring into question the value of retaining a second appeal. Even by the standards of the English bench, Atkinson was not a distinguished law lord.

In terms of background it is perhaps strange to classify Sumner as a political appointee. After all, he was one of Haldane's two "nonpolitical" appointments following the 1913 legislation. He had never been a Member of Parliament,[106] but as John Hamilton, he had from humble beginnings achieved success at the Commercial Bar and sat in both the King's Bench Division and the Court of Appeal. In this sense he was clearly a "professional" appointee. Yet, as a Lord of Appeal he was seriously considered as an alternative to Buckmaster as Lord Chancellor in 1915 and to Cave in 1922. In legislative debates,[107] he increasingly became the active spokesman of "stern, unbending, Tories." In addition to his defense of Dyer after the Amritsar Massacre, he opposed the 1922 Irish Treaty and insisted that general strikes were illegal.[108]

Politically he was a vigorous combatant, but on the bench he was able to achieve most of his goals, as were most conservative judges anxious to stem the tide of change, by hewing closely to the declaratory theory, noting in one case that "the argument that your Lordships should discover under this ancient form of action some principle hitherto undetected is really an appeal to this House in its legislative and not in its judicial capacity."[109] He even went so far as to suggest that interstitial development of the law was no longer open to the House. "The fact is that a body of law, which, like ours, has grown through a long period of

106. John Hamilton, Lord Sumner; b. 1859; father, iron merchant; educ., Manchester Grammar School and Balliol College, Oxford (First, "Greats"); called to bar, 1883; Judge, King's Bench Division, 1909–12; Lord Justice, 1912–13; Lord of Appeal, 1913–30; d. 1934; *Dictionary of National Biography 1931–1940*, at 392.

107. Sumner was a regular speaker in the debating chamber; taking the view, shared by Carson and Phillimore, that the law lords were free to speak in debates on all subjects; 49 *Parl. Deb.*, H.L. (5th ser.), cols. 715–17 (22 Mar. 1922) (Irish Free State Agreement Bill).

Sumner was still imbued with nineteenth-century laissez-faire principles; see, e.g., his opposition to the Registration of Firms Bill. "No doubt it may seem a strange thing, in these days when we are too loaded with fetters of legislation, that a mere lawyer should venture to say one word in favour of the ordinary right of a man to mind his own business and manage it in his own way"; 21 *Parl. Deb.*, H.L. (5th ser.), col. 435 (30 Mar. 1916).

108. Of Haldane and his supporters, he submitted, "They are deliberately prepared to undermine the peaceful Constitution under which we live, in order that they may be able to say to their followers, the trade unionists: 'We have defended your last privilege, your most absurd privilege, your most deplorable privilege to the very last breath in our bodies' "; 68 *Parl. Deb.*, H.L. (5th ser.), col. 146 (5 July 1927) (Trades Disputes and Trades Union Bill).

109. *Admiralty Comm'rs v. S.S. Amerika (Owners)*, [1917] A.C. 38, 60 (1916). "It is not for us to dispute settled law"; *J. C. Houghten & Co. v. Northard Lowe & Wills, Ltd.*, [1928] A.C. 1, 19–20 (1927).

intensely conservative and unsystematic development, is sure to contain gaps—blemishes, if you will—which a philosopher or a nomothete would have contrived to avoid. It cannot be helped. It is too late for law courts to improve or explain them away. That is for the Legislature."[110] He argued that all prior decisions had to be followed, no matter how inadequately reported.[111] He was equally convinced that with respect to statutes, the courts could only "construe" and not "amend";[112] and he purported to be unmoved by morality[113] or personal feelings,[114] which he insisted were irrelevant to judicial work.

An examination of Sumner's work over time, however, inevitably reflects trends and predispositions. He was tough on politically motivated local councillors[115] and trade unionists[116] and concerned not to

110. *Rodriguez* v. *Speyer Bros.*, [1919] A.C. 59, 133 (1918).

111. See *Palgrave, Brown & Co.* v. *S.S. Turid (Owners)*, [1922] 1 A.C. 397, on whether to overrule a Court of Appeal decision that had only been reported in *The Times*. "[I]f it had not been reported at all, it would still have been a decision which, when brought to light by any means, must have been regarded as authority"; ibid. 413. See also *Egyptian Delta Land & Inv. Co.* v. *Todd*, [1929] A.C. 1, 30 (1928): "I venture to submit that a long current of judicial expressions, whether technically obiter or not, the general agreement of the most valuable textbooks and the course taken in argument by so many law officers of the Crown afford sufficient warrant for saying that the rule is settled and ought not to be disturbed."

112. "[T]he Legislature alone can make law"; *Egyptian Delta Land & Inv. Co.* v. *Todd*, [1929] A.C. 1, 34 (1928). For similar comments, see *Leeds Industrial Co-op Soc'y Ltd.* v. *Slack*, [1924] A.C. 851, 872: "I think this kind of reasoning is really an argument for a modern amending Act, framed in accordance with the notions of 1924, not for a construction of this Act according to the words used in 1858."

He realized, however, that his predecessors had not always been so careful in limiting their functions. See *Spencer* v. *Hemmerde*, [1922] 2 A.C. 507, 519: "Still less do I imagine it to be possible to extract anything that deserves to be called a principle from the decisions of three centuries, which have been directed to what is after all the task of decorously disregarding an Act of Parliament [i.e., the Statute of Limitations]."

For other views on statutory interpretation, see *Farmer* v. *Cotton's Trustees*, [1915] A.C. 922, 941 (Scot.), and *Gosse Millerd* v. *Canadian Gov't Merchant Marine, Ltd.*, [1929] A.C. 223 (1928).

113. "[N]either can I find any guidance in applying the rule in Lord Mansfield's words, 'decency, morality and public policy.' The last tells us nothing. All our law, even statute law, is supposed to rest on public policy, but as public policy is an evolving not to say an unstable thing, the public policy of one century may not be quite the same as that of the next but one. In a matter like the present the word morality tells us nothing, for what moralists condemn the law ignores"; *Sorrell* v. *Smith*, [1925] A.C. 700, 743.

114. "It is, of course, impossible not to be very fully alive to the fact that this case excites and will continue to excite warm feelings of sympathy, commiseration and chivalry. . . . I recognise that such sensibilities are respectable and deep, but they do not concern the law. . . . The questions raised in this appeal are pure questions of law, difficult but dry, on which it is impossible to dogmatise and useless to be perturbed"; *Russell* v. *Russell*, [1924] A.C. 687, 730.

115. *Roberts* v. *Hopwood*, [1925] A.C. 578, 609–10. There is also a hint of political condescension in his dissent in *Salford Guardians* v. *Dewhurst*, [1926] A.C. 619, 629.

116. *Amalgamated Soc'y of Carpenters* v. *Braithwaite*, [1922] 2 A.C. 440, 466, requiring a very high standard of drafting in the rules of a trade union.

expand the coverage of workmen's compensation legislation out of any sentimental feelings for workmen.[117] In the area of tax law, however, he made perhaps his most significant contribution, for it was the law lords of this period who finally moved the interpretation away from the Edwardian one of viewing such legislation in the light of parliamentary policies, through a stage when the legislation was given its "ordinary meaning," to a position where tax law, being "penal in nature," was construed restrictively.

In this progression Sumner played a leading part. He not only felt that "statutory language cannot be construed by asking which construction will most benefit the Revenue,"[118] but he was even outraged when the Court of Appeal used the normal method of legal reasoning by analogy in a tax situation.[119] It was also Sumner who announced that "[i]t is trite law that His Majesty's subjects are free if they can to make their own arrangements so that their cases may fall outside the scope of the taxing Acts. They incur no legal penalties and strictly speaking, no moral censure if, having considered the lines drawn by the legislature for the imposition of taxes, they make it their business to walk outside them."[120] A leading English academic lawyer recently commented, "This principle has been repeatedly reaffirmed by other eminent judges, and its major importance, from the standpoint of personal freedom, cannot be exaggerated, more especially having regard to the extent and severity of modern taxation. It is the foundation of all modern estate planning, and without it, the last bastion of private property in a collectivist society would have been destroyed."[121]

117. For example, in *Mersey Docks & Harbours Bd. v. Procter*, [1923] A.C. 253, Sumner, with the majority of the House, held that failure to keep up the chains around a floating dock was not a breach of any duty owed to a workman who was drowned while falling from the floating dock on a foggy night. "How can a workman extend the Board's liabilities, indicated by this term 'invitation,' by making a mistake of his own and getting lost in a fog? What legal reason can there be for the Board's inviting him to go somewhere in a fog, where he does not want to go at all and would certainly not be invited to go in clear weather, and where moreover, the Board has no interest or desire to invite him at any time? There is none: the suggestion is a mere impulse of compassion"; ibid. 273.

Sumner staunchly refused to be moved by compassion from a path that he considered to be logically correct: "I would like to add that, if I have not dwelt on the melancholy circumstances of this accident, it is not that I am not sincerely sorry for the widow or that I mean in any way to blame the deceased, but merely that, in a question of law, which is not without its difficulties, I only find myself embarrassed by considerations distressing in themselves, which every lawyer knows to be logically irrelevant"; ibid. 278.

118. *Brown v. National Provident Institution*, [1921] 2 A.C. 222, 260. It was also in this decision that Sumner arrogantly asserted, "Most of the operative clauses are unintelligible to those who have to pay the taxes and in any case derive such clarity as they possess from the judges, who have interpreted them"; ibid. 257.

119. "[T]he Crown does not tax by analogy"; *Ormond Inv. Co. v. Betts*, [1928] A.C. 143 (1927).

120. *Levene v. IRC*, [1928] A.C. 217.

121. George W. Keeton, *English Law* 357–58. It may, in fact, be unfair somewhat to

Sumner, however, should be given his due. He possessed a first-rate analytical mind. His opinions were often long, more because of his attention to detail and authority than because of general verbosity. They remain strictly on point, clear,[122] and certainly not lacking in common or business sense.[123] In matrimonial cases, Sumner was sensitive to changes in mores.[124] Yet his juristic stance made it difficult for him to be regarded as a distinguished appeal judge, even as an advocate of judicial restraint. He was yet another law lord whose jurisprudential assumptions made nonsense of a second appeal. It is clear that his powerful intellect led his opinions to be studied with care by the practitioners of his time;[125] his reluctance to spell out an appellate stance was unfortunate in terms of the contribution he might have made.

The third of the Conservative law lords—Lord Carson[126]—was clearly a politician. Indeed, he was in many ways too much of a politician, having been named a Lord of Appeal upon the death of Moulton in 1920, many felt,[127] in order to buy his silence on the Irish question. A

---

give so much credit to Sumner. Occasionally Sumner looked to the substance of the transaction. See his dissent in *IRC* v. *Blott*, [1921] 2 A.C. 171, 217; and his reluctant following of *Blott* in *IRC* v. *Fisher's Executors*, [1926] A.C. 395, 412.

122. See, e.g., his opinions in *Weld-Blundell* v. *Stephens*, [1920] A.C. 956, 986; *Spencer* v. *Hemmerde*, [1922] 2 A.C. 507; *Sorrell* v. *Smith*, [1925] A.C. 700; *Edwards* v. *Porter*, [1925] A.C. 1 (1924).

Sumner had a similar ability to cut issues down to size and render them dry. See his remarks on the Solicitors (Qualification of Women) Bill, 24 *Parl. Deb.*, H.L. (5th ser.), col. 270 (2 Feb. 1917): "This presents itself to my mind as a very simple and I should have thought rather obvious reform attended with no great results, either in the way of dangers or benefits." See also on Equal Franchise Bill, 71 *Parl. Deb.*, H.L. (5th ser.), col. 190 (21 May 1928), arguing that the majority of voters were bored by politics.

123. See, e.g., his opinion in *Produce Brokers Co.* v. *Olympia Oil & Cake Co.*, [1916] 1 A.C. 314, 332 (1915): "A construction which would have conferred on the Appeal Committee a true arbitral function as to the interpretation and performance of the printed contract, and a provisional and appealable function over so important a matter as the customs of the trade itself, would have been equally anomalous and inconvenient."

124. For example, he took the minority view in *Russell* v. *Russell*, [1924] A.C. 687, recognizing the great change in matrimonial law since 1857 and refusing to extend the well-established rule that neither spouse may give evidence that would bastardize a child in divorce proceedings. He considered it most important that the court should have before it all the relevant evidence.

125. As a study of the case notes in the *Law Quarterly Review* of this period shows. See, especially, "Note," 46 *Law Quarterly Review* 143 (1930).

He was personally a bitter man, who resented his humble beginnings and early disappointments. He was widely disliked; *Dictionary of National Biography 1931–1940*, at 392. Buckmaster noted that only Sumner's wife attended his funeral; Heuston, *Lives* 307.

126. Edward Henry Carson; b. 1854; father, engineer; educ., Portalington School and Trinity College, Dublin; called to Irish bar, 1877, English Bar, 1893; M.P. for Dublin University, 1892–1918; Solicitor-General for Ireland; Solicitor-General of England, 1900–1905; Attorney-General of England, 1915–16; First Lord of Admiralty, 1916–18; Lord of Appeal, 1921–29; d. 1935; *Dictionary of National Biography 1931–1940*, at 146. See also Edward Majoribanks and Ian Colvin, 1–3 *The Life of Lord Carson*; and H. Montgomery Hyde, *Carson*.

127. Majoribanks and Colvin, 3 *Life of Carson* 415.

conservative Dublin Protestant, he had risen to be Solicitor-General of England by 1905 and, after the fall of the Conservatives, became a prominent member of the opposition who was even considered as leader of the Conservatives in 1911. A ferocious supporter of the Ulster Covenant and the Ulster Volunteer Force, with the outbreak of World War I Carson threw his weight behind the government, becoming Asquith's Attorney-General in 1915, Lloyd George's First Lord of the Admiralty in 1916, and in 1917 a member of the War Cabinet. In 1918, however, when the rumor broke that Lloyd George planned to introduce Home Rule, Carson resigned and fought the new legislation until he saw no alternative but to accept partition of Ireland.

Carson was never entirely clear whether he was a lawyer or politician,[128] but his devotion to the Union was unquestioned.[129] Perhaps inevitably, by 1922 Carson—not surprisingly, in the light of the events surrounding his own elevation—had become the center of a heated debate about the part law lords should play in party politics.[130] Birkenhead tried to repress Carson's urge to speak out on all manner of political issues. Carson's response was that if the Lord Chancellor sat in the House of Lords as a judge and was at the same time a member of the government without tainting justice, then he (Carson) would not be muzzled. With a certain amount of logic, Carson also pointed out that if party politics were going to influence a judge, which he denied even happened,[131] preventing him from airing his political views in public would not terminate such influence. The debate had no effect on Carson, who continued his campaign for the Union, nor did it temper his criticism of the unions[132] or his hostility to reform of the Prayer Book of the Church of England.

Carson's politics did not, it is true, intrude noticeably into his deci-

128. "I have remained a lawyer first and a politician afterwards"; Hyde, Carson 1. "I died on the day I left the House of Commons and the bar"; Majoribanks and Colvin, 3 Life of Carson 399.

129. "From the day I first entered Parliament up to the present, devotion to the union has been the guiding star of my political life"; Dictionary of National Biography 1931–1940, at 147. He turned down many tempting offers and opportunities because of his work for the Union, e.g., Lord Chancellorship in 1916 (Hyde, Carson 413); the Presidency of the Probate, Divorce and Admiralty Division in 1905 (Majoribanks and Colvin, 1 Life of Carson 324). In 1916 he was even suggested as Prime Minister (3 ibid. 140).

130. 49 Parl. Deb., H.L. (5th ser.), col. 94 (8 Feb. 1922). "In 1921 Sir Edward Carson joined the Supreme Court of Appeal, and reinforced the critics of the Government's Irish Policy with a vigor which no judicial considerations could repress"; Charles Mallet, Lord Cave 251.

131. He reasserted this at 90 Parl. Deb., H.L. (5th ser.), col. 1057 (1 Mar. 1934).

132. Of the 1906 Trade Disputes Act, he said, "Why bring in a long Bill of this sort? Why not bring in a simple Bill: the king can do no wrong neither can a Trade Union"; 65 Parl. Deb., H.L. (5th ser.), cols. 75–76 (20 July 1926) (his words quoted by Dunedin). See also "Note," 25 Law Quarterly Review 3 (1909).

sions,[133] perhaps because the questions on which he felt strongest did not arise in the cases in which he was called on to sit. As can be seen in his handling of the workmen's compensation cases, however, his conservative outlook swayed his judgment at times.[134] Fascinated by the idea of upholding voluntary contracts,[135] he was reluctant to take into account the inequality of bargaining power between an employer and a worker;[136] and unlike many of the law lords, he was not prepared to mold the often ambiguous and pliable phrases of the Workmen's Compensation Acts in the light of the intent to compensate workers with a minimum amount of formality.[137]

In fairness to Carson, however, he was right when he claimed that, although a politician, there was little to distinguish him from his fellow law lords. Although it could be argued that his conservatism underlay his apparent hostility to government departments in various decisions,[138] it is equally consistent with a concern to prevent injustice. Overall, his was politically and intellectually a conservative approach,[139] but the overrid-

133. See, e.g., *Roberts v. Hopwood*, [1925] A.C. 578, 618, a case where one might have expected him to have strong views. See also *Murphy v. Hurley*, [1922] 1 A.C. 369, 398 (Ire. 1921); *Spencer v. Hemmerde*, [1922] 2 A.C. 507, 540; *S.S. Strathfillan (Owners)* v. *S.S. Ikala (Owners)*, [1929] A.C. 196, 208 (1928).

134. See, e.g., *Welsh Navigation Steam Coal Co. v. Evans*, [1927] A.C. 834, 843.

135. In *Glasbrook Bros. v. Glamorganshire County Council*, [1925] A.C. 270 (1924), he held that the bargain was not voluntary. "When the emergency arises, the subject who asks for protection would be entirely at the mercy of the police if payment were demanded. He would not be contracting as a free agent, as, taking for example the present case, he would have no option, and indeed in this case he was given no option but to enter into a contract of payment or lose his property"; ibid. 299.

136. He alone dissented in *Russell v. Rudd*, [1923] A.C. 309, 331, holding that without clear words an act of Parliament could not "tak[e] away the inherent right of compromising legal claims."

137. See, e.g., *Shotts Iron Co. v. Curran*, [1929] A.C. 409, 421, 426 (Scot.) (dissenting alone and insisting on the "natural meaning"); *Bevan v. Nixon's Navigation Co.*, [1929] A.C. 44, 63 (1928) (in majority: employer not an insurer of work); *Mersey Docks & Harbours Bd. v. Procter*, [1923] A.C. 253, 281 (in majority against worker). He was with the majority in deciding against the worker in *St. Helens Colliery v. Hewitson*, [1924] A.C. 59, 99 (1923):

I do not share the anxieties felt by my noble and learned friend [Shaw] as to the results of the decision proposed by his Lordship from the Woolsack . . . nor do I feel in a position to join in his recommendations to the Legislature. I have no information before me to lead me to a conclusion as to what would be the effect of putting an end to or interfering with voluntary arrangements for providing greater conveniences for workmen going to their employment. However, that does not appear to be a matter on which I am competent or bound to express any opinion.

138. See, for instance, his dissents in *Glasbrook Bros. v. Glamorganshire County Council*, [1925] A.C. 270, 292 (1924); and in *Duff Dev. Corp. v. Government of Kelantan*, [1924] A.C. 797, 835. See also, for example in private law, his speeches in *Matthey v. Curling*, [1922] 2 A.C. 180, 241–42; and *Medway Oil & Storage Co. v. Continental Contractors, Ltd.*, [1929] A.C. 88, 105 (1928).

139. He shared the increasingly pervasive hostility to tax legislation. "I think it is open to comment that the learned judge who heard this case was of one opinion and in the Court of Appeal two of the three Lords Justices were of a different opinion, whilst in your

ing sense derived from reading Carson's opinions is that, just as he had doubts about being a lawyer, he was not particularly happy as a law lord or interested in the appellate work. Blanesburgh recorded that "[t]he juristic side of the work . . . did not appeal to him . . . [t]he judicial office which did (come his way) was not really according to his humor,"[140] and this lack of interest showed through. In his early years it gave the impression that he lacked confidence,[141] although clearly he did not lack technical skills.[142] As the years passed, he showed greater willingness to dissent[143] and even to adopt a rather casual approach to stare decisis.[144]

Carson was, however, never at home on the bench and made no lasting contribution to the concept of the House of Lords as a judicial body unless it was to highlight the schizophrenic roles the law lords played in the British Constitution. That contribution was probably true of all the political law lords. Their days were, however, numbered; frequently appointed for the wrong reasons and at the wrong time, the political law lords were becoming second-class citizens. The professional law lord had acquired the prestige that had once belonged to political appointees.

Lordships' House two noble and learned Lords differ from the other three. That shows how unfortunate the Legislature has been in its attempt to clearly impose a tax upon the subject"; *Wankie Colliery Co.* v. *IRC*, [1922] 2 A.C. 51, 71 (Scot.).

140. Hyde, *Carson* 481. Miss Stevenson, then Lloyd George's mistress, confirmed that "Carson has not found Lord of Appeal a very exciting job"; Lord Beaverbrook (Max Aitkin), *The Decline and Fall of Lloyd George* 118.

141. It was not uncommon for him to say merely "I concur," e.g., *Fitch* v. *Dewes*, [1921] 2 A.C. 158, 170; *Sutters* v. *Briggs*, [1922] 1 A.C. 1 (1921); *Amalgamated Soc'y of Carpenters* v. *Braithwaite*, [1922] 2 A.C. 440; *Elder, Dempster & Co.* v. *Paterson, Zochonis & Co.*, [1924] A.C. 522; or to adopt the judgments or large portions of speeches of others, e.g., *Russell* v. *Rudd*, [1923] A.C. 309, 334–35 and *Poplar Assessment Comm.* v. *Roberts*, [1922] 2 A.C. 93, 126.

142. His career at the bar made him well equipped to understand the technicalities of presenting a case (see, e.g., *Rainham Chem. Works* v. *Belvedere Fish Guano Co.*, [1921] 2 A.C. 465, 492) and had also made him a great believer in the capability of the jury or first instance judge to decide all questions of fact correctly. "[I]n many cases of the vilest and most unfounded charges, trial by jury has hitherto proved the only efficacious protection for the subject attempted to be implicated"; *Russell* v. *Russell*, [1924] A.C. 687, 749. In that case he therefore refused to be a party to throwing any doubt on the jury's verdict as the majority had done. See also *Rutherford* v. *Richardson*, [1923] A.C. 1, 15 (1922); *Mersey Docks & Harbours Bd.* v. *Procter*, [1923] A.C. 253, 282.

143. E.g., *Wankie Colliery Co.* v. *IRC*, [1922] 2 A.C. 51, 71 (Scot.) (with Dunedin); *Russell* v. *Russell*, [1924] A.C. 687, 749 (with Sumner); *Fairman* v. *Perpetual Inv. Bldg. Soc'y*, [1923] A.C. 74 (1922) (on the effect of the evidence not the law); *Russell* v. *Rudd*, [1923] A.C. 309, 330 (alone); *Duff Dev. Corp.* v. *Government of Kelantan*, [1924] A.C. 797, 830 (alone); *Glasbrook Bros.* v. *Glamorganshire County Council*, [1925] A.C. 270, 830 (1924). See also his dissent in *Shotts Iron Co.* v. *Curran*, [1929] A.C. 409, 426 (Scot.).

144. *Wankie Colliery Co.* v. *IRC*, [1922] 2 A.C. 51, 72 (Scot.). Relying, *inter alia*, upon a dictum in a dissenting judgment in *S.S. Celia (Owners)* v. *S.S. Volturno (Owners)*, [1921] 2 A.C. 544, 568, he summarily dismissed the line of precedents relied on in the lower courts.

The period between 1912 and 1940 at last brought the professional tradition to the final court of appeal. For both England and Scotland, a Lordship of Appeal might be seen as the final stepping-stone in the judicial hierarchy. There was not, of course, one monolithic professional tradition, any more than the concept of liberal or conservative or even the concept of formalism had clearly defined, unchanging contents. The Scottish approach during these years was different from the English and perhaps, among the English judges, the commercial lawyers tended to belong to a different tradition.

The Scottish Tradition

If one assumes that the work of appellate judges is not entirely passive, then Scottish judges have at least two marked advantages over English judges. The Faculty of Advocates is far less specialized than the English bar, and there is less specialization on the bench. Scottish law lords therefore have a more "generalist" approach than do English law lords. Second, while the Scots tend to complain bitterly that the substance of Scottish law has been tainted by the common law,[145] the civilian style is still alive—if not in perfect health—in Scotland. Although the traditional statement that Scottish lawyers are more concerned with principle than precedent may be somewhat simplistic, it undoubtedly contains a germ of truth. Dworkin's attempt to distinguish principles from rules,[146] for instance, is more comprehensible, if still somewhat unrealistic, when analyzed in the light of the speeches of Scottish law lords rather than those of the typical English law lord. In short, while Scottish law lords undoubtedly take on some camouflage from their surroundings, their training and style may well be better adapted to a flexible model of the appellate process than is the English barrister's training. This assertion is borne out by examining the three professional[147] Scottish judges of the period—Dunedin, Macmillan, and Thankerton. Although an increasing anglicization did perhaps take place, the Scottish tradition undoubtedly survived.

Lord Dunedin[148] was one of the two judges appointed under the

145. E.g., T. B. Smith, *British Justice*.

146. Ronald Dworkin, "The Model of Rules."

147. Shaw, one of those classified as a "political" law lord, was, in many respects, very much in the Scottish tradition.

148. Andrew Graham Murray; b. 1849; father, Writer to the Signet and Crown Agent for Scotland; educ., Harrow, Trinity College Cambridge, and Edinburgh University; Faculty of Advocates, 1874; 1888, Senior Advocate Depute; 1891, Conservative M.P. for Buteshire; 1891, 1895–96, Solicitor-General for Scotland; 1903–5, Secretary of State for Scotland; 1905, Lord Justice-General of Scotland and Lord President of the Court of Session; 1913–32, Lord of Appeal; d. 1942; *Dictionary of National Biography 1941–1950*, at 608–11.

Appellate Jurisdiction Act of 1913. In some respects he was a politician, having been not only a Conservative M.P. but also Secretary of State for Scotland, with a seat in the cabinet, for two years. Yet, by the time he became a law lord, he had been President of the Court of Session for eight years and owed his promotion to the Liberals Asquith[149] and Haldane. These positions apparently underscored his own natural instincts to regard himself primarily as a lawyer,[150] an emphasis that was borne out during his nineteen years as a Lord of Appeal.[151] Perhaps Dunedin was at his best—and certainly at his most articulate—when he was contrasting English and Scottish law. He actively despised what he considered the English law's obsession with form and remedy at the expense of substance and right,[152] and he was not above improving English law

149. Asquith did not find it easy to lure Dunedin from Edinburgh to London. See letters from Dunedin to Asquith: "You will not think me affected if I say that there are considerations on both sides" (28 Aug. 1913); "In truth I have found it very hard indeed to decide what I ought to do" (9 Sept. 1913); Asquith Papers, 13/141-145, Bodleian Library, Oxford.

150. At his death he was described as a lawyer rather than a politician; Obituary, 92 *Law Journal* 317 (1942).

151. He remained a politically sensitive judge, siding with Birkenhead against Carson and Sumner during the 1922 debates on the relationship of the law lords and party politics. 49 *Parl. Deb.*, H.L. (5th ser.), col. 949 (29 Mar. 1922). Their Lordships knew that the law lords could detach themselves from politics when on the bench, but "I cannot help thinking that the man in the street will not have the same complete confidence in one's impartiality if one mixes oneself up in political questions"; ibid. 950. In fact, after this Dunedin spoke more often in debates, generally on request in connection with technicalities of Scottish law; e.g., 58 *Parl. Deb.*, H.L. (5th ser.), col. 150 (2 July 1924), but also sometimes on more controversial subjects. He opposed the Trade Disputes Act of 1906 (Repeal) Bill, although he declared that he was not giving his own views but merely taking his stand on the Report of the Royal Commission on Trade Unions of 1906, of which he had been chairman; ibid., col. 691 (17 July 1924); 61 ibid., col. 61 (6 May 1925); and 65 ibid., col. 65 (20 July 1926). See also Report of the Royal Commission on Trade Disputes and Trade Combinations, Cd. 2825 (1906).
    Despite this background, in the two quasi-labor cases he was called on to decide, he effectively avoided implementing his prejudices. In *Larkin v. Long*, [1915] A.C. 814 (Ire.), he took the easy way out by merely concurring, though he may have thought that he had been too closely associated with the passage of the Trade Disputes Act to give a separate judgment. In *Sorrell v. Smith*, [1925] A.C. 700, the 1906 act was not relevant, and Dunedin gave a long judgment with the professed aim of trying to draw some clear principle from the chaos of cases. In the course of the judgment he said that he believed that there could not be a civil conspiracy on facts that fell short of a criminal conspiracy; ibid. 725. Still avoiding all trouble, he expressly excluded disputes between employers and workmen from the scope of his decision; ibid. 731.

152. Lord Dunedin (Andrew Graham Murray), *The Divergencies and Convergencies of English and Scottish Law*. See also *Dunlop Pneumatic Tyre Co. v. Selfridge & Co.*, [1915] A.C. 847, 855: "I confess that this case is to my mind apt to nip any budding affection which one might have had for the doctrine of consideration"; and *Weld-Blundell v. Stephens*, [1920] A.C. 956, 977: "If I may put aside for the moment my duty of considering English law alone in this, an English case, and may look at it with eyes which are always open to consider the English law as a foreign system, I think it is a cumbersome curiosity of English law." See also *North Staffordshire Ry. v. Edge*, [1920] A.C. 254, 264 (1919).

by importing Scottish concepts.[153] Nowhere was this more elegantly exemplified than in *Sinclair v. Brougham*,[154] in which he began, "Now I think it is clear that all ideas of natural justice are against allowing A. to keep the property of B., which has somehow got into A.'s possession without any intention on the part of B. to make a gift to A." Proceeding from that point and surveying Roman and Scottish authorities, he declared, "Is English equity to retire defeated from the task which other systems of equity have conquered?"[155] Having reached his decision in favor of *B.*, he confessed, "I have dealt with the whole matter rather on principle than on authority."[156]

Of Dunedin, it could clearly be said that he was happier when untrammeled by authority.[157] Of course, he sometimes found himself reluctant to outflank authority.[158] Yet, a sense of balance characterized his approach. When Dunedin spoke out about the law's presumptions in favor of civil liberties, he appreciated the implications of what he was saying.[159] His speeches reflect his sense of the relationship among legislature, executive, and judiciary.[160] Thus, even though in *Halliday*'s case Dunedin underlined the absolute nature of parliamentary sovereignty,[161] he was not unconcerned by the consequences of the interpretation

153. E.g., *Duff Dev. Corp.* v. *Government of Kelantan*, [1924] A.C. 797, 821 (an aside about Roman law); *Ward* v. *Van der Loeff*, [1924] A.C. 653, 669.

154. [1914] A.C. 398, 431.

155. Ibid. 435.

156. Ibid. 439.

157. "I have said that I have formed my opinion not without hesitation; but that hesitation is due to one fact only. Had there been no authorities to deal with, and I were to approach the matter from the point of view of legal principle alone, I do not think I should have felt much difficulty"; *Bowman* v. *Secular Soc'y, Ltd.*, [1917] A.C. 406, 432–33. See also *Hole* v. *Garnsey* [1930] A.C. 472.

158. "I think the only safe course is to keep close to the well-established rule that the domicile of a husband and wife . . . is one and the same"; *Lord Advocate* v. *Jaffrey*, [1921] 1 A.C. 146, 164 (Scot. 1920). See also *Ertel Bieber & Co.* v. *Rio Tinto Co.*, [1918] A.C. 260, 273: "I take my view of what is against public policy from what has been said in a series of cases."

159. See, e.g., "[I]t is a cardinal principle of the law of England, ever jealous for personal liberty, that when once a person has been held entitled to liberty by a competent Court there shall be no further question"; *Secretary of State for Home Affairs* v. *O'Brien*, [1923] A.C. 603, 621.

160. Other cases in which the executive was involved include *Attorney-General* v. *De Keyser's Royal Hotel, Ltd.*, [1920] A.C. 508, 522, holding that the Crown must pay compensation for confiscation; *Minister of Health* v. *R., ex parte Yaffé*, [1931] A.C. 494, 501–2, allowing the executive wide but not unbounded powers.

161. "It is pointed out that the powers, if interpreted as the unanimous judgement of the Courts below interprets them, are drastic and might be abused. That is true but the fault, if fault there be, lies in the fact that the British Constitution has entrusted to the two Houses of Parliament, subject to the assent of the King, an absolute power untrammelled by any written instrument obedience to which may be compelled by some judicial body"; *R.* v. *Halliday, ex parte Zadig*, [1917] A.C. 260, 270–71.

adopted.[162] He was not prepared to relinquish judicial responsibility entirely, for he realized the weakness of the conception of the legislature as an all-seeing and all-perfect body,[163] a stance that enabled him to take a balanced view toward statutory interpretation.

Dunedin never doubted that factors other than pure logic went into deciding a final appeal. He could admit that his analysis went beyond the words used in a statute and could even advocate that such a practice be more widespread.[164] This is particularly noticeable in the field of workmen's compensation cases where he appeared to undergo, over the years, something of a conversion from a strict, literal approach[165] to a broader, sympathetic one.[166] His centralist approach also came through

162. See *Hearts of Oak Assurance Co.* v. *Attorney-General*, [1932] A.C. 392, 405: "I think that every consideration of good taste and proper feeling point to the advisability of an inquiry of this sort being held in private. . . . But the statute does not say whether it is to be in public or in private, and therefore I cannot see how a Court of law can have power to say that it must be in private." See also *Sharpness New Docks & Gloucester & Birmingham Navigation Co.* v. *Attorney-General*, [1915] A.C. 654, 663: "I wish . . . to state explicitly my opinion that the whole question necessarily depends upon the proper construction of the statute; and that where the statute deals with the subject its provisions form a code on that subject, and cannot be added to by what has been called a common law doctrine." See also *Russell* v. *Rudd*, [1923] A.C. 309, 327.

163. "Now it is often argued when dealing with different sections of the same Act that if so and so had been meant, the draftsman would have expressed himself in one section as he had in another. But a parliamentary draftsman is not a being of immaterial [*sic*] conception, he is a mere mortal that varies from year to year, and to argue that because the draftsman of 1912 said so and so, is, I think, to put too great a strain on the argument"; *R.* v. *Commissioners of Customs & Excise*, [1928] A.C. 402, 408.

164. See especially ibid. 409:

My Lords, in the judgements in this case, and still more in those of *Watney, Combe's* case there were stern warnings to those who in order to read in words into a statute which are not there, or to divert words used from their ordinary and natural meaning, permitted themselves to speculate as to what the aim and attainment of the Act was likely to be. Your Lordships will have noticed that I have based my opinion on the words of the statute and on them alone, but with all deference to those opinions, with which indeed I cordially agree, I think it is quite legitimate when it comes to a question of construction without addition or diversion of words to see what the aim of the statute would turn out according to the one interpretation or the other.

See also *Whitney* v. *IRC*, [1926] A.C. 37 (1925), and *Forth Conservancy Bd.* v. *IRC*, [1931] A.C. 540, 547 (Scot.).

165. See early cases such as *Trim Joint Dist. School Bd.* v. *Kelly*, [1914] A.C. 667, 685–86 (Ire.), dissenting with Atkinson and Parker; *Charles R. Davidson & Co.* v. *M'Robb*, [1918] A.C. 304, 319 (Scot.); *A. G. Moore & Co.* v. *Donnelly*, [1921] 1 A.C. 329, 343 (Scot. 1920); *Kerr* v. *Ayr S.S. Co.*, [1915] A.C. 217, 240 (Scot. 1914) dissenting with Atkinson and Parmoor.

166. In *Ocean Coal Co.* v. *Davies*, [1927] A.C. 271 (1926), Atkinson, Wrenbury, Carson, and even Shaw held that the arbitrator had no jurisdiction to award any payment after the incapacity had ceased. Dunedin's was the only dissenting voice, and he confessed to having some difficulty in justifying his decision:

My difficulty does not arise in what I think is the intendment of the statute. It arises on the consideration of whether the words used have been adequate to carry out the intention of the statute and, I confess after much hesitation, I have come to be of the opinion that they are.

I have said before that I think in interpreting a statute a Court must take it that the statute is meant

in tax cases. While he would castigate the Crown if he thought the tax authorities were overreaching themselves,[167] he made a conscious effort to make the Finance Acts work.[168] Equally, in common law matters he would make a reasonable search for a *ratio decidendi*, but he did "not think it is part of the tribunal's duty to spell out with great difficulty a *ratio decidendi* in order to be bound by it."[169] Of course, whether the matter was statutory or common law, he found himself "bound" by certain decisions,[170] and he could make conservative judicial noises with the best of them.[171]

Dunedin perhaps fell short of being a great appeal judge, but he was certainly an honorable, thoughtful, and competent one. No doubt he had

to work, and that it should not allow the statute to be defeated unless the words used are quite inadequate to have the desired effect. [Ibid. 278]

See also *Shotts Iron Co.* v. *Curran*, [1929] A.C. 409, 416 (Scot.): "I think it necessary first of all firmly to grasp the fact that the scheme of the Act entirely gives the go-by to notions of legal liability."

167. "I am bound to say that I do not think I have ever been called on to decide a more useless appeal than this appeal. . . . It does not matter one whit which way this case is decided, because there is no general principle involved. . . . [I]t really is high time—and I say this insistently—that those who advise the Crown in these matters should make up their minds that the Crown can be wrong, and not think it absolutely necessary to bring every case to this House, however trivial, simply because the Crown has been found wrong in that particular one"; *Fry* v. *Burma Corp.*, [1930] A.C. 321, 326.

In a House of Lords debate he reasserted this view and suggested that if the Crown lost in the Court of Appeal it should normally only be given leave to appeal if it paid the expenses of a second appeal; 76 *Parl. Deb.*, H.L. (5th ser.), col. 1227 (3 Apr. 1930).

168. See *IRC* v. *Blott*, [1921] 2 A.C. 171, 202 (dissenting); and *Whitney* v. *IRC*, [1926] A.C. 37, 52 (1925): "A statute is designed to be workable and the interpretation thereof by a Court should be to secure that object, unless crucial omission or clear direction makes that end unattainable."

169. "Now, when any tribunal is bound by the judgement of another Court, either superior or co-ordinate, it is, of course, bound by the judgement itself. And if from the opinions delivered it is clear—as is the case in most instances—what the *ratio decidendi* was which led to the judgement, then that *ratio decidendi* is also binding. But if it is not clear, then I do not think it is part of the tribunal's duty to spell out with great difficulty a *ratio decidendi* in order to be bound by it"; *Great Western Ry.* v. *The Mostyn (Owners)*, [1928] A.C. 57, 73 (1927).

170. "[I]t is with the greatest reluctance that I find myself compelled to concur with your Lordship in the judgement proposed: I say this, not only because were it not for authority I should wish to decide the case otherwise, but still more because I think that the effect of the judgement will be disastrous to the proper efficiency of the statutory body concerned, and will, to a great extent, defeat the object for which the Act of Parliament under which they exist was passed"; *Forth Conservancy Bd.* v. *IRC*, [1931] A.C. 540, 547 (Scot.).

171. "My Lords, I candidly regret that I do not see my way to differ from the opinion that has just been expressed because I cannot help having the moral feeling that this money is probably going to the society to which, if we could have asked him, the testator would not have sent it. But that is not the question for a Court of Law; the question for a Court of Law is, taking the will as it stands, . . . what is the meaning of the words used"; *National Society for Prevention of Cruelty to Children* v. *Scottish National Society for Prevention of Cruelty to Children*, [1915] A.C. 207, 214 (Scot. 1914). See also *Russell* v. *Russell*, [1924] A.C. 687, 720; *Dunlop Pneumatic Tyre Co.* v. *Selfridge & Co.*, [1915] A.C. 847.

his failings,[172] but he continued the tradition begun by Watson and Shaw of the superior Scottish command of the purposes of the appellate process. The reputation he had established was furthered by Macmillan,[173] who became a Lord of Appeal in 1930, although, in some ways, Macmillan was less anglicized in his approach than Dunedin.

It is not easy to pass judgment on Macmillan. While classified as a professional judge, Macmillan had not sat as a judge until he was appointed a Lord of Appeal at the relatively early age of fifty-six. Although he had been a Unionist candidate, he served the Labour government of 1924 as Lord Advocate and, by adroit mending of fences, he felt he had a commitment from both Baldwin and MacDonald that ultimately he would be appointed a Lord of Appeal.[174] Thus, after the fall of the first MacDonald administration, instead of returning to the Scottish bar, he stayed in London to practice at the Parliamentary Bar, and his regular appearances in the House of Lords led to his appointment as standing counsel to both the Canadian and the Australian governments.[175]

When Macmillan was ultimately appointed by Sankey and MacDonald to replace Sumner as a Lord of Appeal,[176] Sumner warned the new law lord that "judging is always a stodgy job."[177] Macmillan purported not to find it so,[178] but perhaps he paid a high price. His problem was acutely diagnosed by Dunedin who, in writing to Hailsham in 1935, described Macmillan as "[v]ery able, but you cannot put your best into law if you have as many irons in the fire as he has."[179] Macmillan's irons were extensive. He was a collector of the famous,[180] and even though he

172. See the anti-Semitic tone of his speech in *Glicksman* v. *Lancashire & Gen. Assurance Co.*, [1927] A.C. 139, 143 (1926).

173. Hugh Pattison Macmillan; b. 1873, Glasgow; educ., Collegiate School Gagrock, Edinburgh University, Glasgow University; Faculty of Advocates, 1897; K.C., 1912; Lord Advocate, 1924; Lord of Appeal, 1930–47; Minister of Information, 1939–40; d. 1952. On Macmillan, see especially Hugh Macmillan, *Law and Other Things* and *A Man of Law's Tale*. Note also Bernard Lloyd Shientag, *Moulders of Modern Legal Thought*, chap. 6; obituary, *The Times*, 6 Sept. 1952.

174. See *Man of Law's Tale* 101–2; *Law and Language*; and "Scots Law as a Subject of Comparative Study" 477.

175. Macmillan, *Man of Law's Tale* 140.

176. For the mechanics of this, see ibid. 141–42.

177. " . . . even if you enliven it by being in a minority of one and insisting that you are right all the same"; ibid. 145.

178. "I enjoyed it"; ibid. 149. During his fifteen years on the bench, he delivered "about 152 written judgements in the House of Lords and about seventy-seven in the Privy Council"; ibid. 147.

179. Heuston, *Lives* 481.

180. See, for instance, the lists of those entertained at the country house he bought in Surrey (Moon Hall); Macmillan, *Man of Law's Tale* 158–59. The list is preceded by the remark, "I sometimes wish we had kept a visitor's book at Moon Hall, at least during the years when it was still possible to practice the pleasant art of hospitality and before the austerities of war and the welfare state turned us all into social isolationists."

was personally engaging,[181] those who met him found him increasingly tiresome as the years passed.[182] He fancied himself for the Lord Chancellorship in 1938,[183] and in 1939 he resigned as a Lord of Appeal to become an unsuccessful Minister of Information.[184] By 1941 he was back as a Lord of Appeal.

There is something in Macmillan's background that prevents one from being surprised at the divergence between his rhetoric and his performance, a divergence that became more noticeable with time. Typical of his remarks were announcements that "the high province of a Supreme Court is to control and develop the law so as to enable it to keep pace with and yet moderate the changing social and economic conditions of the nation."[185] He admired and restated Holmes' finest phrases about the growth and life of the law. He speculated about law, ethics, and the judicial process:

> Judges, as they often remind us, have to administer the law as they find it, but all the time they are slowly shaping and developing it. In almost every case, except the very plainest, it would be possible to decide the issue either way with reasonable legal justification. It must be so in view of the large number of decisions which are arrived at only by a majority of judicial votes, for I assume that the dissenting judges are just as convinced of the soundness of their law as are their brethren in the majority. It is thus clear that the judiciary are constantly confronted with the necessity of making a choice among the doctrines of the law alleged to be applicable to the particular case, and the choice which they make in the particular instance results inevitably in the expansion or restriction of the doctrine applied or rejected. It is at this point that what may, I think, quite properly be called ethical considerations operate and ought to operate. I hope I shall be acquitted of any suggestion that judges should allow themselves to be swayed by sentiment to twist the law, and I should deprecate as strongly as any the admission of the motives of the social reformer into the counsels of the Bench. . . . But when, as happens from time to time, the law itself presents a choice, and when it is a question whether one or other principle is to be applied, then it seems to me impossible, as it is undesirable, that the decision should not have regard to the ethical motive of promoting justice.[186]

This rhetoric, with its echoes of Shaw's functional approach, was also reflected in Macmillan's early judgments. In a workmen's com-

---

181. He could, however, be both vicious and unfair. See especially his patronizing (and probably unfair) portrait of Shaw in *Dictionary of National Biography 1931–1940*, at 806.

182. See, for instance, the view of the Secretary of the Cabinet; Thomas Jones, *A Diary with Letters: 1931–1950* (London, 1954), 522–23.

183. Macmillan, *Man of Law's Tale* 155–56.

184. Even Macmillan admitted, "I was not much of a success as the first Minister of Information in the Second World War"; ibid. 163.

185. Macmillan, *Law and Other Things* 220.

186. Ibid. 49.

pensation case in 1931 he declared that precedents in that area should "be stepping-stones rather than halting places."[187] Macmillan was also equally willing to congratulate his colleagues when, faced with precedents of which they disapproved, he noted, "I am glad that it has proved possible to surmount this difficulty in a manner so satisfactory."[188] Indeed, when he wished, Macmillan could manipulate precedent, or torpedo rules with principles, with a felicity of which Cardozo would not have been ashamed. In *Penman* v. *Fife Coal Company*, Macmillan distinguished out of existence a decision of Herschell's.[189] A similar skill was exhibited when the House came to consider whether the arbitration clause of a contract could be enforced after a contract was frustrated. The Privy Council had already decreed that it could not[190] and there were strong dicta in the House by Haldane,[191] among others, to the same effect. In other areas and with other law lords, such dicta would almost certainly have been treated as binding. They provided no stumbling block for Macmillan. He conceded that "in view of their high authority," they were entitled to the most careful consideration; but what had been enough to convince the Privy Council was not enough to move Macmillan. He argued simply that he did "not think they constitute pronouncements in law by this House such as to be binding on your Lordships."[192]

Macmillan was most adept at manipulating "two competing doctrines," and he was willing "to consider and accommodate" their respective "spheres of operation."[193] He was in the majority in *Donoghue* v. *Stevenson* and it was he who, with Atkin, was largely responsible for the wide *ratio* that later judges attributed to the decision.[194] Indeed some understandably prefer his speech, for it again faced the concept of competing doctrines[195] and had the grand sweep of the Scottish judge accustomed to prefer principle to precedent:[196]

187. *Birch Bros.* v. *Brown*, [1931] A.C. 605, 631.
188. *Richards* v. *Goskar*, [1937] A.C. 304, 325 (1936).
189. [1936] A.C. 45 (Scot. 1935). The Herschell decision was *Hewlett* v. *Allen*, [1894] A.C. 383; the legislation, the Truck Act of 1831.
190. *Hirji Mulji* v. *Cheong Yue S.S. Co.*, [1926] A.C. 497 (P.C.).
191. *Jureidini* v. *National British & Irish Millers Ins. Co.*, [1915] A.C. 499, 505 (1914).
192. *Heyman* v. *Darwins, Ltd.*, [1942] A.C. 356, 372 (1941).
193. *Wilsons & Clyde Coal Co.* v. *English*, [1938] A.C. 57, 74 (Scot. 1937).
194. [1932] A.C. 562 (Scot.).
195. "[I]n discussion of the topic which now engages your Lordship's attention two rival principles of law find a meeting place where each has contended for supremacy. On the one hand, there is the well established principle that no one other than a party to a contract can complain of a breach of that contract. On the other hand, there is the equally well established doctrine that negligence apart from contract gives a right of action to the party injured by that negligence . . . [used] in its technical legal sense, implying a duty owed and neglected"; ibid. 609.
196. Ibid. 609 ff., 618.

Now I have no hesitation in affirming that a person who for gain engages in the business of manufacturing articles of food and drink intended for consumption by members of the public in the form in which he issues them is under a duty to take care in the manufacturing of these articles. That duty, in my opinion, he owes to those whom he intends to consume his products. He manufactures his commodities for human consumption; he intends and contemplates that they shall be consumed. By reason of that very fact he places himself in a relationship with all the potential consumers of his commodities, and that relationship which he assumes and desires for his own ends imposes upon him a duty to take care to avoid injuring them. He owes them a duty not to convert by his own carelessness an article which he issues to them as wholesome and innocent into an article which is dangerous to life and health.[197]

Throughout his career as a law lord, Macmillan showed signs of this early position—a willingness to treat negligence flexibly[198] and a reluctance to defer automatically to the policy of stare decisis.[199] But as the years passed, the divergence between rhetoric and reality became more obvious and he had less and less impact on the law. He was of course sometimes in the majority with Atkin and Wright in vital decisions, but he was rarely in the lead. He was aware of the need to develop the law for reasons that ranged from justice[200] to business convenience,[201] but he appeared to lack the spirit to push his views. His essentially apolitical nature led him to stand increasingly for the status quo. This tendency appeared to be especially strong after his term as Minister of Information[202] and was evident to its fullest extent in *Liversidge* v. *Anderson*, where he showed himself one of those judges whom Atkin described as "more executive-minded than the executive." Macmillan deferred to the views of Atkinson in *Halliday*'s case[203] and stated his own views in much the same terms. It was not an elegant performance.

Academic lawyers probably overestimate the importance of *Liversidge* v. *Anderson*, but in terms of the purpose of the nation at large it is

197. Ibid. 620.

198. See, e.g., *Read* v. *J. Lyons & Co.*, [1947] A.C. 156 (1946).

199. See his views in the rating case of *Robinson Bros. (Brewers), Ltd.* v. *County of Durham Assessment Comm.*, [1938] A.C. 321, 339–40: "The case is not a favourable one for the application of the doctrine of *stare decisis*. The decision on behalf of which it is invoked is both embarrassing and unjust—embarrassing, because even the experienced counsel who appeared at your Lordship's bar had considerable difficulty in explaining precisely what it decided and what evidence it ruled out . . . unjust, because the unduly low valuation of public-houses to which it has given rise places an unjustifiable burden on the occupiers of other hereditaments."

200. His contribution to *Beresford* v. *Royal Ins. Co.*, [1938] A.C. 586, 601, was sympathetic. There the House refused to allow beneficiaries of an insurance policy to collect where the insured had committed suicide while sane.

201. See, e.g., his approval of the developing concepts of frustration in *Denny, Mott & Dickson, Ltd.* v. *James B. Fraser & Co.*, [1944] A.C. 265, 272 (Scot. 1943).

202. Heuston, *Lives* 562–63.

203. [1942] A.C. 206, 247 (1941).

impossible not to note Macmillan's increasingly destructive approach to tax legislation. Despite his views on precedent he often adopted a formalistic approach toward statutory interpretation.[204] In the *Duke of Westminster*'s case, although going by no means as far as Tomlin and Russell in promoting tax avoidance, he was "fully conscious of the anomalous consequences which might conceivably arise in other connections from the course adopted by the respondent." He refused, however, to concern himself with anything but "the technical question whether the respondent has brought himself within the language of the income tax rule."[205]

Moreover, Macmillan, who began to specialize in the increasingly frequent tax appeals, continued to develop this highly artificial approach. In *Inland Revenue Commissioners* v. *Ayrshire Employers Mutual Insurance Association*,[206] when Parliament had clearly intended to make the annual surpluses of mutual insurance companies subject to tax, Macmillan found a particularly formalistic argument to show that this had not been the effect of section 31 of the Finance Act of 1933. He was then happily able to announce, "[T]he Legislature has plainly missed fire."[207] Of this decision, Lord Diplock was later to say that "if, as in this case, the Courts can identify the target of Parliamentary legislation their proper function is to see that it is hit: not merely to record that it has been missed. Here is judicial legislation at its worst."[208] Yet it was Macmillan who, addressing the Canadian Bar Association on "Law and Order," talked at length about the unsatisfactory state of legislative drafting in England,[209] while his speeches in tax cases could only force Parliamentary Counsel's Office to draft in an increasingly narrow and formalistic way. It was a vicious circle that he did little to ameliorate. If Macmillan began as the bright hope of the House of Lords, he contributed to what

---

204. *Barras* v. *Aberdeen Steam Trawling & Fishing Co.*, [1933] A.C. 402, 447 (Scot.). See also *R. & W. Paul, Ltd.* v. *Wheat Commission*, [1937] A.C. 139, 154 (Scot. 1936).

205. *IRC* v. *Duke of Westminster*, [1936] A.C. 1, 28 (1935). Macmillan conceded the efficacy of what he termed the "collateral documents," i.e., that they embodied an agreement that the employee would not expect or be entitled to any further payment from the respondent (ibid. 26–27), but he concluded that the "absolute obligation to pay irrespective of employment remains unaffected by the collateral documents"; ibid. 27. He finally consoled himself with the thought, "It is not likely that many other employers will follow the respondent's example, for few employers would care to take the risk to which the respondent has left himself exposed—namely, that his servants may quit his employment and take their services elsewhere and yet continue to exact the covenanted weekly payments from him"; ibid. 28.

206. [1946] 1 All E.R. 637 (H.L., Scot. 1945).

207. "Its failure is perhaps less regrettable than it might have been for the subsection has the less laudable design of subjecting to tax what the law has consistently and emphatically declared not to be profit"; ibid. 641.

208. Sir Kenneth Diplock, *The Courts as Legislators* 10.

209. Macmillan, *Law and Other Things* 29–30.

Diplock was to call "the high-water mark of the narrow semantic approach."[210]

Thankerton,[211] the third of the Scottish law lords, had actually been appointed a year before Macmillan, on the resignation of Shaw in 1929.[212] The son of Lord Watson, Thankerton had also been a Unionist (Conservative) Member of Parliament, and at different times had been Solicitor-General and Lord Advocate of Scotland. It was only to be expected that promotion, in time, would follow, but when it came his was not a popular appointment.[213] It would seem that Thankerton's court manner was responsible for some of this lack of popularity, and he apparently made few attempts to overcome his failings,[214] although he continued to sit—by then the senior Lord of Appeal—until 1948.

Thankerton was the least Scottish of the three Scottish law lords under discussion. Unlike the other Scottish law lords he took a rather English "declaratory" approach to the law, yet, again unlike the others, he never felt at home with the common law. The result was that his contributions were often negative, although in some cases his speeches showed signs of Scottish breadth. In the field of restrictive trade practices, for instance, he was loath to find that agreements or actions, directed toward the safeguarding of vested interests, were outside the law.[215] He retained some of the flexible Scottish approach to negligence and was a

---

210. Diplock, *Courts as Legislators* 10.

211. William Watson; b. 1873; father, Baron Watson of Thankerton (law lord); educ., Winchester and Jesus College, Cambridge (Third, Law); admitted to Faculty of Advocates, 1899; K.C., 1914; M.P. (Unionist) S. Lanarkshire, 1913–18, Carlisle, 1924–29; Advocate Depute, 1919; Procurator Chief of Scotland, 1918–22; Solicitor-General for Scotland, 1922; Lord Advocate, 1922–24, 1924–29; P.C., 1922; Lord of Appeal, 1929–48; d. 1948; *Dictionary of National Biography 1941–1950*, at 929.

212. Thus, for a brief while, three (Dunedin, Macmillan, and Thankerton) of the seven law lords were Scottish judges.

213. "The appointment was not unexpected but was received with no great warmth"; *The Times*, 14 June 1948.

214. "Lord Thankerton had a habit of arguing with counsel with some aggressiveness and heat. As so often happens, with the years talkativeness on the bench did not decrease." Dunedin noted in 1935, "Doing well as to work and law, but making himself a veritable nuisance by excessive talking. I was asked to speak to him, and did quite lately. He took it quite well, but I hear . . . that instead of being better he is worse than ever"; Heuston, *Lives* 481. In later years he also irritated some counsel by practicing his hobby of knitting while on the bench.

215. In *Thorne v. Motor Trade Ass'n*, [1937] A.C. 797, 810, he considered, as settled law, that "the use of the 'Stop List' by an association in good faith and in furtherance or protection of its legitimate trade interests is legal," and that the alternative offer, to pay a fine, was intended to be more favorable to the offending person, against whom the "stop list" could be invoked.
Being wedded to this view that actions based on the protection of vested interests were legitimate, it was not surprising that he found the alleged conspiracy in *Crofter Hand Woven Harris Tweed Co. v. Veitch*, [1942] A.C. 435, 437 (Scot. 1941), to have been nothing more than the legitimate promotion of interests.

member of the majority in *Donoghue* v. *Stevenson*;[216] but his speech there was limited to a finding that a duty was owed and that there had been breach and damage.[217] While certainly some evidence showed that his was not an isolated approach to negligence,[218] Thankerton played no major role, as might have been expected of a judge trained in the civilian tradition, in broadening the concept of negligence. Indeed, it could even be argued that his being party to the judicial legislation in *Donoghue* v. *Stevenson* was an aberration.

During the almost twenty years when Thankerton sat on the court, he reflected a sense of stability, or, to use the looser phraseology of the American courts, he at best represented the "swing vote." With respect to workmen's compensation he adopted a generally balanced approach.[219] While he did not show any aversion to those for whom such legislation had been enacted, he gave no impression of being aware of the evolutionary processes going on, which were reflected in the type of case coming by way of appeal.[220] This interpretation of his approach to the work of the courts was also reflected in his decisions on the doctrine of

216. [1932] A.C. 562, 601 (Scot.).

217. Perhaps he was just overawed by Atkin. He considered Atkin's judgment and "so entirely agree with it that I cannot usefully add anything to it"; ibid. 604. One of the "ifs" of modern legal history is posed by the question of what might have happened if he had joined Tomlin and Buckmaster. As it was, Atkin was able to carry both Scottish law lords with him.

218. In *East Suffolk Rivers Catchment Bd.* v. *Kent*, [1941] A.C. 74, 94 (1940), Thankerton was again prepared to find that the appellants owed a duty to the respondents to use such reasonable care as would avoid causing damage to the respondents' property, but felt that "the respondents have failed to make a case . . . to establish the essential link between the breach of duty . . . and the main damage"; ibid. 96. In *Bourhill* v. *Young*, [1943] A.C. 92, 97 (Scot. 1942), Thankerton reiterated his belief in the concept of negligence, yet was not prepared to accept Lord Justice Kennedy's views on the area of "potential danger" as conclusive and was against any idea of laying down any "hard and fast rule" on the question of remoteness. Finally, Thankerton again found that the situation in *Glasgow Corp.* v. *Muir*, [1943] A.C. 448, 454–56 (Scot.), did not warrant the finding that the tea shop manageress and the urn carrier, although under a duty of care in some circumstances, were in a position to foresee the harm resulting as a natural and probable consequence of this particular act.

219. A good example of Thankerton's objectivity can be seen in his speech in *Wilsons & Clyde Coal Co.* v. *English*, [1938] A.C. 57, 62, 67 (Scot. 1937), where he held that when the doctrine of common employment held such terrors for workmen, "[I]t appears clear, then, that, when the workman contracts to do the work, he is not to be held as having agreed to hold the master immune from the latter's liability for want of due care in the provision of a reasonably safe system of working." The case decided that in regard to some duties owed by an employer to employees, the employer could not comply with his duty merely by showing delegation to a competent servant. See R. F. V. Heuston, ed., *Salmond on the Law of Torts* 140–42.

220. See *Nokes* v. *Doncaster Amalgamated Collieries, Ltd.*, [1940] A.C. 1014, 1034. On the other hand, in *McLaughlin* v. *Caledonia Stevedoring Co.*, [1938] A.C. 642, 649 (Scot.), he gave what appears in retrospect to be a beneficial interpretation of § 1(1) of the Workmen's Compensation Act of 1931. In the following year in *Harris* v. *Associated Portland Cement Mfrs., Ltd.*, [1939] A.C. 71, 80 (1938), he concurred in limiting the effect

public policy in contract. In *Fender* v. *St. John-Mildmay*[221] Thankerton announced that the proper function of the court with regard to questions on public policy is "to expound, and not to expand, such policy."[222] Nor did his caution end there,[223] although finally he was able to adjust his decision to what was generally regarded as a commonsense solution.

If one requires any further evidence of Thankerton's judicial caution, it is provided by his decisions concerning judicial control of the executive; and if anything, that caution became more noticeable as the years passed. In the *Yaffé* case in 1931,[224] on the vexed question of when and to what extent a court can interfere with a minister's power given to him by delegated legislation, Thankerton held that unless Parliament had expressly excluded the jurisdiction of the courts, "the Court has the right and duty to decide whether the Minister has acted within the limits of his delegated power."[225] He further held, however, that where the minister had been given a "discretionary power, the exercise of that power within the limits of the discretion will not be open to challenge in a Court of law."[226]

Some fifteen years later Thankerton had to decide a similar point connected with a minister's power under delegated legislation in *Franklin* v. *Minister of Town and Country Planning*[227] and he gave what was, in effect, the judgment of the court. In *Franklin* Thankerton found that no judicial function whatsoever was cast upon the minister under the Labour government's planning legislation and that the most he had to do was to "consider" reports and "objections." Unless a plain dereliction of that duty was manifest, the courts could not impeach the minister's action. Both decisions were a reflection of the man. Both were no doubt "right" in a technical and political sense, yet neither showed any sense of judicial strategy or the limits and advantages of the appellate process. The insistence that pieces of delegated legislation, like statutes them-

of the added peril doctrine, although he did not, as one might have predicted, go so far as Atkin.

221. [1938] A.C. 1, 22 (1937).

222. Ibid. 23. On the other hand, he conceded, "That does not mean that they are precluded from applying an existing principle of public policy to a new set of circumstances, where such circumstances are clearly within the scope of the policy. Such a case might well arise in the case of safety of the State, for instance. But no such case is suggested here"; ibid.

223. Ibid.; "the Courts must be watchful not to be influenced by their view of what the principle of public policy, or its limits, should be." Thankerton concluded, however, that he was unable to find "immoral tendencies" in the present case and that "[p]ublic policy is not concerned with tendencies that may exist in a very limited number of cases"; ibid. 25.

224. *Minister of Health* v. *R., ex parte Yaffé*, [1931] A.C. 494, 531.

225. Ibid. 532.

226. Ibid. 533.

227. [1948] A.C. 87 (1947).

selves,[228] had to be given their surface meaning was a less-than-satisfactory basis for developing what passed in England for administrative law. Yet perhaps Thankerton's strength was that he would not have comprehended that criticism.

228. He was rightly suspicious of the phrase "intention of Parliament." See *London & North Eastern Ry.* v. *B. A. Collieries, Ltd.*, [1945] A.C. 143, 171 (1944), with particular reference to "compensation" legislation. He argued that the only true interpretation of a statute lay in the words as they appeared. See *Wicks* v. *DPP*, [1947] A.C. 362, 367 (1946): "I would like to add that the intention of Parliament is not to be judged by what is in its mind, but by its expression of that mind in the statute itself."

NINE

Vying Professional Approaches

If Thankerton represented a move toward substantive formalism on the part of the Scottish judges, by 1940 substantive formalism—the belief in legal formalism as an end in itself—was the norm for the English judges. For the most part, the English judiciary moved from a stage of political amateurism to a stage of high formalism without the intervening stage of the Grand Style. As Mr. Justice Holmes said, however, "[T]o generalize is to omit." There were exceptions to the trend, the two most distinguished being Atkin and Wright. They, especially during the 1930s, brought a powerful touch of the Grand Style to the English judicial scene. Understandably, they often spoke the language of the declaratory theory and they were not distinguished constitutional lawyers; yet, as common lawyers, they were supreme masters of the appellate process and, while complementing some of the Scottish judges, they provided an increasingly stark contrast to the substantive formalists.

It is interesting to speculate why, shortly before the most conservative intellectual period in the history of the court, two outstanding appeal judges such as Atkin and Wright should have emerged. Their appearance cannot have been unrelated to the fact that they were both commercial lawyers. When the Commercial Court (or List) was reestablished within the Queen's Bench Division in the 1890s,[1] it was claimed to have "brought back learning to the common law"; and such a claim was borne out by such early practitioners as Scrutton,[2] whose pupils both Atkin and Wright were at the bar. Their master, who made many enemies, lived to see them both appointed to the House of Lords while he was still in the Court of Appeal. No doubt this was a bitter blow to him. Yet his legacy to English law was great. Scrutton had been an outstanding com-

---

1. T. E. Scrutton, *Charter Parties and Bills of Lading*, Appendix.
2. To balance the pro view of the Commercial Bar in the early twentieth century, see the con view in William Beveridge, *Power and Influence* 10–12.

mercial lawyer[3] and was a creative judge. He was acutely aware of the delicate balancing process in which the courts, particularly the appeal courts, were forced to indulge.[4] Atkin and Wright carried that sensitivity to the highest court.

The Commercial Tradition: Atkin

Between 1930 and 1940, no law lord had greater influence in the House of Lords than Lord Atkin of Aberdovey.[5] After a slow start at the bar, he ultimately built up an impressive practice, particularly in commercial and workmen's compensation cases, and was appointed a puisne judge by Haldane. After a period in the Court of Appeal, Atkin was appointed to replace Atkinson as Lord of Appeal in 1928. Almost at once, his speeches became the focus of considerable deference,[6] and his was the chief influence on the House until Simon was made Lord Chancellor in 1940.[7] Wright said that during these years a remarkable number of the cases considered involved "policy"; therefore the period "is a striking illustration of the judicial exercise of the legislative power."[8] It would seem more likely that it was Atkin's approach that turned ordinary cases into instances that appeared to involve problems of policy, and where interstitial legislation in the Holmesian sense was inevitable. In every respect Atkin was a great common lawyer.

Around all outstanding judges, myths begin to develop. Atkin, in his

3. Karl N. Llewellyn, *The Common Law Tradition.* On Scrutton see also C. H. S. Fifoot, *Judge and Jurist in the Reign of Victoria* 29.
4. Scrutton, for instance, wrote of the difficulties of securing judicial impartiality:

This is rather difficult to attain in any system. I am not speaking of conscious partiality; but the habits you are trained in, the people with whom you mix, lead to your having a certain class of ideas of such a nature, that, when you have to deal with other ideas, you do not give as sound and accurate judgments as you would wish. This is one of the great difficulties at present with Labour. Labour says: "Where are your impartial judges? They all move in the same circle as employers, and they are all educated and nursed in the same ideas as the employers. How can a Labour man or a trade unionist get impartial justice?" It is very difficult sometimes to be sure that you have put yourself in a thoroughly impartial position between two disputants, one of your own class and one not of your class. Even in matters outside trade-unionist cases (to some extent in workmen's compensation cases) it is sometimes difficult to be sure, hard as you have tried, that you have put yourself in a perfectly impartial position between the two litigants. [T. E. Scrutton, "The Work of the Commercial Courts" 6-8]

5. James Richard Atkin; b. 1867; father, member of Queensland Legislative Assembly; educ., Christ College, Brecon and Magdalen College, Oxford (Second, "Greats"); Judge, King's Bench Division, 1913-19; Lord Justice, 1919-28; Lord of Appeal, 1928-44; d. 1944; *Dictionary of National Biography 1941-1950,* at 27.
6. Obituary, *The Times,* 26 June 1944.
7. As has been seen, Hailsham complained that "Atkin is naturally apt to be followed by his fellow law lords of the Chancery or Scottish Bar in a Common Law Point"; R. F. V. Heuston, *Lives of the Lord Chancellors 1885-1940,* at 531. Dunedin's complaint was rather different. "Clever, and a good common lawyer. But obstinate if he had taken a view and quite unpersuadable"; ibid. 481.
8. Lord Wright (Robert Anderson), "Lord Atkin of Aberdovey: In Memoriam" 307.

private life, was not a particularly interesting person nor were his interests particularly intellectual ones. He made no extrajudicial contribution to the appellate process. The Report of the Committee on Legal Education, which he chaired, was uninspiring.[9] His work in interpreting Commonwealth constitutions, during the time he sat in the Privy Council, was undistinguished. It was Atkin who presided in the crucial series of decisions striking down the Canadian "New Deal" legislation,[10] and it was Atkin who presided in the 1931 appeal from Kenya about whether public sale of Crown lands in towns could be limited to whites. While he did not blindly accept parliamentary supremacy in the latter case, Atkin announced that "[q]uestions of policy . . . are not matters for the legal tribunal."[11] This attitude was not the mark of a great constitutional lawyer.

In more general public law, Atkin was stronger, although that is not to suggest that he had any interest in competing directly with decisions of the executive.[12] Yet he had a sense of civil liberties and was reluctant to extend the contempt power; as he said in a Privy Council decision, "[J]ustice is not a cloistered virtue."[13] He was opposed to the privileged form of trial for members of the House of Lords. On Sankey's motion that the trial of peers had outlived its usefulness, Atkin declared, "I think nobody can deny that the privilege which peers enjoy, if it be a privilege, which I very much doubt, is in fact a violation of the ordinary principle that all men are deemed to be equal in the eyes of the law."[14] It was this same

9. Report of the Legal Education Committee, Cmd. 4663 (1934).

10. See chap. 6, at 202–3. Defenders have fairly pointed out that this group of decisions and the related ones in the Privy Council in general upheld decisions of the Supreme Court of Canada. In that the Supreme Court had been following earlier Privy Council decisions, it could be argued that the criticism should be directed more at Watson and Haldane than Atkin. Yet, a constitutional lawyer, comfortable with the "organic growth" of a constitution, would have been less inhibited than Atkin.

11. *Commissioner for Local Gov't Lands & Settlement* v. *Kaderbhai*, [1931] A.C. 652, 654 (P.C.). With this, however, should be contrasted *Gallagher* v. *Lynn*, [1937] A.C. 863 (N. Ire.), an appeal from Northern Ireland to determine whether the Milk and Milk Products Act was an act that the Northern Ireland Parliament was competent to pass. Atkin insisted that a broad view had to be taken. "[Y]ou look at the 'true nature and character of the legislation' . . . the pith and substance of the legislation"; ibid. 870.

12. Where a matter such as sovereign immunity was involved, he was insistent that it was not a matter for the courts. "Our State cannot speak with two voices on such a matter, the judiciary saying one thing, the executive another. Our Sovereign has to decide whom he will recognise as a fellow sovereign in the family of States; and the relations of the foreign State with ours in the matter of State immunities must flow from that decision alone"; *Spanish Republican Government* v. *S.S. "Arantzazu Mendi,"* [1939] A.C. 256.

13. *Ambard* v. *Attorney-General for Trinidad & Tobago*, [1936] A.C. 322, 335 (P.C.).

14. 99 *Parl. Deb.*, H.L. (5th ser.), col. 406 (4 Feb. 1936) (trial of peers by peers): "The question really seems to be one rather of the equal administration of justice than of the maintenance of the dignity of privileges of the House. I think nobody can deny that the privileges which peers enjoy . . . [are] . . . a violation of the ordinary principle that all men are ordained to be equal in the eyes of the law."

belief in the spirit of the Rule of Law that led to his famous dissent in *Liversidge* v. *Anderson.*[15]

In that case, Atkin did basically what Shaw had done during World War I in *Halliday*'s case; namely, he insisted that delegated legislation be read narrowly when it provided for imprisonment without trial. In a society that has no written constitution or entrenched provisions, with only the most amateur tradition of discussing presumptions of interpretation, it is not easy to evaluate such dissents. To what extent do they represent courage and to what extent obstinacy?[16] In the case of Liversidge's imprisonment, Atkin refused to concede that the words in the regulation—"has reasonable cause to believe"—implied a purely subjective test on the part of the executive. " 'Reasonable cause to believe' is just as much a positive fact capable of determination by a third party as is a 'broken ankle or a legal right.' "[17] He supported this position by showing "that this meaning of the words has been accepted in innumerable legal decisions for many generations, that 'reasonable cause' for a belief when the subject of legal dispute has been always treated as an objective fact to be proved by one or other party and to be determined by the appropriate tribunal."[18] Having established to his own satisfaction that this interpretation was true and that the objections to allowing the reasons for detention to be revealed on the grounds of public interest were "greatly exaggerated,"[19] Atkin proceeded to support his decision in terms of liberty of the subject.[20]

15. [1942] A.C. 206 (1941).

16. Of the speech, Heuston, for instance, says, "Lord Atkin's judgment, though obviously attractive to anyone who believes in personal liberty, suffers from the flaw that it erects a question of fact into a question of law. Atkin started from the belief that words in a statute must always have one particular meaning, but as Maugham's judgment showed, the true question is what is the meaning of these words in this context"; Heuston, *Lives* 566. For sympathetic criticisms of Atkin's view in *Liversidge* v. *Anderson*, Lord Wright (Robert Anderson), "Lord Atkin of Aberdovey" 332; and *Dictionary of National Biography 1941–1950*, at 27.

17. *Liversidge* v. *Anderson*, [1942] A.C. 206, 228 (1941).

18. Ibid.

19. Ibid. 240.

20. "I view with apprehension the attitude of judges who on a mere question of construction when face to face with claims involving the liberty of the subject show themselves more executive minded than the executive. Their function is to give words their natural meaning, not, perhaps, in war time leaning towards liberty, but following the dictum of Pollock, C.B. in *Bowditch* v. *Balchin*, cited with approval by my noble and learned friend Lord Wright in *Barnard* v. *Gorman*: 'In a case in which the liberty of the subject is concerned, we cannot go beyond the natural construction of the statute.' In this country, amid the clash of arms, the laws are not silent. They may be changed, but they speak the same language in war as in peace. It has always been one of the pillars of freedom, one of the principles of liberty for which on recent authority we are now fighting, that the judges are no respecters [sic] of persons and stand between the subject and any attempted encroachments on his liberty by the executive, alert to see that any coercive action is justified in law. In this case I have listened to arguments which might have been addressed acceptably to the Court of King's Bench in the time of Charles I"; ibid. 244.

To those accustomed to a written constitution and a tradition of legal protection of civil liberties stronger than that of England, such a position would appear to be unexceptionable. Yet Atkin dissented alone. More than that, he was put under pressure by Simon, the Lord Chancellor, who had not sat, to change the tone if not the content of his speech before it was delivered.[21] When Atkin refused,[22] Maugham, who had presided, made a bizarre attack on him in a legislative session,[23] and the law lords refused to eat with Atkin in the House of Lords or, at one point, even to speak to him. Many felt he never really recovered from this treatment before his death in 1944.

Atkin's approach in *Liversidge* v. *Anderson* was related to his attitude toward statutory interpretation. Unlike some law lords, he did not pontificate about the "correct" canons of statutory construction, nor on the "plain meaning" of some phrase; but for all this he attempted to give effect to the wishes of Parliament in interpreting statutes. This effort was especially true in workmen's compensation decisions; in many respects he again inherited the mantle of Shaw in such cases. Atkin emphasized the compensatory nature of the Workmen's Compensation Acts[24] and was prepared to look at the needs of the workmen in the context of market conditions rather than solely in terms of physical incapacity.[25] He opposed interpretations that involved a "diminution of the rights of the

21. Letter from Simon to Atkin, 31 Oct. 1941. In particular Simon wanted the paragraph about Alice in Wonderland's view of the meaning of words, [1942] A.C. 206, 245 (1941), removed. Simon conceded, "Of course it is entirely for you"; but he concluded, "I at any rate feel that neither the dignity of the House, nor the collaboration of colleagues, nor the force of your reasoning would suffer from the omission"; cited, R. F. V. Heuston, "*Liversidge* v. *Anderson* in Retrospect" 43.

22. "The present cases as I see them do not merely involve questions of the liberty of the particular persons concerned but involve the duty of the courts to stand impartially between the subject and the executive. I feel strongly about the matter, and am not dismayed that at present I stand alone.

"I have the highest esteem for my colleagues: If I had not I could have used very different language to what I have used. I have not the slightest intent to ridicule them. . . . I cannot think therefore that there are sufficient grounds for allowing this proposed omission. I cannot think that the dignity of the House will suffer"; Letter from Atkin to Simon, 1 Nov. 1941.

Simon replied, "I wrote [not] only as an onlooker, but from a friendship which unites me to all my colleagues." At the end of the letter, however, Simon reiterated his view. "I wish you saw your way to omit the jibe!" Letter from Simon to Atkin, 3 Nov. 1941.

23. Heuston, "*Liversidge* v. *Anderson* in Retrospect" 45–46, 43.

24. E.g., *Tannoch* v. *Brownieside Coal Co.*, [1929] A.C. 642, 647 (Scot.); *Birch Bros.* v. *Brown*, [1931] A.C. 605, 617. "Once you have found the work which he is seeking to do to be within his employment the question of negligence, great or small, is irrelevant: and no amount of negligence in doing an employment job can change the workman's action into a non-employment job. . . . The fact is that the workman's negligence in doing his job is one of the most fruitful causes of injury; and, if it would in any degree preclude compensation, the benefits of the Act would be seriously impaired"; *Harris* v. *Associated Portland Cement Mfrs., Ltd.*, [1939], A.C. 71, 76–77 (1938).

25. E.g., *White* v. *London & North Eastern Ry.*, [1931] A.C. 52, 65 (1930).

workman existing in relation to ordinary accidents."[26] He took an equally liberal view of the breadth of "the course of his employment,"[27] as well as to the general administration of the acts.[28] Yet Atkin went further than that. With Wright, he helped to integrate workmen's compensation into the expanding concepts of tort liability by requiring employers to provide a safe system of work.[29] If the British workingman felt by 1940 that he was increasingly receiving a fair deal from the courts, considerable credit for this must belong to Atkin.[30]

In the general area of public law, Atkin also made an effort to prevent the most flagrant avoidance devices in tax law. In particular, dissenting in the *Duke of Westminster*'s case,[31] Atkin refused to be bound

26. *Richards v. Goskar*, [1937] A.C. 304, 323 (1936). For the application of this approach to a statutory change, see *McLaughlin v. Caledonia Stevedoring Co.*, [1938] A.C. 642 (Scot.), where the House was called upon to interpret the 1931 Workmen's Compensation Act on the question of where the burden of proving that a workman had taken reasonable steps to find work lay. In reversing the Court of Session, Atkin spoke out most clearly against a decision which involved altering "the negative form of the proviso and turning a negative proviso into a condition precedent"; ibid. 648. His interpretation suggested that he was fully conversant with the debates during the 1931 bill, and, what was more, while citing no legislative history, he firmly enforced the intention of the government spokesman at the time of the bill. See the Commons debates, especially 244 *Parl. Deb.*, H.L. (5th ser.), col. 2030, 2036–37 (14 Nov. 1930).

27. E.g., *Blee v. London & North Eastern Ry.*, [1938] A.C. 126, 132 (1937): "In my opinion the case is not free from doubt; but I have come to the conclusion that there were special facts in this case."

28. E.g., *Lissenden v. C. A. V. Bosch, Ltd.*, [1940] A.C. 412, 423 (1939): "That a workman who has been held to be entitled to some compensation withheld from him in the past should not be entitled to exercise his statutory right to appeal so as to ask for more without forgoing the receipt of the compensation admittedly and undoubtedly due until his appeal is heard would, I think, appear to most people a rule unjust and entirely opposed to the scheme of the Act."

29. See *Wilsons & Clyde Coal Co. v. English*, [1938] A.C. 57, 59 (Scot. 1937), where he did not deliver a speech, since he had read the other Lords' speeches beforehand and felt he could "add nothing."

30. Additionally, as a corollary to his development of the tort of negligence, Atkin was instrumental in curbing the worst excesses of contributory negligence and common employment. In *Caswell v. Powell Duffryn Ass'd Collieries, Ltd.*, [1940] A.C. 152, 166 (1939), for instance, where the House held that the defense of common employment was available, Atkin suggested that "a different degree of care may well be expected from a workman in a factory or a mine from that which might be taken by an ordinary man not exposed continually to the noise, strain, and manifold risks of factory or mine." So, too, when it was suggested that the doctrine of common employment applied to two employees of a bus company, when two buses collided on a public highway, Atkin and the House firmly refused to apply the doctrine of common employment, for to apply the notion in such a situation, would be, as Atkin put it, "implied contract run riot"; *Radcliffe v. Ribble Motor Servs., Ltd.*, [1939] A.C. 215, 232.

It is arguable that Stafford Cripps also helped to curb the worst excesses of common employment. Speaking of the Radcliffe case, which Cripps, as a member of the bar, took *pro bono*, his biographer said, "Cripps almost persuaded their Lordships to rule that the doctrine of common employment did not exist." In any event, he obtained an "entirely new interpretation of the doctrine of common employment"; Patricia Strauss, *Cripps, Advocate Extraordinary* 215.

31. *IRC v. Duke of Westminster*, [1936] A.C. 1, 7 (1935).

by the mere form of the tax avoidance device. He had no difficulty with the basic idea that a taxpayer had "the legal right so to dispose of his capital and income as to attract upon himself the least amount of tax,"[32] and he was equally willing to accept that "[t]he only function of a court of law is to determine the legal results of his [the taxpayer's] dispositions so far as they affect tax."[33] Yet, after a functional analysis of the whole tax avoidance scheme,[34] Atkin concluded that "the facts and the terms of the letter indicate that the transaction was intended to have, and had, far more substantial results than the interchange of unnecessary assurances between master and servant . . . [that] the document was intended to be contractual is a conclusion that I find irresistible."[35]

Atkin's speeches give the overall impression that he was anxious to make the relationship between the judiciary and the other branches of government an intelligent and responsible one. In dealings with the legislature this effort was particularly apparent. When he felt that the law as it stood could not legitimately be remedied by the House as a judicial body, he clearly stated the problem and invited the legislature to intervene.[36] Within the more strict ambit of common law decisions, Atkin's judicial skills had full scope. He by no means ignored the by then firmly established judicial style that required a full examination of all the precedents. He made no effort to revert to the nineteenth-century House of Lords style that permitted a general statement of principle illustrated by a sample of decisions. His was not even the broad sweep in the Scottish tradition. Atkin allowed himself no such shortcuts. Even one of his outstanding judgments like *Donoghue* v. *Stevenson*[37] was painstaking and at times highly technical in its examination of precedents. Only when this process was finished was he ready to articulate the general statements that were to have such an impact on the law of England.

His intellectual distinction lay in his ability to handle precedents and rules in such a way that he could lay down principles; his attitude toward such a process was perhaps most neatly summarized in his response to a

32. Ibid. 8.

33. Ibid.

34. He analyzed the effects of the deed of covenant were it to come into force without any further agreement and concluded that there were numerous "embarrassments" that he felt the respondent did not intend. Atkin felt that he could not contemplate so many servants consciously making such bargains. "The better construction appears to be that the servants were never asked to abandon the existing contractual rate"; ibid. 14. The arrangement "would inevitably be understood by the recipient and would be intended by the writers to be understood as a representation that he [the employee] was being asked to make a contract in terms of the document"; ibid. 13.

35. Ibid.

36. See, for instance, *English Ins. Co.* v. *Official Receiver & Liquidator of Nat'l Benefit Assurance Co.*, [1929] A.C. 114, 125–26 (1928).

37. [1932] A.C. 562 (Scot.). For the typical techniques in a dissenting speech, see *Hole* v. *Garnsey*, [1930] A.C. 472, 493.

doctrine established to meet the requirements of the forms of action. "When these ghosts of the past stand in the path of justice clanking their medieval chains the proper course for the judge is to pass through them undeterred."[38] It is all strangely reminiscent of Holmes' call to lure the "dragon" of legal history out of the cave and "on to the plain and in the daylight," where he might be either tamed or made "a useful animal."[39]

Atkin's facility with precedents was a source of wonder even to other law lords. In one case Russell said of Atkin's speech that "it has opened up a way through what I feared was an impasse," by reconciling authorities when he had "thought it impossible so to do."[40] What appeared to Russell as a remarkable feat was to Atkin a commonplace.[41] This direct realization of the power of manipulation of precedent as a means of developing doctrine would have been of little value had Atkin not been committed at the same time to the idea that the final court of appeal had a duty to develop the law along intelligent lines. On matters of public policy, he had no doubt that the courts had a duty to be creative.[42] In all appropriate cases, he sought to go to the substance of the matter and to apply his concept of the basic end toward which the law ought to develop different areas of the common law.

Some of those areas are well known. Atkin was primarily responsible for developing a duty of care that took negligence beyond occupier's liability into a more generalized sphere. He began the process in *Oliver* v. *Saddler and Company* [43] and carried it a stage further in *Excelsior Wire Rope Company* v. *Callan*,[44] again developing a wider test than the other law lords.[45] The famous test in *Donoghue* v. *Stevenson*[46] was a logical

---

38. *United Australia, Ltd.* v. *Barclays Bank, Ltd.,* [1941] A.C. 1, 29 (1940).

39. Oliver Wendell Holmes, Jr., *Collected Legal Papers* 186–89.

40. *Richards* v. *Goskar,* [1937] A.C. 304, 325 (1936).

41. For his day-to-day handling of precedent, see, e.g., *Birch Bros.* v. *Brown,* [1931] A.C. 605, 617–23.

42. He described Halsbury's view in *Janson* v. *Dreifontein Consol. Gold Mines,* [1902] A.C. 484, 500, that the categories of public policy are closed as "too rigid a doctrine." *Fender* v. *St. John-Mildmay,* [1938] A.C. 1, 21 (1937): "It appears to me to be wrong to assume that the doctrine of public policy applies to any class of contract without regard to the public mischief on which the decision or decisions are based."

43. [1929] A.C. 584, 592 (Scot.). The majority of the law lords placed considerable emphasis on the "special circumstances" of the case, but Atkin based his judgment on the wider concept that "the stevedore firm owed a duty to the porters to take reasonable care to see that the sling was in fit condition to take the load"; ibid. 596.

44. [1930] A.C. 404.

45. While most of the other law lords were emphasizing the duty owed to invitees, Atkin specifically rejected the idea that the liability for injury to children playing on a machine had anything to do with this, since the defendants were not occupiers of the land. He then proceeded to spell out a far wider test of duty of care: "to take reasonable precautions to see that the children were not injured by the occasional use to which the owners put that dangerous machine"; ibid. 413.

46. [1932] A.C. 562, 578 (Scot.).

conclusion. Having deferred both to justice[47] and to common sense,[48] Atkin nevertheless established what was a comprehensive duty of care, at least so far as manufactured goods were concerned, through the sophisticated skills of a legal craftsman.[49] The development of this broad test has been accepted in an ever-expanding tradition. On occasion Atkin clearly would have preferred its development to be rather speedier,[50] but despite the pace, his contribution to generalizing the duty of care was of historic importance.

The attempt by Atkin to develop the common law along the lines he felt were needed by modern society can be seen in all branches of the law. In tort, not only did Atkin help to confirm the independent tort of negligence, but he also sought to move the emphasis in tort further from fault toward compensation. This progress is reflected in his gradual absorption of workmen's compensation concepts into the expanding areas of common law liability such as the safe system of work, while at the same time limiting doctrines like contributory negligence.[51] Atkin tried to emphasize the compensatory approach through other devices as well. In *Rose v. Ford*,[52] for example, the House of Lords used a statute that allowed a right of action to pass to the representatives of the deceased[53] to undermine the rule that death gave rise to no cause of action, by allowing damages to be given for the shortening of the expectation of

47. "I do not think so ill of our jurisprudence as to suppose that its principles are so remote from the ordinary needs of civilised society and the ordinary claims it makes upon its members as to deny a legal remedy where there is so obviously a social wrong"; ibid. 583.

48. "It will be an advantage to make clear that the law in this matter, as in most others, is in accordance with sound common sense"; ibid. 599.

49. For excerpts from Atkin's speech, see chap. 6, at 215.

50. See especially Atkin dissenting in *East Suffolk Rivers Catchment Bd. v. Kent*, [1941] A.C. 74 (1940). The majority (Simon, Thankerton, Romer, Porter) held that no action in negligence lay when a public authority negligently fulfilled a discretionary duty to repair a sea wall. Atkin, in his dissent, said he did "not wish to refer in detail to *Donoghue v. Stevenson*, but I venture to think that the principles there accepted by the majority of this House give guidance on this part of the case"; ibid. 92. On the general problem, Atkin's views were clear:

[N]ow quite apart from a duty owed to a particular individual which is the question in this case I suggest that it would be difficult to lay down that a duty upon a public authority to act without negligence or not carelessly or improperly does not include a duty to act with reasonable diligence by which I mean reasonable dispatch. I cannot imagine this House affording its support to a proposition so opposed to public interests where there are so many public bodies exercising statutory powers and employing public money upon them. I myself have been unable to think of any case where a duty to perform a continuous operation with reasonable care, i.e., without negligence, does not involve an obligation to perform it with reasonable dispatch. Of course, what is reasonable means reasonable in all circumstances of the particular case. [Ibid. 90–91]

51. *Radcliffe v. Ribble Motor Servs., Ltd.*, [1939] A.C. 215, 232.

52. [1937] A.C. 826.

53. Law Reform (Miscellaneous Provisions) Act of 1934.

life. Again Atkin was in the lead in this piece of "judicial legislation,"[54] although he lived to see some weakening of the development by the House.[55]

This same approach—the relating of the law to the problems of society—characterized Atkin's attitude toward other problems. In commercial cases he was able to bring to bear his wide knowledge of the City and commercial affairs.[56] He insisted on the enforcement of contracts, at least those concluded between businessmen dealing at arm's length.[57] He would allow no sentimentality to interfere with what he conceived of as the best overall approach for the business community.[58] At the same time he believed that contracts should be made to work. He was equally willing to chastise businessmen for their haphazard business practices[59]

54. *Mayne and MacGregor on Damages*, 12th ed. (London, 1961), 786. For Atkin's basic thrust, see *Rose v. Ford*, [1937] A.C. 826, 834. "I see no reason for extending the illogical doctrine of *The Amerika* to any case where it does not clearly apply." Of the doctrine that *actio personalis moritur cum persona*, Atkin said, "If the rule is really based on the relevant death being due to felony, it should long ago have been relegated to a museum: for deaths by negligence are often not felonious, and where they happen more than a year and a day after the wrongful act cannot be"; ibid.

55. See *Benham v. Gambling*, [1941] A.C. 157 (1940).

56. R. W. Harding, "Lord Atkin's Judicial Attitudes and Their Illustration in Commercial Law and Contract" 434.

57. It was not enough that goods were merchantable; they had to measure up to the contract description. E.g., *Arcos v. Ronaasen & Son*, [1933] A.C. 470, 480: "[T]he conditions of a contract must be strictly performed." Some have argued that this decision is inconsistent with the broad approach in *Hillas & Co. v. Arcos, Ltd.*, [1932] All E.R. 494 (H.L.). The answer to this would seem to be in commercial rather than legal terms. "It will be found that most of the cases that admit any deviation from the contract are cases where there has been an excess or deficiency in quantity which the Court has considered negligible. But apart from this consideration the right view is that the conditions of the contract must be strictly performed." (I.e., he is talking about performance rather than intention to be bound as was the issue in *Hillas v. Arcos*.) Atkin continued:

If a condition is not performed the buyer has a right to reject. I do not myself think that there is any difference between business men and lawyers on this matter. No doubt, in business, men often find it unnecessary or inexpedient to insist on their strict legal rights. In a normal market if they get something substantially like the specified goods they may take with or without grumbling and claim for an allowance. But in a falling market I find that buyers are often as eager to insist on their legal rights as courts of law are ready to maintain them. No doubt at all times sellers are prepared to take a liberal view as to the rigidity of their own obligations, and possibly buyers who in turn are sellers may also dislike too much precision. But buyers are not, as far as my experience goes, inclined to think that the rights defined in the code are in excess of business needs. [*Arcos v. Ronaasen & Son*, [1933] A.C. 470, 480]

58. *Bell v. Lever Bros.*, [1932] A.C. 161, 210 (1931). "The implications to be made are to be no more than are necessary for giving business efficacy to the transaction"; ibid. 226. "The result is that in the present case servants unfaithful in some of their work retain large compensation which some will think they do not deserve. Nevertheless, it is of greater importance that well established principles of contract should be maintained than that a particular hardship should be redressed; and I see no way of giving relief to the plaintiffs in the present circumstances except by confiding to the Courts loose powers of introducing terms into contracts which would only serve to introduce doubt and confusion where certainty is essential"; ibid. 229.

59. "[I]t is difficult to understand why businessmen persist in entering upon considerable obligations in old fashioned forms of contract which do not adequately express the

or to invite the government to legislate on some point in order to make sense of a business arrangement.[60] What he realized—a realization that few other English judges have been able to share—was that the rigorous rules of contract applied to parties dealing at arm's length may not be appropriate when there is little savoring of equality of opportunity or equality of bargaining power.[61]

Atkin was equally able to take a balanced view toward divorce. He strongly supported the court's power to award maintenance at the time of divorce, notwithstanding a covenant by the wife not to petition for maintenance in excess of that provided by the deed of separation.[62] In the 1937 debates on the Matrimonial Causes Act, he spoke in the legislative debates in the House advocating progressive reforms,[63] and he was prepared to adopt the same attitude in the judicial work of the House. In *Fender v. St. John-Mildmay*,[64] in holding that there was nothing contrary to public policy in finding valid a promise of marriage made by a person between the date of the decree nisi and the decree absolute, Atkin was not convinced that the decision would induce "sexual immorality" nor contravene the obligations that are recognized as owing from a husband and a wife. "I can only say that if the lady yields to a promise with such an indefinite date, she is probably of a yielding disposition, and it would appear difficult to predict that immorality is either facilitated or accelerated by the promise."[65] "The whole notion of any danger to public interest seems to me fanciful and unreal."[66]

In short, Atkin was concerned not only with the intricacies of legal doctrine, but also with the impact of the law on the society in which he lived. His greatest contribution came during the ten years between 1930

---

true transaction. The traditional form of marine policy is perhaps past praying for; but why insurance of credits or contracts, if insurance is intended, or guarantees of the same, if guarantees are intended, should not be expressed in appropriate language, passes comprehension"; *Trade Indemnity Co. v. Workington Harbour & Dock Bd.*, [1937] A.C. 1, 17 (1936).

60. E.g., *English Ins. Co. v. Official Receiver & Liquidator of Nat'l Benefit Assurance Co.*, [1929] A.C. 114, 125 (1928).

61. See also his broad and balanced view toward company law in *Hunter v. Hunter*, [1936] A.C. 222, 261 (1935); and *Russian & English Bank v. Baring Bros. & Co.*, [1936] A.C. 405, 428.

62. *Hyman v. Hyman*, [1929] A.C. 601, 625.

63. E.g., on the clause to prohibit a divorce petition for the first five years of marriage: "You have got to make up your mind whether or not it is or is not for the advantage of the community that there should be divorce, and if, as I think, it is of vital importance to the community that divorce should be possible within the first five years—sometimes these are the very worst cases of all—then there is no reason why you should adopt a reactionary proposal such as this"; 105 *Parl. Deb.*, H.L. (5th ser.), col. 758. (24 June 1937) (Marriage Bill).

64. [1938] A.C. 1 (1937); see Harding, "Atkin's Judicial Attitudes" 437.

65. *Fender v. St. John-Mildmay*, [1938] A.C. 1, 21 (1937).

66. Ibid. 15–16.

and 1940. He led the House intellectually, and the other law lords rarely mustered a majority to overrule him. He consciously developed many areas of the law and provided an outstanding decade of judicial history. Although Hailsham's efforts to muzzle him failed, with the appointment of Simon as Lord Chancellor, Atkin's power over the House began to wane. Simon's speeches often represented the judgment of the whole House; and particularly after Atkin's death, Simon's new appointments as Lords of Appeal were men with an attitude toward the role of the appeal process alien to Atkin's. Yet, the fact that the English courts emerged from the troubled period of the thirties with their reputations relatively untarnished politically as well as strengthened intellectually must be attributed to the outstanding English appeal judge of the inter-war period—Atkin.

The Commercial Tradition: Wright

Scrutton's other distinguished pupil, Lord Wright,[67] had a career similar to Atkin's. Wright too served in both the King's Bench Division and the Court of Appeal before becoming a Lord of Appeal in 1932, some four years after Atkin. He remained a Lord of Appeal for three years after Atkin's death, resigning in 1947. As with Atkin, Wright's chief contributions came in the 1930s; the apparent importance of his work in the 1940s was to a large extent a distortion reflecting the lack of distinction of his later colleagues. That Wright did not equal Atkin's genius as a common lawyer may be readily argued. Although Wright expressed his views about precedent and the role of the judiciary more openly than Atkin, he was not such a subtle master of the art of doctrinal manipulation or, to put it more conventionally, of legal craftsmanship. Nor perhaps had Wright the same urge to be so. Wright had had a more conventional background than Atkin, he had less inclination to relate the law to the needs of society, and he did not press causes with Atkin's relative passion. At the same time the difference between the two was not so great as some have implied. When it came to the interpretation of constitutions, Wright was probably more sophisticated than Atkin. It is arguable that Wright had absorbed Scrutton's warning about the dif-ficulties of impartiality when class interests are involved even better than had Atkin;[68] certainly, in later years Wright's sophistication in commer-

---

67. Robert Anderson Wright; b. 1869; educ., privately and Trinity College, Cambridge (First, Classics and Moral Science); called to bar, 1900; K.C., 1917; Judge, King's Bench Division, 1925–32; Lord of Appeal, 1932–35, 1937–47; Master of the Rolls, 1935–37; d. 1962.

68. Of course, he may have learned this lesson not from his time at the Commercial Bar but from his early experience as a lecturer in industrial law at the London School of Economics. He had also been a fellow of Trinity College, Cambridge.

cial cases tended to overshadow Atkin's earlier preeminence.[69]

Jurisprudentially, Wright began from the same premise as Atkin: that major policy choices were for the legislature or executive.[70] Thus foreign affairs were the sole responsibility of the government; but he went further than Atkin in deferring to the omniscience of Parliament. Wright felt that the protection of civil liberties[71] was not essentially the responsibility of the courts, and he was more prepared to accept the assumptions of parliamentary government. "The safeguard of British liberty is in the good sense of the people and in the system of representative and responsible government which has been evolved," said Wright, concurring with the majority in *Liversidge v. Anderson*.[72]

For all this, however, he was acutely conscious of the power and responsibility of the courts in interpreting statutes, and here he visualized an important role for the judges. He disapproved of the traditional English legislative drafting technique by which every point was elaborated in detail.[73] He would have preferred to see judges exercising a more creative approach in interpretation. Statutes should be construed, if possible, not to derogate from the common law,[74] and it was for the judges to determine whether a statute had retrospective effect.[75] Within the statutes, if

69. Robert Anderson Wright, *Some Developments of Commercial Law in the Present Century*.

70. E.g., on the question of the recognition of foreign governments, "The Court is, in my opinion, bound without any qualification by the statement of the Foreign Office, which is the organ of His Majesty's Government for this purpose in a matter of this nature"; *Spanish Republican Government v. S.S. "Arantzazu Mendi,"* [1939] A.C. 256, 267–68.

71. He did, however, hold that the Potato Marketing Board was not a government department and therefore could not claim Crown privilege; *Rowell v. Pratt*, [1938] A.C. 101, 104 (1937). But although he talked of the need to protect the liberty of the subject, he found that the Customs Act of 1876 gave the customs authorities an immunity from suit where they had reasonable grounds for suspecting someone of smuggling. "It is the duty of the court in construing sections of this nature to balance the two conflicting principles, the one that the liberty of the subject is to be duly safeguarded; the other that the expressed intention of the legislature to give powers of arrest beyond those existing at common law should not be too narrowly construed"; *Barnard v. Gorman*, [1941] A.C. 378, 389.

72. [1942] A.C. 206, 261 (1941). He later justified his views in these terms:

[T]he strength of the Government's case lay largely in the provisions of the Regulations for an advisory committee which was established under the presidency of so powerful a judge as Mr. Justice Birkett. It is true that the Committee's powers were advisory and did not bind the secretary to obey them or even involve them, but that, with the whole context of the Regulation and the circumstances of the time, was held sufficient to justify a construction of the Regulation in the sense claimed by the Government and thus to legalize the man's detention. [Wright, "Atkin of Aberdovey" 307]

73. See his speech on the Public Order Bill of 1936. "After a somewhat long and tedious experience of construing Acts of Parliament, I have come to the conclusion that one of the greatest difficulties in draftsmanship is too much elaboration, too much definition"; 103 *Parl. Deb.*, H.L. (5th ser.), col. 840 (15 Dec. 1936).

74. "A statute must not be construed as changing the common law, unless a clear intention to do this is shown, and then only to the extent to which the intention to change is clearly shown"; *Lochgelly Iron & Coal Co. v. McMullan*, [1934] A.C. 1, 24 (Scot. 1933).

75. *New Brunswick Ry. v. British & French Trust Corp.*, [1939] A.C. 1, 33 (1938).

the words were absolutely clear they must be obeyed by the courts;[76] but Wright allowed the final appeal court considerable leeway. The process was by no means a mechanical one. Even in *Liversidge* v. *Anderson* he tempered his view that the power of the Home Secretary could be found only "by scrutinising the language of the enactment . . . in the light of the circumstances and the general policy and object of the measure."[77]

It was this broad approach to statutory interpretation, together with a greater interest in affairs outside England, that led Wright to be regarded in retrospect as a good, and reflective, constitutionalist. It is accepted that Wright fought one of the more outrageous of the Privy Council's 1937 decisions striking down the Bennett "New Deal." *Attorney-General for Canada* v. *Attorney-General for Ontario*[78] decided that since section 92 of the 1867 British North America Act gave "property and civil rights" to the provinces, the dominion was not entitled to enact legislation implementing the labor provision in the ILO treaty, and in this way enact minimum wage legislation. The Privy Council, by holding that the treaty-making power was not vested exclusively in the federal government achieved the stultifying situation that the Bricker Amendment sought to achieve in the United States in the 1950s. Wright was suitably frustrated and in effect later conceded that he dissented.[79] Moreover, even when in interpreting section 92 of the Australian constitution he had written the opinion of the Judicial Committee, he was later prepared to have doubts about the wisdom of his decision.[80]

As to the more general powers of the judges in molding the common law, Wright took an articulate stand. He considered at some length the question of when it was legitimate for the House to overrule the decisions of the lower courts that had stood for a number of years.[81] He would

76. E.g., *Milne* v. *Commissioner of Police for City of London*, [1940] A.C. 1, 38–39 (1939).

77. [1942] A.C. 206, 261 (1941). This theme had been more fully spelled out in an earlier case, where Wright argued that "if the words of an enactment are fairly capable of two interpretations, one of which seems to be in harmony with what is just, reasonable and convenient, while the other is not, the Court will prefer the former." At the same time he insisted that if the words were not ambiguous, then they must be enforced, although the Court "feels that the result is not in accordance with the ordinary policy of the law or with what seems to be reasonable." But even in reaching this conclusion, he reaffirmed that "[a] statute must be construed as a whole and with some regard to its apparent purpose and object"; *Rowell* v. *Pratt*, [1938] A.C. 101, 105 (1937).

78. [1937] A.C. 326 (P.C.).

79. Robert Anderson Wright, "Obituary for Rt. Hon. Sir Lyman Poore Duff, G.C.M.G." 1123, 1126. For the literature on this article, see Edward McWhinney, *Judicial Review in the English Speaking World* 54. In this case the board consisted of Atkin, Thankerton, Macmillan, Wright, and Mr. Justice Rowlatt. The "swing vote" may well have been that of Rowlatt, a not particularly distinguished tax judge.

80. *James* v. *Australia*, [1936] A.C. 578 (P.C.); Robert Anderson Wright, "Section 92—A Problem Piece" 145.

81. "It is impossible to lay down precise rules according to which this power will be

have been happy to see this power to overrule given to the House with respect to its own decisions, on the ground that "there is greater public inconvenience in perpetuating an erroneous judicial opinion, than the inconvenience to the Court of having a question, disposed of in an earlier case, re-opened."[82] He saw, however, the flexibility in the existing concept of precedent and was not afraid to articulate and discuss the "perpetual erosion of authorities."[83] Indeed, so long as the rule of stare decisis survived, Wright was much concerned with the problem of distinguishing earlier House of Lords precedents and with the question of overturning lines of cases in the lower courts.

Nowhere were these two problems better illustrated than in the series of cases on common employment, a doctrine that appealed little to Wright. In such situations, he started from the assumption that only Parliament could overrule a doctrine so firmly established by the House;[84] but having paid deference to the limits that must be placed on the common law in its efforts to adapt to new situations, he somehow found himself in a position to counterattack. In *Wilsons and Clyde Coal Company* v. *English*[85] it was a direct counterattack. Thus Wright's new con-

---

exercised. But in general this House will adopt this course only in plain cases where serious inconvenience or injustice would follow from perpetuating an erroneous construction or ruling of law"; *Admiralty Comm'rs* v. *S.S. Valverda (Owners)*, [1938] A.C. 173, 194 (1937). In another case he made the duty seem a more active one: "[T]his House has the duty to reconsider it when at last it is brought before it and to set it aside if it is seen to be contrary to justice and convenience"; *Lissenden* v. *C. A. V. Bosch, Ltd.*, [1940] A.C. 412, 432 (1939). See also *Fibrosa Spolka Akcyjna* v. *Fairbairn Lawson Combe Barbour, Ltd.*, [1943] A.C. 32, 72 (1942): "If the doctrine is, as I think it clearly is, wrong and unjust, it is the duty of this House, exercising its function of finally declaring the law, to reverse it, unless there are very special circumstances."

82. Robert Anderson Wright, "Precedents" 118, 145.

83. Robert Anderson Wright, *Legal Essays and Addresses*, at xviv.

84. "Your Lordships have been invited by counsel for the appellants to say that the rule is based on industrial and social conditions which have changed. Therefore it is said, as it is the duty of the common law to mould and adapt itself from time to time so as to do justice under new and changing conditions, this is a case in which that duty should be fulfilled. It is indeed true that the common law is flexible and progressive, but it is so only subject to definite limitations. One is that this House is bound by its own decisions. It may . . . refuse to act upon expressions of opinion or matters of observation stated in opinions of members of the House. But in a matter of clear and precise decision such as the doctrine of common employment, it is well settled by established authority that the decision of the House is final and that the rule can only be changed by the Legislature. . . . This House cannot usurp the function of the Legislature in a matter of this nature"; *Radcliffe* v. *Ribble Motor Servs., Ltd.*, [1939] A.C. 215, 245–46.

85. "The rule is explained on the ground that the employee by his contract of employment agrees with his employer to assume the risk of his fellow-servant's negligence. The principle is stated, with little regard to reality or to modern ideas of economics or industrial conditions, to be that this particular risk is included in the agreed remuneration. This result is stated rather as a dogma to flow logically from the relation of master and servant. Notwithstanding repeated expressions of disapproval, the doctrine has survived, largely

cept of the employer's duty to provide a safe system of work was excused from the ravages of common employment. Even in more general areas of negligence, having stated how narrowly confined was the House's power to limit common employment, he was able to claim that "these considerations make it more important to state the rule precisely and to determine its exact limits, which have sometimes been in danger of being overlooked."[86] Here too, then, he was able to curb common employment.

In general, Wright played a rather different role from Atkin as far as liability in tort was concerned. While Atkin became famous for his development of a generalized duty of care, Wright's contribution was more subtle. It was he who in *Liesbosch* put some limit on the impact of the direct consequences test in tort and so established boundaries of liability in damages. "The law cannot take account of everything that follows a wrongful act."[87] Wright was also a member of the House that found that the concept of negligence did not establish a duty of care on the part of a motorcyclist toward a road user not within the area of potential danger.[88] He used the occasion to restate the principle of the duty of care in a way that appealed to his concept of the role of the common law. "This general concept of reasonable foresight as the criterion of negligence or breach of duty (strict or otherwise) may be criticised as too vague, but negligence is a fluid principle, which has to be applied to the most diverse conditions and problems of human life. It is a concrete, not an abstract, idea. It has to be fitted to the facts of a particular case."[89]

In other areas of negligence, Wright and Atkin worked more obviously together. Building on their speeches in *Lochgelly Iron and Coal Company* v. *McMullan*, Wright in *Wilsons and Clyde Coal Company* v. *English*[90] clearly spelled out the obligation of an employer to provide a

---

because of statutory remedies given to employees to minimise what to modern ideas appears to be its obvious injustice. But it has never been carried to the extremity of excluding all remedy against employers or all duty in the employers so long as they have exercised care in the selection of managers or foremen. It is difficult to see what that duty would mean in the case of an absentee or infant or inexpert employer, or what it would mean in the case of a great modern industrial concern. But in truth the employer's obligation, as it has been defined by this House, is personal to the employer, and one to be performed by the employer per se or per alios"; [1938] A.C. 57, 80 (Scot. 1937).

86. *Radcliffe* v. *Ribble Motor Servs., Ltd.*, [1939] A.C. 215, 246. There Wright found that the doctrine did not apply because the workmen were not employed in common work.

87. *Liesbosch (Owners of the Dredger)* v. *The Edison*, [1933] A.C. 449, 460. In *Overseas Tankship (U.K.), Ltd.* v. *Morts Dock & Eng'r. Co. (The Wagon Mound)*, [1961] A.C. 388, 424 (P.C.), which refused to follow the "direct test" rule laid down *in re Polemis*, Simonds said of *Liesbosch*, "Here was the opportunity to deny the rule or to place it secure upon its pedestal. But the House of Lords took neither course; on the contrary, it distinguished Polemis on the ground that in that case the injuries suffered were the 'immediate physical consequences' of the negligent act."

88. *Bourhill* v. *Young*, [1943] A.C. 92 (Scot. 1942).

89. Ibid. 107.

90. [1938] A.C. 57, 76 (Scot. 1937).

safe system of work independent of any liability under the Workmen's Compensation Acts. He insisted that if the employer appointed an agent to provide the safe system, the doctrine of common employment did not apply between the agent and an ordinary workman.[91] Wright also joined Atkin in minimizing the full impact of contributory negligence in cases involving statutory negligence.[92]

If Wright did not play quite such an original role as Atkin in the development of tort, he probably played a more important role in the development of commercial law. His attitude was most clearly expressed in a case in 1939, in which he declared, "Commercial law has always been ready, so far as possible to sacrifice pedantic logical consistency in favor of convenience in the conduct of business."[93] The strength of Wright's view was shown when, shortly after his appointment to the Lords, he delivered his famous speech in *Hillas and Company v. Arcos*.[94] In balancing the points that a court should look for in deciding whether a contract had in fact been concluded between businessmen, he declared it to be "the duty of the court to construe such documents fairly and broadly, without being too astute or subtle in finding defects; but, on the contrary, the court should seek to apply the old maxim of English law, *Verba ita sunt intelligenda ut res magis valiat quam pereat*."[95]

In *Luxor (Eastbourne), Limited v. Cooper* he spoke out strongly against any attempt to formulate strict rules of interpretation to be applied in every case of disagreement on the contract.[96] He refused to put the doctrine of public policy on a pedestal and claimed that it was a "dispensing power which judges have exercised or may exercise under the name of public policy, which I regard as something within the general principles of the common law, not something outside and above them."[97] Indeed, in almost all areas of commercial law, Wright made speeches

91. "The well-established, but illogical, doctrine of common employment is certainly one not to be extended, and indeed has never in its long career been pushed so far as the Court of Appeal sought to push it"; ibid. 79.

92. *Caswell v. Powell Duffryn Ass'd Collieries, Ltd.*, [1940] A.C. 152, 178 (1939). "What is all-important is to adapt the standard of what is negligence to the facts, and to give due regard to the actual conditions under which men work in a factory or mine, to the long hours and the fatigue, to the slackening of attention which naturally comes from constant repetition of the same operation, to the noise and confusion in which the man works, to his pre-occupation in what he is actually doing at the cost perhaps of some inattention to his own safety." See also *Flower v. Ebbw Valve Steel, Iron & Coal Co.*, [1936] A.C. 206, 210 (1935). There also Wright appeared to require more than ordinary negligence to amount to contributory negligence to defeat a claim for statutory negligence.

93. *Northumbrian Shipping Co. v. Timm & Son*, [1939] A.C. 397, 409.

94. [1932] All E.R. 494 (H.L.).

95. Ibid. 514. For a rather different approach on his part, see *Scammell & Nephew, Ltd. v. Ouston*, [1941] A.C. 251, 269 (1940): "[T]heir agreement was inchoate and never got beyond negotiations."

96. *Luxor, Ltd. v. Cooper*, [1941] A.C. 108, 130 (1940).

97. Wright, *Legal Essays and Addresses*, at xxxvi. For speeches by Wright on public

during this period, and in many cases his views resulted in a lucid exposition of the general principles involved.[98]

Perhaps Wright's most permanent contribution to commercial law was his expansion of the doctrine of frustration of contract during World War II. By the time most of these cases were decided, the shock of *Liversidge* v. *Anderson* apparently had robbed Atkin of his urge to fight for new principles. It was therefore Wright who led the campaign to develop this area of commercial law, and he insisted on taking a realistic approach. He rejected the idea that frustration could be determined solely by the pretense that the courts were only interpreting contracts and implying a term.[99] He felt that while frustration involved the construction of the contract,[100] the real power was the dispensing power of the court's and he saw no point in disguising it.[101] After all, the doctrine was originally an instance of judicial legislation's giving the courts power to vary a contractual obligation; to apply it was therefore up to the courts. "In short, in ascertaining the meaning of the contract and its application to the actual occurrences, the court has to decide, not what the parties actually intended, but what as reasonable men they should have intended. The court personifies for this purpose the reasonable man . . . I have quoted these statements of law to emphasise that the court is exercising its powers when it decides that a contract is frustrated, in order to achieve a result which is just and reasonable."[102] He was there able to take the view best suited for commercial convenience. "No detailed absolute rules

---

policy, see *Fender* v. *St. John-Mildmay*, [1938] A.C. 1, 35 (1937); *Admiralty Comm'rs* v. *S.S. Valverda (Owners)*, [1938] A.C. 173, 180 (1937).

98. E.g., his analysis of misrepresentations in *Spense* v. *Crawford*, [1939] 3 All E.R. 271, 288 (H.L.): "A case of innocent misrepresentation may be regarded rather as one of misfortune than as one of moral obliquity. There is no deceit or intention to defraud. The court will be less ready to pull a transaction to pieces where the defendant is innocent, whereas in the case of fraud the court will exercise its jurisdiction to the full in order, if possible, to prevent the defendant from enjoying the benefit of his fraud at the expense of the innocent plaintiff"; or his views on the interpretation of contracts, e.g., *Luxor, Ltd.* v. *Cooper*, [1941] A.C. 108, 130 (1940).

99. *Denny, Mott & Dickson, Ltd.* v. *James B. Fraser & Co.*, [1944] A.C. 265, 275 (Scot. 1943).

100. E.g., *Heyman* v. *Darwins, Ltd.*, [1942] A.C. 356, 378 (1941).

101. "The court has formulated the doctrine by virtue of its inherent jurisdiction just as it has developed the rules of liability for negligence, or for the restitution or repayment of money where otherwise there would be unjust enrichment. I find the theory of the basis of the rule in Lord Sumner's pregnant statement (Hirji Mulji v. Cheong Yue S.S. Co., Ltd.), that the doctrine of frustration is really a device by which the rules as to absolute contracts are reconciled with the special exceptions which justice demands"; *Denny, Mott & Dickson, Ltd.* v. *James B. Fraser & Co.*, [1944] A.C. 265, 275 (Scot. 1943).

102. *Joseph Constantine S.S. Line, Ltd.* v. *Imperial Smelting Corp.*, [1942] A.C. 154, 185–86 (1941). See also, in the *Fibrosa* case, "The court is thus taken to assume the role of the reasonable man, and decides what the reasonable man would regard as just on the facts of the case. The hypothetical 'reasonable man' is personified by the court itself. It is the court which decides"; [1943] A.C. 32, 70 (1942).

can be stated. A certain elasticity is essential."[103] Wright, in short, did not subscribe to that modern English whim that rigid rules necessarily lead to predictability.

In matters of legislation and litigation involving workmen, Wright was perhaps less prominent than Atkin in helping to restore the confidence of the working classes in the courts, but he certainly made a major contribution in the attempt to do so. His efforts in protecting workmen's compensation and developing statutory duties, while restricting common employment and contributory negligence have already been noted. Like others of the law lords, Wright regretted the flow of litigation on the words "out of and in the course of his employment"[104] in workmen's compensation cases. He remained on the lookout to see that justice was done and would sometimes sympathize with workmen who, to some, appeared scarcely to deserve sympathy.[105] In the law's relations with the unions, he went even further. Wright's was perhaps the most important speech in the case that was thought at the time to have put trade union officials, when acting on behalf of the union, finally out of the reach of the courts. In *Crofter Hand Woven Harris Tweed Company* v. *Veitch*,[106] the House refused to apply the tort of conspiracy to the behavior of trade union officials who instructed their members not to handle certain cargoes of yarn. Wright's speech in the House dealt more clearly than did those of the other law lords with the implications of the concept of the tort of

103. *Denny, Mott & Dickson, Ltd.* v. *James B. Fraser & Co.*, [1944] A.C. 265, 274 (Scot. 1943).

104. E.g., *Dover Navigation Co.* v. *Craig*, [1940] A.C. 190, 199 (1939): "It is not legitimate to seek to write into the section definitions and limitations which the Legislature have not thought fit to insert." See also *Noble* v. *Southern Ry.*, [1940] A.C. 583, 600: "If I attempt to repeat myself I shall only again add to the number of phrases or paraphrases which have accumulated round the Act, and have furnished material for the ingenuity of advocates and the embarrassment of county court judges. I have often reflected with sadness that the Act was intended to be administered with as little technicality as possible. Yet thousands of reports have accumulated around it and fresh ones are likely to go on accumulating so long as the Act remains in the present form."

Such an approach by Wright was not unique. In *Lissenden* v. *C. A. V. Bosch, Ltd.*, [1940] A.C. 412, 431 (1939), he felt "a shock to one's sense of justice. Here is a working man, who in order to seek relief has to come to this House as a pauper because he has been held to be barred from his statutory right of appeal not by anything in an Act of Parliament but by a judicial decision." In *Steele* v. *Robert George & Co.*, [1942] A.C. 497, 503 (N. Ire. 1941), Wright expressed sympathy with a workman who refused to undergo a surgical operation to minimize the effect of an accident, although the House held that his refusal broke the chain of causation.

105. "I feel no doubt that the action of the legislature is denying to the Courts the power (in the case of death, etc.) to exclude a claim on the ground that the man was infringing a prohibition, and the action of this House in making it clear that the workman's negligence by adding a risk did not bar his claim so long as the accident arose out of and in the course of his employment, have done much to change the general attitude of the Courts in considering these cases"; *Noble* v. *Southern Ry.*, [1940] A.C. 583, 602.

106. [1942] A.C. 435 (Scot. 1941).

conspiracy that they were spelling out;[107] nor would Wright weaken any such basic right by invoking a concept of malice.[108]

Other sides to Wright's work and character deserve mention. Where substantive law was concerned, Wright shared many of Atkin's urges to import a broad reasonable view of the law. He delivered the only dissent in the famous *Diplock* case, refusing to hold that the use of the words "charitable or benevolent" instead of "charitable and benevolent" in directions to executors was sufficient to justify the court's finding that the trust was not charitable and so holding that it failed for indefiniteness.[109] On occasion, however, Wright was satisfied with the form rather than the substance, as in the *Duke of Westminster*'s case.[110] Yet in some ways Wright shared Atkin's enthusiasm for what, by the standards of the law lords, were liberal causes. He strongly supported A. P. Herbert's Matrimonial Causes Act in 1937,[111] and he refused to take seriously the suggestion that it should be contrary to public policy for a man who had not yet been granted a final decree of divorce to become engaged in such a way that he might be sued for breach of promise.[112]

Wright was a distinguished judge who deserves to be considered in a class with Atkin. Judicial fashions, of course, change. Wright's speeches are now regarded as too generalized to be authoritative, at least by some members of the bar. That he was sometimes guilty of unnecessary verbosity is true;[113] but the fact that he is currently out of fashion may be more a reflection of the present outlook of the English legal profession than of the distinction of Wright as a judge.[114]

The Growth of Substantive Formalism

If the attitudes of the Lord Chancellors and the Scottish law lords revealed an increasing trend toward formalism, then that acceleration can be seen more clearly still in the work of the typical English professional law lord. The Macmillans, Atkins, and Wrights were, intellectually, more

107. Ibid. 463.
108. Ibid. 468.
109. *Chichester Diocesan Fund & Bd. of Fin., Inc.* v. *Simpson*, [1944] A.C. 341.
110. *IRC* v. *Duke of Westminster*, [1936] A.C. 1 (1935). Atkin and Wright only infrequently delivered speeches in revenue cases. This may be one of the reasons that the tax cases of the 1930s are out of line with the Grand Style that typified many common law areas.
111. "I fervently support his Bill. I think it will promote domestic happiness"; 105 *Parl. Deb.*, H.L. (5th ser.), col. 838 (28 June 1939).
112. *Fender* v. *St. John-Mildmay*, [1938] A.C. 1 (1937): "These new relationships are not in their nature bad on the ground of immorality or likely to lead to immorality any more than the engagement of affectionate couples who have not suffered the miseries of an ill-assorted union."
113. E.g., *Vita Food Prods., Inc.* v. *Unus Shipping Co.*, [1939] A.C. 277, 283 (P.C.).
114. See also Arthur L. Goodhart, "Lord Macmillan and Lord Wright" 259.

often than not in a minority. At the beginning of the period, Parker and Wrenbury, while clearly professional judges, valued their moments of creativity and felt that law and politics were not entirely separate spheres. By the middle of the period, theirs was becoming a rare view. Russell in some way stepped in as the conservative member of the court, but behind the cultured mask of the declaratory theory. More typical were Blanesburgh and Tomlin, competent technicians who appeared to have little sense of the appellate process and less of what role a second appeal might fulfill. A similar approach characterized those like Phillimore and Warrington—peers who were not Lords of Appeal—as well as Maugham and Roche.

Parker and Wrenbury, of course, had the advantage of arriving in the Lords before Birkenhead announced the convention that law lords did not speak on controversial topics in legislative debates. Both were Chancery men; but already the Chancery Bar, which in the mid-nineteenth century had been regarded as the home of broad principles, was beginning to take on the concern with narrow rules that had been viewed as more characteristic of the common law bar. Thus, to later writers both men are something of an enigma.

Lord Parker[115] was chosen as Macnaghten's successor as a Lord of Appeal and sat until 1918. While Loreburn regarded Parker as a Liberal,[116] Asquith opined that "his politics are, I suspect, those of an equity draftsman."[117] In one sense, perhaps, both Loreburn and Asquith were right. While it was assumed that law lords were supposed to have some general input into legislative debates, Parker spoke out in a liberal direction in favor of profit sharing in industry[118] and in favor of the League of Nations.[119] Unfortunately, his political acumen was such that he made

115. Robert John Parker; b. 1857; father, clergyman; educ., Westminster, Eton, King's College, Cambridge (First, Classics); called to bar, 1883; Judge, Chancery Division, 1906–13; Lord of Appeal, 1913–18; d. 1918; *Dictionary of National Biography 1912–1921*, at 421.

116. If Parker was a liberal, he was not noticeably a radical. In *Bowman v. Secular Soc'y, Ltd.*, while by implication restricting the crime of blasphemy, he allowed himself—the son of the Rector of Claxby—some snide digs of humanism; [1917] A.C. 406, 445. In *Larkin v. Long*, [1915] A.C. 814, 833 (Ire.), he declared that the Trade Disputes Act of 1906, since it cut down the subject's right to sue, must be construed strictly. "[T]o hold that every dispute in which the officials of a union chose to interfere must be a trade dispute would, in my opinion, unduly extend the immunity from liability conferred by the Act and, therefore, unduly curtail the common law rights of other persons." While he sometimes found himself on the "liberal" wing in workmen's compensation cases, he was careful not to be caught tampering with the "ordinary" meaning of words.

117. Heuston, *Lives* 148.

118. 20 *Parl. Deb.*, H.L. (5th ser.), col. 609 (14 Dec. 1915); "If the beginning of their new period in our history be coincident with a permanent peace between Capital and Labour even the war itself may have been worth-while."

119. Ibid., col. 616; 27 ibid., col. 548 (14 Jan. 1918); ibid., col. 1194–96 (29 Jan. 1918) (Representation of the People Bill). In addition to asserting that in the modern world

the first of these speeches during a munitions crisis and the second during a major German advance.[120] Yet there can be no doubt that Parker was viewed as an excellent Chancery judge when he sat in that division between 1906 and his appointment to the Lords in 1913.

Parker articulated the declaratory approach to law. He thought the courts should take the most formalistic approach to statutory interpretation,[121] and he deferred obsequiously to stare decisis. When it was suggested that Ellenborough's decision in *Bolton* v. *Baker*, holding that there could be no action arising out of death, be reversed, Parker announced, "If it were any part of the functions of this House to consider what rules ought to prevail in a logical and scientific system of jurisprudence, much might no doubt be said for this criticism; . . . This House, however, is bound to administer the law as it finds it. The mere fact that the law involves some anomaly is immaterial unless it be clear that the anomaly has been introduced by erroneous judicial decision."[122] Yet despite announcements such as these, within Parker was a residual sense of the nineteenth-century Chancery practitioner. He was a master of using history to change what had been thought to be the accepted doctrine, and this approach allowed him, when the circumstances in his eyes merited it, to look at the reasons for the principle cited before transposing the principle from one situation to another.

Thus, while Parker himself subscribed to the "hands off" aspects of laissez-faire with respect to the economy,[123] he used the historical ap-

---

there was no place for neutrality, he outlined a detailed scheme to prevent future wars and also argued that the basis of law was not force but a sense of mutual obligation that could not be imposed but that had its roots in the distant past. For a sympathetic interpretation of this speech by Sumner, see *Dictionary of National Biography 1912–1921*, at 421, 422. In fairness, also, Parker presided competently at the Committee of Enquiry in the Marconi Scandal; ibid.

120. He supported the claim of women who had passed the examinations that qualified men for a university degree to vote in the university constituencies; 27 *Parl. Deb.*, H.L. (5th ser.), col. 548 (14 Jan. 1918).

121. See, for instance, his dissent in *Trim Joint Dist. School Bd.* v. *Kelly*, [1914] A.C. 667, 713 (Ire.), vigorously deprecating the more humane but rather strained interpretation put by the majority on the word "accident" in the Workmen's Compensation Acts. "[This argument] not only abandons the principle of interpreting the Act according to the ordinary meaning of the words used, but substitutes a method of interpretation based upon what in the opinion of individual judges, the Legislature may be reasonably supposed to have intended, a method which, in my judgement, is without any justification at all"; ibid. 717.

122. *Admiralty Comm'rs* v. *S.S. Amerika (Owners)*, [1917] A.C. 38, 47–48 (1916). See also, on Parker's strict approach to stare decisis even in workmen's compensation cases, *Parker* v. *S.S. Black Rock (Owners)*, [1915] A.C. 725, 729: "It is a line of decisions which lays down a distinctly workable rule upon the construction of an Act, the obscurity of which is exceedingly great, and I should be unwilling in any way to interfere with it."

123. E.g., *North-Western Salt, Ltd.* v. *Electrolytic Alkali Co.*, [1914] A.C. 461, 479–80: "The competition between salt producers within the area covered by the agreement . . . either *inter se* or with salt producers outside this area may have been so drastic that some

proach to see that when Equity concepts and common law concepts competed, businessmen did not use Equity's refusal to allow any clog on the equity of redemption to frustrate the reasonable expectations of businessmen making a contract.[124] It was this teleological approach that enabled him in the *Daimler* case to refuse to apply the full rigor of the rule in *Salomon*'s case to wartime conditions;[125] and it was the wartime work of the Privy Council in prize cases that gave Parker an opportunity to restate the role of the judiciary[126] and the primacy of international law.[127] Parker, in short, had many of the marks of an acute appellate judge, despite his articulated commitment to substantive formalism.

In terms of personal interest, however, Parker was overshadowed by Wrenbury,[128] who, although never a Lord of Appeal (he was better known

---

combination limiting output and regulating competition within the area so as to secure reasonable prices may have been necessary, not only in the interests of the salt producers themselves, but in the interests of the public generally, for it cannot be to the public advantage that the trade of a large area should be ruined by a cut-throat competition."

See the similar views he expressed in *Attorney-General for Australia* v. *Adelaide S.S. Co.*, [1913] A.C. 781 (P.C.). There is also evidence of a "hands-off" approach in his speeches in frustration cases; e.g., *F. A. Tamplin S.S. Co.* v. *Anglo-Mexican Petroleum Prods. Co.*, [1916] 2 A.C. 397, 422.

124. "They [the defendants] can state no intelligible principles underlying this alleged equity, but contend that your Lordships are bound by authority. That the Court should be asked in the exercise of its equitable jurisdiction to assist in so inequitable a proceeding as the repudiation of a fair and reasonable bargain is somewhat startling, and makes it necessary to examine transactions"; *G. & C. Kreglinger* v. *New Patagonia Meat & Cold Storage Co.*, [1914] A.C. 25, 46 (1913). Parker was prominent in the leading equity appeals during this period.

125. E.g., *Sinclair* v. *Brougham*, [1914] A.C. 398; *Stickney* v. *Keeble*, [1915] A.C. 386, 415 (1914).

My Lords, the truth is that considerations which govern civil liability and rights of property in time of peace differ radically from those which govern enemy character in time of war. . . . The ideal of joint-stock enterprise, that with limited liability the more unlimited the trading the better, is an ideal of profound peace. The rule against trading with the enemy is a belligerent's weapon of self-protection. I think that it has to be applied to modern circumstances as we find them, and not limited to the applications of long ago, with as little desire to cut it down on the one hand as to extend it on the other beyond what those circumstances require. . . . To my mind the rule would be deprived of its substantial justification, and be reduced to a barren canon, if it were held, in circumstances such as these that it had no application by reason of the mere fact that the company is registered in London. [*Daimler Co.* v. *Continental Tyre & Rubber Co.*, [1916] 2 A.C. 307, 344]

The *Law Quarterly Review* considered his reasoning to be most satisfactory; "Note," 32 *Law Quarterly Review* 340 (1916).

126. "The idea that the King in Council, or indeed any branch of the Executive, has power to prescribe or alter the law to be administered by Courts of Law in the country is out of harmony with the principles of our Constitution"; *The Zamora*, [1916] 2 A.C. 77, 90 (P.C.).

127. "If the Court is to decide judicially in accordance with what it conceives be the law of nations, it cannot, even in doubtful cases, take its directions from the Crown, which is a party to the proceedings"; ibid. 97. Parker's work in that division of the Privy Council given over to prize cases was of considerable importance. See also, for instance, *The Roumanian*, [1916] 1 A.C. 124, 129 (P.C. 1915).

128. Henry Burton Buckley; b. 1845, London; father, clergyman; educ., Merchant

as Lord Justice Buckley), was given a peerage when he retired from the
Court of Appeal in 1915 and continued to sit regularly for more than ten
years. Like Parker, Wrenbury adhered to the declaratory theory of law.
In *Halliday*'s case he restated the formal rule in statutory construction,[129]
and he was a dissenter in *Bourne* v. *Keane*[130] in favor of maintaining stare
decisis even where the lower court decision stood alone. He could uphold
the best traditions of the bench, as he did with his detached approach in
Roberts v. *Hopwood*.[131] Although his career at the Chancery Bar had
been closely related to the growth of the limited liability company,[132] he
did not approach tax law from a narrowly partisan viewpoint.[133] It is
true that he was jealous about his expertise in Equity,[134] and throughout
his judicial career he retained an ability to state a legal problem with
remarkable clarity.[135]

Taylor's, Christ's College, Cambridge; Fellow Christ's, 1868–82; called to bar, 1869;
Q.C., 1886; Judge, Chancery Division, 1900–6; Lord Justice, 1906–15; cr. Lord Wrenbury, 1915; d. 1935; *Dictionary of National Biography 1931–1940*, at 118.

129. R. v. *Halliday, ex parte Zadig*, [1917] A.C. 260, 307: "There is room for difference of opinion whether what I may call legislation by devolution is expedient; whether a
statute ought to be self-contained; whether it is desirable that a statute should provide that
regulations made by a defined authority or in a defined matter shall themselves have the
effect of a statute. But I think it clear that this statute has conferred upon His Majesty in
Council power to issue regulations which, when issued, will take effect as if they were
contained in the statute."

130. [1919] A.C. 815, 924–25. The cynic might think that Wrenbury's enthusiasm for
stare decisis in this case was not unrelated to his lack of enthusiasm for the Roman Catholic
Church.

131. [1925] A.C. 578, 612.

132. See, e.g., Henry B. Buckley, *The Law and Practice under the Companies Act
(1873)*. See also his participation in debates in the House, e.g., on the Companies (Foreign
Interest) Bill, 24 *Parl Deb.*, H.L. (5th ser.), col. 779 (29 Mar. 1917), and Companies
(Particulars as to Directors) Bill, 25 ibid., col. 749 (3 July 1917).

133. He took a relatively impartial line, if anything, favoring the Revenue. See,
e.g., *Whitney* v. *IRC*, [1926] A.C. 37, 54 (1925), even though he said on one occasion, "I
defy anybody reading the Income Tax Acts, involved, complicated, and numerous as
they are, to rise from his studies with anything but a headache"; 29 *Parl. Deb.*, H.L. (5th
ser.), col. 186 (28 Feb. 1918) (Income Tax Bill). In that year, he was a member of the Joint
Committee of Lords and Commons for Consolidating the Tax Acts.

134. See, for example, his dissenting speech in *Russian Commercial & Indus. Bank* v.
British Bank for Foreign Trade, Ltd., [1921] 2 A.C. 438, 463: "My Lords, I have felt my
responsibility in this case to be the greater because not one of the four judges before
whom this case has come below is a judge who has been trained in Courts of Equity,
and (a fact which is to myself the keenest matter of regret) no one of your Lordships
with whom I am privileged to sit in deciding this case has been so trained either. Under
these circumstances, I feel my voice to be indeed a voice crying in the wilderness but I
have felt bound to cry even though I cry in vain."

135. See, for example, in *Amalgamated Soc'y of Carpenters* v. *Braithwaite*, [1922] 2
A.C. 440, 469: "The matter may be stated tersely, I think, by saying that it is not
enforcing an agreement against a party to grant an injunction to restrain him from
tearing it up. When the injunction is granted and obeyed, the result is simply to leave
the relations between the parties in *status quo ante* without enforcing them at all."

See also *Weld-Blundell* v. *Stephens*, [1920] A.C. 956, 998: "Weld-Blundell did an

What was particularly noteworthy about Wrenbury, however, was his iconoclasm and his refusal to be browbeaten. He held a then-unfashionable belief in birth control, which no doubt encouraged him to dissent in *Sutherland* v. *Stopes*.[136] Although, as a good lawyer would, he insisted that his own views on birth control were irrelevant,[137] he indirectly met the snide remarks on the subject by his colleagues by pointing out the personal, public, and national importance of the subject.[138] Having failed, moreover, to persuade his colleagues on the bench to adopt his view of the law, he then, typically, carried the issue to the debating chamber of the House.[139] Nor did he hesitate to clash with the powerful. In the *Viscountess Rhondda* case[140] he was among the few dissenters in the Committee for Privileges who would have allowed a peeress in her own right to sit in the Lords. Refusing to be intimidated by Birkenhead[141] and openly criticizing the way in which the matter had been hurried through without proper time for consideration of the law,[142] he adopted a strict lawyer's approach to the construction of the Sex Disqualification (Removal) Act.[143] To take the sweetness out of Birkenhead's success he concluded by declaring, "It remains, however, that in no Court of Justice from the lowest to the highest, including your Lordships' House, can this case hereafter be cited as any authority upon the proper construction of the statute. This Committee is a mixed tribunal of laymen and of those generally styled 'learned in the law.' The former did not, before giving their vote, even wait to receive such assistance as their legal colleagues could give them in applying the law to that which is a purely legal question."[144]

Wrenbury and Parker, then, belonged to the breed of law lord who assumed that, although they had obligations to be technically proficient

---

unlawful act in libelling Lowe and Comins. He cannot by legal process reimburse himself for the consequences and throw the cost upon another."

136. [1925] A.C. 47 (1924).

137. Ibid. 86.

138. Ibid. 85. He also stressed that the jury had found that the comments about Stopes had not been fair; ibid. 94.

139. 63 *Parl. Deb.*, H.L. (5th ser.), col. 1046 (28 Apr. 1926). He followed a similar course after his defeat in the Court of Appeal in the *Daimler* case. See also 20 ibid., col. 583 (19 Dec. 1915) (Companies of Enemy Character Bill).

140. *In re Viscountess Rhondda*, [1922] 2 A.C. 339.

141. Ibid. 401.

142. Ibid. 393.

143. That is, he strongly denied that reference could be made to its parliamentary history.

144. *In re Viscountess Rhondda*, [1922] 2 A.C. 399, 400–1. One senses that Birkenhead was not amused: "It is no part of my duty to allay my noble and learned friend Lord Haldane's fears or to deprive my noble and learned friend Lord Wrenbury of any of the satisfaction which alleviates the circumstance that upon this occasion he finds himself in so inconsiderable a minority"; ibid. 376.

as judges, the role of a law lord was at least partly a political one. After the convention was established early in the twenties, however, that law lords should not speak out on political issues, the traces of the political role of judges, both on and off the court, became more difficult to discover. Lords Blanesburgh and Tomlin were typical of this newer group.

As Robert Younger, Blanesburgh[145] had become a reasonably successful Chancery practitioner, a Chancery judge in 1915, in 1919 a member of the Court of Appeal, and a Lord of Appeal in 1923. Obviously, in his personal life Blanesburgh was an attractive man, cultured and urbane.[146] Yet, as an appellate judge he represented ever more clearly the growing tradition of substantive formalism that fewer and fewer English judges appeared willing or able to fight. Blanesburgh's speeches make it difficult to believe that he saw any serious rationale in having a second appeal court. Of course there was no question of Blanesburgh's technical competence, although a comparison of his later speeches with his earlier ones and with his judgments in the Court of Appeal may lead to the conclusion that well before his resignation he was past his prime. Indeed, Dunedin crisply advised Hailsham, when he became Chancellor in 1935, "Blanesburgh, you will not as Sankey did, refuse his resignation."[147] In fact Blanesburgh did not resign until 1937.

Despite his fourteen years in the final court of appeal there is little to say about Blanesburgh. He exhibited all the traditional rhetoric (and, in his case, reality) of searching for a *ratio decidendi* in the *Adamson* case so that it might bind the House in the *Mostyn*.[148] Blanesburgh was certainly not totally impervious to the implications of his decisions. In *Harnett v. Fisher*[149] he was worried about his decision holding that limitation had run against a man negligently certified as insane. Yet he consoled himself with the thought that "[i]f this appeal fulfills no other useful purpose, it will at least have served to draw the attention of those engaged in the amendment of the Lunacy Laws to a matter which is not unworthy of consideration."[150] He was concerned by what he saw as the

---

145. Robert Younger; b. 1861; father, brewer; educ., Edinburgh Academy, Balliol College, Oxford (Second, Law); called to English bar, 1884; Q.C., 1900; Judge, Chancery Division, 1915–19; Lord Justice, 1919–23; Lord of Appeal, 1923–37; d. 1946; *Dictionary of National Biography 1941–1950*, at 985.

146. "Full of buoyant gusto and emotional bonhomie"; Hugh Macmillan, *A Man of Law's Tale* 149.

147. Heuston, *Lives* 481.

148. "I agree, of course, at once, that by the *ratio decidendi* of that case—if it can be discovered—and by the decision itself—whether its *ratio decidendi* can be discovered or not—your Lordships are as much bound as is at least every English Court"; *Great Western Ry. v. The Mostyn (Owners)*, [1928] A.C. 57, 99 (1927).

149. [1927] A.C. 573, 596.

150. Ibid. 603. See also his suggestions of the courses still open to the injured worker in *Nimmo & Co. v. Connell*, [1924] A.C. 595 (Scot.). As Blanesburgh's was a

need to protect "blacklegs" in the *Glasbrook* case,[151] but again he saw the limits of the Lords' role as being to draw attention to an unsatisfactory state in the law.[152] He made some effort to comprehend what was happening, going so far in one tax case as to do the un-English thing of looking at legislative history to understand what a section meant.[153] Such isolated eccentricities, however, scarcely justify treating Blanesburgh as a significant appellate judge. It is difficult to believe that he added anything of moment to the decisions already arrived at by the Court of Appeal or the Court of Session.

Blanesburgh's colleague, Tomlin,[154] was scarcely stronger, although the perceptive Dunedin rather surprisingly said, in evaluating the seven Lords of Appeal in 1935 (the year Tomlin died, incidentally) that he was "[t]o my thinking the best of the bunch."[155] He had certainly had a meteoric rise, being appointed in 1929 directly from a puisne judgeship in the Chancery Division. Yet, the judgments of this pupil of Parker's lacked his master's breadth; they represented yet another confirmation of the imminent flowering of substantive formalism. Uthwatt wrote of Tomlin, perhaps euphemistically, that "[i]t is a curious fact—due perhaps to Tomlin's continuous care and wide knowledge—that few of his judgments stand out from the others." Uthwatt added that Tomlin "never seemed to leave the firm ground of fact" and that "he had but little of that speculative interest in the history and philosophy of the law which was so marked in the mind of his master Parker."[156] Denning was less kind. In criticizing Tomlin's dissent in *Donoghue* v. *Stevenson*, Denning classified

---

dissenting judgment, it was not necessary for the employee to pursue these suggestions.

151. "The men exhibited notable moral courage in returning to work at all, and it must be remembered that although they had in preserving the mines the same real interest as the strikers they were under no higher duty in that matter than any other of His Majesty's subjects. Why, then, should any exceptional exhibition of physical hardihood be expected or required of them?" *Glasbrook Bros.* v. *Glamorganshire County Council*, [1925] A.C. 270, 303 (1924).

152. "[T]his case will, I cannot doubt, be of great public advantage if it attracts the attention of those concerned to a practice so far unregulated, but which, if not carefully circumscribed, is readily open to unwitting abuse . . ."; ibid. 308.

153. The decision in *R.* v. *Commissioners of Customs & Excise*, [1928] A.C. 402, turning on the construction of § 46 of the Finance Act of 1910: "I therefore thought it right for my own satisfaction to examine the Finance Bill of 1909–10, as presented to this House in 1909 and then rejected, in order to see whether § 46 had any counterpart in that Bill"; ibid. 423.

154. Thomas James Chesshyre Tomlin; b. 1867; father, barrister; educ., Harrow, New College, Oxford; called to bar, 1891; K.C., 1913; Judge, Chancery Division, 1923–29; Lord of Appeal, 1929–35; d. 1935; *Dictionary of National Biography 1931–1940*, at 866. See also obituary, *The Times*, 14 Aug. 1935.

155. Heuston, *Lives* 481.

156. *Dictionary of National Biography 1931–1940*, at 866.

him as one of those "timid souls who were fearful of allowing a new cause of action."[157]

In retrospect Tomlin seems not only to be overshadowed by Atkin, Wright, and Macmillan, but to belong more properly with Blanesburgh than with Russell and Thankerton. As already noted, judicial styles do change. Tomlin was a model judge of the orthodox school,[158] the touchstone of whose life was conformity.[159] One can, however, see how Dunedin was led to what in retrospect seems an extravagant claim. Like so many English judges, out of court Tomlin was prepared to discuss social and political views and the nature of the judicial process in a meaningful way. He was apparently a balanced civil libertarian.[160] His private papers reveal that he was in favor of radical reform of legal education, including the merging of training for barristers and solicitors. He thought the House of Lords should have power to overrule its own decisions. Although he had dissented in *Donoghue* v. *Stevenson*, apparently he strongly approved of the decision and, in a speech to the American Bar Association, extolled it as an example of the wisdom of the common law's adaptation to new situations.[161]

Yet, to the legal historian, who is limited almost primarily to Tomlin's writings in his judgments, the picture is of a competent conventional judge, using as his standard the internal logic of the common law and giving the impression of being out of his depth on the few occasions when he strayed beyond those boundaries.[162] These limitations were clear in *Donoghue* v. *Stevenson*[163] itself. Tomlin viewed the acceptance of an independent concept of negligence as leading to "alarming consequences" and concluded that in his opinion there was "no material from which it is

157. Sir Frederick Pollock thought Buckmaster and Tomlin (the two dissenters in *Donoghue* v. *Stevenson*) "the last men one would have suspected of timidity"; R. F. V. Heuston, "*Donoghue* v. *Stevenson* in Retrospect" 1, 3–4.

158. Tomlin chaired various governmental committees and commissions—perhaps the most important being his chairmanship of the Royal Commission on the Civil Service, 1929–31. See *Report*, Cmd. 3909.

159. In his obituary in *The Times* it was reported that Tomlin "entered with enthusiasm into the country life and became village squire in the truest sense of the term, being an ideal landlord and taking an interest in all village activities." See also In Memoriam—"Lord Tomlin of Ash" 51 *Law Quarterly Review*, 567 (1935).

160. For a discussion of Tomlin's "Liberty under the Common Law," see Hugh Macmillan, *Law and Other Things* 10.

161. Address to the American Bar Association, Thomas J. Tomlin, "Case Law" 594. Some of the schemes he put forward in this speech for keeping the common law flexible—e.g., that fewer cases should be reported—strike a somewhat unsatisfactory note; Tomlin Papers, *passim*, private possession, Cambridgeshire.

162. Even at his most outspoken, he was careful to emphasize that such conduct must be "without violation of essential principle"; see *Hillas & Co.* v. *Arcos, Ltd.*, [1932] All E.R. 494 (H.L.).

163. [1932] A.C. 562, 599 (Scot.).

legitimate for your Lordships' House to deduce such a principle."[164] He had already concluded that "in my opinion the decision in *Winterbottom v. Wright* . . . is directly in point against the appellant."[165] In other words, Tomlin felt that either contract or a fiduciary relationship was essential for a successful action for negligence.[166] Again, in *Liesbosch*[167] he was content to concur. It would seem that the common law was not a sphere that Tomlin either entered or left with any distinction.

Outside the common law, Tomlin was most prominent in litigation concerned with workmen's compensation and taxation. In workmen's compensation cases, he saw little need to look to the purpose of the legislation,[168] but merely interpreted the words as they stood.[169] Although, in general, Tomlin sought neutral principles in workmen's compensation, he refused to apply neutral principles in tax law; there he insisted on applying, in an extreme form, the judicially created presumption that taxation must be treated as penal legislation. In terms of this approach, Tomlin's greatest triumph was undoubtedly in the *Duke of Westminster*'s case,[170] in which he overthrew whatever may have survived of the "substance" doctrine. Of the doctrine he said, "The sooner this misunderstanding is dispelled, and the supposed doctrine given its *quietus*, the better it will be for all concerned, for the doctrine seems to involve substituting 'the incertain and crooked cord of discretion' for 'the golden

164. Ibid. 601.
165. Ibid. 600.
166. His real fear, with Buckmaster, was where the line would ultimately be drawn. "I think that if the appellant is to succeed it must be upon the proposition that every manufacturer or repairer of any article is under a duty to everyone who may thereafter legitimately use the article to exercise due care in the manufacture or repair. It is logically impossible to stop short of this point"; ibid. 599.
In some ways it is difficult to imagine that Tomlin was seriously dissenting, since his speech ran for only one and a half pages and cited only one authority. Moreover, for a judge who had such an aversion to the concept of duty and breach, he spoke, in another case, with remarkable latitude about the duty of a client to disclose irregularities to his bank, although, in fairness, it is difficult to deduce from the case whether the claim was in contract or tort; *Greenwood v. Martins Bank, Ltd.*, [1933] A.C. 51, 57 (1932).
167. *Liesbosch (Owners of the Dredger) v. The Edison*, [1933] A.C. 449.
168. But see *Simpson v. London, Midland & Scottish Ry.*, [1931] A.C. 351, 366 (Scot.), where he deduced from the authorities the rule applicable to unexplained accidents, which the courts must apply when considering § 1 of the 1925 Workmen's Compensation Act. He was adamant on the function of the court in such cases in appeals from an arbitrator. "It is not for the Court to treat the case as one for fresh decision where the conclusion of . . . the arbitrator, though unimpeachable in law, does not command itself to the judgment of the Court"; ibid. 367.
169. Contrast for instance, Tomlin's concurrence on the "added peril" doctrine in *Rosen v. S.S. Quercus (Owners)*, [1933] A.C. 494, with Atkin, who accepted the existence of the "added peril" doctrine in *Harris v. Associated Portland Cement Mfrs., Ltd.*, [1939] A.C. 71, 75 (1938), and then confined it to a nonoperative "context."
170. *IRC v. Duke of Westminster*, [1936] A.C. 1 (1935).

and straight metwand of the law.' "[171] But Tomlin was not content to let the matter rest there; he continued:

Every man is entitled if he can to order his affairs so as that the tax attaching under the appropriate Acts is less than it otherwise would be. If he succeeds in ordering them so as to secure this result, then however unappreciative the Commissioners of Inland Revenue or his fellow taxpayers may be of his ingenuity, he cannot be compelled to pay an increased tax. This so-called doctrine of "the substance" seems to me to be nothing more than an attempt to make a man pay notwithstanding that he has so ordered his affairs that the amount of tax sought from him is not legally claimable.[172]

Few would disagree with Tomlin's view that a person is entitled to minimize his tax, but if the commissioners may look only at what he says he has done and not in fact what he has done, the result may be a somewhat unbalanced approach. Tax legislation had become highly technical before *Westminster*, but it was all but hypocritical of Tomlin (as it was of some of the other law lords) to deny the substance doctrine and yet criticize the legislative devices that the literal method of construction forced on the Treasury.[173] After these decisions, there was even less chance that the courts could play an intelligent role in handling tax law. The taxation process degenerated into a complex form of a crossword puzzle with the Treasury and Parliamentary Counsel's Office on one side and tax counsel (and frequently, so it seemed, the judges) on the other. Thus, in this, as in other areas, it is difficult to describe Tomlin as other than a conventional, uninspiring, and occasionally destructive judge.

At least Lord Russell[174] was not particularly conventional from a juristic point of view, although it was becoming almost too late for a law lord not to endorse the declaratory theory. Russell came to the bench through the by then approved route of the High Court and the Court of Appeal. Son of a Lord Chief Justice who had briefly been a Lord of Appeal, he had taken no part in politics but had achieved the professional eminence that "justified" his promotion. Although no professional politician, his political views were clear. He was conservative (if not Conservative) politically, socially, and religiously. His personal assumption

171. Ibid. 19.

172. Ibid. 19–20.

173. See, for example, *Neumann* v. *IRC*, [1934] A.C. 215, 222, where Tomlin was highly critical of tax legislation that had complicated the issues because "the amendments . . . to the Income Tax Acts, directed as they frequently are to stopping an exit through the net of taxation freshly disclosed, are too often framed without sufficient regard to the basic scheme upon which the Acts originally rested."

174. Francis Xavier Joseph Russell; b. 1867; father, Lord of Appeal, then Lord Chief Justice; educ., Beaumont and Oriel College, Oxford (First, Law); called to bar, 1893; K.C., 1908; Judge, Chancery Division, 1919–28; Lord Justice, 1928–29; Lord of Appeal, 1929–46; d. 1946.

that all change was for the worse was translated to the judicial sphere. He appeared to care little for the development of the law, but if it were to be developed he preferred that it follow conservative policies. He saw no merit in the House's looking to the substance of any transaction; the task of the law was to enforce legal arrangements. If the application of legal standards led to an unjust result, if the worse came to the worst, then the legislature, that excrescence of democracy, might always intervene.[175]

The public image of Russell is associated chiefly with his view in workmen's compensation cases, in which he took on the mantle of Atkinson and Carson as the defender of employers against the collectivist encroachments of the state on behalf of the workers. Contrary to the views of almost all his brother law lords, he saw nothing wrong with the judicially developed "added peril" doctrine,[176] and he was anxious at all times to keep other aspects of the "scope of employment" doctrine within narrow bounds.[177] In his treatment of commercial matters he showed a similar regard for laissez-faire individualism. At almost any cost, government had to be prevented from intervening. When the motor trade established a system of private courts to prevent price cutting in the industry, he was shocked when the regular courts were invited to hold that the fines exacted by the private court from a retailer in lieu of being put on the "stop list" in effect amounted to blackmail.[178] In the area of contract, he was noticeably less attracted to the idea of frustration than were the other law lords;[179] it was not for the courts to intervene and make bargains for the parties.

Not unnaturally, he was a staunch supporter of property rights. While not customarily willing to set the regular courts up in opposition to the legislature or the executive, he took this line in *Minister of Health v. R., ex parte Yaffé*.[180] Even though all the other law lords were prepared to hold that the minister had, by his order, cured any defects there might have been in a slum clearance scheme, Russell delivered a vigorous dissent on the ground that a statute taking away property had to be construed

---

175. For a rather different interpretation, see Dunedin: "Quick, first-rate but occasionally inclined to be narrow in outlook"; cited, Heuston, *Lives* 481.

176. E.g., see his dissent in *Harris v. Associated Portland Cement Mfrs., Ltd.*, [1939] A.C. 71, 81 (1938).

177. E.g., *Alderman v. Great Western Ry.*, [1937] A.C. 454, 457; *Knowles v. Southern Ry.*, [1937] A.C. 463, 466. In fairness to Russell, some of his later speeches were more sensitive to the needs of workmen; e.g., *Victoria Spinning Co. v. Matthews*, [1936] 2 All E.R. 1359 (H.L.).

178. "I am wholly unable to understand how it can be suggested that this was not an eminently reasonable thing to do"; *Thorne v. Motor Trade Ass'n*, [1937] A.C. 797, 812.

179. Unlike Simon and Wright, he felt that frustration could never apply to a lease; *Cricklewood Property & Inv. Trust, Ltd. v. Leighton's Inv. Trust, Ltd.*, [1945] A.C. 221, 233 (1944).

180. [1931] A.C. 494, 536.

narrowly even if it involved the court in overruling the policy of a central department.[181] Similarly, a man's income was clearly part of his property, and the state must be kept away from it if at all possible. Russell's view of taxation was made clear in the *Duke of Westminster* case,[182] and in a similar spirit, he was able to construe narrowly a number of tax provisions.[183] Even when he was not able to find for the taxpayer, he was often prepared to offer him sympathy.[184]

Russell projected other important views into his decisions on the matter of divorce. Unlike most of the other law lords, as a Roman Catholic he vigorously opposed the Matrimonial Causes Act of 1937. "It is a Bill mainly and essentially to extend the grounds for divorce, and that is the reason why I, who am fundamentally opposed to divorce in any shape or form, must vote against this Bill."[185] His views expressed in legislative debates were transferred to his judicial functions and are perhaps best seen in *Fender v. St. John-Mildmay*.[186] He dissented vigorously from the idea that a man might contract to marry between the time of a divorce decree nisi and absolute.[187] Although, perhaps, it was only in tax cases that Russell was able to see that his personal views accorded wide acceptance, his attitude toward the judicial functions of the House was to have

181. "The Act under consideration enables a local authority to take away property compulsorily, and in many cases to pay for it less than full compensation. It is, therefore, essential that all the provisions leading up to the exercise of such a power should be strictly observed according to the language of the statute. Non-compliance with any such provision would, in my view, be fatal to the Minister's power to make a confirmation order"; ibid. 537.

182. [1936] A.C. 1, 24 (1935): "I confess that I view with disfavour the doctrine that in taxation cases the subject is to be taxed if, in accordance with a Court's view of what it considers the substance of transaction, the Court thinks that the case falls within the contemplation or spirit of the statute. The subject is not taxable by inference or analogy, but only by the plain words of the statute applicable to the facts and circumstances of his case." In keeping with this narrow approach to interpretation he also took a narrow approach to the arrangement involved: "I can find nothing in the letter and acknowledgement which constitutes or resembles a contract . . . But if I am wrong . . . and some contract dehors the deed was brought into existence by means of the letter and acknowledgement, it can be no more than a contract by [the gardener] that his remuneration for future services shall not be full remuneration but only the additional sum referred to in the letter"; ibid. 23.

183. E.g., *Christie v. Lord Advocate*, [1936] A.C. 569 (Scot.).

184. E.g., *Dewar v. IRC*, [1931] A.C. 566. There the House held that when a father set up a trust in favor of his daughter, tax paid by the father could not be recovered by the daughter. See Russell's comments at ibid. 573. See also his dissent in *IRC v. Crossman*, [1937] A.C. 26, 62 (1936). In fairness to Russell, it must be noted that during World War II he was more sympathetic to the activities of the Revenue authorities; e.g., *FPH. Fin. Trust, Ltd. v. IRC*, [1944] A.C. 285, 309 (1943).

185. 106 *Parl. Deb.*, H.L. (5th ser.), col. 579 (19 July 1937). He also argued the Roman Catholic position during the debates on the 1944 Education Act.

186. [1938] A.C. 1 (1937).

187. Russell felt that "the duty . . . to refrain from sexual intercourse with others, surely continues" and leaned heavily on the fact that the marriage still exists until the decree is made absolute; ibid. 28.

an important bearing upon the future development of the attitudes of the law lords.

The Russell position in terms of both juristic technique and policy preferences was generally supported by Lord Roche[188] during his brief tenure as a Lord of Appeal (1935–38). He was said to have had a considerable reputation as a King's Bench judge, especially in criminal law cases.[189] As an appeal judge (he served one year in the Court of Appeal before going to the Lords) he continued to behave as a good judge of first instance.[190] He was anxious not to intervene in economic issues;[191] he followed Hailsham's interpretations in tax cases;[192] and although he went along with the majority in *Rose* v. *Ford*,[193] he was obviously unhappy in a situation where the House, caught between two competing principles, had no choice but to make law.[194] Thus, it was not surprising to find him dissenting in *Fender* v. *St. John-Mildmay*,[195] not on the sanctity of marriage point that motivated Russell,[196] but because he adopted a Halsburian view of public policy. He considered that "to evolve new heads of public policy or to subtract from existing and recognised heads of public policy if permissible to the Courts at all, which is debatable, would in my judgement certainly only be permissible upon some occasion as to which the legislature was for some reason unable to speak and where there was substantial agreement within the judiciary and where circumstances had fundamentally changed. None of those conditions

188. Alexander Adair Roche; b. 1871; father, physician; educ., Ipswich Grammar School, Wadham College, Oxford (First, "Greats"); called to bar, 1896; K.C., 1912; Judge, King's Bench Division, 1917–34; Lord Justice, 1934–35; Lord of Appeal, 1935–38; d. 1956; *Dictionary of National Biography 1951–1960*, at 846.

189. *The Times* called him "one of the most efficient judges of his time"; Obituary, 24 Dec. 1956. He took the role of High Court judges seriously. See his opposition to increasing the number of King's Bench judges for fear their prestige might be diminished; Brian Abel-Smith and Robert Stevens, *Lawyers and the Courts* 270.

190. Although some of the early concurrences were no doubt out of deference to his senior colleagues, he rarely seemed to contribute his own speeches.

191. E.g., *Thorne* v. *Motor Trade Ass'n*, [1937] A.C. 797, 823.

192. E.g., *IRC* v. *Crossman*, [1937] A.C. 26, 71 (1936).

193. [1937] A.C. 826, 853.

194. The competing principles were the rule in *Baker* v. *Bolton*, holding that death gave rise to no cause of action and the Law Reform (Miscellaneous Provisions) Act of 1934 that allowed certain causes of action to survive death. Roche understandably feared that damages for loss of expectation of life might achieve a "frequency and prominence in litigation far greater than is warranted in fact . . . [and] may result in the inflation of damages in undeserving cases"; ibid. 861–62. In *Rose* v. *Ford* he was still unable to convince himself of where his responsibility lay, "but on a consideration of that matter I am unable to see that it is the duty or the right of your Lordships, sitting in a judicial capacity, either to enter upon a task of rendering the law uniform and consistent where lack of uniformity or of consistency may manifest itself at present, or for the sake of uniformity to extend the rule to cases and circumstances not actually within its scope"; ibid. 857.

195. [1938] A.C. 1, 51 (1937). Roche did, however, oppose the Matrimonial Causes Bill.

196. Although see Roche at ibid. 53.

seem to me to exist here."[197] He was convinced that in the handling of public policy "the management that is most useful is one that is most consistent and uncapricious."[198] Such an attitude, while appropriate for a trial judge, seemed strange for a judge in the final court of appeal, especially when he expressed displeasure because "this House is again asked to allow an innovation by taking something away from a rule sanctioned by a decision."[199]

This growing movement toward substantive formalism, especially on the part of English judges, was occasionally ameliorated, especially in the earlier years, by the addition of peers who were not Lords of Appeal. In their different ways Parmoor and Wrenbury added to the wisdom of the House, but the standard of their successors' contributions was not consistently high.

Phillimore,[200] who was almost a contemporary of Parmoor and Wrenbury, was a weak judge, except perhaps in those civilian areas of the law where he had practiced.[201] Indeed, he owed his promotion to the High Court not to ability but to the fact that Salisbury, having remonstrated with Halsbury about the excessive number of Conservative M.P.'s being appointed to the High Court bench, was placated with the appointment of Phillimore, who was a rich Liberal.[202] He survived, however, to reach the Court of Appeal, and Sankey later said, graciously, that "he became a better judge every year he sat."[203] Yet, there is little in the Appeal Cases to confirm that judgment. They portray Phillimore as a man obsessed with finding a *ratio decidendi* in order to apply stare decisis.[204] He rarely led the House,[205] and in Viscountess Rhondda's claim allowed himself to be bullied by Birkenhead into an intellectual

197. Ibid. 54–55.
198. Ibid. 56.
199. Ibid. 54.
200. Walter George Frank Phillimore; b. 1845; father, baronet and Admiralty judge; educ., Westminster, Christ Church, Oxford; called to bar, 1868 (Ecclesiastical and Admiralty law); Judge, Queen's Bench Division, 1897–1913; Lord Justice, 1913–16; peer, 1918; d. 1929; *Dictionary of National Biography 1922–1930*, at 677.
201. E.g., his restatement of diplomatic immunity in *Engelke* v. *Musmann*, [1928] A.C. 433, 448. He was Chairman of the Naval Prize Tribunal and Chairman of the committee considering early schemes for the League of Nations. He was also a member of the committee working out the constitution of the Permanent Court of International Justice at the Hague.
202. Heuston, *Lives* 56–58.
203. *Dictionary of National Biography 1922–1930*, at 677–78.
204. E.g., his efforts—along, it must be said, with those of other law lords—to make sense of *Adamson's* case in *Great Western Ry.* v. *The Mostyn (Owners)*, [1928] A.C. 57, 94 (1927). Dissenting with Dunedin, he noted, "[I]t seems to me that the *ratio decidendi* in your Lordships' House is to be found in the adoption of the latter view of Lord Cairns L.C., by Lord Blackburn and, in very hesitating terms, by Lord Hatherley and not expressly dissented from by Lord O'Hagan."
205. Although in the important contract case of *Rose & Frank Co.* v. *Crompton &*

position of which he clearly disapproved.[206] When he sat in tax cases, he took the mechanical approach, although in one case, in leaving Parliament to repair a hole that his opinion would have torn in the legislation, he hinted that Parliament might use the opportunity to rethink whether the wealthy were not taxed too heavily.[207]

Lord Warrington,[208] who was given a peerage after his retirement from the Court of Appeal in 1927, sat for an even longer period, indeed until his death in 1937. Here was yet another judge of whom it was said "the higher he went, the better he got." The basis for such a claim, however, is not immediately obvious from his judgments, which display a tendency, even those that might be thought to raise fundamental legal issues, toward an unhelpful brevity.[209] In at least two leading commercial cases—*Bell* v. *Lever Brothers* and *Banco de Portugal* v. *Waterlow and Sons*—Warrington dissented against Atkin, and in retrospect it is not Warrington's speeches that appear distinguished.[210]

Bros., [1925] A.C. 445, 450 (1924), he gave the only opinion, with Buckmaster, Atkinson, Birkenhead, and Sumner concurring.

206. "Upon the whole, and after reflection, I think it would not be right to give to general words of the statute, followed as they are by words of particular application, the incidental effect of creating this important right"; [1922] 2 A.C. 339, 405. He also allowed himself a protest against the suggestion that it was permissible to look at the legislative history of an Act of Parliament; ibid. 404.

207. See his dissent in *Whitney* v. *IRC*, [1926] A.C. 37, 62 (1925): "I think that, as the law at present stands, the appellant is not liable to super tax, and I see no great harm in coming to that conclusion. If it is desired, it would be easy for Parliament to express the liability in plain language and direct the necessary modification in the procedure. Meanwhile there would be no harm, in my humble judgement, in giving to those responsible for the finances of the country the opportunity of considering the familiar saying about the bird with the golden eggs."

208. Thomas Rolls Warrington; b. 1851; father, in silver business; educ., Rugby, Trinity College, Cambridge; called to bar, 1875. Q.C., 1895; Judge, Chancery Division, 1904–15; Lord Justice, 1915–26; cr. peer, 1926; d. 1937; *Dictionary of National Biography 1931–1940*, at 893.

209. E.g., *Minister of Health* v. *R.*, *ex parte Yaffé*, [1931] A.C. 494, 513. See also his cursory judgment in *Lochgelly Iron & Coal Co.* v. *McMullan*, [1934] A.C. 1, 12 (Scot. 1933), and his simple concurrence in *Feist* v. *Société Intercommunale Belge d'Electricité*, [1934] A.C. 161, 165 (1933).

210. In *Bell* v. *Lever Bros.*, [1932] A.C. 161, 200 (1931), Warrington's thesis was that the negotiations and agreements as to the premature termination of the service agreements and the question of compensation, although this was not part of the service agreements, were "as fundamental to the bargain as any error one can imagine"; ibid. 208.

Banco de Portugal v. *Waterlow & Sons*, [1932] A.C. 452, raised even more dramatically the issue of how far the courts were prepared to allocate risk in major international commercial transactions. The bank sued the printers of currency for breach of contract for allowing an impostor to obtain possession of a large quantity of bank notes, which were subsequently put into circulation by the criminal. As a result, the bank had to withdraw the issue and reimburse all holders of the notes. The main question for decision was: what was the measure of damages? The majority (Sankey, Atkin, and Macmillan) decided that the correct measure was the exchange value expressed in

Certainly Warrington was a humane man;[211] yet he represented the waning importance attributed by the English legal establishment to the final appeal court. It was seen, perhaps increasingly, as a kind of retirement ground, without any clearly defined role. In such an atmosphere, its approach at best tended to be a rehashing of the Court of Appeal approach, at worst a restatement of the assumptions and simplistic restatement of rules that judges had acquired and articulated while sitting at first instance. The worst excesses of such a system were hidden during the 1930s while men of the caliber of Atkin, Macmillan, and Wright sat and dominated the proceedings, but as their influence evaporated the absence of any serious purpose or rationale for the final appeal court in the English legal culture became painfully obvious.

---

sterling of genuine currency given by the bank in exchange for the spurious notes (some £600,000). Warrington decided that the printers were liable only for the expense of printing the notes that the bank had to issue to exchange for the spurious notes (some £9,000).

211. One of the few cases in which Warrington articulated dissatisfaction was in the workmen's compensation case of *Thomas* v. *Ocean Coal Co.*, [1933] A.C. 100, 126 (1932), where he politely rebuked the Court of Appeal judges for invoking the "added peril" doctrine in circumstances expressly provided for by the statute.

THE ERA OF
SUBSTANTIVE FORMALISM
1940–1955

In modern American legal thought, formalism has enjoyed something of a revival. Alienated by the nihilism of realism and the pretentiousness and excesses of the social and policy sciences, the process school,[1] having absorbed some of the intellectual rigor of the linguistic philosophers, now praises the virtues of formalism. Duncan Kennedy, for instance, has argued that the formalists seek not only to remove discretion by providing detailed rules, but as part of that process, to eliminate arbitrariness in rule identification by deducing these rules from the fundamental principles of the common law and liberal political theory. From an Anglo-American vantage point, Ronald Dworkin has argued that such fundamental principles have a binding force, not customarily associated with the discretion inherent in the usual statement on formalism or even in the utilitarian formulae that call for a balancing of interests.[2]

Such analyses may, conceivably, turn out to fit the approach of the more distinguished law lords of the 1960s and 1970s. For the 1940s and for much of the 1950s, there were no obvious signs that the law lords had developed rules out of broader principles of the common law or the liberal state. Indeed, there was virtually no acceptance of an element of

1. For a useful analysis of recent developments in American legal thought see Bruce Ackerman, "Law and the Modern Mind" 119.

2. Duncan Kennedy, "Legal Formality" 323; Ronald M. Dworkin, "Hard Cases," *passim.* For the outstanding recent analysis of the utilitarian balancing process, see John Rawls, *A Theory of Justice.*

discretion, let alone a utilitarian balancing of interests. The process, at best, fell into Karl Llewellyn's category of judicial formalism, with opinions written "in deductive form with an air of expression of single-line inevitability."[3] At worst, the process was a restatement of the declaratory theory in such extreme form that it denied any purpose for a second appeal court. Legal rationality became an end in itself. The literal meaning of words was to be the only criterion of statutory interpretation. It was a period that can be most aptly described as one of substantive formalism.

Beneath the rise of substantive formalism were understandable political pressures; indeed, the student of realpolitik might find such posturing to be evidence of sophisticated political maneuvers. Yet for the years between 1940 and 1955, to suggest such political sophistication may be as misleading as it is unnecessary. The need to play possum was obvious even to the least politically minded of the judges. In 1940 Britain was in a state of crisis; democracy had given way to a form of generally benevolent dictatorship; it was not the best time for the judges to stand on ceremony or pretend to power. With the end of the state of crisis in 1945, the electorate overwhelmingly returned a Labour government committed to a program of social and political legislation that, while no doubt distasteful to many of the judges, could be challenged only with extreme danger. Even when Churchill and the Conservatives were returned to power in 1951, the situation did not change appreciably. Churchill, at the age of seventy-seven, was primarily interested in foreign affairs, and he left domestic matters largely to R. A. Butler, whom he disliked, but who was a democrat with views not particularly different from at least those of the right wing of the Labour party. Again it was not an atmosphere in which judges might have been expected to show or to take initiatives.

Thus for these fifteen years the judges, in public law, under the guise of an extreme form of the declaratory theory, played the role of total deference to the executive. This approach naturally spilled over into the area of private law. Substantive formalism became a way of life. In a few brief years the court that had boasted of Atkin and Wright came to regard itself not only as incapable of major judicial legislation, but also as incapable of the most trivial of judicial legislation, even when the inexorable logic of common law appeared to leave a gap. It was in this atmosphere that the value of a second appeal began to be seriously questioned politically. A second appeal, in the absence of any rationale, appeared increasingly to be no more than a subsidy to the legal profession and a burden to litigants. Moreover, with the professionalization of

3. Karl Llewellyn, *The Common Law Tradition* 38.

the Lords of Appeal the law lords no longer included politicians of standing to act as apologists for the appellate function.

Although in 1955 the days of the second appeal appeared to be numbered, things slowly changed. It was about that time that the businessmen and technocrats who had run the domestic side of the Conservative party began to give way to a new breed of Conservative politician who looked back to the more hierarchical and historical days of the 1930s and before;[4] slowly the assumption that modern toryism accepted "naked democracy" came to be challenged. In 1954, Simonds, a professional judge, was replaced as Lord Chancellor by Kilmuir, who was far less interested in retaining a clear separation between law and politics; the rising leaders Eden, Macmillan, and Home—in different ways all seen as men of the Right—helped to blur this separation. Moreover, while the Suez disaster of 1956 curbed the foreign pretensions of the renovated traditional Tory outlook, it served if anything, as evidence that the urge to restore traditional values and attitudes should be channeled into domestic matters.

4. "Butler's prestige fell when the boom had to be stopped in October, 1955. He became Lord Privy Seal and was replaced at the Treasury by Harold Macmillan; in the party the modernizers and businessmen began to lose ground, and the people who wanted to get back to 'before the war' made their opinions heard more loudly than they had done for some time. They may have felt this was electorally safer once the 1955 election was won, and they were also encouraged by the signs that Butler's power was less than it had been and that modern Conservatism was on the retreat"; Trevor O. Lloyd, *Empire to Welfare State* 335.

The Politics of
Substantive Formalism

The Appellate Function

The period from 1940 to 1955 was not an expansive period in the judicial work load of the House of Lords. In 1939, the House had heard forty-five cases, about the average after the abolition of the absolute right of appeal in 1934.[1] During World War II the number of appeals heard declined,[2] although there was a modest rise immediately after the war.[3] After that, another decline set in; in 1950, the House heard thirty-one cases and by 1953 the number had fallen to nineteen. The number of appeals increased to thirty-four in 1955, but dropped again until 1959.[4]

Although the House had, for much of the nineteenth century, been predominantly a Scottish court, its effect in that jurisdiction had weakened by the middle of the twentieth. Moreover, the type of case heard from England was changing; especially after the passage of the Legal Aid and Advice Act in 1949, the charge could legitimately be levied against the House that it was predominantly a rich man's court. While legal aid was rapidly provided in the Court of Appeal and High Court, it was not extended to the House of Lords.[5] The Lords were, it is true, more lenient

1. From English courts, 41; from Scottish, 4.
2. Although it did so only modestly: 1940, 28; 1941, 38; 1942, 34; 1943, 31; 1944, 39; 1945, 28.
3. To 45 in 1946 and 53 in 1947.
4. It should be noted, however, that during these years the House was tough on those seeking leave to appeal under the 1934 legislation. In 1950, for instance, the Appeals Committee allowed 2 petitions for leave to appeal and rejected 18. The figures for 1955 were 7 and 26.
5. "For general economic reasons," as the government put it.

in allowing in forma pauperis proceedings,[6] but these were of limited use; increasingly, the House seemed to be a court only for the affluent. This irony in a period when many thought they were witnessing a major social revolution was remarkable.

In 1952, for instance, the House handed down twenty-three decisions, of which nine were basically tax-related;[7] in 1955, of the thirty-four decisions given, thirteen were tax-related.[8] In short, more than a third of the House's work was tax-oriented and, with the exception of negligence cases (five in 1952 and four in 1955), which were normally financed by the unions on one side and the insurance companies on the other, the remaining cases were scattered over the generally more affluent areas of the law.[9] In line with this trend, the pace of the House was changing. In the years before the war it took about 2 days, or a little more, to hear an appeal.[10] By the 1950s, it was taking more than 3 days to hear an appeal. In 1950, 100 days were required to hear thirty-one cases; in 1951, 121 days to hear thirty-nine; in 1952, 71 to hear twenty-four; in 1953, 62 to hear nineteen; and, in 1954, 91 days to hear twenty-one cases. By that year, the average of the 4-day case had arrived.[11]

This increase may explain why the Appellate Jurisdiction Act of 1947 raised the maximum number of Lords of Appeal from seven to nine, for the change could certainly not have been caused by the manpower needs of the Judicial Committee of the Privy Council. During the 1930s, the Judicial Committee had averaged 100 appeals a year. This figure declined during the early years of the war, but by 1944 the number was up to 90 again and for the next three years hovered around 100.

6. In 1950, for instance, 2 of the 3 petitions for leave to appeal in forma pauperis were allowed; in 1955, all 4 such applications were allowed. Of the 8 bills taxed in 1952, the average cost of an appeal by the losing party was £1,073.

7. Regular tax cases accounted for 6, 2 involved the definition of charities for tax purposes, and 1 concerned a trust point revolving around taxation.

8. Regular tax cases accounted for 10, 1 was a charity case, 1 involved taxation of damages, and 1 concerned the tax aspects involved in the interpretation of a will.

9. In 1952, cases in the following areas were decided: 2 international law cases, 2 family law, 1 false imprisonment (tort), 1 on trade union membership, 1 contract, 1 compulsory purchase, 1 libel, and 1 criminal. Two of the negligence cases, the trade union membership case, and 1 of the family law cases were in forma pauperis proceedings.

In 1955, cases in the following areas were decided: 3 patent cases, 1 involving a will, 1 international law, 1 compulsory purchase, 2 landlord and tenant, 1 trade union, 2 family law, 1 involving procedure, 2 contract, and 3 admiralty decisions. The trade union case and one of the family law decisions were in forma pauperis proceedings.

10. In 1936, 49 cases took 112 days; in 1937, 35 cases took 77 days; in 1938, 42 cases took 91 days.

11. There appeared, however, to be a change in the affirm/reverse ratio. In appeals from the Court of Appeal, in 1936, 18 were affirmed, 11 reversed, and 2 varied. The figures for 1937 were 11, 14, 0; and for 1938, 24, 12, 2. The figures for 1952 were 12, 4, 1; for 1953, 11, 5, 0; and for 1954, 8, 4, 1.

Then, with the ending of appeals from India, Canada, and South Africa[12] in 1949 the situation changed dramatically. It was as if the Judicial Committee was trumpeting the end of the empire. For the law lords it was certainly a changed world. In 1931 the two final appeal courts had heard 169 appeals; in 1951, although by then two more Lords of Appeal had been appointed, the two courts heard only 67 cases.[13]

Outside the law courts the law lords were not idle. They continued to speak in the legislative sessions of the Lords[14] and were particularly active in the capital punishment debate in the late forties and in the Liberties of the Subject Bill in 1950. Both were somewhat strangely regarded as lawyer's bills and therefore as apolitical. Yet in terms of actual power and influence, the law lords were most influential not in the judicial or legislative work of the Lords, but in their chairmanship of Royal Commissions and similar bodies that, during the 1940s, came to rival the great nineteenth-century "Blue Books" as indicators of social ferment and change. Between 1945 and 1969, judges—mainly law lords—chaired 7 of the 24 Royal Commissions and 118 of the 358 departmental committees.[15] Du Parcq, for instance, headed the Royal Commission on the Justices of the Peace,[16] Cohen shared the Royal Commission on Taxation of Profits and Income with Radcliffe,[17] Morton chaired the Royal Commission on Marriage and Divorce,[18] and Uthwatt chaired the

12. The Irish Free State had abolished all appeals during the 1930s, and Canada had done so with respect to criminal appeals. See chap. 6. In 1940, after the Cahan Bill had been referred to it, the Supreme Court of Canada held that the Canadian Parliament could abolish appeals altogether. The appeal to the Judicial Committee from this reference was not heard until 1946, when the Privy Council agreed that abolition of appeals to London would be *intra vires* § 91; *Attorney-General for Ontario* v. *Attorney-General for Canada*, [1947] A.C. 127 (P.C. 1946).

On the mechanics of abolition after this, see Coen G. Pierson, *Canada and the Privy Council*, chap. 7.

13. Total Number of Appeals to the Privy Council Decided after a Hearing for 1930–1949

1930	100	1940	59
1931	117	1941	61
1932	93	1942	64
1933	108	1943	69
1934	88	1944	90
1935	94	1945	105
1936	98	1946	104
1937	122	1947	97
1938	81	1948	55
1939	96	1949	76

14. Law lords still continued to dominate the Committee for Privileges (3 of its 20 members are required to be law lords), while a law lord by custom chaired the Committee on Consolidation.

15. T. J. Cartwright, *Royal Commissions and Departmental Committees in Britain* 72.

16. *Report*, Cmd. 7463 (1948).

17. *Report*, Cmd. 9474 (1955).

18. *Report*, Cmd. 9678 (1955).

Committee on Leaseholds.[19] Moreover, while sitting as lower court judges on their way to the Lords during this period, Asquith,[20] Cohen,[21] Evershed,[22] Jenkins,[23] and Devlin[24] chaired commissions or committees. These lists do not begin to exhaust chairmanships, let alone deal with membership on commissions and committees or membership in the innumerable standing bodies that the law lords staffed.[25] Although the law lords were declaring themselves to be eunuchs in judicial affairs, outside the courts their virility remained evident. In the case of the Lord Chancellor the political element was inevitable.

Lord Simon

It is difficult to write fairly about John Simon.[26] He was undoubtedly a remarkably intelligent man who clearly understood the nature of the judicial process. He was also Lord Chancellor at a politically inopportune moment. He was not a member of the War Cabinet, and understandably the courts were not viewed as particularly important during the period of his Chancellorship. Yet, even taking this into account, there was something profoundly disquieting about his Chancellorship with respect to the appellate process. An obvious reason for this unrest was that Simon, despite his understanding of the process, threw his weight not behind the appellate role as defined by Atkin and Wright, but rather behind the substantive formalism of an increasing number of the less distinguished judges. Similarly, where public law was concerned, Simon chose to stifle what remained of the courts' residual concerns with personal freedom. Both of these positions might have been more tenable had not Simon publicly been an advocate of a creative role for the judicial process and had he not, at times, displayed a public obsession with civil liberties.

19. *Report*, Cmd. 7982 (1950).
20. Royal Commission on Equal Pay; *Report*, Cmd. 6937 (1946).
21. Committee on Company Law Amendment; *Report*, Cmd. 6659 (1945).
22. Committee on Port Transport Industry, 1945.
23. Committee on Intermediaries; *Report*, Cmd. 7904 (1949).
24. Committee on Port Transport Industry; *Report*, Cmd. 9813 (1956).
25. The judiciary also provided 5 members of Royal Commissions (a further 11 were Q.C.'s) and 108 members of departmental committees (a further 74 were Q.C.'s); Cartwright, *Royal Commissions and Departmental Committees* 76.
26. John Allsebrook Simon; b. 1873, Manchester; father, Congregational minister; educ., Fettes College, Wadham College, Oxford; called to bar, 1899; K.C., 1908; M.P. (Lib.) Walthamstow, 1906–18, Spen Valley, Yorks, 1922–40; Solicitor-General, 1910–13; Attorney-General, 1913–15; Secretary of State for Home Affairs, 1915–16; Deputy Leader of Commons, 1935–37; Chancellor of Exchequer, 1937–40; Lord Chancellor, 1940–45; d. 1954; *Dictionary of National Biography 1951–1960*, at 892. "It is paradoxical that at the end of the long public career Simon should have been more successful as a lawyer than as a politician"; ibid. 894.

Perhaps the result of such conflicting positions was that people were always uncertain as to where Simon stood on any issue. To many he was a paradigmatic lawyer, able to speak on any side of an issue and frequently reputed to hold views in favor of both sides. Thus, Lord Beaverbrook claimed that Simon was threatening resignation in 1914 on pacifist grounds while he was a member of the war party in the cabinet;[27] and then illogically he did resign from the cabinet over conscription in 1916.[28] Birkenhead, not exactly the best role model, criticized Simon's professional ethics.[29] It is indeed remarkable that a man who held the offices of Home Secretary, Foreign Secretary, Chancellor of the Exchequer, and Lord Chancellor should have been regarded in much the same way that Dryden regarded Buckingham;[30] and it may not have been entirely flattering that the obituary in *The Times* concluded that the Lord Chancellorship was his natural habitat,[31] although politics had remained his first love.[32]

Beginning life as a member of the Liberal party,[33] Simon had had a distinguished career at the bar, and as early as 1915, he had been offered

---

27. Lord Beaverbrook (Max Aitkin), *Politicians and the War* 20, 22.

28. C. Maurice Bowra, *Memories 1898–1939*, at 191–92. This and other passages in the Bowra autobiography are particularly revealing of Simon's character.

It should come as no surprise that Simon was an appeaser even after World War II had begun. Some even thought Ambassador Kennedy's negative attitude was influenced by Simon; William Stevenson, *A Man Called Intrepid* 84.

29. R. F. V. Heuston, *Lives of the Lord Chancellors 1885–1940*, at 382. They had been at Wadham College, Oxford, together, as undergraduates.

30. A man so various, that he seemed to be
    Not one, but all Mankind's Epitome,
    Stiff in opinions, always in the wrong;
    Was everything by starts and nothing long.

    [John Dryden, *Absalom and Achitophel*]

31. "With his accession to the Woolsack in 1940, both friendly and hostile critics will agree that Lord Simon entered upon the most successful phase of his varied career since the days when he had led the English Bar"; Obituary, *The Times*, 12 Jan. 1954. The obituary took the view that "in the law courts he was pre-eminent; at the Home Office excellently placed, at the Treasury a somewhat disappointing Chancellor; in foreign affairs, for all his qualities, a failure—he presented, in fact, an almost perfect example of the limitations as well as the uses of the legal mind. . . . It was for the Woolsack to redeem his fading reputation."

Dalton explained Labour's refusal to join Chamberlain's War Cabinet on the ground that his party had no confidence in Simon or his abilities as Chancellor of the Exchequer; Martin Gilbert and Richard Gott, *The Appeasers* 330. Aneurin Bevan shared the view that Simon was "the worst Foreign Secretary since Ethelred the Unready"; Michael Foot, 2 *Aneurin Bevan* 211.

32. Carl Eric Roberts, *Sir John Simon, Being an Account of the Life and Career of Sir John Simon* 311. The impression is borne out by reading Simon's autobiography, *Retrospect*; chap. 14, on his Lord Chancellorship, is particularly empty.

33. Salisbury offered the rather remarkable thought that "liberalism was his creed, and he never swerved from it"; 185 *Parl. Deb.*, H.L. (5th ser.), col. 262 (19 Jan. 1954).

the Lord Chancellorship.[34] He had chosen to remain in active politics and had always regarded "the bar as a stepping-stone to politics."[35] After serving as Home Secretary under Lloyd George, he spent some years in the political wilderness, to return first as Foreign Secretary and then as Home Secretary and Chancellor of the Exchequer in the National governments of the 1930s. There was no evidence, however, that he was any more trusted in these roles. Conservatives often distrusted him because of his middle-class background and Liberal antecedents,[36] while Labour hated him for his famous speech in which he declared that the General Strike was illegal.[37] The Left was not enthusiastic, either, about his hostility to the closed shop,[38] especially when he insisted that it was "absurd" to compare the closed shop with the situation in certain professions—including the law; and it was little comfort to Labour politicians of the late 1940s to be reminded that Simon had supported the Trade Disputes Act in 1906.[39]

In truth, all of Simon's dealings evidenced a coldness[40] that many took for cynicism or opportunism.[41] His liberal friends found it difficult to explain why he characterized the suggestion that the death penalty be abolished as a "preposterous proposal";[42] and about most of his activities there seem to have been two possible interpretations. He no doubt, for example, felt that he was performing an immense public service in serving as Chairman of the India Commission (always known as the

34. Heuston, *Lives* 265.

35. *Dictionary of National Biography 1951–1960*, at 893. "His talents were those of the efficient chief of staff rather than of the inspiring commander-in-chief, and he was neither responsible for, nor even showed any, desire to introduce any major legislative reform"; ibid. 894.

36. Simon, *Retrospect*, chap. 1.

37. "It would be lamentable if the working classes of this country were to go on with this business without understanding that they are taking part in a novel and an utterly illegal proceeding"; John Simon, *The General Strike* 4. For Goodhart's answer to this, see Arthur L. Goodhart, "The Legality of the General Strike," in *Essays in Jurisprudence and the Common Law* 226. See generally Julian Symons, *The General Strike* 114–23.

38. 140 *Parl. Deb.*, H.L. (5th ser.), cols. 929–45 (30 Apr. 1946).

39. Ibid., col. 945.

40. E.g., "God, what a toad and a worm Simon is!" Harold Nicolson, *Diaries and Letters 1939–1945*, at 407.

41. But see, for example, Lord Alexander of Hillsborough: "I must say, however, from my own personal experience of him that behind all that apparent coldness was one of the most human and feeling personalities it would be possible to meet"; 185 *Parl. Deb.*, H.L. (5th ser.), col. 264 (14 Jan. 1954).

42. 157 ibid., cols. 1055–60 (29 July 1948). He did, however, suggest the Crown Proceedings Act, which allowed litigants to sue the Crown without having to bring a petition of right. He put down a parliamentary question after *Adams v. Naylor*, [1946] A.C. 543; 145 *Parl. Deb.*, H.L. (5th ser.), cols. 392–94 (4 Feb. 1947). He also introduced a bill to make the Crown liable as an occupier; ibid., col. 348 (4 Feb. 1947). See also Crown Proceedings Act of 1948.

Simon Commission) and in submitting the recommendations that ultimately led to the India Act of 1935.[43] Yet, many have argued that far from seeing this as a step on the road to freedom for India, Simon was chiefly interested in putting a brake on independence by building up the princes.[44] If this latter skepticism is fair, his claim that "there is no country in the world that has a greater sympathy for a genuine national movement than my country of Britain" will not stand serious investigation.[45]

It was within this political and personal context that Simon's judicial activities were conducted. The combination of his intellectual and political power was forbidding.[46] He worked intensely[47] and sat with remarkable frequency during his tenure as Chancellor.[48] Other law lords dissented from his speeches only with some trepidation,[49] and even when he was not sitting he did not hesitate to put pressure on judges—for instance, in his efforts to persuade Atkin to modify his judgment in *Liversidge* v. *Anderson*.[50]

43. Perry Spear, *India* 370–71, 383. For a description of Simon's sacrifice, see Heuston, *Lives* 437.

44. For a less favorable appraisal of the achievements of the Simon Commission, see Jawaharlal Nehru, *The Discovery of India* 368–74; and John Morris-Jones, *The Government and Politics of India*, London, 1967, p. 19.

45. John Simon, "Some Aspects of the Indian Problem" 648. For the conventional nonsense to which English judges almost always subject American audiences, see John Simon, "Our Common Inheritance of Law" 449.

46. For example, he was no mean legal historian. See, for instance, his investigation into the development of the doctrine of "waiving a tort" in *United Australia, Ltd.* v. *Barclays Bank, Ltd.*, [1941] A.C. 1, 11ff. (1940). Many of his speeches had admirable clarity, and his facility in handling doctrine was indeed impressive. Porter said of him, "So far as is humanly possible he always left the subject of his speeches absolutely clear and their meaning unmistakable. . . . If the duty of a judge is to make certain that he has followed and appreciated an argument, given it due weight and felicitously expressed the reasons for his decision, Lord Simon will stand high in the ranks of those who sit to clarify the law"; 185 *Parl. Deb.*, H.L. (5th ser.), cols. 267–68 (19 Jan. 1954). For an example of his ability to crystallize an issue, see *Denny, Mott & Dickson, Ltd.* v. *James B. Fraser & Co.*, [1944] A.C. 265, 269 (Scot. 1943).

47. Simonds said of Simon, "[A] long and wide experience in the law, a scholar's passion for accuracy, and a compelling sense of the judicial oath drove him to sustained and unremitting efforts in the preparation of judgements which will, as I said the other day, be his most enduring monument. I sometimes thought that in that work he found his greatest happiness"; 185 *Parl. Deb.*, H.L. (5th ser.), col. 275 (19 Jan. 1954).

48. He also sat with some regularity after he ceased to be Chancellor in 1945.

49. See, for example, his speech in *Benham* v. *Gambling*, [1941] A.C. 157, 160 (1940), severely restricting *Rose* v. *Ford*. Similarly, see *Duncan* v. *Cammell, Laird & Co.*, [1942] A.C. 624.

50. R. F. V. Heuston, "*Liversidge* v. *Anderson* in Retrospect" 43, letter from Simon to Atkin, 31 Oct. 1941:

I *do* hope you will not resent it if I write this private and friendly note. I asked . . . to . . . see . . . the speeches prepared for the 18B judgements on Monday. . . . My eye catches your very amusing citation from Lewis Carroll. Do you really on final reflection think this is necessary? I fear that it may be regarded as wounding to your colleagues who take the view you satirise and I feel sure you

Simon was undoubtedly fully aware of the function of law in society and of the potential for lawmaking in the final appeal court.[51] He was also aware of the advantages of the declaratory theory of law. This theory helped to break the General Strike,[52] and it was intended to convince the Canadians that the Privy Council was merely interpreting a statute literally when deciding constitutional cases.[53] Thus, during his time on the Woolsack, utilitarian functions of the House were sacrificed for the limited benefit of political acceptability. Simon publicized the legal platitudes about certainty.[54] He publicly endorsed the orthodox mystique of the judicial process and of the inevitability of precedent, an endorsement he passed on to less talented and less perceptive colleagues.

In private law, Simon cared neither for the approach nor for the policies pursued by the leaders of the House in the 1930s. His innate ability allowed him to breathe new life into technical concepts when the spirit moved him,[55] but in general, he saw little need to refine the com-

---

would not willingly seek to hold them up to ridicule. I am all in favour of enlivening judgements with literary allusion but I would venture to ask you whether the paragraph should be retained. Of course it is entirely for you . . . I at any rate feel that neither the dignity of the House nor the collaboration of colleagues nor the force of your reasoning would suffer from the omission."

51. See, for instance, John Simon, *The Limits of Precedent*. While articulating a narrow judicial function in the House, he declared that "[a] wise judge, therefore, takes the greatest pains to guard against the danger of laying down a proposition of law in too wide terms"; ibid. 5. At ibid. 7, he accepted the broad power of developing the law through distinguishing certain decisions. See also John Simon, Introduction to *The Case of Requisitions*, by L. Scott and A. Hildesby, at xxi.

52. In referring to Mr. Justice Astbury's much criticized dictum in *National Sailors' & Firemen's Union of Great Britain* v. *Reed*, holding the General Strike illegal, Simon called it an "opportune judicial pronouncement," and praised it both for declaring what all had suspected the law already was and for helping to break the strike; Simon, *General Strike*, at xiv.

53. For a rather terrifying view of Simon's vision of the Commonwealth, see John Simon, *Crown and Commonwealth*.

54. E.g., "What the House of Lords lays down judicially as being the law is the law, however wrong the law lords may afterwards think the decision to have been, and, upon the whole, I think that it is better so, for by no other means can legal certainty be established"; Simon, *Limits of Precedent*.

55. E.g., "Every case in this branch of the law [common employment] depends on its own facts"; *Glasgow Corp.* v. *Bruce*, [1948] A.C. 79, 83 (Scot. 1947). See also his thoughts on the last opportunity rule, where he adopted the view of the Law Revision Committee; *Report*, Cmd. 6032, at 16 (1939): "In truth, there is no such rule—the question, as in all questions of liability for a tortious act, is not who had the last opportunity of avoiding the mischief, but whose act caused the wrong?" *Boy Andrew (Owners)* v. *St. Rognvald (Owners)*, [1948] A.C. 140, 149 (Scot. 1947).

During his Chancellorship he also helped to develop the concept of commercial frustration. E.g., *Joseph Constantine S.S. Line, Ltd.* v. *Imperial Smelting Corp.*, [1942] A.C. 154 (1941); and especially *Heyman* v. *Darwins, Ltd.*, [1942] A.C. 356, 368 (1941). He also left open the possibility of applying frustration to leases. See *Cricklewood Property & Inv. Trust, Ltd.* v. *Leighton's Inv. Trust, Ltd.*, [1945] A.C. 221, 227 (1944). In his later years, however, he vigorously opposed the idea that the frustration concept was based on a

mon law. Thus the development of the tort of negligence was slowed,[56] if not reversed, and the protection of workmen that the House had seen as its special responsibility waned.[57]

Yet, in terms of both creativity and the exercise of policy preferences, Simon occasionally allowed himself full rein. In one of his first reported decisions, the *United Australia* case, Simon noted that, "while admiring the subtlety of the old special pleaders, our Courts are primarily concerned to see that rules of law and procedure should serve to secure justice between parties."[58] So, too, when he felt strongly enough he could say bluntly that "the present question is not, in my opinion, one in which this House is required, on the ground of public interest, to maintain a rule which has been constantly applied but which it is convinced is erroneous."[59] Equally, he was aware that the criminal law of each generation was shaped by the standards of that generation, and he did not hesitate to apply his own standards.[60] The political animal in Simon was strong, and there is no doubt that he sometimes steered the House wisely. He dissuaded the law lords from developing the law of conspiracy with respect to trade unions.[61] His views in construing wills[62] and handling divorce cases[63] reflected sound common sense, and in such areas he

---

"just and reasonable" solution rather than on an implied term; *British Movietonews, Ltd. v. London & Dist. Cinemas, Ltd.,* [1952] A.C. 166, 181, 195 (1951).

56. E.g., *East Suffolk Rivers Catchment Bd. v. Kent,* [1941] A.C. 74, 88 (1940): "In my opinion the respondents equally have no claim when the appellants do intervene, save in respect of such damage as flows from their intervention and as might have been avoided if their intervention had been more skillfully conducted." Also *Benham v. Gambling,* [1941] A.C. 157 (1940), and *Read v. J. Lyons & Co.,* [1947] A.C. 156, 165 (1946).

57. He did not seek to curb the general willingness of the House to help workmen, but at the same time he felt no enthusiasm for weakening doctrines such as common employment. "According to a doctrine which has been established in our law for more than a hundred years, and which nothing short of an Act of Parliament can alter, the sufferer in such a case must be regarded as having entered into a contract with his employer that he will not hold him liable for the other workman's fault"; *Colfar v. Coggins & Griffith (Liverpool), Ltd.,* [1945] A.C. 197, 201 (1944). Cf. *Doudie v. Kinneil Cannel & Coking Coal Co.,* [1947] A.C. 377, 381 (Scot. 1946).

58. *United Australia, Ltd. v. Barclays Bank, Ltd.,* [1941] A.C. 1 (1940).

59. *Perrin v. Morgan,* [1943] A.C. 399, 414 (1942).

60. See his concluding thoughts in *Holmes v. DPP,* [1946] A.C. 588, that the "application of common law principles in matters such as this must to some extent be controlled by the evolution of society"; ibid. 600. His conclusion, however, was basically unsympathetic to the serviceman returning to the adulterous wife.

61. *Crofter Hand Woven Harris Tweed Co. v. Veitch,* [1942] A.C. 435, (Scot. 1941). See Wolfgang Friedmann, "The Harris Tweed Case and Freedom of Trade" 1.

62. E.g., *Perrin v. Morgan,* [1943] A.C. 399, 414 (1942): "It is far more important to promote the correct construction of future wills in this respect than to preserve consistency in misinterpretation."

63. E.g., *Blunt v. Blunt,* [1943] A.C. 517, 525, as to the exercise of discretion where the petitioner confessed to adultery. While Simon stressed the consideration of "the interest of the community at large, to be judged by maintaining a true balance between respect for

helped the common law avoid head-on collisions with the changing mores of the community.[64]

Yet the policies he pursued in other areas did much to undermine the usefulness of the courts and the common law. Simon, in his public statements, was a vigorous defender of his version of civil liberties. He opposed the "contracting out" aspects of the unions' political levy on the ground that it was a danger to individual liberty.[65] He was a vigorous supporter of the somewhat hysterical Liberties of the Subject Bill in 1950, having stated, "We are governed more by subordinate regulations than by the law of the land,"[66] and he was opposed to the profits tax since it was an unfair burden on shareholders.[67] Indeed, he revealed as his inarticulate premise that "I have a horrid prejudice in favour of liberty."[68] Yet, where the state was concerned,[69] in his judicial work, he gave the lie to his own claim that of the great freedoms, "all really proceeded from the interpretation and application of the law by the judges themselves."[70] He advocated civil liberties and the importance of the independence of the judiciary, but he subordinated their significance to that of the legislature and the executive in a way that, in terms of power, made the courts increasingly appear to be but an arm of the executive.

His Chancellorship was, of course, during a time of war and massive national emergency,[71] but the concept of Crown privilege was almost entirely his work in *Duncan v. Cammell, Laird and Company*.[72] Despite

---

the binding sanctity of marriage and the social considerations which make it contrary to public policy to insist on the maintenance of a union which has utterly broken down."

64. This was another reason that it was convenient to embrace the declaratory theory of law. E.g., see Simon's support for the Legal Aid and Advice Bill. "In this way we shall diminish very much, I hope that occasional sense of bitterness which really arises from a misunderstanding of the elementary idea that the law of England is a sensible thing. If it is not sensible, it is the fault of Parliament, because Parliament has not made it as sensible as it ought to be"; 163 *Parl. Deb.*, H.L. (5th ser.), col. 321 (27 June 1949).

65. 140 ibid. cols. 929–45 (30 Apr. 1946).

66. 167 ibid., cols. 1087–90 (28 June 1950).

67. 165 ibid., cols. 903–11 (22 Nov. 1949).

68. 167 ibid., col. 1090 (28 June 1950).

69. His only noted concern with civil liberty was exhibited in *Christie* v. *Leachinsky* [1947] A.C. 573, 581 (1946).

70. 167 *Parl. Deb.*, H.L. (5th ser.), cols. 1087–90 (28 June 1950).

71. Of World War I, Simon wrote, "[P]ublic opinion and the House of Commons generally recognized as inevitable the claim of the Authorities to interfere drastically in the interests of national defense with individual rights, and the conduct of the Crown's advisors was not regarded as opposed to the interests of citizens but rather as representing the claims of the whole body politic against some individual member"; Introduction to Scott and Hildesby, *Case of Requisition*, at x.

72. [1942] A.C. 624. In delivering the only speech, he noted, "In framing my opinion, I have had the advantage of consultation with, and contribution from, the six noble and learned Lords who sat with me at the hearing of the appeal, and while what I am about to

a nominal deference to the power of the judiciary in privilege cases, the rule Simon established was in fact a broad and absolute one. "That the interest of the state must not be put in jeopardy by producing documents which would injure it is a principle to be observed in administering justice, quite unconnected with the interests or claims of the particular parties in litigation."[73] In *Barnard* v. *Gorman*,[74] while paying elaborate deference to the concept of civil liberties,[75] he in fact found that, on the wording of an act of 1876, the customs authorities had a wide power to detain persons whom they suspected of an offense, and those detained had no right to bring an action for false imprisonment. Most sinister of all, however, was his behavior in *Liversidge* v. *Anderson*.[76] Although he was not sitting in that case, Simon, as has been seen, sought to modify the dissenting speech that Atkin had prepared,[77] and he no doubt would have been happy to see the whole speech withdrawn.

A similar ambivalence, in terms of both style and content, surrounds Simon's approach to statutory interpretation, and, once again, there are some situations that might be mistaken for hypocrisy. It was not that he in any way failed to appreciate the alternatives available to the House in construing statutes. In one of his earliest speeches, he balanced narrow and broad approaches in a highly elegant, if somewhat elliptical, passage.[78] He was far better able to analogize and to sense the underlying

---

say is the expression of my own view, I have reason to think that it also expresses the judgement of my colleagues"; ibid. 629.

73. Ibid. 642.

74. [1941] A.C. 378.

75. "The question is a very serious one, for on the one hand, it is rightly stressed that the liberty of the subject is involved and if an innocent man is detained under official authority his personal freedom is for the time being interfered with, even though he may be treated with all consideration and may, in fact, have suffered little from being in temporary custody. . . . We must not give the statutory words a wider meaning merely because on a narrower construction the words might leave a loophole for frauds against the revenue. If, on the proper construction of the section, that is the result, it is not for judges to attempt to cure it. That is the business of Parliament"; ibid. 383–84.

76. [1942] A.C. 206 (1941).

77. Heuston, "*Liversidge* v. *Anderson* in Retrospect" 33, 43.

78. "The principles of construction which apply in interpreting such a section are well established; the difficulty is to adapt well established principles to a particular case of difficulty. The golden rule is that the words of a statute must prima facie be given their ordinary meaning. We must not shrink from an interpretation which will reverse the previous law, for the purpose of a large part of our statute law is to make lawful that which would not be lawful without the statute, or conversely, to prohibit results which would otherwise follow. Judges are not called upon to apply their opinions of sound policy so as to modify the plain meaning of statutory words, but where, in construing general words the meaning of which is not entirely plain, there are adequate reasons for doubting whether the legislature could have been intending so wide an interpretation as would disregard fundamental principles, then we may be justified in adopting a narrower construction. At the same time, if the choice is between two interpretations, the narrower of which would fail to achieve the manifest purpose of the legislation, we should avoid a construction which

policies of acts than were almost all of his contemporaries.[79] He was by
no means incapable of reinterpreting the meaning of a statute through
the subtle use of the canons of construction[80] or by applying tests of
changed social conditions.[81] Yet his articulated views helped to crystallize the highly rarefied stance toward statutory interpretation adopted by
the law lords during the following period. In tax cases, for instance, his
subtle changes in interpretation convinced many that his judicial work
reflected his political fortunes. Under Churchill during the war, he refused
to take a technical approach to tax law[82] and pursued the policy that all
were under an obligation to pay their fair share.[83] Under the postwar
Labour administration, however, not only did Simon legislatively oppose
such measures as a profits tax, but, judicially, he returned to an approach
to tax law in keeping with the *Duke of Westminster*'s case—a position
that, in the long run, could help only the particularly affluent.[84] Indeed,

---

would reduce the legislation to futility and should rather accept the bolder construction
based on the view that Parliament would legislate only for the purpose of bringing about an
effective result"; *Nokes* v. *Doncaster Amalgamated Collieries, Ltd.*, [1940] A.C. 1014,
1022.

79. See, for example, *Hill* v. *William Hill Park Lane, Ltd.*, [1949] A.C. 530, 548 ff.

80. E.g., *Westminster Assessment Comm.* v. *Conservative Club*, [1944] A.C. 55, 60
(1943).

81. *Blyth (Mirrielee' Trustees)* v. *Lord Advocate*, [1945] A.C. 32 (Scot. 1944). The
question was whether a member of the Home Guard was a "common soldier" within the
meaning of the estate duty exemption in § 8(1) of the Finance Act of 1894. Although no
such body as the Home Guard existed in 1894, the House decided that the deceased fell
within the words of the statute and £64,000 of estate duty was excused.

82. E.g., in *Commissioners for General Purposes of Income Tax for City of London* v.
Gibbs, [1942] A.C. 402, 414 (1941), "It is these considerations which have made it necessary for me to look further into the statutory history and possible application of rule 9, not
because I have any doubt of the correctness of the proposition of English law as to the
nature of a partnership firm, but because our duty in construing a statute such as this is to
find out what the legislature must be taken to have really meant by the expressions which it
has used, without necessarily attributing to the legislature a precise appreciation of the
technical appropriateness of its language."

83. His main attack on the earlier approach was in *Latilla* v. *IRC*, [1943] A.C. 377,
381 (1942):

My Lords, of recent years much ingenuity has been expended in certain quarters in attempting to devise
methods of disposition of income by which those who were prepared to adopt them might enjoy the
benefits of residence in this country while receiving the equivalent of such income without sharing in the
appropriate burden of British taxation. Judicial dicta may be cited which point out that, however
elaborate and artificial such methods may be, those who adopt them are "entitled" to do so. There is, of
course, no doubt that they are within their legal rights, but that is no reason why their efforts, or those of
the professional gentlemen who assist them in the matter, should be regarded as a commendable exercise
of ingenuity or as a discharge of the duties of good citizenship.

84. E.g., *Russell (Inspector of Taxes)* v. *Scott*, [1948] A.C. 422 (N. Ire. 1948), where,
Simon noted, "I must add that the language of the rule is so obscure and so difficult to
expound with confidence that—without seeking to apply any different principle of construction to a Revenue Act than would be proper in the case of legislation of a different
kind—I feel that the taxpayer is entitled to demand that his liability to a higher charge
should be made out with reasonable clearness before he is adversely affected. In the present

several of the decisions that helped develop the new profession of tax planners came from the Simon pen.[85] Here, as elsewhere, the difference between Simon's articulated and actual positions threw doubt on his own distinction and a pall on the final appeal court.

Politically the approach worked. Following Simon's skill in deferring to the executive in matters of public law and that of Jowitt in refusing to give any hint that the slightest degree of judicial control might be exerted in private law, the House was able to avoid any serious weakening of its status during the postwar Labour administration. A strict approach to stare decisis at the turn of the century had been the Conservative's way of attempting to freeze the common law as it then existed—drawn, as Weber would have argued, largely in favor of those already in power. A similar mechanical approach to the common law was used in the 1940s and early 1950s in an effort to convince those in power (by this time a different group) that the judges were not doing anything of importance. Prestige was traded for power. Soon left-wing writers were heartily endorsing this asexual attitude. The wheel had indeed come full circle; the orthodox approach was fully established.

Lord Jowitt

The articulated position of Simon's regime was deliberately assumed as the official stance of the House by Jowitt when he became Chancellor in the Attlee government in 1945. Jowitt[86] was, in some ways, in a more difficult position than his predecessor. A right-wing member of the new Labour administration, he was faced by a group of political colleagues whose views may well have chilled his legal spine. No doubt recalling some of the decisions of the Court of Appeal in the 1930s and of the House of Lords earlier in the century, Aneurin Bevan made it quite clear that the new Labour government would allow no judicial sabotage of its

---

instance, this reasonable clearness is wanting"; ibid. 433. See also his speech in *Trinidad Petroleum Dev. Co.* v. *IRC*, [1946] 1 All E.R. 497 (H.L.), a case concerning the computation of excess profits under § 17(1) of the Finance Act (No. 2) of 1939. He announced, "We are not entitled to improve upon the section in order to produce what might seem a more just result: our duty is merely to interpret the words used"; ibid. 499.

85. "The liability of the subject under a taxing statute ought not to be arrived at by a course of subtle and sophisticated argument and, even in the case of the most learned judicial pronouncement, it is well to recognise that on rare occasions bonus dormitat Homerus"; *D'Avigdor-Goldsmid* v. *IRC*, [1953] A.C. 347, 362 (1952).

86. William Allen Jowitt; b. 1885; father, Anglican clergyman; educ., Marlborough, New College, Oxford; called to bar, 1909; K.C., 1922; M.P. (Lib.), Hartlepools, 1922–24, (Lab.) Preston, 1929–31, Ashton-under-Lyme, 1939–45; Attorney-General, 1929–32; Solicitor-General, 1940–42; Paymaster-General, 1942; Minister without Portfolio, 1942–44; Minister of National Insurance, 1944–45; Lord Chancellor, 1945–51; d. 1957; *Dictionary of National Biography 1951–1960*, at 562.

legislation.[87] Bevan[88] and many of the leading members of the new administration had little time for Jowitt, who was an alien in the Labour camp. Jowitt had left the Liberal party in 1929[89] to become the Labour Attorney-General and would have stayed on in the National Administration had he not been defeated in the ensuing election. Readmitted to the Labour party in 1936, he served as a minister in the National government during World War II and seemed a natural choice for Lord Chancellor in 1945. Yet he had little in common with the leading Labour supporters, and though he remained a member of the party until his death in 1957, he increasingly shared much of the skepticism about socialism of men like Hartley Shawcross. Indeed, Jowitt ranks as one of those lawyers who, while being Labour supporters, seemed to the outside world to be more conservative than many Conservative M.P.'s. He certainly gave the impression of being more devoted to the law than he was to socialism.

On the other hand, there is no doubt that Jowitt was a committed law reformer. The Austin Jones Committee on the County Courts and the Evershed Committees on Civil Procedure both originated during Jowitt's term. He was Chancellor at a time when Parliament abolished common employment, mitigated contributory negligence, and made it possible as of right to sue the Crown for civil wrongs.[90] He did not hesitate to abolish flogging,[91] and, although his sentiments may not have been felicitously expressed, he showed little of the customary reluctance to appoint enough judges to meet the demands of litigation.[92]

Yet it was with respect to the judiciary that Jowitt felt the greatest tension between his position as a lawyer and his position as a member of the Labour party. He told the American Bar Association that "perforce the most important task of all is when I have to appoint the judges"; and

87. Speech by Aneurin Bevan, 425 *Parl. Deb.*, H.L. (5th ser.), col. 1982 (23 July 1946).

88. When, in January 1943, Churchill appointed Jowitt as one of the three men charged with post-war planning, Bevan was less than charitable about the appointments. "They have entrusted further egg laying to a number of carefully selected and hopefully infertile hens"; Foot, *Aneurin Bevan* 408–9.

89. He was elected as a Liberal in 1929, but appeared to have few qualms about joining a Labour administration. His behavior caused intense resentment at the bar; *Dictionary of National Biography 1951–1960*, at 562.

90. On these reforms, see generally, Brian Abel-Smith and Robert Stevens, *Lawyers and the Courts* 247–56.

91. Although he remained an advocate of capital punishment during the Labour administration of 1945–51: "When the Criminal Justice Act was before this House, I was one of those who took the view and, I say quite frankly, advised behind the scenes, that we should insist upon the retention of capital punishment. All I say now is that the more I think about the matter, the more worried I become and the more uncertain I feel"; 185 *Parl. Deb.*, H.L. (5th ser.), cols. 149–50 (16 Dec. 1952).

92. "[I]t is far better to have extra judges even though on occasion they have to go and play a round of golf, than that Her Majesty's lieges should be kept waiting for justice in the law courts"; 190 ibid., cols. 47–48 (1 Dec. 1948).

he boasted that he had "never let political considerations weigh with me to the slightest degree in trying to get the fittest man," adding "I have never appointed, incidentally, a member of my own party."[93] While that may have impressed his American audience, it did not sit well with the members of his own party. An inherent hostility toward the High Court and appeal judges flourished in the Labour party and, while intellectually there was some opposition to appointing for political purposes and while the number of senior lawyers who were Labour supporters was limited, the idea that not any of the new appointees to the bench were socialists was upsetting. The rank and file harrassed Jowitt by refusing to increase judicial salaries[94] and, as the radicals had done with the earlier Liberal Chancellors Herschell and Loreburn,[95] Jowitt was given a hard time about the political balance on local benches of justices of the peace.[96]

Such conflicting pressures no doubt accounted for some of the strange inconsistencies Jowitt exhibited in his judicial role. He was particularly sensitive about the Labour party and "liberty"[97] and the Labour party and the Rule of Law.[98] At a personal level, he felt that morals and the criminal law should not necessarily overlap;[99] it was natural for him to assume that a clear line existed between law and policy.[100] It also seemed natural to him that certainty of doctrine inevitably led to predictability of

93. William Allen Jowitt, "Message from Britain" 177.

94. "[U]nless we promise a reasonable remuneration for our Judges, there is a danger that we may not recruit the right sort of man. . . . [I]f we are to have, as thank God we have had for many years, justice properly and well administered. . . . I honestly believe that justice is better administered in this country than in any other country in the world—we must draw the right sort of man"; 186 *Parl. Deb.*, H.L. (5th ser.), cols. 1023–24 (6 Apr. 1954). He also, of course, felt obliged to defend the judiciary against criticism. "Nothing annoys me more than for people to brush on one side the opinions of judges on any question of this sort by saying, 'Look what Ellenborough said. The judges have always been against any reform of the law.' That, of course is completely and farcically untrue"; 185 ibid., col. 150 (16 Dec. 1953).

95. Heuston, *Lives* 114–17, 153–58.

96. This led to the Royal Commission on the Justice of the Peace; *Report*, Cmd. 7463 (1948).

97. 177 *Parl. Deb.*, H.L. (5th ser.), col. 1227 (16 July 1952).

98. See especially his speech to the American Bar Association: "Never has there been a time when the rule of law has been more firmly entrenched in my country. Never has there been a time when the acts of the Executive are more completely subject to the opinions of an entirely independent judiciary"; Jowitt, "Message from Britain" 1178.

A Canadian audience was comforted with the thought that "[y]ou need have no worry but that an independent Bar will be preserved, and we shall continue to have a fair Press. We shall maintain the right to criticise and we shall maintain the principle of trial by jury. . . . I believe the task which confronts our legislature is to work out some kind of synthesis between a planned economy on the one hand, which for better or for worse, we are surely going to try, and the rights of the individual on the other hand"; William Allen Jowitt, "Address to Canadian Bar Association" 117.

99. See his speech when demanding the establishment of a committee on that "very great evil, homosexuality"; 187 *Parl. Deb.*, H.L. (5th ser.), cols. 745–46 (19 May 1954).

100. 177 ibid., col. 1227 (16 July 1952).

result. Accordingly, he was bitterly opposed to "flexibility," which he regarded as the antithesis of law. In 1953, for instance, he claimed that "the history of law has always been that in primitive society law tends to be and must be flexible. The magistrate sits as a Cadi under a palm tree and administers what he thinks is right and just; but, as system develops, the law tends to become less and less flexible." He also justified the growth of "fixed" rules in Equity as "an inevitable tendency in civilised society."[101]

In short, Jowitt put himself in the position of regarding substantive formalism as "the heir of all the ages past." Judges, as helpless pawns in some mechanical operation over which they had no control, were perceived as impartial and objective and, of necessity, independent. From this basic assumption it was not difficult to hold that the House never had the option to consider in which direction the law should move. This view was most forcefully stressed when, in Australia, Jowitt was asked what the House might do if *Candler* v. *Crane, Christmas and Company*[102] were appealed from the Court of Appeal. He answered:

I am in a somewhat delicate position because if *Candler's* Case did come up in the House of Lords I might find myself presiding, and therefore I do not desire to express any very definite opinion. However, I do want to tell you quite shortly how the House of Lords would proceed to consider that case, because it seems to me that some of the speeches today have completely lost sight of this. We should regard it as our duty to expound what we believe the law to be, and we should loyally follow the decisions of the House of Lords if we found there was some decision which we thought to be in point.

It is really not a question of being a bold or timorous soul; it is a much simpler question than that. You know there was a time when the earth was void and without form, but after these hundreds of years the law of England, the common law, has at any rate got some measure of form in it. We are really no longer in the position of Lord Mansfield who used to consider a problem and expound it *aequa et bona*—what the law ought to be—and it is a long time since Lord Hardwicke's time. . . .

I do most humbly suggest to some of the speakers to-day that the problem is not to consider what social and political conditions do today require; that is to confuse the task of the lawyer with the task of the legislator.

It is quite possible that the law has produced a result which does not accord with the requirements of today. If so, put it right by legislation, but do not expect every lawyer, in addition to all his other problems, to act as Lord Mansfield did, and decide what the law ought to be. He is far better employed if he puts himself

---

101. 185 ibid., col. 152 (16 Dec. 1953). Presumably his concern to codify the law (a concern that is endemic among Labour Lord Chancellors) was related to this: "One of the great points of consolidation ought to be not merely that the law may be found set out together in a convenient place, but that it may be so stated that, so long as he brings a reasonable mind to bear upon it, he who reads may understand what he is reading"; 190 ibid., col. 48 (1 Dec. 1954).

102. [1951] 2 K.B. 164 (C.A.). Effectively overruled by *Hedley Byrne & Co.* v. *Heller & Partners*, [1964] A.C. 465 (1963).

to the much simpler task of deciding what the law is. It may be that the law is that an innocent misrepresentation, altogether outside the field of contract, and altogether outside the field of statute, does give rise to a right of action. I express no opinion except to say that certainly our legislature did not seem to think so, because, if I remember rightly, legislation was expressly introduced to avoid some of the consequences of the *Derry v. Peek* decision. It may be that that is so, but please do not get yourself into the frame of mind of entrusting to the judges the working out of a whole new set of principles which does accord with the requirements of modern conditions. Leave that to the legislature, and leave us to confine ourselves to trying to find out what the law is. If this case does come to the House of Lords, if we examine it and discover that there is a case which is precisely in point, then whether we like the decision or whether we do not, whether we think it accords with modern requirements and conditions or whether we think it does not, we shall follow loyally the decision which has already been come to. In that way and that way only can we introduce some certainty into the law.[103]

Jowitt's acceptance of substantive formalism may have been as politically wise as it was intellectually unsatisfactory. This is particularly true if one bears in mind the attitudes displayed by many members of his own party toward the Lord Chancellor and his "patronage." How could his colleagues look on the judges with anything but favor when the judges did nothing but declare the law as it had always been, when the judiciary decided solely legal issues and eschewed political or policy decisions. No Labour M.P. could take umbrage when the bench based its decisions solely on the letter of some statute or the logic of the common law —representing, as they did, nothing but an objective, impartial legal analysis, untrammeled by any difficulties (or discretion) represented by the open-textured nature of language, or any inarticulate premises underlying the decision-making process. Although such a position may have been politically sound, practically it destroyed the rationale of the final appeal.

Strangely enough, there is little evidence of Jowitt's own inclinations in handling appellate work. He sat in a few leading cases in both final appeal courts.[104] The extensive legislative program of the Attlee administration might have made it difficult for Jowitt to sit regularly for appeal work in any event, but one of the lasting effects of World War II was that the Lords' chamber. In 1948, the noise caused by repairing the Palace of Westminster forced the law lords to move from the chamber to a committime available for judicial work of the House, which was still carried on in the Lords' chamber. In 1948, the noise caused by repairing the Palace of Westminster forced the law lords to move from the chamber to a commit-

103. W. K. Fullagar, "Liability for Representatives at Common Law" 296.

104. See, for instance, his judgment upholding Canada's right to abolish appeals to the Privy Council; *Attorney-General for Ontario* v. *Attorney-General for Canada*, [1947] A.C. 127 (P.C. 1946).

tee room. This led to the establishment of an Appellate Committee,[105] a move, incidentally, that was vigorously opposed by Simon.[106] The net effect of the change, however, was that, since the House might now sit concurrently in its legislative and judicial capacities—after 1948 judgment being given only in the chamber itself—the Lord Chancellor had to choose between presiding as Speaker of the House and his judicial functions. Jowitt and most of his successors opted for the Speakership.

Thus Jowitt had little opportunity to show his talents in operating substantive formalism. During his Chancellorship he delivered two judgments in family law matters that froze existing patterns. In *Baxter* v. *Baxter*,[107] he refused to hold that a marriage had not been consummated when birth control devices had been used and, in *Weatherley* v. *Weatherley*,[108] he held that, so long as cohabitation continued, a refusal to have sexual intercourse did not amount to constructive desertion. Yet despite his claim that sitting as a judge was the duty "which interests me most,"[109] most of Jowitt's significant appeals were heard in the last few months of his life, not only after Labour had lost office, but also after he had ceased to be active as an opposition spokesman.[110]

Despite all the assumptions of substantive formalism, in at least two of the cases in which Jowitt took part, it can be argued that there was an unsatisfactory excess of judicial legislation. Jowitt presided in *Joyce* v. *Director of Public Prosecutions*, in which he had some difficulty reconciling his articulated statements about the judicial process with his inclination to extend the definition of treason and to uphold "Lord Haw-Haw's" conviction. "It is not for His Majesty's judges to create new offences or to extend any penal law and particularly the law of high treason, but new conditions may demand a reconsideration of the scope of the principle. It is not an extension of a penal law to apply its principle to circumstances unforeseen at the time of its enactment, so long as the case is fairly brought within its language."[111]

Jowitt also presided in another notable example of judicial legisla-

105. To be distinguished from the Appeals Committee, which hears petitions for leave to appeal and petitions to bring in forma pauperis proceedings.

106. Louis Blom-Cooper and Gavin Drewry, *Final Appeal* 111–12.

107. [1948] A.C. 274, 290 (1947). See L. C. B. Gower, "Baxter v. Baxter in Perspective" 176.

108. [1947] A.C. 628.

109. "Note," 30 *Canadian Bar Association Journal* 109, 115 (1948).

110. E.g., the 1956 *Appeal Cases* report him sitting in *British Transp. Comm'n* v. *Gourley*, (at 185), *Esso Petroleum Co.* v. *Southport Corp.* (at 218), *Institute of Fuel* v. *Morley* (at 245), and *Attorney-General* v. *Parsons* (at 421). All these cases were decided in 1955.

111. *Joyce* v. *DPP*, [1946] A.C. 347, 366 (1945). See "Note," 62 *Law Quarterly Review* 105 (1946). See also J. A. Cole, *Lord Haw-Haw and William Joyce*, chaps. 31 and 32.

tion, *British Transport Commission* v. *Gourley*,[112] in which the House held that income tax payments had to be taken into account when assessing damages in tort. In that case Jowitt was forced to admit that "[i]t is a strange fact that until 1933 the question whether the tax position of the injured person should be taken into account in assessing damages had, so far as I can ascertain, never been raised."[113] Ultimately, even Jowitt had to consider the underlying policy issue—at least in a general way—for he concluded, "My Lords, I agree with Lord Simon in thinking that to ignore the tax element at the present day would be to act in a manner which is out of touch with reality."[114] This decision in *Gourley*, many would argue, was even more out of touch with reality in that it arbitrarily reduced damages awarded in negligence cases—damages that, it was felt, were already calculated without sufficient precision and without reflecting the "real" costs of accidents. It was not self-evident that substantive formalism either prevented judicial legislation or made it more rational.

Jowitt had the problem of persuading Labour M.P.'s, especially those of the Left, that no further power should be taken away from the judges or the regular courts. In large part he succeeded. Although the National Insurance (Industrial Injuries) Act of 1946 put an end to the old system of workmen's compensation and lawyers were effectively not involved in its successor system, the profession successfully lobbied to allow workmen to continue to pursue whatever claims they might also have at common law. While much other new "social" legislation excluded recourse to the courts, normally giving such disputes as there were to tribunals, the day-to-day work of lawyers was not affected except in the sense that, after the establishment of legal aid, in economic terms the central government was subsidizing the private practice of law. In this regard, Jowitt was regarded as highly successful in protecting the judiciary and the profession.

Lord Simonds

Simonds, who was Chancellor for the first three years of the Churchill administration, should have been in theory under no such political restraints. During his six years in opposition, Churchill had railed against the use of tribunals and the exclusion of the courts from supervision of new social programs. Once in office, however, Churchill was primarily interested in foreign matters. The preeminence of tribunals was con-

---

112. [1956] A.C. 185 (1955); and see Olive Stone, "The Tax Element in Damages Reconsidered" 334.

113. *British Transp. Comm'n* v. *Gourley*, [1956] A.C. 185, 198 (1955).

114. Ibid. 203.

tinued by the new Tory technocrats who ran domestic policy in what the *Economist* called the spirit of "Butskillism," suggesting that there was not much difference between Butler and Gaitskell.[115] The technocrats still appeared to be in power, and despite the murmurings on the Right, Churchill showed his only real interest in the judges when he agreed to increase their salaries.[116] Accordingly, in his search for a Lord Chancellor, Churchill showed scant originality. He offered the job first to one Lord of Appeal, Asquith, for the rather insubstantial reason that Churchill had served in Asquith's father's cabinet. When Asquith refused, Churchill then offered the post to another law lord, Simonds, whom the Prime Minister had never met and probably had never heard of, and whom his successor as Lord Chancellor, Kilmuir, described as being as innocent of politics as "a newly baptised baby."[117] Simonds' choice to continue the technocratic device of substantive formalism could thus be explained partly as a function of the political atmosphere and partly as the result of personal necessity.

Simonds,[118] however, did not merely maintain substantive formalism; he elevated it to new levels. Indeed, he became the High Priest of the new orthodoxy. In this respect, his contribution was more important than those of either of his predecessors during the period. Not only was he more intellectually impressive than Jowitt and more personally attractive than Simon, but also, in addition to his prestige as Lord Chancellor,[119] he had been (and would be again) an active Lord of Appeal—and a particularly powerful one—from 1944 until his retirement in 1962. During the time that the House was dominated by Simonds, its purpose, intellectually and practically, remained the preservation of the status quo.

Some of Simonds' positions were articulated with the greatest vigor when they were beginning to be challenged, toward the end of his tenure as a Lord of Appeal, primarily by Denning who by the early 1950s was rising to dominate the Court of Appeal. When Denning sought to embrace the mischief rule of interpretation and suggested that appeal courts should look to the purpose of legislation when a lacuna was discovered, Simonds was beside himself:[120]

115. Arthur Marwick, *Britain in the Century of Total War* 373–74.

116. To enable them "to maintain a modest but dignified way of life suited to the gravity, and indeed the majesty, of the duties they discharge"; 525 *Parl. Deb.*, H.C. (5th ser.), col. 1063 (23 Mar. 1954).

117. *Political Adventures* 194.

118. Gavin Turnbull Simonds; b. 1881; educ., Winchester, New College, Oxford (First, "Greats"); called to bar, 1906; K.C., 1924; Judge, Chancery Division, 1937–44; Lord of Appeal, 1944–51, 1954–62; Lord Chancellor, 1951–54; d. 1971.

119. While he held the office of Lord Chancellor (1951–56), he rarely sat judicially.

120. "[T]he criticism which I venture to make of the judgement of the learned Lord Justice is not directed at the conclusion that he reached. . . . But it is on the approach of the

The part which is played in the judicial interpretation of a statute by reference to the circumstances of its passing is too well known to need restatement: it is sufficient to say that the general proposition that it is the duty of the court to find out the intention of Parliament—and not only of Parliament but of Ministers also—cannot by any means be supported. The duty of the court is to interpret the words that the legislature has used; those words may be ambiguous, but, even if they are, the power and duty of the court to travel outside them on a voyage of discovery are strictly limited. . . . What the legislature has not written, the court must not write. This proposition, which restates in a new form the view expressed by the Lord Justice . . . cannot be supported. It appears to me to be a naked usurpation of the legislative function under the thin disguise of interpretation. And it is the less justifiable when it is guess work with what material the legislature would, if it had discovered the gap, have filled it in. If a gap is disclosed, the remedy lies in an amending Act.[121]

It was also Denning,[122] in one of his moves to expand the rights of third-party beneficiaries, who spurred Simonds to a vigorous restatement of the role of the House in common law appeals. After quoting Haldane's dictum that English law "knows nothing of a *jus quaesitum tertii* arising

---

Lord Justice to what is a question of construction and nothing else that I think it desirable to make some comment; for at a time when so large a proportion of the cases that are brought before the courts depend on the construction of modern statutes it would not be right for this House to pass unnoticed the propositions which the learned Lord Justice lays down for the guidance of himself and presumably of others"; *Magor & St. Mellons RDC v. Newport Corp.*, [1952] A.C. 189, 190 (1951).

    121. Ibid. 191.
    For a further restatement of the "natural meaning" approach to statutory interpretation by Simonds, see *George Wimpey & Co. v. British Overseas Airways Corp.*, [1955] A.C. 169 (1954).
    For a clash between the two approaches, see *Galloway v. Galloway*, [1956] A.C. 299 (1955), where in a divorce proceeding, a wife was seeking custody of an illegitimate child born before her marriage to the respondent. The lower courts held that they had no jurisdiction to award custody to her since the word "children" in § 26(1) of the Matrimonial Causes Act of 1950 must be presumed to mean only legitimate children. The majority of the House (Oaksey, Radcliffe, and Tucker) held that it meant all children. Simonds, dissenting with Cohen, could accept only the historical meaning. Simonds continued:

The common law of England did not contemplate illegitimacy and, shutting its eyes to the facts of life, described an illegitimate child as "filius nullius." This prima facie meaning may in certain circumstances be displaced and a wider meaning given to the words, and it is said that those circumstances are present if the wider meaning is more consonant with the policy of the statute in which the words are found. . . . This is not, I think, an entirely happy phrase, for it appears to suggest that the court begins its consideration of the statute with an impartial mind towards either meaning. It is, moreover, capable of leading and, I think, has led the court to find the policy of the Act in its own predilections of a later age rather than in the provisions of the Act itself. [Ibid. 310–11]

    122. For examples of other disputes with Denning, note the disagreement over the basis of frustration. Denning was an advocate of the "just and equitable" approach, Simonds a rather stern advocate of the "implied term" theory. See *British Movietonews, Ltd. v. London & Dist. Cinemas, Ltd.*, [1952] A.C. 166, 188 (1951); *Davis Contractors, Ltd. v. Fareham UDC*, [1956] A.C. 696, 715–16. See also Simonds' horror at the idea that, in a hire-purchase case, "there is a general principle of equity which justifies the court in relieving a party to any bargain if in the event it operates hardly against him"; *Bridge v. Campbell Discount Co.*, [1962] A.C. 600, 614.

by way of contract," Simonds evaluated the invitation to overrule the earlier principle:

> To that invitation I readily respond. For to me heterodoxy, or, as some might say, heresy, is not the more attractive because it is dignified by the name of reform. Nor will I easily be led by an undiscerning zeal for some abstract kind of justice to ignore our first duty, which is to administer justice according to law, the law which is established for us by Act of Parliament or the binding authority of precedent. The law is developed by the application of old principles to new circumstances. Therein lies its genius. Its reform by the abrogation of these principles is the task not of the courts of law but of Parliament. . . . I would cast no doubt upon the doctrine of stare decisis, without which law is at hazard.[123]

In view of the conflicting posturing about stability and certainty that surrounds the appeals system in England and to some extent in all countries that make use of the common law, it is easy to dismiss such statements as mere rhetoric. There is, however, considerable evidence that Simonds sought to effect the theory that he espoused. Perhaps the most extreme example of this was *Jacobs* v. *London County Council*,[124] where the plaintiff claimed she was an invitee. Statements made by some of the law lords in an earlier case[125] indicated that in such circumstances she would be a licensee. Despite the fact that for many years judges had assumed such earlier statements were obiter,[126] Simonds was quite clear as to what should happen. "There is in my opinion no justification for regarding as obiter dictum a reason given by a judge for his decision, because he has given another reason also. If it were a proper test to ask whether the decision would have been the same apart from the proposition alleged to be obiter then a case which ex facie decided two things would decide nothing."[127] He continued, "As I have already said, I recognise that the dividing line is difficult to draw, but it would, I think, be to deny the importance, I would say the paramount importance, of certainty in the law to give less than coercive effect to the unequivocal statement of the law made after argument by the members of this House

123. *Midland Silicones, Ltd.* v. *Scruttons, Ltd.*, [1962] A.C. 446, 467–69 (1961).

124. [1950] A.C. 361, 368.

125. *Fairman* v. *Perpetual Inv. Bldg. Soc'y*, [1923] A.C. 74 (1922).

126. E.g., Lord Justice Scott in *Haseldine* v. *C. A. Daw & Son*, [1941] 1 K.B. 343 (C.A.).

127. "It is not, I think, always easy to determine how far, when several issues are raised in a case and a determination of any one of them is decisive in favour of one or other of the parties, the observations upon other issues are to be regarded as obiter. That is the inevitable result of our system. For while it is the primary duty of a court of justice to dispense justice to litigants, it is its traditional role to do so by the means of an exposition of the relevant law. Clearly, such a system must be somewhat flexible, with the result that in some cases judges may be criticised for diverging into expositions which could by no means be regarded as relevant to the dispute between the parties; in others critics may regret that an opportunity has been missed for making an oracular pronouncement upon some legal problem which has long vexed the profession"; *Jacobs* v. *LCC*, [1950] A.C. 361, 368–69.

in *Fairman*'s case. Nor, perhaps I may add, are your Lordships entitled to disregard such a statement because you would have the law otherwise. To determine what the law is, not what it ought to be, is our present task."[128] It should come as no surprise that although Simon had still maintained that the Privy Council was "not absolutely bound by previous decisions of the Board,"[129] Simonds took the view that, for practical purposes, stare decisis was as "effective in the Privy Council as it is in the House of Lords."[130]

No doubt Simonds' judicial technique, which generally led to the freezing of the status quo, produced an outcome that was politically attractive to him. Where his policy preferences were clear, they almost uniformly fell on the conservative side of the spectrum.[131] For example, Simonds felt no political discomfort when, as a result of his years of dominance, any serious concept of public law in England was finally extinguished. His view of the role of the judiciary made it essential for him to accept the law-policy dichotomy propounded by the Committee on Ministers' Powers;[132] he was shocked when Denning suggested that quasi estoppel might apply to a government department;[133] he saw nothing wrong with the Simon view of Crown privilege;[134] and he was only too anxious to keep the courts entirely out of the process of supervising executive procedures, even if mala fides were involved.[135] While he paid

---

128. Ibid. 373. On this decision, and critical of Simonds, see Arthur L. Goodhart, "The 'I Think' Doctrine of Precedent" 374.

129. *Attorney-General for Ontario* v. *Canadian Temperance Ass'n*, [1946] A.C. 193, 206 (P.C. 1945).

130. *Bakhshuwen* v. *Bakhshuwen*, [1952] A.C. 1, 11 (P.C. 1951).

131. On the hand, Simonds also opposed the reintroduction of corporal punishment as "panic legislation, a step backward over 130 years"; 178 *Parl. Deb.*, H.L. (5th ser.), col. 907 (22 Oct. 1952).

132. E.g., *Labour Relations Bd. of Saskatchewan* v. *John East Iron Works, Ltd.*, [1949] A.C. 134, 149 (P.C. 1948).

133. *Howell* v. *Falmouth Boat Constr. Co.*, [1951] A.C. 837, 845. Denning, in the Court of Appeal, had sought to weaken the *Amphitrite* doctrine, which basically allowed the Crown to break any executory contract with impunity, in a series of cases beginning with *Robertson* v. *Minister of Pensions*, [1949] 1 K.B. 227 (1948).

134. "Nobody who had had any judicial experience would quarrel with the view that it is not for the Judge but for the Minister ultimately to decide whether or not it is in the public interest that documents should be disclosed"; 146 *Parl. Deb.*, H.L. (5th ser.), col. 932 (31 Mar. 1947).

135. *Smith* v. *East Elloe RDC*, [1956] A.C. 736, 750–51:

My Lords, I think that anyone bred in the tradition of the law is likely to regard with little sympathy legislative provisions for ousting the jurisdiction of the Court, whether in order that the subject may be deprived altogether of remedy or in order that his grievance may be remitted to some other tribunal. But it is our plain duty to give the words of an Act their proper meaning and, for my part, I find it quite impossible to qualify the words of the paragraph in the manner suggested. It may be that the legislature had not in mind the possibility of an order being made by a local authority in bad faith or even the possibility of an order made in good faith being mistakenly, capriciously or wantonly challenged. This is a matter of speculation. [Ibid.]

lip service to civil liberties,[136] he was not ready to see the courts seriously involved in their protection.[137]

In private law, his penchant for the established order was clear from the first. One week after he was appointed a law lord Simonds was sitting in the *Diplock* case,[138] and the speech he gave there set the tone of his judicial career. He had no doubt that a testator, in requiring executors to use the residue of his estate for "charitable or benevolent" purposes, had failed to establish a valid charitable gift. Benevolent was not a "term of art," and he could not treat the word "or" conjunctively rather than disjunctively. Benevolent purposes might be noncharitable ones and, therefore, the bequest could not take advantage of the immunity accorded to charities[139] with respect to uncertainty of objects. The estate thus passed to a distant relative of whom the testator had never heard, rather than to the charities that he had intended.[140] While Simonds accepted that the objects Caleb Diplock had wanted were clear, he had not achieved this by "the plain meaning of the testator's words."[141] Simonds'

136. "My Lords, the liberty of the subject and the convenience of the police or any other executive authority are not to be weighted in the scales against each other. This case will have served a useful purpose if it enables your Lordships once more to proclaim that a man is not to be deprived of his liberty except in due course and process of law"; *Christie* v. *Leachinsky*, [1947] A.C. 573, 595 (1946).

137. In a criminal case, he dissented in favor of upholding the conviction; the majority felt that the prosecution had not fully proved its case. See *DPP* v. *Head*, [1959] A.C. 83, 96 (1958), where the other members of the House agreed that the Court of Criminal Appeal had rightly quashed a conviction of a man accused of having carnal knowledge of a mental defective, when there was no evidence in the certificates that she was a moral defective.

Simonds saw no reason to expand the court's supervision of extradition and deportation proceedings. See, e.g., *Zacharia* v. *Republic of Cyprus*, [1963] A.C. 634, 655 (1962) (dissenting on whether there was jurisdiction for the House to hear appeals under the Fugitive Offenders Act of 1881).

138. *Chichester Diocesan Fund & Bd. of Fin., Inc.* v. *Simpson*, [1944] A.C. 341, 362.

139. One cannot but admire Simonds' clarity. "The question is whether, in the context in which they are found in this will, these words give to the executors a choice of objects extending beyond that which the law recognises as charitable. If they do not that is the end of the matter. The trust is a good charitable trust. If they do, it appears to be conceded by counsel for the appellant institution that the trust is invalid"; (ibid. 368).

140. When Simonds talked of "effect," he meant the effect of the meaning in law, not the practical effects of the decision. He refused to consider as relevant the fact that all the money had already been distributed to charitable institutions. "Equally irrelevant are the facts which are brought to your Lordships' attention that the estate is a large one, that the next-of-kin are not near relatives, that the discovery of a possible flaw in the will was fortuitous and that the proceedings were belated. The construction of this will is the same, whether its invalidity brings an unexpected windfall to distant relations or its validity disappoints the reasonable hopes of a dependent family"; ibid. 367.

141. "For I approach this will, as I approach any other will, with the resolve to find the testator's intention from the language that he has used. When I have found it, I consider its effect. If there is an ambiguity, it may be that I am at liberty to choose that construction which will give legal effect to the instrument rather than that which will invalidate it. Where the testator's words would, if no question of invalidity arose, leave no doubt in my mind, I am not at liberty to create an ambiguity in order then to place what is sometimes called a benignant construction on the will"; ibid. 367–68.

position was so unshakable that he purported to be dismayed by the argument the Attorney-General had addressed to the House.[142] To Simonds the resort to the intent of the testator was near to intellectual treason, while a suggested change in the law implied a resort to an analysis of the effects of such changes in practice, to a reexamination of earlier authorities, and even to a consideration of the basic policy involved. All this was beyond the province of the House sitting in its judicial capacity.[143] Thus when, during a legislative debate in the House some years later, Denning attacked the House's handling of *Diplock*, alleging that it had all sprung from a typist's error, Simonds responded to the charge, defending the decision warmly.[144] Substantive formalism was at the core of the Simonds approach.

In terms of both style and substance, it comes as no surprise that, with respect to tax law, Simonds led the return to the high formalism of the prewar period as represented by the *Duke of Westminster*'s case after the more balanced "patriotic" viewpoint used during the years of World War II. He was not amused by the attempts of the Finance Acts of 1938 to counter various tax avoidance devices

142. "My Lords, it may not have come as so rude a shock to some of your Lordships as it did to me to hear it suggested that there could be any doubt but that it is utterly invalid, but, in fact, the learned Attorney-General, if I understood his argument, categorically invited your Lordships to hold that a bequest for charitable or benevolent objects simpliciter is in English law a good and effective bequest, and urged that *In re Jarman's Estate* which decided the contrary be overruled"; ibid. 370.

143. The principle involved was taken to its logical conclusion in *Minister of Health* v. *Simpson*, [1951] A.C. 251 (1950), where the House held that the next of kin had a claim in equity against the residuary beneficiaries when they had exhausted their remedy against the personal representatives. The only speech was by Simonds, the other law lords merely concurring. He refused to restrict the remedies of the next-of-kin. "[I]t would be a strange thing if the Court of Chancery, having taken upon itself to see that the assets of a deceased person were duly administered, was deterred from doing justice to creditor, legatee or next of kin because the executor had done him wrong under a mistake of law. If in truth this were so, I think that the Father of Equity would not recognise his child"; ibid. 270.

144. See debate on the Charities Bill of 1960; 222 *Parl. Deb.*, H.L. (5th ser.), cols. 530–35 (31 Mar. 1960). Judicially, Simonds continued his domination of the Lords' thinking in the law of charities. Indeed, Simonds dominated the field of charity law for 20 years. His general attitude, as has already been seen, was to limit the scope of charity, as in *Oppenheim* v. *Tobacco Sec. Trust Co.*, [1951] A.C. 297, 307 (1950), whether he was considering the desirability of vivisection or the efficacy of prayer; *Gilmour* v. *Coats*, [1949] A.C. 426, 446. As the composition of the House changed, his approach to the different issues of charity appeared to become increasingly arid. See, for instance, *Institution of Mechanical Eng'rs* v. *Cane*, [1961] A.C. 696, 707 (1960), where he insisted that the purposes of an organization must be deduced solely from the words in the charter. Cf. the speeches of Denning (ibid. 723–24), Radcliffe (ibid. 719), Simonds (ibid. 708), and Reid (ibid. 713–18). But Simonds remained faithful to his basic policies even if he was prepared to see some rationalization. E.g., *IRC* v. *Badderley*, [1955] A.C. 572, 583 (1954): "To determine, whether the privileges, now considerable, which are accorded to charity in its legal sense, are to be granted or refused in a particular case, is often a matter of great nicety, and I think that this House can perform no more useful function in this branch of the law than to discourage a further excess of refinement where already so many fine distinctions have been made."

because the ways of those who would avoid liability to tax are often devious and obscure, the Sections are framed in language of the widest and most general scope, and in the case of one of the Acts ... the operative Subsections are reinforced by a provision which appears to exhort the assessing authority, and presumably the Court, to let the balance, wherever possible, be weighted against the taxpayer. But, this notwithstanding, I think that it remains the taxpayer's privilege to claim exemption from tax unless his case is fairly brought within the words of the taxing section.[145]

He repeatedly took the position that it was not part of the House's duty to help the Crown collect revenue for "a transaction which, had the legislature thought of it, would have been covered by appropriate words."[146] Similarly, in *Potts' Executors* v. *Inland Revenue Commissioners*, Simonds was unconcerned when he allowed tax on settlements to be avoided by arranging for a company to make advances, pointedly adding, "It was kindly urged by learned counsel for the respondents that if this appeal is allowed, an easy way of evading tax will be open to the taxpayer. This is an argument which is of no weight whatever. The question is what is the fair meaning of the words in a taxing statute."[147] Form had to prevail over substance.[148]

The Simonds approach would have been readily intelligible if any danger of allowing the Revenue a discretionary power to tax had existed. The situation was, however, far from that. While Simonds talked of the "fair meaning," the approach in fact required not that the government prove that on a "fair meaning" of the words the transaction should be taxed; but instead the government had the much harsher burden of showing that exact words in the statute covered the specific form of the transaction.[149] If the courts refused to look at the purpose and policy of the transaction or even to reason from analogy, the chance of "hitting"

145. *Vestey's Executors* v. *IRC*, 31 Tax Cas. 1, 80 (H.L. 1949).

146. "It was urged that the construction that I favour leaves an easy loophole through which the evasive taxpayer may find escape. That may be so, but I will repeat what has been said before. It is not the function of a court of law to give to words a strained and unnatural meaning because only thus will a taxing section apply to a transaction which, had the Legislature thought of it, would have been covered by appropriate words"; *Wolfson* v. *IRC*, 31 Tax Cas. 141, 169 (H.L. 1949).

147. [1951] A.C. 443, 452 (1950).

148. "I am not in the construction of such a statute, entitled to say that, because the legal or business result is the same whether on the one hand I borrow money from the company and with it make certain payments, or on the other hand the company at my request makes certain payments on my implied promise to repay, therefore it is immaterial what words are in the statute if that result is attained. The answer must be found according to the ordinary fair meaning of the words"; ibid. 455.

149. On this see, for instance, *Russell* v. *Scott*, [1948] A.C. 422, 433–34 (N. Ire. 1948): "My Lords, there is a maxim of income tax law which, though it may sometimes be overstressed, yet ought not to be forgotten. It is that the subject is not to be taxed unless the words of the taxing statute unambiguously impose the tax upon him. It is necessary that this maxim should on occasion be reasserted and this is such an occasion. . . . For it appears

the form rather than the substance of the transaction was limited. It is difficult not to conclude that Simonds derived some pleasure from his intellectual devices for thwarting the Crown's efforts to collect taxes from the wealthy. In the *Ayrshire* case, for instance, he concluded, "It is at least clear what is the gap that is intended to be filled and hardly less clear how it is intended to fill that gap. Yet, I can come to no other conclusion than that the language of the section fails to achieve its apparent purpose and I must decline to insert words or phrases which might succeed where the draftsmen failed."[150] One of the law lords of the 1970s later described this as "the high-water mark of the narrow semantic approach."[151]

Throughout his long career, Simonds did not seem to waiver in his attitudes.[152] Butskillite tax reform was eviscerated. When Parliament tried to stop the more scandalous aspects of dividend stripping, Simonds helped muster a majority to undermine the legislation. "[I]t appears to me to be wholly immaterial, so long as the transaction is not a sham . . . what may be the fiscal result or the ulterior fiscal object of the transaction."[153] His reluctance to deviate from the exact wording of legislation remained as strong as ever,[154] but nevertheless Simonds did not always find for the taxpayer. His method of rigid interpretation forced him to give some victories to the Revenue,[155] but at times it looked as if he took pains in impeding the work of the commissioners.[156] Worst of all, he gave the

to me that here is a case in which the subject is entitled to say that the words of the section under which it is sought to tax him do not do so with the clarity which the subject matter demands."

See also *St. Aubyn* v. *Attorney-General*, [1952] A.C. 15, 32 (1951):

Lord Halsbury adds that in a Taxing Act it is impossible to assume any intention or governing purpose in the Acts to do more than take such tax as the statute imposes: it must be seen whether the tax is expressly imposed. This is true doctrine which I must bear in mind as I listen to the constant refrain of learned counsel for the Crown that this or that is just the transaction at which this or that section is aimed. The question is not at what transaction the section is, according to some alleged general purpose, aimed but what transaction its language, according to its natural meaning, fairly and squarely hits. [Ibid. 32]

150. [1946] 1 All E.R. 637, 641 (H.L., Scot. 1945).
151. Kenneth Diplock, *The Courts as Legislators* 10.
152. Perhaps it is possible to detect a different approach where the taxation of foreign income was involved. See, for example, *Countess of Kenmare* v. *IRC*, [1958] A.C. 267, 276 (1957), and *Collco Dealings, Ltd.* v. *IRC*, [1962] A.C. 1, 19, (1961).
153. *Griffiths* v. *J. P. Harrison (Watford), Ltd.*, [1963] A.C. 1, 12 (1962). See the powerful dissents by Reid (ibid. 12) and Denning (ibid. 17).
154. Ambiguity was given a restricted meaning; *Kirkness* v. *John Hudson & Co.*, [1955] A.C. 696, 705.
155. E.g., *IRC* v. *Rolls-Royce, Ltd.*, [1962] 1 W.L.R. 425 (H.L.).
156. See *Public Trustee* v. *IRC*, [1960] A.C. 398, 415 (1959), suggesting that the Revenue authorities had caused confusion by sometimes relying on Macnaghten's dictum and sometimes opposing it. On the use of the commissioner's powers, see *Edwards* v. *Bairstow (Inspector of Taxes)*, [1956] A.C. 14, 32 (1955).

impression that tax interpretation was a game and that he saw nothing wrong or discreditable in involving the judicial process in the sport.[157]

In terms of looking at the basic Simonds approach, another provocative area for analysis was presented by those cases involving the protection of workers. Simonds certainly did not share the hostility to workers that, for example, motivated Atkinson, but he refused to take the position that Atkin and Wright, among others, had adopted, which assumed that workmen's compensation[158] and factory legislation should be read in the light of the original purpose of the legislation, namely, the protection of workmen. In the area of the Factories Act, Simonds announced, ex cathedra, in *Nicholls v. F. Austin (Leyton), Limited*, that "[t]he fence is intended to keep the worker out, not to keep the machine or its product in."[159] That remark was to cause considerable hardship; once let loose, it was a hare that could not be captured.[160]

In common law negligence cases, Simonds was an inglorious dissenter in *Paris v. Stepney Borough Council*.[161] He held that an employer owed no special duty to a one-eyed employee to provide and ensure the use of goggles, and, with the remainder of the House, Simonds held that the employer in *Davie v. New Merton Board Mills, Limited*[162] had discharged his duty by purchasing from a reliable source the tool that caused the injury. In *Lister v. Romford Ice and Cold Storage Company*[163] Simonds' decision, allowing the employer's insurance company to recover damages for the employee's negligent driving from the employee on the

---

157. "But this [argument based on the scheme of the Acts] is a principle which can easily be pressed too far in the consideration of a body of legislation such as that now under review, in which, if any prevailing motive can be found, it is in the attempt, as each loophole for escape from taxation is discovered, to close it as firmly as possible"; *Fendoch Inv. Trust Co. v. IRC*, 27 Tax Cas. 53, 68 (H.L. 1945).

No discussion of Simonds' attitude on tax would be complete without a mention of *Chapman v. Chapman*, [1954] A.C. 429, where the House (including Simonds) held that the Chancery Division judges, who had long been varying trusts in favor of infant beneficiaries to avoid taxes and were claiming an inherent power in the court to do this even if there was no power in the trust instrument, were held to have no such authority. Simonds, however, strongly supported the Variation of Trusts Act, which overruled *Chapman v. Chapman*. In the debates on the legislation he suggested that the bill contain a clause specifically allowing the courts to sanction tax avoidance schemes—"an object from which I, for one, do not dissent in any way"; 210 *Parl. Deb.*, H.L. (5th ser.), col. 377 (30 June 1958).

158. See his speech in one of the last of the workmen's compensation cases; *Railway Executive v. Culkin*, [1950] 2 All E.R. 637, 638 (H.L.).

See also his refusal to encourage alternative remedies under workmen's compensation; *Young v. Bristol Aeroplane Co.*, [1946] A.C. 163, 192 (1945).

159. [1946] A.C. 493, 505.

160. Similarly, Simonds did not share the earlier enthusiasm for curbing common employment. E.g., *Alexander v. Tredegar Iron & Coal Co.*, [1945] A.C. 286, 302 (1944).

161. [1951] A.C. 367, 374 (1950).

162. [1959] A.C. 604, 617 (1958).

163. [1957] A.C. 555 (1956). See K. W. Wedderburn, *The Worker and the Law* 71–72.

ground of breach of an implied term of a contract of employment, was made in the absence of any overt discussion of the insurance implications. In *Davie*, Simonds vigorously protested the suggestion that the insurance situation and implications should be taken into account;[164] in *Lister*, in almost Victorian tones, Simonds justified his position that the House should uphold the sanction of the law on the rationale that it would force employees to perform their duties carefully[165]—an argument that, taken to its logical conclusion, might well hold most contracts of insurance to be contrary to public policy.

To dismiss Simonds' attitude toward worker protection in purely class terms would not be accurate, for he was opposed to the extension of liability in many areas of tort.[166] Normally, this premise remained inarticulate since its purpose could be served by the rigorous application of substantive formalism, which ensured the application of a policy of status quo.[167] Yet occasionally the premise became articulate. This occurred most obviously in Simonds' Privy Council decision in the *Wagon Mound*. There the Judicial Committee made a valiant effort to restore foresee-

164. "I will only say that this is not a consideration to which your Lordships should give any weight at all in your determination of the rights and obligations of the parties. The legislature has thought fit in some circumstances to impose an absolute obligation upon employers. The Factories Acts and the elaborate regulations made under them testify to the care with which the common law has been altered, adjusted and refined in order to give protection and compensation to the workman. It is not the function of a court of law to fasten upon the fortuitous circumstance of insurance to impose a greater burden on the employer than would otherwise lie upon him"; [1959] A.C. 604, 627 (1958).

165. In fairness to Simonds, under different fencing provisions, in *John Summers & Sons v. Frost*, he held that "it appears to me to be an illegitimate method of interpretation of a statute, whose dominant purpose is to protect the workman, to introduce by implication words of which the effect must be to reduce that protection"; [1955] A.C. 740, 751.

Similarly, he was sympathetic to the employee's position when it was suggested that there might be a hiatus between the Workmen's Compensation Act and the National Insurance Act, "a result clearly to be avoided if the language of the Act fairly admits of any other construction"; *Mobberley & Perry, Ltd. v. Holloway*, [1952] A.C. 133, 139 (1951).

166. It was basically this narrow view of the scope of tort that led him to reject the American concept that, in an ultrahazardous activity, an occupier acts at his peril; *Read v. J. Lyons & Co.*, [1947] A.C. 156, 181–82 (1946). Similarly, he embraced with enthusiasm the most formalistic distinctions in occupiers' liability; e.g., *Jacobs v. LCC*, [1950] A.C. 361, 368.

167. There was no reason to think that, in any other torts, Simonds was concerned to see any extension of liability. See, e.g., *Speidel v. Plato Films, Ltd.*, [1961] A.C. 1090, 1124: "In effect, therefore, the plea of the appellants was that the law was not what it ought to be. That is a plea to which this House is not inclined to listen when it is sitting as a supreme appellate tribunal, and perhaps I should ignore it. But I cannot refrain from observing how emphatically I dissent from the view that the law should be altered to the advantage of those who make defamatory statements about others." The same held true in most other areas. Definitions in evidence were not to be extended; e.g., *Davies v. DPP*, [1954] A.C. 378, 401. In conflicts, the general approach was not expansionist; e.g., *National Bank of Greece & Athens S.A. v. Metliss*, [1958] A.C. 509, 521 (1957); *Rahimtoola v. Nizam of Hyderabad*, [1958] A.C. 379, 392 (1957); *Adams v. National Bank of Greece S.A.*, [1961] A.C. 255, 271 (1960).

ability as a test not only for liability in negligence but also for the extent and remoteness of damages.[168] The matter was so clear to Simonds that his opinion started from the premise that the test of damages should be based on fault and foreseeability, unless precedents forced him to decide otherwise. His assumption that the whole area was based on fault allowed him to treat *Polemis* as "illogical and unjust."[169] To him the position was quite clear. "[W]hy should that test [reasonable foreseeability] be rejected which . . . corresponds with the common conscience of mankind?"[170] In this decision there was little doubt that Simonds accepted the law lords as the repository of the basic policies to be applied.

These policies became articulate only when Simonds' premises could not be implemented by the application of substantive formalism. When the literal interpretation of a 1705 statute would have led virtually all the minor royalty of Europe, including the pretenders to the German throne, to become British subjects, Simonds extolled the virtues of the contextual approach to statutory interpretation.[171] In common law, too, Simonds occasionally found himself rejecting the need to search for precedents. In *National Bank of Greece and Athens* v. *Metliss*[172] he announced that "the question is rather one of principle and analogy, though analogies are dangerous and principles difficult to state with precision."[173] In isolated instances he grew even more rash. "[I]n the absence of authority binding this House, the question is simply: What does justice demand in such a case as this? . . . If I have to base my opinion on any principle, I would venture to say it was the principle of rational justice."[174] This position was a significant way from the rationalization of the House's task expressed so vigorously in *Jacobs* v. *London County Council*, of discovering "what the law is, not what it ought to be."

Using *Jacobs* as a touchstone, it is also clear that Simonds by no means always deferred to the "considered dicta" that had loomed so large in his interpretation of the *Fairman* case. In *Davies* v. *Director of Public Prosecutions*, he dismissed observations by Atkinson in the *Christie*

168. *Overseas Tankship, Ltd.* v. *Morts Dock & Eng'r Co.*, [1961] A.C. 388 (P.C.).
169. Ibid. 424.
170. Ibid. 423. On this decision see the symposium *The Foresight Saga*, published by the Haldane Society.
171. *Attorney-General* v. *Prince Ernest Augustus of Hanover*, [1957] A.C. 436, 461 (1956): "I conceive it to be my right and duty to examine every word of a statute in its context, and I use 'context' in its widest sense, which I have already indicated as including not only other enacting provisions of the same statute, but its preamble, the existing state of the law, other statutes in pari materia, and the mischief which I can, by those and other legitimate means, discern the statute was intended to remedy."
172. [1958] A.C. 509 (1957).
173. Ibid. 524.
174. Ibid. 525.

case as "unnecessary."[175] Also in contrast with his position in *Jacobs*, when Simonds found there had been two binding reasons for the earlier decision, he by no means always regarded himself as bound by both of them. In *Public Trustee v. Inland Revenue Commissioners*[176] he was faced with an inconvenient dictum of Macnaghten's[177] and resorted to all the devices of the most creative of judges. "I have come to the conclusion . . . that the time has come to re-examine, not indeed, any decision of this House nor any reasoning that was strictly necessary to such a decision, but certain observations upon the interrelation of sections 1 and 2 which, as I humbly think, were made without full consideration of their consequences."[178] Nor did Simonds exactly redeem himself with his closing thoughts. "I believe that I yield to no one in the importance that I attach to the rule of precedent. But this case stands alone in my experience."[179]

That particular decision was not, however, to be unique. In his last year as a Lord of Appeal, in an area where even the most ardent judicial activist counsels restraint—the criminal law—Simonds dominated a decision—*Shaw v. Director of Public Prosecutions*,[180] that, by virtually everyone's standards,[181] created a new crime of conspiracy to corrupt public morals.

In the sphere of criminal law I entertain no doubt that there remains in the courts of law a residual power to enforce the supreme and fundamental purpose of the law, to conserve not only the safety and order but also the moral welfare of the State, and that it is their duty to guard it against attacks which may be the more insidious because they are novel and unprepared for. That is the broad head (call it public policy if you wish) within which the present indictment falls. It matters little what label is given to the offending act. To one of your Lordships it may appear an affront to public decency, to another considering that it may succeed in its obvious intention of provoking libidinous desires it will seem a corruption of public morals. Yet others may deem it aptly described as the creation of a public mischief or the undermining of moral conduct. . . . When Lord Mansfield, speaking long after the Star Chamber had been abolished, said that the Court of King's Bench was the *custos morum* of the people and had the superintendency of offences *contra bonos mores*, he was asserting, as I now assert, that there is in

175. [1954] A.C. 378, 399. The decision is also interesting for Simonds' explanation of how a "practice" (corroboration) may become a "rule of law"; (ibid. 396.).

176. [1960] A.C. 398 (1959).

177. In *Earl Cowley v. IRC*, [1899] A.C. 198, 210 (Macnaghten's dictum on charging clauses).

178. [1960] A.C. 398, 409 (1959).

179. Ibid. 415–16.

180. [1962] A.C. 220 (1961).

181. "Judicial folly" per J. E. Hall Williams, "Notes on Cases," 24 *Modern Law Review* 626, 631 (1961); "an egregious performance" per D. Seaborne Davies, "The House of Lords and Criminal Law" 105. Cf. Arthur L. Goodhart, "The Shaw Case" 560, 567: "important contributions to the development of the criminal law."

that court a residual power, where no statute has yet intervened to supercede the common law, to superintend those offences which are prejudicial to the public welfare. Such occasions will be rare, for Parliament has not been slow to legislate when attention has been sufficiently aroused. But gaps remain and will always remain since no one can foresee every way in which the wickedness of man may disrupt the order of society. . . . Let it be supposed that at some future, perhaps, early, date homosexual practices between adult consenting males are no longer a crime. Would it not be an offence if even without obscenity, such practices were publicly advocated and encouraged by pamphlet and advertisement? Or must we wait until Parliament finds time to deal with such conduct? I say, my Lords, that if the common law is powerless in such an event, then we should no longer do her reverence. But I say that her hand is still powerful and that it is for Her Majesty's judges to play the part which Lord Mansfield pointed out to them.[182]

By any standards Simonds' speech was remarkable. Jowitt had banished the ghost of Mansfield lest he be thought to encourage an action for negligent statement leading to financial loss, but Simonds resurrected the spirit to prevent the nation from being corrupted by the publication of a directory listing the names of prostitutes.[183] Such was a measure of the intellectual underpinnings of substantive formalism.

The Impact of the System

The changing role of the Lord Chancellor in general politics and the politics of law remains a matter for debate, yet it would be surprising if the concepts of law expounded by Simon, Jowitt, and Simonds had not been reflected in the appointments and attitudes of the Lords of Appeal of the period. This expectation is more than fulfilled. Most of the law lords were undoubtedly technically competent, yet almost none seemed to sense any role for the House except to declare the law by detecting defects in the reasoning of judges of first instance, a task already canvassed —presumably adequately—by the Court of Appeal. Sensing a role merely as the refiner of the already refined, and either consciously or unconsciously aware of the political dangers of any move that might be seen in the political world as judicial legislation, the law lords of the period were distinguished largely by their lack of distinction. In their defense it must be said that their weaknesses were often those of the system, rather than of the persons themselves.

Whatever concept of the appellate process the judges may have, the brief terms of service of many meant that the opportunity to express

182. [1962] A.C. 220, 267–69 (1961). He concluded with an analysis of the "vagueness" issue. "There are still, as has recently been said, 'unravished remnants of the common law.'

So in the case of a charge of conspiracy to corrupt public morals the uncertainty that necessarily arises from the vagueness of general words can only be resolved by the opinion of twelve chosen men and women. I am content to leave it to them"; ibid. 269.

183. On *Shaw* generally, see H. L. A. Hart, *Law, Liberty and Morality*, Lecture 1.

attitudes or policies was limited. From the earlier period Lords Romer and Porter, both appointed in 1938, remained Lords of Appeal until 1944 and 1954, respectively. Porter's fourteen years as a Lord of Appeal, however, were to represent a record, with the exception of Reid[184] and Radcliffe.[185] With the advent of the war began what appeared almost as a policy of appointing Lords of Appeal who had little chance of continuing as law lords for any appreciable period. Lord Goddard sat for a couple of years (1944–46) and Uthwatt (1946–49) and du Parcq (1946–49) for little more.

With retirements and the expansion of the number of Lords of Appeal in 1947, four new law lords were appointed: Normand (1947–53), Oaksey (1947–57), Morton (1947–59), and MacDermott (1947–51). Even then the average length of service was only seven years—short, for instance, by the standards of the Supreme Court of the United States. The generation of judges that succeeded them served for an average of one less year: Greene (1949–50), Tucker (1960–61), Asquith (1951–54), and Cohen (1950–61). Moreover, some of these law lords, especially Cohen, Morton, and du Parcq, had major interruptions in their service as law lords while acting as chairmen of Royal Commissions. This discontinuity, coupled with the servicing of two courts (the Lords itself and the Privy Council) as well as the panel system by then applicable in the Lords as well as the Privy Council, makes it difficult to examine the work of such judges, whether from the point of view of legal historian, sociologist, or jurisprude.

Cumulatively, however, some evaluation can be made. The eleven judges to be discussed here were all professional judges. Only three had served less than eight years on the bench when they reached the Lords (Porter, four; Uthwatt, five; and MacDermott, three), and only three more less than twelve.[186] Only one Lord of Appeal reached the Lords before he was sixty,[187] and several were appointed when they were over sixty-five (Romer, Goddard, Uthwatt, du Parcq, Oaksey, and Greene).[188] Some of the objections to the advanced ages of the law lords, which had figured so prominently in nineteenth-century criticism, still appeared to have relevance in the twentieth century.

Some of the promotions to the bench also hinted at the need to allow judges to serve out their fifteen-year terms in order to qualify for a pension—the system that applied until the 1960s. Little attempt was made to disguise these moves. For instance, Greene's biographer attri-

184. Reid (1948–75).
185. Radcliffe (1949–64).
186. Goddard, 11; Morton, 9; Cohen, 8.
187. MacDermott, at 51.
188. Romer had been appointed at 72.

butes his promotion to a Lordship of Appeal to the fact that he had become totally exhausted in the Court of Appeal; he was promoted to the Lords in the hope that his strength would return.[189] The Lords was also at times seen as a training ground; during this period, after brief terms in the Lords, Goddard went to be Chief Justice of England and MacDermott to be Chief Justice of Northern Ireland. Meanwhile, Simonds oscillated between the positions of Lord Chancellor and Lord of Appeal.[190] The use of the final appeal court either as a retirement center or as a training ground is not necessarily wrong, but it scarcely suggests that those holding the reins of power attributed a high priority to the House of Lords.

Since appointment as a Lord of Appeal was, by this period, largely depoliticized, it is not surprising that among the judges actual experience of politics was limited. Only two of the eleven, Normand and MacDermott, had been in the legislature, both of them as Unionists (Conservatives).[191] Perhaps the tone was set by Morton, who said of himself, " I think I am an ordinary, typical British lawyer of the type who has kept to professional work and has never had anything to do with politics."[192] Some exceptions to that "ordinary, typical British lawyer" mold did, however, exist. Goddard had stood as an independent Conservative candidate, according to some accounts because he found the "regular" Conservative candidate too liberal;[193] du Parcq was reputedly a Liberal supporter and Uthwatt a Labour one. But for the most part, Morton was right; the Lords of Appeal were basically passive supporters of the status quo, conservatives with a lowercase rather than a capital c.[194]

189. *Dictionary of National Biography 1951–1960*, at 428. This was not the first time the legal establishment had come to his assistance. During the 1920s and 1930s, Greene had led a virtually charmed life. He was said to have had one of the largest practices ever seen at the bar, and by the end limited himself to appearing in the House of Lords and Privy Council, in the meantime sitting on many major commissions and committees. When, in 1935, he seemed on the verge of a breakdown, he was appointed to the Court of Appeal and two years later he was made Master of the Rolls, Wright having "left the seat warm for him." When, in 1949, he again showed signs of total exhaustion, he was made a Lord of Appeal; it was hoped that his strength would return. It did not, and he resigned in 1950; ibid.

190. Lord of Appeal, 1944–51; Lord Chancellor, 1951–54; Lord of Appeal, 1954–61.

191. MacDermott's experience was in the Northern Ireland legislature at Stormont, not at Westminster.

192. Fergus Durly Morton, "The Dual Function of the House of Lords" 889, 900. In a similar vein, he stated, "I am no politician, and have never been one, and I have never had to do with what is sometimes called 'big business'"; "Address Given during the Thirty-first Annual Meeting (Proceedings)" 116.

193. E.g., John Paine, "Labour and the Lawyers" 44.

Goddard regarded himself as apolitical. He noted that he was the first Chief Justice since Tenterden who had not been an M.P.; Rayner Goddard, "Politics and the British Bench" 124, 130.

194. A strange, unverified, exception to this, is D. N. Pritt's assertion that in 1949 he was sounded out about becoming a law lord ("for which I urged the appointment of Cyril

Professional competence, especially competence in the Court of Appeal, was the standard for promotion. Although a few Lords Justices were regarded as "good" by the profession in the Court of Appeal and did not make it to the Lords, that situation was generally the exception. Luck and connections did, however, help. Asquith was a perfect example. The son of the Prime Minister, he was a Lord of Appeal from 1951 to 1954. Cyril Asquith was a kind, rather shy man[195] who achieved great distinction as a classicist at Oxford but had only limited success at the common law bar. It came as a surprise to the bar (and caused Chief Justice Hewart considerable anger) when he was appointed a High Court judge by Lord Chancellor Maugham in 1938, only two years after becoming a King's Counsel. In 1946 he was promoted to the Court of Appeal by Jowitt in whose chambers he had been, and as a Lord Justice he produced a number of elegant, if doctrinally conservative, decisions.[196] Jowitt's influence also led to Asquith's promotion to the Lords in 1951, but in the same year, he was offered even greater preferment. On the fall of the Labour government, Churchill offered the Lord Chancellorship to Asquith, under whose father Churchill had served as a cabinet member. As already noted Asquith declined and Simonds became Chancellor.[197]

These were not a group of Lords of Appeal who might be expected to swim against the tide of their de facto appointers—Simon, Jowitt, and Simonds. For the most part they acquiesced in the articulated jurisprudential views of (and normally the actual policies pursued by) the Lord Chancellors. Nowhere were the phrases of substantive formalism more elegantly expressed than in Lord Greene's Haldane lectures.[198] "[T]he function of the legislature is to make the law, the function of the administration is to administer the law and the function of the judiciary is to interpret and enforce the law. The judiciary is not concerned with policy. It is not for the judiciary to decide what is in the public interest. These are the tasks of the legislature, which is put there for the purpose, and it is not right that it should shirk its responsibility."[199] The idea of judges in

Radcliffe, who was duly given the position"); D. N. Pritt, 2 *Autobiography* 46. Pritt was a fellow traveler, who was expelled from the Labour party for his pro-Communist and pro-Soviet line.

195. For a touching example of his generosity, see his stepmother's autobiography; Margot Asquith, 2 *Margot Asquith* 211–13.

196. E.g., *Victoria Laundry Windsor, Ltd. v. Newman Industries, Ltd.*, [1949] 2 K.B. 528 (C.A.); *Thurogood v. Van Der Berghs & Jurgens, Ltd.*, [1951] 2 K.B. 537, 550 (C.A.); *Candler v. Crane, Christmas & Co.*, [1951] 2 K.B. 164, 185 (C.A.).

197. *Dictionary of National Biography 1951–1960*, at 41.

198. Wilfred Arthur Greene; b. 1883; father, solicitor; educ., Westminster School and Christ Church, Oxford (First, "Greats"); called to bar, 1908; Lord Justice, 1935–49; Lord of Appeal, 1949–50; d. 1952; *Dictionary of National Biography 1951–1960*, at 428–29.

199. Wilfred Greene, "Law and Progress" 349, 351.

a democracy, where more than one political party applied principles of public policy, being themselves involved in policymaking, appalled him. "The consideration of 'public policy' is in truth an excrescence on the law. Its existence has been deplored; its extension has been prohibited; and few people would nowadays be found to deny the proposition that it is appropriate for the Legislature and not the judiciary to determine whether or not a particular course ought to be taken as being in the national interest or a particular act prohibited as being against public policy."[200]

Needless to say, Greene denied that the courts could make new law,[201] relying on the common assumption that stare decisis automatically led to certainty. He opposed legislation that left a discretion to the judiciary. "The whole tradition and practice of legal administration makes it extremely difficult for the judges to administer a law by which the tribunal is to grant or withhold rights according as they think it just or reasonable so to do."[202]

He castigated those who would not apply the canons of construction rigidly to all types of legislation. The idea that such canons should be relaxed in the field of what he termed "social legislation" merely to try to avoid an undesirable or unjust result was totally unacceptable.[203] Indeed,

200. Wilfred Greene, *The Judicial Office* 16–17.

201. "I do not suppose that anyone nowadays would contemplate inventing a new equity in order to remedy a defect of the common law or some legal fiction to remedy a defect of equity. The recognised method of dealing with such defects in modern times is legislation, which in principle is a far preferable and a more honest method, though the slow and deliberate operation of parliamentary machinery is not too well adapted to the purpose"; ibid. 5.

202. Greene, "Law and Progress" 365.

203. "But that is no reason for doing what this new school would have done, namely, that the judges should depart from the language used by Parliament in order to produce what may appear to them a juster result or one which they may think Parliament would have intended if its attention had been called to the point. Who are the judges that they should set up as arbitors of policy or claim power to change the directions of Parliament in some particular case if they happen to consider them unsuitable, unjust or against the public interest? . . . Policy is not the concern of the judges save insofar as the manifest objects of the statute, as appearing on its face, may provide a context pointing to one interpretation rather than another"; ibid. 351.

Thus, in the Court of Appeal during the war, Greene, like Simon, adopted an anti-tax avoider attitude in tax cases. E.g., "It scarcely lies in the mouth of the taxpayer who plays with fire to complain of burnt fingers"; *Lord Howard de Walden* v. *IRC*, [1942] 1 K.B. 389, 397 (C.A.). The same was not true later. In a series of Privy Council cases he restated the rules of construction that presumed the absence of a taxing power. See *Messrs. Mohanlal Hargovind of Jubbulpore* v. *Commissioner of Income Tax, Central Provinces and Berar, Nagpur* [1949] A.C. 521, 527 (P.C.); *Attorney-General for British Columbia* v. *Esquimalt & Nanaimo Ry.*, [1950] A.C. 87, 107 (P.C. 1949); *Mohindar Singh* v. *The King*, [1950] A.C. 345, 353 (P.C.); *Executors of Will of Hon. Patrick Burns* v. *Minister of National Revenue*, [1950] A.C. 213, 219 (P.C. 1949).

Greene sat for such a short while as a law lord that it is hardly fair to attempt an evaluation of his work. But see *Hill* v. *William Hill, Ltd.*, [1949] A.C. 530, 552–59. There he seemed to have rather less difficulty overruling a 40-year precedent than one might have

if one took Greene at his face value, so restricted was his view of the judicial process that it is difficult to understand the need not only for a second appeal court, but, carrying the argument to its logical conclusion, even for an independent judiciary. At some point, the rhetoric of substantive formalism had to come face-to-face with reality.

expected in light of his public statements, although the approach to § 18 of the Gaming Act of 1845 was predictably narrow. See especially ibid. 552, 555.

The Mechanics of Substantive Formalism

The Scope of the Problem

For the most part, the role the House had cast for itself meant there was little to distinguish one law lord from another or indeed little worth noting about the law made during this period. The aura of substantive formalism was not conducive to independent lines of thought among the appellate judges. Yet, on closer analysis, trends do appear, particularly in legislative speeches and when some law lord also sat in another court. Thus one can see a law-and-order group, which emerged with the increase in crime after World War II and was most closely associated with Lords Oaksey and Goddard.

Son of a High Court judge, Oaksey was appointed to the House in 1947, after moving through the usual route of High Court and Court of Appeal,[1] and remained a Lord of Appeal for ten years. He was not a notable law lord. The high spot in his career had probably been his appointment as the President of the International Tribunal at Nuremberg in 1945. This position, combined with his work on assize while he was a King's Bench Division judge, had made him a severe disciplinarian. His views in international matters—"England is always inclined, it seems to me, to be too generous or too casual and too undisciplined in dealing with her conquered foes"[2]—were not very different from his views in municipal matters.

1. Geoffrey Lawrence; b. 1880; father, Lord Chief Justice; educ., Hailebury and New College, Oxford (Third, "Greats"); called to bar, 1906; K.C., 1925; Judge, King's Bench Division, 1932–44; Lord Justice, 1944–47; Lord of Appeal, 1947–57; President of International Tribunal, Nuremberg, 1945.

2. Lord Oaksey (Geoffrey Lawrence), *The Nuremberg Trials and the Progress of International Law* 14. At Nuremberg, Lawrence was regarded as "a ruddy and cheerful

He took an active part in the debates of the House dealing with crime and punishment. He was a strong supporter of the reintroduction of corporal punishment[3] and an opponent of the abolition, partial or total, of capital punishment.[4] Although many of his brethren on the bench agreed with him on these points, his approach tended to be rather more assertive. Dismissing those who opposed capital punishment as persons "who relied upon statistics, emotion and political views," the Oaksey view was unique. He maintained that the judges, the police, and prison officers[5] were the only persons who really understood the position.[6] Such an outlook was not calculated to make his views particularly palatable to those who held contrary opinions. He was, to say the least, an unsophisticated penologist, holding that the objects of punishment were first the protection of the public, and second, retribution.[7] Nor, by North American standards, would he be thought of as a civil libertarian in his judicial capacity. In *Harris* v. *Director of Public Prosecutions*[8] Oaksey dissented alone, arguing that under the "similar facts" rules of evidence, details of seven previous larcenies, of which the accused was acquitted, were admissible as evidence that the accused had committed an eighth.[9]

Outside the area of "law and order," however, there was little to separate Oaksey from the group of fellow law lords, except possibly his propensity to dissent, which appeared to be related to his need to show that he had made up his own mind.[10] Occasional policies do, however,

---

embodiment of John Bull . . . with a gift for compromise, regardless of doctrine or theory"; Bradley F. Smith, *Reaching Judgment at Nuremberg* 4–5. Lawrence "loved the courtroom," but the hard work of legal analysis and drafting fell to the junior British judge, Birkett; ibid. 118–19.

3. "I adhere to the opinion that flogging has a deterrent effect"; 166, *Parl. Deb.*, H.L. (5th ser.), col. 345 (21 Mar. 1950); see also 178 ibid., col. 882 (22 Oct. 1952).

4. "If imprisonment is a deterrent . . . then the greater penalty of death must be a deterrent"; 198 ibid., col. 625 (9 July 1956); 157 ibid., cols. 1047–48 (20 July 1948).

5. On the other hand, he opposed putting the whole of administration of punishment into the hands of prison officials, since they had only seen the prisoner behind bars and not as a criminal; 178 ibid., col. 882 (22 Oct. 1952).

6. 198 ibid., col. 624 (9 July 1956).

7. "It is all wrong to say that punishment has nothing to do with retribution. There are certain cases which shock the conscience of every ordinary man. . . . This clause [for abolishing capital punishment] flouts the opinion of the electorate, and flouts the opinion of every ordinary man"; 157 ibid., col. 1047–48 (20 July 1948).

8. [1952] A.C. 694, 713.

9. In other areas of the law, his concern for the forces of law and order led him to dissent on the issue of the definition of charity in *IRC* v. *City of Glasgow Police Athletic Ass'n*, [1953] A.C. 380, 397 (Scot.). He dissented, arguing, not on any basic legal ground, but because "the efficiency of a police force is largely dependent upon the activity and physical fitness of its members, and athletic and other sports ought to be and are encouraged by those responsible for such forces. It is clear, too, that the efficiency of the police is a matter of public importance."

10. E.g., "Do not allow your judgment to be affected too much by the judgment of others"; Oaksey, *Nuremberg Trials* 15.

show through. While the Labour government was in the legislative process of making contributory negligence on the part of plaintiffs a discretionary rather than an absolute bar, Oaksey, judicially, continued to take a tough approach. He was, naturally, with the majority in denying recovery in *London Graving Dock Company* v. *Horton*,[11] but he also dissented against any weakening of contributory negligence, whether the plaintiff was a workman[12] or a corporation.[13] Yet, by 1957, when he retired at the age of seventy-seven, he had ceased to be a law lord of any consequence.

The other main proponent of the law-and-order school was Lord Goddard.[14] Far better known as Lord Chief Justice (1946–58) than as a Lord of Appeal (1944–46), the tone he set was similar, particularly since he continued to sit occasionally in criminal cases in the Lords while he was Lord Chief Justice. Goddard was an ardent supporter of capital and corporal punishment and of more severe sentences for criminals.[15] He attacked J.P.'s for being too lenient[16] and insisted that homosexuality be met with the full force of the law.[17] Throughout the many legislative debates in the Lords on the question of capital punishment, he stuck to his guns. He even declared that the general dispensation to convicted murderers given by the Home Secretary after the rejection of Sidney Silverman's abolition bill in 1956 was "unconstitutional" under the Bill of Rights.[18]

Indeed, for many, Goddard embodied the antiintellectual, somewhat sadistic, tone of the English judiciary in the 1940s and 1950s.[19] In criminal

11. [1951] A.C. 737, 757.

12. E.g., *Grant* v. *Sun Shipping Co.*, [1948] A.C. 549, 568 (Scot.). See, however, his decisions in *General Cleaning Contractors, Ltd.* v. *Christmas*, [1953] A.C. 180, 189 (1952); *Stapley* v. *Gypsum Mines, Ltd.*, [1953] A.C. 663, 677; *National Coal Bd.* v. *England*, [1954] A.C. 403, 420.

13. E.g., "It is, in my opinion, a fundamental principle of justice and not merely a rule of the common law, that no one can take advantage of his own wrong . . . and this principle is just as much applicable to the construction of statutes as it is to any other branch of law. . . . The appellants cannot, therefore, claim for damage to their harbour caused in part by their own failure to fulfill their obligations"; *Workington Harbour & Dock Bd.* v. *Towerfield (Owners)*, [1951] A.C. 112, 150 (1950).

14. Rayner Goddard; b. 1877; educ., Marlborough and Trinity College, Oxford (Second, Law); called to bar, 1899; K.C., 1923; Judge, King's Bench Division, 1932–38; Lord Justice, 1938–44; Lord of Appeal, 1944–46; Lord Chief Justice of England, 1946–58.

15. E.g., 157 *Parl. Deb.*, H.L. (5th ser.), cols. 1029 ff. (20 July 1948); 178 ibid., cols. 852 ff. (22 Oct. 1952); 185 ibid., col. 174 (1953 Dec.); 198 ibid., col. 735 (10 July 1956); 201 ibid., col. 1199 (21 Feb. 1957).

16. E.g., 216 ibid., col. 923 (10 June 1959).

17. It is a "crime which has always been treated in this country as one of the gravest crimes that can be committed"; 266 ibid., col. 664 (24 May 1965). "You have to take those who practice it as being as responsible as any others who come before the courts."

18. "If the law is not to take its course then, in Heaven's name, let us abolish the whole thing altogether"; 201 ibid., col. 1202 (21 Feb. 1957).

19. Nowhere was this more vividly illustrated than at the time of his death in 1971.

appeals to the Lords, Goddard not surprisingly "strengthened" the criminal law.[20] Yet Goddard liked to think of himself as a civil lawyer,[21] and in some respects that is not an unfair claim. At a time when most of the law lords were mesmerized by substantive formalism, in private law cases Goddard's speeches suggest a more realistic appreciation of the potential role of appeal judges,[22] although this reality was frequently concealed by the fact that, in policy terms, his inclinations were toward the preservation of the status quo. Thus in keeping with his approach, he was opposed to the extension of the doctrine of commercial frustration to interests in land,[23] and he rejected the idea that the protection of the "consortium" of a wife, long enjoyed by husbands, should be extended to a wife when her husband was injured and no longer able to have intercourse with her.[24] In this latter decision, Goddard also allowed himself to expound about the

---

Bernard Levin, no friend of "do-gooders" but a certified intellectual, vigorously attacked Goddard's memory in *The Times* ("Goddard, as Lord Chief Justice, was a calamity"); while the more establishmentarian members of the legal profession rushed to Goddard's defense. The result was an unsubtle clash between the latent hostility toward law and lawyers on the one hand and a blind defense of the status quo and resentment of any criticism of the judiciary on the other. For a discussion of the events of 1971, see Shimon Shetreet, *Judges on Trial* 184–85. For a recent adulatory biography of Goddard, see Fenton Bresler, *Lord Goddard*.

20. See, for instance, his concurrence in *DPP* v. *Smith*, [1961] A.C. 290, 335 (1960), tightening the concept of criminal responsibility. For another typical example, see *Attorney-General for Northern Ireland* v. *Gallagher*. "[T]here was not, in my opinion, any evidence of insanity: at the most, evidence only of self-imposed drunkenness. I will assume the respondent was an aggressive psychopath but no one suggested that such a condition of itself amounted to insanity. I will assume that on one who suffers from that mental condition alcohol can have an explosive effect. This means no more than that drink would, or at most might, result in a loss of self-control"; [1963] A.C. 349, 368 (N. Ire. 1961). See also his reaffirmation of the misdemeanor of misprision of felony in *Sykes* v. *DPP*, [1962] A.C. 528, 565 (1961).
    He opposed the extension of the right of appeal from the Court of Criminal Appeal to the House of Lords; 222 *Parl. Deb.*, H.L. (5th ser.), cols. 276–77 (24 Mar. 1960). His concern to allow the Court of Criminal Appeal to order a new trial was motivated by the fear that if that court quashed a conviction on legal grounds, it would be unable to order the accused retried; 176 ibid., col. 759 (8 May 1952).

21. He is reported to have said that "he felt that while in the Court of Appeal and the House of Lords he may have made a modest contribution to lawyer's law"; Arthur Smith, *Lord Goddard* 203. Goddard was in the Court of Appeal from 1938 to 1944.

22. "[The common law] has been developed by judicial decision in your country and in mine to meet the changed habits and conditions of the age and the environment in which it existed"; Rayner Goddard, "Recollections of a Lawyer's Life" 336, 338.

23. *Cricklewood Property & Inv. Trust, Ltd.* v. *Leighton's Inv. Trust, Ltd.*, [1945] A.C. 221, 243 (1944). He sat on two other commercial appeals in this period: *Larrinaga S.S. Co.* v. *The King*, [1945] A.C. 246, 263 (1944), in which he concurred with Porter; and *Scherling, Ltd.* v. *Stockholms Enskilda Bank Aktiebolag*, [1946] A.C. 219, 267–70 (1945), in which he joined Thankerton and Porter against Russell and Macmillan in holding that the war merely suspended and did not abrogate a contract entered into prior to it.

24. *Best* v. *Samuel Fox & Co.*, [1952] A.C. 716, 729–34. His basic legal argument was that "never during the many centuries that have passed since reports of the decisions of English courts first began has the recovery of damages for such injury been recorded."

sexual relations of husband and wife in a tone reminiscent of Victorian mythology.[25]

That Goddard could expound doctrine in a creative way was clear in *Carmarthenshire County Council v. Lewis.*[26] More often, his instinct was to restrict liability in negligence, and in this respect he became involved in limiting the scope of the Factories Acts by a strict interpretation of the legislation.[27] His support of the decision in *Gourley,*[28] holding that tort damages must be reduced by the amount the plaintiff would have had to pay by way of income tax, may also be seen as reflecting a reluctance to see concepts of compensation develop too dramatically.[29]

It may well have been that if Goddard had had a longer period as a law lord, he would have developed an appellate style and purpose of his own. He was not committed to the trappings of substantive formalism. He did not view the partnership between Parliament and the courts as requiring the appeal courts to be eunuchs, and there is evidence that he sought to implement parliamentary purpose in various areas of social legislation.[30] The type of administrative law that Goddard was moving to develop might well have been conservative, but he would not have shared his colleagues' position that he was helpless when faced with the task of balancing the rights of citizen and state. In keeping with the relative positions accorded by British society to appeal judges, however, Goddard naturally moved to the Chief Justiceship when it was proffered, and his

25. "There may be loss of affection but provided the spouses continue to live together as man and wife it seems to me it still exists however different life may be from the days of the honeymoon"; ibid. 733. Cf. Walter Houghlin, *The Victorian Frame of Mind* 341 ff.

26. [1955] A.C. 549. There the House had to decide whether the case of a child's running out into a public highway from a school yard, causing a lorry driver to swerve and crash, should be treated by analogy with the law relating to animals straying onto the highway. The House refused to use the analogy and applied the general test of negligence. Goddard, in a succinct opinion noted, "Now, once a doctrine has become a rule of law it is the duty of the courts to apply and follow it without regard to its origin, but if to follow it would be to extend it, in my opinion it is not only legitimate but essential to examine the origin and reason for it if it be known"; ibid. 560.

27. See especially *Close v. Steel Co. of Wales,* [1962] A.C. 367, 389–90 (1961). Goddard joined Morton and Guest in the majority; Denning and Morris dissented.

28. *British Transp. Comm'n v. Gourley,* [1956] A.C. 185, 204–10 (1955).

29. For some of the difficulties the decision caused, see P. S. Atiyah, *Accidents, Compensation and the Law* 178–79.

A year later, in *West Suffolk County Council v. W. Rought, Ltd.,* [1957] A.C. 403 (1956), the House, which again included Goddard, extended the Gourley principle to compensation on compulsory purchase of land.

30. E.g., *Mobberley & Perry, Ltd. v. Holloway,* [1952] A.C. 133, 140 (1951), containing the National Insurance Industrial Injuries Act of 1946; *Langford Property Co. v. Batten,* [1951] A.C. 223, 235 (1950), dissenting in favor of a landlord in a Rent Restriction Act case; *Contract & Trading Co. v. Barbey,* [1960] A.C. 244, 253–54 (1959); *Earl Fitzwilliam's Wentworth Estates Co. v. Minister of Housing & Local Gov't,* [1952] A.C. 362, 379–81 (1951), construing the powers of the Central Land Board under the Town and Country Planning Act of 1947.

potential as an appeal judge evaporated in the rhetoric of retribution.

In this sense, however, Goddard was an exception to the pervasive norm, for the norm was substantive formalism. No one better illustrated that phenomenon than Lord Normand. A Scottish Lord of Appeal from 1947 to 1953 (although until 1962 he continued to sit occasionally), Normand managed both to articulate the traditionally rather broader approach often found among Scottish judges and yet, in practice, to apply substantive formalism with Sassenach enthusiasm. It was Normand who praised Scottish law whose "strength lies, even today, in principle more than in precedent"[31]; and he had no difficulty recognizing the fallacy in the argument that there is a fixed rule governing each new case, which needed only to be discovered. "It is really a fiction and each new application of the precedent enlarges its meaning and modifies the law."[32] Yet, despite these stated positions and his earlier experience as a politician,[33] his appellate work showed scarcely a hint of judicial sophistication, at least so far as English appeals were concerned.[34]

Normand was clearly a complex man. For a man who had been Solicitor General of Scotland and who believed that judges, far from holding up reform, were the sine qua non of all reform,[35] it seemed odd that he apparently distorted the purpose of the Factories Acts for fear that the cost of accident prevention might be too onerous for the manufacturers.[36] If later generations, however, were to find his Factories Act

---

31. He continued, "That does not mean that precedent and case law are unimportant, but that they are to be handled with care and that they should be consciously brought to the test of principle"; Wilfred Normand, *"The Equipment of an Advocate," Scots Law Times* 245, 246 (1935).

32. Wilfred Normand, *Scottish Judicature and Legal Procedure*, 41.

33. Wilfred Guild Normand; b. 1884; educ., Fettes College, Edinburgh Univ., Oriel College, Oxford; admitted, Faculty of Advocates, 1910; K.C., 1925; Unionist M.P., 1931–35; Solicitor-General for Scotland, 1929, 1931–33; Lord Advocate, 1933–35; Lord Justice-General and Lord President, Court of Session, 1935–47; Lord of Appeal, 1947–53; d. 1962.

34. For his protective view of Scottish law, see 178 *Parl. Deb.*, H.L. (5th ser.), col. 319 (28 July 1952); Normand, *Scottish Judicature and Legal Procedure, passim*. For appeals where he emphasized the difference between Scottish and English law, see, for instance, *Hill v. William Hill, Ltd.*, [1949] A.C. 530, 559–68; and *Jamieson v. Jamieson*, [1952] A.C. 525, 537 (Scot.).

35. "The legal mind is essentially critical, and the critical spirit is the beginning of all sound reform. It is that critical faculty that traces to their source the injustices and oppressions of which men complain, and it is also that critical faculty which rejects plausible remedies, or remedies which touch symptoms only, or which do damage to what is sound and healthy"; "Equipment of an Advocate" 249.

36. *Carroll v. Andrew Barclay & Sons*, [1948] A.C. 477, 487 ff. (Scot.).

In *Parvin v. Morton Mach. Co.*, [1952] A.C. 515 (Scot.), although arguing it was a "novel question," Normand held that the Factories Act did not apply to machinery manufactured in the factory; ibid. 522. Normand naturally found himself with the majority in Horton's case, [1951] A.C. 737, 750, declaring himself unable to depart from the line of precedent.

cases conservative from a policy point of view, his tax decisions represented the height of substantive formalism.[37] He was an opponent of the "substance of the transaction" doctrine,[38] and he purported to take an objective approach, as if tax legislation were a giant crossword puzzle. "I do not rely on the comparative equity of the rival contentions of parties."[39] Yet at the same time Normand actually started from the premise that owed its heritage to Halsbury's later days—the idea that taxation, being "penal," had to be construed like criminal legislation lest there be some violation of civil liberties. "Tax avoidance is an evil, but it would be the beginning of much greater evils if the courts were to overstretch the language of the statute in order to subject to taxation people of whom they disapproved."[40] The net effect of these strange conflicts was Normand's conclusion that the courts had no responsibility for seeing that tax law was either effective or workable. Bearing in mind the percentage of the House's work that by this time fell within that category, it was a strangely destructive position. While his work in other areas is perhaps less open to criticism,[41] it is surprising to find *The Times* concluding that "[t]he rough and tumble of professional life at the Bar did not appeal to his fastidious mind, and it was as a Judge, particularly in the House of Lords and Privy Council, that he reached his full stature."[42]

In talking about the influence of "the system" on the appellate bench in the period after World War II, it would be naive to assume that the absence of political experience or commitment was the only problem leading the law lords to give the impression of having lost their sense of

37. This approach led him almost invariably to decide in favor of the taxpayer. Cf., however, *Thomas* v. *Marshall (Inspector of Taxes)*, [1953] A.C. 543, 552; *IRC* v. *Reid's Trustees*, [1949] A.C. 361, 373 (Scot. 1948); *Smith's Potato Estates, Ltd.* v. *Bollard (Inspector of Taxes)*, [1948] A.C. 508, 529. He even went so far as to dissent in favor of the Revenue in *St. Aubyn* v. *Attorney-General* [1952] A.C. 15, 41 (1951).

38. "[I]n construing a taxing Act . . . [t]he court is not entitled to say that for the purposes of taxation the actual transaction is to be disregarded as 'machinery' and that the substance or equivalent financial results are the relevant consideration"; *Potts' Executors* v. *IRC*, [1951] A.C. 443, 548 (1950).

39. *IRC* v. *John Dow Stuart, Ltd.*, [1950] A.C. 149, 168 (Scot. 1949).

40. *Vestey's Executors* v. *IRC*, 31 Tax Cas. 1, 90 (H.L. 1949). This passage is quoted by G. S. A. Wheatcroft, *The Law of Income Tax, Surtax and Profits Tax* 1040, where he describes it as the best expression of the then-current approach to tax legislation.

41. For example, on the law of negligence: *Bolton* v. *Stone*, [1951] A.C. 850, 860; *Caminer* v. *Northern & London Inv. Trust, Ltd.*, [1951] A.C. 88, 99 (1950); *Workington Harbour & Dock Bd.* v. *Towerfield (Owners)*, [1951] A.C. 112, 136 (1950).

On private international law: *Boissevain* v. *Weil*, [1950] A.C. 327; *Kahler* v. *Midland Bank, Ltd.*, [1950] A.C. 24, 29 (1949).

On company law: *Scottish Ins. Corp.* v. *Wilsons & Clyde Coal Co.*, [1949] A.C. 462, 493 (Scot.); *Prudential Assurance Co.* v. *Chatterley-Whitfield Collieries, Ltd.*, [1949] A.C. 512.

On matrimonial law: *Baxter* v. *Baxter*, [1948] A.C. 274 (1947); *King* v. *King*, [1953] A.C. 124, 127 (1952); *Jamieson* v. *Jamieson*, [1952] A.C. 525, 533 (Scot.).

42. *The Times*, 8 Oct. 1962.

purpose. Normand had had political experience; Uthwatt equally was thought to have political commitment—to the Labour party in his case; and indeed his *Report on Compensation and Betterment of Land*, published in 1942,[43] was by most standards viewed as a socialist document.[44] In his judicial work, however, there is little to suggest that Uthwatt had any more sense of judicial strategy than did his contemporaries. In "policy" terms he was indistinguishable from other law lords.[45] He was as enthusiastic as his fellow law lords in limiting the fencing provisions of the Factories Acts.[46] In handling tax legislation, he refused to consider the historical reasons for a provision,[47] and on occasion he also refused to "impute" to the legislature "any intention to go beyond the necessities of the case."[48]

In short, little in Uthwatt's style, purpose, or distinction sets him apart from his colleagues. If he took a position on precedent or the role of the courts in interpretation, these views were not explicit and do not emerge even from a careful study of his speeches. His rise through the ranks of the High Court and the Court of Appeal apparently had driven out any sense of appellate purpose.[49] Doctrinally, some of his decisions in tort have been termed "useful,"[50] but his leading contracts judgment has

---

43. Cmd. 6291. The Conservatives opposed the Uthwatt proposal when his report came out. See Lord Kilmuir (David Maxwell-Fyfe), *Political Adventures* 75.

44. The recommendations of the report were partially implemented, though with considerable changes, by the Town and Country Planning Act of 1947. The recommendations were more fully implemented by the Land Commission Act of 1966.

45. Although it is perhaps not surprising to find him concurring with Thankerton in *Franklin* v. *Minister of Town & Country Planning*, [1948] A.C. 87 (1947), that the decision of the Minister of Town and Country Planning was not open to review.

46. As a party to the decision in *Nicholls* v. *F. Austin, Ltd.*, [1946] A.C. 493, 505, he refused to accept the contention that "the obligation imposed by the subsection . . . is to fence the machine, viewed as a single operating unit, so as to avoid the possibility of danger arising to the worker from its operation"; ibid. 506. Instead, relying on the general scheme of the act and the fact that the Secretary of State had power to make specific regulations requiring the fencing of materials that are dangerous when in a machine, he decided against the worker. Again, in *Read* v. *J. Lyons & Co.*, [1947] A.C. 156 (1946), he decided against an injured munitions inspector, regarding *Rylands* v. *Fletcher* as laying down a principle applicable only between occupiers in respect of their lands; ibid. 186; and unlike du Parcq, who, as will be seen, dissented vigorously in favor of the working-class tenants in *Shelley* v. *LCC*, [1949] A.C. 56, 67 (1948), Uthwatt was content to let the local authority have a free hand in evicting tenants, in the course of carrying out its duty.

47. *Nugent-Head* v. *Jacob (Inspector of Taxes)*, [1948] A.C. 321, 327.

48. *Berkeley* v. *Berkeley*, [1946] A.C. 555, 585.

49. Augustus Andrewes Uthwatt; b. 1879; father, landowner; educ., Ballarat, Melbourne University, Balliol, Oxford; called to bar, 1904; Judge, Chancery Division, 1941–46; Lord of Appeal, 1946–48; d. 1949; *Dictionary of National Biography, 1941–1950*, at 898–99.

50. E.g., *Adams* v. *Naylor*, [1946] A.C. 543, 553; *Mersey Docks & Harbours Bd.* v. *Coggins & Griffith (Liverpool), Ltd.*, [1947] A.C. 1, 20 (1946); *London Passenger Transp. Bd.* v. *Upson*, [1949] A.C. 155, 172 (1948).

been questioned.[51] In other words, Uthwatt's time as a Lord of Appeal from 1946 to 1949 was consistent with the tenor of that period. A left-wing reputation could easily be subsumed within substantive formalism.

The Norm

The absence of a rationale for the appellate function was reflected, in different ways, in virtually all of the law lords. Romer,[52] for instance, was a Lord of Appeal from 1938 to 1944,[53] after spending twenty years in the Chancery Division and the Court of Appeal.[54] Clearly a likable man,[55] Romer apparently perceived his role as a Lord of Appeal as no different from his role as a Lord Justice in the Court of Appeal. His speeches show little or no sense of any creative function or even of the idea that a final appeal court might be a convenient forum for restating basic doctrines.[56] Romer took a strict view of construction and inter-pretation,[57] although in *Liversidge* v. *Anderson* he seemed prepared to go to any lengths to support the executive's actions.[58] A similar view appeared in common law cases. In tort, for instance, he expressed his

51. *Winter Garden Theatre (London), Ltd.* v. *Millennium Prods., Ltd.*, [1948] A.C. 173, 198 (1947). See the comments of Devlin in *Australian Blue Metal, Ltd.* v. *Hughes*, [1963] A.C. 74 (P.C. 1962).

52. A near contemporary of Romer's was Clauson, who, while he never became a Lord of Appeal, was created a peer on resigning from the Court of Appeal in 1942. His opinions were usually limited to simple concurrences, although he sat on a number of important cases, e.g., *Duncan* v. *Cammell, Laird & Co.*, [1942] A.C. 624; *Blunt* v. *Blunt*, [1943] A.C. 517. One of the few occasions on which Clauson gave a speech was in *Glasgow Corp.* v. *Muir*, [1943] A.C. 448 (Scot.), which was little more than a simple concurrence and was in his own words a "humble judgement"; ibid. 468. Clauson, of course, sat mainly in the war years when the House was under the domination of Simon. See *Dictionary of National Biography 1941–1950*, at 154–55; *The Times*, 16 Mar. 1946.

53. Mark Lemon Romer; b. 1866; father, Lord Justice; educ., Rugby, Trinity College, Cambridge (Second, Mathematics); called to bar, 1890 (Chancery); Judge, Chancery Division, 1922–29; Lord Justice of Appeal, 1929–38; Lord of Appeal, 1938–44; *Dictionary of National Biography 1941–1950*, at 734–36.

54. *The Times*, somewhat unenthusiastically, described him as "solid, learned," whose promotion was "entirely justified"; *The Times*, 19 Aug. 1944. Romer had the good fortune of being brother-in-law of Lord Chancellor Maugham.

55. Ibid.

56. A possible exception is *Cohen* v. *Cohen*, [1940] A.C. 631, 635, on the issue of desertion under the Matrimonial Causes Act of 1937.

57. E.g., *Perrin* v. *Morgan*, [1943] A.C. 399, 420 (1942).

58. "[W]e are dealing here with an Act passed and regulations made under it in times of great national emergency, and in view of this circumstance and of the objects which that Act and those regulations so plainly had in view, the courts should, in my opinion, prefer that construction which is the least likely to imperil the safety of this country"; [1942] A.C. 206, 280 (1941).

"Whether or not the acts of some individual appear to be of this description is a question of which the Secretary of State must plainly be a better judge than any court of law can be"; ibid. 281.

A further sense of Romer's views on individual liberties may be obtained from *Nokes* v. *Doncaster Amalgamated Collieries, Ltd.*, [1940] A.C. 1014, 1037. See especially at 1045, quoting Herschell: "[A] sense of the possible injustice of legislation ought not to

judicial duty in *Earl Fitzwilliam's Collieries Company v. Phillips*. "[L]oy-alty to the decision of your Lordships' House in *Elliott v. Burn* . . . de-mands that this feeling [of limited duty] should be sternly repressed."[59]

Such a judicial philosophy was by no means unique to Romer. Des-pite the fact that he was offered the Chancellorship by Churchill, Asquith was in many ways a lame duck by the time he reached the Lords.[60] The charitable have said "the higher he went the better he got,"[61] but there is little to show that he was any more distinguished as a Lord of Appeal than he had been as a Lord Justice[62] or, for that matter, as a High Court judge or a barrister. While Asquith undoubtedly appreciated the nature of the judicial process in the common law world,[63] he had virtually no impact on the Lords. The fact that he rarely dissented[64] is almost the only characteristic that distinguished him from his brethren. In legislative debates he advocated capital[65] and, while on the bench, corporal[66] pun-ishment and appeared to be out of sympathy with the problems of injured workmen,[67] although in fact it was more likely that he was out of touch with them. His views on the criminal law offered nothing unique.[68] In tax cases Asquith was often content merely to concur or deliver a short speech,[69] and he did nothing to unwind the tangled web of revenue law.[70]

---

induce your Lordships to do violence to well settled rules of construction" and concluding, "I cannot, consistently with well settled rules of construction, so read the sections as to avoid causing the alleged injustices to which I have referred." See also *Barnard v. Gorman*, [1941] A.C. 378, 396.

59. [1943] A.C. 570, 583. See also *East Suffolk Rivers Catchment Bd. v. Kent*, [1941] A.C. 74, 96 (1940).

60. Cyril Asquith, b. 1890; father, Prime Minister; educ., Winchester and Balliol College, Oxford (First, "Greats"); called to bar, 1920; K.C., 1936; Judge, King's Bench Division, 1938–46; Lord Justice, 1946–51; Lord of Appeal, 1951–54; d. 1954.

61. E.g., *Dictionary of National Biography 1951–1960*, at 40.

62. E.g., his rather dated view in *Buchler v. Buchler*, [1947] 25.

63. "Nor, speaking more generally, does English jurisprudence start from a broad principle and decide cases in accordance with its logical implications. It starts with a clean slate, scored over, in course of time, with ad hoc decisions. General rules are arrived at inductively, from the collation and comparison of these decisions: the rules do not pre-exist them"; *Chapman v. Chapman*, [1954] A.C. 429, 470.

64. But see *King v. King*, [1953] A.C. 124, 146 (1952); *Stapley v. Gypsum Mines, Ltd.*, [1953] A.C. 663, 685.

65. 185 *Parl. Deb.*, H.L. (5th ser.), cols. 172–74 (16 Dec. 1953).

66. 178 ibid., cols. 873–76 (22 Oct. 1952).

67. See *Parvin v. Morton Mach. Co.*, [1952] A.C. 515, 523 (Scot.) *Latimer v. AEC, Ltd.*, [1953] A.C. 643, 660.

68. He concurred in the wide definition of accomplice in murder; *Davies v. DPP*, [1954] A.C. 378.

69. E.g., *Nash (Inspector of Taxes) v. Tamplin & Sons Brewery (Brighton)*, [1952] A.C. 231 (1951); *Coutts & Co. v. IRC*, [1953] A.C. 267 (1952); *Morgan v. Tate & Lyle, Ltd.*, [1955] A.C. 21 (1954).

He delivered short opinions in *Stainer's Executors v. Purchase (Inspector of Taxes)*, [1952] A.C. 280, 290 (1951); and *Barron (Inspector of Taxes) v. Littman*, [1953] A.C. 96, 121 (1952).

70. He was, however, a party to the important estate duty decision, *D'Avigdor-*

In landlord and tenant legislation, his contribution generally amounted merely to concurring,[71] although he exhibited a conventional view of statutory interpretation.[72] Again, one seeking a rationale for the second appeal would look in vain in the speeches of Asquith.

It might be possible to dismiss the lack of contributions by Romer and Asquith in terms of their relatively short service on the bench, but one cannot grant the same leniency to Lord Tucker. Appointed a Lord of Appeal in 1950 after seventeen years in the lower courts, Tucker continued to sit until his retirement in 1961 and occasionally thereafter.[73] In general, however, his speeches are not much different from those of the other law lords, although it would be surprising if, during his eleven years, some individualistic traits had not appeared. Two are perhaps worth pursuing—his attitude toward criminal law and his view of workmen's cases.

Like many of his brethren, Tucker was in favor of the death penalty, but his position was based more on the cruelty of life imprisonment than, for instance, the rather hysterical opposition of judges like Oaksey.[74] Yet overall, Tucker's was a strict approach to criminal law. Not only did he regard the death penalty as a "unique deterrent,"[75] but he did not want to encourage defenses based on drunkenness, even though the condition might induce insanity[76] and automatism.[77] At the same time he was able both to demand a harsh "objective" test in murder and to assume and expand customary crimes like conspiracy to corrupt public morals,[78] which had been thought to be lost in the mists of time.

Yet Tucker gave the impression of searching for a judicial approach in various matters; and there is some evidence that his positions did

---

Goldsmid v. IRC, [1953] A.C. 347 (1952), in which he said in rather pedantic style, "Disengaged from certain clinging and obscuring draperies, the point seems to me a short one. . . . If I buy an apple tree and it subsequently bears fruit, I am beneficially interested in the fruit from the start"; ibid. 377–78.

71. E.g., Capital & Provincial Property Trust, Ltd. v. Rice, [1952] A.C. 142 (1951); Moodie v. Hosegood, [1952] A.C. 61 (1951); Preston & Area Rent Tribunal v. Pickavance, [1953] A.C. 562.

72. E.g., East End Dwellings Co. v. Finsbury Borough Council, [1952] A.C. 109, 132 (1951).

73. Frederick James Tucker; b. 1888; educ., Winchester and New College, Oxford (Second, Jurisprudence); called to bar, 1914; K.C., 1933; Judge, King's Bench Division, 1937–45; Lord Justice, 1945–50; Lord of Appeal, 1950–61.

74. Kilmuir thought his speech and Salisbury's in favor of retention of the death penalty in 1956 were the two most powerful; Kilmuir, Political Adventures 265. For the speeches, see 198 Parl. Deb., H.L. (5th ser.), cols. 561 ff. (9 July 1956).

75. Ibid., col. 812 (10 July 1956).

76. Attorney-General for Northern Ireland v. Gallagher, [1963] A.C. 349, (N. Ire. 1961).

77. Bratty v. Attorney-General for Northern Ireland, [1963] A.C. 386, 408 (N. Ire. 1961).

78. DPP v. Smith, [1961] A.C. 290, 335 (1960).

change over time.[79] In industrial injury cases, for instance, as time went on, both his approach and his attitude altered. In his early years as a law lord he seemed reluctant to enforce statutory duties of care rigorously against employers lest they appear as absolute duties,[80] but as time went on, his acceptance of a broader system of compensation appeared to grow.[81] The position should not, however, be overstated, for Tucker was a party to the decision in both *Davie* v. *New Merton Board Mills, Limited*[82] and *Lister* v. *Romford Ice and Cold Storage Company*,[83] refusing in the latter case to give an employee the "licence to be as negligent as he liked."[84] In this context, it proves difficult to escalate Tucker above the mediocre uniformity that characterized the period of substantive formalism.[85]

The Unexploited Potential

Although the House was in the grip of substantive formalism—an influence that pervaded the performance of all the law lords, including, to a limited extent, even Radcliffe and Reid, during this period—beneath

79. Compare his dissents in favor of the taxpayer in *St. Aubyn* v. *Attorney-General*, [1952] A.C. 15, 59 (1951); and in favor of the Revenue in *Morgan* v. *Tate & Lyle, Ltd.*, [1955] A.C. 21, 60 (1954).

80. E.g., *Parvin* v. *Morton Mach. Co.*, [1952] A.C. 515, 523 (Scot.); and *Richard Thomas & Baldwins, Ltd.* v. *Cummings*, [1955] A.C. 321, 331.

On common law duty of care: "[I]t appears to me desirable in these days, when there are in existence so many statutes and statutory regulations imposing absolute obligations upon employers, that the courts should be vigilant to see that the common law duty owed by a master to his servants should not be gradually enlarged until it is barely distinguishable from his absolute statutory obligations"; *Latimer* v. *AEC, Ltd.*, [1953] A.C. 643, 658. See also *General Cleaning Contractors, Ltd.* v. *Christmas*, [1953] A.C. 180, 194–95, 198 (1952).

81. "[The risk] was obvious, its consequences were likely to be calamitous, and the remedy was simple and available. I do not consider that it is imposing too high a standard of care upon a master to require that he should take the precaution suggested, notwithstanding, that no such accident had occurred before in his experience"; *Morris* v. *West Hartlepool Steam Navigation Co.*, [1956] A.C. 552, 576 (1955).

"A member of the crew is one of the factory maintenance staff and if his work requires him to be in the danger area I can see no reason why he should not be entitled to the benefit of this particular safety regulation"; *Canadian Pacific S.S., Ltd.* v. *Bryers*, [1958] A.C. 485, 508 (1957).

82. [1959] A.C. 604, 646 (1958).

83. [1957] A.C. 555, 594 (1956). He said, "It would, I think, require very compelling evidence of some general change in circumstances affecting master and servant to justify the court in introducing some quite novel term into their contract."

84. Ibid. 593.

85. Nor during this period were the peers who were not law lords likely to do much to leaven the tone of the proceedings.

Lord Merriman, President of the Probate, Divorce and Admiralty Division—and incidentally a former Conservative M.P.—sat mainly in appeals emanating from that division. He tended to restate long-established rules and well-established interpretations. See, first, his proposed dissent quoted by Hodson in *Ross Smith* v. *Ross Smith*, [1963] A.C.

"the system" the potential for more distinguished appellate judges existed. In a different ambience, Tucker might have felt more free to develop an appellate style of his own. Morton and du Parcq were to show greater evidence of appellate skills, while Porter and MacDermott could justly be treated as serious appellate judges.

Before turning to them, however, it is instructive to look at the impact the system had on the potential of Lord Cohen, who in many common law systems might have been expected to develop into a serious appellate judge.[86] After a successful practice at the Chancery Bar and relatively short stays in the Chancery Division and the Court of Appeal, Cohen served as a Lord of Appeal from 1951 to 1960. For virtually all those years, however, his primary energies were elsewhere. While he was on the Chancery bench, he had presided over the Company Law Amendment Committee[87] (whose report was largely implemented by the Companies Act of 1947) and by the time he became a Lord of Appeal he was Chairman of the semipermanent Royal Commission on Awards to Inventors (from 1946 to 1956); early in 1951 he also assumed the joint Chairmanship of the Royal Commission on the Taxation of Profits and Income, which remained active until 1955. No sooner was that work finished than Cohen was called upon in 1957 to become Chairman of the Committee on Prices, Productivity, and Income—the "three wise men" who were to implement Harold Macmillan's attempt to curb inflation.[88] This proved virtually a full-time appointment, yet he resigned from this post only shortly before the end of his term as a Lord of Appeal.

Thus to write of Cohen as a law lord is to write of an almost hypothetical figure. His relatively rare appearances meant that he never achieved, judicially, the dominance one would have expected even in company and tax matters.[89] He was certainly aware of the potential for

280, 332 (1962); and second, *Riverstone Meat Co.* v. *Lancashire Shipping Co.*, [1961] A.C. 807, 849 (1960).

86. Lionel Leonard Cohen; b. 1888; father, City (knighted); educ., Eton, New College, Oxford (First, History/Law); called to bar, 1913; K.C., 1929; Judge, Chancery Division, 1943–46; Lord Justice, 1946–51; Lord of Appeal, 1951–60; d. 1973.
Other aspects of Cohen's career are interesting and worth reporting. For instance, he was working as a temporary civil servant in the Ministry of Economic Warfare when he was appointed to the Chancery bench. On a more personal level, he was a convert to the abolition of capital punishment. Cf. 202 *Parl. Deb.*, H.L. (5th ser.), cols. 363, 364 (7 Mar. 1957); and 268 ibid., cols. 1257–58 (27 July 1965).

87. Cmd. 6659 (1945). *First Report*, Cmd. 8761 (1953); *Second Report*, Cmd. 910 (1954); *Final Report*, Cmd. 9474 (1955).

88. Harold Macmillan, *Riding the Storm* 352.

89. Almost immediately after his appointment in 1951, Cohen gave the principal speech in *IRC* v. *Gordon*, [1952] A.C. 552, 562 (Scot.), which revealed a tax avoidance loophole for a taxpayer with foreign remuneration. This expansive decision received, as Cohen himself described it in a latter case, a "sudden death" by § 24 of the Finance Act of

lawmaking provided by a second appeal,[90] although his preferred form of law reform was undoubtedly legislation rather than litigation.[91] Nevertheless, his outside commitments prevented any serious "bucking" of substantive formalism.

At first blush it may seem strange to include Morton among those whose potential judicial strengths were smothered by substantive formalism, for much about him did fit into the typical mold. Morton described himself as a "typical British lawyer,"[92] and his career, until becoming a law lord, was the by then highly conventional professional judge route.[93] A successful Chancery practitioner, he reflected many of the prejudices of the English judiciary in the period of substantive formalism. He indulged publicly in platitutdes about the role of law;[94] he announced that he had "a profound mistrust of nonjudicial tribunals, however . . . well meaning they may be";[95] he joined in that conservative excursus into judicial lawmaking, *Lister* v. *Romford Ice and Cold Storage Company*;[96] and he was shocked when Denning suggested that statutes might be interpreted

1953. See *Thompson (Inspector of Taxes)* v. *Moyse*, [1961] A.C. 967, 1002 (1960). Although this was not the last time he gave the principal speech in tax and commercial cases (see, for instance, *Union Corp.* v. *IRC*, [1953] A.C. 482, 494; and *Parke Davis & Co.* v. *Comptroller-General of Patents, Designs & Trade Marks*, [1954] A.C. 321, 328), he tended, on his isolated appearances, not to give the impression of dominating even his chosen fields. See, however, his perceptive dissents, both with Radcliffe, in *Oughtred* v. *IRC*, [1960] A.C. 206, 229 (1959) and in *The Aello*, [1961] A.C. 135, 177 (1960).

90. "The House, being a part of Parliament, is not in theory so strictly bound by precedent as is the Court of Appeal, though it naturally treats with great respect and rarely disturbs earlier decisions of its own and it hesitates to disturb a long-established rule, even if that rule rests on the decision of a lower court"; Lionel Cohen, "The Jurisdiction, Practice and Procedure of the Court of Appeal" 3, 13–14.

91. In *National Provincial Bank, Ltd.* v. *Ainsworth*, [1965] A.C. 1175, both his opinion in the case ["[T]he existing law I think is in an unsatisfactory state, particularly as regards the position of the deserted wife and of the third parties"; ibid. 1228] and in the legislative debate in the House following the case ["I hope that the Government will find it possible to afford greater protection than our Judgement leaves with the truly deserted wife"; 266 *Parl. Deb.*, H.L. (5th ser.), col. 284 (25 May 1965)] demonstrate that he had the inclination to provide a remedy for injustice. Yet, sitting judicially, he concurred with his brethren in reversing the Court of Appeal's decision in favor of the wife.

92. See chap. 10, n. 192.

93. Fergus Durly Morton; b. 1877 (Scotland); father, stockbroker; educ., Kelvinside, St. John's, Cambridge (First, Law); called to English bar, 1912; K.C., 1929; Judge, Chancery Division, 1938–44; Lord Justice, 1944–47; Lord of Appeal, 1947–59.

94. Fergus Durly Morton, "The Dual Function of the House of Lords" 889. For a more rigorous analysis in connection with the War Damage Bill of 1965, see 265 *Parl. Deb.*, H.L. (5th ser.), cols. 289 ff. (13 Apr. 1965).

95. Morton, "Dual Function" 889, 890. In *Smith* v. *East Elloe RDC*, [1956] A.C. 736, 753, however, he held that the courts' jurisdiction to question the validity of a compulsory purchase order was ousted by the words of the statute: "[I]t does not seem to me inconceivable, though it does seem surprising, that the legislature should have intended to make it impossible for anyone to question in any court the validity of a compulsory purchase order on the ground that it was made in bad faith"; ibid. 756.

96. [1957] A.C. 555, 580 (1956).

in the light of their policies.[97] Even his extrajudicial work has been much criticized.[98]

Nevertheless, during his period as a Lord of Appeal (1947–59), Morton at times showed a sense of judicial strategy and appellate responsibility that was lacking in most of his contemporaries. Despite later criticisms of his Royal Commission on Marriage and Divorce, in matrimonial appeals Morton was prepared to take a relatively advanced view. In *Ross Smith* v. *Ross Smith*[99] he joined with the majority in deciding that the 103-year-old decision in *Simonin* v. *Mallac*[100] should be overruled, thus going further than was strictly necessary in order to decide the question before him; while in *Godfrey* v. *Godfrey*[101] he advocated the death of the doctrine of "once connivance, always connivance."[102] Morton's more balanced spirit, was, however, shown chiefly in tax cases, when he refused to abandon the idea that the courts had a responsibility for keeping law reasonably coherent and in line with the will of Parliament. Thus, Morton was far more shocked than his contemporaries by the idea of giving courts the inherent power to vary trusts in order to minimize tax.[103] In some ways more remarkable, however, was Morton's

97. "In so far as the intention of Parliament or of Ministers is revealed in Acts of Parliament or Orders, either by the language used or by necessary implication, the courts should, of course, carry these intentions out; but it is not the function of any judge to fill in what he conceives to be the gaps in an Act of Parliament. If he does so, he is usurping the function of the legislature"; *Magor & St. Mellons RDC* v. *Newport Corp.*, [1952] A.C. 189 (1951).

98. E.g., Royal Commission on Marriage and Divorce. See especially O. R. McGregor, *Divorce in England*. He vigorously denied that the commission was (or could have been) dominated by its lawyer members and considered it was remarkable how unanimous the report in fact had been. "It was impossible to prove anything one way or the other; it was just a matter of what was the best thing"; 199 *Parl. Deb.*, H.L. (5th ser.), col. 985 (24 Oct. 1956). In 1963 when Leo Abse tried to introduce a qualified type of divorce by consent, Morton stood firm on the decision of his commission against this. The commission, as he pointed out, had after all taken "a good deal of trouble"; 250 ibid., col. 1548 (21 June 1963). He was particularly concerned about the unfairness to a wife who wanted to safeguard her marital status and who would have to go through the ordeals of appearing before a judge whose discretion would render the outcome uncertain; ibid., col. 1549. See also 199 ibid., col. 983 (24 Oct. 1956). He was also opposed to the legitimation of children born as the result of an adulterous relationship; 218 ibid., cols 331–32 (21 July 1959); he was equally opposed to the legalization of marriage to a divorced wife's sister; 199 ibid., col. 983 (24 Oct. 1956).

He supported the death penalty; 201 ibid., cols. 1202–4 (21 Feb. 1957).

99. [1963] A.C. 280 (1962).

100. [1860] 2 Sw. & Tr. 67.

101. [1965] A.C. 444 (1964).

102. Ibid. 457. He dissented, however, in *Blyth* v. *Blyth*, [1966] A.C. 643 (165), a decision involving the 1963 Matrimonial Causes Act's abolition of the presumption of condonation arising from sexual intercourse, and held that on the evidence intercourse did amount to condonation. He placed a higher burden of proof on the petitioner than did the majority, who were probably more in tune with the spirit of the 1963 legislation.

103. "[I]f the court had power to approve, and did approve, schemes such as the present scheme, the way would be open for a most undignified game of chess between the Chancery Division and the legislature. The alteration of one settlement for the purposes of

response to Parliament's attempts to develop anti-tax avoidance devices. When, in *Potts' Executors* v. *Inland Revenue Commissioners*,[104] the House had to construe section 40 of the 1938 act, the majority decided for the taxpayer, citing Tomlin's formalistic statements in the *Duke of Westminster*'s case. Morton alone refused to ignore the intent of the legislature, giving various examples of how surtax could easily be avoided if the majority's view were accepted. He concluded that it seemed "a very strange and capricious result, and incidentally it reveals an extremely simple way of making the section wholly ineffective."[105] By this time, of course, the other law lords were firmly committed to the notion that they must not take into account anything so extraneous as the effect of their decision.[106]

To defend Morton solely on isolated decisions in tax and family law may impose some historical strains,[107] yet in the period of substantive formalism, Morton does seem somewhat out of the ordinary. The same may be said of Lord du Parcq, who sat as a Lord of Appeal from 1946 to 1949.[108] Indeed, du Parcq's deviation from the norm was perhaps even greater, for although he talked of the need for certainty in the law[109] and emphasized the importance of settled rules,[110] du Parcq opposed the

---

avoiding taxation already imposed might well be followed by scores of successful applications for a similar purpose by beneficiaries under other settlements. The legislature might then counter this move by imposing fresh taxation upon the settlements thus altered. The beneficiaries would then troop back to the Chancery Division. . . . So the game might go on"; *Chapman* v. *Chapman*, [1954] A.C. 429, 468.

His fears, however, were shared neither by the Law Reform Committee, which in 1957 recommended that the position should be restored to what it had been thought to have been previously nor by the Conservative administration of the period, which implemented the committee's recommendations. See Variation of Trusts Act of 1958.

104. [1951] A.C. 443 (1950).

105. Ibid. 463.

106. For other examples of his independence of spirit in the tax field, see *Kirkness* v. *John Hudson & Co.*, [1955] A.C. 696, 714; and *Morgan* v. *Tate & Lyle, Ltd.*, [1955] A.C. 21, 35 (1954).

107. Although a party to the Diplock decision, *Minister of Health* v. *Simpson*, [1951] A.C. 251 (1950), he also spoke legislatively in favor of a general provision rectifying all intended charitable trusts affected by the decision; 201 *Parl. Deb.*, H.L. (5th ser.), col. 1202 (21 Feb. 1957).

108. Herbert du Parcq; b. 1880; father, bookseller; educ., Victoria College, Jersey and Exeter College, Oxford (Second, "Greats"); called to bar, 1906 (common law); K.C., 1926; Judge, King's Bench Division, 1932–38; Lord Justice, 1938–46; Lord of Appeal, 1946–49; d. 1949; *Dictionary of National Biography, 1941–1950*, at 228–29.

109. "[T]he worth of a body of law may be tested by asking whether, given any agreed statement of facts, a skilled lawyer can give a clear and definite answer to the question: what in the circumstances does the law say? . . . Our own common law stands the test fairly well, but it is sometimes ignominiously defeated"; Herbert du Parcq, *Aspects of the Law* 4–5.

110. Ibid. See also *Tyne Improvement Comm'rs* v. *Armament Anversois S/A*, [1949] A.C. 326, 350 (1948). See also his skeptical view of development through equity: "We cannot . . . now look to Equity for any fresh alleviation, if that be needed, of the rigours of the common law if any such exist. That venerable institution has begotten a healthy and

splitting of legal hairs[111] as well as logic for logic's sake. He claimed justice as a goal.[112] The model was definitely not Simonds. Outside the courts, du Parcq spoke in almost post-Realist terms about the judicial process. "Circumstances are so infinitely various that, however carefully general rules are framed, they must be construed with some liberality, and not too rigidly applied." It was necessary "to lay down principles lest juries should be persuaded to do injustice by imposing an undue, or perhaps an inadequate, liability on a defendant. The court must be careful, however, to see that the principles laid down are never so narrowly interpreted as to prevent a jury, or judge of fact, from doing justice between the parties."[113] Yet what distinguished du Parcq from many of his contemporaries was that he attempted to apply this approach in his work in the Lords. At a time when this connection was often denied, he not only started from, but was prepared to admit, the basis from which his concept of statutory interpretation operated. "There is an inevitable interaction between the methods of parliamentary drafting and the principles of judicial interpretation."[114] He made intelligent comments about canons of construction[115] and appealed to Parliament to include a statement of intent in statutes.[116] In the meantime he worked toward a balanced approach.[117]

---

vigorous family of principles, but its days of procreation are over. So it is that we must look to Parliament, at the promptings of the Law Revision Committee, to make by statute such changes in the law as it may find the leisure to enact"; du Parcq, *Aspects of the Law* 9.

111. "Law is for the protection and the government of men. Its language must be plain. . . . [J]ustice is never achieved by splitting hairs"; ibid. 19–20.

112. "Justice, in the sense of fair dealing between man and man, is always the aim. If that aim be attained, it matters little that the law is not always logical or consistent or trim and tidy"; ibid. 7.

113. Ibid. While Porter may have been a little unrealistic in his belief about the masses' concern with the judicial functions of the House, there was an element of truth when he said of du Parcq "that the people at large felt that here was one who appreciated their problems and was anxious that justice as they understood it should be done"; cited, Peter E. Jones, "In Memoriam" at ix.

114. *Cutler v. Wandsworth Stadium, Ltd.*, [1949] A.C. 398, 411.

115. "I do not regret . . . the fact that . . . so-called rules of construction 'have fallen into some disfavor.' It must be recognised, however, that the courts have laid down, not indeed rigid rules, but principles which have been found to afford some guidance when it is sought to ascertain the intention of Parliament"; ibid. 410.

116. "To a person unversed in the science or art of legislation it may well seem strange that Parliament has not by now made it a rule to state explicitly when its intention is in a matter which is often of no little importance, instead of leaving it to the courts to discover by a careful examination and analysis of what is expressly said, what that intention may be supposed probably to be. There are no doubt reasons which inhibit the legislature from revealing its intention in plain words. I do not know, and must not speculate, what those reasons may be. I trust, however, that it will not be thought impertinent, in any sense of that word, to suggest respectfully that those who are responsible for framing legislation might consider whether the traditional practice, which obscures, if it does not conceal, the intention which Parliament has, or must be presumed to have, might not safely be abandoned"; ibid.

117. See, for instance, *Shelley v. LCC*, [1949] A.C. 56, 71 (1948); *Amalgamated*

In common law matters, du Parcq showed a similar sense of judicial strategy. His sophisticated mind could avoid the apparently "binding" precedent by dubbing it an "exception."[118] In Factories Act cases, his opinions, even when representing the majority, allowed for the possibility of future development.[119] At least some evidence indicates that du Parcq was prepared to accept the mantle of Atkin and Wright in protecting the workingman.[120] In common with the other law lords, however, he was heavily involved with administrative tasks for two of his four years on the bench, as Chairman of the Royal Commission on the Justices of the Peace,[121] and then he died in office before he was seventy. Once again the "system" seemed to triumph.

Other isolated law lords did, however, triumph over their environment. In terms of the general quality of the appellate bench, Lord Porter, a Lord of Appeal from 1938 to 1954,[122] stood out. Porter differed from his colleagues in several ways. His background was at the Commercial Bar with its reputation for a less rarefied approach to problems than in many branches of the law. Porter was also far less a product of the *cursus honorum* than many of his brethren; he had served only four years as a King's Bench judge when he went to the Lords. Finally, having reached the Lords at the relatively early age of sixty-one, he was able to serve for sixteen years, years, incidently, that were far less interrupted by other public service than was common for law lords during this period. Indeed,

---

Anthracite Collieries, Ltd. v. *Wilds*, [1948] A.C. 440, 456.

118. "[W]ith the greatest respect for the Court of Session, that their opinion that they were, as Lord Carmont put it . . . 'really bound by the case of *Wardlaw's Trustees*' . . . is an unhappy example of the use of precedent. . . . The will now before your Lordships bears the imprint of the lawyer's hand, and I do not find its meaning obscure. It would, I think, be unfortunate if a benevolent interpretation, which the ill-chosen language of a layman may have justified, were henceforth to be regarded in Scotland as a rigid canon of construction, and if it were thus suggested to conveyancers that they might take Mr. Wardlaw's method of expression as a model. This would be to mistake an exception for a rule"; *MacKintosh* v. *Gerrard*, [1947] A.C. 461, 482–83 (Scot.).

119. Thus, while siding with the majority in *Carroll* v. *Andrew Barclay & Sons*, [1948] A.C. 477 (Scot.), he restated *Nicholls* v. *F. Austin, Ltd.*, [1946] A.C. 493, in such a way that it restricted the Simonds ratio. See especially [1948] A.C. 477, 486–87.

120. In *Grant* v. *Sun Shipping Co.*, [1948] A.C. 549, 556 (Scot.), in which he gave his longest speech, he decided that the shipowners were in breach of their duty to provide a safe working place and that the injured stevedore was not guilty of contributory negligence. Du Parcq went even further than the other law lords and held that there had also been a breach of the relevant Docks Regulations; he was prepared to apply a more restrictive view of contributory negligence to the doctrine of a safe system of work than to the common law generally (see especially ibid. 567). On this latter point see also the "common man's approach" reflected in *London Passenger Transp. Bd.* v. *Upson*, [1949] A.C. 155, 176 (1948).

121. Report, Cmd. 7463 (1948).

122. Samuel Lowry Porter; b. 1887; educ., Perse School, Emmanuel College, Cambridge (Second, Law); called to bar, 1905; K.C., 1925; Judge, King's Bench Division, 1934–38; Lord of Appeal, 1938–54; d. 1956.

Porter must rank as one of the few law lords who perhaps sat too long.

To suggest that Porter had a sense of purpose as an appellate judge in no way should be taken as meaning that he saw his role as an expansionist one in all areas. Indeed, in negligence, he pursued the policy of restricting rather than expanding liability. In *Horton*[123] he refused to accede to an argument based on *Donoghue* v. *Stevenson*. His leading judgment in *Edwards* v. *Railway Executive*[124] is an example of a decision restricting occupiers' liability. Porter's name appeared with remarkable frequency in cases where negligence was held not to have been proved.[125] Porter also was obviously unenthusiastic about strict liability, firmly refusing in *Read* v. *J. Lyons and Company*[126] to allow any extension of the rule in *Rylands* v. *Fletcher*. "[T]he liability is itself an extension of the general rule and, in my view, it is undesirable to extend it further."[127] Yet, while his personal predispositions leaned toward restricting liability, his approach to legislation protecting workingmen was remarkably free of preconceptions. One of the first Workmen's Compensation Act[128] appeals in which he sat, and in which he gave the leading opinion, contained an apt illustration of his approach. "The Act was not meant to effect its result by formal methods. Settlement by agreement was the object primarily aimed at."[129] There is evidence, however, that in interpreting the Factories Acts he fell under the spell of his more formalistic colleagues.[130]

123. *London Graving Dock Co.* v. *Horton*, [1951] A.C. 737, 744–50.

124. [1952] A.C. 737, 738.

125. E.g., *Caminer* v. *Northern & London Inv. Trust, Ltd.*, [1951] A.C. 88, 92 (1950); *Bolton* v. *Stone*, [1951] A.C. 850, 857; *Bourhill* v. *Young*, [1943] A.C. 92, 112 (Scot. 1942); *East Suffolk Rivers Catchment Bd.* v. *Kent*, [1941] A.C. 74, 103 (1940).

126. [1947] A.C. 156, 175 (1946).

127. Ibid. 177–78. Another example of Porter's unwillingness to innovate is found in *Glasgow Corp.* v. *Bruce*, [1948] A.C. 79, 83 (Scot. 1947). The doctrine of common employment "has often been considered and sometimes criticised, but it is firmly established and its principles must be followed where they are applicable"; ibid. 83–84.

128. Of the legislation, he said, "No finality is ever likely to be reached. . . . From time to time new aspects the meaning of the section will come to light and the facts to be adjudicated upon will be marshalled afresh. Moreover, the Court will always have to adjust the balance to one side or the other in circumstances where the arguments are evenly matched—and such conditions are likely to recur. The line, says the layman, should be clear, definite, and easily understood by any moderately intelligent man. The lawyer tries to make it so and to simplify the problems. He would do better if only the facts with which he has to deal were less complex"; Samuel L. Porter, *Case Law in the Interpretation of Statutes* 31.

129. *Dobson Ship Repairing Co.* v. *Burton*, [1939] A.C. 590, 599. In *Young* v. *Bristol Aeroplane Co.*, [1946] A.C. 163, 185 (1945), he took the view (shared by Simon and Russell, but not by Macmillan and Simonds), that a worker should not be deemed to have exercised his statutory option between taking compensation or claiming damages until he was fully aware of the alternatives—the test of his knowledge being subjective, not objective. Indeed, apart from a perhaps rather harsh decision in *Amalgamated Anthracite Collieries, Ltd.* v. *Wilds*, [1948] A.C. 440, Porter emerges from all these cases as the friend of the worker and an intelligent interpreter of the legislation.

130. See especially *Carroll* v. *Andrew Barclay & Sons*, [1948] A.C. 477, 482 (Scot.);

Indeed, when one discusses Porter's major contributions, it must be admitted that they generally occurred early in his period as a law lord. His courageous and unpopular dissent in *Joyce* v. *Director of Public Prosecutions* was given in 1945.[131] Porter dissented from the conclusion of his colleagues on the ground that the renewal of his passport by Joyce was a fact from which a jury could infer only that he had retained his allegiance and that the act did not give rise to a presumption that allegiance continued until disclaimed or withdrawn. The matter, in Porter's view, should have been put to the jury for them to decide as a fact, rather than having been the subject of a positive ruling by the judge.[132] Like Atkin, he refused to let the exigencies of war corrupt the law that would also have to be applied under normal conditions. Many of his finest commercial judgments were given during World War II,[133] as were his important observations on statutory interpretation. In this regard he showed keen insight into the difficulty of drafting statutes. The uncertainty of their application was not a fault of language but "a condition of life."[134]

By the late 1940s, however, Porter's iconoclasm was taking a more petulant direction. He saw himself increasingly as a conservative doubting the value of civil liberties[135] and as an antiintellectual, expressing relief, when discussing academic lawyers, that "[i]f it were not for the mercy of God, they might be judges themselves."[136] Yet the measure of the man

---

Latimer v. *AEC, Ltd.*, [1953] A.C. 643, 652; *Richard Thomas & Baldwins, Ltd.* v. *Cummings*, [1955] A.C. 321, 330 (1954).

131. [1946] A.C. 347, 374–86 (1945).

132. See especially ibid. 381–82.

133. For his important contributions to the frustration of contract doctrine, see *Joseph Constantine S.S. Line, Ltd.* v. *Imperial Smelting Corp.*, [1942] A.C., 154, 196 (1941); *Heyman* v. *Darwins, Ltd.*, [1942] A.C. 356, 389 (1941); *Fibrosa Spolka Akcyjna* v. *Fairbairn Lawson Combe Barbour, Ltd.*, [1943] A.C. 32, 76 (1942); *Denny, Mott & Dickson, Ltd.* v. *James B. Fraser & Co.*, [1944] A.C. 265, 281 (Scot. 1943); *Cricklewood Property & Inv. Trust, Ltd.* v. *Leighton's Inv. Trust, Ltd.*, [1945] A.C. 221, 241 (1944). See also his important speech in *Crofter Hand Woven Harris Tweed Co.* v. *Veitch*, [1942] A.C. 435, 480 (Scot. 1941).

134. Porter, *Case Law* 10. Porter generally took a reasonable view of statutory provisions trying, if possible, to find the intent of Parliament. "In the case of an argument so evenly balanced I should not myself have felt justified in differing from the majority of the Court of Appeal. But as your Lordships take a different view I am not prepared to dissent from the opinions which have been expressed. I am the more ready to accept this view, as I cannot but believe that whatever its wording may express, the intention of the Act was to limit the right of action to a term of three years in all cases"; *Caxton Publishing Co.* v. *Sutherland Publishing Co.*, [1939] A.C. 178, 201 (1938).

135. See especially Samuel L. Porter, "English Procedure and Practice" 13.

136. This remark was made in one of Porter's speeches in House of Lords debates on the Defamation Bill, which gave effect to the proposals of the committee of which he was chairman. A dispute arose between Jowitt and Porter as to whether the distinction between libel and slander should be abolished. Porter took some umbrage at Jowitt's suggestion that he had ignored the opinions of academics. Porter retorted, "I have the greatest regard for

was larger than this. While Porter would have passed unnoticed on the bench of a competent American state appellate court, in the midst of substantive formalism, his willingness to take an independent line meant that he stood out from and above most of his colleagues.

Of the judges dealt with in this chapter, however, none stood out from the norm more noticeably than Lord MacDermott. His difference in background from his contemporaries could not have been clearer.[137] The first Ulsterman to be appointed a Lord of Appeal since Partition, MacDermott had had considerable political experience (he had been both a Northern Irish cabinet minister and the Attorney-General at Stormont) but little judicial experience (three years as a High Court judge in Northern Ireland). There were, however, other unique qualities. At the time of his appointment as a Lord of Appeal (1947) MacDermott was, at fifty-one, the youngest man ever to hold the post;[138] moreover, MacDermott was the first law lord since Wright who had been an academic lawyer.[139] It is perhaps not surprising, therefore, that in his four years as a Lord of Appeal, MacDermott should have had a considerable impact, which was occasionally revived in the subsequent twenty years.

Although an Ulster Unionist, in policy terms he was, by the standards of his contemporaries, not a conservative. His political and provincial experience apparently made him aware of constitutional implications and nuances that eluded others. Indeed, such viability as constitutional law has had in Northern Ireland is owed to his post-law lord period as Chief Justice.[140] In terms of the temper of the times, however, it was his jurisprudential approach that set him apart most clearly. Unlike his contemporaries, MacDermott did not see the role of the final appeal court as one of further refining the previously refined. Instead he sought to construe statutes with legislative intent in mind, to restate common law principles broadly, and to prevent the law from deviating too noticeably from common sense or the current political and social developments of modern Britain. MacDermott's greatest contribution to the law was

---

their ability, knowledge, research and impartiality, but they have not to make the law work. This is the difficulty and the difference between us and them." It was at that point that Porter added his comment about academic lawyers; 117 *Parl. Deb.*, H.L. (5th ser.), col. 1109 (15 July 1952).

137. John Clarke MacDermott; b. 1896; father, cleric; educ., Campbell College, Queen's University, Belfast (First, Law); called to Irish bar, 1921; K.C., (N. Ire.), 1936; Northern Ireland M.P. (Unionist), 1938–44; Minister, 1940–41; Attorney-General for Northern Ireland, 1941–44; Judge, High Court of Northern Ireland, 1944–47; Lord of Appeal, 1947–51; Lord Chief Justice, Northern Ireland, 1951–71.

138. The following year, Radcliffe was appointed at 50.

139. In addition to practicing at the bar, MacDermott was Lecturer in Jurisprudence at Queen's University, Belfast, from 1931 to 1935.

140. Harry Calvert, *Constitutional Law in Northern Ireland, passim.* For his more recent writing, see John C. MacDermott, *Murder in 1963.* He continued to sit occasionally in the House; e.g., *R. v. Turner,* [1974] A.C. 357, 368 (1973).

probably that he was always aware of the realities of the situation and the practical results of his decisions. He refused to sit back complacently and merely extol the virtues of the existing legal system.

It was perhaps in the area of public law that MacDermott's inherent sense of the relationship of the legislature and the courts made the clearest contribution. Unlike most law lords, MacDermott articulated for himself a model of civil liberties.[141] It was certainly not a model that would appeal to all. Concerned about the power of unions, he would have taken away much of the protection of the 1906 act and prohibited the closed shop.[142] Yet he was also concerned with "natural justice" in its broadest forms,[143] and his belief in civil liberties in general led him, extrajudicially, to criticize the wartime decisions like *Liversidge* v. *Anderson* and *Duncan* v. *Cammell, Laird and Company,* the abandonment during the 1950s of judicial control over procedural due process in *Nakkuda Ali* v. *Jayaratne* and *Smith* v. *East Elloe Rural District Council,* and the strange (yet almost contemporary) expansion of criminal law in *Shaw* v. *Director of Public Prosecutions.* He regretted the growth of what he called the "literal" school but, perhaps somewhat cynically, expressed the hope that the broader approach based in *Shaw* (the "Ladies' Directory" case) might be applied to construction generally.[144]

MacDermott was naturally concerned about what had happened to the process of statutory construction during the period of substantive formalism. He put forward the ideas of mandatory "liberal" construction, preambles, "clause-tasters" and subsidized litigation about legislation, all at a time when Jowitt and Simonds were the Lord Chancellors.[145] Above all, MacDermott was anxious to give effect to the intentions of Parliament.[146] Thus, in tax law, MacDermott was sometimes found insisting that the Revenue be required to show fair play[147] and, at other

141. John C. MacDermott, *Protection from Power under English Law.*

142. Ibid. 180, 193. He had some chance of putting his views into effect in *Bonsor* v. *Musicians' Union,* [1956] A.C. 104 (1955). See especially his dismissal of the argument that a member could not sue the union because it was his "agent"; ibid. 149.

143. MacDermott, *Protection from Power* 83: "The categories of natural justice are not closed: they may alter slowly, but they must always be capable of reflecting changed circumstances and prevailing standards."

144. John C. MacDermott, "Some Requirements of Justice" 103 ff.

145. MacDermott, *Protection from Power* 68–69.

146. E.g., *Tyne Improvement Comm'rs* v. *Armament Anversois S/A,* [1949] A.C. 326, 358 (1948); *Smith* v. *London Transp. Executive,* [1951] A.C. 555, 580 (1950).

147. In *Potts' Executors* v. *IRC,* [1951] A.C. 443, 464 (1950), he did not accede the Crown's argument on the meaning of "loan" in the antiavoidance provisions of the Finance Act of 1938. One of the Crown's arguments was that to hold as the majority proposed to do would lead to easy circumvention of the statute. MacDermott's reply to this was that the section attempted to prevent certain forms of tax evasion in a manner that would harm innocent people: "Tax evasion often places the draftsman in great difficulty and it may not always be possible to avoid hurting the guiltless. But § 40 seems capable of involving straightforward transactions to such a considerable extent that a decision which may encourage the substitution of something better need not be a matter for regret"; ibid. 466.

times, insisting that common sense be applied to prevent the wealthy being given a naked opportunity to avoid paying their taxes.[148]

In terms of construing legislation, however, perhaps MacDermott's interventions were most dramatic in the area of the Factory Acts. He was obviously distressed as he saw the law lords turning the Factory Acts into a formalistic obstacle course.[149] In his dissent in *Sparrow* v. *Fairey Aviation Company*,[150] MacDermott refused to be bound by what he argued were mere dicta in earlier cases and urged a return to the actual words of section 14 of the Factories Acts, in which there was no evidence of limitation "to the prevention of contact between the actual body of the workman and the dangerous part."[151] As MacDermott made clear, "[s]tare decisis is a doctrine to be honoured in the interests of consistency and certainty; but to apply it here would be to break new ground without advancing those interests, and to reach a point where the intention of Parliament could suffer erosion by a sort of judicial inadvertence which even the most anxious circumspection cannot entirely avoid."[152]

It was also in a case concerning workmen that MacDermott articulated his general approach to the development of policy within common law doctrines. In *London Graving Dock Company* v. *Horton*,[153] the House was offered the opportunity of protecting workmen through the development of occupiers' liability. The legal position was resolved into whether the invitor owed a "duty to take reasonable care to protect his invitee from the relevant danger" or "no duty to an invitee who has knowledge or due notice of the relevant danger."[154] The majority based

148. In *IRC* v. *Lord Rennell*, [1964] A.C. 173, 197 (1963), MacDermott dissented. The majority held that an exemption from estate duty of "gifts made in consideration of marriage" might include persons other than those getting married. MacDermott refused to construe the concept so broadly:

I am far from convinced that, for the ordinary reader who is content to take the language of the statute as he finds it, the expression in question would have this meaning. I doubt if such a reader would know it as an expression used in common speech. . . . [T]he purpose and history of the relevant legislation seem to me to lead to the conclusion that a gift "made in consideration of marriage" . . . must be a gift which confers some actual or enforceable benefit of value on one or more of those within the marriage consideration. To begin with, the exemption was obviously aimed at benefiting a special and deserving class, such as those entering upon the married state and the obligations which that condition entails. [Ibid. 198]

149. See also *Glasgow Corp.* v. *Bruce*, [1948] A.C. 79, 85 (Scot. 947); *Galashiels Gas Co.* v. *O'Donnell*, (1949) A.C. 275, (Scot. 1948); *Paris* v. *Stepney Borough Council*, [1951] A.C. 367, 387 (1950). He decided against the injured workman in *Harrison* v. *National Coal Bd.*, [1951] A.C. 639 (1950), the last Lords' decision on the doctrine of common employment.

150. [1964] A.C. 1019, 1034–48 (1962).

151. Ibid. 1039. The majority, relying on *Close* v. *Steel Co. of Wales*, [1962] A.C. 367 (1961), held that the duty to fence did not include a duty to fence against a tool which the operator was using coming into contact with dangerous parts of the machine.

152. [1964] A.C. 1019, 1048 (1962).

153. [1951] A.C. 737.

154. Ibid. 761.

their speeches principally on the much-quoted judgment of Willes in *Indermaur v. Dames.* MacDermott was not happy about following this earlier decision slavishly; he regarded it as a judgment "which, however outstanding, was certainly never intended to take its place in the statute book."[155] With the competing policy choice before him, MacDermott argued:

> In applying the common law to a given state of facts upon which there is no binding authority it is permissible and proper, in choosing between two possible views, to have regard to the reasonable requirements of the community which the law has to serve. . . . Such a process demands great caution and is not necessarily conclusive. But if one view leads to a narrow and unreasonable rule and the other does not, it is a point in favour of the latter. . . . Your Lordships' decision will establish what was not established before, and that, as it seems to me, makes a comparison between the broad merits of the rival contentions both relevant and right.[156]

Finally MacDermott chose the first alternative,[157] suggesting that he had little time for "that love of precedent which reduces responsibility and eases decision."[158]

MacDermott managed to bring this sense of balanced creativity and policymaking to various areas of the law. He was prepared to question deference to the laws of foreign nations in conflicts,[159] and in charity law he was willing to examine earlier precedents and state a new principle, as well as calling for amending legislation.[160] He helped resolve apparent conflict between the established law of contracts and agreements relating to land.[161] In handling such matters, he admitted that his criterion was not precedent but "the tradition of the spirit of the law," the "tradition distilled from the talk, the example, the sense of truth and justice and duty of the generations, the tradition that comes as a legacy to the novice

155. Ibid. 762.

156. Ibid. 765–66.

157. "It respects the settled distinction between sciens and volens in this branch of jurisprudence, a distinction which the appellants' contention would, in effect, obliterate. It provides a rational criterion of responsibility over a wider range of circumstance, being equally applicable to avoidable and unavoidable dangers and to invitees of all kinds and degrees. And, not least, though in a sense this is but to enlarge on what I have just said, it applies to a relationship which, as already observed, is infinitely varied in character, a test of liability which is correspondingly flexible and adoptable. . . . And lastly, I see nothing in all this to bear harshly on the occupier. He controls the premises he serves his own interest by the invitation, he has left to him all the pleas open to one accused of negligent conduct. Why should he be exonerated, or partly exonerated, from the duty of taking reasonable care? I have been unable to find any satisfactory answer to that question in principle or authority"; ibid. 772–73.

158. MacDermott, *Protection from Power* 41.

159. *Kahler v. Midland Bank, Ltd.,* [1950] A.C. 24, 36 (1949).

160. *National Deposit Friendly Soc'y Trustees v. Skegness UDC,* [1959] A.C., 293, 314–15 (1958).

161. *Winter Garden Theatre, Ltd. v. Millennium Prods., Ltd.,* [1948] A.C. 173, 203 (1947).

and informs him, in due course and better than lectures or books, of what he must strive to attain."[162] To those accustomed to a sophisticated appellate bench, such observations may seem trite. In the era of Jowitt and Simonds they were profoundly important in keeping the common law tradition alive.

Private Law

The nature of private law was, however, changing; the common law concepts were giving way to statutory solutions. Substantive formalism in the judiciary was being balanced by legislative intervention. In the area of landlord and tenant, the 1936 Housing Act had reversed, at least with respect to less expensive housing, the centuries-old common law doctrine that implied no terms of fitness of habitation in a lease,[163] while, by the earlier legislation, the vast majority of rental housing in the private sector had been subjected to rent restriction.[164] Yet when statutes did not intervene, the tendency in common law areas such as crime, family law, and conflicts was to accept the implications of the status quo.

In criminal law the House, during World War II, gave the impression of having little concept of the problems or the difficulties facing either accused or prosecution, and it generally chose rather visceral authoritarian solutions.[165] In the postwar years these views seemingly mellowed slightly, although it was held that a man might be charged with a

162. MacDermott, *Protection from Power* 41.

163. For a liberal interpretation of this, see *Summers* v. *Salford Corp.*, [1943] A.C. 283, 285 (1942); a jammed window in a small house was a breach of the implied undertaking to keep it "in all respects reasonably fit for human habitation."

164. The early postwar decisions on this legislation appeared reasonable. See Simon delivering the judgment of the House on the meaning of "attendance" and "furniture," the two mystical matters that might take rented accommodation out of the ambit of the Rent Acts; *Palser* v. *Grinling*, [1948] A.C. 291 (1947). At least at first, an effort was made to allow rent to be increased in appropriate cases; *Asher* v. *Seaford Court Estates, Ltd.*, [1950] A.C. 508. The local authorities were also given reasonable flexibility in interpreting their scope; *Shelley* v. *LCC*, [1949] A.C. 56 (1948). But as time went on, it is arguable that the House began to misconstrue the intent of Parliament and to allow rents to be raised where Parliament had not thought it appropriate; *Langford Property Co.* v. *Batten*, [1951] A.C. 223 (1950). On the other hand, the House did extend the protection to widows of contractual tenants in addition to widows of statutory tenants, specifically included in the 1935 act; *Moodie* v. *Hosegood*, [1952] A.C. 61 (1951). See also *Capital & Provincial Property Trust, Ltd.* v. *Rice*, [1952] A.C. 142 (1951), apportioning the base of statutory rent when two flats had originally been let as a single unit. See also *Preston & Area Rent Tribunal* v. *Pickavance*, [1953] A.C. 562.

165. E.g., *Mancini* v. *DPP*, [1942] A.C. 1 (1941); Southern Europeans expected to behave with *sang froid* of the "reasonable man," when provoked and a "hot-blooded" response did not justify the reduction of murder to manslaughter. The Appeal Cases for 1946 included *Joyce* v. *DPP*, [1946] A.C. 347 (1945) (failure of American citizen to divest himself entirely of British passport made him available for charge of treason), and *Holmes* v. *DPP*, [1946] A.C. 588 (returning serviceman not entitled to kill wife and then plead provocation when the latter confessed adultery—must catch same in flagrante delicto).

violation of the Defense Regulations committed during the war, after the regulations had expired.[166] While rejecting a claim for false imprisonment, however, the House put limitations on the right to arrest without warrant in *Christie* v. *Leachinsky*.[167] Patriotism and authoritarianism, however, rapidly reasserted themselves. The crime wave, so it was said, had to be stopped. Accordingly, in the 1950s the law of evidence with respect to accomplices was extended to convict Davies of the Clapham Common murders,[168] and when Mau Mau threatened in Kenya, the Privy Council could find no reason why the illegal obtaining of evidence should justify the quashing of the death penalty imposed on a Kikuyu youth.[169] In other words, the sense of hierarchy and authority led to an instinctive support of government, a result similar to that brought about by the judicial reluctance to become involved in administrative law and civil liberties.

In family law, one can perhaps see a slight trend in the other direction. During the war there was an effort to relax family law a little,[170] although the post war period was noted for the importance of the decisions rather than for their distinction.[171] Indeed, in each area the House seemed to approach problems looking only backward, giving precedents undue weight and largely ignoring principles, with little or no sense of any responsibility for adapting the common law to new and changing surroundings. For instance, the House after 1945 seemed unable to mold private international law concepts, even gingerly, to meet the demands of the Cold War[172] or, domestically, to adapt the concepts of company law

166. *Wicks* v. *DPP*, [1947] A.C. 362 (1946).

167. [1947] A.C. 573 (1946).

168. *Davies* v. *DPP*, [1954] A.C. 378.

169. *Kuruma, Son of Kaniu* v. *The Queen*, [1955] A.C. 197 (P.C. 1954). The Judicial Committee did express the hope that the sentence would not be carried out.

170. E.g., *Blunt* v. *Blunt*, [1943] A.C. 517, dealing with the court's exercise of discretion when the petitioners have confessed to adultery. For a more conventional decision, see *Henderson* v. *Henderson & Crellin*, [1944] A.C. 49 (1943).

171. Including, on consummation, *Baxter* v. *Baxter*, [1948] A.C. 274 (1947), a series of decisions on cruelty, including *Jamieson* v. *Jamieson*, [1952] A.C. 525 (Scot.), and *King* v. *King*, [1953] A.C. 124 (1952); some thoughts on proof of adultery, *Preston-Jones* v. *Preston-Jones*, [1951] A.C. 391 (1950); the impact of insanity on desertion, *Crowther* v. *Crowther*, [1951] A.C. 723; and a somewhat odd case raising a conflicts recognition problem, *Starkowaski* v. *Attorney-General*, [1954] A.C. 155 (1953).

172. On the Cold War, see, e.g., *Kahler* v. *Midland Bank, Ltd.*, [1950] A.C. 24 (1949); and *Zivnostenska Banka National Corp.* v. *Frankman*, [1950] A.C. 57 (1949). See also *United States of America & Republic of France* v. *Dollfus Mieg et Cie S.A. & Bank of England*, [1952] A.C. 582 (1951); *Gdynia-Amerijka Linie,* v. *Boguslawski*, [1953] A.C. 11 (1952); *Bank voor Handel en Scheepvaart N.V.* v. *Administrator of Hungarian Property*, [1954] A.C. 584 (1953). For disputes arising out of other international crises, see *Boissevain* v. *Weil*, [1950] A.C. 327 (loan during World War II in violation of Defense Regulations of 1939) and *Arab Bank, Ltd.* v. *Barclays Bank*, [1954] A.C. 495 (Arab-Israeli conflict, 1948). In *Indian Government* v. *Taylor*, [1955] A.C. 499 (1954), the House carried into the conflicts field its basic view of tax law and refused to enforce an Indian tax claim in an English court.

to an environment that was rather less receptive to private enterprise.[173]

Yet for all the changes, tort and contract were still the staple of private law. Throughout the fifteen-year period, the instinct to impose liability in tort was far less strong than in the 1930s. During the war, the House, in a series of cases, the most notable being *East Suffolk Rivers Catchment Board v. Kent*,[174] *Bourhill v. Young*,[175] and *Glasgow Corporation v. Muir*,[176] appeared to limit the scope of the duty of care in negligence, while in *Benham v. Gambling*,[177] the law lords restricted the concept of loss of expectation of life developed in *Rose v. Ford*.[178] This reluctance to impose liability continued in the postwar period. The doctrine of *res ipsa loquitur* was construed narrowly;[179] *Read v. J. Lyons and Company*[180] showed that the House was not going to smile on liability in the absence of fault. Owners of animals, trees, and cricket balls were not to be liable for accidents caused by their possessions.[181] Statutes were normally construed to deny a private person a right of action,[182] and a person had to be unlawfully detained for an unreasonable time before receiving damages for false imprisonment.[183] Wives

173. On company law generally, see *Southern Foundries (1926), Ltd. v. Shirlaw*, [1940] A.C. 701; *Morris v. Kanssen*, [1946] A.C. 459; and *Scottish Ins. Corp. v. Wilsons & Clyde Coal Co.*, [1949] A.C. 462 (Scot.). See also *Regal (Hastings), Ltd. v. Gulliver*, [1942] 1 All E.R. 378 (H.L.) and on the liability of directors, see *Westburn Sugar Refineries, Ltd., ex parte* [1951] A.C. 625 (Scot.), allowing a company under § 66(1)(c) of the Companies Act of 1948 to reduce its capital, by giving assets to shareholders, when threatened with nationalization.

174. [1941] A.C. 74 (1940), holding (Atkin dissenting) that a statutory body could not be held liable for failing to exercise its statutory powers or exercising them in a dilatory manner.

175. [1943] A.C. 92 (Scot. 1942). A unanimous House held that a motorcyclist who, as the result of his own negligence, killed himself, did not owe a duty of care to an eight-month-pregnant fishwife who was standing on the far side of a tramcar and suffered nervous shock as the result of the crash, later producing a stillborn child.

176. [1943] A.C. 448 (Scot.). The House refused to allow children to recover for burns received when a tea urn fell on them while they were in a tea shop buying ice cream. The refusal to allow recovery was based not on the absence of a duty of care, but on the fact that the tea was being carried by picnickers whom the manageress had allowed to walk through the shop. In these circumstances she was not expected to foresee the danger that might have led her to order the children out of the hall; in any event, there was no explanation of how the accident had been caused. In fairness, on the facts, it is difficult to see how the House could have found liability.

177. [1941] A.C. 157 (1940).

178. [1937] A.C. 826.

179. *Woods v. Duncan*, [1946] A.C. 401 (1945). This represented further litigation arising out of the *Thetis* disaster and took a limited view of *res ipsa loquitur*, holding that it only shifted the evidential burden of proof.

180. [1947] A.C. 156 (1946).

181. *Searle v. Wallbank*, [1947] A.C. 341 (1946) (animals), *Caminer v. Northern & London Inv. Trust, Ltd.*, [1951] A.C. 88 (1950) (tree); and *Bolton v. Stone*, [1951] A.C. 850 (cricket ball).

182. *Cutler v. Wandsworth Stadium, Ltd.*, [1949] A.C. 398. This should be contrasted with *Workington Harbour & Dock Bd. v. Towerfield (Owners)*, [1951] A.C. 112 (1950).

183. *John Lewis & Co. v. Tims*, [1952] A.C. 676.

were not to be compensated for losing the consortium of their husbands.[184] The high point of these trends, however, was undoubtedly *Jacobs* v. *London County Council*.[185] This decision, together with the *Horton* case,[186] brought a harsh rigidity to the categories of persons to whom an occupier owed responsibility, rigidities that only legislation was able to eradicate.[187] The other responsibilities of occupiers also seemed to be minimal.[188] Only at the very end of the period, in line with the changes in responsibility toward workers, did a hint of a broader approach toward liability appear.[189]

In commercial law, the changes in style and substance reflected more obviously the changes in the style of the law lords. During the war the last fetters of the medieval simplicities of the equity of redemption were shaken off in *Knightsbridge Estates Trust, Limited* v. *Byrne*,[190] and the House grappled intelligently with the issue of commissions on sales[191] even if its skirmishes with the making of contracts were rather less productive.[192] World War II, however, as all wars, also exacerbated another important problem—the frustration of contracts.[193] In the *Constantine* case, where the vessel in question was so badly damaged that it could not perform the charterparty, Wright began a series of speeches[194] designed to strike a balance between contract modification and the sanctity of contract.[195] In these changes Wright was assisted by Simon—who, as was his custom, hedged his bets[196]—and rather less effectively by Macmillan.[197] This trio was able to remold the face of frustration so noticeably that even the strict purveyors of orthodoxy who came after them were not entirely able to destroy their work.[198]

184. *Best* v. *Samuel Fox & Co.*, [1952] A.C. 716.

185. [1950] A.C. 361.

186. *London Graving Dock Co.* v. *Horton*, [1951] A.C. 737.

187. See Arthur L. Goodhart, "The 'I think' Doctrine of Precedent" 374. A test of reasonableness was ultimately introduced by the Occupiers' Liability Act of 1957.

188. E.g., *Edwards* v. *Railway Executive*, [1952] A.C. 737 (occupier not liable to 9-year-old boy who had trespassed on railway line).

189. *Carmarthenshire County Council* v. *Lewis*, [1955] A.C. 549.

190. [1940] A.C. 613.

191. *Luxor, Ltd.* v. *Cooper*, [1941] A.C. 108 (1940).

192. *Scammell & Nephew, Ltd.* v. *Ouston*, [1941] A.C. 251 (1940).

193. *Joseph Constantine S.S. Line, Ltd.* v. *Imperial Smelting Corp.*, [1942] A.C. 154 (1941); *Heyman* v. *Darwins, Ltd.*, [1942] A.C. 356 (1941); *Fibrosa Spolka Akcyjna* v. *Fairbairn Lawson Combe Barbour, Ltd.*, [1943] A.C. 32 (1942); *Denny, Mott & Dickson, Ltd.* v. *James B. Fraser & Co.*, [1944] A.C. 265 (Scot. 1943); and *Cricklewood Property & Inv. Trust, Ltd.* v. *Leighton's Inv. Trust, Ltd.*, [1945] A.C. 221 (1944).

194. See *Constantine* at 185, *Fibrosa* at 70, and *Denny, Mott* at 274.

195. "No detailed absolute rules can be stated. A certain elasticity is essential"; *Denny, Mott* at 274.

196. E.g., ibid. 270.

197. Macmillan's speech in *Heyman* at 369, is far from satisfactory.

198. In *Heyman* the House also established the logically questionable but practically convenient principle that an arbitration clause might survive an allegedly frustrating event

With the war over, however, and especially after Wright's resignation in 1947, the direction and tone of commercial cases changed. Some useful decisions were made in shipping and related matters,[199] and the *Winter Garden Theatre, Limited v. Millennium Productions, Limited*[200] must rank as an important decision in eliminating some of the strange notions of land law that had crept into contract. With Atkin and Wright gone, however, the cases tended to take on a more formalistic cast,[201] a process seen most clearly in *British Movietonews, Limited v. London and District Cinemas, Limited*,[202] where the House categorically rejected the approach of Denning, L.J., who was attempting to keep alive Wright's flexible motions of frustration. If critics insist that Denning was trying to expand these concepts as well, then it may be that he was merely setting the stage for the final—or rather most recent—period of the House's history.

Public Law

To identify substantive trends over a fifteen-year period is never easy. Especially in the English context, reliable trend spotting may take rather longer. Moreover, between 1940 and 1955 there were other problems, particularly the paucity of decisions and the expansion in the numbers of Lords of Appeal. Tone can, however, be set in relatively few decisions during a limited period, and the few constitutional cases that were heard in these fifteen years revealed a surprising unity of interest among Simon, Jowitt, and Simonds. All in different ways took the view that parliamentary sovereignty implied that there should be no serious

---

so that an arbitrator might determine whether the contract that justified his sitting was in fact no longer in existence. The decision, however, did require some intellectual gymnastics in order to distinguish earlier House of Lords and Privy Council decisions. Cf. especially *Hirji Mulji v. Cheong Yue S.S. Co.*, [1926] A.C. 497 (P.C.).

More dramatic in some ways was the *Fibrosa* decision. Even Webber, the staid author of *The Effect of War on Contracts*, saw this case as clear "judicial legislation." There the House was concerned with reexamining the rule laid down in *Chandler v. Webster*, [1904] 1 K.B. 493 (C.A.), that, where there had been frustration, the economic loss lay where it fell. In overruling the earlier Court of Appeal decision, and by making use of quasi contract, the House allowed at least a certain balancing of the equities. It was not the perfect solution—the legislature still had to intervene [see the Law Reform (Frustrated Contracts) Act of 1943]—but something vital had been accomplished.

199. E.g., *Morrison S.S. Co. v. Greystoke Castle*, [1947] A.C. 265 (1946) (direct action by cargo owners for share of general average against ship that was partially responsible for event); *Monarch S.S. Co. v. Karlshamns Oljefabriker (A/B)*, [1949] A.C. 196 (Scot. 1948) (war risk clause, unseaworthiness, commercial implications); and *Comptoir d'Achat et de Vente du Boerenbond Belge S.A. v. Luis de Ridder Limitada (The Julia)*, [1949] A.C. 293 (1948) (c.i.f. contracts).

200. [1948] A.C. 173 (1947).

201. Perhaps this can first be detected in *Hill v. William Hill, Ltd.*, [1949] A.C. 530.

202. [1952] A.C. 166 (1951).

judicial questioning not only of acts of Parliament, but of decisions of the Civil Service, which, by 1940 may well have been the strongest force in government, although committed to a judgelike insistence that it was uninvolved in policymaking.[203] The responsible system of government, however, which made ministers both legislators and heads of departments in the executive, de facto gave greatest power to the senior civil servants who had security of tenure.

During World War II, a quartet of cases suggested that there was no room at all for judicial review of any act of the central government. The writing was on the wall in *Barnard* v. *Gorman*,[204] in which customs officers were held not liable for an action for false imprisonment and malicious prosecution when they claimed reasonable grounds for detaining someone, even if he turned out to be innocent. This attitude was carried to its extreme in two cases decided in November 1941: *Liversidge* v. *Anderson*[205] and *Greene* v. *Secretary of State for Home Affairs*.[206] In *Liversidge*, an action for false imprisonment was brought against the Home Secretary, who had imprisoned the appellant under regulation 18B, par. (1) of the Defense (General) Regulations of 1939, which provided that "[i]f the Secretary of State has reasonable cause to believe any person to be of hostile origin or associations . . . he may make an order against that person dictating that he be detained." Only Atkin felt that the words "has . . . cause" were not synonymous with "thinks he has cause"—in other words, that the executive had to offer some proof. The remaining law lords were prepared to admit that habeas corpus had been sunk without trace by regulations made under the Emergency Powers (Defense) Act of 1939, a decision confirmed by the *Greene* case. The final decision in the quartet concerned the right of the executive to claim Crown privilege. It was understandable that, in an action brought in time of war alleging defects in a submarine, the Admiralty should be reluctant to produce documents, and the claim of privilege on the facts involved might well have been justified. In *Duncan* v. *Cammell, Laird and Company*,[207] however, Simon went far beyond these limited justifications in a

203. Of the role of the Civil Service during the Labour administration of 1945–51, Marwick comments that Attlee "had a colossal respect for the traditions of British government; having been born into the same kind of upper-middle-class family as had most senior civil servants, he was not the sort of man to invite a direct confrontation with them. Later Attlee penned a somewhat fulsome tribute to the civil servants who had cooperated loyally with the Labour government; sometimes one has the impression that it was rather the government which cooperated loyally with the civil servants"; Arthur Marwick, *Britain in the Century of Total War* 329.

204. [1941] A.C. 378.

205. [1942] A.C. 206 (1941).

206. [1942] A.C. 284 (1941). For a useful background to this case, see John M. Blum, *V Was for Victory* 167–72. The British treatment of Jewish refugees in these years left something to be desired.

207. [1942] A.C. 624.

speech concurred in by the other six law lords. Once again the precedents were far from clear. Some, Simon chose to ignore; others, he treated in a way that caused concern even to the most ardent advocates of the declaratory theory. As a result, for the following twenty years, it was assumed that the Crown (that is, the Civil Service) had an absolute right not only to claim privilege, but also to determine that privilege for itself.

A decision like *Liversidge* inevitably leads to a certain amount of public soul-searching, not all of it particularly profound.[208] There was, after all, no fundamental law to prevent the suspension of habeas corpus by the Crown (or at least Parliament); the most the courts could require was that the proper words be used. Since 1688, the concept of judicial review of fundamental law as such was dead in England. The battle was about the residual elements of fundamental law—the presumptions of fairness in civil liberties and procedural due process on which the judges might base their legal reasoning; and what these four cases held was that, at least during wartime, no such premises or assumptions were operative. Yet, although liberals, somewhat courageously, protested *Liversidge*, the case reflected assumptions about the primacy of an omnipotent executive that were far from unique. During the 1930s, in interpreting the Indian Constitutional Act of 1915, the Privy Council accorded absolute powers to the Governor-General. "[I]t cannot be disputed that an emergency existed and that [the Governor-General's actions] are for the peace and good government. . . . Those are matters of which the Governor-General is the sole judge; he is not bound to give any reasons."[209] This approach was confirmed in a series of Privy Council cases following *Liversidge*.[210]

Perhaps the greatest significance of the *Liversidge* approach was the impact it had on Commonwealth and former Commonwealth countries. The idea that the judiciary might in any sense be ultimate guardians of civil liberties or responsible for procedural due process was reserved for professional conferences; it rarely appeared on the bench. Thus during

208. On the case, see the defense by A. L. G[oodhart], "Note," 58 *Law Quarterly Review* 3 (1942); and the criticism by Carleton Kemp Allen, "Regulation 18B and Reasonable Cause" 232. ("In the light of this decision it is enough for the Home Secretary merely to think that he has reasonable cause.") See also Arthur L. Goodhart, "A Short Replication," ibid. 243.

For a later evaluation, see Julius Stone, *The Province and Function of Law* 193–94. See also MacDermott:

In fact, both the majority and the minority justices in *Liversidge v. Anderson* seem to have resorted to policy factors right from the outset in order to determine that the provision there in question was ambiguous: in the case of the majority, the policy of according the widest possible latitude of discretion to the executive at the height of a great War; in the case of the minority, the policy bound up with Dicey's rule of law concept of resisting of the utmost executive encroachments upon individual liberties. [*Protection from Power* 48]

209. *Bhagat Singh* v. *King-Emperor*, 58 Indian Appeals 169 (P.C. 1931).
210. See especially *King-Emperor* v. *Benoari Lal Sarma*, [1945] A.C. 14 (P.C. 1944). But see also *King-Emperor* v. *Sibnath Baerji*, 72 Indian Appeals 241 (P.C. 1945).

World War II the Japanese-Canadians[211] and the IRA (Irish Republican Army)[212] received short shrift. After 1945, the influence of the *Liversidge* mentality on the one hand made it difficult for Commonwealth countries fumbling toward judicial review to implement it,[213] and at the same time gave the executives in such countries a legal framework to establish autocratic forms of government. If one were to stop the clock in 1977, one would find that in countries as disparate as Northern Ireland, India, Uganda, Southern Rhodesia, and Nigeria, imprisonment without trial was justified in terms of either the letter or the spirit of *Liversidge*.

In this light it would not have been surprising that, whatever government had been returned in 1945, the law lords would have been unlikely to seek a battle with the executive. As it was, they were politically astute enough to know that, with a huge Labour landslide, it would have been uncomfortable to give any hint of a concern even with procedural due process. This area shows a parallel with the Supreme Court of the United States, particularly with Mr. Dooley's observation that the Court "reads the election returns." Canada saved any embarrassment by abolishing appeals to the Privy Council. In Australian constitutional appeals, the Judicial Committee appeared satisfied to follow the line of least resistance and uphold the High Court of Australia.[214] Nor was the Privy Council concerned to develop administrative law even in those countries that had a written constitution. In *Nakkuda Ali* v. *Jayaratne*,[215] the Judicial Committee refused to issue certiorari against the decision of the Controller of Textiles in Ceylon, on the ground that in refusing to issue a license, he was not acting judicially. On the facts the decision may have been correct, but the reasoning made it seem as if the courts were effectively excluding themselves from playing any role, constructive or otherwise, in the future of public law.

Meanwhile, the House of Lords, through the senior Lord of Appeal, Thankerton, refused to concede in *Franklin* v. *Minister of Town and*

211. The Japanese-Americans were merely interned; the Japanese-Canadians, irrespective of nationality, were liable to deportation as the result of delegated legislation under the National Emergency Transitional Powers Act of 1945; *Co-operative Committee on Japanese-Canadians* v. *Attorney-General for Canada*, [1947] A.C. 87 (P.C. 1946). Wright relied, *inter alia*, on *King-Emperor* v. *Sibnath Baerji*, 72 Indian Appeals 241 (P.C. 1945).

212. See the interpretation of the Offences against the State Act of 1940, in *re Article 26 of the Constitution; and in re Offences against the State (Amendment) Bill*, 1940, [1940] Ir. R. 470. The case was, of course, decided before *Liversidge*.

213. E.g., *Baffour Osii Akoto*, Civil Appeal 42/61 (Ghana 1961), discussed in William B. Harvey, *Law and Social Change in Ghana* 288 ff.

214. E.g., *Australia* v. *Bank of New South Wales*, [1950] A.C. 235 (P.C. 1949). At 310 the committee even conceded that in such appeals (here the issue of bank nationalization) "the problem to be solved will often be not so much legal as political, social or economic." On this point, see Edward McWhinney, *Judicial Review in the English Speaking World*.

215. [1951] A.C. 66 (P.C. 1950).

Country Planning[216] that the courts had any role in supervising the procedure followed under the New Towns Act. The following year, in the *Fitzwilliam* case the House once again confirmed that not only was it disinterested in policy issues (or substantive due process, if one prefers), but also it could see no role for itself in supervising procedural due process.[217] The nadir in this series of cases, however, came early in 1956 with the decision in *Smith* v. *East Elloe Rural District Council*.[218] There the majority held that, although the plaintiff was alleging bad faith both in the making and in the confirmation of a compulsory purchase order, he had no opportunity to question it either under the act concerned or in any other manner. By this time, however, the political mood was beginning to shift and, on different points, Morton, Reid, Radcliffe, and Somervell all dissented.

Thus, throughout the fifteen-year period covered by this study the House washed its hands of constitutional law per se. In this sense there was consistency. But other areas of public law were characterized by swings of the pendulum—the most obvious, in tax law, already noted in the discussions of Simon and Simonds. A review of the cases of the war years shows how remarkably strong and consistent was the theme that all were under an obligation to pay a fair share and that the affluent should not be entitled to stand on the form of their transaction.[219] Justice,

216. [1948] A.C. 87 (1947). The action sought to question an order of the Minister of Town and Country Planning that designated Stevenage a new town site. The main ground on which the appellants based their case was that under the act the minister had a judicial or quasi-judicial function in scrutinizing the scheme and the many objections to it. They alleged that he failed to do this and called in evidence a press report and speech of the minister that, they contended, demonstrated that he had prejudged the issue (before the bill had received its Second Reading and some months before the statutory committee of inquiry). The basic issue in litigation was the function and duties of the minister under the act and the decision as to whether he had contravened these duties. None of the duties was found to be of such a nature that, if they were not followed, the courts might intervene.

217. *Earl Fitzwilliam's Wentworth Estates Co.* v. *Minister of Housing and Local Government*, [1952] A.C. 362 (1951), construed § 43 of the Town and Country Planning Act of 1947, on the point of whether the Central Land Board had validly made an order and was thus authorized by the minister to acquire part of the applicant's land compulsorily. The board could acquire land under the section if the minister was "satisfied that it was expedient in the public interest . . . and that the Board is unable to acquire the land by agreement on reasonable terms. . . . Once acquired the land may be disposed of by the Board in accordance with such direction as may be given to them in that behalf by the Minister." Shawcross, in his argument for the minister, stated, "The Courts cannot inquire into the motives of the Minister . . . it is not a matter for the courts but rather for parliamentary control"; ibid. 373. This was basically the argument that the House adopted.

For a more workmanlike approach to the Town and Country Planning Acts, admittedly on a politically less explosive point, see *LCC* v. *Marks & Spencer, Ltd.*, [1953] A.C. 535.

218. [1956] A.C. 736.

219. Just as World War II was about to begin, the House decided that the whole of the dividend of a company was taxable, even if part of that dividend itself represented an already-taxed dividend of some other company; *Barnes* v. *Hely Hutchinson*, [1940] A.C.

of course, demanded that many decisions went in favor of the taxpayer.[220] The point was that both the canons of construction and the literal rule of interpretation that had been at the very heart of the *Westminster* case had in five years been almost entirely abandoned; and Simon's speech in *Latilla*[221] in 1943 was the mirror image of Russell's in *Westminster*.[222]

The change in tax interpretation after the war, particularly the reintroduction of the presumption against a section's application unless the transaction was covered by its actual words, together with the overall literal interpretation of the legislation, has been discussed in connection with Simonds, who played such an important role in these changes. It was not difficult to see what pressures lay behind the shifts. While the rates of income tax and supertax (paid by those with particularly large incomes) had seemed not unreasonable in wartime,[223] the fact that supertax actually rose after the war seemed intolerable.[224] The 1948 Cripps

---

81 (1939). Once the war had begun, there was perhaps an even greater effort to appear to be doing justice to all sections of the community. In at least one case, what would now be called a "golden handshake" was held to be assessable for income, although where a portion of it was in commutation of pension, it was treated as capital; see *Cameron* v. *Prendergast*, [1940] A.C. 549; and *Tilley* v. *Wales*, [1943] A.C. 386 (1942). Later cases may have cut back on this; e.g., *Beak* v. *Robson*, [1943] A.C. 352 (1942). But directors of English companies, no matter where they were legally resident, were held liable to tax under Schedule E; *McMillan* v. *Guest*, [1942] A.C. 561. In computing profits for the national defense contribution it was held that profits from a controlling interest in a company not itself liable to the contribution were taxable; *British-American Tobacco Co.* v. *IRC*, [1943] A.C. 335 (1942). In a rather different area, interest due to a mortgagee that was added to capital was held still to attract income tax; *IRC* v. *Oswald* [1945] A.C. 360. At the time, the decision was described as "revolutionary"; "Note," 61 *Law Quarterly Review* 334 (1945).

220. In that wilderness between capital and income, for instance, reversionary interests were treated as capital; *Hughes (Inspector of Taxes)* v. *Ulting*, [1940] A.C. 463. The House put reasonable limitations on the situations where the commissioners might make a surtax direction; *Thomas Fattorini, (Lancashire), Ltd.* v. *IRC*, [1942] A.C. 643, although in applying the rule (or discretion) the law lords seemed sometimes to give questionable decisions. For example, *FPH Fin. Trust, Ltd.* v. *IRC*, [1944] A.C. 285 (1943), held that an appellant was not an investment company and therefore not liable to a surtax directions. In *Absalom* v. *Talbot*, [1944] A.C. 204 (1943), the House refused to sanction the Revenue's arguments that a speculative builder, who advanced money on a second mortgage repayable by installments, should be liable to tax on such transactions.

221. *Latilla* v. *IRC*, [1943] A.C. 377 (1942). See especially the sentiment about tax avoidance devices: "[O]ne result of such methods, if they succeed, is, of course, to increase *pro tanto* the load of tax on the shoulders of the great body of good citizens who do not desire, or do not know, how to adopt these maneuvers. Another consequence is that the legislature has made amendments to our income tax code which aim at nullifying the effectiveness of such schemes"; ibid. 391.

222. During the war, even Russell was found dissenting in a tax case decided in favor of the taxpayer; *FPH Fin. Trust, Ltd.* v. *IRC*, [1944] A.C. 285 (1943).

223. The year 1940 saw the imposition of purchase tax (sales tax), which affected all segments of the community, as well as a combination of surtax and income tax that could rise to a combined rate of 97.5 percent and an excess profits tax that could reach 100 percent; Trevor O. Lloyd, *Empire to Welfare State* 253.

224. Under Dalton between 1945 and 1947; ibid. 292.

budget was even more threatening, providing a rate that could rise above 100 percent on "unearned incomes"—in effect, a capital levy.[225] The needs of Korea led Gaitskell, in his 1951 budget, to raise the standard rate yet again,[226] and it was only after the return of the Conservatives later that year that the rate began to fall. Yet, the biggest threat was not so much to those with large incomes as it was to those with capital. Although at the time there was no capital gains tax, there were, on paper, ferocious death duties (estate tax). It was here, however, that the "tax planners" had done their work most effectively, and the percentage of revenue from death duties had fallen dramatically. Thus the first 1947 budget raised the rate of duty and tried to close some of the loopholes. At first the move worked, but "the improvement did not last for long; mainly because of the increasing ingenuity of property-owners in handing on their money before death."[227] This ingenuity—and the Revenue's efforts to counteract it—was to consume much of the House's time and to receive a good deal of encouragement.

Labour had been in for only a few months when the House decided *Inland Revenue Commissioners* v. *Ayrshire Employers Mutual Association.*[228] This was the case in which Macmillan boasted about the legislature's "misfiring."[229] A more dramatic undermining of the tax program under the guise of substantive formalism was, however, still to come. Wheatcroft has singled out Normand's speech in *Vestey's Executors* (1949)[230] as the height of the proavoidance spree of the Lords.[231] In retrospect, however, there seems to be little difference between Normand's speech and Simonds' in that case; or indeed between the ap-

225. Ibid. 293.

226. 9s. 6d. in the £1; ibid. 311.

227. Ibid. 292.

228. [1946] 1 All E.R. 637 (H.L.), 27 Tax Cas. 331 (H.L., Scot. 1945). The question before the House was whether a surplus realized by a mutual insurance society as a result of transactions between the members was taxable as a profit. Decisions of the House of Lords dating from 1889 held that where there was complete identity between contributors and participators any profit made was not taxable. The Crown, however, maintained in *Ayrshire* that these decisions had been reversed by § 31(1) of the Finance Act of 1933. The Lords held that, despite this statutory provision, the surplus was still not taxable, as the earlier decisions turned on the mutual nature of the transactions, not on whether the parties were or were not members of the association with which § 31(1) had been concerned.

229. 27 Tax Cas. 331, 347 (H.L., Scot. 1945): "The legislature has plainly misfired. The failure perhaps is less regrettable than it might have been for the Sub-Section has not the meritorious object of preventing evasion of taxation but the less laudable design of subjecting to tax as profit what the law has consistently and emphatically declared not to be profit."

230. *Vestey's Executors* v. *IRC*, 31 Tax Cas. 1 (H.L. 1949). The House was called on to construe the antiavoidance provisions contained in § 18 of the Finance Act of 1936 and § 38 of the Finance Act of 1938, which attempted to counteract some of the tax advantages gained by the manipulation of settlements and the transfer of assets abroad. Its decision was a remarkably narrow one.

231. G. S. A. Wheatcroft, *The Law of Income Tax, Surtax and Profits Tax* 1040.

proach they took there and the attitude Simonds exhibited in *Wolfson* v. *Inland Revenue Commissioners*[232] or, indeed, that showed by Normand in *Bray Inspector of Taxes* v. *Colenbrander*.[233] Similarly, both law lords appeared to take rather extreme positions in *Potts' Executors* v. *Inland Revenue Commissioners*, a decision interpreting yet another of the anti-avoidance devices in the 1938 legislation.[234] Both Normand and Simonds cited with approval Tomlin's speech in the *Westminster* case.[235] Even more was to come. Whereas, in *Potts'*, the corporate form was used to avoid sur- or supertax, in *D'Avigdor-Goldsmid* v. *Inland Revenue Commissioners*,[236] it was finally held that, for practical purposes, the worst "excesses" of estate duty could be avoided through an insurance policy.

Thus the House slowly undermined the force of estate duty with respect to particularly wealthy persons and gave those with large incomes some, although by no means so generous, support. The latter group was helped most effectively by the basis of British tax, that is, a rather narrowly defined concept of residence, as opposed to nationality. Even the concept of residence was avoided by the ingenious, since the tax authorities until the 1970s allowed a rather generous use of the strange English phenomenon of having "ordinary residence" elsewhere.[237] Thus, some support was offered by the House to those who were able to prove foreign residence or foreign income, although the loopholes developed by their lordships were by and large closed by the succeeding Finance Acts.[238]

232. 31 Tax Cas. 141 (H.L. 1949).

233. [1953] A.C. 503. The question in the case was whether remuneration paid abroad by a non-U.K. resident employer to a U.K. resident in respect of duties performed wholly in the U.K. were taxable in toto or only on so much as was remitted to the U.K. The House came down in favor of the latter interpretation. The decision was to cause political problems for Mr. Heath's government in the Lonrho affair in the early seventies.

234. [1951] A.C. 443 (1950). This was the first case on § 40(1) of the Finance Act of 1938, an antiavoidance section aimed at the avoidance of surtax by the manipulation of settlements and companies. The principal question in the case was the meaning of the words "sums paid by way of loan."

235. Simonds fell back on the words of Tomlin (ibid. 454), and adopted them (ibid. 457). See also the decision of the House in *IRC* v. *Wesleyan General Assurance Soc'y*, 30 Tax Cas. 11 (H.L. 1948), especially Simon, where Tomlin's principle was again cited with approval (ibid. 25). See also Uthwatt: "man may live by borrowing; but that habit does not attract income tax"; ibid. 27.

236. [1953] A.C. 347 (1952). In 1934, a settlor appointed a policy of insurance on his life, originally taken out in 1904, together with other settled property, to his son absolutely. From that time on, the son paid the premiums, which his father had previously paid. In time, the settlor died and estate duty was claimed on the monies received by the son under the policy, under the 1894 Finance Act, § 2(1)(d). The House, reversing the decision by the Court of Appeal, unanimously held that there was no estate duty payable, since from 1934 "the beneficial interest" in the policy belonged to the son and no "beneficial interest" in it accrued or arose on the death of the settlor.

237. To this should be added the fact that, unlike the United States, in England there is no self assessment in the American sense; it is primarily up to the Revenue to discover income rather than a duty to report it. Prosecutions for tax evasion are rare.

238. E.g., *Nugent-Head* v. *Jacob*, [1948] A.C. 321, showing the advantages of keeping

In general, the House was less enthusiastic about companies' avoiding tax, and they continued the narrow definition of the deductible business expense.[239] The only major exception was the almost bizarre case of *Morgan v. Tate and Lyle, Limited*.[240] The same House that had rejected by a majority both foreign taxes and the legal costs of fighting an excess profits assessment as not being legitimate business expenses[241] allowed a company engaged in sugar refining to deduct the expenses of a propaganda campaign opposing the threatened nationalization of the industry.[242] The width of this decision surprised even the *Law Quarterly Review*, which conceded that the implications of the decision were such that legislation along American lines might be needed to curb such contributions.[243] At least at times the mask of conscious irrelevance, which characterized so much of this period of substantive formalism, slipped.

The Worker and the Law

The House's work with respect to unions and workingmen showed some of the same trends as its involvement with tax law. During the war, in *Crofter Hand Woven Harris Tweed Company v. Veitch*,[244] the House

---

a wealthy American wife resident abroad (reversed by 1952 Income Tax Act, § 36). See also *IRC v. Gordon*, [1952] A.C. 552, (Scot.), where, by a series of manipulations, the taxpayer succeeded in having his foreign income tax free. The loophole was closed by the 1953 Finance Act, § 24.

239. See, for instance, the restrictive decisions on the deduction of business expenses in *Smith's Potato Estates, Ltd. v. Bollard*, [1948] A.C. 508 (Simon and Oaksey dissenting); *Rushden Heel Co. v. Veene*, 30 Tax Cas. 298 (H.L. 1948). The House even refused to allow taxes paid in Eire to be deducted as a business expense; *IRC v. Dowdall, O'Mahoney & Co.*, [1952] A.C. 401 (1951). This decision led to a series of double taxation treaties.
    The exception to this trend was *Nash v. Tamplin & Sons Brewery*, [1952] A.C. 231 (1951). After effectively distinguishing out of existence *Usher's Wiltshire Brewery, Ltd. v. Bruce*, [1915] A.C. 433 (1914), the House held that brewers might deduct as business expenses the notional rents they could have obtained for leasing their pubs on the open market, and not merely the more nominal sums they received from their "tied" tenants. If there was one area during those years in which the House did seem rather harsh on the taxpayer, it was in cases involving foreign companies. See *Canadian Eagle Oil Co. v. The King*, [1946] A.C. 119 (1945), and *IRC v. Reid's Trustees*, [1949] A.C. 361 (Scot. 1948). On the first of these cases, however, see "Note," 62 *Law Quarterly Review* 326 (1954).

240. [1955] A.C. 21 (1954).

241. Morton, Reid, and Asquith. Tucker and Keith dissented.

242. Nationalization might have taken one of two forms, either the acquisition of the assets of the company by a national body or the acquisition of the company's share capital by a national body. In the latter case, the same company would still be carrying on the trade. The majority, however, accepted that *Morgan v. Tate & Lyle* had in mind the former type of nationalization and that it was sufficient that the expenditure was incurred to preserve the company's trade as distinct from the industry's, which would of course continue, whether nationalized or not. The minority held that the expenditure was merely to help the trader keep the profits of the trade for himself, which was neither what the statute nor Davey's famous gloss meant.

243. A. Farnsworth, "Note," 70 *Law Quarterly Review* 457 (1954). For a political scientist's viewpoint, see Richard Rose, "Money and Election Law" 2.

244. [1942] A.C. 435 (Scot. 1941).

refused to allow the tort of conspiracy to be used against trade union officials in an industrial dispute.[245] Although some of the harsh nineteenth-century antilabor prejudice was thus ameliorated,[246] the mood of the House was perhaps best reflected in the approach to the compensation of injured workers. Either the inexorable inherent logic of the common law or the need to minimize labor disputes during a world war[247] led the House to continue and even accelerate its willingness to give the working-man a "fair shake" when it came to compensation for injuries. Time and again the statutory duty of care was strictly enforced by the Lords,[248] with the Court of Appeal being reversed. Occupiers' liability was found to be a convenient method of compensating workmen since, among other things, it avoided the issue of contributory negligence.[249] Atkin and Wright, needless to say, made every effort to keep contributory negligence out of the new areas of liability, particularly the doctrine of the safe system of work,[250] although in this enterprise they were unsuccessful.[251] Similarly, while it was impossible to keep common employment entirely out of statutory negligence and the employer's duty of care,[252] at least the Truck Acts were applied beneficially in favor of the workmen.[253]

The Workmen's Compensation Acts were also interpreted in a broad manner. The basic presumption that the accident had arisen in the course of the employment unless the employer was able to prove otherwise became even more clearly the norm.[254] Workmen were given far greater

245. Specifically, the House upheld the right of trade union officials on the island of Lewis to instruct their members not to handle yarn being imported to the islands, which could be woven into tweed at a price lower than that of yarn spun on Lewis. Although most of the law lords spoke in terms of rationalizing the unsatisfactory state of the tort of conspiracy, it was Wright's speech that carried the greatest weight and brought the unions most satisfaction, particularly his remark that "[t]he right of workmen to strike is an essential element in the principle of collective bargaining"; ibid. 463.

246. See, especially, *Nokes* v. *Doncaster Amalgamated Collieries, Ltd.*, [1940] A.C. 1014, holding that a workman's contract of service was not automatically transferred by the amalgamation of the company for which he worked with another, even if such amalgamation agreement purported to transfer such contracts. Thus the workman could not be successfully prosecuted for absenting himself from work contrary to § 4 of the Employers and Workmen Act of 1875.

247. Strikes, surprisingly, were a serious problem during World War II. See A. J. P. Taylor, *English History 1914–1945*, at 566–67.

248. E.g., *Caswell* v. *Powell Duffryn Ass'd. Collieries, Ltd.*, [1940] A.C. 152 (1939).

249. *Thomson* v. *Cremin*, [1956] 1 W.L.R. 103n (H.L. 1941).

250. Ibid.; see especially Wright at 109.

251. E.g., *Lewis* v. *Denye*, [1940] A.C. 921.

252. *Alexander* v. *Tredegar Iron & Coal Co.*, [1945] A.C. 286 (1944).

253. *Pratt* v. *Cook, Son & Co.*, [1940] A.C. 437 (1939) (reduction of cost of meals from wages held to violate 1831 Truck Act).

254. E.g., *Dover Navigation Co.* v. *Craig*, [1940] A.C. 190 (1939) (contracting yellow fever in West Africa); *Noble* v. *Southern Ry.*, [1940] A.C. 583 (presumption that servant walking along track was engaged on employer's business), *Weaver* v. *Tredegar Iron & Coal Co.*, [1940] A.C. 955 (use of platform in mine presumed to be for purpose of employer).

latitude before the courts than they had previously enjoyed; no longer would the courts hold that the acceptance of an amount of compensation precluded workmen from suing under the acts.[255] Employees were given greater rights of decision with respect to undergoing medical operations;[256] the function of the doctor's certificate and of the medical assessor were noticeably circumscribed;[257] and a liberal view toward earnings was taken.[258] As the war dragged on, it may be that sympathy ebbed a little,[259] but the overall wartime pattern was clear—considerable support for the workman.

Just as tax law moved back to a clearly premised position after World War II, so did cases concerning factory accidents. It was, of course, not a clear-cut question; radical change in the whole setup of compensation for workmen was underway after the war. The National Insurance (Industrial Injuries) Act of 1946 abolished the tarnished workmen's compensation system.[260] The manual unions, the consumers of the system, wanted to see national insurance as the sole remedy, but the legal profession, one of the most powerful unions of all, lobbied vigorously against that suggestion, and the Monckton Committee recommended that alternative remedies should be retained, a compromise given statutory authority by the Law Reform (Personal Injuries) Act of 1948. Meanwhile, employees suing at common law acquired two new important rights: the Law Reform (Contributory Negligence) Act of 1945 had converted contributory negligence to comparative negligence, and the 1948 act abolished the defense of common employment.[261] In this rapidly

255. E.g., *Lissenden v. C. A. V. Bosch, Ltd.*, [1940] A.C. 412 (1939); *London Brick Co. v. Robinson*, (1943] A.C. 341 (1942) (widow recovered under Fatal Accidents Acts and therefore could not recover under the Workmen's Compensation Acts. However, infant's claim was allowed under the latter acts.).

256. *Steele v. Robert George & Co.*, [1942] A.C. 497 (N. Ire. 1937), holding that the burden of proof was on the employer to show that an employee was unreasonable in refusing to undergo an operation.

257. *Edinburgh Collieries Co. v. Flockhart*, [1940] A.C. 566 (Scot.); *Richardson v. Redpath, Brown & Co.*, [1944] A.C. 62 (1943).

258. *McMahon v. David Lawson, Ltd.*, [1944] A.C. 32 (Scot. 1943).

259. E.g., *Jones v. Amalgamated Anthracite Collieries Ltd.*, [1944] A.C. 14 (1943) (Wright dissenting); *Young v. Bristol Aeroplane Co.*, [1946] A.C. 163 (1945) (cutting back workmen's right of election between common law and workmen's compensation remedies).

260. Of the final cases decided by the House on workmen's compensation, see *Young v. Bristol Aeroplane Co.*, [1946] A.C. 163 (1945), a case whose *ratio decidendi* is far from clear, but which was presumably intended to protect the workmen with respect to alternative remedies; and *Doudie v. Kinneil, Cannel & Coking Coal Co.*, [1947] A.C. 377 (Scot. 1946), where the House settled conflicting English and Scottish decisions relating to the statutory maximum compensation payable when a second accident resulted in total incapacity. The final decision the House delivered on workmen's compensation, *Amalgamated Anthracite Collieries, Ltd. v. Wilds*, [1948] A.C. 440, appeared to reflect an increasing hostility to workmen's claims.

261. While the House pointed up the absurdity of the whole principle in the two

changing atmosphere, it was predictable that the House would proceed with caution, but there were moments when the law lords appeared to start from the assumption that it was the workmen and not the lawyers who insisted on retaining the alternative remedy.[262]

With workmen's compensation out of the courts and a reluctance to allow general negligence actions for an unsafe system of work, the emphasis turned toward an interpretation of the Factories Acts by which workmen could found their causes of action before the regular courts. Yet in the late 1940s and early 1950s, the law lords, who might have integrated the Factories Acts with the concept of a safe system of work that Atkin and Wright had been developing, in fact chose to limit the right of recovery under the acts within narrow bounds. In *Nicholls v. F. Austin, Limited*,[263] and *Carroll v. Andrew Barclay and Sons*,[264] the House decided that the fencing provisions had no application if products flew out of the machine or if the machine itself broke. The House also held that the fencing provisions did not apply to machines manufactured in a factory and not firmly part of the manufacturing process,[265] and it narrowly construed the requirement that the fencing was required when the machinery was "in motion or in use."[266] The House took a similarly

---

Glasgow Corporation cases, *Graham v. Glasgow Corp.*, [1947] A.C. 368 (Scot. 1946) and *Glasgow Corp. v. Bruce*, [1948] A.C. 79 (Scot. 1947), it made no last minute effort to ameliorate the memory of that harsh common law doctrine. It did, however, refuse to accept the argument that because the Essential Work Order prevented miners' leaving their employment, the whole contract of service had been so changed that the safe system of work doctrine should no longer apply; *Alexander v. Tredegar Iron & Coal Co.*, [1945] A.C. 286 (1944). The earlier attempts to keep common employment out of this newly developed doctrine had been aborted, e.g., in *Colfar v. Coggins & Griffith, Ltd.*, [1945] A.C. 197 (1944), although Reid entered a lone dissent in *Harrison v. National Coal Bd.*, [1961] A.C. 639 (1960), arguing that a Mine Regulation imposed an absolute duty on the owner, preventing the latter from relying on the doctrine.

262. On the transitional provisions, see the helpful decision in *Hales v. Bolton Leathers, Ltd.*, [1951] A.C. 531 (1950), and the remarkable decision in *Mobberley & Perry, Ltd. v. Holloway*, [1952] A.C. 133 (1951), where the House happily blessed the idea that there might be a "hiatus" between the two acts.

263. [1946] A.C. 493, 505. A piece of wood flew out of a circular saw that the plaintiff was operating. It was here that Simonds opined that "[t]he fence is intended to keep the worker out, not to keep the machine or its products in."

264. [1948] A.C. 477 (Scot.). There was a five-foot fence between the motor and the operator, but the belt of the lathe broke and lashed out over the fence, injuring the operator. Again the Lords held that the duty to fence was a duty to keep the operator away from the machine and that the act did not have in mind the danger of machinery breaking.

265. *Parvin v. Morton Mach. Co.*, [1952] A.C. 515 (Scot.). The appellant, a minor, was instructed to clean a dough-broke that had been manufactured and assembled in the respondent's yard. The guard on the broke had been removed, and the appellant caught his hand in the machinery.

266. In *Richard Thomas & Baldwins, Ltd. v. Cummings*, [1955] A.C. 321, a fitter was injured while he was helping another workman make adjustments in electric power-driven grinding machinery. The motor power had been shut off, and he was moving the machine by hand when he crushed his finger. His claim was rejected.

narrow view of the statutory duty to maintain factory floors in an efficient state[267] and, under the Mines Regulations, to ensure that the roof
and sides of working places be made secure.[268]

The Factories Acts, related legislation, and the regulations issued
under them were often ambiguous;[269] this vagueness caused the law
lords ultimately to rely on their premises that, during this period, were
not expansionist. The general attitude was spelled out, in the *Carroll*
case,[270] by Normand. "In the absence, therefore, of any clear positive
indication that the obligation to fence securely has the meaning attributed to it by the appellant, the implications of the material sections as a
whole must be considered, and practicability becomes relevant to the
construction of the obligation." By "practicability" the law lords primarily meant commercial practicability; on this basis, they decided that
the cost of taking the measure advocated would be prohibitive. They
were also able to console themselves since employers in default under the
regulations could be prosecuted criminally; indeed, the fact that the legislation was "penal" was one of the reasons that the law lords felt justified
in construing it narrowly.[271]

Thus, while plaintiffs covered by the national insurance system had
been given the right to continue to bring actions in the regular courts,
that right was somewhat hollow, since the courts not only construed the
Factories Acts narrowly but normally disallowed common law actions
based on an unsafe system of work.[272] Nor did the House offer any
encouragement that other areas of tort might be of help to the injured
employee. In *Read v. J. Lyons and Company*,[273] the House strongly

267. In *Latimer v. AEC, Ltd.*, [1953] A.C. 643, the factory floor was flooded after an
unusually heavy rainstorm, and an oily cooling moisture became mixed with the flood
waters. When the waters subsided, a film of the oil remained, leaving the floor slippery.
Sawdust was spread so far as supplies would allow, but some areas were left untreated. A
workman slipped and fell while working on an untreated area. The House held, first, that
the employers had not been negligent at common law, having done all that a reasonable
employer could have been expected to do, and, second, that there was no breach of the
statutory duty to see that floors were maintained in an efficient state, this condition being
too transient and exceptional.

268. E.g., *Marshall v. Gotham Co.*, [1954] A.C. 360.

269. Of an Explosives in Coal Mines Order, Porter said, "The regulations are numerous and lack precision. They were intended, I fancy, as a working guide and their exact
meaning left to elucidation by a court of law in case any dispute arose"; *Harrison v.
National Coal Bd.*, [1951] A.C. 639, 652 (1950).

270. *Carroll v. Andrew Barclay & Sons*, [1948] A.C. 477 (Scot.).

271. E.g., Normand's speech in ibid. 489, and Morton's in ibid. 493.

272. E.g., *Latimer v. AEC, Ltd.*, [1953] A.C. 643.

273. [1947] A.C. 156 (1946). The plaintiff, who had been placed in that job by the
Labour Exchange, was injured in the course of her duties as an inspector by the explosion
of a shell that was being manufactured. No negligence could be proved, and it was held that
those operating the factory were not liable. According to the House, *Rylands v. Fletcher*
could not be applied because there was no "escape" of the dangerous "thing" from the
premises. While this was the basis of the decision, there were also dicta that the rule did not

resisted the attempt of a factory inspector to recover for injuries on some extension of the strict liability theories of *Rylands* v. *Fletcher*. Equally hostile to the workman was *London Graving Dock Company* v. *Horton*,[274] in which an unsuccessful attempt was made by a workman to recover against an employer for breach of the latter's responsibilities as an occupier of premises.

The attitude, while indubitable, was not unambiguous. Even in the late forties, some isolated decisions ran against the tide;[275] by the early fifties, especially during the period when Simonds was serving as Lord Chancellor and not sitting regularly, a change of heart was beginning to be apparent. In a series of three cases the House seemed appreciably less interested in the "commercial feasibility" of the employer's providing protection. In *Stapley* v. *Gypsum Mines, Limited*,[276] the House exhibited the full potential of the Factories Acts freed from the restrictions of common employment and contributory negligence, a process taken further in *National Coal Board* v. *England*.[277] Both *Stapley* and *England*

---

apply to personal injuries (e.g., Macmillan at 170–71, 173, refusing to follow earlier Court of Appeal decisions) and that the making of munitions in wartime was a "non-natural" use of land (see per Simon). Overall, there was a general reluctance to extend strict liability under the rule any further, and arguments based on logical grounds were firmly resisted. (See, e.g., per Macmillan.) On *Read* v. *Lyons*, see Francis H. Newark, "The Boundaries of Nuisance" 171.

274. [1951] A.C. 737. The injured man, an experienced welder and the employee of ship repairers (subcontractors), was injured on the ship under repair, without negligence on his part, because of the inadequacy of certain staging. He knew of this danger and had made many complaints to the ship repairer, but to no effect. The House held, Reid and MacDermott dissenting, that the welder had no remedy against the ship repairers as occupiers of the ship. The majority view was that the welder, or invitee, had full knowledge of the risk. He was *sciens* and it was unnecessary for the defense to show he was also *volens*. The House was not concerned with the position of the invitee vis-à-vis as his own ultimate master. The law lords further rejected an attempt to apply *Donoghue* v. *Stevenson*.

275. In 1949 the House (including both Reid and MacDermott) decided *Galashiels Gas Co.* v. *O'Donnell*, [1949] A.C. 275 (Scot. 1948), which, while by no means a landmark case, did seem to take a more neutral view toward the Factories Acts. The House held that the duty to see that every lift is properly maintained in efficient working order was a continuing absolute duty and that neither intention nor lack of care need be shown to prove breach.

276. [1953] A.C. 663. Two miners of equal status, S and D, reported to the foreman that part of the mine roof was dangerous. The foreman told them to fetch it down. After trying unsuccessfully to bring the roof down, by joint decision, S and D resumed work. The roof fell, and S was killed. His widow sued the mine owners for negligence and breach of their duty under the Mines Regulations. The trial judge decided that S was half responsible for his own death and the Court of Appeal that he was solely responsible. By a majority the House held that D's fault contributed 20 percent to the death. The majority gave S the full benefit of the abolition of the doctrine of common employment and of contributory negligence as an absolute bar, taking the realistic view that if D had refused to disobey orders, S was unlikely to have done so.

277. [1954] A.C. 403. Here, the mine worker was injured by the premature explosion of a detonator. The shot firer had admittedly committed a breach of the regulation by not ascertaining that all persons had taken proper cover, but the injured worker was also in

were 3–2 decisions. The third case, *John Summers and Sons, Limited* v. *Frost*,[278] heard in 1955, was a unanimous decision, and the House included Simonds. This slow change of heart was also visible in areas outside the Factories Acts. The vigorous dissents by Reid and MacDermott in *Horton*'s case were a pointer. A few months earlier, MacDermott had mustered a majority in *Paris* v. *Stepney Borough Council*[279] putting Simonds and Morton into a minority, although in theory only on the facts. The decision is important, however, because it revived the prewar common law creation of a safe system of work, which had become somewhat submerged as an independent cause of action during the period of restrictive interpretation. Finally, in *General Cleaning Contractors, Limited* v. *Christmas*, the House unanimously held there had been a breach of a safe system of work even though specific evidence of a negligent act was somewhat vague.[280] By 1955, then, indications were that the spirit of the 1930s was reviving, a spirit that would be reflected both in substance and in style.

---

breach because he had agreed with the shot firer to carry out one of the shot firer's duties. The House, with the same composition as in *Stapley*, decided that the worker was only contributorily negligent and that his own breach of statutory duty did not debar him from suing.

278. [1955] A.C. 740 (Simonds, Reid, Keith, Oaksey, and Morton). A maintenance fitter injured his thumb when it came into contact with a grinding wheel. The upper part of the machine was guarded by a fixed hood, but part of the stone was unguarded. The fitter claimed there had been a breach of the duty to fence under § 14. The House held that the duty was absolute and that there had been a breach. The fact that compliance might render the machine unusable did not absolve the factory owner from that duty.

279. [1951] A.C. 367 (1950).

280. [1953] A.C. 180 (1952). An experienced window cleaner had to work on a narrow ledge cleaning a dangerous defective window. He made no complaint. While he was working the sash fell, the cleaner lost his balance and fell. Although safety belts were made available by the window cleaning company, they were not used because there were no hooks for them on these premises. The House held that the employers had negligently failed in their duty to devise a reasonably safe system of work and to provide for an obvious danger, since they had not given instructions to ensure that windows should be tested before cleaning nor did they provide wedges to prevent windows from closing. The cleaner had pleaded that the negligence lay in not providing hooks or requiring the use of ladders, but the House held there was insufficient evidence to establish this. The House was happy to remedy this defect. "It cannot, in my opinion, be that as a matter of law a plaintiff cannot succeed in such a case unless he proves the particular system in which the work can be performed safely"; per Oaksey, ibid. 190–91, disputing dicta of Simon in *Colfar* v. *Coggins & Griffith, Ltd.*, [1945] A.C. 197, 203 (1944).

PART FOUR

MODERN TIMES
1956–1976

The English way, so it is said, is evolution and not revolution. To look for massive or radical change in the British scene is to look for the unlikely, if not the impossible, whatever the rhetoric of the moment. Yet the twenty years between 1956 and 1976 did represent a remarkable change in the social and political environment. In 1956, with the Suez invasion, Britain made what proved its last serious attempt to behave as if it were a major power;[1] in 1976 Britain appeared to many as the "sick man of Europe."[2] In international power terms, the country not only had seen the British Empire evolve into the British Commonwealth, but also had witnessed the latter cease to have serious political meaning. The decline in the "special relationship" with the United States had not, at least by the mid-seventies, been offset by any obvious increase in British influence in the European Economic Community. This inability to influence the Common Market may have been no more than a reflection of the fact that Britain, in 1950 the second most affluent nation in Europe in terms of gross national product, had become one of the poorest; and it was still unclear to what extent North Sea oil would redress the balance.

Whether the relative decline in the standard of living compared with other industrialized nations was balanced by a certain "quality of life" was a matter of dispute; what was clear was that the shifts in international power and economics could not leave Britain entirely untouched. In a

1. E.g., Hugh Thomas, *Suez*; Anthony Nutting, *No End of a Lesson*.
2. Hudson Institute, *The United Kingdom in 1980, passim.*

society where the gross national product showed little or no growth, the redivision of the economic pie was likely to put great pressure on the class lines that still retained their late-nineteenth-century flavor. These tensions were further exacerbated in the decades under discussion by the social and intellectual revolution in the developed countries, reflected in a spectrum of changes ranging from the widespread acceptance of birth control to the burgeoning of the social sciences. While these pressures grew, Britain seemed strangely ambivalent about how to handle the aristocracy of talent that the 1944 Education Act had theoretically produced. By the mid-1970s, it was still unclear to what extent such persons were a part of the established class system and to what extent they were expected to operate outside it.

It was in the light of such movements that established institutions in England seemed to come under greater stress. The Monarchy was subject to serious criticism for the first time in a century; the peerage (with hereditary peers no longer being created) was reduced to little more than a curiosity. Yet even those who held power had to grow accustomed to a level of analysis and criticism not until then directed at the British system of government or its institutions.[3] The power of the Civil Service was openly recognized and evaluated. The weaknesses of Parliament were subjected to a spate of analyses from commentators of both the Right and the Left. Prime Ministers, cabinets, the effectiveness of question time as the manifestation of responsible government, and similar matters were all seen, both by academics and by social commentators, to be legitimate grist for the critical mill. These same observers were also questioning a situation in which the Conservative party had generally abandoned the ideology of the free market and the Labour party its basic socialist doctrines. Some saw both a political and an intellectual vacuum.

Those writing over the decades about the then-current state of England have always overestimated the imminence of radical change. Yet even in that most conservative of areas—the legal system—there was increasing evidence that serious change was taking place. During the twenty years under discussion, the judges of first instance saw their status reduced to something much more akin to that of regular civil servants, while appeal judges began to appreciate their potential power to develop legal doctrine. The House of Lords as a judicial body was still, jurisprudentially, a pale shadow of the Supreme Court of the United States,[4]

3. For a cross-section of the criticism of British central government by political scientists, see Brian Chapman, *British Government Observed*; Bernard Crick, *The Reform of Parliament*; Wladyslaw J. Stankiewitz, *Crisis in British Government*; and William J. L. Wallace, *The Foreign Policy Process in Britain*.

4. During the period there were, from time to time, somewhat emotional demands for the Americanization of the English judiciary. E.g., Kenneth C. Davis, "The Future of Judge-

but in one clear regard the English legal process had been Americanized: in keeping with the Monarchy, the Church of England, and other established institutions, the law had been significantly demystified.

To write about the present is, inevitably, difficult, yet not so difficult as it might have been, for the House of Lords in the last twenty years has shown signs of life after a period of judicial catatonia. Since the period coincided with a call for the total abolition of appeals to the Lords, the cynic might suggest that the period is no more than an example of Samuel Johnson's general principle, "Depend on it, Sir, when a man knows he is to be hanged in a fortnight, it concentrates his mind wonderfully." Had the law lords not found some rationale for their existence between 1956 and 1976, they might well have been consigned exclusively to the realms of legal history. In fact efforts have been made by the law lords to consider what the appellate process entails and, indeed, why it exists. Simplistic belief in substantive formalism has, in general, given way to a willingness to admit a limited interstitial legislative role, even if the rationale of that role has not been clarified. Meanwhile, the caliber of the law lords (or at least their willingness to address the rationale of the appellate process) has been strengthened. Although these changes have brought criticism, they have also made a continued future for the House (at least as an appellate body) far more probable.

Made Public Law in England" 201. For a more balanced view, see Louis L. Jaffé, *English and American Judges as Lawmakers*. For a recent analysis of the different English and American approaches from a relatively conservative viewpoint, see Patrick Devlin, "Judges and Lawmakers" 1.

Political Change and the Lord Chancellors

The Political Climate

By the mid-1950s the Conservative government was, philosophically speaking, in the hands of the Tory Old Guard,[1] a blend of upper-class confidence and nostalgia. Sir Anthony Eden had taken over the Conservative party and led it to a wider margin of success in the 1955 election. Emotionally the return to the "good old days" engendered considerable support, but economically and socially any real return to the past was impossible. Not only was 1956 the year of Suez, it was also the year in which the play *Look Back in Anger*—John Osborne's attack on the smugger aspects of the English class system—proved a stunning success. The British Empire was dwindling visibly. In the late forties India and Pakistan had become independent. In 1957 Ghana became the first African colony to gain independence, and by the mid-sixties almost all the former British colonies were independent, even formerly white-dominated areas such as Kenya and Jamaica.

Harold Macmillan, who succeeded Eden as Prime Minister after the Suez fiasco, while in appearance and style more than acceptable to the Old Guard, sympathized politically with the modernizers in the party. The economy, released from the last vestiges of wartime controls and benefiting from the relatively low prices of primary products, showed its one major burst of energy in the post-1945 world,[2] enabling Macmillan to win another election handsomely in 1959.[3] Yet the economic gains of

1. Trevor O. Lloyd, *Empire to Welfare State* 355.
2. Richard E. Caves and Associates, *Britain's Economic Prospects, passim.*
3. David E. Butler and Richard Rose, *The British General Election of 1959.*

the fifties did not filter down to the ordinary workers,[4] and during the sixties what became known as the English malaise set in.[5] With Hugh Gaitskell's death in 1963, Harold Wilson became leader of the Labour party, while the Profumo scandal later that year hastened the replacement of Macmillan as leader of the Conservative party (and thus as Prime Minister) by Sir Alec Douglas-Home. Most interpreted this change as a move toward the Right within the party.

The Labour party under Wilson was able to capitalize on the serious economic and frustrating social situations; Labour barely won the 1964 election[6] and slightly increased its lead in the 1966 election.[7] Yet by 1970 the Conservative party, revitalized under the more liberal leadership of Edward Heath, succeeded in ousting the Labour administration.[8] As a result of Heath's showdown with the miners, Labour was returned in both elections of 1974,[9] although early in 1976 Wilson resigned, to be replaced by James Callaghan—the Conservative opposition being, by then, led by Margaret Thatcher. No matter which party was in power, however, and no matter what the rhetoric, there seemed little ability to control the shape of social or economic change. Rapid inflation, rather than socialist legislation, de facto redistributed wealth to those who were best organized. Pessimists saw the country becoming more and more unstable; even the modern additions to the establishment—the unions and the welfare state—appeared to have lost their sacred status.

These political, social, and economic upheavals undoubtedly encouraged a willingness to challenge fundamentals that had not been challenged before. The element of skepticism that had been marked at the beginning of the period by *Look Back in Anger* gave way in the sixties to television satire "That Was the Week That Was," while by the 1970s the satirical magazine *Private Eye* was seen as an important commentary on modern England. Yet there had indeed been change. Commercial television and comprehensive schools were by the mid-seventies as essentially English as they had once been thought of as exclusively American. Lobbies had become a part of the British way of life,[10] as had motorways and the supermarket. Massive immigration, curbed partially by the Immigration Act of 1962 and later legislation, led to difficult new problems of

4. Lloyd, *Empire to Welfare State* 358–59.
5. Ibid., chap. 13.
6. David E. Butler and Anthony King, *The British General Election of 1964*.
7. David E. Butler and Anthony King, *The British General Election of 1966*.
8. David E. Butler and Michael Pinto-Duschinsky, *The British General Election of 1970*.
9. David E. Butler and D. Kavanagh, *The British General Election of February, 1974*. This election brought in a minority Labour government. The October election provided a small overall majority.
10. E.g., H. H. Wilson, *Pressure Group*. See also Samuel E. Finer, *Anonymous Empire*.

race relations, tackled for the first time by the Race Relations Act of 1965 and then by a series of further pieces of legislation ending with the Race Relations Act of 1976.[11] By 1969 a religious or class war, depending on one's perspective, had broken out in Northern Ireland; undoubtedly, this civil war on Britain's doorstep added to the sense of disintegration that characterized Westminster and Whitehall.[12] Indeed, few sacred shibboleths survived the twenty years without question. Some of the most vexing social issues of earlier decades had been settled. Capital punishment was abolished;[13] homosexuality had been decriminalized.[14] The public schools had been investigated,[15] the new universities and other elements in higher education had gone some distance toward challenging the social dominance of Oxford and Cambridge, and even these two institutions slowly admitted the existence of more recent developments in the social sciences.

Perhaps the most dramatic factor, however, was that by the mid-seventies between 60 and 70 percent of the GNP was consumed by the government. Conservatives had always been concerned by "bigness" in government, but now liberals in all three parties were beginning to reflect some of this concern. Those who regarded themselves as social democrats began talking once again about the Rule of Law, civil liberties, and even an entrenched Bill of Rights.[16] The Conservative party specifically endorsed the establishment of a judicially controlled Bill of Rights,[17] a subject both debated in the House of Commons[18] and discussed by the Chairman of the Law Commission—the Labour party's answer to law reform.[19] Britain's adherence to the European Convention on Human Rights added some credence to possible developments in that area,[20] while the various proposals for devolution within the United Kingdom

11. See Anthony Lester and Geoffrey Bindman, *Race and Law*; Eliot J. Rose, et al., *Colour and Citizenship*. The first attempt to deal with sexual discrimination was the Sex Discrimination Act of 1975.

12. Richard Rose, *Governing without Consensus*.

13. James B. Christoph, *Capital Punishment and British Politics*.

14. Lloyd, *Empire to Welfare State* 413.

15. *First Report of the Public Schools Commission*, HMSO, 1968. No effort, however, was made to implement this report.

16. For academic support, see Hood Phillips, *Reform of the Constitution*, chap. 7. In 1960, Canada took the first step toward the establishment of an entrenched Bill of Rights. See Walter S. Tarnopolsky, *The Canadian Bill of Rights*. In England, in a reverse of nineteenth-century stances, a Bill of Rights was endorsed by the *Economist* and questioned by *The Times*. See *Economist*, 12 July 1975, at 25.

17. See especially the speech of Sir Keith Joseph to the Society of Conservative Lawyers; *The Times*, 18 Mar. 1975, at 3. The Liberal party also attempted to jump on the bandwagon; ibid., 16 July 1975, at 6.

18. "Note," 125 *New Law Journal* 687 (1975).

19. Leslie Scarman, *English Law—The New Dimension*, parts 6 and 7.

20. See Michael Zander, *A Bill of Rights?*; and Frank Stacey, *A New Bill of Rights for Britain*.

again raised the specter of judicial review of parliamentary legislation.[21]

Moving from the realm of possibility to the realm of fact, remarkable changes took place in British government during these twenty years. In the House of Commons the specialist committee had at last appeared.[22] For the first time in a hundred years a major effort had been made to restructure the Civil Service.[23] As the defects in question time were recognized, some of the traditional gaps in control over the executive were remedied by the establishment of an ombudsman, known as the Parliamentary Commissioner.[24] Moreover, as the result of a series of Royal Commissions,[25] the whole of local government was reorganized.[26] Such a dramatic series of radical changes had not been evident for a century— since the fifties, sixties, and early seventies of the nineteenth century.

Change and the Legal System

Twenty years of political and social development were to have a profound effect on the legal system, both institutionally and psychologically. The expanding cult of modernization meant that liberals in each of the major parties would endeavor to complete the political and legal reforms begun by Disraeli and Gladstone. Not only legal institutions, but private law as well, were increasingly the concern of this movement. In terms of law, probably the most important manifestation of the movement was the establishment of the Law Commission in 1965. Within a rapid space of time, this permanent body of commissioners, charged with proposing reforms in those areas that most English lawyers thought of as "lawyers' law," had helped to bring about legislative reform in areas as varied as land and family law, while forcing reconsideration of approaches in areas as diverse as planning and statutory construction.[27]

Whether one looks at the legislation itself or the approach to the legislation, the twenty years in question are revealing. For the first time in modern English legal history, there was serious debate about the role of the courts in interpreting statutes. The Law Commission's *Report on*

21. For the Kilbrandon report itself, see *Report of the Royal Commission on the Constitution*, Cmnd. 5460 (1973). For the government proposals contained in the White Paper, see *The Times*, 28 Nov. 1975, at 1, 4–5. For the possible constitutional role of the judiciary in determining issues of ultra vires, see Leader, *The Times*, 15 Jan. 1976, at 15.

22. Frank Stacey, *British Government 1966–1975*, chap. 3.

23. See especially the Fulton Report: *Report of the Committee on the Civil Service*, Cmnd. 3638 (1968). See also Stacey, *British Government 1966–1975*, chap. 7.

24. See Frank Stacey, *The British Ombudsman*.

25. See especially *Report of the Royal Commission on Local Government in Greater London*, Cmnd. 1164 (1960) and *Report of the Royal Commission on Local Government in England*, Cmnd. 4040 (1969).

26. See especially the Local Government Act of 1972.

27. John H. Farrar, *Law Reform and the Law Commission*.

Statutory Interpretation in 1969[28] suggested a rather broader approach to the judicial interpretation of legislation, but this was apparently too threatening, and the government appointed an "outside" committee under Sir David Renton, which felt more comfortable with accepted approaches to the literal or natural meanings of words.[29] The idea that the interpretation of legislation involves two steps—the cognitive one of discovering meaning and the creative one of applying the section of the law as written to the facts in issue—although accepted by virtually all American writers, was still regarded as "dangerous" in England.[30] The strides toward a more creative judicial role had been relatively limited ones; only in the English context did they seem dramatic. Yet these advances should not be underestimated; there were important changes in both substance and approach.

Taxation, for instance, which by the mid-fifties took a substantial part of the judicial time of the House of Lords, experienced changes in content and style that were of considerable significance to the appellate process in general. Legislation in 1960 introduced the first effective postwar tax avoidance device, and in 1962 the Conservative government established the first capital gains tax covering short-term capital gains, a change that eventually led to Selwyn Lloyd's fall.[31] Both of these changes, but especially the former, were destined to affect the appeal process. Moreover, with the return of the Labour government in 1964, the capital gains tax was generalized in the Callaghan budget of 1965[32] and there-

28. Report No. 21, 11 June 1969.

29. *Preparation of Legislation*, Cmnd. 6053 (1975).

30. "A person who . . . examines the two . . . recent reports on statutory interpretation may be struck by the fact that nowhere does the report expressly recognize the courts' creative function in the application of statutes. In so sophisticated a report, what is the significance of the omission? Was it oversight? Was it a repudiation of the view that 'statutory interpretation' includes judicial creation?

"The answer to the last two questions seems to be no. The authors of the report were fully aware of the distinction and there is no indication that they would repudiate it. The simple fact is that in current British judicial thinking all judicial action with respect to statutes is still officially subsumed under the term 'interpretation,' presumably in its authentic, cognitive sense. Although it is now conceded that British courts make common law, it is not yet acknowledged that they make law in supplementation of statutes. The authors were therefore reluctant to couch their report in terms that most British readers would have considered dangerously revolutionary"; Reed Dickerson, *The Interpretation and Application of Statutes* 32–33.

Dickerson was referring to the two (English and Scottish) Law Commission Reports.

31. Lloyd, *Empire to Welfare State* 379–80.

32. Callaghan said, "The failure to tax capital gains is widely regarded . . . as the greatest blot on our existing system of direct taxation . . . [T]here is no doubt that the present immunity from tax of capital gains has given a powerful incentive to the skilled manipulator of which he has taken full advantage to avoid tax . . . [W]e shall only make headway against tax avoidance of this sort when capital gains are also taxed"; 710 *Parl. Deb.*, H.C. (5th ser.), col. 245, (6 Apr. 1965).

after became acceptable in the litanies of both parties.[33] In the early 1970s, the Conservative party merged surtax and income tax into a more coherent system,[34] while in 1972 the value added tax (VAT) replaced purchase tax, as Britain prepared to join the Common Market.[35] With the return of the Labour administration in 1974, VAT was made variable in order to tax luxuries more heavily,[36] while the capital transfer tax in effect provided Britain with a form of gift tax that carried a connotation of a capital levy.[37]

Each change made the British tax system more complex and forced a continuing series of detailed statutory interpretations. Moreover, the rapid expansion of the tax bite,[38] by no means to everyone's liking, emphasized the need for equity,[39] which was at least partially undermined by the traditional formalistic approach to tax cases. Finally, in 1975, the law lords, in the words of *The Times*, affirmed a "wide interpretation of tax avoidance law."[40] This decision was given amid the threat by the Labour government of the imposition of a vigorous wealth tax.[41]

The acceptance of a functional approach to statutory interpretation in tax cases was evidence that the judiciary was aware of the effects of demystification of the legal process. Other examples drove home this point. In 1956 the Restrictive Practices Court had been established by the Conservative government to determine whether restrictive agreements, including price fixing between manufacturers, were in the public interest. In Parliament the proposal for a new court, which was to include both High Court judges and lay members, caused the utmost controversy and highlighted the English approach to this role of law and the legal process. On the issue of justiciability, the Labour party spokesmen

33. The tax base for individuals is 30 percent. See Commerce Clearing House, 1 *British Tax* 3503.

34. John Chown and Peter Rowland, "The Finance Bill" 133.

35. R. S. Nock and M. A. Pickering, "The Shape of the Value Added Tax" 70.

36. H. H. Mainprice, "Multi-rate VAT in the United Kingdom" 201.

37. See especially G. S. A. Wheatcroft, "First Thoughts on the Capital Transfer Tax" 265.

38. In 1965–66, taxes represented 28.4 percent of the GNP; by 1975–76, they represented an estimated 36.7 percent. See John Jeffrey-Cook, "Ten Traumatic Tax Years" 1038.

39. See especially A. R. Ilersic, "National Tax Reform" 371; N. W. Spicer, "New Approaches to the Problem of Tax Evasion" 152.

40. *IRC v. Joiner*, [1975] 1 W.L.R. 690 (H.L.), for an analysis of the antievasion provisions of the Finance Act of 1960 and the Corporation Taxes Act of 1970.

41. For a negative reaction, see Graeme MacDonald, "The Wealth Tax" 283. The concept of a wealth tax was referred, among other things, to the Royal Commission on the Distribution of Income and Wealth, chaired by Lord Diamond, appointed in 1974. Its *First Report*, Cmnd. 6171 (1975), was surprisingly moderate, but this may have been in keeping with changed Labour party thinking. Shortly before his resignation early in 1976, Mr. Wilson appeared to be emphasizing the need for private capital formation and investment.

insisted that litigation under the act would involve "policy" and the decisions should therefore be taken by a minister responsible to Parliament, while Conservatives argued that since the rules had been drafted narrowly, the matter was appropriate for independent, impartial judges.[42]

The narrow constructionist role was by no means the only acceptable model for the judiciary. Certainly any criticism that the Restrictive Practices Court stirred did not deter later Conservative Prime Ministers from making use of the judiciary to produce "impartial" solutions to thorny political issues. In 1957, when inflation seemed totally out of control, Cohen was imported to chair the Committee on Prices, Productivity, and Incomes;[43] Macmillan used Devlin, perhaps unfairly, in an effort to whitewash the British government's handling of the Nyasaland crisis in 1959.[44] Perhaps the most ostentatious use of a judge during these years was the Denning inquiry into the Profumo scandal.[45] So long as the judges continued to behave "scientifically" in the regular courts, it was not politically difficult to assign them as "impartial arbiters" of delicate social and economic issues outside the courts. This had always been more difficult in the United States where there was less acceptance of the scientific approach by the leading judges and greater skepticism about impartiality among the public. Moreover, the separation of powers meant that the use of Mr. Justice Murphy as prosecutor at Nuremberg and Chief Justice Warren to investigate the Kennedy assassination were regarded with concern by many constitutional authorities. In England, however, the judges, and especially the law lords, were seen partially as professional arbitrators of public issues, even those involving the most complex policies.

The role of public arbitrators could be maintained, with limited difficulty, during the period of substantive formalism. As the judges, *qua* judges, were used to resolve more obviously socially and politically complex issues in the courts, their utility as scientific public arbiters declined. In the long run it was the Heath government's decision to apply the model of the Restrictive Practices Court to the unions, with the passage of the National Industrial Relations Act of 1971[46] that was to bring the judiciary under the most glaring and often unfavorable publicity. A significant segment of the Labour party in Parliament became committed to

42. For a detailed analysis of the debates, see Robert Stevens and Basil Yamey, *The Restrictive Practices Court*, chap. 3.

43. Harold Macmillan, *Riding the Storm* 352.

44. Ibid. 737.

45. *Denning Report*, Cmnd. 2152 (1963). See also Clive Irving, et al., *Anatomy of a Scandal*.

46. R. W. Rideout, "The Industrial Relations Act, 1971" 655; for a defense of the use of the court see Lord Hailsham (Quintin McGarel Hogg), *The Door Wherein I Went* 292–94.

the removal of the President of the Industrial Relations Court, Sir John Donaldson, and although the return of the Labour party in 1974 heralded the end of that court,[47] the demystification of the judiciary had reached an important new stage. The question raised by *The Times* when the Restrictive Practices Court had been established had proved prophetic: "Will judges who have been watched in the new tribunals weighing the highly controversial questions of expediency, however closely their terms of reference are limited, carry back to the Queen's Bench or Chancery quite the same unassailable reputation for detachment from political considerations that they have hitherto enjoyed?"[48] The answer, especially after the Donaldson affair, was "no."

Of course, it was not only the Conservative party that designated judges for these extra chores.[49] The Labour party used judges not only to chair Royal Commissions, but also in an effort to solve the problem of London's third airport;[50] and both parties called up the judiciary extensively in an effort to pour oil on the troubled waters of Northern Ireland, where the virtues of impartiality were partially compromised by apparently conflicting advice.[51]

More obviously, over the twenty years the mystique attached to limited numbers had been diluted.[52] In 1937 there had been seven Lords of Appeal, five Lords Justices, and twenty-nine High Court judges. By 1955 the number of High Court judges had crept up to thirty-nine, by 1965 to sixty, and by 1976 to seventy-three. In 1976 there were fifteen Lords Justices and eleven Lords of Appeal authorized. The general effect of the Courts act of 1971 had been to extend considerably the number, power, and influence of what had been the County Court judges and the recorders, and the new Crown and circuit courts had spread all levels of

---

47. For a discussion of the operation of the court, see J. A. Farmer, *Tribunals and Government* 79–82. For a retrospective view of the Court, see Michael Moran, *The Politics of Industrial Relations*, passim.

48. Cited, Stevens and Yamey, *Restrictive Practices Court* 38.

49. For the use of the judges in extrajudicial activities, see Fred L. Morrison, *Courts and Political Process in England*, chap. 8; and Shimon Shetreet, *Judges on Trial* 354–63. *Report of the Royal Commission on Tribunals of Enquiry*, Cmnd. 3121 (1966) recommended against further use of judges in the way Denning had been used in the Profumo affair.

50. *Report of the Commission on the Third London Airport*, HMSO, 1971 (Mr. Justice Roskill).

51. Those used included Searman, Parker, Cameron, Diplock, Gardiner, and Widgery. On this, see especially Gavin Drewry, "The Judge as Political Anodyne" 531. John Griffith has argued that the Diplock and Gardiner reports were in "open disagreement"; John A. G. Griffith, *The Politics of the Judiciary* 48. For some further concern about the use of judges in this way, see Hailsham, *Door Wherein I Went* 203–4.

52. Criticism of specific judges was by then far more frequent in both Parliament and the press; e.g., "The Week," 125 *New Law Journal* 687 (1975).

courts across the country.[53] Courts were seen increasingly as a social service.

Indeed, attitudes toward the profession itself had changed. In the late fifties and early sixties the conservatism and apparently increasing irrelevance of the judiciary had been much criticized.[54] In the later sixties that criticism was translated into more concrete forms. The legal profession was examined by the Monopolies Commission[55] and legal education by a government committee,[56] while in 1976 a Royal Commission was established to investigate the profession as a whole. Yet the profession, too, had changed. In 1955 there had been eighteen thousand solicitors and two thousand barristers in practice. By 1976 the relative numbers were twenty-nine thousand solicitors and thirty-seven hundred barristers.[57] The increase in the number of law students and law teachers was even more dramatic, as was the fact that the profession was deriving an ever-growing share of its income from the public fisc through the legal aid scheme. Academic criticism of the profession became widespread. These political and professional factors ultimately affected the operation of the House of Lords as a judicial body.

The Appellate Process, 1956–1976

The appellate process experienced considerable tensions during the period. World politics was causing a gradual decline in the work of the Judicial Committee of the Privy Council, and at least some reformers had serious doubts about whether, domestically, a second appeal to the House of Lords was justified. At the same time many were questioning the continued existence of the Lords as a political body. For the Judicial Committee of the Privy Council these two decades represented the gradual closing of an era. The only moment of renewal came when Gerald Gardiner, somewhat illogically, suggested that although the House of Lords should be abolished to save litigants' money, a peripatetic Commonwealth Court should be established to hear second appeals.[58] Once Lord Chancellor, Gardiner, with limited support from Parliament,[59] floated

53. For an analysis of the criticism, see Brian Abel-Smith and Robert Stevens, *Lawyers and the Courts*, part 3.

54. Thus it became normal to expect newly appointed judges to undergo training; see Brian Abel-Smith and Robert Stevens, *In Search of Justice*, chap. 6.

55. See *Report of the Monopolies Commission on Professional Services*, Cmnd. 4463 (1970).

56. *Report of the Committee on Legal Education*, Cmnd. 4595 (1971).

57. "What the Attorney-General Said," 126 *New Law Journal* 147 (1976).

58. Gerald Gardiner and Andrew Martin, *Law Reform* NOW 16.

59. For details of the parliamentary motion, see *The Times*, 25 May 1965, at 12.

the idea at the Commonwealth Conference of 1965, only to see it fail.[60] Later the same year the idea collapsed at the Commonwealth and Empire Law Conference.[61]

Meanwhile, the work of the Judicial Committee continued to diminish. In 1938, 107 appeals had been lodged with the Judicial Committee; in 1956 the number was 28. Although the number of appeals lodged actually increased around 1960,[62] the overall decline continued through the sixties and seventies.[63] Reflected in cases actually decided after a hearing, this represented a decrease from the two high years of 1961 (52 cases) and 1964 (59 cases) to the annual case load of 27, 24, and 30, for the years 1972, 1973, and 1974, respectively.[64] Meanwhile, the number of jurisdictions from which appeals might be taken also dropped,[65] and had not Gough Whitlam been removed as Prime Minister of Australia in 1975, there might well have been no further appeals from that country, which was, by the 1970s, with Malaysia, the chief client of the court.[66]

Both Malaysia and Australia apparently had their peculiar reasons for retaining appeals to the Privy Council,[67] based on political jealousies embodied in their federal constitutions.[68] For example, Malaysia main-

60. The only major support appeared to be from Malaysia; *The Times*, 10 June 1965, at 8. The story of the collapse appears in the news and correspondence columns of *The Times* for May and June 1965.

61. Held in Sydney. Despite the fact that the English Attorney-General was "confident" that the conference would endorse a Commonwealth Court, it was reported that the issue "has been widely regarded as a non-starter"; *The Times*, 1 Sept. 1965, at 1, 7.

62. 55 in 1959; 11 in 1960; and 54 in 1961; *Civil Judicial Statistics, England and Wales*.

63. 38 in 1969; 54 in 1970; 33 in 1971; 41 in 1972; and 35 in 1973; ibid.

64. The increase for 1974 was reflected by an increase in U.K. appeals: 1 concerning the suspension of a medical practitioner and 6 relating to the disposal (or other arrangement) for redundant churches. These latter appeals came from the ecclesiastical courts under the 1883 legislation.

65. For a useful survey of countries from which appeals might be taken in 1974 see A. M. Finlay, "A Pacific Regional Court of Appeal?" 493, 494.

66. Of the 38 cases heard in 1962, 10 were from Ceylon, 7 from the East African Court of Appeal, and 9 from Malaysia. By 1972, of the 27 cases heard (26 from the Commonwealth), Australia provided 7 and Malaysia 4. The remainder were from Bahamas, 2; Ceylon, 1; Guiana, 1; Hong Kong, 3; Jamaica, 3; New Zealand, 2; Singapore, 2; Trinidad and Tobago, 1. There was 1 ecclesiastical appeal. Of the 23 Commonwealth cases heard in 1974, 7 were from Australia, 3 from New Zealand, and 5 from Malaysia; *Civil Judicial Statistics, England and Wales, passim*.

67. In this connection, it has been said, "New Zealand is the only stable and autonomous Commonwealth country with a firmly established local bar and a tradition of independent courts to continue the appeals to London"; B. J. Cameron, "The Future of Appeals to the Judicial Committee of the Privy Council, a Symposium: New Zealand" 172, 184.

68. It would be unfair to dismiss out of hand the Privy Council's contribution to the constitutional law of new nations. While in general formalistic and undistinguished, see the activist and constitutionally creative approach in *Akar v. Attorney-General of Sierra Leone*, [1970] A.C. 853 (P.C. 1969); *Olivier v. Buttigieg*, [1967] 1 A.C. 115 (P.C. 1966); *Kanda v. Government of Malaya*, [1962] A.C. 322 (P.C.).

tained a somewhat fictional independence, whereby the Privy Council was technically used only to advise the Malaysian Yang di-Pertuan Agong.[69] The Australian commitment was even more complex. Politically, the Labour party found the idea of having the final appeal court in London degrading, while the County Liberal party urged the retention of appeals after the Statute of Westminster, on condition that they were heard only by Lords of Appeal and not by mere law lords or privy councillors.[70] Meanwhile the Australian judges, who were already unhappy with some of the decisions of the House of Lords, felt some disenchantment with the Judicial Committee.[71] In particular, although the categories of Commonwealth judges eligible to sit had been considerably broadened in 1928, the Australian judges refused to participate in the Judicial Committee until dissenting opinions were allowed.[72]

This complaint, going back almost as far as 1878 when Selborne had reimposed the old rule of a single opinion,[73] was finally remedied by Gardiner in 1966,[74] after another attempt by the Australian Federal Parliament to limit appeals.[75] The exact effect of the Judicial Committee (Dissenting Opinion) Order in Council is unclear.[76] One distinguished academic, L. C. B. Gower, has argued that allowing dissents has destroyed the major purpose of the Judicial Committee—a limited unity of substantive law across the legal systems, while Lord Reid insisted that the order greatly improved the quality of Privy Council judgments.[77]

Undoubtedly a relationship existed between the work of the Lords

69. Ahmad Ibrahim, "The Future of Appeals to the Judicial Committee of the Privy Council, a Symposium: Malaysia and Singapore" 163, 165.

70. One of the political reasons for this solution was that some members of the Australian cabinet were unwilling to have cases heard by the nonwhites eligible to sit in the Privy Council.

71. The Australian courts refused to follow *DPP* v. *Smith*, [1961] A.C. 290 (1960). See per Sir Owen Dixon in *Parker* v. *R.*, 111 Commw. L.R. 610, 632 (1963).

72. Although in 1962, after the Commonwealth Conference of that year, 6 Australian judges were made privy councillors, along with 1 judge each from Nigeria, the Federation of Rhodesia and Nyasaland, and New Zealand; Michael Nash, "Privy Council" 1171.

73. The authenticity of this has now been questioned. See D. B. Swinfen, "Single Judgment in the Privy Council 1833–1966" 153. The article also describes the earlier attempts to allow dissents.

74. Gardiner held a meeting of the law lords and polled the ex-law lords. The decision to allow dissents was a majority one.

75. G. Sawer, "The Future of Appeals to the Judicial Committee of the Privy Council, A Symposium: Australia" 138, 142.

76. For a list of dissents up to 1971, see Louis Blom-Cooper and Gavin Drewry, *Final Appeal* 111.

77. "If you compare the quality of Privy Council judgments with speeches in the House of Lords for a long time back, I think you will agree that from the point of view of developing the law Privy Council judgments have been much inferior. . . . The reason is that a single judgment must get the agreement of at least all in the majority so it tends to be no more than the highest common factor in their views"; James S. C. Reid, "The Judge as Law Maker" 22, 29.

and the Privy Council, but in general for the Lords these were bullish years in terms of work load. Despite the talk of abolition, Gardiner actually increased the statutory allowable limit of Lords of Appeal to eleven in the Administration of Justice Act of 1968.[78] Such additions proved justified not only by the outside demands on the law lords, especially Donovan's Chairmanship of the Royal Commission on Trade Unions and Employers' Associations and Pearson's Chairmanship of the Royal Commission on Civil Liability and Compensation for Personal Injury, but also in terms of the number of appeals. Whereas between 1947 and 1959 the House of Lords heard an annual average of thirty-three appeals, for the period 1960 to 1972 they heard an average of forty-three.[79] By the early 1970s each appeal took an average of three days to hear.[80]

The reasons for this expansion of work are complex, partly related to the overall revival in litigation in the first of the two ten-year periods under discussion.[81] Yet more important were two specific changes. First, the Administration of Justice Act of 1960 extended the right of appeal in criminal cases virtually assimilating it to that in civil cases. In the same year, the government extended legal aid to the House of Lords,[82] a

78. In fact, it does not appear that there have ever been 11 Lords of Appeal, although there were 10 at one point. By the end of 1975 there were again 9. The Judicial Pensions Act of 1958 had imposed a retiring age of 75 for any newly appointed judges, including Lords of Appeal.

79. In 1973 the House heard 50 cases and in 1974, 29. For a detailed breakdown of the work of the House between 1958 and 1960, see Blom-Cooper and Drewry, *Final Appeal*, part B.

Between 1952 and 1968 the House heard 512 appeals: 349 from the Court of Appeal (Civil); 102 from the Court of Session; 15 from the Court of Appeal of Northern Ireland; 27 from the Court of Criminal Appeal, the Court of Appeal (Criminal), and the Courts-Martial Appeal Court; 17 from the Divisional Court of Queens's Bench; and 2 from the Court of Criminal Appeal in Northern Ireland. Of the 512 appeals, 183 civil and 12 criminal were allowed or allowed in part; ibid. 242. During that same period the Appeals Committee sat for 171 days to hear 639 petitions for leave to appeal, of which 143 were allowed; ibid. 126.

The 466 civil cases between 1952 and 1968 included 127 revenue and rating cases, 90 "fault liability" cases, 52 commercial cases, 13 labor law cases, 58 land law cases, 16 wills and trusts, 5 company, 4 defamation, 28 patent copyright and trademark cases, 18 cases in the general area of practice and procedure, 11 administrative law, 12 family law, 11 international law, 8 constitutional law, 2 transport law, and 13 miscellaneous; ibid. 246.

Of these appeals, 358 were unanimous; 55 had 1 dissent, and 53, 2; ibid. 187. For the details of the costs of bringing appeals, see ibid., chap. 11. The tradition of separate judgments survived in both civil and criminal cases. During this period, in 35 percent of decisions each law lord gave a judgment, and in 74.3 percent the majority of law lords gave separate judgments; ibid. 184.

80. 1971 the House heard 49 cases in 155 days; in 1972, 50 in 146 days; *Judicial Statistics 1971*.

81. Abel-Smith and Stevens, *Lawyers and the Courts* 262–75.

82. The Administration of Justice Act of 1969 allowed the process of "leapfrogging," in certain circumstances, directly from the trial court to the House of Lords. Its effect on

decision that undoubtedly affected the volume of appeals. The situation may even have been exacerbated by the 1966 Practice Statement on Precedent:

Their Lordships regard the use of precedent as an indispensable foundation upon which to decide what is the law and its application to individual cases. It provides at least some degree of certainty upon which individuals can rely in the conduct of their affairs, as well as a basis for orderly development of legal rules.

Their Lordships nevertheless recognise that too rigid adherence to precedent may lead to injustice in a particular case and also unduly restrict the proper development of the law. They propose, therefore, to modify their present practice and, while treating former decisions of this House as normally binding, to depart from a previous decision when it appears right to do so.

In this connection they will bear in mind the danger of disturbing retrospectively the basis on which contracts, settlements of property and fiscal arrangements have been entered into and also the especial need for certainty as to the criminal law.

This announcement is not intended to affect the use of precedent elsewhere than in this House.[83]

The impact of this statement is relevant to the whole of Part IV of this book. Yet whatever the impact may have been elsewhere, no sudden change occurred in the role of the law lords as legislators.[84] When the overall reform of the House of Lords as a legislative body again became a live issue in the late 1960s,[85] the White Paper on the House of Lords appeared to preserve the legislative prerogatives of the law lords,[86] who by this time were regarded as an integral and influential part of the nonpartisanship that the Lords as a whole liked to claim for themselves.[87] Indeed, as has happened at least twice in the previous hundred years, it is possible to argue that the existence of the law lords helped to preserve the upper house as a whole.

---

the House and its work is unclear, but see Gavin Drewry, "Judgment on Leapfrogging" 698; Gavin Drewry, "Leapfrogging—and a Lord Justice's Eye View of the Final Appeal" 260.

83. *Practice Direction (Judicial Precedent)*, [1966] 1 W.L.R. 1234 (H.L.). On this, see especially W. Barton Leach, "Revisionism in the House of Lords" 797, 813.

84. For an excellent study of the law lords as legislators, see Blom-Cooper and Drewry, *Final Appeal*, chap. 10.

85. Stacey, *British Government 1966–1975*, chap. 5.

86. "There should be a place in the reformed House of Lords for law lords and bishops"; *Reform of the House of Lords*, Cmnd. 3799, at 29 (1968). This view was not shared by all speakers on the Parliament Bill. See Gavin Drewry, "Judges in Parliament" 431. It should be noted, however, that the Lords' judicial functions were to remain untouched by the proposals in the 1975 White Paper on Devolution; *The Times*, 28 Nov. 1975, at 5.

87. "The rest of the House respects the Law Lords' strong conviction of political neutrality, both for its own sake and for the implication that it preserves some mysterious essence of non-partisanship that pervades the Lords as a whole"; Janet P. Morgan, *The House of Lords and the Labour Government 1964–1970* (Oxford, 1975), at 103.

Yet if the Lords of Appeal had managed to maintain neutrality, they did so during twenty years that produced five Lord Chancellors who were generally aggressive with respect to the role of law. It can, for instance, be argued that the secularization or demystification of the law began in earnest with the appointment of Kilmuir as Chancellor in 1954. Kilmuir, as will be seen, thought the law should be used and not simply put on a pedestal. He commended judicial lawmaking and thought politics and law should not be divorced. Typical of his innovations were the establishment of the Restrictive Practices Court, the rapid expansion of legal aid (including aid to the House) and the extension of the criminal work of the Lords. In 1962 on the "Night of the Long Knives," Kilmuir was replaced as Lord Chancellor by Dilhorne, who represented something of a throwback to the substantive formalists. In 1964, with the arrival of a Labour administration, Gardiner became Lord Chancellor. Although his concept of the role of the law and of the legal profession was more conventional than that of his two predecessors, he was a strong believer in law reform and he was even prepared to allow this belief in reform to interfere with his otherwise conventional view of the judicial process. Thus, in addition to establishing the Law Commission "to reform lawyers' law," it was Gardiner who also formally allowed the Lords to overrule their own earlier decisions. In 1970, with the return of the Conservatives, Gardiner was replaced by Quintin Hogg, the second Lord Hailsham and the son of an earlier Lord Chancellor. In this appointment the Tory tradition of a politically robust Chancellor was patently continued, reflected most strongly in Hailsham's establishment of the Industrial Relations Court in an effort to curb the power of the unions. By 1977 there was no evidence that the Labour Lord Chancellor since 1974, Elwyn Jones, was of a retiring disposition, although his view of the judicial process may have been rather conventional.

Lord Kilmuir[88]

Kilmuir did not think of himself as a great lawyer,[89] a view shared by many members of the profession. Yet he deserves to rank as one of the most important figures in twentieth-century English law, for it was during the Kilmuir Chancellorship (1954–62) that the first major effort to halt the decline of the courts' importance was made. In this regard, it is

88. David Maxwell-Fyfe; b. 1900; educ., George Watson's College, Edinburgh, Balliol College, Oxford; called to bar, 1922; Q.C., 1934; M.P. (Cons.), Liverpool (West Derby), 1935–54; Solicitor-General, 1942–45; Attorney-General, 1945; Home Secretary, 1951–54; Lord Chancellor, 1954–62; d. 1967.
89. See Lord Kilmuir (David Maxwell-Fyfe), *Political Adventures*.

difficult to imagine a more dramatic contrast between Kilmuir and his predecessor, Simonds.

In many ways, Kilmuir was a typical Conservative M.P. of the interwar years, advancing through social and educational contacts, rather than climbing up some ladder open primarily to talent. Like Harold Macmillan, however, in whose administration he served, he did have a social conscience.[90] His was not merely a jingoistic belief in the past nor an entirely naive belief in judicial activism, for to Kilmuir must go a considerable share of the credit for shaking off the judicial catatonia that Jowitt and Simonds had allowed to settle on the English legal system. Kilmuir believed that lawyers should be important in the modern state.[91] It was he, for instance, who set up the Restrictive Practices Court[92] and was responsible for the passage of the Tribunals and Enquiries Act. Moreover, Kilmuir intended that these acts should make English law more relevant. In his autobiography he wrote, "I have always been anxious that the law should not be regarded as a treasured antique, to be taken down, admired, and replaced exactly as before. It must play its part in the modern scientific state."[93] As Lord Chancellor he had argued, "I believe that the law is as effective a dynamic force in modern problems as it is soundly based on these historical roots. Therefore, I believe that the law should be brought in to help in the solution of the great problems of the modern State."[94]

90. Lord Kilmuir (David Maxwell-Fyfe), "The Shaftesbury Tradition in Conservative Politics" 70.

91. "The lawyer may not be the key-stone of the political arch, but if he is the cement of the political stability then in a troubled world, he has carried a burden and achieved a result with which he need never be ashamed to face his fellow citizens or posterity"; Lord Kilmuir (David Maxwell-Fyfe) "Lawyer Statesman" 939, 1013.

92. During the debates he said, "I have come to the conclusion that the questions at issue are not inappropriate for judicial determination within the framework laid down in the Bill. . . . The Government do not deny that some element of economic judgement will be demanded of the Court, and that is why it will be a mixed one, and the expertise and experience of practical affairs of the lay members will contribute to its judgements"; 198 *Parl. Deb.*, H.L. (5th ser.), cols. 18–19 (26 June 1956).

93. Kilmuir, *Political Adventures* 263.

94. 199 *Parl. Deb.*, H.L. (5th ser.), col. 350 (26 July 1956). See also Lord Kilmuir (David Maxwell-Fyfe), "The State, the Citizen and the Law" 172, 173:

[T]he function of the law is constantly changing; I do not merely mean that it is constantly being amended but that the whole purpose of our machinery of law is gradually but uninterruptedly developing.

The law is not to be compared to a venerable antique, to be taken down, dusted, admired and put back on the shelf; rather it is like an old but still vigorous tree—firmly rooted in history; but still putting out new shoots, taking new grafts and from time to time dropping dead wood. That process has been going on, now and will continue.

After all, law is not an end in itself. It is a means whereby the State can develop and regulate in an orderly and just manner the social system which it desires. It follows that, as the social problems of the day are constantly changing the law must adapt itself to meet them.

Kilmuir ought equally to be praised for his concern with law reform,[95] although his goal of one piece of law reform each year may sound a trifle simplistic.[96] In addition to his innovations in restrictive practices and administrative law, Kilmuir introduced, often in the face of considerable opposition, some ten acts concerned with family law. He also revised the rules relating to occupiers' liability, established Crown Courts in Liverpool and Manchester, extended the jurisdiction of the County Courts and provided for legal aid there, as well as in appeals to the Lords, and effectively extended the House's jurisdiction in criminal cases. He courageously increased the number of High Court judges, and he even managed to establish a retirement age for the senior judiciary.[97] Moreover, he made it clear that service as an M.P. would count in appointments to the High Court bench.

As a judge, Kilmuir probably had no sophisticated notions about the judicial process,[98] and the idea of "judicial strategies" would probably have meant little to him. Yet his bluff approach shook substantive formalism to its roots. He specifically commended *Bonsor* v. *Musicians' Union*[99] as a "notable" example of judicial lawmaking,[100] and publicly declared, "I am glad the judges have by extending old rules to new sets of circumstances produced what were, in effect, new rules."[101] At the same

95. He described law reform as a subject "particularly close to my heart"; Lord Kilmuir (David Maxwell-Fyfe), "Law Reform" 75. He took the view that "[o]rganic growth aided now and then by pruning and grafting is generally to be preferred to complete uprooting and replanting"; ibid. 76.

96. Kilmuir, *Political Adventures* 302.

97. Ibid. 299–302.

98. He was, however, more willing to articulate his views than his predecessors had been. For the benefit of an American audience, he willingly trotted out the accepted formulae: "Parliament may make or change any law it please. When once a judge has ascertained the law which governs an issue, he has no choice but to apply it. . . . Parliament at the behest of the Executive makes the statutes and the judges interpret them"; Lord Kilmuir (David Maxwell-Fyfe), "The British Courts and Parliament" 373.

He was also well aware of how little all this could mean: "[A]lthough the House of Lords, sitting judicially, cannot reverse its own earlier decisions, it can distinguish them and has done so on innumerable occasions in the legal field"; 203 *Parl. Deb.*, H.L. (5th ser.), col. 272 (1 May 1957). See also his arguments on the Occupiers' Liability Bill. "Inflexibility and refinements may bring about hard cases and injustice, even where the law is not fundamentally unsound, for an injured person may have all the merit on his side and yet be unable to bring himself within a rigid and narrow classification. Uncertainty in the law tends to multiply litigation . . . or to discourage injured persons from seeking redress which is properly theirs. The object of this Bill will be to make a limited but undoubtedly important part of our law less rigid and to remove from it some of the complexities and uncertainties with which it has become overlaid"; ibid., cols. 258–59.

99. [1956] A.C. 104 (1955).

100. Lord Kilmuir, Foreword to Arthur Citrine, *Trade Union Law* at vii.

101. He continued, "I have based legislation on judicial invocation of the doctrine of public policy in order, for example, to declare contracts void, as against public interest, for I liked its label that it was 'the prevailing opinion of wise men as to what is for the public good' and I know that such a rule must change with changing conditions of society. Yet at

time, he accepted much of Dicey's simplistic view on the role of the judges as the defenders of civil liberties.[102] The man who as Home Secretary deported Dr. Cort[103] unencumbered by any judicial review, was still obsessed with the notion that "this modern world has become so complicated that no legislature could stop all the holes, and Parliament itself relies on the judges to safeguard our freedom."[104] This same mentality led Kilmuir to the dangerous argument that "the whole of our system is based on the assumption that these freedoms exist so that they do not need to be guaranteed."[105] Everything was in order, providing the judges were objective[106] and the English judges were obviously independent.[107] Yet, despite the rhetoric, when it came to a matter like Crown privilege, there was little evidence that, in balancing the public and the private interest, Kilmuir was prepared to entrust the protection of civil liberties to the judges.[108]

---

the end of the day I do not think one needs a notice-board to tell one when interpretation ceases and legislation begins"; Lord Kilmuir (David Maxwell-Fyfe), "Judicial Qualities" 112, 113.

102. Kilmuir may have been the last Lord Chancellor to take Dicey at face value. His appointment of the Franks Committee on Administrative Tribunals was apparently inspired by his implicit belief in Dicey's concept of the Rule of Law and he did not hesitate to adopt, as his own, the dichotomy between legal and policy questions of the Committee on Ministers' Powers. See Kilmuir, "State, Citizen and Law" 172, 179: "bad law administered by good judges." See also his argument that since special tribunals were here to stay every effort should be made to get them to adopt the true legal process and a judicial attitude; ibid. 178.

For a more balanced view, see

[I]t is my faith that the State exists for man and the benefit of its citizens. I recognise that in this country public needs must on occasion surmount private rights in order to provide houses, schools, hospitals, nuclear power stations, weapon sites or "what have you." If, however, the true value of human individuality is to be maintained, then the individual must be given a fair and open opportunity of putting his objection and his case; and further, we must put into this procedure all that we have learned in the way of justice and protection for private citizens from the great social service of the Common Law, which is followed by a third of the population of the world. If, when we have translated into reality the spirit of the Franks Report, we can then feel that we have done something on the threshold of this new, complicated scientific age, our time will not have been spent in vain. [206 *Parl. Deb.*, H.L. (5th ser.), cols. 591–92 (27 Nov. 1957)]

103. See Kilmuir, *Political Adventures* 228.

104. Lord Kilmuir (David Maxwell-Fyfe), "Individual Freedom under an Unwritten Constitution" 629, 644.

105. Ibid. 632.

106. "It is a condition of individual freedom that the judiciary should not only be independent but should attract men who can display the essential judicial qualities of abandonment of prejudices, learning in the law, quick appreciation of facts, objectivity and wise silence"; ibid. 642.

107. "The absence of political pressure upon my predecessors and myself is one of the most remarkable phenomena of the Government of Great Britain. This bulwark of freedom stands firm"; ibid. 642–43.

108. He took the view that the minister, not the judge, must decide the issue; 197 *Parl. Deb.*, H.L. (5th ser.), col. 743 (6 June 1956). He did, however, make a few minor changes in the procedures to be followed by the executive.

On specific policies, therefore, it is not surprising that liberals found themselves out of sympathy with Kilmuir. During his period as Home Secretary, Tom Driberg described Kilmuir as "the man who rations mercy," for allowing Bentley to go to the gallows.[109] Kilmuir's attempt to find a via media with respect to capital punishment in the Homicide Act of 1957 was scarcely a triumph, although he may have been right in saying that "even if it does not go exactly where we want it to lead, it leads in the right direction."[110] Judicially, his handling of criminal cases was not a success. In the disastrous *Director of Public Prosecutions* v. *Smith* decision he gave the only speech, assuming it was obvious that there must be an objective test of responsibility for murder,[111] although he was to find that many other common law countries did not share such an assumption. He took an equally undifferentiated view of the defense of automatism, although on the facts of *Bratty* he may have been justified.[112] Moreover, although he was anxious to use law and the courts constructively and to extend their responsibilities in various directions, he drew the line at using the law to discourage racial discrimination.[113]

As a judge, Kilmuir sat in relatively few appeals. Yet those civil cases in which he sat revealed something attractive about his commonsense approach to the judicial process. In one case he conceded that generally he was attracted by "rugged simplicity."[114] In the area of commercial

109. For Kilmuir's defense of his actions in this case, see *Political Adventures* 206.

110. 202 *Parl. Deb.*, H.L. (5th ser.), col. 626 (19 Mar. 1957).

111. [1961] A.C. 290, 326–27 (1960): "This purely subjective approach involves this, that if an accused said that he did not in fact think of the consequences, and the jury considered that that might well be true, he would be entitled to be acquitted of murder.

"My Lords, the proposition has only to be stated thus to make one realise what a departure it is from that upon which the courts have always acted."

112. *Bratty* v. *Attorney-General for Northern Ireland*, [1963] A.C. 386, 403 (N. Ire. 1961).

113. Boast as he might of the important role law might play in the modern state, he felt that "[l]egislation could not, in itself, prevent discrimination on the part of individuals in their private dealings with coloured people, and indeed the Bill makes no attempt to do so. But from these personal and private dealings between neighbours, workmates and children, arise the public attitude and behaviour towards coloured people in general, which the Bill seeks to control. In the Government's view, this problem is not solvable by legislation"; 240 *Parl. Deb.*, H.L. col. 519 (14 May 1962).

He took a rather similar view with respect to sexual offenses. See, for instance, his reasons for refusing to accept the recommendations of the Wolfenden Committee with respect to homosexuality. "It is not the function of the law to attempt to cover all the fields of sexual behaviour. But when we seek to define the proper scope of the law, and to say what is the sphere in which the State, acting through the criminal law, has a duty to impose general standards, there are wide and deep differences of opinion. There are cases . . . when it may well be the duty of a Government to lead rather than to follow public opinion, but in a matter of this kind the general sense of the community, particularly as expressed in Statutes which have been left undisturbed for long periods, is an important feature; and the community is entitled to its view as to what affects society as a whole"; 206 ibid., cols. 771, 773 (4 Dec. 1957).

114. *LCC* v. *Wilkins*, [1957] A.C. 362, 370 (1956).

law, his speeches, while lacking Simonds' learning, also lack the latter's pedantry and formalism.[115] Some administrative and labor lawyers have reservations about his decisions, but to the generalist they are attractive,[116] as are his speeches on factory accidents, sitting both legislatively[117] and judicially.[118] The same may also be true with respect to taxation,[119] although, as with other areas of the law, there are too few decisions to make any reliable predictions of what he might have done had he sat regularly. In this regard it was unfortunate that he chose to spend his last years working in the City rather than sitting as an appeal judge.[120]

Kilmuir fits into no clear category. He was lucky to reach the Woolsack, but probably no luckier than most of the Lord Chancellors of this century. It was unfortunate that he was axed by Macmillan as part of the latter's strategy to save his administration after the Profumo scandal. Yet Kilmuir deserves to rank high on the list of Chancellors during this century: he had shaken the complacency of the system.

115. *A. V. Pound & Co. v. M. W. Hardy & Co.*, [1956] A.C. 588; *G. H. Renton & Co. v. Palmyra Trading Corp.*, [1957] A.C. 149 (1956).

116. E.g., *LCC v. Wilkins*, [1957] A.C. 362 (1956); *Vine v. National Dock Labour Bd.*, [1957] A.C. 488 (1956).

117. See also his legislative speeches, e.g., "I thought the original system of workmen's compensation was an admirable one. My opinion was completely changed on that point. . . . It is, I feel, extremely valuable that we should keep an open mind and consider how these problems are affected by the changing conditions of the modern world"; 197 *Parl. Deb.*, H.L. (5th ser.), col. 180 (3 May 1956).

118. E.g., "If one were in doubt as to the construction of a regulation, it might be legitimate to lean to an interpretation which made the regulation *intra vires, ut magis valeat quam pereat.* That is a very different thing from saying that the construction of a regulation can change automatically by reason of an extension in the *vires* of the enabling Act"; *Canadian Pacific S.S., Ltd. v. Bryers*, [1958] A.C. 485, 501 (1957). "In my opinion, it would require express words to prevent the Minister from making regulations in favour of all persons employed in the factory"; ibid. 502. "Apart from authority, I would be of opinion that the regulations enure for the benefit of a member of the crew"; ibid. 503.

See also *Cade v. British Transp. Comm'n*, [1959] A.C. 256 (1958); and *Wigley v. British Vinegars, Ltd.*, [1964] A.C. 307, 324 (1962): "In my view the true distinction is between those who are to work for the purposes of the factory and those who are not. . . . Window cleaning is part of the maintenance of the factory and in my view the deceased was within the protection afforded by section 26. I am happy to arrive at this conclusion, which appears to me to be in accordance with common sense and the intention of the Act."

119. E.g., *Verdin v. Coughtrie*, [1961] A.C. 880. Cf., however, his speeches on the Variation of Trusts Bill. "[I]t is far more undesirable that in seeking the right solution to a problem of this kind, Parliament should perpetuate injustices as between one taxpayer and another because of some rigid theory that nothing should be done which might conceivably injure the Revenue"; 209 *Parl. Deb.*, H.L. (5th ser.), col. 851 (12 June 1958). "Of course it is true that the judge may form a view of a particular application which would not be shared by another judge. But, of course, that is no new thing; it is a matter of constant occurrence whenever judicial discretion is involved; and long may it continue"; ibid., col. 852.

120. He sat in twenty-four appeals to the Lords during his Chancellorship, but thereafter sat not at all; Blom-Cooper and Drewry, *Final Appeal* 180.

Lord Dilhorne

The "Night of the Long Knives" brought Dilhorne to the Wool-sack.[121] Sir Reginald Manningham-Buller, Lord Dilhorne, belonged to a younger generation than Kilmuir and had worked his way through the party's hierarchy, including periods as Solicitor-General and Attorney-General. He had, however, more than his share of detractors in the party,[122] and his appointment as Lord Chancellor was not greeted with any particular enthusiasm. Yet, arriving at the Lords at the relatively early age of fifty-four, without any judicial experience, he gradually developed a reputation as a solid, workaday judge, but one consistent with the rather more flexible approach that has characterized the House of Lords over the last twenty years.

Dilhorne's two years as Lord Chancellor (1962–64) were too short to justify any fair judgment about his ability in that office.[123] Once out of office, his position was ambiguous. In political debates he gave only cursory support to Gardiner's plans for a Law Commission.[124] Yet with Lord Carrington as the Conservative leader of the Lords, Dilhorne found himself underemployed. He therefore threw himself into sitting as an ex officio law lord[125] while taking a politically outspoken conservative view-point in legislative debates.[126] His enthusiasm as an ex officio law lord

121. Reginald Manningham-Buller; b. 1905; father, soldier (baronet); educ., Eton and Magdalen College, Oxford (Third, Jurisprudence); called to bar, 1927; K.C., 1946; M.P. (Cons.), Daventry, 1949–50, South Northamptonshire, 1950–62; Solicitor-General, 1951–54; Attorney-General, 1954–62; Lord Chancellor, 1962–64; Lord of Appeal, 1969–.

122. He was not particularly popular with the judiciary, either. He was seen as the éminence grise behind the government's rejection of the Devlin Report on Nyasaland. He certainly made a provocative speech in the House of Commons, although the Prime Minister also took advice from Kilmuir and Julian Amery before rejecting the Devlin Report; Macmillan, *Riding the Storm* 737–38.

123. He sat in 7 appeals during his 27 months as Chancellor; Blom-Cooper and Drewry, *Final Appeal* 180.

It was as a member of the government that Dilhorne threatened the Burmah Oil Company that if it won compensation in the courts he would take it away by statute. The company did win, in *Burmah Oil Co.* v. *Lord Advocate*, [1965] A.C. 75 (Scot. 1964); and Dilhorne's successor, Gardiner, introduced the War Damages Bill, which Dilhorne supported; 264 *Parl. Deb.*, H.L. (5th ser.), col. 749 (25 Mar. 1965). See also Blom-Cooper and Drewry, *Final Appeal* 368–74.

124. While nominally accepting that there was need for reform, he warned, "[W]e have just cause to be proud of both English and Scottish law, and it does no service to seek to denigrate either." He would not accept Gardiner's premises. "I think that in his enthusiasm for this subject he has painted a wholly exaggerated picture of the state of our law, and that is what I want to rebut"; 264 *Parl. Deb.*, H.L. (5th ser.), col. 1161, 1164 (1 Apr. 1965).

125. In addition to sitting extensively in the Judicial Committee of the Privy Council, Dilhorne sat in 26 appeals between 1964 and 1968; Blom-Cooper and Drewry, *Final Appeal* 180.

126. He attended 85 percent of the legislative debates between 1963 and 1968; ibid. 211.

led to some lobbying for his appointment as a Lord of Appeal and, after his successor as Lord Chancellor (Gardiner) had changed the rules so that former Lord Chancellors no longer automatically presided,[127] Dilhorne was appointed a Lord of Appeal in 1969. Thus the third stage in his judicial career began.[128]

In many ways there was a remarkable similarity in the judicial work of the three Conservative Chancellors of this period. Although Dilhorne was less popular than Kilmuir and less of an intellectual than Hailsham, their judicial styles were not dissimilar. Although Dilhorne in his later years veered back, all three represented some weakening of the substantive formalism of Jowitt and Simonds, yet they lacked the intellectualism of a Diplock or a Wilberforce and were far from achieving the subtle sense of the appellate process represented by a Reid or a Radcliffe. Their similarity in outlook is no doubt partly due to the fact that all three Tory Chancellors were basically general common lawyers, who had faced the "real world" in circuit practice. Thus while all three accepted (or at least mouthed) the usual platitudes about the mechanistic nature of the common law,[129] their experience told them that logic was only one ingredient in the judicial decision. Moreover, their lack of experience as trial judges, coupled with their political experience, meant that they could not maintain, intellectually, the extremes to which substantive formalism had been taken, even if that had been their political inclination.

Dilhorne's contribution was essentially that of the experienced "knockabout" common lawyer who had been transferred to the final appeal court.[130] In common law cases, Dilhorne's energy was directed toward "ascertaining the facts" and then "applying the law." In his hands, "ascertaining the facts," was at times, an impressive performance.[131] The same cannot be said of his "applying the law." When

---

127. Ibid. 181, n. 1.

128. After that he spoke mainly on bills relating to criminal and civil law and procedure. But see his interventions in the Badgers Bill, 338 *Parl. Deb.*, H.L. (5th ser.), col. 1710 ff. (15 Feb. 1973), and the Protection of the Environment Bill, 348 ibid., col. 1349 ff. (22 Jan. 1974) and ibid., cols. 1602 ff. (24 Jan. 1974).

129. For Dilhorne's views on the rule of law, see Lord Dilhorne (Reginald Manningham-Buller), "The Rule of Law" 1015, 1016–18.

130. In the early part of his career as a Lord of Appeal he showed some conscious tendency to dissent, but as he gained seniority this trait appeared to evaporate. For his first three years as a Lord of Appeal, in reported cases, his dissent rate was as high as 24 percent; in the ensuing years it ranged around 10 percent.

131. For useful examples of his handling of facts, see *East Ham Corp.* v. *Bernard Sunley & Sons*, [1966] A.C. 406 (1965); *Wheat* v. *E. Lacon & Co.*, [1966] A.C. 552; *Boardman* v. *Phipps*, [1967] 2 A.C. 46 (1966); *British Rys. Bd.* v. *Liptrot*, [1969] 1 A.C. 136 (1967); *James Miller & Partners* v. *Whitworth Street Estates (Manchester), Ltd.*, [1970] A.C. 583; *National Westminster Bank Ltd.* v. *Halesowen Presswork, Ltd.*, [1972] A.C. 785. Sometimes his dissents appear to turn more on the facts than the law; e.g., *Johnson* v. *F. E. Callow (Engineers), Ltd.*, [1971] A.C. 335, 353 (1970).

Dilhorne was unable to settle the issue by determining material facts, his examination of authorities did not reveal great sophistication. In some ways the master of the construction of a contract or document, Dilhorne seemed reluctant to accept any responsibility even for restating the law in commercial areas,[132] although his inclination in tort appeared to be to restrict liability.[133] Only occasionally did some "development" in the law slip through.[134]

The result of this approach was that, after an effective analysis of the factual situation, Dilhorne's judgments often read as little more than a digest of cases.[135] The contrast was particularly striking when, as was the situation in the mid-seventies, the House had a number of strong law lords. In a period of increased flexibility, he often regarded it as his duty to chastise those who wished to develop the common law.[136] His general approach when faced with a patent lacuna in the law was to ask Parliament to "clarify the law."[137] Even in those common law areas where all of the modern generations of law lords accepted some responsibility for reworking the law, Dilhorne remained skeptical. In *Dorset Yacht Company v. Home Office*, in dissent, he argued, "No doubt very powerful arguments can be advanced that there should be such a duty. . . . However this may be, we are concerned not with what the law should be but with what it is. The absence of authority shows that no such duty now exists. If there should be one, that is, in my view, a matter for the legislature and not for the courts."[138]

Some have found more flexibility in Dilhorne's view of statutory interpretation; certainly his use of the statutory scheme approach has been an important step away from the purely literal approach.[139] In an early decision on tax law, for example, he refused to restrict the scope of

132. E.g., *Suisse Atlantique Société d'Armament Maritime S.A. v. N.V. Rotterdamsche Kolen Centrale*, [1967] 1 A.C. 361, 397 (1966): "In my view it is not right to say that the law prohibits and nullifies a clause exempting or limiting liability for a fundamental breach or breach of a fundamental term. Such a rule of law would involve a restriction of freedom of contract and in the older cases I can find no trace of it."

133. E.g., *Dorset Yacht Co. v. Home Office*, [1970] A.C. 1004; *Wheat v. E. Lacon & Co.*, [1966] A.C. 552; *Naylor v. Yorkshire Elec. Bd.*, [1968] A.C. 529 (1967). See also his dissent in *Henderson v. Henry E. Jenkins & Sons*, [1970] A.C. 282, 293 (1969).

134. *Norwich Pharmacal Co. v. Commissioners of Customs & Excise*, [1974] A.C. 133, 182 (1973), where Dilhorne appeared to allow the extension of patent law on the principle of effectiveness.

135. E.g., *R. v. Smith*, [1975] A.C. 476, 504–5 (1973).

136. E.g., his criticism of Denning and Buckley for failing to "adhere to the law" in *IRC v. Mills*, [1975] A.C. 38, 52–53 (1974).

137. *Suisse Atlantique Société d'Armament Maritime S.A. v. N.V. Rotterdamsche Kolen Centrale*, [1967] 1 A.C. 361, 390 (1966).

138. [1970] A.C. 1004, 1045.

139. E.g., *Donaghey v. Boulton & Paul, Ltd.*, [1968] A.C. 1 (1967); *Cleary v. IRC*, [1968] A.C. 766 (1967); *DPP v. Carey*, [1970] A.C. 1072 (1969).

the antiavoidance provisions.[140] Yet he always stopped short of accepting the mischief rule,[141] and perhaps, in later years he deviated somewhat from his statutory scheme approach. In *Argyle Motors (Birkenhead), Limited* v. *Birkenhead Corporation*, he reminded his fellow law lords that "[e]xtension of the right to compensate is a matter for Parliament and not for judicial decision."[142] His approach was the more conventional one that "our task is to say what in our opinion, the law is, not what it should be."[143] He generalized this view by citing with approval Maxwell on the *Interpretation of Statutes*, to the effect that the court "must bear in mind that its function is jus dicere, not jus dare: the words of the statute must not be overruled by the judges, but reform of the law must be left in the hands of Parliament."[144]

As long as it was limited to criminal cases, there was some sympathy for Dilhorne's approach, but by the mid-1970s his view seemed out of line with those of the other Lords of Appeal. For Dilhorne, it was none of the appellate court's business to consider the severity of sentences as it was for Salmon in *R.* v. *Doot*.[145] Unlike Reid or Denning, Dilhorne

140. In *IRC* v. *Parker*, [1966] A.C. 141, 160 (Scot. 1965), one of the first cases on § 28 of the Finance Act of 1960 to reach the Lords, and a decisive case for setting the future judicial attitude to the section, Dilhorne refused to restrict the provision. "The view was expressed in the Court of Appeal that Section 28 was directed to dividend stripping and that the objective of the company in this case was not of this character. I think I should make it clear that, in my opinion, this is taking too narrow a view of section 28. That section was, in my view, directed to tax avoidance taking place in certain circumstances and one has to consider whether in a particular case the circumstances specified exist. In my opinion, in this case they did." See also *Luke* v. *IRC*, [1963] A.C. 557, 571–72 (Scot.); and, on § 28, *Cleary* v. *IRC*, [1968] A.C. 766 (1967).

141. *IRC* v. *Parker*, [1966] A.C. 141 (Scot. 1965).

142. *R.* v. *Hyam*, [1975] A.C. 55, 85 (1974).

143. [1975] A.C. 99, 134 (1973). See also *Maunsell* v. *Olins*, [1975] A.C. 373, 384 (1974). He argued that altering the law "involves questions of policy and all we have to do is to decide whether the sections apply in this case."

There were, inevitably, earlier examples of this approach. See, for example, *Westminster Bank, Ltd.* v. *Zang*, [1966] A.C. 182, 218 (1964): "If the protection given to the drawer by section 3 is inadequate, that is a matter for Parliament to rectify." See also *Fisher* v. *Raven*, [1964] A.C. 210 (1963), although, since that was a criminal case, different considerations may have applied.

Dilhorne took an even stricter view of judicial legislation when criminal law was involved. See *R.* v. *Doot*, [1973] A.C. 807, 822: "[I]f the law be as the Court of Appeal held it was, that law can only be changed by Parliament. This House in its judicial capacity cannot alter the law." See also *R.* v. *Marcus*, [1976] A.C. 35, 59 (1975): "I appreciate that the appellant escapes the punishment he deserves . . . [but that] should not lead to anything other than a strict construction of this penal statute" (dissenting).

For narrow statements of the courts' role in statutory construction see *Tesco Supermarkets, Ltd.* v. *Nattrass*, [1972] A.C. 153, 183–84 (1971); *Albert* v. *Motor Insurers' Bureau*, [1972] A.C. 301, 324 (1971); *Ealing London Borough Council* v. *Race Relations Bd.*, [1972] A.C. 342, 360 (1971); *R.* v. *Sakhuja*, [1973] A.C. 152, 175 (1972).

144. *Kammins Ballrooms Co.* v. *Zenith Invs. (Torquay), Ltd.*, [1971] A.C. 850, 869.

145. See Dilhorne at [1973] A.C. 807, 821.

resisted any urge to develop "natural justice."[146] Unlike Simon of Glaisdale, Dilhorne used precedents as answers, rather than as pointers; he saw the Lords' role as reconciling earlier decisions but not as explaining, clarifying, or developing the law.[147] Dilhorne, unlike Radcliffe, had no difficulty with the fact that "the law" might vary with whichever government was in power,[148] something with which the House in its judicial capacity could scarcely be concerned:

As I understand the judicial functions of this House, although they involve applying well established principles to new situations, they do not involve adjusting the common law to what are thought to be the social norms of the time. They do not include bowing to the wind of change. We have to declare what the law is, not what we think it should be. If it is clearly established that in certain circumstances there is a right to exemplary damages, this House should not, when sitting judicially, and indeed, in my view, cannot properly abolish or restrict that right. . . . If the power to award such damages is to be abolished or restricted, that is the task of the legislature.[149]

Such shades and reality of substantive formalism carried over into all spheres of the appellate process. Dilhorne in statutory construction cases emphasized, at a general level, the mechanical role left to the courts; at a different level it forced him back to the interpretive devices that were the hallmarks of the substantive formalists.[150] In *Norwich Pharmacal Company* v. *Customs and Excise Commissioners*, he upheld an earlier decision, while admitting his difficulties in establishing a *ratio decidendi*.[151] Rather than overruling earlier decisions he announced that, properly understood, the doctrines did not conflict;[152] the "ordinary and natural"[153] and "ordinary natural meaning"[154] were once more staple fare. Thus having appeared in his earlier years as the natural successor to Kilmuir, Dilhorne increasingly appeared as a Conservative exponent of substantive formalism.

146. *Athanassiadis Government of Greece (Note)*, [1971] A.C. 282, 291.
147. E.g., *E. L. Oldendorff & Co. G.m.b.H.* v. *Tradax S.A.*, [1974] A.C. 479, 552 (1973).
148. *British Oxygen Co.* v. *Board of Trade*, [1971] A.C. 610, 631 (1970).
149. *Broome* v. *Cassell & Co.*, [1972] A.C. 1027, 1107.
150. He also shared the substantive formalists' level of criticism. In *Smedleys, Ltd.* v. *Breed*, Dilhorne criticized the government for bringing an action for violating public health legislation when no harm had resulted. "What this litigation has cost I dread to think. A great deal of time of the courts has been occupied. I cannot see that any advantage to the general body of consumers has or will result, apart, perhaps from the exposition of the law"; [1974] A.C. 839, 857 (1972).
151. [1974] A.C. 133, 188 (1973).
152. E.g., *R.* v. *Sakhuja*, [1973] A.C. 152, 180–81 (1972).
153. Ibid. 174.
154. *Cozens* v. *Brutus*, [1973] A.C. 854, 865 (1972).

Lord Gardiner

When Harold Wilson formed his first administration in 1964 he chose as his Lord Chancellor Gerald Gardiner[155] who, although a member of the Labour party, had not been active in party politics as such. Gardiner was in many ways the archetypal liberal intellectual in the Labour party, with all the inherent contradictions involved, and his strengths and weaknesses were in the tradition of Herschell, Loreburn, Haldane, and Sankey. Gardiner said of himself that he had "an instinctive reaction to injustice. Whenever I saw something in the law which seemed to me to be causing injustice, I always wanted to put it right."[156] His record in terms of the reform of what he described as "lawyers' law"[157] could scarcely be questioned. In 1963, under the auspices of the Society of Labour Lawyers, he had published *Law Reform NOW*, a statement that called for sweeping changes in many branches of the law, most of which were achieved, after the return of the Labour administration, by the Gardiner-created Law Commission: a five-lawyer permanent law reform committee. As a result of the commission's activities, few areas of doctrine were not recommended for some kind of change, and a significant number of reforms were actually carried into law by Parliament.[158]

155. Gerald Austin Gardiner; b. 1900; father, knighted; educ., Harrow and Magdalen College, Oxford; called to bar, 1925; K.C., 1948; Lord Chancellor, 1964–70.

156. Gerald Gardiner, "The Role of the Lord Chancellor in the Field of Law Reform" 326. In *Who's Who* for 1972 Gardiner's recreations were described as "Law Reform and the Theatre."

He reported that, while practicing at the bar, he was a member of the Medico-Legal Society, the Howard League for Penal Reform, the Institute for the Study and Treatment of Delinquency, the Divorce Law Reform Association, the Abortion Law Reform Association, and the Lord Chancellor's Law Reform Committee. As a member, he attended 330 meetings of the Evershed Committee on the Practice and Procedure of the Supreme Court, and as Chairman of the Bar Council, he pushed that organization into the business of law reform; Gardiner, "Role of Lord Chancellor" 328. See also Gerald Gardiner, "Comparative Law Reform" 1021.

157. Acceptance of the distinction between "lawyers' law" and "law involving policy" permeated Gardiner and Martin, *Law Reform* NOW. After experience with the Law Commission, however, even Gardiner appeared to doubt the division. In discussing the Law Commission's position on divorce law, he noted, "There is no such thing as lawyer's law reform. We all know that some property bills are quite technical, but you cannot divide up the subject in that way. There are but few law reform bills, or I suppose, any bills which do not raise questions on which laymen may disagree. I respectfully defy anyone to write down on paper any precise, workable definition of what you mean by 'lawyers' law reform'; and if the Law Commission were confined to highly technical property subjects we might as well not have it"; 303 *Parl. Deb.*, H.L. (5th ser.), col. 316 (30 June 1969). See also Gerald Gardiner, "Methods of Law Reform" 3; Gerald Gardiner, "Some Aspects of Law Reform" 171.

158. Gardiner, "Role of the Lord Chancellor" 332. For other examples of Gardiner's pride in the work of the Law Commission, see 317 *Parl. Deb.*, H.L. (5th ser.), cols. 798–99 (4 Apr. 1971); with respect to the Nullity of Marriage Bill, 305 ibid., col. 479 (6 Nov. 1969), noting that the Matrimonial Proceedings and Property Bill "demonstrates, perhaps better than any other measure we have so far discussed, the value and operation of the Law

Apparently Gardiner was somewhat surprised by his successes in law reform. Despite all his work in law reform during his years in practice, he reported, "What I had to discover when I became Lord Chancellor was how large and effective the role of the Lord Chancellor in the field of law reform could be made to be."[159] Although piloting the Law Commission Bill through Parliament was no easy task, particularly since his predecessor and some of the law lords were not enthusiastic, Gardiner was more than satisfied with the success of his brainchild. By the time he had left office the commission had produced twenty reports, of which fourteen had been implemented.[160] It was little wonder that he concluded a public lecture with the observation, "We certainly started a period of massive law reform. I am naturally delighted that it appears to be continuing. It may in time die out. Whether it dies will mainly depend on the personal approach to law reform of the Lord Chancellor."[161]

Although an advocate of law reform through the Law Commission, Gardiner's view of judicial creativity through litigation was less clear.[162] In *Law Reform NOW*, he had argued in favor of abolishing the second appeal, a position he was to restate in later legislative debates.[163] Yet it was Gardiner who engineered the Practice Statement of 1966, formally freeing the House from its strict position on stare decisis. One senses, however, that he expected relatively little creativity to result.[164] This in some ways is not surprising, for despite his enthusiasm for reform of

---

Commission." He continued, "My lords, the subject is a complicated one and reform in this field has necessitated a degree of consultation and intensive discussion. Without the Law Commission I doubt very much whether such a study would have been practicable"; ibid., col. 480.

159. Gardiner, "Role of the Lord Chancellor" 328.

160. See, generally, Farrar, *Law Reform, passim.*

161. Gardiner, "Role of the Lord Chancellor" 337.

162. His assumptions about "lawyers' law"—at least in his early statements as Lord Chancellor—and the benefits of codification suggest a relatively formalistic approach to the legal process.

163. "Whilst it is usually thought in the interest of the litigant to have an appeal, it is very doubtful whether, having regard to the desire for certainty, the desire to arrive at a decision within a given time, more than one appeal is really in the litigant's interest"; 299 *Parl. Deb.*, H.L. (5th ser.), col. 41 (4 Feb. 1969). It has been argued that he became more ambiguous about his position after his appointment as Chancellor. See Blom-Cooper and Drewry, *Final Appeal* 14–15. He certainly opposed abolishing the functions of the House as a legislative body. See the debate on the White Paper on House of Lords Reform, especially 297 *Parl. Deb.*, H.L. (5th ser.), col. 641 (19 Nov. 1968).

164. "It would not be extraordinary to expect that men trained from youth in the habit of appeal to precedent should be reluctant to accept innovations"; Gerald Gardiner, "The Judicial Attitude to Penal Reform" 196, 197. Legislatively, however, after the Practice Statement of 1966 he noted that the "noble and learned Lords of Appeal have decided not to follow their previous rule of practice by which they consider themselves bound by previous decisions, and one of the consequences of that has been to enable them recently to decide the case of *Conway v. Rimmer*"; 302 *Parl. Deb.*, H.L. (5th ser.), col. 1044 (18 June 1969).

lawyers' law and the court structure,[165] Gardiner was in many ways a conventional lawyer. Not only was he a believer in preserving the House of Lords at least as a legislative body,[166] but he viewed with alarm the growing power of the executive,[167] a concern not generally felt by fellow members of the Labour party. Similarly, although he sometimes qualified his remarks, many of his views were conventional in the sense that he was often complacent toward established institutions. For instance, although Gardiner argued in favor of abolition of the second appeal in order to spare the litigant expense, he simultaneously argued in favor of a second appeal to a Commonwealth Court as a contribution to keeping the remnants of the Empire intact.[168] He also applauded the British police as "the best in the world";[169] he did "not think there was any doubt that our system of legal aid is the best in the world";[170] and he argued in Parliament that "the English legal system is probably the best legal system in the world."[171]

Substantive law, then, was the focus of Gardiner's interest in reform. He was uncomfortable with suggestions for change that affected the traditional approach of the profession. He was most unwilling to admit any serious analogy between the National Health Service and the social service aspects of law.[172] He supported the work of lay justices of the peace and opposed their replacement by stipendiary magistrates.[173] What agitated him most, however, was any suggestion that the divided legal profession be altered. Both in public lectures and in legislative debates he reaffirmed his total belief in the distinction between barristers and solici-

165. Gardiner, for instance, was a strong supporter of the Beeching Commission; *Report of the Royal Commission on Assizes and Quarter Sessions*, Cmnd. 4153 (1969). Of the Courts Act of 1971, implementing many of the recommendations of the report, he said, "[I]t is a radical and spectacular reform; it is the biggest reform in the administration of justice which has taken place in this century, and possibly at any time in our legal history"; 312 *Parl. Deb.*, H.L. (5th ser.), col. 1255 (19 Nov. 1970).

166. 297 ibid., col. 641 (19 Nov. 1969).

167. "I have watched this for twenty years, some outside Parliament, some in Government and some in Opposition, and all the time over the last twenty years Parliament has been losing power to the Executive. I do not believe that this is for the good of our country. . . . This continual increase in the powers of the Executive over Parliament is not right"; 334 ibid., col. 931 (17 Aug. 1972).

168. Gardiner and Martin, *Law Reform* NOW, chap. 1.

169. "[T]hey are also, of course, the most powerful and least controlled"; 338 *Parl. Deb.*, H.L. (5th ser.), cols. 1564–80, at 1570 (14 Feb. 1973).

170. 305 ibid., cols. 1276–83, at 1281 (26 Nov. 1969).

171. 302 ibid., col. 311 (20 May 1969). He added, however, "Of course, like all legal systems, it has its better points and its worse points. Its best part, perhaps, lies in the integrity and ability of the Judges and its worst point in the form of its law."

172. See especially Gerald Gardiner, "An Interview with the Lord Chancellor" 2. He was also convinced that while foreigners thought some aspects of English law "mad," they thought that English judges were "the best in the world"; 264 *Parl. Deb.*, H.L. (5th ser.), col. 1141 (1 Apr. 1965).

173. 338 ibid., col. 404 (29 Jan. 1973).

tors,[174] and he fought strongly against proposals to open up any further judicial appointments to solicitors.[175] Nor was Gardiner particularly impressed with innovations developed in other legal systems. He was opposed to both small claims courts[176] and neighborhood legal centers.[177]

It was not surprising that under these circumstances Gardiner should object to both a written constitution[178] and a Bill of Rights.[179] Yet no doubt he was a far more convinced civil libertarian than is customary among either the judiciary or Labour party members. From his earliest years at the bar he was opposed to the death penalty.[180] He maintained that it was important for newspapers to feel free to criticize the quality of justice.[181] He spoke in favor of the right of privacy and the Universal Declaration of Human Rights.[182] He spoke out strongly against the Elev-

174. E.g., Gerald Gardiner, "Two Lawyers or One?" 1.

175. "I feel very strongly that the great reputation which English justice has elsewhere is due at least partly and I think very greatly, to the fact that we have a divided profession instead of, as in America, every lawyer trying to do everything. For the reasons I then explained, I regret that the dividing line between the professions has for the last quarter of a century always moved one way. I do not think there has ever been a case of barristers being allowed to do any of the things of which solicitors have always had a monopoly, but gradually solicitors have been allowed to do things which hitherto have been the province of the Bar"; 338 *Parl. Deb.*, H.L. (5th ser.), col. 404 (29 Jan. 1973).

Of the judiciary, he said at another point, "We are, I think, in grave danger of taking the very high standard of integrity too much for granted, and I believe that the standard is entirely due to our divided profession. . . . It is not, of course, that barristers are intellectually, morally or socially any better than solicitors—of course not. It is the system. From his earliest years in Chambers a barrister has the ethics of the profession drummed into him"; 313 ibid., cols. 702–3 (3 Dec. 1970).

176. 305 ibid., col. 1278 (26 Nov. 1969).

177. Ibid., col. 1279: "We in this country have a proper system of legal aid, and there is no legal aid in the United States. I think that the answer is simply that we should extend legal aid and advice."

178. "Personally I think we are lucky not to have a written Constitution. It seems to me that those who have written constitutions like the United States find great difficulties in altering them"; 297 ibid., col. 645 (19 Nov. 1968).

179. "I would agree that the Universal Declaration of Human Rights as a goal to which we should all be aiming, is a great document, but we cannot simply turn it into an Act of Parliament"; 302 ibid., cols. 1045–46 (18 June 1969). See also ibid., col. 1092, and Gardiner, "Interview with the Lord Chancellor."

180. His views on capital punishment were well known. He was Joint Chairman of the National Campaign for the Abolition of Capital Punishment; see, e.g., all by Gerald Gardiner, "The Purposes of Criminal Punishment" 117; *Capital Punishment as a Deterrent and the Alternative*; and "The Judicial Attitude to Penal Reform" 196, disputing Jowitt's estimate of the high place held by the judges among the great reformers of criminal law.

181. "[T]he administration of justice in this country is insufficiently criticised."; 274 *Parl. Deb.*, H.L. (5th ser.), col. 1439 (25 May 1966). "Anybody is entitled to express his honest opinion about a sentence and about the way in which the judge has conducted a case, though it is desirable that it should not overstep the bounds of courtesy and should not be a virulent personal attack on a judge. But, subject to that, the administration of justice is not, as Lord Atkin once said, a cloistered virtue, and anybody is entitled to express his honest opinion about it. I have tried for about thirty years to persuade newspapers that this is the law. They will not believe it"; ibid., cols. 1438–39.

182. "It has been my view for 12 years and more that we need a general right of

enth Report of the Criminal Law Revision Committee with its tentative suggestions for the abolition of the accused criminal's right of silence and the easier admission of previous convictions.[183] Yet it must be remembered that it was also Gardiner who piloted through the Lords the War Damage Act, which took away the plaintiff's victory in *Burmah Oil Company v. Lord Advocate*. While some of the opposition to this measure may have been intemperate, the Gardiner defense was not profound.[184]

This odd combination of intellectual radicalism and professional conservatism may have been the chief reason for the contempt for Gardiner felt by many of his colleagues in the Labour cabinet. For instance, he was anathema to Dick Crossman, who regarded him as "an extraordinarily inept politician" who "nearly failed to get the Law Commission Bill through Cabinet."[185] Yet even Crossman admitted that Gardiner was highly regarded by Wilson,[186] and the Prime Minister made considerable use of him at the time of the Unilateral Declaration of Independence in Southern Rhodesia[187] as well as in the abortive attempt by Britain to gain entry to the Common Market.[188] Gardiner's successor as Lord Chancellor, Hailsham, was later to dismiss Gardiner's participation in these and other activities "as a sort of interdepartmental housemaid, sweeping up the debris after some kind of mess or scandal had occurred."[189]

Such activities kept Gardiner from sitting regularly as a law lord

---

privacy incorporated into our law. This would be in accordance with the United Nations Covenant on Human Rights, and with the United Nations Covenant on Civil and Political Rights to which the Government of the United Kingdom are a party and which so provides"; 343 ibid., col. 114 (6 June 1973).

183. 338 ibid., cols. 1564–80 (14 Feb. 1973). He was also the author of the Rehabilitation of Offenders Bill of 1974, designed to protect former offenders from being forced to disclose, or having disclosed, earlier convictions; ibid., cols. 708 ff. (11 Feb. 1974).

184. "The trouble with any question of ethics, at least I have always found, is that there is no principle which we should all accept which can be literally applied 100 per cent"; 264 ibid., col. 810 (25 Mar. 1965). He had already stated that, in his opinion, retrospective legislation was against the rule of law; ibid. In justification of the retrospective element in the case, he said, "[I]t has to be observed that although what your Lordships' House decides is what the law is, out of the nine Appeal Judges who heard the matter, six were of the opinion that the case was so clear that, whatever the facts might prove to be at the trial, the action ought to be dismissed *in limine*, because the *Burmah Oil Company*'s case was hopeless. So the point, to put it very mildly, is one of very considerable doubt"; ibid., col. 809. See also Gardiner's somewhat convoluted support of the closed shop under the Trade Union and Labour Relations (Amendment) Bill of 1975; Gerald Gardiner, "Rule of Law Repudiated" 1077–78.

185. Richard Crossman, 1 *The Diaries of a Cabinet Minister* 56. Elsewhere Crossman described him as a "political innocent" (ibid. 131) and "completely ineffective" (ibid. 395). See also at 258–59.

186. Ibid. 131.

187. Harold Wilson, *A Personal Record*. Gardiner visited Salisbury in February 1965; ibid. 143, 146.

188. Ibid. 387.

189. Hailsham, *Door Wherein I Went* 250.

during his term in office, especially because he also took seriously his responsibilities for presiding over the House of Lords in its legislative capacities (and of making partisan speeches, which the Chancellor may do if he moves from the Woolsack). Indeed, in his six years in office he sat only twice in judicial appeals.[190] Many felt that he took the Speakership too seriously,[191] although he did make adequate arrangements for presiding officers in the various appellate tribunals.[192] Yet since he sat in only a few cases after his retirement as Chancellor,[193] there is no way of knowing whether, overtly or covertly, Gerald Gardiner would have been as successful a law reformer judicially as he was legislatively.

Lord Hailsham

Hailsham,[194] who was Lord Chancellor in the Heath administration (1970–74), was a man of a totally different stamp from Gardiner, somewhat akin to Dilhorne but closer to Kilmuir. Hailsham was in fact a party workhorse. The son of a Lord Chancellor, he had a distinguished career at Oxford, ultimately becoming a fellow of All Souls. He entered Parliament in 1938 as M.P. for Oxford, where he was seen by his opponents as a supporter of Chamberlain and appeasement, although he was to abandon Chamberlain in the crucial Norwegian debate in 1940,[195] thereby helping to bring about the Prime Minister's fall. After serving during the war, Hailsham returned and became active in party affairs,

190. He delivered his own speech only once, in *R. v. Button*, [1966] A.C. 591 (1965). See also Gavin Drewry, "Lord Chancellor as Judge" 855.

191. Anthony Sampson, *The New Anatomy of Britain* 359. This is supported by his comments in the 1968 Holdsworth Lecture saying that administrative and political duties made it possible for a Lord Chancellor to sit for only about a fortnight in January and a fortnight in October. See Gerald Gardiner, *The Trials of a Lord Chancellor* 3, 5, 9–10.

192. It was also Gardiner who introduced the system whereby, in the absence of the Lord Chancellor, the Appellate Committee and the Judicial Committee would be presided over by the senior law lord and not by the senior ex-Lord Chancellor or by the ranking peer, on the alleged ground that "when a Lord Chancellor gives up the woolsack he may, and indeed almost certainly will, have had very little experience of sitting judicially unless he happens to have held judicial office"; "The Office of Lord Chancellor" 517. See also 302 *Parl. Deb.*, H.L. (5th ser.), col. 469–70 (22 May 1969).

193. *Car Owners' Mutual Ins. Co. v. Treasurer of the Commonwealth of Australia*, [1970] A.C. 527 (P.C. 1969); *Commissioner of Valuation for Northern Ireland v. Fermanagh Protestant Bd. of Educ.*, [1969] 1 W.L.R. 1708 (H.L., N. Ire.); *Johnson v. F. E. Callow, Ltd.*, [1971] A.C. 335 (1970); *Rugby Joint Water Bd. v. Shaw-Fox*, [1973] A.C. 202 (1972); *Lep Air Servs., Ltd. v. Rollowins Invs., Ltd.*, [1973] A.C. 331 (1972).

194. Quintin McGarel Hogg; b. 1907; father, Lord Chancellor; educ., Eton, Christ Church, Oxford (First, "Greats"); called to bar, 1932; Q.C., 1956; M.P. (Cons.), Oxford, 1938–50, St. Marylebone, 1963–70; First Lord of the Admiralty, 1956–57; Minister of Education, 1957; Lord President of the Council, 1957–59, 1960–64; Lord Privy Seal, 1959–60; Minister for Science and Technology, 1959–64; Lord Chancellor, 1970–74.

195. Hailsham, *Door Wherein I Went*, chaps. 19–20.

more as a representative of the Old Guard than of the modernizers in the Conservative party.[196]

Many, including Quintin Hogg himself, had hoped to see him ultimately as leader of the Conservative party, but, at the death of his father in 1950, he was translated to the Lords, where he served as Leader of the Lords and Chairman of the party. With the Peerage Act of 1963, however, Hailsham renounced his peerage and, as Quintin Hogg once again, made a run to succeed Harold Macmillan as party leader.[197] Failing in that effort, he served in Sir Alec Douglas-Home's cabinet, then spent the remainder of the 1960s as a vigorous member of the Opposition. For this he was rewarded with the Lord Chancellorship in the Heath administration of 1970, once again returning to the Lords with the title of Lord Hailsham. Yet he remained a popular politician and was much in demand at political rallies after Heath's fall in early 1974,[198] a period during which he continued to sit as a law lord.

Despite his intellectual credentials, Hailsham is best known as an ardent and strident politician. His most characteristic attribute was his outspoken insistence on the maintenance of moral standards,[199] and his outbursts both on television and in Parliament about the Profumo scandal had a lasting effect on his career.[200] His blustery style was proverbial,[201] and he personally espoused a commitment to a moral order in a way that had become unfashionable by the mid-twentieth century.[202] This manner

196. See, for instance, Lord Hailsham (Quintin McGarel Hogg), *The Case for Conservatism.*

197. Hailsham, *Door Wherein I Went,* chap. 32.

198. E.g., "Tory Women Cheer Lord Hailsham on Freedom," *The Times,* 21 May 1975.

199. Remarks attributed to Hailsham include both "Politics and morality cannot be divorced" and "The wisest Conservatives are Christians." See "Lord Hailsham's Convictions" 38. For a more coherent exposition of his moral attitudes, see Hailsham, *Door Wherein I Went,* chaps. 2–14.

200. Described at length (as a Pharisee) in Bernard Levin, *Run It Down the Flagpole* 63–66. For a defense of his behavior, see *Door Wherein I Went,* especially at 197: "I am afraid that as the result of a television programme in which I appeared with Bob MacKenzie, I have acquired the reputation for being a bit of a prude about sexual morality." In *The Times* Lord Balfour noted, "Surely such a proud and powerful Christian could have shown some element of Christian charity in his denunciation of a man with a shattered life"; *The Times,* 17 June 1963, at 3.

201. Lord Byers, the Liberal whip in the Lords, said of Hailsham's attack on Lord George-Brown during the debates on the Industrial Relations Bill, "It has given the noble and learned Lord the Lord Chancellor an opportunity to enjoy himself. I must say that I thoroughly appreciated his *tour de force.* I would calculate it at about Force Eight; it is nice to see him in full sail"; 312 *Parl. Deb.,* H.L. (5th ser.), col. 447 (4 Nov. 1970).

202. Perhaps his most articulate statement of this approach came in Lord Hailsham (Quintin McGarel Hogg), *The Need for Faith in a Scientific Age:*

When I survey the emotional, the intellectual, the moral, the political, even the physical litter and chaos of the world today, when truth has almost ceased to be regarded as objective, when kindness is made to

carried over to the law so that, unlike "liberals" like Devlin, or more "detached" conservatives like Radcliffe, Hailsham was able to proclaim that "to divorce law from morality is the dictator's charter."[203] Similarly Hailsham had no doubt that "capitalism" was "an intrinsic part of the movement to freedom."[204]

Other approaches also identified Hailsham as a conservative. He was somewhat skeptical about the extension of legal aid to tribunals.[205] Although he established the Pearson Commission, he had serious doubts about whether a comprehensive insurance or compensation scheme along New Zealand lines was a good solution.[206] He was doubtful about the value of looking at committee and commission reports to construe amending clauses.[207] It was not surprising that he favored a Bill of Rights[208] although, at another time, he appeared to suggest that such a bill or constitutional statute would merely imply certain assumptions.[209]

---

depend on political class, or racial affiliations, when only the obvious stands in need of publicity; when I look at popular pin-ups, play-boys, millionaires, and actresses with the bodies of gods and goddesses and the morals of ferrets lurching from one demoralising emotional crisis to another and never guessing the reasons; when I view the leaders of great states, the masters of immense concentrations of power and wealth, gesticulating like monkeys and hurling insults unfit for fishwives; when I reflect on the vapidity of so much that is popular in entertainment, the pretenses of so much that passes for profundity, the pointlessness and frustration in the popular mood on one side, and the brutality and cynicism on the other; after I consider all this, I can only reflect, without complacency but with a profound sense of thankfulness and peace, not that I am not as other men are, but that being as other men are I have become a citizen of no mean city, where decency and orderliness prevail, where objective truth is honoured, beauty admired, and kindness and human feeling universalised to cover the whole compass of suffering humanity, with a mission to carry on into the modern world the traditions nurtured and fostered in Greece, Rome and Jerusalem, which I hold sacred, believing that these alone at least in my own experience, can sanctify and therefore civilise the restless and destructive spirit of chaos and mutual hatred which allowed to develop uncontrolled in modern conditions, could well annihilate the human species upon the planet, or alternatively undo the process of evolution itself and plunge mankind back into the anerial status from which it arose.

203. Lord Hailsham (Quintin McGarel Hogg), *The Problems of Being a Lord Chancellor* 15.

204. 343 *Parl. Deb.*, H.L. (5th ser.), cols. 782–88 (13 June 1973).

205. 332 Ibid., cols. 525–31 (23 June 1972).

206. 337 ibid., col. 976 (19 Dec. 1972).

207. 336 ibid., col. 876 (16 Nov. 1972).

208. Lord Hailsham (Quintin McGarel Hogg), *Some Proposals for Constitutional Reform*. Reported in *The Times*, 16 Apr. 1969, at 6. He returned to the theme in a series of articles in *The Times* in 1975. See the issues of 12, 16, 19, and 20 May 1975. For his most vigorous restatement of this see his 1976 Dimbleby lecture, "Elective Dictatorship" 693.

209. Of a Bill of Rights, he said, "My difficulties were two in general character. In the first place, I thought—and up to a point still think—that it is an anachronism in the 20th century to talk in terms of legislation of this sort. The second objection is a more technical one: that under the British Constitution as it has developed there is a logical contradiction involved in legislation of this kind"; 313 *Parl. Deb.*, H.L. (5th ser.), col. 256 (26 Nov. 1970).

But he was prepared to consider a constitutional statute:

I am not prepared to say that I should be against a Constitutional Statute which gave us some of the features of a controlled constitution—on the contrary, I have advocated it and I made two positive suggestions towards it. I thought it would be possible to allow Parliament to enact by an Act of

On individual civil rights Hailsham was not always an advocate of traditional values. He was strongly critical of the right to silence, and he
appeared to favor the admissibility of previous convictions in certain
circumstances.[210] In short, Hailsham was a vigorous supporter of law
and order. Contempt for authority, such as throwing eggs at cabinet
ministers, was irrebuttable evidence of a sick society.[211] He was appalled
by student protesters, whom he likened to "the baboons of the I.R.A.,"[212]
and he was convinced that it was the permissive society,[213] and not
legitimate social grievances,[214] that was causing the rapid rise in crime.
Such views were put forward forcefully and frequently courageously. The
Hailsham approach to judicial decision making was not substantially
different: "robust common sense" was applied robustly.

In terms of approach, Hailsham was less concerned with the niceties
of substantive law reform than Gardiner had been,[215] yet he was far
more interested in sitting as a judge than his predecessor had been. As
soon as he became Lord Chancellor, Hailsham appointed a series of
Deputy Speakers so that he would not need to preside regularly in the
legislative debates of the Lords.[216] Moreover, he brought to the judicial
work many of the positions he had articulated politically, for he had
complete confidence in the English system of justice[217] and the tradi-

---

Parliament that a ritual phrase could be used before certain fundamental rights were infringed: an
interpretation clause by which courts would assume that an Act of Parliament did not have that intention unless the ritual phrase appeared in its text. And thirdly, a self-denying ordinance by one or both of
the Houses of Parliament whereby if the ritual phrase was used it might be treated as a hybrid Bill."
[Ibid., col. 268]

See also 302 ibid., col. 1090 (18 June 1969).

210. 338 ibid., col. 1596 (14 Feb. 1973). Nor were his views on race relations particularly progressive. "I hold the view that in general race relations are better not made the
subject of Acts of Parliament. . . . In practice, the 1965 Act, has proved wholly ineffective
as I always thought it would. It was nevertheless less objectionable than the 1968 Act";
Hailsham, *Door Wherein I Went* 230.

211. *The Times*, 12 Mar. 1968, at 2.

212. Ibid., 24 Apr. 1972, at 2.

213. "The climate of permissiveness generally has, I believe, a far bigger influence on
society in general and therefore on crime and the criminal than the criminal courts and the
police put together"; ibid., 13 May 1972, at 3.

214. "Legitimate social grievance does not drive people to rob trains or go 'queer
bashing.' Law is not a thing you can pick and choose about. Law is something you have a
duty to obey in a free society"; ibid., 18 Feb. 1970, at 31.

215. Gerald Gardiner, "Law Reform—Not Now?" 1065. See also Hailsham, *Problems of Being Lord Chancellor* 4.

216. Hailsham, *Door Wherein I Went* 249–50. See also *The Listener* 13 July 1972.
Hailsham's energy was proverbial. "When at the War Office, I shared a desk with a
portly amiable captain who coped tirelessly and uncomplainingly with the mountainous
paper work—Quintin Hogg—now Lord Chancellor of Great Britain"; David Niven, *The
Moon's a Balloon* 222.

217. "There are a number of things in Britain that have been devalued in my time. Our
power as a great power has been devalued. Parliament has, perhaps been devalued. The

tional concepts of judicial objectivity[218] and law.[219] Yet such a position did not prevent Hailsham from being an admirer of his new wave of creative judges,[220] and he did not share Dilhorne's reluctance to be seen making law in his judicial capacity.

Thus Hailsham's robust approach helped to continue the restoration of sanity to section 14(1) of the Factories Act in *Johnson v. F. E. Callow, Limited*.[221] While Hailsham had harbored some doubts about whether the section had actually intended to give a civil remedy,[222] he had no difficulty in defining "machine" broadly[223] and he was concerned to base relief broadly.[224] Thus while he talked of the "gap" in the legislation,[225] he went a significant way toward closing it. Nor was he moved by eloquent pleas about civil liberties when a taxpayer was denied a right to be heard before a tax commissioner made an initial decision on tax liability.[226]

---

pound has been devalued, and lots of other things: but one thing has not been devalued, I think and that's the quality of British justice. Our judges are still upright and incorruptible, so is our legal profession, both branches of it, and abroad, in some very great countries, this is not so"; Lord Hailsham (Quintin McGarel Hogg), "Lord Hailsham on the Law" 76.

218. "One's life, in the main, is giving people advice as to whether they're likely to lose. Judges are advocates of experience who have succeeded, and the essence of being a good counsel is that you give competent advice. The way in which you give competent advice is being able to form an unprejudiced view of the facts of a case as you were given it, and apply legal principles which you know; and when you become a judge you do it in public, after having spent a life-time of experience in chambers"; ibid. 77.

219. "The whole basis of law is a set of objective rules to carry moral conviction to the Government"; "Lord Hailsham's Convictions," *The Listener*, 11 July 1974, at 38.

220. "Another topic which is of immense importance at the present time is the revival of the Courts themselves under the influence of a series of distinguished contemporary judges as a dynamic feature in the development of English Law. When I was called to the Bar in 1932 the development of judge-made law seemed almost to have come to a standstill. But, during the forty years which have elapsed since that time Parliament and the judges have co-operated in a continuous stream of decisions and enactments giving a whole set of new remedies both against the Crown, and subordinate authority. I do not think either could have acted effectively without co-operation from the other. If the judges had over-stepped the mark by becoming political, Parliament would, I think, have curbed their power. But in some fields legislation has opened the door to new fields of judicial activity"; Hailsham, *Problems of Being Lord Chancellor* 6.

221. [1971] A.C. 335 (1970). Hailsham was somewhat irritated that the case had not come up as a common law unsafe system of work case; see at 348.

222. Ibid. 342.

223. E.g., ibid. 349.

224. E.g., ibid. 341.

225. "It is however too late for the courts to close the gap. The gap can only be closed by legislation or to some extent by the use of the regulatory powers of the Minister. It has however to be said that I for one would be slow to enlarge the gap or to extend the ambit of the criticised decisions beyond the limits required by the facts of the cases concerned and the reasoning of the judgments in them"; ibid. 343.

226. *Pearlberg v. Varty*, [1972] 1 W.L.R. 534, 537 (H.L.): "Despite the majestic conception of natural justice on which it was argued, I do not believe that this case involves any important legal principle at all. On the contrary, it is only another example of the general proposition that decisions of the courts on particular statutes should be based in the

In many areas a similar view was to be seen. Hailsham did not hesitate to interfere with an umpire's award in an arbitration when it appeared to weaken the concept of consideration by a dubious extension of estoppel, a doctrine that he thought was in need of major reexamination.[227] He was not about to accept any sophisticated notions of the situs of an obligation;[228] and, while relying on his common sense (and the actual words of the statute), he held that in an adoption it was permissible for the trial judge to put the best interests of the child ahead of the legal rights of the natural parents.[229]

Yet, although not publicly articulating it, in criminal cases Hailsham took the position that the law should not be expanded.[230] This could reflect either the judicial policy that it is for Parliament rather than the courts to develop new crimes or, alternatively a commitment to the civil liberty that would not allow a person to be prosecuted for a crime about which he could not know. The Hailsham position, however, seems more clearly related to his commitment to "law and order." In *R. v. Hyam*,[231] he refused to overrule *Director of Public Prosecutions* v. *Smith*,[232] which had opened up an objective test of intent in murder.[233] At the same time,

---

first instance on a careful, even meticulous, construction of what the statute actually means in the context in which it was passed."

227. *Woodhouse A.C. Israel Cocoa, Ltd. v. Nigerian Produce Mkt. Co.*, [1972] A.C. 741, 758: "I desire to add that the time may soon come when the whole sequence of cases based on promissory estoppel since the war, beginning with *Central London Property Trust Ltd. v. High Trees House Ltd.* . . . may need to be reviewed and reduced to a coherent body of doctrine by the courts. I do not mean to say that they are to be regarded with suspicion. But as is common with an expanding doctrine they do raise problems of coherent exposition which have never been systematically explored."

228. *Westminster Bank Executor & Trustee Co. (Channel Islands) v. National Bank of Greece S.A.*, [1971] A.C. 945, 953 (1970).

229. *In re W (An Infant)*, [1971] A.C. 682, 692.

230. See, for instance, his series of speeches in criminal cases reported in 1975. In *R. v. Hyam*, [1975] A.C. 55 (1974), while conducting an extensive discussion, he regarded the subject as one of "fairly narrow compass"; ibid. 66. In *R. v. Smith*, [1975] A.C. 476 (1973), his treatise-like speech attempted to clear up the confusion about *actus reus* "[b]efore the understanding of the Latin tongue has wholly died out of these islands"; ibid. 492.

Hailsham managed, however, to give the impression that he was reluctant to restate the principles of law he actually did restate. In *R. v. Boardman*, [1975] A.C. 421 (1974), he complained, "[T]he variety of human circumstances is infinite, and the fertility of ingenuity in counsel considerable, and in the present case we were constrained once more to traverse the pitted battlefield of 'similar fact' evidence. . . . Nevertheless, since it springs eternal in the human breast, I, for one, cannot resist expressing once more the hope that this case at least may give a quietus to the series of cases on this topic reaching the highest tribunal"; ibid. 445. Again in *R. v. Smith*, he complained, "This would be enough to decide the results of this appeal, but both counsel invited us to take a wider view of our obligations, and since the question was discussed by the Court of Appeal in general terms and since I believe that the result of our decision is to overrule a number of decided cases . . . I feel bound to accede to this invitation"; [1975] A.C. 476, 490 (1973).

231. [1975] A.C. 55 (1974).

232. [1961] A.C. 290 (1960).

233. "At the end of the day there are, I think, two reasons against formally overruling

however, he restricted the intention test in a way that might be thought to satisfy many of the critics of *Smith*.[234] He did, however, insist that a "guilty mind" be proved before conviction, and he was not enthusiastic about statutory offenses that dispensed with mens rea.[235] At the same time he was not opposed to expanding the criminal law as such, holding, for instance, that a single person might be convicted of an affray.[236] Similarly, when a group of Sierra Leonean students occupied their High Commission, Hailsham had no doubt that a conspiracy to commit the tort of trespass was indictable.[237] He added, "I do not regard the categories of conspiracy to effect a public mischief as closed, or even as capable of being closed,"[238] and concluded, "the categories here are not closed, and I have no doubt that they include a combination to trespass upon or occupy a foreign embassy or a Commonwealth High Commission, the inviolability of which her Majesty's Government are under an

---

Smith [1961] A.C. 290 (1960) in virtue of our practice direction as suggested by the authors of Smith and Hogan. The first is that in view of the diversity of interpretation it is difficult to know exactly what one is overruling. Indeed, if the extreme minimalising interpretations be adopted, there is little or nothing to overrule or indeed little enough to require the intervention of Parliament in 1967. The second is that there are at least two passages in *Smith* of permanent value which on any view ought not to be overruled"; [1975] A.C. 55, 72 (1974).

Illogically, in rape, he appeared to demand that the accused had affirmative knowledge that the woman was not consenting to the act; *R. v. Morgan*, [1976] A.C. 182, 2041 (1975).

234. "I do not think that foresight as such of a high degree of probability is at all the same thing as intention and, in my view, it is not foresight but intention which constitutes the mental element in murder. . . . But what are we to say of the state of mind of a defendant who knows that a proposed course of conduct exposes a third party to a serious risk of death . . . ? In that case, if my analysis be correct, there is not merely actual foresight of the probable consequences, but actual intention to expose his victim to the risk of those consequences whether they in fact occur or not"; [1975] A.C. 55, 77 (1976).

235. See especially *Smedleys, Ltd. v. Breed*, [1974] A.C. 839 (1972).

There are other examples of Hailsham's restating traditional common law concepts, e.g., refusing to hold that dishonest intention necessarily amounted to an attempt where goods, originally stolen, had returned to the custody of the police and were therefore no longer stolen, but were part of a police trap, in *R. v. Smith*, [1975] A.C. 476 (1973). See also *R. v. Kilbourne*, [1973] A.C. 729, on corroboration. See also his commonsense views of the interpretation of the Road Safety Act of 1967, with respect to breathalizer tests; *R. v. Sakhuja*, [1973] A.C. 152 (1972).

236. *R. v. Taylor*, [1973] A.C. 964 (1972). Gardiner had extended the same crime in *R. v. Button*, [1966] A.C. 591 (1965), by holding it need not be committed in a public place.

237. *R. v. Kamara*, [1974] A.C. 104, 122–23 (1973): "I have no hesitation myself in adding the present type of case to this list. . . . since this was a conspiracy to trespass by invading a foreign embassy or Commonwealth High Commission and, with the Court of Appeal, I consider that a public interest is directly involved in such an act." See also ibid. 128: "I am for myself not prepared to say with complete confidence that Lawton L.J. was wholly wrong in claiming that all combinations to commit trespass are therefore indictable."

238. Ibid. 123. He continued, "[B]ut extension should be very closely and jealously watched by the courts, owing to the difficulty of riding the horse of public policy and the danger of applying the subjective criteria of individual judges to the concept."

obligation to protect. I feel certain, too, that there are many other public buildings owned by the authorities in this country to which the same considerations would apply."[239]

If Hailsham had little objection to judicial development of the common law, however, he was not minded to tolerate rapid changes in the law by those not authorized to make them. Perhaps his most vigorous speech in a judicial proceeding was in *Broome* v. *Cassell and Company*,[240] a libel case in which the Court of Appeal, led by Denning, had decided to ignore much of the authority on exemplary damages that the House had developed in *Rookes* v. *Barnard*. Hailsham was furious. First of all, the behavior of the Court of Appeal had allegedly been an insult to the litigants.[241] Yet more outrageous was the behavior of the Court of Appeal in suggesting that it was free to ignore decisions of the Lords.[242] Hailsham then proceeded to show what he meant by constitutional propriety, by refusing to interfere with the damages awarded by the jury, although he thought them much too large.[243] It was characteristic of the

239. Ibid. 126.
240. [1972] A.C. 1027.
241. "Private litigants have been put to immense expense, of which most must be borne by the loser, discussing broad issues of law unnecessary for the disposal of their dispute"; ibid. 1053.
242. "I am driven to the conclusion that when the Court of Appeal, described the decision in *Rookes* v. *Barnard* as decided '*per incuriam*' or 'unworkable' they really only meant that they did not agree with it. But, in my view, even if this were not so, it is not open to the Court of Appeal to give gratuitous advice to judges of first instance to ignore decisions of the House of Lords in this way and, if it were open to the Court of Appeal to do so, it would be highly undesirable. The course taken would have put judges of first instance in an embarrassing position, as driving them to take sides in an unedifying dispute between the Court of Appeal or three members of it . . . and the House of Lords. But, much worse than this, litigants would not have known where they stood. None could have reached finality short of the House of Lords, and, in the meantime, the task of their professional advisers of advising them either as to their rights, or as to the probable cost of obtaining or defending them, would have been, quite literally, impossible. Whatever the merits, chaos would have reigned until the dispute was settled, and, in legal matters, some degree of certainty is at least as valuable a part of justice as perfection.

"The fact is, and I hope it will never be necessary to say so again, that, in the hierarchical system of courts which exists in this country, it is necessary for each lower tier including the Court of Appeal, to accept loyally the decisions of the higher tiers"; ibid. 1054.
243. "A number of factors lead me, however, to the belief that the verdict should not be disturbed. The first, and paramount, consideration in my mind is that the jury is, where either party desires it, the only legal and constitutional tribunal for deciding libel cases, including the award of damages. . . . The point is that the law makes the jury and not the judiciary the constitutional tribunal, and if Parliament had wanted the roles to be reversed in any way, Parliament would have said so at the time of the Administration of Justice (Miscellaneous Provisions) Act 1933, since section 6 of that Act expressly excepts defamation actions . . . from the change it then authorised. . . .

"It may very well be that on the whole, judges, and the legal profession in general, would be less generous than juries in the award of damages for defamation. But I know of no principle of reason which would entitle judges, whether of appeal or at first instance, to

man. He certainly had his vigorous critics; yet Hailsham, together with Kilmuir and Gardiner, had in different ways breathed a new life into the appellate process. More important, Hailsham had reasserted the judicial responsibilities of the Lord Chancellor.

---

consider that their own sense of the proprieties is more reasonable than that of a jury, or which would entitle them to arrogate to themselves a constitutional status in this matter which Parliament has deliberately withheld from them, for ought we know, on the very ground that juries can be expected to be more generous on such matters than judges"; ibid. 1065–66.

THIRTEEN

Four Interpretations

Choosing the four Lords of Appeal who have had the greatest influence—or even those who are representative of the competing approaches—during the last twenty years inevitably involves some invidious distinctions. During the period, the quality of the judiciary in the House changed, not only in intellectual terms but, more interestingly, in terms of judicial style, particularly with respect to appellate strategy. The choice of the four for discussion here was made within that context.

In terms of the length of service, if on no other basis, Radcliffe (1949–64) and Reid (1948–74) would have to be included. A discussion of both could be justified on other grounds: Radcliffe as one of the strongest analytical minds ever appointed to the Lords and Reid as yet another Scot who became the gentle custodian of the finest traditions of the common law. Denning and Devlin deserve inclusion for different reasons. Neither served particularly long as a Lord of Appeal (Denning, 1957–62; Devlin, 1961–64), yet both had important effects on the legal system in the period between 1956 and 1976. For much of that time Denning, sitting as Master of the Rolls—the presiding judge of the Court of Appeal—led a one-man Realist crusade. Devlin's work and intellectual influence, on the other hand, was mainly outside the courts. As chief apologist for the nineteenth-century liberal intellectual tradition, he sought to keep the role of the courts, including the appeal courts, within narrow bounds.

Lord Radcliffe

Indicative of his peculiar stamp on the House of Lords as a judicial body is the fact that, of all the post–World War II English judges, Radcliffe[1] has had more impact in the United States than any other.[2] This is not surprising, for Radcliffe did not hesitate to reject the approach of the advocates of substantive formalism, a doctrine not only incomprehensible, but largely inconceivable, to American judges. Radcliffe believed in the common law and the principles underlying it as a force in itself. Insofar as this position was akin to the American acceptance of a form of fundamental law, it ran the inherent danger of being antidemocratic. Yet, whatever the political perspectives of the observer, the willingness to articulate such basic assumptions on the part of an English judge was stimulating, even though the directions in which Radcliffe would have liked to see the law move and his actual role in the appellate process were disappointing to some.

In order to comprehend Radcliffe's attitudes and contributions, it is essential to consider the role he played in English life during the period in question. While he deplored the use of the word "Establishment,"[3] no man was more obviously a member of it. He read "Greats" at Oxford and was a fellow of All Souls before his meteoric rise at the Chancery Bar. Although he had not been a politician in the strict sense before becoming a law lord, Radcliffe had been Director-General of the Ministry of Information during a significant part of World War II and in the year he became a judge he negotiated the boundary between the newly independent India and Pakistan.[4] Appointed to the bench directly as a Lord of Appeal, he was at once in great demand for all kinds of public service. In fiscal affairs he was both Chairman of the Royal Commission on the Taxation of Profits and Income[5] and Chairman of the Committee of Enquiry into the Monetary System.[6] His work on the boundary disputes

1. Cyril John Radcliffe; b. 1899; educ., Haileybury and New College, Oxford (First, Honours, "Greats"); called to the bar, 1924; Q.C., 1935; Director-General of Ministry of Information, 1941–45; Lord of Appeal, 1949–64; d. 1977.

2. See, for example, Chief Judge Wyzanski's view that the *Law and Its Compass* is "a work not one whit inferior in imagination and idealism to Cardozo's *The Nature of the Judicial Process*"; Charles E. Wyzanski, Jr., *The New Meaning of Justice* 147.

3. "Let a fairy grant me three wishes, I would gladly use them all in one prayer only, that never again should anyone using pen or typewriter be permitted to employ the inane cliché 'Establishment'"; Cyril John Radcliffe, *Not in Feather Beds* 175. See also at 178: "[T]he trouble in this country may be not that we have an Establishment but that we have too many people who talk about the Establishment without knowing what they mean." Cf. Sir Alan Herbert's quip about "government by Radcliffery"; noted in Cartwright, *Royal Commissions and Departmental Committees* 69.

4. "Radcliffe was chosen on the grounds that he would be an impartial judge—in other words he had never set foot on Indian soil and had had no previous dealings with the country. His briefing at the Colonial Office is said to have lasted no more than thirty minutes, and he left England with no more than this information and a couple of maps"; John Higgins, "Partition in India," in *The Age of Austerity 1945–1951*, ed. Michael Sissons and Philip French at 200.

5. 1951–55; *Report*, Cmd. 9474 (1955).

6. 1957–59; *Report*, Cmnd. 827 (1959).

in the Punjab and Bengal were the basis of his appointment as Constitutional Commissioner for Cyprus in 1956, another crisis that ended in *de facto* partition. Radcliffe was perhaps best known, however, for his various inquiries into security problems and his speech in the Lords, when the Wilson government rejected his Report on D-Notices, was described by Richard Crossman in his *Diaries* as "the most effective quiet rebuke of a P.M. by a public servant of modern time."[7] He also served as Chairman of the British Museum, as well as on the British Broadcasting Corporation Advisory Committee, the Board of Governors or Trustees of various colleges of London University, and as Chancellor of Warwick University, in addition to his legislative work in the House of Lords.[8] In short, as had become the norm for the most talented of the appeal judges, Radcliffe's most creative urges were channeled outside the appellate process.[9]

It is nevertheless tempting to speculate that his constant jostling with the outside world had an important impact on Radcliffe's judicial style. When one realizes that Radcliffe was appointed by Jowitt and served under Simonds, his view of the judicial process shows a refreshing bluntness. "[T]here was never a more sterile controversy than that upon the question whether a judge makes law. Of course he does. How can he help it? . . . Judicial law is always a reinterpretation of principles in the light of new combinations of facts. . . . [J]udges do not reverse principles, once well established, but they do modify them, extend them, restrict them and even deny their application to the combination in hand."[10]

---

7. Richard Crossman, 2 *The Diaries of a Cabinet Minister* 414.
    For Radcliffe's other work in the area of security and privacy, see especially his Chairmanship of the Committee on Security Procedures in the Public Service, (*Report*, Cmnd. 1681 [1961]); and Vassal Tribunal of Enquiry, (*Report*, Cmnd. 2009 [1962]). For a similar inquiry, chaired by Radcliffe, see *Report of the Committee of Privy Councillors on Ministerial Memoirs*, Cmnd. 6386 (1976). For Radcliffe's view on this committee, see *The Times*, 4 Nov. 1976.
    8. Radcliffe was not particularly active in the legislative work of the House. He spoke only 4 times during one twelve-and-a-half-year period in the Lords; Louis Blom-Cooper and Gavin Drewry, *Final Appeal* 205. His early contributions to debates in the House were on broadcasting. See, e.g., 172 *Parl. Deb.*, H.L. (5th ser.), cols. 1261 ff. (25 July 1951); 176 ibid., cols. 1401 ff. (26 May 1952). But in addition to his speech on security referred in fn. 7, see also his various contributions to the British Museum debate, *Government by Contempt: Whitehall's Way with Parliament and People* (London, 1968).
    9. As Radcliffe noted in retirement, "I cannot help feeling a little saddened, when I survey my 'collected works,' by the realization that so much of my total literary output is submerged in the reports of Committees of which I have been chairman and in legal judgments"; Radcliffe, *Not in Feather Beds* at x.
    10. Quoted in 110 *Solicitor's Journal* 733 (1966). See also:

Would anyone now deny that judicial decisions are a creative, not merely an expository, contribution to the law? There are no means by which they can be otherwise, so rare is the occasion upon which a decision does not involve choice between two admissible alternatives. Put it at its least contentious, a judge might commend himself to the most rigid principles of adherence to precedent, might close his

Radcliffe questioned the at that time apparently unshakable belief in the irresistible force of legal logic that underlay the position of substantive formalism:

> A professor of logic would find in even famous judgments some sad howlers —the undistributed middle, transference of meaning in the use of the same word, questions begged until they are in rags. And not only the professor of logic. Ask an intelligent member of the public to make a critical study of some well-known judgment and to give his comments. He would find much to admire—a good, if rather dessicated, style of prose, clarity of exposition, economy of expression, and a reassuring air of detachment: but what I do not believe is that he would be impressed or convinced by is the reasoning itself. . . . In particular, the distinctions upon which the result seems to turn often present themselves as somewhat unreal, not so much points of substance as fine points of verbal distinction.[11]

In short, Radcliffe had moved from a formalist position to accept that factors other than pure reason went into a man's thinking,[12] although he remained skeptical of the value of attempts by social scientists to study the nonanalytical aspects of the judicial process.[13]

---

day's work every evening in the conviction that he had said nothing and decided nothing that was not in accordance with what his predecessors had said or decided before him: yet, even so, their words, when he repeats them, mean something materially different in his mouth, just because twentieth-century man has not the power to speak with the tone or accent of the man of the seventeenth or the eighteenth or the nineteenth century. The context is different; the range of reference is different; and, whatever his intention, the hallowed words of authority themselves are a fresh coinage newly minted in his speech. In that limited sense time uses us all as the instrument of innovation. [*Not in Feather Beds* 271]

11. *Not in Feather Beds* 73.

12. "There was a time . . . when I believed that a man possessed a separate intellectual or logical power, his reasoning faculty, independent of his other powers or dispositions, and that it was his highest duty as a man to accord preeminence to that power—*un roseau pensant*, etc. That belief has not persisted with me. It seems to me that thinking is a function of the whole of one's personality, with all the interplay of emotions and experiences that in time claim and receive recognition from one's reason: so that reason either becomes a term so comprehensive that it embraces everything that conditions one's thought or else remains an isolated analytic and deductive faculty which does not in practice determine by any means all one's opinions or views"; ibid., at xvi.

13. "Once we begin to talk about society's changes and the conditions governing the law's response to them, we find we have to make some assessment of the Judge as maker of law in his own right, lawgiver by virtue of his office. His duties and his failures in this capacity contribute very much a contemporary theme, although I doubt whether its elaboration is not likely to prove more a curse than a blessing. It is so easy to start, and it seems so hard to know where to stop. . . . It is much more important to analyse the relative truth of an idea so far reaching; because unless the analysis is strict and its limitations observed, there is real danger in its elaboration. We cannot run the risk of finding the archetypal image of the judge confused in men's minds with the very different image of the legislator. We cannot run the risk that an institution which societies such as ours have never known how to do without should be destroyed merely through an untimely eagerness to be all things to men. . . . Personally, I think, that judges will serve the public interest better if they keep quiet about their legislative function. . . . The judge who shows his hand, who advertises what he is about, may indeed show that his is a strong spirit, unfettered by the past; but I doubt very much whether he is not doing more harm to general confidence in the law as a constant, safe in the hands of the judges, than he is doing good to the law's credit as a

Nevertheless, having once himself departed from the position of substantive formalism, Radcliffe was intellectually bound to explain what, then, were the goals and motive forces of the law toward which judges should strive. His explanations were not always satisfactory. "Judicial decisions, no matter who gives them, must always be related to certain basic beliefs about the nature and purpose of a human being which are held by another human being. In that sense he may not be objective, but he can be honest and fair." Despite his suggestion that such questioning might be harmful, Radcliffe appeared to regard "real" law as something separate from both legislation and judge-made law.[14] In this sense his approach was akin to Coke's, at least in those passages that postulated the notions of fundamental law, so attractive to the American Federalists in the early years of the Republic. Radcliffe saw law as needing to contain some element enabling it to "justify itself . . . and justify itself afresh to each new generation, as the bond of a society of free men."[15] To give substance to a position that may well have seemed obvious to him, Radcliffe proposed turning to some sort of natural law,[16] which would be a contributor to national character.[17] Based on custom or the "established way,"[18] he claimed it could nourish each individual spirit.[19] "We must never, then, lose touch with the idea of Natural Law or give up the belief that all positive law bears some relation to it."[20]

Radcliffe saw the most obvious example of natural law, at least

---

set of rules nicely attended as the sentiment of the day. I do take sides on this. I do not think that the law's comparative inflexibility is a cause of any deep dissatisfaction in the public. I do think that the intellectual mind has a tendency to criticise a reality that it resents"; ibid. 270–71, 273.

14. "There is really not much to be said for Law unless it is thought of as representing absolute standards of right and wrong, even at a far remove. But then that means that its fundamental rules, whatever they are, stand above and independent of social needs and aspirations of the day. The function of the lawyer, you might say, is to reconcile the demands of human nature to the acceptance of those rules. There are periods of historical development when men prize very highly such a service of reconciliation. I do not think that this is one of those periods"; ibid. 81–82.

15. Cyril John Radcliffe, *Law and the Democratic State* 3. He asked, "[H]ave we not come to a time when we must find another name for statute law than Law itself?"; ibid. 4.

16. "I fear this tendency to isolate the law and to insist that it should treat itself as a self-sufficient value, something inherently different from those deeper values that express themselves in morals or religion"; Cyril John Radcliffe, *Law and Its Compass* 56.

17. Cyril John Radcliffe, "Some Reflections on Law and Lawyers" 361. He cited the English theory of contract as "a symbol of the great emancipation of the human spirit"; ibid. 365.

18. Ibid. 366. "In truth a healthy society is sustained as much by loyalty to its institutions as by calculations of material gains or visions of immortal logic"; ibid. 364.

19. *Law and Its Compass* 63–66.

20. *Ibid.* 93. An obstacle to getting "Natural Law in at the front door," as Mansfield had failed to do, is that "precedent. . . . however much of its uses may be abused, is the necessary hostage surrendered by every system of jurisprudence to the public confidence in its 'serene impartiality'"; ibid. 33.

natural law in the common law, in the concept of public policy in the law of contract. In his view the concept of public policy "stands at any rate for this, that there are some things that the law will not stand for. So regarded it must express those inner convictions that sustain the system itself."[21] While he admitted that there was a "marked reluctance to make use of it which has now become a feature of English judicial utterance,"[22] he maintained that, as the judge could never be really free of public policy considerations, "he should make a more intensive effort to analyze what its basic requirements are and to train himself to become a sounder exponent of their intrinsic nature."[23]

Intellectually, Radcliffe was concerned both with civil liberties, and, especially in his later years, with the apparent process of erosion of authority.[24] For this reason, not only intellectually but also politically, he thought it undesirable that the judiciary should either shackle or expose itself by conceding what it was about. On the one hand there are Radcliffe's words, evocative of Maine and Pollock, describing the judicial process: "The law has to be interpreted before it can be applied, and interpretation is a creative activity. The law was not there until that particular decision was given. Once it has been given, the whole enormous component which is the body of the law, has changed its composition by the addition of a new element, significant or insignificant, which in some degree modifies the whole."[25]

Yet on the other hand there is political caution. "[I]f judges prefer to adopt the formula—for that is what it is—that they merely declare the law and do not make it, they do no more than show themselves wise men in practice. Their analysis may be weak, but their perception of the nature of law is sound. Men's respect for it will be the greater, the more imperceptible its development."[26] If public opinion might lose respect for

21. Ibid. 37.
22. Ibid. 45–46.
23. Ibid. 47.
24. "Our national tradition greets the errors of Authority with not much more sophistication than that with which a small boy is supposed to welcome an elderly gentleman slipping on the pavement. Out of the few institutions of this country that ought to be accorded national status, one blindly perpetuates a radical myth that finds its natural enemy in all authority, and the other clings to an outmoded formula that denies the acceptance of any law beyond that of its own will. . . . Indeed, it is a serious question whether England is not rapidly becoming, in the strict sense, an ungovernable country." Radcliffe is presumably referring to the Labour party and the Trade Union Congress; *Not in Feather Beds* 226.
See also ibid. 236: "[A]t all levels of society we need more persons of experience and authority to speak and act boldly and sincerely, without deference to the subtleties of public relations or the imputed susceptibilities of youth or of egalitarian opinion."
25. Ibid. 213.
26. *Law and Its Compass* 39. See also, "The legislature and the judicial process respectively are two complementary sources of law-making, and in a well ordered state each has to understand its respective functions and limitations. Judicial law is always a

creative judges, Parliament certainly would. "I think that the judge needs to be particularly circumspect in the use of his power to declare the law, not because the principles adopted by Parliament are more satisfactory or more enlightened than those which would commend themselves to his mind, but because it is unacceptable constitutionally that there should be two independent sources of law-making at work at the same time."[27] Karl Llewellyn has described the process that Radcliffe espoused as being like that of a "Victorian virgin tubbing in her nightgown." Certainly, a covert operation such as that proposed by Radcliffe made the analysis of the goals toward which judges might be working of considerable interest.

What were these fundamental principles that Radcliffe advocated and judges were apparently free to cultivate?[28] Radcliffe noted, "We badly need to develop a modern philosophy of authority for future use instead of just chanting the old choruses of rebellion."[29] He also opined that there are "ideas of equity and wisdom which most men would wish to see imprinted on the fabric of society."[30] The views of "most men" seem appreciably different from the populist notions that were to concern Devlin. Indeed, Radcliffe was to a large extent silent about what the "fundamental principles of equity and wisdom"—running his two themes together—were. The nearest he came to articulating these principles was in a lecture entitled "The Dissolving Society," in which he confirmed that "[i]n our history the single great public philosophy has been a belief in the truths of the Christian religion."[31] It would seem that the fundamental principles of the law were closely associated with the fundamental tenets of a public philosophy that, like the former, had suffered a singular decline in the twentieth century.

While it is possible to suggest that, by Radcliffe's own standards, such a guiding force lacks rigor, his awareness of the possibilities of creativity in the appellate process was clear. The need to avoid advertising such a process to the legislature led Radcliffe to handle discussions of the judicial process with considerable skill.[32] Adopting the approach

---

reinterpretation of principles in the light of a new combination of facts, of which very relevant ones, unprovable by evidence, are the current beliefs of the society in which those facts occur"; *Not in Feather Beds* 215.

27. Ibid. 216.

28. "After fifteen years in a final appeal court I suspect I have changed my views very much. . . . More and more I am impressed by the inescapable personal element in the judicial decision. . . . Say indeed, that a judge must be fair, or that he must be impartial: that is essential. He must strip himself of all prejudices, certainly; except I ought to add, those prejudices which on consideration he is prepared to stand by as his sincere convictions"; ibid. 212.

29. Ibid. 178.

30. *Law and the Democratic State* 8.

31. *Not in Feather Beds* 243.

32. "It has been a pity, I think, that so much of judicial opinion in this country has

of the Scottish judges, he claimed that rather than emphasizing principle, "there is a tendency today to give too much importance to particular decisions, and by so doing to discover leading cases before they have proved that they have in them the quality to lead."[33] In the light of this, it is scarcely surprising that Radcliffe was at his best in developing basic common law concepts. He moved slowly.[34] He remained anxious that not every precedent be transferred into a principle.[35] Yet he was acutely conscious of the teleological possibilities. "[I]t sometimes helps to assess the merits of a decision, if one starts by noticing its results and only after doing that allots to it the legal principles upon which it is said to depend."[36]

Bearing this injunction in mind, one can say that Radcliffe left his mark on a significant number of areas of the common law. In erudite, elegant speeches he restated a narrow conception of the doctrine of frustration in contract,[37] an approach in keeping with his observation that the courts had persuaded themselves that "in the name of good order they have some primary duty to uphold freedom of contract, rather than a duty to work out a theory of contract as a whole which started from the necessity of a fundamental decency in private relations."[38] In the same vein, while agreeing in another case to the striking down of a penalty

---

been conveyed by the method of logical deduction. . . . [S]yllogistic reasoning is only conclusive if you first import your chosen meaning into the words of the premise you start with. It is only a demonstration of a truth if you have already been converted to the truth. In our history of judgment-making too many decisions have begun by insisting that particular words have one particular meaning and then deducing that, if they have, certain consequences must necessarily follow. . . . It is the unexpressed assumptions, which are nevertheless very much present, that are often the real hinges of decisions"; ibid. 214–15.

33. Ibid. 216.

34. "No one really doubts that the common law is a body of law which develops in process of time in response to the developments of the society in which it rules. Its movement may not be perceptible at any distinct point of time, nor can we always say how it gets from one point to another; but I do not think that, for all that, we need abandon the conviction of Galileo that somehow, by some means, there is a movement that takes place"; *Lister* v. *Romford Ice & Cold Storage Co.*, [1957] A.C. 555, 591–92 (1956).

35. In the "rotten elm tree" case, *Caminer* v. *Northern & London Inv. Trust, Ltd.*, [1951] A.C. 88, 110 (1950), he was not happy with the majority decision but was not prepared to dissent. He would not differ on the principle but on the application of it to the facts for "the truth is that the evidence is not in a satisfactory state for the purposes of an appellate court. There is too much ambiguity in some of the questions, and there are too many inconclusive answers that were left unresolved." Accordingly, he advised against the citation of this decision as a precedent; ibid. 111. In *Esso Petroleum Co.* v. *Southport Corp.*, [1956] A.C. 218 (1955), Radcliffe emphasized that the decision was being based solely upon the way the case had been pleaded, rendering its precedential value, at best, uncertain; ibid. 241.

36. *Imperial Chem. Indus., Ltd.* v. *Shatwell* [1965] A.C. 656, 676 (1964).

37. *Davis Contractors, Ltd.* v. *Fareham UDC*, [1956] A.C. 696, 724; *Tsakiroglou & Co.* v. *Noblee Thorl G.m.b.H.*, [1962] A.C. 93, 120 (1961).

38. Radcliffe, *Law and Its Compass* 63. In keeping with this, he praised the theory of contract as having taught men to look out for themselves; "Some Reflections on Law and Lawyers" 364.

clause in a hire purchase agreement, he warned of the dangers of treating the doctrine of unconscionability as a "panacea."[39] Yet, in shipping cases Radcliffe was prepared to admit that "[t]he corpus of commercial law has been built up largely by this process of supplying from the common usage of the trade what is the unexpressed intention of the parties."[40] Accordingly, he refused to be drawn into the sterile speculations of less sophisticated judges. "I do not believe that . . . it is possible or right to analyse very precisely where law begins and fact ends."[41]

The same elegant, intelligent—if sometimes cautious—perception of and silent resolve on directions also characterized the Radcliffe approach to tort. In workmen's cases he saw his role as the balancing of values,[42] while believing that fault had to remain as the essential basis of liability.[43] His approach appeared at its strongest in *Lister v. Romford Ice and Cold Storage Company.*[44] When an employer sued an employee to recover for damages incurred by the latter's negligent driving, Radcliffe felt compelled to dissent from the majority's view allowing recovery. The novelty of the claim and the realities of the situation did not deter him,[45] and he had no doubt that the common law ought to have risen to the occasion.[46]

39. " 'Unconscionable' must not be taken to be a panacea for adjusting any contract between competent persons when it shows a rough edge to one side or the other, and equity lawyers are, I notice, sometimes both surprised and discomforted by the plenitude of jurisdiction, and the imprecision of rules that are attributed to 'equity' by their more enthusiastic colleagues"; *Bridge v. Campbell Discount, Co.,* [1962] A.C. 600, 626.

40. *Tsakiroglou & Co. v. Noblee Thorl G.m.b.H.,* [1962] A.C. 93, 122 (1961). See also, *Riverstone Meat Co. v. Lancashire Shipping Co.,* [1961] A.C. 807 (1960), where he had to construe the Hague rules and fell back on the history of the rules and the settled interpretation before the High Court and Court of Appeal had diverged from it; ibid. 868; and *The Aello,* [1961] A.C. 135 (1960), especially at 161, 177, where Radcliffe advocated "a clear general rule" in this "tangled branch of commercial law."

41. *Tsakiroglou & Co. v. Noblee Thorl G.m.b.H.,* [1962] A.C. 93, 124 (1961).

42. "[T]he courts should be circumspect in filling out that duty [the master's duty of care] with the much vaguer obligation of encouraging, exhorting or instructing workmen or a particular workman to make regular use of what is provided. Properly to measure that obligation as a legal duty requires a fuller knowledge of the circumstances of the factory and of the relations between employers and workmen and their representatives than was available at any rate in the present case"; *Qualcast (Wolverhamptom), Ltd. v. Haynes,* [1959] A.C. 743, 753.

43. In *Brown v. National Coal Bd.,* [1962] A.C. 574, 591 (1961), he was unwilling to turn the mine manager "into a blind guarantor of the desired consequences, however casual or unforeseeable the cause of the accident," although he admitted that Parliament could in theory impose absolute liability; ibid. 595. Radcliffe also sat on the *Shatwell* appeal that revived the defense of *volenti non fit injuria* in the employer and employee relationship. He, however, was able to decide the case on the basis of causation, as he held that each guilty party emerged as the author of his own injury.

44. [1957] A.C. 555 (1956).

45. Society "has been almost revolutionised by the growth of all forms of insurance"; ibid. 591.

46. In deciding this "very difficult point," he started from the basis that someone had to ensure against third-party risks and that the natural person to do so would be the

As one moves away from private law,[47] however, the Radcliffe approach becomes more complex. In public law, it was not his sophisticated view of the judicial process that was generally apparent, but rather his internal conflict between the needs for order and the support of authority on the one hand and his instinct for civil liberties on the other. He had argued extrajudicially that "the art of political theory is hardly begun with the rules for ascertaining and enforcing the wishes of a majority: the real art lies in analysing and expounding the circumstances and occasions upon which, whatever the wishes of a majority, they ought not to be given effect at the expense of a minority, large or small."[48] As to the civil libertarian position, Radcliffe argued in favor of the special protection of certain relationships. "We all feel that there are relationships arising out of human institutions which deserve special protection from outside invasion or even voluntary relinquishment: marital and parental relationships, freedom of religious worship, freedom of association, freedom of labour, and freedom of artistic and productive expression."[49]

In that same passage Radcliffe called on the law to "nourish and enrich the growth of each individual human spirit"; however, commitments to minority rights and personal freedom ultimately seemed swamped by Radcliffe's increasing concern to buttress authority. In his Carr-Saunders lecture entitled "Some General Reflections on Immigration and Settlement," Radcliffe attacked Parliament for its "lordly outburst of indictment or remedy-making" and particularly the passage of the Race

---

employer. This term would be implied in the service agreement. He had little sympathy for the insurers, "I do not at all understand the idea that it is somehow hard on the insurers that they should be affected by an implied term that bound the person to whose rights they are claiming to be subrogated"; ibid. 589. In reply to the argument that the risk in this case was not a compulsory one, he said, "I do not think that the term postulated should be tied down to all the complications and qualifications which arise on a strict interpretation of the Act. What mattered to the parties was that, while the lorry was being driven on the employer's business, someone might be injured in circumstances that entitled him to recover damages from either employer or employee or both of them"; ibid. There were also "almost intolerable anomalies" involved in the respondent's argument. If the employee were sued by the third party, the employee could have called on the insurance company for the cover that the employer had brought him. Whereas, in the present circumstances, "I should be very much interested to know how the premium required by an insurance company is adjusted to the risk of these alternative situations"; ibid. 590.

47. For his decisions on libel, see *Associated Newspapers, Ltd.* v. *Dingle*, [1964] A.C. 371 (1962); *Speidel* v. *Plato Films, Ltd.*, [1961] A.C. 1090. In the field on conflicts, see *Boissevain* v. *Weil*, [1950] A.C. 327; *Kahler* v. *Midland Bank, Ltd.*, [1950] A.C. 24 (1949); *Adams* v. *National Bank of Greece S.A.*, [1961] A.C. 255 (1960); *In re United Rys. of Havana* v. *Regla Warehouses, Ltd.*, [1961] A.C. 1007 (1960). In *United States & Republic of France* v. *Dollfus Mieg et Cie S.A. & Bank of England*, [1952] A.C. 582, 616 (1951), he said of the question of sovereign immunity, "[T]his is not a field in which the law can be set at rest by a neat combination of words."

48. Radcliffe, *Not in Feather Beds* 245.

49. Radcliffe, *Law and Its Compass* 66.

Relations Act of 1968.[50] He deplored Parliament's attempt to shape moral attitudes, especially since "prejudice and discrimination do not carry any ordinary association of moral ill-doing."[51] Nor was Radcliffe any more comfortable with developments in the universities in the late sixties. While his investigation into Warwick University[52] was lauded by many, there was something ironic in the proponent of the maintenance of values—if necessary, by a minority of "right-thinking" men—also concluding that he retained some doubts "whether there may not be teachers so far committed to particular socio-political systems as to disqualify them from the objective analysis of their subject that the university tradition itself assumes."[53]

The conflict between libertarianism and authoritarianism was apparent in Radcliffe's public law decisions. While he had applauded Atkin's dissent in *Liversidge* v. *Anderson*,[54] he was reluctant to interfere with administrative discretion if he perceived that a statutory code of conduct existed, even when mala fides was alleged.[55] Arguments based on "justice" could play no part in the development of administrative law.[56] Even

50. On this, see especially Anthony Lester, "The Broken Compass" 443.

51. Then Lord Radcliffe objects that the concept of racial discrimination is too vague to be capable of having precise legal meaning; he "wrote down four different descriptions of definitions of it and" [as one might have foreseen!] "none of them was the same as another." He continues: "I cannot . . . imagine how juridicial notions can be founded on such vague conceptions. The conduct of human life consists of choices, and it is a very large undertaking indeed to outlaw some particular grounds of choice. . . . I try to distinguish in my mind between an act of discrimination and an act of preference, and each time my attempt breaks down. Either, I think both are outlawed by the Act of 1968, or else the one merges indistinguishably into the other"; ibid. 444.

52. Warwick University, *Report of the Rt. Hon. Viscount Radcliffe, G.B.E., as to the Procedures followed in the university with regard to Receiving and Retaining Information about Political Activities of the Staff and of Students*.

53. Cited, E. P. Thompson, "A Report on Lord Radcliffe" 737.

54. With Radcliffe's defense of authority, contrast his letter to Atkin after *Liversidge* v. *Anderson*: "I only wanted to say how entirely I agree with every line of your judgment"; he went on to say that he hoped that Atkin's view should "somehow prevail before things go much further"; R. F. V. Heuston, "*Liversidge* v. *Anderson* in Retrospect" 33, 52.

55. The act had provided "a complete statutory code for regulating the extent to which, and the conditions under which, courts of law might be resorted to for the purpose of questioning the validity of a compulsory purchase order within the protection of the Act"; *Smith* v. *East Elloe RDC*, [1956] A.C. 736, 768.

56. "They are not reflections which are capable of determining the construction of the Act once it has been passed, unless there is something that one can lay hold of in the context of the Act which justifies the introduction of the exception sought for. Merely to say that Parliament cannot be presumed to have intended to bring about a consequence which many people might think to be unjust is not, in my opinion, a principle of construction for this purpose. In point of fact, whatever innocence of view may have been allowable to the lawyers of the eighteenth and nineteenth centuries, the twentieth century lawyer is entitled to few assumptions in this field. It is not open to him to ignore the fact that the legislature has often shown indifference to the assertion of rights which courts of law have been accustomed to recognise and enforce, and that it has often excluded the authority of courts of law in favour of other preferred tribunals"; ibid. 769.

though Radcliffe mused that "lawyers are at heart anarchists, in that by training they believe all executive power to be evil,"[57] his own decisions rarely went against the executive. He could insist that he had "searched in vain for a principle of construction as applied to Acts of Parliament which would enable the appellant to succeed,"[58] yet in only one leading case did he find that the executive—in this situation once again a local authority—had exceeded its authority.[59]

The *Burmah Oil* case, where the majority allowed compensation for property destroyed in time of war, is perhaps the sharpest example of this conflict, settled in favor of authority—partly, no doubt, in keeping with Radcliffe's concept of the silent role of the judiciary. After stating the doctrinal difficulties,[60] he argued that public policy demanded that the right to compensation be left to the executive.[61] He concluded, "None of this is an argument against the propriety or, indeed, urgent desirability of the state providing compensation schemes to take care, so far as possible, of all war damage of person or property. But it is for those who fill and empty the public purse to decide when, by whom, on what conditions and within what limitations such compensation is to be made available."[62] The judges were to maintain a low profile.

In fairness to Radcliffe, where personal freedoms were involved

57. Radcliffe, "Some Reflections on Law and Lawyers" 361–62.
58. [1956] A.C. 770.
59. In *Chertsey UDC v. Mixnam's Properties, Ltd.*, [1965] A.C. 735 (1964), he reluctantly held that the local authority had exceeded its power under the Caravan Sites and Control of Development Act of 1960, in that "permissible conditions must relate to the user of the licensed site, not to the user of the licensee's legal powers of letting or licensing caravan spaces"; ibid. 757. Also on control by the courts over delegated legislation, see *Belfast Corp. v. O.D. Cars, Ltd.*, [1960] A.C. 490 (N. Ire. 1959).
60. "As we know only vaguely what this prerogative is and have even vaguer information as to when and on what occasions it has been asserted throughout history, I have become more and more uncertain what it is that we are really talking about"; *Burmah Oil Co. v. Lord Advocate*, [1965] A.C. 75, 113 (Scot. 1964).
"Whether the law itself, and I mean by that the common law administered by the judges without any statutory authority to assist them, can compel the provisions of compensation at the public expense when a subject has suffered from some exercise of this prerogative is the question that we have to decide in this case. A priori, I do not know that I should have expected the common law to have charge of such a matter"; ibid. 118.
61. "[W]here war damage is concerned, the long-standing absence of any recognition that there is jurisdiction in the courts to award compensation is based on sound considerations of public policy. Such damage is a matter being unpredictable in extent and range, that must be controlled by that department of the sovereign power that is responsible for the raising and expenditure of public money. There is not a legal line between those divisions of that damage that carry a legal right to compensation and those that do not"; ibid. 134.
62. Ibid. However, although the common law should not be concerned in this matter when the actions of the Crown were admittedly lawful, there is something "which may, by a permissible transfer of language, be called a public law which requires the careful attention of the state to damage thus inflicted and calls upon it to make such provision as the recognised . . . equity in favor of compensation may demand"; ibid. 135.

there was more evidence that he was able to push the law in the directions represented by his libertarian leaning. It was Radcliffe, for instance, who, in the Privy Council,[63] delivered a serious body blow to the decision in *Liversidge* v. *Anderson*.[64] Still more revealing is his speech in *Zacharia* v. *Republic of Cyprus*[65] where he dissented on the ground that to send Zacharia back to Cyprus would be oppressive and unjust.[66] He felt no similar libertarian sentiments, however—or was able to repress them—when English protesters immobilized an air base.[67]

If the appellants in *Chandler* v. *Director of Public Prosecutions* fell into Radcliffe's category of attackers of authority, his approach to legislation as a source of law involved in theory even greater conflicts. With his vision of "true" law bearing many of the hallmarks of fundamental law, Radcliffe had some difficulty in accepting statute law as "real" law.[68] He publicly suggested that statute law be treated as some form of "sub-law," since statute law had lost sight of the fundamental principles of real law. He found it scarcely surprising that legislation frequently lacked "values" when, "in order to be elected at all, each party must devise for the electorate a programme of action calculated to appeal to the material interests of the greater number."[69] To put it in other terms, Radcliffe was unimpressed by the modern attitude of many. "The law of their country can never be to such persons in any sense their master: it is either an impediment to be got rid of or a servant to execute their or-

63. *Nakkuda Ali* v. *Jayaratne*, [1951] A.C. 66, 73 (P.C. 1950).

64. [1942] A.C. 206 (1941).

65. [1963] A.C. 634, 664 (1962).

66. He was not impressed by the argument that there should be a presumption that it would not be unjust to return a prisoner in response to a demand by a Commonwealth government or a friendly power. In this case Zacharia was "the object of an implacable vendetta" and "plainly, he will be in great danger of his life, and I do not think that it really matters under what precise authority his enemies are acting"; ibid. 668, 673.

For a libertarian definition of political offense, see *R.* v. *Governor of Brixton Prison, ex parte Schtraks*, [1964] A.C. 556, 585 (1962). See C. F. Amerasinghe, "The Schtraks Case" 28.

See also *Rumping* v. *DPP*, [1964] A.C. 814, 835 (1962), where Radcliffe dissented, holding that the implications of allowing as evidence intercepted communications between spouses was "overwhelmingly distasteful"; ibid. 845.

67. "[I]f a man is shown to the satisfaction of the jury to have approached an airfield with the direct purpose of obstructing its operational use, a verdict of guilty must result, provided that they are also satisfied that the airfield belongs to Her Majesty and was at the relevant date part of the defence system maintained by the Crown for the protection of the realm"; *Chandler* v. *DPP*, [1964] A.C. 763, 796 (1962).

68. "[I]s law to be thought of as an expression of the general will of society, the better the law the more flexibly it changes in response to that changing will; or may we, however imperfectly, try to relate it to some other more constant, less mundane, authority?" Radcliffe, *Law and the Democratic State* 9–10.

69. Ibid. 8. See also at 9, and Radcliffe, "*Some Reflections on Law and Lawyers*" 365: "[W]hat law is not, in essence, is the command of a ruler. And what law more and more tends to become in England is the command of a ruler, even if he be according to the democratic canon but an emanation of ourselves."

ders."[70] Although Radcliffe assumed that "the intended purpose of statute law is to correct or supplement the common law when it is inadequate or has gone astray,"[71] as a result of widespread modern legislation "[l]aw as it is in our present time is not quite the kind of thing that we want to regard as Law."[72]

Such sentiments might be thought evidence of a hostile frame of mind, yet ironically, it was this very skepticism that enabled Radcliffe to interpret statutes in a less wooden way than the substantive formalists.[73] The breadth of Radcliffe's intellect became clearest in tax cases. There is little reason to think that Radcliffe was a believer in radical or even liberal schemes of taxation.[74] He regarded tax law, however, as one of those areas in which, as far as possible, decisions should be restricted to their facts and should not pass into the law as precedents.[75] His numerous decisions were characterized by a sense of balance. While he used his skills and information acquired in various commissions and committees to point out unfair elements in tax administration,[76] in *Independent Television Authority and Associated-Rediffusion, Ltd.* v. *Inland Revenue Commissioners,*[77] he pointed out possible untapped sources of stamp duty revenue, while in *Inland Revenue Commissioners* v. *Frere*[78] he added some critical remarks about the system of extrastatutory concessions that

---

70. Radcliffe, *Not in Feather Beds* at xi.

71. *Law and the Democratic State* 5.

72. Ibid. 10.

73. Thus, while he held that "words . . . in the Act must be understood in the light of any established legal interpretation that prevailed at the date of the passing of the Act," in *Welham* v. *DPP*, [1961] A.C. 103, 123 (1960), he had no difficulty with the idea that Parliament could legislate away common law principles. See especially *Workington Harbour & Dock Bd.* v. *Towerfield (Owners)*, [1951] A.C. 112, 159 (1950); and *Galloway* v. *Galloway*, [1956] A.C. 299, 313, 323 (1955). For dicta justifying a broad approach, see *St. Aubyn* v. *Attorney-General*, [1952] A.C. 15, 52 (1951); for those justifying a narrow approach, see *Goodrich* v. *Paisner*, [1957] A.C. 65, 90 (1956).

74. In a letter to *The Times* in 1974, he vigorously attacked the wealth tax proposed by the Wilson administration; e.g., "the profound absurdity of the whole proposal"; "intellectual fraud"; *The Times*, 3 July 1974, at 17.

75. See especially *Nash* v. *Tamplin & Sons Brewery, Ltd.*, [1952] A.C. 231, 256 (1951), and *IRC* v. *Dowdall, O'Mahoney & Co.*, [1952] A.C. 401, 422 (1951). See also *Unit Constr. Co.* v. *Bullock (Inspector of Taxes)*, [1960] A.C. 351 (1959), criticizing precedents on residence of company (especially at 367–68). In *Sanderson* v. *IRC*, [1956] A.C. 491, 500 (1955), Radcliffe began the process of undermining Macnaghten's dictum in *Earl Cowley* v. *IRC*, [1899] A.C. 198.

76. For example, he demanded a review of tax penalties. "Such a review has been called for both in the Report of the Income Tax Codification Committee—and the Final Report of the most recent Royal Commission on Income Tax—and the recommendation has no doubt reached the destination usually reserved for advice invited by governments from such committees"; *IRC* v. *Hinchy*, [1960] A.C. 748, 777. A new code of tax penalties was introduced by the Finance Act of 1960.

77. [1961] A.C. 427, 438 (1960).

78. [1965] A.C. 402, 416 (1964).

play such an important part in the United Kingdom tax system.[79] In English terms, such an approach was evidence of a judge who was sensitive to the relationship of the judiciary and the executive. Had Radcliffe come to the House of Lords fifteen years later, he would have been the natural leader of the group of law lords seeking to work out a more comprehensive rationale for the final appeal court, particularly the relationship between the judiciary and the legislature.

Lord Devlin

Devlin forms a nice contrast with Radcliffe. Like Radcliffe, Devlin had publicly discussed the judicial process[80] and, superficially, both judges had emphasized similar points: the relationship between law and morality and the downplaying of the judicial contribution to the law. Yet the similarities are deceptive, for Devlin's morality was that of the majority, almost a populist viewpoint, and his skepticism about judicial creativity seemed to spring more from his ascent up the judicial *cursus honorum* rather than from the sophisticated political skepticism exhibited by Radcliffe. For Devlin, after abandoning a possible vocation as a Jesuit priest, carved out a career for himself at the Commercial Bar and then sat as a puisne judge in the King's Bench Division and briefly in the Court of Appeal before spending his three years as law lord.[81]

Devlin's observations on morality and the judicial process, although again superficially similar to Radcliffe's, involved a wider jurisprudential controversy over the relationship between law and morality, with Devlin being opposed to J. S. Mill on the one hand and H. L. A. Hart on the other. The two basic Devlin themes appear to be first, that there is no private realm of morality into which the law cannot enter[82] and second, that the morality that the law enforces must be popular morality. On the first, Devlin might have had Radcliffe's support; on the second, he would not, for Radcliffe was not primarily interested in the beliefs held by the ordinary reasonable man or "the man in the jury box," as Devlin put

79. "I have never understood the procedure of extra-statutory concessions in the case of a body to whom at least the door of Parliament is opened every year for adjustment of the tax code"; ibid. 429. See also *Unit Constr. Co. v. Bullock*, [1960] A.C. 351 (1959), as the test of residence of a company. "I think that a statutory code could have been provided and on the whole I regret that it has not"; ibid. 365.

80. See especially, all by Patrick Devlin, *Trial by Jury; The Criminal Prosecution in England; Law and Morals; Samples of Lawmaking;* and *Enforcement of Morals.*

81. Patrick Arthur Devlin; b. 1905; educ., Stonyhurst College, Christ's College, Cambridge (Second, Law); called to bar, 1929; K.C., 1945; Judge, Queen's Bench Division, 1948–60; President, Restrictive Practices Court, 1956–61; Lord Justice, 1960–61; Lord of Appeal, 1961–64.

82. One of the potential confusions is that Devlin frequently uses the word "law" as concerning both judge-made law and legislation, while Radcliffe, at least in the works discussed in this chapter, uses law to refer primarily to judge-made law.

it.[83] Whereas Radcliffe saw as his guiding principles the belief of right-thinking men, Devlin asserted, "[W]hat the lawmaker has to ascertain is not the true belief [of right and wrong] but the common belief."[84] Such deference to the masses was alien to Radcliffe, but it was much more acceptable to Devlin, who was, perhaps, less skeptical of majority rule. Devlin believed that in a democracy only Parliament should change the law.[85] Insofar as judges did make law, he saw them as servants of society, "whose business it is to fashion rules for the service of a community whose needs are subject to change."[86] Such a subservient role for both judges and the law would not have been acceptable to Radcliffe.

Indeed, Devlin's years on the bench, in a period when the Lords was dominated by Simonds, appear to have given him the feeling not only that the period of judicial creativity was over, but that there were almost no dying embers. "I doubt if judges will now of their own motion contribute much more to the development of the law,"[87] he wrote in 1962; and after the establishment of the Law Commission, he predicted, "It will result also in the appellate courts playing a much less important part in the life of the law."[88] Although Devlin was conscious that "[t]he judges always have been and still are fashioners of law, not creators, out of material that is supplied to them,"[89] he predicted that even if the House of Lords were to abandon its belief in infallibility, the practical effect would be limited. "If the House of Lords did not treat itself as bound by its own decisions, it might do its own lopping and pruning . . . and perhaps even a little grafting, instead of leaving all that to the legislature. But it could not greatly alter the shape of the tree."[90] Thus, even

83. *Enforcement of Morals* 90.

84. Ibid. 94.

85. *Samples of Lawmaking* 22. Thus Devlin claimed it was not "too strong a sense of pride that has led the House of Lords to rely on its own infallibility" but the acceptance of this constitutional principle: "In the House of Lords the judicial process exhausts itself. The law that is there pronounced may not even at the time be the best rule for the needs of society that could be devised; and certainly, if it is, it will not always remain so. But it is the best that can be produced by development and without abrupt change. Change is for the legislature"; ibid. 21–22.

86. Ibid. 21.

87. Ibid. 23. "In the early days of the common law the judges had to do much of their own spinning; today the legislative mills turn out the yarn in large quantities and in varying qualities, but it still has to be woven into cloth"; ibid. 3. See also *The Listener*, 20 Aug. 1964, at 261–63: "Judges as law-makers live on sufferance. Not only can the territory that is left to them be invaded at will, but any decision that they give, if it is unwelcome, can be set aside."

88. Cited, Leslie Scarman, *Codification and Judge-Made Law* 11.

89. Devlin, *Samples of Lawmaking* 3.

90. Ibid. 116. On the previous page, Devlin expounded his concept of precedent:

The common law has grown by the formation of precedents and the division and multiplication of precedents until a complete organism is formed. Thus precedent is both the life force of the common law and the factor that controls its development. Without precedent there would be no law at all; each case

though he occasionally criticized the cautious behavior of judges (who "have become too much like priests to whom alone the oracle speaks . . . [I]f they saw themselves only as craftsmen they would make less fuss about discarding the outmoded"),[91] he appeared to feel that such an approach was inevitable in an arena bounded by the English judiciary and a constitutional democracy.

It was perhaps this conflicted view of the role of the judiciary in a parliamentary democracy that left the impression that Devlin was least comfortable with those decisions involving an element of public law. In his writings he noted that the fact that the influence of the common law over the executive was receding was "not due to any timidity in the face of advances by the executive but rather to voluntary withdrawal in the field of public policy as a whole."[92] "The common law has put the control of the executive into the safe keeping of Parliament. They cannot now withdraw their endowment even if they would."[93] Indeed, in terms of civil liberties he was forced to concede that "[t]he executive knows that in dealing with the liberty of the subject it must not do anything which would seriously disturb the conscience of the average member of Parliament or of the average juryman. I know of no other real checks that exist to-day upon the power of the executive."[94]

Devlin's reluctance to impinge on the executive's power can be sensed in *Zacharia* v. *Republic of Cyprus*.[95] Devlin held not only that those accused of political offenses could be imprisoned under the Fugitive Offenders Act of 1881 but also that the political nature of the offense was not even a factor to be taken into account. "The court could not exercise its discretion in that way without trespassing upon matters of policy."[96]

---

would be decided by the opinion of the judge and not according to rule. But precedent could not make a rule if any judge could alter it. So precedent, when finally established, becomes as rigid as the branch of a tree. There are still young shoots that can be trained this way or that but the branch itself can only be lopped or pruned. Once the tree is fully grown the area which it can shade is determined and cannot be extended. [Ibid. 115]

91. Ibid. 21.
92. Ibid. 115.
93. Ibid. 119.
94. Devlin, *Trial by Jury* 162. Devlin was in general an admirer of the jury system. The great value of juries, he considered, was that in the criminal law particularly, they helped to keep the judges from constructing a mystique and they were also "an insurance that the criminal law will conform to the ordinary man's idea of what is fair and just"; ibid. 160. In this discussion, Devlin refused to accept many basic English assumptions. "There is no difference in origin between questions of fact and questions of law; there is simply a point at which a particular way of dealing with the facts in order to produce justice becomes sufficiently well recognised to be adopted as a general rule and so to become law"; ibid. 150.
95. [1963] A.C. 634, 681 (1962).
96. Ibid. 688. Perhaps his strongest position in favor of civil liberties was *Glinski* v. *McIver*, [1962] A.C. 726, 765, holding that the police were entitled to no special privileges when sued in tort for malicious prosecution. See especially at 776–77.

Similarly, although he voted with the majority in *Ridge* v. *Baldwin*,[97] his view that a breach of the rules of natural justice rendered a decision of the Watch Committee voidable and not void would have meant (if he had not found a breach of the police regulations as well) that the Home Secretary's confirmation of the dismissal settled the question. In that sense the decision was less of a strengthening of civil liberties than might at first appear, although Devlin's speech itself contains strong dicta in favor of natural justice.[98]

Moreover, other examples, the best known being the *Chandler* case, show that Devlin's dicta seemed to outrun the breadth of his decision.[99] In *Chandler* the high-flown constitutional rhetoric[100] boiled down, in short, to little more than a statement that factual issues should be left to the jury.[101] In terms of the criminal process, his arguments that relevance was the true test of admissibility of evidence in a criminal trial were not alien to his early authoritarian training. Indeed, in public law in its widest sense, Devlin underlined the mechanical and the subservient aspects of the law.[102]

97. [1964] A.C. 40, 136 (1963).

98. See ibid. 140–41.

99. *Chandler* v. *DPP*, [1964] A.C. 763, 801 (1962).

100. "The Attorney-General submitted that, while it is a question of fact for the jury whether the entry was for a purpose prejudicial, once it was proved that the purpose was to interfere with a prohibited place and to prevent its operating, then a judge should be entitled to direct a jury to return a verdict of guilty. With great respect I think that to be an unconstitutional doctrine. It is the conscience of the jury and not the power of the judge that provides the constitutional safeguard against perverse acquittal"; ibid. 803–4. He noted that the arguments

have embraced big constitutional questions concerning the right to trial by jury and not by judge, and the extent to which the courts can question statements on political matters by the executive. All such questions which concern the liberty of the subject need great care in their consideration. It is to me a special inducement to the exercise of care that these appellants have not traded their liberty for personal gain but for what they sincerely, and however mistakenly, believe to be the safety of the world. Furthermore (their own expressed determination to break the law notwithstanding), it is the duty of this House to see that men and women who have a creed they want to preach in no case pay any penalty for their faith unless they have taken themselves out of the protection of the law by doing that which the law forbids. [Ibid. 811–12]

He also commented, "There is no rule of common law that whenever questions of national security are being considered by any court, for any purposes, it is what the Crown thinks to be necessary or expedient that counts, and not what is necessary or expedient in fact. If there were, the reasoning in *Liversidge v. Anderson* would, in effect, be part of the common law instead of the exegesis of an emergency regulation"; ibid. 811.

101. The rhetoric fizzled out in reality:

I must confess that I find it difficult to see how a sensible jury could have acquitted. In saying that, I do not mean to offer any opinion on the wisdom or otherwise of nuclear disarmament. That is a matter of policy on which differing views are held. . . . But so long as the contrary view is held by the majority and the policy of the country thus determined, I cannot see how it can be otherwise than prejudicial to the State to obstruct the execution of that policy. To have a nuclear weapon and also to have divided counsels about its use, which are pressed to the point of sabotage, seems to add one class of peril to another already sufficiently great. [Ibid. 803]

102 . In *Jones v. DPP*, [1962] A.C. 635, 690 (1961), he took the ahistorical—albeit

Like other appeal judges, Devlin found rhetoric and reality not always consistent. In *Jones* v. *Director of Public Prosecutions*, he refused to give the words of the act their literal meaning. While defending stare decisis,[103] in the words of one commentator, Devlin made "[t]he most revolutionary suggestion concerning previous authority."[104] Similarly, in respect to statutory construction, extrajudicially Devlin could emphasize the existence[105] or the absence[106] of power on the part of the judges, in construing legislation.[107] In *Associated Newspapers, Limited* v. *Registrar of Restrictive Trading Agreements*,[108] on the construction of the Restrictive Trade Practices Act of 1956, however, Devlin did not hesitate to use his experience in the Restrictive Practices Court to interpret broadly the intentions of Parliament.[109] Nor should it be forgotten that Devlin,

---

rational—position that the ascertainment of truth was the basic purpose of the criminal trial.

He refused to accept the exact and literal construction of proviso (f) of § 1 of the Criminal Evidence Act of 1898, because "a rule so framed appears to me to be so irrational that it is impossible to suppose that it could have been intended by Parliament"; ibid. 696. One reason was that it "puts the ascertainment of truth which is the object of the criminal trial at the mercy of chance"; ibid. 697.

Similarly, in *Connelly* v. *DPP*, [1964] A.C. 1254, 1339, Devlin refused to import the concept of issue estoppel into the criminal law to protect an accused when *autrefois acquit* was not available. He suggested, however, that protection might be provided by alterations in the rules for drafting indictments; ibid. 1359–60.

103. Stare decisis, he said, "is a useful principle and based on an essential characteristic of our law, namely, that it is developed not merely for elegance and correctitude but for use in practice. If mistakes have been made, if the correct thing has not always been done, but if the result produced is a sensible one that has established itself in the practice of the law let it be left alone. . . . There is much to be said for leaving such a state of affairs undisturbed; there is nothing at all to be said for overthrowing some parts of it while clinging to others"; *Jones* v. *DPP*, [1962] A.C. 635, 711 (1961).

104. Rupert Cross, "The Criminal Evidence Act, 1898, and the House of Lords as a Court of Criminal Appeal" 407, 414.

105. "The law is what the judges say it is. If the House of Lords were to give to an Act of Parliament a meaning which no one else thought it could reasonably bear, it is their construction of the words used in preference to the words themselves that would become the law"; Devlin, *Samples of Lawmaking* 2.

106. See *The Listener*, 20 Aug. 1964, at 261, on the duty of the judge where the words of a statute are obscure: "The duty of the judge in such a case is simply to find the right meaning. He is not, if there are two or more meanings, given an option to pick the one he likes best. He must give preference to the meaning which he thinks was intended or which would have been intended if the case had been foreseen; and he must ascertain the intention by looking beyond the section he is interpreting to the language and effect of the statute as a whole."

107. *Essex County Council* v. *Essex Inc. Congregational Church Union*, [1963] A.C. 808, 829, especially at 833, 835, on giving a meaning to difficult provisions in an act.

108. [1964] 1 W.L.R. 31 (H.L. 1963).

109. "The legal determination of an agreement does not necessarily mean that the parties have made up their minds forever to abandon the restrictive practices embodied in it. After all, they will have entered into the agreement knowing it to be prohibited unless justifiable under § 21; and so it is not surprising if, when they bring it to an end without waiting to justify it, Parliament wants to look below the surface. Therefore, the Act is designed to put their real intentions to the test"; ibid. 61–62.

while a King's Bench judge, volunteered for the presidency of the Restrictive Practices Court, an institution developed by Kilmuir to make "the law" more relevant, through the administration of flexible standards that made it impossible to draw clear lines between law and policy.[110]

The greatest irony, however, is that during his limited term in the House Devlin was a creative judge in traditional areas of the common law. Except in tax cases,[111] he seldom concurred, but delivered long, reasoned, and lucid speeches that, at least in some cases, Karl Llewellyn would have included under the rubric of the Grand Style. Whether or not one agrees with the directions in which he took it, one can scarcely deny that he did develop the law.[112]

This is clear throughout his decisions. In *Bridge* v. *Campbell Discount Company*,[113] involving a penalty clause in a hire purchase agreement, Devlin cut through to the salient point.[114] He warned businessmen about the dangers of allowing form and practice to diverge too noticeably;[115] he also thought through, with far greater clarity than most, the concept of "loss of expectation of life,"[116] in an effort to prevent its

110. See Robert Stevens and Basil Yamey, *The Restrictive Practices Court.*

111. For a tax decision, see *IRC* v. *Littlewoods Mail Order Stores, Ltd.*, [1963] A.C. 135 (1962).

112. For his view that changes in the law might be obtained by procedural alterations, see *Connelly* v. *DPP*, [1964] A.C. 1254, 1339. See also, *in re K (Infants)*, [1965] A.C. 201, 236 (1963), where he described procedural rules as determined by the "collective wisdom" of the judges; ibid. 237. He continued, "[A] principle of judicial inquiry, whether fundamental or not, is only a means to an end. If it can be shown in any particular class of case that the observance of a principle of this sort does not serve the ends of the justice, it must be dismissed; otherwise it would become the master instead of the servant of justice"; ibid. 238.

113. [1962] A.C. 600, 632.

114. See ibid. 634: "I do not see how an agreement can be genuine for one purpose and a sham for another. If it is a sham, it means that it was never made and does not exist; if it does not exist, it must be ignored altogether; it cannot be a part of Clause 9 when that clause is applied by virtue of Clause 6 or Clause 8 and not a part of it when it is applied by virtue of Clause 7."

115. "I should not wish the House to dictate to commercial men how they should frame their documents, but they must appreciate that in the end disputes have to be determined according to the language used. However liberal a court of law may be in giving effect so far as it can to practice, usage and custom, it is the words in the charterparty that must ultimately determine the issue. The confusion that has been created by the divergence between practice and language appears to me to be now so great as to call for some reconsideration of the terms in which the lay time clause is usually expressed"; *Reardon Smith Line, Ltd.* v. *Ministry of Agriculture, Fisheries and Food*, [1963] A.C. 691, 745.

116. *H. West & Son, Ltd.* v. *Shephard*, [1964] A.C. 326, 353 (1963). In English law, he held, "[t]he elements to be compounded have been called the objective and the subjective. The loss of property element is objective; it requires some sort of valuation that is in no way dependent on the victim's sense of loss. The other element is subjective because it depends entirely on mental suffering actually experienced"; ibid. 355. For Devlin's perceptive observations as to compensation, see ibid. 356–57. ("compensation that is fair and yet not full").

appearing "repugnant to common sense."[117] Moreover, even though the basis of Devlin's speech in *Rookes* v. *Barnard* has been criticized, especially for his alleged hostility to the unions,[118] few have denied the sophistication (or the originality) of his comprehensive "reclassification" of the law on exemplary damages.[119] Examples of Devlin's work in handling common law flexibly abound. He had no qualms about having the torts of conspiracy and intimidation, considerably strengthened by *Rookes* v. *Barnard*, applied uniformly in all areas of society.[120] He clarified the legal and colloquial concepts of innuendo in libel,[121] and in *Hedley Byrne and Company* v. *Heller and Partners, Limited*[122] he helped make the law for an area in which he had already discerned a vacuum that needed to be filled. "The emergence of negligence has divided the law of torts into two parts. One part covers every form of physical injury and makes a coherent whole. The other part continues to deal with all injury that is not physical in the haphazard manner that formerly characterized the whole of the law of torts. . . . This part of the law still awaits a unifying principle."[123] His speech in *Hedley Byrne* was an attempt to provide such a unifying principle for this area of the law, one in line with modern needs. At the beginning he announced the policy he thought the law ought to pursue;[124] he "made it plain" that he would "not in this matter yield to

117. Ibid. 361. He had another attempt at the concept in *Naylor* v. *Yorkshire Elec. Bd.*, [1968] A.C. 529, 547 (1967), where he again probed the basic issue: "The law has endeavoured to avoid two results, both of which it considered to be undesirable. The one is that a wrongdoer should have to pay large sums for disabling and nothing at all for killing; the other is that the large sum appropriate to total disablement should come as a windfall to the beneficiaries of the victim's estate. . . . It would, I think, be a great improvement if this head of damage was abolished and replaced by a short Act of Parliament fixing a suitable sum which a wrongdoer whose act has caused death should pay into the estate of the deceased"; ibid. 550.

118. [1964] A.C. 1129, 1203. See especially his reluctance to pay deference to anything but the actual words of the statute; ibid. 1219.

119. It was, of course, to cause immense problems in *Broome* v. *Cassell & Co.*, [1972] A.C. 1027.

He also drew fascinating new lines. He considered that to draw a line between lawful and unlawful coercion rather than physical and economic coercion was "right, natural and logical" for the "universal purposes of the common law." In the field of industrial disputes "it may be that pragmatically and on grounds of policy the line should be drawn between physical and economic pressure. But that is for Parliament to decide"; ibid. 1220.

120. Ibid. 1218.

121. *Lewis* v. *Daily Telegraph, Ltd.*, [1964] A.C. 234, 277 (1963).

122. [1964] A.C. 465, 514 (1963).

123. Devlin, *Samples of Lawmaking* 8.

124. "[B]efore I examine the authorities, I shall explain why I think that the law, if settled as [counsel for the respondents] Mr. Foster says it is, would be defective. As well as being defective in the sense that it would leave a man without a remedy where he ought to have one and where it is well within the scope of the law to give him one, it would also be

persuasion but only to compulsion."[125] Then, in a speech that appeared to be modeled on and in fact cited Atkin's in *Donoghue* v. *Stevenson*,[126] he went on to find that a duty of care was owed, although effectively disclaimed on the facts.[127]

Enough has been said to suggest that Devlin was a highly complex man and judge. No doubt, as with others, his views underwent change; certainly without such an explanation it would be difficult to comprehend his various claims, which oscillated between those of a substantive formalist and at the other limit gave hints of a Cardozian realism. Perhaps the nearest rationalization of his views came in the Chorley lecture.[128] After carefully and understandably distinguishing the roles of the English and American judges within their respective "constitutions," his concern emerged as a dual one that few would deny—that a dynamic activist judiciary is out of keeping with both the British tradition and reality,[129] and that the opportunity for real lawmaking by the judges occurs in a limited number of cases.[130] In fact, Devlin then admitted that there is "quite a large field for judicial activity"[131] and made what in America would be almost a classic defense of judicial restraint—perhaps allowing greater latitude to the judges in common law matters[132] and a rather

---

profoundly illogical"; *Hedley Byrne & Co.* v. *Heller & Partners, Ltd.*, [1964] A.C. 465, 516 (1963).

125. Ibid. 517.

126. "I should consider the result a grave defect in the law and so contrary to principle that I should hesitate long before following any decision to that effect which had not the authority of this House"; ibid. 516. In examining *Donoghue* v. *Stevenson*, Devlin made clear his feelings about how judges should push forward the boundaries of the law. He repeated Atkin's warning "against the danger of stating propositions of law in wider terms than is necessary, lest essential factors be omitted in a wider survey and the inherent adaptability of English law be unduly restricted"; ibid. 524. He also emphasized the distinction Atkin had drawn between the general concept of proximity and the specific proposition of law formulated by the use of that concept; namely, in the circumstances of *Donoghue* v. *Stevenson*, the liability of a manufacturer to an ultimate consumer. To attempt to extend the law by talking in terms of proximity, Devlin explained, was "a misuse of a general conception and it is not the way in which English law develops"; ibid. The general conception is used "to open up a category of cases giving rise to a special duty.... What *Donoghue* v. *Stevenson* did may be described either as the widening of an old category or as the creation of a new and similar one. The general conception can be used to produce other categories in the same way. An existing category grows as instances of its application multiply, until the time comes when the cell divides"; ibid. 524–25.

127. Devlin approved the disclaimer on the ground that responsibility could attach "only if the doing of [the] act implied a voluntary undertaking to assume responsibility"; ibid. 529.

128. Patrick Devlin, "Judges and Lawmakers" 1.

129. E.g., ibid. 1–2, 5–6.

130. Although he conceded that the opportunity existed "most of the time" in the House of Lords; ibid. 4.

131. Ibid. 8.

132. Devlin, for instance, would have been happy to see common employment or the fellow servant rule reversed by judicial fiat; ibid. 13. This is something that State Supreme

narrow role in statutory interpretation.[133] If such a philosophy is a settled one, then one may speculate that Devlin, in his own way, was a casualty of substantive formalism. The intellectual shallowness and practical frustrations of that approach led to equally irrational outbursts against it. These reactions both irritated Devlin[134] and apparently contributed to his own schizophrenic view of the appellate process. If he had been sitting during the mid-seventies, when both sides have moderated their rhetoric, his would have been a commanding voice.

In short, Devlin was one of the most powerful minds to sit on the appellate bench in the post-1945 period. Within the narrow confines delegated by the British Constitution to the judges, Devlin was a masterful operator. On occasion, an intellectual advocate of a populist tradition that would make judges eunuchs, Devlin in fact "developed" the common law with grace and elegance. Yet he was a mystical figure. He seemed unable to produce a satisfactory philosophy of the judicial process until long after he retired. Despite the reserve surrounding the English judiciary, he managed to convey a feeling of being bored both as a High Court judge and as a law lord. Taxation, the staple diet of the final appeal event, was clearly not to his taste, and his dispute with Sir Reginald Manningham-Buller (Lord Dilhorne) over the Nyasaland Report provided, it is said, the excuse for his retirement. Yet, waspish barbs from the sidelines[135] were a poor substitute for the serious work of a law lord at a

---

Courts in the United States have felt unable to do. See Fowler V. Harper and James Fleming, Jr., *The Law of Torts*, § 22.11. Only in Illinois has the Supreme Court considered whether such a fundamental change in the law might be made by the judiciary, ultimately concluding that such a fundamental change in the law belonged to the legislature; *Maki v. Frelk*, 85 Ill. App. 2d 439, 229, N.E.2d 248 (1967). On this see William L. Prosser, *Handbook of the Law of Torts* 434.

133. Devlin, "Judges and Lawmakers" 13–16.

134. "There are progressives who like moths outside a lighted window are irresistibly attracted by what they see within as the vast unused potential of judicial lawmaking. They would surmount the obstacle of a reactionary judiciary by reconstructing it"; ibid. 7.

135. Devlin, on his retirement, took over the Chairmanship of the Press Council. When he retired from that position, *The Times*, in an editorial, claimed that that body had "grown in authority" under Devlin; "A Just Chairman," *The Times*, 15 Jan. 1969.

Devlin also took a prominent part in Justice, the English branch of the International Commission of Jurists. In this role he attacked the judges for taking up the cause of law and order. "It is quite wrong for the judiciary to think they are responsible for the moral health of the community in some way. . . . I am not even sure judges are regarded by the country in general as being . . . wholly independent." He reaffirmed his view that the law must follow changes in morals and customs. "It is for the legislature to decide when the time has come to consolidate new ideas into the consensus and likewise expel the old." The judiciary must be "impartial narrators of what the law is saying"; *The Times*, 28 June 1972.

In a broadcast, Devlin tilted at other sacred cows, notably the adversary system and the insistence on oral evidence, both of which added to the heavy cost of litigation. He took the view that there could be no worthwhile saving in cost "so long as we accept it as the inalienable right of every litigant to have the whole of his evidence and argument presented by word of mouth"; *The Times*, Nov. 1968, at 8.

time when the House was emerging from the damaging implications of the period of substantive formalism.[136]

Lord Reid

If Devlin tended to fight the battles of the judicial process from the sidelines, Reid[137] was in the center of the battle; yet, in so many ways he was the exemplar of Devlin's "craftsman." In the period between 1948 and the end of 1974, and especially after he became the senior Lord of Appeal in 1962, Reid was the most influential judge in the House of Lords.[138] Whether the issue was one of common law or statute, Reid's judgment was almost invariably the most sophisticated treatment and the one that commanded the most respect. As a Scottish lawyer he brought to the common law a sense of principle and breadth[139] generally lacked by those who dominated the House when he arrived. Although he was comfortable putting the bulk of his effort into his judicial work rather than into extrajudicial public service,[140] as a former politician he had an innate sense of the relationship of the legislature and the courts—something often denied to more "courageous or timorous" souls.[141]

Again, no doubt as a result of his Scottish background, Reid was largely unconcerned about the inevitability of the contribution the House had to make to the development of both common law and statute law.[142]

In 1974 he completed a book on President Woodrow Wilson, *Too Proud to Fight*. In 1976, his report on identification parades was published; *Report of the Departmental Committee on Evidence of Identification in Criminal Cases*, House of Commons Paper, 338 (1976).

136. After his retirement he sat in three cases in the Lords, although he made some "notable appearances" in the Privy Council; Blom-Cooper and Drewry, *Final Appeal* 182.

137. James Scott Cumberland Reid; b. 1890; father, farmer; educ., Edinburgh Academy and Jesus College, Cambridge (First, Law); called to Scottish Bar, 1914; M.P. (Unionist) Sterling and Falkirk, 1931–35, Millhead (Glasgow), 1937–48; Solicitor-General for Scotland, 1936–41; Lord Advocate, 1941–44; Dean of Faculty of Advocates, 1945–48; Lord of Appeal, 1948–74; d. 1975.

138. There was some thought that he might become Lord Chancellor when the Conservatives were returned in 1951—on the assumption that that office may be held by a Scottish judge. As Simon of Glaisdale, a former Conservative Solicitor-General noted, however, by 1951 Reid "had hardly . . . had sufficient opportunity to demonstrate fully the formidable juristic powers which have contributed so notably to the development of the law in the last two decades"; Jocelyn Simon, "Review" 289, 294.

139. For one of his last restatements of the view that principles not rules underlie law, see *R. v. Smith*, [1975] A.C. 476, 500 (1973).

140. Although he did serve as Chairman of the Malayan Constitutional Commission in 1956–57, he spoke in legislative debates on average less than twice a year; Blom-Cooper and Drewry, *Final Appeal* 205.

141. Reid believed there should be more former politicians serving as Lords of Appeal. "They know how the machinery of government works and are able to understand better issues concerning the administration"; Marcel Berlins, "The One Judge We Will Really Miss," *The Times*, 14 Jan. 1975.

142. "The law is what the judge says it is. Before a point of law has been decided in

Since he took the position that "the purpose of an appeal to the House of Lords is not so much to benefit the parties to a dispute but to clarify the law as a matter of public importance,"[143] he felt that all appeals to the Lords should be paid out of public funds. For the same reason he welcomed the advent of legal aid to the Lords and thought that the increase in the number of criminal appeals had had a good effect on that branch of the law, since the House had had an opportunity to restate various doctrines.[144]

Reid was neither an unthinking Realist nor an advocate of some blind orgy of judicial lawmaking. With respect to the common law his philosophy was simple:[145]

I suppose that almost every doctrine of the common law was invented by some judge at some period in history, and when he invented it he thought it was plain common sense—and indeed it generally was originally. But, with the passage of time more technically minded judges have forgotten its origin and developed it in a way that can easily cause injustice. In so far as we appellate judges can get the thing back on the rails let us do so; if it has gone too far we must pin our hopes on Parliament.[146]

Reid was well aware that the relative functions of the courts and Parliament would have to vary in different areas.[147] "When we are dealing

---

court, counsel must be guarded in advising his client. But after a decision he will rely on it for the answer—perhaps with a note of caution that a higher court may reach a different decision. . . .

"There was a time when it was thought almost indecent to suggest that judges make law—they only declare it. Those with a taste for fairy tales seem to have thought that in some Aladdin's cave, there is hidden the Common Law in all its splendour and that on a judge's appointment there descends on him knowledge of the magic words Open Sesame. Bad decisions are given when a judge muddles the pass word and the wrong door opens. But we do not believe in fairy tales anymore.

"So we must accept the fact that for better or for worse judges do make law, and tackle the question how do they approach this task and how should they approach it"; James S. C. Reid, "The Judge as Law Maker" 22.

143. Berlins, "One Judge We Will Really Miss," *The Times*, 14 Jan. 1975.

144. This was one of the reasons that he felt uncomfortable with the "leapfrog" process. See debates on the Administration of Justice Bill of 1968.

145. "Unlike most supreme tribunals this House holds itself bound by its own previous decisions. . . . I have on more than one occasion stated my view that this rule is too rigid and that it does not in fact create certainty. . . . But I am bound by the rule until it is altered.

"But I can find no invariable practice with regard to *rationes decidendi*. . . .

"I would certainly not lightly disregard a departure from any *ratio decidendi* of this House. But there are at least three classes of cases where I think we are entitled to question or limit it: first, where it is obscure, secondly where the decision itself is out of line with other authorities of established principles, and thirdly, where it is much wider than was necessary for the decision so that it becomes a question of how far it is proper to distinguish the earlier decision"; *Midland Silicones, Ltd. v. Scruttons, Ltd.*, [1962] A.C. 446, 475–77 (1961).

146. James S. C. Reid, "The Law and the Reasonable Man" 193, 194–95.

147. "I think we must treat different branches of the law in different ways"; ibid. 193. In some regards, the Reid view of judicial creativity was the antithesis of Radcliffe's:

with property and contract it seems right that we should accept some degree of possible injustice in order to achieve a fairly high degree of certainty."[148] But he saw no such underlying policy when it came to tort.[149] Criminal law, on the other hand, was not to be extended by the judges, although they might remain guardians of the requirement of mens rea. Yet, subject to these reservations, Reid had no doubt that lawyers' law—by which he meant the basic areas of common law delegated to the judiciary—was best developed by the final appeal court. "If you think in months, want an instant solution for your problems and don't mind that it won't wear well, then go for legislation. If you think in decades, prefer orderly growth and believe in the old proverb more haste less speed, then stick to the common law. But do not seek a middle way by speeding up and streamlining the development of the common law."[150]

Unlike many appeal judges, Reid, toward the end of his life, clarified his theory of the criteria for judicial development of the law. First, the direction in which the law should be developed was to be tested by the criterion of common sense, something that was "not static," but that prevented "technically minded judges [from pressing] precedents to their logical conclusions."[151] Common sense appeared to serve Reid as a humanist substitute for the Christian base on which Radcliffe and Denning ultimately purported to rely.[152] Second, the new law had to take into account principle, although not narrow, notions of precedent.[153] "Rigid

---

Whatever views may have prevailed in the last century, I think it is now widely recognised that it is proper for the courts in appropriate cases to develop or adopt existing rules of the common law to meet new conditions. . . . [W]e ought to recognise a difference between cases [of] "lawyer's law" and cases . . . dealing with matters which directly affect the lives and interests of large sections of the community and which raise issues . . . on which laymen are as well able to decide as are lawyers. On such matters it is not for the courts to proceed on their view of public policy, for that would be to encroach on the province of Parliament. [*Pettitt* v. *Pettitt*, [1970] A.C. 777, 794–95 (1969)]

148. Reid, "The Law and The Reasonable Man" 197. Even here, however, Reid had thought out judicial strategies. "Yet, we must even tackle the problem of standard printed conditions. The big man may be able to insist on making his own bargain but the small man cannot—he must take it or leave it. And, I have no ready-made solution to offer you. Can we in the next few years devise a principle or method whereby unfair contracts can be modified without at the same time opening the flood-gates of litigation?" Ibid. 196.

149. "A man knows quite well that what he intends to do may injure his neighbour; he may even intend such injury. Would the law be defective if his lawyer could not tell him with the same degree of certainty just how far he can go without having to pay damages?" Ibid. 197.

150. "Judge as Law Maker" 28.

151. Ibid. 25–26.

152. See, for instance, his Holmesian position in one of his last decisions. "I would not, however, decide the matter entirely on logical argument. The life blood of the law has not been logic but common sense." He went on to reject an argument because "[t]he law may be an ass but it cannot be so asinine as that"; *R. v. Smith*, [1975] A.C. 476, 500 (1973).

153. "We have to avoid, on the one hand, the rock Scylla where sits the austere figure of Austin and on the other the whirlpool Charybdis where some modern theorists for ever

adherence to precedent will not do. And paying lip service to precedent while admitting fine distinctions gives us the worst of both worlds. On the other hand, too much flexibility leads to intolerable uncertainty."[154] Finally, judicial developments in the law had to be tested against public policy. While avoiding those cases where public opinion was sharply divided—to be left to Parliament[155]— judges should no longer be afraid of public policy. "So long as the powers that be can see to it that the new race of judges are not mere technicians, but are men of the world as well, we can—indeed, we must—trust them to acquaint themselves with public policy and apply it in a reasonable way to such new problems as will arise from time to time."[156] Indeed, by the end of his judicial career, Reid was a master of the art of balancing the conflicting policy goals involved in the decisions of the House.[157]

Yet, from the earliest part of his career he refused to be a slave to precedent.[158] He was committed to the idea that "[t]he common law ought never to produce a wholly unreasonable result, nor ought existing authorities to be read so literally as to produce such a result in circumstances never contemplated when they were decided."[159] The same attitude characterized his approach when he found little authority. "To my mind the best way of approaching this question is to consider the consequences of a decision in either sense. The circumstances are such that no decision can avoid creating some possible hard cases, but if a decision in one sense will on the whole lead to much more just and reasonable results, that appears to me to be a strong argument in its favour."[160]

It was this sense of the realities of the judicial process that led Reid

---

go round in circles. But we must get rid of the idea which still seems to animate some of our pedestrian confreres, that law is a congeries of unrelated rules. That results in the dreary argument that the case is similar to A v. B and C v. D but is distinguished from X v. Y and *in re* Z. That way lies confusion and uncertainty. We must try to see what was the principle or reason why A v. B should go one way and X v. Y the other"; "Judge as Law Maker" 26.

154. Ibid.

155. Ibid. 23.

156. Ibid. 27.

157. See, for instance, F. *Hoffman-LaRoche & Co. A.G. v. Secretary of State for Trade & Indus.*, [1975] A.C. 295 (1973), where Reid articulated the conflicting goals of drug manufacturers and society and then attempted to balance the interests. He concluded that process by deciding that tradition and balancing required that an interim injunction be granted, but without the Crown's giving an undertaking on damages, adding, "[I]f I thought that the appellants had a strong case on the merits I would try to stretch a point in their favour to protect them from obvious injustice though I would find difficulty in doing so"; ibid. 342.

158. See, for instance, his dissent in *London Graving Dock Co. v. Horton*, [1951] A.C. 737, 786: "I have come to the conclusion that to hold there was such a duty would infringe no principle and would conflict with no binding or well-recognised authority."

159. *Cartledge v. E. Jopling & Sons*, [1963] A.C. 758, 772.

160. *Starkowaski v. Attorney-General*, [1954] A.C. 155, 170 (1953).

to be more skeptical than others about some of the reforms suggested during the 1960s. He had doubts about the value of the Law Commission and especially about Gardiner's commitment to codify the law.[161] Reid did not share the view, which appealed to both Simonds and Gardiner in different ways, that strict deference to precedent and careful drawing of narrow rules ensured certainty in the law. Indeed, Reid thought that rigid rules, as opposed to principles, might have precisely the opposite effect.[162] The aim of an effective final appeal court was to strike a balance between rigidity and flexibility,[163] based on the type of problem being faced.

In the light of this background, Reid was less interested in and less influenced by the 1966 Practice Statement than some expected.[164] He had, on the one hand, never felt as constrained as others, nor was he as convinced as some of the direct value of overruling cases, although he conceded that "[o]n balance, it seems to me that overriding such a deci-

161. "Personally, I am no believer in codes. I believe that the Common Law method is better." He took the view that the House ought to be discussing "how do we develop the law as a matter of legal principle"; 258 *Parl. Deb.*, H.L. (5th ser.), cols. 1066–67 (11 June 1964). "[I]t is dangerous to represent to people that they can easily understand the law in its new guise. They will get into trouble. . . . But, I am not going to oppose experiments. I belong to the school of thought which believes that an ounce of fact is better than a ton of theory"; 264 ibid., cols. 1196–97 (1 Apr. 1965).

162. See especially his dissent in *London Graving Dock Co.* v. *Horton*, [1951] A.C. 737, 785: [T]his case will decide whether an invitor's duty is determined by a rule, which seems to me to have no foundation in principle, that he can, while continuing to hold out an invitation, always relieve himself of his duty to take care by giving notice. I do not deny that fixed rules have advantages: cases can be more readily decided and people interested can perhaps forecast more accurately what the decision will be in any case. But in the realm of negligence, at least, rigid rules give rise to what I believe to be avoidable injustice. I see no reason to depart unnecesarily from the simple method of asking in any case what would a reasonable man in the shoes of the defendant have done.

163. In *Gollins* v. *Gollins*, [1964] A.C. 644, 660 (1963), he drew a subtle distinction between the need "to reduce tests, rules and presumptions to a minimum," and the danger of leaving the matter "at large," for that puts "too great a burden on the trial judge and . . . [is] likely to lead to a multitude of appeals."

164. He was, on the other hand, much in favor of allowing dissents in the Privy Council. He felt that one-judge decisions both gave a false air of certainty and prevented development of the law; Reid, "Judge as Law Maker" 29. See also his explanation in *Broome* v. *Cassell & Co.*, [1972] A.C. 1027, 1085:

My main reason is that experience has shown that those who have to apply the decision [*Rookes v. Barnard*] to other cases and still more those who wish to criticise it seem to find it difficult to avoid treating sentences and phrases in a particular speech as if they were provisions in an Act of Parliament. They do not seem to realise that it is not the function of noble and learned Lords or indeed of any judges to frame definitions or lay down hard and fast rules. It is their function to enunciate principles and much that they say is intended to be illustrative or explanatory and not to be definitive. When there are two or more speeches they must be read together and then it is generally much easier to see what are the principles involved and what are merely illustrations of it.

For similar warnings about treating earlier statements as if they were statutory rules, see *Strick* v. *Regent Oil Co.*, [1966] A.C. 295, 313 (1964).

sion will promote and not impair certainty of the law."[165] Reid remained, however, to the end a little cautious about directly upsetting stare decisis unless it was absolutely essential.[166]

In part this hesitancy no doubt reflected Reid's sense of balance, which guided not only the scope of judicial lawmaking as such, but also the relationship between the appellate judiciary and the lawmaking role of Parliament. Reid had no doubt that, at a certain point, either because of the strength of the earlier precedent or because of the subject matter of the appeal, radical change was the province of Parliament. Thus, in *Cartledge v. E. Jopling and Sons, Limited*, where the plaintiff did not discover he had pneumoconiosis until the limitation period had expired, so that Reid felt obliged to dismiss the appeal, he announced that "some amendment of the law is urgently necessary";[167] Parliament obliged almost at once.[168] So too, in holding that car manufacturers' records of cylinder block registration numbers were inadmissible under the hearsay rule in *Myers v. Director of Public Prosecutions* Reid announced, "[W]e cannot introduce arbitrary conditions or limitations; that must be left to legislation."[169] In Reid's view judicial legislation should be limited to "the development and application of fundamental principles."[170] While both

165. *Jones v. Secretary of State for Social Servs.*, [1972] A.C. 944, 966 (1971). He had, however, expressed support for the change:

There are in the Commonwealth a number of courts which have the power to re-examine their past decisions. . . . I would only instance the Court of Session in Scotland with which I am most familiar. I have never noticed any ill effects from the fact that the Court has that power; nor do I think anyone could say that there has been any tendency to use it too freely. Of course, the justification for the present rule is that it is supposed to lead to certainty in the law—a most desirable thing, if one can achieve it. But a good deal could be said to the effect that it has exactly the contrary effect. There is, indeed, some evidence of that in the Report of the Law Reform Committee. Possibly the classical example is that of the law of Workmen's Compensation, and it would hardly be too much to say, with regard to that branch of the law, that as decisions become more numerous, so the law becomes more uncertain. [203 *Parl. Deb.*, H.L. (5th ser.), col. 262 (2 May 1957)]

166. See, for instance, *Herrington v. British Rys. Bd.*, [1972] A.C. 877, 892; *Broome v. Cassell & Co.*, [1972] A.C. 1027, 1083; *Knuller (Publishing Printing and Promotions), Ltd. v. DPP*, [1973] A.C. 435, 454 (1972).

167. [1963] A.C. 758, 773.

168. Limitation Act of 1963. On this incident, see Blom-Cooper and Drewry, *Final Appeal* 361.

169. [1965] A.C. 1001, 1021 (1964). See Blom-Cooper and Drewry, *Final Appeal* 362. Reid's position was attacked by Jaffé; Louis L. Jaffé, *English and American Judges as Lawmakers* 28–29. In fairness it should be noted that Parliament responded to Reid's plea by passing the Criminal Evidence Act of 1965.

170. *Myers v. DPP*, [1965] A.C. 1001, 1021–22 (1964):

I have never taken a narrow view of the function of this House as an appellate tribunal. The common law must be developed to meet changing economic conditions and habits of thought, and I would not be deterred by expressions of opinion in this House in old cases. But there are limits to what we can or should do. If we are to extend the law it must be by the development and application of fundamental principles. We cannot introduce arbitrary conditions or limitations: that must be left to legislation. And if we do in effect change the law, we ought, in my opinion, only to do that in cases where our decision

of these cases were decided before the 1966 Practice Statement, the approach he exhibited in them probably continued to reflect his basic approach.[171]

Certainly Reid had a more developed sense than the other law lords about areas where it was inappropriate for the judiciary to legislate even interstitially. In the *Shaw* case, where Simonds led the attack to reactivate and extend the concept of criminal conspiracy, Reid countered:

> Even if there is still a vestigial power of this kind it ought not, in my view, to be used unless there appears to be general agreement that the offence to which it is applied ought to be criminal if committed by an individual. Notoriously, there are wide differences of opinion today as to how far the law ought to punish immoral acts which are not done in the face of the public. Some think the law already goes too far, some that it does not go far enough. Parliament is the proper place, and I am firmly of the opinion the only proper place, to settle that. When there is sufficient support from public opinion, Parliament does not hesitate to intervene. Where Parliament fears to tread it is not for the courts to rush in.[172]

Courts might conclude that Parliament had misunderstood the law;[173] they were not free to question Parliament directly.[174]

---

will produce some finality or certainty. If we disregard technicalities in this case and seek to apply principle and common sense, there are a number of other parts of the existing law of hearsay susceptible of similar treatment, and we shall probably have a series of appeals in cases where the existing technical limitations produce an unjust result. If we are to give a wide interpretation to our judicial functions, questions of policy cannot be wholly excluded, and it seems to me to be against public policy to produce uncertainty. The only satisfactory solution is by legislation following on a wide survey of the whole field, and I think that such a survey is overdue. A policy of make-do and mend is no longer adequate. The most powerful argument of those who support the strict doctrine of precedent is that if it is relaxed judges will be tempted to encroach on the proper field of the legislature, and this in my opinion offers a strong temptation to do that which ought to be resisted.

In criminal law, Reid maintained this distance. See, for instance, *R. v. Smith*, [1975] A.C. 476, 500 (1973): "The accused in the present case may be as deserving of punishment as he would have been if the goods had still been stolen goods. But such a radical change in the principles of our law should not be introduced in this way even if it were desirable."

171. The approach remained a "balanced" one. See, for instance, his reactions in *Broome* v. *Cassell & Co.* on the issue of penal damages: "[F]ull argument . . . has convinced me that I and my colleagues made a mistake in concurring with Lord Devlin's speech in *Rookes* v. *Barnard*"; [1972] A.C. 1027, 1084.

172. *Shaw* v. *DPP*, [1962] A.C. 220, 275 (1961).

173. E.g., *West Midland Baptist Trust Ass'n* v. *Birmingham Corp.*, [1970] A.C. 874, 898 (1969).

174. In *British Rys. Bd.* v. *Pickin*, [1974] A.C. 765, the House was invited to disregard a private act of Parliament, on the ground that the act had been obtained by fraud. Reid announced:

The function of the court is to construe and apply the enactments of Parliament. The court has no concern with the manner in which Parliament or its officers carrying out its Standing Orders perform these functions. Any attempt to prove that they were ruled by fraud or otherwise would necessarily involve an inquiry into the manner in which they had performed their functions on dealing with the Bill which became the British Railways Act 1968. . . .

For a century or more both Parliament and the Courts have been careful not to act so as to cause conflict between them. Any such investigations as the respondent could easily lead to such a conflict, and I would only support it if compelled to do so by clear authority. But it appears to me that the whole trend of authority for over a century is clearly against permitting such an investigation. [Ibid. 787–88]

This position in no sense meant that the courts were to treat the construction and interpretation of statutes as a mechanical process.[175] Reid believed that rules of construction "are not rules in the ordinary sense of having some binding force . . . we must look at all the relevant circumstances."[176] Thus, Reid would look to the trimmings of legislation —the long title,[177] the side-notes and the cross-headings.[178] This Reid justified on the ground that, in many cases, the provisions to be construed had not been discussed in either Commons or Lords.[179] Yet, even though he was prepared to look to the "mischief which it [the act] must have been intended to remedy," he, in general, refused to go so far as to look at Hansard or at the reports of the committees.[180]

Perhaps the most important aspect of Reid's approach to statutes, however, was his sense of realism based on the inevitability of uncertainty both linguistically[181] and politically. He put it perhaps most strongly in a tax case, *Greenberg* v. *Inland Revenue Commissioners*, interpreting section 28 of the Finance Act of 1960:

175. E.g., *Associated Newspaper, Ltd.* v. *Registrar of Restrictive Trading Agreements*, [1964] 1 W.L.R. 31 (H.L. 1963). See also Robert Stevens, "Statutory Interpretation, Restrictive Practices and the 'New' House of Lords" 337.

176. *Maunsell* v. *Olins*, [1975] A.C. 373, 382 (1974).

177. *British Oxygen Co.* v. *Board of Trade*, [1971] A.C. 610, 621 (1970). On this general approach see also *Chertsey UDC* v. *Mixnam's Properties, Ltd.*, [1965] A.C. 735, 746 (1964).

178. *R.* v. *Schildkamp*, [1971] A.C. 1, 10 (1970).

179. "[I]t may be more realistic to accept the Act as printed as being the product of the whole legislative process, and to give due weight to everything found in the printed Act. I say more realistic because in very many cases the provision before the court was never even mentioned in debate in either House, and it may be that its wording was never closely scrutinised by any member of either House. In such a case it is not very meaningful to say that the words of the Act represent the intention of Parliament but that punctuation, cross-headings and side-notes do not.

"So, if the authorities are equivocal and one is free to deal with the whole matter, I would not object to taking all these matters into account, provided that we realise that they cannot have equal weight with the words of the Act"; ibid. 10.

180. *Smith* v. *Central Asbestos Co.*, [1973] A.C. 518, 529 (1972).

[I]t would be misleading to look at their recommendations without also looking at *Hansard* to see how the problem was presented to Parliament. I have on more than one occasion stated the grave practical difficulties of doing that. Not only would it substantially increase the work of counsel and therefore the cost to litigants but in many cases it would be impracticable to obtain access to reports of the committee stage in Select Committees of the House of Commons where useful material would be most likely to be found. [Ibid. 529–30]

However, in *R.* v. *Warner*, [1969] 2 A.C. 256, 279 (1968), Reid suggested there might be exceptions to the general rule "where examining the proceedings in Parliament would almost certainly settle the matter immediately one way or the other."

181. "I blame not so much the individual draftsman as the modern involved style of drafting. If only lawyers would realize that no language is a precision tool and that short simple sentences, though they may look less precise, are really much more likely to have a clear meaning than the kind of jargon which is now fashionable . . ."; Reid, "Judge as Law Maker" 28. See also *Hartnell* v. *Minister of Housing & Local Gov't*, [1965] A.C. 1134, 1153; *Rosenbaum* v. *Burgoyne*, [1965] A.C. 430, 439 (1964).

I am inclined to think that the real explanation of these verbal difficulties may be that, in legislation of such extreme complexity as we have here, it is not humanly possible for a draftsman to preserve that consistency in the use of language which we generally look for. Indeed, I sometimes suspect that our normal meticulous methods of statutory construction tend to lead us astray by concentrating too much on verbal niceties and paying too little attention to the provisions read as a whole.[182]

Reid had come a long way from his earliest position to *Greenberg*, in which he noted, with respect to the broad tax avoidance provision in issue, that if the House did not interpret such provisions broadly, Parliament would enact something more sweeping that would catch "the ordinary well-intentioned person."[183] In 1949 Reid's approach to tax cases, both in terms of presumption and attitude, were barely distinguishable from Normand's or Simonds'.[184] Slowly, however, Reid began approaching cases, not with the presumption that tax legislation was penal legislation to be construed narrowly, but on the assumption that it was neutral legislation.[185] Moreover, before long, he was publicly considering the reasons that the House found its diet of tax cases tasteless,[186] and he sought to make it more palatable by making the approach more balanced.

In a series of decisions Reid interpreted various tax avoidance legislation in favor of the Revenue and so brought tax law back toward the via media.[187] He vigorously dissented in *Griffiths v. J. P. Harison, Limited*,[188] where Simonds and the majority, flouting the will of the legislature, invited the dividend stripper to continue his activities. Reid had no doubt that, in such circumstances, the courts might look to the substance of the transaction.[189] In his efforts to balance the equities, Reid sometimes found

182. *Greenberg v. IRC*, [1972] A.C. 109, 138 (1971). Where criminal law was concerned, he stated the scope of the courts' work more narrowly; *Jones v. DPP*, [1962] A.C. 635, 622 (1961).

183. [1972] A.C. 109, 137 (1971).

184. E.g., *IRC v. John Dow Stuart, Ltd.*, [1950] A.C. 149, 183 (Scot. 1949):

[T]he fact that a word is ambiguous does not entitle a court to select another meaning which it is plain that no reasonable man could have intended. . . . It might be that an equitable result or even a reasonable result could only be reached by attributing to a phrase in a statute a meaning which no reasonable man would attach to it. But to attribute such a meaning to a phrase would in effect be legislating and not construing the statute and it is beyond the province of a court of law. If by processes of construction no meaning can be found which is equitable or even reasonable then the matter can only be put right by further legislation.

185. This was beginning to be clear by the time of *IRC v. Dowdall, O'Mahoney & Co.*, [1952] A.C. 401, 410 (1951).

186. *Nash v. Tamplin & Sons Brewery, Ltd.*, [1952] A.C. 231, 250 (1951).

187. E.g., *Countess of Kenmare v. IRC*, [1958] A.C. 267, 293 (1957), where Reid gave a broad reading to the antiavoidance provision [§ 38(2) of the 1938 Finance Act], finding that surtax directions might apply to settlements without overseas trustees. See also *Jamieson v. IRC*, [1964] A.C. 1445, 1461 (1963).

188. [1963] A.C. 1, 12 (1962).

189. E.g., ibid. 13.

himself in the position of giving decisions that were harsh toward tax-payers,[190] but on some occasions the taxpayer received a somewhat unexpected benefit,[191] normally accompanied by a Reid appeal for amending legislation.[192] Yet, even these barriers seemed to crumble after section 28 passed in 1960. Reid increasingly gave the impression that the House in its judicial and parliamentary capacities had complementary responsibilities.[193] Moreover, by being by far the most prolific law lord in the field, Reid ensured that his would be the dominant approach.[194]

One would, of course, expect some evolution of thought over time, and in most areas Reid demonstrated a sense of open-mindedness that made change possible during his tenure of more than twenty-five years as a Lord of Appeal. For example, Reid was among those, in Factories Act cases, refusing to concede that the fencing requirements of section 14 were intended to do any more than keep the workman out, with the result that flying objects from the machines were not included in the prohibition. In *Sparrow* v. *Fairey Aviation Company*,[195] although he regretted the earlier decisions, he felt that he was not in a position to depart from them,[196]

190. E.g., *IRC* v. *Bates*, [1968] A.C. 483, 501 (1966). In such circumstances, Reid normally called for amending legislation. See ibid. 508.

191. In *in re Pilkington Will Trusts*, [1964] A.C. 612 (1962), the House in deciding that the power of advancement given by § 32 of the Trustee Act of 1925, could be exercised for the purpose of saving estate duty and surtax by means of a resettlement once more opened up a path to tax avoidance. Reid was reluctant to do this but was even more reluctant to legislate. "[I]f it is thought that the power which Parliament has conferred is likely to be used in ways of which Parliament does not approve then it is for Parliament to devise appropriate restrictions of the power"; ibid. 629–30. See also the ad valorem loophole exposed in *Wm. Cory & Son* v. *IRC*, [1965] A.C. 1088.

192. Reid justified this because "[s]o long as one adheres to the natural meaning of the charging words the law is certain, or at least as certain as it is possible to make it. But if courts are to give to charging words what is sometimes called a liberal construction, who can say just how far this will go. It is much better that evasion should be met by amending legislation. One is familiar with this in the realm of income tax, and if the ingenuity of taxpayers' advisers is now turning to the Stamp Act no doubt that in time will be met in the same way"; *Wm. Cory & Son* v. *IRC*, [1965] A.C. 1088, 1107. The decision was in fact nullified by the Finance Act of 1965, § 90.

193. "We seem to have travelled a long way from the general and salutary rule that a subject is not to be taxed except by plain words. But I must recognize that plain words are seldom adequate to anticipate and forestall the multiplicity of ingenious schemes which are constantly being devised to evade taxation. Parliament is very properly determined to prevent this kind of tax evasion and, if the courts find it impossible to give very wide meanings to general phrases, the only alternative may be for Parliament to do as some other countries have done, and introduce legislation of a more sweeping character which will put the ordinary well-intentioned person at much greater risk than is created by a wide interpretation of such provisions or those which we are now considering"; *Greenberg* v. *IRC*, [1972] A.C. 109, 137 (1971).

194. Between 1952 and 1970 there were 133 revenue appeals and 23 rating appeals. Reid delivered speeches in over half the cases (66 majority opinions and 8 dissents); Blom-Cooper and Drewry, *Final Appeal* 322.

195. [1964] A.C. 1019 (1962).

196. The *Close* decision, [1962] A.C. 367 (1961), he held, "must be treated as a

meanwhile legislatively chastising those who arrogated this freedom to themselves.[197] Considerable evidence indicates that by the mid-sixties, however, he was working judicially to undermine the rigidity of the earlier decisions.[198] Again then Reid tried to see that the Lords held a balanced view. On the one hand employers were not allowed to rely on the fact that other firms did not take precautions to prevent foreseeable accidents;[199] on the other, workmen could not be expected readily to prove that industry-wide precautions were inadequate. Similarly, Reid sought to balance the compensatory aspects of the Factories Acts with the safety aspects,[200] frequently showing more subtlety than the legislation in weighing

---

positive decision that the only duty under the statute is to fence against contact of the worker with dangerous parts of a machine"; ibid. 1033. "It is too late to question the rule which this House laid down in *Close's* case, and we must do our best to apply it in a practical way"; ibid. 1034.

197. In discussing the *Fairey* case later, he said that he did not withdraw any of his observations there. He also took the view that Denning, who had dissented in *Close*, ought to have been constrained in this case to follow *Nicholls* v. *F. Austin, Ltd.*, [1946] A.C. 493. "I have said more than once that I should be happy to see a modification of that very strict rule, but unlike my noble and learned friend, I take the view that so long as a rule lasts we ought to obey it"; 248 *Parl. Deb.*, H.L. (5th ser.), cols. 1337–38 (25 Apr. 1963).

198. E.g., *Midland & Low Moor Iron & Steel Co.* v. *Cross*, [1965] A.C. 343, 363 (1964): "The purpose of this legislation is to promote the safety of workmen when they are at work and I would find it very surprising if the Act requires us to disregard dangers which arise out of the ordinary working of the machine, and only to have regard to dangers which can arise when the machine is running light before normal working begins." See also *John G. Stein & Co.* v. *O'Hanlon*, [1965] A.C. 890, 902 (Scot.). There, Reid insisted that a manager must take one or other of the steps required in the regulations and not merely provide a method that he thought best. "[T]hat ... would make evasion of the statute easy"; ibid. 905. See also *Imperial Chem. Indus., Ltd.* v. *Shatwell*, [1965] A.C. 656, 670 (1964); *Donaghey* v. *Boulton & Paul, Ltd.*, [1968] A.C. 1 (1967) and *British Rys. Bd.* v. *Liptrot*, [1969] 1 A.C. 136, 156 (1967); *J. & F. Stone Lighting & Radio, Ltd.* v. *Haygarth*, [1968] A.C. 157, 170 (1966); and *Nimmo* v. *Alexander Cowan & Sons*, [1968] A.C. 107, (Scot. 1967).

199. E.g., *Morris* v. *West Hartlepool Steam Navigation Co.*, [1956] A.C. 552, 574 (1955).

200. See, e.g., *Grant* v. *National Coal Bd.*, [1956] A.C. 649, 660–62 (Scot.); *Brown* v. *National Coal Bd.*, [1962] A.C. 574, 587 (1961): "[T]he primary purpose of these provisions is to prevent accidents rather than to deal with compensation to those who receive injuries, and it does not at all follow that the effect of the new provisions will be to leave untouched all the old methods of obtaining compensation or damages. So I must examine the new section with at most an inclination to seek a meaning which would preserve the old remedies." See also *Nimmo* v. *Alexander Cowan & Sons*, [1968] A.C. 107, 113 (Scot. 1967), emphasizing the criminal nature of statutory liability. For a later contrast between Reid's compensatory and safety approaches, cf. *British Rys. Bd.* v. *Liptrot*, [1969] 1 A.C. 136, 156 (1967), and *Haigh* v. *Charles W. Ireland, Ltd.*, [1974] 1 W.L.R. 43 (H.L., Scot. 1973). "Lawyers are inclined to regard the Factories Act as something which gives damages to work people. But that is not really its purpose. The primary purpose of the Factories Act is to prevent accidents, and paying damages after accidents have happened is only second best." 248 *Parl. Deb.*, H.L. (5th ser.), col. 1338 (25 Apr. 1963). Reid suggested that the remedies lay in making the act wide enough to authorize comprehensive regulations and in giving practical guidance to employers and factory inspectors.

gross inconvenience to employers against the need to protect workmen.[201]

It was with this same balanced approach that Reid looked at other areas of the law that concerned the protection (and compensation) of workmen. In 1951, in *London Graving Dock Company* v. *Horton* he gave a powerful dissent in an effort to allow workmen to be given a remedy in occupiers' liability—refusing to accept that the fact that they knew of the danger (*sciens*) was the same thing as accepting the risk (*volens*).[202] By 1953, he found himself leading a majority in *Stapley* v. *Gypsum Mines, Limited*,[203] in rejecting the return of common employment or the fellow servant rule through the back door in workmen's cases. Nor did this urge to provide a centralist position leave Reid. Toward the end of his career, Reid led the House toward a broad interpretation of the Limitation Act of 1963, holding that failure on the part of a plaintiff to realize the existence of a legal claim prevented the time for issuing the writ from beginning to run.[204]

The balancing of interests may have been the keynote of Reid's approach to the protection of workmen, but in the generalized areas of tort that came before the House he was more willing to impose liability than were many of his contemporaries. In his early days, in the *Horton* case he sought to expand the scope of an invitor's duty,[205] but even after the passage of the Occupiers' Liability Act of 1957,[206] he continued to

201. See *Marshall* v. *Gotham Co.*, [1954] A.C. 360, 373, where Reid, while ultimately finding against the workman, did not consider that "practicable" and "reasonably practicable" were synonymous, but "as men's lives may be at stake it should not lightly be held that to take a practicable precaution is unreasonable." See also *John Summers & Sons* v. *Frost*, [1955] A.C. 740, 764. In *Gough* v. *National Coal Bd.*, [1959] A.C. 698, 709, Reid argued, "I would agree with this argument to the extent that Parliament cannot have intended altogether to prevent the winning of coal, and that nothing in the Act can be read in such a way as to produce this result. But before coming to what I think is the true interpretation of the section, I think it well to look at some of the consequences of reading it in the way in which it has been read." For another "balancing" act, see *Morris* v. *West Hartlepool Steam Navigation Co.*, [1956] A.C. 552, 574 (1955).

202. [1951] A.C. 737, 783–84.

203. [1953] A.C. 663, 679. See also *National Coal Bd.* v. *England*, [1954] A.C. 403, 422; and *Harrison* v. *National Coal Bd.*, [1951] A.C. 639, 672 (1950); cf. *Marshall* v. *Gotham Co.*, [1954] A.C. 360, 373. He was also anxious to prevent the fellow servant rule from reappearing in common law remedies; *Stavely Iron & Chem. Co.* v. *Jones*, [1956] A.C. 627, 640. In interpreting Commonwealth Workmen's Compensation legislation, he took a liberal tack. See, e.g., *Sunshine Porcelain Potteries Pty.* v. *Nash*, [1961] A.C. 927, 937 (P.C.), allowing the retroactive application of a new Limitation Act.

204. *Smith* v. *Central Asbestos Co.*, [1973] A.C. 518, 528 (1972).

205. *London Graving Dock Co.* v. *Horton*, [1951] A.C. 737, 785.

206. Of the Occupiers' Liability Bill, he said, "To my mind, the Bill to a large extent restores the Common Law against certain unfortunate decisions which have been given in the last half century or so, and the reason why it is necessary for this House now to deal with those matters, is the existence of a rule whereby the House, sitting in a Judicial capacity, has no power to re-examine past decisions of the House"; 203 *Parl. Deb.*, H.L. (5th ser.), col. 262 (2 May 1957).

wrestle with the liability of occupiers toward trespassers, ultimately imposing a subjective test of "humanity" based on the ability of the defendant to pay.[207] In the more general area of negligence,[208] Reid had no
doubt that school authorities had a duty to keep children in[209] or that
borstal authorities owed a similar duty to keep inmates in its institutions
or to pay damages.[210] In determining this latter issue, Reid argued that
although Atkin's statement in *Donoghue* v. *Stevenson* should not be
treated as statutory definition, "the time has come when we can and
should say it ought to apply unless there is some justification or valid
explanation for its exclusion."[211]

While Reid was willing to find that public policy excluded the right
to sue a barrister for negligent advocacy,[212] his overall approach emphasized the compensatory nature of the tort of negligence.[213] Such an as-

207. In *Herrington* v. *British Rys. Bd.*, [1972] A.C. 877, Reid made it clear that the
law that had grown up around *Addie & Sons* v. *Dumbreck*, [1929] A.C. 358 (Scot.),
especially with respect to child trespassers, was less than satisfactory. The only objection to
the House's reforming the law was, as he saw it, the failure of the 1957 act to deal with
trespassers, leaving the problem of "to what extent this House sitting in its judicial capacity
can do what Parliament failed to do in 1957. I dislike usurping the functions of Parliament"; ibid. 897–98. Reid, after holding that the House could not "dismiss this appeal
without holding that *Addie's* case was wrongly decided" (ibid. 898), nevertheless went on
to transform the duty not to act recklessly in Addie's case into a subjective test of "culpa-
bility," based on "humanity":

[A]n occupiers' [*sic*] duty to trespassers must vary according to his knowledge, ability and resources....

So the question whether an occupier is liable in respect of an accident to a trespasser on his land
would depend on whether a conscientious humane man with his knowledge, skill and resources could
reasonably have been expected to have done or refrained from doing before the accident something
which would have avoided it....

It would follow that an impecunious occupier with little assistance at hand would often be excused
from doing something which a large organisation with ample staff would be expected to do. [Ibid. 899]

208. In keeping with his approach to the Factories Acts, Reid was, however, more
cautious in developing statutory negligence; e.g., *Cutler* v. *Wandsworth Stadium, Ltd.*,
[1949] A.C. 398, 415.

209. *Carmarthenshire County Council* v. *Lewis*, [1955] A.C. 549, 562.

210. *Dorset Yacht Co.* v. *Home Office*, [1970] A.C. 10004. While Reid agreed that in
general, one could not be liable for the acts of another who was not his servant or agent, he
said that "here the ground of liability is not responsibility for the acts of the escaping
trainees; it is liability for damage caused by the carelessness of these officers in the knowledge that their carelessness would probably result in the trainees causing damage of this
kind"; ibid. 1027.

211. Ibid.

212. "I would not expect any counsel to be influenced by the possibility of an action
being raised against him to such an extent that he would knowingly depart from his duty to
the court or to his profession; but although the line between proper and improper conduct
may be easy to state in general terms, it is by no means easy to draw in borderline cases . . .
it would be a grave and dangerous step to make any change which would imperil in any
way the confidence which every court rightly puts in all counsel who appear before it";
Rondel v. *Worsley*, [1969] 1 A.C. 191, 228 (1967).

For a criticism of the policy that Reid applied in this case, see Brian Abel-Smith and
Robert Stevens, *In Search of Justice* 285–86.

213. "Damages are awarded not to punish the wrongdoer but to compensate the
person injured." Moreover, he argued that "compensation should be based much less on

sumption possibly explains why Reid found it easier than some of the judges both to accept a wide concept of *res ipsa loquitur*[214] and, more important, to encourage the development of liability for negligent statements. In *Hedley Byrne and Company v. Heller and Partners, Limited* Reid admitted that negligent statements must be treated in a different way from physical injury,[215] but he nevertheless built up a concept of basic liability in the field.[216] Shortly before his retirement, for example, Reid was able to find, with little difficulty, that architects supervising building work were not protected from liability merely because they were required to act "fairly."[217]

---

the nature of the injuries than on the extent of the injured man's consequential difficulties in his daily life"; *H. West & Son v. Shephard*, [1964] A.C. 326, 342 (1963).

Rather surprisingly, Reid supported the multiplier method rather than more scientific actuarial calculation when awarding damages; e.g., *Taylor v. O'Connor*, [1971] A.C. 115, 128–29 (1970). Reid was prepared to take the possibility of inflation into account, but "we should not assume the worst"; ibid. 130. Reid also convinced the House to hold that pensions, whether discretionary or received as of right, had to be ignored in awarding damages in line with the treatment of insurance payments; *Parry v. Cleaver*, [1970] A.C. 1, 13 (1969).

214. *Henderson v. Henry E. Jenkins & Sons*, [1970] A.C. 282 (1969). When a truck's brakes failed on a hill it was up to the defendants "to prove that in all the circumstances which they knew or ought to have known that they took all proper steps to avoid danger"; ibid. 291. For an example of holding an employer liable for an unexplained accident, see *Morris v. West Hartlepool Steam Navigation Co.*, [1956] A.C. 552, 574 (1955). For an interesting example of Reid's views on causation, see *Baker v. Willoughby*, [1970] A.C. 467, 489 (1969).

215. [1964] A.C. 465, 480 (1963).

[I]t would be going very far to say that he [the maker of a negligent statement] owes a duty to every ultimate "consumer" who acts on those words to his detriment. . . .

So it seems to me that there is good sense behind our present law that in general an innocent but negligent misrepresentation gives no cause of action. There must be something more than a mere misstatement. . . . The most natural requirement would be that expressly or by implication from the circumstances the speaker or writer has undertaken some responsibility, and that appears to me not to conflict with any authority which is binding on this House. [Ibid. 483]

216. In discussing the principle to be applied, Reid rejected the idea that *Donoghue v. Stevenson* was of direct help: "That is a very important decision, but I do not think that it has any direct bearing on this case. That decision may encourage us to develop existing lines of authority, but it cannot entitle us to disregard them"; ibid. 482. His attitude was reflected in the note he took of Haldane's remark that the obligations in this area are based on "principles which the judges have worked out in the fashion that is characteristic of a system where much of the law has always been judge-made and unwritten"; ibid. 485. It was with this spirit that he concentrated his attention on the relationship between *Derry v. Peek* and *Nocton v. Lord Ashburton*. After a searching examination of Haldane's speech in the latter decision, he concluded, "Lord Haldane did not think that a duty to take care must be limited to cases of fiduciary relationship in the narrow sense. . . . He speaks of other special relationships, and I can see no logical stopping place short of all those relationships where it is plain that the party seeking information or advice was trusting the other to exercise such a degree of care as the circumstances required, where it was reasonable for him to do that, and where the other gave that information or advice when he knew or ought to have known that the inquirer was relying on him"; ibid. 486.

217. *Sutcliffe v. Thackrah*, [1974] A.C. 727, 737: "There is nothing judicial about an architect's function in determining whether certain work is defective. There is no dispute."

In other areas of tort, too, Reid took a "strong" position. His opinions in the important labor cases of the mid-sixties brought little satisfaction to the unions. In *Rookes v. Barnard* he made it clear that, in his view, intimidation was sufficiently offensive that it more than justified giving rise to a tort;[218] and in *J. T. Stratford and Son, Limited v. Lindley*, Reid concluded that "it must have been obvious to them [the union officials] that failure to return the barges was a breach of contract."[219] In a similar spirit Reid made a sweeping assault on punitive damages in the libel case of *Broome v. Cassel* as "confusing the function of the civil law which is to compensate with the function of the criminal law which is to inflict deterrent and punitive penalties."[220]

In the area of commercial law, Reid took the position that "the law should be kept up to date in accord with contemporary business practices."[221] In line with this, in *Heron II*[222] Reid injected an element of tort into the theory of contract damages while formally restating *Hadley v. Baxendale*.[223] In *Suisse Atlantique v. N.V. Rotterdamsche*, on the other hand, he felt unable to hold that an exclusion clause could never relieve from liability for fundamental breach of contract.[224] In commercial law,

218. [1964] A.C. 1129, 1164.

Threatening a breach of contract may be a much more coercive weapon than threatening a tort, particularly when the threat is directed against a company or corporation, and, if there is no technical reason requiring a distinction between different kinds of threats, I can see no other ground for making any such distinction. . . . Intimidation of any kind appears to me to be highly objectionable. The law was not slow to prevent it when violence and threats of violence were the most effective means. Now the subtler means are at least equally effective I see no reason why the law should have to turn a blind eye on them. We have to tolerate intimidation by means which have been held to be lawful but these I would stop. [Ibid. 1169]

In this case Reid also joined in interpreting the second limb of § 3 of the Trade Disputes Act virtually out of existence by deciding that Parliament had made a mistake in 1906 as to the existence of a tort of interference with business; ibid. 1174.

219. [1965] A.C. 269, 323 (1964).

220. [1972] A.C. 1027, 1086. Reid argued that while the House had felt obliged to award punitive damages in *Rookes v. Barnard*, "I still think it well within the province of this House to say that undesirable anomaly should not be permitted in any class of case where its use was not covered by authority"; ibid. 1086.

"Any diminution or abolition of the functions of a jury in libel cases can only come from Parliament. If this case brings nearer the day when Parliament does take action I for one shall not be sorry"; ibid. 1091.

221. Interview with Reid, 25 Oct. 1967 (notes corrected for accuracy by Lord Reid).

222. *Koufos v. C. Czarnikow, Ltd.*, [1969] 1 A.C. 350, 381 (1967). This may have been one of the first cases to be affected, indirectly at least, by the 1966 Practice Statement.

223. Reid felt that the law as stated by Lord Justice Asquith in *Victoria Laundry v. Newman Indus., Ltd.* was wrong. The new (or renewed) test was, "[t]hat the loss was sufficiently likely to result from the breach of contract to make it proper to hold that the loss flowed naturally from the breach or that loss of that kind should have been within his contemplation"; *Koufos v. C. Czarnikow, Ltd.*, [1969] 1 A.C. 350, 385. See also at 388: "to have a very substantial degree of probability." On this, see Grant Gilmore, *The Death of Contract* 83–84. On the mitigation of damages, see *White & Carter (Councils), Ltd. v. McGregor*, [1962] A.C. 413, 425 (Scot. 1961).

224. *Suisse Atlantique Société d'Armament Maritime S.A. v. N.V. Rotterdamsche*

however, Reid's creativity can perhaps best be seen in the restraint of trade cases, holding, for instance, that tied garages or what a chemist might sell had to be decided by modern notions of freedom of contract and current concepts of public policy.[225] In keeping with this approach, he found his attitude toward frustration closer to that of Wright than that of Simonds.[226] In fact, Wright would no doubt have approved of Reid's pronouncement that "[i]t is never satisfactory to construe a commercial document purely on a meticulous examination of its language."[227]

The creative balancing process was carried into family law and conflicts as well.[228] In debates on the reform of divorce, Reid took a humane posture,[229] and judicially he had already insisted on a subjective approach to cruelty.[230] In terms of property settlements between spouses Reid was prepared to see reasonable development by the judges.[231] If

---

Kolen Centrale, [1967] 1 A.C. 361, 405–6 (1966):

In my view no such rule of law ought to be adopted. I do not take that view merely because any such rule is new or because it goes beyond what can be done by developing or adapting existing principles. Courts have often introduced new rules when, in their view, they were required by public policy. In former times when Parliament seldom amended the common law, that could hardly have been avoided. And there are recent examples although, for reasons which I gave in *Shaw v. Director of Public Prosecutions* [[1962] A.C. 220 (1961)], I think that this power ought now to be used sparingly. But my main reason is that this rule would not be a satisfactory solution of the problem which undoubtedly exists.

For a similar reluctance to change the harsh, albeit straightforward, rule of *non est factum*, see *Gallie v. Lee*, [1971] A.C. 1004, 1015 (1970). Although not so rigid, Reid was less willing than some to tamper with privity of contract; *Hepburn v. A. Tomlinson (Hauliers), Ltd.*, [1966] A.C. 451, 470–71; *Beswick v. Beswick*, [1968] A.N. 58, 70 (1967).

225. *Esso Petroleum Co. v. Harper's Garage (Stourport), Ltd.*, [1968] A.C. 269 (1964). He refused to treat earlier judicial statements about restraint of trade as "definitions"; and, in deciding which agreements were in the public interest, he thought it "legitimate to supplement it [the evidence] from a considerable body of reported cases regarding solus agreements and from facts found in the Report of the Monopolies Commission"; ibid. 301. See also, in this decision, his view that the doctrine of public policy must depend on practical effects and his view of "freedom of contract." Ibid. 298.

In *Dickson v. Pharmaceutical Soc'y of Great Britain*, [1970] A.C. 403, 420 (1968), Reid declared, "[I]t appears to me that if a member of a profession can show that a particular restriction on his activities goes beyond anything which can reasonably be related to the maintenance of professional honour or standards, the court must be able to intervene."

For an analysis of the related concept of "public interest" in the definition of charities, see *IRC v. City of Glasgow Police Athletic Ass'n*, [1953] A.C. 380, 402–3 (Scot); *Scottish Burial Reform & Cremation Soc'y, Ltd. v. Glasgow Corp.*, [1968] A.C. 138, 145 (Scot. 1967).

226. E.g., *Tsakiroglou & Co. v. Noblee Thorl G.m.b.H.*, [1962] A.C. 93, 117–18.

227. *Union of India v. Compania Naviera Aeolus S.A.*, [1964] A.C. 868, 881 (1962).

228. On conflicts, see also *In re United Rys. of Havana & Regla Warehouses, Ltd.*, [1961] A.C. 1007, 1050 (1960).

229. *The Times*, 1 and 16 July and 14 Oct. 1969.

230. *Gollins v. Gollins*, [1964] A.C. 644, 660 (1963); *Williams v. Williams*, [1964] A.C. 698, 720 (1963).

231. E.g., *Pettitt v. Pettitt*, [1970] A.C. 777, 792 (1969), where Reid was content to see the presumption of advancement (with respect to work done on a house) weakened, since it

jurisdiction with respect to foreign decrees was involved, he was prepared to go even further. In *Indyka v. Indyka* he noted, "[O]bviously we cannot revise an Act of Parliament: the most we can do is to suggest matters which might be borne in mind when an amending Bill is being drafted and passed. But, Parliament has rarely intervened in the matter of recognition of foreign matrimonial decrees. The existing law is judge-made and I see no reason why that process should stop."[232]

On the other hand, Reid saw every reason for the process to stop in criminal law. His speech in *Shaw* is one of the classic statements of judicial restraint.[233] His approach also required that evidentiary rules and burdens be clearly established by statute[234] and that changes in the rules of evidence be left to Parliament.[235] In general he construed statutory offenses narrowly,[236] and whether in dissent or majority he refused to interpret drug offenses as being cases of absolute liability.[237] He even

---

had been developed when a wife was economically dependent on her husband. "These considerations have largely lost their force under present conditions and, unless the law has lost all flexibility so that the courts can no longer adapt it to changing conditions, the strength of the presumption must have been much diminished"; ibid. 793. On the other hand, he stopped short of developing anything approaching community property. "I would therefore refuse to consider whether property belonging to either spouse ought to be regarded as family property for that would be introducing a new conception into English law and not merely developing existing principles"; ibid. 795. For a further example of his reaching toward a fair solution of property rights, refusing to draw a distinction between direct and indirect contribution, see *Gissing v. Gissing*, [1971] A.C. 886 (1970).

232. [1969] 1 A.C. 33 (1967). The decision was in line with *Ross Smith v. Ross Smith*, [1963] A.C. 280, 292–94 (1962), where Reid had effectively undercut *Simonin v. Mallac*, 2 Sw. & Tr. 67; 164 Eng. Rep. 917 (1860).

233. *Shaw v. DPP*, [1962] A.C. 220, 269 (1961).

234. E.g., *Armah v. Government of Ghana*, [1968] A.C. 192, 224 (1966); *Commissioners of Customs & Excise v. Harz*, [1967] 1 A.C. 760, 813 (1966).

235. *Myers v. DPP*, [1965] A.C. 1001, 1018 (1964).

236. E.g., *R. v. Treacy*, [1971] A.C. 537, 550 (1970), refusing to find that the offense of blackmail had been committed in England (Interpreting the Theft Act of 1968).

237. Under the Drugs (Prevention of Misuse) Act of 1964, he dissented in *R. v. Warner*, [1969] 2 A.C. 256 (1968). The severity of the sentence and the social stigma "makes me hesitate to impute to Parliament an intention to deprive persons accused of these offences of the defence that they had no mens rea. . . .

"I dissent emphatically from the view that Parliament can be supposed to have been of the opinion that it could be left to the discretion of the police not to prosecute, or that if there was a prosecution justice would be served by only a nominal penalty being imposed. . . .

"I think the general view still is that it is better that ten guilty men should escape than that one innocent man should be convicted"; ibid. 278.

In *Sweet v. Parsley*, [1970] A.C. 132 (1969), he was in the majority and able to take a more relaxed approach:

Our first duty is to consider the words of the Act: if they show a clear intention to create an absolute offence that is an end of the matter. But such cases are very rare. Sometimes the words of the section which creates a particular offence make it clear that mens rea is required in one form or another. Such cases are quite frequent. But in a very large number of cases there is no clear indication either way. In such cases there has for centuries been a presumption that Parliament did not intend to make criminals

showed a reluctance to hold corporations guilty in strict liability statutory offenses.[238] Yet, occasionally Reid deviated. In *R. v. Taylor*[239] he joined his colleagues in expanding the concept of affray; in *R. v. Knuller,* although he in no way had changed his view that the earlier decision had been wrong, he felt the House was bound to follow *Shaw* in a case on criminal conspiracy.[240]

Any doubts about Reid's place as a great appeal judge would be dispelled by examining his record in the area of public law, for even in this area where so few British judges shine, he achieved distinction. In procedural control of the executive, he built on his dissent in *Smith v. East Elloe Rural District Council,* where he refused to accept that Parliament had intended to exclude the jurisdiction of the courts even if mala fides were present.[241] In *Padfield v. Minister of Agriculture, Fisheries and Food,*[242] Reid, presiding, went some distance not only in developing a presumption that a minister must exercise his discretion in accordance with the purposes of an act,[243] but also that a minister could not avoid his re-

---

of persons who were in no way blameworthy in what they did. That means that whenever a section is silent as to mens rea there is a presumption that, in order to give effect to the will of Parliament, we must read in words appropriate to require mens rea. [Ibid. 148]

238. E.g., *Tesco Supermarkets, Ltd. v. Nattrass,* [1972] A.C. 153, 167 (1971).

239. [1973] A.C. 964, 988 (1972).

240. *R. v. Knuller, Ltd.,* [1973] A.C. 435, 455–56 (1972):

I dissented in *Shaw's* case. On reconsideration I still think that the decision was wrong and I see no reason to alter anything which I said in my speech. But it does not follow that I should now support a motion to reconsider the decision. I have said more than once in recent cases that our change of practice in no longer regarding previous decisions of this House as absolutely binding does not mean that whenever we think that a previous decision was wrong we should reverse it. In the general interest of certainty in the law we must be sure that there is some very good reason before we so act. We are informed that there had been at least 30 and probably many more convictions of this new crime in the ten years which have elapsed since *Shaw's* case was decided, and it does not appear that there has been manifest injustice or that any attempt has been made to widen the scope of the new crime. I do not regard our refusal to reconsider *Shaw's* case as in anyway justifying any attempt to widen the scope of the decision and I would oppose any attempt to do so. But, I think that however wrong or anomalous the decision may be it must stand and apply to cases reasonably analogous unless or until it is altered by Parliament.

... I said in *Shaw's* case ... and I repeat that Parliament and Parliament alone is the proper authority to change the law with regard to the punishment of immoral acts. Rightly or wrongly the law was determined by the decision in *Shaw.* Any alteration of the law as so determined must in my view be left to Parliament.

241. [1956] A.C. 736, 760. See also at 766:

It is said that Parliament may have intended that even cases of gross dishonesty should be excluded from duress because otherwise it would be embarrassing to deal with allegations of this kind after a long interval, and, if the case was proved, a local authority and ultimately the ratepayers might be involved in grievous loss. I am not entirely satisfied that the law is powerless to deal justly with such situations. But, even if that were a possible consequence, I would hesitate to attribute to Parliament the view that considerations of that kind justify hushing up a scandal.

242. [1968] A.C. 997, 1032.

243. "Parliament must have conferred the discretion with the intention that it should be used to promote the policy and objects of the Act; the policy and objectives of the Act

sponsibilities by refusing to give reasons.[244] This position was taken even further in *Anisminic, Limited* v. *Foreign Compensation Commission.*[245] In that latter case judicial review of "determinations" was expressly excluded by the Foreign Compensation Act of 1950, but the House, again led by Reid, held that determinations beyond the jurisdiction of the commission were not covered by the words forbidding their being called "in question in any court of law."[246] Finally, in laying down how discretion was to be applied, Reid held in *British Oxygen Company* v. *Board of Trade* that "[t]here are two general grounds on which the exercise of an unqualified discretion can be attacked. It must not be exercised in bad faith, and it must not be so unreasonably exercised as to show that there cannot have been any real or genuine exercise of the discretion."[247]

The second of these grounds basically required the person exercising the discretion to hear—directly or indirectly—the party involved.[248] This aspect of the concept of discretion built on Reid's earlier decisions on natural justice, particularly *Ridge* v. *Baldwin*, holding as wrongful the dismissal of a chief constable when the Watch Committee had failed to give him an adequate right to be heard.[249] In addition to demanding high

---

must be determined by construing the Act as a whole and construction is always a matter of law for the court. In a matter of this kind it is not possible to draw a hard and fast line, but if the Minister, by reason of his having misconstrued the Act or for any other reason, so uses his discretion as to thwart or run counter to the policy and objects of the Act, then our law would be very defective if persons aggrieved were not entitled to the protection of the court"; ibid. 1030.

244. "I do not agree that a decision cannot be questioned if no reasons are given. If it is the Minister's duty not to act so as to frustrate the policy and objects of the Act, and if it were to appear from all the circumstances of the case that that has been the effect of the Minister's refusal, then it appears to me that the court must be entitled to act"; ibid. 1032–33.

245. [1969] 2 A.C. 147, 167 (1968).

246. "It cannot be for the commission to determine the limits of its powers . . . if they reach a wrong conclusion as to the width of their powers, the court must be able to correct that—not because the tribunal has made an error of law, but because as a result of making an error of law they have dealt with and based their decision on a matter with which, on a true construction of their powers, they had not to deal"; ibid. 174.

See also *Kingsway Invs. (Kent), Ltd.* v. *Kent County Council*, [1971] A.C. 72, 86 (1969), refusing to give the words allowing planning permission to be granted "subject to such conditions as they think fit" their natural meaning.

247. [1971] A.C. 610, 624 (1970).

248. "The general rule is that anyone who has to exercise a statutory discretion must not 'shut his ears to an application.' . . . what the authority must not do is to refuse to listen at all"; ibid. 625.

249. [1964] A.C. 40, 63 (1963). In holding that dismissal to be wrongful, Reid argued that 30 or 40 years ago there would have been no difficulty about the plaintiff's recovering, but that later cases had taken a more restricted view when ministers' duties were involved. Reid, however, was prepared to set the law off in a new direction. *Liversidge* v. *Anderson*, [1942] A.C. 206 (1941), was described as a "very peculiar decision," and various other cases were explained away. Of *Nakkuda Ali* v. *Jayaratne*, [1951] A.C. 66 (P.C. 1950), Reid said:

standards of natural justice from central government departments or police authorities, Reid expected the same standards from other agencies, whether they were the Commissioners of Inland Revenue[250] or Scottish education authorities.[251]

Yet the right to sue government departments, whether at the central or local level, was of little value unless the odds were fair. Thus, Reid's judgment in *Conway* v. *Rimmer*[252] put an end to Crown privilege, at least as represented by Simon's judgment in *Duncan* v. *Cammell, Laird*.[253] Reid had no doubt that "it is proper to prevent the use of any document, wherever it comes from, if disclosure of its contents would really injure the national interest. . . . But in this field it is more than ever necessary that in a doubtful case the alleged public interest in concealment should be balanced against the public interest that the administration of justice should not be frustrated."[254] Thus Reid's solution was to have the government departments produce doubtful documents to the judge, without

---

This House is not bound by decisions of the Privy Council, and for my own part nothing short of a decision of this House directly in point would induce me to accept the position that, although an enactment expressly requires an official to have reasonable grounds for his decision, our law is so defective that a subject cannot bring up such a decision for review however seriously he may be affected and however obvious it may be that the official acted in breach of his statutory obligation. [Ibid. 77]

His general approach, however, was clearly spelled out:

We do not have a developed system of administrative law—perhaps because until fairly recently we did not need it. So it is not surprising that in dealing with new types of cases the courts have had to grope for solutions, and have found that old powers, rules and procedure are largely inapplicable to cases which they were never designed or intended to deal with. But I see nothing in that to justify our thinking that our old methods are any less applicable today than ever they were to the older types of case. And, if there are dicta or modern authorities which point in that direction, then in my judgement, they should not be followed. [Ibid. 72–73]

250. "Natural justice requires that the procedure before any tribunal which is acting judicially shall be fair in all the circumstances, and I would be sorry to see this fundamental general principle degenerate into a series of hard-and-fast rules. For a long time the courts have, without objection from Parliament, supplemented procedure laid down in legislation where they have found that to be necessary for this purpose. But before this unusual kind of power is exercised it must be clear that the statutory procedure is insufficient to achieve justice and that to require additional steps should not frustrate the apparent purpose of the legislation"; *Wiseman* v. *Borneman*, [1971] A.C. 297, 308 (1969).

251. "An elected public body is in a very different position from a private employer. Many of its servants in the lower grades are in the same position as servants of a private employer. But many in higher grades or 'offices' are given special statutory status or protection. The right of a man to be heard in his own defence is the most elementary protection of all and, where a statutory form of protection would be less effective if it did not carry with it a right to be heard, I would not find it difficult to imply this right"; *Malloch* v. *Aberdeen Corp.*, [1971] 1 W.L.R. 1578, 1582 (H.L., Scot.).

252. [1968] A.C. 910, 937 (1967).

253. [1942] A.C. 624, 629. In keeping with his style, he refused to overrule the earlier decision, but merely held that Simon had misunderstood the earlier dicta, [1968] A.C. 910, 948.

254. Ibid. 950. For another example of balancing of the public interest see *Chandler* v. *DPP*, [1964] A.C. 763, 790–91 (1962).

showing them to the other party.[255] Nor did Reid hesitate to bring out the implications of *Conway* v. *Rimmer* in a series of later cases.[256]

It was in this same spirit that Reid refused to allow the plea of act of state to be used in an action by a British subject.[257] Perhaps most dramatic of all was Reid's view that contempt of court should not be used to "gag" the press. In the litigation involving the articles in the *Sunday Times*, that urged the manufacturers of thalidomide to settle the actions brought by parents of deformed children, he saw nothing wrong with urging the settlement but felt that the article discussing the merits of the actual case might be enjoined.[258] Such prior restraint, perhaps narrow by the traditions of civil liberties in North America, represented a distinct step forward in the British judicial tradition.[259] Britain may still, for comprehensible political reasons, be far from an entrenched Bill of Rights, but at least in Reid there was an appellate judge who understood the process of balancing interests,[260] a process essential to the introduction of such a document. His cautious introverted common lawyerism, however, was in stark contrast to the extroverted beliefs of his contemporary, Denning.

"Thank God for Lord Denning"[261]

Denning is certainly the most interesting and possibly the most important English judge of the twentieth century.[262] His approach was not

255. [1968] A.C. 910, 953.

256. E.g., *R.* v. *Lewes Justices, ex parte Secretary of State for Home Affairs*, [1973] A.C. 388, 399 (1972); *Norwich Pharmacal Co.* v. *Commissioners of Customs and Excise*, [1974] A.C. 133, 173 (1973). See also, on a different point, *Atkinson* v. *United States of America*, [1971] A.C. 197, 232 (1969): "It is now well recognised that the court has power to expand procedure laid down by statute if that is necessary to prevent infringement of natural justice and is not plainly contrary to the intention of Parliament."

257. *Nissan* v. *Attorney-General*, [1970] A.C. 179, 205 (1969).

258. *Attorney-General* v. *Times Newspapers, Ltd.*, [1973] Q.B. 710 (C.A.):

The law on this subject is and must be founded entirely on public policy. It is not there to protect the private rights of parties to a litigation or prosecution. It is there to prevent interference with the administration of justice and it should in my judgement be limited to what is reasonably necessary for that purpose. Public policy generally requires a balancing of interests which may conflict. Freedom of speech should not be denied to any greater extent than is necessary but it cannot be allowed where there would be real prejudice to the administration of justice.

259. It strongly influenced the Phillimore Committee. See *Report of the Committee on Contempt of Court*, Cmnd. 5794, paras. 103–11 (1974).

260. See also his reluctance to accept that there might be a taking without compensation: *Hartnell* v. *Minister of Housing & Local Gov't*, [1965] A.C. 1134, 1157; *Burmah Oil Co.* v. *Lord Advocate*, [1965] A.C. 75, 101, (Scot. 1964). Note also his discussion of the European Convention on Human Rights and the Universal Declaration on Human Rights to justify his refusal to apply an act of Parliament retrospectively in a deportation case; *R.* v. *Miah*, [1974] 1 W.L.R. 683 (H.L.).

261. Leader, *The Times*, 28 June 1975, at 13, discussing the attempt by the Labour government to prevent publication of the Crossman Diaries. See, now, Hugo Young, *The Crossman Affair*, passim.

262. Alfred Thompson Denning; b. 1899; father, "gentleman"; educ., Andover Gram-

only the antithesis of substantive formalism, but he exhibited few of the qualms of judicial restraint that characterized Radcliffe, Devlin, and Reid. Not only did he have no doubt that appeal judges make law, but he believed that they should actively make law. He regarded certainty in the law as an overrated virtue and had a remarkable effect on the development of substantive law. Arriving on the bench at a time when outside forces were beginning to demystify the English legal system, Denning, a self-styled iconoclast,[263] was only too ready to offer assistance. A highly intelligent man, he lacked the intellectualism of Radcliffe and Devlin, but he also lacked the former's feeling that judicial legislation should go unnoticed and any hint of the latter's lamentation that judicial legislation was dead. At the same time he did not savor the subtle sense of the relationship between Parliament and the law lords that characterized Reid at his best.

Even without his distinctive embracing of the Grand Style, the very length of Denning's tenure as an appeal judge would have made him significant. Appointed a High Court judge in 1944, he was promoted to the Court of Appeal in 1948, becoming a Lord of Appeal in 1957. In 1962, he returned to preside over the Court of Appeal as Master of the Rolls, an office he still held in 1977.[264] Indeed, much of his most creative work was done in the Court of Appeal, which he was convinced was a more important appeal court than the Lords. Moreover, he did not hesitate to make his division of that court the one to which he assigned potential lawmaking cases.[265] Thus, in discussing his work it is necessary to look at a selection of decisions from both of his terms in the Court of Appeal, even at the risk of distorting his contributions as a law lord.[266]

---

mar School and Magdalen College, Oxford (First, Jurisprudence and Mathematics); called to bar (Common Law), 1923; K.C., 1938; Judge, King's Bench Division, 1946–48; Lord Justice, 1948–57; Lord of Appeal, 1957–62; Master of Rolls, 1962–.

263. See Alfred Denning, "The Way of an Iconoclast" 77, 89: "What then is the way of an iconoclast? It is the way of one who is not content to accept cherished beliefs simply because they have been long accepted. If he finds that they are not suited to the times or that they work injustice, he will see whether there is not some competing principle which can be applied to the case in hand. He will search the old cases, and the writers old and new, until he has found it." This article contains a summary of the cases decided by Denning at first instance and in the Court of Appeal that he considered of most importance.

264. Compared with an average of 50 or 60 cases a year in the Lords, the Court of Appeal altogether hears an average of 800. While the court is divided into 4 divisions, the Master of the Rolls both presides in one of the 3-man divisions and controls the flow of work to the others. It is here, free of the 5-judge panels (and effectively freed of the criminal law) with which Denning had to deal in the Lords, that he set an important pace.

265. Hugo Young, "England's Most Revolutionary Judge," *Sunday Times*, 17 June 1973, at 33.

266. In terms of public service, he is perhaps best known for his report on the Profumo affair; *Denning Report*, Cmnd. 2152 (1963). But he has served in many other capacities. See, for instance, his secret report for the government on the relations between the Jamaican government and Fyffes. The government apparently rejected the report; *Sunday Times*, 24 Jan. 1971, at 5.

He was also the most loquacious of the law lords in legislative debates.[267]

Abraham Goldstein has argued[268] that the English legal system is intelligible to Americans only if it is appreciated that as yet, no Realist revolution has occurred in England. It is equally true, however, that insofar as there has been a Realist movement in England, it has been largely synonymous with the name of Denning. In contradistinction to the Radcliffe approach, Denning trumpeted the law-making potential of the judiciary from the rooftops.[269] He constantly reminded public audiences[270] and his fellow judges[271] that stare decisis was a recent development. He had no doubt that the Scottish system of emphasizing principle rather than precedent was to be preferred to the English system.[272]

Denning's consistent refrain, however, was the inevitably creative element in the judicial, and especially the appellate, process:

The truth is that the law is uncertain. It does not cover all the situations that may arise. Time and again practitioners and judges are faced with new situations, where the decision may go either way. No one can tell what the law is until the courts decide it. The judges do every day make law, though it is almost heresy to say so. If the truth is recognized then we may hope to escape from the dead hand of the past and consciously mold new principles to meet the needs of the present.[273]

He had no doubt of its implications for the final appeal court. "If the law is to develop and not to stagnate, the House must, I think recapture this vital principle—the principle of growth. The House of Lords is more

267. Between 1953 and 1968, he spoke 79 times in debates (an average of 6.83 a year). Parker came nearest to him during that period in number of speeches (39) and Wilberforce in average per year (5.04); Blom-Cooper and Drewry, *Final Appeal* 205.

268. Abraham S. Goldstein, "Research into the Administration of Criminal Law" 27, 37.

269. He regularly announced his belief in the fact that judges could still remedy injustice. See, for instance, on the right to privacy: "I am not in despair. The judges may well do it. There is nothing in any decision of this House, judicially, which prevents it, in that whenever any grievous cases come up we find that the lawyers produce a remedy"; 229 *Parl. Deb.*, H.L. (5th ser.), col. 639 (13 Mar. 1961).

In discussion of the Law Commission Bill, Denning also showed his preference for judge-made law over legislation in many areas; 264 ibid., cols. 1210–11 (1 Apr. 1965).

It was also Denning who reminded other judges of the implications for English law of both the style and the substance of common market law. On "matters with a European element the treaty is like an incoming tide. It flows into the estuaries and up the rivers. It can not be held back"; *H. P. Bulmer, Ltd. v. J. Bolinger S.A.*, [1974] ch. 401, 418 (C.A.).

270. Alfred Denning, *From Precedent to Precedent* 31–32: "The modern convention has only grown up during the last 100 years and can be departed from just as any other practice of the House can be."

271. He never ceased to remind his fellow judges that "this 'fundamental principle' [of binding precedent] was a discovery of the nineteenth century . . . it was carried to the most extravagent lengths"; *Midland Silicones, Ltd. v. Scruttons, Ltd.*, [1962] A.C. 446, 483 (1961).

272. Alfred Denning, *Borrowing from Scotland* 30.

273. Alfred Denning, "The Reform of Equity" 31.

than another court of law. . . . It acts for the Queen as the fountain of justice in our land."[274] In short, Denning was the apologist for an activist role for the judiciary. He did not allow himself the excuses of others: "It cannot be helped. The Law will have it so." "We are only concerned with what the law is, not with what it ought to be." "If this leads to an unjust result, it is a matter for Parliament, not for us."[275] The existence of injustice or a state of the law with which he disagreed was invariably a challenge.

As may well be imagined, his views about the function of the judiciary did not make him popular with the other law lords. Simon dissociated himself from Denning's view about frustration of contract in the *British Movietonews* case.[276] Simonds, however, was perhaps Denning's leading antagonist. They disagreed in legislative debates about the absurdity of the *Diplock* decision;[277] Simonds was at odds with Denning about the latter's efforts to extend frustration and castigated him for his attempts to develop a broad policy approach to the interpretation of statutes.[278] They disagreed, again both judicially and in legislative debates, about the House's role in cases dealing with section 14 of the Factories Act,[279] while Denning almost precipitated a constitutional crisis in *Broome* v. *Cassell and Company*[280] by refusing in the Court of Appeal to follow a decision of the House that he believed to be wrong.[281]

As Master of the Rolls, Denning had already gone out of his way to emphasize the flexibility involved in handling earlier precedents.[282] During the late sixties he pushed these claims further and further. He took

274. Denning, *From Precedent to Precedent* 34.

275. Alfred Denning, *The Road to Justice* 1.

276. *British Movietonews, Ltd.* v. *London & Dist. Cinemas, Ltd.,* [1952] A.C. 166 (1951). "[I]t is desirable, in order to remove the possibility of misunderstanding hereafter, to refer to certain passages in the judgement delivered by Denning, L.J. where phrases occur which give us some concern"; ibid. 181.

"I do not agree that there has been a recent change as the result of which the courts now exercise a wider power in this regard than they previously used. . . . The general principle upon which the court acts is now settled; so Lord Finlay, L.C. stated in *Bank Line Ltd.* v. *Arthur Capel & Co.*"; ibid. 183.

277. 222 *Parl. Deb.,* H.L. (5th ser.), cols. 981, 989–93 (12 Apr. 1960).

278. *Magor & St. Mellons RDC* v. *Newport Corp.,* [1952] A.C. 189, 191 (1951).

279. 248 *Parl. Deb.,* H.L. (5th ser.), cols. 1332–36 (25 Apr. 1963).

280. [1971] 2 Q.B. 354 (C.A.).

281. On this, see especially Hailsham, in *Broome* v. *Cassell & Co.,* [1972] A.C. 1027, 1054: "[I]t is not open to the Court of Appeal to give gratuitous advice to judges of first instance to ignore decisions of the House of Lords in this way. . . .

"[I]t is necessary for each lower tier, including the Court of Appeal, to accept loyally the decisions of the higher tiers. . . . Even this House, since it has taken freedom to review its own decisions, will do so cautiously." See also ibid. 1136.

282. In the light of this, it is perhaps not surprising that Denning had serious doubts about allowing "certified" cases to be "leapfrogged" from the High Court to the House of Lords; 297 *Parl. Deb.,* H.L. (5th ser.), col. 470 (12 Nov. 1968).

the 1966 Practice Statement, designed for the House of Lords, more seriously than any of the Lords of Appeal. While *Conway* v. *Rimmer* was in the Court of Appeal, he refused to be bound by *Duncan* v. *Cammell, Laird*,[283] announcing that "the doctrine of precedent has been transformed by the recent statement of Lord Gardiner L.C. This is the very case in which to throw off the fetters."[284] He applied the same flexibility to earlier Court of Appeal decisions. In *Boys* v. *Chaplin* he took the view that the court was not bound by earlier decisions in interlocutory appeals.[285] Later that year, in *W. and J. B. Eastwood, Ltd.* v. *Herrod*, Denning went further and held that where case A had been distinguished in case B, case C was free to ignore precedent A altogether, since there were "conflicting tests." "The cynic can comment on this process if he likes. It is a way round the strict doctrine of precedent. But I prefer it to the endless task of distinguishing the indistinguishable and reconciling the irreconcilable. That is the way we had to do it in the past, and in doing so we have made confusion worse confounded. It is better to make a clean cut and to depart from a prior precedent if we are satisfied that it is wrong."[286]

He returned to the attack in *Gallie* v. *Lee* where, when his colleagues in the Court of Appeal refused to ignore what they conceived to be a binding precedent, Denning reasoned, "We are, of course, bound by the decisions of the House, but I do not think we are bound by prior decisions of our own, or at any rate, not absolutely bound. We are not fettered as it was once thought. It was a self-imposed limitation; and we who imposed it can also remove it. The House of Lords have done it. So why should we not do likewise?"[287] Yet, the coup de grace was still to come. It was two years later, in *Broome* v. *Cassell*, that Denning an-

283. *Duncan* v. *Cammell, Laird & Co.*, [1942] A.C. 624.
284. He continued:

Crown privilege is one of the prerogatives of the Crown. As such it extends only so far as the common law permits. It is for the judges to define its ambit; and not for any government department, however powerful. And when I say "the judges," I mean not only the judges of England. I include the judges of the countries of the Commonwealth. The Queen is their Queen, as she is ours. Crown prerogative is the same there as here. At least it should be. When we find that the Supreme Courts of those countries, after careful deliberation, decline to follow the House of Lords—because they are satisfied that it is wrong—that is excellent reason for the House to think again. It is not beneath its dignity, nor is it now beyond its power, to confess itself to have been in error. Likewise with this court. We should draw on the wisdom of those overseas, as they in the past have drawn on ours. Thus we shall do our part to keep the common law a just system—yes, a just and uniform system—throughout its broad domain. [[1967] 1 W.L.R. 1031, 1037 (C.A.)]

His fellow Lords Justices did not agree.
285. [1968] 2 Q.B. 1, 23 (C.A. 1967). He also warned that, in non-interlocutory appeals, "I foresee the time may come when we have to reconsider the self-imposed limitations stated in Young's case, especially in view of the recent change in the practices of the House of Lords"; ibid. 24.
286. [1968] 2 Q.B. 923, 934 (C.A.).
287. [1969] 2 Ch. 17, 37 (C.A.).

nounced he was prepared to ignore a House of Lords precedent that he regarded as wrongly decided.

The House's decision with respect to the doctrine of exemplary damages in *Rookes* v. *Barnard*[288] had not been followed in many Commonwealth countries,[289] which led Denning to conclude that "[t]his wholesale condemnation justifies us, I think, in examining this new doctrine for ourselves; and I make so bold as to say that it should not be followed any longer in this country. I say this primarily because the common law of England on this subject was so well settled before 1964 —and, on such sound and secure foundations—that it was not open to the House of Lords to overthrow it. It could only be done by the legislature."[290] Lest this outburst be attributed to a sudden commitment to fidelity to precedent,[291] Denning supported his position by noting that earlier cases had been ignored by the House and "finally, I say that the new doctrine is hopelessly illogical and inconsistent."[292] After this, a battle with Lord Chancellor Hailsham was inevitable.[293]

The incursions into the field of precedent dramatically underscore the Denning approach. Throughout his judicial career, Denning was gnawing at doctrines that he felt to be wrong. As early as *Robertson* v. *Minister of Pensions*,[294] Denning, as a judge of first instance, was arguing

288. [1964] A.C. 1129.

289. E.g., *Australian Consol. Press, Ltd.* v. *Uren*, [1969] A.C. 590 (P.C.).

290. *Broome* v. *Cassell & Co.*, [1971] 2 Q.B. 354, 380–81 (C.A.).

291. For a delightful example of Denning's use of conventional concepts of precedent, see *Fawcett Properties, Ltd.* v. *Buckingham County Council*, [1961] A.C. 636, 675 (1960). Cf. his dissent in *London Transp. Executive* v. *Betts*, [1959] A.C. 213, 246 (1958) on the force of *Potteries Elec. Traction Co.* v. *Bailey*, [1931] A.C. 151 (1930): "The decision may be binding on your Lordships if there is another such paint shop anywhere, but it is not, in my opinion, binding for anything else."

292. *Broome* v. *Cassell & Co.*, [1971] 2 Q.B. 354, 381 (C.A.). He continued:

In the result I would hold that, even if *Rookes v. Barnard* . . . is binding on us, we should so construe it as not to invalidate the verdict in this case.

This case may, or may not, go on appeal to the House of Lords. I must say a word, however, for the guidance of the judges who will be trying cases in the meantime. I think the difficulties presented by *Rookes v. Barnard* are so great that the judges should direct the juries in accordance with the law as it was understood before *Rookes v. Barnard*. Any attempt to follow *Rookes v. Barnard* is bound to lead to confusion. [Ibid. 384]

293. Denning, however, was not easily repressed. See, for instance, his judgment in *in re Harper* v. *National Coal Bd. (intended action)*, [1974] Q.B. 614 (C.A.). In discussing a then recently decided House of Lords case, *Smith* v. *Central Asbestos Co.*, [1973] A.C. 518 (1972), he noted, "there is no discernible ratio among the majority of the House of Lords. In these circumstances I think we are at liberty to adopt the reasoning which appears to us to be correct. In my opinion we should adopt the reasoning which was accepted in the court in the long line of cases before the decision of the House of Lords"; ibid. 780. See also Denning's continued willingness to treat the House's decisions as given per incuriam; *Schorsch Meier G.m.b.H.* v. *Hennin*, [1975] Q.B. 416 (C.A. 1974).

294. [1949] 1 K.B. 227, 231 (1948).

that the doctrine of the *Amphitrite*,[295] which appeared to allow government contracts to be broken at will, should be drastically curtailed. In his first case as a Lord of Appeal, *Rahimtoola v. Nizam of Hyderabad*, he argued strongly in favor of a reworking of the doctrine of sovereign immunity.[296] Such a position was scarcely surprising from a man who, in 1953, saw fit to publish a volume entitled *The Changing Law*.[297] Yet, in keeping with the tradition of the English bench, it was in private law, especially in tort and contract,[298] that Denning was at his strongest. In those areas he attempted to make his most obvious mark, and he was by no means unsuccessful.

In contract, it has already been seen that he attempted to open up the concept of frustration.[299] He was, however, after bigger game. He wished to weaken the strong position that consideration had acquired in English law, by developing a concept of equitable estoppel.[300] He fought equally vigorously against the narrow English view that only a party to a contract might sue on it.[301] The English position that one party to a contract might so limit his liability by exception clauses that he might have no basic responsibilities appalled him.[302] After a series of cases in

295. *Rederiaktiebolaget Amphitrite v. The King*, [1921] 3 K.B. 500, 503–4 (Mr. Justice Rowlatt).

296. "[S]overeign immunity should not depend on whether a foreign government is impleaded, directly or indirectly, but rather on the nature of the dispute. . . . If the dispute brings into question, for instance, the legislative or international transactions of a foreign government, or the policy of its executive, the court should grant immunity if asked to do so, because it does offend the dignity of a foreign sovereign to have the merits of such a dispute canvassed in the domestic courts of another country, but if the dispute concerns, for instance, the commercial transactions of a foreign government . . . there is no ground for granting immunity"; [1958] A.C. 379, 422 (1957).
The other law lords specifically dissociated themselves from this position. See, e.g., Simonds, ibid. 398.
In later years, as Master of the Rolls, Denning had greater latitude in developing the principle of sovereign immunity. In *Thai-Europe Tapioca Serv., Ltd. v. Government of Pakistan*, [1976] 1 Lloyd's List L.R. 1 (C.A. 1975), Denning relied on his dicta in *Rahimtoola*, justifying the principle in the light of subsequent U.S. decisions.

297. Alfred Denning, *The Changing Law*. For examples of Denning's manipulation of precedent as a law lord, see his efforts to save the earlier precedent in *Midland Silicones, Ltd. v. Scruttons, Ltd.*, [1962] A.C. 446, 483, 492 (1961). For examples of vigorous attacks on earlier precedents, see for instance, *Blyth v. Blyth*, [1966] A.C. 643, 667 (1965), where he refused to follow a doctrine of MacDermott's about the burden of proof in matrimonial cases; and *Betty's Cafés, Ltd. v. Phillips Furnishing Stores, Ltd.*, [1959] A.C. 20, 49 (1958).

298. For a brief outline of such cases see Denning, "The Way of the Iconoclast."

299. *British Movietonews, Ltd. v. London & Dist. Cinemas, Ltd.*, [1952] A.C. 166 (1951).

300. *Central London Property Trust, Ltd. v. High Trees House, Ltd.*, [1947] K.B. 130 (1946); *Combe v. Combe*, [1951] 2 K.B. 215 (C.A.); *Tool Metal Mfg. Co. v. Tungsten Elec. Co.*, [1954] 1 W.L.R. 862 (C.A.).

301. *Midland Silicones, Ltd. v. Scruttons, Ltd.*, [1962] A.C. 446, 481 (1961); *Beswick v. Beswick*, [1968] A.C. 58 (1967).

302. E.g., *Adler v. Dickson*, [1955] 1 Q.B. 158 (C.A. 1954).

which he attempted to limit the right to "contract out" by a particularly narrow construction of exemption clauses, he developed the concept of "fundamental breach."[303] This, in time, was largely eviscerated by the House of Lords[304] although Denning returned to the assault in an effort to resuscitate it.[305]

In that other basic staple of the common law, torts, Denning was equally at home and equally anxious for rapid judicial change. Early in his life in the Court of Appeal, in *Candler v. Crane, Christmas and Company*[306] he called for an extension of negligence to cover financial loss resulting from negligent statements, but he was unable to persuade his fellow Lords Justices to be "bold" rather than "timorous."[307] In this same area of negligence Denning sought to introduce such notions as the "family car."[308] In some ways it was style as much as substance that Denning added to his forays into tort. He sought to weaken the stricter aspects of the Limitation Acts.[309] Unlike most other English judges he took the insurance aspect of the situation into consideration,[310] and he

303. *Karsales (Harrow), Ltd. v. Wallis,* [1956] 1 W.L.R. 936 (C.A.).

304. *Suisse Atlantique Société d'Armament Maritime S.A. v. N.V. Rotterdamsche Kolen Centrale,* [1967] 1 A.C. 361 (1966).

305. *Harbutt's "Plasticine," Ltd. v. Wayne Tank & Pump Co.,* [1970] 1 Q.B. 447 (C.A.). For a good example of his flexible approach to the interpretation of contracts, see *British Crane Hire v. Ipswich Plant Hire,* [1975] Q.B. 303 (C.A. 1974). For his views of penalty clauses in hire purchase agreements, see *Bridge v. Campbell Discount Co.,* [1962] A.C. 600, 631–32: "[T]he courts have power to grant relief against the penal sum contained in this 'minimum payment' clause no matter for what reason the hiring is terminated. . . . Now that equity and law are one, the hire-purchase company should recover its actual damage, and such damage should be assessed according to the realities and not according to any fiction."

306. [1951] 2 K.B. 164 (C.A.).

307. "On the one side there were the timorous souls who were fearful of allowing a new cause of action. On the other side there were the bold spirits who were ready to allow it if justice so required." Referring, at 178, to *Donoghue v. Stevenson,* [1932] A.C. 562 (Scot.). In considerable part, his position was accepted by the House in *Hedley Byrne & Co. v. Heller & Partners,* [1964] A.C. 465 (1963). Denning, however, still pushed forward. See, for example, *Dutton v. Bognor Regis UDC,* [1972] 1 Q.B. 373 (C.A. 1971).

308. *Launchbury v. Morgans,* [1971] 2 Q.B. 245 (C.A.). In parallel developments in conflicts law, Denning sought to develop such doctrines as "the proper law of the tort." See especially *Boys v. Chaplin,* [1968] 2 Q.B. 1, 20, 24–26 (C.A. 1967); and *Sayers v. International Drilling Co.,* [1971] 1 W.L.R. 1176, 1180 (C.A.). On the recent development of the doctrine in England, see Albert Venn Dicey and John H. C. Morris, *Conflict of Laws* 936.

309. See especially *Goodchild v. Greatness Timber Co.,* [1968] 2 Q.B. 372 (C.A.) and *in re Pickles v. National Coal Bd. (intended action),* [1968] 1 W.L.R. 997 (C.A.). It is unclear what effect the House's decision in *Central Asbestos Co. v. Dodd,* [1973] A.C. 518 (1972), had on Denning's efforts. Cf. L. J. Watmore, "Personal Injuries" 672; Antony D. Woolf, "Personal Injury Limitation" 824. See also *in re Harper v. National Coal Bd. (intended action),* [1974] Q.B. 614 (C.A.).

310. E.g., *Post Office v. Norwich Union Fire Ins. Soc'y, Ltd.,* [1967] 2 Q.B. 363, 375 (C.A.): "We assume that the defendant in an action of tort is insured unless the contrary appears." See also *Morris v. Ford Motor Co.,* [1973] Q.B. 792, 800 (C.A.), "Their insurance company has received the premiums and should bear the loss."

did not hesitate to criticize decisions like *Lister* v. *Romford Ice*,[311] in which the majority of law lords were content to ignore the reality of the insurance situation. He was prepared, however, to go even further than this. In discussing the extension of the duty of care in negligence, he opined, "[I]t seems to me that it is a question of policy which we, as judges, have to decide." Whatever the situation in the United States, such a position was unique in England.[312]

In attempting to give a balanced view of Denning's contributions to the development of doctrines outside tort and contract, it is not easy to know which areas of law to consider or which periods to cover. If one limits discussion to the few years that Denning spent in the Lords, then only in a small number of areas were there sufficient decisions to discuss his work meaningfully. If one attempts to span his thirty years on the bench, the element of selectivity invariably leads to distortion. Since Denning was one of the few English judges who clearly merits an extensive intellectual biography, the problem of choice and fairness becomes particularly acute.

Because it tells us about the man and his willingness to do battle, it is perhaps important to discuss his not entirely deserved reputation[313] as

311. *Lister* v. *Romford Ice & Cold Storage Co.*, [1957] A.C. 555 (1956). He described *Lister* as "an unfortunate decision. Its ill effects have been avoided only by an agreement between insurers not to enforce it. It should not be extended to this case. I would apply this simple principle: where the risk of a servant's negligence is covered by insurance, his employer should not seek to make that servant liable for it"; *Morris* v. *Ford Motor Co.*, [1973] Q.B. 792, 800 (C.A.).

312. "This case is entirely novel. Never before has a claim been made against a council or its surveyor for negligence in passing a house. . . . The time has come when, in cases of new import, we should decide them according to the reason of the thing.

"In previous times, when faced with a new problem, the judges have not openly asked themselves the question: what is the best policy for the law to adopt? But the question has always been there in the background. It has been concealed behind such questions as: Was the defendant under any duty to the plaintiff? Was the relationship between them sufficiently proximate? Was the injury direct or indirect? Was it foreseeable, or not? Was it too remote? And so forth.

"Nowadays we direct ourselves to considerations of policy"; *Dutton* v. *Bognor Regis UDC*, [1972] 1 Q.B. 373, 397 (C.A. 1971).

He then proceeded to attempt to balance the policies involved in granting a building certificate.

313. His decision in *Close* v. *Steel Co. of Wales*, [1962] A.C. 367, 380 (1961), was against the employee, as was his decision in *Brown* v. *National Coal Bd.*, [1962] A.C. 574, 595 (1961), in which he held that even under the 1911 act the employer's duty was not absolute. In *Qualcast, Ltd.* v. *Haynes*, [1959] A.C. 743, although parts of his speech sound favorable to the employee, "what is 'a proper system of work' is a matter for evidence, not for law books. It changes as the conditions of work change. The standard goes up as men become wiser. It does not stand still as the law sometimes does"; ibid. 760–61. He decided *Gough* v. *National Coal Bd.*, [1959] A.C. 698, 715, in favor of the worker.

His labor cases did not always meet with enthusiasm from the unions. His decisions in the Court of Appeal interpreting the Trade Disputes Act and related legislation attempted to strike a balance between (an admittedly vague) concept of civil liberty and the right of

the champion of the worker. The reputation stemmed from his partial dissent in the Factories Act decision in *Close* v. *Steel Company of Wales*[314] on the effect of the *Nicholls*[315] and *Carroll*[316] cases, which the majority held to be binding on the point in issue. He strenuously denied that these cases covered the facts at all.[317] The dispute was carried into the debating chamber of the House, where Denning clashed with Reid.[318] Denning had some strong words to say about the House's decisions: "The law at the moment is illogical, inconsistent and absurd. . . . I am afraid one has to face the fact that it is the fault of the interpretation which has been put on it by this House sitting judicially, which is infallible, which never makes a mistake and which can never correct itself."[319] In other respects, however, Denning was not thought of as being especially concerned with workmen's problems.

In terms of permanent contributions the Denning approach to statutory interpretation—particularly the application of the mischief rule[320]

---

the unions to exercise their powers to the full. E.g., *Crouch* v. *Post Office*, [1973] 1 W.L.R. 766 (C.A.); *Edwards* v. *Society of Graphical & Allied Trades*, [1971] Ch. 354 (C.A.); *Heatons Transp., Ltd.* v. *Transport & General Workers' Union (T & GWU)*, [1973] A.C. 15 (C.A. 1972); *Hill* v. *C. A. Parsons & Co.*, [1972] Ch. 305 (C.A. 1971).

314. [1962] A.C. 367, 380 (1961).

315. *Nicholls* v. *F. Austin, Ltd.*, [1946] A.C. 493.

316. *Carroll* v. *Andrew Barclay & Sons*, [1948] A.C. 477 (Scot.).

317. "The doctrine that your Lordships are bound by a previous decision of your own is, as I have always understood it, limited to the decision itself and to what is necessarily involved in it. It does not mean that you are bound by the various reasons given in support of it, especially when, they contain 'propositions wider than the case itself required.' . . . I fail to see how any speeches in this House can bind your Lordships to hold that a dangerous part of machinery need not be fenced, when the statute expressly says it shall be"; *Close* v. *Steel Co. of Wales*, [1962] A.C. 367, 388–89 (1961).

318. 248 *Parl. Deb.*, H.L. (5th ser.), col. 1332 (25 Apr. 1963).

319. Ibid., cols. 1332–33. He put much of the blame onto Simonds. "My noble and learned friend Lord Simonds, in an arresting aphorism, said that the purpose of the fence was to keep the worker out, not to prevent pieces of the machines or its products from flying out at him. Well, as I have said, it sounds very arresting but it is not good sense. They are both equally dangerous parts of the machinery and ought to be securely fenced"; ibid., col. 1334. He concluded, "It is a disgrace to the law that it should remain unremedied; and if the decisions of this House judicially, as is our convention, are absolutely binding on successors, and if the House sitting judicially cannot correct its own mistakes, then it is imperative in the law that legislatively this House, sitting as a Legislative Chamber, should immediately take steps to remedy defects in the law when they are exposed"; ibid., col. 1336.

320. In his writings he even succeeded in finding a religious basis for this rule. When the judges were influenced by the teachings of the Bible, "[t]he statutes were to be interpreted, not only according to the language used, but also with regard to the mischief which Parliament sought to remedy, so as to give 'force and life' to the intention of the legislature"; Denning, *Changing Law* 106.

The religious principle in question was "truth." "I cannot help thinking that this literal interpretation of contracts or statutes is a departure from real truth. It makes words the masters of men instead of their servants"; ibid. 105. "[I] fear that the judges are too often inclined to fold their hands and blame the legislature, when really they ought to set to work

—may be almost as important as the shake-up that Denning administered to the concept of precedent.[321] One of his earliest clashes with Simonds came when he announced, in 1950:

> I have no patience with an ultra-legalistic interpretation which would deprive the appellants of their rights altogether. . . . We do not sit here to pull the language of Parliament and of Ministers to pieces and make nonsense of it. That is an easy thing to do, and it is a thing to which lawyers are too often prone. We sit here to find out the intention of Parliament and of Ministers and carry it out, and we do this better by filling in the gaps and making sense of the enactment than by opening it up to destructive analysis.[322]

He did not hesitate to return time and again to this theme, and it led him to demand a "better balance" in corporate tax[323] and rating

---

and give the words a reasonable meaning, even if this does involve a departure from the letter of them"; ibid. 106.

321. Denning was, of course, capable of making the classic English statements on statutory interpretation. In 1949, for instance, he wrote, "In these days no reproach can be levied at the judges that they do not keep pace with the times. The judges of England have no politics and always carry out the intentions of Parliament as expressed in the statutes or to be inferred therefrom"; Alfred Denning, *Freedom under the Law* 84.

"The judges, of course, administer the law, good or bad, as they find it. The law which they administer is made in great part by Parliament, and so they must act in accordance with what Parliament says. They should show proper respect for, and confidence in, what Parliament has decided and should always carry out faithfully the intentions of Parliament"; Alfred Denning, *The Independence of the Judges* 10.

322. *Magor & St. Mellons RDC v. Newport Corp.*, [1950] 2 All E.R. 1226, 1236 (C.A.). The Simonds reply was direct: "This proposition . . . cannot be supported. It appears to me to be a naked usurpation of the legislative function under the thin disguise of interpretation"; [1952] A.C. 189, 191 (1951). Earlier, Denning had said:

A judge, believing himself to be fettered by the supposed rule that he must look to the language and nothing else, laments that the draftsmen have not provided for this or that, or have been guilty of some or other ambiguity. It would certainly save the judges trouble if Acts of Parliament were drafted with divine prescience and perfect clarity. In the absence of it, when a defect appears, a judge cannot simply fold his hands and blame the draftsman. He must set to work on the constructive task of finding the intention of Parliament and he must do this not only from the language of the statute, but also from a consideration of the social conditions which gave rise to it, and other mischief which it was passed to remedy, and then he must supplement the written word so as to give "force and life" to the intention of the legislature. [*Asher v. Seaford Court Estates, Ltd.*, [1949] 2 K.B. 481, 499–500 (C.A.)]

His views did not change. See, for instance, *Croft v. Land Comm'rs*, [1971] R.V.R. 174 (C.A.): "It may be that there is a gap left by Parliament in the statute. But I would say, as I have said on previous occasions, it is open to this Court in a proper case to fill in the gaps. We can do what the legislators would have done if they had thought about it."

323. It was in the field of tax law that the mischief rule found its clearest exposition. His speech in *Escoigne Properties, Ltd. v. IRC* provided a forum for his exposition of the rule. "A statute" he announced, "is not passed in a vacuum." To determine what Parliament had in view, "[a]ll that the courts can do is to take judicial notice of the previous state of the law and of other matters generally known to well-informed people"; [1958] A.C. 549, 565–66.

In short, he refused to take a formalistic approach to tax law. "The whole field of revenue law is simply one of Parliament enacting words in a Statute so as to impose taxes or duties, and of accountants, solicitors and barristers all of them—finding ways round these cases.[324] Although, as in so many areas of Denning's work, the policy directions in which the law was to be developed were rough-hewn rather than sophisticated, he sensed that a stricter approach to interpretation might be justified in criminal statutes.[325] Beyond those general guidelines he had apparently not sought to rethink the nineteenth-century assumptions that underlay the current canons of construction.

Indeed, if one were to criticize Denning's courageous assault on the citadels of substantive formalism generally it would be in terms of a lack of sophistication. This observation should in no way cloud his remarkable contribution to the debates about law and justice over this extended period, but as one moves away from the "pure" common law areas, the inherent weaknesses of the Denning style of lawmaking become more obvious. In criminal law, for instance, Denning appeared erratic. In general he seemed to assume, if not to articulate, that criminal law had greater need for stare decisis and strict construction than many other areas of the law, but at times he needlessly confused settled doctrines.[326] In policy terms, it often seemed that a muscular Christian belief in "law

---

words, finding gaps in the Act, so that the provisions do not apply"; 264 *Parl. Deb.*, H.L. (5th ser), col. 1212 (1 Apr. 1965).

He opined, for example:

My Lords, I am almost shy of attaching so much weight to Section 58(4): for I am well aware that the Master of the Rolls found it inelegant and obscure. Its language was, he said, almost offending. And even Romer L.J. found it bewildering. So be it. If it is to be approached literally, I would find the same. But where I differ is that I think we should not place so much emphasis on the literal wording of it. We should seek rather to find the objective which Parliament had in mind when it enacted it. And this I have no doubt about. The object was to make sure that, whenever the Act referred to a single person doing something or other, it covered him also when he was one of several doing it jointly. Seeing that is its object, I would do my best to effectuate it, even in a taxing statute, especially when the contrary view leads to such untoward results. [*Barclays Bank Ltd.* v. *IRC*, [1961] A.C. 509, 544 (1960)]

But compare *Hochstrasser (Inspector of Taxes)* v. *Mayes*, [1960] A.C. 376, 397 (1959), where he rejected the Crown's definition of profits. "It would, if accepted, put a greater burden on the taxpayer than ever the statute warrants, and it would introduce more confusion into a subject where enough already exists."

In interpreting tax situations, he looked to substance rather than to form. E.g., *Littlewoods Mail Order Stores, Ltd.* v. *McGregor*, 45 Tax Cas. 519, 536 (C.A. 1969): "I think we should look at the Fork Manufacturing Co., Ltd. and see it as it really is—the wholly-owned subsidiary of Littlewoods. It is the creation, the puppet of Littlewoods in point of fact; and it should be so regarded in point of law."

324. E.g., *Imperial Tobacco Co.* v. *Pierson*, [1961] A.C. 463, 477, where Denning dissented. "[I] am a little suspicious of the literal rule in this case, because it leads to such surprising results."

325. E.g., in *Jones* v. *DPP*, [1962] A.C. 635, 666 (1961), dissenting with Devlin, on the construction of the Evidence Act of 1898, taking the time-honored broad view of the provisions of § 1.

326. E.g., *DPP* v. *Head*, [1959] A.C. 83, 104 (1958). The House unanimously dismissed the appeal, but whereas the majority did so because they considered the Court of Criminal Appeal had been correct, Denning considered the lower court wrong but argued that it would not be fair in the circumstances to restore the conviction. See especially at 111–14.

and order"[327] was at least as much responsible for his goals as any developed notion that laws should be "clear" in the criminal area. Denning was a party to *Director of Public Prosecutions v. Smith*,[328] although he later tried to explain away the novelty of his decision,[329] and the idea of responsibility found in *Smith* is also evident in his decisions on automation[330] and drunkenness.[331] In general, Denning took a tough line against the criminal.[332] He was not swayed by arguments that the offense of misprision of felony that the House resurrected was too wide, and he would not allow close family or personal ties to justify the refusal to report an offense, adopting an objective test for deciding whether a person had knowledge of an offense.[333]

Indeed, in Denning's makeup ran a strong streak of nineteenth-century morality that sometimes emerged in criminal cases and, for him, rapidly became entwined in rather emotional aspects of personal morals.[334] This same tendency affected his outlook in some aspects of family

327. Denning also exhibited uncritical observations about the virtues of the English courts and police. With respect to the courts, see, for example, his advocacy of "forum shopping" (provided the forum was England) in Young, "England's Most Revolutionary Judge" 30. On the police, see, for instance, 219 *Parl. Deb.*, H.L. (5th ser.), col. 434 (5 Nov. 1959), and 220 ibid. cols. 736–38 (27 Jan. 1960).

328. [1961] A.C. 290 (1960).

329. See Alfred Denning, *Responsibility before the Law* 30, where he agreed that perhaps the House did not stress that the objective test was only a test and that a subjective proposition underlay the whole discussion. However, he argued, the law holds every man responsible for his actions and it cannot admit of excuses that would render the due administration of the law impossible or ineffective.

Rather strangely, he was also on record as saying, "In order to hold a person individually responsible for his crime, so as to be liable to punishment, it is obviously necessary that he should have a guilty mind. . . . In order that an act should be punishable, it must be morally blameworthy. It must be a sin"; Denning, *Changing Law* 112. He stressed, however, that the M'Naughten Rules were concerned with a "man's knowledge not . . . his will power"; ibid. 113.

330. See *Bratty v. Attorney-General for Northern Ireland*, [1963] A.C. 386, 408 (N. Ire. 1961).

331. *Attorney-General for Northern Ireland v. Gallagher*, [1963] A.C. 349, 379–80 (N. Ire. 1961), where he restated the law of drunkenness as a crime:

My Lords, this case differs from all others in the books in that the accused man, whilst sane and sober, before he took to the drink, had already made up his mind to kill his wife. This seems to me to be far worse—and far more deserving of condemnation—than the case of a man who, before getting drunk, has no intention of killing, but afterwards in his cups, whilst drunk kills another by an act which he would not dream of doing when sober. Yet by the law of England in this latter case his drunkenness is no defence even though it has distorted his reason and his will-power. So why should it be a defence in the present case? And, is it any better by saying that the man is a psychopath?

332. See also, *DPP v. Head*, [1959] A.C. 83, 104 (1958), and *Welham v. DPP*, [1961] A.C. 103, 129 (1960), where he rejected the views of modern scholars on the meaning of "with intent to defraud." Characteristically, he continued, "Seeing, therefore, that the words of the statute are of doubtful import, it is, I think, legitimate to turn for guidance to the previous state of the law before the Act"; ibid. 131.

333. *Sykes v. DPP*, [1962] A.C. 528, 563–64 (1961).

334. Denning, for instance, was reluctant to enforce rules of national justice rigidly when a woman student had allowed a man to stay overnight in her room at a Teachers

law. Undoubtedly he achieved much in this area. He fought a vigorous, if legally inconvenient, battle to provide a matrimonial home for deserted spouses, until the House of Lords killed the concept in *National Provincial Bank, Limited* v. *Ainsworth*.[335] He was also instrumental in preventing unreasonable hurdles being put in the way of divorce petitions,[336] and legislatively he supported a more flexible divorce law.[337] Yet publicly he felt a need to pontificate on morality, an aspect of the English judicial style that alarmed Devlin. Denning saw the divorce reform legislation and the Abortion Act as evidence of a weakening commitment to chastity and thereby as a step toward the destruction of family life. "It is time for all good folk to take a stand; else the permissive society will soon become the decadent society."[338] Moreover, although his views appeared to oscillate somewhat, Denning at different times appeared to see the legalization of homosexual acts between consenting adults,[339] the abolition of the death penalty,[340] and the extension of criminal legal aid[341] as further evidence of the decadent society.

Perhaps the element of self-perceived morality also played some part in Denning's judicial decisions in the area of constitutional and administrative law. His approach showed much of the civil libertarian—for example, his insistence that newspapers were free to criticize the courts,[342]

College. In overlooking procedural niceties in her dismissal, he noted: "This is a fine example to set for others! And she a girl training to be a teacher! I expect the governors and staff all thought she was an unsuitable person. . . . She would never make a teacher. No person would knowingly entrust their child to her care"; *Ward* v. *Bradford Corporation*, 70 L. G. R. 27 (C.A. 1972).

335. [1965] A.C. 1175. The legislature ultimately intervened to produce a Denningesque solution; Matrimonial Homes Act of 1967. Even then Denning helped develop a right of a mistress to a matrimonial home; *Eves* v. *Eves*, [1975] 1 W.L.R. 1338 (C.A.).

336. E.g., *Blyth* v. *Blyth*, [1966] A.C. 643, 667 (1965).

337. For his support of the "irretrievable break-down of marriage" test provided by the Divorce Reform Act of 1969, see *The Times*, 1 Oct. 1971. For Denning's earlier views on divorce, see *Changing Law* 120–22. "The only real remedy is the growth of a strong public opinion condemning divorce, and, I would add, condemning infidelity. It is the concern of everyone who has the welfare of the country at heart"; ibid. 121–22 and 250 *Parl. Deb.*, H.L. (5th ser.), cols. 405–7 (22 May 1963), warmly welcoming the Matrimonial Causes and Reconciliation Bill.

338. *The Times*, 1 Oct. 1971.

339. He strongly opposed the reforms of the law relating to homosexuals suggested by the Wolfenden Committee. "Natural sin is of course deplorable, but unnatural vice is worse because as the law says, it strikes at the integrity of the human race"; 206 *Parl. Deb.*, H.L. (5th ser.), col. 807 (4 Dec. 1957).

340. He opposed the abolition of capital punishment; 268 ibid., cols. 678–81 (20 July 1965). He still considered it a deterrent and believed that the objects of punishment were retributive as well as deterrent and reformatory. Denning was later to vote against any extension in the experimental period for the abolition of the death penalty; *The Times*, 20 Dec. 1969.

341. *The Times*, 13 Jan. 1972.

342. For his earlier views, see Denning, *Freedom under the Law*, and for later views, see his evidence (with Salmon) to the Phillimore Committee on Contempt of Court; *Report*

a view that opened up the possibility of serious criticism of the judicial process in the thalidomide case.³⁴³ It was also he who, in a series of courageous decisions, sought to interpret the Race Relations Acts of 1965 and 1968 broadly, only to see his efforts in the Court of Appeal reversed in the House of Lords.³⁴⁴ He also attempted to make the National Industrial Relations Act more palatable to the unions.³⁴⁵ In general terms, he believed in the right to privacy;³⁴⁶ and in public law, he took tentative pseudo-eighteenth-century steps toward a doctrine that might question parliamentary motives and reintroduce a form of judicial review, at least with respect to the passage of private legislation.³⁴⁷ Neither was he reluctant to curb the discretion of either ministers or law officers.³⁴⁸

Yet, alongside these iconoclastic approaches ran more conventional views. In the House sitting in its legislative capacity, Denning took a large part in the debates following the Franks Committee *Report on Tribunals and Enquiries*³⁴⁹ and spoke at length, often in conventional Diceyian terms,³⁵⁰ about the constitutional principles involved.³⁵¹ His

---

of the Committee on Contempt of Court, Cmnd. 5794, at 98 (1974). See also *Fraser v. Evans,* [1969] 1 Q.B. 349 (C.A. 1968).

343. *Attorney-General v. Times Newspapers, Ltd.,* [1973] Q.B. 710 (C.A.). His narrow view of contempt was not accepted by the House, [1974] A.C. 273 (1973).

344. See, for instance, in *Charter*: "To my mind the members of the Conservative Club are 'a section of the public.' They are Conservative. That is the one quality which is common to them all. It is the *sine qua non.* It is essentially an impersonal quality"; *Race Relations Bd. v. Charter,* [1972] 1 Q.B. 545, 556 (C.A.). He tried again in the *Dockers' Club* case: "Here numbers count. . . . The number of associates is so large that they cannot be regarded as private body. They are to my mind a section of the public"; *Race Relations Bd. v. Dockers' Labour Club & Institute, Ltd.,* [1974] 1 Q.B. 503, 511 (C.A.).

345. *Heatons Transp. (St. Helens), Ltd. v. T & GWU,* [1973] 15 A.C. (C.A. and H.L. 1972), on the liability of unions for acts of their officials.

346. 229 *Parl. Deb.,* H.L. (5th ser.), col. 639 (13 Mar. 1961): "The courts of the United States have founded a complete doctrine of the right of privacy. . . . Why cannot we do something similar? I am not in despair."

347. *Pickin v. British Rys. Bd.,* [1973] Q.B. 219 (C.A. 1972). See, for instance, Denning: "[S]uppose the court were satisfied that this private Act was improperly obtained, it might well be the duty of the court to report that finding to Parliament, so that Parliament itself could take cognisance of it." For the House of Lords decision, see *British Rys. Bd. v. Pickin,* [1974] A.C. 765.

348. See *Secretary of State for Educ. & Science v. Tameside Metropolitan Borough Council,* [1977] A.C. 1014, 1020 (C.A. 1976); and his de facto dissent in *Gouriet v. Union of Post Office Workers,* [1977] Q.B. 729, 733 (C.A.).

349. Cmnd. 218 (1957).

350. Denning could be as trite as the next judge; see, for example, *Freedom under the Law* 58: "The common law of England is, on the whole, in full accord with the good sense of the people. The judge states it simply and clearly to the jury and they loyally accept it from him," and, "[s]o long as the judges hold the balance there will be no police state in England"; ibid. 31. "Secure from any fear of removal, the Judges of England do their duty fearlessly, holding the scales even, not only between man and man, but also between man and the State"; *Independence of Judges* 7.

351. See 206 *Parl. Deb.,* H.L. (5th ser.), cols. 544–49 (27 Nov. 1957); 208, ibid., cols.

basic theme was that tribunals ought to be part of the judicial system without any responsibility to the executive.[352] It was thus important to establish an appeal from them to the courts on all points of law[353] and to require that tribunals give their reasons for their decisions.[354] The whole argument suggested a lack of analysis of the different types of tribunals involved. Denning later took the view that control over tribunals had been achieved,[355] although he wanted to see more control over inquiries and over what he termed "maladministration."[356] He frequently argued against a written constitution on the ground that the common law and the judiciary were a better bulwark,[357] but the argument sometimes appeared to be based on a simplistic view of politics and the administrative process.

In short, Denning, an outstandingly able and intelligent lawyer, may fairly be described as primarily a "visceral" appeal judge. Perhaps his approach was exactly what the English legal system needed as an antidote to the period of substantive formalism. As the majority of appeal judges began to move away from the image of high formalism, Denning came through as a judge who shot from the hip and who, despite his prominence, gave scant thought either to the juristic techniques available to him or to the constitutional implications of his approach. His commitment to judicial legislation was clear, but the public nuances of judicial restraint and activism were overlooked in the hectic judicial life. This lack of defined purpose becomes even more obvious when a systematic effort is made to examine his concept of the relationship of law and justice.

600–6 (1 Apr. 1958); 236 ibid., cols. 204–9 (7 Dec. 1961); and 233 ibid., cols. 175–81 (12 July 1961).

352. [The Franks Report] "contains and reaffirms a constitutional principle of the first importance—namely, that these tribunals are not part of the administrative machinery of government under the control of departments. They are part of the judicial system of the land under the rule of law"; 206 *Parl. Deb.*, H.L. (5th ser.), col. 544 (27 Nov. 1957). "These tribunals form as valuable and indispensable a part of our judicial system as justices of the peace; their work is just as valuable, and they should be held in high regard"; ibid., col. 549.

353. "I would ask that, if appeals are to be limited to points of law, a liberal interpretation should be given as to what constitutes a point of law"; 206 ibid., col. 548 (27 Nov. 1957).

354. 208 ibid., col. 600 (1 Apr. 1958).

355. 233 ibid. col. 176 (12 July 1961): "May I say that the Council on Tribunals, from their Reports, have done a really magnificent job in seeing that the rules of procedure will be governed by the rules of ordinary fair play?"

356. Ibid., especially at col. 180. He considered that rather than introduce an ombudsman the sphere of control by the Council on Tribunals could be extended; 236 ibid., cols. 204–9 (7 Dec. 1961). Ultimately, Parliament did introduce an ombudsman (parliamentary commissioner) by the Parliamentary Commissioner Act of 1967.

357. "We regard judges as standing between the individual and the state, protecting the individual from any interference with his freedom which is not justified by the law"; Denning, *Independence of Judges* 1.

Inevitably, underlying Denning's demands for changing the law were certain assumptions about the policies to be pursued in making those changes. In general, Denning was less articulate about his goals than his discussion of the opportunities to work toward them. He was not, however, entirely silent. "Each generation has its duty to keep the law in conformity with needs of the time. Indeed, its function, as I would see it, is just to see that justice is done according to the law. The law should be such that it meets with the approval of right-thinking members of the community."[358] But who are "right-thinking people"? From Denning's words, it is far from easy to know, but they are apparently, preferably, Christians. "Although religion, law and morals can be separated, they are nevertheless still very much dependent on each other. Without religion there can be no morality, and without morality there can be no law."[359] At root, then, Denning differs little from Radcliffe: "The common law of England has been molded for centuries by judges who have been brought up in the Christian faith. The precepts of religion, consciously or unconsciously, have been their guide in the administration of justice."[360] Indeed, he feared for English law, "[i]f religion perishes in the land, truth and justice will also. We have already strayed too far from the faith of our fathers. Let us return to it, for it is the only thing that can save us."[361] It was little wonder that Denning, the lawmaker, felt impelled to speak out so freely on moral issues.[362]

In the American context a judicial activist like Denning would be expected to have both a more clearly articulated and balanced view of the judicial process and a more sophisticated concept of the underlying purposes toward which he was developing the law. Ultimately, the future of

358. "[O]nly second to that would I put certainty. But certainty, I am afraid, can rarely be achieved to the degree which we should like, because when you are legislating you cannot foresee the innumerable circumstances which may arise"; 229 *Parl. Deb.*, H.L. (5th ser.), col. 639 (13 Mar. 1961). See also Denning, *Road to Justice* 4–5, on the theme of how to define justice. Cf. Geoffrey Marshall, *Constitutional Theory* 90.

359. Denning, *Changing Law* 99.

360. Ibid. 109.

361. Ibid. 122.

362. In addition to the subjects already discussed, see his welcome to the Suicide Bill. "This bill heralds the end of a long chapter in our English Law"; 229 *Parl. Deb.*, H.L. (5th ser.), col. 266 (2 Mar. 1961). He voted for the Second Reading of the Abortion Bill, 270 ibid., cols. 1181–84 (30 Nov. 1965); and opposed the reintroduction of corporal punishment; 230 ibid., cols. 1119–23 (1 May 1961): "We should not, on our collective responsibility, do an act which individually I believe no one of us would be prepared to do or even to witness." He supported the Street Offences Bill but was a little disturbed at the use of the word "common prostitute," which he considered implied guilt before trial. He also wanted to see male prostitutes equally subject to the law. "These men loiter as much as women . . . . They are loitering for this purpose too"; 216 ibid., cols. 779–83 (9 June 1959), and 217 ibid., cols. 1198–99 (14 July 1959). He considered that the Obscene Publications Act was not vigorous enough against pornography; 216 ibid., cols. 503–7 (2 June 1959).

the judicial role in England, even in its reaction to substantive formalism, may lie far more with subtle use of judicial restraint than with scattershot judicial activism. Despite this caution, few would deny that Denning was the most important judge sitting in 1977.

When the history of the twentieth-century judiciary comes to be written, Denning's name may well be the most prominent, not so much for what he did, but for what he showed was possible. Indeed, all four law lords discussed in this chapter posed fundamental questions about the role of the appeal process. Once substantive formalism was left behind, the questions of what guided the law and in which direction could no longer be ignored. For Radcliffe the guide was a kind of fundamental or natural law; for Devlin, a *Volksgeist* to be derived from basically democratic sources. Reid, more of a craftsman and less of a philosopher, preferred to apply a concept of common sense behind the shroud of judicial restraint. Judicial restraint was not something that came easily to Denning. He saw few political or intellectual reasons why, in the areas where litigation took place, the appeal judges should not be lawgivers. These four partly competing concepts may well reflect the lines of battle along which discussion of the appellate process could take place in the later 1970s and the 1980s.

FOURTEEN

The Law Lords: The First Decade

The groping toward and gradual development of a rationale for the final appeal court was not, of course, the work of four law lords, however outstanding their careers; it was the effort of a large number of Lords of Appeal over a twenty-year period. In addition to the increase in the number of law lords in 1948 and 1968,[1] the rate of their turnover continued to be rapid, at least during the early years under discussion. These were obviously transitional years, and however one tries to separate the law lords into categories, there are elements of arbitrariness. Nevertheless, the internal pressures between the waning influence of the substantive formalists and the growing power of those who advocated a creative (albeit limited) role for the final appeal court are perhaps best illustrated by looking at the law lords of this period through the categories of the Scottish, political, Chancery, and divorce traditions.

1. An effect of the increased numbers, however, was that fewer law lords were created who were not Lords of Appeal or Lord Chancellors. The three leading exceptions during this period were Lords Merriman, Parker of Waddington, and Birkett.

Merriman (1880–1962) was a former Conservative M.P. (1924–33), Solicitor-General (1928–29 and 1932–33), and President of the Probate, Divorce and Admiralty Division (1933–62), who sat occasionally in the House between 1948 and 1962, mainly in matrimonial appeals. See, e.g., *Baxter* v. *Baxter*, [1948] A.C. 274 (1947); and *Jamieson* v. *Jamieson*, [1952] A.C. 525 (Scot.). He also sat in Admiralty and maritime appeals. See, e.g., *The Empire Jamaica*, [1957] A.C. 386 (1956); and *Riverstone Meat Co.* v. *Lancashire Shipping Co.*, [1961] A.C. 807 (1960).

Merriman's approach was generally conservative. See, for instance, his dissent with Hodson in *Ross Smith* v. *Ross Smith*, [1963] A.C. 280 (1962). Although Merriman apparently sat in only 7 cases, he made 26 speeches in legislative proceedings.

Parker, who was Lord Chief Justice from 1958 to 1971, sat only once in the House while he held office, to concur in *DPP* v. *Smith*, [1961] A.C. 290 (1960). He did, however, sit occasionally in the Privy Council after his retirement. See Louis Blom-Cooper and Gavin Drewry, *Final Appeal* 181.

Parker was, however, a frequent speaker in legislative debates. He spoke on 39 occasions between 1958 and 1968; ibid. 205. See, for instance, his attempt to dispel the notion that judges were "reactionary"; 258 *Parl. Deb.*, H.L. (5th ser.), cols. 1071–74 (11 June 1964); and his vigorous opposition to the War Damage Bill: "about as blatant a piece of confiscatory legislation as it is possible to imagine"; 264 ibid., col. 777 (25 Mar. 1965).

The Scottish Tradition

As Scottish Lords of Appeal, Keith (1953–61) and Guest (1961–71) were overshadowed by their contemporary, Reid, and successor, Kilbrandon. Yet Keith had a well-deserved reputation as an iconoclast and was no mean appeal judge, while Guest, for reasons that are unclear, became perhaps the most anglicized of the Scottish law lords and almost as comfortable with substantive formalism as Normand.

Lord Keith of Avonholm was appointed as a Scottish "representative" to replace Normand in 1953.[2] Said to be loath to leave Scotland,[3] Keith made it plain in his speeches and his contributions to the legislative debates of the House that he had a higher opinion of Scottish than of English law.[4] He probably made his greatest contribution to the law when he was sitting as a Lord Ordinary in Scotland, not in the House of Lords[5] where he so often held the minority view.[6] Indeed, it can be

---

In attempting to dispel the idea that judges had opposed reform, Parker spelled out his philosophy:

For centuries the judges made the law and extended the law to meet the changing needs of society. Indeed in doing so, they gave decisions involving a very high degree of policy.

It is only in this century and the last that the judge-made law has shrunk and shrunk; and now the position is that the judges sit day by day in court, they see where the shoe pinches and they see where the law which they have to administer appears to work injustice. I venture to think that the judges have done a lot to accelerate reform. . . .

[W]hile being a reformer at heart I feel very strongly, that especially in the law, great care should be taken to see that what you are seeking to put in its place is better than what was there before. . . . Above all, care should be taken not to reform for reform's sake or to carry out reform which is purely window dressing. [258 ibid., cols. 1072, 1074]

Birkett (1883–1962), a former Lord Justice (1950–57), was given a peerage in 1958. An attractive man, he was better known (and perhaps happier) as a man of letters and an advocate than he was as a judge. He appears to have sat in only 7 appeals in the Lords, in only 2 of which he gave judgment: *National Deposit Friendly Soc'y Trustees* v. *Skegness UDC*, [1959] A.C. 293 (1958) (rating); and *Winter* v. *IRC*, [1963] A.C. 235 (1961) (taxation). During that same period he made at least 10 speeches in debates. See generally H. Montgomery Hyde, *Norman Birkett*, and Dennis Bardens, *Lord Justice Birkett*.

2. James Keith; b. 1886; father, businessman (knighted); educ., Hamilton Academy, Glasgow University (First, History); Advocate, 1911; K.C., 1926; Senator, College of Justice, 1937–53; Lord of Appeal, 1953–61; d. 1964.

3. Obituary, *The Times*, 1 July 1964, at 14, col. 5.

4. See, e.g., The Death Penalty (Abolition) Bill; 198 *Parl. Deb.*, H.L. (5th ser.), col. 641 (9 July 1956), and 216 ibid., col. 1171 (16 June 1959). Occupiers' Liability (Scotland) Bill: "One of the purposes of this bill is, of course, to return to what was the old law in Scotland before it was affected by the decisions of the House sitting in its judicial capacity." See also James Keith, *The Spirit of the Law of Scotland*.

5. He was appointed Dean of the Faculty of Advocates in 1936 and in 1937 a Senator: "The appointment was warmly approved by the profession, and on the bench he worthily sustained the reputation he had made at the Bar. . . . As a Lord Ordinary in the Outer House and in the Inner House where he sat under Lord Cooper's presidency his opinions were marked by their freshness and independence. Lord Cooper was an innovator of independent mind, but in the Division Lord Keith for other reasons and from a different approach frequently dissented. They both put life into the law of Scotland"; Obituary, *The Times*, 1 July 1964.

6. No fewer than 22 percent of his full opinions were dissents. For Denning, in second place, the figure was 16 percent; Blom-Cooper and Drewry, *Final Appeal* 179.

argued that Keith viewed the House of Lords sitting in its judicial capacity as an alien body interfering with the orderly development of Scottish law and overturning traditional doctrines. He clearly felt this in the field of negligence,[7] and he was obviously relieved that the House had never been allowed to tamper with Scottish criminal law.[8] In other areas as well, he did not hesitate to point to the inherent advantages in the Scottish system.[9]

Keith had been a dissenter as a Lord Ordinary and carried this practice into the House of Lords sitting in both its legislative[10] and its judicial capacities.[11] For instance, as a legislator, he had no difficulty espousing causes long before they were acceptable to other members of the judiciary. He supported the abolition of capital punishment as early as 1956,[12] and in 1959 supported legislation allowing children born as a result of an adulterous union to be legitimated by subsequent marriage of their parents.[13]

7. "Left to itself the law of negligence in Scotland would no doubt have developed easily along a well-defined course and have achieved results in most cases not materially different from those achieved, with perhaps more difficulty or ingenuity, in England, in the development of the law of tort"; *Spirit of the Law of Scotland* 9. He felt this to be especially true of the law of occupiers' liability; ibid. 14.

8. "Criminal administration in Scotland is a highly efficient, satisfactory and enlightened system and the criminal law, as developed by the Scottish judges, from whom no appeal lies to the House of Lords, presents some features that are opposed to settled doctrine in England"; ibid. 30.

9. It was, therefore, probably with a considerable amount of satisfaction that he could say, in an English appeal, *National Bank of Greece & Athens S.A.* v. *Metliss*, [1958] A.C. 509, 530 (1957), concerned with the nationalization of a Greek bank and succession to another person's rights and obligation: "The term 'universal successor' may be foreign to English law but it cannot be regarded as strange in this House for the doctrine is part of the common law of Scotland, though now affected by statute, and till within the last hundred years had important consequences to the heir in a succession."

This approach proved useful when the House had to consider the Greek government's countermove following the *Metliss* case; *Adams* v. *National Bank of Greece S.A.*, [1961] A.C. 255 (1960).

In *Midland Silicones, Ltd.* v. *Scruttons, Ltd.*, [1962] A.C. 446, 479 (1961), he had to apply the English rules of privity of contract, which are alien to Scots law. See *Spirit of the Law of Scotland* 24.

10. Keith spoke an average of once a year; Blom-Cooper and Drewry, *Final Appeal* 205.

11. "[I]n the highest court his contributions were fresh, individual and often dissenting. Despite his years, he seemed in the House of Lords to have the freshness and vigour of youth in 1953. When he was appointed it was written of him—and truly written of him: 'as a person there is a kind of perennial youth about Lord Keith. The years seem to pass him by unscathed . . . he gives the impression that he walks alone. Independent in thought and direct in speech his mind is always alive to consider and weigh an argument, and there is nothing superficial in his legal thinking'"; Obituary, *The Times*, 1 July 1964, at 14.

12. 198 *Parl. Deb.*, H.L. (5th ser.), cols. 641–43 (9 July 1956).

13. 217 ibid., col. 694 (2 July 1959): "Of course, I recognise that this proposal is contrary to the Canon Law, to the law of Scotland, and to the law of England as it at present exists. But we are faced here with a real problem." Simonds rejoined, "I am sure of one thing in the world, that my noble and learned friend Lord Keith of Avonholm would

Judicially Keith dissented more frequently than any other law lord of the period, and his dissents, sometimes based on a disagreement about goals, were more often those of the Scottish judge committed to principle, opposing the then-fashionable English obsession with precedent. Keith refused to weaken the concept of mitigation of damages in contract.[14] In *British Transport Commission* v. *Gourley*,[15] Keith was not at all disturbed that he dissented alone against six law lords:[16] he could find neither reason nor authority to justify a deduction of income tax when assessing damages in tort. His opinion was brief and to the point.[17] He emphasized that it was impossible to make an accurate estimate of the "notional" tax. The existing rule "has been adopted for generations and creates the minimum of trouble."[18] Keith alone of the law lords emphasized that the party who should be benefiting if tax were to be taken into account, namely the government, would be unaffected by the decision.[19] Only the defendant stood to benefit.

In an era still dominated by formalism, Keith's was a voice arguing for realism. The artificial arguments favored by both counsel and judiciary did not appeal to him.[20] He was not blinded by legal logic, whether

---

not dare to get up in Scotland and make, in regard to the law of Scotland, a proposal that he is prepared to sanction in England"; ibid., col. 703.

14. *White & Carter, Ltd.* v. *McGregor*, [1962] A.C. 413, 434 (Scot. 1961), on the election of remedies in contract, was a Scottish appeal in which Keith dissented. The majority view involved overruling a previous decision of the First Division to which Keith had been a party; *Langford & Co.* v. *Dutch*, [1952] Sess. Cas. 15 (1951). Keith was willing to reconsider his decision, but his ultimate view was unchanged. The logical result of the majority's decision "is not, in my opinion, in accordance with principle or authority, and cuts across the rule that where one party is in breach of contract the other must take steps to minimise the loss sustained by the breach"; *White & Carter, Ltd.* v. *McGregor*, at 442. Later writings have generally applauded the Keith position.

15. (1956) A.C. 185, 216 (1955).

16. Jowitt, Goddard, Reid, Radcliffe, Tucker, and Somervell.

17. He began: "My Lords, after listening to the full and able arguments for both sides in this case, I have considered afresh the opinion I expressed in *Blackwood* v. *Andre*. With some regret, knowing the views of your Lordships, I have found myself unable to change my opinion"; [1956] A.C. 185, 216 (1955). The core of his presentation was at 216–17: "I do not ignore the fact that B may need the damages more than A and the difference may seem to introduce a measure of equity as between A and B, to the advantage of the wrongdoer, but the law has not yet reached the state of assessing damages for a legal wrong on the basis of need."

18. Ibid. 217.

19. "If there is a case for thinking that assessing damages on the basis of gross earnings in actions for personal injuries, or for wrongful dismissal, enables the individual to escape his fair contribution to the national revenue, the position, in my opinion, should be rectified by legislation"; ibid. 218. In *West Suffolk County Council* v. *W. Rought, Ltd.*, [1957] A.C. 403, 415 (1956), he felt bound to apply the *Gourley* principle to compensation for loss of profit on compulsory purchase, but he added, "I reserve entirely my opinion on how far the ratio of *Gourley*'s case can be applied to assessing the value of land"; ibid. 416.

20. For example, "The suggestion that *The Aello* failed to get a berth because of the failure of the charterers to have a cargo ready is, in the circumstances, quite unreal";

the issue was one of "lifting the corporate veil"[21] or handling the political aspects of conflicts law.[22] Even in the area of the House's heaviest traffic—tax law—Keith was prepared to be the iconoclast. At a time when the model for interpretation seemed to many to be the crossword puzzle, Keith was willing to look at the substance of the transaction. In *Inland Revenue Commissioners* v. *Saunders*[23] he said, "The Act[24] is not concerned in my opinion with subtleties of conveyancing" and "the reality of the transaction in my opinion, was that the settler made two provisions."[25] When applying a profits tax provision, he was faced with the position that "[i]f the respondents' contentions and the judgement of the court below, as well as the determination of the commissioners, are right there is a gap in the legislation which prevents that intention, in present circumstances, from taking effect."[26] From that point he sought, and found, an interpretation that would not defeat that intention.[27] In-

---

dissenting in *The Aello*, [1961] A.C. 135, 198 (1960). "[I] find it somewhat unreal to imagine a landlord, spurred by the request of a tenant for a new tenancy suddenly to bethink himself of a scheme of reconstructing or substantially altering his premises"; dissenting in *Betty's Cafés, Ltd.* v. *Phillips Furnishing Stores, Ltd.*, [1959] A.C. 20, 47–48 (1958).

See also *Vine* v. *National Dock Labour Bd.*, [1957] A.C. 488, 507 (1956), on the effect of the National Dock Labour Scheme: "The Scheme gives the dock worker a status. Unless registered he is deprived of the opportunity of carrying on what may have been his lifelong employment as a dock worker, and he has a right and interest to challenge any unlawful act that interferes with this status. If the actions here complained of were a nullity, the plaintiff, in my opinion, has a clear right to have that fact declared by the Court"; ibid. 508–9.

21. E.g., "In law the society and the company were, it is true, separate legal entities, [but] the company was in substance, though not in law, a partnership consisting of the society, Dr. Meyer and Mr. Lucas"; *Scottish Co-operative Wholesale Soc'y* v. *Meyer*, [1959] A.C. 324, 361 (Scot. 1958) (a case where relief was given to an oppressed minority under § 210, Companies Act of 1948). "The Section introduces a wide power to the court to deal with such a situation in an equitable manner"; ibid. 364. See also *Lyle & Scott, Ltd.* v. *Scott's Trustees*, [1959] A.C. 763, 786 (Scot.): "There must reside in the courts some power to enforce observance of the article, unless the rights of the shareholders are to be defeated."

22. Dissenting in *Bank voor Handel en Scheepvaart N.V.* v. *Administrator of Hungarian Property*, [1954] A.C. 584, 632 (1953), he maintained that the Custodian of Enemy Property could not claim the Crown's immunity from tax. He alone of the law lords seemed to appreciate that the ultimate benefit of the exemption would be received by the person entitled to the income in question at the end of the war. "It would be a somewhat remarkable result that an immunity could be claimed which was of no benefit to the Crown and was indeed to its detriment"; ibid. 637.

23. [1958] A.C. 285 (1957).

24. § 38, Finance Act of 1938.

25. *IRC* v. *Saunders*, [1958] A.C. 285, 299–300 (1957).

26. *IRC* v. *South Georgia Co.*, [1958] A.C. 599, 613 (Scot.).

27. "There is nothing in the proviso which excludes such an interpretation and such a reading is consistent with the whole object of the statute. As already indicated, the formula of the proviso is designed to secure that any draft from past undistributed income to make up a distribution of dividend should bear its proper share of the distributional charge. This object would be entirely defeated if a company which operated in any year at a loss and paid a dividend out of past profits were to pay no distribution charge. An application of the

deed, in most areas of tax law he sought to return revenue law to a via media.[28]

While Keith could be critical of parliamentary reluctance to bring order to statutory chaos,[29] his general approach to statutes was to seek the intent of Parliament, by looking at the framework of the legislation.[30] When Parliament in 1955 granted rate relief not only to charitable bodies but also to those whose "main objects . . . are . . . concerned with . . . social welfare," Keith proved himself a sophisticated operator in the interstitial development of legislation; the same approach characterized his work in the area of the Factories Acts and related legislation. He thought that legislation designed to protect the worker should be interpreted in his favor where doubt existed.[31] When dealing with the employer's common law duty to his employee, he was anxious to avoid putting glosses on the principle that the employer must take reasonable care for the safety of each of his workmen individually. "In the sphere of negligence where circumstances are so infinite in their variety it is rarely, if ever, that one case can be binding authority for another."[32] On the

---

formula in the proviso to such a case, by taking profits as nil, involves, I think, no straining of the statutory language"; ibid. 616.

28. He was party to *Grey v. IRC*, [1960] A.C. 1 (1959); *Oughtred v. IRC*, [1960] A.C. 206 (1959); and *Parker v. Lord Advocate*, [1960] A.C. 608 (Scot. 1959), all favorable to the Revenue.

Of course he did not invariably find for the Revenue. See, e.g., *Westminster Bank, Ltd. v. IRC*, [1958] A.C. 210 (1957). In characteristic vein, Keith dissented in *Morgan v. Tate & Lyle, Ltd.*, [1955] A.C. 21, 63 (1954), since he took the view that expenses incurred in an antinationalization propaganda campaign were not deductible expenses.

See also his decision in *Regazzoni v. K. C. Sethia (1944), Ltd.*, [1958] A.C. 301, 328 (1957), where he agreed with the view of some of his brethren that the time-honored propositon that "no country ever takes notice of the revenue laws of another" was too widely expressed.

29. E.g., *IRC v. Hinchy*, [1960] A.C. 748, 785. The more irrational aspects of the penalty provisions were remedied by the Finance Act of 1960.

30. *National Deposit Friendly Soc'y Trustees v. Skegness UDC*, [1959] A.C. 293, 307 (1958), interpreting the Rating and Valuation (Miscellaneous Provisions) Act of 1955. The House held that the charitable element of altruism must exist. Keith was worried about going too far too soon; ibid. 311.

In a subsequent case, *General Nursing Council for England & Wales v. St. Marylebone Borough Council*, [1959] A.C. 540, Keith construed the Nurses Act of 1957 to find that the objects of the General Nursing Council were not "directed" to the advancement of social welfare. "We are not concerned with indirect consequences nor entitled to speculate on what ultimate purposes, if any, Parliament had in view"; ibid. 561. In the third case on these provisions, *Skegness UDC v. Derbyshire Miners' Welfare Comm.*, [1959] A.C. 807, he merely concurred. The committee was held to be within the exemption.

31. *Hamilton v. National Coal Bd.*, [1960] A.C. 633, 647 (Scot. 1959). See also *Grant v. National Coal Bd.*, [1956] A.C. 649, 667 (Scot.): "I can deduce from the language used only that the section was passed for the protection of workmen and that if a workman is injured by a breach of the statute he has a remedy in damages against his employer." See also *John Summers & Sons v. Frost*, [1955] A.C. 740, 776.

32. *Qualcast, Ltd. v. Haynes*, [1959] A.C. 743, 755, rejecting the employee's claim. See also *Cavanagh v. Ulster Weaving Co.*, [1960] A.C. 145, 166 (N. Ire. 1959), upholding

other hand, he refused to accept that liability was absolute. In *Davie* v. *New Merton Board Mills, Limited,* he rejected the appellant's claim, noting that "[f]or all practical purposes the appellant's case involves [holding] that an employer is bound to warrant the sufficiency and safety of the tools used by his servants."[33]

In this regard, as in others,[34] Keith revealed an element of conservatism. Yet what survives about him is not conservatism or liberalism but an innate sense of the creative element in the appellate process. Keith would have attributed this approach to his Scottish background. "Principle rather than precedent has always appealed to the Scottish lawyer and the rule of *stare decisis* has held less sway over his mind than in the case of his English neighbour."[35] In developing the law within this approach, Keith manifested eminent good sense[36] in a period when a significant number of law lords apparently had given up the search for a rationale for the appellate process. Compared with Reid, Keith was more Scottish and more outspoken, giving, indeed, the impression that he wished to be thought of primarily as an iconoclast. Had that not been his image and had he remained on the court longer, his influence might well have ranked with Reid's.

The same could not be said of Lord Guest,[37] who replaced Keith in

---

the employee's claim, and questioning Dunedin's observations in *Morton* v. *Wm. Dixon, Ltd.,* [1909] Sess. Cas. 807: "Lord Dunedin cannot, in my opinion, have intended to depart from or modify the fundamental principle that an employer is bound to take reasonable care for the safety of his workmen."

33. [1959] A.C. 604, 652 (1958).

34. For example, Keith refused to join in demolishing Macnaghten's dictum in *Earl Cowley* v. *IRC* that the two sections on estate duty charging in the Finance Act of 1894 were mutually exclusive: "It is impossible to say what effect a departure from a practice based on this pronouncement may have on the future development of estate duty law, but it could be, I should think, not inconsiderable and may lead to the building up of a new body of estate duty decisions. . . . I am not convinced that what has been accepted as settled law should now be reversed and a new chapter of estate duty law entered upon afresh"; *Public Trustee* v. *IRC,* [1960] A.C. 398, 429 (1959). "This may seem contrary to the spirit of the law of Scotland but the spirit must yield to settled precedent"; Keith, *Spirit of the Law of Scotland* 16. Note also *Independent Television Authority & Associated-Rediffusion, Ltd.* v. *IRC,* [1961] A.C. 427, 451 (1960). See also *IRC* v. *Wood Bros. (Birkenhead),* [1959] A.C. 487, 513 (1958), where Keith dissented with Simonds, relying on the old adage that "income tax is a tax on income." "It is said that a change has taken place in the outlook of income tax legislation, and that all receipts which are subject to tax are not necessarily income receipts. . . . But a particular exception . . . does not, in my opinion, detract from the general principle to which I have referred"; ibid. 515.

35. Keith, *Spirit of the Law of Scotland* 18.

36. It was said of Keith that "his advocacy was marked by integrity, perception, and contempt for the verbose." These traits were also manifested in his judicial pronouncements. His opinions were in general concise and clearly argued. It is the exception rather than the rule to find an opinion whose ratio is not clearly expressed. His opinion in *Bonsor* v. *Musicians' Union,* [1956] A.C. 104, 149 (1955), was one of these exceptions.

37. Christopher William Graham Guest; b. 1901; father, J.P.; educ., Merchiston Castle, Cambridge (Second, Law) and Edinburgh; called to Scottish Bar, 1925; Q.C., 1945;

1961 and at once took on the camouflage of substantive formalism at the very time the leading English judges were beginning to talk in more instrumental terms. Guest emitted occasional indications of the Scottish tradition of interest in principle rather than precedent, but these signs were rare.[38] Nor did his experiences as a Conservative candidate in 1945 appear to have given him any wider view of the judicial process.[39]

Guest had no reluctance in falling back on precedent in cases raising difficult issues. For example, in *Close* v. *Steel Company of Wales*,[40] he had no inhibition in applying Simonds' dictum in *Nicholls* v. *F. Austin, Limited*[41] that "the fence is intended to keep the worker out, not to keep the machine or its products in" or in concluding, "[i]t is implicit, in my view, in the decision that the scope of the section only extended to protecting the operator against contact with the dangerous part."[42] Similarly, in *Beswick* v. *Beswick*,[43] although by no means alone, he would not consider departing from the "respectable" line of authority to the effect that a person who is not a party to a contract cannot sue on it. In *Boys* v. *Chaplin*, he insisted on deciding the case on the narrow point that heads of damages were a procedural problem to be determined by the lex fori, totally rejecting the Denning position that the courts should adopt the "proper law of the tort" position.[44] Similarly in *Henderson* v. *Henry E. Jenkins and Sons*,[45] he dissented in favor of a narrow view of *res ipsa loquitur* and so, in effect, in favor of a narrow view of liability.[46]

In approaching tax cases, Guest carried his substantive formalism

---

unsuccessful Conservative (Unionist) candidate, Kirkcaldy, 1945; Dean, Faculty of Advocates, 1955–57; Senator, College of Justice, 1954–61; Lord of Appeal, 1961–71.

38. E.g., *Hughes* v. *Lord Advocate*, [1963] A.C. 837 (Scot.); *Ross Smith* v. *Ross Smith*, [1963] A.C. 280 (1962), where he favored overruling a hundred-year-old decision.

In *Nimmo* v. *Alexander Cowan & Sons*, [1968] A.C. 107 (Scot. 1967), a problem of the Scottish rules of pleading and the Factories Act, Guest adopted a rather broader view of statutory interpretation. See also a rare dissent in *Chertsey UDC* v. *Mixnam's Properties, Ltd.*, [1965] A.C. 735, 760 (1964), giving a "benevolent interpretation" to the discretion to be exercised by the Council.

39. See, for instance, the simplistic article comparing the U.S. Supreme Court and the Appellate Committee of the House of Lords, in which Guest noted of the former, "The court also has a political flavour which has certainly not existed in this country since the days of the Stuarts"; C. W. G. Guest, "The Supreme Court of the United States" 245.

40. [1962] A.C. 367, 408 (1961).

41. [1946] A.C. 493.

42. [1962] A.C. 367, 409 (1961). See also *Sparrow* v. *Fairey Aviation Co.*, [1964] A.C. 1019, 1053–54 (1962), and also the somewhat unrealistic remark, "The section [14(1) of Factories Act of 1961] may assume that the man will be clothed. It does not necessarily assume that he will be holding a tool"; ibid. 1053.

43. [1968] A.C. 58, 83 (1967).

44. [1971] A.C. 356, 380 (1969).

45. [1970] A.C. 282 (1969).

46. See especially ibid. 292. Guest showed similar reluctance to expand this concept of libel. See *Morgan* v. *Odhams Press, Ltd.*, [1971] 1 W.L.R. 1239 (H.L.), dissenting where there was no internal evidence linking the plaintiff to the statement.

into the area of statutory interpretation. On the knotty problem of tax avoidance or evasion he began his term as a law lord by giving the taxpayer the benefit of every possible doubt. In the "dividend stripping" case of *Griffiths* v. *J. P. Harrison, Limited*, Denning (dissenting with Reid) was in favor of upholding the decision of the special commissioners. "[T]he Commissioners were entitled to see these people as they really are, prospectors digging for wealth in the subterranean passages of the Revenue, searching for tax repayments."[47] Guest, agreeing with Simonds and Morris, refused to indulge in any process that involved looking at the substance rather than the form. "In my opinion one has to look at the transaction itself irrespective of the object, irrespective of the fiscal consequences."[48] In the later case of *Inland Revenue Commissioners* v. *Lord Rennell*, he refused to accept the Revenue's interpretation of the phrase "parties within the marriage consideration" because the words "are plain and clear and must be interpreted in the way ordinary words of the English language are used. To read them as the Revenue would have them read is not construction, but judicial paraphrase. It is probably not profitable to surmise upon what the intention of the Parliament in 1910 was in enacting Section 59(2)."[49] The effect of this decision was to provide an excellent loophole for those anxious to avoid estate duty who were fortunate enough to have relatives who were marrying.

In other areas too, Guest appeared in the tradition of substantive formalism. In public law he talked a bold line[50] and seemed to take delight in the idea that "the Executive has recently had its claws pared."[51] The War Damages Act, reversing the *Burmah Oil* case, he castigated as a cynical example of retrospective legislation at its worst.[52] Yet his own

47. [1963] A.C. 1, 22 (1962).

48. Ibid. 26. In fairness, after the legislature had stepped in with a broad antiavoidance device (§ 28, Finance Act of 1960), Guest was prepared to give full effect to it, although, typically, he refused to consider the anomalies his decision might create; *IRC* v. *Parker*, [1966] A.C. 141 (Scot. 1965). For another typical decision, see *Luke* v. *IRC*, [1963] A.C. 557, 586 (Scot.), where his instincts led him to side with the taxpayer, but his formalism led him to dissent, holding that the sums were perquisites of office and therefore taxable. "I therefore approach this legislation from the point of view that, if possible, on a fair construction of the section, some mitigation must be found to the extreme results of the contentions for the Revenue." However, he felt compelled "although most unwillingly" to dissent.

49. [1964] A.C. 173, 208 (1963).

50. "[L]ong before the Law Commissions had reported, there could be detected in the judicial decisions over the past few years a tendency to give the courts a greater control over the Executive"; C. W. G. Guest, "The Executive and the Judiciary" 113.

51. Ibid. 118.

52. Ibid. 116. Guest had apparently been the legal adviser to Burmah Oil before he went on the Scottish bench and had advised the company that it had a good claim in this particular case. In the debates in the House he argued on the one hand, "The courts declare what the law is. Parliament can always change the law if it so wishes, and that is what is proposed in Clause 7 (7) and upon that matter, which is a political question, I express no

decisions in the area were not particularly bold, nor did they show any great or subtle understanding of appellate strategy. In *McEldowney* v. *Forde*, a case that began before the Ulster emergency, he made it clear that he would not interfere with the discretion of ministers responsible for Northern Ireland,[53] despite his extrajudicial admiration[54] for *Padfield* v. *Minister of Agriculture*[55] and *Anisminic* v. *Foreign Compensation Commission*[56] because of their efforts in curbing discretion. Similarly, although he was an admirer of *Ridge* v. *Baldwin*[57] and an advocate of the position that Parliament must be presumed not to have interfered with natural justice, he allowed the Commissioners of Inland Revenue considerable leeway in reducing the right of *audi alterem partem* in proceedings under section 28 of the Finance Act of 1960.[58] When the Privy Council approached the Sierra Leonean constitution as an organic document rather than strictly as an act of Parliament, Guest was vigorous in his dissent, accusing his fellow members of the Judicial Committee of looking behind the face of a statute in an effort to discover its purpose.[59] Even Watson, who frequently used a positivistic stand to forward the

---

view at all," and, on the other, "A vital question of principle is here concerned, and it affects the rule of law and, as I have hoped to show, the independence of the Judiciary"; 264 *Parl. Deb.*, H.L. (5th ser.), cols. 787–90 (25 Mar. 1965).

Guest was a reasonably frequent contributor to House of Lords debates. He was the fifth most active participant on average between 1953 and 1968; Blom-Cooper and Drewry, *Final Appeal* 205. He often intervened to state the Scottish position; e.g., Licensing Bill, 232 *Parl. Deb.*, H.L. (5th ser.), cols. 1307–10 (4 July 1961); Trusts (Scotland) Bill, 233 ibid., cols. 547–48 (18 July 1961); Criminal Justice (Scotland) Bill, 244 ibid., cols. 561–64 (15 Nov. 1962). And see his exchange with Lord Greenhill, ibid., cols. 1338–40 (29 Nov. 1962); Criminal Procedure (Right of Reply) Bill, 257 ibid., col. 254 (9 Apr. 1964).

After becoming a law lord, Guest had few extrajudicial appointments, but he was Chairman of the Scottish Licensing Law Committee from 1959 to 1963. For the controversy surrounding the recommendations, see Blom-Cooper and Drewry, *Final Appeal* 208.

53. "In such a case as this the discretion entrusted to the Minister to make regulations for the preservation of peace and the maintenance of order in Northern Ireland is a very wide power and his discretion will not lightly be interfered with. The court will only interfere if the Minister is shown to have gone outside the four corners of the Act or has acted in bad faith"; [1971] A.C. 632, 649 (N. Ire. 1969).

54. "Executive and Judiciary" 116. He was also more willing than the two dissenting judges (Reid and Upjohn) to hold planning permission *intra vires* the enabling legislation (Town and Country Planning Act of 1947) in *Kingsway Invs., Ltd.* v. *Kent County Council*, [1971] A.C. 72 (1969). See especially ibid. at 105: "The power under § 14 (1) is to impose such conditions as the planning authority think fit. . . . So long as the condition relates to the implementation of planning policy then, in my view, the condition is valid."

55. [1968] A.C. 997.

56. [1969] 2 A.C. 147 (1968).

57. [1964] A.C. 40 (1963). "This decision is a milestone in the history of judicial pronouncement and was of far-reaching effect"; "Executive and Judiciary" 116.

58. *Wiseman* v. *Borneman*, [1971] A.C. 297, 310 (1969).

59. *Akar* v. *Attorney-General of Sierra Leone*, [1970] A.C. 853, 871 (P.C. 1969). The majority held that legislation attempting to limit Sierra Leone on citizenship to children of African fathers was unconstitutional in that it violated the antiracial clause of the constitution.

policies he preferred in the Canadian constitution, would not have understood this extreme form of substantive formalism. In Guest, the broad Scottish tradition had given way to an approach that was almost more English than the English.[60]

The Political Tradition

During the post-1945 period, the political law lord made a comeback. Reid and MacDermott had been successful politicians, and both Simonds and Dilhorne served as Lords of Appeal after being Lord Chancellor. Goddard, Guest, and Wilberforce had all been unsuccessful Conservative candidates, and Morris an unsuccessful Liberal candidate. Finally, two Lords of Appeal in the immediate period under discussion—Somervell and Donovan—had been M.P.'s, the first, Conservative and the second, Labour. These two formed an important link between the Simonds and the Reid courts.

Lord Somervell[61] had held office as both Solicitor-General and Attorney-General and had been Home Secretary in Churchill's caretaker government of 1945, before spending nine years in the Court of Appeal and then serving from 1954 to 1960 as a Lord of Appeal. It was during these latter years that the ideology of substantive formalism represented by Simonds was assaulted by Denning's colorful criticisms, ultimately making possible the balanced Reid approach that was to come into its own in the sixties. It would not be fair to view Somervell as a leader in the development of a more flexible style. He spoke not at all in the House in its legislative capacity, and he delivered full dissents in only four cases.[62] Yet, the Somervell style was an important step along the route of the House toward the development of a more clear rationale.[63]

In interpreting statutes, Somervell was skeptical of the positivist stand of those who had spent their lives solely in the Temple and the law courts; he was well aware that the meaning of a word might differ

---

60. Guest was, for instance, not particularly comfortable with the 1966 Practice Statement. In *Pook v. Owen*, [1970] A.C. 244 (1969), he chose to distinguish *Ricketts v. Colquhoun*, [1926] A.C. 1 (1925), rather than overrule it as Pearce, for instance, did. Guest's overall approach may explain why he became an increasingly frequent dissenter; Blom-Cooper and Drewry, *Final Appeal* 179.

61. Donald Somervell; b. 1889; father, public school master; educ., Harrow, Magdalen College, Oxford (First, Chemistry); K.C., 1929; Unionist M.P., 1931–45, Crewe Division, Cheshire; Solicitor-General, 1933–36; Attorney-General, 1936–45; Home Secretary, 1945; Lord Justice, 1946–54; Lord of Appeal, 1954–60; d. 1960.

62. Blom-Cooper and Drewry, *Final Appeal* 205, 176.

63. "[T]he kindness and courtesy that had distinguished him at the Bar made him the pleasantest of judges to encounter on the Bench. As befitted a fellow of All Souls, his judgements had distinction of style, and his scientific training gave them conciseness and precision"; Obituary, *The Times*, 21 Nov. 1960, at 17, col. 1.

radically depending on the context,[64] and he was prepared to use a broad technique of interpretation, whether the subject matter was rating[65] or factory legislation.[66] At a time when it was still fashionable to treat tax law in the tradition of narrow "penal" interpretation, Somervell refused to be bound by such constraints. Once having discovered the purpose of the particular provision, from an analysis of what anomaly or gap the provision was intended to remedy, he did his best to fulfill the intention of Parliament. Subtle conceptual distinctions were to be avoided,[67] although Somervell realized that the House had to examine publicly the possible implications of the decision.[68]

Similar traits are evident in Somervell's handling of common law issues. While he could play the accepted English game of searching for the "right" precedent, he also shared a Scottish preference for principle. In *Indian Government* v. *Taylor*, for example, in deciding whether the Indian government could prove in a voluntary liquidation for tax owed by a United Kingdom registered company, Somervell announced with some obvious relief, "There is no decision binding on your Lordships' House and the matter therefore fails to be considered in principle."[69] Similarly, he sought to treat as much as possible in earlier precedents as

64. "It is unreal to proceed as if the court looked first at the provision in dispute without knowing whether it was contained in a Finance Act or a Public Health Act. The title and the general scope of the Act constitute the background of the contest. When a court comes to the Act itself, bearing in mind any relevant extraneous matters, there is, in my opinion, one compelling rule. The whole or any part of the Act may be referred to and relied on"; *Attorney-General* v. *Prince Ernest Augustus of Hanover*, [1957] A.C. 436, 473 (1956).

65. *General Nursing Council for England & Wales* v. *St. Marylebone Borough Council*, [1959] A.C. 540, where he dissented, holding that the General Nursing Council had, as its main objects, "the advancement of social welfare. . . . [I]t does not matter whether those objects are charitable in the legal sense or not. I would assume the subsection was framed so that valuation officers could apply it without getting embogged in the technicalities of the law relating to charities"; ibid. 564.

66. E.g., *Grant* v. *National Coal Bd.*, [1956] A.C. 649, 661 (Scot.); *Cavanagh* v. *Ulster Weaving Co.*, [1960] A.C. 145, 167 (N. Ire. 1959): "I do not pretend to have considered every gloss on 'reasonable care' which may from time to time have been cited as helpful, but speaking for myself I think the fewer the formulas the better will be the administration of this branch of the law in which circumstances in one case can never be precisely similar to those in another."

67. "Having regard to the intention of the section to be gathered from its terms and to the statutory background, the words should be given, in my opinion, a wide construction. I wholly reject the distinction sought to be drawn between the management and the carrying on of the business"; *Sun Life Assurance Soc'y* v. *Davidson (Inspector of Taxes)*, [1958] A.C. 184, 208 (1957).

68. "If one considers consequences, the results of the taxpayer's construction would be remarkable. . . . Benevolent as at times financial provisions may be, it is impossible to believe that such capricious benevolence could have been intended"; *Income Tax Special Comm'rs* v. *Linsleys (Established 1894), Ltd.*, [1958] A.C. 569, 597. See also *Wheeler* v. *Mercer*, [1957] A.C. 416, 434–35 (1956).

69. [1955] A.C. 491, 513 (1954).

fact rather than law,[70] thereby making the precedential process more flexible.

Somervell was also less uncomfortable than many of his colleagues in handling the conflicting policy issues that underlay the competing doctrines of the common law.[71] His dissent in *Lister* v. *Romford Ice and Cold Storage Company* was a model of this approach. He accepted the first step in the majority's reasoning, namely that there is an implied term in contracts of service that an employee in the performance of his duty should take care; but Somervell implied a further term that the employer would see that the driver was protected by insurance and, thus, neither the employer nor his insurers could sue the driver in respect of the driver's liability.[72] Somervell faced the fact that his decision would have far-reaching consequences, but so, he considered, had the opposing view. "The public interest has for long tolerated owners being so immune, and it would, I think, be unreasonable if it was to discriminate against those who earned their living by driving. Both are subject to the sanction of the criminal law as to careless or dangerous driving. The driver has a further sanction in that accidents causing damage are likely to hinder his advancement."[73]

Somervell opposed refinements in the law and the development of concepts as ends in themselves. Subtle distinctions between void and

70. "Now that negligence cases are mostly tried without juries, the distinction between the functions of judge and jury is blurred. A judge naturally gives reasons for the conclusion formerly arrived at by a jury without reasons. It may sometimes be difficult to draw the line, but if the reasons given by a judge for arriving at the conclusion previously reached by a jury are to be treated as 'law' and citable, the precedent system will die from a surfeit of authorities"; *Qualcast, Ltd.* v. *Haynes*, [1959] A.C. 743, 757. See also at 759: "I will not elaborate these reasons or someone might cite my observations as part of the law of negligence." See also *Davis Contractors, Ltd.* v. *Fareham UDC*, [1956] A.C. 696, especially at 735.

71. E.g., in *National Bank of Greece & Athens S.A.* v. *Metliss*, [1958] A.C. 509, 525 (1957), he concurred with the atypical Simonds position that, in the absence of authority, the question was simply "[w]hat did justice demand in such a case as this?"

72. [1957] A.C. 555 (1956).

Nothing was said in this case and I dare say nothing is usually said. If, when such a contract was being negotiated, the question had been raised, it is obvious, I think, that the driver would have stipulated for the usual cover that an owner driver provides for himself. If nothing is said it is, in my opinion, for the employer to see that the driver's resources are protected by insurance. It is inconsistent with such an obligation that the employer should seek by action to make the driver personally liable as in the present case. . . .

"[U]nreasonable" would be too mild an epithet if the owner had protected his own resources if he was negligent but had failed to ensure the protection of his driver or, of course, made it clear that he must insure himself. . . .

I find it easier to imply this term than the obligation of the driver to take care. [Ibid. 599]

Much play had been made by the majority with the impreciseness of the alleged term. Somervell's response was that "It would, I think, be as precise as the 'i' or the 'f' in a c.i.f. contract. . . . [I]f a policy is taken out in the ordinary terms that is sufficient"; ibid.

73. Ibid. 601.

voidable executive orders were not for him. "The distinction between void and voidable is by no means a clear one, as a glance at the entry under 'void' in Stroud's Judicial Dictionary shows. I am not satisfied that the question whether a man should go or not go to prison should depend upon the distinction."[74] Similarly, when he had to decide upon the juristic nature of a trade union[75] he would not resort to legalistic concepts. "The position in law of trade unions under the various Acts of Parliament is a special one. To import into the subject such general phrases as 'legal personality,' 'legal entity,' 'quasi corporation,' whatever 'quasi' may mean, may well serve to obscure that which is not in any case particularly easy to discern."[76]

In the area of public law, Somervell's political career provided a particularly useful background. Somervell, as wartime Attorney-General, had been counsel in *Liversidge* v. *Anderson*,[77] a fact that may have haunted him somewhat. Certainly, as a law lord he was reluctant to accept parliamentary ouster of the jurisdiction of the courts. Thus in *Smith* v. *East Elloe Rural District Council*, he joined Reid in dissent, arguing that the jurisdiction of the courts was not ousted by the compulsory purchase provisions before the court. He started from the premise that "ultra vires and mala fides are, prima facie matters for the courts. If the jurisdiction of the courts is to be ousted it must be done by plain words."[78] He could not believe that Parliament had indirectly retracted

---

74. *DPP* v. *Head*, [1959] A.C. 83, 104 (1958). See also *Regazzoni* v. *K. C. Sethia, Ltd.*, [1958] A.C. 301, 329 (1957), holding that the distinction between what is wrong and what is prohibited is not important.

75. *Bonsor* v. *Musicians' Union*, [1956] A.C. 104, 155 (1955).

76. See also *Vine* v. *National Dock Labour Bd.*, [1957] A.C. 488 (1956): "The phrase 'quasi-judicial' suggests that there is a well-marked category of activities to which certain judicial requirements attach. An examination of the cases shows, I think, that this is not so. The court has to consider whether a Minister, tribunal or board has to act 'judicially' in some respect and has failed to do so"; ibid. 511. He found the solution to the delegation problem not in the distinction between judicial and administrative functions, but in the practical effects of the exercise of its power; ibid.

77. For his views on Regulation 18B, see Donald Somervell, "Acts of Attainder" 306, 312: "If the powers that be decided that an arbitrary act is necessary, is it better to clothe it with some legal form, to make it look as if the rules were being observed, or to make its arbitrariness, the departure from the rule of law, as obvious as did 18B?" See also Donald Somervell, "Law and Liberty" 547. "The principle that private rights and normal procedure must give way to national safety is a principle enshrined in the law as laid down by the judges irrespective of parliamentary sanction. The fundamental difference, of course, is that, whereas at Common Law each interference would or might have to be justified on evidence in a court of law as reasonably necessary, the Act gives power to provide a statutory code and statutory sanction for such interferences as the Executive thinks necessary or expedient"; ibid. 548.

78. [1956] A.C. 736, 772. He proceeded, "The jurisdiction of the court under paragraph 15 is ousted after six weeks. If Parliament had intended that this should apply in the case of a person defrauded it would have made it plain, and not left it to be derived from a

the right of resort to the courts. "In other words, Parliament, without ever using words which would suggest that fraud was being dealt with has deprived a victim of fraud of all right of resort to the courts, while leaving the victim of a bona fide breach of a regulation with such a right. If Parliament has done this it could only be by inadvertence. . . . The Act, having provided machinery for access to the courts in cases of ultra vires, cannot have intended to exclude altogether a person defrauded. General words, therefore, should not be construed as effecting such an exclusion."[79] As to the convenience argument, he merely noted that "if there is a possibility of bad faith in matters of this kind, I would think it much more inconvenient to the administration, national and local, as a whole that a person defrauded should be deprived of any remedy in the courts."[80]

Dissents such as those in *Lister* and *East Elloe* advertised Somervell as different from the typical law lord in terms of his concept of the appellate process. Yet his less spectacular work in mundane common law and statutory areas may in the long run have been at least as important. In many decisions Somervell in style and conclusion was indistinguishable from the substantive formalists; yet, overall, the advantage for law lords of some training in politics seemed confirmed. Further confirmation, although some would argue less clear, was provided by Lord Donovan, who was a Labour M.P. before becoming a High Court judge and then, from 1963 to 1971, a Lord of Appeal.[81]

For various reasons, it is more difficult to be conclusive about Donovan's accomplishments. By far the most important reason is that for almost half of his tenure as a Lord of Appeal—from 1965 to 1968—he was Chairman of the Royal Commission on Trade Unions and Employers' Associations,[82] an effectively full-time occupation;[83] this position

---

doubtful syllogism which would certainly not occur to a layman and would not, I think, occur ordinarily to a lawyer"; ibid.

79. Ibid. 772.

80. Ibid. 773.

81. Terence Norbert Donovan; b. 1898; father, teacher; educ., Brockley Grammar School; called to bar, 1924; civil servant, 1920–32; K.C., 1945; Labour M.P., Leicester (East), 1945–50; Leicester (North East), 1950; Judge, King's Bench Division, 1950–60; Lord Justice, 1960–63; Lord of Appeal, 1964–71; d. 1971.

82. See the commission's *Report*, Cmnd. 3623 (1967). For a review of its main recommendations, see K. W. Wedderburn, "Report of the Royal Commission on Trade Unions and Employers' Associations" 674.

83. For Donovan's "defense" of the report during the debates on the Labour government's White Paper (*In Place of Strife*), see 300 *Parl. Deb.*, H.L. (5th ser.), cols. 848–54 (18 Mar. 1969); and for his reactions to the Industrial Relations Bill, see 318 ibid., cols. 39–46 (5 Apr. 1971), especially at col. 40, discussing the history of the employees' view of the law. "[W]orkers came to regard the law as their natural enemy . . . if they were to improve their conditions they could not rely upon the law being changed in Parliament; they had to rely upon their own industrial strength expressed in combinations." With respect to the enforceability provisions, he said, "[I]t would be wrong not to express the

was not his only extrajudicial government work.[84] A lesser reason is, perhaps, that some members of the Labour party were disappointed with some of his attitudes as a judge. While ultimately they were to regard his views on the relationship of the law and the unions as moderate—he was, for instance, opposed to making collective bargaining agreements legally enforceable—there had been earlier disappointments. Some thought Donovan, as a High Court judge, had not been sufficiently sympathetic to workmen's claims, and although in the Court of Appeal he was in favor of the union position in *Rookes* v. *Barnard*,[85] his speech in the Lords in *J. T. Stratford and Son* v. *Lindley* restricted the definition of "trade dispute" and thus weakened the protection of the Trade Disputes Act of 1906.[86] Meanwhile, the intellectual wing of the Labour party was disappointed by his lack of concern with civil liberties.[87] In particular, Donovan delivered the most important speech in the first of the Race Relations Act cases, setting the tone for a narrow, formalistic interpretation of the legislation.[88]

While Donovan was in some situations reluctant to go along with "expansions" in the law,[89] as a law lord he was generally sympathetic to

---

anxieties that some of us feel about the proposed permanent intrusion of the High Court into this sensitive field where all its decisions of fact will be final"; ibid., col. 45. See also 321 ibid., col. 843 (6 July 1971) and 322 ibid., col. 891 (20 July 1971).

84. For Donovan's earlier extrajudicial governmental work, see Blom-Cooper and Drewry, *Final Appeal* 203. While a Lord of Appeal, he was also Chairman of the Interdepartmental Committee on the Court of Criminal Appeal; *Report*, Cmnd. 2755 (1965). This report was implemented by the Criminal Appeal Act of 1966. For Donovan's contributions to the debates, see 274 *Parl. Deb.*, H.L. (5th ser.), cols. 1338–41 and 1351–52 (24 May 1966).

85. [1963] 1 Q.B. 623 (C.A. 1962). Later, sitting in the House, he justified this view:

I was a party to the decision in favour of the defendants in *Rookes v. Barnard* when that case came before the Court of Appeal. I took the view as regards Section 3 that Parliament intended to enact that something which was unlawful before should not be unlawful in the future in the context of a trade dispute: since there would be no point in declaring that *lawful* acts should no longer be actionable. But it transpires that, together with my colleagues, I was wrong: and the prospect, therefore, of finding out from an election address just how the law stands with regard to trade disputes is a prospect which I find attractive but not very likely. [*J. T. Stratford & Son* v. *Lindley*, [1965] A.C. 269, 340 (1964)]

86. Ibid.

87. This may be unfair, but he certainly preferred decorum in the courts to freedom of the media. In a legislative debate on the future of television he intervened to say, "I know it is somewhat unusual for a law lord to intervene in a debate of this character, but this is an opportunity I cannot lose to protest as strongly as I can see against the re-trial of criminal cases on television"; 302 *Parl. Deb.*, H.L. (5th ser.), cols. 444–45 (21 May 1969).

88. By distinguishing between "nationality" and "national origins" (discrimination on the basis of the latter's being prohibited) he held it was not a violation of the statute to discriminate against Polish nationals in housing lists. "The Act itself contains no definition of 'national origins.' It must, I think, mean something different from mere nationality, otherwise there would be no reason for not using that one word, as indeed the Act does in later provisions"; *Ealing London Borough Council* v. *Race Relations Bd.*, [1972] A.C. 342, 354 (1971).

89. See, for instance, his response in *Boys* v. *Chaplin*, [1971] A.C. 356, 383 (1969): "I

a broad approach to both common law and statutory construction. As he put it, dissenting in *Myers*, "[T]he common law is molded by the judges and it is still their province to adapt it from time to time so as to make it serve the interests of those it binds."[90] Thus, in negligence,[91] if not in other areas of tort,[92] Donovan's instinct was to expand liability. Whatever his reputation may have been in the courts of first instance, in Factories Act cases he adopted a sympathetic approach to the worker and a "commonsense" construction of the relevant legislation. In particular, he approached the notorious section 14 with the intention of giving that section reasonable scope to ensure the overall protection of workmen.[93] In working with tax legislation, Donovan appeared increasingly concerned to see that tax statutes were interpreted in the light of their policies. While some of his early decisions in this field were thought to reflect a formalistic tendency, his mature approach was more balanced.[94] If *Wiseman* v. *Borneman*[95] confirmed the view of some of Donovan's critics that he did not have an instinct for civil liberties, at least it demonstrated his interest in establishing an equitable tax system; and Donovan appeared to have an increasing concern with the final appeal court as the balancer of interests. Again it seemed that the arrangement that called for the leading law lords to spend a significant part of their time on extrajudicial work had taken its toll of another potentially strong

---

do not think we should adopt any such doctrine as 'the proper law of the tort' with all its uncertainties. There is no need here for such a doctrine—at least while we remain a United Kingdom. Nor would I take the first steps towards it in the name of flexibility." On the other hand, see *Lupton* v. *F.A. & A.B., Ltd.*, [1972] A.C. 634, 657 (1971), where Donovan held that *Griffiths* v. *J. P. Harrison, Ltd.*, [1963] A.C. 1 (1962) had been wrongly decided and should be overruled.

90. "Particularly is this so in the field of procedural law"; *Myers* v. *DPP*, [1965] A.C. 1001, 1047 (1964).

91. He was one of the majority in *Henderson* v. *Henry E. Jenkins & Sons*, [1970] A.C. 282 (1969), where a heavy burden of proof was put on the defendant to show that he was not responsible for the defective brake in the lorry. See especially at 300.

92. He dissented (with Reid) in *Morgan* v. *Odhams Press, Ltd.*, [1971] 1 W.L.R. 1239 (H.L.), refusing to hold that the alleged libel was clearly referable to the plaintiff.

93. "[T]he plain purpose of Section 14 (1) of the Factories Act is to reduce danger and increase safety in favour of workmen in factories containing machinery. One cannot, therefore, construe the words 'dangerous part of any machinery' except in the context of workmen being in the vicinity of the machinery and thereby running the risk of injury unless dangerous parts are fenced. The obvious case of workmen being in the vicinity is in the course of their work"; *Midland & Low Moor Iron & Steel Co.* v. *Cross*, [1965] A.C. 343, 374 (1964). Cf. *Imperial Chem. Indus., Ltd.* v. *Shatwell*, [1965] A.C. 656 (1964), where Donovan supported the introduction of *volenti non fit injuria* into the realm of statutory duty.

94. See, for instance, *Wm. Cory & Son* v. *IRC*, [1965] A.C. 1088; *in re Ralli's Settlement: Rally Bros.* v. *IRC*, [1966] A.C. 483; *in re Kirkwood: Public Trustee* v. *IRC*, [1966] A.C. 520; *Lupton* v. *F.A. & A.B., Ltd.*, [1972] A.C. 634, 657 (1971). Cf. *Pook* v. *Owen*, [1970] A.C. 244, 259 (1969).

95. *Wiseman* v. *Borneman*, [1971] A.C. 297, 312 (1969).

Lord of Appeal. Nevertheless, the overall style of Somervell and Dono-van suggested that political experience was likely to provide a sound basis for handling the creative elements inherent in the work of appellate judges. Such experience was also likely to provide political wisdom as to the directions in which the law should be developed.

The Chancery Tradition

During these earlier years, there were also three judges who were most closely associated with what might be called the Chancery tradi-tion. Lord Jenkins was a Lord of Appeal from 1959 to 1963, Lord Evershed from 1962 to 1965, and Lord Upjohn from 1963 to 1971. Among them they suggested that the Chancery Division, although it had moved some distance from the substantive formalism of Simonds, never-theless lacked the intellectual distinction of the best of the common law-yers and the legal vigor of the Scottish or political traditions.

To discuss Jenkins[96] is not simple, since, although he sat in some forty-four appeals, he had seemingly already lost much of his energy and earlier incisiveness[97] by the time he reached the Lords. His usually long speeches[98] generally took a moderate line, whether the issue was one of factory legislation[99] or wardship proceedings.[100] When faced with tax legislation, he attempted to banish presumptions in favor of either the Revenue or the taxpayer,[101] placing the responsibility for unfairness or anomalies resulting from this approach on the shoulders of Parliament.[102]

96. David Llewelyn Jenkins; b. 1889; father, Indian civil servant (knighted); educ., Charterhouse, Balliol College, Oxford (Second, "Greats"); called to bar, 1923; K.C., 1938; Judge, Chancery Division, 1947–49; Lord Justice, 1949–59; Lord of Appeal, 1959–63; d. 1969.

97. From January 1960 to May 1962 he was also partly unavailable while presiding over the Company Law Committee. See *Report of the Company Law Committee*, Cmnd. 1749, 1962. The report was partially implemented—for example, on insider trading—by the Companies Act of 1967. See Tom Hadden, *Company Law and Capitalism* 251–52.

98. E.g., *Pyx Granite Co.* v. *Minister of Housing & Local Gov't*, [1960] A.C. 260, 292 (1959); *Hamilton* v. *National Coal Bd.*, [1960] A.C. 633, 651 (Scot. 1959); *Fawcett Properties, Ltd.* v. *Buckingham County Council*, [1961] A.C. 636, 681 (1960).

99. E.g., *Hamilton* v. *National Coal Bd.*, [1960] A.C. 633, 658 (Scot. 1959).

100. Here Jenkins showed that he would not blindly apply the principles of natural justice to every type of judicial proceeding: "[A]ny attempt to formulate general pro-nouncements applicable in all cases will be likely to create more difficulties than it solves"; *in re K (Infants)*, [1965] A.C. 201, 232 (1963).

101. E.g., *Jamieson* v. *IRC*, [1964] A.C. 1445 (1963), at 1466:

The sections upon which this case turns may be thought unnecessarily obscure and in the circumstances to bear somewhat heavily on the respondent. But your Lordship's task as in any other revenue case, is to construe the provisions of the taxing enactment according to the ordinary and natural meaning of the language used and then to apply that meaning to the facts of the case. If by the application of this process the taxpayer is brought fairly within the net, he is caught. Otherwise he goes free, but there must be no straining of language either way.

102. E.g., his dissent in *Luke* v. *IRC*, [1963] A.C. 557, 582 (Scot.); *IRC* v. *Lord*

Nevertheless, the overall impression is that Jenkins had little impact on the operation of the House as a judicial body.

Of far greater importance was another Chancery practitioner,[103] Evershed,[104] although again it can be argued that he was past his prime when he exchanged the Mastership of the Rolls and a Lordship of Appeal with Denning in 1962. In his last years in the Court of Appeal, the dispatch of business had slowed and Evershed—who had been one of the youngest Q.C.'s ever at the Chancery Bar—gave increasingly convoluted judgments. On reaching the House, perhaps due to increasing ill health, he became the great doubter of the court. Seldom did the issue before the court appear to him as clear-cut or simple as it did to the other law lords.[105] Yet Evershed rarely dissented formally. He was more likely to state the arguments against the majority's decision and their inherent weaknesses but then conclude by concurring with the majority.[106] In *Rookes* v. *Barnard*, for instance, when he came to deal with the provisions of the 1906 Trade Disputes Act, he obviously had doubts and could muster strong arguments in support of the proposition that section 3 of the act should protect the defendants and although he expressed his faith in the sense of responsibility of the trade unions,[107] he would not dissent formally.

That pseudodissent, however, does reflect the inherent inconsisten-

---

Rennell, [1964] A.C. 173, 204 (1963): "On the point of construction, I feel constrained—though I confess not without some regret—to uphold the views unanimously expressed in the courts below.

"The exemption in the form in which it now stands may be open to criticism as unduly wide, and as applicable to cases for which it can hardly have been intended; but if that is thought to be the case, then surely the proper remedy lies in amending legislation."

103. "I have spent my professional life in what is, I think your Lordships will admit, the more respectable branch of the law, known as the Chancery Division"; 256 *Parl. Deb.*, H.L. (5th ser.), col. 244 (5 Mar. 1964).

104. Francis Raymond Evershed; b. 1899; father, solicitor; educ., Clifton, Balliol College, Oxford (Second, "Greats"); called to bar, 1923; K.C., 1933; Judge, Chancery Division, 1944–47; Lord Justice, 1947–49; Master of the Rolls, 1949–62; Lord of Appeal, 1962–65; d. 1966.

105. E.g., *Henning* v. *Church of Jesus Christ of the Latter-Day Saints*, [1964] A.C. 420, 430 (1963); *Haley* v. *London Elec. Bd.*, [1965] A.C. 778, 795 (1964): "My Lords, I must confess to having felt greater difficulty than some of your lordships in concluding that in the present case the respondent board must be held liable to the appellant—though not, I hope, on account of any desire to adhere to my own decision in the Court of Appeal in the case of *Pritchard* v. *Post Office*." See also *Williams* v. *Williams*, [1964] A.C. 698 (1963).

106. His health was not the only thing at stake here. Evershed disliked dissents; Raymond Evershed, "The Judicial Process in 20th Century England" 761, 768. He was, moreover, a man of intellectual humility. He was quick to acknowledge the assistance obtained by him from other judges and also from outside sources such as academic writers. See, e.g., his expression of indebtedness to an article by A. L. Goodhart in the *Law Quarterly Review*, in *Williams* v. *Williams*, [1964] A.C. 698, 733 (1963).

107. "[I] hope and believe that the trade unions in our country are sufficiently responsible and influential to see that acts done by their members in the course of trade disputes are not wholly irresponsible"; [1964] A.C. 1129, 1196.

cies that Evershed brought to the Lords. He was too intelligent to take seriously the myth of substantive formalism and too human not to want to develop the law in more modern directions. Yet he had, as a young man, been influenced by the liberal tradition that the courts should not interfere with the work of Parliament, and he was an admirer of Greene, whose views on judicial restraint could not have been more extreme. Thus, one can see in Evershed's opinions, speeches, and writings, themes that appear to be inconsistent: a deference to the legislature, yet at the same time a plea that the courts be more creative in both common law and statutory situations.

For example, in *Ridge* v. *Baldwin* he was driven to a real dissent because he feared the courts were using the concept of natural justice to undermine parliamentary sovereignty.[108] Yet, in a debate in the House on the Factories Act decisions, he argued:

Our rule of precedent in this country has become over-strict. It was not so strict half a century ago. It is not so strict in other parts of the English speaking world and other parts of the Commonwealth. May I express the hope that this House might at some time consider this matter and perhaps pass legislation limiting in some way the strict application of the rule of precedent?

[I] hope that this House would find occasion to give time . . . also to the very strict or literal interpretation of Statutes which in this case, perhaps, has led to some of the difficulty, and to differences between this country and other members of the Commonwealth.[109]

Yet, when Kenneth Culp Davis of the University of Chicago leveled a broadside at the role of the judiciary in England, it was Evershed who was deputized to answer the charges. This he did by arguing on the one hand that the law was "a living part of the whole social structure" and "must be applied to novel social conditions" and that "there should reside in the highest tribunal a flexibility sufficient to enable anomalies to be removed and such adjustment made of the effect of previous decisions as may make them better conform to changes in the conceptions and

108. I do not wish at all to denigrate the principles of natural justice or of their proper invocation in the courts. On the other hand, we have, as I have already many times pointed out, the very wide terms of the Act of Parliament here in question, and the body in which was invested this wide discretion was an entirely responsible body. To insist, as I venture to think, on the invocation of these principles whenever anyone is discharged from some office seems to me to involve a danger of usurpation of power on the part of the courts and under the pretext of having regard to the principles of natural justice to invoke what may often be in truth little more than sentiment; and on occasions when the courts, though having necessarily far less knowledge of all the relevant circumstances, may be inclined to think that, had the decision rested with them, they would have decided differently from the body in question. [*Ridge* v. *Baldwin*, [1964] A.C. 40, 96 (1963)]

See also *in re K (Infants)*, [1965] A.C. 201, 218 (1963), where Evershed delivered a long speech holding that the rules of natural justice should not necessarily be applied strictly in wardship proceedings.

109. 248 *Parl. Deb.*, H.L. (5th ser.), col. 1342 (25 Apr. 1963).

conditions of a rapidly moving world";[110] yet, on the other hand, he made an extreme plea for parliamentary supremacy and opposed judicial legislation on the ground that it was un-English.[111]

In total, Evershed heard only forty-one appeals in the Lords, and many suffered the defects of convolution. The policies pursued in general reflected his liberal humanitarianism. He explained legislatively how, in the Court of Appeal, he had fought the extreme Simonds decisions in the Factories Act cases[112] and proceeded to seek to restrict them when he reached the Lords.[113] As a law lord he also insisted that "Equity was not presumed to be of an age past childbearing."[114] While he could warn of the dangers of "palm tree justice,"[115] he could also expound judicially, in the most elegant terms, the inherently creative function of the common law[116] and in his writings point to the Rent Restriction Acts as an area in which the judges had creatively construed legislation.[117] Evershed was also a man anxious to see the procedure of the High Court reformed.[118]

110. Evershed, "Judicial Process" 761, 772, 790. He once again argued in favor of a reformulation of the rules of statutory interpretation; ibid. 789–90.

111. E.g., ibid. 765.

112. "We in the Court of Appeal thought it would perhaps be a good thing if this House were to say that *Nicholls* had not gone so far as it might appear to have done. To the disappointment of my colleagues and myself, only my noble and learned friend Lord Denning and one colleague were of that opinion. . . . To me and my colleagues the result was, to say the least, somewhat illogical and not very good sense"; 248 *Parl. Deb.*, H.L. (5th ser.), col. 1341 (25 Apr. 1963).

113. When § 14 again came up for decision before the House in *Midland & Low Moor Iron & Steel Co.* v. *Cross*, [1965] A.C. 343 (1964), he allowed the *Nicholls* case little scope as a precedent; ibid. 368.

114. See *Simpson's Motor Sales (London), Ltd.* v. *Hendon Corp.*, [1964] A.C. 1088 (1963), at 1126–27: "I should, I hope, be the last to suggest that the proper application and, where necessary, extension of equitable principles in the present day and age, when so much human activity is governed and controlled by legislation, should be restricted and I have in mind the picturesque language once used by Harman L.J. when he said that he thought equity was not presumed to be of an age past child-bearing."

115. Ibid. 1127.

116. In *Haley* v. *London Elec. Bd.*, [1965] A.C. 778, 800–801 (1964), where, despite typical doubts, in agreeing that a statutory authority obstructing a pavement owed a duty of care to a blind pedestrian, he justified the decision in the following terms:

If it be said that your Lordships are making new law, that is only because, whatever may have been the facts and circumstances reasonably to be contemplated a hundred years or more ago, at the present time it must be accepted as one of the facts of life that appreciable numbers of blind persons, having had the requisite training, are capable of using or use in fact public footpaths. . . . [I] derive assistance . . . from the principle that the ancient rules of the English common law have—and have as one of their notable virtues—the characteristic that in general they can never be said to be finally limited by definition, but have rather the capacity of adaptation in accordance with the changing circumstances of succeeding ages.

117. Raymond Evershed, *The Influence and Importance of Practice and Procedure in the Supreme Court* 23–24; Evershed, "Judicial Process" 774–76.

118. His Committee on Supreme Court Practice and Procedure—see *First Interim Report*, Cmd. 7764 (1949); *Second Interim Report*, Cmd. 8176 (1951); *Third Interim Report*, Cmd. 8617 (1952); and *Final Report*, Cmd. 8878 (1953)—for instance, undoubt-

In short, there is little doubt that Evershed's instincts were to develop a rationale for the final appeal court.[119] His tragedy was that, like so many Lords of Appeal "with potentional," he arrived in the Lords already a tired man and, in any event, sat for too short a time to make an impact. Such an ambience was unlikely to produce either good appeal judges or a reason for their existence.

A certain touch of jurisprudential inconsistency also characterized the third of the Chancery law lords—Upjohn.[120] At the time of the appointment of the law commissioners he had announced that "[a]s a judge he felt that certainty in the law was of paramount importance and he saw his duty to be to declare the law as it is; he deprecated judicial legislation."[121] Yet, he was also capable of attempting to back both horses and to see both flexibility and certainty in the common law system.[122]

---

edly produced the most important report in the legal system in fifty years until it was overshadowed by the Beeching Report. Yet, Evershed was shabbily treated for his pains. His report was not taken seriously. See Brian Abel-Smith and Robert Stevens, *Lawyers and the Courts*, chap. 10.

119. His considered position was in favor of abolishing the House of Lords and reverting to the Selborne scheme of an expanded "First Division" of the Court of Appeal; Blom-Cooper and Drewry, *Final Appeal* 14.

120. Gerald Ritchie Upjohn; b. 1903; father, K.C.; educ., Eton, Trinity College Cambridge (First, Law/Engineering); called to bar, 1929; K.C., 1943; Judge, Chancery Division, 1951–60; Lord Justice, 1960–63; Lord of Appeal, 1963–71; d. 1971.

121. 109 *Solicitors' Journal* 247 (1965).

122. "I am a great believer in following precedent and the maintenance of existing principles, even if they are not quite perfect; if they are not, then let them be altered by Parliament.

"I expect I am wrong—I hope so—but I think there has been a tendency perhaps over the last ten years to draw fine distinctions between earlier cases, in order to do what is called justice in a particular case; by which I mean what is fair and proper on the facts of that particular case so as to avoid what seems a hardship upon someone which ought not in fairness to be imposed upon him. I may be old-fashioned but I deplore that attitude. Let us remember that the law is really administered by solicitors in their offices, assisted where necessary by counsel's opinion. For every case reported in the courts, there must be hundreds not reported and thousands settled out of court upon the advice of solicitors acting upon a view of the law, sometimes contained in a statute, but very frequently expressed in some judicial observations.

"We all know (and after all I was at the Bar for many years) that however clear the principle may be, almost every case, however simple, contains circumstances which prevent it being a completely text book case, and requires the exercise of an experienced and well informed mind on the part of the solicitor. So it is the duty of judges, so far as is humanly possible, to declare the law for the guidance of the profession, and not to find distinctions unless it is really necessary to do so. Of course, they are always making new laws by applying old principles to new circumstances, which, with the vast progress of every kind now going on in the every day life of the ordinary man and woman, arise today. I believe judges are the best persons to apply old principles to entirely new circumstances: they have the knowledge, the experience and the wisdom to do it. . . . So I hope judges will in the future stick to broad principles, avoiding unnecessary distinctions, and to put it vulgarly, no palm tree justice nor esoteric views upon the welfare of mankind. Let precedent, sensibly applied, continue to reign, and I have no doubt it will"; Gerald Upjohn, "Twenty Years On" 657.

This apparent inconsistency in his jurisprudential approach was also reflected in his judicial work. Sitting as a Chancery judge, he thought the formalistic tax approach represented by the *Duke of Westminster* case the appropriate model for the registration of restrictive agreements;[123] yet as a judge of the Restrictive Practices Court from 1956 to 1960 he generally took an instrumental view of his task.[124] The apparent inconsistency was more general. While in theory he was in favor of the relaxation of precedent by the 1966 Practice Statement,[125] he found it unnecessary to overrule *Duncan* v. *Cammell, Laird and Company* in *Conway* v. *Rimmer*, taking a line of argument that some might dismiss as specious.[126] Certainly it can be argued that reworking public policy (cast as the public interest) can be at least as creative judicially as overruling an earlier decision;[127] and there is little doubt that Upjohn was adept at avoiding unfortunate precedents.[128] Similarly, his speech in *Beswick* v. *Beswick*[129] suggested that he was neither an iconoclast, as some styled themselves,

123. *In re Austin Motor Car Co.'s Agreements*, L.R. 1 R.P. 6 (Ch. 1957).

124. E.g., *in re Federation of British Carpet Mfrs. Agreement*, L.R. 1 R.P. 472, 540 (1959).

125. Upjohn, "Twenty Years On" 657.

126. "My lords, apart altogether from our recent liberation from some of the chains of precedent, which for my part I think should only be exercised rarely and sparingly, I do not think that the *Cammell, Laird* case governs this case for a number of reasons.

"First, it is now quite clear that per incuriam the House misunderstood the law of Scotland as now explained and enunciated in *Glasgow Corporation* v. *Central Land Board*.

". . . Secondly, I do not think that the observations of Lord Simon were intended to bind or did bind the courts to reach the conclusion that in every case (save where honesty or bona fides were challenged) the affidavit of the Minister claiming privilege is conclusive. . . .

". . . Thirdly, I think that there is a broader ground on which your lordships can re-examine this matter"; *Conway* v. *Rimmer*, [1968] A.C. 910, 990–91 (1967).

The broader ground was that of public interest, which had changed considerably since *Duncan's* case.

127. "My lords, feeling as I do unfettered by any necessity for a strictly textual adherence to Lord Simon's words, I think that the principle to be applied can be very shortly stated. On the one side there is the public interest to be protected; on the other side of the scales is the interest of the subject who legitimately wants production of some documents which he believes will support his own or defeat his adversary's case. Both are matters of public interest, for it is also in the public interest that justice should be done between litigating parties by production of all documents which are relevant and for which privilege cannot be claimed under ordinary rules. They must be weighed in the balance one against the other"; ibid. 992.

For a similar balancing of interests in the area of public policy, see *Rondel* v. *Worsley*, [1969] 1 A.C. 191, 281–82 (1967).

128. Dissenting with Reid in a tax case, for example, on the question of whether the House was bound by a somewhat obscure Macmillan opinion, he said, "My lords, we are not bound to follow a case merely because it is indistinguishable on the facts. A decision, even in your Lordships' House, is binding on your Lordships only because it lays down some principle of law or for its reasoning on some particular facts. . . . The fact that in the *Central London Railway* case taxed profits were sufficient to cover both interest and dividends must per incuriam have been overlooked"; *Chancery Lane Safe Deposit & Offices Co.* v. *IRC*, [1966] A.C. 85, 128 (1965).

129. [1968] A.C. 58, 94 (1967).

nor a rigid conservative. While refusing to make an inroad into the rule of privity of contract because "whatever may have been the state of the law before *Tweddle v. Atkinson*, it is difficult to see how your lordships can go back over one hundred years in view of the decision in this House of *Dunlop Pneumatic Tyre Co. Ltd. v. Selfridge & Co. Ltd.*, and *Scruttons Ltd. v. Midland Silicones, Ltd.*,"[130] he could still find a solution to the problem facing the House by appealing to equity. "It is in such common sense and practical ways that equity comes to the aid of the common law, and it is sufficiently flexible to meet and satisfy the justice of the case in the many different circumstances that arise from time to time."[131]

In both a general and a specific sense, then, there are examples of Upjohn's concern with justice.[132] In the area of public law, Upjohn supported the development of an embryonic form of procedural due process.[133] In interpreting the Factories Acts to determine whether someone was "employed" in "manual labour," for instance, Upjohn denied that the authorities could give any binding guidance and concluded that "the general concept of manual labour coupled to common sense points wholly in one direction in this particular case and no authority really is of great assistance in its solution." The worker was then held to be protected by the factory legislation.[134]

130. Ibid. 95. See also his refusal to develop the law further in *National Provincial Bank, Ltd. v. Ainsworth*, [1965] A.C. 1175.

131. [1968] A.C. 58, 98 (1967). For another example of his concern to do justice, see his dissenting speech in *Boardman v. Phipps* on the application of the doctrine that a trustee cannot profit from his trust; [1967] 2 A.C. 46, 128 (1966). See also his view, "Rules of equity have to be applied to such a great diversity of circumstances that they can be stated only in the most general terms and applied with particular attention to the exact circumstances of each case"; ibid. 123.

132. E.g., his speech on the Misrepresentation Bill; 274 *Parl. Deb.*, H.L. (5th ser.), cols. 942–46 (17 May 1969); *Armah v. Government of Ghana*, [1968] A.C. 192, 262 (1966).

133. "[T]he use of that adjective [unfettered], even in an Act of Parliament, can do nothing to unfetter the control which the judiciary have over the executive, namely that in exercising their powers the latter must act lawfully and that is a matter to be determined by looking at the Act and its scope and object in conferring a discretion on the Minister rather than by the use of adjectives"; *Padfield v. Minister of Agriculture*, [1968] A.C. 997. On a substantive level, he was among the majority in *Burmah Oil Co. v. Lord Advocate*, [1965] A.C. 75, 163 (Scot. 1964).

134. *J. & F. Stone Lighting & Radio, Ltd. v. Haygarth*, [1968] A.C. 157, 183 (1966). See also *Nimmo v. Alexander Cowan & Sons*, [1968] A.C. 107, 125 (Scot. 1967): "My Lords, it is not in doubt that the whole object of the Factories Act is to reinforce the common law obligation of the employer to take care for the safety of his workmen." Also on the theme of "common sense" see *Naylor v. Yorkshire Elec. Bd.*, [1968] A.C. 529, 552 (1967): "Over the years the conventional sum to be awarded for such head of damage rises no doubt, but by fits and by starts rather than by any estimation of the purchasing power of the pound, and in my view so it should be. This is a matter which is better and safely left to the experience and common sense of judges who day by day have to judge of these matters."

Although prepared to interpret private agreements in the light of what he saw the public interest to be,[135] Upjohn was less prepared to apply his "common sense" touchstone to revenue legislation,[136] and he seemed less comfortable than some in applying the broad antiavoidance devices developed by the 1960 Finance Act.[137] Upjohn could thus be regarded as a transitional figure. He was more vigorous than either Jenkins or Evershed, his tenure was longer (he also undertook little extra-judicial work), and there may well have been an evolution in his style. In his earlier years his words were often those of the substantive formalists, but his actions, especially in the later years, coincided more often with Reid's than with Simonds'.[138] Overall, Upjohn, with Evershed and Jenkins, had begun the process of reassociating Chancery with principle, rather than precedent.

The Divorce Tradition

The divorce bar, centered as it was until the early seventies on the old Probate, Divorce, and Admiralty Division (when the Family Division appeared), was not noted for its intellectual distinction. It is possible that intellectually it ranked above the criminal bar, but in prestige it ranked lower than the Chancery and specialized bars and its practitioners were rarely thought of as leaders of the profession. Yet during the twenty years under discussion two members of the divorce bar reached the House— Lord Hodson (1960–71) and Lord Pearce (1962–69).

Hodson[139] was, in many respects, a throwback to an earlier period —a man of strong views especially with respect to the family, but also a man who as a judge was a believer in substantive formalism. Hodson had

---

135. See, for example, *Sefton v. Tophams, Ltd.*, [1967] 1 A.C. 50 (1966); *Suisse Atlantique Société d'Armament Maritime S.A. v. N.V. Rotterdamsche Kolen Centrale*, [1967] 1 A.C. 361, 427 (1966). At times, however, some of his early scientific training appeared to come through in his approach to commercial issues. See, for instance, the distinction between damages in tort and contract, and the "four questions to be answered"; *The Heron II*, [1969] 1 A.C. 350, 420 (1967).

For more evidence of his scientific training, see his work in patent cases, Blom-Cooper and Drewry, *Final Appeal* 301–3.

136. See, e.g., *Chancery Lane Safe Deposit & Offices Co. v. IRC*, [1966] A.C. 85, 124 (1965), dissenting in favor of the Revenue; *Public Trustee v. IRC*, [1960] A.C. 398 (1959); and *in re Ralli's Settlement*, [1966] A.C. 483, giving the principal speech against the Crown. See also *Cleary v. IRC*, [1968] A.C. 766, 791 (1967), where he took the line that when the words of Parliament were literally satisfied, however harsh the conclusion, responsibility rested with Parliament for the harsh result.

137. See *IRC v. Brebner*, [1967] 2 A.C. 18, 30 (Scot.).

138. He was, incidentally, a supporter of the second appeal to the Lords. Blom-Cooper and Drewry, *Final Appeal* 14.

139. Francis Charlton Hodson; b. 1895; father, clergyman; educ., Cheltenham, Wadham College, Oxford (war degree); called to bar, 1921; K.C., 1937; Judge, Probate, Divorce, and Admiralty Division, 1937–51; Lord Justice, 1951–60; Lord of Appeal, 1960–71.

already sat as a judge for twenty-three years when he reached the Lords, and the idea that the Lords might be performing a different role from the lower courts was not congenial to him. In a public lecture he quoted with approval Baron Parke's pronouncement that "[i]t is the province of the judge . . . not to speculate upon what is best, in his opinion, for the advantage of the community";[140] in keeping with this position, he publicly chastised the House for attempts to remake the hearsay doctrine[141] and doubted whether Equity had any element of creativity remaining.[142] Hodson's approach ensured that, at least in the later years, although he often presided over a panel in the Lords, he rarely influenced his fellow law lords.

While he restated the classic formulation of substantive formalism, in matters of family law one did not have to search far for the policies Hodson was pursuing in deciding cases. As was appropriate for the son of a Gloucestershire parson, Hodson staunchly opposed the two major divorce law reforms of the period—Leo Abse's 1963 Matrimonial Causes and Conciliation Act and the more far-reaching Divorce Reform Act of 1969, which finally allowed "no fault" divorce. Far from believing that divorce should be allowed when the marriage had "irretrievably broken down," Hodson was a firm adherent to the concept of matrimonial fault. He therefore fought every change in 1963, whether it concerned reconciliation procedures[143] or condonation of adultery.[144] When the 1969 Divorce Reform Bill appeared, Hodson's outrage was even greater, and he participated vigorously in the debates in favor of the status quo.[145] His opposition conformed to his perceptions of the judicial role. If judges

140. Francis Hodson, *Judicial Discretion and Its Exercise* 20–21.

141. "Hedge the extension about with safeguards as you will, this surely would be judicial legislation with a vengeance in an attempt to introduce reform of the law of evidence which if needed can properly be dealt with only by the legislature"; *Myers v. DPP*, [1965] A.C. 1001, 1034 (1964).

142. "Equity had in fact crystallised and has not shown any sign of decrystallisation since"; Hodson, *Judicial Discretion and Its Exercise* 10. See also his opinion in *White & Carter, Ltd. v. McGregor*, [1962] A.C. 413, 443 (Scot. 1961); cf. "Equity may not be past the age of child-bearing but an infant of the kind suggested would lack form or shape"; *National Provincial Bank, Ltd. v. Ainsworth*, [1965] A.C. 1175, 1224.

143. He opposed the reconciliation provisions of clause 2. "To introduce formality of this kind, and technicality and legality into the relations of husband and wife is to me still revolting"; 251 *Parl. Deb.*, H.L. (5th ser.), col. 1579 (12 July 1963). Rather surprisingly, he did not find it "revolting" that correspondence between spouses could be intercepted and used in evidence against one of them on a charge of murder; *Rumping v. DPP*, [1964] A.C. 814, 861 (1962).

144. E.g., 251 *Parl. Deb.*, H.L. (5th ser.), cols. 1553, 1578 (12 July 1963). Hodson had one success with the bill: His amendment to make condoned adultery unrevivable was accepted. See Matrimonial Causes Act, § 3.

145. E.g., 303 *Parl. Deb.*, H.L. (5th ser.), cols. 1236–37, 1272, 1274, 1314, 1315, 1317, 1329, 1332, 1384, 1385 (10 & 11 July 1969); 304 ibid., cols. 162, 163, 165 (15 July 1969).

were to be forced to decide whether "the marriage had utterly broken down," he argued, "[t]his would reduce the judicial function to a farce. . . . A judge is trained to try cases according to law, and he is no better qualified than a doctor or any other member of the community to say whether a marriage should be dissolved on the ground that it has utterly or hopelessly broken down. One would suppose the parties themselves were as good judges of this as anyone else might be."[146] For similar reasons, he had vigorously opposed the 1963 solution of making collusion between the pair a discretionary rather than an absolute bar to a divorce decree. "I for my part think it is to the good that in the courts of this country the exercise of judicial discretion is confined within narrow lines, which if not clearly defined at least are not wholly capricious boundaries."[147]

With such views on the sanctity of marriage, it is not surprising that when Hodson came to decide appeals under the then-existing categories of matrimonial offense, he should have been in favor of maintaining the status quo. Nowhere was this more clear than in his dissents in two cruelty cases—*Gollins* v. *Gollins*[148] and *Williams* v. *Williams*.[149] In *Gollins* he strongly opposed the idea that magistrates could, in effect, determine cruelty as a question of fact,[150] while in the *Williams* case, he drew a strong analogy with criminal law,[151] holding not only that an insane person could not be cruel but also that the M'Naughten Rules were the most convenient to apply. The majority, however, was satisfied that the time had come to base cruelty on an objective standard. This reluctance to tamper with existing family law doctrines characterized Hodson's other opinions, on both matrimonial offenses[152] and jurisdiction.[153] It was no surprise that Hodson was the senior member in the House in the *Ainsworth* case,[154] when Denning's efforts to develop an

---

146. Hodson, *Judicial Discretion and Its Exercise* 7.

147. Ibid. 19. See also 250 *Parl. Deb.*, H.L. (5th ser.), col. 1541 (21 June 1963).

148. [1964] A.C. 644, 677 (1963).

149. [1964] A.C. 698, 743 (1963).

150. "There is no indication that this husband ever had the smallest intention of doing any harm to anyone, least of all his wife. In what way then was he cruel? . . . [T]he question must always be: was the conduct, be it positive or negative, cruel according to the meaning of that word as understood by ordinary people?" [1964] A.C. 644, 684 (1963).

151. "There may be different considerations applicable in civil cases generally, but there is this parallel between divorce cases . . . and criminal proceedings in that the standard of proof is to all intents and purposes the same"; [1964] A.C. 698, 745 (1963).

152. In keeping with his belief in the indissolubility of marriage, in *Godfrey* v. *Godfrey*, [1965] A.C. 444, 461 (1964), Hodson held that the husband's original connivance at his wife's adultery had not been spent.

153. In *Ross Smith* v. *Ross Smith*, [1963] A.C. 280, 323 (1962), he alone held not only that the narrow jurisdiction represented by *Simonin* v. *Mallac* was still good law in the case of void marriages but also that it should be extended to voidable marriages.

154. *National Provincial Bank, Ltd.* v. *Ainsworth*, [1965] A.C. 1175. Again the tone

equitable interest in the matrimonial property in favor of a deserted wife were negatived.[155]

Hodson's concern to retain what he perceived as Christian values with respect to marriage was by no means limited to that area of the law. While opposed to judicial discretion in the granting of divorces, Hodson announced in a lecture, "Whether they are applying the law or exercising their discretion the judges have a duty to perform in their independent search for truth and justice, and a contribution to make towards the maintenance of true religion and virtue in the land."[156] Thus, despite his admiration for Baron Parke and substantive formalism, Hodson was quite able to go along with the majority in *Shaw* v. *Director of Public Prosecutions*. "Even if Christianity is not part of the law of England yet the common law has its roots in Christianity and has always regarded the institution of marriage as worthy to be supported as an essential part of the structure of the society to which we belong. I do not see any reason why a conspiracy to encourage fornication and adultery should be regarded as outside the ambit of a conspiracy to corrupt public morals."[157] The courts or, in a criminal case, the jury still had the function of *custos morum*. "In the field of public morals it will thus be the morality of the man in the jury-box that will determine the fate of the accused, but this should hardly disturb the equanimity of anyone brought up in the traditions of our common law."[158]

Outside family law, however, by reason of both attitudes and attributes, Hodson was a follower rather than a leader, or, at least, a vain dissenter. He opposed changes in equity[159] and conflicts.[160] In the field of

---

of his speech was designed to discourage judicial discretion. For instance, at 1221, he talked of "palm tree justice."

155. Hodson and Denning, however, then joined forces to ensure a statutory solution to the problem, the Matrimonial Homes Act of 1967; see Blom-Cooper and Drewry, *Final Appeal* 209–10.

Despite this, the tone of Hodson's support was not entirely friendly. Hodson spoke

as one of the wicked men who was member of that section of your Lordships' House which came to the decision which my noble and learned friend Lord Denning dislikes so much. . . . My noble and learned friend Lord Denning moves us to tears every time he mentions a deserted wife, the poor woman he has been protecting in the Court of Appeal for years. But there are not many of them. Then he comes to this House and, in sepulchral tones says, "When the House of Lords got the case of a bank, what did they do then? They protected the bank."

But let us not get our feet off the ground. We are not dealing with thousands and thousands of deserted wives. We are dealing with thousands and thousands of poor people who want to raise money on their houses, when perhaps a man has to move because his job has moved. [275 *Parl. Deb.*, H.L. (5th ser.), cols. 649, 650 (28 June 1966)]

156. Hodson, *Judicial Discretion and Its Exercise* 24.
157. [1962] A.C. 220 (1961).
158. Ibid. 294.
159. E.g., *McPhail* v. *Doulton*, [1971] A.C. 424, 437 (1970), dissenting in opposition to the Wilberforce view that powers and trust powers might be assimilated.
160. E.g., *Boys* v. *Chaplin*, [1971] A.C. 356, 373 (1969).

commercial law,[161] Hodson in general supported a nineteenth-century concept of freedom to contract. Parties in default were not to be heard to complain about damages,[162] and he saw no need to limit the rights of the parties to "contract out."[163] Hodson opposed third parties' being able to sue on covenants running with land[164] or on contracts themselves.[165] Even when he sought to stake out a new line, fate seemed to ensure that Hodson would be overshadowed by his colleagues. In *Hedley Byrne* v. *Heller*,[166] for instance, his speech treating liability as based on an extension of *Donoghue* v. *Stevenson*, while in some ways the most radical, proved not as significant as the more sophisticated and subtle speeches of Reid and Devlin.[167] In *Heron II*, where the Lords were involved in adapting (and probably extending) the concept of damages in contract, Hodson found solace in concepts specifically rejected by other law lords as meaningless and misleading.[168] In *Rookes* v. *Barnard*, his adoption of the "limited" rather than "licentious" view of section 3 was not a significant move.[169]

The inherent difficulties in Hodson's jurisprudential stance are most easily discerned in the area of public law. Like all law lords, Hodson felt the need to give notice that he believed in "the liberty of the subject."[170]

161. Hodson was a member of the Permanent Court of Arbitration at the Hague and sat on a number of the shipping appeals in the House. E.g., *Riverstone Meat Co.* v. *Lancashire Shipping Co.*, [1961] A.C. 807 (1960); *Tsakiroglou & Co.* v. *Noblee Thorl G.m.b.H.*, [1962] A.C. 93 (1961); *Union of India* v. *Naviera Aeolus S.A.*, [1964] A.C. 868 (1962).

162. E.g., *White & Carter, Ltd.* v. *McGregor*, [1962] A.C. 413 (Scot. 1961). Cf. his willingness to take account of the public interest in the freedom of trade in *Esso Petroleum Co.* v. *Harper's Garage, Ltd.*, [1968] A.C. 269 (1966).

163. "So long as one remembers that one is construing a document and not applying some rule of law superimposed on the law of contract so as to limit the freedom of the parties to enter into any agreement they like within the limits which the law prescribes, one can apply one's mind to each contract as it comes up for consideration"; *Suisse Atlantique Société d'Armament Maritime S.A.* v. *N.V. Rotterdamsche Kolen Centrale*, [1967] 1 A.C. 361, 410 (1966).

164. E.g., *Sefton* v. *Tophams, Ltd.*, [1967] 1 A.C. 50 (1966). See especially at 65. It is, perhaps, significant that dissenting judgments were written by Reid and Wilberforce.

165. *Beswick* v. *Beswick*, [1968] A.C. 58 (1967).

166. *Hedley Byrne & Co.* v. *Heller & Partners*, [1964] A.C. 465, 504 (1963).

167. And perhaps illogically, Hodson was prepared to allow the bank to exempt itself from liability. "In the case of a person giving a reference I see no objection in law or morals to the giver of the reference protecting himself by giving it without taking responsibility for anything more than the honesty of his opinion"; ibid. 511. Cf. *Gallie* v. *Lee*, [1971] A.C. 1004 (1970), restricting the doctrine of *non est factum*.

168. Referring to the *Victoria Laundry* case, where Asquith had "suggested the phrase 'liable to result' as appropriate to describe the degree of probability required. This may be a colourless expression, but I do not find it possible to improve on it. If the word 'likelihood' is used, it may convey the impression that the chances are all in favour of the thing happening, an idea which I would reject"; *The Heron II*, [1969] 1 A.C. 350, 410 (1967).

169. [1964] A.C. 1129, 1202–3.

170. "The decision in this appeal depends on a very short point which, though tech-

Yet, Hodson's natural instinct was to side with the executive. He would offer no protection to Zacharia when the government of Cyprus demanded his return.[171] In *Burmah Oil* he dissented with Radcliffe in favor of the Crown.[172] The extent to which Hodson was prepared to go in supporting the executive, however, was seen fully only in *McEldowney v. Forde*:[173] with Reid absent, Hodson presided and led a majority (with Pearce and Diplock dissenting) in a direction that seemed to undermine the developments in public law during the 1960s.[174] Hodson refused to find an inelegantly drafted regulation banning " 'republican' clubs or any like organizations howsoever described" ultra vires the enabling legislation. In so doing, he was forced to develop a somewhat tenuous distinction between the legislative and executive powers of the minister[175] and to admit, but ignore, the possibility of abuse.[176]

In rather the same vein, despite the continuing rhetoric of substan-

---

nical, is decisive in favour of the respondent if well founded, since where the liberty of the subject is concerned the formalities required must be strictly observed"; *R. v. Metropolitan Police Comm'r, ex parte Hammond*, [1965] A.C. 810, 837 (1964).

171. "[I] see no reason why this application for return should not be treated as what on the face of it is, namely, an application by the Cyprus Government acting responsibly in the interests of justice"; *Zacharia v. Republic of Cyprus*, [1963] A.C. 634, 681 (1962).

In *R. v. Governor of Brixton Prison, ex parte Schtraks*, [1964] A.C. 556 (1962), he ordered that the prisoner be returned to Israel under the Extradition Act of 1870, holding that the charges were not of a political character. "In some modern States politics and justice may be inextricably mixed, and it is not always easy, for example, to say what amounts to a revolt against the Government. No special feature appears to exist in this case, and I find no substance in the contention that extradition should be refused because of the political character of the offences charged"; ibid. 612.

172. Radcliffe's was clearly by far the more powerful speech. Rather surprisingly, Hodson relied heavily on policy arguments; *Burmah Oil Co. v. Lord Advocate*, [1965] A.C. 75 (Scot. 1964). See especially at 140–41.

173. [1971] A.C. 632 (N. Ire. 1969).

174. Blom-Cooper and Drewry, *Final Appeal* 266–67.

175. "In my opinion there is a distinction between the powers given by Section 1 subsection (1) and those given by subsection (3) [power to make new regulations] of the same section, in that the former are executive and the latter legislative powers. The Minister is not restricted by the language relating to his executive powers when executing his legislative powers though no doubt he will not be unmindful of the language of Parliament in the whole Act"; *McEldowney v. Forde*, [1971] A.C. 632, 645 (N. Ire. 1969).

176. "Accepting that the word 'republican' is an innocent word and need not connote anything contrary to law, I cannot escape the conclusion that in its context, added to the list of admittedly unlawful organisations of a militant type, the word 'republican' is capable of fitting the description of a club which in the opinion of the Minister should be proscribed as a subversive organisation of the type akin to those previously named in the list of admittedly unlawful organisations. The context in which the word is used shows the type of club which the Minister had in mind and there is no doubt that the mischief aimed at is an association which has subversive objects. On this matter, in my opinion, the court should not substitute its judgement for that of the Minister, on the ground that the banning of 'republican clubs' is too remote. I agree that the use of the words 'any like organisation however described' lends some support to the contention that the regulation is vague and for that reason invalid, but on consideration I do not accept the argument based on vagueness"; ibid. 645.

tive formalism, nothing suggested that Hodson was anything but pleased with arrangements whereby crimes were developed by analogy or implication,[177] or the prosecution made use of illegally obtained evidence.[178] Even when Hodson found against the Crown or local authority there was often a feeling that he was unhappy interfering with the established order. Although finding for the plaintiff in *Ridge* v. *Baldwin*, he was not comfortable.[179] His speech in *Conway* v. *Rimmer*[180] was less than elegant. It was unclear whether he was distinguishing or overruling *Duncan* v. *Cammell, Laird*, and his distinction between "contents" and "class" threw some doubt on whether his decision was actually supported by his reasoning.[181] A similar unsatisfactory element characterized his approach in *Padfield* v. *Minister of Agriculture*,[182] where Hodson held both that the minister had "complete discretion" whether to refer a complaint to a committee of investigation,[183] and that he had acted unlawfully in refusing to do so.[184] Such decisions are not the stuff that might provide an effective modern administrative law. Yet, the weaknesses revealed by these opinions pervade other areas of Hodson's work, ranging from revenue[185] to industrial accidents.[186] One has the decided feeling that

177. *R.* v. *Treacy*, [1971] A.C. 537 (1970).

178. Thus, although the Jamaican constitution prohibited unlawful searches and seizures, judges still had discretion to admit evidence obtained through an illegal search, holding "it was not such a case in which the evidence had been obtained by conduct of which the Crown ought not to take advantage"; *King* v. *The Queen*, [1969] 1 A.C. 304 (P.C. 1968).

179. "It may be that I must retreat to the last refuge of one confronted with as difficult a problem as this, namely, that each case depends on its own facts, and that here the deprivation of a pension without a hearing is on the face of it a denial of justice which cannot be justified upon the language of the section under consideration"; [1964] A.C. 40, 133 (1963). It is perhaps not without significance that Hodson failed to prevent Faramus from losing his union status and thus his job in *Faramus* v. *Film Artistes' Ass'n*, [1964] A.C. 925 (1963).

180. [1968] A.C. 910 (1967).

181. See especially ibid. at 979.

182. [1968] A.C. 997, 1045.

183. Ibid. 1046.

184. Ibid. 1049.

185. E.g., he dissented with Tucker in *re Sutherland decd.: Winter* v. *IRC*, [1963] A.C. 235 (1961), supporting the Revenue's construction of "contingent liability" and with Morton against the Revenue in *IRC* v. *Parker*, [1966] A.C. 141 (Scot. 1965), on the question of when the benefit arose. He did, however, accept that a wide interpretation should be given to § 28, Finance Act of 1960; ibid. 165.

186. Although in *Imperial Chem. Indus., Ltd.* v. *Shatwell*, [1965] A.C. 656, 682 (1964), he supported the reintroduction of the defense of *volenti* into the field of master and servant on the ground that

[i]t is manifestly unjust that each brother who has acted in defiance of orders and of regulations made by the employer should be able to sue the employer and recover damages on the ground that the master is vicariously liable for the wrongful act of the servant committed in the course of his employment.

In a situation such as this it seems to me that the pull of public policy is in a direction opposite from that taken in those cases . . . where the statutory duty is imposed directly on the employer.

Hodson would have felt more comfortable in Simonds' than in Reid's court.

The same cannot be said of Pearce.[187] A good analytical lawyer, if not an intellectual, Pearce was basically a divorce lawyer.[188] Yet, coming from a relatively conventional judicial career, he was willing to acknowledge the inevitably creative role in the final appeal court and, within the narrow English constraints, to put himself at the activist rather than the restraint end of the judicial spectrum. Thus, while Pearce was careful to insist that Parliament had the responsibility for remedying injustices in specific decisions,[189] he had little doubt that the final appeal court had the duty to keep law in line with fairness and justice. His aim was "to create and develop broad principles that can be reasonably modified to meet an endless diversity of facts." A combination of these approaches ensured both creativity and publicity about such creativity that would have left Radcliffe uncomfortable.

Nevertheless, Pearce provided an invaluable ally for Reid, as the latter assumed dominance over the House. In the area of statutory interpretation Pearce could not be accused of too mechanical an approach,[190] although of course he worked within the parliamentary limitations as he saw them,[191] while refusing to be bound by the more irrational bans on legislative history.[192] The interpretation of statutes, however, gave Pearce little scope either for the restating of his policy premises or for his views on the judicial role.

187. Edward Holroyd Pearce; b. 1901; father, teacher; educ., Charterhouse, Corpus Christi College, Oxford (Third, "Greats"); called to bar, 1925; Q.C., 1945; Judge, Probate, Divorce, and Admiralty Division, 1948–54; Queen's Bench Division, 1954–57; Lord Justice, 1957–62; Lord of Appeal, 1962–69.

188. "Too close a judicial self-analysis is not helpful in deciding the issue. And when a judge begins to doubt whether or not he has reasonable doubts it obscures rather than clarifies his difficult task"; *Blyth* v. *Blyth*, [1966] A.C. 643, 674 (1965).

189. E.g., *Cartledge* v. *E. Jopling & Sons*, [1963] A.C. 758, 784.

190. E.g., *Rookes* v. *Barnard*, [1964] A.C. 1129, 1237; *Henning* v. *Church of Jesus Christ of the Latter-Day Saints*, [1964] A.C. 420, 440–41 (1963), presuming that "considerations of fairness and public benefit" must have weighed with Parliament in providing rating relief; *Pfizer Corp.* v. *Ministry of Health*, [1965] A.C. 512, 549–50, dissenting; and *IRC* v. *Brebner*, [1967] 2 A.C. 18, 26 (Scot.) on § 28(1) of the Finance Act of 1960.

191. E.g., *De Vigier* v. *IRC*, [1964] 1 W.L.R. 1073, 1079 (H.L.), where he was compelled unwillingly to find for the Revenue on the construction of § 408 of the Income Tax Act of 1952. In *Luke* v. *IRC*, [1963] A.C. 557 (Scot.), especially at 589, he was able to avoid the "injustice" he saw in the Revenue's argument. See also *Imperial Chem. Indus., Ltd.* v. *Shatwell*, [1965] A.C. 656, 686 (1964), admitting that he approached the defense of *volenti non fit injuria* in connection with master and servant with suspicion, although in that case he held it applicable.

192. E.g., *Beswick* v. *Beswick*, [1968] A.C. 58 (1967), construing § 56 of the Law of Property Act of 1925. He went so far as to look at Haldane's preface to Cherry's *Lectures on the New Property Acts*, giving an account of the genesis and birth of the bill in order to attempt to discover Parliament's intent; ibid., 93–94.

In family law, for instance, Pearce saw the Lords' function as a humanizing one, and the policies he advocated were in contrast to Hodson's strong belief in the concept of matrimonial offense.[193] Pearce emphasized that the courts were granting relief provided by Parliament and that religious concepts such as "for better, for worse," which were tied up with the indissolubility of marriage, were of little help.[194] "I cannot accept the argument that divorce is partly punitive and should, therefore, look to the criminal law for guidance. The dissolution or permanent interruption of a union which is in theory life-long and indissoluble cannot be justified by any logic. But the frailties of humanity produce various situations which demand practical relief, and the Divorce Acts owe their origin to a merciful appreciation of that demand."[195] Similarly, in *Indyka* v. *Indyka* he fully accepted that it was the duty of the courts to do their best to reduce the "unhappiness" caused by "limping" or "unilateral" marriages.[196]

In areas of private law, generally, this urge to adapt and develop the law was clear, although the lines it took were sometimes strange. In *Hedley Byrne* v. *Heller*, Pearce, rather than seeking generalized standards of liability, sought to impose duties of care on specific categories or groups and was obviously disappointed not to be able to impose liability in that particular case.[197] Similarly, Pearce had little difficulty accepting

193. Pearce had been a member of the Royal Commission on Marriage and Divorce, 1951. Apart from the Rhodesia Referendum in 1971–72, he does not appear to have been widely used for extrajudicial duties during his time as a Lord of Appeal. Similarly, he rarely spoke in legislative debates; Blom-Cooper and Drewry, *Final Appeal* 205.

194. *Gollins* v. *Gollins*, [1964] A.C. 644, 694 (1963).

195. "Any extension of the area of relief has always been advocated on the ground that there are situations of hardship that must be alleviated, and has been contested on the ground that to extend relief would create corresponding hardship to the other party and would weaken the important and sacred institution of matrimony. Never does an intention to punish enter into the debate; nor is an extension of the grounds of divorce ever advocated or opposed on the ground that it will extend the area of punishment of errant spouses. . . . [The Divorce Acts] appear to intend a practical alleviation of intolerable situations with as little hardship as may be upon the party against whom relief is sought"; *Williams* v. *Williams*, [1964] A.C. 698, 752–53 (1963).

On this occasion the need to protect the spouse was paramount. "It may be that to know all is to pardon all; but the court cannot act on the maxim"; ibid. 762. For a further example of his approach to human problems see *Blyth* v. *Blyth*, [1966] A.C. 643, 671 (1965): "[T]he divorce courts have to deal very often with persons who have little self-control, and whose minds and bodies are not always co-ordinated. In dealing with such persons one has to be careful not to cause injustice by drawing mental inferences more suitable to persons who are better co-ordinated and more self-controlled."

196. [1969] 1 A.C. 33, 77 (1967).

197. [1964] A.C. 465, 540 (1963). Robert Stevens, "*Hedley Byrne* v. *Heller*" 121, 144. In intellectual terms, his opinion in this case is overshadowed by Reid and Devlin. Reid's speech was also clearly more important in the *Heron II*, where Pearce insisted, rather woodenly, on a distinction between damages in tort and contract; [1969] 1 A.C. 350, 413 (1967).

responsibility for balancing policies[198] or developing a more up-to-date version of the public interest.[199] Occasionally, he appeared as a surprise advocate—for instance, by taking a proinventor position at the time the trend in the House was to restrict patents,[200] and at other times his vigor might be thought to be the cause of later embarrassment. His insistence, on policy grounds, in *Rondel v. Worsley*[201] on immunity for barristers in whatever work they are doing may well have gone too far,[202] while he felt the need in *J. T. Stratford and Son v. Lindley*[203] to try to explain away some of the House's apparent antilabor bias in *Rookes v. Barnard.*[204]

The Pearce style was perhaps better suited to the undoubted renaissance of public law during the 1960s.[205] His reluctance to hide his assumptions and predispositions contrasted markedly with those operating in the sphere of public law in the fifties. He had no doubt that the courts had to administer the law "above the executive and even against them."[206]

198. For further examples of his conscious balancing of policies, see, for instance, *Rumping v. DPP*, [1964] A.C. 814, 865 (1962); and *Myers v. DPP*, [1965] A.C. 1001, 1037 (1964).

199. In the "Solus Sites" case he argued, "[I] consider that the courts require on such a matter full guidance from evidence of all the surrounding circumstances and of relevant commercial practice. . . . Without such guidance they cannot hope to arrive at a sensible and up-to-date conclusion on what is reasonable"; *Esso Petroleum Co. v. Harper's Garage, Ltd.*, [1968] A.C. 269, 323 (1966).

200. E.g., dissenting in *Rodi & Weinenberger A.G. v. Henry Showell, Ltd.*, [1969] Pat. Cas. 637, 387 (H.L.).

201. "So far as concerns providing a spur to the advocate by the possibility of actions for negligence, this is unnecessary. Both solicitors and counsel are always keen to win a case and, incidentally, to give satisfaction to their clients so far as this is compatible with their duty to the court and to their professional standards. This is an inevitable part of their human makeup as is the ambition of every judge to decide his cases right. Their danger rather lies in that they may be too keen to win. Thus, to provide a spur is bad rather than good"; [1969] 1 A.C. 191, 272 (1967).

202. Brian Abel-Smith and Robert Stevens, *In Search of Justice* 283–87.

203. "It was suggested . . . that *Rookes v. Barnard* went a long way further than it was, in my opinion, intended to go. It was, for instance, suggested by [counsel for the respondents] that it withdrew from the protection of Section 3 [of the Trade Disputes Act of 1906] the threats of a trade union official to the employer to call a strike in breach of the contract of employment. It certainly does not do that"; [1965] A.C. 269, 366 (1964).

204. Rather surprisingly, in the Judicial Committee of the Privy Council, Pearce's contributions in public law were undistinguished. Perhaps his political instinct was to keep the "English" courts out of disputes in the colonies and former colonies. But see his dissent in *Madzimbamuto v. Lardner-Burke*, [1969] 1 A.C. 645, 731 (P.C. 1968), upholding the right of the Smith regime to continue, de facto, to rule Rhodesia after the Unilateral Declaration of Independence. Presumably this dissent made Pearce sufficiently "politically acceptable" to chair the commission to test Rhodesian approval of the proposed British-Rhodesian settlements, 1971–72.

205. See for the "policy" basis of Pearce's judgment in *Rookes v. Barnard*, [1964] A.C. 1129, 1234–35.

206. E. H. Pearce, "The Law as a Whole" 411, 412. He distinguished the English and American positions. "We have studiously avoided any interference with policy decisions

In *Burmah Oil*, then, his stance was clear. "It is plainly just and equitable that when the State takes or destroys a subject's property for the general good of the State it shall pay him compensation. Are there good grounds of authority or theory or practice for saying that in England the prerogative had no such general duty to compensate?"[207] This approach was consistent with his robust restatement of the courts' responsibility to maintain procedural due process in *Padfield*.[208] More courageous in its way was Pearce's dissent in the "Irish Republican Clubs" case, rather than giving the minister carte blanche to ban any organization.[209] The line of the dissent has reminded some commentators of Atkin in *Liversidge* v. *Anderson*.[210] The House, said Pearce,

> cannot take the easy course of "passing by on the other side" when it seems clear to it that the Minister is using a power in the way in which Parliament, who gave him that power, did not intend. . . . But if it seems clear on grounds of rationality and common sense that he was exceeding the power with which Parliament was intending to clothe him to further the purposes of the Act, the courts have a duty to interfere. The fact that this is not an easy line to draw is no reason why the courts should give up the task and abandon their duty to protect the citizen.[211]

It will come as no surprise then to discover that the 1966 Practice Statement was attractive to Pearce. While most other law lords still attempted to distinguish earlier cases in the House rather than overruling them, few inhibitions gripped Pearce.[212] For this reason, his is perhaps the most satisfactory speech in *Conway* v. *Rimmer*.[213] Pearce had no difficulty in weighing the respective policy that overruling and developing new law involved.[214] Indeed, in *Myers* v. *Director of Public Prose-*

---

and confined our power to curbing only those acts of the executive that are a breach of statutory power or a breach of the rules of natural justice.'

207. *Burmah Oil Co.* v. *Lord Advocate*, [1965] A.C. 75, 149 (Scot. 1964).

208. "I do not regard a Minister's failure or refusal to give any reasons as a sufficient exclusion of the courts' surveillance. If all the prima facie reasons seem to point in favour of his taking a certain course to carry out the intentions of Parliament in respect of a power which it has given him in that regard, and he gives no reason whatever for taking a contrary course, the court may infer that he has no good reason and that he is not using the power given by Parliament to carry out its intentions"; *Padfield* v. *Minister of Agriculture*, [1968] A.C. 997, 1053.

209. *McEldowney* v. *Forde*, [1971] A.C. 632 (N. Ire. 1969).

210. Blom-Cooper and Drewry, *Final Appeal* 266.

211. [1971] A.C. 632, 653 (N. Ire. 1969).

212. E.g., in *Pook* v. *Owen*, [1970] A.C. 244 (1969), of the majority of three (Guest, Pearce, Donovan), only Pearce "overruled" the earlier House decision in *Ricketts* v. *Colquhoun*, [1926] A.C. 1 (1925).

213. [1968] A.C. 910 (1967).

214. Pearce argued,

The Ministry puts forth the rigid general claim [of privilege]. The court accepts it. The litigant ruefully leaves the lists a victim of an injustice, great or small. In some cases this injustice is a necessary evil for the public good, in others unnecessary. Yet, the court has not weighed the balance or considered whether

cutions,[215] Pearce made it clear that he was prepared to develop the law of evidence when Reid and a majority felt changes in the law of hearsay should be made only by Parliament. On other occasions, however, Pearce was able to push forward the law of evidence.[216] Here, as elsewhere, his successes may have been ephemeral, but if the revolution wrought by Reid and others in renewing the life and purpose of the House of Lords in fact survives the seventies, Pearce's name will be remembered, not perhaps as an intellectual leader, but as a vital foot soldier, and as a divorce judge in marked contrast to Hodson.

The Class of 1975

In 1971 Guest, Donovan, and Upjohn ceased to be Lords of Appeal; in 1975 not only Reid, but Lords Morris, Pearson, and Cross retired. These three came from a mix of tradition; their careers clarify the changing mores of the House in the sixties and early seventies. Morris had sat since 1960, Pearson since 1965, and Cross since 1971. Each, in his own

---

the public interest in the well-being or routine of the Ministry or the public interest in the fair administration of justice should have prevailed in that particular case. . . .

In my view, it is essential to leave the vague generalities of wide classes and get down to realities in weighing the respective injuries to the public of a denial of justice on the one side and, on the other, of a revalation of government documents which were never intended to be made public and which might be inhibited by an unlikely possibility of disclosure.

[T]he court should consider whether the document is relevant and important in a reasonable action so that one may fairly say that the public interest in justice requires its disclosure. It must consider whether the disclosure will cause harm administratively, either because of the undesirability of publishing the particular contents or because of the undesirability of making public a particular class of documents. . . . [Ibid. 985–88]

215. "I use the words machinery of justice, because the question how far a court will admit evidence and what weight it will give to it is part of the judicial process. It is the method of extracting the truth to which the law is to be applied and it cannot be considered in vacuo without regard to social conditions. The main argument against any change in principles of law is not applicable to the method of ascertaining the truth. When principles of law are disturbed, many persons who have ordered their affairs on the basis of existing legal authority may suffer injustice. There may be unforeseen repercussions in other branches of the law which may lead to confusion and injustices. The admission of records such as those in question can produce no such effect and lead to no injustice"; [1965] A.C. 1001, 1037 (1964).

216. See *Murdoch* v. *Taylor*, [1965] A.C. 574, where he disagreed, in part, on whether the judge should or should not have a discretion whether to allow any cross-examination as to previous convictions or bad character. "It is certainly not an easy problem. But the difficult burden of holding the scales fairly, not only as between the prosecution and defendants, but also as between the defendants themselves and of doing his best thereby to secure a fair trial for all concerned, falls inevitably on the trial judge and is generally achieved in practice with considerable success. The use of a judicial discretion under Section 1(f)(iii) as between co-defendants would be but an addition to the judge's existing burden"; ibid. 587. "In such a difficult matter which may not infrequently arise in borderline cases, the judge, who sees the general run of the case as it unfolds before him, can produce a fairer result by the exercise of a judicial discretion than by the strict and unfettered application of an arbitrary rule of law"; ibid. 587–88.

way, had provided a link in the gradual development of a new concept of the role of the final appeal court, and the sum of their contributions helped mold the House as a total court. If history will not designate any of them as great appeal judges, Lord Morris of Borth-y-gest[217] at least had a significant impact during his fifteen years on the bench.

In one sense Morris was a caricature of the career judge—serving for a total of thirty years on the bench, after successful practice as an advocate in general common law work. Yet Morris had another side. He had been a Liberal candidate and was the first Lord of Appeal to have attended the Harvard Law School—or indeed any American law school, and he was considerably in demand as an arbiter of wage claims.[218] He was, in the same way as many of his contemporaries, a link between the emphasis on formal logic that underlay substantive formalism and the more sophisticated view of judicial strategy that was afoot in the early seventies. Yet, although Morris outshone many of his contemporaries, he was neither an intellectual in the manner of Wilberforce and Diplock, nor a creative lawyer in the Reid or the Simon of Glaisdale style. He appeared to reflect the tone of the other law lords, rather than becoming a leader in his own right.

Morris was certainly well aware that the appellate role was a potentially creative one. He admitted the limitation on judicial legislation[219] but also insisted that "the law is never something fixed and static, like a monument of stone, but is something live and virile. It grows and evolves

---

Blom-Cooper and Drewry, *Final Appeal* 280, have described Pearce's speech in *Toohey v. Metropolitan Police Comm'r*, [1965] A.C. 595, as "an unheralded decision touching on the nature of testimony, [which] may prove to have been, sociologically, the most decisive step forward, if not the nearest approach to a revolution in criminal jurisprudence yet achieved." It was in that case that Pearce said, "Human evidence shares the frailty of those who give it. It is subject to many cross-currents such as partiality, prejudice, self-interest and, above all, imagination and inaccuracy. . . . If a witness purported to give evidence of something which he believed he had seen at a distance of fifty yards, it must surely be possible to call the evidence of an oculist to the effect that the witness could not possibly see anything at a greater distance than twenty yards"; ibid. 608.

217. John William Morris; b. 1896; father, bank manager; educ., Liverpool Institute, Trinity Hall, Cambridge (Second, Law), Harvard Law School; called to bar, 1921; K.C., 1935; Liberal Candidate, Ilford 1923 and 1924; Judge, King's Bench Division, 1945–51; Lord Justice, 1951–60; Lord of Appeal, 1960–75.

218. E.g., Chairman, Court of Enquiry into the Engineering and Shipbuilding Wage Dispute, 1954; referee to decide wage questions in settlement of railway strike, 1955; Chairman, National Reference Tribunal under Coal Mining Industry Conciliation Scheme, 1955–65.

While a Lord of Appeal, he chaired the Committee on Jury Service; *Report*, Cmnd. 2627 (1965). On this, see William Cornish, *The Jury, passim*. He was the fourth most active participator in the legislative debates of the House of Lords; Blom-Cooper and Drewry, *Final Appeal* 205.

219. E.g., "It is not our style to give judges a kind of roving commission of untutored benevolence"; John W. Morris, *Law and Public Opinion* 1.

as men's ideas flourish and as men's affairs develop."[220] Toward the end of his career he put the idea more broadly:

We must, I think, recognize that daily in the judicial sphere there has to be recourse to a personally built conception of what the judge thinks is fair. The judge is sworn to administer justice according to law. If it is clear what the law is, or if it is categorically laid down—as in an enactment—the judge must follow it. But there is so much that is nowhere written down in black and white, and then the judge must do what is just.[221]

It was consistent, then, that Morris and Pearce became the first judges to make use of the 1966 Practice Statement when they refused to follow *Duncan v. Cammell, Laird*[222] in *Conway v. Rimmer*;[223] but it was also typical of Morris that he justified the overruling—unlike Pearce—in terms of the fact that the 1942 decision was doctrinally incorrect in view of the earlier precedents.[224] So too, when Morris refused to follow *Addie and Sons v. Dumbreck*[225] in *Herrington v. British Railways Board*,[226] the Morris approach was a convoluted one. He first distinguished the factual situation,[227] then argued that "on its facts, the decision in *Addie's* case should in my view have been the other way."[228] At the same time he claimed that "[i]t would not, in my view, be fitting for us to make fundamental changes in the law, according to our view as to what its terms and policy should be, when Parliament, apparently deliberately, has refrained from making such changes";[229] but nevertheless he concluded that Addie's case was "wrongly decided."[230]

Therefore, it is not surprising to find Morris refusing to use the 1966 Practice Statement in some other cases. Although not unsympathetic to the view that the law of exemplary damages worked better before the decision in *Rookes v. Barnard*, he was not about to consider overruling it

220. John W. Morris, "The Equipment of the Lawyer" 881.

221. John W. Morris, "Natural Justice" 1.

222. [1942] A.C. 624.

223. [1968] A.C. 910, 958 (1967): "Though precedent is an indispensable foundation upon which to decide what is the law, there may be times when a departure from precedent is in the interests of justice and the proper development of the law. I have come to the conclusion that it is now right to depart from the decision in *Duncan*'s case."

224. Ibid. 970.

225. [1929] A.C. 358 (Scot.).

226. [1972] A.C. 877.

227. "In the present case a question arises whether some duty may be owed to a person before he becomes a trespasser. In that case a question arose whether a duty was owed to someone who was already a trespasser"; ibid. 902.

228. Ibid. 911.

229. "We can, however, assure that the tide of development of the common law is not unwarrantably impeded"; ibid. 904.

230. Ibid. 911.

in *Broome* v. *Cassell.*[231] Rather more surprising, perhaps, was his vigorous refusal to reconsider *Shaw* in *R.* v. *Knuller.*[232] He arrived at this position by insisting that *Shaw* had not made new law, that "in my view *Shaw*'s case was correctly decided,"[233] and that the 1966 Practice Statement "drew attention to the especial need for certainty as to the criminal law."[234] In evaluating that view, however, one must take into account the fact that Morris had been a party to *Shaw* v. *Director of Public Prosecutions.*[235]

Morris' decision is surprising in that his enthusiasm for conspiracy ran counter to his more-enlightened-than-average view of the criminal law and law reform. He had been in favor of abolition of the death penalty[236] and had supported the establishment of the Law Commission.[237] He had spoken out in favor of reforms in the criminal law[238] and opposed the anti-civil libertarian aspects of the Eleventh Report of the Criminal Law Revision Committee.[239] Yet in the House itself, as in the *Knuller* case, he appeared to allow himself to be heavily influenced by other law lords. In *Warner* v. *Metropolitan Police Commissioner,*[240] although paying deference to the idea that mens rea ought to be an ingredient of a crime unless Parliament specifically excluded it, Morris appeared to exclude it by implication.[241] In a differently constituted

231. "I do not think that power that was referred to in the statement of July 26, 1966 . . . was intended to encourage a tendency periodically to chop and change the law. In branches of the law where clarification becomes necessary there may well be decisions which as a matter of policy are not universally welcome or where some may think that some variant of the decision one way or another would have been more acceptable. But this does not mean that decisions of this House should readily be reviewed whenever a case presents itself which is covered by a decision. There must be something much more"; [1972] A.C. 1027, 1098.

232. [1973] A.C. 435 (1972).

233. Ibid. 463.

234. Ibid.

235. [1962] A.C. 220, 229 (1961).

236. 268 *Parl. Deb.*, H.L. (5th ser.), cols. 535–38 (19 July 1965): "Whatever view your lordships may hold in regard to retribution as such, I hope you will reject the idea that the death penalty is to be endorsed as a measure of retribution. Our abhorrence and condemnation of taking life is not well expressed if we must adopt that which we condemn."

237. "No big commercial concern these days could fail to falter if it did not revise its plans, renew its plants, modernise and keep its development plans up to date. The law is worthy of equally tender care"; 269 ibid., col. 1214 (1 Apr. 1965). See also his support of the Limitation Bill of 1963, reversing *Cartledge* v. *Jopling*; 251 ibid., cols. 1282–83 (8 July 1963).

238. E.g., his speeches on the Criminal Justice Bill of 1961, 230 ibid., cols. 1096–98 (1 May 1961), and the Compensation for Victims of Crimes of Violence Act of 1964, 257 ibid., cols. 1832–86 (7 May 1964).

239. "I have many reservations or very serious apprehensions about some of the recommendations"; 338 ibid., col. 1627 (14 Feb. 1973).

240. [1969] 2 A.C. 256 (1968).

241. "All the indications are that . . . Parliament decided to forbid possession abso-

panel in *Sweet* v. *Parsley*, another drug case a year later, however, Morris delivered a vigorous speech requiring mens rea "unless Parliament has by the statute enacted that guilt may be established in cases where there is no *mens rea*."[242]

This same almost inconsistent approach, depending on the composition of the panels, appeared in tax cases, especially the early cases in which he sat dealing with dividend stripping.[243] In matrimonial cases, too, Morris appeared to be less predictable than the other lords, voting with the majority while preserving the idea of implied intention of cruelty in *Gollins*,[244] dissenting in *Williams*,[245] but being willing to change the basis of the rules of recognition in *Indyka*.[246] In *Close* v. *Steel Company of Wales*,[247] he dissented vigorously with Denning on the fencing provisions of the Factories Act, while in later cases he voted with the majority.[248]

The enigmatic aspects of Morris came to the fore in various ways. On the one hand he could narrow issues remarkably; on the other he could engage in bold developments of the law. In respect to the former, he frequently indulged in phrases such as "[t]he issue calling for decision depended . . . simply and solely upon the interpretation of the contract made by the parties."[249] When Morris adopted this narrowing process it enabled decisions to be taken in what seems a simple way. "In a system of law not contained in any formal code decision is reached by applying settled or recognised principle to particular ascertained facts."[250] He also

---

lutely. . . . The intention of Parliament is revealed by the words used in their context in the Act"; ibid. 295 ff. Yet, in *Armah* v. *Government of Ghana*, [1968] A.C. 192 (1966), one of the few cases where the House refused to deport a fugitive offender on a de facto political charge, Morris dissented. Cf. *Commissioners of Customs & Excise* v. *Harz*, [1967] 1 A.C. 760 (1966), where Morris played a significant part in holding inadmissible the answer to a compulsory interrogation.

242. [1970] A.C. 132, 152 (1969).

243. Cf. especially his speeches in *Griffiths* v. *J. P. Harrison, Ltd.*, [1963] A.C. 1 (1962), and *Finsbury Securities* v. *IRC*, [1966] 1 W.L.R. 1402 (H.L.). In support of the Revenue, see also his speech in *Cleary* v. *IRC*, [1968] A.C. 766 (1967).

244. *Gollins* v. *Gollins*, [1964] A.C. 644, 674 (1963).

245. *Williams* v. *Williams*, [1964] A.C. 698, 733 (1963).

246. *Indyka* v. *Indyka*, [1969] 1 A.C. 33 (1967).

247. [1962] A.C. 367, 407 (1961).

248. E.g., *Sparrow* v. *Fairey Aviation Co.*, [1964] A.C. 1019, 1050 (1962). He was on the whole sympathetic to the workman in interpreting factory legislation. E.g., *Midland & Low Moor Iron & Steel Co.* v. *Cross*, [1965] A.C. 343 (1964); *J. & F. Stone Lighting & Radio, Ltd.* v. *Haygarth*, [1968] A.C. 157 (1966).

249. *Modern Eng'r (Bristol), Ltd.* v. *Gilbert-Ash (Northern), Ltd.*, [1974] A.C. 689, 702 (1973). See also *Parry* v. *Cleaver*, [1970] A.C. 1, 23 (1969); *Dorset Yacht Co.* v. *Home Office*, [1970] A.C. 1004, 1033; *Lynall* v. *IRC*, [1972] A.C. 680, 699; *F. Hoffman-LaRoche & Co. A.G.* v. *Secretary of State for Trade & Indus.*, [1975] A.C. 295, 353 (1973).

250. *Esso Petroleum Co.* v. *Harper's Garage, Ltd.*, [1968] A.C. 269, 304 (1966).

adopted a related approach in dealing with statutory interpretation—beginning with linguistics[251] and then handling glosses.[252] The analysis of policy, whether in case law or legislative interpretation, tended, if it came at all, to come last.[253]

This approach, owing something historically to substantive formalism, has to be contrasted with Morris' occasional bold developments of doctrine—particularly when sitting with a creative panel of law lords. Generally heavily supported by doctrine and not as intellectually vigorous as other speeches, these outbursts, in their own way, were an important contribution. Although eager to show he was only applying a settled principle, Morris was a party to *Hedley Byrne* v. *Heller.*[254] In *Rondel* v. *Worsley* he considered authorities from 1742 in finally upholding the immunity of barristers from negligence actions, while concluding, "It would be a retrograde development if an advocate were under pressure unwarrantably to subordinate his duty to the court to his duty to the client."[255] In *Dorset Yacht Company* v. *Home Office* the technique was the same: a narrow statement of the issue,[256] heavy reliance on precedents and existing principles,[257] and then what was in effect a bold decision.[258] In leading contracts cases his style seemed similar.[259]

Two strong interests should be noted in a discussion of Morris: his faith in the jury and his belief in natural justice. He allowed his faith in the jury to buttress his decision in *Shaw*. "Even if accepted public standards may to some extent vary from generation to generation, current

251. E.g., *in re Holmden's Settlement Trusts*, [1968] A.C. 685, 703.

252. E.g., *BSC Footwear, Ltd.* v. *Ridgeway*, [1972] A.C. 544, 558 (1971).

253. E.g., *The Tojo Maru*, [1972] A.C. 242, 275–76 (1971).

254. [1964] A.C. 465 (1963). See especially at 502: "My Lords, guided by the assistance given in *Nocton v. Lord Ashburton*, I consider that it ought not to have been held in *Le Lievre v. Gould* that *Cann v. Willson* was wrongly decided."

255. [1969] 1 A.C. 191, 251 (1967).

256. [1970] A.C. 1004, 1033: "It is therefore . . . important to remember that we are only asked to decide whether . . . there was some duty of care."

257. "The principle expressed in . . . *Donoghue v. Stevenson* . . . would seem to be directly applicable"; ibid. 1034.

258. "I doubt whether it is necessary to say, in cases where the court is asked whether in a particular situation a duty existed, that the court is called upon to make a decision as to policy. Policy need not be invoked where reason and good sense will at once point the way"; ibid. 1039.

259. On restraint of trade, for instance, while he called for consideration of the public interest, it was circumscribed by narrower concepts. E.g., *Dickson v. Pharmaceutical Soc'y of Great Britain*, [1970] A.C. 403, 422 (1968); *Esso Petroleum Co. v. Harper's Garage, Ltd.*, [1968] A.C. 269 (1966), especially at 304: "[I]n some situations more than one principle may be relevant and important. Particularly is this so where principles have, as their foundation, the dictates of public policy."

In *The Heron II*, [1969] 1 A.C. 350 (1967), Morris was both more sympathetic to the *Victoria Laundry* case than were his colleagues (ibid. 399), and more willing to stay with general phrases, such as holding the party in breach responsible for damages "liable to result or at least not unlikely to result"; ibid. 406.

standards are in the keeping of juries, who can be trusted to maintain the corporate good sense of the community and to discern attacks upon values that must be preserved."[260] He confirmed that confidence in upholding *Shaw* in *Knuller*.[261] Such was his belief in the infallibility of the jury[262] and the standards of "right-thinking citizens"[263] who adhere to "what reasonable and well-disposed people would regard as rational, necessary and wise,"[264] that he even championed the jury in civil cases— a rare phenomenon in modern English law.[265]

Morris' belief in the jury was not unrelated to his commitment to the principles of natural justice, "the principles of fair play so deeply rooted in the minds of modern Englishmen,"[266] and to the sense of justice as the "intuitive and instinctive sense of what is fair and seemly."[267] These views, expressed fairly early in his career, did not weaken. In a public lecture in 1973, he predicted a glowing future for natural justice in all areas of the law,[268] and his speech in *Ridge* v. *Baldwin*[269] had undoubtedly been significant in the development of procedural due process in the 1960s. It was typical of the man. After all, nearing eighty, he was the lone dissenter in favor of a broad interpretation of the Race Relations Act in *Race Relations Board* v. *Charter*.[270] While he agreed that law was

260. [1962] A.C. 220, 292 (1961). For similar sentiments, see *Sykes* v. *DPP*, [1962] A.C. 528, 572 (1961).

261. [1973] A.C. 435, 462 (1972): "[P]arliament has fairly and squarely assigned such a task to a jury . . . with the knowledge that there is every likelihood that the collective view of a body of men and women on a jury will reflect the current view of society."

262. Morris, *Law and Public Opinion* 22.

263. John W. Morris, "The Rich Heritage of the Law" 57, 59.

264. Ibid.

265. *Broome* v. *Cassell & Co.*, [1972] A.C. 1027, 1097. The other law lords in this case were less enthusiastic about the use of juries in libel cases. Morris even had some sympathy with the use of juries in personal injury cases; *Law and Public Opinion* 14.

266. John W. Morris, "Courts and Domestic Tribunals" 318, 324.

267. John W. Morris, *The Spirit of Justice* 4.

268. "We can, I think, take pride in what has been done in recent periods and particularly in the field of administrative law by involving and applying these principles which we may broadly classify under the designation of natural justice. Many testing problems as to their application yet remain to be solved. But I affirm that the area of administrative action is but one area in which the principles are to be deployed. Nor are they to be invoked only when procedural failures are shown. Does natural justice qualify to be described as a majestic conception? I believe it does. Is it just a rhetorical but vague phrase which can be employed when needed, to give a gloss of assurance? I believe that it is very much more. If it can be summarised as being fair play in action—who could wish that it would ever be out of action? It denotes that the law is not only to be guided by reason and by logic but that its purpose will not be fulfilled if it lacks more exalted inspiration"; Morris, "Natural Justice" 1, 16.

269. [1964] A.C. 40 (1963). See Blom-Cooper and Drewry, *Final Appeal* 262.

270. "[B]y enacting the Race Relations Acts, 1965 and 1968, Parliament introduced in the law of England a new guiding principle of fundamental and far-reaching importance. It is one that affects and must influence action and behaviour in this country within a wide-ranging sweep of human activities and personal relationships. . . . In one sense there results

not "fixed and static," and that there must be no "mystique" of the law,[271] he generally left leadership to his colleagues and to Parliament.[272] Yet Morris was an important infantryman in the redeployment of judicial forces.

If Morris' contribution is compared with that of Pearson and Cross, however, its importance is magnified. While Morris was not generally a leader, he clearly enjoyed being a member of the Reid court and saw the importance of the House as a judicial body. This was not the style of Pearson or Cross. Lord Pearson[273] had been thought of as a constructive member of the Court of Appeal and a good President of the Restrictive Practices Court,[274] and his early decisions as a law lord appeared to have a sense of boldness.[275] As a former Chairman of the Law Reform Committee, he was particularly concerned with criminal law[276] and almost at once appeared to be influential in criminal appeals.[277] By the time of his retirement, however, Pearson seemed to be one of the narrowest and most unimaginative of the law lords, uncomfortable in the atmosphere that dominated the Reid court in the late sixties and early seventies.

Yet Pearson, if indeed the transformation is accurately described,

---

for some people a limitation on what could be called their freedom: they may no longer treat certain people, because of their colour, race or ethnic or national origins, less favourably than they would treat others. But in the interests of the same cause of freedom . . . Parliament has . . . prescribed discrimination . . . as being unlawful"; [1973] A.C. 868, 889.

271. Morris, "Equipment of the Lawyer" 868, 865. See also, "There is a quality of robust common sense in the people of our land. We must see that our law always has that same robust vigour"; Morris, "Rich Heritage" 435.

272. See his insistence, in some of his decisions, that Parliament had to settle policy: *Race Relations Bd.* v. *Applin,* [1975] A.C. 259, 273 (1974); *F. Hoffman-LaRoche & Co.* v. *Secretary of State for Trade & Indus.,* [1975] A.C. 295, 342 (1973).

273. Colin Hargreaves Pearson; b. 1889; father, barrister; educ., St. Paul's, Balliol College, Oxford (Second, "Greats"); called to bar, 1924; K.C., 1949; Judge, Queen's Bench Division, 1951–61; Lord Justice, 1961–65; Lord of Appeal, 1965–75.

274. See Robert Stevens and Basil Yamey, *The Restrictive Practices Court, passim.*

275. See, for instance, his dissent in *in re Ralli's Settlement,* [1966] A.C. 483, 516, where he looked at the substance of a tax avoidance device and concluded, "Examining the clause realistically in search of its true nature and effect, I cannot take it at its face value"; his view in *J. & F. Stone Lighting & Radio, Ltd.* v. *Haygarth,* [1968] A.C. 157, 187 (1966), that "the Factories Act, 1961, should be regarded as a beneficial rather than a penal statute." In *Indyka* v. *Indyka,* [1969] 1 A.C. 33, 107 (1967), he accepted that the change in conditions had rendered the former basis of jurisdiction "unrealistic and disadvantageous," and he therefore joined in its restructuring.

276. See, for instance, his conversion to the view that the Court of Criminal Appeal be reorganized; 274 *Parl. Deb.,* H.L. (5th ser.), cols. 822–26 (12 May 1960).

277. For instance, he delivered the opinion of the court in *Armstrong* v. *DPP,* [1965] A.C. 1262, on the issue of postal bingo and *Verrier* v. *DPP,* [1967] 2 A.C. 195 (1966), concerning the common law power to sentence for misdemeanors.
He also gave the leading judgments in some civil appeals early in his term of office. E.g., *Garnac Grain Co.* v. *H. M. F. Faure & Fairclough, Ltd.,* [1968] A.C. 1130, 1133 (1967), on the repudiation of contract; and *Fluflon, Ltd.* v. *William Frost & Sons,* [1968] Pat. Cas. 508 (H.L.), on the construction of a patent license.

must be treated as a victim of the system of using judges heavily for extrajudicial work. Even before becoming a law lord, Pearson had, in 1964, chaired a Committee of Inquiry into the Dispute in the Electricity Industry; and, after becoming a Lord of Appeal, he was at times treated more like a labor arbitrator than a judge. Thus shortly after becoming a law lord, the Minister of Labour, Ray Gunther, persuaded Pearson to chair a Committee of Inquiry into the Dock Strike.[278] It was a demanding inquiry, with the Prime Minister claiming that the strike was Communist-inspired,[279] and Pearson's report was, not unnaturally, controversial,[280] nearly splitting the cabinet.[281] Nevertheless, Pearson remained active in the negotiations even after the publication of the report.[282] His performance clearly impressed the Wilson government; the following year (1967) he was brought in to arbitrate the dispute in civil aviation and the next year (1968) to handle the dispute in the steel industry. He was chairman of the committee investigating the dock strike in 1970 and chairman of the tribunal looking at teachers' pay in 1971 and 1972. Finally, in 1973, Pearson was appointed—this time by the Heath administration—as Chairman of the Royal Commission on Civil Liability and Compensation for Personal Injury. This effectively full-time occupation de facto terminated Pearson's judicial career two years before his formal retirement.

It is no doubt appropriate to view the bulk of Pearson's judicial work in the light of these extraordinary extrajudicial demands, for after early hints that he might be a powerful appellate judge, Pearson increasingly resembled a conventional law lord of the older generation. His mature view was that judges, even appeal judges, had little, if any, discretion. He saw his role as limited to the discovery of existing law;[283] certainty in the law was the primary purpose of the judicial function,[284]

278. Harold Wilson, *A Personal Record* 232.

279. Ibid. 236–39.

280. Pearson had unsuccessfully urged the union to return to work while the inquiry was going on. The report when it appeared was highly critical of the union, whose executive rejected it; ibid. 233.

281. In cabinet George Brown and James Callaghan took the "not-a-penny-beyond-the-Pearson-proposals" approach; Frank Cousins, Barbara Castle, and Dick Crossman were for compromising; Richard Crossman, 1 *The Diaries of a Cabinet Member*, 537–38.

282. After the publication of the report on 8 June 1966, Pearson chaired the negotiations among the employers, the union, and the Trade Union Congress in late June; Wilson, *Personal Record* 240.

283. "That is, I think the existing state of the law, and it is sufficient for the decision of the present case. I see the attractions of the new interpretation which . . . Lord Hailsham . . . and Viscount Dilhorne have placed upon . . . the Act of 1967. . . . This might or might not be desirable as a matter of policy, but it is not necessarily what Parliament intended . . . and it conflicts with . . . *Pinner v. Everett.* . . . [S]tare decisis is an important principle, and it seems preferable to maintain the law as it has been developed hitherto"; *R. v. Sakhuja*, [1973] A.C. 152, 190 (1972).

284. E.g., *Boys v. Chaplin*, [1971] A.C. 356, 400, 406 (1969).

and this allowed little room for judicial "variance."[285] In terms of the constitutional approach, the Pearson view was characterized in *Pook* v. *Owen*. "Although the result is unfair, I do not think it can be properly corrected without a change in the system."[286]

The style and impact of this approach are themselves predictable. Issues were narrowed rather than generalized,[287] and cases were decided on precedent rather than principle. Only if there were no case "actually in point" did the search turn to principle.[288] As he put it in *Dorset Yacht Company* v. *Home Office*, "Can such a duty be held to exist on the facts alleged here? On this question there is no judicial authority except the one decision in the Ipswich County Court. . . . In this situation it seems permissible, indeed almost inevitable, that one should revert to the statement of basic principle by Lord Atkin in *Donoghue v. Stevenson*."[289] As one would expect, a similar approach was maintained toward statutory construction; words were to be given their "natural and probable" meaning,[290] and parliamentary policy was to be derived from the interstices of the sections and clauses.[291]

Since Pearson saw the main purpose of judicial policy making to be the restating of existing law, his opinions appear as the narrow restating

---

285. E.g., *R.* v. *Ludlow*, [1971] A.C. 29, 38 (1970); *The Tojo Maru*, [1972] A.C. 242, 289 (1971). See also *Taylor* v. *O'Connor*, [1971] A.C. 115, 140 (1970): "It is desirable for the sake of uniformity and certainty that the same general method should be employed for assessing damages in fatal accident cases, whenever it is reasonably possible to do so, adjustments being made for special features in particular cases."

286. [1970] A.C. 244, 266 (1969).

287. E.g., *Slough Estates, Ltd.* v. *Slough Borough Council (No. 2)*, [1971] A.C. 958, 971; *Woodhouse A.C. Israel Cocoa, Ltd.* v. *Nigerian Produce Mkt. Co.*, [1972] A.C. 741, 762. Extrinsic factors were, as far as possible, excluded; *R.* v. *Sakhuja*, [1973] A.C. 152, 182 ff. (1972); *R.* v. *Governor of Brixton Prison, ex parte Keane*, [1972] A.C. 204, 212 ff.

288. E.g., "It seems to me that *Gourley's* case affords ample guidance for the decision of the present question"; *Parry* v. *Cleaver*, [1970] A.C. 1, 48 (1969); *Kammins Ballrooms Co.* v. *Zenith Invs., Ltd.*, [1971] A.C. 850, 877: "In my opinion that cogent reasoning of a strong court is applicable and should be applied in the construction of the phrase." See also *Nimmo* v. *Alexander Cowan & Sons*, [1968] A.C. 107, 137 (Scot. 1967): "Obviously the question is difficult, because there is a conflict of judicial opinion."

289. [1970] A.C. 1004, 1053.

290. E.g., *Slough Estates, Ltd.* v. *Slough Borough Council (No. 2)*, [1971] A.C. 958, 970. See also *J. & F. Stone Lighting & Radio, Ltd.* v. *Haygarth*, [1968] A.C. 157, 188 (1966): "There is no need to construe the Act restrictively, though equally there is no need to extend it beyond its natural meaning."

291. E.g., *Torr* v. *Torr*, [1973] A.C. 254, 268 (1972); *R.* v. *Governor of Pentonville Prison, ex parte Azam*, [1974] A.C. 18, 68 (1973). For earlier examples where Pearson seemed to bow to the minutiae of statutory interpretation, see *Armah* v. *Government of Ghana*, [1968] A.C. 192, 263 (1966) and *DPP* v. *Whyte*, [1972] A.C. 849, 866 (on the meaning of "persons"). The limits of his willingness to develop the law in statutory cases is perhaps reflected in *British Rys. Bd.* v. *Liptrot*, [1969] 1 A.C. 136, 167 (1967), on the issue of whether § 14 of the Factories Act applied to mobile parts of a crane: "I would agree to this extent, that for the very simple reasons of common sense there must be some limitation of Section 14 in relation to vehicles and mobile machines."

of existing principles, frequently refusing to extend them to a new situation. Thus, in *Rondel* v. *Worsley*, "for more than a hundred years" it had been settled that a barrister-client relationship was not a "legally binding arrangement."[292] In *Gallie* v. *Lee* "the principle" of *non est factum* "can and should be applied so as to confine the scope of the plea . . . within narrow limits."[293] The compensation concept based on the family car fell foul of the limited role of the judiciary in *Launchbury* v. *Morgans*. "It seems to me that these innovations, whether or not they may be desirable, are not suitable to be introduced by judicial decision."[294] Public law in particular appeared to make Pearson uncomfortable. He was party to the Irish Republican Clubs case—*McEldowney* v. *Forde*—and while he was prepared to concede that theoretically the minister might make orders ultra vires the clause giving him power with respect to "the preservation of peace and the maintenance of order," he was unmoved by the arguments of vagueness of the regulation in question or the fact that there was no evidence that the club in question was seditious.[295]

Even where the House appeared to be breaking new ground, the line was a cautious one. Judgments are heavy with somewhat dated references to causation[296] and causes.[297] It was not a fertile ground in which to expect the 1966 Practice Statement to take root. "[T]here is the principle of *stare decisis*. A decision of this House has had the distinctive advantage of being final both in the sense that it put an end to the litigation between the parties and in the sense that it established the principle embodied in the ratio decidendi. . . . This distinctive advantage of finality should not be thrown away by too ready use of the recently declared liberty to depart from previous decisions."[298] Yet in *Herrington* Pearson went along with the other law lords in concluding, after a generally formalistic statement of the problem, that *Addie and Sons* v. *Dumbreck* was "not now adequate or defensible as applying to modern conditions."[299] His new test of "humanity" did not, however, find favor with

292. [1969] 1 A.C. 191, 287 (1967).
293. [1971] A.C. 1004, 1034 (1970).
294. [1973] A.C. 127, 142 (1972).
295. [1971] A.C. 632, 655–57 (N. Ire. 1969).
296. E.g., *Baker* v. *Willoughby*, [1970] A.C. 467, 496 (1969).
297. E.g., *Dorset Yacht Co.* v. *Home Office*, [1970] A.C. 1004, 1053: "The essential feature of this case is not the 'escape' (whatever that may have amounted to) but the interference with the boats."
298. *R.* v. *National Ins. Comm'r, ex parte Hudson*; see *Jones* v. *Secretary of State for Social Servs.*, [1972] A.C. 944, 996 (1971), refusing to reconsider *Dowling*'s case "in the absence of any demonstration that it was arrived at per incuriam or is for some other reason clearly unmaintainable."
299. *Herrington* v. *British Rys. Bd.*, [1972] A.C. 877, 927. See also:

It seems to me that the rule in *Addie's* case has been rendered obsolete by changes in physical and social conditions and has become an incumbrance impeding the proper development of the law. With the

the Law Commission when it examined the decision.[300] In short, while Pearson would have complemented Simonds, he was not in step with the style of a Reid or Morris, a Wilberforce or Diplock.

Even more out of step with the image of the House in the early seventies was Lord Cross of Chelsea, who was a Lord of Appeal from 1971 to 1975.[301] An elegant Chancery lawyer,[302] Cross was perhaps the clearest adherent of the declaratory theory of law to sit in the Lords in recent times. Although—or perhaps because—he had begun life as an academic lawyer, he seemed uncomfortable in the judicial role.[303] For Cross the 1966 Practice Statement was effectively a dead letter. Change in the law had to come from Parliament.[304] Thus in *Albert* v. *Motor*

---

increase of the population and the larger proportion living in cities and towns and the extensive substitution of blocks of flats for rows of houses with gardens or back yards and quiet streets, there is less playing space for children and so a greater temptation to trespass. There is less supervision of children, so they are more likely to trespass. Also with the progress of technology there are more and greater dangers for them to encounter by reason of the increased use of, for instance, electricity, gas, fast-moving vehicles, heavy machinery and poisonous chemicals. There is considerably more need than there used to be for occupiers to take reasonable steps with a view to deterring persons, especially children, from trespassing in places that are dangerous for them. [Ibid. 929]

300. *Report of the Law Commission*, No. 70, Cmnd. 6428 (1976).

301. Arthur Geoffrey Neale Cross; b. 1904; educ., Westminster, Trinity College, Cambridge; called to bar, 1930; K.C., 1949; Judge, Chancery Division, 1960–69; Lord Justice, 1969–71; Lord of Appeal, 1971–75.

302. See, for instance, *Dingle* v. *Turner*, [1972] A.C. 601, on trusts for the relief of poverty; *in re Westbourne Galleries, Ltd.*, [1973] A.C. 360 (1972) on the rights of minority shareholders. See also Geoffrey Cross, "Some Recent Developments in the Law of Charity" 187.

303. He was a fellow of Trinity College, Cambridge, from 1927 to 1931. See, e.g., *Alphacell, Ltd.* v. *Woodward*, [1972] A.C. 824, on the interpretation of the Rivers (Prevention of Pollution) Act of 1951. Cross "found this a difficult case" (at 845), while Wilberforce (at 834) found "the present case comparatively simple." Sometimes Cross would confess to not following all of counsel's arguments. E.g., *R.* v. *Hyam*, [1975] A.C. 55, 97 (1974). In that same case he wavered in agreeing with Kilbrandon that there should be but one grade of homicide; he also found the view of Diplock attractive. "On the other hand, my noble and learned friend, Viscount Dilhorne . . . thinks his [opinion] is wrong . . . and he may be right in so thinking. All that I am certain of is that I am not prepared to decide between them without having heard the fullest possible argument on the point"; ibid. 97–99. In *R.* v. *Governor of Pentonville Prison, ex parte Sotiriadis*, [1975] A.C. 1 (1974), Cross expressed doubts about the propriety of a change in construction, although he concluded, "But as all of your lordships are clearly of opinion that the construction suggested . . . ought to be adopted . . . I am not prepared to register a dissent"; ibid. 32. For a further example of his vacillating style, see *F. Hoffman-LaRoche & Co. A.G.* v. *Secretary of State for Trade & Indus.*, [1975] A.C. 295, 371–72 (1973).

304. Although see *Miliangos* v. *George Frank (Textiles), Ltd.*, [1976] A.C. 443 (1975), where he stressed that "the fact that no lawyer regards previous decisions of this House as absolutely binding does not mean that whenever we think that a previous decision was wrong we should reverse it. In the general interest of certainty in the law we must be sure that there is some very good reason before we so act"; ibid. 496. Eventually he agreed with Wilberforce that "the 'foreign exchange' situation generally and the position of sterling in particular" justified allowing judgments in English courts to be given in foreign currencies. See also *Launcbury* v. *Morgans*, [1973] A.C. 127, 144 (1972).

Insurers' Bureau he was unable to accept a distinction accepted by the other law lords because he felt it intruded on Parliament's right to decide what the law was.[305] In *British Railways Board* v. *Pickin*, he vigorously rejected any attempt to analyze the words at issue in the light of legislative history.[306] Interpretation began and ended effectively with "prima facie" meanings,[307] and Parliament was chastised if legislation required the judges to give content to a phrase.[308] Indeed, his most ambitious decision was one of his last—*the Philippine Admiral*. There, presiding over a strong Privy Council, he spoke for the Judicial Committee when it took an important step in bringing the law of immunity of foreign sovereigns more into line with modern conditions.[309]

More in keeping with his general approach was his tendency to draw issues narrowly and, if possible, to postpone them.[310] Precedent was piled on precedent. At the same time, rather in the Pearson model, Cross attempted to allocate responsibility outside the judicial arena. He supported a "strong" view of contempt.[311] In criminal cases the reasonableness of the jury was invoked as a standard,[312] and rather surprisingly, in race relations cases, that of the "man in the street."[313] In the criminal

305. [1972] A.C. 301, 341 (1971).

306. "We do not and cannot know whether the question of giving them notice was raised during the passage of the Bill. It may have escaped attention; on the other hand, Parliament may have addressed its mind to the point and decided that in all the circumstances the giving of notice was not necessary. That is a matter into which it is impossible for us to inquire"; *Pickin* v. *British Rys. Bd.*, [1974] A.C. 765, 802–3.

307. *R.* v. *Selby*, [1972] A.C. 515, 544 (1971); *R.* v. *Sakhuja*, [1973] A.C. 152, 194 (1972).

308. E.g., *Race Relations Bd.* v. *Charter*, [1973] A.C. 868, 904.

309. [1977] A.C. 373 (P.C. 1975). See especially at 403:

[C]ounsel for the appellant could and did argue with force that granted that the restrictive theory was to be preferred, the courts should leave it to the government to ratify the 1926 and 1972 Conventions and to introduce the legislation necessary to make them part of our law and should not tamper with the law as so far declared in England by applying the restrictive theory to actions in rem. But their lordships—while recognising that there is force in that argument—are not prepared to accept it. Thinking as they do that the restrictive theory is more consonant with justice they do not think that they should be deterred from applying it so far as they can by the thought that the resulting position may be somewhat anomalous.

310. E.g., *National Dock Labour Bd.* v. *John Bland & Co.*, [1972] A.C. 222, 240 (1971); *R.* v. *Patents Appeal Tribunal, ex parte Beecham, Group, Ltd.*, [1974] A.C. 646, 687–88 (1973). See also *Alfred Crompton Amusement Machs., Ltd.* v. *Commissioners of Customs & Excise (No. 2)*, [1974] A.C. 405, 432 (1973): "One day it may be necessary for this House to consider the point but in my judgement it does not arise for decision in this case."

311. "Nowadays when sympathy is readily accorded to anyone who defies constituted authority the very name of the offence predisposes many people in favour of the alleged offender. Yet the due administration of justice is something which all citizens, whether on the left or on the right or in the centre, should be anxious to safeguard"; *Attorney-General* v. *Times Newspapers, Ltd.*, [1974] A.C. 273, 322 (1973).

312. E.g., *Stafford* v. *DPP*, [1974] A.C. 878, 906 (1973).

313. *Ealing London Borough Council* v. *Race Relations Bd.*, [1972] A.C. 342, 366 (1971): "His reaction would probably be 'once a Hun always a Hun' or 'once a Jap always

area, at least, this approach led to technical decisions, including the conviction of the vendors of pornographic literature[314] and the freeing of a rapist who unreasonably thought the woman had no objection to intercourse.[315] While some commentators understandably feel that Parliament has attempted to "shuffle off" its responsibilities onto the courts in recent years, the Cross view suggests that some judges, even at the appeal level, were prepared to "shuffle off" their responsibilities onto Parliament.

When one considers the fact that nine or ten Lords of Appeal sat in up to three panels in the House, with each law lord still normally producing an uncoordinated speech or judgment, as well as helping to staff the Judicial Committee of the Privy Council, it is perhaps surprising that trends appeared at all. Lord Chancellors, however, still assigned law lords to particular cases—normally in panels of five—and the Chancellors of the post-1955 period tended to be stronger men than their predecessors. So too law lords of the caliber of Reid and Radcliffe (discussed in chapter 13) and Wilberforce, Diplock, and Simon of Glaisdale (discussed in chapter 15) ensured that important new approaches were taken and that, despite the panel system, trends could be projected and analyzed. As the House returned more to issues of public law, Prime Ministers were thought to have taken more interest in the appointments of Lords of Appeal. In short, life had been discovered in a body that in 1955 had shown considerable evidence of terminal irrelevance.

---

a Jap.'" See also *Race Relations Bd.* v. *Charter*, [1973] A.C. 868, 907, where he analogized from charity cases in an effort to give meaning to "a section of the public."

314. *DPP* v. *Whyte*, [1972] A.C. 849.

315. *R.* v. *Morgan*, [1976] A.C. 182 (1975).

FIFTEEN

The Last Decades

By 1977, the senior law lords were Lord Wilberforce, who had sat since 1964, and Lord Diplock, who had sat since 1968. Both were senior not only in terms of service, but also in typifying two of the leading forces in the House. Many would say that after the retirement of Reid at the end of 1974 Wilberforce and Diplock were the two most important voices in the House, as well as providing the leadership in the Judicial Committee of the Privy Council. Wilberforce and Diplock justify individual treatment both because they had been sitting since the 1960s and because they had both assumed leadership roles. This chapter, however, also considers the Hailsham and Elwyn-Jones appointees—assuming that, despite the legal requirements of the 1876 act, it is the Lord Chancellor rather than the Prime Minister who is de facto the appointing authority so far as Lords of Appeal are concerned.[1]

The Senior Law Lords: Wilberforce

Wilberforce[2] in many senses represented a meeting of various traditions of judicial expertise. A fellow of All Souls, he achieved great success in the rarefied regions of the law known as the Chancery Division,[3] yet

---

1. It should also be noted that Lord Parker, Lord Chief Justice from 1958 to 1971 (and the son of Parker of Waddington) sat in one appeal, concurring in *DPP* v. *Smith*, [1961] A.C. 290 (1960). His successor, Lord Widgery, had by 1976 apparently not sat as a lord. In *Arenson* v. *Arenson*, [1977] A.C. 405 (1975), Lord Wheatley, a Senator of the College of Justice, sat. He had been created a life peer in 1970.

2. Richard Crane Wilberforce; b. 1907; father, Indian judge; educ., Winchester and New College, Oxford (First, "Greats"); called to bar, 1932; Q.C., 1954; Judge, Chancery Division, 1961–64; Lord of Appeal, 1969–.

3. He practiced mainly in revenue law, restrictive practice, and private international law, as well as having an extensive practice before the Privy Council; Richard C. Wilberforce, "Educating the Judges" 254, 260.

he was also an internationalist, having represented the United Kingdom in various international activities.[4] As a judge he felt comfortable discussing Freud[5] and the relationship of law and economics,[6] while insisting that judges were human beings.[7] Becoming a Lord of Appeal after only three years as a judge of first instance (he leapfrogged the Court of Appeal), Wilberforce showed more interest than his predecessors in reforming the procedures of the final appeal court. He argued publicly in favor of Treasury-financed litigation before the Lords,[8] while behind the scenes he ensured that the Lords of Appeal were provided with offices and secretarial help. He was believed to favor such Americanized notions as law clerks and written briefs. Moreover, after Denning, he was the most active law lord in legislative debates.[9]

Unlike some of the law lords, Wilberforce welcomed the establishment of the Law Commission,[10] since his general feeling was that "our law, in many respects, is not up to date at all, it reflects the standards of the Victorian period of the nineteenth century, in such matters as family relations, in many economic matters, in many social matters."[11] He was even a supporter of the "right kind" of codification, which would drive the judges back to principle rather than leave them enmeshed in precedent,[12] but he remained aware that the making of law was a subtle blend

4. These concerns have remained. He has a wide knowledge of Commonwealth practice, e.g., *Broome* v. *Cassell & Co.*, [1972] A.C. 1027, 1113; he was also conversant with American law (e.g., ibid. 1112–15), as well as European law. See, for instance, 297 *Parl. Deb.*, H.L. (5th ser.), col. 1193 (1 Apr. 1965). In the discussion of the Law Commission Bill, he argued, "I should like to have seen stated positively, as an objective of the Bill, the bringing into line of English law with the law of our neighbours"; 264 ibid., col. 1177.

5. Wilberforce, "Educating the Judges" 260.

6. Richard C. Wilberforce, *Law and Economics*.

7. Wilberforce, "Educating the Judges" at 260.

8. See *Broome* v. *Cassell & Co.*, [1972] A.C. 1027, 1113.

9. Participating on an average of 5 times a year; Louis Blom-Cooper and Gavin Drewry, *Final Appeal* 205.

On the other hand, he has been used less for public inquiries than some law lords. His 1972 Report on Miners' Pay was thought by many to have been too generous to the workers. E.g., "Living with Wilberforce," *Economist*, 19 Feb. 1972, at 61; "The People We Think We Are," ibid., 26 Feb. 1972, at 15. See, now, both with respect to Wilberforce's inquiry into miners' pay and his inquiry into the electric supply industry, John A. G. Griffith, *The Politics of the Judiciary* 42–44.

10. "What it seeks to do is really to enter into a new dimension of law reform rather than to expand the existing methods; and that, I believe, is what the present age requires"; 264 *Parl. Deb.*, H.L. (5th ser.), cols. 1172 (1 Apr. 1965). This was his maiden speech in the House.

11. Ibid., cols. 1173–74.

12. "By presenting to the courts legislation drafted in a simple way by definition of principles, we may restore to the judges what they have lost for many years to their great regret; the task of interpreting law according to statements of principle, rather than by painfully hacking their way through the jungles of detailed and intricate legislation. So I believe that a process of codification, intelligently carried out, will revive the spirit of the Common Law rather than militate against it"; ibid., cols. 1175–76.

of judicial and legislative input. He was, for instance, party to *Ainsworth*,[13] where the House refused to put its imprimatur on Denning's "equity" in the matrimonial home in favor of deserted spouses. Yet in the debates on the Matrimonial Homes Bill, in which he supported legislative change, he explained that the bill exemplifed "in a rather striking and interesting way the difference, the dividing line, between cases where the law can be reformed by decisions of the courts, and other cases where intervention by the legislature is concerned."[14]

Such a sentiment in no way implied that Wilberforce was unconcerned or restrictive about the role of the final appeal court in the lawmaking process, but he was an articulate exponent of judicial restraint. In his own judicial work, however, Wilberforce used various creative techniques. Deciding in favor of the Revenue in *Pook* v. *Owen*,[15] he chose to distinguish precedent vigorously, rather than to overrule it entirely. In restating various areas of private and public international law, he developed new doctrines, sometimes by adopting American solutions,[16] sometimes by being prepared to accept existing solutions subject to overriding social policies.[17] Yet he could march more boldly and publicize the lawmaking role when he felt it was appropriate. In *Indyka* v. *Indyka* he helped rewrite the rules for the recognition of foreign decrees.[18] In changing the rules for payment of damages in foreign currencies he declared, "It is entirely within the House's duty . . . to give the law a new direction . . . where, on principle and in reason, it appears right to do so."[19]

13. [1965] A.C. 1175.

14. 275 *Parl. Deb.*, H.L. (5th ser.), col. 28 (14 June 1966). See also: "There was undoubtedly some disappointment felt when your Lordships' House, in a Committee of which I was a member, decided in the *Ainsworth* case that that was not the right road and, as some of us thought, that the right road was that of legislation. When one looks at this Bill and sees the number of matters with which it had to deal in some detail . . . one may well think that that approach was right and that this is a case for intervention by legislative enactment"; ibid., col. 29. See also Blom-Cooper and Drewry, *Final Appeal* 363.

15. [1970] A.C. 244, 261 (1969). For a similar technique, see *Chancery Lane Safe Deposit & Offices Co.* v. *IRC*, [1966] A.C. 85 (1965), especially the conclusion at 136.

16. *Carl-Zeiss Stiftung* v. *Rayner & Keeler, Ltd.* (No. 2), [1967] 1 A.C. 853, 950 (1966), on the issue of the status of a nonrecognized government.

17. *Boys* v. *Chaplin*, [1971] A.C. 356 (1969), accepting the rule of *lex loci delictus* as the basis of the law of conflict in tort, but subject to overriding English social policy. See especially at 391.

18. "If the principles of recognition of foreign decrees of divorce are placed on the more general basis which I have suggested (rather than being governed by the quasi-mathematical application in reverse of domestic legislation) I have no fears that uncertainty will be introduced into the law. The courts are well able to perform the task of examining the reality of the connection between the resident petitioner wife and the jurisdiction invoked, bearing in mind, but not being rigidly bound by, the developments of domestic jurisdiction. In so acting, I am convinced that they are more likely to reach just, and to avoid artificial, results"; [1969] 1 A.C. 33, 106–7 (1967).

19. *Miliangos* v. *George Frank, Ltd.*, [1976] A.C. 443, 469 (1975). With this should

If Wilberforce did not always demonstrate creativity, this absence may be attributed as much to his innate modesty and to his idiosyncratic view of the goals of the law as to any serious reluctance to use the lawmaking power of the Lords in a sophisticated and restrained way. He was, for instance, far more willing to concur in judgments than some members of the Lords, even when he had doubts,[20] and he freely admitted when he had difficulty making up his mind.[21] There was, it is true, a reluctance to question even the context of recent legislation, a caution perhaps best exemplified in *Director of Public Prosecutions* v. *Whyte*, in which Wilberforce joined Pearson and Cross in the majority (Simon of Glaisdale and Salmon dissenting) in interpreting the new definition of obscenity in the Obscene Publications Act in a formalistic way.[22] Yet even here, the approach is partially explained by the areas of interest that appeared to activate Wilberforce; in contract and tort, for instance, where his goals were not the same expansionary ones as those of many of his colleagues.

In contract the concept of fundamental breach was not particularly attractive to him.[23] Yet he knew full well that "English law, having

---

be contrasted his decision on *forum non conveniens* where he refused to bring the English rule in line with the decisions in other common law countries. "It is clear . . . that for some 100 years the law of England has rather a divergent path. . . . The arguments in favour of 'forum non conveniens' . . . are not so overwhelming that we should now make a radical change of direction"; *The Atlantic Star*, [1974] A.C. 436, 464 (1973).

20. E.g., "[A]s the point is one of construction and as the arguments in favour of the limitation . . . have been clearly and forcefully put . . . I see no purpose in diluting them by observations of my own. I must however rank myself as *dubitans*"; *IRC* v. *Carran Co.*, [1967] Sess. Cas. 47, 61 (1966, H.L.). See also *Westwood* v. *Post Office*, [1974] A.C. 1, 9 (1973): "I defer to this unanimity of view though I have to say that, unaided, I should have difficulty in reaching the same conclusion"; *R.* v. *Boardman*, [1975] A.C. 421, 445 (1974): "[T]he present case is, to my mind, right on the border line. . . . These matters lie largely within the field of the judge's discretion, and the jury's task."

21. "My opinion . . . I have only reached with hesitation, and . . . I fear is largely one of impression"; *Argyle Motors, Ltd.* v. *Birkenhead Corp.*, [1975] A.C. 99, 132 (1973). See also *Maunsell* v. *Olins*, [1975] A.C. 373, 389–90 (1974).

22. "The Act . . . has replaced the common law definition or conception, of obscenity by one of its own. . . . Both the policy and the language of the Act have been plentifully criticised; the former we cannot question, and with the latter we must do our best"; *DPP* v. *Whyte*, [1972] A.C. 849, 859. But see also: "I have serious doubts whether the Act will continue to be workable in this way, or whether it will produce tolerable results. The present is, or in any rational system ought to be, a simple case, yet the illogical and unscientific character of the Act has forced the justices into untenable positions"; ibid. at 862.

See also *Sweet* v. *Parsley*, [1970] A.C. 132, 161 (1969): "On this admittedly prosaic interpretation of the subsection, I do not embark upon a wider examination of the problem of absolute offences, or of guilty intention." For another somewhat unsatisfactory case of statutory interpretation when Wilberforce presided, see *Heatons Transp., Ltd.* v. *T&GWU*, [1973] A.C. 15 (1972).

23. E.g., "An act which, apart from the exceptions clause, might be breach sufficiently serious to justify refusal of further performance, may be reduced in effect, or made not a

committed itself to a rather technical and schematic doctrine of contract, in application takes a practical approach, often at the cost of forcing the facts to fit uneasily into the marked slots of offer, acceptance and consideration."[24] More significant, however, in terms of goals, was his view of the role of tort. While he by no means saw it in static terms,[25] Wilberforce was unconvinced that compensation was its only purpose.[26] Hence, in rejecting the suggestion that automobile liability might be founded on the "family car,"[27] Wilberforce, while accepting the inevitable element of judicial creativity in the Lords' work,[28] argued that "liability and insurance are so intermixed that judicially to alter the basis of liability without adequate knowledge (which we have not the means to obtain) as to the impact this might make on the insurance system would be dangerous, and, in my opinion, irresponsible."[29] In this context, it is not surprising that Wilberforce, in his early years, voted with Reid in an effort to find some middle ground in Factories Act cases,[30] but by the 1970s he sensed that perhaps some aspects of the legislation had been pushed too far by the judiciary.[31]

---

breach at all, by the terms of the clause"; *Suisse Atlantique Société d'Armament Maritime S.A. v. N.V. Rotterdamsche Kolen Centrale*, [1967] 1 A.C. 361, 431 (1966). In keeping with his view of the binding nature of contract, see his dissent in *Sefton v. Tophams, Ltd.*, [1967] 1 A.C. 50, 83–84 (1966). Cf., on implied terms, *Liverpool City Council v. Irwin*, [1977] A.C. 239 (1976).

24. *New Zealand Shipping Co. v. A. M. Satterthwaite & Co.*, [1975] A.C. 154, 167 (P.C. 1974), where Wilberforce, presiding in the Judicial Committee, revived the idea of the unilateral contract in order to permit vicarious immunity—i.e., allowing a third party to rely on exemption clauses inserted by others.

25. See, for example, *Herrington v. British Rys. Bd.*, [1972] A.C. 877, especially at 912: "It is often the fate of clear pronouncements—in law as in science—to be treated in this way, with consequences more and more strained as different cases are forced within them by the use of fictions and other devices until there is a busting at the seams and a cry that this case as a statement of the law must be overruled."

26. E.g., "It cannot lightly be taken for granted, even as a matter of theory, that the purpose of the law of tort is compensation, still less that it ought to be"; dissenting in *Broome v. Cassell & Co.*, [1972] A.C. 1027, 1114.

27. *Launchbury v. Morgans*, [1973] A.C. 127, 133 (1972). It is difficult to reconcile Wilberforce's concept of implied authority in this case with his use of it in *Heatons Transp., Ltd. v. T&GWU*, [1973] A.C. 15 (1972).

28. "I think, too, though counsel for the appellant argued eloquently to the contrary, that some adaptation of the common law rules to meet these new problems of degree is capable of being made by the judges"; *Launchbury v. Morgans*, [1973] A.C. 127, 136 (1972).

29. Ibid. 137. He also rejected the use of prospective overruling. "Any new direction, and it may be one of many alternatives, must be set by Parliament." See also *Argyle Motors, Ltd. v. Birkenhead Corp.*, [1975] A.C. 99, 130 (1973): "[A] generous policy of compensation . . . involves too great a shift in financial burden . . . to be suitable for introduction by judicial decision."

30. E.g., dissenting with Reid in *Nimmo v. Alexander Cowan & Sons*, [1968] A.C. 107 (Scot. 1967). But see also *John G. Stein & Co. v. O'Hanlon*, [1965] A.C. 890, 911 (Scot.); *Christopher Hill, Ltd. v. Ashington Piggeries, Ltd.*, [1972] A.C. 441, 494 (1971).

31. E.g., *Westwood v. Post Office*, [1974] A.C. 1, 9 (1973).

In general, Wilberforce was far more comfortable than most law lords in handling statutes.[32] This ease was particularly significant in his handling of tax cases. Sympathetic to the complexity of the legislation,[33] he took the view that the courts had done well in dealing with "the mounting pile of precedents."[34] As part of his overall approach, he insisted that tax avoidance provisions be given the wide meaning that Parliament intended. Thus early in his career he refused to limit section 28 of the Finance Act of 1960, to the area of dividend stripping,[35] while in *Inland Revenue Commissioners* v. *Joiner* in 1975 he gave the concept of "tax advantage" under section 460(b) of the 1970 Finance Act a wide ambit.[36] So, too, although interfering with contract by developing such concepts as fundamental breach was not particularly attractive to him,[37]

---

32. His approach has included both a reluctance to become involved with "a radical interference with statutory words," *John G. Stein & Co.* v. *O'Hanlon*, [1965] A.C. 890, 911 (Scot.), and, at the same time, a willingness to look at "the whole structure of the Act," *Minister of Social Security* v. *Amalgamated Eng'r Union (AEU)*, [1967] 1 A.C. 725, 753 (1966). While comfortable with a wide judicial supervision over the *vires* of subordinate bodies, e.g., *Hartnell* v. *Minister of Housing & Local Gov't*, [1965] A.C. 1134, 1172–73 (1964), he insisted on limits on the power of judicial construction:

To accept this seems to me to go far beyond such a logical extension of the Crown's rights as a liberal process of judicial interpretation may properly accept: it gives to those rights another dimension altogether which it is the province of the legislature to define on a fresh consideration of the respective interests of the public and inventor. I suggest that a more limited interpretation of the subsection is open to your Lordships and that a dividing line can be drawn which avoids these consequences. [*Pfizer Corp.* v. *Ministry of Health*, [1965] A.C. 512, 568.

33. "Of course the laws are very complicated, but so long as we have complicated taxes and a complicated economy, it is useless to suppose one would ever get really simple tax legislation"; 264 *Parl. Deb.*, H.L. (5th ser.), col. 1173 (1 Apr. 1965).

34. *Strick* v. *Regent Oil Co.*, [1966] A.C. 295, 347 (1964). See also Wilberforce, *Law and Economics* 15: "[W]ith very little help from the legislature—whose main effort has often been directed merely to stopping up holes—the courts have had to deal with these developing complexities [of commercial, financial, and private life] as best they can. And they have had to do so, as always, from case to case, with no control over the order in which new situations have to be considered, with very little means of sensing the direction in which the next development is likely to occur." For early cases, where Wilberforce refused to read precedent narrowly in the tax field, see also *Chancery Lane Safe Deposit & Offices Co.* v. *IRC*, [1966] A.C. 85, 136 (1965).

35. *IRC* v. *Parker*, [1966] A.C. 141, 176–77 (Scot. 1965).

36. [1975] 1 W.L.R. 1701 (H.L.). See also his dissent in *Europa Oil (N.Z.), Ltd.* v. *IRC*, [1976] 1 W.L.R. 464.

He managed however to maintain a "balanced" view. See, for instance, his partial dissent in *Taylor* v. *Provan*, [1975] A.C. 194, 213 (1974), and his call for clarification in *IRC* v. *Bates*, [1968] A.C. 483, 521 (1966).

37. "The principle that the contractual intention is to be ascertained—not just grammatically from words used, but by consideration of those words in relation to commercial purpose (or other purpose according to the type of contract)—is surely flexible enough, and, though it may be the case that adhesion contracts give rise to particular difficulties in ascertaining or attributing a contractual intent, which may require a special solution, those difficulties need not be imported into the general law of contract nor be permitted to deform it"; *Suisse Atlantique Société d'Armament Maritime S.A.* v. *N.V. Rotterdamsche Kolen Centrale*, [1967] 1 A.C. 361, 434 (1966).

Wilberforce was concerned with maintaining a competitive economy[38] and ensuring that the law of contract was stated in terms of principles rather than rules.[39]

In public law, also, Wilberforce added strength to the development of procedural due process.[40] Yet he was prepared to go along with narrow decisions in the Race Relations Act,[41] and he felt no overwhelming issue of civil liberties in most deportation cases.[42] The arguments in *Pickin* left him entirely cold. "How can we know how Parliament understood the recital. . . . [B]y no process short of summoning . . . persons

38. "We lawyers need to reorientate our thinking in this whole field in the interest of the survival of capitalism, as a system combining modernity and obvious justice—through recognition of the completely changed nature of the function of the limited companies"; Wilberforce, *Law and Economics* 13. See especially his views on restraint of trade, and particularly his speech in *Esso Petroleum Co.* v. *Harper's Garage, Ltd.*, [1968] A.C. 269, 330 (1966).

39. He was less than fully enthusiastic about the Misrepresentation Bill, regarding it as premature in view of the Law Commission's then current plans for codification of contract. "What it does is to attempt the rather ambitious task of putting into statutory language matters which normally are dealt with by judicial development of the Law"; 274 *Parl. Deb.*, H.L. (5th ser.), cols. 946–55 (17 May 1966). See also *Gallie* v. *Lee*, [1971] A.C. 1004, 1027 (1970).

For a similar view of the law of charities as "a moving subject," see *Scottish Burial Reform & Cremation Soc'y, Ltd.* v. *Glasgow Corp.*, [1968] A.C. 138, 154 (Scot. 1967).

40. E.g., *Anisminic, Ltd.* v. *Foreign Compensation Comm'n*, [1969] 2 A.C. 147, 207 (1968):

Although, in theory perhaps, it may be possible for Parliament to set up a tribunal which has full and autonomous powers to fix its own area of operation, that has, so far, not been done in this country. The question, what is the tribunal's proper area, is one which it has always been permissible to ask and to answer, and it must follow that examination of its extent is not precluded by a clause conferring conclusiveness, finality or unquestionability upon its decisions. These clauses in their nature can only relate to decisions given within the field of operation entrusted to the tribunal. They may, according to the width and emphasis of their formulation, help to ascertain the extent of that field, to narrow it or to enlarge it, but unless one is to deny the statutory origin of the tribunal and its powers, they cannot preclude examination of that extent.

Wilberforce was also more willing than his colleagues to grant a temporary injunction against the Crown, feeling that such was in keeping with the Crown Proceeding Act of 1947. Dissenting in *F. Hoffman-LaRoche & Co. A.G.* v. *Secretary of State for Trade & Indus.*, [1975] A.C. 295 (1973).

41. Indeed, Wilberforce was a dissenter in the one case where the Lords upheld a finding of unlawful discrimination; *Race Relations Bd.* v. *Applin*, [1975] A.C. 259, 276 (1974).

42. E.g., his decision while presiding in *R.* v. *Governor of Pentonville Prison, ex parte Sotiriadis*, [1975] A.C. 1 (1974). But cf. the approach in *R.* v. *Governor of Pentonville Prison, ex parte Cheng*, [1973] A.C. 931; *R.* v. *Governor of Pentonville Prison, ex parte Azam*, [1974] A.C. 18, 63 (1973): "[I] would not wish to decide this point on a dry interpretation of the words alone. It is necessary to try to understand the Parliamentary intention." See also at 59: "To these bare facts I would add that there lie behind each case human stories of hardship and struggle of which the learned judges who have heard these applications have been fully aware. They are not directly relevant to these appeals. . . . But it is right . . . to bear in mind that the legal provisions . . . operate in their nature upon the way of life and basic rights of individuals and their families." See also *Suthendran* v. *Immigration Appeal Tribunal*, [1977] A.C. 359 (1976).

and examining their records can we find out. . . . To do so involves . . . a potential clash with Parliament and . . . a series of steps which can lead to no result."[43] In this, as in so many other regards, Wilberforce appears as successor to Radcliffe. A first-rate analytical mind, Wilberforce adapted the more secretive view of judicial restraint, which Radcliffe harbored in the Simonds era of the fifties, to the more open system that characterized the Reid court in the seventies. While Wilberforce undoubtedly believed that it was "within the House's duty . . . to give the law a new direction," the "principle" and "reason" that were to activate that process for him belonged to the Radcliffe tradition of judicial restraint.

The Senior Law Lords: Diplock

Lord Diplock,[44] appointed a Lord of Appeal when Gardiner was Lord Chancellor, belonged to a somewhat similar tradition, sharing both the intellectual ability, and some of the Radcliffe values that characterized Wilberforce. Diplock, however, showed less of the modesty and caution that Wilberforce exhibited, was more of a judicial activist and more outspoken about it, as well as holding different views about the goals that the law should pursue. Perhaps some of these traits were attributable to the different types of practice followed by Wilberforce and Diplock. Diplock was a particularly successful common lawyer who, in his final years at the bar, in addition to a successful commerical practice, was involved in a series of major constitutional cases in Pakistan[45] and represented the Kabaka of Buganda in his dealings with the Governor of Uganda, Sir Andrew Cohen, and the Colonial Office.[46]

As a judge in the lower courts, Diplock was regarded as analytically outstanding, iconoclastic, and outspoken. His view of the common law was not kept hidden; he claimed that its beauty was that "it is a maze not a motorway."[47] As President of the Restrictive Practices Court, he challenged economic learning on "transaction costs," holding that "the costs of doing business" might outweigh the advantage of competition that was embodied as a presumption in the balancing test that that court was required to operate under the 1956 act.[48] As a junior Lord Justice,

---

43. *British Rys. Bd. v. Pickin*, [1974] A.C. 765, 796.
44. William John Kenneth Diplock; b. 1907; father, solicitor; educ., Whitgift, University College, Oxford (Second, Chemistry); called to bar, 1932; K.C., 1948; Judge, Queen's Bench Division, 1956–61; Lord Justice, 1961–68; Lord of Appeal, 1968–.
For an example of his extrajudicial public service during his period as a Lord of Appeal, see *Report of the Commission to Consider Legal Procedures to Deal with Terrorist Activities in Northern Ireland*, Cmnd. 5185 (1972).
45. E.g., W. Ivor Jennings, *Constitutional Problems in Pakistan* 253–55.
46. E.g., Mutesa II, King of Buganda, *Desecration of My Kingdom* 135–36.
47. *Morris v. C. W. Martin & Sons*, [1966] 1 Q.B. 716, 730 (C.A. 1965).
48. *In re Cement Makers' Federation Agreement*, L.R. 2 R.P. 241 (1961); discussed in

he exercised his judicial humor at the expense of his more senior col-leagues.[49] Whether flippant or acerbic, this tendency continued on[50] and off the bench; and he showed no reluctance to speak out, even on con-troversial issues. Thus although Chairman of both the Council of Legal Education and the Institute of Advanced Legal Studies, Diplock argued against potential lawyers' studying law in the universities.[51] Legislatively, he led the law lords in their attempt to retain existing law whereby damages, awarded to widows for the deaths of their husbands, were assessed by judges partly on the ground of what they thought, having seen the widow, were her chances of remarriage. For his pains, Diplock was accused by Lady Summerskill of exercising coldly calculated logic devoid of humanity.[52]

It was no doubt consonant with his style that Diplock should have entitled his Holdsworth lecture *The Courts as Legislators*.[53] Diplock did not share Radcliffe's view about the importance of the covert nature of judicial legislation.[54] Rather, he announced that "no lawyer really supposes that such decisions as *Rylands v. Fletcher* in the last century and *Donoghue v. Stevenson* in this did not change the law just as much as the Law Reform (Contributory Negligence) Act."[55] He also argued, however, that "implicitly" every judgment delivered "not under a palm tree but in a court bound by the rules of precedent speaks to the future and speaks generally."[56] He was aware that the "courage and imagination" of an earlier period had passed.[57] "Yet if Law Reform

---

Robert Stevens and Basil Yamey, *The Restrictive Practices Court* 206–22. See also Kenneth Diplock, *The Role of the Judicial Process in the Regulation of Competition*.

49. In *Hughes* v. *Hughes*, Bar Library Transcript 117a/1966 (C.A.), he sat with Den-ning, M.R., and Harman, L.J., both of whom gave judgments allowing the appeal. Diplock merely said, "For the reasons given by my brother Harman I would dismiss the appeal." See Blom-Cooper and Drewry, *Final Appeal* 87.

50. E.g., *Ferguson* v. *IRC*, [1970] A.C. 442, 464 (Scot. 1969): "[T]he question is not untrammelled by authority—and very remarkable trammels they are." See also his return from time to time to the Shylock-Antonio analogy, e.g., in *Attorney-General* v. *Times Newspapers, Ltd.*, [1974] A.C. 273, 313 (1973).

51. Kenneth Diplock, "Introduction to a Discussion of the Wilson Report" 193.

52. For the debate, see 318 *Parl. Deb.*, H.L. (5th ser.), cols. 521 ff. (6 May 1971), and cols. 1527 ff. (14 May 1971) and see Blom-Cooper and Drewry, *Final Appeal* 213–25.

53. Diplock, *The Courts as Legislators* (Birmingham, 1965).

54. "My purpose this afternoon is to examine the judicial process first to show that courts by the very nature of their functions are compelled to act as legislators and secondly to make some suggestions as to how they should approach that task"; ibid. 2.

55. Ibid.

56. Ibid. 3.

57. "Where do you find the sources of the common law today? In the bold imaginative judgments delivered by a great generation of judges between the sixties and the nineties of the last century. . . . Yet somehow at the turn of the century the courts seemed to have lost their courage . . . what in the nineteenth century was done by judges to adapt the common law and equity to the needs of contemporary society has in the last thirty years had to be

Acts . . . reflect past failures of the courts to fulfill their proper functions they have given us today a fresh chance."[58] He admitted that there were justifiable complaints about judge-made law—that it was in arrears, complex, and reactionary, but in different ways Diplock saw all these problems as surmountable.[59]

The Diplock claims were, of course, not unlimited:

[I]n a highly complex swiftly changing society most changes are organizational and involve the creation of new or the adaption of existing administrative organs to carry them out. This Parliament alone can do. . . . The Courts could never have created the Welfare State. In any event it is not the business of judges in a democracy to decide how society shall be organized; whether, for instance, steel shall be nationalized or not. But organizational changes do not destroy human relationships, they only alter the framework in which the individual, whether within the organization or outside, performs his duty to his neighbour. It is the regulation of those human relationships within the new framework that I suggest is the proper field of judge-made law.[60]

Diplock thus saw parliamentary and judicial lawmaking as complementary. Statutory interpretation, even in the dreariest tax case,[61] was not a purely mechanical function. Parliament should draft more broadly,[62] and the courts should seek to implement parliamentary purpose from the principles laid down, eschewing the narrow semantic approach. To boast, as Macmillan had in *Inland Revenue Commissioners* v. *Ayrshire Employers Mutual Insurance Company*,[63] that "the legislature has plainly

---

done by the Law Reform Committee, upon whose reports nearly a score of Law Reform Acts have been passed to alter judge-made rules of common law and equity. Each of these acts announces the twentieth-century failure of the judges to show courage and imagination"; ibid. 20–21.

58. Ibid. 21.

59. Ibid. 16 ff. Of the Law Commission, he wrote, "There is a new interest in law reform. New machinery is being created to hasten it. This is all to the good. But I believe there still remains a wide field of law reform in which the old machinery of the judicial process still has a valuable if unspectacular part to play"; ibid. 23.

60. Ibid. 15.

61. On the one hand he admitted, "It no more lies within the field of morals than does a crossword puzzle. I would rather do a crossword puzzle than try a revenue appeal. It calls for much the same mental agility and the solution is more rewarding." That did not, however, mean that the courts' responsibility was at an end:

Whenever the court decides that kind of dispute it legislates about taxation. It makes a law taxing all gains of the same kind or all documents of the same kind. Do not let us deceive ourselves with the legal fiction that the court is only ascertaining and giving effect to what Parliament meant. Anyone who has decided tax appeals knows that most of them concern transactions which members of Parliament and the draftsman of the Act had not anticipated, about which they had never thought at all. Some of the transactions are of a kind which had never taken place before the Act was passed. They were devised as a result of it. The court may describe what it is doing in tax appeals as interpretation. So did the priestess of the Delphic oracle. But whoever has final authority to explain what Parliament meant by the words that it used makes law as if the explanation it has given were contained in a new Act of Parliament. It will need a new Act of Parliament to reverse it. [Ibid. 5–6]

62. Ibid. 16.

63. [1946] 1 All E.R. 637 (H.L., Scot. 1945).

missed-fire" was "judicial legislation at its worst," which came "at the
high-water mark of the narrow semantic approach." If these modern
judges "can identify the target of parliamentary legislation their proper
function is to see that it is hit: not merely to record it has been missed."[64]

Few judges have come to the Lords with such a publicly stated view
of the judicial process, and considerable evidence indicated that Diplock,
after his appointment as Lord of Appeal in 1968, attempted to give effect
to his articulated view. Thus, where it seemed appropriate, he did not
hesitate to discuss the policy implication of extending a principle of law.
In *Dorset Yacht Company v. Home Office* he said:

This is the first time that this specific question has been posed at a higher judicial
level than that of a county court. Your Lordships in answering it will be performing a judicial function similar to that performed in *Donoghue v. Stevenson*
and more recently in *Hedley Byrne & Co. Ltd. v. Heller and Partners, Ltd.* . . .

This function, which judges hesitate to acknowledge as law-making, plays at
most a minor role in the decision of the great majority of cases. . . .

It will be apparent that I agree with the Master of the Rolls that what we are
concerned with in this appeal "is . . . at bottom a matter of public policy which
we, as judges, must resolve."[65]

At the same time, Diplock bore in mind his own injunctions about institutional competence. Thus where extensive investigation was needed before the law could be changed, he argued in favor of a parliamentary
solution.[66]

This bifurcated approach naturally raises curiosity about Diplock's
attitude to the 1966 Practice Statement. While dissenting in *Broome* v.
Cassell on the exemplary damages point, Diplock did not urge the overruling of *Rookes v. Barnard*.[67] Also, in an Australian appeal he made it
clear that "the fact that the court considers its previous decision to have
been plainly wrong is a prerequisite to discarding it," but is "by no means
a decisive reason for doing so."[68] Yet at a certain point his caution
evaporated. The point was clearly passed in *Herrington*. "[A]ll nine
judges who have been concerned with the instant case . . . are convinced
that the plaintiff's claim ought to succeed; and, if I may be permitted to
be candid, are determined that it shall. The problem of judicial technique

64. Diplock, *Courts as Legislators* 10.
65. [1970] A.C. 1004, 1058.
66. E.g., *in re Vandervell Trustees*, [1971] A.C. 912, 944.
67. [1972] A.C. 1027.
68. *Geelong Harbour Trust Comm'rs v. Gibbs Bright & Co.*, [1974] A.C. 810, 818
(P.C.); he continued: "The law laid down by a judicial decision, even though erroneous,
may work in practice to the satisfaction to those who are affected by it, particularly where
it concerns the allocation of the burden of unavoidable risks between parties engaged in
trade and commerce and their insurers. If it has given general satisfaction and caused no
difficulties in practice, this is an important factor to be weighed against the more theoretical
interests of legal science in determining whether the law so laid down ought now to be
changed by judicial decision."

is how best to surmount or to circumvent the obstacle presented by . . . *Addie's* case."[69] In *Knuller*, Diplock went even further, dissenting alone and vigorously in favor of overruling *Shaw*.[70] In some ways these were easier cases for Diplock, for he believed both *Shaw*[71] and *Addie*[72] to have been wrong in doctrinal terms at the time they had been decided.

When the courts pushed forward the law, either by expanding the scope of a doctrine or by overruling an earlier decision, Diplock's own values were involved and he did not refuse, when he felt it appropriate, to discuss what he believed to be morally right. In *R. v. Hyam* he said, "[I]f a decision of this House is founded upon a proposition of law which is erroneous in a respect which makes it bear too harshly upon a defendant . . . I have no doubt that your Lordships are entitled to correct that proposition . . . to leave the error uncorrected would offend concepts of what is right";[73] and this element of morality appeared elsewhere in his decisions.[74] He developed a balancing test to see where the public interest lay in contempt of court in *Attorney-General v. Times Newspapers, Limited*;[75] and, again in the area of public law, he did not hide his belief that the bold and courageous judge would move toward a procedural code based on certiorari.[76] With that in mind, it is possible to understand more easily Diplock's vigorous dissent in the Irish Republican Clubs

---

69. *Herrington v. British Rys. Bd.*, [1972] A.C. 877, 931. See also at 936:

A formula which is both exclusive and expansive seems to me, as a matter of linguistics, to be a contradiction in terms. For my part I would not follow the alternative route thus hinted at by which an amelioration of the law in favour of meritorious trespassers might be attained. I think it preferable to seek to identify the underlying principles which had been tacitly accepted in *Addie's* case as justifying exclusion from the category of intruders to whom the *Addie* test applies, those persons to whom judges have hitherto managed to ascribe the status of licensee without acknowledging the fictitious character of their imputed "licence" from the occupier.

70. [1973] A.C. 435 (1972).

71. "The consideration that the defendants in the instant case may have been undeservedly lucky if Shaw's case is overruled ought not . . . to deter this House from correcting an unfortunate mistake as to the common law"; ibid. 481. See also at 469: "To bow to the decision yet to deny the legal reasoning upon which it was based is to draw the kind of distinction which reflects discredit on the English legal system. To deliver the Law Lords from the temptation to do this was one of the objects of the change of policy announced in July 1966."

72. Of the *Addie* case, he said, "Even at that time it offended against what Lord Atkin . . . was to call 'a general public sentiment of moral wrongdoing for which the offender must pay.' . . . I well recall the disappointment with which it was received by those who thought that previous cases in this House had shown in the common law as moving towards a less draconian treatment of those who trespassed innocently"; [1972] A.C. 877, 931.

73. [1975] A.C. 55, 94 (1974).

74. *R. v. Treacy*, [1971] A.C. 537, 565 (1970); *Broome v. Cassell & Co.*, [1972] A.C. 1027, 1129; *Stafford v. DPP*, [1974] A.C. 878, 906 (1973).

75. [1974] A.C. 273, 308 (1973).

76. Kenneth Diplock, "Judicial Control of the Administrative Process" 1.

case, where he applied in effect a "void for vagueness" doctrine to the Northern Ireland minister's use of delegated power.[77]

Diplock in general kept to his ambition to apply his "principled" approach to both the common law and statutory issues. In interpreting legislation, not only did he look to the scheme of the act,[78] but he sought to use the meaning of the man in the street[79] and common sense.[80] It was inevitable, too, that he should question the canons of construction. In *Pettitt* v. *Pettitt*, in reviewing the share in the matrimonial home under the Married Women's Property Act of 1882, Diplock argued, "It would, in my view, be an abuse of the legal technique for ascertaining or imputing intention to apply to transactions between the post-war generation of married couples 'presumptions' which are based upon inferences of fact which an earlier generation of judges drew as to the most likely intentions of earlier generations of spouses belonging to the propertied classes of a different social era."[81] Moreover, his interpretation of the Road Traffic Act in *Director of Public Prosecutions* v. *Carey* emphasized that, rather than having a curiosity about whether Parliament misfired, he was anxious to see that legislative targets were hit. As Blom-Cooper and Drewry had put it, "[B]y giving flexibility to the statutory provisions relating to the administration of the breath test, [he] restored public confidence in the law and made amending legislation unnecessary."[82]

Like all judges, Diplock was erratic. He tried to make judge-made law less complex, as far as possible, by agreeing with his fellow law lords rather than delivering a separate concurring opinion.[83] Indeed, both he

77. *McEldowney* v. *Forde*, [1971] A.C. 632 (N. Ire. 1969). See at 665: "A regulation whose meaning is so vague that it cannot be ascertained with reasonable certainty cannot fall within the words of delegation."

For another Northern Irish decision where Diplock (with Reid) appeared to inject a civil libertarian purpose, see *Kennedy* v. *Spratt*, [1972] A.C. 83 (N. Ire. 1971).

78. E.g., *DPP* v. *Carey*, [1970] A.C. 1072, 1091 (1969); this was, however, not to be confused with the "mischief rule" approach; *DPP* v. *Bhagwan*, [1972] A.C. 60 (1970).

79. E.g., *Heaton* v. *Bell*, [1970] A.C. 728, 762 (1969); *R.* v. *Treacy*, [1971] A.C. 537, 565 (1970): "The Theft Act 1968 makes a welcome departure from the former style of drafting in criminal statutes. It is expressed in simple language as used and understood by ordinary literate men and women. It avoids so far as possible those terms of art which have acquired a special meaning understood only by lawyers."

For concern with straightforward language, see also *R.* v. *Hester*, [1973] A.C. 296, 327–28 (1972): "[T]o incorporate in the summing up a general disquisition upon the law of corroboration in the sort of language used by lawyers may make the summing up immune to appeal upon a point of law, but it is calculated to confuse a jury of laymen and, if it does not pass so far over their heads that when they reach the jury room they simply rely upon their native common sense, may, I believe . . . have the contrary effect to a sensible warning couched in ordinary language directed to the facts of the particular case."

80. *Ferguson* v. *IRC*, [1970] A.C. 442 (Scot. 1969).

81. [1970] A.C. 777, 824 (1969).

82. "Lord Diplock's analysis of statutory construction was, in addition, a masterly judicial exposition"; Blom-Cooper and Drewry, *Final Appeal* 391.

83. In his first 64 appearances, he gave sole judgments 6 times, assenting judgments 27

and Wilberforce appeared to favor an Opinion of the Court along the lines of the Supreme Court of the United States, rather than the traditional free-for-all of House of Lords speeches. Yet he also sometimes gave the impression of inserting an unnecessary historical discussion.[84] At times, too, Diplock appeared to lapse into a formalistic "discovering" of the law by applying the literal (or ordinary meaning) rules of interpretation,[85] and, despite his pronouncements, he still seemed to see much of the crossword puzzle in tax cases—even those interpreting anti-avoidance devices.[86]

Perhaps the greatest conflicts in Diplock's judicial career, however, came in the area of civil liberties. In some areas Diplock was firm and courageous. Not only did he argue in favor of overruling *Shaw* in *Knuller*, but in *Withers* he delivered another assault on the whole notion of "conspiracy to effect a public mischief."[87] Yet Diplock was less concerned than many of the law lords about the recommendations of the *Eleventh Report of the Criminal Law Revision Committee*.[88] On contempt of court he seemed ambivalent, and on race relations neither his interest in

---

times, dissents on 6 occasions, and formal concurrences on 25 occasions. Even Professor Gower complimented him for his restraint; L. C. B. Gower, "Reflections on Law Reform" 257, 259.

In a reverse trend, toward the end of his career, Reid appeared willing to concur in Diplock's leading judgments; e.g., *Haigh* v. *Charles W. Ireland, Ltd.*, [1974] 1 W.L.R. 43 (H.L., Scot. 1973).

84. E.g., After a discussion of spending power, inflation and interest rates, he concluded, "[T]he only practicable course . . . is to leave out of account the risk of further inflation . . . and the high interest rates. . . . In estimating the amount of the annual dependency in the future . . . money should be treated as retaining its value at the date of the judgement, and in calculating the present value of annual payments which would have been received in future years, interest rates appropriate to times of stable currency . . . should be adopted"; *Mallett* v. *McMonagle*, [1970] A.C. 166, 176 (N. Ire. 1969). See also the discussion of the history of evidence in *R.* v. *Hester*, [1973] A.C. 296, 326 (1972).

85. E.g., *Gallaher, Ltd.* v. *Commissioners of Customs & Excise*, [1971] A.C. 43, 69 (1970).

86. Cf., for instance, his rather formal judgment with the broad Wilberforce approach in *IRC* v. *Joiner*, [1975] W.L.R. 1701 (H.L.). But cf. *Seramco, Ltd. Superannuation Fund Trustees* v. *Income Tax Commissioner*, [1977] A.C. 287 (P.C., 1976).

87. "It would be disingenuous to try to conceal my personal conviction that this branch of the criminal law of England is irrational in treating as a criminal offence an agreement to do that which, if done, is not a crime; and that its irrationality becomes injustice if it takes days of legal argument and historical research on appeal to your Lordships' House to discover whether any crime has been committed even though the facts are undisputed. I welcome the fact that this reproach to our criminal jurisprudence is enjoying the urgent attention of the Law Commission"; *R.* v. *Withers*, [1975] A.C. 842, 862 (1974). See also his reasons on the right to silence; *Hall* v. *The Queen*, [1971] 1 W.L.R. 298, 301 (P.C.).

88. "I commend the greater part of this Bill, with a number of reservations, on the grounds that it brings some rationality, some common sense, into a part of the law in which, however proud we may be of it, we must recognise that a great deal is today quite irrational nonsense"; 338 *Parl. Deb.*, H.L. (5th ser.), cols. 1649–50 (15 Feb. 1973).

hitting the parliamentary target nor his concern with civil liberties was activated. Indeed, in contrast with the concern expressed by Kilbrandon and Simon of Glaisdale, he assumed that the Race Relations Act only undermined the civil liberties of the majority:

This is a statute which, however admirable its motives, restricts the liberty which the citizen has previously enjoyed at common law to differentiate between one person and another in entering or declining to enter into transactions with them. . . .

The arrival in this country within recent years of many immigrants from disparate and distant lands has brought a new dimension to the problem of the legal right to discriminate against the stranger. If everyone were rational and humane—or, for that matter, Christian—no legal sanction would be needed to prevent one man being treated by his fellow man less favourably than another *simply upon the ground of his colour, race or ethnic or national origins.* But in the field of domestic or social intercourse differentiation in treatment of individuals is unavoidable. No one has room to invite everyone to dinner. The law cannot dictate the choice of one's friends. . . .

Thus, in discouraging the intrusion of coercion by legal process in the fields of domestic or social intercourse, the principle of effectiveness joins force with the broader principle of freedom to order one's private life as one chooses.[89]

The idea that the judiciary might protect the civil rights of a minority was not attractive. Every judge, in his own way, is a product of his age. This was especially true of Wilberforce and Diplock. Promoted to the Lords by a Labour Lord Chancellor, they nevertheless clearly represented the broader and bolder view of the judicial process and the function of the courts first propounded by Kilmuir.

The Hailsham and Elwyn-Jones Appointees

As Lord Chancellor from 1970 to 1974, Hailsham made four appointments as Lords of Appeal: Simon of Glaisdale, Kilbrandon, Cross, and Salmon. Of these, all but Cross were still sitting in 1976 (although Kilbrandon retired that year and Simon in 1977). Simon, Kilbrandon, and Salmon, together with their seniors, Reid, Wilberforce, and Diplock provided the powerhouse of a renewed House of Lords during the 1970s. Perhaps never before had there been such a sizable group of distinguished Lords of Appeal available at one time.

By 1977 Elwyn-Jones had made five appointments during his Chancellorship: Edmund-Davies, Fraser of Tullybelton, Russell, and to replace Kilbrandon and Simon, Keith of Kinkel and Scarman. These five could represent a more "conservative" series of appointments that might have the effect of dampening the flexible approach of the Hailsham appoin-

89. *Dockers' Labour Club & Institute, Ltd. v. Race Relations Bd.*, [1976] A.C. 285, 295–96 (1974).

tees. Such an event was unlikely to happen while Wilberforce and Diplock continued the more flexible traditions of Reid and, at least in 1977, it was too early to make any predictions about the later appointments.

Lord Simon of Glaisdale[90] served extensively in all three branches of government before becoming a Lord of Appeal. He was a junior cabinet member in both the Home Office and Treasury before becoming Solicitor-General in the Macmillan administration. Then after presiding in the Probate, Divorce, and Admiralty Division for nearly a decade,[91] he was appointed a Lord of Appeal in 1971. Almost at once he became influential in the council of the law lords. With broad interests,[92] he developed what might well be described as a new style in the Lords. In decisions that he considered important he expounded at length (and numerically) on what judicial strategy he believed the court should follow.[93] While his was not a strongly activist approach, his analysis of the limited areas within which he believed the Lords, in its judicial capacity, should operate, made a significant contribution to the understanding of the scope of judicial legislation and ensured Simon's lasting importance as an appeal judge.

Ironically, however, while he may be best known for his pronouncements on judicial strategy, his greatest facility may well be in the manipulation of conventional judicial weapons. Whether handling case law or statute, Simon conveyed the impression of attempting to relate the concept of law to the reality of the situation. "I am far from holding that a judicial decision should be arrived at solely by an abstract judicial dialectic, without regard to those reasons of the heart of which the reason has

90. Jocelyn Edward Salis Simon; b. 1911; educ., Gresham's School, Holt, Trinity Hall, Cambridge; called to bar, 1934; Q.C., 1951; M.P. (Cons.) Middleborough West, 1951–62; Joint Parliamentary Under-Secretary of State, Home Office, 1957–58; Financial Secretary to the Treasury, 1958–59; Solicitor-General, 1959–62; President, Probate, Divorce, and Admiralty Division, 1962–71; Lord of Appeal, 1971–77.

91. Where his reputation was that of a conservative in matrimonial matters. See especially Leo Abse, "The Inevitability of the Matrimonial Offence" 205. At one point, Simon appeared to be arguing that no divorce should be allowed where there were children; *Sunday Times*, 2 May 1965, at 1; *The Times*, 3 May 1965, at 7. For Simon's views, see Jocelyn Simon, "*With All My Worldly Goods. . . .*"

92. See, for example, by Jocelyn Simon, "English Idioms from the Law"; "Shakespeare's Legal and Political Background" 33; "Some Reflections on Legal Education," 8 *Journal of the Society of the Public Teachers of Law* 89 (1964); and, with J. V. D. Webb, "Consolidation and Statute Law Revision," *Public Law* 285 (1975).

93. E.g., in *Ealing London Borough Council v. Race Relations Bd.*, [1972] A.C. 342, 363 (1971), Simon exhaustively examined 5 different approaches to statutory interpretation; in *Jones v. Secretary of State for Social Servs.*, [1972] A.C. 944, 1016 (1971), he carefully subdivided his argument 7 ways, an approach also followed in *R. v. Governor of Pentonville Prison ex parte Cheng*, [1973] A.C. 931, 947 ff.; in *Miliangos v. George Frank, Ltd.*, [1976] A.C. 443, 470 (1975), he offered 5 general and 8 specific reasons to prove that it was an inappropriate case to overrule an earlier decision.

at best an indifferent understanding."[94] He was aware that doctrine might have to be "stretched" to achieve "equity."[95] Thus he made use of both history[96] and "common sense,"[97] a combination that led him to emphasize the issue of competing doctrines inherent in any decision. "Since every obverse has its reverse, each has its concomitant disadvantage."[98] His position also made it easier for him to open up discussions of public policy and yet link them to precedent.[99] Thus Simon criticized the fallacies in legal reasoning and emphasized the fact that the *ratio decidendi* of a decision reflected historical evolution rather than the single decision itself:

A judicial decision will often be reached by a process of reasoning which can be reduced into a sort of complex syllogism, with the major premise consisting of a pre-existing rule of law (either statutory or judge-made) and with the minor premise consisting of the material facts of the case under immediate consideration.

The conclusion is the decision of the case which may or may not establish new law—in the vast majority of cases it will be merely the application of existing law to the facts judicially ascertained. Where the decision does constitute new law, this may or may not be expressly stated as a proposition of law: frequently the new law will appear only from subsequent comparison of, on the one hand, the material facts inherent in the major premise with, on the other, the material facts which constitute the minor premise. As a result of this comparison it will often be apparent that a rule has been extended by an analogy expressed or implied. . . . In this way, legal luminaries are constituted which guide the wayfarer across uncharted ways.

But where a legal rule is not extended by analogy, but the previous authority has been distinguished, the appropriate metaphor is no longer the single luminary, but rather those binary stars each part of which lives within the field of the other and is essentially influenced by it. Sometimes it seems as if the twin has been formed by the breaking away of a substantial part of the original mass.[100]

In this context Simon approached the more relaxed trends in stare decisis. In handling authorities, he employed existing tools to achieve

94. *Attorney-General v. Times Newspapers, Ltd.*, [1974] A.C. 273, 315 (1973). Simon was conscious of occasions when emotion might sway him. See, for instance, *Smith* v. *Central Asbestos Co.*, [1973] A.C. 518, 546 (1972).

95. E.g., *Rugby Joint Water Bd.* v. *Shaw-Fox*, [1973] A.C. 202, 222 (1972).

96. E.g., *Ealing London Borough Council* v. *Race Relations Bd.*, [1972] A.C. 342, 361, 362 (1971).

97. In *Rugby Joint Water Bd.* v. *Shaw-Fox*, [1973] A.C. 202, 241 (1972), one counsel's argument was rejected because it was so "artificial, legalistic and destructive of the fundamental principles on which compensation is assessed." See also *Thomson* v. *Gurneville Securities, Ltd.*, [1972] A.C. 661, 678 (1971); and *Wickman Machine Tool Sales, Ltd.* v. *L. Schuler A.G.*, [1974] A.C. 235, 269 (1973).

98. *The Atlantic Star*, [1974] A.C. 436, 471 (1973).

99. "The foregoing seems to me to arise from the very nature of the judicial process and its function in society. But it is powerfully supported by judicial authority"; *Attorney-General v. Times Newspapers, Ltd.*, [1974] A.C. 273, 316 (1973).

100. *Lupton v. F.A. & A.B., Ltd.*, [1972] A.C. 634, 658–59 (1971).

much,[101] but obviously at a certain point he was brought face-to-face with the 1966 Practice Statement. Perhaps his very success in the more conventional areas of common law judicial creativity made him cautious of frontal overruling. In *Jones v. Secretary of State for Social Services* Simon, in interpreting statutory language that had been before the House previously, was "clearly of the opinion that it would be wrong now to seek to depart from that decision."[102] For Simon, "the most satisfactory outcome of these appeals would have been to have allowed them on the basis that they were governed by the decision in Dowling's case, but to have overruled that decision prospectively."[103] In *Knuller*, where the House was invited to overrule *Shaw*, Simon described the 1966 Practice Statement as a convention of the Constitution, as the term was used by Dicey.[104] On the merits, however, and particularly on the 1966 Practice Statement's proviso about not introducing uncertainty, Simon refused to accept the argument that the concept of a conspiracy's affecting public morals was itself uncertain.[105] He was not prepared to follow Diplock,

---

101. "The last hundred years have seen many examples of relaxation of the stance of regarding contractual rights and obligations as sacrosanct and exclusive of other considerations: though these examples do not compel equity to follow—certainly not to the extent of overturning established authorities—they do at least invite a more liberal and extensively based attitude on the part of courts which are not bound by these authorities. I would therefore hold myself that equity has an unlimited and unfettered jurisdiction to relieve against contractual forfeitures and penalties"; *Shiloh Spinners, Ltd. v. Harding*, [1973] A.C. 691, 726 (1972).

102. [1972] A.C. 944, 1023 (1971).

103. "In this country it was long considered that judges were not makers of law but merely its discoverers and expounders. The theory was that every case was governed by a relevant rule of law, existing somewhere and discoverable somehow, provided sufficient learning and intellectual rigour were brought to bear. But once such a rule had been discovered, frequently the pretense was dropped that the rule was pre-existing. . . . Nevertheless the theory, however unreal, had its value—in limiting the sphere of lawmaking by the judiciary (inevitably at some disadvantage in assessing the potential repercussions of any decision, and increasingly so in a complex modern industrial society), and thus also in emphasising that central feature of our constitution, the sovereignty of Parliament. But the true, even if limited, nature of judicial lawmaking has been more widely acknowledged of recent years; and the declaration of July 20, 1966, may be partly regarded as of a piece with that process. It might be argued that a further step to invest your lordships with the ampler and more flexible powers of the Supreme Court of the United States would be no more than a logical extension of present realities and of powers already claimed without evoking objection from other organs of the constitution. But my own view is that, though such extension should be seriously considered, it would preferably be the subject matter of parliamentary enactment"; ibid. 1026.

For a further espousal of prospective overruling, see *Miliangos v. George Frank, Ltd.*, [1976] A.C. 443, 490 (1975).

104. [1973] A.C. 435, 484 (1972).

105. "[T]he type of uncertainty invoked by the appellant is not that with which the declaration of July 26, 1966 . . . was concerned. The context was the doctrine of precedent. The declaration was, in other words, concerned with that certainty which comes from following rules of law already judicially determined not with any such certainty as may come from the abrogation of those judicially determined rules of law which involve issues

and *Shaw* survived, for Simon also felt that the rule had not led to any "injustice." This theme reappeared in his dissent in *Miliangos*, where Simon admitted that "I might be tempted to join in overruling the *Havana* case if I were convinced that it would on balance conduce to justice."[106]

Thus, while Simon discussed the 1966 Practice Statement, or at least its implications, on several occasions,[107] he only once used it to overrule an earlier decision, doing so then on the ground that the earlier decision was doctrinally incorrect.[108] In addition to being unconvinced of the "justice" of change and to being heavily influenced by the need for certainty, Simon was obviously concerned chiefly with the parliamentary and constitutional problems of such obvious lawmaking. Simon had no qualms about overruling lower court doctrines, even if well established, if they were concerned with "lawyers' law,"[109] but in most cases his response was similar to that in *Director of Public Prosecutions for Northern Ireland* v. *Lynch*. "This branch of the law is closely bound up with matters of policy relating to public safety. Such matters are far more fitly weighed in Parliament on the advice of the executive than developed in courts of law."[110] His concern about changing the criminal law of duress was even more apparent in *Knuller*. Simon's speech savored of

---

of fact and degree. *Shaw v. Director of Public Prosecutions* laid down with certainty that the offence of conspiracy to corrupt public morals was part of our criminal law. Parliament, in the Theatres Act 1968, recognised that this had been so established. A number of persons have been prosecuted and convicted on this basis. It was not contended that the rule had led to any injustice"; ibid. 488.

106. *Miliangos* v. *George Frank, Ltd.*, [1976] A.C. 443, 488 (1975).

107. E.g., *Blathwayt* v. *Lord Cawley*, [1976] A.C. 397, 427 (1975): "I must not be taken thereby to be implying that it is for the courts of law to embark on an independent and unfettered appraisal of what they think is required by public policy on any issue. Courts are concerned with public policy only in so far as it has been manifested by parliamentary sanction or embodied in rules of law having binding judicial force. As to such rules of law your Lordships have the same power to declare, to bind and to loose as in regard to any other judicial precedent." See also *L. Schuler A.G.* v. *Wickman Machine Tool Sales, Ltd.* v. *L. Schuler A.g.*, [1974] A.C. 235, 263 (1973); *DPP for N. Ire.* v. *Lynch*, [1975] A.C. 653, 685 (N. Ire.); *R.* v. *Withers*, [1975] A.C. 842, 862 (1974); *DPP* v. *Shannon*, [1975] A.C. 717, 762 (1974); *Taylor* v. *Provan*, [1975] A.C. 194, 218 (1974).

108. In *E. L. Oldendorff & Co. G.m.b.H.* v. *Tradax Export S.A.*, [1974] A.C. 479, 562 (1973); Simon said, "[T]he *Aello* incorrectly interpreted *Leonis v. Rank* . . . and laid down an inadmissible, commercially irrelevant and inconvenient test of whether a ship is 'arrived.' . . . [I] think that this is a case where your Lordships should exercise the power envisaged in the Practice Statement of July 26, 1966, and, holding *The Aello* to be wrongly decided, decline to follow it."

109. E.g., "The technical foundation of the rule is apparent, and so is the purpose which it served for so many years. But its irrationality and practical inexpediency are also apparent, and so is the fact that it is no longer needed to serve its former purpose. On the contrary, the present case illustrates its absurdity, inconvenience and injustice"; *DPP* v. *Shannon*, [1975] A.C. 717, 767 (1974).

110. *DPP for Northern Ireland* v. *Lynch*, [1975] A.C. 653, 697 (N. Ire.).

Reid's efforts to persuade his colleagues not to invent or expand conspiracy as they had done in *Shaw*. In agreeing with his colleagues that *Shaw* should not be overruled, Simon reminded them that "your lordships are concerned with highly controversial issues, on which there is every sign that neither public nor parliamentary opinion is settled. . . . Of course, courts of law do not shrink from decisions which are liable to be controversial when judicial duty demands such decisions, but your lordships are here in a field where the decisions—at any rate, policy decisions—are better left to Parliament, if such is possible."[111]

The institutional arguments were elaborated in *Miliangos* in which Simon argued basically that "the instant appeal raises questions, the answer to which imperatively demands the contribution of expertise from far outside the law—on monetary theory, public finance, international finance, commerce, industry, economics—for which judges have no training and no special qualification merely by their aptitude for judicial office." Law, in Simon's view was "too serious a matter to be left to judges."[112] On this same issue he said:

By contrast, the training and qualification of a judge is to elucidate the problem immediately before him, so that its features stand out in stereoscopic clarity. But the beam of light which so illuminates the immediate scene seems to throw surrounding areas into greater obscurity: the whole landscape is distorted to the view. A penumbra can be apprehended, but not much beyond; so that when the searchlight shifts a quite unexpected scene may be disclosed. The very qualifications for the judicial process thus impose limitations on its use. This is why judicial advance should be gradual. "I am not trained to see the distant scene: one step enough for me" should be the motto on the wall opposite the judge's desk. It is, I concede, a less spectacular method of progression than somersaults and cartwheels; but it is the one best suited to the capacity and resources of a judge. We are likely to perform better the duties society impose on us if we recognise our limitations. Within the proper limits there is more than enough to be done which is of value to society.[113]

111. *R. v. Knuller, Ltd.*, [1973] A.C. 435, 489 (1972); he continued, "Certainly it is the sort of matter on which it is most undesirable that there should be in effect, an appeal from one Appellate Committee of your Lordships' House to another. In default of any decision by Parliament to reverse the judgment in *Shaw v. D.P.P.* the determination in particular cases is in the hands of that microcosm of democratic society, the jury."

112. [1976] A.C. 443, 481–82 (1975). He had already argued:

All such experience as I have had of decision making within and without the law convinces me that the resolution of this issue demands a far greater range of advice and a far more generally based knowledge than is available to a court of law—even one assisted—by the most meticulous, cogent and profound arguments of counsel. Law is too serious a matter to be left exclusively to judges.

. . . I am sure that an expert committee, including or taking evidence from departmental officials, would apprehend a great number of not immediately apparent repercussions of the decision which my noble and learned friends propose to take. Such a committee might conclude that the repercussions make the decision unacceptable or they might suggest some means of mitigating any adverse effect. Or they might advise that the repercussions were on balance acceptable. But at least the crucial decision would be taken in the light of all the consequences involved. [Ibid. 481]

113. Ibid. 824–25.

To support this general approach, Simon offered various particular reasons to suggest why on the merits, the overruling of the *Havana* case made little sense—in law and justice.

The conclusion of Simon's speech in *Miliangos* was, however, also significant. As a kind of afterthought, he offered three observations about the role of judicial legislation which suggested a rapidly changing sense of the appellate process. First, he admitted, "I would be more ready to go along with my noble and learned friends if the decision had prospective effect only." Second, he suggested that "the type of law reform by judiciary which is here exemplified" ought to be done by "the Lords of Appeal sitting *in banc*," at least with respect to overruling recent decisions. (The implications of this would be that the House, in such situations, would operate much like the Supreme Court of the United States.) Third, he argued that "if courts are to undertake legislative responsibilities . . . something must be done to equip them better for the type of decision-making which is involved. Official advice and a balanced executive view might be made available by a law officer or his counsel acting as *amicus curiae.*"[114] There is little doubt that Simon's preference was for the more traditional and less obvious forms of judicial lawmaking,[115] yet his analysis of the political implications of judicial lawmaking were by far the most dramatic made in the judicial forum itself. The idea that a Lord of Appeal might discuss publicly—let alone from the bench—and analyze the concepts of prospective overruling, *in banc* decisions, and an executive *amicus* brief would have come close to causing a constitutional crisis twenty years earlier.

Simon's willingness, however, to indulge in more conventional forms of judicial creativity was clear from his approach to statutory interpretation. As most English judges, he, from time to time, spoke of the task as being to interpret words in "their ordinary meaning,"[116] "their natural, ordinary and grammatical meaning"[117] and "their ordinary, natural and literal sense."[118] Indeed, Simon occasionally referred to this approach as "the primary and golden rule."[119] Yet, for him, this was a place to start rather than the finishing point. Thus, in moving toward a decision in other cases, he rejected the "plain words" argument "simply because the words are not plain," having observed, "I think it unlikely that the

114. Ibid. 832.
115. E.g., his unwillingness to distinguish *R. v. Dudley & Stephens* in *DPP for Northern Ireland v. Lynch*, [1975] A.C. 653 (N. Ire.); and his willingness to depart from *Dharmasena v. The King* in *DPP v. Shannon*, [1975] A.C. 717 (1974).
116. *Ealing London Borough Council v. Race Relations Bd.*, [1972] A.C. 342, 361, (1971).
117. *Race Relations Bd., v. Applin*, [1975] A.C. 259 (1974).
118. *R. v. Governor of Pentonville Prison, ex parte Cheng*, [1973] A.C. 931, 951.
119. Ibid.

instant situation was within the draftsman's contemplation at all."[120] The idea of equity, no doubt related to Simon's concept of justice, also entered in: "[B]efore accepting results so astonishing, so inconvenient, so subversive of established principle and so unjust to defendants I should require to find an intention that this should be so expressed in plain words. I find no such thing."[121] So too, Simon had no qualms about using Law Commission and other official reports to discover intent, and he lobbied, "in the really clinching case," to have parliamentary debates admitted.[122]

Moreover, the statements of Simon's version of the "golden rule" have to be balanced against his different approaches in other cases. While he sometimes resorted to "linguistic analysis," his wide-ranging analysis emphasized the open-textured nature of language and significantly undermined the pretentions of the "plain meaning" rule.[123] He sometimes admitted that he reached his conclusion "on a functional analysis. But this is borne out by linguistic analysis."[124] Moreover, in keeping with his analysis of the institutional purposes of the courts in terms of the 1966 Practice Statement, he on various occasions analyzed, at length, the courts' role in construction and interpretation of statutes. He addressed the "internal" modes of interpreting statutes in *R.* v. *Governor of Pentonville Prison ex parte Cheng*.[125] Then, in *Ealing London Borough Council* v. *Race Relations Board*, after excluding examination of *travaux préparatoires* in general, he addressed the issue of the basic approach that the courts should take toward the interpretation of statutes.[126]

---

120. *Rugby Joint Water Bd.* v. *Shaw-Fox*, [1973] A.C. 202, 234 (1972).

121. *Smith* v. *Central Asbestos Co.*, [1973] A.C. 518, 550 (1972).

122. *Race Relations Bd.* v. *Charter*, [1973] A.C. 868, 900; and *Dockers' Labour Club & Institute, Ltd.* v. *Race Relations Bd.*, [1976] A.C. 285, 299 (1974). In this latter case Simon noted that "the fact that debates in Congress are freely cited to the courts of the United States suggests that there is no fundamental rule of the common law prohibiting the practice." At 300 he suggested that if the promoter of the bill or the minister introducing it made specific representations about how it should operate, by "constitutional convention" these should become part of the act. See also *Crouch* v. *McMillan*, [1972] 1 W.L.R. 1102, 1119 (H.L.). Cf., however, *Ealing London Borough Council* v. *Race Relations Bd.*, [1972] A.C. 342, 361 (1971):

Though this may sometimes be useful, it is open to abuse and waste: an individual legislator may indicate his assent on an assumption that the legislation means so-and-so, and the courts may have no way of knowing how far his assumption is shared by his colleagues, even those present. Moreover, by extending the material of judicial scrutiny the cost of litigation is inevitably increased. Finally, our own constitution does not know a pure legislature; the sovereign is the Queen in Parliament and the legislative history of a statute stretches back from the parliamentary proceedings—by successive drafts of a bill, heads of instruction to the draftsman, departmental papers and minutes of executive committees . . . into the arcana imperii."

123. E.g., *Jones* v. *Secretary of State for Social Servs.*, [1972] A.C. 944, 1015 (1971).

124. *Fleming* v. *Associated Newspapers, Ltd.*, [1973] A.C. 628, 648 (1972).

125. [1973] A.C. 931, 947 ff.

126. [1972] A.C. 342 (1971); also, see the following:

In view of the consciousness of the Simon approach to judicial creativity, it is particularly interesting to analyze the assumptions and values from which he began. He shared the view of his fellow law lords—with the exception of Denning, Kilbrandon, and Morris—that the Race Relations Act should be construed narrowly.[127] On the other hand, in tax cases Simon read legislation broadly in order to prevent tax avoidance.[128] In terms of civil liberties, Simon early made it clear that he was opposed to Crown privilege on a blanket[129] although not on a selective[130] basis. While he had a few qualms about a strong law of contempt of court,[131] he was concerned about the taking of property when the purpose appeared largely unrelated to the enabling legislation.[132] Not willing to overrule *Shaw* in *Knuller*, he opposed the suggestions in the earlier case that judges were free to invent new crimes or "still had some role to play in the general superintendence of morals."[133] Moreover, his general concern with civil liberties appeared to underlie his dissents in deportation[134] and obscenity[135] cases.

At heart, however, Simon was a constitutionalist. In *Pickin*, he criticized counsel for drawing a clear line between public and private acts,[136] but his basic concern was to maintain the existing separation of powers:

In the absence of such material the courts have five principal avenues of approach to the ascertainment of the legislative intention: (1) examination of the social background, as specifically proved if not within common knowledge, in order to identify the social or juristic defect which is the likely subject of remedy; (2) a conspectus of the entire relevant body of the law for the same purpose; (3) particular regard to the long title of the statute to be interpreted (and, where available, the preamble) in which the general legislative objectives will be stated; (4) scrutiny of the actual words to be interpreted, in the light of the established canons of interpretation; (5) examination of the other provisions of the statute in question (or of other statutes in pari materia) for the illumination which they throw on the particular words which are the subject of interpretation. [Ibid. 361]

127. E.g., *Race Relations Bd.* v. *Charter*, [1973] A.C. 868, 902, construing "section of the public" narrowly: "Notwithstanding the paramount objective of discouragement of racial discrimination, I find it impossible to believe that Parliament would willingly have countenanced the implications involved in the wider contention made on behalf of the board. I think 'a section of the public' in Section 2 (1) was used to denote a group of persons in their public capacities or roles, in contrast to a group of persons in their private capacities or roles." But, by the time of *Dockers' Labour Club & Institute, Ltd.* v. *Race Relations Bd.*, [1976] A.C. 285, 298–300 (1974), Simon seemed to feel that the narrowness had gone too far, although he felt unable to dissent.

128. E.g., *Fleming* v. *Associated Newspapers, Ltd.*, [1973] A.C. 628 (1972).

129. Jocelyn Simon, "Evidence Excluded by Considerations of State Interest" 62.

130. E.g., his protection of the sources of police information in *R.* v. *Lewes Justices, ex parte Secretary of State for Home Affairs*, [1973] A.C. 388, 407–8 (1972).

131. *Attorney-General* v. *Times Newspapers, Ltd.*, [1974] A.C. 273 (1973). See especially at 315–16 and 319.

132. *Rugby Joint Water Bd.* v. *Shaw-Fox*, [1973] A.C. 202 (1972). See especially at 222.

133. *R.* v. *Knuller, Ltd.*, [1973] A.C. 435, 490 (1972).

134. *R.* v. *Governor of Pentonville Prison, ex parte Cheng*, [1973] A.C. 931.

135. *DPP* v. *Whyte*, [1972] A.C. 849.

136. *British Rys. Bd.* v. *Pickin*, [1974] A.C. 765, 800.

It is well known that in the past there have been dangerous strains between the law courts and Parliament—dangerous because each institution has its own particular role to play in our constitution, and because collision between the two institutions is likely to impair their power to vouchsafe those constitutional rights for which citizens depend on them. So for many years Parliament and the courts have each been astute to respect the sphere of action and the privilege of the other—Parliament for example, by its sub judice rule, the courts by taking care to exclude evidence which might amount to infringement of parliamentary privilege. . . . It would be unthinkable that two proceedings—one parliamentary and the other forensic—should proceed concurrently, conceivably arriving at different conclusions.[137]

Simon of Glaisdale may well have been the most constitutionally conscious of the Lords of Appeal in a century.

Lord Salmon,[138] who became a Lord of Appeal in 1972, was a different kind of judge. More outspoken outside the courtroom than Simon, he was involved in various civil libertarian causes and while in the Court of Appeal he had had a reputation as a creative judge,[139] frequently siding with Denning.[140] In the House these traits reappeared, although perhaps not as strongly as many had expected, particularly in view of the earlier extrajudicial pronouncements.

In terms of civil liberties, perhaps most dramatic was Salmon's concern with contempt of court. Although the Interdepartmental Committee on the Law of Contempt as It Affects Tribunals of Inquiry,[141] which he chaired, recommended retention of a modified form of contempt, Salmon grew increasingly impatient with the broad English approach. When asked by the Phillimore Committee on Contempt of Court when contempt should start in a civil proceeding, he answered, "Nowhere, because I would not have any contempt. I say never. Certainly never in a judge-alone case. I think the law of libel takes care of anything you may

137. Ibid. 799, 800.

138. Cyril Barnet Salmon; b. 1903; educ., Mill Hill, Pembroke College, Cambridge; called to bar, 1925; K.C., 1945; Judge, Queen's Bench Division, 1957–64; Lord Justice, 1964–72; Lord of Appeal, 1972–.

139. "a judge noted for robust assertions of individual rights"; Stanley A. de Smith, *Constitutional and Administrative Law*, 458–59.

For examples of typical decisions in the Court of Appeal, see *Morris v. C. W. Martin & Sons*, [1966] 1 Q.B. 716 (C.A. 1965); *Charnock v. Liverpool Corp.*, [1968] 1 W.L.R. 1498 (C.A.); *R. v. Savundranayagan*, [1968] 1 W.L.R. 1761 (C.C.A.); and *Gallie v. Lee*, [1969] 2 Ch. 17 (C.A.). 140. "The Court of Appeal is not, however, and never has been bound by obiter dicta however august. Naturally it treats them with the greatest respect and usually follows them. If convinced however that they are wrong, the court is entitled and indeed obliged to decide the case in accordance with its over view of the law and justice." He then cited *in re Grosvenor Hotel, London (No. 2)*, where he, Denning, and Harman reviewed the earlier authority and held the speech of Simon in *Duncan v. Cammell, Laird* to be obiter and wrong; Salmon, "The Last Bulwark of Individual Liberty" 749.

141. Cmnd. 4078 (1969).

say about a civil case, and if a judge is going to be affected by what is written or said he is not fit to be a judge."[142] No doubt this same spirit led him, as a law lord, to restrict judicial immunity for arbitrators, holding that an architect issuing an interim certificate might be sued for negligence, despite the quasi-arbitral aura of the work.[143]

Salmon's feeling that different rules applied when a jury sat (restricted today de facto in civil actions to defamation and in criminal cases to pleas of "not guilty") did not suggest that he had any serious doubts about the jury. Indeed, he strongly supported both the idea and the wisdom of the typical criminal jury.[144] He was incensed when the *Eleventh Report of the Criminal Law Revision Committee* urged reducing the procedural defenses available to defendants. In his maiden speech in the House, he attacked the proposals to extend the admissibility of previous convictions and hearsay evidence.[145] Not only did he take issue with the Edmund-Davies Report, but he also disagreed with the view of the metropolitan police commissioner, which he characterized as "the suggestion that since nowadays the danger of convicting an innocent man can involve no more than wrongfully depriving him of his liberty, that danger would be accepted as necessary in order to ensure that no guilty man may escape conviction."[146] Despite this "modern . . . dangerous philosophy, the liberty of the subject is something which the law still jealously guards."[147] He added in *R. v. Boardman*, "Evidence against an accused which tends only to show that he is a man of bad character with a disposition to commit crimes . . . is inadmissible . . . I do not pause to discuss the philosophic basis for this fundamental rule. It is certainly not founded on logic, but on policy. To admit such evidence would be unjust and would offend our concept of a fair trial."[148]

In the criminal law proper, Salmon indeed demonstrated a concern for procedural fairness. He diagnosed the problem of a rising crime rate, not as being weakness on the part of the judiciary or juries, but rather as a problem of police effectiveness. "Whilst the detection rate remains as it is, ten to one in favour of the perpetrators of serious crime not being brought to trial, the conviction rate must be wholly irrelevant so far as

142. *Report*, Cmnd. 5794, at 98 (1974).
143. *Sutcliffe* v. *Thackrah*, [1974] A.C. 727, 757. See now also *Arenson* v. *Arenson*, [1977] A.C. 405, 440 (1975), rejecting immunity of auditors in negligence, even when acting in a quasi-public capacity. See especially: "I find it difficult to discern any sensible reason, on grounds of public policy or otherwise, why such an arbitrator with such a limited role, although formally appointed, should enjoy a judicial immunity which so called quasi-arbitrators in the position of the respondents certainly do not."
144. Cyril Salmon, *Crime and Punishment* 5–6.
145. 338 *Parl. Deb.*, H.L. (5th ser.), cols. 1603–10 (14 Feb. 1973).
146. Salmon, *Crime and Punishment* 5.
147. *The Times*, 28 June 1974, at 3.
148. [1975] A.C. 421, 461 (1974).

the volume of crime is concerned."[149] But Salmon was not totally unwilling to help in the "War on Crime." In *R*. v. *Doot*,[150] he not only consciously extended the law of conspiracy,[151] but he also criticized the lower courts for imposing drug-offense sentences that he felt were too light. On the other hand, he dissented in a Jamaican appeal, holding that since a death penalty for those over eighteen was provided by legislation, that legislation should be read narrowly to keep from the gallows someone who murdered at seventeen and was convicted at eighteen.[152] In other areas of personal freedom, Salmon also pursued a civil libertarian goal. In the leading pornography case of the period, he dissented with Simon. While deploring "the role of such books," he concluded, "It is evident from the case stated that the justices found in effect that the likely readers of the books were dirty minded old men who were already in such a state of depravity and córruption that there were grave doubts as to whether they could be further depraved or corrupted by the books in question."[153] So too in a series of deportation cases he exhibited a concern for personal freedom.[154]

Rather surprisingly, the Salmon concern did not spill over to racial discrimination. Although Salmon had criticized those countries where "large sections of the population are prevented from earning their living and subjected to intolerable indignities solely because of their ethnic origins or political convictions,"[155] he nevertheless was *dubitans* in the

149. Salmon, *Crime and Punishment* 2.
150. [1973] A.C. 807.
151. "I recognise that if your Lordships were to hold that our courts are invested with jurisdiction in circumstances such as the present your Lordships would in a sense be extending the application of the criminal law since such a case as the present has never yet been decided in our courts. . . .

"There may, however, be most exceptional cases, and I think that this is one of them, in which a new point falls to be decided and accordingly a development of the law in accordance with principle becomes permissible and indeed necessary. The crime of conspiracy is the creation of the common law and peculiar to it"; ibid. 832.
152. *Baker* v. *The Queen*, [1975] A.C. 774, 790 (P.C.): "Looking at Section 29 (1) in isolation I have no doubt that it is reasonably capable of bearing either of the meanings to which I have referred; nor have I any doubt that to adopt the meaning which makes it mandatory for anyone who may commit murder at any time between the ages of 8 and 18 to be hanged for a crime providing that he is not sentenced to death until after he has attained 18 years of age leads to shocking and indeed barbarous results." See also at 796 for his hope that the prerogative of mercy would be exercised.
153. *DPP* v. *Whyte*, [1972] A.C. 849, 872.
154. E.g., *R*. v. *Governor of Pentonville Prison, ex parte Cheng*, [1973] A.C. 931, 963, where he announced his conclusion was "dictated alike by reason, principle and justice." See also *R*. v. *Governor of Pentonville Prison, ex parte Azam*, [1974] A.C. 18 (1973), especially at 70.
155. Cyril Salmon, *The Law and Individual Liberty* 9. At 8, he stressed the (historically inaccurate) fact that the English courts had always set their face against slavery. On this, see F. O. Shyllon, *Black Slaves in Britain, passim*.

only race relations case where the House found for the Race Relations Board.[156] Nor was Salmon particularly sympathetic to picketing, which was guaranteed by section 134 of the Industrial Relations Bill of 1971. When a picket stopped a man for nine minutes to argue, Salmon concluded that that, "to my mind, was about as clear a wilful obstruction of the highway without lawful authority or excuse as it is possible to imagine and to which Section 134 of the Act of 1971 can afford no shadow of a defence."[157] Perhaps more in keeping with his civil libertarian image was his legislative battle in 1975 to protect the right of the courts to ensure that they had jurisdiction in cases of "arbitrary or unreasonable discrimination" where a union had a closed shop.[158] So too, Salmon continued to strike a balance between the needs of government and the requirements of justice with respect to Crown privilege, insisting always that "it is ultimately for the court to decide whether or not it is in the public interest for the document or information to be disclosed."[159]

Contrasted with Simon, however, Salmon, who might have been expected to be more creative judicially and more articulate about the judicial process, had in fact—at least by 1977—been less so. Salmon, for instance, took a formalistic approach to causation, assuming that there is normally only one causal event.[160] He "deprecated litigation the purpose of which is to influence political decisions."[161] He dissented in *Smith* v. *Central Asbestos Company*, holding the plaintiff to the very letter of the Limitation Act of 1963;[162] while in *Launchbury* v. *Morgans*, the litmus-paper test of judicial restraint, he seemed to turn his back on his col-

156. *Race Relations Bd.* v. *Applin*, [1975] A.C. 259, 282 (1974).

157. *Hunt* v. *Broome*, [1974] A.C. 587.

158. The Trade Union and Trade Disputes Act of 1974 had legalized the closed shop. The Trade Union and Labor Relations (Amendment) Bill of 1975 proposed taking away any redress in the courts from those discriminated against by the closed shop. Salmon argued that "for a man to be expelled by his trade union is infinitely more damaging than for him to be unfairly dismissed by his employer for after all, there are other employers"; "Note," 125 *New Law Journal* 273 (1975).

159. *R.* v. *Lewes Justices, ex parte Secretary of State for Home Affairs*, [1973] A.C. 388, 412 (1972). In the area of public law, Salmon was also Chairman of the Interdepartmental Committee on the Law of Contempt as It Affects Tribunals of Inquiry; *Report*, Cmnd. 4078 (1969). He also became a slow convert to a Bill of Rights; *Law and Individual Liberty* 9. He was also Chairman of the Royal Commission on Corruption, which was set up at the time of the Poulson scandals. See *Report of the Royal Commission on the Standards of Conduct in Public Life*, Cmnd. 6524 (1976). See also Gavin Drewry, "Poulson and Parliament" 1079.

160. *Alphacell, Ltd.* v. *Woodward*, [1972] A.C. 824, 847–48; although see at 847: "that what or who has caused a certain event to occur is essentially a practical question of fact which can best be answered by ordinary common sense rather than by abstract metaphysical theory." See also *Hunt* v. *Broome*, [1974] A.C. 587, 603.

161. *The Times*, 23 Apr. 1974, at 16.

162. [1973] A.C. 518, 551 (1972).

leagues and his reputation in the Court of Appeal.[163] The decisions discussed earlier could not, of course, have been achieved without a strong element of flexibility, but there is a surprising note of judicial conservatism even when Salmon said, "[Y]our lordships are, therefore, free to redirect the common law on to its true course if your lordships are convinced that in the past it has diverged from it."[164] The conservatism could, however, be overcome. "This appeal is . . . the first occasion upon which your Lordships' House has had an opportunity of deciding whether or not the doctrine is good law. Clearly it is not a doctrine to be lightly overthrown, however fragile its foundations. Nevertheless I am convinced that . . . it is contrary alike to principle, sound authority, reason and justice and that therefore we are obliged to overthrow it."[165]

Lord Kilbrandon came out of Scottish tradition,[166] replacing Guest as one of the Scottish Lords of Appeal in 1971 and, in turn, being replaced by Keith in 1977. Kilbrandon had been active in both public service and law reform while serving as a Scottish judge. In addition to being a Senator of the College of Justice, he had served as Chairman of the Scottish Law Commission for six years,[167] as well as Chairman of the Royal Commission on the Constitution,[168] which recommended devolution for Scotland and Wales. It may have been this heavily Scottish focus that caused Kilbrandon to tread softly during his years as a law lord. His speeches were replete with modest comments about his inability to con-

---

163. [1973] A.C. 127 (1972). See at 151:

[A]pplying the principles of law hitherto accepted, the circumstances of this case cannot justify the judgement against Mrs. Morgans. The question is, however, whether that principle ought to be extended by accepting the proposition favoured by Lord Denning. . . . No doubt the proposition . . . may have much to commend it on the grounds of public policy. . . . I have always recognised that it is an important function of this House to develop and adapt the common law to meet the changing needs of time. . . . In the present case, however, the proposed "development" constitutes such a radical and far-reaching departure from accepted principle that it seems to me to smack of naked legislation. . . . [T]his is essentially a matter for the legislature.

164. *DPP* v. *Shannon*, [1975] A.C. 717, 770 (1974). As befitted his view of the appellate process, Salmon also believed that his decisions should offer clear guidance to the courts below. In *R.* v. *Sakhuja*, [1973] A.C. 152, 201 (1972), where he wanted the court to "set . . . the seal of this House's approval" on a decision so the court "finally lays down" the rule of law. See also *Woodhouse A. C. Israel Cocoa, Ltd.* v. *Nigerian Produce Mkt. Co.*, [1972] A.C. 741, 770.

165. *Sutcliffe* v. *Thackrah*, [1974] A.C. 727, 757.

166. Charles James Dalrymple Shaw; b. 1906; father, County Clerk of Ayrshire; educ., Charterhouse, Balliol College, Oxford, Edinburgh University; Faculty of Advocates, 1932; K.C., 1949; Dean, Faculty of Advocates, 1957–59; Senator, College of Justice, 1959–71; Lord of Appeal, 1971–76.

167. The commission had called for a model Code of Evidence along American lines; *The Times*, 10 Nov. 1968, at 3. See also Lord Kilbrandon (C.J.D. Shaw), "The Scottish Law Commission" 193.

168. *Report*, Cmnd. 5460 (1973). For the government's reaction, see *Democracy and Devolution: Proposals for Scotland and Wales*, Cmnd. 5732 (1974).

tribute to English law and his relief that, on some points,[169] English and Scottish law appeared to be identical.[170]

Despite this apparent diffidence, Kilbrandon gave the impression of a powerful judge, but one who found it somewhat difficult to comprehend the English style of judgment and adapt his own style to it. Some of his opinions seem to have been written at two levels, with broad Scottish discussions of principle but narrow English *rationes decidendi*.[171] At times, indeed, Kilbrandon sounded faintly apologetic that his speeches were short and, by the standards of a Wilberforce or a Diplock, relatively free of precedent; at other times his speeches hinted that he was uncomfortable with the declaratory theory.[172] So too, again perhaps out of a civil law tradition or perhaps out of his rationale of a final appeal court, he offered advice to lower courts before giving judgment.[173]

In many respects, however, his judicial style conformed to the centrality of principle that Reid restored to the Lords. Kilbrandon was more willing than some English law lords to explore the impact of decisions. He was critical of earlier decisions where findings on fact or standards of behavior appeared to have been elevated to principles of law.[174] In line

169. E.g., "since it is unlikely that any contribution of mine would be regarded as of value in clarifying the law of England"; *Broome v. Cassell & Co.*, [1972] A.C. 1027, 1132. Or, "I think I can greatly shorten what I have to say on this topic, which is of a technical character involving an expert knowledge of English legal history in the nature of things denied to me"; *Norwich Pharmacal Co. v. Commissioners of Customs & Excise*, [1974] A.C. 133, 201 (1973).

170. E.g., *Lep Air Servs., Ltd. v. Rolloswin Invs., Ltd.*, [1973] A.C. 331, 359 (1972); *National Westminster Bank, Ltd. v. Halesowen Presswork, Ltd.*, [1972] A.C. 785, 824. See, generally, Kilbrandon, *Other People's Law*.

171. See, for example, *R. v. Knuller, Ltd.*, [1973] A.C. 435, 496 (1972): "I have dealt with this part of the case on a narrow front, not only because it has been more widely and carefully considered by the noble Lords who preceded me, but also because I think that as far as possible it is expedient to do so." See also *Norwich Pharmacal Co. v. Commissioners of Customs & Excise*, [1974] A.C. 133, 203–4 (1973): "The most attractive way to state an acceptable principle intellectually at least, may be as follows. . . . But it is not necessary, in such a case as is being figured, to go as far as this."

172. For example, he often noted a conflict within the authorities. "The authorities are not in a condition entirely satisfactory for the drawing of confident conclusions"; *National Westminster Bank, Ltd. v. Halesowen Presswork, Ltd.*, [1972] A.C. 785, 822. See also *Alfred Crompton Amusement Machs., Ltd. v. Commissioners of Customs & Excise (No. 2)*, [1974] A.C. 405, 435 (1973); *Norwich Pharmacal Co. v. Commissioners of Customs & Excise*, [1974] A.C. 133, 201 (1973). Kilbrandon then lamented the uselessness of an older authority that could offer guidance but that was reported in 3 different places, on each occasion with significant differences; ibid. 202. His speech in *Heath v. Drown*, [1973] A.C. 498, 516 (1972), further illustrated the carefully scrutinized use of authority.

173. In *R. v. Governor of Pentonville Prison, ex parte Sotiriadis*, he noted that "in my judgement the correct procedure to be adopted on a provisional warrant has heretofore been misapprehended by the authorities at Bow Street." He then explained the proper procedure. At the end of his advice, he noted, "I now turn to the three parts of the question before your Lordships"; [1975] A.C. 1, 35–36 (1974).

174. E.g., *Cozens v. Brutus*, [1973] A.C. 854, 866–67 (1972); *Alfred Crompton*

with this, he made it clear that "I do not myself find the quotation of dictionary definitions helpful."[175] Whether the issue was one of statuory or contractual construction, he took a balanced view.[176] Kilbrandon admitted to a "purposive construction" of statutes,[177] and, dissenting in the first important race relations case, he held that the act prohibited discrimination, not only on the grounds of "national origins," but also on the grounds of nationality.[178]

In this case, however, Kilbrandon made it clear that he felt Parliament, or the system of statutory construction, left much to be desired by failing either to give specific guidance or to allow the judges to have the

---

Amusement Machs., Ltd. v. *Commissioners of Customs & Excise (No. 2)*, [1974] A.C. 405, 435 (1973).

175. *Cozens* v. *Brutus*, [1973] A.C. 854, 867 (1972).

176. "One must, above all other considerations . . . in a case where the agreement is in obscure terms, see whether an interpretation proposed is likely to lead to unreasonable results, and if it is, be reluctant to accept it. The grotesque consequences of an insistence on a right to rescind on *any* breach of clause 7(b) do not require emphasis"; *Wickman Mach. Tool Sales, Ltd.* v. *L. Schuler A.G.*, [1974] A.C. 235, 272 (1973). For an example of this approach applied to statutes, see *Westwood* v. *Post Office*, [1974] A.C. 1, 14, (1973): "It was suggested by counsel that this was perhaps an oversight by Parliament, which Parliament would one day get around to putting right. I prefer the interpretation which has the effect that when the authorised attendant goes to the telephone exchange he goes to office premises, and is still working in office premises when he is working in the dangerous lift motor room." See also *Brown* v. *Allied Ironfounders, Ltd.*, [1974] 1 W.L.R. 527 (H.L. Scot.). Both of these decisions on statutory duty were based on interpretations favorable to workmen.

177. *Heath* v. *Drown*, [1973] A.C. 498, 517 (1972).

178. "The arguments in favour of either interpretation are finely balanced. I would not accept the view that there is some presumption here in favour of freedom from liability; the race relations code does, of course, contain some criminal sanctions, and it restricts liberty, but, on the other hand, it is conceived as a measure of social reform and relief of distress. Not much help is to be got from the presumptions either for freedom or in favour of benevolent interpretations. I have come to the conclusion that on a consideration of the Acts as a whole the interpretation contended for by the respondents leads to a result less capricious and more consistent with reality than that proposed by the appellants, although, as I have said, the language used, and the limitations on the assistance permissible, do not encourage confidence in the expressing of an opinion"; *Ealing London Borough Council* v. *Race Relations Bd.*, [1972] A.C. 342, 369 (1971).

While he went along with the majority in *Dockers' Labour Club & Institute, Ltd.* v. *Race Relations Bd.*, [1976] A.C. 285 (1974), he noted "[T]he appellant club is run on racialist lines. . . . when a club operates a racialist policy, coloured people will know this. They will accordingly not put up for membership, nor will members expose them to insult by inviting them in as guests." After discussing the work of the House with respect to the Race Relations Act, he concluded, "It is not necessary to emphasise the need for some authoritative examination of possible remedies for this constitutional infirmity;" ibid. 300–301. See also his civil libertarian dissent in *Suthendran* v. *Immigration Appeal Tribunal*, [1977] A.C. 359, 369 [1976].

For another view on public law, see *Broome* v. *Cassell & Co.*, [1972] A.C. 1027, 1132: "[S]ince all commercial publication is undertaken for profit, one must be watchful against holding the profit motive to be sufficient to justify punitive damages; to do so would be seriously to hamper what must be regarded, at least since the European Convention was ratified, as a constitutional right to free speech."

tools to do the job.[179] This outburst may well reflect the evolution of a Kilbrandon view of the relationship of the House of Lords and Parliament. On the one hand he implored Parliament to reconsider the law of bankruptcy[180] and conspiracy,[181] while readily admitting, "I do not suppose that anyone now sitting down to draft a civil code would include an article providing for punitive damages. But the doctrine exists."[182] Thus his approach to the 1966 Practice Statement was generally cautious. While in *R. v. Knuller* he thought it unnecessary to overrule *Shaw* in order to allow the appeal, he also felt "it would in any event be a strong step indeed to hold that a pronouncement on principle in a criminal matter made so recently and so authoritatively was wrong, but for my part I would find such a course impossible to contemplate in view of an even more recent Act of the legislature."[183]

His later view was more complex. In *Director of Public Prosecutions v. Lynch*,[184] he argued, "If there is one lesson which has been learned since the setting up of the Law Commissions it is this, that law reform by lawyers for lawyers (unless in exceptionally technical matters) is not socially acceptable. An alteration in a fundamental doctrine of our law . . . could not properly be given effect to save after the widest reference to interests, both social and intellectual, far transcending those available in . . . your Lordships' House." Such a view apparently accepted the peculiarly English notion, recently replanted by Gardiner and apparently accepted by Reid,[185] that there is such a thing as "lawyers' law." Within that limited mythical realm, however, it was apparently acceptable for the courts to legislate, for in *R. v. Hyam*, Kilbrandon said, "It is because I regard the adoption of a fresh definition of the intention . . . necessary to support a charge of murder as inevitably called for by the

---

179. "That one should be left groping for, or even speculating about, the meaning of a key phrase used in a recent Act of Parliament designed to remedy social grievances by assuring large groups of citizens of the protection of the law, and at the same time imposing criminal sanction, is an unhappy feature of our present rules for the interpretation of Statutes"; *Ealing London Borough Council v. Race Relations Bd.*, [1972] A.C. 342, 367 (1971).

180. *National Westminster Bank, Ltd. v. Halesowen Presswork, Ltd.*, [1972] A.C. 785, 824.

181. *R. v. Doot*, [1973] A.C. 807, 830.

182. *Broome v. Cassell & Co.*, [1972] A.C. 1027, 1136.

183. [1973] A.C. 435, 496 (1972).

184. [1975] A.C. 653, 700 (N. Ire.), also commenting:

It is an impermissible, or at least an undesirable, mode of law reform to use the occasion of an appeal in a decided case for the purpose of declaring that changing conditions and enlarging opinions have rendered the *ratio decidendi* of the lower court obsolete and therefore susceptible of being set aside. . . . It would in my opinion be a necessary preliminary to the reform of that generally accepted version of the common law that consultations, on a far wider basis than discussions among lawyers, including the arguments of counsel before the highest tribunal, should have taken place and been seriously considered.

185. E.g., *Pettitt v. Pettitt*, [1970] A.C. 777, 794–95 (1969).

passing into law of the Homicide Act 1957 that I have come to the conclusion that this House is entitled to declare the common law basis upon which the rule laid down by Parliament rests, rather than leaving it to Parliament itself to do so."[186] That statement may suggest an emphasis on principle or it may convey a commitment to latent rather than patent legislation—an approach of which Radcliffe would have approved. It may, however, merely imply that Kilbrandon's position was not at that point fully formed, but, if that were so, it also meant that with his retirement at the end of 1976, a fully formulated view would never appear.

Even if the Kilbrandon jurisprudential approach is assumed to have been narrower than Diplock's, for example, it may be that in the future it will seem broad in comparison with the early Lords of Appeal appointed by the Labour Lord Chancellor from 1974 on—Lord Elwyn-Jones.[187] While the Conservative Hailsham favored the appointment of political law lords who might be expected to take a broad approach, professionally, the new Labour Lord Chancellor was a conservative. Elwyn-Jones was, for instance, opposed to the establishment of a Royal Commission on the profession.[188] The conservatism was thought by some to have carried over to his early appointments of Lords of Appeal. The *New Statesman*, the organ of the intellectual wing of the Labour party, argued that in the House of Lords "only one of its judges (Lord Salmon) could be described as a liberal, and a Labour Lord Chancellor ought to have redressed the balance. Instead Elwyn Jones tipped the balance the other way by choosing his old friend Lord Edmund Davies, the most reactionary member of the Court of Appeal. . . . Instead of making a second appointment, Elwyn Jones permitted Lord Hailsham, whose judgments sometimes read like his speeches to associations of conservative ladies, to remain on the bench."[189]

The strong words about Edmund-Davies,[190] a former head of the chambers from which the Lord Chancellor came, were based mainly on the *Eleventh Report of the Criminal Law Revision Committee*, which he chaired.[191] This report, in a general survey of criminal evidence, as has

186. [1975] A.C. 55, 98 (1974).

187. Frederick Elwyn Jones; b. 1909; educ., Llanelli Grammar School, University of Wales, Gonville and Caius, Cambridge; called to bar, 1935; Q.C., 1953; M.P. (Lab.) West Ham, 1945–74; Attorney-General, 1964–70; Lord Chancellor, 1974–.

188. *The Times*, 13 Feb. 1976, at 1. For an important decision by Elwyn Jones, holding that recklessness in getting drunk was sufficient mens rea for offenses committed "under the influence," see *DPP* v. *Majewski*, [1977] A.C. 443, 467 (1976).

189. John Paine, "Labour and the Lawyers" 44.

190. Herbert Edmund-Davies; b. 1906; educ., Mountain Ash Grammar School, King's College, London, Exeter College, Oxford; called to bar, 1929; K.C., 1943; Judge, Queen's Bench Division, 1958–66; Lord Justice, 1966–74; Lord of Appeal, 1974–.

191. Cmnd. 4991 (1972).

been seen, called for changes that included restricting the right of an individual to remain silent both in a police station and in court, abolition of the standard police caution at the time of arrest, as well as extension of the admissibility of hearsay and previous convictions. The report received "strongly critical" notices, not only from Devlin, Dilhorne, Gardiner, Morris, Reid, and Salmon during the debates in the Lords, but even from such normally conservative bodies as the Bar Council and the British Legal Association.[192]

However, it is unclear whether Edmund-Davies' reputation was fully justified. In *Morgan*—in which the House appeared to hold that rape could not be committed if the accused, even unreasonably, thought the woman had consented—Edmund-Davies joined Simon in dissenting from a court dominated by Hailsham.[193] On the other hand, although Simon dissented because of the policy implications of the decision,[194] Edmund-Davies made it clear that he would have preferred to go with the majority but felt obliged to dissent "in accordance with established law."[195] He then went on to urge the legislature to reform "this part of the law,"[196] which would suggest that judicial creativity, at least, did not come naturally to the new law lord.[197] Yet, in a public lecture, he took some umbrage at Professor Louis Jaffé's claim that "There have been great Judges in England [but] the great English Judge [is] a relic of the past."[198] Assimilating judicial creativity and judicial independence, Edmund-Davies responded that "our contemporary Law Reports contain many proofs that it remains a sturdy and flourishing plant. And if there ever was a menopause in judicial law-making, all that I can say is that it must have been of a truly remarkable kind. For not only is it over and done with, but conception has resumed and is clearly proceeding at a brisk pace."[199]

---

192. "Note," 71 *Law Society's Gazette* 954 (1974).

193. [1976] A.C. 182 (1975).

194. "The policy of the law in this regard could well derive from its concern to hold a fair balance between victim and accused. It would hardly seem just to fob off a victim of a savage assault with such comfort as he could derive from knowing that his injury was caused by a belief, however absurd, that he was about to attack the accused. A respectable woman who has been ravished would hardly feel that she was vindicated by being told that her assailant must go unpunished because he believed, quite unreasonably, that she was consenting to sexual intercourse with him"; ibid. 221.

195. Ibid. 235.

196. Ibid. The government responded by agreeing to establish a committee to investigate the law of rape.

197. This assertion is supported by *Miliangos* v. *George Frank, Ltd.*, [1976] A.C. 443 (1975). While agreeing to overrule the *Havana* case, he appeared to justify the overruling partly on the ground that he was dealing with a "rule of procedure"; ibid. 840.

198. Louis L. Jaffé, *English and American Judges as Lawmakers* 1–2.

199. Herbert Edmund-Davies, "Judicial Activism" 1, 14. See also at 13: "[W]hatever a judge does, he will most surely have his critics. If, in an effort to do justice, he appears to

Whatever the long-term implications of the biological analogies, there is probably no reason to expect greater creativity from the second English appointee, Lord Russell.[200] A grandson of the Lord Chief Justice (who had himself been a Lord of Appeal for a few months) and son of the conservative Lord of Appeal in the 1930s, the new Russell had a reputation as a judicial conservative in the Court of Appeal[201] and had in fact been overtaken in the promotion "race" from the Chancery Division by both Wilberforce and Cross.[202] Thus, in both the Edmund-Davies and the Russell appointments, Elwyn-Jones reverted to the earlier tradition of appointing law lords late in life (both were nearly seventy at the time of appointment, relatively close to the now-mandatory retirement age of seventy-five) with almost two decades' experience in the lower courts. Neither had had any political experience.

To fill Reid's place, however, Lord Fraser of Tullybelton[203] was appointed; he was younger, had some political experience and only a decade on the bench. Lord Keith of Kinkel[204] (to be distinguished from his father, Keith of Avonholme), had been a Senator of the Court of Session for some six years when he was appointed at 56 to replace Kilbrandon. Moreover, the replacement for Simon of Glaisdale, Lord Scarman,[205] had been regarded as an outstanding member of the Court of Appeal. Moreover, not only had he served as chairman of the Law Commission, he had also publicly analyzed the judicial implications of a Bill of Rights. Thus while the Elwyn-Jones appointees could cause a swing of the judicial pendulum toward a narrower view of the judicial process, it would be unfair to attempt any such generalization at this stage.

---

make new law, there will be cries that he is overweaning, and that he has rendered uncertain what had long been regarded as established legal principles. On the other hand, if he sticks to the old legal rules, an equally vocal body will charge him with being reactionary, a slave to precedent, and of failing to apply the law to changing social needs."

200. Charles Ritchie Russell; b. 1908; educ., Beaumont, Oriel College, Oxford; called to bar, 1931; K.C., 1948; Judge, Chancery Division, 1960–62; Lord Justice, 1962–75; Lord of Appeal, 1975–.

201. E.g., his position in *Gallie* v. *Lee*, [1969] 2 Ch. 17, 37 (C.A.), taking a narrower view of precedent than Salmon and especially Denning.

202. Richard Roe, "Personal Angle" 119 *Solicitors' Journal* 677 (1975).

203. Walter Ian Reid Fraser; b. 1911; educ., Repton, Balliol College, Oxford, University of Glasgow; Advocate, 1936; Q.C., 1953; (Unionist) Candidate, East Edinburgh, 1955; Dean of the Faculty of Advocates, 1959–64; Senator, College of Justice, 1964–75; Lord of Appeal, 1975–.

204. Henry Shanks Keith; b. 1922; father, Lord of Appeal; educ., Edinburgh Academy, Magdalen College, Oxford, Edinburgh University; Advocate, 1950; Q.C., 1962; Senator, College of Justice, 1971–76; Lord of Appeal, 1976–.

205. Leslie George Scarman; b. 1911; educ., Radley College, Brasenose College, Oxford (First, "Greats"); called to bar, 1937; Q.C., 1957; Judge, Probate, Divorce and Admiralty Division (later Family Division), 1961–73; Chairman, Law Commission, 1965–73; Lord Justice, 1973–77; Lord of Appeal, 1977–.

SIXTEEN

Conclusions and Reflections

The change in judicial style, amounting almost to a change in the nature of the judicial process over the last twenty years, might be expected to have a significant impact on the law. Indeed, it is when one comes to record the changes in substantive law between the mid-fifties and the mid-seventies that the subtlety and importance of the shifts in the approach to the appellate process become increasingly evident. Solicitors in their office might continue to give advice and barristers in their chambers to give opinions on the assumption that legal logic was ten-tenths of the law. No doubt this approach was both proper and economically efficient. Even High Court judges were, however, somewhat more flexible than before, while the Court of Appeal, presided over by Denning for more than half the period, was an obvious source of law.

The House of Lords was in a more ambiguous position than the other courts of law. Except to the cognoscenti, Reid, Wilberforce, and Diplock were unknown, and Kilbrandon, Salmon, and Simon were scarcely household words. Yet within the profession there was a subtle change in perception of the responsibilities of the House; by the mid-seventies it was no longer regarded as the restater of accepted doctrines, bur rather as the incremental developer of new doctrines. The process and progress were not uniform. Any system that allowed a dozen judges to sit in up to three panels with frequent substitutions in personnel was unlikely to give one immutable image. Yet the overall picture had altered, and while the belief in the predictability of "clear rules" was no doubt still stronger than in any other common law jurisdiction, the belief in the anonymity and irrelevance of the judicial contribution had largely evaporated. If the psychological and sociological bases of these changes had still to be probed, the reality of the changes was nevertheless remarkable.

Private Law

Naturally the developments varied with the period and the subject at issue; the move from substantive formalism came primarily after the retirement of Simonds in 1962. From 1963 on, with the ebb and flow to be expected when decisions were made by the fluctuating panels of law lords[1] and when panels were still sometimes constituted with the hope of producing certain results[2] both public and private law showed important signs of change. Substantive formalism gave way to a more natural operation of the judicial process[3] so that it became meaningful to talk in terms of judicial restraint and judicial activism, while the law lords more often discussed the policies they should pursue and the needs of society outside the courts. In private law the rate of change varied considerably. Contract took some while to regain a via media; in tort, despite Radcliffe's skepticism,[4] the movement was decidedly perceptible; in family law, there was rapid progress before Parliament rendered most of the developments moot.

In contract law, in the late fifties and early sixties a number of decisions appeared to confirm the approach that had dominated the House during the Chancellorships of Simon, Jowitt, and Simonds. Among these decisions would have to be included *Davis Contractors, Limited v. Fareham Urban District Council* where the House restated both a narrow role and a rule for the doctrine of frustration.[5] In the *Suisse Atlantique* case,[6] the House largely undid the doctrine of fundamental

---

1. .For a typical example of this, contrast *Hedley Byrne & Co.* v. *Heller & Partners*, [1964] A.C. 465 (1963), where a panel of 5 law lords (Reid, Morris, Hodson, Devlin, Pearce) expanded *Donoghue* v. *Stevenson* to cover at least some elements of negligent misstatements, with *Commissioner of Rys.* v. *Quinlan*, [1964] A.C. 1054, 1084 (P.C.), where a panel of 5 law lords sitting in the Privy Council thought the *Donoghue* v. *Stevenson* principle a "somewhat overworked shorthand"; R. F. V. Heuston, ed., *Salmond on the Law of Torts* 202.

2. See, for instance, the vicissitudes in the composition of the panel in *Hedley Byrne & Co.* v. *Heller & Partners*, [1964] A.C. 465 (1963); Robert Stevens, "*Hedley Byrne v. Heller*" 121.

3. For a litany of the relative roles of creativity at the different levels of the judicial hierarchy, see Brian Abel-Smith and Robert Stevens, *In Search of Justice* 171–72.

4. In *Lister* v. *Romford Ice & Cold Storage Co.*, [1957] A.C. 555, 591–92 (1956), Radcliffe said: "No one really doubts that the common law is a body of law which develops in process of time in response to the development of the society in which it rules. Its movement may not be perceptible at any distinct point in time, nor can we always say how it gets from one point to another; but I do not think that, for all that, we need abandon the conviction of Galileo that somehow, by some means, there is a movement that takes place."

5. [1956] A.C. 696. In *Tsakiroglou & Co.* v. *Noblee Thorl G.m.b.H.*, [1962] A.C. 93 (1961), the House held that the closure of the Suez Canal during the Suez crisis did not frustrate a c.i.f. contract to buy groundnuts at Port Sudan for shipment to Hamburg.

6. [1967] 1 A.C. 361 (1966). See also *G. H. Renton & Co.* v. *Palmyra Trading Corp.*, [1957] A.C. 149 (1956), where an exception clause, which enabled the carrier to discharge

breach of contract, developed by Denning[7] and others[8] as a means of preventing a party's contracting out of all responsibility under a contract.[9] On the other hand, while attempting to "develop" rather than "restrict" a doctrine, in this case the role of penalty clauses in hire purchase contracts, the House managed to impose some order into the law in *Bridge* v. *Campbell Discount Company*[10] holding that in that case the clause in an automobile hiring was in fact a penalty.[11]

That much in the area of contract and commercial law was conservative, in the sense of restating the basic doctrines that had been laid down in the nineteenth century, must be readily admitted. In the area of damages, the *Heron II*[12] superficially reaffirmed *Hadley* v. *Baxendale*, although *White and Carter, Limited* v. *McGregor*[13] weakened the responsibility of the innocent party to mitigate damages after breach. The speeches were, however, lacking in coordination. The House seemed equally unable or unwilling to move away from fixed notions of privity of contract, rejecting the concept of "vicarious immunity" in *Midland Silicones, Limited* v. *Scruttons, Limited*[14] and a frontal assault on privity in *Beswick* v. *Beswick*,[15] and it showed little more initiative in implying

---

timber in Hamburg instead of at an English port, was held not repugnant to the main object or intention of the contract and not null and void under the Hague Rules.

7. In addition to Denning's activities in the lower courts before the *Suisse Atlantique* decision, e.g., *Olley* v. *Marlborough Court Hotel*, [1949] 1 K.B. 552; *Adler* v. *Dickson*, [1955] 1 Q.B. 158 (C.A. 1954), see his post-decision activities. E.g., *Anglo-Continental Holidays* v. *Typaldos Lines London, Ltd.*, [1947] Lloyd's List L.R. 61 (C.A.). See also the Malaysian appeal, *Sze Hai Tong Bank, Ltd.* v. *Rambler Cycle Co.*, [1959] A.C. 576 (P.C.), and the comment on this in G. H. Treitel, *The Law of Contract* 189–90.

8. E.g., Parker in *Karsales, Ltd.* v. *Wallis*, [1956] 1 W.L.R. 936 (C.A.). On this see Louis Blom-Cooper and Gavin Drewry, *Final Appeal* 292.

9. Reid argues, [I]n the earlier cases I do not find any reliance on any rule of law that a party guilty of a breach going to the root of the contract can never rely on clauses excluding his liability"; [1967] 1 A.C. 361, 400 (1966). The effect of Reid's speech appears to be to "reduce" the concept of fundamental breach from a rule of law to a doctrine of construction; ibid. 399. See *Harbutt's "Plasticine," Ltd.* v. *Wayne Tank & Pump Co.*, [1970] 1 Q.B. 447 (C.A.), for the difficulties of interpreting *Suisse Atlantique*. See also P. N. Leigh-Jones and M. Pickering, "Fundamental Breach" 515.

10. [1962] A.C. 600. On this, see G. C. Cheshire, C. H. S. Fifoot, and M. P. Furmston, eds., *The Law of Contract* 604–5.

11. The speeches were, however, lacking in coordination. On the point of whether the contractual sum would have been enforceable if the hirer had exercised his option to determine the agreement, the answers were varied and confusing. Simonds and Morton held that if he had exercised his option he would not have been entitled to relief. Denning and Devlin considered that the court had power to grant relief, however the contract was determined. Radcliffe left the question open.

12. [1969] 1 A.C. 350 (1967). See C. J. Hamson, "Contract and Tort" 15.

13. [1962] A.C. 413 (Scot. 1961). See Arthur L. Goodhart, "Liability for Negligent Misstatements" 263.

14. [1962] A.C. 446 (1961).

15. [1968] A.C. 58 (1967). On this see generally, Treitel, *Law of Contract*, chap. 15. But see now *New Zealand Shipping Co.* v. *A. M. Satterthwaite & Co.*, [1975] A.C. 154 (P.C. 1974).

terms[16] except possibly in the area of sales.[17] The House was, however, happier in construing contracts,[18] and undoubtedly some of its restatements, like that of *non est factum* were justified even in modern terms.[19]

The House did not, however, limit its activities to restating basic nineteenth-century concepts of contract, with isolated excursions into penalty clauses and construction of contracts.[20] On the one hand it showed an almost casual willingness to extend the concept of restrictive covenants,[21] while at the same time vigorously reactivating the public interest element in restraint of trade cases in *Esso Petroleum Company* v. *Harper's Garage, Limited*.[22] Moreover, by 1975 the House was prepared to abrogate its own earlier rule and allow judgments to be given in foreign currencies.[23]

On balance, then, the House regarded itself as less involved in developing contract than other areas of the law. Perhaps it was felt that the program of the Law Commission, particularly its utilitarian urge to codify the law of contract, made serious reforms either unnecessary or impolite.[24] Or perhaps the Simonds assertions were difficult to live down. Whatever

16. In *Trollope & Colls, Ltd.* v. *North West Metropolitan Regional Hosp. Bd.*, [1973] 1 W.L.R. 601 (H.L.), the House appeared to hold that the expectation of reasonable men was not enough to imply a term.

17. E.g., *Hardwick Game Farm* v. *Suffolk Agricultural Poultry Producers Ass'n*, [1969] 2 A.C. 31 (1968); *B. S. Brown & Son* v. *Craikes, Ltd.*, [1970] 1 W.L.R. 752 (H.L. Scot.); *Christopher Hill, Ltd.* v. *Ashington Piggeries, Ltd.*, [1972] A.C. 441 (1971).

18. *Adamastos Shipping Co.* v. *Anglo-Saxon Petroleum Co.*, [1959] A.C. 133 (1958); *East Ham Corp.* v. *Bernard Sunley & Sons*, [1966] A.C. 406 (1965); *Wickman Mach. Tool Sales, Ltd.* v. *L. Schuler A.G.*, [1974] A.C. 235 (1973).

19. *Gallie* v. *Lee*, [1971] A.C. 1004, 1039 (1970).

20. It may well be that the two most important events in the substantive law of contract during the period were the abolition of the Statute of Frauds by the Law Reform (Enforcement of Contracts) Act of 1954 (see Cheshire, Fifoot, and Furmston, *Law of Contract* 172–75) and the passage of the Misrepresentation Act (see Treitel, *Law of Contract*, chap. 9).

21. *Sefton* v. *Tophams, Ltd.*, [1967] 1 A.C. 50 (1966).

22. [1968] A.C. 269 (1966). See J. D. Heydon, "The Frontiers of the Restraint of Trade Doctrine" 229. The House, in this case, was even prepared to look to a report of the Monopolies Commission to determine what amounted to the "public interest." For another vigorous decision in this area, see *Amoco Australian Pty.* v. *Rocca Bros. Motor Eng'r Co.*, [1975] A.C. 561 (P.C.). See also the appeal from the Restrictive Trade Practices Court in *Associated Newspapers, Ltd.* v. *Registrar of Restrictive Trading Agreements*, [1964] 1 W.L.R. 31 (H.L. 1963), where it was held that the Court had jurisdiction to entertain a reference in regard to terminated (as well as subsisting) agreements. See especially the speeches of Devlin (at 61) and Pearce (at 62), who noted that the intent of Parliament in passing the Restrictive Trade Practices Act of 1956 could otherwise be evaded. On this, see Robert Stevens and Basil Yamey, *Restrictive Practices Court* 180–92.

23. *Miliangos* v. *George Frank, Ltd.*, [1976] A.C. 443 (1975).

For another important creative decision, see *Steadman* v. *Steadman*, [1976] A.C. 536 (1974), where Reid led the House of Lords in relaxing the rules of part performance. For a criticism of the decision, see H. W. R. Wade, "Part Performance" 433.

24. See also the Fair Trading Act of 1973 and the Consumer Credit Act of 1974, both in their different ways aimed at the issue of equality of bargaining power.

the reason, contract made a dramatic contrast with tort, for in areas of general liability as well as responsibility under the Factories Acts, dramatic shifts occurred from the mid-fifties to the mid-seventies.

The early period in tort still showed a hint of the glory of fault that found its chief outlet in the decision in the *Wagon Mound*, in which Simonds delivered the judgment of the Judicial Committee of the Privy Council.[25] Moreover, throughout the period the House seemed uncomfortable with its handling of the issue of limitation in personal injury actions.[26] It also exhibited reluctance to modernize in the area of damages,[27] beginning with the early decision in *British Transport Commission* v. *Gourley*[28] holding that computation of damages in accidents had to take into account the notional tax that would have been paid, to the later decisions refusing to use modern actuarial methods for the computation of damages.

25. *Overseas Tankship, Ltd.* v. *Morts Dock & Eng'r. Co. (The Wagon Mound)*, [1961] A.C. 388 (P.C.). It was in this decision that Simonds announced that "justice" and the "common conscience of mankind" justified a move away from the compensatory approach to liability; ibid. 423.

See, generally, Haldane Society, *The Foresight Saga*; P. S. Atiyah, *Accidents, Compensation and the Law* 126. See also *Overseas Tankship (U.K.), Ltd.* v. *Miller S.S. Co. (The Wagon Mound No. 2)*, [1967] 1 A.C. 617 (P.C. 1966), where, on similar facts, the Judicial Committee appeared to come to an inconsistent decision. See R. W. M. Dias, "Trouble on Oiled Waters" 62.

26. In *Cartledge* v. *E. Jopling & Sons*, [1963] A.C. 758, the House held that time ran from the moment the injury was suffered, even if the plaintiff was unaware that it had occurred. See also the *Report of the Committee on Limitation of Action in Cases of Personal Injury*, Cmnd. 1829 (1962) and the Limitation Act of 1963. In *Smith* v. *Central Asbestos Co.*, [1973] A.C. 518, 529 (1972), Reid said that the act "has a strong claim to the distinction of being the worst drafted Act on the statute book." See now Law Reform (Miscellaneous Provisions) Act of 1971 and the Limitation Act of 1975.

27. See, for example, *Mallett* v. *McMonagle*, [1970] A.C. 166, 176 (N. Ire. 1969), where the House endorsed the game of guessing whether a widow had the chance of remarrying and argued that "money should be treated as retaining its value at the date of judgment." Although, in *Taylor* v. *O'Connor*, [1971] A.C. 115 (1970), the law lords were willing to take inflation into account, they refused to be scientific about it. This strange unwillingness to face the realities of damages appeared in other decisions. While there was logic in the decision that the first tortfeasor should not pay less merely because there had been a second tort in *Baker* v. *Willoughby*, [1970] A.C. 467 (1969), coupled with *Naylor* v. *Yorkshire Elec. Bd.*, [1968] A.C. 529 (1967), where "loss of expectation of life" damages were held almost to nominal ones, the House gave the impression it was not happy as arbiter of compensation for personal injuries. E.g., *H. West & Son* v. *Shephard*, [1964] A.C. 326 (1963) (the plaintiff survived as a vegetable; dispute primarily over general damages); *Parry* v. *Cleaver*, [1970] A.C. 1 (1969) (whether a noncontributory pension was to be treated as insurance or taken into account in assessing damages). More impressive was *Mulholland* v. *Mitchell*, [1971] A.C. 666 (1970), where the House upheld the Court of Appeal's decision to admit additional evidence of rising costs of medical care.

28. [1956] A.C. 185 (1955). The law lords voted 6–1 to reduce the potential award from £37,720 to £6,695. The principle was later extended to compensation for loss of profit for the compulsory purchase of business premises: *West Suffolk County Council* v. *W. Rought, Ltd.*, [1957] A.C. 403 (1956), and to certain libel damages, *Lewis* v. *Daily Telegraph, Ltd.*, [1964] A.C. 234 (1963).

In the area of liability as a whole there was no such reluctance to adapt the law. *Hedley Byrne and Company* v. *Heller and Partners*,[29] developing liability for certain negligent statements, was an outstanding example of judicial creativity; *Hughes* v. *Lord Advocate*,[30] provided an important break with some of the limitations of the forseeability requirement in the tort of negligence; *Henderson* v. *Henry E. Jenkins and Sons*[31] and *Dorset Yacht Company* v. *Home Office*[32] pointed toward the development of some theory of strict liability; and *Herrington* v. *British Railways Board*,[33] building on the Occupiers' Liability Act of 1957, extended a duty of care toward child trespassers that "should send a shiver of disquiet through every occupier of land in the country."[34] Within the context of the somewhat erratic nature of the common law, with aberrant policy decisions like *Rondel* v. *Worsley*[35] in which the House exempted the bar from the full rigors of the law of negligence, the trend toward liability was remarkably consistent, reflecting what was apparently a coherent judicial approach to the field.[36]

In terms of change of position between the mid-fifties and mid-seventies there could be no more provocative area than the general area of "master-servant" law, specifically the Factories Acts. It was in the early years of this period that, in *Lister* v. *Romford Ice*[37] the House held

29. [1964] A.C. 465 (1963). On this see Stevens, *"Hedley Byrne v. Heller"* 121.

30. [1963] A.C. 837 (Scot.).

31. [1970] A.C. 282 (1969). (Where a lorry ran downhill as result of an unexplained failure of the brakes, it was up to the owner to disprove negligence.)

32. [1970] A.C. 1004 (duty of care to keep borstal boys under supervision).

33. [1972] A.C. 877. For the earlier period before the 1957 act, see A. C. *Billings & Sons* v. *Riden*, [1958] A.C. 240 (1957).

34. I. S. Stephenson, "Trespassers and Judicial Innovation" 663.

35. [1969] 1 A.C. 191 (1967). See also the refusal to extend the concept of vicarious liability through "the family car"; *Launchbury* v. *Morgans*, [1973] A.C. 127 (1972).

36. This must be looked at in the whole context of liability. See Atiyah, *Accidents, Compensation and the Law*, chap. 3.

The period was also marked by considerable libel litigation. In favor of protecting the plaintiff, the House held in *Speidel* v. *Plato Films, Ltd.*, [1961] A.C. 1090, that evidence of particular acts of misconduct by the plaintiff could not be given in mitigation, the court being concerned with established reputation, not with actual character nor with deserved reputation. In *Associated Newspapers, Ltd.* v. *Dingle*, [1964] A.C. 371 (1962), it was held that the court should not take into account the effect of the publication of the same libel by other persons on other occasions and should not reduce the damages because the plaintiff's reputation had already been tarnished by a privileged parliamentary report. On the other hand, in *Lewis* v. *Daily Telegraph, Ltd.*, [1964] A.C. 234 (1963), it was held that a statement that someone was being investigated by the Fraud Squad did not, in its ordinary meaning, imply that the plaintiff was guilty of fraud. *Morgan* v. *Odhams Press, Ltd.*, [1971] 1 W.L.R. 1239 (H.L.) dealt with the requirement that the defamatory matter had clearly to refer to the plaintiff, while *Broome* v. *Cassell & Co.*, [1972] A.C. 1027, faced the thorny issue of exemplary damages.

37. [1957] A.C. 555 (1956); see K. W. Wedderburn, *The Worker and the Law* 71–72. The drastic consequences implied by this case for drivers were averted by a "gentleman's"

that if an employer had suffered loss as a result of being held vicariously liable for the negligence of an employee in driving the employer's vehicle, the employer might recover all the damages from the employee by virtue of an implied term in the contract of service to the effect that the driver would perform his duties with due care. So too, in determining the responsibilities of an employer toward his employee at common law, the House unanimously rejected in *Davie* v. *New Merton Board Mills, Limited* the view that an employer whose system of maintenance and inspection was not at fault and who had bought the tool from a reputable dealer should be liable for injury caused by a latent defect in the tool.[38]

Also at the beginning of this period a series of decisions reflected the Simonds approach to the Factories Acts.[39] In *Close* v. *Steel Company of Wales*[40] the appellant was operating an insecurely fenced electric drill when the bit shattered; he was struck and injured in the eye when the pieces flew out. The House unanimously demolished his case by holding that the risk of grave injury was not forseeable and that, therefore, the bit was not a dangerous part of the machine. The majority argued that, in any event, the claim failed because the decisions in *Nicholls*[41] and *Carroll*[42] had held that the duty was confined to preventing the workman from coming into contact with the machine and did not extend to injury caused by pieces ejected by the machine. In *Close*, the Court of Appeal had in effect asked that the implications of *Nicholls* be limited by the House in keeping with various Court of Appeal decisions attempting to ameliorate the position. The House chose, instead, to declare the Court of Appeal decisions to be wrong. The ball was smashed back into the legislature's court. Some law lords appreciated that *Close* was an unfor-

---

agreement among insurers not to take advantage of the decision. An Interdepartmental Committee appointed by the Minister of Labour in 1957 suggested that legislative reform was not needed. See Gerald Gardiner, "*Lister* v. *The Romford Ice and Cold Storage Company, Ltd.*" 652.

38. [1959] A.C. 604 (1958). See Simonds at 627: "It is not the function of a court of law to fasten upon the fortuitous circumstance of insurance to impose a greater burden on the employer than would otherwise lie upon him." Wedderburn, *Worker and Law* 185–86, points out that the nonliability of the employer is critical if, for example, the supplier is not known, if he is bankrupt, or if two different tools disintegrate and the employee cannot tell which is defective.

On the other hand, the House reaffirmed that no such defense is open to a shipowner in respect of the negligence of independent contractors in response to a claim for not exercising "due diligence" in making a ship seaworthy, when injury to goods was at stake. See *Riverstone Meat Co.* v. *Lancashire Shipping Co.*, [1961] A.C. 807 (1960).

39. Especially § 14: "Every dangerous part of any machinery . . . shall be securely fenced."

40. [1962] A.C. 367 (1961).

41. *Nicholls* v. *F. Austin, Ltd.*, [1946] A.C. 493.

42. *Carroll* v. *Andrew Barclay & Sons*, [1948] A.C. 477 (Scot.).

tunate decision, while politicians were not beyond reminding them of this.[43] Yet the House proceeded to hold itself bound by *Close* in *Sparrow v. Fairey Aviation Company*.[44]

The "ladder" cases from this same period confirm the reluctance of the House of Lords to take a compensatory approach to the Factories Act.[45] The matter was by no means easy. The strange compromises made in the late forties, at the time of the abolition of workmen's compensation and the establishment of a comprehensive system of insurance, left both common law and statutory negligence in an odd kind of limbo. Even in the light of this, some decisions were difficult to follow. In 1965, after an earlier series of decisions clarifying the common law duty of care owed by an employer,[46] the House in *Imperial Chemical Industries, Limited v. Shatwell*[47] went some distance toward undermining the statutory reforms in industrial accident law that had been made in the post-1945 period. While under the Law Reform (Contributory Negligence) Act of 1945, contributory negligence could still be held to amount to 100 percent and therefore the defendant might be refused recovery, this was not possible where two fellow employees had both been negligent, since the common employment (fellow servant) rule had been abolished by the Law Reform (Personal Injuries) Act of 1948. Yet in *Shatwell* the House

43. In the Lords, Lord Shepherd claimed "that . . . it has been the decisions of the House of Lords in its Judicial capacity that have eroded the protection enjoyed by the factory workers for 68 years"; 248 *Parl. Deb.*, H.L. (5th ser.), col. 1326 (25 Apr. 1963).

44. [1964] A.C. 1019 (1962). See also Reid's speech, 248 *Parl. Deb.*, H.L. (5th ser.), col. 1338 (25 Apr. 1963).

In *Sparrow*, the blade of the tool the appellant was using caught against the dangerous part of the lathe and flung his hand against the chuck of the lathe (a nondangerous part), injuring his finger. He alleged a breach of the duty to fence. The majority held that the House was bound by the *Close* case and that there was no duty to fence against the possibility that the tool the operator was using might come into contact with such dangerous parts. Reid noted, "It is too late to question the rule which this House laid down in Close's case, and we must do our best to apply it in a practical way"; [1964] A.C. 1019, 1034.

For later "fencing" cases going the other way, see *Irwin v. White Tomkins & Courage, Ltd.*, [1964] 1 W.L.R. 387 (H.L., N. Ire.); *Gardiner v. Admiralty Comm'rs*, [1964] 1 W.L.R. 590 (H.L.).

45. E.g., *Wigley v. British Vinegars, Ltd.*, [1964] A.C. 307 (1962); *McWilliams v. Sir William Arrol & Co.*, [1962] 1 W.L.R. 295 (H.L., Scot.). Blom-Cooper and Drewry, *Final Appeal* 297, agree that "[t]he high-water mark of judicial exoneration of employer-liability came in *McWilliams v. Sir William Arrol & Co. Ltd.*"

Wedderburn cites two possible causes of these general trends: first, a general middle-class feeling that the workers were doing pretty well and that the employers needed some protection; and second, the addition of legal aid to already available trade union assistance enabled all employees to attempt to enforce their rights in court; *Worker and Law* 210.

46. See *Morris v. West Hartlepool Steam Navigation Co.*, [1956] A.C. 552 (1955); *Qualcast, Ltd. v. Haynes*, [1959] A.C. 743; *Cavanagh v. Ulster Weaving Co.*, [1960] A.C. 145 (N. Ire. 1959).

47. [1965] A.C. 656 (1964). See Paul Brodetsky, "Employees' Joint Breach of Statutory Duty" 733.

announced that the plaintiff could still be prevented from recovering by the application of the doctrine of *volenti non fit injuria*,[48] which most assumed had passed from the stage.

There is evidence, however, that in the late sixties the House attempted to achieve more of a balance by adopting a more compensatory approach to industrial injuries. In *John G. Stein and Company v. O'Hanlon*[49] the House provided considerable protection for the workman by reading the Mines and Quarries Act of 1954 literally. Similarly when the House had difficulty holding for the plaintiff in *Westwood v. National Coal Board*,[50] the law lords unanimously found that there was a breach of duty in common law negligence;[51] while, in *Donaghey v. Boulton and Paul, Limited*,[52] the House unanimously allowed the plaintiff, who had fallen through a hole, to recover against the owner of a hangar for a violation of the Buildings Regulations, when the plaintiff's employer turned out to be a man of straw.

In *Nimmo v. Alexander Cowan and Sons, Limited*,[53] the House appeared to have put the burden of proof on the employer under the Factories Act to show that "every such place shall, so far as is reasonably practical, be made and kept safe for any person working there."[54] In *British Railways Board v. Liptrot*,[55] the House held that a crane was a dangerous machine under the Factories Act and there was therefore an obligation to fence. In a later fencing case, *Johnson v. F. E. Callow Limited*,[56] the plaintiff recovered after his hand was injured by being trapped between a lathe and a boring-bar. Finally, in *Westwood v. Post Office*,[57] the majority of the House applied the Office, Shops, and Railways Act of 1963 to an area of the building where the plaintiff was clearly a trespasser.[58]

48. For a similar development, where the duty was imposed on both employer and employee and the House had to curb somewhat the use of *volenti*, see *Ross v. Associated Portland Cement Mfrs.*, [1964] 1 W.L.R. 768 (H.L.); and *Boyle v. Kodak, Ltd.*, [1969] 1 W.L.R. 661 (H.L.). On *Ross*, see R. W. L. Howells, "A Positive Safety Policy" 738.

49. [1965] A.C. 890 (Scot.).

50. [1967] 1 W.L.R. 871 (H.L.).

51. There were, of course, many borderline cases, most of which might be distinguished as trivial. In *Price v. Claudgen, Ltd.*, [1967] 1 W.L.R. 575 (H.L.), a man working on neon tubes attached to a cinema was held not to be working on a building. In *J. & F. Stone Lighting & Radio, Ltd. v. Haygarth*, [1968] A.C. 157 (1966), a television repair shop was held to be a factory.

52. [1968] A.C. 1 (1967).

53. [1968] A.C. 107 (Scot. 1967).

54. In *Jenkins v. Allied Ironfounders, Ltd.*, [1970] 1 W.L.R. 304 (H.L. 1969), however, the House held that there was no violation of the duty under § 28(1) of the Factories Act to keep floors free from any obstruction.

55. [1969] 1 A.C. 136 (1967).

56. [1971] A.C. 335 (1970).

57. [1974] A.C. 1 (1973).

58. See also *McGhee v. National Coal Bd.*, [1973] 1 W.L.R. 1 (H.L., Scot. 1972),

The second decade of the period had thus somewhat redressed the balance of the first. Yet any inconsistencies in approach were at least as much the responsibility of Parliament as of the law lords. With the coming of comparative negligence, the argument for strict liability for statutory duties was less clear. Indeed, the Monckton Committee on Alternative Remedies in 1946 effectively recommended that there no longer be strict liability, after compensation was automatically provided by the Industrial Injuries Act of 1946.[59] In this respect, the law lords of the mid-seventies were still seeking to strike a balance, a process most obvious in Diplock's speech in *Haigh* v. *Charles W. Ireland, Ltd.*[60]

The pattern of development was rather different in family law. In the early sixties cruelty was consciously redefined in *Gollins*[61] and *Williams*[62] so as to exclude the necessity of an intention to hurt on the part of the so-called offender; but other evidence pointed to a relaxation of attitudes apparently in conformity with changing social mores. Despite the generally conservative strictures of the Royal Commission on Marriage and Divorce that reported in 1956,[63] in *Blyth*[64] earlier authority, suggesting that the proof of adultery required in a divorce case was akin to the criminal standard of proof, was rejected.[65]

Yet in jurisprudential if not in social terms the most significant decision to the area of family law was probably *Indyka*.[66] A few years earlier in *Ross Smith*,[67] the House had seemed unwilling to expand the traditionally narrow view of jurisdiction in matrimonial cases, but in *Indyka* a new attitude appeared to be afoot. A wife who retained both Czechoslovakian nationality and residence was held to have gained a Czech divorce legally despite her husband's residence in England. In so holding the House took the view that, since *Le Mesurier* v. *Le Mesurier*[68]— establishing as it did a jurisdictional test of domicile—was judge-made law, the House was entitled to relax the rule in appropriate circum-

---

holding that the causation element in negligence might be provided by a breach of duty that materially increased the risk of injury (in that case the nonprovision of washing facilities by the employer at a brickworks, which increased the risk to the employee of dermatitis), even though it be not proved exactly *how* the breach of duty caused the damage.

59. Atiyah, *Accidents, Compensation and the Law* 146–50.
60. [1974] 1 W.L.R. 43, 54–55 (H.L., Scot. 1973).
61. [1974] A.C. 644 (1963).
62. [1964] A.C. 698 (1963).
63. Cmnd. 9678 (1956).
64. [1966] A.C. 643 (1965).
65. The decision, *inter alia*, threw doubt on the House's decision in *Preston-Jones* v. *Preston-Jones*, [1951] A.C. 391 (1950). But see also *Godfrey* v. *Godfrey*, [1965] A.C. 444 (1964), where it was held that the causal connection between connivance and adultery still remained.
66. [1969] 1 A.C. 33 (1967).
67. [1963] A.C. 280 (1962).
68. [1895] A.C. 517 (No. 2) (P.C.).

stances. In effect, then, the House did what Parliament had refused to do in 1959.[69] This judicial legislation was ultimately overtaken by parliamentary reform. The overall effect of the Divorce Reform Act of 1969[70] was to take the "law" largely out of the divorce "business," and the House was left with other aspects of family law.[71] In general, however, the House had few problems in adapting the general principles to rapidly changing family mores.[72]

Public Law

If, in private law, the House moved the law back to a new central position and assumed greater responsibility for remolding doctrine, the scene in public law was appreciably more dramatic. Between 1956 and 1976 tax law was transformed from a game of formal rules to the point where some saw the House as the partner of the Commissioners of Inland Revenue; in labor law, the House sometimes on its own and sometimes following parliamentary mandates, made various incursions into the field; in the area of constitutional law proper, the House made bold efforts to develop a meaningful English administrative law; and, beginning in 1961, the House became heavily involved with criminal law.

69. See the Matrimonial Causes (Jurisdiction) Bill of 1959.

70. The basic ground on which a divorce was thereafter granted was that the "marriage has broken down irretrievably." See Jennifer Levin, "The Divorce Reform Act, 1969" 633. See now also the Matrimonial Causes Act of 1973. The only reported case appears to be *Skone* v. *Skone*, [1971] 1 W.L.R. 812 (H.L.), although even this was primarily a case on the law of evidence.

71. E.g., *Pettitt* v. *Pettitt*, [1970] A.C. 777 (1969), interpreting the Married Women's Property Act of 1882; *Gissing* v. *Gissing*, [1971] A.C. 886 (1970), and *Tarr* v. *Tarr*, [1973] A.C. 254 (1972), interpreting § 1(2) of the Matrimonial Homes Act of 1967, passed to alleviate *National Provincial Bank, Ltd.* v. *Ainsworth*, [1965] A.C. 1175; *O'Connor* v. *A. & B.*, [1971] 1 W.L.R. 1227 (H.L., Scot.) and *S.* v. *McC.*, [1972] A.C. 24 (1970), both on adoption without the natural parents' consent; *J.* v. *C.*, [1970] A.C. 668 (1969), on guardianship.

72. This study seriously glosses over various aspects of private law. For trademark, patent, and copyright cases, see Blom-Cooper and Drewry, *Final Appeal* 298–307; for charity cases, see *Glasgow Corp.* v. *Johnstone*, [1965] A.C. 609 (Scot. 1964); *Scottish Burial Reform & Cremation Soc'y, Ltd.* v. *Glasgow Corp.*, [1968] A.C. 138 (Scot. 1967); *in re Resch's Will & Trusts*, [1969] 1 A.C. 514 (P.C. 1967); and *Dingle* v. *Turner*, [1972] A.C. 601.

There were important conflicts cases during the period. See, for instance, the early case, *Regazzoni* v. *K. C. Sethia, Ltd.*, [1958] A.C. 301 (1957), where the House held that on the grounds of public policy and international comity the English courts would not enforce an English contract the performance of which involved an act in a foreign and friendly state, violating the law of that state. Other conflict cases are *Rahimtoola* v. *Nizam of Hyderabad*, [1958] A.C. 379 (1957), where the House held that a bailee of a foreign sovereign's property could plead sovereign immunity; in *in re United Rys. of Havana & Regla Warehouses, Ltd.*, [1961] A.C. 1007 (1960), it was held, *inter alia*, that the rate of exchange when the sum in question fell due and was not paid should be taken as the conversion rate of a debt into sterling. Cf. now *Miliangos* v. *George Frank, Ltd.*, [1976] A.C. 443 (1975).

In many ways the most dramatic change of direction during the period was in tax law. This was significant not only because roughly a third of the House's work was in tax[73] and there was a constant interaction between the House's decisions and subsequent Finance Acts,[74] but also because tax law was the most extreme example of the retreat from substantive formalism. In 1960, for instance, when the influence of Simonds was still strong, the House decided *Public Trustee* v. *Inland Revenue Commissioners*,[75] where it was held that the two sections of the 1894 Finance Act describing estate duty charges were not mutually exclusive; and so allowed settlors an opportunity of avoiding tax. In the same year (1962) that the House was deciding *Griffiths* v. *J. P. Harrison, Limited*,[76] where the majority of law lords appeared to approve of "dividend stripping," it was also deciding *in re Pilkington Will Trusts*,[77] where it was held that the power of advancement conferred by section 32 of the Trustee Act of 1925 could be validly exercised for the purpose of saving estate duty and surtax by means of a resettlement. In the following year, in *Inland Revenue Commissioners* v. *Lord Rennell*,[78] the House allowed a large class of beneficiaries, and not merely the "happy couple," to be counted as beneficiaries of a marriage settlement and thereby avoid the tentacles of estate duty.[79]

Despite these decisions and some concern about earlier tax avoidance schemes,[80] the arrival of cases concerning section 28 of the 1960 Finance

73. Between 1952 and 1968, out of 466 appeals the House heard 127 revenue cases and 23 rating cases. Between 1952 and 1970, of the 133 revenue appeals, 54 percent were concerned with income tax, 16 percent with estate duty, 10 percent with surtax, 8 percent with stamp duty, 8 percent with profits and excess profits tax, and 4 percent with excess profits levy, Selective Employment Tax, etc.; Blom-Cooper and Drewry, *Final Appeal* 246, 322.

74. Between 1952 and 1970 the legislature reversed 27 (of the 133) House of Lords tax decisions: on 18 occasions when the Crown lost and 9 when the Crown had won; ibid. 323.

For examples from early in this period, see *in re Ralli's Settlement*, [1966] A.C. 483, nullified by the Finance Act of 1966, § 90; *Wm. Cory & Son* v. *IRC*, [1965] A.C. 1088, nullified by the Finance Act of 1965, § 90; *Whitworth Park Coal Co.* v. *IRC*, [1961] A.C. 31 (1960), retrospectively nullified by the Finance Act of 1960, § 39. The House appealed for remedial legislation in *IRC* v. *Hinchy*, [1960] A.C. 748, which came in the Finance Act of 1960.

75. [1960] A.C. 398 (1959). This case delivered the death blow to Lord Macnaghten's "dictum" in *Earl Cowley* v. *IRC*, [1899] A.C. 198, that the two sections were mutually exclusive. These dicta had already been weakened by Radcliffe's remarks in *Sanderson* v. *IRC*, [1956] A.C. 491, 500 (1955).

76. [1963] A.C. 1 (1962). In *Collco Dealings, Ltd.* v. *IRC*, [1962] A.C. 1 (1961), however, the House had refused to sanction "dividend stripping" through the use of Irish residents.

77. [1964] A.C. 612 (1962).

78. [1964] A.C. 173 (1963).

79. Section 408 of the 1952 Finance Act, for instance, was not enthusiastically received by the law lords. See, for instance, *De Vigier* v. *IRC*, [1964] 1 W.L.R. 1073 (H.L.); *Bates* v. *IRC*, [1968] A.C. 483 (1966).

80. The change of approach around 1960 was heralded by a gradual weakening of

Act caused a change in attitudes.[81] Reid, for instance, in *Pilkington*[82] and other cases still took a conservative, although by no means extreme, position.[83] Yet in the first decision under section 28, Wilberforce stated a broad position. "I do not find it possible to discern in this Act any indication that it was the purpose of the legislature to limit it to any specific form of tax avoidance. The scheme and drafting, not only of Section 28 but of the preceding sections, is far too general to admit of the suggested restriction and I do not think that interpretation should seek to narrow this generality."[84]

Yet this was apparently an area in which any residual doubts about approach were eased by the 1966 Practice Statement. On the same day that the House announced that it would no longer be bound by its own prior decisions, it decided *Bishop (Inspector of Taxes) v. Finsbury Securities, Limited*,[85] which, while not overruling *Griffith v. Harrison*, appeared to distinguish it out of existence. This approach was developed in *Cleary v. Inland Revenue Commissioners*,[86] where the House had no difficulty in finding a "tax advantage" when sisters engaged in selling the shares of one company, which they controlled, to another controlled company. The law lords continued this tone in their approach to section 28 cases. In *Greenberg v. Inland Revenue Commissioners*,[87] the House applied the section to partially completed avoidance devices, while *Lupton v. F. A. and A. B., Limited*[88] put an end to the forward dividend strip.[89]

In artificial tax avoidance devices not covered by the antiavoidance

---

substantive formalism, reflected by an increasing emphasis on the facts of the particular appeal.

See, e.g., cases on the definition of trading revenue and expenditure that reduced the precedential value of each decision to virtually zero: *Strick v. Regent Oil Co.*, [1966] A.C. 295 (1964); *Moriarty v. Evans Medical Supplies, Ltd.*, [1958] 1 W.L.R. 66 (H.L. 1957); *Constr. Co. v. Bullock*, [1960] A.C. 351 (1959); and especially the Reid and Upjohn dissents in *Chancery Lane Safe Deposit & Offices Co. v. IRC*, [1966] A.C. 85, 101, 124 (1965).

81. Although see *IRC v. Brebner*, [1967] 2 A.C. 18 (Scot.) (where the device was held to be a bona fide commercial transaction); *Bates v. IRC*, [1968] A.C. 483 (1966) (construing another antiavoidance device in § 408 of the Income Tax Act of 1952).

82. [1964] A.C. 612, 630 (1962).

83. "So long as one adheres to the natural meaning of the charging words the law is certain, or at least as certain as it is possible to make it. But if courts are to give to charging words what is sometimes called a liberal construction, who can say just how far this will go. It is much better that evasion should be met by amending legislation"; *Wm. Cory & Son v. IRC*, [1965] A.C. 1088, 1107.

84. *IRC v. Parker*, [1966] A.C. 141, 176 (Scot. 1965). Wilberforce also stressed the independence of § 28 from all other income tax legislation; ibid. 180.

85. [1966] 1 W.L.R. 1402 (H.L.). And see J. G. M[unroe], "Judicial Precedent" 77.

86. [1968] A.C. 766 (1967).

87. [1972] A.C. 109 (1971).

88. [1972] A.C. 634 (1971). Although Morris was able to distinguish *Griffiths v. Harrison*, it was doubted by Dilhorne.

89. Followed in *Thomson v. Gurneville Securities, Ltd.*, [1972] A.C. 661 (1971).

sections, it was also possible to see a growing sense on the part of the law lords that the community at large had ultimately to pay for the excessive greed of individual taxpayers and that a more balanced policy approach might involve a more flexible attitude toward interpretation and doctrine. In *Campbell* v. *Inland Revenue Commissioners*[90] the House refused to allow a business and a charity to be run in such a parallel way that effectively the charity would recover from the Inland Revenue Commission the amounts paid by the company by way of tax. The same—or perhaps an even stronger—approach characterized *Inland Revenue Commissioners* v. *Mills*,[91] where a film star was employed at a salary of four hundred pounds per year for five years by a company that sold her services to Walt Disney for an appreciably greater sum. The difference was then paid out to shareholders who were trustees of a trust, the sole beneficiary of which was the actress herself. While "lifting the veil" in such cases might not strike an outsider as particularly dramatic, in terms of the attitudes reflected in the *Duke of Westminster*'s case (and many decisions that followed it) the new attitude was remarkable.[92]

There is no suggestion, of course, that the Revenue always won. Far from it.[93] Yet a dramatic change had taken place. In the mid-fifties the

90. [1969] A.C. 77 (1968).
91. [1975] A.C. 38 (1974).
92. The sympathy for the problems of the Revenue authorities seemed to go further than this. Even where there was no artificial transaction involved, but a genuine transaction dressed up to minimize tax, the House looked carefully. E.g., *Land Securities Inv. Trust, Ltd.* v. *IRC*, [1969] 1 W.L.R. 604 (H.L.) (rent charges treated as capital). The House similarly showed little interest in weakening the old rule that travel expenses between a man's home and his place of work were not deductible under Schedule E, although in *Pook* v. *Owen*, [1970] A.C. 244 (1969), they held that expenses were deductible. The doctor was held to have two places of work: the hospital to which he was attached and the town in which he practiced. But cf. *Heaton* v. *Bell*, [1970] A.C. 728 (1969), where gross income, before the deduction for use of a firm's car, was the basis of taxable income; and *Fleming* v. *Associated Newspapers, Ltd.*, [1973] A.C. 628 (1972), limited deductions of business expenses for payments by a newspaper to informers and contacts.

The House also seemed generous toward the Revenue in allowing it to substitute its own methods of valuing stock-in-trade rather than the commercially acceptable methods used by the taxpayer; *B.S.C. Footwear* v. *Ridgeway*, [1972] A.C. 544 (1971). See also a similar requirement in connection with the double taxation convention; *Bowater Paper Corp.* v. *Murgatroyd (Inspector of Taxes)*, [1970] A.C. 266 (1969). See also *IRC* v. *Helical Bar, Ltd.*, [1972] A.C. 733.

The House even went so far as to limit the taxpayer's right to be heard when assessments were being made. E.g., *Wiseman* v. *Borneman*, [1971] A.C. 297 (1969), where the House held that there was no right to be heard before the commission when a taxpayer was assessed under § 28. Similarly, in *Pearlberg* v. *Varty*, [1972] 1 W.L.R. 534 (H.L.), the House held that there was no right to be heard where an assessment was made, under § 6(1) of the Income Tax Management Act of 1964, where the taxpayer had failed to file returns for several years.

93. For a good example of a case where the Revenue might have been expected to win and did not, see *IRC* v. *Brander & Cruickshank*, [1971] 1 W.L.R. 212 (H.L., Scot. 1970). The Revenue failed in its efforts to have payments made to a company secretary by way of

accepted approach to tax legislation was that, being penal in nature, the legislation had to be read narrowly and unless the actual transaction or income was "charged," i.e., covered by the exact words of this section, taxation was not payable. By the mid-1960s the situation had changed noticeably. Led by Reid, whose own views apparently had been modified, the House had come to read tax legislation like other legislation and while still chary of taxing by analogy, the law lords sought the meaning of tax provisions by looking to the whole purpose of the section or the act, rather than at the actual words used.

No doubt section 28 of the 1960 Finance Act—the broad anti-avoidance section—had had its impact. Yet in turn this section was dramatically strengthened by sections 460 and 467 of the Income and Corporation Taxes Act of 1970. While optimistic "tax planners" still hoped the tide would turn,[94] by the mid-seventies a headline in *The Times* announced, "Lords Affirm Wide Interpretation of Tax Avoidance Laws."[95] This item referred to Wilberforce's speech in *Inland Revenue Commissioners* v. *Joiner*,[96] in which he traced the dramatic changes in tax law, particularly after 1960. No doubt the pendulum may swing again in the following decades, but it is unlikely that the legislature and judiciary will ever again—at least in tax law—take the position of positive indifference to one another that characterized their relationships in the mid-fifties.

The swing of the pendulum would be an inappropriate analogy to describe the House's involvement with labor law; "incursions" seems a more appropriate word. After thirteen years of Conservative government, the House in 1964, in expanding the tort of intimidation in *Rookes* v. *Barnard*,[97] coupled it with a narrow interpretation of the Trade Disputes Act of 1906,[98] a combination of factors that made it appear at the

---

compensation for loss of office treated under Schedule D (taxable) rather than Schedule E (where "golden handshakes" under £5,000 were not taxable).

94. See especially J. B. Morean, "Tax Avoidance" 83. The author of that article purported to see some of the spirit of the *Duke of Westminster* case in *Ransom* v. *Higgs*, [1974] 1 W.L.R. 1594 (H.L.).

95. The Times Law Report, 26 Nov. 1976, *The Times*, 27 Nov. 1965, at 9.

96. [1975] 1 W.L.R. 1701, 1703 (H.L.). Wilberforce accepted that Reid's speech in *Greenberg* v. *IRC* had "called for a different method of interpretation from that traditionally used in taxing Acts. For whereas it is generally the rule that clear words are required to impose a tax, so that the taxpayer has the benefit of doubts or ambiguities, Lord Reid made it clear that the scheme of the sections, introducing as they did a wide and general attack on tax avoidance, required that expressions which might otherwise have been cut down in the interest of precision were to be given the wide meaning evidently intended, even though they led to a conclusion short of which judges would normally desire to stop."

97. [1964] A.C. 1129. Actually the return of the House to labor law was first seen in *Bonsor* v. *Musicians' Union*, [1956] A.C. 104 (1955).

98. In particular, the House interpreted § 3 of the 1966 act narrowly by holding that

time as if union officials would effectively be liable once again for damages resulting from strikes.[99] Even though the decision was quickly reversed by the newly elected Labour government,[100] the threat posed by the decision to the immunity of unions in general and the closed shop in particular was apparently underlined by *J. T. Stratford and Company* v. *Lindley*, conceding a remedy in tort where barges had been "blacked."[101] The overall impact of these two decisions led to Harold Wilson's appointment of the Donovan Commission and, indirectly, to the attempt to curb some of the power of the unions in the Industrial Relations Bill of 1970.[102]

Although Wilson ultimately withdrew from a potential battle with the unions, the Heath administration had no such qualms, and the Industrial Relations Act of 1971 provided for appeals to the Lords from the new Industrial Relations Court. The new act,[103] besides providing a presumption that collective bargaining agreements were legally enforceable, made numerous other changes, including the development of something that might be described as a statutory tort—the unfair industrial practice. In *Heatons Transport, Limited* v. *Transport and General Workers' Union*, the House was faced with the question of whether what was agreed to be an unfair industrial practice (the "blacking" of lorries) had been committed by the union or only by its officers. Freed by the Industrial Relations Act from the strict rules of evidence, the House, in a "joint judgement" read by Wilberforce, found the union liable, overruling the Court of Appeal.[104]

During this period the House also had to interpret other labor legislation. The provision in the Redundancy Payments Act of 1965 exonerating the employer from making a redundancy payment if he had made to the employee "an offer in writing to renew his contract of employment, or to re-engage him under a new contract" was tested in *McCreadie* v.

Parliament had failed to appreciate the existence of a tort of interference with business; [1964] A.C. 1129; see especially Reid, at 1174, and Devlin, at 1215–16. Devlin, in particular, was not prepared to let the act "hobble the common law in all classes of disputes lest its range is too wide to suit industrial disputes or to give the statute a wider scope than it was ever intended to have"; ibid. 1218.

99. For the various interpretations, see especially K. W. Wedderburn, "Intimidation and the Right to Strike" 257; L. Hoffman, "*Rookes* v. *Barnard*" 116.

100. Trade Disputes Act of 1965. See, for instance, the speech of Gardiner, 267 *Parl. Deb.*, H.L. (5th ser.), cols. 76–83 (15 June 1965).

101. [1965] A.C. 269 (1964). See K. W. Wedderburn, "*Stratford & Son, Ltd.* v. *Lindley*" 205.

102. Harold Wilson, *A Personal Record* 537–39, 640–49.

103. Now largely repealed by the Trade Union and Labour Relations Act of 1974. See, generally, Michael Moran, *The Politics of Industrial Relations*.

104. [1973] A.C. 15, 94 (1972). The joint judgment seemed to hold that the union would be liable unless the shop stewards had been ordered to stop the "blacking."

Thompson and MacIntyre (Patternmakers), Ltd.,[105] while *Fitzgerald v. Hall, Russell and Company*[106] was concerned with the Contracts of Employment Act of 1963. In terms of the judicial process, however, the cases concerning expulsion from a union were more important. While the law lords at times seemed harsh in their treatment of unions battling employers, they seemed relatively lax in requiring high standards of unions vis-à-vis their own members.[107] Yet again the tide may have turned, although the legislature remained reluctant to allow the law lords to develop their own concepts of labor law.

While the legislature moved to intervene when the law lords had undertaken to rework areas of labor law, Parliament showed no such urge to rework the law lords' efforts in reintroducing a limited concept of procedural due process. There was, of course, a long way to go. The period began with *Smith* v. *East Elloe Rural District Council*, in which the majority was prepared to hold that an order made in bad faith could not be quesitoned when the jurisdiction of the courts had been excluded by the enabling legislation;[108] but from that point onward, the emphasis in procedural due process grew steadily. In *Pyx Granite Company* v. *Ministry of Housing and Local Government*,[109] although the decisions of the minister were said to be "final,"[110] the House held that this did not exclude the jurisdiction of the court to grant declarations. "It is a principle not by any means to be whittled down that the subject's recourse to Her Majesty's courts for the determination of his rights is not to be excluded except by clear words."[111] This concept slowly grew stronger. In *Anisminic, Limited* v. *Foreign Compensation Commission*[112] the House held that the words in the Foreign Compensation Act of 1950 providing that the determination of any application to the Foreign Compensation Commission "should not be called in question in any court of law" did not apply when a determination was made partly on an irrele-

---

105. [1971] 1 W.L.R. 1193 (H.L., Scot.).

106. [1970] A.C. 984 (Scot. 1969). The House also had to examine the Dock Labor Scheme. E.g., *National Dock Labour Bd.* v. *John Bland & Co.*, [1972] A.C. 222 (1971); *National Dock Labour Bd.* v. *British Steel Corp.*, [1973] 1 W.L.R. 89 (H.L. 1972). In *Bonsor v. Musicians' Union*, [1956] A.C. 104 (1955), the House held that in such a case even an unregistered trade union might be sued, but what else the case decided is unclear.

107. In *Faramus* v. *Film Artistes' Ass'n*, [1964] A.C. 925 (1963), a unanimous House held that a union was entitled to expel a member for failing to disclose a criminal offense committed in German-occupied Jersey.

In terms of the importance of union membership, however, cf., *Annamunthodo* v. *Oilfields Workers' Trade Union*, [1961] A.C. 945 (P.C.).

108. [1956] A.C. 736. A majority would apparently have allowed an action to be brought if it had been commenced within the 6 weeks provided by statute.

109. [1960] A.C. 260 (1959).

110. Town and Country Planning Act of 1947, § 17.

111. [1960] A.C. 260, 286 (1959), per Simonds.

112. [1969] 2 A.C. 147 (1968). *East Elloe* was criticized but not specifically overruled.

vant factor and therefore was not actually a determination at all. Increasingly there was a willingness to expect ministers to exercise their discretion according to law and, more importantly, to intervene to ensure that that occurred. Thus in *Padfield* v. *Minister of Agriculture*,[113] the House granted mandamus against the minister who had discretion to consider price differentials or not but who, in the eyes of the court, had exercised his discretion in such a way as to frustrate the policy of the act.[114]

In part this procedural due process was to assure an appropriate hearing, a purpose made clear in *Ridge* v. *Baldwin* where the firing of a chief constable was quashed for failure to follow the rules of natural justice,[115] in an appeal that characterized *Liversidge* v. *Anderson* as a "very peculiar decision"[116] and distinguished *Nakkuda Ali* v. *Jayaratne*.[117] The Privy Council later built on *Ridge* v. *Baldwin* to require ministers in Ceylon to hold hearings before taking over the assets of a denominational school[118] or before dissolving a municipal corporation.[119] While in the United Kingdom the doctrine in *Ridge* v. *Baldwin* appears to have been limited to those dismissable for cause, it has been held to apply to the dismissal of a Scottish teacher.[120]

Part of the issue of procedural due process was to prevent taking without an appropriate hearing or the imposition of a series of unreasonable conditions on land, and in the early sixties the House wrestled with this issue.[121] The assumptions in favor of no taking without com-

113. [1968] A.C. 997.
114. See also *Kingsway Invs., Ltd.* v. *Kent County Council*, [1971] A.C. 72 (1969).
115. [1964] A.C. 40 (1963).
116. Ibid. 73.
117. [1951] A.C. 66 (P.C. 1950).
118. *Board of Trustees of the Maradana Mosque* v. *Mahmud*, [1967] 1 A.C. 13 (P.C. 1965).
119. *Durayappah* v. *Fernando*, [1967] 2 A.C. 337 (P.C.).
120. *Malloch* v. *Aberdeen Corp.*, [1971] 1 W.L.R. 1578 (H.L., Scot.). Note the refusal to apply the doctrine to the Commissioners of Inland Revenue; *Wiseman* v. *Borneman*, [1971] A.C. 297 (1969).
121. E.g., in *Chertsey UDC* v. *Mixnam's Properties, Ltd.*, [1965] A.C. 735 (1964), it was held that conditions attached to a caravan site license relating to the licensee's powers of letting the sites were ultra vires and void. In *Hartnell* v. *Minister of Housing & Local Gov't.*, [1965] A.C. 1134, the House struck down conditions attached to a caravan site license that, although not so onerous as to amount to a refusal, nevertheless materially cut down, without compensation, the preexisting right of a site owner. The House argued that a statute should not be held to take away private rights of property without compensation unless it did so in clear and unambiguous language.
   Compare *Belfast Corp.* v. *O. D. Cars, Ltd.*, [1960] A.C. 490 (N. Ire. 1959), in which it was held that the right to use property in a particular way was not itself a property right and, therefore, legislation excluding the right to compensation for injurious effect when planning permission was refused on certain grounds was not a contravention of the Government of Ireland Act of 1920, prohibiting laws that took any property without compensation. See also *Fawcett Properties, Ltd.* v. *Buckingham County Council*, [1961] A.C. 636 (1960), where conditions requiring the occupancy of certain cottages by agricultural workers and their dependents only were held enforceable.

pensation grew gradually stronger and then, finally, in 1964, in *Burmah Oil Company* v. *Lord Advocate*,[122] by a majority of three to two, the House held that the Crown was legally liable for damage when exercising its prerogative rights of taking or destroying property even in time of war or imminent danger, short of actually fighting the enemy.[123] The effect of the decision was traumatic, but neither the outgoing Conservative government nor the incoming Labour government was prepared to allow the courts to develop this kind of protection of property. In what some saw as a vindictive move and many as a violation of the Rule of Law, the War Damage Act, finally passed in 1965, not only changed the rule of law as laid down by the House (something that, after all, happened almost annually in the Finance Acts) but actually overruled the decision itself so that the plaintiff collected nothing.[124] The time was obviously not yet ripe for the development of any general theory of compensation.[125]

Burmah Oil no doubt served to remind the law lords that they were "lions under the mace." In *McEldowney* v. *Forde*, on facts arising before the emergency in Ulster, the House went to considerable lengths to make sense of a badly drafted regulation outlawing republican clubs rather than hold it was ultra vires the Northern Ireland Civil Authorities (Special Powers) Act of 1922.[126] In *British Railways Board* v. *Pickin* the House refused even to examine an allegation that mala fides had been used

---

In *Essex County Council* v. *Essex Inc. Congregational Church Union*, [1963] A.C. 808, the local authority was held not to be entitled to raise as a fresh ground for refusal to purchase property pursuant to a purchase notice the fact that the property was exempt from rates, after service of the counter notice in which the point had not been raised. The House was, however, unable to assist the owner of property that had been under the threat of compulsory purchase for seven years in *Simpson's Motor Sales, Ltd.* v. *Hendon Corp.*, [1964] A.C. 1088 (1963). It was held that the delay was not sufficient and there was no intention to abandon by the acquiring authority; the courts could only interfere if the authority's conduct was against good conscience.

122. [1965] A.C. 75 (Scot. 1964). The majority consisted of Reid, Pearce, and Upjohn; Radcliffe and Hodson dissented.

123. In the absence of any clear authority on this point and with a choice before them, the majority relied upon the practice of the Crown to give compensation, civil law authorities and also upon justice from the point of view of the property owner, while the minority gave considerable weight to the rights of the public and relied on American rather than civil law decisions.

124. Parker, the Lord Chief Justice, opined that "we shall soon be without any laws at all"; 269 *Parl. Deb.*, H.L. (5th ser.), col. 778 (25 Mar. 1969). Shepherd, the government spokesman, argued that "Her Majesty's Government believe that, as a matter of public policy, the Common Law, as it was understood, should be restored, and that no individual should stand in a privileged position above all the other claimants"; 266 ibid., col. 744 (25 May 1965). This view was shared by Dilhorne; ibid., col. 749 and Gardiner, ibid., col. 809. For a full study of the debates, see Blom-Cooper and Drewry, *Final Appeal* 368–74.

125. In *Nissan* v. *Attorney-General*, [1970] A.C. 179 (1969), the House held that "Act of State" was not available against a citizen of the United Kingdom for an act done in an independent state (burning of a hotel in Cyprus).

126. [1971] A.C. 632 (N. Ire. 1969).

to obtain a private act of Parliament. Remedies for that kind of problem lay elsewhere.[127] On the other hand the House had no qualms about restricting the claim of executive privilege when the Crown pleaded it in litigation. In *Conway* v. *Rimmer*[128] what had been thought of as the blanket privilege in *Duncan* v. *Cammell, Laird* was dramatically restricted.[129]

If one moves from customary English areas of constitutional and administrative law to the general area of civil liberties, it is less easy both to detect trends and to make claims that the House has carved out a position for itself over the last twenty years. In American terms, *Attorney-General* v. *Times Newspapers, Limited*[130] represented a clash between the First Amendment and the Sixth Amendment, and although the House was more concerned with freedom of speech than has been customary in the English courts, a wide area of protection from publicity was still maintained even for sub judice civil actions. Thus an injunction was granted to prevent the publication of an article about the thalidomide

127. [1974] A.C. 765. In the Court of Appeal, Master of the Rolls Denning had held that the issue was a justiciable one; *Pickin* v. *British Rys. Bd.*, [1973] Q.B. 219 (C.A. 1972). See Peter Wallington, "Sovereignty Regained" 686.
    On the other hand, the Privy Council had shown fewer qualms when Commonwealth and colonial legislatures were concerned. In *Bribery Comm'r* v. *Ranasinghe*, [1965] A.C. 172 (P.C. 1964), a remedy was given in a Ceylonese appeal where, although the Royal Assent had been given to the legislation, the Speaker's Certificate had never been obtained. On the power of the courts over the procedure of colonial legislatures, see *Rediffusion (Hong Kong), Ltd.* v. *Attorney-General of Hong Kong*, [1970] 2 A.C. 1136 (P.C.). Perhaps the most remarkable case of all was *Hinds* v. *R.*, [1976] 2 W.L.R. 366 (P.C.), where Diplock led the board to hold the Gun Court Act of 1974 unconstitutional because the composition of the Court violated the separation of powers doctrine implicit in the Jamaican constitution.
    128. [1968] A.C. 910 (1967). The earlier doctrine had already been weakened in *Glasgow Corp.* v. *Central Land Bd.*, [1956] Sess. Cas. 1 (H.L., Scot. 1955).
    129. Reid and Upjohn thought it unnecessary to overrule the earlier case; Morris thought differently. See generally Mauro Capeletti and C. J. Golden, Jr., "Crown Privilege and Executive Privilege" 836.
    For a later curbing of some of the apparent developments in *Conway* v. *Rimmer*, see *R.* v. *Lewes Justices*, [1973] A.C. 388 (1972). "[T]here is clearly all the difference in world between the question whether the public interest requires that mundane communications between all persons in the government service should be immune from discovery and the question whether the public interest requires that communications received by the Gaming Board should be immune from discovery"; ibid., Salmon at 414. (In *Rogers* the communication was a letter from a Chief Constable to the Gaming Board.)
    In *Norwich Pharmacal Co.* v. *Comm'rs of Customs & Excise*, [1974] A.C. 133 (1973), however, the customs authorities were forced to disclose details of shipments of a particular chemical when the plaintiff had reasonable cause to believe that they provided the evidence that his patents were being infringed. On the other hand, in *Alfred Crompton Amusement Machs., Ltd.* v. *Comm'rs of Customs & Excise*, [1974] A.C. 405 (1973), documents passing between the divisions of the commissioners were held covered by professional privilege and others by Crown privilege.
    130. [1974] A.C. 273 (1973). See Harvey Teff and Colin Munro, *Thalidomide: The Legal Aftermath*, especially chap. 3. The Lords' decision was later appealed to the European Court of Human Rights, alleging a violation of Article 10 of the European Convention.

tragedy, although the litigation was effectively dormant. A similar reluctance to engage in "balancing" the public interest led the House in criminal cases, especially those involving conspiracy, to refuse to determine the "interests of the state."[131]

The House was equally reluctant to become embroiled in immigration, extradition, or deportation cases. No doubt some of the appeals to the Lords were those of desperate men who deserved little sympathy, legally or morally. Yet at times the deference to the executive appeared extreme. In *Zacharia* v. *Republic of Cyprus*,[132] the House held that under the Fugitive Offenders Act the fact that the crimes involved a political offense was irrelevant and the applicant was therefore extradited; questions of policy were not for the House to decide.[133] The same approach was taken when persons pleaded that they were being sent back to Greece[134] and Ireland[135] in theory for crimes of violence, but in practice for political crimes. Similarly, technical claims about whether the "real" crime to be punished was not the one for which indictment was sought[136] and whether the political offense was actually committed in a third country[137] were not encouraged.[138] Indeed, the most significant case in which deportation was refused was in *Armah* v. *Government of Ghana*,[139] in which the House refused to extradite a former supporter of Nkrumah after the coup that brought Busia to power.[140]

A similar approach characterized the House's approach to immigration questions.[141] By the Commonwealth Immigrants Acts of 1962 and 1968 some immigrants who had entered the country illegally became immune from prosecution by passage of time. An outcry from liberals

---

131. In *Chandler* v. *DPP*, [1964] A.C. 763 (1962), where the question was whether the action of the "Committee of 100" in demonstrating at Wethersfield Airfield was "prejudicial to the safety or interests of the State," the House was content to leave the decision to the Crown alone. It would not venture into the field of policy. "Anyone," said Reid, "is entitled, in or out of Parliament, to urge that policy regarding the armed forces should be changed; but until it is changed, on a change of government or otherwise, no one is entitled to challenge it in court"; ibid. 792.

132. [1963] A.C. 634 (1962).

133. E.g., Devlin: "It is unreasonable to expect the competent authorities of a sovereign independent republic to submit to cross-examination on such matters in the courts of another country; and if they were to state in public and on oath what precautions they intended to take, that in itself might defeat the object of their plans. These are matters which must be the subject of governmental and not of judicial investigation"; ibid. 690.

134. *R.* v. *Governor of Brixton Prison, ex parte Kotronis*, [1971] A.C. 250 (1969).

135. *R.* v. *Governor of Brixton Prison, ex parte Keane*, [1972] A.C. 204 (1971).

136. *Atkinson* v. *United States*, [1971] A.C. 197 (1969).

137. *R.* v. *Governor of Pentonville Prison, ex parte Cheng*, [1973] A.C. 931.

138. Although in the *Cheng* case both Wilberforce and Simon dissented; ibid. 941, 947.

139. [1968] A.C. 192 (1966).

140. Morris and Pearson dissenting. Ibid. 236, 263.

141. *Azam* v. *Secretary of State for Home Affairs*, [1974] A.C. 18 (1973).

was therefore inevitable when such persons were considered illegal immigrants for the purpose of the Immigration Act of 1971.[142] Similarly, liberals were not particularly enthusiastic about the House's four decisions under the Race Relations Acts of 1965 and 1968. In giving content to the new phases in the innovative legislation, the law lords emphasized their assumption that the state should if possible be excluded from a man's private activities.

Thus, in *Ealing London Borough Council* v. *Race Relations Board*,[143] the House held that the refusal by a borough council to put a Polish citizen on its public housing list did not amount to the discrimination prohibited by the act on the grounds of "color, race or ethnic or national origins." The House then faced two "club" cases. When a political club operated a racial barrier (the East Ham South Conservative Club accepted only whites), the House held there had been no breach of the act, since it was a real club (an admission procedure was followed) and was not therefore "a section of the public" within the meaning of the legislation.[144] Yet, even when a more casual type of club was involved with a vastly greater number of members, the result was similar.[145] Indeed, the only "success" the Race Relations Board achieved in the Lords was *Race Relations Board* v. *Applin*,[146] in which the board issued a complaint on the ground that members of the National Front had put pressure on neighbors of a family who made a practice of fostering children to adopt a "white only" policy. The House held that the parents were providing a public service and the children were "a section of the public" and therefore protected by the legislation. It was in this context that the government pushed through a new Act in 1976 to strengthen the legislation, overruling the three House of Lords cases where the board had lost.

While race relations litigation was still moving forward slowly, by

---

142. For the liberal response see, for example, "Did MP's Blunder into Doublecross of Immigrants?" *Sunday Times*, 17 June 1973, at 6.

One of the first acts of the new Labour government of 1974 was to announce an (unpopular) amnesty for such immigrants, although, through an oversight, the amnesty apparently did not apply to a significant number of them.

143. [1972] A.C. 342 (1971).

144. *Race Relations Bd.* v. *Charter*, [1973] A.C. 868.

145. In *Dockers' Labour Club & Institute, Ltd.* v. *Race Relations Bd.*, [1976] A.C. 285 (1974), the subject of the complaint was a member of one of 4,000 workingmen's clubs. One of the privileges of such membership was being able to enter affiliated clubs. Sherrington attempted to enter one of the affiliated clubs and was asked to leave because he was black. The law lords unanimously held that this act was no violation of the act. The one million associates were not a "section of the public" within the meaning of § 2(1) of the Race Relations Act of 1968.

146. [1975] A.C. 259 (1974). See now R. M. Whitel, "The Last Trump for Clubs?" 1104. For an analysis of the House's decisions leading up to the Race Relations Act of 1976, see Anthony Lester, "Fundamental Rights in the United Kingdom" 350–56.

the mid-seventies the House had had fifteen active years of criminal work since the jurisdiction was opened up in 1961.[147] Some would argue that this was still too short a time to judge the quality of the House as a final appeal court, although Blom-Cooper and Drewry have made the claim that the House began with a trio of rightly maligned cases—*Shaw*,[148] *Sykes*,[149] and *Smith*[150]—but then pulled itself together. "The Smith-Shaw-Sykes judicial syndrome has been halted in its tracks. A study of the criminal jurisdiction since 1961 discloses two main strands in the judicial texture: a growing awareness of the preponderance of prosecution power in the criminal process, and a distaste for the over-technical rules (relics, perhaps, of the writ era) that have cosseted the accused and tend only to deflect the court from the attainment of an abstract idea of sensible criminal justice."[151]

Certainly the first three decisions had an almost uniformly bad press. *Director of Public Prosecutions* v. *Smith* appeared to substitute the concept of the reasonable man for the test of mens rea in murder.[152] The effect of the decision was not only to bring down the wrath of the academic community but also to cause the High Court of Australia to announce that, in future, it would feel free not to follow decisions of the House.[153] In *Shaw* v. *Director of Public Prosecutions* the majority, claiming a residual right in the courts to be *custos morum*, held that a conspiracy to corrupt public morals (in this case by publishing a directory of prostitutes and the types of services they offered) was a common law misdemeanor. This time the outcry from criminal lawyers and intellectuals was even louder.[154] In *Sykes* v. *Director of Public Prosecutions*, the House gave a new lease of life to the common law misdemeanor of misprision of felony.[155] The argument that the limits of this offense re-

---

147. The House became a serious criminal court after 1960 when the fiat of the Attorney-General was no longer needed to bring an appeal under § 1 of the Administration of Justice Act of 1960.

148. [1962] A.C. 220 (1961).

149. [1962] A.C. 528 (1961).

150. [1961] A.C. 290 (1960).

151. Blom-Cooper and Drewry, *Final Appeal* 278.

152. It was argued that the logical extension of the rule of this case "must inevitably reintroduce the forms of constructive malice purported to be abolished by Section 1 of the Homicide Act, and indeed give them in some respects a wider extension than they possessed under the old law"; Glanville Williams, "Constructive Malice Revisited" 605. See also Rupert Cross, "The Need for a Redefinition of Murder" 278.

For the defense that the objective test was merely a matter of evidence and did not affect the substance of the crime, see Alfred Denning, *Responsibility before the Law*.

153. Blom-Cooper and Drewry, *Final Appeal* 277. For the different reaction in Ghana, where the decision was given "respectful approval," see L. C. B. Gower, *Independent Africa* 96.

154. E.g., Rupert Cross and A. Jones, *An Introduction to Criminal Law* 122; H. L. A. Hart, *Law, Liberty and Morality* 6–12.

155. [1962] A.C. 528 (1961). Having decided that it was not obsolete, they held that

mained vague and impossibly wide did not sway the House;[156] the decision itself was ultimately superceded by the Criminal Law Act of 1967.[157]

Although it is difficult to dissent from the first part of the Blom-Cooper/Drewry theory, it is less clear how far the House went toward achieving a balance between prosecution power and antiquated defenses. Later cases suggest a toughening of attitudes toward crimes of violence[158] coupled with an extension of crimes related to it,[159] and by no means a tender view of civil liberties when violence was involved.[160] So too, in *Hyam*,[161] Hailsham refused specifically to overrule *Smith*, assuming it had survived. Moreover, *Shaw* continued to show signs of life in *Knuller*,[162] where the publishers of a homosexual directory were convicted for a conspiracy to corrupt public morals and the House also conceded (while quashing) the existence of a conspiracy to outrage public decency. Even Reid, as has been seen, felt it was too late to overrule *Shaw*.[163]

A closer reading of the later conspiracy cases suggests a greater sense

---

concealment of the felony did not necessarily involve a positive act; mere omission to inform the authorities of a felony of which the defendant knew, was sufficient. Further, the accused need not convert the concealment into a source of emolument to himself.

156. E.g., ibid. per Denning at 564. This was not the only occasion when this argument opposing uncertainty, which many have thought should have the utmost weight in the field of criminal law, had been rejected by the House during the period. See especially *Shaw v. DPP*, [1962] A.C. 220 (1961). See also *Cox v. Army Council*, [1963] A.C. 48 (1962).

157. Blom-Cooper and Drewry, *Final Appeal* 277–78.

158. See, for example, the two appeals from Northern Ireland, *Attorney-General for Northern Ireland v. Gallagher*, [1963] A.C. 349 (N. Ire. 1961), where a psychopath, prior to making himself drunk, in which state he murdered his wife, evinced his intention to kill her. The judge directed the jury to apply the M'Naughten Rules to the moment prior to the taking of alcohol, not the time of the killing. The House held that there had been no misdirection. The defense of automatism was pleaded in *Bratty v. Attorney-General for Northern Ireland*, [1963] A.C. 386 (N. Ire. 1961). It failed on the evidence and the rejection by the jury of the plea of insanity, there being no other evidence of a cause of the automatism.

159. E.g., the crime of affray; *Button v. DPP*, [1966] A.C. 591 (1965).

160. See *Connelly v. DPP*, [1964] A.C. 1254. The appellant, having been acquitted on a charge of murder, was then tried on the robbery charge. His plea of autrefois acquit was rejected by the House, which required very great similarity, if not complete identity, between the two crimes.

In *R. v. Desmond*, [1965] A.C. 960, it was held that robbery with violence could be committed in two stages, first violence used to remove the human obstacle and second for the theft.

There had been considerable debate in preceding years on the problems of violence. See, e.g., 198 *Parl. Deb.*, H.L. (5th ser.), col. 581 (10 July 1956); Death Penalty (Abolition) Bill, 201 ibid., col. 21 (21 Feb. 1957); Homicide Bill, 268 ibid., col. 119 (27 July 1965); Murder (Abolition of Death Penalty) Bill, ibid., col. 480 (19 July 1965).

161. [1975] A.C. 55 (1974). See at 71 ff. Illogically, Hailsham refused to apply an objective test to rape, requiring affirmative evidence of mens rea; *R. v. Morgan*, [1976] A.C. 182 (1975). See now the Sexual Offences (Amendment) Act of 1976.

162. [1973] A.C. 435 (1972). Diplock dissented. See C. T. Emery, "After OZ-IT" 199.

163. The crime of conspiracy remained an active one during the period. E.g., in *Board of Trade v. Owen*, [1954] A.C. 602, a conspiracy to commit a crime abroad was held not

of balance. In *R.* v. *Kamara*,[164] although Sierra Leonean students were convicted of conspiracy to trespass, the House nevertheless limited such conspiracies to public places. In *R.* v. *Bhagwan*[165] the House refused to hold that a conspiracy to avoid an act of Parliament was inevitably criminal in the absence of some specific criminal act. Finally, in *R.* v. *Withers*,[166] the House, reacting against the earlier decisions, held that there was no generalized offense of conspiracy to effect a public mischief and that the House had no power to create new offenses.[167] Similar hints of a more mellow approach in other directions[168] included a greater concern to ensure that mens rea was required. In two cases involving possession of drugs, the House in effect imported the requirement of mens rea although the statute appeared to be absolute;[169] a similar approach was used in cases relating to the Trade Descriptions Act of 1908[170] and the Food and Drugs Act.[171]

To claim that the House had reached a via media in balancing the rights of the prosecution and defense[172] or in determining when, if ever, judicial legislation was justified in the criminal law would probably be naive; but the House had come a long way since *Smith*, *Shaw*, and *Sykes*. It was impossible to deny that the Lords played an important role in criminal law, and there was at least some evidence that it was playing a positive role in clarifying doctrine. No doubt this was in part the result of the more aggressive view of the judicial process by the law lords. At the

---

indictable in this country unless the contemplated crime was one for which an indictment would lie here. In *Verrier* v. *DPP*, [1967] 2 A.C. 195 (1966), it was held that there was jurisdiction at common law to sentence to imprisonment for a common law misdemeanor, the sentence being at large and in the discretion of the court. Therefore, in exceptional circumstances a person convicted of conspiracy, but not attempt, could be sentenced to a longer term than could be ordered for the substantive offence. In *R.* v. *Doot*, [1973] A.C. 807, an agreement made abroad to smuggle cannabis into England was held an indictable conspiracy.

164. [1974] A.C. 104 (1973).

165. [1972] A.C. 60 (1970).

166. [1975] A.C. 842 (1974).

167. But cf. *Scott* v. *Metropolitan Police Comm'r*, [1975] A.C. 819 (1974), holding, *inter alia*, that deceit was not an integral part of conspiracy to defraud at common law.

168. Mellowness did not extend in all directions. *Taylor* v. *DPP*, [1973] A.C. 964, extended affray still further; *Lawrence* v. *Metropolitan Police Comm'r*, [1972] A.C. 626 (1971), interpreted § 15 of the Theft Act of 1968 broadly. Indeed, there was a general reluctance to allow technical defenses under the act. E.g., *R.* v. *Turner*, [1974] A.C. 357 (1973).

169. *Warner* v. *Metropolitan Police Comm'r*, [1969] 2 A.C. 256 (1968); *Sweet* v. *Parsley*, [1970] A.C. 132 (1969).

170. *Tesco Supermarkets, Ltd.* v. *Nattrass*, [1972] A.C. 153 (1971).

171. *Smedleys, Ltd.* v. *Breed*, [1974] A.C. 839 (1972).

172. For instance, there are no clear patterns in the House's application of criminal evidence. Cf. *Rumping* v. *DPP*, [1964] A.C. 814 (1962); *Jones* v. *DPP*, [1962] A.C. 635 (1961); *Murdoch* v. *Taylor*, [1965] A.C. 574; *Toohey* v. *Metropolitan Police Comm'r*, [1965] A.C. 595; *Myers* v. *DPP*, [1965] A.C. 101 (1964).

same time it is difficult not to speculate that, had the law lords been even more willing to articulate a role for the final appeal court and to state more general goals for the criminal process, their functions might have been far more effectively pursued.

The House and Its Operations

During the twenty years under discussion, the House as a judicial body underwent various administrative and political changes. Despite the former, even in the mid-seventies many aspects of its operation were amateur. Not all the House's cases were reported in either the official or the unoffical reports.[173] The panel system still injected an element of chance into the outcome of decisions,[174] and although law lords were by then provided with offices and secretarial help (something vouchsafed to only the senior law lords in the mid-fifties), there was nothing akin to the law clerks or law secretaries known in other common law countries. This amateur quality was reflected in the judgments themselves. An opinion of the whole House, while more frequent, was still rare; more usual was a series of individual judgments—in many cases reiterations, with respect to both fact and law—of what was said by other law lords. This overlapping arrangement helped to keep the law flexible by restating points in slightly different ways, but the overall impression was not one of efficiency or, in some respects, even seriousness.[175] So, too, the tradition of complete orality remained. Printed "cases," which amounted to little more than pleadings, were exchanged before argument, but not written briefs. Counsel continued the tradition of reading in toto cases cited in argument. So long as the House decided relatively few cases, this arrangement was reasonably satisfactory. Yet if the House were ever to achieve a more central place in British government, the ever-increasing length of hearings might have to be curbed by the use of written briefs.[176] Such a development might also require the curtailment of the extensive use of the law lords for such extrajudicial work as chairing Royal Commissions and for the other all-purpose functions of Lords of Appeal—for example,

173. For a list of 25 unreported cases between 1956 and 1966, see Blom-Cooper and Drewry, *Final Appeal* 250–51.

174. Although administratively it is not easy to pack panels, an element of this sometimes occurs. In *Kamara* v. *DPP*, [1974] A.C. 104 (1973), which might have annulled *Shaw*, only 4 law lords sat—all known to favor an extension of the doctrine of conspiracy, while 6 other law lords, some of whom had less clear views, were not used to make up a quorum of 5; A. A. Paterson, "Judges: A Political Elite?" 118, 127.

175. For an extended analysis of this phenomenon, see Blom-Cooper and Drewry, *Final Appeal*, chap. 5.

176. The length of hearing was also directly related to the escalating costs of appeals; ibid., chap. 11.

to relieve congestion in the Court of Appeal.[177] Complaints about amateurism in British government were scarcely novel, but the ambiguous status of the law lords at times seemed to fuel confusion about their primary role.

Yet if one moves from the administrative to the political and jurisprudential area, the twenty-year period saw remarkable changes. Undoubtedly the House of Lords in its judicial capacity was seen as an increasingly integral part of the legislative process.[178] The sense of this relationship grew during the 1960s in such a way that a literature began to develop that made possible a more sophisticated approach to the judicial process itself. Until these relationships were examined publicly it had been difficult to discuss when it was appropriate for the courts to call for parliamentary intervention and when to intervene themselves to remedy some defect. Blom-Cooper and Drewry discovered fourteen examples, between 1952 and 1968, when the law lords sitting judicially called on Parliament to remedy some defect in the law that had been revealed by litigation, and in seven of these instances, amending legislation resulted.[179] More frequently, Parliament intervened without invitation; for instance, between 1952 and 1970 the legislature intervened no less than twenty-seven times to reverse the principle underlying the decision of the Lords in tax cases, during a period when the House decided 133 revenue appeals.[180] The frequency of reversals by the annual Finance Acts could not but affect the nature of the judicial process in revenue cases.[181]

Revenue cases were, however, in some respects unique. For the most part, the very interaction of the final appeal court and Parliament seemed to emphasize the inherent lawmaking power of the House of Lords as a judicial body. When Radcliffe announced, "[T]here was never a more sterile controversy than that upon the question whether a judge makes law. Of course he does. How can he help it?"[182] he was stating the obvious. The final appeal court's work consists of choosing between

177. In 1967, for instance, Pearson sat in the Court of Appeal on 5 occasions; Upjohn and Pearce, 4 times; and Wilberforce, 2; ibid. 182.

178. For an early analysis along these lines, see Louis L. Jaffé, *English and American Judges as Lawmakers* 5.

179. Blom-Cooper and Drewry, *Final Appeal* 209. A paradigm of this is Reid's statement in *Cartledge v. E. Jopling & Sons*, [1963] A.C. 758, 773. "[O]ne thing at least is clear. The fact that the present law requires us to dismiss the appeal shows that some amendment of the law is urgently necessary." While the case was still being heard the government set up the Committee on Limitation of Action in Areas of Personal Injury, 1962; the law was rapidly amended by the Limitation Act of 1963. See Blom-Cooper and Drewry, *Final Appeal* 361.

180. Ibid. 322–23.

181. Ibid., chap. 15.

182. Cyril John Radcliffe, "Law and Order" 821.

competing doctrines and competing interpetations and construction. If there were not, indeed, some element of choice in any appeal (although logically or psychologically the preferences may be in one direction or the other) one would have to assume that inefficiency, mendacity, or dishonesty were rampant at the English bar, which allowed the appeal to be taken. Radcliffe's statement and similar statements he made in the early sixties, by pinpointing the existence of such choice, helped to undermine the aura of judicial automatism that had pervaded the era of substantive formalism.

Yet the question of just what law should be made by judges still evoked a feeling of discomfort that was by no means confined to the law lords themselves. There was, of course, a sense of outrage when Parliament intervened to overrule not only the law but the actual outcome of a case in the War Damage Act of 1965;[183] yet that same period saw cases like *Myers* v. *Director of Public Prosecutions*, in which the law lords felt it was not appropriate for them to intervene to modify the hearsay rules,[184] and *National Provincial Bank, Limited* v. *Ainsworth*, in which the House finally decided to leave to the legislature the protection of the deserted wife.[185] When in that very same year, Parliament established a permanent Law Commission, charged with keeping all branches of "lawyers' law" (as Gardiner called it) under review, it might have seemed as if judicial creativity would, if anything, continue the sheltered, demure existence it had traditionally lived in England.

For a series of reasons this did not occur. One obvious reason, which Radcliffe articulated, lay in the greater intellectual curiosity afoot in England in the 1960s, especially with respect to the operation of established institutions.[186] A series of articles emphasized the creative element in various of the House's decisions of the early sixties, especially cases like *Midland Silicones* v. *Scruttons*[187] and *Hedley Byrne* v. *Heller*.[188] Although such decisions were often applauded,[189] the same was not necessarily true for the other obviously creative decisions in the early 1960s in criminal law (*Shaw, Sykes, Smith*) or in labor law (*Rookes* v.

183. Blom-Cooper and Drewry, *Final Appeal*, chap. 16.
184. [1965] A.C. 101 (1964).
185. [1965] A.C. 1175. See the Matrimonial Homes Act of 1967.
186. See generally chap. 12.
187. [1962] A.C. 446 (1961).
188. [1964] A.C. 465 (1963).
189. E.g., Gerald Dworkin, "*Stare Decisis* in the House of Lords" 163; Stevens, "*Hedley Byrne* v. *Heller*" 121; and "The Role of a Final Appeal Court in a Democracy" 509; Wolfgang Friedmann, "Judicial Law Making in England," in *Law, Justice and Equity*, ed. R. H. C. Holland and R. G. Schwartzenberger, at 9.

Barnard, Stratford v. *Lindley*),[190] yet the cumulative effect of these decisions was to focus on the creativity of the House and, in particular, on the work of the individual judges.

The Practice Statement of 1966 should be viewed in this context. Although, in the first ten years, the Practice Statement was discussed rigorously in only half a dozen cases and perhaps only two decisions of the House had been clearly overruled, the psychological impact had been considerable. By 1976 the House was far less concerned about restricting and avoiding earlier decisions, even if it could rarely bring itself to overrule the earlier cases.[191] On the surface, there has been caution in the approach to the 1966 Statement. In *Broome* v. *Cassell* Hailsham argued that the power to overrule earlier decisions should be used "cautiously" and "sparingly."[192] In *Conway* v. *Rimmer*, Upjohn thought the power should only be used "sparingly." In *Jones* v. *Secretary of State for Social Services*, Dilhorne said that in order to preserve certainty in the law, the new procedure should be used "only in rare cases."[193] Simon of Glaisdale noted that since the Lords lacked the resources to legislate, they should use "restraint" by exercising their power only infrequently.[194] Reid could be firmest of all. He argued that the statement should not be used for statutory interpretation since there is no "right decision."[195] He also refused to overrule *Shaw* (in which he had dissented) in *Knuller*, on the ground that "[a]ny alteration of the law . . . must . . . be left to Parliament."[196] It is true that in the *Miliangos* case Wilberforce spoke more broadly of the power of overruling,[197] but in general the formal implementation of the 1966 Practice Statement was restrained.

Put another way, the formal overruling of earlier precedents had been strictly limited. In *Conway* v. *Rimmer*[198] only Morris clearly thought *Duncan* v. *Cammell, Laird* should finally be overruled, yet with *Conway* decided there was precious little left of the earlier precedent; it had been

---

190. See K. W. Wedderburn, *The Worker and the Law*, passim.

191. On the 1966 Practice Statement see R. W. M. Dias, "Precedents in the House of Lords" 153; A. L. G[oodhart], "Note," 82 *Law Quarterly Review* 441 (1966); John Langbein, "Modern Jurisprudence in the House of Lords" 807; W. Barton Leach, "Revisionism in the House of Lords" 797; Julius Stone, "1966 and All That . . . ," 1172. For later reactions, see Julius Stone, "On the Liberation of Appellate Judges" 449; Rodney Brazier, "Overruling House of Lords Criminal Cases" 98.

192. [1972] A.C. 1027, 1055.

193. [1972] A.C. 944, 993 (1971).

194. *Miliangos* v. *George Frank, Ltd.*, [1976] A.C. 443 (1975).

195. *Jones* v. *Secretary of State for Social Servs.*, [1972] A.C. 944, 966 (1971).

196. *Knuller* v. *DPP*, [1973] A.C. 435, 445 (1972).

197. [1976] A.C. 443, 467–70 (1975).

198. [1968] A.C. 910 (1967). See especially Morris at 970.

distinguished in a way that would have been appreciably more difficult before 1966.[199] In *Lupton* v. *F.A. and A.B., Limited*,[200] Donovan and Dilhorne were prepared to overrule *Griffiths* v. *Harrison*,[201] but the majority, led by Simon, preferred to regard it "as a very narrow decision indeed."[202] In *Pook* v. *Owen*[203] only Pearce out of the majority was prepared to overrule *Ricketts* v. *Colquhoun*;[204] Guest and Wilberforce preferred to distinguish the decision. In *Jones* v. *Secretary of State for Social Services*,[205] while four out of the seven law lords felt that the *Dowling* case[206] was wrongly decided, only three (Wilberforce, Dilhorne, and Diplock) were prepared to overrule it.[207] In *Knuller*, Diplock was ready to overrule *Shaw*, taking the position that "[t]o bow to the decision yet to deny the legal meaning on which it was based is to draw the kind of distinction which reflects discredit on the English legal system. To deliver the law lords from the temptation to do this was one of the objects of the change of policy announced in July 1966."[208] The majority of the law lords, however, was much more cautious.[209] Thus while in *Broome* v. *Cassell*[210] counsel was prepared to argue the direct overruling issue—a possibility apparently recognized by the seven-judge panel now customarily convened when the printed case calls for reconsideration of an earlier case—only Hailsham specifically referred to the Practice Statement.[211] Much of the influence the statement has had—and it may not have been insubstantial—has been indirect.

199. See Stone, "1966 and All That . . ." 1201. The prediction that the new statement would legitimate procedures already used had been made at the time of its promulgation. See A. L. G[oodhart], "Note," *Law Quarterly Review* 441 (1966); Julius Stone, "The Lords at the Crossroads" 483, 489.

200. [1972] A.C. 634 (1971).

201. [1963] A.C. 1 (1962).

202. *Lupton* v. *F. A. & A. B., Ltd.*, [1972] A.C. 634, 658 (1971).

203. [1970] A.C. 244 (1969).

204. [1926] A.C. 1 (1925).

205. [1972] A.C. 944 (1971).

206. *Minister of Social Security* v. *Amalgamated Eng'r. Union*, [1967] 1 A.C. 725 (1966).

207. Simon refused to go along. Reid, Morris, and Pearson thought the case rightly decided.

208. *Knuller, Ltd.* v. *DPP*, [1973] A.C. 435, 469 (1972).

209. It was in this case that Reid, who had dissented in *Shaw*, said, "[O]ur change of practice in no longer regarding decisions of the House as absolutely binding does not mean that whenever we think that a previous decision was wrong we should reverse it. In the general interest of certainty in the law we must be sure that there is some very good reason before we so act"; [1973] A.C. 435, 455 (1972).

210. [1972] A.C. 1027; see especially 1055. See David Fleming, "Better the Devil You Know . . ." 232; Arthur L. Goodhart, "Precedent in the Broome and Herrington Cases" 305.

211. [1972] A.C. 1027, 1083: "We cannot depart from *Rookes* v. *Barnard* here. It was decided neither per incuriam nor ultra vires this House; we could only depart from it by tearing up the doctrine of precedent, and this was not the object of this House in assuming the powers adopted by the Practice Statement."

The interaction between the 1966 Practice Statement and the pre-existing tradition of judge-made law appeared most elegantly in *Herrington* v. *British Railways Board*,[212] in which the House revisited the issue of the responsibility of an occupier toward child trespassers. The possibility of overruling *Addie and Sons* v. *Dumbreck*[213] was obvious to both counsel. Counsel for the appellant argued that the 1966 Practice Statement "while freeing the House from the absolute chain of precedent did not turn it into a body of legislators,"[214] while counsel for the appellees argued that the statement "allows the House of Lords to depart from earlier decisions if it is necessary to assume the proper development of the law."[215] Each of the law lords who made up the panel chose his own line of development, reflected most obviously in the views of Reid, Pearson, and Diplock.

Reid, for instance, chose the line that would have appealed most to Radcliffe—the expansion of public policy. "Legal principles cannot solve the problem. How far occupiers are to be required by law to take steps to safeguard such children, must be a matter of public policy."[216] For Pearson, the issue was the more general one of change in social conditions. "[T]he *Addie* v. *Dumbreck* formulation of the duty of occupier to trespasser is plainly inadequate for modern conditions, and its rigid and restrictive characteristic has impeded the proper development of the common law in this field. It has become an anomaly and should be discarded."[217] It was left to Diplock to make the sole judicial reference to the 1966 Statement; his speech highlighted the strong underlying psychological change that had taken place, despite the tepid superficial reference. "[T]his House has since 1966 abandoned its former practice of adhering rigidly to the ratio decidendi of its previous decisions. There is no longer any need to discuss whether to discard the fiction of a so-called license to enter granted by the occupier of land to the person who suffers personal injury on it, should be characterised as overruling Addie's case or as doing no more than explaining its reasoning in terms which are in harmony with the general development of legal concepts since 1929 as to the source of one man's duty to take steps for the safety of another."[218]

Thus, by 1975, when the House overruled *in re United Railways of Havana and Regla Warehouses, Limited*[219] in *Miliangos* v. *George Frank*,

212. [1972] A.C. 877.
213. [1929] A.C. 358 (Scot.).
214. [1972] A.C. 877, 884.
215. Ibid. 890.
216. Ibid. 897.
217. Ibid. 930.
218. Ibid. 934–35.
219. [1961] A.C. 1007 (1960).

Limited,[220] Wilberforce, presiding, felt a need to make only passing reference to the 1966 Statement.[221] His basic conclusion was firm. "I would say that, difficult as the whole matter undoubtedly is, if once a clear conclusion is reached as to what the law now ought to be, declaration of it by this House is appropriate. The law on this topic is judge-made; it has been built up over the years from case to case. It is entirely within this House's duty, in the course of administering justice, to give the law a new direction in a particular case where on principle and in reason, it appears right to do so."[222] Although Simon of Glaisdale, in dissent, analyzed the 1966 Practice Statement in a relatively narrow way,[223] the concurring law lords were concerned with whether the justifications for the policy underlying the earlier case had changed. This they expressed under the maxim *Cessante ratione cessat ipsa lex*; or, as Cross put it, "I ask myself, therefore, whether there has been any change of circumstances since 1961 sufficiently great to justify us in saying that the rule which in the *Havana* case was accepted on all sides without question and which formed an essential foundation for the judgements delivered ought now to be considered to be no longer an existing rule of our law."[224]

In this sense the law lords had come a long way in fifteen years. When in the 1960 Rosenthal lectures, Radcliffe opened the discussion of the legislative function of judges and expressed "surprise that so much pen and ink has been employed by commentators in demonstrating this fairly obvious conclusion,"[225] he went far toward making the discussion of judicial creativity respectable, even if this result was the antithesis of

220. [1976] A.C. 443 (1975). See David Fleming, "Precedent and the Judicial Function in the House of Lords" 17.

221. "This brings one to the declaration made by this House in 1966. Under it, the House affirmed its power to depart from a previous decision when it appears right to do so, recognising that too rigid adherence to precedent might lead to injustice in a particular case and unduly restrict the proper development of the law. My Lords, on the assumption that to depart from the *Havana Railways* case would not involve undue practical difficulties, that a new and more satisfactory rule is capable of being stated I am of opinion that the present case falls within the terms of the declaration. To change the rule would, for the reasons already explained, avoid injustice in the present case. To change it would enable the law to keep in step with commercial needs and with the majority of other countries facing similar problems"; [1975] A.C. 443, (1976).

222. Ibid. continuing:

I cannot accept the suggestion that because a rule is long established only legislation can change it—that may be so when the rule is so deeply entrenched that it has infected the whole legal system, or the choice of a new rule involves more far-reaching research than courts can carry out. . . . I would not think it necessary or right here [to wait for legislation]. Indeed, from some experience in the matter, I am led to doubt whether legislative reform, at least prompt and comprehensive reform, in this field of foreign currency obligation, is practicable. Questions as to the meaning of debts or of damages depend so much on individual mixtures of facts and merits as to make them more suitable for progressive solutions in the courts.

223. Ibid. ff.
224. Ibid.
225. Cyril John Radcliffe, *The Law and Its Compass* 39.

his purpose. This progress in turn was reflected in the work of the House. For all the excursions of Denning, there were workaday developments by the law lords as a whole. Even during 1966 the lawmaking functions of the lords became increasingly widely accepted. In that year, in *Chancery Lane Safe Deposit Company* v. *Inland Revenue Commissioners*[226] the House distinguished almost out of existence one of its own earlier cases; while, as has been seen, on the very day the Practice Statement was issued, the House decided *Bishop* v. *Finsbury Securities, Limited*,[227] which largely eviscerated a case decided only four years earlier.[228] Nor was this creativity hidden from the commentators; scholars who might be regarded as jurisprudentially conservative were well aware of the trend.[229]

The importance of the 1966 Practice Statement, however, was largely psychological,[230] adding legitimacy to a process that had been going on since the late fifties and was accelerating in the early sixties. The statement seemed to confirm that Parliament had no objection to the judges' making law in those areas of society primarily entrusted to dispute settlement in the courts. Thus it is not surprising that, although rarely mentioned, the statement encouraged a greater flexibility of approach and, in particular, an emphasis on principle rather than rule and precedent and a noticeably greater inclination to talk about policy. By 1972 Reid spoke in far more bold terms than Radcliffe had done twelve years earlier. "There was a time when it was thought almost indecent to suggest that judges make law—they only declare it. Those with a taste for fairy tales seem to have thought that in some Aladdin's cave there is the hidden the Common Law in all its splendour and that on a judge's appointment there descends on him knowledge of the magic words Open Sesame. Bad decisions are given when the judge has muddled the password and the wrong door opens. But we do not believe in fairy tales anymore."[231] The battle had moved on. The pressing issues of the mid-1970s were the institutional competence of courts (especially appeal courts) and the gradations of judicial restraint and activism.[232]

226. [1966] A.C. 85, 111 (1965).

227. [1966] 1 W.L.R. 1402 (H.L.).

228. *Griffiths* v. *J. P. Harrison, Ltd.*, [1963] A.C. 1 (1962).

229. E.g., Allen's analysis of the whittling away of stare decisis; Carleton Kemp Allen, "Precedent Limps On" 36; and Rupert Cross, "Stare Decisis in Contemporary England," 203, 214: "[T]he foregoing summary [of cases] makes one wonder whether the spectacle of an English judge labouring under the brutal fetters of a rigid doctrine of precedent is not something which, if it exists at all, exists only in the minds of academic lawyers."

230. "Lord Gardiner's announcement is the essential prerequisite . . . because it implies a crucial change in attitude toward the role of the courts and decisional law in the enterprise of government"; Langbein, "Modern Jurisprudence in House of Lords" 813.

231. James S. Reid, "The Judge as Law Maker" 22.

232. E.g., Michael D. A. Freeman, "Standards of Adjudication, Judicial Law Making and Prospective Overruling" 166.

Toward the Future

The last twenty years, then, have seen a greater willingness to see the courts as an integral part of the governmental process, but that change should not be overestimated. Politicians and political scientists writing about the English scene still normally ignore the courts as an integral part of government,[233] and the wide acceptance of distinction between law and policy (closely associated with the idea of Rule of Law) still allows the judiciary (and even the legal profession) a measure of immunity from criticism, which judges (and lawyers) in other nations might well envy.

The support for the traditional view of law and the courts, however, is by no means limited to politicians or indirectly to those who describe and analyze the system. A substantial element in the legal profession is not unhappy with a system that emphasizes logic, certainty, and predictability and downplays discretion and creativity. Thus Sir Henry Fisher, a former High Court judge,[234] recently attacked the 1966 Practice Statement arguing that judges "should refrain from broad statements of principle and from *obiter dicta*. They should also be scrupulous to apply the law as it exists even if they think it to be wrong or unfair or unjust and should resist the temptation to twist the law to conform with their sympathies or theories, as the proper instrument for the reform of the law is Parliament, aided where necessary by the Law Commission, a Law Reform Committee, or Royal or departmental commissions."[235]

The more traditional approach has also been endorsed by other than the leaders of the practicing profession. The utilitarian-liberal tradition of limiting judicial creativity by the rigorous logic of the common law has remained strong. Professor L. C. B. Gower has recently argued, in urging the virtues of the Law Commission as a change agent, that "[t]he House of Lords . . . has never shone as a law reforming agency and now has ceased to perform the only other justifiable role for an expensive third-tier appeal court—to settle important questions of law clearly and unambiguously. . . . As a result of . . . prolixity it is sometimes impossible to tell what legal principle was decided."[236] The depth of this criticism was

233. E.g., Herbert Morrison, *Government and Parliament*; Samuel H. Beer, *Modern British Policies*; Richard Rose, ed. *Policy-Making in Britain*; R. G. S. Brown, *The Administrative Process in Britain*; Richard Rose, *Politics in England*. When Harold Wilson resigned in 1976, he wrote *The Governance of Britain*. The book made no mention either of the courts or of judges.

234. Currently President of Wolfson College, Oxford.

235. He continued, "They are not trained to legislate, although they may sometimes have to do so when they have to deal with legal questions not precisely covered by statute or previous decisions. Instead of welcoming such occasions as opportunities they should reduce them as much as possible and 'legislate' with the minimum disturbance and with the closest possible analogy to established law"; *Law Society's Gazette*, Dec. 1975; "Note," 119 *Solicitors' Journal* 854 (1975).

236. L. C. B. Gower, "Reflections on Law Reform" 257, 258; he continued, "This, of

further reflected in the 1976 Law Commission's Report on Occupiers' Liability.[237] The report criticized the speeches in *Herrington* v. *British Railways Board*[238] because they did not produce "a clear principle applicable to the generality of cases" and "it is not entirely clear what standard of duty the concept of humanity imposes." Thus a judicial decision that many common law jurisdictions would regard as a useful example of judicial legislation would, if the Law Commission had its way, be replaced by a statutory test.[239] Such an approach was consistent with the traditional intellectual atmosphere to English law. While scholars appreciated the fact that factors other than rules went into decisions, these outside factors were consciously deemphasized.[240] A positivistic approach to the analysis of doctrine thus remained the norm despite the intellectual changes of the period and the psychological implications of the 1966 Practice Statement.

Yet, in spite of these factors, by the mid-1970s forces were gathering and trends were developing that in the long run were likely to accentuate the creative force of the final appeal court. It became increasingly accepted that judges were applying policies just as much when they refused to apply a principle as when they extended one and in a different kind of way when they decided a case by analogizing from one rule rather than

course, delights the Master of the Rolls when, as occurs not infrequently, it is he that is being reversed, for it enables him to go on his own sweet way despite the reversal. But it gives little comfort to protagonists of judge-made law."

For a more tolerant approach, see the view of the first Chairman of the Law Commission, Lord Scarman:

[W]hatever course the development of our law takes, the problem of co-existence of codified law with judicial decision has to be faced. Were it possible, which it is not, for a universal code to leap overnight, like Athena armed and fully-grown, from the head of our parliamentary Zeus, Bentham's noble conception of a code as a complete digest of the laws superceding the decisions of the Judges might be momentarily achieved: I say momentarily because the very first judicial decision interpreting a section of the code would begin the reinstatement of judicial decision as a law-shaping force.

Those of us, therefore, who are considering the question whether codification has any advantages to offer to our legal system must accept that part of our task is to the problem of a code's relationship with judge-made law: it is a question not of total war involving the destruction of one or the other, but a study in co-existence. [Leslie Scarman, *Codification and Judge-Made Law* 4–5]

237. *Reports of the Law Commission*, No. 75, Cmnd. 6928 (1976).
238. [1972] A.C. 877.
239. See "Void for Uncertainty" 349, 350.
240. See, for instance, the work of H. L. A. Hart. In the *Concept of Law*, he readily admits, "In most important cases there is always a choice" (at 12), yet his overriding approach appears at 150: "Here, at the very fringe of these very fundamental things, we should welcome the rule-sceptic, as long as he does not forget that it is at the fringe that he is welcome; and does not blind us to the fact that what makes possible these striking developments by courts of the most fundamental rules is, in great measure, the prestige gathered by courts from their questionably rule-governed operations over the vast, central areas of the law." For a criticism of Hart's position, although from an arguably narrower perspective, see Ronald Dworkin, "The Model of Rules" 14. For Dworkin's general position, see now Ronald Dworkin, *Taking Rights Seriously*.

by applying a competing rule.[241] By English standards the approach to precedent evidenced rapid changes. After 1966 even the more conventional law lords began to talk the language, if not the litany, of judicial creativity. When overruling, the House talked less about the errors of legal logic made in the prior case and more about the underlying policies that had changed since the earlier decision.

In 1955, roughly at the end of the period of substantive formalism, lawmaking by judges had been seen in simplistic terms—it either competed with Parliament or it did not, and it was either good or bad. That has been largely abandoned. Various North American influences helped inject into English thinking the American concepts of judicial restraint and judicial activism[242]—that there are shades of desirability of lawmaking. Rather than the competition between legislature and judiciary that had so concerned Radcliffe, it was increasingly argued that "[t]he organs of government are partners in the enterprise of lawmaking."[243] Out of this, perhaps influenced by the "institutional competence" aspects of the American "process" school, grew a much greater awareness of when judicial legislation was appropriate, not only among academics[244] but also among law lords. From the rudimentary reluctance by Reid to legislate in Shaw,[245] because of the nature of the subject matter, the House reached the detailed hypotheses about judicial creativity by Simon of Glaisdale in Miliangos.[246]

The pressure toward accepting the final appeal court as an integral part of government is not likely to lessen. English law is being increasingly influenced by European law where judicial legislation or at least judicial activism is the order of the day. The European Convention on Human Rights has already been influential,[247] while the Court of the European Commission has been described as "hell-bent on teleological interpretation and a master at creation of new doctrine."[248] When, in 1976, a working group of the Labour party put up a discussion paper urging a Bill of Rights,[249] it confirmed that all three parties were moving in the

241. E.g., William Twining and David Miers, *How to Do Things with Rules*. For a statement of the accepted "rules" for precedent, see Rupert Cross, *Precedent in English Law*, 2d ed., *passim*.

242. E.g., Jaffé, *Judges as Lawmakers* 28–29, discussing *Myers* v. *DPP*, [1965] A.C. 1001 (1964).

243. Ibid. 20.

244. E.g., Freeman, "Standards of Adjudication" 166.

245. *Shaw* v. *DPP*, [1962] A.C. 220 (1961).

246. *Miliangos* v. *George Frank, Ltd.*, [1976] A.C. 443 (1975). See especially at 823–25 for the five tests for overruling.

247. *R.* v. *Miah*, [1974] 1 W.L.R. 683 (H.L.); see Peter Wallington, "The European Convention on Human Rights and English Law" 9.

248. Freeman, "Standards of Adjudication" 166.

249. It would incorporate the European Convention on Human Rights into English law. See *The Guardian*, 16 Feb. 1976. See also Michael Zander, *A Bill of Rights?*

direction of some partially entrenched provisions of the constitution with their inevitable hint of judicial review and even more obvious judicial involvement with policy.

Much, of course, will depend not only on the political turn of events but also on the type of law lord who is appointed. In the past twenty years there has been some resurgence of the political law lord.[250] It is now known, for instance, that both Hartley Shawcross and Walter Monckton toyed with law lordships.[251] Elwyn-Jones, Lord Chancellor, at first appeared to prefer to promote conventional judges, although pressed to appoint younger and more liberal law lords, directly from practice and politics if necessary, by the left-wing press.[252] If labor and race matters—indeed, most public law matters—are to be handled by the judiciary, then some greater flexibility may be necessary in the type of appointments.[253] By 1977 there was some evidence of response to that perceived need.

This would, however, be only the beginning. The trend toward dispersion in decision making will almost certainly send more issues to the courts;[254] and while the idea that the House makes law only in "hard

250. In 1974, 5 of the 10 law lords had political experience. Yet the logic assumed here is by no means always carried into practice. In an appeal on the National Industrial Relations Act—*Heatons Transp., Ltd.* v. *T&GWU*, [1973] A.C. 15 (1972)—the Lord Chancellor (Hailsham) announced a week before the case was decided that no law lord with political experience would sit on the panel. The case was then heard with almost indecent speed; A. A. Paterson, "Judges: A Political Elite?" 118, 126, 127.

251. Although apparently as stepping-stones to the Lord Chief Justiceship. Lord Birkenhead, *Walter Monckton* 303–5.

252. John Paine, "Labour and the Lawyers" 44.

253. E.g., Fleming, "Precedent and the Judicial Function" 17, 20.

254. There was further evidence of this in the summer of 1976, during the so-called Tameside case, where the courts intervened with respect to the minister's discretionary powers in phasing out grammar schools in the Tameside local authority. *The Times* welcomed the decision of the lower courts editorially (*The Times*, 7 July 1976) and reported that the Court of Appeal decision "will have utterly evaporated the force of the 1976 Education Bill and made it much more likely that grammar schools will remain in one-fifth of England"; ibid., 28 July 1976. In holding that the minister had "misdirected" himself, Denning, in the Court of Appeal, purported to treat *Liversidge* v. *Anderson* as having no precedential value; *Secretary of State for Educ. & Science* v. *Tameside Metropolitan Borough Council* [1977] A.C. 1014 (C.A. and H.L. 1976). The Times Law Report, 26 July 1976, *The Times*, 27 July 1976.

Although on a Monday the Court of Appeal refused leave to appeal, on Thursday the House gave leave to appeal and the following day heard the appeal. Early the following week it announced its decision, unanimously upholding the Court of Appeal, although delaying the giving of formal judgments. The *Sunday Times* commented that, "no doubt" the Lord Chancellor had "told them to get on with the decision" (1 Aug. 1976), while the *Observer* noted that "with so many legal luminaries clashing it is not surprising that the Lords appointed a specially strong committee of five law lords"; (1 Aug. 1976).

More generally, the *Sunday Times* published an article by Hugo Jones entitled "The Judges Begin to Fight Back" (1 Aug. 1976), while in discussing another case at first instance, *Laker Airways* v. *Department of Trade*, [1977] Q.B. 643, 696 (1976). *The Times* editorialized with respect to ministerial discretion that "any sign that the courts are ready

cases" will not die easily,[255] the impetus will be not only toward passing more issues to the courts, but also toward accepting the reality of creativity in the judicial process. Rather than following the apostles of the declaratory theory into sophisticated semantic distinctions between principles and policies and principles and rules, the law lords may be expected to return to a twentieth-century Mansfieldism involving a merger of the traditional elegance of English doctrinal analysis and less-than-scientific analysis of the competing policies, represented by the competing doctrines that are inevitably at stake by the time a case reaches the House of Lords. Such a change, with its inherent antidemocratic tendencies, would in time develop its own literature by way of apologia.[256]

Assuming that this development continues, it will not be rapid; but it may be derivative. Constitutionally the changes may come from the experiences of Canada and Australia, and more frequently from the Common Market countries. The increasing influence of American concepts in English academic law have already had an important impact on the analysis of the legal, and especially the judicial, process. Devlin, recently decrying the relevance of the Supreme Court of the United States to the English experience, wrote, "The Supreme Court like the vines of France is not for transplantation. The soil and climate in which it flourishes are not those of Britain; the hands that tend it have now like the Bordeaux vignerons acquired unique skills."[257] Yet the vines of California were imported from France and grafted onto local roots, only to be reexported to France when phylloxera destroyed the strength of the French vine in the 1880s and the 1890s.[258] The *vignerons* of Bordeaux today tend a plant that is basically American. The common lawyer of tomorrow may well be tending a common law that has been exported and reimported, perhaps with European grafts implanted.

Where the vineyard analogy will lead, however, is not clear. Although the substantive formalists believed that the answer to any question lay

to act decisively to prevent its arbitrary use and to test it against principles of natural justice can only be welcomed." Only Professor John Griffith appeared to sound a cautionary note during the period. "Some judges are advocating the institution of a Bill of Rights to protect us from the power of Ministers. It should not be overlooked that the result of so doing would be to give more power to the judges who are responsible and accountable to no one"; John A. G. Griffith, "Power of Judges," *Sunday Times*, 8 Aug. 1976. See also John A. G. Griffith, "The Tameside Opinion" 589.

255. For the most sophisticated defense of the declaratory theory, see Ronald M. Dworkin, "Hard Cases" 1057. The core of Dworkin's distinction is at 1067: "Principles are propositions that describe rights; policies are propositions that describe goals." Dworkin's position, although superficially more "open" than Hart's, would, in the end, deny any discretion to the judiciary, by claiming that in every judicial decision there is some binding principle (even if no rule) applicable.

256. For an attempt to outline the process of alternative model building, see Robert Stevens, "The Role of a Final Appeal Court in a Democracy" 509.

257. Patrick Devlin, "Judges and Lawmakers" 1, 6.

258. Hugh Johnson, *The World Atlas of Wine* 18–19.

within the four corners of the common law, most formalists and positivists have allowed some element of discretion to the judges. Those of a utilitarian bent have called for, or expected, the judiciary to weigh the relative social, political, and economic merits in making these decisions. That tradition, represented most elegantly by Radcliffe, has seen the solution for such lacunae in the application of a kind of natural law still nestling in the breasts of the judges. Some latter-day positivists—taking a position likely to find favor with those who have little confidence in the political sagacity or predelictions of the British judiciary—have argued that, properly understood, the principles (as opposed to the rules) of the common law itself can settle any disputes between competing rules of the law.

In short, while the existence of an area of apparent discretion has become more obvious and accepted, the lack—until recently—of discussion of the judicial process in the British context has meant that serious discussion of competing judicial roles has only just begun. The influence of Continental and American ideas will no doubt influence these analyses as the British rethink the role of the judges—and more especially the appeal judges—in the light of the changing political, social, and economic realities. The Treaty of Rome may already have led to a broader approach to statutory interpretation; a Bill of Rights would demand a more principle-oriented rather than precedent-oriented approach to law in general. Yet whatever the quality of the judges, such a revolution will not be possible as long as apologists seek to restrict the judicial role to one circumscribed by the logic of the law or by some compelling principles of the common law.

The future will lie in an acceptance of the element of discretion in the final appeal process, coupled with a responsibility to articulate the purposes and goals of different branches of the law. The courts in Britain are never likely to compete with the legislature; such a possibility runs counter to four hundred years of political and intellectual history. Complementarity with the legislature is, however, essential; and complementarity involves intelligent creativity. The next decade will show whether the appeal judges are capable of providing a rationale that will at a minimum make them an essential element in the British Constitution and, ideally, raise the issue of whether they might not appear as the junior partners of Parliament in the lawmaking process.

APPENDIXES
BIBLIOGRAPHY
INDEX OF CASES
INDEX

❧ Appendixes

Comparative Analysis of Business of
Selected State and British Courts, 1925

	New York	Wisconsin	Colorado	House of Lords	Privy Council
Administrative Law	10	3	5	1	0
Admiralty	0	0	0	1	0
Bankruptcy	0	0	0	1	0
Commercial Arbitration	6	1	0	0	0
Common Law Topics					
1. Agency	4	1	6	0	0
2. Bills and Notes	8	5	6	0	0
3. Contract and Sale	69	23	34	5	1
4. Corporations and Partner-ships	14	7	9	2	0
5. Criminal Law	35	7	13	0	0
6. Damages	2	1	2	0	1
7. Domestic Relations	9	9	6	2	0
8. Evidence	6	13	20	0	0
9. Insurance	16	5	5	2	1
10. Municipal Corporations	8	11	6	0	1
11. Property	33	22	31	2*	1
12. Quasi-Contract	1	3	0	0	0
13. Suretyship	2	3	2	0	0
14. Torts	71	51	15	3	1
15. Trusts	8	4	3	0	0
16. Water Rights	3	0	6	0	0
17. Wills and Administration	14	15	6	0	0
Constitutional Questions	9	8	5	0	5
Disbarment	2	1	0	0	0

APPENDIX I continued

International Law, War and Peace	3	0	0	0	0
Jurisdiction	3	1	6	0	0
Practice, Pleading and Procedure	81	24	56	0	1
Public Utilities	5	10	1	0	0
Search and Seizure	0	6	1	0	0
Statutory Construction	14	23	6	3	6
Taxation	23	10	8	7	0
Workmen's Compensation	21	21	13	1	1
TOTALS	480	288	271	30	19

*This figure embraces one case involving a claim to peerage.

SOURCE: Felix Frankfurter and James M. Landis, *The Business of the Supreme Court: A Study in the Federal Judicial System* 304 (New York, 1928).

APPENDIX II

Comparative Analysis on Percentage Basis of Business of Selected State and British Courts, 1925

	New York %	Wisconsin %	Colorado %	House of Lords %	Privy Council %
Administrative Law	2.5	1.0	1.8	3.3	0
Admiralty	0	0	0	3.3	0
Bankruptcy	0	0	0	3.3	0
Commercial Arbitration	1.3	.3	0	0	0
Common Law Topics					
1. Agency	.8	.3	2.2	0	0
2. Bills and Notes	1.7	1.7	2.2	0	0
3. Contract and Sale	14.4	8.0	12.5	16.7	5.3
4. Corporations and Partnerships	2.9	2.4	3.4	6.7	0
5. Criminal Law	7.3	2.4	4.8	0	0
6. Damages	.4	.3	.7	0	5.3
7. Domestic Relations	1.9	3.1	2.2	6.7	0
8. Evidence	1.3	4.5	7.4	0	0
9. Insurance	3.3	1.7	1.8	6.7	5.3
10. Municipal Corporations	1.7	3.8	2.2	0	5.3
11. Property	6.9	7.6	11.4	6.7	5.3
12. Quasi-Contract	.2	1.0	0	0	0

APPENDIX II continued

13. Suretyship	.4	1.0	.7	0	0
14. Torts	14.8	17.7	5.5	10.0	5.3
15. Trusts	1.7	1.4	1.1	0	0
16. Water Rights	.6	0	2.2	0	0
17. Wills and Administration	2.9	5.2	2.2	0	0
Constitutional Questions	1.9	2.8	1.8	0	26.3
Disbarment	.4	.3	0	0	0
International Law	.6	0	0	0	0
Jurisdiction	.6	.3	2.2	0	0
Practice, Pleading and Procedure	16.9	8.3	20.7	0	5.3
Public Utilities	1.0	3.5	.4	0	0
Search and Seizure	0	2.1	.4	0	0
Statutory Construction	2.9	8.0	2.2	10.0	31.4
Taxation	4.8	3.5	3.0	23.3	0
Workmen's Compensation	4.4	7.3	4.8	3.3	5.3

SOURCE: Felix Frankfurter and James M. Landis, *The Business of the Supreme Court: A Study in the Federal Judicial System* 305 (New York, 1928).

✑ Bibliography

BOOKS

Abel-Smith, Brian, and Stevens, Robert. *In Search of Justice: Society and the Legal System*. London, 1968.
_____. *Lawyers and the Courts: A Sociological Study of the English Legal System 1750–1965*. London, 1967.
Allen, Carleton Kemp. *Law in the Making*. 7th ed. London, 1958.
Allen, H. C., and Thompson, Roger, eds. *Contrast and Connection: Bicentennial Essays in Anglo–American History*. Athens, Ohio, 1976.
An Annual Register of World Events. 1842–.
Arnstein, Walter L. *The Bradlaugh Case*. Oxford, 1965.
Asquith, Margot. *Margot Asquith: An Autobiography*. 2 vols. New York, 1920.
Atiyah, P. S. *Accidents, Compensation and the Law*. 2d ed. London, 1975.
Atkinson, A. B. *Unequal Shares*. London, 1972.
Atlay, J. B. *Victorian Chancellors*. 2 vols. London, 1908.
Ayers, Gwendoline. *England's First State Hospitals and the Metropolitan Asylums Board, 1867–1930*. London, 1971.
Bagehot, Walter. *Bagehot's Historical Essays*. Edited by Norman St. John-Stevas. Cambridge, 1968.
_____. *The English Constitution*. Garden City, 1961.
Bagnell, P. S. *The Railwaymen*. London, 1963.
Ballentine, Sargeant. *Some Experiences of a Barrister's Life*. London, 1883.
Bardens, Dennis. *Lord Justice Birkett*. London, 1963.
Bayliss, F. *British Wage Councils*. Oxford, 1962.
Beaverbrook, Lord (Max Aitken). *The Decline and Fall of Lloyd George*. London, 1966.
_____. *Politicians and the War*. London, 1960.
Beer, Samuel H. *Modern British Policies*. London, 1965.
Beveridge, William. *Power and Influence*. London, 1953.
Bickel, Alexander M. *The Least Dangerous Branch: The Supreme Court at the Bar of Politics*. Indianapolis, 1962.
Birkenhead, Lord. *The Life of F. E. Smith, First Earl of Birkenhead*. London, 1959.
_____. *Walter Monckton: The Life of Viscount Monckton of Brenchley*. London, 1969.

Blackstone, William. *Commentaries on the Law of England*. Boston, 1799.

Blake, Robert. *The Conservative Party from Peel to Churchill*. London, 1970.

Blom-Cooper, Louis, and Drewry, Gavin. *Final Appeal: A Study of the House of Lords in Its Judicial Capacity*. Oxford, 1972.

Blum, John M. *V Was for Victory*. New York, 1976.

Bond, Maurice F., ed. *The Manuscripts of the House of Lords*. London, 1965.

Boswell, James. *Life of Johnson*. Oxford, 1953.

Bowra, C. Maurice. *Memories 1898–1939*. Cambridge, Mass., 1967.

Bowyer, George. *The Appellate Jurisdiction of the House of Lords and the New Court of Appeal*. London, 1873.

Bresler, Fenton. *Lord Goddard: A Biography*. London, 1977.

Bromhead, P. A. *The House of Lords in Contemporary Politics*. London, 1958.

Brown, R. G. S. *The Administrative Process in Britain*. London, 1971.

Browne, G. P. *The Judicial Committee and the British North America Act*. Toronto, 1967.

Bryce, James. *The American Commonwealth*. 3d ed. London and New York, 1909.

Buckley, Henry B. *The Law and Practice under the Companies Act (1873)*. 13th ed. London, 1957.

Bullock, Alan. *The Life and Times of Ernest Bevin*. London, 1960.

Butler, David E., and Kavanagh, D. *The British General Election of February, 1974*. London, 1974.

Butler, David E., and King, Anthony. *The British General Election of 1964*. London, 1965.

————. *The British General Election of 1966*. London, 1966.

Butler, David E., and Pinto-Duschinsky, Michael. *The British General Election of 1970*. London, 1971.

Butler, David E., and Rose, Richard. *The British General Election of 1959*. London, 1960.

Calvert, Harry. *Constitutional Law in Northern Ireland: A Study in Regional Government*. London, 1968.

Campbell, John. *Life of Lord Campbell*. 2 vols. London, 1881.

————. *Lives of the Lord Chancellors*. 8 vols. London, 1869.

Candozo, Benjamin. *The Nature of the Judicial Process*. New Haven, 1921.

Cave, A. *Three Journeys*. London, 1928.

Caves, Richard E., and Associates. *Britain's Economic Prospects*. Washington, D.C., 1968.

Cecil, David. *Melbourne*. London, 1955.

Chapman, Brian. *British Government Observed*. London, 1963.

Chapman, Gerald W. *Edmund Burke: The Practical Imagination*. Cambridge, Mass., 1967.

Charley, William T. *The Crusade Against the Constitution: An Historical Vindication of the House of Lords*. London, 1895.

————. *Mending and Ending the House of Lords*. London, 1900.

Cheshire, G. C.; Fifoot, C. H. S.; and Furmston, M. P. *The Law of Contract*. 8th ed. London, 1972.

Christoph, James B. *Capital Punishment and British Politics: The British Movement to Abolish the Death Penalty 1947–1957*. London, 1962.

Citrine, Arthur. *Trade Union Law*. 2d ed. London, 1960.

Clegg, H. A.; Fox, Alan; and Thompson, A. F. *A History of British Trade Unionism since 1899*. Oxford, 1964.

Cole, J. A. *Lord Haw-Haw and William Joyce.* New York, 1963.

Commerce Clearing House. *British Tax.* New York, 1973.

Cooper, Charles P. *A Brief Account of Some of the Most Important Proceedings in Parliament, Relative to the Defects in the Administration of Justice in the Court of Chancery, the House of Lords and the Court of Commissioners of Bankruptcy.* London, 1828.

Cornish, William. *The Jury.* Harmondsworth, 1968.

Creighton, Donald. *Canada's First Century 1867–1967.* Toronto, 1970.

Crick, Bernard. *The Reform of Parliament.* London, 1964.

Cripps, Charles (Lord Parmoor). *Do Well and Right and Let the World Sink.* London, 1915.

————. *A Retrospect.* London, 1936.

Cross, Rupert. *Precedent in English Law.* 1st ed. Oxford, 1961; 2d ed. Oxford, 1968.

Cross, Rupert, and Jones, A. *An Introduction to Criminal Law.* 5th ed. London, 1964.

Crossman, Richard. *The Diaries of a Cabinet Minister.* Vol. 1. London, 1975; Vol. 2. London, 1976.

Cullen, Tom. *Maundy Gregory.* London, 1974.

Cunningham, Henry Stewart. *Lord Bowen: A Biographical Sketch.* London, 1897.

Dangerfield, George. *The Strange Death of Liberal England.* London, 1935.

Defoe, Daniel. *History of the Union of Great Britain.* Edinburgh, 1709.

Denison, Charles M., and Scott, Charles H. *The Practice and Procedure of the House of Lords.* London, 1879.

Denning, Alfred. *Borrowing from Scotland.* Glasgow, 1963.

————. *The Changing Law.* London, 1953.

————. *Freedom under the Law.* London, 1949.

————. *From Precedent to Precedent.* London, 1959.

————. *The Independence of the Judges.* Holdsworth Lecture. Birmingham, 1950.

————. *Responsibility before the Law.* Cohen Lecture. Jerusalem, 1961.

————. *The Road to Justice.* London, 1955.

de Smith, Stanley A. *Constitutional and Administrative Law.* Harmondsworth, 1971.

Devlin, Patrick. *The Criminal Prosecution in England.* Yale, 1958.

————. *Enforcement of Morals.* Oxford, 1970.

————. *Law and Morals.* Holdsworth Lecture. Birmingham, 1961.

————. *Samples of Lawmaking.* Oxford, 1962.

————. *Too Proud to Fight: Woodrow Wilson's Neutrality.* London, 1975.

————. *Trial by Jury.* London, 1956.

Dicey, Albert Venn. *Introduction to the Study of the Law of the Constitution.* 8th ed. London, 1915; 10th ed. London, 1959. Reprinted 1973.

————. *Lectures on the Relation between Law and Public Opinion in England during the Nineteenth Century.* London, 1905. Reprinted 1914, 1962.

Dicey, Albert Venn, and Morris, John H. C. *Conflict of Laws.* 9th ed. London, 1973.

Dickerson, Reed. *The Interpretation and Application of Statutes.* Boston, 1975.

Dictionary of National Biography. 26 vols. Oxford, 1917–.

Diplock, Kenneth. *The Courts as Legislators.* Holdsworth Lecture. Birmingham, 1965.

————. *The Role of the Judicial Process in the Regulation of Competition.* Cohen Lecture. Jerusalem, 1967.

Dunedin, Lord (Andrew Graham Murray). *The Divergencies and Convergencies of English and Scottish Law.* Glasgow, 1935.

du Parcq, Herbert. *Aspects of the Law.* Holdsworth Lecture. Birmingham, 1948.

Dworkin, Ronald M. *Taking Rights Seriously.* London, 1977.

Ensor, R. C. K. *England 1870–1914.* Oxford, 1936.

Evershed, Raymond. *The Influence and Importance of Practice and Procedure in the Supreme Court.* Birmingham, 1957.

Fairfield, Charles. *A Memoir of Lord Bramwell.* London, 1898.

Farmer, J. A. *Tribunals and Government.* London, 1974.

Farrar, John H. *Law Reform and the Law Commission.* London, 1974.

Fifoot, C. H. S. *Judge and Jurist in the Reign of Victoria.* London, 1959.

Finer, Samuel E. *Anonymous Empire: A Study of the Lobby in Great Britain.* 2d ed. London, 1966.

Finlayson, Geoffrey B. A. M. *Decade of Reform: England in the Eighteen Thirties.* New York, 1970.

Fitzroy, Almeric. *Memoirs.* 2 vols. London, 1925.

Fleming, Donald, and Bailyn, Bernard, eds. *Law in American History.* Boston, 1971.

Foot, Michael. *Aneurin Bevan.* Vols. 1 and 2. London, 1962 and 1973.

Frankfurter, Felix, and Landis, James M. *The Business of the Supreme Court: A Study in the Federal Judicial System.* New York, 1928.

Freund, Paul. *The Supreme Court of the United States.* Cleveland, 1961.

Friedman, Lawrence M. *A History of American Law.* New York, 1973.

Friedmann, Wolfgang. *Law in a Changing Society.* Harmondsworth, 1963.

Gardiner, Gerald. *Capital Punishment as a Deterrent and the Alternative.* London, 1956.

————. *The Trials of a Lord Chancellor.* Holdsworth Lecture. Birmingham, 1968.

Gardiner, Gerald, and Martin, Andrew. *Law Reform* NOW. London, 1963.

Gibb, Andrew. *Law from Over the Border.* Edinburgh, 1950.

Gilbert, Martin, and Gott, Richard. *The Appeasers.* Boston, 1963.

Gilmore, Grant. *The Death of Contract.* Columbus, 1974.

Gilmore, Grant, and Black, Charles. *Law of Admiralty.* 2d ed. New York, 1975.

Ginsberg, Morris, ed. *Law and Opinion in England in the 20th Century.* London, 1959.

Goodhart, Arthur L. *Essays in Jurisprudence and the Common Law.* Cambridge, 1931.

Gordon, J. W. *The Appellate Jurisdiction of the House of Lords and of the Full Parliament.* London, 1903.

Gough, J. W. *Fundamental Law in English Constitutional History.* Oxford, 1955.

Gower, L. C. B. *Independent Africa: The Challenge to the Legal Profession.* Cambridge, Mass., 1967.

————. *Modern Company Law.* London, 1954.

Graves, Robert, and Hodge, Anthony. *The Long Week-End.* London, 1940.

Greene, Wilfred. *The Judicial Office.* Holdsworth Lecture. Birmingham, 1938.

Gwyn, William B. *Democracy and the Cost of Politics in Britain.* London, 1962.

Hadden, Tom. *Company Law and Capitalism.* London, 1972.

Hailsham, Lord (Quintin McGarel Hogg). *The Case for Conservatism.* London, 1975.

_____. *The Door Wherein I Went*. London, 1975.

_____. *The Need for Faith in a Scientific Age*. Glasgow, 1960.

_____. *The Problems of Being a Lord Chancellor*. Holdsworth Lecture. Birmingham, 1972.

_____. *Some Proposals for Constitutional Reform*. London, 1969.

Haldane, Richard Burdon. *An Autobiography*. London, 1929.

Haldane Society. *The Foresight Saga: A Symposium*. London, 1965.

Hale, Matthew. *The Jurisdiction of the Lord's House*. London, 1796.

Hancock, William K., ed. *Survey of British Commonwealth Affairs*. London, 1937.

Hanes, David. *The First British Workmen's Compensation Act, 1897*. New Haven, 1968.

Harding, Alan. *A Social History of English Law*. Baltimore, 1966.

Harkness, D. W. *The Restless Dominion: The Irish Free State and the British Commonwealth of Nations, 1921–1931*. New York, 1970.

Harper, Fowler V., and Fleming, James, Jr. *The Law of Torts*. 2 vols. Boston, 1956.

Harris, Richard, ed. *Reminiscences of Sir Henry Hawkins*. London, 1904.

Hart, H. L. A. *Concept of Law*. Oxford, 1961.

_____. *Law, Liberty and Morality*. Stanford, 1963.

Harvey, William B. *Law and Social Change in Ghana*. Princeton, 1966.

Haynes, Freeman Oliver. *The Supreme Court of Judicature Act, 1873*. London, 1874.

Herschell, Farrer. *The Political Situation*. London, 1895.

Heuston, R. F. V. *Lives of the Lord Chancellors 1885–1940*. Oxford, 1964.

_____, ed. *Salmond on the Law of Torts*. 16th ed. London, 1973.

Hewart, Gordon B. *The New Depotism*. London, 1929.

Hodson, Francis. *Judicial Discretion and Its Exercise*. Holdsworth Lecture. Birmingham, 1962.

Hoffman, J. S., and Levack, Paul, eds. *Burke's Politics*. New York, 1949.

Hohfeld, Wesley. *Fundamental Legal Conceptions*. New Haven, 1919.

Holdsworth, William S. *History of English Law*. Vols. 1–17. London, 1903–72.

Holland, R. H. C., and Schwartzenberger, R. G., eds. *Law, Justice and Equity*. London, 1967.

Hollander, Barnett. *Colonial Justice: The Unique Achievement of the Privy Council's Committee of Judges*. London, 1961.

Holmes, Oliver Wendell, Jr. *Collected Legal Papers*. New York, 1921.

Houghlin, Walter. *The Victorian Frame of Mind*. New Haven, 1957.

Howe, M. de W., ed. *Holmes-Pollock Letters*. London, 1953.

_____, ed. *Holmes-Laski Letters*. London, 1953.

Hudson Institute. *The United Kingdom in 1980*. London, 1974.

Hughes, Graham, ed. *Law, Reason and Justice: Essays in Legal Philosophy*. New York, 1969.

Hughes, Hector. *National Sovereignty and Judicial Autonomy in the British Commonwealth of Nations*. London, 1931.

Hurst, James W. *Law and Conditions of Freedom in the Nineteenth Century United States*. Madison, 1956.

Hyde, H. Montgomery. *Carson*. London, 1953.

_____. *Norman Birkett*. London, 1964.

Irving, Clive, et al. *Anatomy of a Scandal*. New York, 1963.

Jackson, R. M. *The Machinery of Justice in England*. Cambridge, 1940.

Jaffé, Louis L. *English and American Judges as Lawmakers*. Oxford, 1969.

James, Robert Rhodes. *The British Revolution, 1880–1939*. New York, 1977.

Jenkins, Roy. *Asquith*. New York, 1964.

Jennings, W. Ivor. *Constitutional Problems in Pakistan*. Cambridge, 1957.

Johnson, Hugh. *The World Atlas of Wine*. New York, 1971.

Jones, W. J. *The Elizabethan Court of Chancery*. Oxford, 1967.

Keeton, George W. *English Law: The Judicial Contribution*. Newton Abbot, 1974.

————. *A Liberal Attorney-General*. London, 1949.

Keith, James. *The Spirit of the Law of Scotland*. Holdsworth Lecture. Birmingham, 1957.

Kilbrandon, Lord (C. J. D. Shaw). *Other People's Law*. London, 1966.

Kilmuir, Lord (David Maxwell-Fyfe). *Political Adventures: The Memoirs of the Earl of Kilmuir*. London, 1964.

Koss, Stephen E. *Lord Haldane: Scapegoat for Liberalism*. New York, 1969.

Landon, Michael. *The Triumph of the Lawyers: Their Role in English Politics 1678–1689*. University, Ala., 1970.

Laski, Harold. *Essays in Law and Government*. London, 1932.

Laskin, Bora. *Canadian Constitutional Law*. Toronto, 1951.

Lawson, F. H. *The Oxford Law School 1850–1965*. Oxford, 1968.

Lester, Anthony, and Bindman, Geoffrey. *Race and Law*. Cambridge, Mass., 1972.

Levin, Bernard. *Run It Down the Flagpole*. New York, 1971.

Llewellyn, Karl N. *The Common Law Tradition: Deciding Appeals*. Boston, 1960.

Lloyd, Trevor O. *Empire to Welfare State: English History 1906–1967*. Oxford, 1970.

Loomis, Dwight, and Calhoun, J. Gilbert. *The Judicial and Civil History of Connecticut*. Boston, 1895.

MacDermott, John C. *Murder in 1963*. Holdsworth Lecture. Birmingham, 1963.

————. *Protection from Power under English Law*. Hamlyn Lectures. London, 1957.

MacDonagh, Oliver. *A Pattern of Government Growth: The Passenger Acts and Their Enforcement*. London, 1961.

McGregor, O. R. *Divorce in England*. London, 1957.

McLeod, Ian. *Neville Chamberlain*. London, 1961.

Macmillan, Harold. *Riding the Storm*. London, 1971.

Macmillan, Hugh. *Law and Language*. Holdsworth Lecture. Birmingham, 1931.

————. *Law and Other Things*. Cambridge, 1937.

————. *A Man of Law's Tale*. London, 1952.

MacQueen, John F. *The Appellate Jurisdiction of the House of Lords and Privy Council*. London, 1842.

————. *A Letter to Lord Lyndhurst*. London, 1856.

————. *Report of the Debates on the Life Peerage Question in the House of Lords*. London, 1856.

McWhinney, Edward. *Judicial Review in the English Speaking World*. 2d ed. Toronto, 1960.

Maine, Henry. *Ancient Law*. New York, 1864.

Maitland, Frederick W. *The Constitutional History of the House of Lords*. London, 1894.

————. *Justice and Police: The English Citizen, His Rights and Responsibilities*. London, 1885.

Majoribanks, Edward, and Colvin, Ian. *The Life of Lord Carson*. 3 vols. London, 1932–36.

Mallet, Charles. *Lord Cave: A Memoir*. London, 1931.

Marriott, John A. R. *English Political Institutions*. Oxford, 1910.

————. *Modern England 1885–1932: A History of My Own Times*. London, 1934.

————. *Second Chambers*. Oxford, 1910.

Marsden, Philip. *In Peril before Parliament*. New York, 1965.

Marshall, Geoffrey. *Constitutional Theory*. Oxford, 1971.

Martin, Kingsley. *Harold Laski*. London, 1953.

Martin, Theodore. *Life of Lord Lyndhurst*. London, 1884.

Marwick, Arthur. *Britain in the Century of Total War*. Boston, 1968.

Maugham, F. H. *At the End of the Day*. London, 1954.

————. *The Problem of Judicial Proof*. Holdsworth Lecture. Birmingham, 1939.

————. *The Truth about the Munich Crisis*. London, 1954.

Maugham, Robin. *Somerset and All the Maughams*. New York, 1966.

Maurice, Roderick. *Haldane: The Life of Viscount Haldane of Cloan*. 2 vols. London, 1937.

Megarry, Robert. *Miscellany-at-Law*. London, 1955.

Mitchell, B. R. *Abstract of British Historical Statistics*. Cambridge, 1971.

Monson, Edward. *Builders of Our Law during the Reign of Queen Victoria*. 2d ed. London, 1904.

Monypenny, William F., and Buckle, George. *Life of Disraeli*. 6 vols. London, 1929.

Moran, Michael. *The Politics of Industrial Relations: The Origins, Life, and Death of the 1971 Industrial Relations Act*. London, 1977.

Morgan, John Hartman. *The House of Lords and the Constitution*. London, 1910.

Morley, John. *Life of William Ewart Gladstone*. 3 vols. London, 1903.

Morris, John W. *Law and Public Opinion*. Holdsworth Lecture. Birmingham, 1958.

————. *The Spirit of Justice*. Haldane Lecture. London, 1954.

Morris-Jones, John. *The Government and Politics of India*. London, 1967.

Morrison, Fred L. *Courts and Political Process in England*. Beverly Hills, 1973.

Morrison, Herbert. *Government and Parliament*. 3d ed. Oxford, 1964.

Moulton, F. *Life of Lord Moulton*. London, 1922.

Mowat, C. L. *Britain between the Wars, 1918–1940*. London, 1962.

Mutesa II, King of Buganda. *Desecration of My Kingdom*. London, 1967.

Nash, Thomas A. *Life of Lord Chancellor Westbury*. London, 1888.

Nehru, Jawaharlal. *The Discovery of India*. London, 1956.

New, Chester W. *The Life of Henry Brougham to 1830*. Oxford, 1961.

Nicolson, Harold. *Diaries and Letters 1939–1945*. London, 1967.

Nightingale, J. *Report of the Proceedings before the House of Lords . . . against Her Majesty Caroline*. London, 1821.

Niven, David. *The Moon's A Balloon*. London, 1971.

Normand, Wilfred. *Scottish Judicature and Legal Procedure*. Holdsworth Lecture. Birmingham, 1940.

Nutting, Anthony. *No End of a Lesson: The Story of Suez*. New York, 1967.

Oaksey, Lord (Geoffrey Lawrence). *The Nuremburg Trials and the Progress of International Law*. Holdsworth Lecture. Birmingham, 1947.

O'Brien, R. Barry. *The Life of Lord Russell of Killowan*. London, 1902.

Palley, Claire. *The Constitutional History and Law of Southern Rhodesia 1888–1965 with Special Reference to Imperial Control*. Oxford, 1966.

Parker, Charles S., ed. *Sir Robert Peel: From His Private Papers*. London, 1899.

Pelling, Henry. *America and the British Left*. London, 1956.

―――. *A History of British Trade Unionism*. London, 1966.

Phillips, Hood. *Reform of the Constitution*. London, 1970.

Pierson, Coen G. *Canada and the Privy Council*. London, 1960.

Pinson, Barry. *Revenue Law*. London, 1971.

Plucknett, Theodore F. *Concise History of the Common Law*. 5th ed. London, 1956.

Poirer, P. *The Advent of the Labour Party*. London, 1958.

Pollock, Frederick. *Essays in Jurisprudence and Ethics*. London, 1882.

Porter, Samuel L. *Case Law in the Interpretation of Statutes*. Holdsworth Lecture. Birmingham, 1939.

Potter, Harold. *Historical Introduction to English Law*. 4th ed. Edited by Albert Kiralfy. London, 1958.

Powell, J. Enoch, and Wallis, Keith. *The House of Lords in the Middle Ages*. London, 1968.

Pritt, D. N. *Autobiography*. 3 vols. London, 1966.

Prosser, William L. *Handbook of the Law of Torts*. St. Paul, 1971.

Radcliffe, Cyril John. *Law and the Democratic State*. Holdsworth Lecture. Birmingham, 1955.

―――. *The Law and Its Compass*. London, 1960.

―――. *Not in Feather Beds*. London, 1968.

Rawls, John. *A Theory of Justice*. Cambridge, Mass., 1971.

Rheinstein, Max, ed. *Max Weber on Law in Economy and Society*. Cambridge, Mass., 1954.

Roberts, Carl Eric. *Sir John Simon, Being an Account of the Life and Career of Sir John Simon*. London, 1938.

Robertson, James Patrick. *The Duty of Educated Intellect to the State*. London, 1895.

Romilly, Samuel. *Life of Romilly*. London, 1840.

Rose, Eliot J., et al. *Colour and Citizenship*. London, 1969.

Rose, Richard. *Governing without Consensus: An Irish Perspective*. Boston, 1971.

―――. *Politics in England*. 2d ed. Boston, 1974.

―――, ed. *Policy-Making in Britain*. New York, 1969.

Rowland, Peter. *The Last Liberal Government: The Promised Land 1905–1910*. London, 1968.

―――. *The Last Liberal Government: Unfinished Business 1911–1914*. London, 1971.

Russell, Edward Frederick Langley. *The Royal Conscience*. London, 1961.

Salmon, Cyril. *Crime and Punishment*. Holdsworth Lecture. Birmingham, 1974.

―――. *The Law and Individual Liberty*. Haldane Lecture. London, 1970.

Sampson, Anthony. *The New Anatomy of Britain*. London, 1971.

Scarman, Leslie. *Codification and Judge-Made Law*. Holdsworth Lecture. Birmingham, 1966.

―――. *English Law—The New Dimension*. London, 1974.

Schuster, Claud. *Haldane of Cloan, the Man and His Work*. London, 1928.

Scott, L., and Hildesby, A. *The Case of Requisitions*. Oxford, 1920.

Scrutton, T. E. *Charter Parties and Bills of Lading*. 17th ed. London, 1964.

Selborne, Lord (Roundell Palmer). *Memorials Personal and Political 1865–1895*. 4 vols. London, 1896.

A Selection of Lord Macnaghten's Judgments 1887–1912. London, 1951.

Shaw, A. *Thomas Shaw*. London, 1937.

Shaw, Thomas. *Law of the Kinsmen*. London, 1923.

———. *Legislature and Judiciary*. London, 1911.

———. *Letters to Isabel*. London, 1921 and 1936.

———. *The Other Bundle*. London, 1927.

Shetreet, Shimon. *Judges on Trial*. Amsterdam, 1976.

Shientag, Bernard Lloyd. *Moulders of Modern Legal Thought*. New York, 1943.

Shyllon, F. O. *Black Slaves in Britain*. Oxford, 1974.

Simon, Jocelyn. "*With All My Worldly Goods. . . .*" Birmingham, 1964.

Simon, John. *Crown and Commonwealth*. Oxford, 1953.

———. *The General Strike*. London, 1926.

———. *The Limits of Precedent*. Holdsworth Lecture. Birmingham, 1943.

———. *Retrospect*. London, 1952.

Sissons, Michael, and French, Philip, eds. *The Age of Austerity 1945–1951*. London, 1963.

Smith, Arthur. *Lord Goddard: My Years with the Lord Chief Justice*. London, 1959.

Smith, Bradley F. *Reaching Judgment at Nuremberg*. New York, 1977.

Smith, J. H. *Appeals to the Privy Council from the American Colonies*. New York, 1950.

Smith, John C., and Hogan, Brian. *Criminal Law*. 3d ed. London, 1973.

Smith, T. B. *British Justice: The Scottish Contribution*. London, 1961.

Spear, Perry. *India: A Modern History*. Ann Arbor, 1961.

Stacey, Frank. *British Government 1966–1975: Years of Reform*. Oxford, 1975.

———. *The British Ombudsman*. Oxford, 1971.

———. *A New Bill of Rights for Britain*. Newton Abbot, 1973.

Stallybrass, W. T. S., ed. *Salmond's Law of Torts*. 10th ed. London, 1945.

Stankiewitz, Wladyslaw J. *Crisis in British Government*. London, 1967.

Stephens, W. R. W. *Memoirs of Lord Hatherley*. 2 vols. London, 1883.

Stevens, Robert, and Yamey, Basil. *The Restrictive Practices Court: A Study in the Judicial Process and Economic Policy*. London, 1965.

Stevenson, William. *A Man Called Intrepid: The Secret War*. New York, 1976.

Stone, Julius. *The Province and Function of Law: Law as Logic, Justice and Social Control: A Study in Jurisprudence*. Sydney, 1950.

Strachey, Lytton, and Fulford, Roger, eds. *The Greville Memoirs 1814–1860*. London, 1938.

Strauss, Patricia. *Cripps, Advocate Extraordinary*. New York, 1942.

Symons, Julian. *The General Strike*. London, 1957.

Tarnopolsky, Walter S. *The Canadian Bill of Rights*. 2d ed. Toronto, 1975.

Taylor, A. J. P. *English History 1914–1945*. Oxford, 1965.

Teff, Harvey, and Munro, Colin. *Thalidomide: The Legal Aftermath*. Westmead, 1976.

Thomas, Hugh. *Suez*. London, 1967.

Titmuss, Richard M. *Income Distribution and Social Change*. London, 1962.

Treitel, G. H. *The Law of Contract*. 3d ed. London, 1970.

Turberville, Arthur Stanley. *The House of Lords in the Eighteenth Century*. Oxford, 1927.

Twining, William, and Miers, David. *How to Do Things with Rules*. London, 1976.

Twiss, Horace. *The Public and Private Life of Lord Chancellor Eldon*. London, 1844.

Urquhart, Thomas Malory. *The Experienced Solicitor in Proceedings under the Appellate Jurisdiction of the Right Honorable the House of Lords on Appeals and Writs of Error, and the Jurisdiction Exercised by the House in Matters of Peerage*. London, 1773.

Veall, Donald. *The Popular Movement for Law Reform 1640–1660*. Oxford, 1970.

Veeder, Van Vechten, ed. *Selected Essays in Anglo-American Legal History*. 3 vols. Boston, 1907.

Wallace, William J. L. *The Foreign Policy Process in Britain*. London, 1976.

Warren, Samuel. *Ten Thousand a Year*. Philadelphia, 1840.

Webber, George J. *The Effect of War on Contracts*. London, 1940.

Wedderburn, K. W. *The Worker and the Law*. Harmondsworth, 1965.

Weston, Corrine C. *English Constitutional Theory and the House of Lords 1556–1832*. London, 1965.

Wetter, J. Gillis. *The Styles of Appellate Judicial Opinions*. Leyden, 1960.

Wheatcroft, G. S. A. *The Law of Income Tax, Surtax and Profits Tax*. London, 1962.

Wilberforce, Richard C. *Law and Economics*. Holdsworth Lecture. Birmingham, 1966.

Wilson, Charles E. *Haldane and the Machinery of Government*. London, 1956.

Wilson-Fox, A. *The Earl of Halsbury*. London, 1929.

Wilson, H. H. *Pressure Group: The Campaign for Commercial Television*. London, 1961.

Wilson, Harold. *The Governance of Britain*. London, 1976.

————. *A Personal Record: The Labour Government 1964–1970*. London, 1971.

Wilson, Philip W., ed. *The Greville Diary*. New York, 1927.

Woodward, E. L. *The Age of Reform 1815–1870*. Oxford, 1938.

Wright, Robert Anderson. *Legal Essays and Addresses*. Cambridge, 1939.

————. *Some Developments of Commercial Law in the Present Century*. Holdsworth Lecture. Birmingham, 1936.

Wynne, Maud. *An Irishman and His Family*. London, 1937.

Wyzanski, Charles E., Jr. *The New Meaning of Justice*. New York, 1966.

Yale, David E. C., ed. *Lord Nottingham's 'Manual of Chancery Practice' and 'Prolegomena of Chancery and Equity.'* Cambridge, 1965.

Young, Hugo. *The Crossman Affair*. London, 1976.

Zander, Michael. *A Bill of Rights?* London, 1975.

ARTICLES

Abse, Leo. "The Inevitability of the Matrimonial Offence." *Law Society's Gazette* 205 (1965).

Ackerman, Bruce. "Law and the Modern Mind." 103 *Daedalus* 119 (1974).

Allen, Carleton Kemp. "Precedent Limps On." 81 *Law Quarterly Review* 36 (1965).

————. "Precedent and Logic." 41 *Law Quarterly Review* 320 (1925).

————. "Regulation 18B and Reasonable Cause." 58 *Law Quarterly Review* 3 (1942).

Amerasinghe, C. F. "The *Schtraks* Case, Defining Political Offences and Extradition." 28 *Modern Law Review* 28 (1965).

Beven, Thomas. "The Appellate Jurisdiction of the House of Lords." 17 *Law Quarterly Review* 155 and 357 (1901).

Blom-Cooper, Louis, and Drewry, Gavin. "House of Lords: Reflections on the Social Utility of Final Appellate Courts." 32 *Modern Law Review* 262 (1969).

_____. "The Use of Full Courts in the Appellate Process." 34 *Modern Law Review* 364 (1971).

Brazier, Rodney. "Overruling House of Lords Criminal Cases." *Criminal Law Review* 98 (Feb. 1973).

Brodetsky, Paul. "Employees' Joint Breach of Statutory Duty: *Volenti* Not Barred." 27 *Modern Law Review* 733 (1964).

Cameron, B. J. "The Future of Appeals to the Judicial Committee of the Privy Council, a Symposium: New Zealand." 2 *Otago Law Review* 172 (1970).

Capeletti, Mauro, and Golden, C. J., Jr. "Crown Privilege and Executive Privilege: A British Response to an American Controversy." 25 *Stanford Law Review* 836 (1974).

Chorley, Theo. "Liberal Trends in Present Day Commercial Law." 3 *Modern Law Review* 272 (1940).

Chown, John, and Rowland, Peter. "The Finance Bill." *British Tax Review* 1972.

Cohen, Lionel. "The Jurisdiction, Practice and Procedure of the Court of Appeal." 11 *Cambridge Law Journal* 3 (1951).

Cross, Geoffrey. "Some Recent Developments in the Law of Charity." 72 *Law Quarterly Review* 187 (1956).

Cross, Rupert. "The Criminal Evidence Act, 1898, and the House of Lords as a Court of Criminal Appeal." 78 *Law Quarterly Review* 407 (1962).

_____. "The Need for a Redefinition of Murder." 7 *Criminal Law Review* 278 (1960).

_____. "Stare Decisis in Contemporary England." 82 *Law Quarterly Review* 203 (1966).

Davies, D. Seaborne. "The House of Lords and Criminal Law." 6 *Journal of the Society of the Public Teachers of Law* 104 (1961).

Davis, Kenneth C. "The Future of Judge-Made Public Law in England: A Problem of Practical Jurisprudence." 61 *Columbia Law Review* 201 (1961).

Denning, Alfred. "The Way of an Iconoclast." 5 *Journal of the Society of the Public Teachers of Law* 77 (1959).

Devlin, Patrick. "Judges and Lawmakers." 39 *Modern Law Review* 1 (1976).

Dias, R. W. M. "Precedents in the House of Lords." *Cambridge Law Journal* 153 (1966).

_____. "Trouble on Oiled Waters." *Cambridge Law Review* 62 (1967).

Dicey, Albert Venn. "The Development of Administrative Law in England." 31 *Law Quarterly Review* 148 (1915).

Dilhorne, Lord (Reginald Manningham-Buller). "The Rule of Law: Its Status in the Modern World." 36 *American Bar Association Journal* 373 (1946).

Diplock, Kenneth. "The Courts as Legislators." *Law Guardian* 8 (Jan. 1966).

_____. "Introduction to a Discussion of the Wilson Report." 9 *Journal of the Society of the Public Teachers of Law* 193 (1966).

_____. "Judicial Control of the Administrative Process." 22 *Current Legal Problems* (1971).

Drewry, Gavin. "The Judge as Political Anodyne." 124 *New Law Journal* 531 (1974).

————. "Judges in Parliament." 119 *New Law Journal* 431 (1969).

————. "Judgment on Leapfrogging." 122 *New Law Journal* 698 (1972).

————. "Leapfrogging—and a Lord Justice's Eye View of the Final Appeal." 89 *Law Quarterly Review* 260 (1973).

————. "Lord Chancellor as Judge." 122 *New Law Journal* 855 (1972).

————. "One Appeal Too Many: An Analysis of the Functions of the House of Lords as a Final Court of Appeal." 19 *British Journal of Sociology* 445 (1968).

————. "Poulson and Parliament." 126 *New Law Journal* 1079 (1976).

Duman, Daniel. "A Social and Occupational Analysis of the English Judiciary: 1770–1790 and 1855–1875." 17 *American Journal of Legal History* 353 (1973).

du Parcq, Herbert. "The Final Court of Appeal." 2 *Current Legal Problems* 1 (1949).

Dworkin, Gerald. "*Stare Decisis* in the House of Lords." 25 *Modern Law Review* 163 (1962).

Dworkin, Ronald M. "Hard Cases." 88 *Harvard Law Review* 1057 (1975).

————. "The Model of Rules." 35 *University of Chicago Law Review* 14 (1967).

Edmund-Davies, Herbert. "Judicial Activism." *Current Legal Problems 1975* 1.

Emery, C. T. "After OZ-IT." 30 *Cambridge Law Journal* 199 (1972).

Evershed, Raymond. "The Judicial Process in 20th Century England." 61 *Columbia Law Review* 761 (1961).

Finlay, A. M. "A Pacific Regional Court of Appeal?" *New Zealand Law Journal* 493 (1974).

Fleming, David. "Better the Devil You Know." 30 *Cambridge Law Journal* 232 (1972).

————. "Precedent and the Judicial Function of the House of Lords." 32 *Cambridge Law Journal* 17 (1976).

Frank, Jerome. "When 'omer Smote 'is Bloomin' Lyre." 51 *Yale Journal* 367 (1942).

Freeman, Michael D. A. "Standards of Adjudication, Judicial Law Making and Prospective Overruling." 26 *Current Legal Problems* 166 (1973).

Friedman, Lawrence M. "On Legalistic Reasoning—A Footnote to Weber." *Wisconsin Law Review* 148 (1966).

Friedmann, Wolfgang. "The Harris Tweed Case and Freedom of Trade." 6 *Modern Law Review* 1 (1943).

————. "Judicial Law Making in England." In *Law, Justice and Equity*, edited by R. H. C. Holland and R. G. Schwartzenberger. London, 1967.

————. "Modern Trends in the Law of Torts." 1 *Modern Law Review* 39 (1938).

Fullagar, W. K. "Liability for Representatives at Common Law." 25 *Australian Law Journal* 278 (1951).

Gadbois, G. H. "Evolution of the Federal Court of India: An Historical Footnote." 5 *Journal of the Indian Law Institute* 19 (1963).

Gardiner, Gerald. "Comparative Law Reform." 52 *American Bar Association Journal* 1021 (1966).

————. "An Interview with the Lord Chancellor." 120 *New Law Journal* 2 (1970).

————. "The Judicial Attitude to Penal Reform." 65 *Law Quarterly Review* 196 (1969).

————. "Law Reform—Not Now?" 71 *Law Society's Gazette* 1065 (1974).

————. "*Lister* v. *The Romford Ice and Cold Storage Company, Ltd.*" 22 *Modern Law Review* 652 (1959).

————. "Methods of Law Reform." 13 *St. Louis University Law Journal* 3 (1969).

————. "The Office of Lord Chancellor." 119 *New Law Journal* 517 (1969).

————. "The Purposes of Criminal Punishment." 21 *Modern Law Review* 117 (1958).

————. "The Role of the Lord Chancellor in the Field of Law Reform." 87 *Law Quarterly Review* 326 (1971).

————. "Rule of Law Repudiated." 125 *New Law Journal* 1077 (1975).

————. "Some Aspects of Law Reform." *New Zealand Law Journal* 171 (1969).

————. "Two Lawyers or One?" 23 *Current Legal Problems* 1 (1970).

Goddard, Rayner. "Politics and the British Bench." 43 *Journal of the American Judicature Society* 124 (1959).

————. "Recollections of a Lawyer's Life." 57 *Virginia State Bar Association* 336 (1946).

Goldstein, Abraham S. "Research into the Administration of Criminal Law: A Report from the United States." 1966 *British Journal of Criminology* 27.

Goodhart, Arthur L. "The 'I Think' Doctrine of Precedent: Invitors and Licensors." 66 *Law Quarterly Review* 374 (1950).

————. "Liability for Negligent Misstatements." 78 *Law Quarterly Review* 263 (1969).

————. "Lord Macmillan and Lord Wright." 63 *Law Quarterly Review* 259 (1947).

————. "Precedent in the Broome and Herrington Cases." 88 *Law Quarterly Review* 305 (1972).

————. "The Shaw Case: The Law and Public Morals." 77 *Law Quarterly Review* 560 (1961).

Gower, L. C. B. "*Baxter* v. *Baxter* in Perspective." 11 *Modern Law Review* 176 (1948).

————. "Reflections on Law Reform." 23 *University of Toronto Law Journal* 257 (1973).

Greene, Wilfred. "Law and Progress." 94 *Law Journal* 349 (1944).

Griffith, John A. G. "The Tameside Opinion." *New Statesman* 589 (29 Oct. 1976).

Guest, C. W. G. "The Executive and the Judiciary." 18 *Juridical Review* 113 (1973).

————. "The Supreme Court of the United States." *Scots Law Times* 245 (1973).

Hailsham, Lord (Quintin McGarel Hogg). "Elective Dictatorship." 120 *Solicitors Journal* 693 (1976).

————. "Lord Hailsham on the Law." *The Listener* 76 (18 July 1974).

————. "Lord Hailsham's Convictions." *The Listener* 38 (11 July 1974).

Haldane, Richard Burdon. "The Labourer and the Law." 83 *Contemporary Review* 362 (1903).

————. "The Work for the Empire of the Judicial Committee of the Privy Council." 1 *Cambridge Law Journal* 143 (1921–23).

Hamson, C. J. "Contract and Tort: Measure of Damages." 26 *Cambridge Law Journal* 15 (1969).

Harding, R. W. "Lord Atkin's Judicial Attitudes and Their Illustration in Commercial Law and Contract." 24 *Modern Law Review* 434 (1964).

Hazard, Geoffrey. "Review." 18 *American Journal of Legal History* 259 (1974).

Heuston, R. F. V. "*Donoghue* v. *Stevenson* in Retrospect." 20 *Modern Law Review* 1 (1957).

————. "*Liversidge* v. *Anderson* in Retrospect." 86 *Law Quarterly Review* 33 (1970).

Heydon, J. D. "The Frontiers of the Restraint of Trade Doctrine." 85 *Law Quarterly Review* 229 (1969).

Hoffman, L. "*Rookes* v. *Barnard*." 81 *Law Quarterly Review* 116 (1965).

Holdsworth, William S. "Case Law." 50 *Law Quarterly Review* 180 (1934).

————. "The New Rules of Pleading of the Hilary Term, 1834." 1 *Cambridge Law Journal* 261 (1921–23).

Holmes, Oliver Wendell, Jr. "The Path of the Law." 10 *Harvard Law Review* 457 (1896–97).

Howells, R. W. L. "A Positive Safety Policy." 27 *Modern Law Review* 738 (1964).

Ibrahim, Ahmad. "The Future of Appeals to the Judicial Committee of the Privy Council, a Symposium: Malaysia and Singapore." 2 *Otago Law Review* 163 (1970).

Ilersic, A. R. "National Tax Reform." 164 *Accountant* 371 (1971).

Jeffrey-Cook, John. "Ten Traumatic Tax Years." 125 *New Law Journal* 1038 (1975).

Jennings, W. Ivor. "Appeals to the Privy Council and the Statute of Westminster." 52 *Law Quarterly Review* 173 (1936).

————. "Constitutional Interpretation—The Experience of Canada." 51 *Harvard Law Review* 1 (1937).

Jones, Maldwyn A. "Immigrants, Steamships and Governments: The Steerage Problem in Transatlantic Diplomacy, 1868–74." In *Contrast and Connection*, edited by H. C. Allen and Roger Thompson. Ohio. 1976.

Jones, Peter E. "In Memoriam." 2 *Current Legal Problems* ix (1969).

Jowitt, William Allen. "Address to Canadian Bar Association." 30 *Canadian Bar Association Journal* 109 (1948).

————. "Message from Britain." 33 *American Bar Association Journal* 177 (1947).

Kahn-Freund, Otto. "Labour Law." In *Law and Opinion in England in the 20th Century*, edited by Morris Ginsberg. London, 1959.

Keith-Lucas, Brian. "Popularism." *Public Law* 1962 52.

Kennedy, Duncan. "Legal Formality." 2 *Journal of Legal Studies* 320 (1973).

Kilbrandon, Lord (C. J. D. Shaw). "The Scottish Law Commission." 2 *Georgia Law Review* 193 (1968).

Kilmuir, Lord (David Maxwell-Fyfe). "The British Courts and Parliament: The Judiciary in the British Constitution." 35 *American Bar Association Journal* 373 (1949).

————. "Individual Freedom under an Unwritten Constitution." 45 *Virginia Law Review* 629 (1959).

————. "Judicial Qualities." 36 *New Zealand Law Journal* 112 (1960).

————. "Law Reform." 4 *Journal of the Society of the Public Teachers of Law* 75 (1958).

————. "Lawyer Statesman." 40 *American Bar Association Journal* 939 (1954).

————. "The Shaftesbury Tradition in Conservative Politics." 3 *Journal of Law and Economics* 70 (1960).

————. "The State, the Citizen and the Law." 73 *Law Quarterly Review* 172 (1951).

Langbein, John. "Modern Jurisprudence in the House of Lords." 53 *Cornell Law Review* 807 (1968).

Leach, W. Barton. "Revisionism in the House of Lords: The Bastion of Rigid Stare Decisis Falls." 80 *Harvard Law Review* 797 (1967).

Leigh-Jones, P. N., and Pickering, M. "Fundamental Breach: The Aftermath of Harbutt's 'Plasticine.'" 87 *Law Quarterly Review* 515 (1971).

Lester, Anthony. "The Broken Compass." 119 *New Law Journal* 443 (1969).

_____. "Fundamental Rights in the United Kingdom: The Law and British Constitution." 125 *University of Pennsylvania Law Review* 337 (1976).

Levin, Jennifer. "The Divorce Reform Act, 1969." 33 *Modern Law Review* 633 (1970).

Lewis, L. "The History of Judicial Precedent." 46 *Law Quarterly Review* 207 (1930); 47 *Law Quarterly Review* 411 (1931); 48 *Law Quarterly Review* 230 (1938).

MacDermott, John C. "Some Requirements of Justice." *Juridical Review* 103 (1964).

MacDonald, Graeme. "The Wealth Tax—The Wrong Tool for the Job." *British Tax Review* 1975.

Macmillan, Hugh. "Scots Law as a Subject of Comparative Study." 48 *Law Quarterly Review* 477 (1932).

Macnaghten, Edward. "The Late Lord Davey." 8 *Journal of the Society of Comparative Legislation* 10 (1908).

Mainprice, H. H. "Multi-rate VAT in the United Kingdom." *1975 British Tax Review.*

Megarry, R. E. "Contemplative Nuns in Eire and England." 63 *Law Quarterly Review* 424 (1947).

_____. "Lay Peers in Appeals to the House of Lords." 65 *Law Quarterly Review* 22 (1949).

Morean, J. B. "Tax Avoidance—Turning of the Tide?" 125 *New Law Journal* 83 (1975).

Morris, John W. "Courts and Domestic Tribunals." 69 *Law Quarterly Review* 318 (1953).

_____. "The Equipment of the Lawyer." 30 *Canadian Bar Review* 881 (1952).

_____. "Natural Justice." 26 *Current Legal Problems* 1 (1973).

_____. "The Rich Heritage of the Law." 31 *New Zealand Law Journal* 57 (1955); 52 *Law Society's Gazette* 435 (1955).

Morton, Fergus Durly. "Address Given during the Thirty-first Annual Meeting (Proceedings)." 32 *Canadian Bar Association* 107 (1949).

_____. "The Dual Function of the House of Lords." 35 *American Bar Association Journal* 889 (1949).

M[unroe], J. G. "Judicial Precedent." *British Tax Review* 1970 77.

Nash, Michael. "Privy Council: Functions and Future of the Judicial Committee of the Privy Council." 24 *New Law Journal* 1171 (1974).

Newark, Francis H. "The Boundaries of Nuisance." 65 *Law Quarterly Review* 171 (1949).

Nock, R. S., and Pickering, M. A. "The Shape of the Value Added Tax." *British Tax Review* 1972.

Paine, John. "Labour and the Lawyers." *New Statesman* 11 July 1975 44.

Parry, David Hughes. "Economic Theories in English Case Law." 47 *Law Quarterly Review* 183 (1931).

Paterson, A. A. "Judges: A Political Elite?" 1 *British Journal of Law and Society* 118 (1974).

Pearce, E. H. "The Law as a Whole." 58 *Law Society's Gazette* 411 (1961).

Porter, Samuel L. "English Procedure and Practice—More Particular in Criminal Matters." 2 *Current Legal Problems* 13 (1949).

Powell, G. H. "*Bunch v. Great Western Railway Company.*" 2 *Law Quarterly Review* 469 (1886).

Radcliffe, Cyril John. "Law and Order." 61 *Law Society's Gazette* 821 (1964).

————. "Some Reflections on Law and Lawyers." 10 *Cambridge Law Journal* 3611 (1950).

Reid, James S. C. "The Judge as Law Maker." 12 *Journal of the Society of the Public Teachers of Law* 22 (1972).

————. "The Law and the Reasonable Man." *Proceedings of the British Academy 1968* 193.

Rideout, R. W. "The Industrial Relations Act, 1971." 34 *Modern Law Review* 655 (1971).

Rose, Richard. "Money and Election Law." 9 *Political Studies* 1 (1961).

Salmon, Cyril. "The Last Bulwark of Individual Liberty." 117 *New Law Journal* 749 (1967).

Sawer, G. "The Future of Appeals to the Judicial Committee of the Privy Council, a Symposium: Australia." 2 *Otago Law Review* 138 (1970).

Scott, F. R. "Labour Conventions Case: Lord Wright's Undisclosed Dissent." 34 *Canadian Bar Review* 114 (1956).

Scrutton, T. E. "War and the Law." 34 *Law Quarterly Review* 116 (1918).

————. "The Work of the Commercial Courts." 1 *Cambridge Law Journal* 6 (1921–23).

Simon, Jocelyn. "English Idioms from the Law." 76 *Law Quarterly Review* 283 (1960) and 78 *Law Quarterly Review* 245 (1962).

————. "Evidence Excluded by Considerations of State Interest." *1955 Cambridge Law Journal* 62.

————. "Review." 81 *Law Quarterly Review* 289 (1965).

————. "Shakespeare's Legal and Political Background." 84 *Law Quarterly Review* 33 (1968).

Simon, John. "Our Common Inheritance of Law." 7 *American Bar Association Journal* 449 (1921).

————. "Some Aspects of the Indian Problem." 16 *American Bar Association Journal* 648 (1930).

Somervell, Donald. "Acts of Attainder." 67 *Law Quarterly Review* 306 (1951).

————. "Law and Liberty." 29 *American Bar Association Journal* 547 (1943).

Spicer, M. W. "New Approaches to the Problem of Tax Evasion." *1975 British Tax Review* 132.

Stephenson, I. S. "Trespassers and Judicial Innovation." 69 *Law Society's Gazette* 663 (1972).

Stevens, Robert. "The Final Appeal: Reform of the House of Lords and Privy Council, 1867–1876." 80 *Law Quarterly Review* 343 (1964).

————. "*Hedley Byrne* v. *Heller*: Judicial Creativity and Doctrinal Possibility." 27 *Modern Law Review* 121 (1964).

————. "Judicial Legislation and the Law Lords: Four Interpretations." 10 *Irish Jurist* 1 and 216 (1975).

————. "The Role of a Final Appeal Court in a Democracy: The House of Lords To-day." 28 *Modern Law Review* 509 (1965).

————. "Some Unexplored Avenues in Comparative Anglo-American Legal History." 48 *Tulane Law Review* 1086 (1974).

————. "Statutory Interpretation, Restrictive Practices and the 'New' House of Lords." 27 *Modern Law Review* 337 (1964).

Stone, Julius. "The Lords at the Crossroads." 46 *Australian Law Journal* 483 (1972).

————. "1966 and All That. . . . " 692 *Columbia Law Review* 1172 (1969).

————. "On the Liberation of Appellate Judges—How Not to Do It." 35 *Modern Law Review* 449 (1972).

Stone, Olive. "The Tax Element in Damages Reconsidered." *1958 British Tax Review* 334.

Swinfen, D. B. "Henry Brougham and the Judicial Committee of the Privy Council." 90 *Law Quarterly Review* 396 (1974).

————. "Single Judgment in the Privy Council 1833–1966." 20 *Juridical Review* 153 (1975).

Thayer, J. B. "The Origin and Scope of the American Doctrine of Constitutional Law." 7 *Harvard Law Review* 129 (1893).

Thompson, E. P. "A Report on Lord Radcliffe." *New Society* 737 (30 April 1970).

Tomlin, Thomas J. "Case Law." 20 *American Bar Association Journal* 594 (1934).

Trubek, David. "Toward a Social Theory of Law: An Essay in the Study of Law and Development." 82 *Yale Law Journal* 1 (1972).

Turberville, Arthur Stanley. "The House of Lords as a Court of Law 1784–1837." 52 *Law Quarterly Review* 189 (1936).

Unger, T. "Silence as Admission of Guilt." 7 *Modern Law Review* 70 (1943–44).

Upjohn, Gerald. "Twenty Years On." 65 *Law Society's Gazette* 657 (1968).

Veeder, Van Vechten. "A Century of English Judicature." In 1 *Selected Essays in Anglo-American Legal History*, edited by Van Vechten Veeder. Boston, 1907.

Wade, E. C. S. "Constitutional Law." 51 *Law Quarterly Review* 235 (1935).

Wade, H. W. R. "Part Performance: Back to Square One." 90 *Law Quarterly Review* 433 (1974).

Wallington, Peter. "The European Convention on Human Rights and English Law." *1975 Cambridge Law Journal* 9.

————. "Sovereignty Regained." 37 *Modern Law Review* 686 (1974).

Watmore, L. J. "Personal Injuries—When Time Runs." 122 *New Law Journal* 672 (1972).

Wedderburn, K. W. "Intimidation and the Right to Strike." 27 *Modern Law Review* 257 (1964).

————. "Report of the Royal Commission on Trade Unions and Employers' Associations." 31 *Modern Law Review* 674 (1968).

————. "*Stratford & Son, Ltd. v. Lindley.*" 28 *Modern Law Review* 205 (1965).

Wheatcroft, G. S. A. "First Thoughts on the Capital Transfer Tax." *British Tax Review 1974*.

Whitel, R. M. "The Last Trump for Clubs?" 126 *New Law Journal* 1104 (1976).

Wilberforce, Richard C. "Educating the Judges." 10 *Journal of the Society of the Public Teachers of Law* 254 (1970).

Williams, Glanville. "Constructive Malice Revisited." 23 *Modern Law Review* 605 (1960).

Williams, J. E. Hall. "The Ladies' Directory and Criminal Conspiracy: The Judge as Custos Morum." 24 *Modern Law Review* 626 (1961).

Woolf, Antony D. "Personal Injury Limitation—House of Lords Interpretation." 122 *New Law Journal* 672 (1972).

Wright, Robert Anderson. "Contributory Negligence." 13 *Modern Law Review* 2 (1950).

―――. "Lord Atkin of Aberdovey." 60 *Law Quarterly Review* 332 (1944).

―――. "Lord Atkin of Aberdovey in Memoriam." 32 *Proceedings of the British Academy* 307 (1944).

―――. "Lord Dunedin." 92 *Law Journal* 317 (1942).

―――. "Obituary for the Rt. Hon. Sir Lyman Poore Duff, G.C.M.G." 33 *Canadian Bar Review* 1123 (1955).

―――. "Precedents." 8 *Cambridge Law Journal* 118 (1943).

―――. "Section 92—A Problem Piece." 1 *Sydney Law Review* 145 (1954).

GOVERNMENT DOCUMENTS

1811   *Report of the Committee Appointed to Inquire into the Causes that Retard the Decision of Suits in the High Court of Chancery. House of Commons Sessional Papers.* Vol. 3.

1811   *Report of the Committee to Inspect the Lords Journals; Appointed March 5, 1811. House of Commons Sessional Papers, 1810–1811.* Vol. 2.

1823   *Report of the Select Committee on the Appellate Jurisdiction of the House of Lords. House of Lords Sessional Papers.* Vol. 10.

1824   *Report of the Commission Inquiring into the Forms of Process in the Courts of Law in Scotland. House of Lords Sessional Papers.* Vol. 4.

1824   *Report of the Lords Commissioners to Report on Procedure in Scotland. House of Lords Sessional Papers.* Vol. 4.

1856   *Report of the Select Committee on the Appellate Jurisdiction. House of Lords Sessional Papers.* Vol. 1.

1872   *Report of the Select Committee of the House of Lords on the Appellate Jurisdiction. House of Lords Sessional Papers.* Vol. 9.

1879   *Report of the Royal Commission to Consider the Law Relating to Indictable Offenses,* Cd. 2345.

1906   *Report of the Royal Commission on Trade Disputes and Trade Combinations,* Cd. 2825.

1907   *Proceedings of the Imperial Conference,* Cd. 3524.

1908   *Reform of the House of Lords,* Cd. 3799.

1911   *Proceedings of the Imperial Conference,* Cd. 5745.

1919   *Report of the Commission on the Coal Industry,* Cmd. 359.

1932   *Report of the Committee on Ministers' Powers,* Cmd. 4060.

1934   *Report of the Legal Education Committee,* Cmd. 4663.

1942   *Report of the Committee on Compensation and Betterment of Land,* Cmd. 6291.

1945   *Report of the Committee on Company Law Amendment,* Cmd. 6659.

1946   *Report of the Royal Commission on Equal Pay,* Cmd. 6937.

1948   *Report of the Royal Commission on the Justices of the Peace,* Cmd. 7463.

1949   *Report of the Committee on Intermediaries,* Cmd. 7904.

1949   *First Interim Report of the Committee on Supreme Court Practice and Procedure,* Cmd. 7764.

1950   *Report of the Committee on Leaseholds,* Cmd. 7982.

1951   *Second Interim Report of the Committee on Supreme Court Practice and Procedure,* Cmd. 8176.

1952   *Third Interim Report of the Committee on Supreme Court Practice and Procedure,* Cmd. 8617.

1953 *Final Report of the Committee on Supreme Court Practice and Procedure.* Cmd. 8878.
1955 *Report of the Royal Commission on Taxation of Profits and Income,* Cmd. 9474.
1956 *Report of the Royal Commission on Marriage and Divorce,* Cmd. 9678.
1956 *Report of the Committee on Port Transport Industry,* Cmd. 9813.
1957 *Report of the Committee on Tribunals and Enquiries,* Cmnd. 218.
1959 *Report of the Committee on Enquiry into the Monetary System,* Cmnd. 827.
1960 *Report of the Royal Commission on Local Government in Greater London,* Cmnd. 1164.
1961 *Report of the Committee on Security Procedures in the Public Service,* Cmnd. 1681.
1962 *Report of the Company Law Committee,* Cmnd. 1749.
1962 *Report of the Committee on Limitation of Action in Cases of Personal Injury,* Cmnd. 1829.
1962 *Report of the Vassal Tribunal of Enquiry,* Cmnd. 2009.
1963 *Denning Report,* Cmnd. 2152.
1966 *Report of the Royal Commission on Tribunals of Enquiry,* Cmnd. 3121.
1967 *Privy Council Inquiry into Daily Express and "D" Notices,* Cmnd. 2209.
1967 *Report of the Royal Commission on Trade Unions and Employers' Associations,* Cmnd. 3623.
1968 *First Report of the Public Schools Commission,* H.M.S.O.
1968 *Report of the Committee on the Civil Service,* Cmnd. 3638.
1968 *Reform of the House of Lords,* Cmnd. 3799.
1969 *Report of the Royal Commission on Local Government in England,* Cmnd. 4040.
1969 *Interdepartmental Committee on the Law of Contempt as It Affects Tribunals of Inquiry,* Cmnd. 4078.
1969 *Report of the Royal Commission on Assizes and Quarter Sessions,* Cmnd. 4153.
1970 *Report of the Monopolies Commission on Professional Services,* Cmnd. 4463.
1971 *Report of the Committee on Legal Education,* Cmnd. 4595.
1971 *Report of the Commission on the Third London Airport,* H.M.S.O.
1972 *Report of the Commission to Consider Legal Procedures to Deal with Terrorist Activities in Northern Ireland,* Cmnd. 5185.
1973 *Report of the Royal Commission on the Constitution,* Cmnd. 5460.
1974 *Report of the Committee on Contempt of Court,* Cmnd. 5794.
1974 *Democracy and Devolution: Proposals for Scotland and Wales,* Cmnd. 5732.
1975 *Report of the Royal Commission on the Distribution of Income and Wealth,* Cmnd. 6171.
1975 *Preparation of Legislation,* Cmnd. 6053.
1976 *Report of the Committee of Privy Councillors on Ministerial Memoirs,* Cmnd. 6386.
1976 *Report of the Departmental Committee on Evidence of Identification in Criminal Cases. House of Commons Papers* 338.
1976 *Report of the Royal Commission on the Standards of Conduct in Public Life,* Cmnd. 6524.

RECURRING GOVERNMENT PUBLICATIONS

Civil Judicial Statistics, England and Wales, 1868–.
House of Commons Sessional Papers, passim.
House of Lords Journal, 1620–.
House of Lords Sessional Papers, passim.
Parliamentary Debates: 3d series, 1830–91; 4th series, 1892–1908; 5th series, 1909–.
Reports of the Criminal Law Revision Committee, 1948–.
Reports of the Law Commission, 1966–.
Reports of the Law Revision (Reform) Committee, 1934–.

ᴥ Index of Cases

Page numbers in boldface reflect detailed discussions of the case.

ᘒ General Index

THE AUTHOR

Born in England, Robert Stevens was educated at Oxford and at Yale and practiced law in New York and in London before becoming professor of law at Yale and later provost at Tulane. In 1978 he became president of Haverford College.

THE BOOK

Typeface: Sabon
Design and composition: The University of North Carolina Press
Paper: 50 lb. Perkins & Squier smooth offset by P. H. Glatfelter Paper Company
Binding cloth: Roxite B 53503 by Holliston Mills, Inc.
Printer and binder: Vail-Ballou Press

Published by The University of North Carolina Press